For reference

Not to be taken from the room.

W9-CAE-603

Great Events from History

The Renaissance & Early Modern Era

1454 - 1600

Great Events from History

The Renaissance & Early Modern Era

1454 - 1600

Volume 2
1534-1600

Editor
Christina J. Moose

SALEM PRESS
Pasadena, California   Hackensack, New Jersey

Editor in Chief: Dawn P. Dawson
Acquisitions Editor: Mark Rehn
Research Supervisor: Jeffry Jensen
Manuscript Editors: Desiree Dreeuws, Andy Perry
Assistant Editor: Andrea E. Miller

Production Editor: Cynthia Beres
Graphics and Design: James Hutson
Editorial Assistant: Dana Garey
Layout: William Zimmerman
Photograph Editor: Philip Bader

Cover photos: Corbis, PhotoDisc
(Pictured left to right, top to bottom: Ming Dynasty warrior, China; 16th century chateau, Loire Valley, France; Blue Mosque in Istanbul, Turkey; Michelangelo's statue of *David*; African Mask from Namibia; fortified granary, Tunisia)

Copyright © 2005, by SALEM PRESS, INC.

All rights in this book are reserved. No part of this work may be used or reproduced in any manner whatsoever or transmitted in any form or by any means, electronic or mechanical, including photocopy, recording, or any information storage and retrieval system, without written permission from the copyright owner except in the case of brief quotations embodied in critical articles and reviews. For information address the publisher, Salem Press, Inc., P.O. Box 50062, Pasadena, California 91115.

∞ The paper used in these volumes conforms to the American National Standard for Permanence of Paper for Printed Library Materials, Z39.48-1992 (R1997).

Some of the essays in this work originally appeared in the following Salem Press sets: *Chronology of European History: 15,000 B.C. to 1997* (1997, edited by John Powell), *Great Events from History: North American Series, Revised Edition* (1997, edited by Frank N. Magill; associate editor, John L. Loos), and *Great Events from History: Modern European Series* (1973, edited by Frank N. Magill; associate editors, Thomas P. Neill and José M. Sánchez).

Library of Congress Cataloging-in-Publication Data

Great events from history. The Renaissance & early modern era, 1454-1600 / editor, Christina J. Moose.
    p. cm.
Some of the essays were previously published in various works.
Includes bibliographical references and index.
    ISBN 1-58765-214-5 (set : alk. paper) — ISBN 1-58765-215-3 (vol. 1 : alk. paper) — ISBN 1-58765-216-1 (vol. 2 : alk. paper)
    1. Fifteenth century. 2. Sixteenth century. 3. History, Modern—16th century. I. Title: Renaissance & early modern era, 1454-1600. II. Moose, Christina J., 1952-

D228.G73 2005
909′.5—dc22

2004028878

First Printing

ACC Library Services
Austin, Texas

PRINTED IN THE UNITED STATES OF AMERICA

CONTENTS

1530's *(continued)*

1540's

1550's

1560's

1570's

1580's

1590's

Appendices

Indexes

KEYWORD LIST OF CONTENTS

List of Maps, Tables, and Sidebars

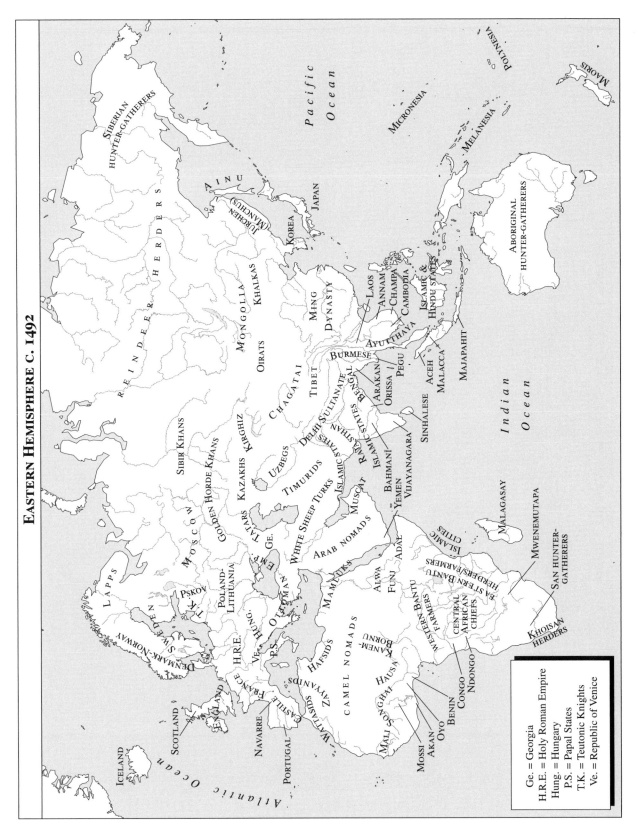

EASTERN HEMISPHERE C. 1492

Ge. = Georgia
H.R.E. = Holy Roman Empire
Hung. = Hungary
P.S. = Papal States
T.K. = Teutonic Knights
Ve. = Republic of Venice

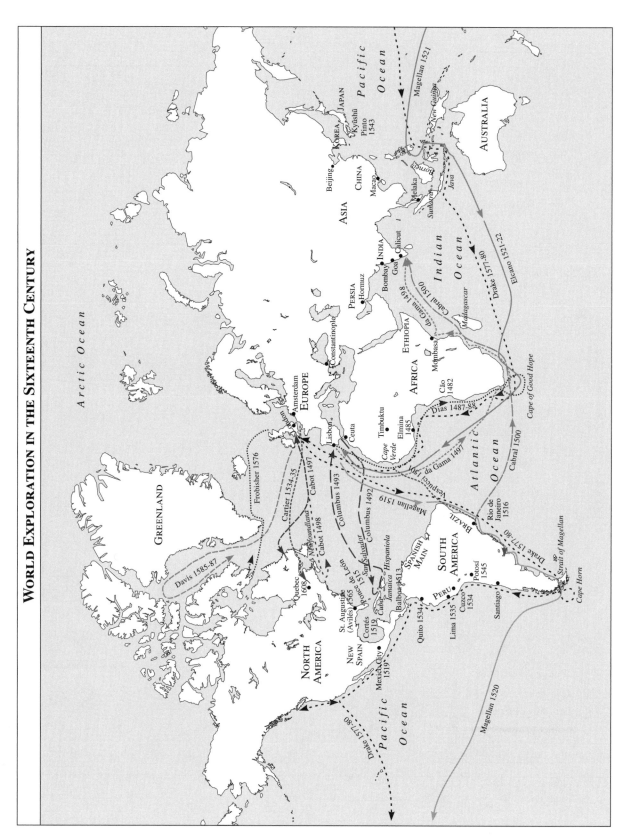

WORLD EXPLORATION IN THE SIXTEENTH CENTURY

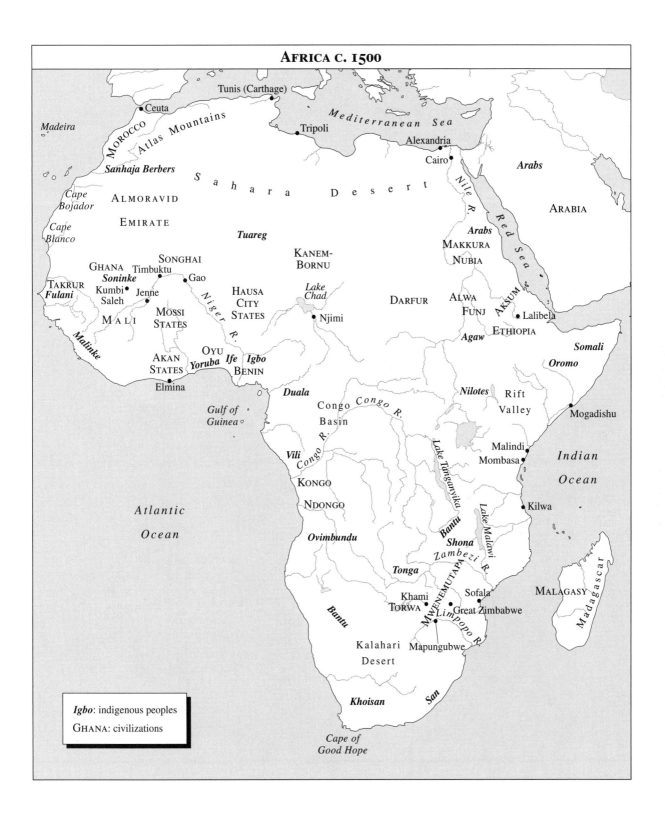

Africa c. 1500

Madeira

Tunis (Carthage)

• Ceuta

Morocco

Atlas Mountains

Mediterranean Sea

• Tripoli

Alexandria •

Cairo •

Arabs

Cape
Bojador

Sanhaja Berbers

Almoravid

Emirate

S a h a r a   D e s e r t

Nile R.

Arabia

Arabs

Cape
Blanco

Tuareg

Kanem-
Bornu

Makkura

Nubia

Red Sea

Takrur

Fulani

Ghana

Soninke

Songhai

Timbuktu

Gao •

Hausa
City
States

*Lake
Chad*

Darfur

Alwa

Funj

Aksum

• Lalibela

Kumbi
Saleh • Jenne

M A L I

Mossi
States

Niger R.

• Njimi

Ethiopia

Agaw

Malinke

Oyu

Yoruba Ife

Igbo

Somali

Akan
States

Benin

Oromo

Elmina

Duala

Congo
Basin

Congo R.

Nilotes

Rift
Valley

*Gulf of
Guinea*

Vili

Congo R.

Mogadishu •

Kongo

Malindi •
Mombasa •

*Indian
Ocean*

Ndongo

Lake Tanganyika

Bantu

Kilwa •

*Atlantic
Ocean*

Ovimbundu

Shona

Lake Malawi

Zambezi R.

Tonga

Madagascar

Malagasy

Khami •
Torwa

Sofala •

Mwenemutapa

Bantu

Great Zimbabwe •

Limpopo R.

Kalahari
Desert

Mapungubwe •

San

Khoisan

Cape of
Good Hope

Igbo: indigenous peoples

Ghana: civilizations

THE AMERICAS: SIXTEENTH CENTURY EUROPEAN SETTLEMENTS

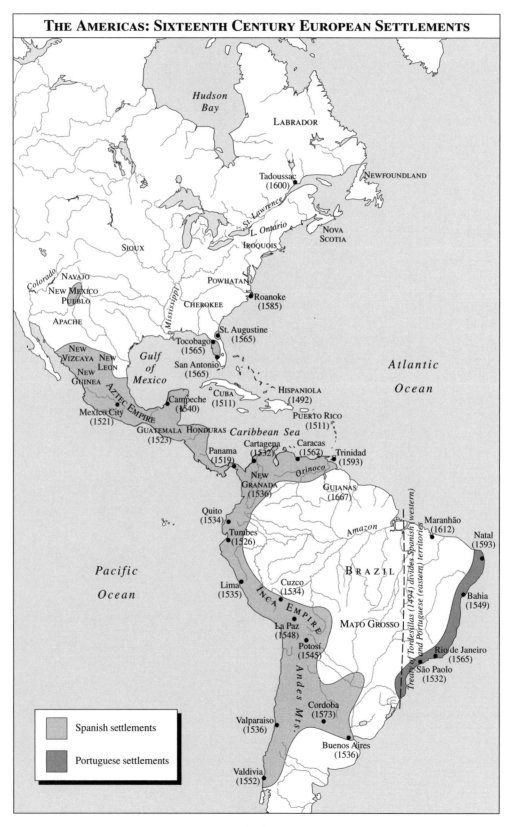

Hudson Bay

LABRADOR

NEWFOUNDLAND

Tadoussac (1600)

St. Lawrence

L. Ontario

NOVA SCOTIA

IROQUOIS

SIOUX

Colorado

NAVAJO

NEW MEXICO

PUEBLO

POWHATAN

Roanoke (1585)

CHEROKEE

APACHE

Mississippi

St. Augustine (1565)

NEW VIZCAYA

NEW LEON

NEW GUINEA

AZTEC EMPIRE

Tocobago (1565)

San Antonio (1565)

Gulf of Mexico

CUBA (1511)

HISPANIOLA (1492)

Atlantic Ocean

Campeche (1540)

Mexico City (1521)

PUERTO RICO (1511)

GUATEMALA (1523)

HONDURAS

Caribbean Sea

Cartagena (1532)

Caracas (1567)

Trinidad (1593)

Panama (1519)

NEW GRANADA (1536)

Orinoco

GUIANAS (1667)

Quito (1534)

Tumbes (1526)

Amazon

Maranhão (1612)

Natal (1593)

Pacific Ocean

Lima (1535)

Cuzco (1534)

B R A Z I L

INCA EMPIRE

Andes Mts.

La Paz (1548)

MATO GROSSO

Bahia (1549)

Potosí (1545)

Rio de Janeiro (1565)

São Paolo (1532)

Cordoba (1573)

Valparaiso (1536)

Buenos Aires (1536)

Valdivia (1552)

Treaty of Tordesillas (1494) divides Spanish (western) and Portuguese (eastern) territories

☐ Spanish settlements

☐ Portuguese settlements

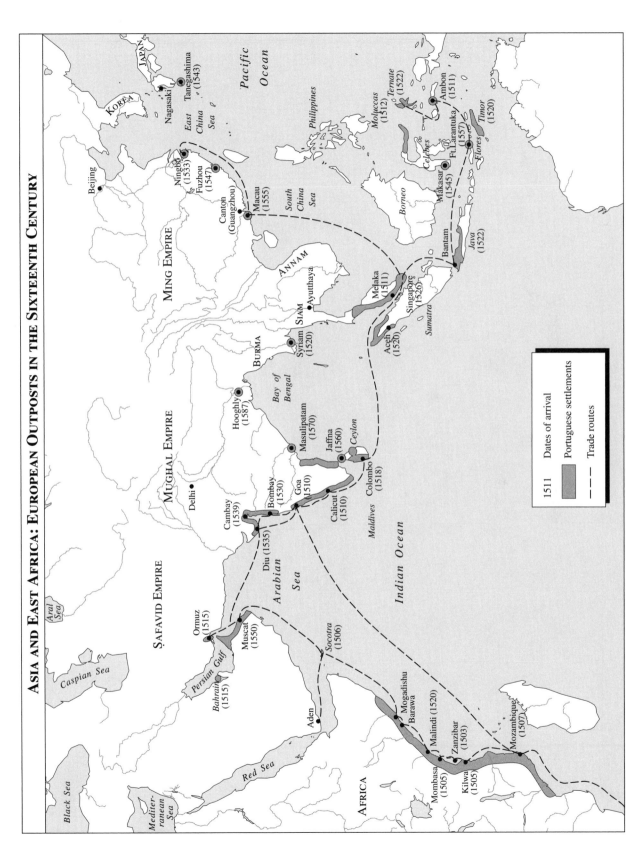

ASIA AND EAST AFRICA: EUROPEAN OUTPOSTS IN THE SIXTEENTH CENTURY

Black Sea

Mediterranean Sea

Caspian Sea

Aral Sea

SAFAVID EMPIRE

Red Sea

Persian Gulf

Bahrain (1515)

Ormuz (1515)

Muscat (1550)

Socotra (1506)

Aden

Arabian Sea

MUGHAL EMPIRE

Delhi

Diu (1535)

Cambay (1539)

Bombay (1530)

Goa (1510)

Calicut (1510)

Colombo (1518)

Ceylon

Jaffna (1560)

Maldives

Masulipatam (1570)

Hooghly (1587)

Bay of Bengal

BURMA

Syriam (1520)

SIAM

Ayutthaya

ANNAM

Indian Ocean

AFRICA

Mogadishu

Barawa

Malindi (1520)

Mombasa (1505)

Zanzibar (1503)

Kilwa (1505)

Mozambique (1507)

MING EMPIRE

Beijing

KOREA

JAPAN

Nagasaki

Tanegashima (1543)

East China Sea

Pacific Ocean

Ningbo (1533)

Fuzhou (1547)

Canton (Guangzhou)

Macau (1555)

South China Sea

Philippines

Melaka (1511)

Singapore (1526)

Aceh (1520)

Sumatra

Borneo

Celebes

Makasar (1545)

Moluccas (1512)

Ternate (1522)

Ambon (1611)

Ft. Larantuka (1557)

Flores

Timor (1520)

Bantam

Java (1522)

1511   Dates of arrival

Portuguese settlements

Trade routes

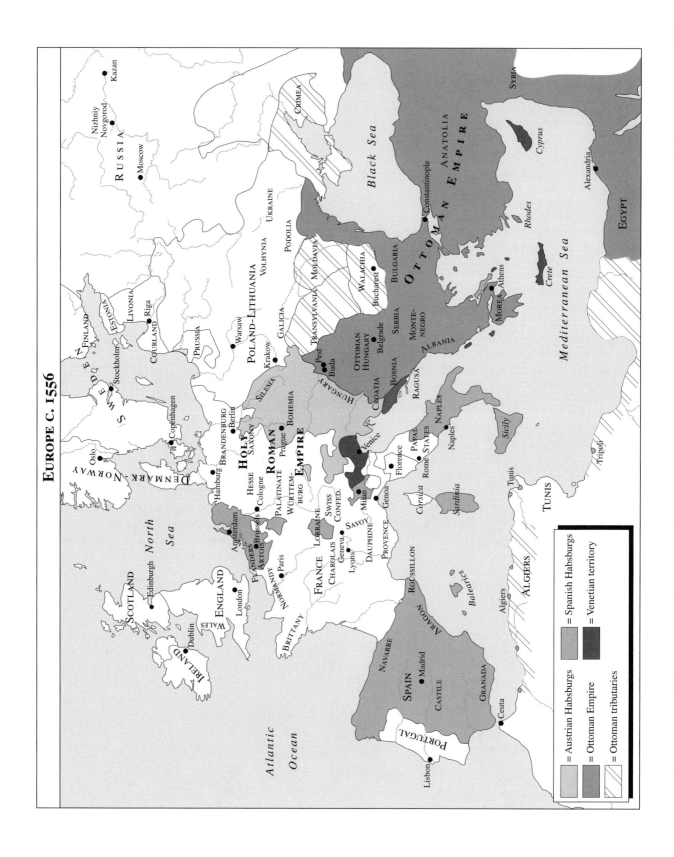

EUROPE C. 1556

Legend:
- = Austrian Habsburgs
- = Ottoman Empire
- = Ottoman tributaries
- = Spanish Habsburgs
- = Venetian territory

RUSSIA — Kazan, Nizhniy Novgorod, Moscow

SWEDEN — Stockholm, FINLAND, ESTONIA, LIVONIA, Riga, COURLAND, PRUSSIA

POLAND-LITHUANIA — Warsaw, Krakow, GALICIA, VOLHYNIA, UKRAINE, PODOLIA

DENMARK-NORWAY — Oslo, Copenhagen, NORWAY

SCOTLAND — Edinburgh
IRELAND — Dublin
WALES
ENGLAND — London

Atlantic Ocean
North Sea
Black Sea
Mediterranean Sea

HOLY ROMAN EMPIRE — Hamburg, BRANDENBURG, Berlin, SAXONY, SILESIA, Prague, BOHEMIA, HESSE, Cologne, PALATINATE, WÜRTTEMBURG, Amsterdam, FLANDERS, Brussels, ARTOIS, Paris, NORMANDY, BRITTANY

FRANCE — LORRAINE, CHAROLAIS, SWISS CONFED., Geneva, SAVOY, Lyons, DAUPHINE, PROVENCE, ROUSSILLON, Milan, Genoa, Venice

PORTUGAL — Lisbon
SPAIN — Madrid, NAVARRE, ARAGON, CASTILE, GRANADA, Ceuta, Balearics

ALGIERS — Algiers
TUNIS — Tunis
Tripoli

Corsica, Sardinia, Sicily, Naples, NAPLES, PAPAL STATES, Rome, Florence

OTTOMAN EMPIRE — Constantinople, ANATOLIA, BULGARIA, WALACHIA, Bucharest, MOLDAVIA, TRANSYLVANIA, SERBIA, Belgrade, MONTE-NEGRO, BOSNIA, CROATIA, HUNGARY, OTTOMAN HUNGARY, Pest, Buda, RAGUSA, ALBANIA, MOREA, Athens, Crete, Rhodes, Cyprus, CRIMEA

SYRIA, Alexandria, EGYPT

1534-1535
OTTOMANS CLAIM SOVEREIGNTY OVER MESOPOTAMIA

In his first military campaign against the Persians, Ottoman sultan Süleyman the Magnificent captured Baghdad and claimed sovereignty over Mesopotamia, the region known today as Iraq. The area remained part of the Ottoman Empire through the early twentieth century.

LOCALE: Primarily Mesopotamia
CATEGORIES: Expansion and land acquisition; wars, uprisings, and civil unrest

KEY FIGURES
Süleyman the Magnificent (1494/1495-1566), Ottoman sultan, r. 1520-1566
Ismāʿīl I (1487-1524), Iranian shah, r. 1501-1524
Ṭahmāsp I (1514-1576), Iranian shah, r. 1524-1576
Selim I (1467-1520), Ottoman sultan, r. 1512-1520
İbrahim Paşa (c. 1493-1536), grand vizier under Süleyman, 1523-1536

SUMMARY OF EVENT
The Ottoman Empire was built on war and steady territorial conquests. Beginning as a small Turkish tribe that migrated to Anatolia (now Turkey) in the fourteenth century, its hereditary rulers, called sultans, achieved a remarkable record of military victory. In 1389, the Ottomans defeated the Serbs in the Balkans, and in 1453, they captured the city of Constantinople (now Istanbul, Turkey), which became their capital.

In the early sixteenth century, the accomplishments of Sultan Selim I included the annexation of Egypt, Palestine, and Syria. The reign of his son, Süleyman I (called "the Magnificent" by Europeans), is remembered as the golden age of Ottoman power and grandeur. In his early campaigns, Süleyman captured Belgrade (1521) and Rhodes (1522), defeated the Hungarians (1526), and laid siege to Vienna (1529).

The expansion of the empire was due in part to its military organization, to the relative weakness and disunity of its opponents, and to its practical policies for governing a large and diverse empire. From the mid-1300's, well-paid professional soldiers called Janissaries included volunteers, war captives, and Christian youths from various parts of the empire. These recruits were converted to Islam, trained with the strictest discipline, and not allowed to marry until they retired from the service.

Despite the Ottomans' reputation for despotism, they allowed a great deal of local autonomy, as long as taxes were paid and order was maintained. In an intolerant age, the Ottomans permitted religious freedom for Christian sects and Jews (called millets), although non-Muslims paid special taxes and were not allowed to serve in the army or hold positions in the central government.

After 1502, the newly founded Ṣafavid Dynasty of Persia (now Iran) became a significant threat to Ottoman interests in southwestern Asia. In 1514, Sultan Selim I, determined to restrain the Ṣafavids, attacked their forces. Prevailing in several battles, he extended the Ottomans' eastern frontier. This began a long-standing rivalry between the two imperial powers. Although the major issue was dynastic hegemony, differences in religion added to the bitterness of the rivalry. The founder of the Ṣafavids, Shah Ismāʿīl I, recognized the Shīʿite form of Islam as the state religion, whereas the Ottomans were committed Sunni Muslims, often claiming the title of caliph (or successor to the prophet) after their conquest of Egypt. Both sects viewed the other's religious doctrines as heretical.

The area that Europeans called Mesopotamia (meaning "between the Tigris and Euphrates Rivers") was the main frontier separating the Ottoman and the Ṣafavid Empires. Mesopotamia therefore became the theater for most of the fighting between the two dynasties. Although almost all Mesopotamians were Muslims, they spoke dialects of the Arabic and Kurdish languages mostly, and they resented external rule by either Turks or Persians. Fragmented into a variety of warring tribes and independent villages, however, the Mesopotamians were in no position to defend themselves against their powerful neighbors.

While Süleyman was busy leading campaigns in the Mediterranean and the Balkans, he was almost powerless to deal with the situation in the east, more than 1,000 miles away. Thus, the Ṣafavid Empire was able to expand its holdings and make additional political alliances. In 1532, Shah Ṭahmāsp I acquired influence over the town of Bitlis in eastern Anatolia, which had been within the Ottoman sphere of influence.

After making a temporary peace with the Habsburg Empire, Süleyman in 1534 gave orders for his army to consolidate eastern strongholds and stop Persian advances. Although it was customary for the sultan to lead the troops into battle personally, Süleyman appointed his trusted vizier, İbrahim Paşa, as commander of an invading army of about 100,000 troops. Süleyman then went on a religious pilgrimage. The Persians, because of their relative weakness, avoided direct confrontations and adopted a scorched-earth strategy. On July 13, İbrahim took control of the mountainous city of Tabrīz in Azerbaijan. Süleyman, always envious of his authority, became disturbed when he received reports that İbrahim was signing himself as sultan. Fearing possible disloyalty, Süleyman hurried eastward to take personal charge of the army.

Arriving in Tabrīz, Süleyman discovered that the enemy's tactics were making it difficult for Ottoman troops to obtain adequate supplies, and he also learned that a Persian ambush had succeeded in killing about ten thousand soldiers. Süleyman decided to move south along the Tigris River and establish a base in Baghdad. When they reached Baghdad, they found it in a state of economic and political weakness. On November 30, the city surrendered without a struggle. The sultan paid respect to its many holy shrines, and he allowed no looting or injury to the inhabitants, which was considered a gracious gesture. One devout Muslim dervish proclaimed that Süleyman had the holy attributes of the Prophet. At just the right moment, a caretaker of the graves claimed to have found the remains of the famous Islamic teacher and jurist Abā Ḥanīfah (c. 699-767). Although the identity of the grave was questionable, both Baghdad citizens and Turkish soldiers appeared to accept the discovery as a sign of Süleyman's divine mission.

After gaining control over Baghdad, Süleyman sent troops to occupy the port city of Basra, which provided naval access to the Persian Gulf. He also made agreements with several local rulers and tribal leaders of Mesopotamia. From his perspective, the great alluvial plain of the Tigris and Euphrates Rivers was important mainly as a frontier stronghold to contain Persian expansion. The potential for taxation was limited because of a long-standing decline in agricultural production—a result of the growing salinization of the soil and reduced irrigation. On April 1, 1535, Süleyman left Baghdad and returned to Tabrīz. Knowing he could not hold such a distant place, he ordered the sacking of the town and destruction of the palace. As his troops marched back to Istanbul, Persian raiders inflicted heavy casualties.

Returning to Istanbul on January 8, 1536, Süleyman remained suspicious of Vizier İbrahim Paşa, whose position was already weakened as a result of his many personal enemies. İbrahim had recently succeeded in having one of his enemies, his chief treasurer, executed on charges of financial malpractice. Before his death, however, the treasurer wrote the sultan a letter admitting his guilt and claiming that İbrahim had joined him in a conspiracy to seize power. It is not known whether Süleyman

believed that the accusation was true. In any case, he invited İbrahim to a private dinner at the Topkapi Palace, where the unsuspecting vizier was strangled by palace executioners.

SIGNIFICANCE

Süleyman had staked out claims to Mesopotamia, but frontier issues would force him to lead two additional campaigns against Persia (in 1548-1549 and 1553-1555). It would take the Ottomans about one century to incorporate Mesopotamia into the empire as three separate provinces, organized around the cities of Baghdad, Basra, and Mosul. Even then, the political situation of the complex region remained fragmented, and the Ottomans never were able to exercise unified control over all of the Arab and Kurdish tribes along the Tigris and Euphrates Rivers. Military leaders of the three provinces, called pashas, would acknowledge the sovereignty of the sultan, but they became increasingly outside his control. Nevertheless, Mesopotamia continued to be a nominal part of the empire until the end of World War I—a period of almost four hundred years.

During Süleyman's long reign, the Ottoman Empire reached almost to its maximum geographical extent. Not long after his death, however, there were clear signs that the empire was beginning a slow process of contraction and decay. There were many factors, including incompetent leadership, internal conflict and corruption, the more-dynamic modernization of European rivals, and growing dissatisfaction on the part of the many ethnic and religious minorities in the empire.

—*Thomas Tandy Lewis*

FURTHER READING

Hourani, Albert. *A History of the Arab Peoples*. Cambridge, Mass.: Harvard University Press, 1991. Written by an outstanding scholar, this readable account includes a great deal of information about Ottoman rule over Iraq and other Arab regions.

Kafadar, Cemal. *Between Two Worlds: The Construction of the Ottoman State*. Berkeley: University of California Press, 1996. Argues that ethnic, tribal, religious, and political affiliations were important to the empire, which saw itself as leader of the world's Muslims and heir to the Eastern Roman Empire.

Kunt, Metin, and Christine Woodhead. *Süleyman the Magnificent and His Age: The Ottoman Empire in the Early Modern World*. Reading, Mass.: Addison-Wesley, 1995. An excellent work that emphasizes the role of Süleyman in the expansion of the empire.

McCarthy, Justin. *The Ottoman Turks: An Introductory History to 1823*. New York: Longman, 1997. A very readable summary of the Ottoman Empire, including a great deal of information about its expansion.

Shaw, Stanford Jay. *Empire of the Gazis: The Rise and Decline of the Ottoman Empire, 1280-1808*. New York: Cambridge University Press. An informed and readable work, controversial because of its emphasis on the empire's toleration and decentralized structures.

Tripp, Charles. *A History of Iraq*. New York: Cambridge University Press, 2000. A general history that includes a useful chapter discussing the Ottomans' conquest and control of the Iraqi region.

SEE ALSO: 1454-1481: Rise of the Ottoman Empire; 1481-1512: Reign of Bayezid II and Ottoman Civil Wars; 1501-1524: Reign of Ismāʿīl I; 1512-1520: Reign of Selim I; 1520-1566: Reign of Süleyman; June 28, 1522-Dec. 27, 1522: Siege and Fall of Rhodes; 1578-1590: The Battle for Tabrīz; 1587-1629: Reign of ʿAbbās the Great; 1589: Second Janissary Revolt in Constantinople; 1593-1606: Ottoman-Austrian War.

RELATED ARTICLES in *Great Lives from History: The Renaissance & Early Modern Era, 1454-1600*: Bayezid II; İbrahim Paşa; Mehmed II; Mehmed III; Süleyman the Magnificent.

April 20, 1534-July, 1543
CARTIER AND ROBERVAL SEARCH FOR A NORTHWEST PASSAGE

Cartier and Roberval led one of the earliest attempts to find a northwest passage to the lucrative Asian trade. Their voyages opened North American exploration and mapped out the principal sites of the future New France, with settlement being the new objective.

LOCALE: Gulf of St. Lawrence and the St. Lawrence River (now in Canada)

CATEGORIES: Exploration and discovery; economics; trade and commerce

KEY FIGURES
Jacques Cartier (c. 1491-1557), master mariner
Jean-François de La Rocque, sieur de Roberval (1500-1561), soldier, courtier, explorer
Donnacona (d. c. 1539), chief of the principal Huron tribe
Francis I (1494-1547), king of France, r. 1515-1547

SUMMARY OF EVENT
From 1492 to about 1534, the exploration of the New World was almost the exclusive domain of Italian sailors. When England and France contested the Spanish and Portuguese monopolies, they employed Italian explorers.

During the 1530's, however, the Italians were replaced by other nationals. John Cabot reported that there were marvelous shoals of fish off the coast of Newfoundland, and word reached the mainland of Europe, prompting fishing boats to brave the hazardous crossings of the North Atlantic to reap the harvest. From these fisheries sprang the beginnings of New France.

Jacques Cartier went to sea early in his life and became an experienced navigator, being awarded the coveted title of master pilot. He evidently visited the Newfoundland fisheries and voyaged to Brazil. In 1534, Cartier was commissioned by the king of France to head an expedition across the Atlantic in search of a northwest passage to Asia. By the time of Cartier's first commissioned trip, Francis I had named him captain and pilot for the king. Cartier's elevated title, as well as his assignment to seek a northwest passage, indicate that the French crown was serious about global exploration.

Politically, French explorations into the Atlantic invited hostile reactions from the colonizers of the Spanish New World and Portuguese Brazil, who, under the earlier terms of the 1494 Treaty of Tordesillas, claimed exclusive rights to all undiscovered areas of the Western Hemisphere. In the economic sphere, Cartier's assignment is part of a broader context of international rivalries that were carried over from before 1492. Just as Cabot's first and second voyages to Newfoundland (1497 and 1498) reflected a strong English desire to gain access to the East Indian spice and Chinese silk trades without passing through foreign intermediaries (traditionally the Italian city-states), Cartier's goal was more than the discovery of new lands. Francis I viewed a possible northwest passage as a potential path to East Asian wealth. What Cartier accomplished during three voyages between 1534 and 1543, although extremely important for the future development of French settlements in the Saint Lawrence Valley, fell considerably short of this goal.

Setting out on April 20, 1534, from Saint-Malo with

two ships, Cartier made landfall on May 10 on an island off the eastern coast of Newfoundland. After exploring the island, he crossed the Gulf of St. Lawrence to Cape Breton and Prince Edward Island, landing on the Gaspé Peninsula. There, upon the pledge that he would return them, he was given two sons of a Huron chief to take to France. From Gaspé, Cartier sailed north to Anticosti Island. Returning to Newfoundland on August 15, he set sail for home and arrived at Saint-Malo on September 5. Although he had not found a northwest passage, Cartier had explored extensively the Gulf of St. Lawrence and its islands.

His own manuscript accounts of the three voyages he made to the Saint Lawrence region provide an extensive narrative of the way of life of the Hurons living in the region, as well as detailed descriptions of flora and fauna. French views of the North American Indians show the biases of this early period of contact between what Cartier called the "civilized" and "savage" societies. Cartier's account of the Hurons during his first expedition left at least two particularly revealing signs of future difficulties the French and other European settlers would face. One was his assumption that the indigenous peoples

were so simple that they could be "moulded in the way one would wish." A second came on July 24, 1534, when his party raised a wooden cross with an added coat of arms marked with the words "Long Live the King of France!" Huron dismay at the French expectation of immediate respect for the symbols of the French state and religion turned into a protest, led by the chief Donnacona. Donnacona met Cartier again under different terms at the end of Cartier's second voyage, when the French forced him and several other American Indians to accompany them as "specimens" on their return to Francis I's court.

As a result of Cartier's favorable reports, French leaders began to think of planting outposts of the kingdom in these new lands. By royal command, the admiral of France commissioned Cartier commander in chief of a second expedition of three ships, which was to sail beyond Newfoundland and discover and occupy lands for France. The little flotilla left Saint-Malo on May 19, 1535. This time, the crossing was imperiled by severe storms, but Cartier reached Blanc Sablon, Newfoundland, on July 15; not until July 26, however, did all three ships assemble there. He had with him the two Ameri-

Jacques Cartier and crew navigate the St. Lawrence River. (Hulton|Archive by Getty Images)

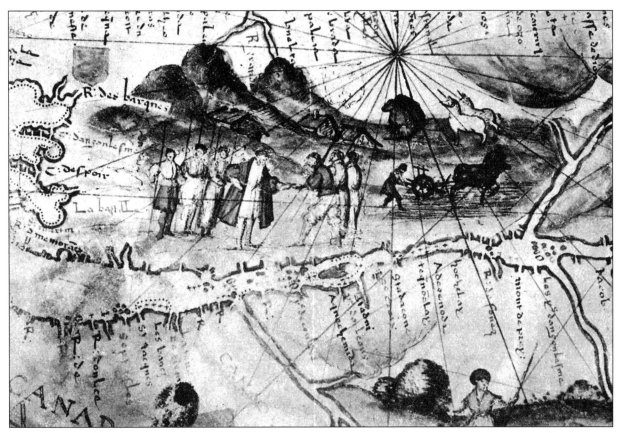

1530's

A sixteenth century map of the St. Lawrence River area, also showing Jacques Cartier and his crew. (Hulton|Archive by Getty Images)

can Indian boys he had taken from Gaspé the previous year. They had learned to speak French and told him of the great river that poured into the Gulf of St. Lawrence, a river he would travel, the first time a European had done so.

As Cartier progressed up the St. Lawrence River, piloted by his two Huron guides, he was welcomed by Indians from the shore. Passing the Island of Orleans, in mid-September, he came to the tribal village of Stadacona (now Quebec City). There he was greeted by Donnacona, who welcomed the return of his two sons but tried to dissuade Cartier from further ascending the river. Donnacona feared the loss of his French ally to the chief of Hochelaga, but ambition and curiosity drove the Frenchman on. He set out on September 19 with the smallest of his vessels, a pinnace, and on October 2 came to Hochelaga (now Montreal, Canada), the metropolis of the North American Indians on the St. Lawrence River. Here the Hurons feasted Cartier and tempted him with hints of a rich kingdom to the west called Saguenay.

From the top of Mont Royal, however, Cartier saw

that the rapids beyond blocked further travel inland, and he returned to Stadacona, above which his men had built a fort. There they wintered rather than risk an unseasonable Atlantic passage. Autumnal brilliance gave way to months of ice and deep snow. Scurvy became rampant but was conquered with an Indian bark remedy.

Musing on the fabled riches of Saguenay, Cartier and his men resorted to treachery. In May of 1536, they kidnapped Donnacona and four other Hurons as evidence to persuade King Francis that further exploration would be profitable. With five other American Indians, who apparently went without force, they set sail for France on May 6. As they came to Newfoundland and passed a group of islands they had named St. Peter's Islands, Cartier's crew realized they were not alone: Boats from France's northwestern seacoast (Brittany) had arrived and begun exploiting the rich North American fishing grounds. On July 15, Cartier was back at Saint-Malo.

From this point on, concern for French settlements, combined with hopes that riches could be gained from finding and conquering Saguenay, tended to replace

507

Francis's original aim of sending explorers to find a northwest passage.

The king, impressed by Cartier's Huron captives, his samples of ores that promised diamonds and gold, and the reports of a land of spices and other abundant resources, determined to develop a colony in the New World—a New France. War between France and Spain interfered with his plans until 1538. Then followed three years of elaborate preparations and diplomatic difficulties. In 1540, Cartier received a royal commission to help lead the undertaking with a grant from the treasury. However, in January, 1541, Jean-François de La Rocque, sieur de Roberval, was given command of the venture, and Cartier's authority could be exerted only in Roberval's absence.

While plans were being drawn up, France's main rival, Charles V, had been informed by the cardinal of Toledo that Francis I was preparing a new fleet for New World exploration and that actions should be taken to thwart its movements. One action suggested was to organize a spy network, including close observation of the port of Saint-Malo. Eventually, two Spanish ships did try, unsuccessfully, to track the French ships sent on the third Cartier mission.

By the spring of 1541, Cartier had procured and equipped five vessels, and on May 23, he sailed from Saint-Malo on his third voyage. Roberval was to follow later. Settlement was now the main aim, although Christian missionary efforts and the search for Saguenay were also important objectives. After a rough Atlantic crossing, the expedition entered the Gulf of St. Lawrence and then proceeded up the river, arriving at Stadacona on August 23. Welcomed by the Hurons despite his earlier kidnapping exploits, Cartier proceeded to settle his colonists beyond Quebec at Cape Rouge for an easier approach to Saguenay. Two of his vessels were sent home with news and samples of spurious minerals. They reached Saint-Malo on October 3. Leaving Vicomte de Beaupré in command, Cartier proceeded to Hochelaga and explored the rapids above it. The events of the winter of 1541-1542 are unknown, except for sailors' gossip later of American Indian attacks, scurvy, and misery.

On April 16, 1542, Roberval, with three ships and perhaps two hundred colonists, sailed from La Rochelle for New France. His delay in leaving to join Cartier had been much longer than he had expected. Part of the problem was the difficulties encountered in acquiring adequate armaments for what had become as much a military mission as a voyage for exploration. In fact, spies for Portugal and Spain had reported that Roberval was prepared to enter Atlantic waters as a pirate and urged the closure of all ports he might try to enter. The ambassador of the English king Henry VIII reported that the French king was uncertain as to Roberval's intentions.

Whatever the circumstances of the splitting of command between Cartier and Roberval, on June 7, 1542, the follow-up expedition entered the harbor of what is now St. John's, Newfoundland.

However, the winter in Canada had been too much for Cartier, and he had abandoned the settlement at Cape Rouge in June and struck out for Newfoundland. At St. John's, he found Roberval's reinforcements. In spite of Roberval's order, he slipped out into the Atlantic and returned to Saint-Malo.

SIGNIFICANCE

The end of Cartier's third voyage marked the effective conclusion of his career as a sea captain and explorer. As for Roberval, he pushed on, ascended the St. Lawrence, and rebuilt Cartier's abandoned settlement. He sent two ships home for reinforcements in September. A difficult winter followed, in which Roberval was forced to resort to drastic disciplinary measures to maintain order. In June, 1543, Roberval began his search for the riches of Saguenay, but he stopped when his boat was wrecked.

By mid-September, 1543, Roberval was back in France, so he probably had given up the settlement in New France by late July. His return marked the end of the first attempt of the French to settle Canada.

Cartier had revolutionized cartographic knowledge by his well-recorded findings, but for the moment neither his nor Roberval's exploits were promising enough to overcome France's European preoccupations.

—*Don R. Gerlach, updated by Byron Cannon*

FURTHER READING

Biggar, H. P. *Collection of Documents Relating to Jacques Cartier and the Sieur de Roberval.* Publications of the Public Archives of Canada 14. Ottawa: Canadian Public Archives, 1930. Combined with the Cartier volume, this collection provides all available information on the voyage.

Cartier, Jacques. *The Voyages of Jacques Cartier.* Toronto, Canada: University of Toronto Press, 1993. A new edition of Cartier's book that attempts to correct misinformation stemming from the earlier translation by H. P. Biggar.

Coulter, Tony. *Jacques Cartier, Samuel de Champlain, and the Explorers of Canada.* New York: Chelsea House, 1993. Brief monograph, geared to younger readers but still informative, detailing the exploration of Canada by the French.

Francis, R. Douglas, Richard Jones, and Donald B. Smith. *Origins: Canadian History to Confederation.* 5th ed. Scarborough, Canada: Nelson Canada, 2004. Textbook on early Canadian history that discusses the cultures and lifestyles of Canadian Indians and Cartier's encounters with them.

Lehane, Brendan. *The Northwest Passage.* Alexandria, Va.: Time-Life Books, 1981. A readable, well-illustrated general history of the long search for the Northwest Passage, placing the significance of Cartier's attempts in broad perspective.

Morison, Samuel Eliot. *The European Discovery of America.* Vol. 2. Reprint. New York: Oxford University Press, 1993. Summarizes the exploits of Cartier

and Roberval in considerable detail. Fine scholarship, detailed bibliographical commentary, and attractive narration.

SEE ALSO: 1490's: Decline of the Silk Road; Oct. 12, 1492: Columbus Lands in the Americas; June 7, 1494: Treaty of Tordesillas; June 24, 1497-May, 1498: Cabot's Voyages; Early 16th cent.: Rise of the Fur Trade; May 28, 1539-Sept. 10, 1543: De Soto's North American Expedition; June 7, 1576-July, 1578: Frobisher's Voyages; Dec. 31, 1600: Elizabeth I Charters the East India Company.

RELATED ARTICLES in *Great Lives from History: The Renaissance & Early Modern Era, 1454-1600:* John Cabot; Jacques Cartier; Charles V; Francis I; Sir Martin Frobisher; Henry VIII; Kalicho; Hernando de Soto.

August 15, 1534
FOUNDING OF THE JESUIT ORDER

The Society of Jesus, popularly known as the Jesuits, was formed as a new monastic order largely in response to influence of the Reformation. It became one of the major institutions of the Catholic Counter-Reformation and sent missionaries to Asia, Africa, and the Americas.

LOCALE: Paris, France
CATEGORIES: Religion; organizations and institutions

KEY FIGURES

Saint Ignatius of Loyola (Iñigo de Oñaz y Loyola; 1491-1556), Spanish aristocrat and founder of the Jesuit Order

Saint Francis Xavier (1506-1552), founding member of the Jesuit order and a missionary in Asia

Peter Faber (Pierre Favre; 1506-1546), founding member of the Jesuit order

Simao Rodríguez (fl. 1534-1540), founding member of the Jesuit order

Diego Laínez (fl. 1534-1540), founding member of the Jesuit order

Alphonse Salmerón (fl. 1534-1540), founding member of the Jesuit order

Nicholas Bobadilla (fl. 1534-1540), founding member of the Jesuit order

Saint Francis Borgia (Francisco de Borja y Aragón; 1510-1572), duke of Gandia and Jesuit priest

Saint Peter Canisius (Pieter Kanius; 1521-1597), Dutch Jesuit theologian

Melchor Cano (c. 1509-1560), Spanish Dominican theologian

Gasparo Contarini (1483-1542), Roman cardinal who championed the Jesuits

Paul III (Alessandro Farnese; 1468-1549), Roman Catholic pope, 1534-1549

Paul IV (Gian Pietro Carafa; 1476-1559), Roman Catholic pope, 1555-1559

Matteo Ricci (Li Madou, Li Ma-tou; 1552-1610), Italian Jesuit missionary in China during the Ming Dynasty

SUMMARY OF EVENT

In the spring of 1521, war broke out between France and Spain over the disputed kingdom of Navarre in the Pyrenees. On May 20, at the Battle of Pamplona, a Spanish knight named Iñigo de Oñaz y Loyola (known as Ignacio or Ignatius since 1537), who was about thirty years old, had his right leg shattered by a cannonball. The French subsequently seized the city and sent Ignatius to physicians who made several unsuccessful attempts to set the leg properly. Ignatius was left with a right leg deformed and shorter than the left. Though a second operation corrected the deformity, it still left him with a limp and consequently ended his military career.

During the long convalescence that followed, the man who would become known as Saint Ignatius of Loyola withdrew to his family castle near Loyola in the Basque provinces of northern Spain. There, he read the few popular works of romance and adventure that were available at the time and out of boredom also took to reading religious literature. In addition to the Scriptures, Ignatius read the German Carthusian Ludolph of Saxony's *Vita Christi* (wr. fourteenth century, pb. 1474; life of Christ) and Jacopo de Voragine's hagiography, *Legenda aurea* (c. 1260, pb. 1470; *The Golden Legend*, 1483).

Until the time of his injury in 1521, Ignatius relates that his life had been wholly worldly and self-seeking. He had been brought up at the court of a great nobleman, where he received little formal education, but where he was thoroughly trained in the military arts, at that time his sole interest. In 1515, he was arrested for brawling. His readings at home in 1521 awakened in him an unfamiliar religious interest.

Toward the end of his convalescence, Ignatius experienced a vision of the Virgin and the Christ child and, by early March, 1522, resolved to go on a pilgrimage to Jerusalem as penance for past sins. He spent some time in retreat at the great Benedictine abbey of Monserrat, and

The Jesuits formed after the first companions of Saint Ignatius of Loyola took vows of poverty and chastity in an abandoned church in Montmarte in 1534. (Frederick Ungar Publishing Co.)

then he went to the town of Manresa near Barcelona, existing as a virtual hermit, begging his daily food, and living in a cell of the Dominican priory or, occasionally, in a cave. He had new mystical experiences and began to sketch out his basic ideas about the religious life, which would by 1548 become the highly influential book *Ejercicios espirituales* (1522-1548; *The Spiritual Exercises of St. Ignatius*, 1736).

Ignatius left Manresa for Rome sometime in late February, 1523, with a view to obtaining papal approval for his trip to the Holy Land. On July 24, he set sail on a Venetian ship and, on September 3, arrived at Jerusalem, only to be persuaded by the Franciscans in charge of the shrines there that no worthwhile work could be accomplished because of the Turks.

He returned home and decided to educate himself. He went to Barcelona, where for two years he attended classes in elementary subjects with the children of the city. In 1526, he enrolled at the University of Alcalá founded by Cardinal Francisco Jiménez de Cisneros. By now, he had acquired three followers who came with him to Alcalá from Barcelona. Although a layperson, Ignatius began to give spiritual advice to those who sought it, and this action aroused the suspicions of the Inquisition, which imprisoned him for a time but did not convict him of heresy.

He was, however, forbidden to teach. To escape this stricture, Ignatius went to the University of Salamanca in July, 1527, where the Inquisition again imprisoned him and again forbade him to teach but acknowledged his orthodoxy. After his release, he walked to Paris, where, in 1528, he enrolled in the University of Paris, first at the Collège de Montaigu and then at the Collège Sainte Barbe. He was desperately poor in Paris and begged for his daily living. He made an extended begging tour of the Netherlands and England to accumulate enough funding for an entire academic year. He received the licentiate in theology in 1534 and an M.A. in 1535. At Sainte Barbe, Ignatius acquired two roommates: Francis Xavier, a fellow Basque, and Peter Faber, a Savoyard. They were to become, with Ignatius himself, the first Jesuits.

By 1534, Ignatius had six followers in Paris: Xavier, Faber, Simao Rodríguez, Diego Laínez, Alphonse Salmerón, and Nicolas Bobadilla. On August 15, the group met in an abandoned church in Montmartre and took vows of poverty and chastity, as members of religious orders customarily did; they also vowed to go to the Holy Land within a year or, if that were not possible, to place themselves in the hands of the pope for whatever purpose he might choose. This meeting is commonly considered to be the moment at which the Jesuit Order was founded, although it did not yet have a name.

Taken gravely ill a few months later, Ignatius returned to Spain and then traveled to Italy, where he settled at Venice to await his companions. Through incredible difficulties, the little group walked from Paris to Venice. A delegation was sent to Rome, where Pope Paul III blessed their pilgrimage, but war between Venice and the Turks made the journey impossible. In 1537, by papal permission, all those in the group who were not yet priests, including Ignatius, were ordained at Venice. At that time they also chose as their title "the Society of Jesus," which is still the official name for the Jesuit Order.

At Rome, where he had gone to obtain Paul III's approval for the new order, Ignatius became immensely popular as a spiritual adviser, but he also attracted animosity for his attacks on a popular preacher of the Augustinian order, whom he accused of preaching Lutheran doctrine. The Inquisition once again investigated Ignatius's case, but again he was acquitted.

The small group at Rome and the others elsewhere in Italy had already embarked on the work of preaching, teaching religion to children, and operating charitable houses. Ignatius and his companions at Rome gave regular theological lectures to Paul III, who came to hold them in high regard.

In 1539, the Jesuits began to draw up their rule, the *Formula Instituti*, which was adopted by a vote of the members. Vows were to be taken and were to be binding under pain of sin, but all members were to have a voice in important policy decisions. There was to be absolute

---

A JESUIT EXERCISE FOR LOVE

The following spiritual exercise written by Saint Ignatius of Loyola shows how one should contemplate "to gain love." Ignatius's exercises include instructions on the type of praying and acting.

Prayer. The usual Prayer.

First Prelude. The first Prelude is a composition, which is here to see how I am standing before God our Lord, and of the Angels and of the Saints interceding for me.

Second Prelude. The second, to ask for what I want. It will be here to ask for interior knowledge of so great good received, in order that being entirely grateful, I may be able in all to love and serve His Divine Majesty.

First Point. The First Point is, to bring to memory the benefits received, of Creation, Redemption and particular gifts, pondering with much feeling how much God our Lord has done for me, and how much He has given me of what He has, and then the same Lord desires to give me Himself as much as He can, according to His Divine ordination. . . .

Second Point. The second, to look how God dwells in creatures, in the elements, giving them being, in the plants vegetating, in the animals feeling in them, in men giving them to understand: and so in me, giving me being, animating me, giving me sensation and making me to understand. . . .

Third Point. The third, to consider how God works and labors for me in all things created on the face of the earth—that is, behaves like one who labors—as in the heavens, elements, plants, fruits, cattle, etc., giving them being, preserving them, giving them vegetation and sensation, etc. Then to reflect on myself.

Fourth Point. The fourth, to look how all the good things and gifts descend from above, as my poor power from the supreme and infinite power from above; and so justice, goodness, pity, mercy, etc.; as from the sun descend the rays, from the fountain the waters, etc.

Source: Excerpted from the online edition of *The Spiritual Exercises of St. Ignatius of Loyola*, by Saint Ignatius of Loyola. Translated by Father Elder Mullan (New York: P.J. Kenedy & Sons, 1914), n.p. U.S. Jesuit Conference. http://www.jesuit.org. Accessed September 28, 2004.

1530's

---

obedience to the pope, but a Jesuit was to deal with the pope only indirectly through his own superiors. Except for houses of study, neither any individual Jesuit nor the order as a whole was to own any property or money beyond what was necessary for immediate needs.

In an important divergence from the practice of all other religious orders, the Jesuits decided that their members would not be required to have communal prayers at specified times of the day, lest this practice interfere with their work in the world. Each Jesuit was instead to pray privately. There was to be no distinctive dress for the order, and no rigorous fasts or penances would be observed, lest such practices undermine the energy that was needed for work in the world.

Despite powerful opposition by two cardinals, the

new order was championed by the most important prelate at the Vatican, Cardinal Gasparo Contarini, and Pope Paul III officially approved it by his bull *Regimini Militantis Ecclesiae* (for the rule of the Church militant) on September 27, 1540. The bull limited the group to sixty members, but this barrier was quickly lifted, and within fifteen years the new order had more than one thousand members. Ignatius was unanimously elected the first general of the order, holding the post until his death on July 31, 1556. He was later proclaimed a saint of the Church. At all times, the order remained faithful to the pope.

From the beginning, the Jesuits were among the leading scholars of Europe, and Alphonse Salmerón and Diego Laínez, early members of the order, were two of the leading theologians of the Council of Trent to argue for taking a strict attitude toward the Protestants, in contrast to the more moderate attitude advocated by the Augustinians and others. Although the Jesuits worked primarily with children and the poor, their high intellectual caliber appealed to the elite. By the end of the sixteenth century, the order had become identified with the education of aristocratic youth at secondary and university levels.

Individual Jesuits also became highly influential as private tutors and confessors to important laymen. Yet, it is important to note that the early Jesuits were slow to become involved in university work because of Ignatius's belief that they should be ready to go on any mission assigned to them and should not be tied to institutions. Their first college for lay students was in the duchy of Gandia in Spain, opened reluctantly at the behest of Duke Francis Borgia, who himself became a Jesuit priest after the death of his wife in 1546 and was eventually made general of the order.

SIGNIFICANCE

The Jesuits soon emerged as powerful opponents of the Protestants. Peter Canisius led a group of Jesuits who were successful in reconverting certain parts of Lutheran Germany to the Catholic Church, and another small group, at great personal risk, was largely responsible for keeping Roman Catholicism alive in Elizabethan England. The order continued to make enemies, including the noted Spanish Dominican theologian Melchor Cano, with whom Laínez once had a bitter quarrel. Pope Paul IV was also unfriendly to the society, although it continued to grow during his pontificate. A protracted quarrel developed between Dominican and Jesuit theologians on the issue of human free will, with the Jesuits

placing greater stress than the Dominicans on the human ability to choose freely their spiritual destiny. Jesuit moralists gained a reputation for laxity in that they usually sought to interpret moral laws in a sense favorable to worldly men.

The phenomenal growth of the Society of Jesus was helped by the period of European expansion, opening up a vast opportunity for accomplishing Christ's commission to "go into all the world and preach the gospel." Because of their early influence on King John III of Portugal, the Jesuits under Father José de Anchieta achieved tremendous success in Brazil and also in Paraguay. They confronted some initial problems, however, in Asia, where there were more complex ancient cultures with established higher religions having their own scriptures and developed religious philosophies. Yet, even in Asia, the initial efforts of Francis Xavier bore fruit in India, Ceylon, Malaya, Melaka, and Japan. The Chinese mission was continued by Father Matteo Ricci. Jesuit missionaries' reports back home—the so-called relations—brought a wealth of reliable information about Asia, Africa, and the Americas to Europe.

By the seventeenth century, the order was one of the largest in the Church and was engaged in virtually every kind of religious activity as well as numerous secular activities. The name of the order became a byword in Europe and America. As Father William Bangert has observed, "apostolic action, Christian Humanism, and the interior ideal of being with Jesus—in order to serve—may help to explicate the singular identity that the Society of Jesus has preserved through over four centuries of history."

—James F. Hitchcock, updated by Narasingha P. Sil

FURTHER READING

Bangert, William V. *A History of the Society of Jesus.* 2d ed., rev. and updated. St. Louis, Mo.: The Institute of Jesuit Resources, 1986. A comprehensive yet concise and reliable history of the society.

Brodrick, James. *The Origin of the Jesuits.* New York: Longmans, Green, 1940. Reprint. Westport, Conn.: Greenwood Press, 1971. Though somewhat dated, this remains a good guide to the early history of the Jesuits.

Conwell, Joseph F. *Impelling Spirit: Revisiting a Founding Experience, 1539.* Chicago: Loyola Press, 1997. Extensive study of the visceral theological experience of the foundation of the Jesuits, based on the founders' proposed papal letter approving the society. Includes bibliographic references and index.

Donnelly, John Patrick. *Ignatius of Loyola: Founder of the Jesuits*. New York: Longman, 2004. A thorough survey of Ignatius's life, work, and ideas; some chapters deal with biographical events, while others focus on Ignatius's thought on a particular issue, such as education or women. Includes illustrations, maps, bibliographic references, glossary, and index.

Dudon, Paul. *St. Ignatius of Loyola*. Translated by William J. Young. Milwaukee, Wis.: Bruce, 1949. A magisterial biography.

Lonsdale, David. *Eyes to See, Ears to Hear: An Introduction to Ignatian Spirituality*. Rev. ed. Maryknoll, N.Y.: Orbis Books, 2000. This classic introduction to Ignatius's spiritual theology and its applicability to contemporary life has been expanded to include a more thorough discussion of gender and a consideration of the nature and meaning of Ignatius's renewed popularity in current society. Includes bibliographic references and index.

Meissner, W. W. *The Psychology of a Saint: Ignatius of Loyola*. New Haven, Conn.: Yale University Press, 1992. A pioneering study of the inner life of Ignatius—his transformation from Iñigo the *hidalgo* to Ignatius the saint—in his gradual identification with Christ through an internalization of the teachings and values of Jesus Christ.

O'Malley, John W. *The First Jesuits*. Cambridge, Mass.: Harvard University Press, 1993. Based squarely on Latin and Spanish sources, a solid scholarly study of the organization of the Society of Jesus.

Ravier, André, *Ignatius Loyola and the Founding of the Society of Jesus*. Translated by Joan Maura and Carson Daly. San Francisco, Calif.: Ignatian Press, 1987. An interpretation of Ignatius and his society. Begins with a chronology of Ignatius and his followers' activities; ends with an analysis of the message and mission of Ignatius. Based on Ignatius's correspondence and his autobiography, letters of some of his close collaborators, and several volumes of the *Monumenta Historica Societatis Jesus*. Contains a bibliography (primarily French sources) and an index.

Young, William J., ed. and trans. *Letters of St. Ignatius of Loyola*. Chicago: Loyola University Press, 1959. Valuable primary material containing 441 letters written by Ignatius between 1524 and 1556.

Young, William J., trans. *St. Ignatius' Own Story as Told to Luis González de Cámara with a Sampling of His Letters*. Reprint. Chicago: Loyola University Press, 1980. First published in 1958, this work is an important primary source on the society and its founder. Ignatius's eleven letters reproduced here are a mine of information.

SEE ALSO: Nov. 1, 1478: Establishment of the Spanish Inquisition; Beginning c. 1495: Reform of the Spanish Church; 1500-1530's: Portugal Begins to Colonize Brazil; 1511-c. 1515: Melaka Falls to the Portuguese; Oct. 31, 1517: Luther Posts His Ninety-five Theses; Aug., 1523: Franciscan Missionaries Arrive in Mexico; July, 1535-Mar., 1540: Henry VIII Dissolves the Monasteries; Mar., 1536: Calvin Publishes *Institutes of the Christian Religion*; 1545-1563: Council of Trent; 1549-1552: Father Xavier Introduces Christianity to Japan; 1550's-c. 1600: Educational Reforms in Europe; 1558-1603: Reign of Elizabeth I; July 21, 1582: Battle of the Tobol River.

RELATED ARTICLES in *Great Lives from History: The Renaissance & Early Modern Era, 1454-1600:* Saint Ignatius of Loyola; Paul III; Matteo Ricci; Saint Francis Xavier.

1530's

December 18, 1534
ACT OF SUPREMACY

The Act of Supremacy declared Henry VIII the head of the Church in England, immediately legitimizing his divorce from Catherine of Aragon, his clandestine marriage to Anne Boleyn, and his subsequent claims to church revenues.

LOCALE: London, England
CATEGORIES: Government and politics; religion; laws, acts, and legal history

KEY FIGURES

Thomas Cromwell (1485?-1540), royal secretary, drafted Act of Supremacy
Henry VIII (1491-1547), king of England, r. 1509-1547
Catherine of Aragon (1485-1536), queen of England, r. 1509-1533
Anne Boleyn (c. 1500/1501-1536), queen of England, r. 1533-1536
Clement VII (Giulio de' Medici; 1478-1534), Roman Catholic pope, 1523-1534
Charles V (1500-1558), Holy Roman Emperor, r. 1519-1556
Thomas Cranmer (1489-1556), archbishop of Canterbury, 1533-1556
John Fisher (1469-1535), bishop of Rochester
Mary I (1516-1558), queen of England, r. 1553-1558
Cardinal Thomas Wolsey (1471/1472-1530), cardinal and Lord Chancellor, 1515-1529

SUMMARY OF EVENT

The break between Rome and the Church in England was brought about by the matrimonial problems of Henry VIII. In 1509, Pope Julius II had granted a dispensation to make it legally possible for Henry to marry Catherine of Aragon. Catherine and Henry did not produce a male heir, and Henry feared that succession of their daughter Mary might cause a disputed monarchy and a return to civil war. Moreover, he was in love with Anne Boleyn, who was not content to be merely the king's mistress.

The ecclesiastical courts could not grant a divorce, only an annulment, and Julius II had made sure that the marriage was valid in the first place. Henry appealed to Rome through his Lord Chancellor, Cardinal Thomas Wolsey, but the new pope, Clement VII, was virtually a prisoner in Rome of Catherine's nephew, the Holy Roman Emperor Charles V. Vacillating between desires to avoid offending both Henry and Charles, Clement appointed Wolsey and an Italian cardinal to hear proceed-

ings in London, but the case was later recalled to Rome.

Disgusted with the long delay, Henry suspected Wolsey of conniving with the pope to prevent a decision from being made and dismissed Wolsey in disgrace. Henry was impatient to marry Anne Boleyn and failed to see why the king of England should have to subject himself to the pope of Rome. He had been orthodox in his religion and had actually received the title of Defender of the Faith from Pope Leo X for a book published in 1521 entitled *Assertio septem sacramentorum adversus Martinum Lutherum* (*Assertio septem sacramentorum: Or, An Assertion of the Seven Sacraments Against Martin Luther*, 1687), which attacked the ideas of church reformer Martin Luther. Thomas Cromwell, a royal secretary, and Thomas Cranmer, a royal chaplain, counseled that there was legal precedent for not acquiescing to the pope's indecisiveness. They suggested that Henry consult on the question of his marriage with the universities of Europe, which saw no impediment to the annulment.

In 1530, Pope Clement VII was free of Charles V's control; he forbade Henry VIII to remarry without his permission and also forbade all general discussion of the matter. Henry's countermove was to arrange for the English nobility to send a letter to the pope urging an annulment and warning that civil war might result if Henry did not beget a legitimate male heir.

In February of 1531, Henry made another move against Rome when he summoned the bishops and threatened them with prosecution under the old law of *praemunire* for having accepted Wolsey as papal legate without his approval. He demanded an enormous fine of 118,000 pounds and extorted from the Convocation of Canterbury a declaration that the king is "only and supreme Lord [of the clergy] and, as far as the law of Christ allows, even Supreme Head." Insertion of the phrase "as far as the law of Christ allows" was made at the insistence of the bishops and rendered the pronouncement ambiguous, but the title Supreme Head was not forgotten.

Meanwhile, Parliament continued with its work of curtailing the independence of the Church in England. Bishops were forbidden to pay "annates," an annual tax, to the pope. Those who had been nominated bishops were to be consecrated even if the pope withheld his approval. The House of Commons complained bitterly about the power of the ecclesiastical courts, and a statute was passed declaring that canon law was subject to the king's approval. Even the bishops acquiesced under pressure.

In August of 1532, William Warham, the archbishop of Canterbury, died. Henry nominated the hitherto obscure Thomas Cranmer to succeed him, and the pope approved in January, 1533. Since at least 1525, Cranmer had been a convinced Protestant and was strongly, though privately, antipapal. He was also secretly married.

Henry had come to realize that he could expect no favorable action from Clement VII on annulment of his marriage, and he submitted the case to Cranmer, who granted a dissolution of the marriage on May 23, 1533. Henry had been secretly married to Anne Boleyn since January of 1533, and she was already pregnant with the future Queen Elizabeth I. When the pope heard about Cranmer's action, he excommunicated Henry, Cranmer, and Anne Boleyn. The following year, the pope gave his final decision on the annulment, which was negative. By that time, however, Henry no longer cared.

Throughout 1533 and early 1534, Parliament continued to enact legislation drafted by Thomas Cromwell. The king alone was given the right to appoint bishops. He could now collect annates and other papal fees. An Act of Succession was passed that declared Mary illegitimate and established the offspring of Anne Boleyn as the true heirs to the throne. The pope was denied all legal jurisdiction in England by the Act in Restraint of Appeals; all appeals from Church courts were to be made to the king's courts. The act declared that "this realm of England is an empire," a formulation intended to imply that the king had virtually unlimited power. Popular pamphlets began to appear that attacked the Papacy and glorified the king.

On November 11, 1534, Parliament voted the Act of Supremacy, the most significant statute of the English Reformation. Formally accepted by Henry on December 18, 1534, the Act of Supremacy did not declare the king Supreme Head of the Church in England but asserted that he already held that position. Although he was not given clerical powers, such as the right to consecrate bishops, the king was given ultimate and full responsibility to maintain doctrinal purity in the Church in England and to supervise the conduct of the clergy. To deny the king this power or to call him a heretic or a schismatic was declared to be treason punishable by death.

Parliament also prescribed an Oath of Succession, which recognized the validity of Henry's marriage to Anne Boleyn and also embodied the title Supreme Head of the Church. The oath could be required of anyone, but it was especially sought from clergy, public officials, lawyers, schoolmasters, and others in sensitive positions. Only one bishop, John Fisher, refused to take the oath;

most of the lower clergy took it and so did most of the laity to whom it was proffered. An exception was Sir Thomas More, who resigned as Lord Chancellor in an effort to avoid taking the oath. He was charged with treason anyway and was executed in 1535, along with Fisher and a number of monks all convicted of the same offense. Throughout 1535, royal commissioners presented the oath throughout the kingdom; the small minority of individuals who refused to take it were ejected from office, and some were fined or imprisoned.

An early rebellion to the Act of Supremacy was the Pilgrimage of Grace, centered in Lincoln and strongest in the north of England. Because it was largely directed at the widely hated Thomas Cromwell, and not at the king, it was controlled quickly.

SIGNIFICANCE

A great consequence of the passing of the Act of Supremacy was Henry's claiming, as head of the Church in England, the revenues that had previously gone to the pope. Also significant was Henry's refusal to bow to any authority outside the English "empire." He adroitly used Parliament to subdue the Church to the Crown by parliamentary statute. The Act of Supremacy demonstrated that the power to make and unmake laws rested exclusively with the king-in-parliament and not the pope in Rome.

—*James F. Hitchcock, updated by Xavier Baron*

FURTHER READING

Dickens, A. G. *The English Reformation.* 2d ed. University Park: Pennsylvania State University Press, 1991. This influential study, recently challenged, presents the English Reformation as rooted in popular dissatisfaction with the Catholic Church.

Elton, G. R. *Reform and Reformation: England, 1509-1558.* London: Edward Arnold, 1977. An account of English Reformation history stressing its lasting impact on legal, cultural, and political life. The chapter on "The Royal Supremacy" is especially informative.

Graves, Michael A. R. *Henry VIII: A Study in Kingship.* New York: Pearson/Longman, 2003. Attempts to separate myth from reality to better understand Henry the man. Good discussion of the relationship between king and Parliament and its historical precedents and effects. Includes bibliographic references and index.

Haigh, Christopher. *English Reformations: Religion, Politics, and Society Under the Tudors.* Oxford, England: Clarendon Press, 1994. The definitive challenge to Dickens's view of the Reformation in En-

1530's

gland. Haigh sees several succeeding Reformation phases imposed by those holding royal and ecclesiastical power and not widely supported by the general population.

McEntegart, Rory. *Henry VIII, the League of Schmalkalden, and the English Reformation.* Rochester, N.Y.: Boydell Press, 2002. Study of Henry's alliance and consultation with the Protestant League of Schmalkalden, analyzing his partial incorporation of German religious ideology into his own theology and the nascent Church of England. Looks at both the evolution of Henry's religious thought and the wider political implications of that evolution. Includes bibliographic references and index.

Marshall, Peter. *Reformation England, 1480-1642.* New York: Oxford University Press, 2003. Extremely detailed, meticulously supported argument that the English Reformation should be understood to begin in the late fifteenth century and to last well into the seventeenth century. Grapples with and explicates the specific meanings of Protestantism and Catholicism to the major players and to laypeople during the Renaissance. Includes bibliographic references and index.

Newcombe, D. G. *Henry VIII and the English Reformation.* London: Routledge, 1995. Intended for students, this history provides an excellent, well-written, and reasonably thorough introduction.

Scarisbrick, J. J. *Henry VIII.* Berkeley: University of California Press, 1968. In this definitive biography, the chapter on "The Royal Supremacy" is full and provocative. Stresses that the English Reformation that resulted from Henry's actions involved a small minority. Official decisions and events were surrounded by English, continental, and Vatican intrigues.

_____. *The Reformation and the English People.* Oxford, England: Basil Blackwell, 1984. This accessible cultural study stresses that the religious changes of the sixteenth century were not initiated by the English laity, but rather accepted often with indifference.

Solt, Leo F. *Church and State in Early Modern England, 1509-1640.* New York: Oxford University Press, 1990. Solidly researched and well-written analysis of royal and parliamentary power that includes detailed examination of the Reformation Parliaments under Henry VIII.

SEE ALSO: 1515-1529: Wolsey Serves as Lord Chancellor and Cardinal; June 5-24, 1520: Field of Cloth of Gold.

RELATED ARTICLES in *Great Lives from History: The Renaissance & Early Modern Era, 1454-1600:* Anne Boleyn; Catherine of Aragon; Charles V; Clement VII; Thomas Cranmer; Thomas Cromwell; Saint John Fisher; Henry VIII; Julius II; Leo X; Mary I; Sir Thomas More; Cardinal Thomas Wolsey.

December 23, 1534-1540
PARMIGIANINO PAINTS *MADONNA WITH THE LONG NECK*

Parmigianino's extraordinary Madonna represents the peak of refinement for Italian mannerist painting while conforming to the dictates of traditional theological beliefs supported by passages from scriptures, Dante, Petrarch, and contemporary poetry. It appeared at a time when values were being questioned throughout Europe in all areas, soon to be followed by a lapse into orthodoxy.

LOCALE: Parma (now in Italy)
CATEGORY: Art

KEY FIGURES
Parmigianino (Girolamo Francesco Maria Mazzola; 1503-1540), Italian painter
Elena Baiardi Tagliaferri (b. 1488), poet Baiardi's sister and wife of the Parma attorney during the papacy of Paul III

Francesco Tagliaferri (d. 1529), her husband, for whose chapel Elena commissioned the painting from Parmigianino
Paul III (Alessandro Farnese; 1468-1549), Roman Catholic pope, 1534-1549

SUMMARY OF EVENT
Elena Tagliaferri, widow of the noted Petrarchan poet Francesco Baiardi, commissioned a painting from Parmigianino on December 23, 1534, to grace the funerary chapel of her husband, Francesco Tagliaferri, with the intention of soliciting prayers to earn indulgences for the temporal release of his soul from suffering in Purgatory. The painting, the *Madonna dal collo lungo*, or *Madonna with the Long Neck*, was installed on the altar in 1542 with an inscription recognizing that it had been left unfinished at the death of the artist two years earlier.

More than thirty surviving drawings indicate that at one stage, the composition had been a traditional Madonna and Child flanked by Saints Francis and Jerome, symmetrically disposed and in normative proportions. Parmigianino modified the composition to reflect changing doctrinal ideas about the subject. Background temples became foreshortened until a single column was emphasized, foreground saints were made smaller and less prominent, angels holding a large vase now crowded the frontal plane, and the central figures became attenuated. A small figure of Saint Jerome holds a scroll in the lower right corner. Parmigianino uses the conventional device of a parted curtain in the upper left-hand corner to alert the viewer to the Madonna as a revelation.

Parmigianino's *Madonna with the Long Neck* emerged not long after Christopher Columbus had sailed west to reach the Americas; when Nicolaus Copernicus was questioning Ptolemy's ideas of planetary motion; when Niccolò Macchiavelli, in *Il principe* (wr. 1513, pb. 1532; *The Prince*, 1640), was recommending a practical approach to politics over old chivalric ideas; and when Andreas Vesalius, in *De humani corporis fabrica* (1543; *On the Fabric of the Human Body*, books I-IV, 1998; better known as *De fabrica*), was questioning the ancient anatomical studies of Galen. Perhaps most important, however, was the recent revolution in religion now known as the Reformation, inaugurated in 1517 after Martin Luther risked charges of

Parmigianino's Madonna with the Long Neck *(1534-1520)*. (Royal Library, Windsor Castle)

heresy to challenge the Catholic Church in the area of dogma, questioning the sale of indulgences, the efficacy of the sacraments, the importance of the priesthood, and the interpretation of Scripture. The overintellection of these decades was followed in the arts by Parmigianino and his contemporaries, who challenged the classical statements of an earlier generation, such as Leonardo da Vinci's *The Last Supper* (1495-1497) and Raphael's *Disputà* (1510-1511; *Dispute over the Sacrament*).

Luther's position on salvation eliminated the need for the Blessed Virgin as intercessor with Christ. Parmigianino's painting, by contrast, supports the Church's position through a vigorous reassertion of Marian imagery. He represents Mary simultaneously in three of her common roles: as *Virgo Lactans* (the nursing Madonna),

Madonna della Misericordia (Madonna of Mercy), and Madonna of the Immaculate Conception. Saint Jerome and Saint Francis (who appears only in some of the preliminary drawings) were strong advocates of Mary's immaculacy, and Francis was also the namesake of the deceased (and of the painter). Jerome was a friend of widows who argued against their remarrying, and also the patron saint of notaries. Consequently, he had a particular resonance for both donor and husband.

The cross on the vase is a reference to the donor, Elena Tagliaferri, whose patron saint was Helena, the mother of the Constantine, who journeyed to the Holy Land in search of the True Cross. It is also a proleptic reference to Christ's crucifixion as Redeemer. The cleaning of the painting in 1982 confirmed art historian Giorgio Vasari's

(1511-1574) memory of it, revealing a palimpsest of the painted cross on the vase held by the angel. The urn is also a reference to Mary's womb as a tabernacle. Such associations are made in many late Gothic writings, such as the *Mirror of Human Salvation* (c. 1324), which relates the Virgin to the Ark of the Covenant, "As the ark contained the golden urn with the manna, so Mary offered us the true manna of heaven."

The Madonna, oversized even as seated although no throne is visible, follows the medieval practice of hierarchic representation for sacred figures and alludes to Mary's sanctity. Her heightened stature is referred to in numerous writings such as Saint Bernard's opening prayer in Canto 33 of Dante's *Il Paradiso* (c. 1320), "surpassing created beings in all lowliness, as in height above them all, Enobler of thy nature...." Parmigianino's Virgin was said to be influenced by passages from the Song of Songs and reflects attitudes expressed in Agnolo Firenzuola's (1493-1543) dialogues on female beauty, but such passages relate to the Virgin with difficulty only as broad metaphors. Parmigianino more likely offered his visual poetry as a response to passages from Petrarch's *Canzoniere* (1470) in praise of his beloved Laura—such as "Some perhaps may think my style is wrong in making her beyond all others gracious, saintly and wise, charming and chaste and lovely," (*Canzoniere* 247: 2-4), or "Your lofty beauty, unequalled in the world . . . seems to adorn and crown the lovely treasures of your chasteness" (*Canzoniere* 263: 12-14)—which echo to a degree Psalm 44:3, "You are beautiful above all humankind."

The painting is often cited as one of the earliest and most prominent forms of a style now known as mannerism, in which the classic proportions of the human form were discarded in favor of elongated limbs, complicated poses, and unnatural proportions. This departure from the normative through distortion of form had a receptive audience at the time, as evidenced in the changes in canons of proportions for the human figure recommended in art treatises after 1530. As the Jansons put it in their history of art, "After 1520, the confidence of the High Renaissance in the almost divine powers of the human spirit was no longer shared by the younger artists; to them, man seemed once again at the mercy of forces over which he had no control." In this respect, mannerism can be seen as an artistic response by southern Europeans to the turmoil of the times and, to some degree, threats from the north that were both religious and political: the Protestant Reformation, beginning in 1517 with Martin Luther's Ninety-five Theses; the sack of Rome in 1527-1528 by the Habsburg emperor Charles V and the attendant gains

for Protestantism and secular authority against the Catholic Church (some historians have even cited this event as marking the end of the Italian Renaissance); and the subsequent erosion of Church authority by monarchs such as Henry VIII with his deliberate reversal of Church authority in favor of monarchial power.

Madonna with the Long Neck is in this respect a quintessential expression of the mannerist reaction to the new crisis of faith and a rejection of the previous generation's use of classic forms to express confidence in the human spirit. Although enlargement was typical for Marys of the *Misericordia* type (it is Mary who is to be interpreted as enlarged, not the lateral figures as diminished), Parmigianino does not represent Mary in normative proportions. Her torso is distended, and even the Christ Child's arms and legs are attenuated, as is the angel's right leg, indicating that sanctity magnifies all who come into contact with it. A litany from Ecclesiastes 24 refers to Mary's growing tall as a metaphor for her increased stature in agreeing to be the Mother of God. Here, Parmigianino's literal interpretation of the passage results in figural distortion. No other Madonna by Parmigianino has such distended proportions. Tallness for the painter was not simply an affectation on his part, but a theme of the painting as a sign of the heightened state of Mary's wisdom in agreeing to be the mother of the promised Messiah.

The column minus its capital reinforces the notion of extension. It is a reference to Mary as a pillar of the Church; a single column is often made prominent in Annunciation and Nativity scenes. It is also a reference to the one who commissioned the work, Elena, because widows were frequently referred to in poems of the times as standing tall "like a column" against the uncertainty of the future. Furthermore, the funerary context of the painting is underscored by the column and vase, two elements often found in ancient cemeteries.

The distended forms give the painting its sense of elegance and refinement, which flatters Mary, because beauty was synonymous with goodness in writings of the time. Its exquisite character also refers to its patrician patron, who would have expected an image of such opulence. Additionally, Mary's modesty is a reflection of her virtue, and her gestures and attitude are those appropriate for a woman as indicated in contemporary treatises on dance. Her eyes downcast in modesty, the gentle placement of her right hand, and the delicate positioning of her foot suggest care and thoughtfulness in the decorum expected of a woman.

In his figure of the Virgin, Parmigianino makes explicit the incipient elegance of Michelangelo's *Libyan Sibyl* in the ceiling of the Sistine Chapel, as Mary's foot becomes a visual fulcrum in the painting. It is the one element that projects beyond the pictorial surface to intrude on spectator space, and it was stimulated by the extended foot of Michelangelo's Madonna in the Medici Chapel. Mary's foot (and her downward glance directing it) conforms with the deliberate measure of space recommended for the female dancer in contemporary dance treatises. The control implied in this detail becomes a signifier of Mary's virtue. This is the same foot that scriptures foretold would "crush the head of the serpent" (Genesis 3:14), an imagery frequently associated with the immaculacy of Mary.

The prominence of Mary's breast as a nursing Madonna, made explicit in Parmigianino's drawings, is a reference to her Son's Incarnation, so necessary a part of God's promise of Redemption. Christ's destiny is alluded to in the cross on the vase, in the column behind as a reference to his scourging, and in his dangling arm, a signifier of morbidity inspired by a relief on a Roman sarcophagus depicting the *Death of Maleager*. The painting thus becomes a proleptic *pietà*, with Michelangelo's Vatican *Pietà* as a frame of reference.

The painting's traditional iconography in combination with its idiosyncratic elements of style place it on the cusp of important aesthetic and cultural transitions besides the general movements mentioned above. The year of the painter's death was also the year of Pope Paul III's approval of the Jesuit order, founded by Saint Ignatius of Loyola. This was followed in 1545 by the pope's consenting to convene the Council of Trent to counter the Protestant reformers. With Paul's reinstatement of the Inquisition by creation of the Holy Office in 1542, this led to a reassertion of orthodoxy and a revitalization of the Church, with Ignatius's Jesuits reclaiming Eastern Europe from Calvinism and extending the faith to India, China, and Japan in the wake of Portuguese merchant fleets.

Significance

Parmigianino's painting inspired numerous copies, attesting to its popularity. It was recorded in engravings by the Florentine Francesco(?) Petrucci (1660-1719) and the Bolognese friar, Giovanni Antonio Lorenzini (1665-1740), and it offered a point of departure for Benedetto Pagni's (1504-1578) *Medici Madonna*, now in Sarasota. But the Emilian cardinal Gabriele Paleotti (1522-1597), in his discourse of 1582 on sacred and profane images, may have had Parmigianino's panel in mind when he

commented that painting the Virgin with "curly hair, pompous and vain garments and ornaments, and even with pearls hanging from her ears . . . turns ones stomach to see."

—*Edward J. Olszewski*

Further Reading

Bambach, Carmen, Hugo Chapman, Martin Clayton, and George Goldner. *Correggio and Parmigianino: Master Draughtsmen of the Renaissance*. London: British Museum Press, 2000. Catalog of an impressive exhibition of Parmigianino's drawings, with five samples of studies for the *Madonna with the Long Neck*.

DeGrazia, Diane. *Correggio and His Legacy*. Washington, D.C.: National Gallery of Art, 1984. Catalog for an exhibition of drawings by Correggio and his followers, with color reproductions. Includes four studies by Parmigianino for the *Madonna with the Long Neck*.

Gould, Cecil. *Parmigianino*. New York: Abbeville Press, 1994. A concise overview of Parmigianino's career and artistic output, with striking illustrations of his paintings and related drawings, accompanied by a catalog of paintings and etchings.

Vaccaro, Mary. *Parmigianino: The Paintings*. Turin, Italy: Umberto Allemandi, 2002. An introductory text that is followed by lavish color illustrations and a catalog of individual works.

See also: 1469-1492: Rule of Lorenzo de' Medici; 1477-1482: Work Begins on the Sistine Chapel; c. 1478-1519: Leonardo da Vinci Compiles His Notebooks; 1495-1497: Leonardo da Vinci Paints *The Last Supper*; c. 1500: Netherlandish School of Painting; c. 1500: Revival of Classical Themes in Art; 1508-1520: Raphael Paints His Frescoes; 1508-1512 and 1534-1541: Michelangelo Paints the Sistine Chapel; Nov. 3, 1522-Nov. 17, 1530: Correggio Paints the *Assumption of the Virgin*; 1532: Holbein Settles in London; 1563-1584: Construction of the Escorial; June, 1564: Tintoretto Paints for the Scuola di San Rocco.

Related articles in *Great Lives from History: The Renaissance & Early Modern Era, 1454-1600:* Andrea del Sarto; Sandro Botticelli; Caravaggio; The Carracci Family; Benvenuto Cellini; Correggio; Lavinia Fontana; El Greco; Catharina van Hemessen; Leonardo da Vinci; Michelangelo; Andrea Palladio; Paul III; Raphael; Tintoretto; Titian; Giorgio Vasari; Paolo Veronese.

1530's

July, 1535-March, 1540
HENRY VIII DISSOLVES THE MONASTERIES

King Henry VIII eliminated the English monasteries in an attempt to place their accumulated wealth at his disposal. He thereby increased the secularization of English society, magnified the already desperate plight of the poor, and significantly changed the cultural landscape of England.

LOCALE: England
CATEGORIES: Government and politics; religion

KEY FIGURES

Henry VIII (1491-1547), king of England, r. 1509-1547
Thomas Cromwell (1485?-1540), chief minister to Henry VIII, 1531-1540, vicar-general of England, 1535-1540, and king's deputy as head of the Church of England, 1536-1540
Robert Aske (d. 1537), leader of the Pilgrimage of Grace
Richard Layton (d. 1544), English priest and royal commissioner for the visitation of monasteries, 1535-1540
Thomas Legh (d. 1545), English priest and royal commissioner for the visitation of monasteries, 1535-1540
John ap Rice (d. 1573?), English lawyer and royal commissioner for the visitation of monasteries, 1535-1540
John London (1486?-1543), English doctor and royal commissioner for the visitation of monasteries, 1538-1540

SUMMARY OF EVENT

In January, 1535, Henry VIII exercised for the first time his newly defined powers as Supreme Head of the Church in England by appointing his chief adviser, Thomas Cromwell, as his ecclesiastical vice-regent with the title of vicar-general. Cromwell had already drafted most of the Reformation acts and had boasted that he would make his royal master the richest prince in Christendom. He proceeded to make good his boast by suppressing 550 religious houses in England.

In July, 1535, Cromwell nominated three lawyers (Richard Layton and Thomas Legh, priests, and John ap Rice, a layman) to a royal commission that was to visit the religious houses, enjoin the inmates to lead stricter lives, and report to the vicar-general on the spiritual and material status of the various monasteries and convents. The commissioners actually went further and dispensed

from vows all religious postulants under the age of twenty-two years and any other monks or nuns who requested dispensations. Religious vows had hitherto been dispensed only by the pope, and the visitors initiated a novel exercise of royal supremacy.

Cromwell studied the reports of the commissioners between November, 1535, and February, 1536. It was a portent of future action when six small houses voluntarily surrendered to the Crown and were suppressed. On March 11, 1536, Parliament passed an act to suppress all religious houses in England with an annual income of less than £200 sterling, which was to affect about 160 monasteries and 60 convents. It was believed that such small houses, having generally fewer than twelve members, could not properly carry out their functions. Furthermore, the commissioners had reported that the moral and spiritual life of the small houses was inferior to that of the large ones.

Members of the suppressed institutions who desired to do so could enter the larger houses of their orders, which had not been suppressed. Others who wished to return to the world were to be given stipends by the Crown; superiors were to be pensioned off with money or lands, while priests were to be permitted to apply for positions as parish clergy. The provisions of the act were carried out quickly and thoroughly by committees of local laymen appointed to assess the worth of the religious houses and arrange for the transfer of inmates.

In October, 1536, a brief uprising in Lincolnshire demanded the restoration of the monasteries together with economic concessions such as the reform of taxation. Most of the rebels were townspeople, but they were joined by some of the gentry and the rural middle class. While the revolt was being put down, a larger rebellion, which came to be known as the Pilgrimage of Grace, took place in Yorkshire. The northern rebels also consisted of townspeople but included several members of the nobility and many of the gentry. Their leader, Robert Aske, sought restoration of the monasteries and the dismissal of Cromwell; he also accused the king of employing suspected Lutherans in his government.

The ranks of the Yorkshire rebels at one point swelled to forty thousand. Representatives of the king promised to summon Parliament to consider the demands of the rebels, and meanwhile issued a general pardon. The rebels dispersed, but all pardons were canceled the following January in the face of several sporadic uprisings. More than two hundred persons were put to death, including Aske and several monks who had been implicated.

Meanwhile, suppression of the smaller houses had proceeded, and Henry VIII and Cromwell began to consider suppressing the larger institutions. Instead of using statutory methods, however, they decided to use coercion. Cromwell brought pressure to bear on superiors to surrender their houses voluntarily; realizing that suppression was inevitable, most cooperated with the Crown in the hope of obtaining favorable settlements. Nearly 250 institutions disappeared in this manner, the last being surrendered on March 23, 1540. Only 3 houses rejected the idea of the Royal Supremacy altogether: the Observant Franciscans of Greenwich, the Carthusians of London, and the Bridgettine nuns of Sion. In these cases, the strongest opponents were put to death and others were scattered.

The majority of religious houses had already sworn to recognize the king as Supreme Head of the Church in England before suppression had begun. Sixteen of the suppressed monasteries survived in other forms: Fourteen were made into cathedral foundations, with the former monks making up the staff and two others became educational centers, although they disappeared soon afterward. The government fulfilled its promise to use the income of the suppressed houses to provide pensions for those who had been ejected, but the lands and other assets enriched the Crown by some 140,000 pounds sterling annually. The Court of Augmentations was created to deal with the many thousands of acres of land acquired in this way, and it gradually sold or leased its acquisitions to private parties.

The reaction to Henry VIII's suppression was rather mild in London, where the early seeds of English Protestantism were being nurtured. The situation in the north, particularly in Yorkshire, was very different, in part due to lingering opposition to the Tudors and a more conservative Catholicism. In 1536, the Pilgrimage of Grace protests took place, attacking both the abolition of papal supremacy (1534) and the confiscation of the smaller monastic properties. The protesters were particularly hostile to Thomas Cromwell. Several thousand men oc-

cupied Lincoln, but they were rebuked and dispersed by Henry VIII. Robert Aske led a gathering in Yorkshire. He was arrested and executed in June, 1537. Martial law was declared in the northern counties, ending any open opposition to the government's religious policies.

SIGNIFICANCE

When Mary ascended the throne of England in 1553 after the brief reign of her sickly brother Edward VI, she restored papal authority but refrained from reclaiming monastic lands. The few religious houses that she refounded were suppressed by her half sister Elizabeth I between 1559 and 1560.

The immediate effect of the suppression of the monasteries was to add considerable wealth and property to the royal treasury. Longer-term impact was more complex. First, the abolition of the prominent role of the clergy in education and government administration encouraged the secularization of society and culture, since the government bureaucracy was no longer composed of minor clergy of the church. Second, it changed the face of England, since the great monasteries were left either to become ruins, like Tintern or Fountains Abbeys, or to become the mansions of the wealthy, like London's

1530's

SUPPRESSION OF THE MONASTERIES

As the self-anointed head of the Church of England, King Henry VIII ordered that monasteries in England be disbanded and their contents inventoried and sold for his gain. Many monasteries were left to ruin and pillage. Presented here is an extract from an account, written about 1591, of one monastery's destruction, as told by the relative of two witnesses.

As soon as the visitors were entered within the gates, they called the abbot and other officers of the house, and caused them to deliver up to them all their keys, and took an inventory of all their goods both within doors and without; for all such beasts, horses, sheep, and such cattle as were abroad in pasture or grange places, the visitors caused to be brought into their presence, and when they had done so, turned the abbot with all his convent and household forth of the doors.

Which thing was not a little grief to the convent, and all the servants of the house departing one from another, and especially such as with their conscience could not break their profession; for it would have made a heart of flint to have melted and wept to have seen the breaking up of these houses and their sorrowful departing, and the sudden spoil that fell the same day of their departure from the house. And every person had everything good cheap, except the poor monks, friars, and nuns, that had no money to bestow on anything. . . .

Source: From *Readings in European History*, by James Harvey Robinson (New York: Athenaeum Press, 1906), pp. 309-310.

Charterhouse. Third, royal seizure of ecclesiastical property endorsed materialistic greed, which the religious houses were at least officially against, but it also vastly reduced the amount of aid available to the poor and homeless since the church, and particularly the monks, nuns, and friars, had been their principal benefactors.

—*James F. Hitchcock, updated by Xavier Baron*

FURTHER READING

Brigden, Susan. *London and the Reformation*. Oxford, England: Clarendon Press, 1990. A brilliant scholarly book on Reformation England that is accessible to the general reader.

Dickens, A. G. *The English Reformation*. 2d ed. University Park: Pennsylvania State University Press, 1991. Challenged by later scholars, this influential study presents a Reformation seen springing from the general populace.

_____. *Thomas Cromwell and the English Reformation*. London: English Universities Press, 1959. This remains an important study, although overly tolerant of an often wily figure.

Dodds, M. H., and R. Dodds. *The Pilgrimage of Grace, 1536-7, and the Exeter Conspiracy, 1538*. Cambridge, England: Cambridge University Press, 1915. Reprint. London: F. Cass, 1971. This older scholarly text is the foundation of later references in general histories of the English Reformation.

Haigh, Christopher. *English Reformations: Religion, Politics, and Society Under the Tudors*. Oxford, England: Clarendon Press, 1994. The definitive challenge to Dickens's view of the Reformation in England. Haigh sees several phases of reformations imposed "from above" and not widely supported by the general population.

Knowles, David. *The Religious Orders in England*. Vol. 3. Cambridge, England: Cambridge University Press, 1959. Knowles acknowledges the corruption of many religious houses but also emphasizes rapacious greed as the principal motivation behind the suppression.

McEntegart, Rory. *Henry VIII, the League of Schmalkalden, and the English Reformation*. Rochester, N.Y.: Boydell Press, 2002. Study of Henry's alliance and consultation with the Protestant League of Schmalkalden, analyzing his partial incorporation of German religious ideology into his own theology and the nascent Church of England. Looks both at the evolution of Henry's religious thought and at the wider political implications of that evolution. Includes bibliographic references and index.

Marshall, Peter. *Reformation England, 1480-1642*. New York: Oxford University Press, 2003. Extremely detailed, meticulously supported argument that the English Reformation should be understood to begin in the late fifteenth century and to last well into the seventeenth century. Grapples with and explicates the specific meanings of Protestantism and Catholicism to the major players and to laypeople during the Renaissance. Includes bibliographic references and index.

Moorhouse, Geoffrey. *The Pilgrimage of Grace: The Rebellion That Shook Henry VIII's Throne*. London: Weidenfeld & Nicolson, 2002. Detailed history of the Pilgrimage of Grace and of Robert Aske, its leader. Includes photographic plates, illustrations, maps, bibliographic references, and index.

Newcombe, D. G. *Henry VIII and the English Reformation*. London: Routledge, 1995. Intended for the schools, this history provides an excellent, well-written, and reasonably thorough introduction.

SEE ALSO: 1515-1529: Wolsey Serves as Lord Chancellor and Cardinal; 1531-1540: Cromwell Reforms British Government; Dec. 18, 1534: Act of Supremacy; Oct., 1536-June, 1537: Pilgrimage of Grace; May, 1539: Six Articles of Henry VIII; Jan. 28, 1547-July 6, 1553: Reign of Edward VI; July, 1553: Coronation of Mary Tudor; 1558-1603: Reign of Elizabeth I; May, 1559-Aug., 1561: Scottish Reformation; Jan., 1563: Thirty-nine Articles of the Church of England; Feb. 25, 1570: Pius V Excommunicates Elizabeth I.

RELATED ARTICLES in *Great Lives from History: The Renaissance & Early Modern Era, 1454-1600*: Thomas Cromwell; Edward VI; Elizabeth I; Henry VIII; Mary I.

1536
TURKISH CAPITULATIONS BEGIN

A series of capitulations, granted to non-Muslims for protection within Muslim lands, were given to France after it requested the military aid of the Ottoman Turks. The Turks capitulated through a binding treaty rather than through a unilateral edict issued by a sultan, and also for the first time explicitly entered a military and political alliance with a Western power.

LOCALE: Ottoman Empire and Europe
CATEGORIES: Diplomacy and international relations; trade and commerce; wars, uprisings, and civil unrest

KEY FIGURES

Süleyman the Magnificent (1494/1495-1566), Ottoman sultan, r. 1520-1566
Charles V (1500-1558), Holy Roman Emperor, r. 1519-1556, and king of Spain as Charles I, r. 1516-1556
Francis I (1494-1547), king of France, r. 1515-1547
İbrahim Paşa (c. 1493-1536), grand vizier, 1523-1536, to Süleyman the Magnificent
Selim II (1524-1574), Ottoman sultan, r. 1566-1574
Mehmed Paşa Sokollu (1505-1579), Ottoman grand vizier, 1565-1579

SUMMARY OF EVENT

Capitulations are based on the Islamic doctrine or custom of *aman*. *Aman* allows a Muslim community or any individual within the community to grant protection to any specified individual or small group of non-Muslims. Only the imam, the religious leader of the community, or the sultan, however, could give protection to groups of unspecified size, such as all diplomats, traders, or citizens of a specified nationality.

Individuals or groups protected under *aman* were allowed to travel or live without harm in Muslim territory and were treated generally as were non-Muslim subjects of the realm. The protection had to be formally requested and required a reciprocal promise of peace and friendship. *Aman* was documented by a *berat*, a document similar to a passport and issued by the sultan or his representative. The issuing officer, or his superior, alone had the right to revoke the *berat*.

From the beginning of the Ottoman Empire, sultans unilaterally granted capitulations to foreigners to promote commerce and to protect the interests of the merchant class. The sultan retained authority to retract a ca-

pitulation whenever he felt that the recipient had broken his pledge of friendship or exceeded the sultan's conception of the prerogatives of the capitulation. Capitulations were, however, granted to serve Ottoman political, economic, or financial needs. In some cases, a capitulation might be granted to enlist a Christian political ally. Commercial rights might be granted to obtain scarce commodities, such as silver bullion, woolen cloth, tin, steel, or paper. In addition, stimulation of trade would increase customs revenues.

Privileges granted under capitulations included the right to establish merchant communities in Ottoman cities, such as the foreign enclave of Pera in Constantinople. Consuls with judicial authority to arbitrate conflicts within these communities also were established.

In the fifteenth century, the Ottomans, combating Venetian dominance of the Levant trade, unilaterally granted capitulations to Genoa, Ragusa, and Florence, in succession. The first French capitulation came in 1517, when earlier capitulations granted by the Mamlūks in Syria and Egypt were allowed to stand after the Ottomans conquered Egypt.

In 1535, war was renewed between Holy Roman Emperor Charles V and King Francis I of France. Francis immediately sought aid from the Ottomans, whose naval forces already were in conflict with the Habsburg Dynasty's fleet. On February 18, 1536, Süleyman the Magnificent and Francis I concluded a treaty negotiation by Grand Vizier İbrahim Paşa that provided a permanent exchange of envoys and a capitulation for the French.

The agreement, modeled on previous arrangements with Venice and Genoa, permitted French merchants to operate under French law in Ottoman territory administered by a French representative in Constantinople. French and Ottoman subjects were granted the right to travel and trade freely in the territories of both nations. They also were granted a favorably low customs duty of only 5 percent on imports and exports.

French consuls were designated to hear all civil and criminal cases arising among French subjects in Ottoman domains without interference by Ottoman court officials. The Ottomans, however, made themselves available to enforce French judgments if requested to do so. Although civil cases involving Muslim Ottomans had to be tried in Ottoman courts, defendants protected under the capitulation were allowed advice from French consular representatives.

In criminal cases involving French citizens, they were excused from appearing before Ottoman judges but were referred to the grand vizier or his agent, where the testimonies of Ottoman and French subjects were to be given equal weight. In contrast, the testimony of non-Muslims had no effect in contradicting Muslim testimony. In addition, the French were allowed complete religious liberty in the Ottoman Empire, with the right to guard the Christian holy places. In effect, this amounted to a French protectorate over all Catholic inhabitants of the Ottoman Empire.

Also, all Christian ships, with the exception of Venetian vessels, were required to fly the French flag for protection in Ottoman waters. The trade agreement was soon followed by a secret military alliance directed against Charles V, the Holy Roman Emperor and king of Spain. Finally, the king of France, alone among European sovereigns, was henceforth treated as an equal by the sultan, to be addressed as *padishah* in the same manner as the sultan, rather than as a *bey*.

The capitulation of 1536, however, was never fully implemented and, after the death of Francis I, Ottoman-French relations cooled. Stress that was attendant on the advent of the Ottoman-Venetian wars of 1570-1573 caused a revival of the Ottoman-French accord. On October 19, 1569, a new capitulatory agreement, negotiated by Mehmed Paşa Sokollu, was signed by Selim II. This agreement restored the former Ottoman-French capitulations, which then persisted, with modifications, suspensions, and renewals, until the sultanate was abolished. Under the 1569 capitulation, all other Western nations were obliged to sail and trade under the French flag. One result of this situation was that, by the beginning of the seventeenth century, Levantine trade accounted for half of all French trade.

SIGNIFICANCE

Capitulations began to infringe on Ottoman sovereignty, however, amounting to special concessions deleterious to the Turkish economy. Still, England was granted a trade monopoly in 1580 between Egypt and Istanbul, and a British consulate was opened in Egypt. Following the Franco-Spanish rapprochement of 1573, the English and Dutch became stronger rivals of the Habsburgs than were the French, leading to their being granted Ottoman capitulations.

The French capitulations again were revised and reenacted in 1739, the most extensive ever granted. In addition, extraordinary and exclusive privileges were granted to French traders in Ottoman territories. Special rights were granted to Roman Catholic monks in the Holy Land and generally to Catholics throughout the Ottoman Empire. Ultimately, these Latin rights in the Holy Land under this capitulation, which had come to be usurped by the Orthodox Church, became a pretense for Louis-Napoleon Bonaparte in helping to precipitate the Crimean War in 1854. The Treaty of Lausanne, however, finally abolished capitulations in 1923.

—Ralph L. Langenheim, Jr.

FURTHER READING

Fisher, Sydney Nettleton, and William Ochsenwald. *The Middle East: A History.* 6th ed. Boston: McGraw-Hill, 2004. Chapter 18 of this well-known general history is entitled "The Ottoman Empire as a World Power." Provides a comprehensive review of the major events of Süleyman's reign.

Goffman, Daniel. *The Ottoman Empire and Early Modern Europe.* New York: Cambridge University Press, 2002. Reconsideration of the Ottoman Empire, arguing that it should be understood as part of Renaissance Europe, rather than as a "world apart," isolated and exotic.

Inalcik, Halıl. *The Ottoman Empire: Conquest, Organization, and Economy.* London: Variorum Reprints, 1978. Includes a concise definition of the nature of a capitulation.

Kinross, Lord. *The Ottoman Centuries: The Rise and Fall of the Turkish Empire.* New York: William Morrow, 1977. A comprehensive history emphasizing cultural and economic factors and political changes.

_____. *The Ottoman Empire: The Classical Age, 1300-1600.* Translated by Norman Itzkowitz and Colin Imber. New Rochelle, N.Y.: Aristide D. Caratazas, 1973. Discusses the politics of capitulations and their effect on Ottoman society.

Kunt, Metin, and Christine Woodhead, eds. *Süleyman the Magnificent and His Age: The Ottoman Empire in the Early Modern World.* New York: Longman, 1995. Anthology of essays covering the genesis of the Ottoman Empire, the policies and problems faced by the empire in the sixteenth century, and Süleyman's reign in the context of those problems.

Marriott, J. A. R. *The Eastern Question: An Historical Study in European Diplomacy.* 4th ed. Reprint. Oxford, England: Clarendon Press, 1958. Covers the character and effects of the capitulations from the reign of Süleyman I to 1916.

Palmer, Alan. *The Decline and Fall of the Ottoman Empire.* New York: Barnes & Noble Books, 1994. Palmer describes the progressively less favorable terms of the capitulations that were offered subsequent to the reign of Süleyman I and examines their destructive consequences.

Richardson, Glenn. *Renaissance Monarchy: The Reigns of Henry VIII, Francis I, and Charles V.* New York: Oxford University Press, 2002. Comparison of Francis I to two other monarchs who helped define Renaissance government and culture. Focuses on their careers as warriors, governors, and patrons. Includes maps, bibliographic references, and index.

Shaw, Stanford. *Empire of the Gazis: The Rise and Decline of the Ottoman Empire, 1280-1808.* Vol. 1 in *History of the Ottoman Empire and Modern Turkey.* Cambridge, England: Cambridge University Press, 1976. Shaw outlines the concept of capitulations, discusses many individual capitulation agreements, and describes the effect of the policy on the Ottoman economy.

SEE ALSO: Dec. 31, 1600: Elizabeth I Charters the East India Company.

RELATED ARTICLES in *Great Lives from History: The Renaissance & Early Modern Era, 1454-1600:* Charles V; Elizabeth I; Francis I; İbrahim Paşa; Süleyman the Magnificent.

1536 and 1543
ACTS OF UNION BETWEEN ENGLAND AND WALES

Acts of unification altered the political and religious structure of England and Wales, giving Wales representation in Parliament. The Acts heralded for Great Britain unexpected, significant, and long-lasting educational, cultural, social, judicial, and economic changes, which have continued into the twenty-first century.

LOCALE: England and Wales

CATEGORIES: Government and politics; expansion and land acquisition; laws, acts, and legal history

KEY FIGURES

Thomas Cromwell (1485?-1540), King Henry VIII's chief minister

Rowland Lee (d. 1543), head of the Council for Wales, 1534-1543

SUMMARY OF EVENT

An independent Wales began its decline when Prince Llywelyn ap Gruffudd signed the Treaty of Montgomery in 1267, acknowledging Henry III of England as his liege (feudal) lord. Rebellions against Edward I and Edward II led to further invasions and subjugation, and English castles and merchants settled at strategic locations. Edward I killed Llywelyn in 1282.

The 1284 Statute of Rhuddlan divided Wales into counties, marcher (border region) lordships, and a principality. It also subjugated Welsh lands to the English crown, voided local traditions, and gave precedence to English law. Edward I proclaimed his heir prince of Wales, and Edward IV established a Council for Wales, which would have broad powers.

In spite of efforts to limit the privileges of the marcher lords by subsequent kings, Wales remained an amalgam of diverse governance and lax enforcement until the English Reformation, England's break with the Papacy and the Catholic Church that started with the Reformation Parliament, which met from 1529 to 1536. A fear of foreign invasion, a desire to consolidate royal control, and a desire to stabilize the administration of justice, combined with a wish to spread the Reformation and pacify Anglo-Welsh borderlands, prompted Henry VIII to unify England and Wales.

Thomas Cromwell, King Henry VIII's chief minister and the architect of both the Union and the English Reformation, sought to end the use of Wales as a refuge for outlaws and to bring the country within English administration under tighter royal control. He appointed Bishop Rowland Lee president of the Council in the Marches of Wales, with orders to pacify the region. Bishop Lee prosecuted thieves, felons, and corrupt officials of all ranks vigorously. He executed several thousand people, including some of the gentry. By 1543, he brought a high degree of "order and quiet" to the circuits he served. Lee was both feared and respected, and his name became a term of approbation among the Welsh.

In 1534, Parliament passed laws allowing for the punishment of jurors committing perjury and laws stopping ferrymen from abetting thieves and fugitives. Other laws were enacted to aid in the enforcement of writs and to

1530's

discourage wrongful imprisonment and attacks on officials. These laws treated the principality, the marches, and the shires as one area; enhanced the powers of the council; curtailed local privileges; and allowed English justices of the peace to intervene in Wales.

The first of the two laws known as the Acts of Union was enacted in 1536. Wales was reconstituted into thirteen counties (from six original counties); small areas were appended to Shropshire, Herefordshire, and Gloucestershire; and Wales initially gained twenty-six seats in the English parliament. English was made the official written and spoken language of all officeholders and in all legal and administrative matters. A chancery and an exchequer were established at Denbigh and Brecknock, and many outdated practices were abolished.

Primogeniture replaced the Welsh practice of subdividing inherited lands among all sons. The shire administration followed that of England with justices of the peace, sheriffs, coroners, and so on. The same taxes and church hierarchy applied to Wales, and Henry VIII's governance of the Church of England was generally acknowledged. The subsidy of 1542 was the first collected in Wales, and it raised more than 4,000 pounds.

The implementation of the act suffered many delays, caused by the lack of adequate officials and difficult boundary disputes. In 1542, the Welsh elected their first parliamentary representatives. The Welsh member arrived in time to hear consideration of the Act for Certain Ordinances in Wales, which constitutes the second part of the Acts of Union, approved in 1543.

This bill approved the transfer of bishoprics, acknowledged more boundary changes, and provided one parliamentary seat for Haverfordwest, which increased Welsh representation to twenty-seven. It also effectively nullified all Welsh penal laws.

The powers of the Council in the Marches of Wales were increased. It became the chief administrative organ in Wales, and it had the power to refer matters to the king. The council changed from a prerogative jurisdiction to a statutory body as well. The Court of Great Session, already extant in three counties of Northwest Wales, was extended by three more circuits to cover all of Wales except Monmouth, which was served by the Oxford Assize Circuit. The Court of Great Session fulfilled the functions of Kings Bench, Common Pleas, and the Assize courts in England, and handled appeals to the king. The act also authorized the Lord Chancellor to appoint eight justices of the peace in each county to hold quarter sessions in each. They became the ruling judicial and administrative body in their respective counties.

A sheriff, nominated by the Council in the Marshes of Wales and chosen by the Privy Council, was appointed for one year and compensated locally. Details for selecting lower-ranked officials from constables to coroners were included in the act, which also introduced the 40 shilling freehold as the basis for voting rights in Wales. These changes effectively shifted loyalties from the locality to the county level and brought a degree of social reorientation. Although Henry had the power to delay or modify all provisions of the act for three years, he did not.

The shire system created by the union survived to 1974, while the council lasted to the Glorious Revolution of 1690; the Court of Great Session continued to 1830. Territorial boundaries were permanently and clearly defined by these acts. They gave both nations a uniform legal system, an expanded national defense, a legislature, similar administrative structures, a common church governed by one monarch, and a more effective administration of justice. The large population increase in Wales in subsequent generations has been attributed to the increased security brought about by these changes.

These changes propelled the major social developments that were extant before the Union. The landed families and the aristocracy benefited from the abolition of the privileges of the marcher lords, the gradual suppression of violence and crime, the increasing reduction in corruption, and the redistribution of ecclesiastical properties. They improved their command of the English language, filled the offices created by the Union, and availed themselves of opportunities in England. There were eighteen English primary schools in Wales by 1603, and Oxford attracted many of their graduates. Jesus College was established in 1471 to assist Welsh students.

It has often been asserted that the working class and the poor, who spoke Welsh only, were cheated and exploited by some of the new officials. The requirement for using English in all official proceedings provided many opportunities for chicanery and opened a divide between Welsh- and English-speaking groups throughout society.

By 1547, William Salesbury's *Dictionary in English and Welsh* was in print and circulating widely, as were an assortment of calendars, ballads, prayers, poems, and primers in both tongues. These helped to bridge the language divide.

Acts of the English Reformation had earlier applied to Wales, but the Union brought greater attention to their enforcement. The Welsh clergy overwhelmingly subscribed to the supremacy oath, though it is doubtful that more than a tiny percentage of them could perform services in English as required by the Union. While in Wales there was sympathy for Queen Catherine and resentment of Queen Anne among the populace, neither the uprising known as the Pilgrimage of Grace (1536-1537) nor protests against the Book of Common Prayer of 1549 had much appeal.

With the development of the Union, a commission was created by Thomas Cromwell to evaluate the status of religious houses and church properties. Five dozen monasteries, nunneries, and friaries—the entire number in the area—were disbanded, their 250 clergy pensioned off, and their property and treasures sold at a discount. The state also sold, rented, or transferred vast amounts of land to the gentry at a fraction of their true value. Endowments and church livings (properties) were used to reward the new servants of the Tudor state, and Wales was deprived of most of its medieval architectural heritage.

Despite this clerical impoverishment, the reformed religion gained adherents in Wales. After 1547, most of the newly appointed bishops were Welsh, the Book of Common Prayer was printed in Welsh (1553), and a popular rendering of the Bible was published in Welsh in 1588. The willingness of the church to ignore the use of Welsh in services and the popularity of Welsh scriptures and hymns usually are credited with inspiring a flowering of Welsh literature and poetry in the Elizabethan era.

SIGNIFICANCE

The Acts of Union opened English educational, military, professional, and government establishments to the Welsh, such as the ambitious Dafydd Seisyllt, whose grandson anglicized his name, attained great office during Edward VI's reign, and achieved fame as Queen Elizabeth's key statesman, William Cecil.

After years of autonomy from the rest of Great Britain and the European continent, the Union, in effect, subdued Wales and aligned it with the English Empire. Welsh scientists and soldiers, intellectuals and laborers, would come to England in the face of a strong tradition of Welsh cultural preservation.

—*Sheldon Hanft*

FURTHER READING

Black, Jeremy. *A New History of Wales*. Stroud, Gloucestershire, England: Sutton, 2000. Black explores the structural and communal changes brought by the acts as part of a thematic explanation of the evolution of modernity and nationalism in Wales.

Davies, John. *The Making of Wales*. Stroud, Gloucestershire, England: Allen Sutton, 1999. A concise account of the union, with illustrations and broader cultural considerations.

Jones, Gareth Elwyn. *Modern Wales: A Concise History*. 2d ed. New York: Cambridge University Press, 1994. A thematic account that evaluates the Union as an aspect of the "Tudor revolution in government" rather than a new initiative on the part of Cromwell or Henry VIII to integrate the two realms.

Williams, Glanmor. *Recovery, Reorientation, and Reformation in Wales, c. 1415-1642*. New York: Oxford University Press, 1987. Chapters 11 to 13 provide a very detailed account of the political, social, and religious events and consequences of the Union.

SEE ALSO: 1531-1540: Cromwell Reforms British Government.

RELATED ARTICLES in *Great Lives from History: The Renaissance & Early Modern Era, 1454-1600:* Anne Boleyn; Catherine of Aragon; Thomas Cromwell; Elizabeth I; Henry VIII.

1530's

March, 1536
CALVIN PUBLISHES *INSTITUTES OF THE CHRISTIAN RELIGION*

Calvin's theology, fundamentally similar to that of Martin Luther, was outlined in his Institutes of the Christian Religion, *the most important book of the Protestant Reformation. Calvin, however, strongly insisted on the import of predestination to Protestant theology and was more critical of the Catholic Church than was Luther. The work stirred into action Protestants throughout Europe.*

LOCALE: Basel, Switzerland
CATEGORIES: Religion; cultural and intellectual history

KEY FIGURES

John Calvin (1509-1564), French Protestant leader who fled from Paris to Switzerland

Nicholas Cop (fl. sixteenth century), rector of the University of Paris in 1533

Francis I (1494-1547), king of France, r. 1515-1547, who was determined to suppress Protestantism

Marguerite de Navarre (1492-1549), sister of Francis, who sympathized with certain Protestants

Martin Luther (1483-1546), German Protestant leader

Huldrych Zwingli (1484-1531), Swiss Protestant leader

Guillaume Farel (1489-1565), French Protestant leader who settled in Geneva

Martin Bucer (1491-1551), German Protestant reformer who later worked in England

SUMMARY OF EVENT

On All Saints' Day, November 1, 1533, a young professor named Nicholas Cop was installed in the honorary post of rector of the University of Paris. In his inaugural address, he spoke of certain abuses in the Catholic Church and called for a return to a simpler, more biblical form of Christianity. The address was not extremely radical, and the so-called Christian humanists had been promulgating similar views for some time, but Francis I, king of France, was determined to suppress all signs of Protestantism in his capital, and Cop's speech caused a sensation. Cop and several of his followers had to flee from Paris, where fifty persons were arrested on suspicion of complicity with him.

Among those who fled was a twenty-four-year-old scholar named John Calvin, a close friend of Cop who may have written the celebrated address for him. Calvin came from a French family that had close business ties with the Church, but his father and his brother had quar-

reled with Church authorities in their native town of Noyon; both died excommunicate. Young John Calvin was apparently destined for the priesthood, but when studying at Paris, he came under the influence of the still relatively new Christian humanism that stressed study of the ancient classics. Calvin studied Latin, Greek, and Hebrew avidly, and he published a commentary on the Roman moralist Seneca.

Probably at his father's behest he also turned his attention to law; he studied both law and classics at Paris Orléans and at Bourges. About the time of Cop's inaugural address, he underwent a religious conversion, which changed his earlier apathy to eager participation in the new evangelical faith of Martin Luther and others.

After fleeing Paris he spent some time at the court of Marguerite de Navarre, the sister of Francis I, who had strong Protestant leanings. There he studied and meditated, formulating his theological position, and after a brief return visit to Paris, he decided to leave France because of continuing persecution.

John Calvin. (R. S. Peale and J. A. Hill)

He went to Basel in Switzerland, a town that was hospitable to a number of prominent religious refugees. There he composed the first edition of his great work, *Christianae religionis institutio* (*Institutes of the Christian Religion*, 1561), which he completed in the summer of 1535 but which was not published until March, 1536.

The original edition of *Institutes of the Christian Religion*, a master work of the Reformation, was a small piece along the lines of a catechism. During the remainder of his life Calvin revised it repeatedly, and the final definitive edition was published in 1559.

In most respects Calvin's theology did not differ materially from that of Martin Luther, whose work Calvin had read and admired. Like Luther, he asserted the total sinfulness and depravity of humans, and denied that humans have free will. Thus, humans can in no way seek their own salvation, and all their works are without value.

These ideas led directly to the concept for which Calvin is most famous—

CALVIN ON FREE WILL AND PREDESTINATION

Protestant reformer John Calvin, a contemporary of Martin Luther, outlined his reformist theology in his highly influential work Institutes of the Christian Religion. *Calvin had strong views on human free will, predestination, and the ultimate power of God's grace.*

"By means of liberty [Saint Augustine said] it came to pass that man fell into sin; but now the penal depravity consequent on it, instead of liberty, has introduced necessity." And whenever the mention of this subject occurs, he hesitates not to speak in this manner of the necessary servitude of sin. We must therefore observe this grand point of distinction, that man, having been corrupted by his fall, sins voluntarily, not with reluctance or constraint; with the strongest propensity of disposition, not with violent coercion; with the bias of his own passions, and not with external compulsion. . . .

We shall never be clearly convinced as we ought to be, that our salvation flows from the fountain of God's free mercy, till we are acquainted with his eternal election, which illustrates the grace of God by this comparison, that He adopts not all promiscuously to the hope of salvation, but gives to some what He refuses to others. Ignorance of this principle evidently detracts from the divine glory and diminishes real humility. But, according to Paul, what is so necessary to be known never can be known, unless God, without any regard to works, chooses those whom He has decreed.

Source: Excerpted in *The Portable Renaissance Reader*, edited by James Bruce Ross and Mary Martin McLaughlin (New York: Viking Press, 1968), pp. 707, 709.

1530's

---

predestination, an idea that is present in Luther's theology but is not stressed as much as it is by Calvin. The concept of predestination sees God as arbitrarily choosing to grant salvation to certain souls, the elect, who have no control over their own destinies. Conversely, the majority of humans are also damned through God's inscrutable will, although by their totally sinful natures they fully deserve eternal punishment in hell.

Calvin went further than Luther in repudiating the Catholic Church. While Luther continued to insist that Christ is physically present in the Eucharist, Calvin called Christ's presence merely spiritual. Luther retained ceremonial worship, but Calvin introduced a simple, austere service in which the sermon was central. Both reformers made the Bible the center of belief and the sole guide to human conduct. *Institutes of the Christian Religion* included a plea to Francis I to cease persecuting the Protestants and sought to convince the king of the rightness of the reformed beliefs.

After publishing his work, Calvin made a last brief visit to Paris, and then set out for the city of Strasbourg, but wartime conditions caused him to travel by way of Geneva, an incident that altered the entire course of his

life. About half of Switzerland was Protestant at that time as a result of the work of Huldrych Zwingli of Zurich, who had been killed in battle in 1531. Protestant reform had been effected in Geneva by Guillaume Farel, a fiery French preacher who had settled there. Farel was impressed with Calvin and urged him to stay in Geneva. Calvin at first refused, but Farel insisted that if he left he would violate God's command for him to stay there. Reluctantly, Calvin agreed to remain as one of the town's clergy.

From the beginning he played a central role, writing incessantly and composing a set of articles for the organization of the Genevan church, which was accepted by the town authorities. Many Genevans opposed Calvin and Farel, however. The city of Berne was attempting to take over leadership of the Swiss Protestant movement, and a majority of the city council of Geneva imposed liturgical changes in conformity to the dictates of Berne. On principle, Calvin and Farel refused to accept such changes, and they were expelled.

Calvin went to his original destination, Strasbourg, at the invitation of Martin Bucer, the influential South German reformer who presided over the Strasbourg church.

Bucer and Calvin became close friends. Calvin was appointed pastor to the French refugees in the city, and it was there that he married. His friends in Geneva continued to agitate for his return, and he tried to stall their demands by saying that the Genevan church was a true church despite its flaws. In the end, his friends succeeded in recalling him to his old pastorate in September, 1541, but Calvin was reluctant to return, and Farel was not recalled with him.

He had received assurances that there would be no unwarranted interference in his work, and from the first day of his return he began remolding the Genevan church. His "Ecclesiastical Ordinances" (1541), though modified in 1561, were adopted by the town, and provided that the ministers would have considerable disciplinary powers over the people, especially through the power of excommunication. The powers of the Church and the state over religion and morals remained closely related in Calvin's Geneva, and the two institutions operated on a basis of close cooperation.

In the years until his death on May 27, 1564, he became celebrated throughout Protestant Europe. *Institutes of the Christian Religion* became a kind of handbook for Protestants and was translated into several languages. It was originally published in Latin but subsequently Calvin published new editions in both Latin and French. Calvin himself became the unofficial leader of the Reformed faith and maintained a voluminous correspondence with Protestants in all parts of the Continent and the British Isles, who constantly sought his advice on many problems.

SIGNIFICANCE

Through his writings and his personal influence, John Calvin molded the character of Protestantism outside Germany and Scandinavia, which retained the original Lutheranism. In Switzerland, France, the Netherlands, and Scotland, the basic form of Protestantism came to be Calvinist, and the movement also spread later into Germany. Calvin's theology greatly influenced the Church of England until about the 1630's, and an academy that he founded at Geneva became the training ground for hundreds of Protestant pastors from all nations.

Calvin attempted to turn Geneva into a city of model Christians, an effort in which he was only partially successful. Strict regulations on conduct were introduced and rigidly enforced, and the church played the dominant role in civic life. Calvin also strongly opposed heresy; in 1553, he was responsible for the burning at Geneva of Michael Servetus, a Spanish physician who denied the Christian doctrine of the Trinity, and others who disagreed with Calvin's theology were expelled from the city.

—*James F. Hitchcock*

FURTHER READING

Calvin, John. *The Institutes of the Christian Religion.* Translated by Henry Beveridge. Reprint. Grand Rapids, Mich.: W. B. Eerdmans, 2001. This paperback edition of Calvin's great work is one of several readily available in English.

Cottret, Bernard. *Calvin: A Biography.* Translated by M. Wallace McDonald. Grand Rapids, Mich.: W. B. Eerdmans, 2000. This biography seeks to recount the history of Calvin's hopes, ideas, and actions. Less focused on Calvin himself than most biographies, this account is more interested in the institutions he created and the effects he has had upon the world.

Harkness, Georgia. *John Calvin: The Man and His Ethics.* New York: Abingdon-Cokesbury Press, 1958. Classic analysis and critic of Calvinism and Calvinist ethics from the point of view of modern Presbyterianism.

MacKinnon, James. *Calvin and the Reformation.* New York: Russell & Russell, 1962. A general survey of the Reformation that emphasizes the part played by Calvin.

Naphy, William G. *Calvin and the Consolidation of the Genevan Reformation.* 1994. Reprint. Louisville, Ky.: Westminster John Knox Press, 2003. This meticulously researched study of the Genevan Reformation includes twenty-seven statistical tables and eleven appendices on Calvin's Geneva. Focuses on the challenges posed to the Reformation by the large number of refugees that flooded into Geneva.

Oberman, Heiko A. *The Two Reformations: The Journey from the Last Days to the New World.* Edited by Donald Weinstein. New Haven, Conn.: Yale University Press, 2003. Posthumous collection of essays by one of the foremost Reformation scholars of the twentieth century. Attempts to recover an adequate picture of Calvin, opposed to the figure historians have created. Argues that medieval religious thought was essential to both Calvin's and Luther's understandings of Christianity.

Parker, Thomas H. L. *The Doctrine of the Knowledge of God: A Study in the Theology of John Calvin.* Edinburgh: Oliver and Boyd, 1952. Attempts to reach the heart of Calvin's theology through his doctrine of humanity's knowledge of God.

Walker, Walliston. *John Calvin: The Organizer of Reformed Protestantism, 1509-1564.* Reprint. New York: Schocken Books, 1969. A still-useful biography that remains one of the best available in English. The reprint edition includes a bibliographical essay by J. T. McNeill.

Wendel, François. *Calvin: The Origins and Development of His Religious Thought.* New York: Harper and Row, 1963. One of the best general accounts of Calvin's theology, with a succinct summary of his life. Credits Calvin with being the first person to systematically apply Humanist methods of literary criticism to the study of the Bible, although his mature theology in *Institutes of the Christian Religion* marked a profound break with Humanism.

SEE ALSO: Oct. 31, 1517: Luther Posts His Ninety-five Theses; Apr.-May, 1521: Luther Appears Before the Diet of Worms; 1523: Gustav I Vasa Becomes King of Sweden; 1550's-c. 1600: Educational Reforms in Europe; May, 1559-Aug., 1561: Scottish Reformation; Apr. or May, 1560: Publication of the Geneva Bible; July 29, 1567: James VI Becomes King of Scotland; Feb. 25, 1570: Pius V Excommunicates Elizabeth I.

RELATED ARTICLES in *Great Lives from History: The Renaissance & Early Modern Era, 1454-1600:* Martin Bucer; John Calvin; Miles Coverdale; Elizabeth I; Francis I; Henry IV; François Hotman; John Knox; Hugh Latimer; Martin Luther; Marguerite de Navarre; Philipp Melanchthon; Philippe de Mornay; Saint Philip Neri; Michael Servetus; Huldrych Zwingli.

October, 1536-June, 1537
PILGRIMAGE OF GRACE

The Pilgrimage of Grace, a widespread revolt against King Henry VIII, Thomas Cromwell, and the Act of Supremacy, which named Henry the head of the Church in England, was the most serious domestic challenge the king faced during his reign.

LOCALE: Northern England

CATEGORIES: Religion; wars, uprisings, and civil unrest; government and politics

KEY FIGURES

Robert Aske (d. 1537), pilgrimage leader
Henry VIII (1491-1547), king of England, r. 1509-1547
Thomas Cromwell (1485?-1540), Henry VIII's chief minister
Thomas Howard (1473-1554), third duke of Norfolk

SUMMARY OF EVENT

By the fall of 1536, there was a great deal of discontent in the north of England. This discontent had many sources, including bad harvests over the previous few years. Heavy royal taxation came with rumors of more taxes, causing further hardship and resentment. There was also a general sense of alienation in the north, the feeling that the south, and the central government based there, neither knew nor cared about the north and its problems.

Most upsetting of all, however, were the religious changes, in particular the dissolution, or closing, of England's monasteries, which had begun that year. As a result of all these factors, and especially the religious one, northern England rose up in a rebellion that was most likely the most serious internal threat faced by King Henry VIII during his reign.

The closing of the monasteries followed the king's repudiation of the Papacy and his assuming the headship of the Church of England in 1534. The architect of this royal supremacy in the church, as well as the dissolution of the monasteries, was Henry's chief minister, Thomas Cromwell, who was well known to favor Protestantism. Although only smaller monasteries were being shut down in 1536, on the ostensible grounds that they were corrupt, it was widely expected that there would be further attacks on monasticism in general.

Moreover, the recently issued Ten Articles, which attempted to define the doctrine of the Church of England for the first time, indicated that the English church was becoming more open to Protestant doctrine, and royal injunctions were already attacking popular Catholic religious practices on the grounds of "superstition." The conservative Catholic north was incensed with this heretical turn of religious policy by a governmental regime whose questionable morality had been on display in the months prior: The first six months of 1536 saw the death of Henry's first wife, Catherine of Aragon, whom he had divorced in 1533; the death of his second wife, Anne Boleyn, whom he had executed in 1536; and his third marriage, this time to Jane Seymour, also in 1536.

These religious grievances, combined with broader discontent, led to a general insurrection, which broke out in Lincolnshire early in October, 1536. The insurrection was sparked by a group of villagers who mistakenly believed their church goods were about to be seized. Eventually numbering about ten thousand rebels, the leaders of the Lincolnshire Rebellion issued articles that, in addition to economic complaints, called on the king to end the dissolution of the monasteries and dismiss bishops they considered heretical. Lasting less than two weeks, the Lincolnshire disturbance ended peacefully before government action could be taken against it.

News of the Lincolnshire Rebellion, however, quickly led to other revolts, so that, by the end of October, the central government was no longer in control of the north, from Yorkshire and Lancashire to the Scottish border. While each of these disturbances reflected economic and local problems, what bound them all together was their opposition to the religious changes under Henry. Like those of the Lincolnshire rebels, articles produced by the other revolts universally condemned the dissolution of the monasteries and heretical bishops, and they also called for the removal of Thomas Cromwell, who was widely viewed as the "evil counselor" responsible for both the king's offensive religious program and his extortionate fiscal program.

The predominance of the religious issue, however, can be seen in the largest of these revolts, in Yorkshire, led by a lawyer named Robert Aske. It was Aske who named the movement the Pilgrimage of Grace, and extensive religious symbolism was employed by the pilgrims to emphasize that this was a crusade for the old religion. At its peak, Aske's Yorkshire rebellion alone numbered about thirty thousand individuals, and the entire pilgrimage probably approached fifty thousand.

Aske's leadership of the pilgrimage indicates the complicity of local elites. The uprisings were, in their origins, genuinely popular movements, and at the start, local elites seem to have been somewhat coerced into participation by the crowds. The northern elites, however, not only disliked the religious changes as much as the common folk, but also had their own grievances against Henry and Cromwell, in particular recent legislation that limited their control over their lands and increased their financial obligations to the Crown. Therefore, elite influence on, and leadership of, the pilgrimage emerged quickly, with these concerns being listed in the articles of complaint.

In the face of these disturbances, Henry dispatched Thomas Howard, third duke of Norfolk, who was religiously conservative but still loyal to the Crown. Howard realized quickly that the pilgrimage was far too large to

be dealt with militarily, so he opted instead to negotiate with the rebels. Norfolk offered pardons and promises of royal attention to the north's grievances, and he successfully got the rebels to disperse.

Henry was furious with this turn of events, but he had no other choice than to accept it in the short run. Howard turned out to be fairly clever. None of his promises or concessions had been put in writing. Moreover, divisions began to appear among the pilgrims, for, while they were fairly certain of what they did not want, they were less certain of what they did want. In this situation, the elites began to gravitate toward the Crown. Aske himself was brought to the royal court for Christmas. The commoners among the pilgrims had been uneasy with the settlement reached with Howard, and they continued to have doubts and suspicions.

Early in 1537, these simmering dissatisfactions flared up again in a handful of further rebellions. The new disturbances played into Henry's hands. Smaller and more dispersed than the earlier pilgrimage, they were within the government's ability to handle, and they provided an excellent justification for revoking all the previous pardons. Norfolk returned to the north, and June saw the last executions for the pilgrimage, including that of Aske.

After the events of 1536-1537, Henry and Cromwell worked to extend central control over the north, undermining the power of the traditional leading families there and instituting a Council of the North. The dissolution of the monasteries continued, and, while the pace of religious change in other regards slowed or even reversed, this was entirely because of the changing inclinations of the king, whose shift toward conservatism after 1539 cost Thomas Cromwell his head as well.

SIGNIFICANCE

The Pilgrimage of Grace illustrates two very important things about early Tudor England. First, the central government's coercive and policing powers were limited. Howard negotiated with the rebels because he had to. Despite King Henry's anger, his government simply did not have the resources to pacify and end such a widespread uprising. It was fortunate for Henry that differences among the pilgrims themselves fractured the movement and alienated many northern elites. If not for these differences, the king might never have been able to extract his vengeance on the pilgrimage's leaders.

The second, and perhaps more significant, aspect of the pilgrimage is the ability of issues concerning religion to ignite open rebellion and the inevitable mixing of religious grievances with those that are secular. Religious rebellion occurred again during the reign of Henry's son, King Edward VI. Edward's more aggressively Protestant religious policy, including the introduction of a new, Protestant worship service, led to uprisings in Devon and Cornwall in 1549. As with the Pilgrimage of Grace, religious concerns were mixed with economic ones, and news of the revolt in the west led to other rebellions, eastward and northward into East Anglia. As the uprising moved farther east, however, religion became less of a factor and complaints about the economy became more of a factor. Indeed, in Norfolk in 1549, Kett's Rebellion made a great show of support for the government's changes in religion and religious practice, while also protesting oppressive landlords. Not nearly as threatening as the Pilgrimage of Grace, all these rebellions were suppressed.

—*Sharon L. Arnoult*

FURTHER READING

Dodds, Madeleine Hope, and Ruth Dodds. *The Pilgrimage of Grace, 1536-1537, and the Exeter Conspiracy, 1538.* 2 vols. London: Frank Cass, 1971. Originally published in 1915, this work remains the most comprehensive study of the events.

Fletcher, Anthony, and Diarmaid MacCulloch. *Tudor Rebellions.* 5th ed. New York: Longman, 2004. This volume sets the pilgrimage within the context of other Tudor revolts, such as the Western Rebellion.

Hoyle, R. W. *The Pilgrimage of Grace and the Politics of the 1530's.* New York: Oxford University Press, 2001. The most scholarly recent work on the pilgrimage, this study reviews the historiography of, and current controversies surrounding, this event, and it analyzes the uprisings.

Moorhouse, Geoffrey. *The Pilgrimage of Grace: The Rebellion That Shook Henry VIII's Throne.* London: Weidenfeld and Nicolson, 2002. This is a well-written narrative of the rebellions and their aftermath.

Shagan, Ethan H. "Politics and the Pilgrimage of Grace Revisited." In *Popular Politics and the English Reformation.* New York: Cambridge University Press, 2003. Shagan focuses on the politics within and without the pilgrimage.

SEE ALSO: Dec. 18, 1534: Act of Supremacy; July, 1535-Mar., 1540: Henry VIII Dissolves the Monasteries; May, 1539: Six Articles of Henry VIII; 1549: Kett's Rebellion.

RELATED ARTICLES in *Great Lives from History: The Renaissance & Early Modern Era, 1454-1600:* Thomas Cromwell; Edward VI; Henry VIII.

1537

POPE PAUL III DECLARES RIGHTS OF NEW WORLD PEOPLES

Pope Paul III declared the rights of New World indigenous peoples in three papal bulls that established the primacy of the Catholic Church in guaranteeing indigenous rights and privileges. The pope hoped also to restore a sense of Christian responsibility to the conquests in the New World.

LOCALE: Spain

CATEGORIES: Laws, acts, and legal history; religion; colonization

KEY FIGURES

Charles V (1500-1558), Holy Roman Emperor, r. 1519-1556, and king of Spain as Charles I, r. 1516-1556

Ferdinand II (1452-1516), king of Aragon, r. 1479-1516, king of Castile, r. 1474-1504, and regent of Castile, r. 1504-1516

Bartolomé de Las Casas (1474-1566), Spanish priest and critic of the exploitation of indigenous peoples of the New World

Paul III (Alessandro Farnese; 1468-1549), Roman Catholic pope, 1534-1549

SUMMARY OF EVENT

When Christopher Columbus first encountered the indigenous peoples of the Caribbean, he likely was interested in them as slaves primarily. In the first decade after the arrival of Columbus, thousands of indigenous peoples were forced to work in mines and in agricultural fields under extremely harsh and brutal conditions. The death rate became so high that Spanish authorities became concerned.

In 1493, Pope Alexander VI assigned responsibility for the peoples of the West Indies to King Ferdinand of Spain, who delegated authority over his new territories to his appointed representatives in the New World. In 1501, Governor Nicolás de Ovando of New Spain proposed a system of forced labor called the *encomienda*, a system of employment that he hoped would reduce the horrors of slavery. Ferdinand approved this labor system, one that was similar to the system found in many parts of Spain, where impoverished peasants were required to work long hours under harsh conditions for their landlords.

Under Ovando's system, Spanish landowners in Mexico, Cuba, and South America, who were called *encomenderos*, were assigned a group of indigenous laborers who were required to work on Spanish-owned estates or in gold or silver mines. The workers were supposed to receive wages and were to be protected and instructed in the Christian faith by their masters. They would officially be "free persons," with all rights belonging to free people, but they were temporarily assigned by the king of Spain, their true lord and master, to work for the *encomenderos*. Thus, in the eyes of legal authorities, the workers were not slaves. In reality, however, little difference existed between the new forced labor system and the old one. Indigenous men, women, and children were

bought, sold, whipped, and otherwise abused by their Spanish masters, who showed little concern for their legal rights as free people. Whatever their status under Spanish law, the indigenous peoples of the New World were still treated as slaves.

Continued harsh treatment of the indigenous peoples led to intense criticism from a number of Spanish missionaries posted in New Spain. King Ferdinand called for a new set of laws to protect the rights of his New World subjects. To help develop these laws, he invited opinions from the best legal minds in Spain. The Dominican friar Matias de Paz responded with a lengthy defense of indigenous rights, which troubled the king deeply. Paz said that the Spaniards surely had a legitimate right to conquer and rule the indigenous peoples, because they were a weak, backward, and godless people. The conquest, however, also imposed great responsibilities on the conquerors. First, the Crown had an obligation to use every means possible to convert indigenous peoples to Christianity. As good Christians, Spaniards were obligated to treat the indigenous as humanely and justly as possible.

Paz's argument inspired the first series of laws aimed at protecting the peoples of the West Indies: the Laws of Burgos of 1512. King Ferdinand realized that little progress had been made in improving the treatment of the Mexican, Central, and South American Indians since the establishment of the *encomienda*. Hence, laws were needed to guide the landowners in their treatment of their indigenous workers.

The protection for the Indians outlined in the new code included limiting the workers to five months of labor in a mine or in agriculture. After that time, *encomenderos* were required to give their workers forty days of rest. The *encomenderos* were also required to provide their workers with cooked meat and other food. In return, the indigenous were to receive instruction in the Catholic faith, conduct themselves as Christians, renounce their practice of having more than one wife, and sleep off the ground in hammocks. The Laws of Burgos went into effect but proved quite difficult to enforce. Many *encomenderos* simply ignored these laws, and royal officials in the New World had neither the time nor the staff to enforce them.

THE PAPACY AND INDIGENOUS RIGHTS

Pope Paul III, in his encyclical (or bull) Sublimis deus *(May 29, 1537), argued that the indigenous peoples of the Americas were rational beings who could receive the Catholic faith if allowed to do so. The following excerpt from the bull decries slavery on the grounds that God created humans—all humans—so that they might have faith in Him and accept His word.*

The sublime God so loved the human race that He created man in such wise that he might participate, not only in the good that other creatures enjoy, but endowed him with capacity to attain to the inaccessible and invisible Supreme Good and behold it face to face. . . .

We, who, though unworthy, exercise on earth the power of our Lord and seek with all our might to bring those sheep of His flock who are outside into the fold committed to our charge, consider, however, that the Indians are truly men and that they are not only capable of understanding the Catholic Faith but, according to our information, they desire exceedingly to receive it. Desiring to provide ample remedy for these evils, We define and declare by these Our letters, or by any translation thereof signed by any notary public and sealed with the seal of any ecclesiastical dignitary, to which the same credit shall be given as to the originals, that, notwithstanding whatever may have been or may be said to the contrary, the said Indians and all other people who may later be discovered by Christians, are by no means to be deprived of their liberty or the possession of their property, even though they be outside the faith of Jesus Christ; and that they may and should, freely and legitimately, enjoy their liberty and the possession of their property; nor should they be in any way enslaved. . . .

Source: Papal Encyclicals Online. http://www.papalencyclicals.net. Accessed September 29, 2004.

Pope Paul III established the rights of indigenous peoples of the New World in three papal bulls. (Hulton|Archive by Getty Images)

Bartolomé de Las Casas, a former slave-owning landlord in Cuba who had become a Catholic priest, criticized the lack of enforcement of laws protecting the Indians. He condemned the general attitude of Spaniards toward them, including the belief that Native Americans were ignorant savages who were better off because the conquest led them to Christianity. In many books and essays, Las Casas argued that the Indians deserved humane treatment, that their lands and freedom should be restored, and that slavery and the *encomienda* should be abolished. Supporters of the *encomienda* system argued that forced labor was necessary for the indigenous peoples because they did not know how to work for themselves; they were considered lazy heathens interested only in sleeping, making war, and eating the remains of their enemies.

The eloquent arguments made by Las Casas had little impact on political policy until the 1530's, when Pope Paul III, an energetic church leader, issued a series of papal bulls, or official messages, that promoted individual rights and legal protection for the indigenous peoples of the Americas. The pope's views were influenced by the writings of Las Casas and of Bernardino de Minayo, a Dominican priest who came to Rome in 1537 to report on the brutal treatment received by the peoples of the West Indies at the hands of Spanish conquerors.

The three papal bulls issued in 1537 reduced the powers of the Spanish monarchs over indigenous peoples and returned these powers to church authorities. In *Altitudo Divini Consilii*, Paul III placed all matters relating to baptism, instruction in Christianity, and other church matters under the guidance and control of church bishops, rather than *encomenderos*. In *Veritas Ipsa*, indigenous slavery was severely condemned by the pope. The pope's third bull, *Sublimis Deus*, condemned as false doctrine the view that Native Americans were subhuman, irrational beings without souls, incapable of receiving the Catholic faith. According to the pope, the American Indians "are truly men and they are not only capable of understanding the Catholic faith, but, according to our information, they desire exceedingly to receive it." He concluded by asserting that

> said Indians and all other people who may later be discovered by Christians, are by no means to be deprived of their liberty or the possession of their property, even though they be outside the faith of Jesus Christ; and that they may and should, freely and legitimately, enjoy their liberty and the possession of their property; nor should they be in any way enslaved.

Father de Minaya took copies of the pope's statements to the New World without notifying or waiting for the approval of the Council of the Indies, the official lawmaking body for the Spanish colonies. He also neglected to notify the new king of Spain, a powerful monarch who also held title to the Holy Roman Empire as Charles V. Imperial authorities in the New World reacted by throwing Father de Minaya into prison, where he languished for two years. Paul III was forced to issue a note in 1538, indicating "that all other briefs and notes issued before in prejudice of the power of Emperor Charles V as king of Spain, and which might disturb the good government of the Indies," were revoked. Charles did not object, however, to better treatment for native peoples, and he issued his own decree: the New Laws of Spain (1542 and 1543).

SIGNIFICANCE

The New Laws granted legal protection and property rights to all Charles's subjects in the New World. As in previous attempts to protect the rights of the indigenous peoples, however, Spanish royal officials found it difficult to enforce these laws. In many places in Mexico,

Peru, and the islands of the Caribbean, indigenous peoples continued to be enslaved and exploited well into the nineteenth century.

—*Leslie V. Tischauser*

FURTHER READING

Elliott, John H. *Imperial Spain, 1469-1716*. Reprint. New York: Penguin, 1990. Includes a detailed history of the legal and philosophical issues raised in the debate over the treatment of native peoples.

Gibson, Charles. *Spain in America*. New York: Harper & Row, 1966. An excellent, brief survey of Spanish relations with native peoples that includes a full discussion of the *encomienda* system and slavery.

Keen, Benjamin. *Essays in the Intellectual History of Colonial Latin America*. Boulder, Colo.: Westview Press, 1998. This collection includes an essay surveying 460 years of Las Casas scholarship and another essay evaluating Las Casas's legacy.

Las Casas, Bartolomé de. *History of the Indies*. Translated and edited by Andree Collard. New York: Harper & Row, 1971. With this translation, Collard has provided an excellent introduction to the famous history written by Las Casas. Provides a vivid description of Indian-Spanish conflicts.

Lupher, David A. *Romans in a New World: Classical Models in Sixteenth Century Spanish America*. Ann Arbor: University of Michigan Press, 2003. Study of the influence of Roman models of empire upon the Spanish imperial project in the Americas.

Parry, John J., and Robert G. Keith, eds. *The New Iberia: The Conquerors and the Conquered*. Vol. 1. New York: Times Books, 1984. Part of a five-volume collection of documents relating to Spain in the New World from the 1490's to the early 1600's. Each document is ably introduced by the editors.

Remesal, Antonio de. *Bartolomé de Las Casas, 1474-1566, in the Pages of Father Antonio de Remesal*. Translated and annotated by Felix Jay. Lewiston, N.Y.: E. Mellen Press, 2002. Translation and commentary upon a life of Las Casas written sixty years after his death.

Shiels, William E. *King and Church: The Rise and Fall of Patronato Real*. Chicago: Loyola University Press, 1961. Describes the background of Pope Paul III's concerns for native rights.

Thomas, Hugh. *Rivers of Gold: The Rise of the Spanish Empire*. London: Weidenfeld & Nicolson, 2003. Decidedly conservative and Eurocentric history of Spanish colonialism.

SEE ALSO: Oct. 12, 1492: Columbus Lands in the Americas; June 7, 1494: Treaty of Tordesillas; 1495-1510: West Indian Uprisings; 1500-1530's: Portugal Begins to Colonize Brazil; Apr., 1519-Aug., 1521: Cortés Conquers Aztecs in Mexico; 1527-1547: Maya Resist Spanish Incursions in Yucatán; Feb. 23, 1540-Oct., 1542: Coronado's Southwest Expedition; 1542-1543: The New Laws of Spain; 1552: Las Casas Publishes *The Tears of the Indians*.

RELATED ARTICLES in *Great Lives from History: The Renaissance & Early Modern Era, 1454-1600:* José de Acosta; Alexander VI; Charles V; Ferdinand II and Isabella I; Bartolomé de Las Casas; Paul III.

September 27-28, 1538
BATTLE OF PRÉVEZA

At Préveza, an Ottoman fleet led by Admiral Barbarossa won a nominal victory over a fleet of the Holy League. While the battle was largely inconclusive, it served to convince Venice that the Ottoman navy was too formidable to be easily defeated, and the republic ceded control of the Mediterranean to the Turks the following year.

LOCALE: Gulf of Arta (Amvrakikós Kólpos), near Préveza (now in western Greece)

CATEGORIES: Wars, uprisings, and civil unrest; expansion and land acquisition

KEY FIGURES

Barbarossa (Khayr al-Dīn; d. 1546), admiral of the Ottoman fleet, 1533-1546

Charles V (1500-1558), Holy Roman Emperor, r. 1519-1556, and king of Spain as Charles I, r. 1516-1556

Andrea Doria (1466-1560), Genoese statesman, prince of Melfi, 1528-1560, and grand admiral of the Holy Roman Empire, 1528-1555

Andrea Gritti (1455-1538), doge of Venice, r. 1523-1538, and organizer of the Holy League

Paul III (Alessandro Farnese; 1468-1549), Roman Catholic pope, 1534-1549

Süleyman the Magnificent (1494/1495-1566), Ottoman sultan, r. 1520-1566

SUMMARY OF EVENT

In 1533, Ottoman sultan Süleyman the Magnificent made the Barbary corsair Barbarossa admiral of his fleet. The already significant naval resources of the Ottoman Empire were placed at Barbarossa's disposal. In return, he added his own pirate fleet to that of the Turkish navy, cobbled the combined ships and crews into a single, well-disciplined force, and used Turkish wealth to build larger and more heavily armed warships. Barbarossa spent the next five years waging a war of Ottoman expansion in the Mediterranean Sea. In 1534, he captured Tunis. In 1537, he pillaged Italy's coast and conducted an unsuccessful siege of Corfu. Over the next year, he added Patmos, Aegina, Ios, Paros, and Skyros to the Ottoman Empire. All five islands had belonged to the Republic of Venice.

Venice, led by Doge Andrea Gritti, was at the time a member of the Holy League, an alliance that also included Pope Paul III and the Holy Roman Empire under Charles V (Spain's Charles I). The league, whose fleet was commanded by Genoa's Andrea Doria, had been re-sponsible for breaking the Siege of Corfu and had retaken Tunis from the Turks in 1535. Süleyman's forces, however, continued to gain territory and influence in the region. Moreover, despite Charles V's trust in Andrea Doria, many members of his fleet remembered that he had fought on the side of the French against the emperor before switching sides in 1528. The disunity of the allies against them served only to strengthen the Ottomans' position, and the Ottoman navy was clearly in the process of becoming the dominant power in the Mediterranean at the time of the Battle of Préveza in late September of 1538.

The league had spent the previous four months assembling a fleet large enough to challenge Barbarossa's corsair navy. Gathered at Corfu, their fleet consisted of 246 craft armed with twenty-five hundred guns and with close to sixty thousand men on board—twenty thousand Germans and the rest Italians and Spaniards. The force included 55 Venetian galleys, 27 papal craft, and 49 of Doria's Genoese vessels. The rest were Spanish warships dispatched by Charles V. Barbarossa had only 150 galleys under his command, and his ships were for the most part less heavily armed than those of the Holy League. They were, however, lighter and more maneuverable as a result.

The Holy League's members were not in agreement over the best strategy to use at Préveza. The Venetians mistrusted the tactics of their longtime Genoese rival, Andrea Doria, so several alternative battle plans were considered. The league planned to attack the Ottoman fleet in the Gulf of Arta, a large inlet on the west coast of Greece with an extremely narrow entrance. The Ottomans had a fortress on the northern shore of the entrance. The initial battle plans called for infantry troops under papal commander Marco Grimani to land and establish an artillery position overlooking the entrance to the gulf. They could either capture the Ottoman fortress at Préveza on the north shore or simply create a makeshift temporary fort at Actium on the south shore. The league also considered sinking a ship at the entrance to the Gulf of Arta, trapping the Ottoman fleet within. When the time for action arrived, however, Doria, anxious to avoid serious losses and as mistrustful of his allies as they were of him, refused to implement any plan.

Pope Paul III had striven to unite Christianity against the Ottomans, a goal to which Andrea Gritti and Charles V also subscribed, but the Holy Roman emperor had participated reluctantly and belatedly in the war in the eastern Mediterranean. One reason for Charles's reluctance was that the pope had remained neutral in Charles's own long-standing feud with another Catholic monarch, France's King Francis I. Furthermore, Charles had little interest in who controlled the eastern Mediterranean, and he was at any rate uncertain about how serious a blow could be dealt to the Ottoman navy under the skillful command of Barbarossa. Charles had sent an emissary to Barbarossa to try to lure him into changing sides. However, the respective terms of agreement—relinquishing of territory by Charles or sabotaging of Ottoman vessels by Barbarossa—proved to be mutually unacceptable, assuming that the negotiations had been at all serious rather than a simple delaying tactic. Whatever the case, on September 20, the negotiations ended and the Holy League's navy prepared to attack the Ottoman fleet in the Gulf of Arta.

The league reached the entrance to the gulf on September 27. Because most of Barbarossa's 150 men-of-war were significantly lighter than the Holy League's castle-like galleons, however, Admiral Doria was leery of trying to negotiate the sand bar at the mouth of the Gulf of Arta. The heavier craft would be sitting ducks: caught in a narrow inlet, unable to maneuver with the sandbar limiting their movements, and incapable of returning fire with their side cannons so long as they were pointed forward. Moreover, the Ottomans would have friendly territory behind them to fall back to if necessary. Once he understood the situation, Doria decided to withdraw. The entire fleet turned around. It anchored the next day, September 28, 30 miles (48 kilometers) south of Préveza.

Assisted by similarly intrepid corsairs such as Turgut Reis (also known as Dragut Reis) and Sidi Ali Reis, Barbarossa set off in pursuit of Doria's fleet and, on catching up, attacked the heavier league galleons head-on. When the Christian fleet attempted to maneuver into formation to repel the Ottoman attack, its ships became separated and uncoordinated, as Doria and the Venetians did little to support one another. The naval tactics followed at this encounter had become standard by then, however, so even without direct cooperation, the fleet managed to stay together.

The two fleets faced each other in line abreast, with a center and two wings, one of which would keep close to, and thus be protected by, the coastline. This tactic, which would later be followed at Lepanto in 1571, was reminiscent of tactics followed in Renaissance land battles. Doria was resolved to maintain his own ships as intact as possible and left the brunt of the fighting to the Venetians

and the papal forces. As it turned out, however, little fighting took place. The toll on both sides was still light, with Doria losing only seven vessels, when a storm threatened. The Genoese admiral decided to withdraw at once and ordered the fleet to return to Corfu. Barbarossa let them go, claiming victory. Indeed, at the end of the day, Barbarossa had outsailed and outmaneuvered his old adversary, even though this was not the fight to the finish that the two older men had expected for so long. Barbarossa was handsomely rewarded for this victory by the sultan.

SIGNIFICANCE

At the Battle of Préveza, the Christian navy failed to engage in serious combat, let alone to defeat, the much smaller and lighter Ottoman navy. Nor did it return to make another attempt to seize control of the eastern Mediterranean. As a result, the Ottomans dominated the region for the next thirty-three years. The battle demonstrated that Andrea Doria, arguably the most brilliant admiral in the Holy League, was nevertheless unable to hold together the forces of an extremely uneasy alliance long enough to defeat their common foe. The complicated political maneuvering of the various members of the alliance meant that Pope Paul III's dream of launching a new Crusade, uniting the Catholic West against the Islamic forces of Sultan Süleyman the Magnificent, was doomed to failure.

In the wake of the battle, Venice, mistrustful of its allies—especially Admiral Doria—and frightened at the possibility of further, retributive Ottoman strikes against its still-extensive territory, sued for peace. The republic signed a humiliating peace treaty with the sultan in 1539 and formally abandoned the Holy League in 1540. Under the peace treaty, the Venetians relinquished Castelnuovo (now Hercegnovi, Yugoslavia) on the Adriatic Coast, a fort controlling the mouth of Cattaro Bay (the Gulf of Kotor) a few miles south. They ceded equally strategic territories in the Aegean Sea as well. Additionally, Venice agreed to pay 300,000 ducats as war indemnity. It was not until the Battle of Lepanto in 1571 that Christendom retrieved the maritime dominance and prestige it had lost at Préveza.

—*Peter B. Heller*

FURTHER READING

Bicheno, Hugh. *Crescent and Cross: The Battle of Lepanto, 1571.* London: Cassell, 2003. This work, which describes Préveza as a "scene-setter" for Lepanto, includes an excellent map showing the lay of the land at Préveza, the Gulf of Arta, and Corfu. Maps, diagrams, chronology, bibliography, appendices, index.

Brummett, Palmira J. *Ottoman Seapower and Levantine Diplomacy in the Age of Discovery*. Albany: State University of New York Press, 1994. Emphasizes the Ottomans' attention to naval power. Glossary, bibliography, illustrations, index.

Clot, André. *Suleiman the Magnificent*. Translated by Matthew J. Reisz. New York: Saqi, 1992. Contains an appendix detailing problems of maritime makeup and personnel. Maps, genealogy, chronology, bibliography, appendices, index.

Imber, Colin. "The Navy of Suleiman the Magnificent." *Archivum Ottomanicum* 6 (1980): 211-282. A highly detailed account of the technology, armaments, makeup, and personnel used by the Ottoman navy at the time of Préveza. Glossary.

Merriman, Roger B. *Suleiman the Magnificent, 1520-1566*. Reprint. Cambridge, Mass.: Harvard University Press, 1966. Includes a short but pointed discussion of the Battle of Préveza. Bibliographical notes, index.

Vucinich, Wayne S. *The Ottoman Empire: The Record and the Legacy*. Princeton, N.J.: Princeton University Press, 1965. Sets the Battle of Préveza into diplomatic context. Bibliography, index.

SEE ALSO: 1463-1479: Ottoman-Venetian War; 1478-1482: Albanian-Turkish Wars End; June 28, 1519: Charles V Is Elected Holy Roman Emperor; 1520-1566: Reign of Süleyman; June 28, 1522-Dec. 27, 1522: Siege and Fall of Rhodes; Feb., 1525: Battle of Pavia; Oct. 20-27, 1541: Holy Roman Empire Attacks Ottomans in Algiers; 1552: Struggle for the Strait of Hormuz; May 18-Sept. 8, 1565: Siege of Malta; July, 1570-Aug., 1571: Siege of Famagusta and Fall of Cyprus; Oct. 7, 1571: Battle of Lepanto.

RELATED ARTICLEs in *Great Lives from History: The Renaissance & Early Modern Era, 1454-1600:* Barbarossa; Charles V; Paul III; Süleyman the Magnificent.

1530's

1539
JIAJING THREATENS VIETNAM

Civil war in Vietnam allowed China to threaten its neighbor with attack and control and to gain a sliver of contested northern Vietnamese border territory. Also, China weakened the Vietnamese state by recognizing two potentates as rulers over a split nation.

LOCALE: Vietnam and China

CATEGORIES: Diplomacy and international relations; expansion and land acquisition; government and politics

KEY FIGURES

Jiajing (reign name, also Chia-ching; personal name Zhu Houzong, Chu Hou-tsung; posthumous name Sudi, Su-ti; temple name Shizong, Shih-tsung; 1507-1567), Ming emperor of China, r. 1522-1567

Mac Dang Dung (d. 1540), self-proclaimed Mac Dynasty emperor of Vietnam, r. 1527-1530

Mac Dang Doanh (d. 1540), second Mac Dynasty emperor of Vietnam, r. 1530-1540

Le Trang Tong (Prince Duy Ninh; d. 1548), first emperor of the restored Le Dynasty in Vietnam, r. 1533-1548

Nguyen Kim (d. 1545), Vietnamese general who fought to restore the Le Dynasty

SUMMARY OF EVENT

In 1539, an imperial Chinese army assembled just within its border with northeastern Vietnam, near the Nam Quan pass, which separates the two nations. The official mission of the Chinese army was to execute an imperial edict by Ming Dynasty emperor Jiajing. Emperor Jiajing's edict called for the capture of Mac Dang Dung, the father of Vietnamese emperor Le Trang Tong. That a Chinese army was poised to invade Vietnam was understandable from a military point of view only because Vietnam had descended into civil war.

The preceding century had seen a great rise in Vietnam's fortune under the newly founded Le Dynasty. The Le family had gained its power by expelling the Chinese, who had invaded and ruled Vietnam from 1407 to 1428, but also previously, for a much longer period of time. Direct Chinese rule in the early 1400's had threatened to end the independence Vietnam had gained in 938, after enduring almost one thousand years of Chinese occupation. In 1471, Vietnam had crushed the rival kingdom of Cham to the south, captured the Cham capital of Vijaya, and annexed vast stretches of Cham land. A series of ineffective Le emperors, however, would bring a Chinese

539

army within reach of again attacking and annexing Vietnam, this time in 1539.

The Le Dynasty's decline, which allowed for Chinese intervention, had begun in 1505 with the incompetent emperor Le Uy Muc. Vietnamese sources describe him as a kind of Caligula, the controversial and unpredictable first century Roman emperor. He had his mother murdered and became a serial killer, strangling court ladies after spending nights with them. The Vietnamese people soon hated him, calling him the devil king. Fearing for his safety, he hired young bodyguards. One of these bodyguards was Mac Dang Dung, whose arrest nearly led China's emperor Jiajing to send an army into Vietnam in 1539. Originally, Mac was a poor fisher boy whose excellent martial arts skills led him to his imperial job.

The emperor's continuing cruelty alienated him from his people, so his cousin deposed him and had him killed. The new emperor proved ineffective, however, and was called the pig king. In turn, he, too, was killed, by one of his generals, one whom the emperor had ordered to be whipped in the middle of a monk's rebellion in 1516. This threw the Le Dynasty into complete disarray.

Rival factions occupied and burned down the capital, Thăng Long (now Hanoi), and the next emperor lived a few days only. Military leaders chose a new emperor, who took the name of Le Chieu Tong. This emperor asked Mac Dang Dung for help, and made him commander in chief.

Mac soon defeated all of the emperor's enemies but turned against him. First, Mac had Le Chieu Tong assassinated around 1525 or 1526 and then enthroned a new emperor. In 1527, he took the throne for himself, and he had the former emperor and his mother killed. To shore up his legitimacy, Mac asked to be recognized as emperor of Vietnam by the Chinese emperor Jiajing. Formally, the Vietnamese emperor was considered a vassal of the Chinese. In 1528, Jiajing considered the request routine and granted it.

Mac Dang Dung reigned for two years only, formally abdicating in favor of his son Mac Dang Doanh. In practice, he continued to rule from his home village of Co Trai, pretending to be a fisherman.

Mac Dang Dung never became popular, either as emperor or as elder statesman. In 1533, the Le family found a new champion in General Nguyen Kim. In exile in neighboring Laos, Nguyen proclaimed Prince Duy Ninh to be Vietnamese emperor, with the name of Le Trang Tong. He was the youngest son of the late emperor Le Chieu Tong. The Le Dynasty had been revived, but the fight for the throne brought the Chinese to Vietnam's borders.

With its rebel army growing, the Le family sent a delegation to Beijing in March of 1537. There, they found themselves in the middle of a court intrigue. Powerful officials around Emperor Jiajing's grand secretary, Xia Yan, looked for a war. When a son was born to Jiajing in November, 1536, Xia Yan counseled against sending a diplomatic mission to Vietnam to announce the news, as was customary. He believed that the Vietnamese had failed, for twenty years, to pay their nominal tribute to China. In addition, Xia Yan argued that the Mac Dynasty was illegitimate. In his view, this gave China the right to military invention. Advised of the high cost of such a military campaign, Emperor Jiajing refused to authorize it in 1536.

The arrival of the Le delegation led to Chinese reconsideration. The Le emissary pleaded his cause, which became welcome news for the Chinese war faction. In May, 1537, Emperor Jiajing agreed to a punitive campaign to arrest Mac Dang Dung and restore Le rule. One family of Vietnam had invited the Chinese to remove their adversary, at severe risk to Vietnamese autonomy. Local Chinese commanders on the ground in Guangdong province (Canton) objected to the high cost of the mission. Suddenly, Jiajing called off the campaign in June, 1537. By September of 1537, Jiajing developed a revised strategy and then approved the campaign once again.

The leaders of the invasion were appointed in April of 1538. Alarmed, Mac Dang Dung reiterated his and his son's allegiance to Jiajing and sent expensive gifts to Beijing. In China, the official in charge of the border area stated that the Vietnamese were to fight fiercely and that the cost of the invasion would surpass two million ounces of silver. Worried, the Chinese ministry of war called for a full session of the imperial court to decide on the issue.

In 1539, the Chinese army loomed just across the border of Vietnam, apparently ready to strike. In early 1540, Mac Dang Dung traveled to the Nam Quan pass, arriving with forty high officials. (Scholars of Vietnamese history debate whether or not his delegation appeared with bare upper torsos and in chains to signal their submission.) Meeting with high-ranking Chinese officers at the pass, Mac Dang Dung fell to his knees and symbolically kowtowed to the emperor, pressing his face on the stony ground of the road. To this humiliating gesture, Mac Dang Dung added more lavish gifts for the emperor. Most important, he also ceded six northeastern Vietnamese border districts around to the Chinese.

In Beijing, Emperor Jiajing had already canceled the attack on Vietnam because it was too costly. Learning of Mac Dang Dung's submission, his gifts, and the transfer of Vietnamese land, Jiajing agreed to recognize Mac Dang Dung but gave him the title of second-class governor. The new land was made part of the territory around the Chinese city of Quinzhou.

SIGNIFICANCE

Because of the decline of Vietnam's Le Dynasty, China was able to capitalize politically at the expense of Vietnam in 1540. Even though the war faction at Jiajing's court did not attack, China had gained tribute, land, and political influence at very little cost.

The Ming Dynasty would never again muster an army against Vietnam and would soon decline as a dynasty itself, but the hostile factions of the civil war in Vietnam would continue to look to China for help. Each side would seek Chinese support for its claims. Since China was under pressure from the Mongols, however, its influence in Vietnam remained symbolic.

After Mac Dang Dung's public submission, Emperor Jiajing felt justified in his cautious, contradictory approach to the campaign. In 1540, he announced to his court that he would seclude himself to find immortality. Grand secretary Xia Yan was forced to retire in 1542, the year in which empress Xiao Lie saved a drunken Jiajing from being killed by his concubines, who were then executed.

In Vietnam, Mac Dang Dung and his son died in 1540. In 1543, General Nguyen and Le Trang Tong conquered the western capital of Thang Hoa. This victory led to a request for imperial recognition by China. In 1545, China recognized two rulers for the divided nation. This parti-

tion of Vietnam was caused not by China, but by feuding Vietnamese families.

The Mac Dynasty would come to an end in 1592, but this did not bring reunification. Instead, until the late 1700's, Vietnam would continue to be split and ruled by two powerful families, both claiming to rule the country in the name of a Le emperor.

—*R. C. Lutz*

FURTHER READING

Chapuis, Oscar. *A History of Vietnam.* Westport, Conn.: Greenwood Press, 1995. Discusses the threatened attack in detail, from a Vietnamese point of view. Maps, bibliography, index.

Mote, Fred. *Imperial China, 900-1800.* Cambridge, Mass.: Harvard University Press, 2000. Comprehensively covers the threatened attack from a Chinese point of view. Illustrations, maps.

Taylor, Keith. "An Evaluation of the Chinese Period in Vietnamese History." *Journal of Asiatic Studies* 23 (January, 1980): 139-164. Argues that China's influence over Vietnamese culture did not arise from military occupation and threats of invasion.

SEE ALSO: 1450's-1471: Champa Civil Wars; Mar. 18-22, 1471: Battle of Vijaya.

RELATED ARTICLE in *Great Lives from History: The Renaissance & Early Modern Era, 1454-1600:* Le Thanh Tong.

1530's

May, 1539
SIX ARTICLES OF HENRY VIII

Henry VIII passed through Parliament and Convocation a set of articles defining the doctrine of the Church of England and instituting severe punishments for anyone who committed heresy against the new church. The Six Articles aligned the English Church with Catholicism and effectively outlawed Protestantism in England for twenty years.

LOCALE: London, England

CATEGORIES: Religion; government and politics; laws, acts, and legal history

KEY FIGURES

Henry VIII (1491-1547), king of England, r. 1509-1547
Thomas Cromwell (1485?-1540), chief minister to Henry VIII, 1531-1540, vicar-general of England,

1535-1540, and king's deputy as head of the Church of England, 1536-1540
Thomas Cranmer (1489-1556), archbishop of Canterbury, 1533-1556
Stephen Gardiner (c. 1493-1555), bishop of Winchester, 1531-1550, and lord chancellor, 1553-1555
Catherine of Aragon (1485-1536), queen consort of England, r. 1509-1533
Anne Boleyn (c. 1500/1501-1536), queen of England, r. 1533-1536
Jane Seymour (c. 1509-1537), queen consort of England, r. 1536-1537
Anne of Cleves (1515-1557), queen consort of England, r. 1540

Catherine Howard (c. 1521-1542), queen of England,
 r. 1540-1542
Catherine Parr (1473-1554), queen of England,
 r. 1543-1547
Thomas Howard (1473-1554), duke of Norfolk and
 earl of Surrey, 1524-1554, and uncle of Anne
 Boleyn and Catherine Howard
Edward VI (1537-1553), son of Henry VIII by Jane
 Seymour and king of England, r. 1547-1553
Mary I (1516-1558), daughter of Henry VIII by
 Catherine of Aragon and queen of England, r. 1553-
 1558
Charles V (1500-1558), king of Spain, r. 1516-1556,
 and Holy Roman Emperor, r. 1519-1556

SUMMARY OF EVENT

Henry VIII was declared Supreme Head of the Church in
England by the Act of Supremacy in 1534, but that act did
not define the nature of the church he was to govern.
Thomas Cranmer, the archbishop of Canterbury appointed by Henry in 1533, was secretly a Protestant, and
so was Thomas Cromwell, the layman Henry had made
vicar-general in 1535. Henry himself, however, remained staunchly Catholic in his views. Pope Leo X had
given him the title Defender of the Faith in 1521 for his
*Assertio septum sacramentum contra Martinum Luth-
erum* (1521; *Defense of the Seven Sacraments*, 1687), in
which the king had attacked Luther's views.

Henry VIII's first apparent deviation from Catholic
orthodoxy came in 1536, when he persuaded Convocation (a body consisting of all English bishops and representatives of the lower clergy) to adopt the Ten Articles.
This ambiguous document mentioned the three sacraments of baptism, penance, and the Eucharist, but it did
not mention the other four, though it did not deny their
existence. The doctrine of transubstantiation was upheld.
Prayers for the dead were defended, though there was no
mention of purgatory. Regarding the vexing question of
justification, the articles took the moderate view that justification is achieved through both faith and charity. The
Ten Articles were the first attempt to define the doctrine
of the Church of England.

In 1537, Henry authorized publication of the *Institutes of the Christian Man*, known as the *Bishops' Book*.
This text upheld all seven sacraments, while according
four of them a lower status. It also emphasized the authority of Scripture and defined the Church as a universal
institution composed of independent national bodies.

In April, 1539, Parliament was asked to formulate official doctrine for the Church in England. A stalemate en-

sued between the reformers, led by Cromwell and
Cranmer, and the more conservative bishops, most notably Stephen Gardiner, bishop of Winchester. On May 16,
the conservative Thomas Howard, duke of Norfolk and a
close ally of the king, was commissioned to break the
deadlock by submitting the Six Articles to Parliament. In
the light of the king's support, they were speedily accepted, passed Convocation, and became the new official
doctrine of the Church in England.

Disgruntled Protestants referred to the Six Articles as
the Whip with Six Strings because of their severity, and
indeed they were the most conservative doctrinal statement of the sixteenth century outside the Roman Catholic Church. Various Catholic beliefs and practices were
upheld by the articles, including transubstantiation, clerical celibacy, the validity of religious vows, confession to
a priest, and privately celebrated masses. The Six Articles prescribed the death penalty for all who denied transubstantiation, even though they might recant. Denial of
other articles made an offender liable to indefinite imprisonment upon a first offense and death following a
second offense.

In effect, the Six Articles outlawed Protestantism in
England and so destroyed the hopes of many Englishmen
who had looked to Henry VIII to effect a full Reformation along Continental lines. Cranmer strongly opposed
the articles at first, but as archbishop of Canterbury, he
was required to assent to them and promise to enforce
them. He had been married for some years, and to escape
prosecution, he had to send his German wife back to her
native country. Some clergy of Protestant inclinations resigned, including two bishops, but most bided their time
and hoped for the reversal that finally came when Elizabeth I assumed the throne.

Although Thomas Cromwell's theological opinions
were muted, he was among those who regarded the Six
Articles as an abomination. Cautiously, he sought to use
his authority as vicar-general to work for a modification
in religious policy. This desire coincided with, and was
reinforced by, his desire to promote an English alliance
with the German Lutheran princes against the Catholic
emperor, Charles V. The keystone of this plan was the
marriage of Henry and the Lutheran princess, Anne of
Cleves, which Cromwell successfully negotiated and
which took place in January, 1540. The divorced Catherine of Aragon had died in January, 1536, and Anne
Boleyn had been beheaded for treason and adultery in
May of the same year. Henry had then married Jane Seymour, who in October, 1537, had given birth to the long-
awaited male heir but had died in childbirth. At the time

of his marriage to Anne of Cleves, then, Henry had thus been a widower for more than two years.

Cromwell had negotiated the marriage largely for political reasons and had given Henry an exaggerated account of Anne's attractiveness. When the king saw his new bride, he was profoundly disgusted and proclaimed her "the Flanders mare." He refused to live with her and within a short time instituted a suit for divorce. His antagonism toward the marriage was intensified by the pressures of Anne's relatives and their German allies for some kind of religious dispensation in England, which Henry was unwilling to grant. Henry's full anger was now turned on Cromwell, whom he accused of treason. The vicar-general was not brought to trial but was convicted by Act of Parliament and executed on July 28, 1540. The reforming party at court seemed to have suffered an irreparable loss.

Meanwhile, the essentially conservative character of Henry's reformation continued. Latin was still the official language of worship. The Mass was retained, along with a celibate priesthood. Certain outspoken Protestants were burned at the stake as heretics. In the month following Cromwell's fall, Henry married his fifth wife, Catherine Howard, niece—like Anne Boleyn—of the duke of Norfolk. The marriage signaled for the time being the complete triumph of the conservative party. The Howard family later returned to the Roman Church, of which they remained members through the beginning of the twenty-first century. However, Catherine was suspected of infidelity to the aging king, and in February, 1542, she was beheaded, the second of Henry's wives to meet that fate. In July, 1543, he was married, for the last time, to Catherine Parr, who was suspected of Protestant leanings.

Thomas Cranmer, a Protestant appointed archbishop of Canterbury by King Henry VIII in 1533, was tried by Catholics after Henry's death—and during a time when England was moving back toward Catholicism—because of his persistent work for Protestantism in England. (Hulton|Archive by Getty Images)

The marriage brought only a slight loosening of official orthodoxy. Cranmer succeeded in passing a revision of the Bishops' Bible that strongly repudiated papal authority but contained little comfort for the Protestants. The revised version came to be known as the King's Bible because it was believed to reflect Henry's own beliefs. In the same year, an Act of Parliament forbade the common people from reading the vernacular Bible but permitted the practice to nobles and gentlemen.

SIGNIFICANCE

The Six Articles of Henry VIII stand as perhaps the clearest indication of the profound ambivalence of Henry's religious reforms. The king had become Supreme Head of the Church in England primarily for reasons of political expediency rather than out of a desire to reform the religious institutions of his nation. Once in that position, however, he had no choice but to create a new statement of religious doctrine for his new church. He attempted in the Six Articles to align himself as nearly as possible with Catholic doctrine and to make clear that his reformation was not connected to the Protestant Reformation. As Henry no doubt realized, however, for any major European power to reject papal authority and found its own national church could not help but stand as a major blow to Catholicism in the context of the growing power of the Protestants.

Henry died on January 28, 1547. To the end, he remained firm in his religious conservatism. However, in his will he directed that the regency of the kingdom be in the hands of Cranmer and the Seymour family until the young King Edward VI, his son by Jane Seymour, should come of age. During Edward's brief reign, the English Church underwent a considerable measure of reform along Protestant lines, only to have Catholicism restored once more in 1553 under Edward's half sister Mary I, the daughter of Henry and Catherine of Aragon. Under Elizabeth I, the daughter of Henry and Anne Boleyn, the Elizabethan Settlement finally stabilized the Church of England.

—*James F. Hitchcock*

FURTHER READING

Ayris, Paul, and David Selwyn, eds. *Thomas Cranmer: Churchman and Scholar.* Rochester, N.Y.: Boydell Press, 1999. Anthology of essays on all aspects of Cranmer's thought and career, including his facility with the English language, his stint as ambassador, his revisions of ecclesiastical canon law, and the relationship of his ideas to those of Erasmus and Luther. In-

cludes illustrations, bibliographic references, index.

Dickens, A. G. *The English Reformation.* 2d ed. University Park: Pennsylvania State University Press, 1991. Like Hughes, Dickens sees the religious history of the latter part of Henry's reign as greatly affected by the conflict between two parties, neither of which had the king's full confidence. Cromwell and Cranmer headed one, Norfolk and Gardiner the other.

_____. *Thomas Cromwell and the English Reformation.* London: English Universities Press, 1959. A sympathetic but objective account.

Gairdner, James H. *The English Church in the Sixteenth Century: From the Accession of Henry VIII to the Death of Mary.* Reprint. New York: AMS Press, [1971?]. Expresses the conservative Anglican viewpoint.

Gee, Henry, and William John Hardy, comps. *Documents Illustrative of English Church History.* Reprint. New York: Kraus Reprint, 1966. Contains the text of the Six Articles.

Hughes, Philip. *The Reformation in England.* 3 vols. Rev. ed. Reprint. Brookfield, Vt.: Ashgate, 1993. Sees Henry VIII as basically conservative in his religious outlook and unwilling to effect changes unless some tangible profit accrued to the Crown, as happened when the monasteries were suppressed.

Hutchinson, Francis E. *Cranmer and the English Reformation.* Reprint. London: English Universities Press, 1965. A brilliant book and a good place to start one's search for an understanding of how the Reformation came to England and Cranmer's role in it.

Loades, David. *Politics and Nation: England, 1450-1660.* 5th ed. Malden, Mass.: Blackwell, 1999. Examination of Cromwell's life and career against the backdrop of the extended power struggle between the Tudors and the aristocracy and Henry VIII's consolidation of power. Includes bibliographic references and index.

MacCulloch, Diarmaid. *Thomas Cranmer: A Life.* New Haven, Conn.: Yale University Press, 1996. Influential and award-winning biography of Cranmer incorporates recently discovered sources. Includes several appendices, illustrations, bibliographic references, and index.

McEntegart, Rory. *Henry VIII, the League of Schmalkalden, and the English Reformation.* Rochester, N.Y.: Boydell Press, 2002. Study of Henry's alliance and consultation with the Protestant League of Schmalkalden, analyzing his partial incorporation of German religious ideology into his own theology and the nascent Church of England. Looks both at the evolution of Henry's religious thought and at the wider political implications of that evolution. Includes bibliographic references and index.

Smith, H. Maynard. *Henry VIII and the Reformation.* London: Macmillan, 1964. Interprets the Six Articles as a layman's measure for church discipline.

Smith, Lacey B. *Tudor Prelates and Politics.* Princeton, N.J.: Princeton University Press, 1953. Cranmer, Gardiner, and other bishops are studied in relation to political and religious changes.

Wilson, Derek. *In the Lion's Court: Power, Ambition, and Sudden Death in the Reign of Henry VIII.* New York: St. Martin's Press, 2002. Vivid study of the perils of Henry VIII's court details the fates of six of its members, including Cranmer and Cromwell. Thematically designed to suggest parallels between the lives of these "six Thomases" and Henry's six wives. Includes illustrations, maps, sixteen pages of plates, bibliographic references, and index.

SEE ALSO: 1515-1529: Wolsey Serves as Lord Chancellor and Cardinal; Oct. 31, 1517: Luther Posts His Ninety-five Theses; June 28, 1519: Charles V Is Elected Holy Roman Emperor; 1531-1540: Cromwell Reforms British Government; Dec. 18, 1534: Act of Supremacy; July, 1535-Mar., 1540: Henry VIII Dissolves the Monasteries; Oct., 1536-June, 1537: Pilgrimage of Grace; Jan. 28, 1547-July 6, 1553: Reign of Edward VI; July, 1553: Coronation of Mary Tudor; 1558-1603: Reign of Elizabeth I; May, 1559-Aug., 1561: Scottish Reformation; Jan., 1563: Thirty-nine Articles of the Church of England; Feb. 25, 1570: Pius V Excommunicates Elizabeth I.

RELATED ARTICLES in *Great Lives from History: The Renaissance & Early Modern Era, 1454-1600:* Anne of Cleves; Anne Boleyn; Catherine of Aragon; Charles V; Thomas Cranmer; Thomas Cromwell; Edward VI; Elizabeth I; Stephen Gardiner; Henry VIII; Catherine Howard; Mary I; Catherine Parr; Jane Seymour.

1530's

May 28, 1539-September 10, 1543
DE SOTO'S NORTH AMERICAN EXPEDITION

De Soto led the first European journey into the interior of North America, with severe and lasting consequences for American Indians. Also, the largest sixteenth century battle on the continent between Europeans and American Indians took place during the expedition in 1540.

LOCALE: Southeastern North America
CATEGORIES: Exploration and discovery; colonization; wars, uprisings, and civil unrest

KEY FIGURES
Hernando de Soto (c. 1496-1542), Spanish governor of Cuba and expedition leader
Luis de Moscoso Alvarado (1505-1551), governor of Florida and expedition leader after de Soto's death
Juan Ortiz (d. c. 1541), Spanish interpreter for de Soto
Tascalusa (c. 1500-1540), Choctaw chief who ambushed de Soto at Mabila
Vitachuco (fl. sixteenth century), Timucuan leader who fought de Soto at Napituca

SUMMARY OF EVENT
Hernando de Soto was a veteran of early Spanish campaigns in the New World, having served in Nicaragua, Panama, and Peru. As Francisco Pizarro's lieutenant, de Soto helped to topple the Incan Empire, acquiring a share of their treasure, which made him a wealthy man. He returned to Spain in 1537, where his drive for more riches led to his appointment as governor of Cuba and *adelantado* of Florida. This gave him Spain's permission to conquer coastal territories from the Gulf of Mexico to Canada.

On May 28, 1539, de Soto landed near Tampa Bay with 622 soldiers, more than 200 horses, and many slaves. They encountered the indigenous town of Ucita, a well-organized compound with the chief's house on an earthen mound at one end and a temple guarded by a gilded-eyed bird at the other. They destroyed these and made camp.

On June 8, a Spanish patrol found Juan Ortiz, a shipwrecked survivor of the ill-fated Pánfilo de Narváez and Álvar Núñez Cabeza de Vaca expedition (1528-1536). Ortiz had escaped death at the hands of Chief Hirrihugua of Ucita when the chief's daughter Ulele interceded on his behalf. Many believe that Captain John Smith was inspired to invent his own salvation from Powhatan by Pocahontas (which he did not report until some twenty years after the event) after reading Ortiz's story in the

1600's. Ortiz's abilities as translator proved invaluable to de Soto.

On July 15, the main army left Ucita in pursuit of gold. Living off native maize, they traversed northern Timucuan territories in late summer. They were continually harassed by ambushes, and a major uprising occurred at Napituca under the leadership of Vitachuco. On September 15, the deaths of hundreds of indigenous peoples made apparent the advantages of Spanish horses, muskets, and war hounds.

Turning west, the entourage arrived at the principal Apalachee town of Anhaica on October 6. Near what is now Tallahassee, this horticultural center of 250 houses and more than one thousand people had rich stores of food, and de Soto decided to winter there. It was there that de Soto's party heard rumors of a golden kingdom to the northeast ruled by a cacica (female chief), and on March 3, 1540, they crossed over into what is now Georgia to find it. Although delayed by pitched battles, the Spaniards extracted directions to the chiefdom of Cofitachequi from reluctant informants after burning

some of them alive. De Soto used both negotiating and cruelty as political tools, resorting to kidnapping, murder, torture, and mutilation as a policy of intimidation.

Reaching Cofitachequi, de Soto received a gift of pearls from the chieftain, and her temples produced hundreds of pounds more. She directed the party to nearby Talomeco, where her ancestors were interred. The five hundred houses of Talomeco had been abandoned as a result of pestilence, possibly caused by the 1526 slave-raiding foray of Lucas Vásquez de Ayllón along the Carolina coast. Talomeco's mound temple was still intact, a 140-foot structure housing bodies of the elite, fine clothes, artworks, weapons, and chests of pearls. Many of de Soto's men wanted to stay in the abundance of Cofitachequi, but when demands for gold and silver produced only copper and sheet mica, de Soto left on May 3, 1540, to continue his treasure quest. Although she later escaped, he kidnapped the cacica to serve as guide.

During the summer of 1540, de Soto marched through the Carolinas and Tennessee, into the southern Appalachians and the Blue Ridge Mountains. He contacted the

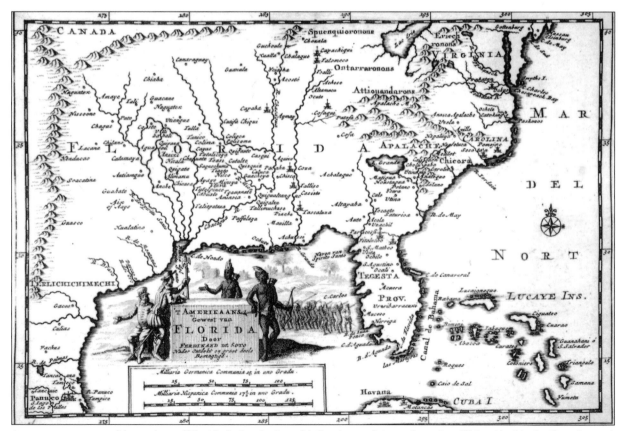

A contemporary map of the territory of Florida during the time of de Soto's expedition to the region. (Hulton\Archive by Getty Images)

DE SOTO'S EXPEDITION, 1539-1543

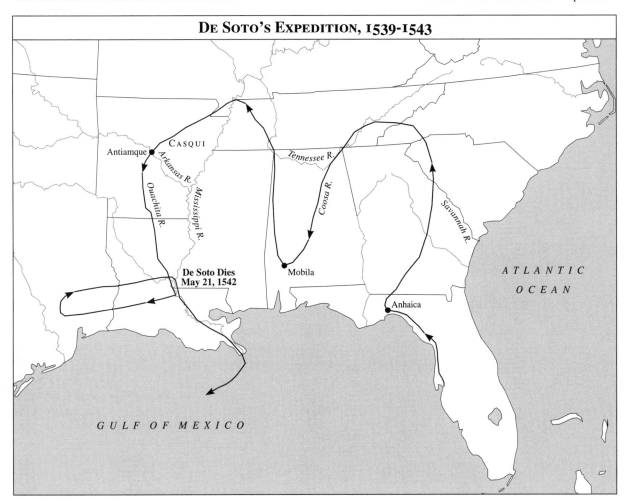

Cherokees at Xuala and Guasili, and then proceeded to the Creek frontier at Chiaha in northern Georgia. When the usual demands for treasure, food, bearers, and women were made, the Chiaha chief told de Soto that riches were to be found farther south, so the expedition continued.

The group passed through western Georgia in mid-July, briefly imprisoning the Coosa chief. It then passed through Itaba and Talisi, reaching Choctaw country in Alabama in early October. Here, the great Tascalusa chief by the same name was taken prisoner. Pressed for four hundred bearers and one hundred women, the chief provided bearers and promised that the women would be available at his town of Mabila. On October 18, 1540, Tascalusa led de Soto into an ambush now called the Battle of Mabila, considered the time's bloodiest battle of the North American continent.

Between four thousand and five thousand warriors attacked the Spaniards, of whom twenty were killed and

150 wounded, including de Soto. Most of their goods—including the Cofitachequi pearls—were lost in the ensuing fire, but Mabila was destroyed and indigenous losses may have been more than three thousand. This loss affected indigenous communities perhaps all the way to Coosa.

De Soto was within reach of his ships in the Gulf of Mexico, but he refused to quit. He turned the battered expedition northwest to invade Chickasaw territory at Apafalaya and Chicaca. They spent a cold winter in 1540-1541 near the Yazoo River in Mississippi. On March 3, 1541, two Chickasaw attacks killed twelve soldiers, sixty horses, and many pigs, and destroyed most of the supplies that had survived at Mabila.

Despite this setback, de Soto continued his spring march to the northwest, reaching the Mississippi River about 10 miles south of what is now Memphis, Tennessee. Crossing in dugout canoes on May 8, 1541, the expe-

Indigenous captives in chains walking before de Soto, who is on horseback, during an expedition through Florida in search of gold. (Hulton Archive by Getty Images)

dition reached the chiefdom of Casqui in Arkansas. De Soto allied with the Casqui chief to jointly attack the rival chiefdom of Pacaha. They stripped the storehouses clean and scattered the bones of the Pacaha elite resting in the sacred mound temples.

De Soto then pressed up the Arkansas River to the very edge of the Great Plains, where he heard of great buffalo herds but little corn and, more important, no gold. Circling back to Casqui, de Soto and his group sought a place to spend the winter, settling at Autiamque, near Little Rock, on November 2, 1541. It was there that Juan Ortiz died, depriving de Soto of invaluable assistance, and the *adelantado* began to show signs of illness and despair.

The spring campaign of 1542 yielded more resistance and few successes, and at Guachoya, on the Mississippi

River, de Soto became feverish. He gave his men a repentant speech about his shortcomings and died of what was probably a European illness on May 21, 1542. Luis de Moscoso Alvarado took command and buried de Soto in the swirling waters of the great river Europeans would credit him with discovering.

Moscoso, after trying an unsuccessful overland trek through Texas, returned to the Mississippi River to attempt a watery route home. His small flotilla set out for the Gulf of Mexico on July 2, 1543. Before he reached the gulf, 700 miles and two weeks later, constant attacks by the indigenous claimed many more lives on both sides. The 311 bedraggled survivors made landfall at Panuco on Mexico's Gulf coast on September 10, 1543.

SIGNIFICANCE

De Soto's precise route is not as important as the lasting impact his expedition had on indigenous cultures, which started their decline soon after de Soto's journey.

Archaeologists have uncovered mass burials and skeletons bearing cuts from European weapons. Razing the mound temples, extinguishing sacred fires, scattering royal ancestral remains, and disrupting the leadership of elite rulers claiming direct descent from the Sun all may have undermined the religious and political fabric of these large and prosperous chiefdoms, sending them into chaos. Tristán de Luna y Arellano, in the 1560's, and Robert Cavelier, sieur de La Salle, in 1682, found only scattered villages where de Soto had described large populations.

The void was so complete that by the 1800's, no one remembered who had built the thousands of earth mounds dotting the waterways of eastern North America. A popular myth attributed them to a "lost race" of mound builders, thereby denying North American Indians their authorship. The Smithsonian scientist Cyrus Thomas disproved this in 1894, citing de Soto's observations and archaeological findings to prove the contrary.

—*Gary A. Olson*

FURTHER READING

Ewen, Charles R., and John H. Hann. *Hernando de Soto Among the Apalachee: The Archaeology of the First Winter Encampment.* Gainesville: University Press of Florida, 1998. Narrative of the discovery, excavation, and interpretation of the only known de Soto camp site. Provides historical background, detailed description of the site and what was learned from it, and new translations of the portions of sixteenth century travel narratives.

Galloway, Patricia, ed. *The Hernando de Soto Expedition: History, Historiography, and "Discovery" in the Southeast.* Lincoln: University of Nebraska Press, 1997. Anthology that seeks to expand traditional studies of de Soto's expedition to discuss its broad cultural implications, focusing on specific details such as the daily routine and health of its members.

Garcilaso de La Vega. *The Florida of the Inca.* Translated by John Grier Varner and Jeannette Johnson Varner. 1605. Reprint. Austin: University of Texas Press, 1988. An early secondhand account based on the experiences of three expedition members.

Hudson, Charles. *Knights of Spain, Warriors of the Sun: Hernando de Soto and the South's Ancient Chiefdoms.* Athens: University of Georgia Press, 1997. Study of the disastrous impact of de Soto's expedition on the North American Indian civilizations he encountered.

Swanton, John R. *Final Report of the United States De Soto Expedition Commission.* 1939. Reprint. Washington, D.C.: Smithsonian Institution Press, 1985. Classic analysis of de Soto's route and the ethnohistorical sources. Contains a new foreword and introduction.

SEE ALSO: Oct. 12, 1492: Columbus Lands in the Americas; 1493-1521: Ponce de León's Voyages; Apr., 1519-Aug., 1521: Cortés Conquers Aztecs in Mexico; 1527-1547: Maya Resist Spanish Incursions in Yucatán; 1528-1536: Narváez's and Cabeza de Vaca's Expeditions; Feb. 23, 1540-Oct., 1542: Coronado's Southwest Expedition; 1542-1543: The New Laws of Spain; Sept., 1565: St. Augustine Is Founded; July 4, 1584-1590: Lost Colony of Roanoke; Jan., 1598-Feb., 1599: Oñate's New Mexico Expedition.

RELATED ARTICLES in *Great Lives from History: The Renaissance & Early Modern Era, 1454-1600:* Christopher Columbus; Ferdinand II and Isabella I; Pedro Menéndez de Avilés; Philip II; Juan Ponce de León; Hernando de Soto; Tascalusa.

1540-1545
SHĒR SHĀH SŪR BECOMES EMPEROR OF DELHI

Shēr Shāh Sūr twice defeated Humāyūn, the second Mughal emperor, and ruled northern India, establishing administrative and political techniques later followed by the emperors of the restored Mughal Dynasty.

LOCALE: Northern India

CATEGORIES: Government and politics; wars, uprisings, and civil unrest; expansion and land acquisition

KEY FIGURES

Shēr Shāh Sūr (1486?-1545), an Afghan who ruled northern India for fifteen years, r. 1540-1545

Humāyūn (1508-1556), second Mughal emperor, r. 1530-1540 and 1555-1556

Islām Shāh Sūr (d. 1553), Shēr Shāh's son and successor, r. 1545-1553

SUMMARY OF EVENT

The time of the Mughal Dynasty of the early sixteenth century marked perhaps the golden age of India. From Bābur's victory over the Lodī sultans at the Battle of Panipat in 1526 until the death of ʿĀlamgīr in 1707, the Mughals dominated the Indian subcontinent as few before them had done. It was an era of glory and great accomplishments, a civilization that melded Indian, Persian, Islamic, and Hindu qualities and characteristics.

India in the sixteenth century, however, could well have taken a different road, with the Mughals a footnote to India's long history. What has appeared inevitable to later generations was not obvious to observers in the 1530's and 1540's, when it appeared likely that the future of India lay in the hands of Shēr Shāh Sūr and not in those of Bābur's heir, his son Humāyūn.

After Bābur's victory at Panipat, it had been likely that many of Bābur's supporters would abandon the Ganges valley plain and the Delhi region to return instead to Afghanistan with loot and glory. Bābur, however, convinced most of his military contingent to remain in India and help to establish an empire. Bābur sent his son and heir Humāyūn to Afghanistan to plan for the conquest of Central Asia's Samarqand region, Bābur's goal for more than two decades. In 1529, informed that his father Bābur was near death, Humāyūn hurried back to Delhi. Bābur

1540's

died the following year and, at the age of twenty-two, Humāyūn became the second Mughal emperor.

Humāyūn would rule his Indian empire for just over ten years between 1530 and 1556, however. Like Bābur, Humāyūn would prove to be a formidable campaigner, but unlike his father, he was easily distracted by the pleasures that power gave him, including an appetite for opium. Less ruthless than Bābur and most of the future Mughal emperors, Humāyūn allowed his younger brothers too much freedom and too much power, and all of them attempted to wrest his empire from him. Future Mughal rulers, however, would confine or execute possible rival family members.

The several Lodī warlords who had survived the Lodī sultan's defeat at Panipat were also a threat to Humāyūn's rule, including the Afghan Shēr Shāh of the Sūr clan, a clan that entered India in the fifteenth century as retainers of the Lodīs. Shār Shāh had served under Bābur but left Mughal service in 1528 and entrenched himself east of Delhi along the banks of the Ganges River at the fortress of Chunar, where he had earlier acquired lands. Before Humāyūn could deal with the threat posed by Shēr Shāh, however, he faced another threat from the sultan of Gujarat. His subsequent campaigns in Gujarat and in Rājasthān and Malwa were successful, but again he made the mistake of allowing his brothers access to political and military authority.

When Humāyūn returned to the east, he attacked Chunar, but even though it fell after a six-month siege, the mobile Shēr Shāh had moved farther east, seizing Bengal and Bihar. In June, 1539, at Chausa, the two opponents finally faced each other on the battlefield. The Mughal emperor suffered a disastrous defeat, with many of Humāyūn's troops either drowned in the Ganges or captured. The following year, in 1540, at the Battle of Kannauj, Shēr Shāh was again victorious. Humāyūn had a numerical advantage, having forty thousand warriors to Shēr Shāh's fifteen thousand, but the latter's cavalry proved decisive and the Mughal emperor barely escaped with his life.

Humāyūn's feckless brothers refused him assistance and he was eventually forced to seek sanctuary in Iran with the Ṣafavid ruler, Shah Ṭahmāsp I.

After his victory at Chausa in 1539, Shēr Shāh took the name for which he is best known and had coins struck in his name. He was in his fifties and his reign would last only five years, but during that brief period Shēr Shāh left his mark on northern India. His empire stretched from the Punjab in the west to the Bay of Bengal in the east. A major accomplishment was his reconciliation of other

Shēr Shāh Sūr, an Afghan, succeeded Humāyūn (pictured above) as the Emperor of Delhi in 1540 after two decisive military victories. (Hulton|Archive by Getty Images)

ambitious Afghan warriors under his rule and solidifying his control over them. His political and administrative endeavors were aimed at avoiding the possible emergence of major rivals to his rule. Instead of relying upon provincial governors, Shēr Shāh divided his territories into districts, which were again divided into civil, military, and religious areas of responsibility, with all officials subject to rotation every two or three years from district to district. This divided and separate administrative structure made it difficult for any single rival to challenge Shēr Shāh's power.

Corruption was always an endemic threat to any Indian government, and during his reign, corrupt officials were removed from office. He was a sincere and pious Muslim who generally tolerated Hinduism and had Hindus appointed to office on occasion, but his campaigns against the Rājputs led to a massacre of Hindus at Raisin in 1542. Military reforms were instituted to ensure that his cavalry of 150,000 and other forces, including 25,000 infantry and 300 elephants, were always ready for war.

Roads were built and improved, notably the Grand Trunk Road, which stretched more than 1,000 miles from eastern Bengal to the Indus River. Trees were planted and post-houses constructed along the roads, and the reduction of duties and taxes upon internal commerce encouraged trade. His silver rupee coins would later form the basis of Mughal coinage. Like so many rulers throughout history, Shēr Shāh was also a builder of note, in Delhi and elsewhere. His most impressive monumental legacy was his own tomb, an octagonal five-story structure at Sarasam, near Varanasi, which would inspire later Mughal emperors.

Shēr Shāh died in 1545, after the successful siege of the Rājput fortress of Kalinjar. A misdirected rocket ignited a series of explosions. Shēr Shāh suffered serious burns and died within a few hours. His son, Islām Shāh Sūr, ascended the throne, but he lacked the disciplined ambition of his father. After Islām Shāh died in 1553, the lands and territories of the Sūrs fell into factional division and terminal weakness. Humāyūn returned from his years of exile in Iran and Afghanistan and reoccupied Delhi by the summer of 1555. The following year he died, and his young son Akbar ascended the Mughal throne.

Significance

The Mughal Dynasty was one of the greatest of the Indian dynasties, and Humāyūn's son Akbar was one of the most notable rulers in world history. The Sūr Dynasty remains almost unknown to those unaware of the history of early modern India.

Shēr Shāh Sūr is at best a footnote to the glories of the Mughals, but in the 1530's and 1540's, it appeared that the Mughals would be the footnote to the Sūrs. The acci-

dental explosion at Kalinjar and other vagaries of history, including incompetent successors, led to the fall of the house of Sūr.

Nevertheless, Shēr Shāh Sūr's influence and impact continued beyond his own lifetime. The Mughals adopted many of his political and administrative approaches and techniques, adopted his silver rupee in their own coinage, and emulated the mausoleum of Shēr Shāh Sūr in the design of their tombs.

—*Eugene Larson*

Further Reading

Bakshi, S. R., ed. *Advanced History of Medieval India.* 3 vols. Rev. ed. New Delhi, India: Anmol, 2003. Volume 2 includes a description of the era of Shēr Shāh Sūr and Humāyūn.

Jayapalan, N. *Medieval History of India.* Delhi, India: Atlantic, 2001. Includes a discussion of the rivalry and accomplishments of Humāyūn and Shēr Shāh Sūr.

Streusand, Douglas E. *The Formation of the Mughal Empire.* New York: Oxford University Press, 1999. An important work of the early decades of the Mughal Empire, including the era of Shēr Shāh and Humāyūn.

Wolpert, Stanley. *A New History of India.* New York: Oxford University Press, 2000. One of the standard Indian history texts, discusses the events surrounding the conflict between Humāyūn and Shēr Shāh.

See also: 1451-1526: Lodī Kings Dominate Northern India; Apr. 21, 1526: First Battle of Panipat; Mar. 17, 1527: Battle of Khānua; Dec. 30, 1530: Humāyūn Inherits the Throne in India; Mar. 3, 1575: Mughal Conquest of Bengal.

Related articles in *Great Lives from History: The Renaissance & Early Modern Era, 1454-1600:* Akbar; Bābur; Humāyūn; Ibrāhīm Lodī; Krishnadevaraya.

1540's

February 23, 1540-October, 1542
CORONADO'S SOUTHWEST EXPEDITION

Coronado conducted the first extensive European exploration of the North American Southwest, which prompted later expeditions and Spanish settlement of the region.

LOCALE: Southwestern North America (now primarily New Mexico) and New Spain (now Mexico)
CATEGORY: Exploration and discovery

KEY FIGURES

Francisco Vásquez de Coronado (1510-1554), expedition leader
Álvar Núñez Cabeza de Vaca (c. 1490-c. 1560), Spanish explorer
Estevanico (d. 1539), Moorish slave who guided the first expedition into the American Southwest
Juan de Oñate (1550-1630), governor and captain general of New Mexico

SUMMARY OF EVENT

The Moors, a nomadic North African tribe, occupied the Iberian Peninsula for several hundred years before being driven out in the late fifteenth century. They contributed much to Spanish culture. They also were part of a myth that would have enduring consequences for North America. Legend had it that oppressed Christians led by seven bishops had fled the Moorish invasion and gone west by sea. These refugees were supposed to have landed on an island called Antilia and established seven cities of fabulous wealth. These cities then formed a utopian commonwealth, later called the Seven Cities of Cíbola.

Spanish explorers, motivated by the New World's promise of wealth, moved quickly to capitalize on its Mexican conquest of the early 1520's by Hernán Cortés. Nuño Beltrán de Guzmán had been appointed governor of the central Mexican province of Panuco in 1527. Guzmán's young American Indian slave, Tejo, told the cruel governor that he had heard stories of seven rich cities to the north and west. In 1529, Guzmán and a force of four hundred soldiers set out to found the province of Nueva Galicia in what is today northwest Mexico just below the Arizona border. He found treacherous terrain, and he killed indigenous peoples along the way. By 1531, he had abandoned his search for the cities of gold.

Then, in 1536, Álvar Núñez Cabeza de Vaca escaped indigenous captivity in Texas and completed an eight-year odyssey from Florida, across south Texas, and across the Rio Grande into Mexico. He and his three companions—two other Spaniards and a Moorish slave named Estevanico, or Estevén—endured much hardship and had many tales to tell. They had not seen the fabulous seven cities but had heard about advanced civilizations to the north. The islanders of Antilia just might have fled to a mainland sanctuary. Thus the rumor was revived.

In August, 1538, twenty-eight-year-old Francisco Vásquez de Coronado was appointed governor of Nueva Galicia. Meanwhile, the viceroy of Mexico, Antonio de Mendoza, was seeking someone to lead an expedition to seek the seven cities. Estevanico was ready and willing, but a slave could not be expected to command Spanish soldiers. Conveniently, two padres arrived who were eager for the adventure. Fray Marcos de Niza and Fray Onarato sought grace in establishing Church authority. Estevanico was ordered along.

The expedition went sour from the beginning. After leaving Nueva Galicia in the spring of 1539, Fray Onarato became ill and had to return. Estevanico ignored Fray Marcos and went on ahead north into present-day Arizona and east across the Gila River into New Mexico. Fray Marcos most likely never got as far as the Arizona country.

Estevanico reached the city of Cíbola (the first use of this term) on Zuñi land in eastern New Mexico. The Zuñis were one of the many settled tribes in the American Southwest that the Spaniards labeled *pueblo* after their sophisticated architectural skills. The Zuñis, however, killed Estevanico and dismembered his body to prove that he was not a god. Fray Marcos reported back to the viceroy that the trek to the land of the Zuñis was gentle, and that all indications were good that the Seven Cities of Cíbola actually existed. These lies spurred further exploration.

In mid-November of 1539, a scouting party led by Melchor Díaz took forty-five soldiers to Cíbola, mounted on the first horses to enter the western part of the continent. Díaz returned with a discouraging report: The terrain was rugged, and no evidence of gold, silver, or jewels was found. Coronado remained undaunted. He was a knight-errant in an exotic land, and his ethos was to serve God and country while serving himself. The Spanish relied on the *adelantado* (military chieftain) to secure new lands for the Crown. This warrior might have to bankroll his own expeditions and the risks were great, but so too were the possible rewards.

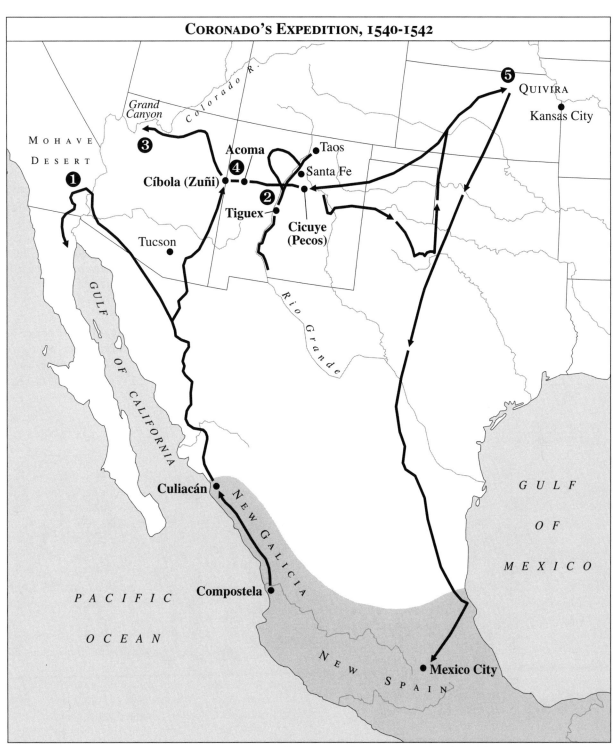

CORONADO'S EXPEDITION, 1540-1542

Grand Canyon

Colorado R.

MOHAVE DESERT

①

③

Acoma

④

Cíbola (Zuñi)

②

Tiguex

Taos

Santa Fe

Cicuye (Pecos)

Tucson

GULF OF CALIFORNIA

Rio Grande

⑤ QUIVIRA

Kansas City

Culiacán

NEW GALICIA

Compostela

PACIFIC OCEAN

NEW SPAIN

GULF OF MEXICO

Mexico City

1540's

Coronado's travels included (1) exploration of the lower Colorado River by a splinter party led by Melchor Díaz; (2) a conflict in which two hundred Tiguex natives were killed; (3) discovery of the Grand Canyon by García López de Cárdenas; (4) Hernando de Alvarado's reconnaissance of the Acoma pueblo, the Rio Grande Valley, and the environs of modern Albuquerque, Santa Fe, and Taos, New Mexico; and (5) Coronado's visit to the fabled area of Quivira (supposed location of the fabled Seven Cities of Cíbola) in eastern Kansas. The great cities that Coronado sought proved to be thatched huts housing poor natives.

Coronado set out on February 23, 1540, from Compostella on Mexico's west coast with 340 soldiers, several hundred American Indians, and a few African servants. He subjugated the Zuñi after a brief fight and sent emissaries ahead to scout the countryside. Captain García López de Cárdenas and his small band went north and became the first Europeans to gaze into the Grand Canyon. Captain Hernando de Alvarado moved east past the mighty fortress of the Acoma pueblos into the Rio Grande Valley and then north through the area that is now Albuquerque, Santa Fe, and Taos, New Mexico. All along, these conquistadores found sophisticated Pueblo settlements with good supplies of maize, turkeys, and beans. They found no gold or silver.

Alvarado then turned east toward what is now the New Mexico-Texas border. There he learned about the slave trade that existed between the Pueblo and Plains tribes. He met a captured Kansas Indian whom the Spaniards called the "Turk" because of his complexion. The Kansas Indian knew what the Spanish craved. To get back to his own country, he concocted a story about pre-

cious minerals aplenty if the Spaniards would head north and east to the Kansas plain and the fabulous city of Quivira. He was taken back to Coronado, who believed him because he wanted to believe.

Scattered fighting had broken out between the Spanish conquistadores and the indigenous inhabitants of New Mexico during the harsh winter of 1540-1541. The Spaniards wanted food, supplies, and clothing, and so they took them. Coronado was nevertheless determined to march to Quivira. He pushed on all the way to eastern Kansas, in the area that is now Wichita, and found mostly grasslands. Coronado had the Kansan Indian "informant" executed, then returned to winter in the Rio Grande Valley before retreating to Old Mexico in the spring of 1542. The exhausted and tattered expedition reached Mexico City sometime before October 13. Coronado felt defeated and disappointed.

SIGNIFICANCE

For forty years, the frontier that Coronado had helped to establish lay neglected by the Spanish authorities. A

Coronado leads an expedition of soldiers, indigenous peoples, and clergy through the arid southwestern United States. (Library of Congress)

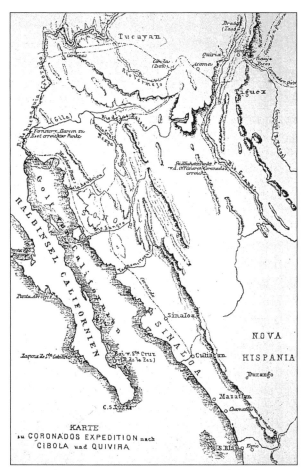

A map of Coronado's expedition in search of the legendary seven cities of fabulous wealth—a utopian commonwealth thought to be in New Spain—which was later called the Seven Cities of Cíbola. (Hulton|Archive by Getty Images)

torture, and extortion. The Franciscans competed with the civil authorities for plunder, until the only difference between the mission *encomiendas* (forced labor arrangements) and those of the governors was into whose pocket went the profits. Oñate established the first settlement, called San Juan, north of Santa Fe. Because the site of Santa Fe had more room, a better defensive position, and a reliable source of water, colonialists began settling the area as early as 1608.

—*Brian G. Tobin*

FURTHER READING

Adorno, Rolena, and Patrick Charles Pautz. *Álvar Núñez Cabeza de Vaca: His Account, His Life, and the Expedition of Pánfilo de Narváez.* 3 vols. Lincoln: University of Nebraska Press, 1999. Volume 1 contains Cabeza de Vaca's own narrative of his adventures. Volumes 2 and 3 provide close readings and interpretations of the narrative together with analyses of the place of the work in literary history and the general history of Spanish exploration in the Americas.

Cabeza de Vaca, Álvar Núñez. *The Narrative of Cabeza de Vaca.* Translated and edited by Rolena Adorno and Patrick Charles Pautz. Lincoln: University of Nebraska Press, 2003. A stand-alone edition of Adorno and Pautz's critically praised translation of Cabeza de Vaca's narrative.

Flint, Richard, and Shirley Cushing Flint, eds. *The Coronado Expedition: From the Distance of Four Hundred Sixty Years.* Albuquerque: University of New Mexico Press, 2003. Anthology studying all aspects of Coronado's expedition, from the names of its members to the technical design of their horseshoes to the interactions with the indigenous peoples.

_____. *The Coronado Expedition to Tierra Nueva: The 1540-1542 Route Across the Southwest.* 1997. Reprint. Niwot, Colo.: University Press of Colorado, 2004. A companion to the above anthology, this multidisciplinary study provides archaeological, ethnographic, historical, and geographic research into the specific route followed by Coronado's expedition. Explains the evidence, details the most likely route, and discusses the importance of these findings.

Forbes, Jack D. *Apache, Navaho, and Spaniard.* Norman: University of Oklahoma Press, 1971. Focuses on Spanish incursions into Arizona, New Mexico, and Texas between 1540 and 1700.

Terrell, John Upton. *Pueblos, Gods, and Spaniards.* New York: Dial Press, 1973. A tribute to Pueblo culture and its resiliency.

combination of internal political squabbling and tribal uprisings preoccupied the viceroy in Mexico City. Gradually, Franciscan missionaries and Spanish miners pushed north and revived interest in Tierra Nueva, as Coronado's men had called the land. The authorities took note, and in 1595 they granted the title of governor and captain general to Juan de Oñate. His job was "to carry out the discovery, pacification, and reconquest of the provinces of New Mexico."

The ruthless and ambitious Oñate went north from El Paso in 1598 and quickly subjugated the Pueblo tribes. He attracted soldier followers by the promise of their becoming Hidalgos, which literally meant "son of someone" and was the lowest rank of Spanish nobility. He became *adelantado* and established a systematic repression of the Pueblo Indians through forced labor, murder, rape,

1540's

Udall, Stewart L. *Majestic Journey: Coronado's Inland Empire.* Rev. ed. Sante Fe: Museum of New Mexico Press, 1995. The former secretary of the U.S. Department of the Interior retraces Coronado's route to demonstrate the historical importance of his expedition.

Webber, David J. *The Spanish Frontier in North America.* New Haven, Conn.: Yale University Press, 1992. Smoothly written synthesis of an important cultural clash.

SEE ALSO: 1493-1521: Ponce de León's Voyages; 1495-1510: West Indian Uprisings; Apr., 1519-Aug., 1521:

Cortés Conquers Aztecs in Mexico; 1528-1536: Narváez's and Cabeza de Vaca's Expeditions; May 28, 1539-Sept. 10, 1543: De Soto's North American Expedition; 1542-1543: The New Laws of Spain; Sept., 1565: St. Augustine Is Founded; Jan., 1598-Feb., 1599: Oñate's New Mexico Expedition.

RELATED ARTICLES in *Great Lives from History: The Renaissance & Early Modern Era, 1454-1600:* Álvar Núñez Cabeza de Vaca; Charles V; Francisco Vásquez de Coronado; Hernán Cortés; Pedro Menéndez de Avilés; Paul III; Juan Ponce de León; Hernando de Soto.

October 20-27, 1541
HOLY ROMAN EMPIRE ATTACKS OTTOMANS IN ALGIERS

Charles V, attempting to reassert his authority in the Mediterranean, assaulted the North African coast, despite the misgivings of some of his top advisers. The attack failed, weakening the Holy Roman Empire and establishing Ottoman domination of the western Mediterranean.

LOCALE: East of Algiers, North Africa
CATEGORIES: Expansion and land acquisition; religion; wars, uprisings, and civil unrest

KEY FIGURES
Barbarossa (d. 1546), renegade Christian corsair and grand admiral of the Ottoman Empire, 1534-1546
Charles V (1500-1558), Holy Roman Emperor, r. 1519-1556, king of Spain, r. 1516-1556 as Charles I
Süleyman the Magnificent (1494/1495-1566), sultan of the Ottoman Empire, r. 1520-1566
Francis I (1494-1547), king of France, r. 1515-1547
Andrea Doria (1466-1560), Genovese soldier of fortune, statesman, and admiral of Charles V's fleet

SUMMARY OF EVENT
The Holy Roman Empire's policy of expansion in North Africa began under Charles V's predecessors: The years 1509-1511 had seen the conquest of Oran, Bugia, and Tripoli, as well as the submission of Algiers. However, the rich prospects of Spanish America had distracted Charles from the empire's energetic expansion southward until North African corsairs of diverse nationalities, especially Barbarossa and his brother ʿArūj, seized Tunis

and Algiers, ruling them as semiautonomous Ottoman provinces. This extension of the Ottoman sultan's power into the western Mediterranean marked the beginning of a long conflict with Habsburg-controlled Spain.

Charles V retook Tunis from Barbarossa in 1535, but he knew that this victory neither guaranteed his empire's naval supremacy nor inflicted permanent damage on the Ottoman-controlled pirates in the western Mediterranean. Charles had therefore planned an expedition against Algiers as early as 1536. By 1541, however, he had become determined to eliminate any Ottoman bases of operations in the Mediterranean Sea, a vital link in the chain of imperial communications. Lurking in the background was the constant threat of Charles's archenemy, France's King Francis I, joining forces with the Ottomans against the extensive Habsburg territories. In fact, such a possibility did occur to both Süleyman I and Francis I. Moreover, in the preceding years, some of the Barbary pirates under Ottoman sponsorship had made raids on the coasts of Spain.

Because of the delay in marshaling German, Spanish, and Italian troops and resources in Genoa in 1541, it was already September when the expedition finally set sail under Charles's personal command. The fleet had missed the season of clement weather, and Andrea Doria strongly urged against the campaign as a result, but Charles could not face the prospect of wasting the cost of recruiting the men, ships, and supplies that he had undertaken over the several previous months. The attack went forward.

A force of twenty-one thousand men was landed

twelve miles east of Algiers on October 20, 1541. Just as their attack was beginning, however, a serious storm arose, preventing them from putting ashore the bulk of Charles's heavy artillery, ammunition, and food. Most of the imperial fleet—perhaps as many as 150 ships—foundered or had to escape out to sea, while the soaked contingents already on shore were barely able to use their compromised ammunition to attack the city.

Algiers's Muslim defenders took advantage of the situation to stage a sortie and attack the imperial forces from October 24 to 26, causing heavy casualties. A hasty, improvised evacuation of Charles's forces mandated the abandonment of all supplies. Charles and fourteen thousand survivors were forced to reembark on the remaining galleys and transports on October 27 and give up the operation to avoid an even greater disaster. The Holy Roman Empire's Tunisian triumph six years earlier had turned into the Algerine rout, not only by virtue of the great losses suffered by Charles's forces but also because Barbarossa's navy now felt free to attack waters vital to Habsburg power throughout the Mediterranean, while Francis I pondered how he could benefit from Charles's predicament. Indeed, by the following year, 1542, the two were again at war.

The attack on Algiers was one of the greatest military setbacks in Charles's career and the last of his important naval endeavors. It was also a major political defeat, for it signified the Holy Roman Empire's relinquishment of the western Mediterranean to the Turks. In addition, Charles's misadventure in Algiers encouraged France's king to renew his alliance with the Ottoman sultan Süleyman the Magnificent against their common enemy, while Süleyman now felt free to attack Habsburg Hungary, annexing the city of Buda that same year.

By 1551, Tripoli in North Africa had fallen to the Ottomans, followed by Jerba (Tunisia) in 1560 and Tunis itself in 1574. Charles, striving to establish a universal, Catholic empire, was also overwhelmed by his conflict with the German Protestants and with others who preferred nationalism as a basis of political organization to Charles's multinational imperialism. Even the popes wavered in their divided loyalty to their Catholic co-religionists, Charles V and Francis I, and those who tried failed to organize a Christian crusade against Muslim Ottoman power.

SIGNIFICANCE

Not even all the gold brought by Spanish galleons from the New World could support the imperialist and religious goals of the Holy Roman Empire. Indeed, part of the delay in getting the Algiers expedition under way earlier in 1541, during more clement weather, had to do with Charles's perennial difficulties raising sufficient funds from the great German banking concerns, such as those of the Fuggers and the Welsers.

During the truces between the four wars between Charles V and Francis I, the Holy Roman Emperor had also tried to convince the French monarch to join him in a Christian crusade against the Muslim Ottomans. This did not happen, but rather, it was the Habsburg sovereign who proved unable to contain the combined power of the Ottomans and their Barbary state allies with France's tacit consent. As a result, the Turks were to retain control of the Mediterranean until the Battle of Lepanto in 1571.

—*Peter B. Heller*

FURTHER READING

Alvarez, Manuel F. *Charles V, Elected Emperor and Hereditary Ruler.* Translated by J. A. Lalaguna. London: Thames and Hudson, 1975. The rise and decline of a king, emperor, statesman, and soldier, as well as his ideals. Maps, genealogy, bibliography, illustrations, index.

Imber, Colin. *The Ottoman Empire, 1300-1650: The Structure of Power.* New York: Palgrave-Macmillan, 2002. A topical approach, ranging from history and chronology to dynasty, geography, law, and institutions. Maps, glossary, bibliography, index.

Lewis, D. B. Wyndham. *Charles V of Europe.* New York: Coward-McCann, 1931. A classic about Charles V's religious ideals and political rivalries. Maps, genealogy, illustrations, index.

Lynch, John. *Spain 1516-1598: From Nation State to World Empire.* Oxford, England: Blackwell, 1991. Covers the reign of three Habsburg monarchs, including Charles V, in chronological fashion. Maps, plates, appendices, bibliographical essay, index.

Schwarzenfeld, Gertrude von. *Charles V: Father of Europe.* Translated by Ruth Mary Bethell. Chicago: Henry Regnery, 1957. A chronological and geographic breakdown of Charles's reign, including an account of Algiers in 1541. Biographical profiles, bibliography, illustrations, index.

Tracy, James D. *Emperor Charles V, Impresario of War: Campaign Strategy, International Finance, and Domestic Politics.* New York: Cambridge University Press, 2002. Biography, history, and military campaigns of the Holy Roman Emperor and the problems of financing his wars. Maps, tables, bibliography, illustrations, index.

1540's

557

1542-1543
THE NEW LAWS OF SPAIN

Charles I issued two laws that prohibited the enslavement of indigenous peoples and countered the colonial aristocracy's attempts to challenge the Crown's authority by misusing the encomienda *system. The New Laws marked the beginning of the end for an abused system intended to entrust indigenous families to the charge of colonists so they could be Christianized and "civilized" but not enslaved.*

LOCALE: Spain and the Spanish New World
CATEGORIES: Laws, acts, and legal history; organizations and institutions; colonization

KEY FIGURES
Charles I (1500-1558), king of Spain, r. 1516-1556, and Holy Roman Emperor as Charles V, r. 1519-1556
Bartolomé de Las Casas (1474-1566), Spanish Dominican missionary
Hernán Cortés (1485-1547), Spanish conqueror of Mexico

SUMMARY OF EVENT
The New Laws of 1542 and 1543 directly addressed the problem of labor supply in the frontier regions that were the Spanish New World. They also reflected an attempt by Charles I, king of Spain, to solve two specific problems. The first dealt with the reconciliation of the Crown's avowed aim to protect indigenous laborers from unscrupulous settlers while guaranteeing a continuance of the economic exploitation of the new lands. The second was the apprehension of the establishment of a Spanish-American neofeudal nobility that could physically challenge royal control of the Spanish colonies.

These problems, as Charles Gibson has indicated, may be traced to the very earliest days of Spanish settlement. The Spaniards as settlers were not willing, and often not able, to produce sufficient goods and services for their own basic needs, so they looked to the indigenous

peoples to support them. The Native Americans at first acquiesced, but when the demands made upon them became intolerable, they revolted.

After a number of clashes, the principle of the *encomienda* was established. This institution had its historical roots in the feudal situation of the Spanish Christian reconquest of the Iberian Peninsula. In America, through a formal grant of *encomienda*, the settlers were said to "hold" designated indigenous families. These families were then entrusted or commended to the charge of a Spanish colonist who thus became the *encomendero*. At first the *encomenderos* were permitted to exact both commodity tribute and labor service from the indigenous people under their control. In this manner, they were able to exploit labor groups without risk or effort. In return, they expected to render military service to the Crown and to Hispanicize the indigenous people committed to their charge.

During the early years of the conquest, the *encomienda* was generally an irregular, uncontrolled, and highly exploitative institution, as was common in frontier situations. Despite insistence that the *encomienda* was a contract with rights, duties, and limitations on each of the contracting parties, the indigenous peoples were treated as slaves.

The problem for the Crown lay in reconciling economic needs with the professed Christian purposes of Spanish imperialism. The monarchy never deviated from its position that the indigenous population was technically free. Native Americans were not chattels, even though granted to an *encomendero*. The principal objects of the *encomienda* were to Christianize pagan peoples through the ministrations of the Spanish Christian *encomendero*, and to "civilize" them by encouraging orderly habits of industry. Royal declarations of indigenous freedom, however, had little connection with the manner in which actual indigenous people continued to be treated in the Americas. To the *encomendero* the encouragement of orderly habits was usually interpreted to mean that permission was given for forced labor.

The excesses of the Spanish settlers were attacked by missionaries in the New World, notably by Dominicans, who made strong humanitarian protests against the actual conduct of the *encomenderos*. The Crown answered the Dominican accusations with the Laws of Burgos (1512), a code of Spanish-indigenous relations that expressed the Spanish government's first considered and official position on the question of *encomienda*. The Laws of Burgos sanctioned the *encomienda* system but sought to surround it with specific directives that would protect the indigenous population from excessive exploitation. However, despite good intentions, it is doubtful whether any *encomendero* modified his conduct as a result of the Burgos legislation.

The *encomienda* continued to flourish despite the misgivings of the Crown. In 1520, Charles I ruled that the entire system of *encomienda* was to come to an end. Hernán Cortés, then conquering the Aztec Empire of Mexico, did not obey the order, however. He granted his soldiers *encomiendas*, and afterward, the institution spread with the soldiers of the conquest.

As Spanish settlement of the new lands became more established, the *encomenderos* made repeated efforts to reinforce their status. Their aim was to transform the *encomienda* system into an instrument for complete and lasting control not only of the indigenous peoples but of the colonies as a whole. To this end, they sought to make *encomiendas* inheritable possessions and to make themselves a perpetual colonial nobility.

While the *encomienda* was becoming an established institution, it had been the monarchy's theoretical contention that the contract establishing an individual *encomienda* was limited to a tenure of a few years or to a single lifetime. The first *encomenderos* proceeded to bequeath their holdings to their heirs, though, and these legacies were not disputed by royal officers. From the Crown's point of view this development was regarded as a bid for power by the incipient colonial aristocracy against the monarchy, and it became the task of Charles I to establish the dominance of royal authority in America. The foremost effort to achieve this goal was the legislation known as the New Laws, promulgated without warning in 1542 and 1543.

The New Laws were actually expressed not in terms of the struggle for power but in terms of humanitarian policy toward indigenous peoples, a policy to which the Crown repeatedly gave theoretical priority. The New Laws prohibited enslavement of the Indians, even as pun-ishment. They forbade the granting of new *encomiendas*. They ordered ecclesiastics and royal officers to relinquish immediately any *encomienda* holdings they might have acquired. Other *encomenderos* were to retain their grants but were not to bequeath them to their heirs. This regulation was calculated to destroy the *encomienda* system within a generation. Tributes taken from indigenous people were to be fixed and regulated, and were not to be exorbitant. The New Laws were far less ambiguous and far more extreme than the earlier Laws of Burgos. The difference in mood between 1512 and 1542 is attributed to the more confident authority of Charles I and to the influence of his humanitarian advisers, especially the Dominican priest Bartolomé de Las Casas.

At most the New Laws could be termed only partially successful. The outcry of the *encomendero* class against them was general throughout the Spanish colonies. Rebellion, which threatened everywhere, erupted seriously in Peru, where it added a further element of disorder to the continuing civil war. The first viceroy of Peru was beheaded by a group of rebellious *encomenderos* when he attempted to enforce the New Laws.

Francisco Tello de Sandoval was the special emissary of Charles, sent from Spain to implement the New Laws in New Spain, but a cautious viceroy tried to restrain him from enforcing the laws in Mexico.

Alarmed at the reaction that the New Laws caused, the Crown made certain changes. The prohibition of inheritance was repealed, and it was decreed that most *encomiendas* then in force should be continued. Such actions in 1545 and 1546 were hailed everywhere in the colonies as a signal victory for the *encomendero* class.

Encomienda was thus given a certain reinforcement and a renewed sanction in the 1540's, despite the New Laws. Although abolition could not be made effective, much restrictive legislation remained in effect, and the strength of the monarchy was everywhere more visible. Royal enactments after the mid-1540's abandoned the effort to terminate *encomienda* immediately and completely. Crown policy was aimed at more attainable goals: control over existing *encomiendas*, the limitation of *encomendero* behavior, and the gradual reduction of *encomienda* so that it might no longer threaten monarchial rule. In law, and to a large extent in practice, the mid-1540's represent the highest point of *encomienda* influence.

SIGNIFICANCE

The New Laws were promulgated at the peak of *encomendero* power and influence. While they were adjusted

1540's

to the realities of the pressure exerted by the colonists, they also mark the beginning of the decline of the *encomienda* system and the collapse of any serious threat to the Crown's absolute power. In the history of the Spanish colonies, the New Laws do not exemplify the most successful legislation enacted by Spain to rule its American colonies. However, the New Laws do serve as a subject for studying the indirect forces that exist and influence the governing policies of the most openly absolutist states.

—*Charles J. Fleener*

FURTHER READING

Cortés, Hernán. *Letters from Mexico*. Translated and edited by Anthony Pagden. Rev. ed. New Haven, Conn.: Yale Nota Bene, 2001. Letters written in the heat of battle by the conquistador, detailing conditions in Mexico during the conquest and giving insight into the character of Cortés.

Díaz del Castillo, Bernal. *The Discovery and Conquest of Mexico, 1517-1521*. Translated by A. P. Maudslay. Edited by Genaro García. Reprint. New York: Da Capo Press, 1996. A classic, riveting, first-person narrative of the conquest recollected by Díaz. Although Díaz believed that he was never given his just due—he was rewarded with a paltry *encomienda* in Guatemala—his account is relatively balanced.

Gibson, Charles. *Spain in America*. New York: Harper & Row, 1966. An excellent survey of the Spanish colonial experience that places the New Laws within the context of Spanish imperial policy.

Hanke, Lewis. *The Spanish Struggle for Justice in the Conquest of America*. 1949. Reprint. Boston: Little, Brown, 1965. The aim of this excellent volume is to recognize that Spain's enterprise in America was to a large extent a spiritual undertaking whose highest significance was the longing for justice that actuated it.

Hazing, C. H. *The Spanish Empire in America*. 1957. Reprint. Harcourt, Brace and World, 1963. Another survey placing the New Laws in relation to Charles I's imperial and colonial projects.

Keen, Benjamin. *Essays in the Intellectual History of Colonial Latin America*. Boulder, Colo.: Westview Press, 1998. This collection includes an essay surveying 460 years of Las Casas scholarship, and another essay evaluating Las Casas's legacy.

Lupher, David A. *Romans in a New World: Classical Models in Sixteenth Century Spanish America*. Ann Arbor: University of Michigan Press, 2003. Study of the influence of Roman models of empire upon the Spanish imperial project in the Americas.

Maltby, William. *The Reign of Charles V*. New York: Palgrave, 2002. Monograph balances biography of Charles with broad analysis of his foreign and domestic policies and their historical consequences.

Simpson, Lesley Byrd. *The Encomienda in New Spain*. Berkeley: University of California Press, 1966. A concise and clearly written survey of the *encomienda* system from the time of Queen Isabella through the sixteenth century.

Thomas, Hugh. *Rivers of Gold: The Rise of the Spanish Empire*. London: Weidenfeld & Nicolson, 2003. Decidedly conservative and Eurocentric history of Spanish colonialism.

SEE ALSO: Oct. 12, 1492: Columbus Lands in the Americas; June 7, 1494: Treaty of Tordesillas; 1495-1510: West Indian Uprisings; 1502-1520: Reign of Montezuma II; 1505-1515: Portuguese Viceroys Establish Overseas Trade Empire; Beginning 1519: Smallpox Kills Thousands of Indigenous Americans; Apr., 1519-Aug., 1521: Cortés Conquers Aztecs in Mexico; Aug., 1523: Franciscan Missionaries Arrive in Mexico; 1527-1547: Maya Resist Spanish Incursions in Yucatán; 1537: Pope Paul III Declares Rights of New World Peoples; Feb. 23, 1540-Oct., 1542: Coronado's Southwest Expedition; 1552: Las Casas Publishes *The Tears of the Indians*; 1565: Spain Seizes the Philippines.

RELATED ARTICLES in *Great Lives from History: The Renaissance & Early Modern Era, 1454-1600*: Charles V; Hernán Cortés; Bartolomé de Las Casas; Paul III.

June 27, 1542-c. 1600
Spain Explores Alta California

The Spanish explored northward from New Spain (modern Mexico), looking for new sources of wealth and locations on which to build military bases and ports for their merchant ships in the Pacific. They successfully mapped much of the coast of California but were unable to establish any significant settlements until the late eighteenth century.

Locale: California, north of the Gulf of California
Category: Exploration and discovery

Key Figures

Juan Rodríguez Cabrillo (c. 1500-1543), Portuguese
 explorer
Sebastián Rodríguez Cermeño (fl. 1590's), Portuguese
 merchant, adventurer, and explorer
Sebastián Vizcaíno (1550?-1616), Spanish explorer
Gaspar de Portolá (c. 1723-1784), Spanish settler and
 explorer
Junípero Serra (1713-1784), father-president of the
 Alta California missions, 1769-1784

Summary of Event

After conquering the Aztec Empire in 1521 and establishing New Spain (Mexico) in its place, the Spanish were eager to expand northward in the hope of finding wealthy civilizations and a strait running through North America that would allow ships to sail directly from Europe to Asia. They also wanted to protect their empire from rival nations and to convert the American Indians to Christianity.

In 1533, a ship sailing from New Spain under the command of Fortún Jiménez landed in a bay, later known as La Paz. The land Jiménez found was thought to be an island and was named California after an imaginary island in a novel. In 1539, Francisco de Ulloa sailed along the west coast of New Spain until it met the coast of California, proving that it was not an island but a peninsula. This peninsula became known as Baja California and the mainland above it as Alta California.

On June 27, 1542, three ships commanded by Juan Rodríguez Cabrillo left the port of Navidad in New Spain. They arrived in a bay, later known as San Diego, on September 28, marking the first time Europeans had landed in Alta California. Cabrillo continued to sail north along the coast, landing several times on the mainland and on nearby islands. He died on January 3, 1543, and the voyage continued under the chief pilot, Bartolomé

Ferrelo, who sailed about as far north as the modern California-Oregon border, then returned to Navidad on April 14.

After Cabrillo's voyage, the Spanish gained new reasons to be interested in settling Alta California. In 1565, Spanish ships began carrying valuable cargo from Manila in the Philippines to Acapulco in New Spain. These ships, known as the Manila galleons, made enormous profits, but the voyage was long and dangerous. A port in Alta California would allow the galleons to take on supplies before continuing down the coast. An additional incentive to secure Alta California came in 1578, when the English privateer Sir Francis Drake entered the Pacific Ocean and began raiding Spanish ships and settlements. In 1584, a Manila galleon commanded by Francisco de Gali observed the coast of Alta California but did not land. In 1587, English privateer Thomas Cavendish captured a Manila galleon, increasing the pressure on the Spanish to protect their territories.

Spanish knowledge of the coast of Alta California increased dramatically around the turn of the seventeenth century. In 1595, a Manila galleon, the *San Agustín*, commanded by Portuguese captain Sebastián Rodríguez Cermeño, explored the northern coast. The ship landed in Drake's Bay (San Francisco) but was destroyed in a storm. Cermeño and his crew made their way down the coast to New Spain in an open boat, continuing to make landings and observations. On May 5, 1602, three ships commanded by Sebastián Vizcaíno left Acapulco and began sailing up the coast of Alta California. Vizcaíno gave new names to places that had been visited previously by Cabrillo and Cermeño. Many of these names, such as San Diego and Santa Barbara, still exist today. On December 16, Vizcaíno sailed into a bay he named Monterey, which he described with some exaggeration as an excellent harbor.

Significance

Despite all the reasons Spain had for settling Alta California, little was accomplished for more than 150 years after Vizcaíno's voyage because of the difficulty of the journey. Settlement began in earnest in 1769, when two ships and two land parties embarked from Baja California. One of the land parties, led by Gaspar de Portolá, included Father Junípero Serra, the founder of the first Alta California missions. These settlement parties created a colony at San Diego—consisting primarily of a mission and a military settlement, or presidio—and reached San Francisco Bay. So many men died of scurvy on the sea voyage north, however, that the initial plans to colonize Monterey Bay had to be scrapped. Large-scale colonization of Alta California remained a vital but impracticable goal.

The sea route to Alta California was long and dangerous because of contrary winds. The settlements in the barren land of Baja California were too poor to supply land parties. A new route had to be found. From 1774 to 1776, Juan Bautista de Anza led explorations north from New Spain and then westward across the Colorado River. The Anza parties established a feasible route to San Gabriel and from there on to San Francisco, where a presidio was founded on September 17, 1776, and a mission on October 9 of that year. Anza's route continued to be the main route into Alta California for later colonists. The first pueblo (town) in Alta California was founded at El Pueblo de San José de Guadalupe (later San Jose) in November of 1777, followed by El Pueblo de Nuestra Señora la Reina de los Angeles de Porciúncula (later Los Angeles) in September of 1781.

At the time of Spanish settlement, Alta California was more densely populated by a greater variety of Native Americans than any other region in North America. Although violent encounters were less common than elsewhere in the Spanish Empire, exposure to European diseases reduced the Native American population drastically.

—*Rose Secrest*

FURTHER READING

Cabrillo National Monument Foundation. *An Account of the Voyage of Juan Rodríguez Cabrillo*. San Diego, Calif.: Cabrillo Historical Association, 1999. An excellent account of the voyage of Cabrillo, including a foldout map of the expedition.

Clavijero, Francisco Xavier. *History of Ancient and Lower California, 1789*. Translated and edited by Felix Jay. Lewiston, N.Y.: E. Mellen Press, 2002. New translation of an eighteenth century survey of California history. Includes bibliographic references.

Daniels, George G., ed. "The Cruel Road to Empire." In *The Spanish West*. New York: Time-Life Books, 1976. Includes a lively, anecdotal account of the settling of Alta California. Intended for general readers.

Emanuels, George. *Early California Voyages*. Sonoma, Calif.: Diablo Books, 2001. Study of the explorers who sailed to California, beginning with Cabrillo. Includes illustrations, bibliographic references, and index.

Kessel, John L. *Spain in the Southwest: A Narrative History of Colonial New Mexico, Arizona, Texas, and California*. Norman: University of Oklahoma Press, 2002. Comprehensive survey of the history of the American Southwest from the 1490's to the mid-nineteenth century. Includes illustrations, maps, bibliographic references, and index.

Kleber, Louis Charles. "California's Spanish Missions." *History Today* 42, no. 9 (September, 1992): 42-47. Discusses the impact of the missions on the Native Americans in Alta California, including the devastating drop in population as a result of disease.

Lyon, Eugene. "Track of the Manila Galleons." *National Geographic* 178, no. 3 (September, 1990): 5-37. A detailed account of the ships that helped promote the settling of Alta California. Colorful maps and photographs.

Rawls, James J., and Walton Bean. "Discovery, Exploration, and Founding" and "Outposts of a Dying Empire." In *California: An Interpretive History*. 8th ed. Boston: McGraw-Hill, 2003. These two chapters provide a clear, concise account of important events in the history of the Spanish settlement of Alta California, with an extensive bibliography.

Weber, David J. *The Spanish Frontier in North America*. New Haven, Conn.: Yale University Press, 1992. An exhaustive, wide-ranging history of the northern borderlands of the Spanish Empire in the New World. Includes detailed accounts of the settling of Alta California.

July 15, 1542-1559
PAUL III ESTABLISHES THE *INDEX OF PROHIBITED BOOKS*

The successes of the Protestant Reformation led the Papacy to reinstate two related yet distinct instruments designed to stop the spread of heresy: the Inquisition and a system of strict censorship of printed material.

LOCALE: Rome, Papal States (now in Italy)
CATEGORIES: Religion; cultural and intellectual history; literature

KEY FIGURES
Paul III (Alessandro Farnese; 1468-1549), Roman Catholic pope, 1534-1549
Paul IV (Gian Pietro Carafa; 1476-1559), Roman Catholic pope, 1555-1559
Pius IV (Giovanni Angelo de' Medici; 1499-1565), Roman Catholic pope, 1559-1565
Pius V (Antonio Ghislieri; 1504-1572), Roman Catholic pope, 1566-1572

SUMMARY OF EVENT
Before the ascension of Alessandro Farnese to the papal throne as Pope Paul III in 1534, the Holy See all but ignored the advances of Lutheranism and other Protestant movements in the Holy Roman Empire and Italy. The new pontiff almost immediately appointed as cardinals men of both great learning and piety. He quickly created a committee to study weaknesses and abuses in the Church and to suggest courses of action. In March, 1537, this committee, led by three of the new cardinals, including Gian Pietro Carafa—the future Pope Paul IV—presented Paul with their report, "Recommendations on Church Reform." Among many suggestions concerning clerical abuses, they wrote, ". . . all princes should be instructed by letter to be on their guard lest any books be printed indiscriminately under their authority. Responsibility in this matter should be given to the [local bishops]." Hoping for reconciliation, Paul delayed taking direct action against Protestants until the imperial Diet of Regensburg (1541) made it clear that no reconciliation was at all likely.

On July 15, 1542, Paul III issued *Licit ab Initio*, the bull establishing the Sacred Congregation of the Inquisition into Heretical Depravity, also known as the Holy Office. Its charge was to investigate and punish heretics and, initially at least, to root out and destroy heretical literature. The Holy Office was the creature of Cardinal Carafa, who sat as its president until he became pope in 1555. Six cardinals generally headed this institution,

though the actual number varied with later popes' preferences. They served as the real judges of the accused. At the outset, they were aided by twenty-seven counselors and three theologians. Carafa was a Dominican priest, and Dominicans dominated the Inquisition both in Rome and in the field, except in Venice and Florence, where a Franciscan had traditionally taken the role of inquisitor.

Ecclesiastical tribunals of inquisition had a long history by the 1540's, and at the time of Paul's bull they were currently active in Spain (since 1478), Portugal (since the 1530's), and the Netherlands (since 1522). In Rome, the Sacred Congregation continued under that name until Pope Sixtus V renamed it the Congregation of the Roman and Universal Inquisition or Congregation of the Holy Office when he reorganized the Papal Curia in 1588 with the constitution *Immensa Aeterna*.

Lists of prohibited books were also an established institution. Such lists had been compiled locally by bishops or civic authorities since the dawn of printing, and they were then current in Louvain, Paris, Lucca, Venice, and Florence. In his bull *Inter Multiplices* (1487), Pope Innocent VIII had given bishops and the Master of the Sacred (Papal) Palace in Rome the right to act as censors of printed materials. Their authority was further confirmed by Pope Alexander VI in 1501, and by the Fifth Lateran Council in 1515, all before Luther ever posted his Ninety-five Theses.

In Spain, Portugal, and the Netherlands, enforcement of the ecclesiastical tribunals' decisions was supported by the authority of the state. The bishops in Italy, however, lacked such a resource of temporal power to aid in the execution of their duty. On July 12, 1543, Paul III's decree *Animadvertentes* removed the duty of censorship from bishops. He placed enforcement instead in the hands of the Holy Office, giving its members the sole right of granting licenses of *imprimatur*—"it may be printed." After 1543, no book in Italy was to be produced without such a license. There was as yet, however, no list of prohibited books.

It was under Paul IV that the first papally approved lists of prohibited books appeared. A tentative catalog of sixty-one works was produced in 1558, and this was followed by the Inquisition's grand *Index librorum prohibitorum* (*Index of Prohibited Books*), which condemned the complete works of nearly 550 writers and a host of individual titles. These included all of the works

HISTORY OF THE *INDEX*

One outgrowth of the interest in church reform begun at the Council of Trent was the compilation of the first edition of the Index librorum prohibitorum, *or* Index of Prohibited Books, *which was initiated under the auspices of the Congregation of the Inquisition.*

1557	Under the authority of Pope Paul IV, the first edition of the *Index of Prohibited Books* is compiled.
1559	The first version of the *Index* is published in a revised and expanded format.
1571	Pope Pius V establishes a special "Congregation of the Index," which is authorized to oversee the list and revise it as necessary.
1664	The *Index* is revised so that books and authors are listed alphabetically.
1753	Pope Benedict XIV develops detailed new rules that govern future compilations of the *Index*.
1757	Pope Benedict XIV authorizes an extensive revision of the *Index* that corrects previous errors.
1897	Pope Leo XII issues the papal bull *Officiorum ac munerum*, outlining the censorship duties of diocesan bishops. As a result of this directive, the *Index* begins to occupy a less prominent place in the affairs of the Roman Catholic Church.
1917	Pope Benedict XV transfers the charge of the *Index* to the Holy Office.
1948	The final edition of the *Index*, containing 4,100 entries, is published.
1966	The Vatican Council II abolishes the *Index*, which becomes a historic document for Roman Catholicism. Church officials retain the authority to prohibit future books that constitute a threat to the faith or morals of Catholics.

of Desiderius Erasmus, a man Paul III had invited to join the College of Cardinals. Though most of the works or authors were Protestant and thus heretical, others were merely obscene or critical of the Church.

The *Index* was widely criticized as draconian and largely ignored after Paul's death in August, 1559. It drew fire from early Jesuit scholars like Peter Canisius ("it is a stumbling block") and Diego Laínez, who declared that even very orthodox Catholics found it too severe. Pius IV issued the decree "Moderation of the *Index*" in 1561, spreading enforcement among the inquisitors and the—presumably more tolerant—bishops.

The formal inquisitorial process was laid out by canon law in the late Middle Ages and had changed little by the sixteenth century. Studies of the Roman practice are few, since the records of the Holy Office have been open to all scholars only since 1998. Nonetheless, it appears that in Roman trials the use of torture was less barbaric, and the procedures resulted in far fewer executions, than in the trials of the Spanish Inquisition. Nevertheless, under Pope Paul IV there was such egregious abuse of the tribunals that even such a champion of Catholicism as the French historian Henri Daniel-Rops was led to characterize them as "an appalling reign of terror." Under Paul's chief inquisitor, the rigid Dominican cardinal Antonio Ghislieri, the procedures were harsh and the punishments brutal. Paul liked to attend the weekly meetings

and called the Holy Office the "apple of my eye and favorite of my heart."

In 1566, Cardinal Ghislieri ascended to the papacy as Pope Pius V. In his first year as pope, he had the ominous Palazzo dello Santo Uffizio (Palace of the Holy Office) built near the Spanish steps in Rome. Here the activities and records of the Inquisition were sacrosanct from all save its own officers. Indeed, no one, except perhaps the pope himself, was outside its jurisdiction. Like the other, national inquisitions, the tribunals' Roman and local trials were held in secret, giving rise to all sorts of gothic imaginings. In fact, the Holy Office had to use diplomatic channels with various Italian states, for example in obtaining extradition of major heretics.

During the eighteenth session of the Council of Trent, beginning in February, 1562, the Augustinian Girolamo Seripando began revising Paul's *Index*. The twenty-fifth session of 1563 produced "Ten Rules Concerning Prohibited Books" as part of its "Decree Concerning Reform." The *Index* was now in the hands of reformist bishops. They produced a more moderate document that addressed many of the criticisms of Paul's list and allowed for expurgation (removal) of objectionable parts of otherwise meritorious works. A third list was conceived in 1572, when Pope Gregory XIII established the Congregation of the *Index*, a standing committee specifically dedicated to censorship. This version of the *Index* remained hidden until March 27, 1596, when it was pro-mulgated by Pope Clement VIII.

SIGNIFICANCE

The _Index_ continued in use through thirty-two editions, until it was suppressed in 1966 after the Second Vatican Council. It had the immediate effect of driving printers out of Rome and into the more liberal Venice, which retained its position as Italian center of progressive publishing. In general, the _Index_ was only as effective as those enforcing it, and this differed widely over the centuries and from place to place in Italy. In the twentieth century, the Inquisition evolved into the Congregation for the Doctrine of the Faith, its official name after December, 1965. The Holy Office and the _Index_ together served to dampen the spirit of exploration and innovation that had made Italy the front-runner of the Renaissance, as they turned against heliocentric astronomers, "immoral" authors, and even artists such as Tintoretto. The Counter-Reformation Papacy's successes against heresy in Italy were bought at the high cost of Italy's place in the intellectual and cultural circles of early modern Europe.

—_Joseph P. Byrne_

FURTHER READING

Del Col, Andrea. _Domenico Scandella Known as Menocchio: His Trials Before the Inquisition, 1583-1599._ Binghamton, N.Y.: Medieval & Renaissance Texts & Studies, 1996. Following a long introduction, Del Col prints the transcripts, in English, of this accused man's two trials, the second of which ended in his execution.

Fragnito, Gigliola, ed. _Church, Censorship, and Culture in Early Modern Italy._ New York: Cambridge University Press, 2001. Collection of articles written since the opening of the Archive of the Congregation for the Doctrine of the Faith in 1998. General introduction to the Congregation in Fragnito's Introduction.

Ginzburg, Carlo. _The Cheese and the Worms: The Cosmos of a Sixteenth-Century Miller._ New York: Penguin Books, 1985. A close study of a single case tried before the Roman Inquisition, that of Scandella (see Del Col above). Provides excellent insights into the inquisitorial process in a provincial area.

Godman, Peter. _The Saint as Censor: Robert Bellarmine Between Inquisition and Index._ Boston: Brill, 2000. Extended introduction to Cardinal Bellarmine and the roles of inquisitor and censor, with ninety documents in original Italian or Latin.

Grendler, Paul F. _The Roman Inquisition and the Venetian Press, 1540-1605._ Princeton, N.J.: Princeton University Press, 1977. The Inquisition and _Index_ had an odd pair of effects on Venetian publishing: printers had to be more careful, but they now got the business previously in the hands of Roman printers.

Tedeschi, John A. _The Prosecution of Heresy: Collected Studies on the Inquisition in Early Modern Italy._ Binghamton, N.Y.: Medieval & Renaissance Texts & Studies, 1991. A widely ranging collection of short papers, each of which focuses on inquisitorial processes in Italy during the sixteenth and seventeenth centuries.

Wright, A. D. _The Counter-Reformation: Catholic Europe and the Non-Christian World._ New York: St. Martin's Press, 1982. Discussion of the _Index_ and Inquisition embedded in broader context of minority religious populations in Europe and in Spanish and Portuguese colonies.

SEE ALSO: 1456: Publication of Gutenberg's Mazarin Bible; 1473-1600: Witch-Hunts and Witch Trials; Nov. 1, 1478: Establishment of the Spanish Inquisition; 1492: Jews Are Expelled from Spain; 1494: Sebastian Brant Publishes _The Ship of Fools_; Oct. 31, 1517: Luther Posts His Ninety-five Theses; Mar., 1536: Calvin Publishes _Institutes of the Christian Religion_; 1543: Copernicus Publishes _De Revolutionibus_; 1545-1563: Council of Trent; 1550's: Tartaglia Publishes _The New Science_; 1550's-c. 1600: Educational Reforms in Europe; 1583-1600: Bruno's Theory of the Infinite Universe.

RELATED ARTICLES in _Great Lives from History: The Renaissance & Early Modern Era, 1454-1600:_ Anne Askew; Nicolaus Copernicus; Miles Coverdale; Francisco Jiménez de Cisneros; Paul III; Pius V; Tomás de Torquemada.

1540's

1543
COPERNICUS PUBLISHES *DE REVOLUTIONIBUS*

Copernicus's work On the Revolutions of the Heavenly Spheres *replaced the ancient Greek idea of an Earth-centered solar system, the geocentric model, with the modern heliocentric model that placed the Sun at the center of the solar system.*

LOCALE: Nuremberg, Germany

CATEGORIES: Astronomy; science and technology; cultural and intellectual history

KEY FIGURES

Nicolaus Copernicus (1473-1543), astronomer

Rheticus (1514-1574), Austrian astronomer and mathematician who encouraged Copernicus to write his major work

Martin Luther (1483-1546), first major religious leader to attack Copernicus's work

SUMMARY OF EVENT

Since at least ancient times, humans have been fascinated with the motion of the objects in the sky. They recog-

Nicolaus Copernicus. (R. S. Peale and J. A. Hill)

nized that most of these objects, the stars in particular, appeared to rotate in circles around the fixed pole star, Polaris, in the Northern Hemisphere, as if the stars were fixed to a rigid sphere that surrounds the earth and that rotates once each day.

More than two thousand years ago, humans recognized there were several unusual objects in the sky, called the wanderers, because they appeared to move relative to the stars. In addition to the Sun and the Moon, these wanderers included five planets visible without telescopes: Mercury, Venus, Mars, Jupiter, and Saturn. The paths of these wanderers were observed and recorded. Astronomers wanted to know what caused the motion of the wanderers and how this motion could be predicted, while astrologers believed the positions of these wanderers influenced the daily lives of individuals on Earth.

Ancient Greek philosophers tried to develop models for the motion of the wanderers that would be in accord with all past measurements and allow prediction of their future positions. The most successful among them, the Greek philosopher Ptolemy (c. 100-178), constructed a model in which all the objects in the sky moved around the earth on progressively larger concentric circles. This model, however, did not accurately predict the motions of the wanderers, so Ptolemy fixed the planets to other circles that rolled around larger concentric circles.

The Ptolemaic model, as it came to be called, was later adopted by Roman Catholic religious leaders because it was consistent with their idea that humans were a "special creation" of God, and thus it seemed appropriate for humankind to occupy a "special position" at the center of all creation. The Ptolemaic model dominated religious thinking in Europe as Europe emerged from the Middle Ages.

This idea that the earth occupied a special position in the solar system was challenged by Nicolaus Copernicus, an astronomer and a Roman Catholic canon of the Church. Copernicus, who was born in the Prussian city of Thorn (modern Toruń, Poland), received his advanced education in Italy, where he studied astronomy, mathematics, and medicine and received a doctor's degree in canon law. Copernicus's long service in the religious office as canon of Ermland made him an odd candidate to defy Church teachings, but his study of astronomy led him on a path of conflict with the Church.

Copernicus was an avid observer who compiled twenty years of observations of the positions of the wanderers in the sky. By combining his observations with those recorded by earlier observers, Copernicus was able to observe flaws in the predictions of Ptolemy's model. By 1513, when Copernicus returned to Poland from Italy, he had formulated his own model of the motion in the solar system, reviving an idea proposed more than seventeen hundred years earlier by Greek astronomer Aristarchus of Samos. In the Copernican model, the Sun was stationary at the center of the solar system, with the earth and the other planets moving around the Sun in concentric circular orbits. Copernicus wrote: "As if seated on a royal throne, the sun rules the family of planets as they circle around him." The earth, in this model, was reduced to the status of one of the several planets circling around the Sun. It held no special status from a location at the center of all creation.

Copernicus circulated his idea among his friends in a manuscript entitled *Commentariolus* (1514; English translation, 1939). This manuscript asserted that "The center of the Earth is not the center of the universe.... All the spheres revolve around the Sun, as if it were in the middle of everything." Copernicus recognized, however, that his idea was contrary to the teaching of the Church, so he refrained from widespread distribution of this manuscript. Nevertheless, Pope Clement VII became aware of *Commentariolus* in 1533 but took no action to suppress Copernicus's idea.

The first serious attack on Copernicus's model came from Protestant religious leaders. Martin Luther said of Copernicus, "This fool wants to turn the whole art of astronomy upside down! But as the Holy Scripture testifies Joshua bade the sun to stand still, not the earth." Luther's appeal to Scripture, and thus faith in the word of God, to explain the behavior of nature, was in sharp contrast to Copernicus's belief that the behavior of natural objects could be understood by a combination of observation or experimentation and of reasoning in what has come to be called the scientific method.

Perhaps because of the attacks by religious leaders, Copernicus did not publish the full description of his idea, in *De revolutionibus orbium coelestium* (1543; *On the Revolutions of the Heavenly Spheres*, 1952; better known as *De revolutionibus*), until 1543. Georg Joachim, called Rheticus, a professor of mathematics, had heard of

The Copernican model of a Sun-centered solar system challenged the prevailing Ptolemaic theory of an Earth-centered universe. The ancient Greek philosopher Ptolemy is shown on the left. (Library of Congress)

Copernicus's idea and then journeyed to Ermland in 1539 to learn more about it from Copernicus himself. Rheticus encouraged Copernicus, who was nearing seventy years of age, to commit his ideas to writing. Copernicus agreed, and he divided the text of *De revolutionibus* into six parts: the first, and most controversial, concerned the arrangement of objects within the solar system; the second contained his new star catalog; the third covered precession, that is, how the motion of the earth's pole causes the fixed star about which the sky appears to rotate to change with time; the fourth discussed the moon's motions; and the fifth and sixth examined the motions of the planets.

The book was typeset in Nuremberg, Germany, initially under the supervision of Rheticus. Andreas Osiander, who took over supervision when Rheticus left Nuremberg, wrote to Copernicus in 1541, urging him to avoid a direct attack on the teachings of the Church about the arrangement of the solar system. Osiander suggested the introduction to *De revolutionibus* should indicate that either the hypothesis of Copernicus or that of Ptolemy could explain the observed planetary motion. Copernicus rejected this, but Osiander removed the introduction Copernicus had written and substituted his own preface, which emphasized that *De revolutionibus* presented a hypothesis. Since Osiander did not sign the new preface, readers generally assumed it was written by Copernicus, who did not see a copy of the printed work until he was near death in 1543.

Osiander's preface might have kept Roman Catholic theologians from attacking the book for some time. *De revolutionibus* was not placed on the *Index librorum prohibitorum* (the *Index of Prohibited Books*) of the Roman Catholic Church until 1616, when the Holy Office in the Vatican began its investigation of the astronomer Galileo Galilei, who had spoken openly of his admiration for the work of Copernicus. At that time the Holy Office pronounced the idea of a Sun-centered solar system to be "foolish and philosophically absurd." In the intervening years, Roman Catholic leaders faced another challenge to the special status of the earth and of humankind. Giordano Bruno, an Italian astronomer, philosopher, and Catholic cleric, was burned alive in 1600 for suggesting that the universe might contain other inhabited worlds.

SIGNIFICANCE

Although Christian religious leaders rejected Copernicus's work, it was widely adopted by astronomers and astrologers throughout Europe as the method to predict planetary positions because of the simplicity of calculating the positions using this method.

The publication of *De revolutionibus* began what is called the Copernican Revolution. Copernicus's work influenced later European astronomers, including Johannes Kepler and Galileo Galilei, and set the stage for the adoption of the Sun-centered model of the solar system by the scientific world. Kepler replaced the concentric circles of the Copernican model with elliptical paths for the planets and removed all the remaining discrepancies between observed planetary positions and the predictions of the Sun-centered model. Galileo, whose *Dialogo . . . sopra i due massimi sistemi del mondo* (*Dialogue Concerning the Two Chief World Systems*, 1953) was published in 1632, firmly established the Sun-centered solar system in the minds of European astronomers.

—*George J. Flynn*

FURTHER READING

Armitage, Angus. *Copernicus.* New York: T. Yoseloff, 1957. A biographical account of Copernicus describing the impact of his ideas on modern science.

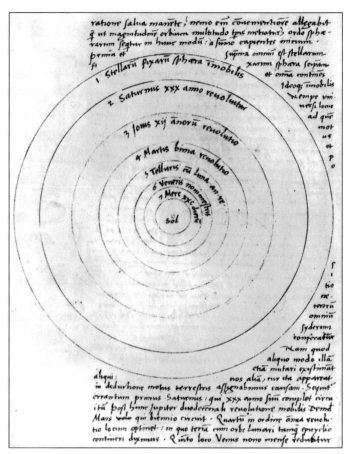

A diagram with commentary, from Copernicus's work concerning the position of the planets in relation to the Sun. (Hulton|Archive by Getty Images)

Barrett, Peter. *Science and Theology Since Copernicus: The Search for Understanding.* Reprint. Poole, Dorset, England: T&T Clark, 2003. Traces the legacy of Copernicus over four hundred years. Traces the history of the debate between science and Christianity, attempting to fashion a philosophical basis for the simultaneous embrace of scientific method and religious faith in the modern world.

Blumenberg, Hans. *The Genesis of the Copernican World.* Translated by Robert M. Wallace. Cambridge, Mass.: MIT Press, 1987. A study of the ideas of the Copernican Revolution with a focus on its impact on European history.

Durham, Frank, and Robert D. Purrington. *Frame of the Universe.* New York: Cambridge University Press, 1983. Traces the evolution of ideas about the arrangement of the solar system, with a two-chapter discussion of the Copernican Revolution.

Gingerich, Owen. *The Book Nobody Read: Chasing the Revolutions of Nicolaus Copernicus*. New York: Walker, 2004. A fascinating and original work of scholarship. Gingerich spent years tracking down and examining every extant copy of the original printing of *De revolutionibus*. Using this bibliographic analysis, he demonstrates who read the work, what they thought of it, and how Copernicus's ideas spread throughout Europe. Includes illustrations, photographic plates, maps, bibliographic references, and index.

Henry, John. *Moving Heaven and Earth: Copernicus and the Solar System*. Cambridge, England: Icon, 2001. Argues that Copernicus's discovery had revolutionary effects for the cultural status afforded to theoretical science and mathematics in Western culture. Asserts that before Copernicus, pure knowledge was believed to come only from the traditions of ancient scholars, whose work was preserved only in fragments. Copernicus demonstrated that abstract mathematics and formal scientific inquiry could produce pure knowledge on their own, thereby transforming the nature of thought and truth in the West.

Kuhn, Thomas S. *The Copernican Revolution*. Cambridge, Mass.: Harvard University Press, 1966. An in-depth account of the ideas of Galileo and their influence on European astronomy.

Ley, Willy. *Watchers of the Skies*. New York: Viking Press, 1966. An excellent account of early astronomy, with a chapter on Copernicus and his major work.

SEE ALSO: 1462: Regiomontanus Completes the *Epitome* of Ptolemy's *Almagest*; c. 1478-1519: Leonardo da Vinci Compiles His Notebooks; 1572-1574: Tycho Brahe Observes a Supernova; 1580's-1590's: Galileo Conducts His Early Experiments; 1582: Gregory XIII Reforms the Calendar; 1583-1600: Bruno's Theory of the Infinite Universe; 1600: William Gilbert Publishes *De Magnete*.

RELATED ARTICLES in *Great Lives from History: The Renaissance & Early Modern Era, 1454-1600:* Sophie Brahe; Tycho Brahe; Giordano Bruno; Nicolaus Copernicus; Leonardo da Vinci; Martin Luther; John Napier; Georg von Peuerbach; Rheticus.

1543
VESALIUS PUBLISHES *ON THE FABRIC OF THE HUMAN BODY*

Vesalius's On the Fabric of the Human Body *produced a new level of accuracy in anatomical studies with its illustrations of the dissected human body. The work presented richly detailed observations and urged the use of the scientific method.*

LOCALE: Basel, Switzerland
CATEGORIES: Health and medicine; biology; science and technology

KEY FIGURES
Andreas Vesalius (1514-1564), professor of anatomy
Titian (Tiziano Vecelli; c. 1490-1576), Renaissance painter
Jan Steven van Calcar (Stephen van Calcar; 1499?-1546?), a pupil of Titian
Bartolommeo Eustachio (c. 1524-1574), anatomist whose ideas rivaled those of Vesalius

SUMMARY OF EVENT
Andreas Vesalius, known as the father of modern anatomy, is also regarded as one of a small group of individuals who initiated the scientific revolution. He was born in Brussels and studied medicine at the Universities of Louvain and Paris, conservative schools that stressed medical teaching according to the writings of Galen (129-c. 199), the Greek physician whose work was regarded as authoritative in Vesalius's time.

Vesalius taught anatomy at the Universities of Pavia, Bologna, and Padua, where he adopted the technique of lecturing along with demonstrations in dissection done by him in person. He became a popular lecturer, and his methods of instruction became the model for the teaching of anatomy in other schools.

In 1543, Vesalius presented his masterpiece, *De humani corporis fabrica* (*On the Fabric of the Human Body*, books I-IV, 1998; better known as *De fabrica*), published in Basel by the printer Johannes Oporinus. In this book, Vesalius followed Galen in many inaccuracies as well as in true observations. The illustrations in the book, however, were accurate to a level never before achieved in the study of human anatomy. Without the drawings, the book would have done little to excite interest in further anatomical research and could not be regarded as a milestone in the history of science. The illustrations were made probably in the studio of the Italian painter Titian, the supervisor of a number of artists including Vesalius and a fellow countryman, Jan Steven van Calcar. Van Calcar previously had collaborated with Vesalius in the production of six large plates illustrating anatomical nomenclature.

The drawings in Vesalius's work achieved more than mere naturalism. They show, among other things, the dissection of muscles, so that the relations between the structure and functions of muscles, tendons, bones, and joints are clearly visible. These drawings were the most detailed and extensive illustrations of the systems and organs of the body up to this time, and they include a large number of new observations the anatomist had made on the veins, arteries, and nerves. In addition, the study of

the brain presented remarkable new insights about that organ.

The work is divided into seven parts or books, each of which is devoted to a group of organs of the human body; Book V, for example, describes the abdominal viscera. The explanations in physiology follow Galen closely, and not all of the books are of equal value. However, included in the text is an emphasis on the need for introducing the scientific method into anatomical studies, and the overall value of the work far outweighed its deficiencies. In 1555, Vesalius produced a new edition, considerably revised, but then he gave up teaching and research to become court physician to Holy Roman Emperor Charles V.

The work of Vesalius was paralleled by a contemporary and rival, Bartolommeo Eustachio, a citizen of Rome. His work, similar to that of Vesalius, was completed in 1552 but was not published until 1714. He was engaged with the same problems as Vesalius, and in some respects his anatomical drawings are more accurate. He introduced the study of anatomical variations, with his most successful work being done on the sympathetic nervous system, the kidney, and the ear. His name has been given to the eustachian tube, the narrow canal connecting the ear and throat.

As has often happened in the history of science, the two men were seeking knowledge in the same area. Had it not been for the fact that Vesalius published his book before Eustachio had even finished his illustrations, the latter might be known today as the father of anatomy.

SIGNIFICANCE

Vesalius insisted that human anatomy be studied through hands-on dissection and observation, an insistence that led to his being included as one of world history's greatest physicians. *De fabrica* is the culmination of Vesalius's observations in all their detail, and it stands as the foundational text in human anatomy.

—*Robert F. Erickson*

FURTHER READING

Ackerknecht, Erwin H. *A Short History of Medicine.* Rev. ed. Baltimore: Johns Hopkins University Press, 1982. A survey that contains many suggestions for further reading.

Castiglioni, Arturo. *A History of Medicine.* Translated and edited by E. B. Krumbhaar. 2d rev. ed. New York: A. A. Knopf, 1958. A standard history containing an English translation of the encyclopedic Italian work by Vesalius.

A detailed illustration of the muscles of the human body from Vesalius's De fabrica *(1543).* (Hulton|Archive by Getty Images)

Andreas Vesalius. (Frederick Ungar Publishing Co.)

Cunningham, Andrew. *The Anatomical Renaissance: The Resurrection of the Anatomical Projects of the Ancients*. Brookfield, Vt.: Ashgate, 1997. This important study of the history of anatomy emphasizes Vesalius's indebtedness to Galenic anatomy and the importance of ancient science to Renaissance thinkers generally. Includes illustrations, bibliographic references, and index.

Friedman, Meyer, and Gerald W. Friedland. *Medicine's Ten Greatest Discoveries*. New Haven, Conn.: Yale University Press, 2000. Vesalius's invention of the modern science of anatomy is the first of the ten discoveries discussed in this book. Includes illustrations, bibliographic references, and index.

Gordon, Benjamin L. *Medieval and Renaissance Medicine*. New York: Philosophical Library, 1959. Examines the history of medicine from the early Middle Ages to the sixteenth century.

Hall, A. Rupert. *The Scientific Revolution, 1500-1750*. 3d ed. New York: Longman, 1983. Compares *De fabrica* with *De revolutionibus orbium coelestium* (1543) by Nicolaus Copernicus. Argues that both works demonstrate the beginnings of the Scientific Revolution.

O'Malley, C. D. *Andreas Vesalius of Brussels, 1514-1564*. Berkeley: University of California Press, 1964. A biography many regard as the definitive English-language work on Vesalius and his time.

Persaud, T. V. N. *A History of Anatomy: The Post-Vesalian Era*. Springfield, Ill.: Charles C Thomas, 1997. Study of Vesalius's legacy and the development of the science of anatomy. Includes illustrations, bibliographic references, and index.

Simmons, John. *The Scientific Hundred: A Ranking of the Most Influential Scientists, Past and Present*. Secaucus, N.J.: Carol, 1996. Simmons ranks Vesalius as the twenty-first most important scientist in world history and explains how he has influenced anatomical science up to the present day. Includes illustrations, bibliographic references, and index.

Singer, Charles. *A Short History of Anatomy and Physiology from the Greeks to Harvey*. New York: Dover, 1957. Includes a survey of developments in anatomical studies during the Renaissance.

SEE ALSO: c. 1478-1519: Leonardo da Vinci Compiles His Notebooks; 1530's-1540's: Paracelsus Presents His Theory of Disease; 1543: Copernicus Publishes *De Revolutionibus*; 1553: Servetus Describes the Circulatory System.

1540's

Autumn, 1543
EUROPEANS BEGIN TRADE WITH JAPAN

In 1543, Portuguese sailors landed on Tanegashima, south of Kyūshū. In the first recorded trade between Europe and Japan, the local lord purchased their harquebuses and made working copies. Domestic musket-making quickly spread and grew. Firearms made traditional samurai warfare obsolete and radically changed the course of history.

LOCALE: Tanegashima, Japan

CATEGORIES: Trade and commerce; exploration and discovery; diplomacy and international relations

KEY FIGURES

Fernão Mendes Pinto (c. 1510-1583), Portuguese adventurer and writer who claimed he was at Tanegashima

Myōsan (fl. mid-sixteenth century), Buddhist priest skilled in making weapons and gunpowder

Shimazu Takahisa (1514-1571), Tanegashima Tokitaka's overlord, the first to employ firearms in combat in Japan

Tachibanaya Matasaburō (fl. mid-sixteenth century), Ōsaka merchant who set up the first private gunsmithing business in Japan

Oda Nobunaga (1534-1582), national warlord, r. 1573-1582, who first used firearms on a large scale in battle

Tanegashima Tokitaka (1528-1579), lord of Tanegashima who made the first Japanese firearms

SUMMARY OF EVENT

Portuguese ships began journeys of exploration down the African coast in the fifteenth century, reaching the Cape of Good Hope in 1487. The Portuguese goal of establishing a maritime trade route to India and beyond was furthered in 1497 by the Treaty of Tordesillas (originally signed in 1494), in which Spain yielded the exploration of India and East Asia to Portugal. The Portuguese founded a settlement at Goa, India, in 1510, and another on the Malay Peninsula in 1511.

Portuguese trading vessels reached Canton in 1517, but incidents provoked by Portuguese sailors caused Portuguese shipping to be officially banned from Chinese ports in 1521, causing Portugal to seek out other trading ports in East Asia. Even so, Portuguese traders continued surreptitious trade along the China coast, anchoring far offshore and transferring cargo to Chinese vessels, which

brought them to the docks. Some Portuguese traders used Chinese ships and crews, keeping out of sight themselves while anchored in Chinese ports.

In the early autumn of 1543, a foreign ship appeared off Tanegashima, a sizable Japanese island south of Kyūshū. Early records do not indicate whether the ship was a Chinese or a Portuguese vessel. Two Portuguese came ashore, each armed with an harquebus (also spelled arquebus). They stayed on the island about ten days and were hosted by the local lord, Tokitaka, who purchased their weapons. The Portuguese adventurer Fernão Mendes Pinto later claimed in his memoirs that he was present, but there is no actual proof that he was.

After taking basic lessons in marksmanship from the Portuguese, Tokitaka had local swordsmiths make copies and produce the proper gunpowder blend. The original Portuguese matchlock harquebuses were then among the most advanced and accurate firearms in the world, and the making of domestic versions of them revolutionized military technology in Japan. A Portuguese ship stopped at Tanegashima the following year, with the latest gunsmithing equipment, which Tokitaka also purchased, after the Portuguese demonstrated how it was used to make firearms.

Tokitaka passed this firearms technology along to his overlord, Shimazu Takahisa. Shimazu hosted Portuguese voyagers who subsequently came to Kagoshima, including the Jesuit missionary Francis Xavier (1506-1552). Shimazu benefited from trade with the Portuguese and obtained more harquebuses from them. The domestic models made by Japanese swordsmiths, however, were regarded by many samurai as superior in performance, workmanship, and materials. Shimazu was the first to employ some troops using harquebuses, in his victory at the Battle of Kajiki Castle, in Kagoshima, in 1549.

The Negoro temple, far to the northeast in Wakayama, had a large network of affiliated Buddhist temples and a strong contingent of defensive warrior monks known as *sōhei*. These monks were famous for their skill in both making and using weapons of all sorts. The senior priest at Negoro, Myōsan, persuaded Tokitaka to send him one of the two Portuguese harquebuses, and his monks were soon making their own versions of the weapon. The Negoro temple subsequently trained and equipped its own force of musketeers, numbering more than one thousand. When the national warlord Oda Nobunaga attacked the Ishiyama Honganji temple in Ōsaka in 1570, the

Negoro temple sent its regiment of musketeers to assist, forcing Oda's troops to withdraw. Negoro and Honganji musketeers were able to keep Oda at bay for another decade after that.

Oda Nobunaga had musketeers of his own, but the 1570 standoff made him more aware of the effectiveness of using them to shoot harquebuses in rotating volleys, maintaining continuous deadly fire to mow down conventionally armed warriors. On June 28, 1575, in the Battle of Nagashino, Oda used three thousand musketeers, shooting from behind wooden barricades, to wipe out samurai cavalry that outnumbered them by three to one. After this, musketeers were regarded as essential for military success and made up at least a third of the armies of most warlords.

Tachibanaya Matasaburō, an enterprising merchant from the Ōsaka area, went to the Negoro temple and learned how to make harquebuses under Myōsan's guidance. He went on to study gunsmithing for more than a year at Tanegashima, before returning home to establish his own firearms business. The success of this private commercial undertaking led to the establishment of similar harquebus-making enterprises all over Japan, and as a result the use of these firearms became relatively commonplace throughout the country.

SIGNIFICANCE

The purchase of Portuguese harquebuses in 1543 was the first recorded instance of trade between Japan and Europe. It created a Japanese demand for Portuguese firearms technology, leading in turn to broader Portuguese-Japanese trade and to growing Portuguese influence in Japan. The harquebuses revolutionized Japanese warfare. Peasants could learn to use them in a relatively short time, as opposed to the years samurai needed to master traditional sword and archery skills.

Ashigaru, light infantry armed with spears, previously easy prey for samurai cavalry, became musketeers who were a threat to traditional mounted samurai. Religious warriors and peasant insurgents supported by firearms could maintain defensive control of their territory for longer periods of time, until they were overcome by superior numbers of samurai aided by *ashigaru* musketeers. These changes in warfare reduced the effectiveness of traditional mounted samurai led by regional warlords, hastening the development of a unified national army with sufficient firepower to keep potential commoner insurgents in check.

Finally, while the purchase of the harquebuses in 1543 led to trade with Portugal for nearly a century, the ability

of the Japanese to make their own firearms set a model for self-sufficiency in other areas. Many regarded the Japanese weapons as superior to the Portuguese originals and had the same view of other imported items, such as eyeglasses, clocks, tobacco, and glassware. Japanese entrepreneurs learned to produce these things themselves, and when Japanese voyages overseas were prohibited in 1635 and Portuguese ships were banned in 1639, imported goods were readily replaced by domestic substitutions. On the other hand, Japanese firearms remained largely frozen in time technologically, until new rifles and handguns arrived in quantity from the West after the arrival of Commodore Matthew Calbraith Perry in 1853.

—Michael McCaskey

FURTHER READING

Chase, Kenneth W. *Firearms: A Global History to 1700.* Cambridge, England: Cambridge University Press, 2003. A study of the worldwide impact of the use of firearms on world civilization, including the way the Japanese developed firearms on their own after European firearms first appeared on Tanegashima.

Collis, Maurice. *The Grand Peregrination: Being the Life and Adventures of Fernão Mendes Pinto.* Manchester, England: Carcanet, 1990. Incorporates all major events, including Pinto's reported Tanegashima experiences, creating a highly readable narrative.

Cooper, Michael. *They Came to Japan: An Anthology of European Reports on Japan, 1543-1640.* Michigan Classics in Japanese Studies 15. Ann Arbor, Mich.: Center for Japanese Studies, University of Michigan, 1995. The experiences of Europeans in Japan in the sixteenth and seventeenth centuries in their own words, including the real or imagined Tanegashima experience of Fernão Mendes Pinto.

Lidin, Olof G. *Tanegashima: The Arrival of Europe in Japan.* Copenhagen: NIAS Press, 2002. A scholarly study of this early encounter between Japanese and Europeans which draws from original sources to analyze subsequent Portuguese arrivals and their effects on sixteenth century Japanese society and culture.

Mendes Pinto, Fernão. *The Travels of Mendes Pinto.* Translated and edited by Rebecca D. Catz. Chicago: University of Chicago Press, 2004. Complete modern English translation with notes that distinguish factual and fictional elements in this sixteenth century Portuguese narrative.

Milward, Peter. *Portuguese Voyages to Asia and Japan in the Renaissance Period: Proceedings of the Interna-*

1540's

tional Conference Held at Sophia University, Tokyo, from September 24-26, 1993, Commemorating the First Arrival of Westerners in Japan (Portuguese Traders on the Island of Tanegashima) on September 23, 1543, Exactly 450 Years Ago. Edited by Peter Milward. Tokyo: Renaissance Institute, Sophia University, 1994. Intended for an academic audience but helpful for general readers who want to gain knowledge from multiple perspectives.

Turnbull, Stephen. *Nagashino 1575.* Oxford, England: Osprey, 2000. Concise account of the Battle of Nagashino, the first in Japanese history in which firearms played the decisive role.

SEE ALSO: June 7, 1494: Treaty of Tordesillas; 16th cent.: Proliferation of Firearms; 1505-1515: Portuguese Viceroys Establish Overseas Trade Empire; 1505-1521: Reign of Zhengde and Liu Jin; 1549-1552: Father Xavier Introduces Christianity to Japan; 1550's-1567: Japanese Pirates Pillage the Chinese Coast; 1550-1593: Japanese Wars of Unification; 1568: Oda Nobunaga Seizes Kyōto.

RELATED ARTICLES in *Great Lives from History: The Renaissance & Early Modern Era, 1454-1600:* Bartolomeu Dias; Vasco da Gama; Hōjō Ujimasa; Ferdinand Magellan; Oda Nobunaga; Tomé Pires; Matteo Ricci; Saint Francis Xavier; Zhengde.

1544-1628
ANGLO-FRENCH WARS

The Anglo-French wars between 1544 and 1628 marked a shift in the relationship between England and France from dynastic to religious struggles and greatly impacted the political and cultural dynamic of early modern Europe.

LOCALE: Calais and Boulogne, France
CATEGORIES: Wars, uprisings, and civil unrest; diplomacy and international relations; religion

KEY FIGURES
Henry VIII (1491-1547), king of England, r. 1509-1547
Henry II (1519-1559), king of France, r. 1547-1559
Edward VI (1537-1553), king of England, r. 1547-1553
First Duke of Somerset (Edward Seymour; c. 1506-1552), Lord Protector of England
Mary I (1516-1558), queen of England, r. 1553-1558
Elizabeth I (1533-1603), queen of England, r. 1558-1603
Henry IV (1553-1610), king of Navarre, r. 1572-1589, and king of France, r. 1589-1610

SUMMARY OF EVENT
From the time of the conquest of England by William the Conqueror, duke of Normandy, in 1066, kings of England held a claim to the throne of France. In the Middle Ages, England held dominion over much of modern-day France, but after the conclusion of the Hundred Years' War in 1453, those holdings had dwindled to the area surrounding the city of Calais. At the beginning of the sixteenth century, England and France each sought simply to conquer the other's territory and to achieve martial glory at the other's expense, but by the 1550's, their con-

flict had shifted from a territorial struggle to a religious one. After England became Protestant in the 1530's, the struggle between France and England became a struggle for dominance between the Catholic and Protestant faiths.

Henry VIII, whose wars in France lasted throughout his reign, sought in 1513, 1523, and 1544 to emulate his ancestor Henry V as a conqueror of French lands. Henry maintained his right to the French throne and sought to have himself crowned king of France, even going so far as to gain a guarantee from Pope Leo X that he would be named "Most Christian King," a traditional title of French kings. Later, in 1521, when Henry VIII's daughter Mary was betrothed to Charles V (king of Spain and Holy Roman Emperor) as part of an alliance between Henry and Charles to go to war against France, Henry stated that his grandson would become "lord and owner . . . of all Christendom."

Henry's military campaigns in France met with little success before 1544, except for the capture of Tournai,

MAJOR BATTLES OF THE ANGLO-FRENCH WARS	
1544	Battle of Boulogne
1549	Siege of Boulogne
1557	Battle of Saint-Quentin
1558	Battle of Calais
1628	Battle of La Rochelle

France, in 1513 (which was returned in 1518). The French wars had cost tremendous amounts of money, so that by 1525, Henry was unable to finance a third invasion. However, with the money he gained from his suppression of the Catholic monasteries and religious houses in the 1530's, Henry made another alliance with Charles V and declared war on France once more. At great cost, they captured the city of Boulogne in 1544. In 1549, King Henry II of France invaded Boulogne in an attempt to regain the territory and the honor he lost with it. England could not sustain the cost of defending Boulogne, especially given the added stress of a war with Scotland, which was aided by the French. Edward Seymour, duke of Somerset and protector of the young King Edward VI, sold the city back to France in 1550 and signed a peace treaty with France the next year.

After Edward VI's death, Mary I became queen of England, returned England to the Catholic faith, and married Charles V's son, King Philip II of Spain. Philip went to war with France over Italian territorial claims and asked for English help, but Mary and her council resisted the renewal of conflict with France. Henry II, however, harbored many English rebels in his country, including Thomas Stafford, a claimant to the English throne. When Stafford invaded England with some French support, Mary and her council were forced to act and declared war on France. Nevertheless, Mary never invoked her claim to the throne of France, nor (since both countries were Catholic at the time) were there any religious overtones to their battles.

Initially, the war went well for England and Spain, and Henry II was soundly beaten at the Battle of Saint-Quentin (1557). Henry, seeking an easy revenge against Mary, became aware that Calais's defenses were weak. The French attacked and easily retook the city in January, 1558. Their largely symbolic victory heralded the end of English territory in France.

When Elizabeth I became queen in 1558, she attempted to reassert English control over Calais by allying herself with the Huguenots (French Protestants) against the French crown. The so-called Newhaven Adventure was an expensive failure, gaining virtually nothing for England, but it was to mark a shift in Anglo-French relations for the remainder of the sixteenth and seventeenth centuries. The Protestant Elizabeth's alliance with Prot-

Henry VIII's visit to France in 1520 secured an alliance with French king Francis I against Holy Roman Emperor Charles V, but the alliance did not last. Henry and Francis were at war within twenty-four years. (R. S. Peale and J. A. Hill)

1540's

estant forces within France against that nation's Catholic monarch renewed and broadened the struggle between Protestant and Catholic Europe.

The Protestant Reformation was already sweeping through Europe, often violently. France fought against the Huguenots, leading to such massacres as the St. Bartholomew's Day Massacre in 1572, while the Spanish fought against Protestant rebels in the Netherlands. Elizabeth I was in the precarious position of being caught between Protestant lords pleading for her military aid against Catholic powers and the fear of Catholic (especially French) invasion in support of Mary, Queen of Scots. Between 1560 and 1580, Elizabeth I tried to keep an uneasy peace between England, France, and Spain. She shunned large-scale military expeditions, instead supporting French Huguenots with loans and secret shipments of munitions, stopping short of outright military aid. She also promised to unite England and France by marrying a member of the French royalty.

By 1585, war had broken out between the Netherlands and Spain, and Elizabeth signed the Treaty of Nonsuch, promising an English army to assist the Dutch rebels against Spain and the Catholic League (an alliance of Catholic powers led by Spain). A few years later, a civil war broke out in France when the French king, Henry III, died leaving a Protestant heir to the throne: King Henry of Navarre became King Henry IV of France. A Protestant king was anathema to many French Catholics, however. Therefore, the Catholic duke of Guise, Henry I of Lorraine, with the support of the Spanish-led Catholic League, sought to usurp the throne to "protect" France from its new Protestant ruler. England, having assisted the Huguenots in France, and already at war with the Catholic League in the Netherlands, was forced into war with the Catholic League on behalf of the Protestant cause in Europe. The war did not end until 1598, when Henry IV was officially crowned king of France and signed the Edict of Nantes, promising toleration for both Catholics and Protestants within France. Thus, the Anglo-French wars ended with England being caught up in the civil wars sweeping Europe as a result of the Protestant Reformation.

SIGNIFICANCE

The European religious conflicts continued well into the seventeenth century. In the 1620's, after the assassination of Henry IV, the Huguenots revolted against the French regency of Marie de Médici. Englishman George Villiers, the first duke of Buckingham, with the blessing of his king, Charles I, came to the Huguenots' aid—a campaign that proved just as costly as all of the other wars with France. The English crown was left in desperate financial straits, which Charles had difficulty remedying, and which eventually led to civil war in England.

The Anglo-French wars were important for two reasons. First, these events were characteristic of the larger struggle between Catholicism and Protestantism taking place throughout Europe in the sixteenth century and had decisive effects upon sixteenth century culture and politics. Many historians have tried to portray England as a country far removed from the wars and intrigues of the Continent. Others have ignored France's decisive impact on English foreign policy during this period. In reality, the Anglo-French wars serve as an example of the complex relationships common to all of Europe during this period. Between 1544 and 1558, both England and

France were part of a system of alliances between royal houses that resulted in military conflict. After 1558, these alliances gave way to a more pressing concern with religion.

The wars also impacted the political history of Europe in several important ways. Because of the cost to England, finances became a pervasive problem throughout the sixteenth and seventeenth centuries, and the government had increasing problems maintaining a proactive policy on the Continent. From the continental side, the Protestant cause would have had difficulty surviving without English aid. England became an important Protestant power, whereas, had it remained Catholic, it might have remained a lesser power, eclipsed by France and Spain, and Protestantism in Germany and especially the Netherlands might have had a very different fate. In all, these wars serve as both an important reflection of early modern society and an important factor in the political and religious landscape of the sixteenth and seventeenth centuries.

—*Shawn Martin*

FURTHER READING

Black, Jeremy. *The Origins of War in Early Modern Europe.* Edinburgh: John Donald, 1987. A seminal collection of essays by leading scholars in the period looking at not only the Anglo-French wars but also warfare in other parts of Europe.

Doran, Susan. *England and Europe in the Sixteenth Century.* New York: St. Martin's Press, 1999. An examination of England's international relations, stressing continuity between the late Medieval and Tudor periods.

Grummit, David, ed. *The English Experience in France c. 1450-1558: War, Diplomacy, and Cultural Exchange.* Hampshire, England: Ashgate, 2002. A survey of the medieval and early modern relationship between England and France focusing on both political and cultural aspects of it.

Holt, Mack P. *The French Wars of Religion, 1562-1629.* Cambridge, England: Cambridge University Press, 1995. A useful survey focusing on the socioeconomic aspects of the French civil wars.

Sutherland, N. M. *Henry IV of France and the Politics of Religion, 1572-1596.* 2 vols. Bristol, Avon, England: Elm Bank, 2002. Extremely detailed account of the role of religion in France's monarchy and political sphere during the late sixteenth century. Each chapter discusses a specific political event or issue from the point of view of the conflict between Protestants and

Catholics. Includes illustrations, map, bibliographic references, and index.

See also: Aug. 29, 1475: Peace of Picquigny; Aug. 22, 1513-July 6, 1560: Anglo-Scottish Wars; Dec. 18, 1534: Act of Supremacy; July, 1535-Mar., 1540: Henry VIII Dissolves the Monasteries; Jan. 28, 1547-July 6, 1553: Reign of Edward VI; July, 1553: Coronation of Mary Tudor; 1558-1603: Reign of Elizabeth I; Jan. 1-8, 1558: France Regains Calais from England; Mar., 1562-May 2, 1598: French Wars of Religion; Jan. 20, 1564: Peace of Troyes; Aug. 24-25, 1572: St. Bartholomew's Day Massacre; July 7, 1585-Dec. 23, 1588: War of the Three Henrys; Aug. 2, 1589: Henry IV Ascends the Throne of France; Apr. 13, 1598: Edict of Nantes.

Related articles in *Great Lives from History: The Renaissance & Early Modern Era, 1454-1600:* Edward VI; Elizabeth I; Henry II; Henry IV; Henry VIII; Mary I; First duke of Somerset.

1545-1548
Silver Is Discovered in Spanish America

Spanish discovery of rich silver veins in the viceroyalties of New Spain and Peru sparked a rush of fortune-seekers from Europe to America, resulting in transformations of the local labor system and dramatic changes to the global economy.

Locale: Potosí, viceroyalty of Peru (now in Bolivia), and Zacatecas, viceroyalty of New Spain (now in Mexico)
Categories: Economics; trade and commerce; environment; exploration and discovery; colonization

Key Figures
Charles V (1500-1558), king of Spain as Charles I, r. 1516-1556, and Holy Roman Emperor, r. 1519-1556
Antonio de Mendoza (c. 1490-1552), first Spanish viceroy of New Spain, 1535-1550, and viceroy of Peru, 1551-1552
Francisco de Toledo (1515-1584), Spanish viceroy of Peru, 1569-1581

Summary of Event
In the mid-sixteenth century, Christopher Columbus's dream of finding great riches in the New World was finally realized. Soon after the fall of the Aztec Empire in 1521, the Spanish conquistadors found small deposits of silver in central Mexico. In the 1540's, however, far more dramatic discoveries took place. By then, Spaniards had traveled south, where they encountered a thriving Inca Empire. In 1545, the first major silver strike occurred in Potosí, in present-day Bolivia, at what came to be called the Cerro Rico (Rich Hill). Rich veins of ore were easily accessible in the upper part of the mountain. Spaniards flocked to the new viceroyalty of Peru, hoping to make

their fortune. At roughly the same time that Potosí began its boom, silver strikes were also made in north-central Mexico. The silver extracted from Zacatecas, where

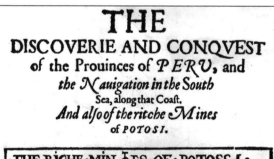

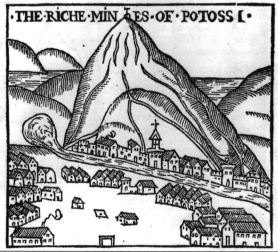

The promise of riches from silver drew many to Potosí in South America and to Zacatecas in Mexico, creating a population boom in New Spain, inflation in the world economy, and increasing tensions between the indigenous and immigrants from Europe. (Hulton|Archive by Getty Images)

strikes were made between 1546 and 1548, contributed to make the viceroyalty of New Spain a thriving colony.

The confirmation that the Spanish possessions in the New World were indeed treasure troves brought major changes in global population movement and in the world economy. It also transformed relations between the colonizers and the indigenous people of Peru and Mexico. Before 1545, the Spaniards who came to America were primarily adventuresome conquerors who hoped to find wealth but were prepared for hardships and even fierce battles with the indigenous population. With the discovery of huge silver deposits, however, businessmen and investors began to find the New World attractive. Those who now came across the Atlantic often expected to stay for a while, and so more and more of them brought their families.

Spain's king, Emperor Charles V, was determined that his American colonies should be governed well. Antonio de Mendoza (viceroy of New Spain from 1535 to 1550) and Francisco de Toledo (viceroy of Peru from 1569 to 1581) proved a credit to their king. They administered the viceroyalties efficiently and fairly, curbed rebellions, and presided over an expansion in mining activities. To discourage smuggling and tax evasion, Charles appointed crown officials who served tours of duty in the New World, where they took charge of minting the silver and collecting the royal tax. Charles also established a fleet system to protect the silver bars from pirate attacks on their journey from America to Spain.

Silver production brought dramatic change to colonial towns. Devout Spaniards contributed a share of their new wealth to the Church, and splendid cathedrals were built in the viceroyalties of New Spain and Peru. Silver funded the coming of more missionaries and the establishment of monasteries and convents in the colonies. The areas around the mines witnessed a tremendous growth in population. Most of the new arrivals were not Europeans, however; they were indigenous peoples recruited to work in the mines. Some of this labor was coerced. In Peru, Francisco de Toledo established a system whereby indigenous communities were responsible for providing a quota of mine workers to Potosí each year. This system, called the *mita*, disrupted indigenous villages. Many of the *mitayos* traveled far from their homes to the mines, so they took with them their wives and children. Once in Potosí, a significant number opted not to return to their villages.

The mines also recruited paid laborers, at wages that were higher than those offered indigenous peoples engaged in any other service. There was a reason for the higher wages: Working in the mines could be very dangerous. Injuries and death on the job were not uncommon. After digging or blasting into the mountain to uncover the veins of ore, miners used pickaxes to extract the silver and then, climbing up precarious ladders, brought out hundreds of pounds of ore on their backs. As more and more

SPAIN'S COLONIAL SILVER MINES

→ Silver shipping routes

indigenous communities resisted their *mita* obligations, wages continued to attract workers to the mines. Since it was also necessary to supply food and clothing for those working in the mines, a cash economy emerged, buttressed by wage labor.

SIGNIFICANCE

Far beyond the regions from which it was extracted, American silver contributed to major transformations in the world economy. It lured Spaniards to America, creating a labor crisis and rising wages and costs in Spain. The increased supply of silver, a common currency in the early modern world, also spurred inflation. American silver thus caused a "price revolution," first in Spain and later throughout Europe, as the silver quickly made its way out of Spain for a variety of reasons. For one, Spaniards used silver to purchase from other Europeans consumer goods and food supplies that were then shipped to the colonies, where they were sold for a profit. Furthermore, King Charles I of Spain was also Holy Roman Emperor Charles V, ruling over the unwieldy Habsburg domain. In response to the political challenge of new Protestant rulers, Charles funded a series of wars in support of Roman Catholicism. These costly wars drained American silver out of Spanish coffers and into the hands of European bankers and suppliers.

Once the wars of religion ended in 1648, competition for New World colonies began in earnest. Now American silver was used to fund nationalist wars, as England, Holland, and France expanded their colonial holdings, while Spain and Portugal attempted to hang on to territory they believed was rightfully theirs. Increased commerce with the East took American silver to the Ottoman Empire, to India, and to China, bringing with it a rise in prices around the globe.

There is a cautionary irony to the story of American silver. The areas where it was mined and to which it was first shipped benefited only temporarily from their windfall. In fact, the wealth from American treasure failed to foster sustained economic growth not only in Potosí and Zacatecas but also in Spain. Although Potosí had become one of the largest and richest cities in the world by 1650, after the more easily accessible silver had been mined the area entered into a steep decline. Spain, controlling the richest silver mines in the world, witnessed a significant downturn in the seventeenth century, when the power of England and France surpassed that of Spain and the source of imperial wealth shifted from the extraction of bullion to the development of plantation agriculture based on African slave labor.

Silver from New Spain was transported to Europe and minted as coinage. (Frederick Ungar Publishing Co.)

1540's

The discovery of silver in New Spain and in Peru confirmed hopes that the New World housed immense treasure. While many benefited from the extraction of silver, however, others, especially the indigenous peoples of America, were exploited. The price increases generated by the rush to the New World and by the increased amount of bullion affected economies and governments all over Europe and as far away as the Middle East and China. The new supply of silver encouraged a growing acceptance of the theories of mercantilism, which called for limited manufacturing in the colonies, and it thereby fostered growing tensions between European mother countries and their colonies.

—*Joan E. Meznar*

FURTHER READING

Bakewell, Peter John. *Miners of the Red Mountain: Indian Labor in Potosí, 1545-1650.* Albuquerque: University of New Mexico Press, 1984. Discusses the richest period of extraction at Potosí, focusing on the use of indigenous labor in the mines.

_____. *Silver Mining and Society in Colonial Mexico:*

Zacatecas, 1546-1700. New York: Cambridge University Press, 2002. Examines the onset and development of a mining industry in Mexico.

Ferry, Stephen. *I Am Rich Potosí: The Mountain That Eats Men.* Introduction by Eduardo Galeano. New York: Monacelli Press, 1999. Exceptional photographs of miners in present-day Potosí.

Galeano, Eduardo. *Open Veins of Latin America: Five Centuries of the Pillage of a Continent.* 25th anniversary ed. Foreword by Isabel Allende. New York: Monthly Review Press, 1997. This passionately written condemnation of the economic exploitation of Latin America includes a good description of the effects of silver mining on the global economy.

Hamilton, Earl J. *American Treasure and the Price Revolution in Spain, 1501-1650.* New York: Octagon Books, 1965. The classic account of how American silver, and the inflation it fostered, transformed Europe's economy and brought on the decline of the Spanish Empire.

Stein, Stanley J., and Barbara Stein. *Silver, Trade, and War: Spain and America in the Making of Early Modern Europe.* Baltimore: Johns Hopkins University Press, 2003. Discusses the effect of American silver on nationalist wars in Europe and on the eventual decline of Spain.

SEE ALSO: Oct. 12, 1492: Columbus Lands in the Americas; Beginning c. 1500: Coffee, Cacao, Tobacco, and Sugar Are Sold Worldwide; 16th century: Worldwide Inflation; 1502: Beginning of the Transatlantic Slave Trade; Jan. 23, 1516: Charles I Ascends the Throne of Spain; Beginning 1519: Smallpox Kills Thousands of Indigenous Americans; Apr., 1519-Aug., 1521: Cortés Conquers Aztecs in Mexico; June 28, 1519: Charles V Is Elected Holy Roman Emperor; Aug., 1523: Franciscan Missionaries Arrive in Mexico; 1532-1537: Pizarro Conquers the Incas in Peru; 1542-1543: The New Laws of Spain.

RELATED ARTICLES in *Great Lives from History: The Renaissance & Early Modern Era, 1454-1600:* Charles V; Christopher Columbus.

1545-1563
COUNCIL OF TRENT

The Council of Trent provided a basis for reform of abuses in the Catholic Church as a response to the Protestant Reformation and defined key Catholic doctrines that remained in effect until Vatican II in the mid-twentieth century.

LOCALE: Trent (now in Italy)
CATEGORIES: Religion; organizations and institutions

KEY FIGURES

Charles V (1500-1558), Holy Roman Emperor, r. 1519-1556, who led the campaign to hold the council

Paul III (Alessandro Farnese; 1468-1549), Roman Catholic pope, 1534-1549, who summoned the council

Julius III (Giovanni Maria Ciocchi del Monte; 1487-1555), Roman Catholic pope, 1550-1555, who convened the second session of the council

Pius IV (Giovanni Angelo de' Medici; 1499-1565), Roman Catholic pope, 1559-1565, who convened the last session

Francis I (1494-1547), king of France, r. 1515-1547, who resisted a council

James Laynez (1512-1565), Jesuit theologian at the council

Jerome Seripando (d. 1563), Augustinian theologian who was influential at the first council

SUMMARY OF EVENT

Protestantism spread rapidly throughout Europe in the sixteenth century, threatening both political and religious stability in central Europe. This led to demands for the internal reform of the Catholic Church. In keeping with an established practice, many people supported the summoning of a general council of all the bishops to consider the needs of the Church. It was generally believed that a council could more readily exert massive pressure for reform than could isolated decrees by the pope or individual bishops.

A general council had met at Rome in 1512-1515, disbanding shortly before Martin Luther posted his Ninety-five Theses in October of 1517. This gathering, the Fifth Lateran Council, anticipating many of the complaints raised by Protestant critics, decreed various reforms, but little was done to implement them.

Support for a general council grew after 1517. The

campaign for a general council was led by the Holy Roman Emperor, Charles V. The Holy Roman Empire was a federation of states including Italy and central Europe united under the tutelage of an emperor elected by the German princes. The empire was to provide religious and political unity. The Protestant Reformation threatened this unity. Charles V especially desired a council to place the weight of the Church behind reform measures that he felt could be used to halt the spread of Protestantism and perhaps be used to convince Protestants to return to the Catholic faith.

The popes, however, showed little initial interest in the project because of an earlier experience with conciliarism, a time period when Church councils stripped the popes of much of their power. Francis I of France also opposed such a council. France, like England, had resisted political control by the Holy Roman Emperor and had worked to limit the Church's interference in state affairs.

In 1537, however, Paul III recognized the need to take steps to counteract the spread of Protestantism, so he appointed a committee of cardinals to study abuses in the Church. Their report was uncompromising in its denunciation of evils and abuses at all levels. For the next few years, as a response to the report, Pope Paul worked for the convening of a council, but it had to be postponed several times. The first session finally met at Trent in northern Italy on December 13, 1545. Attendance was sparse at first, with an overwhelming preponderance of Italian bishops. Two major tasks confronted the council: reform of abuses in the Church and a restatement of Catholic doctrine in clear distinction to Protestantism. Charles V was most concerned with the former and hoped that doctrinal issues would be left undefined so as not to further antagonize Protestants. Pope Paul was most concerned about the latter, hoping for a definitive statement of doctrine that could be used to openly combat Protestant heresy. The bishops agreed to consider both projects simultaneously, but in the first session they were able to agree only on certain points of doctrine.

In matters of faith, the teachings of the Protestants were a strong determinant of the topics that the council discussed. The first point agreed on was the acceptance of the Latin Vulgate as the official Bible of the Catholic Church, including the books of Judith and the Maccabees

One session of the Council of Trent, from a painting by Titian. (Frederick Ungar Publishing Co.)

A DECREE OF THE COUNCIL OF TRENT

The Council of Trent issued decrees that outline a range of Catholic concerns, including responses to Protestant reformers, reiterations and defenses of Catholic Church doctrine, declarations of heresy, and, perhaps most critical, reforms that abolish abuse by clergy and monks and institute strict disciplinary measures against those clergy and monks who are abusive.

It is to be desired that those who undertake the office of bishop should understand what their portion is, and comprehend that they are called, not to their own convenience, not to riches or luxury, but to labors and cares, for the glory of God. For it is not to be doubted that the rest of the faithful also will be more easily excited to religion and innocence if they shall see those who are set over them not fixing their thoughts on the things of this world, but on the salvation of souls and on their heavenly country. Wherefore this holy Council, being minded that these things are of the greatest importance toward restoring ecclesiastical discipline, admonishes all bishops that, often meditating thereon, they show themselves conformable to their office by their deeds and the actions of their lives; which is a kind of perpetual sermon; but, above all, that they so order their whole conversation that others may thence be able to derive examples of frugality, modesty, continency, and of that holy humility which so much commends us to God.

Wherefore . . . this Council not only orders that bishops be content with modest furniture, and a frugal table and diet, but that they also give heed that in the rest of their manner of living, and in their whole house, there be nothing seen which is alien to this holy institution, and which does not manifest simplicity, zeal toward God, and a contempt for vanities.

Source: Excerpted from *Readings in European History*, by James Harvey Robinson, abridged ed. (Boston: Athanaeum Press, 1906), pp. 315-316.

and the Epistle of James, whose worth had been questioned by Luther. This was a response to the Protestant practice of translating the Bible into local vernaculars. The delegates at Trent also affirmed that the ancient traditions of the Church are an authoritative guide to religious truth equal to that of the Bible. Luther had in contrast asserted that the Bible should be "the sole rule of faith."

The most important decree of the first session concerned justification. Protestants taught that a person is wholly sinful and lacks free will so that salvation is totally a gift from God. The Council of Trent, on the other hand, decreed that persons are capable of performing some naturally good works and that they have the capacity to cooperate with God's offer of grace. The reception of this grace, which is unmerited by persons, makes it possible for them to fulfill God's law. Salvation depends in part, then, on works and not just on faith, as the Protestants generally taught.

The major reform considered at the first session was

the requirement that bishops reside in their dioceses. This was a response to a common practice of bishops to reside in the comfort and stimulation of cities far removed from areas where they were to provide oversight. Likewise, this practice allowed some clerics to have control over a number of areas, thus becoming both financially and politically powerful. Virtually everyone accepted the idea of residency in principle, but there was strong pressure to grant exceptions, especially to cardinals and others who were in the direct service of the pope. When a decree on the subject was finally proposed, it was voted down as being too weak, the only decree of the council to meet that fate.

The first session also officially declared that there are seven Catholic sacraments established by Christ. The seven sacraments are baptism, confirmation, Eucharist (communion), marriage, ordination, penance (confession), and extreme unction (last rites). Most Protestants had rejected all sacraments except baptism and the Eucharist. Also, in contrast to the Protestants, the Council of Trent decreed that sacraments confer grace in their physical operation, although the recipient must be well disposed. Most Protestants argued that the sacraments were simply symbolic reenactments and did not directly confer grace.

Attendance at the first session reached a peak of about seventy-five delegates, including a substantial Spanish contingent. The French bishops largely boycotted the first session. Jerome Seripando, head of the Augustinian order to which Luther had belonged, was the most influential voice at the first session. By late 1547, however, attendance had fallen. Citing an outbreak of typhus and a bad climate, the papal legates transferred the council to Bologna. However, few delegates made the trip, and the council was suspended indefinitely.

The second session met at Trent in 1551 and 1552 under Pope Julius III, who had presided over the first session as a cardinal. It declared that Christ is really and physically present in the Eucharist, reaffirming the doctrine of transubstantiation in which the bread and wine are understood to be transformed into the actual body and blood of Christ. In contrast, most Protestants, with the notable exception of Luther, believed that the presence of Christ in the Eucharist is merely symbolic. The second session also issued decrees on the sacraments of penance and extreme unction. The second session ended after Maurice, the duke of Saxony's attack on Charles V placed the town of Trent in danger.

Following the death of Julius, Pope Paul IV assumed office. He was a lifelong reformer but opposed the council as a threat to papal authority. He went forward with certain reform measures, including the strengthening of the Inquisition against heretics and the first edition of *Index librorum prohibitorum* (the *Index of Prohibited Books*), but did not resume sessions of the council.

In 1561, the third session of the council was summoned to Trent by Pope Pius IV. A decree on the Mass was issued, in which it was declared to be the same sacrifice as the sacrifice of Christ in the Crucifixion. A decree on marriage was also issued. The question of the residency of bishops again arose, and with papal support a decree was issued from which there were to be no exceptions. Attempts to control the influence of secular rulers over church offices had to be dropped.

In the haste of the closing days in 1563, the council issued decrees on the existence of purgatory and on the propriety of honoring saints, their relics, and their images. All bishops were also required to set up seminaries in their dioceses in which candidates for the priesthood could be trained adequately. Clerical morality and attention to duty were to be rigorously enforced.

In its doctrinal decrees, the Council of Trent set forth clear statements of Catholic belief and thus provided tools for the Jesuits and others in their attempts to win back Europe to the Catholic Church. James Laynez, a Jesuit theologian, was the most influential presence at the third session.

The last session was the best attended of the three, with a maximum of 255 bishops, slightly more than half of whom were Italians. Although in all three sessions German bishops suggested that Protestant representatives attend the Council of Trent for discussions, they were invited only to the second session. A few appeared, but nothing of importance occurred since they were given no real opportunity to present their views.

SIGNIFICANCE

As a response to the council, Pius IV issued the catechism of the Council of Trent, containing the official doctrines of the Church couched in simple language as a general guide to the layperson. This catechism, coupled with reform of abuses inside the Church, was the foundation for the Counter-Reformation through which the Catholic Church attempted to halt and reverse the spread of Protestantism. The council provided the Church with doctrinal clarity but in the process also defined the rigid doctrinal lines that would separate the Catholic and Protestant churches until Vatican II (1961-1963), when a new Church council would seek to promote a new era of Christian unity and cooperation.

—James H. Forse, updated by Charles L. Kammer III

FURTHER READING

Burns, Edward NcNall. *The Counter Reformation.* Princeton, N.J.: Van Nostrand, 1964. Includes some documents from the council and offers a critical perspective.

Greengrass, Mark. *The Longman Companion to the European Reformation, c. 1500-1618.* New York: Longman, 1998. Places the Council of Trent and the Catholic Reformation within the context of the overall European Reformation.

Jedin, Hubert. *A History of the Council of Trent.* 2 vols. Translated by Ernest Graf. London: Thomas Nelson and Sons, 1961. Comprehensive discussion of the council and the religious and political conflict which informed it.

_____. *The Medieval and Reformation Church: An Abridgment of the History of the Church.* Vol. 5. New York: Crossroad, 1993. Discussion of the council within the context of the Counter-Reformation.

Luebke, David M., ed. *The Counter-Reformation: The Essential Readings.* Malden, Mass.: Blackwell, 1999. Collection of essays surveying Counter-Reformation scholarship in the second half of the twentieth century from the points of view of a variety of disciplines.

Mullett, Michael A. *The Catholic Reformation.* New York: Routledge, 1999. Traces the entire history of the Catholic Reformation, beginning with its roots in the Middle Ages, as well as the impact of the movement on the arts and on daily life. One chapter details the mutual influence of the Papacy upon the Counter-Reformation and of the Counter-Reformation on the Papacy.

Olin, John C. *Catholic Reform from Cardinal Ximenes to the Council of Trent.* New York: Fordham University Press, 1990. Places the Council of Trent in the historical context of the reform movement and includes some documents of the council.

O'Malley, John W. "The Council of Trent: Myths, Misunderstandings, and Misinformation." In *Spirit, Style,*

Story: Essays Honoring John W. Padburg, edited by Thomas M. Lucas. Chicago: Jesuit Way, 2000. Attempts to correct false understandings of the importance of the Council of Trent for Catholic history generally and Jesuit history in particular.

SEE ALSO: Oct. 31, 1517: Luther Posts His Ninety-five Theses; Aug. 15, 1534: Founding of the Jesuit Order;

1550's-c. 1600: Educational Reforms in Europe; 1582: Gregory XIII Reforms the Calendar.

RELATED ARTICLES in *Great Lives from History: The Renaissance & Early Modern Era, 1454-1600:* Charles V; Francis I; Andrea Gabrieli; Gregory XIII; Michel de L'Hospital; Martin Luther; Giovanni Pierluigi da Palestrina; Paul III; Philip II; Pius V; Saint Teresa of Ávila.

February 27, 1545
BATTLE OF ANCRUM MOOR

A Scottish army under the command of Archibald Douglas routed a much larger English force commanded by Ralph Evers and Brian Layton, in retaliation against Henry VIII's Rough Wooing of Mary, Queen of Scots.

LOCALE: Ancrum Moor, north of Ancrum, Scotland
CATEGORIES: Wars, uprisings, and civil unrest; government and politics

KEY FIGURES
Archibald Douglas (c. 1489-1557), sixth earl of Angus, 1514?-1528, 1542-1557, and lieutenant general of southern Scotland, 1544-1557
Ralph Evers (c. 1508-1545), English noble
Walter Scott of Buccleuch (c. 1490-1552), Scottish noble
Brian Latoun (c. 1500-1545), English noble
Henry VIII (1491-1547), king of England, r. 1509-1547
Mary Stuart (1542-1587), queen of Scotland, r. 1542-1567

SUMMARY OF EVENT
The Battle of Ancrum Moor marked the first successful Scottish counterattack against the English king Henry VIII's "Rough Wooing" of Mary, Queen of Scots. After the death, in 1542, of James V (r. 1513-1542), Scotland was left with the infant Mary as queen and her mother, Mary of Guise, as regent. After the Scots rejected Henry VIII's proposed marriage of Mary, Queen of Scots to his son Edward (the future Edward VI), the English attempted to force the Scots into agreeing to the marriage by ordering armies to ravage the Scottish Lowlands, launching an invasion across the Firth of Forth in the spring of 1544. Since May, 1544, the majority of Scottish troops were concentrated on the defense of Edinburgh Castle, allowing English armies to cut a swathe of destruction across southern Scotland.

An English army of roughly three thousand soldiers, under the command of Sir Ralph Evers (also known as Ralph Eure) and Sir Brian Latoun (also known as Bryan Layton), advanced toward Jedburgh in early February, 1545. Evers and Latoun, who had acquired notoriety among the Scots for their particular brutality in the enforcement of the Rough Wooing, were carrying spoils from a savage pillaging of Melrose. At Melrose, the English had destroyed Holyrood Abbey and desecrated the graves of the Douglas lords, a family famed for their power in the Anglo-Scottish borderlands. These acts added to the growing list of English atrocities committed throughout the Lowlands.

English scouts detected signs of Scottish forces in the vicinity, as their armies approached Ancrum Moor, north of the village of Ancrum. Evers and Layton grew confident at the sight of some seven hundred "Assured Scots," Borderers that had allied themselves with England. Their confidence was only increased by intelligence of a small army of Scots, numbering perhaps four hundred men, who were positioned on a hill overlooking the moor.

The Scots were led by the lieutenant general of southern Scotland, Archibald Douglas, the sixth earl of Angus. Douglas had recently rallied troops to his cause through his courageous resistance against English forces that had nevertheless driven off a Scottish army under the command of James Hamilton, the earl of Arran, at Coldingham. Unbeknownst to Evers and Layton, Douglas's scouts had alerted him to the incoming English, and the Scottish commander was already preparing a trap for an overconfident English army that was both weighed down and exhausted by the booty it was bearing from Melrose.

Anticipating an easy victory, the English decided immediately to deploy their forces in the hope of mounting a surprise nighttime attack. However, Douglas, anticipating the English strategy, retreated to even higher ground, both to tire out the impulsive English and to win time for his own reinforcements. Indeed, Douglas's forces were soon joined by approximately five hundred foot soldiers under the command of Sir Walter Scott of Buccleuch, as well as by a cavalry contingent led by Sir Norman Leslie. The Scots now had forces totaling some twelve hundred troops. Even more important, Douglas's sound intelligence about the numbers and movements of the English troops allowed him ample opportunity to prepare the stage for a decisive engagement.

Douglas positioned cavalry at the height of the hill, feigning retreat to lure the English troops uphill. The Scots also planted cavalry traps, digging pits along the marsh-lined Roman road of Dere Street, which cut across Ancrum Moor. Douglas's strategy was to trip up the enemy horses that would pursue them in a second feigned retreat. Scottish soldiers, positioned in "hedgehog" units—square-shaped, densely packed formations of spear-wielding foot soldiers and musketeers—would then ambush the surprised English cavalry.

Using schiltron formations, groups of soldiers packed tightly together with spears pointed forward, the Scots absorbed the first charge of the English troops, who were not only exhausted by their unsuccessful nocturnal advance but also now had to deal with the sun shining in their faces and the bitterly cold winds whipping downhill. In a fierce counterattack, the Scots advanced into the main body of the English army, inflicting heavy losses on the surprised English forces. Douglas's tactics of trapping the English cavalry worked as planned, leading to critical English casualties. Moreover, by drawing many English troops into areas of the moor where Scottish troops were positioned to engage them, Douglas prevented the English from adequately forming their battle lines, leaving the English foot soldiers with no way to defend themselves.

As the Scottish advantage became clear, the Assured Scots allied to the English switched sides, joining the Scots in what would become an almost total rout of the English. There were very few Scottish casualties, while perhaps as many as one thousand English soldiers were killed, with hundreds more taken prisoner. The bodies of Evers and Layton were mutilated by the victorious Scots as revenge for the atrocities their armies had committed throughout the Scottish Lowlands. The Scots had finally retaliated for years of English incursions, driving the remainder of the English forces east, toward the main body of English troops, near Berwick.

A gravestone with a poem commemorating the courageous actions of the Fair Maiden Lilliard, who is pur-

ported to have taken her slain lover's sword and hacked away at the English even after the loss of her legs, stands at the site of the Scots' triumph at Ancrum Moor. However, scholars insist that the stone is probably of eighteenth century construction and that the legend of such an avenging woman itself significantly predates the sixteenth century.

SIGNIFICANCE

The Battle of Ancrum Moor had its most significant effect in rallying the spirits of a Scotland that had been demoralized by years of brutal English military incursions. The Scottish Lowlands had experienced unspeakable pillage and slaughter throughout a period that stretched beyond the Rough Wooing to include the humiliating defeat at Solway Moss in 1542. Emboldened by their success against the latest wave of invasion, the Scots now pressed on with plans to renew their alliance with the French against the English, in the hopes of counterinvading England.

Archibald Douglas was rewarded handsomely by King Francis I of France (r. 1515-1547), receiving four thousand crowns and the Order of Saint Michel. Douglas, who had been distrusted by the Scots for his role in Henry VIII's initial negotiations concerning the marriage of Mary, shored up his reputation as a key military player. Douglas was now well positioned to play a leading role in a Scottish offensive against the hated English war machine.

The Scots' sense of triumph, however, was short-lived. Edward Seymour, the earl of Hertford, who was the commander of Henry VIII's invading forces in Scotland, began soon after Ancrum Moor to mobilize troops for retaliatory strikes against the newly emboldened Scots. After a series of punitive raids in 1545, Hertford, now the duke of Somerset and Lord Protector in the new regime of Edward VI (r. 1547-1553), launched a full-scale invasion of Scotland. In September, 1547, Scottish resistance crumbled with the death of some ten thousand Scots under the command of the earl of Arran at the Battle of Pinkie, near Edinburgh.

—*Randy P. Schiff*

FURTHER READING

Banks, F. R. *Scottish Border Country*. London: B. T. Batsford, 1951. A historical and geographical survey of the Anglo-Scottish borderlands. Offers numerous plates and maps, as well as detailed treatment of key military engagements.

Fissel, Mark Charles. *English Warfare, 1511-1642*. New

York: Routledge, 2001. A survey of English military history, featuring numerous maps and illustrative plates. Includes detailed discussion of military tactics employed by the Scots.

Merriman, Marcus. *The Rough Wooings: Mary Queen of Scots, 1542-1551*. East Linton, East Lothian, Scotland: Tuckwell, 2000. A detailed discussion of Henry VIII's brutal policy of forcing Scotland to accept his plans for Mary, Queen of Scots. Argues that there are two distinct periods of English aggression.

Phillips, Gervase. *The Anglo-Scots Wars, 1513-1550: A Military History*. Rochester, N.Y.: Boydell Press, 1999. A survey of the armed conflicts opened up by the English victory at Flodden, focusing on technical matters of warfare. Features plates and maps.

Sadler, John. *Scottish Battles*. Edinburgh: Canongate, 1996. A survey of key battles throughout Scottish history, featuring numerous tables and maps. The chapter on Ancrum Moor offers detailed discussion of military tactics employed by both armies.

SEE ALSO: Aug. 22, 1513-July 6, 1560: Anglo-Scottish Wars; Dec. 18, 1534: Act of Supremacy; 1544-1628: Anglo-French Wars; Jan. 28, 1547-July 6, 1553: Reign of Edward VI; May, 1559-Aug., 1561: Scottish Reformation; July 29, 1567: James VI.
RELATED ARTICLES in *Great Lives from History: The Renaissance & Early Modern Era, 1454-1600:* Edward VI; Francis I; Henry VIII; Mary, Queen of Scots; Mary of Guise.

1546
FRACASTORO DISCOVERS THAT CONTAGION SPREADS DISEASE

Fracastoro's De contagione et contagiosis morbis et eorum curatione, *in which he postulates that diseases are caused by the spread of "seeds" or "seminaria" that could self-multiply, is generally considered to be the first work to attribute disease to unseen "germs" and helped lay a foundation for modern understanding of infectious disease.*

LOCALE: Verona, Republic of Venice (now Verona, Italy)
CATEGORIES: Health and medicine; biology; science and technology

KEY FIGURES
Girolamo Fracastoro (c. 1478-1553), Italian physician, astronomer, and poet
Paul III (Alessandro Farnese; 1468-1549), Roman Catholic pope, 1534-1549, who summoned the Council of Trent

SUMMARY OF EVENT
Girolamo Fracastoro epitomized the Renaissance thinker. He studied medicine at Padua and became a physician, but he was also a poet, philosopher, a natural historian who developed theories of fossils, and, like his contemporary at Padua Nicolaus Copernicus, an astronomer. He produced a work in 1538 in which he suggested that the Earth and planets traveled in spherical orbits around a fixed point, foreshadowing the later work of his contem-

porary, Copernicus. In the same treatise, Fracastoro discussed superimposing lenses—one of the first descriptions of a telescope. He also observed that all comet tails point away from the Sun, a fact that later was determined to be related to the solar wind.

Medicine, however, is the field in which Fracastoro's contributions are most noted. In the early 1500's, after the return of Spanish explorers from the New World, Europe was experiencing a new, virulent infectious disease. Now known as syphilis, this disease derives its name from a 1,300-verse poem, *Syphilis sive morbus Gallicus* (*Syphilis: Or, A Poetical History of the French Disease*, 1686; better known as *Syphilis*), published by Fracastoro under his Latin name, Hieronymous Fracastorius. This poetic work gives a mythical account of a shepherd, Syphilis, who angers Apollo and is cursed with the disease. In this poem, Fracastoro first articulates his thoughts on contagion and the spread of disease.

Fracastoro argues that nature is complex but understandable through careful study. He suggests that syphilis did not have a single point of origin followed by spread, and he suggests natural causes for the disease. He also suggests that the particles that cause the disease can be carried by air and that they can remain dormant for years before "breaking out."

Fracastoro continued his observations about infectious disease and his studies of syphilis, and in 1546 he published a treatise on infectious diseases, *De*

Religious communities often tended to the sick, injured, and dying in public rooms, or wards, such as the one depicted here (sixteenth century Paris), where diseases often spread easily and rapidly. (Frederick Ungar Publishing Co.)

contagionibus et contagiosis morbis et eorum curatione (1546; *De contagione et contagiosis morbis et eorum curatione*, 1930), in which he is the first person to use the word "contagion." Fracastoro defines contagion as an infection passing from one person to another. He accurately describes the three stages of syphilis: the small genital sore (primary syphilis), lesions and a body rash several months after the initial sore (secondary syphilis), and dementia (caused by brain deterioration) and other organ destruction (tertiary syphilis). He also describes the mode of transmission of syphilis, noting that it is a sexually transmitted disease, and he recognizes the fact that a woman infected with syphilis can pass the disease to her child during pregnancy or after birth through her breast milk.

Fracastoro described the causative agents of syphilis as "seeds" or "seminaria." Since the first microorganisms were not seen until the 1670's and 1680's by Antoni van Leeuwenhoek (1632-1723) and others, it is unlikely that Fracastoro envisioned the seminaria as the microorganisms described by those scientists. However, Fracastoro did propose three modes of transmission of seminaria between individuals. In the 1546 treatise, he states that diseases could be transmitted by direct contact, indirectly by contact with infected objects such as dirty linens, or across a distance by contaminated air.

Fracastoro was able to apply his theories to practical situations. When plague broke out in Verona, Fracastoro left for Lake Garda. There he practiced medicine from his country house and served as physician to Pope Paul III. After the Treaty of Crespi (1544) ended the wars between the Holy Roman Emperor Charles V (r. 1519-1558) and the French king Francis I (r. 1515-1547), Pope Paul III convened the Council of Trent (1545-1563). The purpose of the council was to address important questions of Catholic faith and discipline including the canonization of the Scriptures. The council met seven times, but an outbreak of the plague disrupted the work of the council. Fracastoro urged that the Council of Trent be moved to Bologna to avoid the contagion of the plague. However, members of the council who supported Charles V refused to leave, and Pope Paul III postponed the meeting indefinitely in April, 1547, to avoid a schism within the Church.

SIGNIFICANCE

Fracastoro's description of disease transmission and contagion did not immediately lead to the development of sterile techniques or successful treatments directed at the "seminaria" that he believed caused diseases. In fact, more than three hundred years passed after the 1546 publication of *De contagione et contagiosis morbis et eorum curatione* before the modern germ theory of disease was developed by Robert Koch (1843-1910). The development of the modern germ theory required several technological and intellectual developments, including the design of the compound microscope, with which Leeuwenhoek first observed microorganisms or, as he called them, animalcules.

Additionally, the theory of "spontaneous generation" of organisms had to be disproved before the science modern bacteriology could develop. This theory held that life could arise spontaneously out of inanimate matter (as appeared to be the case when maggots appeared in dead meat); Leeuwenhoek held that life could arise only from life, and eventually Lazzaro Spallanzani (1729-1799) disproved spontaneous generation through experiments he conducted in 1765.

In the early 1860's, Louis Pasteur (1822-1895) concluded that "diseases of wine" were caused by microorganisms, or "germs." Shortly after, Joseph Lister (1827-1912) extended Pasteur's work to show that microorganisms cause infection in wounds, and he developed antiseptic techniques in surgery.

In many ways Leeuwenhoek's theories culminated in the work of Koch, who in 1876 developed the germ theory of disease in which he identified the bacterium (now known as *Bacillus anthraxis*) responsible for causing anthrax. In this work, Koch used four steps to prove that the bacterium caused anthrax. He first isolated the bacterium from all of the infected animals, next he grew anthrax bacteria in "pure culture" in the laboratory, then he infected a healthy animal with the cultured bacteria, and finally he re-isolated the same bacteria from the infected

test animal after it developed the disease. These same steps are followed by twenty-first century epidemiologists as they search for the causes of emerging diseases.
—*Michele Arduengo*

FURTHER READING

Gould, Stephen J. "Syphilis and the Shepherd of Atlantis." *Natural History* 109 (2000): 38-48. An article giving historical perspective and context for Fracastoro's poem "Syphilis and the Shepherd of Atlantis." Compares Fracastoro's poetic documentation of syphilis to the less dramatic completion of the genome sequence of *Treponema pallidum*, the organism that causes syphilis.

Hudson, Margaret M. "Fracastoro and Syphilis: Five Hundred Years On." *Lancet* 348 (1996): 1495-1497. Discusses the spread of syphilis in Europe, Fracastoro's *Syphilis sive morbus Gallicus*, and his contributions to Renaissance science.

Lederberg, Joshua. "Infectious History." *Science* 288 (2000): 287-293. Historical discussion of the control and treatment of infectious diseases from the 1400's to the present day. Includes a time line of infectious diseases.

Thurston, Alan J. "Of Blood, Inflammation, and Gunshot Wounds: The History of the Control of Sepsis." *Australian and New Zealand Journal of Surgery* 70 (2000): 855-861. Describes the contribution of military medicine to the development of control and treatment for wound infections and sepsis.

SEE ALSO: 1517: Fracastoro Develops His Theory of Fossils; Beginning 1519: Smallpox Kills Thousands of Indigenous Americans; 1530's-1540's: Paracelsus Presents His Theory of Disease; 1543: Vesalius Publishes *On the Fabric of the Human Body*; 1546: Fracastoro Discovers That Contagion Spreads Disease; 1553: Servetus Describes the Circulatory System.

RELATED ARTICLES in *Great Lives from History: The Renaissance & Early Modern Era, 1454-1600:* Georgius Agricola; Nicolaus Copernicus; Girolamo Fracastoro; Conrad Gesner; William Gilbert; Paracelsus; Michael Servetus; Andreas Vesalius.

January 16, 1547
CORONATION OF IVAN THE TERRIBLE

Ivan the Terrible, the heir to the principality of Moscow, had himself crowned czar of Russia, formally recognizing the expanded territory and power wielded by the Rurik Dynasty in the wake of Muscovy's expansion.

LOCALE: Moscow, Russia

CATEGORIES: Government and politics; expansion and land acquisition

KEY FIGURES

Ivan the Terrible (1530-1584), grand prince of Moscow, r. 1533-1547, and czar of Russia, r. 1547-1584

Macarius (c. 1482-1564), metropolitan of Russia, 1542-1564

SUMMARY OF EVENT

The coronation of Ivan the Terrible as Czar Ivan IV of Russia on January 16, 1547, marked a major change in the ideology of rulership in Russia. The term *czar* (emperor) was a Russian translation of the Byzantine title of emperor (*basileus*), meant to evoke the ancient Roman title of caesar. Up to this time, the rulers of Russia had been called grand princes, a designation that meant authority over a particular principality within Russia. In the fourteenth and fifteenth centuries, there were several grand princes ruling over different principalities at once. When the grand princes of Moscow assumed the princedom of Vladimir as well, however, they effectively became the titular heads of all the Russian principalities. During the centuries of Mongol rule in Russia (1237-1480), all grand princes were required to have their titles recognized by the Mongol khans of the Golden Horde.

The Russian principalities were brought under Muscovite control during the reigns of Ivan the Great (r. 1462-1505) and Vasily III (r. 1505-1533). Moreover, by the beginning of the sixteenth century, Moscow had emerged as the leading center of Eastern Orthodoxy, becoming both the religious and the political center of Russia. Ivan the Great, though officially called grand prince of Moscow and Russia, frequently used the title czar and, in an effort to imitate the Habsburgs, adopted from the Byzantine emperors the double-headed eagle on his state seals. He also married Sophia Palaeologus, niece to the last emperor of Byzantium.

An important tenet in Eastern Orthodoxy was the belief that true Christianity had moved from the West to the East, but the fall of Constantinople in 1453 raised the possibility of yet another transfer of empire and Orthodoxy. Simeon of Suzdal believed Vasily II, grand prince of Moscow (r. 1425-1462), already represented the true Orthodox ruler. Zosima, the metropolitan (spiritual head) of the Russian Orthodox Church, thought Ivan the Great to be the new Emperor Constantine. In his transcription of the traditional "Tale of the White Cowl," "Povest' o Belom Klobuke" (late fifteenth century), the archbishop of Novgorod, Gennadius, declared Russia the "Third Rome" (after "Second Rome" Constantinople), and this theme was elaborated upon by Filofei of Pskov in 1523. In the *Skazanie o Kniaz'iakh Vladimirskikh* (c. 1530; tale of the princes of Vladimir), the ancestry of Ivan the Terrible was actually traced back to the Roman emperor Augustus. Ivan's coronation was in keeping with the emerging belief in Russia as the new center of Orthodoxy, ruled by the new emperor of a Third Rome, the czar.

In 1498, Ivan the Great crowned his son, Dmitry, in a ceremony intentionally reminiscent of the Byzantine practice of selecting a caesar—usually the emperor's son or relative—to succeed the emperor. It is not clear whether Ivan made use of tenth century Byzantine practice, as found in the Book of Ceremonies, or instead used later imperial rites from a time when the office of caesar had diminished in importance. In any case, unlike the coronation of Ivan the Terrible, the 1498 ceremony did not have direct imperial implications for the ruler. Ivan the Terrible's coronation, on the other hand, was largely based on fourteenth century Byzantine ritual and clearly constituted an assertion of imperial power.

The coronation ceremony of Ivan IV as czar of Russia was the inspiration of Metropolitan Macarius. He was a strong supporter of the Josephites, a religious group that espoused the teachings of Saint Joseph of Volokolamsk (Ivan Sanin; 1439-1515). The Josephites stressed the importance of monastic discipline and Orthodox ritual for worship. Monastic property and wealth were justified on the grounds of dispensing charity and visibly demonstrating God's glory. The Josephites supported state power as necessary for eradicating heresies. Macarius, then, was simultaneously attempting to legitimate state power with religious and nationalist ideology and to yoke state power to the religious institutions of Russia. In other words, he sought to make Ivan an emperor while making the emperor an instrument of the Church. The coronation ceremony was emblematic of these dual goals.

1540's

589

Ivan the Terrible. (Library of Congress)

Ivan was crowned at age seventeen in the Kremlin Cathedral of the Dormition, the traditional site for anointing Russian rulers. At the palace, Ivan assembled the imperial regalia, consisting of a cross, the imperial crown, sword, and shoulder cape (*barmy*), and handed them to an archpriest of the Cathedral of the Dormition and to the state treasurer (*kaznachei*). As the procession arrived at the cathedral to ringing church bells, the regalia were placed on a table before the central or Holy Door (the Royal Door) of the iconostasis—the wall of icons separating the congregation from the altar. The table sat on a dais of twelve steps, symbolizing the twelve apostles, surrounded on both sides by the thrones of Ivan and Macarius.

With the metropolitan seated, Ivan proclaimed that he wished to be crowned as grand prince of Moscow, Vladimir, Novgorod, and all Russia, as had his ancestors before him. Macarius recognized him as such, blessed him with the Cross, and sat him on his throne. Then Ivan again spoke, declaring that he wished to be anointed czar. Macarius recognized the claim, blessed Ivan with the "life-giving Cross" (believed to be made of the wood that held the crucified Jesus), placed the crown and cape of office upon Ivan, and presented him with the imperial

sword. In his prayers, Macarius likened Ivan to King David of Israel and declared him czar of a holy people.

Macarius enjoined Ivan to rule with justice and to minister to the poor. He urged Ivan to respect the Church and its monasteries and to remember that his powers derived from God through the Church. The relationship between church and state was that of the harmony of equals (*symphonia*). After the sermon, Macarius met Ivan in front of the Holy Doors, anointed him with myrrh, and then, after three attempts (symbolic of the Holy Trinity), accorded Ivan the traditional Byzantine imperial privilege to enter into the sanctuary to partake of the Eucharist. With the Mass completed, Ivan proceeded out of the church, and with his younger brother, Yuri, scattering silver three times before him, he went to the Cathedral of the Archangel Michael to render his respect to the tombs of his ancestors. He then continued to the palace for a banquet.

Macarius employed the traditional Russian ceremony for the coronation of Muscovite grand princes, but he added the Byzantine practice of anointing the czar and allowing him to take communion in the sanctuary. The *barmy* had been used as early as the reign of Ivan I Kalita (Moneybag; r. 1328-1341), and the crown, the Golden Cap of Monomakh—believed to be a twelfth century crown given by the Byzantine emperor Constantine Monomachus to the Kievan prince Vladimir Monomakh—was probably fashioned by Central Asian craftspeople in the late thirteenth century. Yet both were given imperial significance, representing the transfer of imperial power from Constantinople to Moscow.

One of the most serious controversies in Russian historiography is the nature and extent of the Mongol conquest. Scholars have noted that Muscovite rulers depended on the khans of the Golden Horde for their political legitimacy and may have incorporated some aspects of Mongol administration, military organization, and diplomatic practice. Yet the coronation of Ivan the Terrible makes it quite clear that sixteenth century political ideas derived from Byzantine and not Tatar precedents. Like a Byzantine emperor, Ivan wore the imperial robe of purple upon which rested his *barmy* and a golden chain; in his right hand he held a cross, and in his left hand a sword; and on his head sat the crown of Monomakh, resembling a Byzantine crown, and a diadem, marking Ivan a warrior in the ancient Roman tradition.

SIGNIFICANCE

Ivan the Terrible's coronation was designed to legitimize his claim to an imperial title by laying upon him layer after layer of the trappings of power. The sheer weight of the symbolism, as Christian Orthodox, Byzantine, Roman, and traditional Russian signs of power accumulated about him, was overwhelming. It was a significant harbinger of things to come, as Ivan would later commit many extreme acts, on both a global and a local scale, with the impunity of a divinely ordained ruler. The terror of his later reign has been analyzed by modern historians as the campaign of someone who believed that it was his God-given prerogative to create for his enemies a Hell on earth.

—*Lawrence N. Langer*

FURTHER READING

Benson, Bobrick. *Fearful Majesty: The Life and Reign of Ivan the Terrible.* New York: G. P. Putnam's Sons, 1987. A popular history of Ivan.

Maurreu, Pierre. *The Image of Ivan the Terrible in Russian Folklore.* New York: Cambridge University Press, 1987. An analysis of the images of Ivan in folklore.

Miller, David. "The Coronation of Ivan IV of Moscow." *Jahrbücher für Geschichte Osteuropas* 15 (December, 1967): 559-574. The most thorough discussion of the coronation in English.

Myerson, Daniel. *Blood and Splendor: The Lives of Five Tyrants, from Nero to Saddam Hussein.* New York: Perennial, 2000. Short but gripping and fully realized biography of Ivan, in a collection that also portrays Nero, Josef Stalin, Adolf Hitler, and Saddam Hussein.

Pavlov, Andrei, and Maureen Perrie. *Ivan the Terrible.* London: Pearson/Longman, 2003. Major reassessment of Ivan's reign that seeks to do away with the stereotypes of Cold War-era historians and achieve a balanced and accurate appraisal of Ivan as neither an evil genius nor a wise and benevolent statesman. Argues that Ivan's campaign of terror was motivated not merely by personal sadism but by a belief in the divine right of the monarch to punish treason on earth in a manner as extreme as the punishments of Hell. Includes maps, genealogical tables, bibliographic references, index.

Platonov, Sergei F. *Ivan the Terrible.* Edited and translated by J. L. Wieczynski. Gulf Breeze, Fla.: Academic International Press, 1974. An excellent translation of a work by a famous Russian historian of the old St. Petersburg school of Russian historiography, which emphasizes facts in making historical interpretations.

Shulman, Sol. *Kings of the Kremlin: Russia and Its Leaders from Ivan the Terrible to Boris Yeltsin.* London: Brassey's, 2002. Ivan is the first of the major Russian leaders profiled in this history of the Kremlin. Includes photographic plates, illustrations, bibliographic references, and index.

Skrynnikov, Ruslan G. *Ivan the Terrible.* Edited and translated by Hugh Graham. Gulf Breeze, Fla.: Academic International Press, 1981. A serious and balanced study by a Soviet historian that presents Ivan and his *Oprichnina* in a nonideological framework. Contains a short bibliography of Russian-language books and articles.

SEE ALSO: 1478: Muscovite Conquest of Novgorod; 1480-1502: Destruction of the Golden Horde; After 1480: Ivan the Great Organizes the "Third Rome"; 1499-c. 1600: Russo-Polish Wars; Jan.-May, 1551: The Stoglav Convenes; Summer, 1556: Ivan the Terrible Annexes Astrakhan; 1581-1597: Cossacks Seize Sibir; July 7, 1585-Dec. 23, 1588: War of the Three Henrys; 1589: Russian Patriarchate Is Established.

RELATED ARTICLES in *Great Lives from History: The Renaissance & Early Modern Era, 1454-1600* Ivan the Great; Ivan the Terrible; Sophia Palaeologus; Vasily III.

1540's

January 28, 1547-July 6, 1553
REIGN OF EDWARD VI

After the strong monarchy of Henry VIII, accession of a child brought government by factions with instability and corruption. Protestantism enjoyed the king's support and that of powerful officials. This reign secured a Protestant presence that withstood Catholic resurgence under the next monarch.

LOCALE: England
CATEGORY: Government and politics

KEY FIGURES

Edward VI (1537-1553), son of Henry VIII and king of England, r. 1547-1553
Edward Seymour (c. 1506-1552), the duke of Somerset and Lord Protector, r. 1547-1549
John Dudley (c. 1502-1553), duke of Northumberland, who replaced Seymour
Robert Kett (1492-1549), rebel leader

SUMMARY OF EVENT

The reign of King Henry VIII (1509-1547) featured a strong monarchy sometimes despotic in character. The king shrewdly preserved the appearances of constitutional government by making Parliament his accomplice in enacting policies that expressed his own will, and so measures that increased royal authority became law through legal means. Henry executed relatively few of his opponents, and even severance of relations with the Papacy involved little bloodshed. England prospered in many ways, so there was no great resistance to authoritarian rule.

The maintenance of this situation would not be possible under the weak monarchy of Edward. At the time of Henry's death, Edward was a child, and the government was relegated to a Council of Regency during the young king's minority. Henry had done little to prepare the councillors, so ambitious noblemen such as Edward Seymour and John Dudley dominated king and council. Relations with Scotland and France were hostile, the economy was in decline, and corruption flourished. At the same time, English Protestantism made great gains, rooted in the anti-Catholic laws and actions of Henry's reign.

The council made Seymour Lord Protector with the prerogative of appointing his supporters to government positions. After gaining this power, Seymour often ignored the council and ruled by decree, which caused animosity that led to his downfall. Edward made Seymour

duke of Somerset with an income of £7,400 per year, but Seymour (now Somerset) regarded the king as a child to control. Eventually, this attitude alienated the intelligent monarch; he correctly perceived that the Lord Protector's paternalism toward him was motivated, at least in part, by his desire to be the actual ruler.

While Somerset was in power (1547-1549), he pursued a rather liberal agrarian policy, one that sought to aid peasants, for whom he had genuine concern. He fixed rents to protect them from exploitation, but that antagonized landlords, whom he could not afford to alienate. In foreign affairs, he tried to exclude French influence from Scotland by arranging the marriage of Edward to Mary Stuart, the daughter of King James V, who was five years younger than Edward. The failure of this scheme led Somerset into a war against the Scots, which in turn led them to consolidate their alliance with France. They sent Mary to Paris for her education, where she became engaged to the heir to the French throne, Francis II. Somerset's failed diplomacy caused war with France in 1549, a conflict that went badly.

The Lord Protector's arrogant manner and disdain for the council finally led, in 1549, to an intrigue against him instigated by John Dudley. Somerset's overthrow occurred after a peasant uprising led by Robert Kett in which the rebels seized control of Norwich until Dudley, as an agent of the council, defeated them. Similar uprisings elsewhere failed, but the disorder brought discredit upon the Lord Protector, who had sympathized with the peasants and had attempted to improve their lot. The affair ended Somerset's career, and the cause of social reform fell with him. After Kett's Rebellion, Dudley organized a plot to make himself ruler. His faction sent Somerset to the Tower of London, and at the end of 1551, he was condemned to death for conspiring against Dudley, whom the king had made duke of Northumberland; his execution took place on January 22, 1552.

Northumberland became the dominant figure in government, but without the title Lord Protector. He was driven by ambition and had little regard for the people his predecessor had tried to help. Unrestrained by moral convictions, he flattered the king and posed as the monarch's servant, a device to gain legitimacy for his position. He secured oppressive laws to deal with troublesome peasants, and in foreign affairs, he made peace with France by ceding Boulogne. To pacify the Scots, he removed English troops from their soil without compensation, measures he deemed necessary to pursue his domestic schemes.

In 1534, during the reign of Henry VIII, the Act of Supremacy had made the monarch head of the Church of England, so the religion of the ruler but was bound to influence the policy of his government. Edward, unlike his father, was a devout Protestant and an enthusiast for continuing reformation. The Council of Regency was weighted toward Protestantism, with twelve of sixteen members of that persuasion, and among Edward's teachers were noteworthy Protestant scholars. The king was a fine student who mastered four languages, to the delight of tutors such as Roger Ascham and John Cheke, distinguished Humanist pedagogues. Under the influence of preachers such as Hugh Latimer and Nicholas Ridley, Edward learned theology and developed the conviction that it was his duty to promote further reforms in both state and church.

The administration of Somerset had repealed the Henrician laws against heresy, and England had opened slowly to Protestant influence. Thomas Cranmer, archbishop of Canterbury under Henry and now Edward, had revealed his Protestant convictions and composed the Book of Common Prayer (1549) to facilitate English-language church services. An Act of Uniformity (1549) required use of the prayer book, and Parliament abolished reliquaries and chantries, prominent features of medieval Catholicism that Henry had retained. During Northumberland's tenure, the government confiscated lands from chantry priests who had prayed for departed souls, a practice Protestants renounced.

Repeal of the heresy laws allowed Protestant theologians from the continent to teach in England, where they urged the government to enact anti-Catholic measures. With royal approval, first Somerset and now Northumberland encouraged the spread of Protestantism, as continental scholars joined their English colleagues in calling for abolition of the Mass, distribution to the laity of the Eucharist in both species, and permission for priests to marry. The success of their endeavors appeared in a revised Book of Common Prayer and the Forty-two Articles of Religion, which Cranmer produced in 1552 and which were published in 1553. These documents show the influence of Martin Bucer of Strassburg, Pietro Martire Vermigli (Peter Martyr) of Italy, and Jan Łaski from Poland. England acquired through them the theological complexion of Reformed doctrine that had originated with Huldrych Zwingli in Zurich and John Calvin in Geneva.

Thomas Cranmer was the central figure in the reform of the Anglican Church, as he guided the government in removing statues from church buildings, closing shrines, and replacing stained-glass windows with clear panes. Confiscations of Catholic endowments brought revenue to the royal treasury and to nobles who supported the pol-

King Edward VI's coronation procession in London, 1547. (Hulton|Archive by Getty Images)

icy. When some bishops opposed these changes, the Lord Protector coerced them at least to refrain from obstructing his program. The second edition of the Book of Common Prayer demonstrated beyond doubt that England's official religion had become Protestant. Edward VI formally approved the revised prayer book and the Articles shortly before he died on July 6, 1553.

Although Protestants gained control of church and state, the population at large had not embraced the new religion. It was strongest in London, but even there only a minority professed the Reformed faith. Many Protestants were, however, people of wealth and political connections, so they exerted greater influence than their numbers might indicate. Somerset depended on Protestant nobles for support, and he and they were zealous to convert the nation to their beliefs. Throughout most of rural England common people remained Catholic, inclined either toward Rome or toward Anglo-Catholicism.

Somerset dealt with religious diversity by prohibiting preaching, except for delivery by licensed ministers of state-approved homilies. The approved sermons attacked the doctrine of purgatory and affirmed justification through faith alone, the cardinal principle of Protestant theology. When Northumberland gained power, he continued state patronage of the reformers, although he lacked fervent commitment to their beliefs. Legislation of 1550 had ordered destruction of any religious service books that the 1549 Act of Uniformity had not approved. A second Act of Uniformity (1552) approved a more overtly Protestant edition of the Book of Common Prayer. This law categorically denied transubstantiation, the Catholic doctrine of Christ's real presence in the Eucharist. The same act eliminated confessions to priests and removed Catholics from the Council of Regency and from bishoprics still in Catholic hands.

Edward became active in state affairs as he grew older and supported Northumberland's measures to make England Protestant, even appealing to his sister Mary Tudor to renounce Catholicism. Perhaps he realized the insecurity of the Reformation and feared a return to Catholicism should Mary succeed him.

By the beginning of 1553, Edward was seriously ill and expected that his reign would end soon. To prevent a reversion to Catholicism, Northumberland persuaded the king to name Lady Jane Grey, Northumberland's daughter-in-law, his heir, an action that negated the will of Henry VIII. Edward signed the official documents only days before tuberculosis took his life in July. The dying monarch regarded himself as God's agent to protect the true faith, so he agreed to the scheme. He expired at Greenwich, as he prayed that God would defend England from papistry.

SIGNIFICANCE

The plot to keep Mary Tudor from the throne failed, and England endured five years of turmoil, as the new monarch tried unsuccessfully to restore Catholicism. Her persecution of Protestants made her unpopular and actually aided the growth of the religion she despised. The reforms initiated in Edward's reign withstood her opposition, and the next queen, Elizabeth I, affirmed the Protestant faith and restored most Edwardian reforms, although with some alterations.

In international affairs, England was still a second-rate power when Edward died. Failed foreign policy and the insecure monarchy left the nation's future in doubt. The reign of Mary I brought additional troubles when she married Philip of Spain and allowed him to control English policy. The name of Tudor had been blemished by two weak monarchs by the time Elizabeth became queen. Against all odds, she would achieve national unity and gain for England the status of a great power.

—*James Edward McGoldrick*

FURTHER READING

Loach, Jennifer. *Edward VI*. New Haven, Conn.: Yale University Press, 1999. Scholarly history that emphasizes social and political aspects of Edward's reign.

MacCulloch, Diarmaid. *The Boy King*. New York: St. Martin's Press, 1999. Excellent coverage of Protestant fortunes during Edward's reign.

Weir, Allison. *The Children of Henry VIII*. New York: Ballantine Books, 1996. Examines the personal lives of the monarchs rather than affairs of state; insightful treatment of Edward VI.

SEE ALSO: May, 1539: Six Articles of Henry VIII; 1544-1628: Anglo-French Wars; Jan. 28, 1547-July 6, 1553: Reign of Edward VI; Jan., 1563: Thirty-nine Articles of the Church of England.

RELATED ARTICLES in *Great Lives from History: The Renaissance & Early Modern Era, 1454-1600:* Martin Bucer; Sebastian Cabot; William Cecil; Thomas Cranmer; Edward VI; Elizabeth I; Sir John Fortescue; Stephen Gardiner; Lady Jane Grey; Edmund Grindal; Richard Hooker; John Knox; Hugh Latimer; Mary, Queen of Scots; Mary of Guise; Mary I; Matthew Parker; Nicholas Ridley; Jane Seymour; First duke of Somerset; The Tudor Family.

1548-1600
SIAMESE-BURMESE WARS

Siam (modern Thailand) and Burma (now Myanmar) were tangled in a series of wars in which Siamese perseverance forced the Burmese to abandon their expansions to the east for a century and a half. The conflicts defined not only a region and its boundaries but also its peoples, who still experience effects of the conflicts.

LOCALE: Southeast Asia, mainly Siam (now Thailand)
CATEGORIES: Wars, uprisings, and civil unrest; diplomacy and international relations; expansion and land acquisition

KEY FIGURES

Tabinshwehti (1512-1550), Burmese king of Toungoo Dynasty, r. 1531-1550, and king of unified Burma, r. 1546-1550
Bayinnaung (1515-1581), Burmese king, r. 1551-1581
Chakrapat (d. 1569?), Siamese king, r. 1548-1569?, and younger brother of King P'rajai
Phra Naret (Black Prince; 1555-1605), Siamese king, reigned as Naresuan, r. 1590-1605
P'rajai (d. 1547?), Siamese king, r. 1534-1547?

SUMMARY OF EVENT

Burmese domination in the late fifteenth century of the area of what is now Myanmar was followed by two centuries of Burmese attempts to subdue Thai kingdoms and add them to Burma's territories. The first period of strife, falling roughly between 1548 and 1600, caused great suffering for Thai and Mon peoples alike, but eventually the conflicts ended in stalemate.

Following the fall of Burma's capital city, Pagan, in 1287, the Burmese and the Mons entered into a period of unrest that lasted more than two centuries, in which both tried to secure dominance in the region. Eventually, the Burmese controlled Myanmar, and by the mid-sixteenth century they dominated the once-powerful Mons completely.

The Burmese king Tabinshwehti began the conquest of Myanmar in the 1530's, first conquering the Kingdom of Pegu, which fell in 1539. The Mon king died after the fall, leading most of the Mon chiefs to Tabinshwehti in an attempt to end the conflict. Although Tabinshwehti made great efforts to unify the Burmese and Mons, including cutting his hair in the Mon fashion and staging coronations using both Burmese and Mon rituals, he also ordered the massacre of large populations of Mons who did not surrender to his rule. The newfound unity and power of the Burmese inspired them to seek expansion into the neighboring Thai kingdoms to the east.

The Burmese and the Thais, living in an area of relatively low population density, sought to enslave captives, thereby making them into a source of revenue. The Thais were divided into several small and competing states, the most powerful of which, Siam, had Ayutthaya as its capital.

Ayutthaya had long struggled to absorb its smaller, northern Thai neighbor of Chiang Mai and to dominate the Chao Phraya River valley. Other Thai peoples, such as those in the Shan states and Laos, played shifting roles in this struggle. After consolidating his power in Myanmar, Tabinshwehti began to plan for the conquest of Ayutthaya.

There were many reasons for the invasion, but a combination of the need for captives to serve as slaves and an unquenchable drive for expansion that had fueled Tabinshwehti's life thus far were the most likely reasons. Both Burma and Siam had long sought to dominate the smaller Thai kingdom of Chiang Mai, but the stated reason for war was more spiritual. White elephants, albinos, were valued strongly in both Thai and Burmese cultures. According to one legend, Buddha had been a white elephant—an animal believed to have magical properties—in a previous incarnation. The Siamese king at Ayutthaya, P'rajai, had a stable of white elephants. Tabinshwehti, demanding two of the elephants, became outraged after the Siamese refused to part with them. Tabinshwehti, however, did not force the issue, but unrest in the Siamese royal family in the 1540's prompted him to invade Siam, with the goal of conquering and annexing the kingdom.

In 1547, after the king of Chiang Mai had died in a hunting accident, Siamese armies (under King P'rajai) arrived at the gates of Chiang Mai intending to conquer the northern Thai kingdom. After they were repulsed, King P'rajai was poisoned by one of his concubines. In the king's absence, his concubine had become pregnant by a commoner. Her nine-year-old son by the king was placed on the throne of Siam's capital, Ayutthaya, and then was sent to a monastery or killed (accounts vary); the concubine and her lover proclaimed the lover king of Ayutthaya. After a reign of two months, Siamese nobles rebelled and killed the usurpers and placed P'rajai's younger brother on the throne, to rule as King Chakrapat.

With the onset of the dry season in 1548, the Burmese began their invasion of Siam. Although the invasion was massive by local standards, it failed to take Ayutthaya by the arrival of the wet season, and the Burmese army had to retreat. Attacks by the Siamese, who hastened the invaders home, caused great losses among Tabinshwehti's forces. Following this setback, Tabinshwehti lost much of his earlier drive, and he neglected affairs. His Mon subjects, who suffered most of the casualties in the invasion, rebelled and, in 1550, killed Tabinshwehti. This rebellion was crushed by Bayinnaung, Tabinshwehti's brother-in-law, who soon dominated the Burmese. Bayinnaung then conquered Chiang Mai and led a punitive expedition into Laos, which had opposed the Burmese conquest of Chiang Mai in 1557. After the defeat of the Laotians in 1559, Bayinnaung controlled most of the Thai peoples to the north of Siam. From this position of power he repeated the demand that Ayutthaya surrender two white elephants to Burma. King Chakrapat of Siam refused.

The second Burmese attack on Siam, from 1568 to 1569, with perhaps 120,000 soldiers, proved more successful for the Burmese. Chakrapat died attempting to defend his capital, and the Burmese ruled the territory of Ayutthaya (which fell in 1569) for the next fifteen years. Thousands of Thais were enslaved and taken to Burma. Following the death of Bayinnaung in 1581, the Thais began to recover their strength and independence. A Siamese prince known as Phra Naret (the Black Prince), who had been living as a hostage in Burma, gained enough acceptance by the Burmese that eventually he married Bayinnaung's sister and was allowed to return to Ayutthaya. Once in his home city, he expelled the Burmese garrison. He then solidified his control over Siam by squashing rebellions in outlying provinces and launching a punitive invasion of Cambodia. The revived Siam then invaded Burma but was able to conquer only parts of the south in 1593. Burmese forces, although taken by surprise by the suddenly revitalized and aggressive Siam, still were able to defend the central kingdom.

The strategic stalemate that ensued was made possible by a balance of power between the two kingdoms. Following more than four decades of war and occupation, the two kingdoms began to focus on new adversaries. The Burmese became more isolationist, although recurring problems on their Chinese border kept them busy. The Siamese found new difficulties, as the French and Dutch began to replace the much more amiable Portuguese in the waters around the Malay Peninsula.

This era of peace lasted until the revival of warfare between the two kingdoms in 1760, which was caused, initially, by the escape of a large population of Mons into Siam following a Burmese capture of the southern Irrawaddy River valley. The cycle of invasions was renewed, lasting several decades after the Burmese sacked Ayutthaya in 1768 and after the collapse of the Ayutthaya Dynasty in Siam. Ayutthaya would not recover from the destruction.

The new Chakkri Dynasty took power in Siam soon after and established its capital farther down the Phra Chat River, across from the modern capital city, Bangkok. Even with the establishment of a new capital and the founding of a new and dynamic royal family, the Burmese invaded Siam four more times between 1785 and 1802, unsuccessfully. Lasting peace did not come until the imperialist era of the late nineteenth century, when Britain displaced the Burmese monarchy and assumed control over Burma.

SIGNIFICANCE

The struggle between Siam and Burma in the last half of the sixteenth century defined a relationship between the Thais and the Burmese that has lasted into the twenty-first century. Although it was the Burmese who most often were the aggressors in the struggles, the Siamese were the ones who absorbed most of the Thai kingdoms and who survived the later imperialist era with the loss of minor peripheral territory only. In the late nineteenth century, the Burmese were conquered by the British and their monarchy was destroyed, whereas the Chakkri Dynasty still reigns in Bangkok.

—*Barry M. Stentiford*

FURTHER READING

Hall, D. G. E. *A History of Southeast Asia*. 4th ed. New York: St. Martin's Press, 1980. A concise and well-organized introductory history of the region and the struggles between China and Burma.

Jumsai, Manich. *Popular History of Thailand*. Bangkok, Thailand: Chalermnit, 2000. A narrative account of Thai history written for the Anglophone reader but based almost entirely on Thai sources.

SarDesai, D. R. *Southeast Asia: Past and Present*. 3d ed. San Francisco, Calif.: Westview Press, 1994. A concise history of Southeast Asia, focusing on the colonial experience and its impact on the region in the postcolonial era.

Wood, W. A. R. *A History of Siam.* 1924. Reprint. Bangkok, Thailand: Wachrin, 1994. Often based as much on legend as on fact, this often-cited work is one of the first English-language works to attempt a scholarly understanding of Siamese history.

Wyatt, David K. *Thailand: A Short History.* 2d ed. New Haven, Conn.: Yale University Press, 2003. A standard academic history of the Thais from their tribal origins through the end of the twentieth century.

SEE ALSO: 1450's-1529: Thai Wars; 1454: China Subdues Burma; 1469-1481: Reign of the Ava King Thihathura; c. 1488-1594: Khmer-Thai Wars; 1505-1515: Portuguese Viceroys Establish Overseas Trade Empire; 1527-1599: Burmese Civil Wars; 1558-1593: Burmese-Laotian Wars; c. 1580-c. 1600: Siamese-Cambodian Wars.

RELATED ARTICLES in *Great Lives from History: The Renaissance & Early Modern Era, 1454-1600:* Afonso de Albuquerque; Tomé Pires; Saint Francis Xavier.

1549
KETT'S REBELLION

Robert Kett, a Norfolk tanner and landowner, and his followers protested the enclosure of pastures for more-profitable grazing—which benefited landowners—instead of for growing crops—which was a necessary form of subsistence for the poor. After taking the city of Norfolk, the rebellion was defeated at the Battle of Dussindale.

LOCALE: Norfolk, England

CATEGORIES: Wars, uprisings, and civil unrest; government and politics

KEY FIGURES

Robert Kett (1492-1549), rebel leader

First duke of Somerset (Edward Seymour; c. 1506-1552), Lord Protector of England

SUMMARY OF EVENT

Kett's Rebellion was the most significant of numerous English uprisings during the summer of 1549. The reasons for the insurrections varied, and there was little coordination between them. Most were minor and short-lived, but two (Kett's Rebellion in the county of Norfolk, and another at the city of Exeter) were far more serious. In Exeter and elsewhere the disquiet was rooted in religious resistance, while other revolts protested economic concerns. The latter was primarily the case in Kett's Rebellion.

The face of agriculture in rural England was changing during the first part of the sixteenth century. The feudal system of land ownership was being replaced by what were called enclosures. In the traditional system, land was owned by the local landlord and farmed by his tenants to produce a harvest that benefited all to a greater or lesser extent. With a growing, global demand for mate-

rial goods, such as clothing, it became more profitable to use land for grazing sheep rather than growing food crops. This, however, required significant amounts of land, and wealthy landowners sought to expand existing properties and fence off, or enclose, these larger pastures solely for the use of grazing sheep. The practice was extremely unpopular with ordinary rural people, many of whom were displaced and unemployed as a result of the enclosures.

It was this steady revolution in agricultural practice that formed the tense backdrop to Kett's Rebellion. In Norfolk, as elsewhere, resentment toward enclosures was high, but Kett's Rebellion is more complicated and, to an extent, a story of a revolt that is difficult to understand fully.

Historians speculate as to exactly why Robert Kett, a relatively wealthy landowner himself, seemingly overnight became a rebellious leader of thousands of men who, under Kett's command, would seize the city of Norwich and then twice defend it against the king's forces. The rebellion provides a revealing glimpse of rural disaffection and economic tension, but it is also a deeply absorbing psychological mystery.

If Kett's motivations are lost to us, the broad outlines of his story, though hazy to begin with, are quite straightforward. In Wymondham, Norfolk, on Tuesday, July 9, 1549, a small group of locals knocked down fences associated with enclosures. One of the landowners the men sought to menace was Kett, but he turned them away and directed them to another landowner's property. The next day, Kett began to march an army of men toward Norwich, seemingly with the goal of taking the city. Estimates of the number of men vary, but most accounts agree that it was between ten thousand and fifteen thousand.

After several days of maneuvering, which included taking a handful of wealthy hostages, the army had worked its way around the city of Norwich and was positioned on Mousehold Heath, east of Norwich. This date, July 11, marks the beginning of a strange standoff between Norwich and Kett's army. According to most historians, it was believed at the time that the army could have taken the city easily, but neither side wanted bloodshed, so deliberations were conducted at the level of diplomacy rather than battle. Accounts show that Kett's men moved freely through Norwich and that the city provided its large, menacing neighbor, Kett's camp, with provisions.

A standard interpretation argues that this delicate balance was broken when a messenger from the king, responding to the city's first plea for help, arrived in Norwich. Once there was an official presence, this view asserts, the city would have appeared to be losing to the hostile force and Kett's army would not have been able to simply sit still once Kett had rejected the government's offer of pardon. Kett's men attacked and took the city, though they remained, mostly, based on Mousehold.

The government, led by Edward Seymour, the first duke of Somerset and lord protector, had to divide its attention between the different uprisings, particularly Exeter and Norwich, as well as address hostilities with Scotland and, increasingly, France. Their response to Kett's Rebellion was to send a force quickly, led by Sir William Parr, the marquess of Northampton. The force, though relatively small, was made up of a significant number of courtly stars. Unfortunately for Northampton, his attempt to hold the city was resisted by Kett's force, which enjoyed a real tactical advantage in the city streets and from Mousehold. The nobles retreated to Cambridge and awaited further direction.

The government had a serious situation on its hands, and it responded seriously. Somerset himself was preparing to lead a larger force to Norwich, though circumstances led him to give the charge to the earl of Warwick, John Dudley. As historians suggest, this change of mind would cost Somerset dearly, perhaps leading directly to his removal from the head of the Privy Council later in the year.

Warwick's force met up with Northampton and progressed to Norwich, where it faced little resistance entering the city. Kett's men tried to retake the city but ended up back at Mousehold, albeit after some initial successes. The situation looked increasingly hopeless for the rebels, who had lost momentum and advantage. On August 26,

by cover of night, the rebels abandoned Mousehold and prepared for an open battle with the royal forces. The battle took place at Dussindale on August 27, quickly becoming the last stand of the insurgents. Warwick executed a number of captives after pardoning other combatants. Kett took flight but was soon captured and taken to the Tower of London. After being held there with his brother, William, who had also been a ringleader of the rebellion, Robert Kett was transported back to Norwich for execution. His fate was a gruesome one, reserved for those found guilty of treason: He was hung, cut down while still alive, then forced to watch his own entrails removed and burned. He was then beheaded and quartered. The strange series of events known as Kett's Rebellion, which began as a rambunctious moment of local dissent six months earlier, was quelled, though not explained, by Kett's trial and violent death.

SIGNIFICANCE

It seems correct to argue that Kett's Rebellion achieved virtually none of its aims in the short or long term. If Kett and his men were motivated by a sense of injustice against unfair and harmful changes to the system of land ownership, these changes were implemented nonetheless. The English economy continued its eventual transformation into a capitalist society, rewarding innovation and individualism rather than preserving traditional, community-based economic systems. Depending on one's own interpretation, then, Kett could appear as a Romantic hero determined to take a stand against practices that he understood to be benefiting the few while causing hardship to the many. He is in this scenario a tragic hero felled by irresistible forces of change.

Alternatively, one could see him as a troublemaker, though a well-intentioned one, who led hundreds of discontented men to their deaths and caused the city of Norwich to become a broken battleground. As with all people, historic figures and ordinary folk, a true understanding of Kett probably lies somewhere between the best and worst descriptions of him.

As Stephen Land and others argue, however, the greatest effect of Kett's Rebellion may have been that it contributed significantly to the downfall of Somerset's protectorship. Given the widespread unrest that Kett's Rebellion came to symbolize, many judged Somerset's domestic policies a failure. Warwick's triumphal return from Norwich, moreover, ensured that he was well positioned to assume the lead of the King's Council once Somerset's fall had been engineered.

—Paul Gleed

FURTHER READING

Beer, Barrett L. *Rebellion and Riot: Popular Disorder in England During the Reign of Edward VI.* Kent, Ohio: Kent State University Press, 1982. This book is useful for understanding the rebellion in relation to other contemporary disturbances, particularly Exeter's.

Bindoff, S. T. *Kett's Rebellion, 1549.* London: Historical Association, 1968. This pamphlet is still considered by many historians to be the preeminent modern account of the rebellion.

Land, Stephen K. *Kett's Rebellion: The Norfolk Rising of 1549.* Ipswich, England: Boydell Press, 1977. A highly readable account of the rebellion that synthesizes past sources nicely. Land stresses the larger contexts of the rebellion, stressing particularly the interwined fates of Kett and Somerset.

Shagan, Ethan. "Protector Somerset and the 1549 Rebellions: New Sources and New Perspectives." *English Historical Review* 114, no. 455 (February, 1999): 34-63. An analysis of Seymour's handling of Kett's Rebellion, along with copies of nine letters related to negotiations with rebel leaders.

SEE ALSO: Early 1460's: Labor Shortages Alter Europe's Social Structure; 1531-1540: Cromwell Reforms British Government; Dec. 18, 1534: Act of Supremacy; July, 1535-Mar., 1540: Henry VIII Dissolves the Monasteries; Oct., 1536-June, 1537: Pilgrimage of Grace; May, 1539: Six Articles of Henry VIII; Jan. 28, 1547-July 6, 1553: Reign of Edward VI.

RELATED ARTICLES in *Great Lives from History: The Renaissance & Early Modern Era, 1454-1600:* Thomas Cromwell; Edward VI; Henry VIII; First duke of Somerset.

1549-1552
FATHER XAVIER INTRODUCES CHRISTIANITY TO JAPAN

Over the period 1549-1552, Jesuit priest Francis Xavier and his colleagues established Christianity in Japan, converting several thousand adherents and introducing European learning and trade.

LOCALE: Kagoshima and Yamaguchi, Japan
CATEGORIES: Religion; diplomacy and international relations

KEY FIGURES

Saint Francis Xavier (Francisco de Jaso y Azpilcueta; 1506-1552), a Jesuit missionary to East Asia
Cosme de Torres (fl. sixteenth century), a Jesuit missionary to East Asia
Juan Fernández (c. 1536-c. 1604), a member of the Jesuit order
Anjirō (Pablo de Santa Fe; fl. sixteenth century), a Japanese samurai warrior
Ōuchi Yoshitaka (1507-1551), a powerful warlord

SUMMARY OF EVENT

To counter the Protestant Reformation of the early sixteenth century, the Catholic Church launched an internal reform known as the Counter-Reformation. At the heart of this movement was a new order of priests, the Society (or Company) of Jesus, popularly known as the Jesuits. Their fundamental mission became the preservation and advancement of Catholic tradition. Their founder, Saint Ignatius of Loyola, was a Spaniard.

It was Spain together with Portugal, bastions of Catholicism, that pioneered maritime discoveries in the fifteenth century that opened trade routes and new lands in Africa, Asia, and the Americas. Supported by the power of the expanding Spanish and Portuguese empires, Jesuits took the forefront in evangelizing the globe for Catholicism. They were particularly dedicated to establishing schools, emphasizing learning as key to solidifying Catholic faith.

One Jesuit, Saint Francis Xavier, became particularly distinguished in advancing Catholicism to the farthest known eastern reaches of the globe, Japan. He was born Francisco de Jaso y Azpilcueta into an aristocratic Basque family in the castle of Xavier near Pamplona, Spain. Studying in Paris, he became the friend of a fellow Basque and Spaniard, Ignatius Loyola. In 1534 Francis and five other students joined Ignatius in organizing what became, with papal approval in 1540, the Society of Jesus.

Father Francis Xavier began his missionary career the same year. Leaving Portugal under royal auspices, he evangelized throughout Asia until he died twelve years later off the coast of China. He labored to establish Catholic missions in Mozambique, India, Sri Lanka, and the

1540's

islands of Indonesia. He operated from Goa, India, the chief center of the Portuguese empire in the East.

At Melaka (now Malacca in Malaysia), he met in 1547 a Japanese samurai (warrior aristocrat) named Anjirō (also known as Anger or Han-Sir), who had come to request that the Jesuit journey to Japan to advance Christianity there. Responding to the request, Francis Xavier traveled to Japan, landing on August 15, 1549, at the port of Kagoshima on Kyūshū, the southernmost of Japan's four major islands. He was accompanied by Anjirō, who was baptized as Pablo de Santa Fe, and two other Jesuits, Father Cosme de Torres and Brother Juan Fernández.

They arrived during a period of exceptional political and religious transition in Japan's history known as the Sengoku Jidai, or Warring States period. These conditions would initially aid but ultimately frustrate their missionary efforts. Japan was experiencing a feudal period after ancient imperial authority had waned. Local authorities or warlords known as daimyo, with mounting military force, had replaced central authority. Changing power relations among local lords created chronic instability and violence. Nonetheless, economic opportunities emerged from the debilitated government and social regulations. Moreover, large religious, philosophical, and cultural questions had opened. Traditional Shinto and Confucian spiritual tenets had been confronting and were absorbing or mixing with newer Buddhist challenges.

In this unstable yet open flux of ideas, relations, and opportunities, the handful of Christians evangelized the gospel. Not speaking Japanese, the Jesuits initially were unable to preach. At Kagoshima until October, 1550, Francis composed, with the aid of translators, a Japanese catechism of basic Catholic doctrine. The presence of the Jesuits was tolerated by the local warlord, Shimazu Takahisa, who hoped they might aid him in attracting Portuguese traders to his province. He calculated that economic bonds could become strategic ones in the endless rounds of warfare that characterized Japanese civil society.

Francis's ambition, however, was to journey to Kyōto, the imperial capital on the main island of Honshū. There he hoped to obtain the permission and support of the emperor for the preaching of Christianity. On his way northward to the capital, he stayed in Yamaguchi from October to December, where he and his fellows were now emboldened to preach.

Using the crossroads of the city as pulpits, they read from their Japanese catechism, denouncing Japanese idolatry and morals. They were often mocked by the street folk because of their ragged appearance and awkward speech. Nevertheless, a segment of the population was sympathetic, particularly to the Christian teaching of compassion. Some local aristocrats invited Francis to their homes, interested in hearing of his travels around the world and his knowledge of trade and technical advances rumored to be emerging from Europe. One of these noblemen, Naito Takaharu, became a patron, protector, and eventually, the Jesuit's most important convert. Moreover, he introduced Francis to the region's most powerful warlord, Ōuchi Yoshitaka.

After finally reaching Kyōto, Francis learned that the Japanese emperor was weak and irrelevant to plans for national conversion. In returning to Yamaguchi in March, 1551, he now saw how Ōuchi held a singular position of regional power. To persuade him to support Christianity, Francis tempered his manner, dressed in better clothing, and offered Ōuchi gifts that had been destined for the emperor. These gifts were meant to impress the Japanese regarding the value of Portuguese trade and technology and the productive intellectual environment that Christianity fostered. The gifts included a clock, a music box, books, spectacles, a mirror, and rich fabrics and tableware. Most alluringly and tellingly for history, one gift was a three-barreled rifle.

Ōuchi responded generously, giving the Jesuits an abandoned monastery, some land, and, together with Naito, financial aid. They also received permission to preach and soon had five hundred converts for their newly constructed church. Their message was particularly effective among the underclass, who responded to the Christian message of brotherly love and who lost no social prestige by adhering to a new religion. A noted convert was a blind lute player who, as Brother Lorenzo, became a lay evangelist of the Jesuits. Francis was even able to convert a Zen Buddhist monk. In talking of the Christian God, Francis used the Latin word *deus*, which unfortunately could be equated by enemies of Christianity with a Japanese word, *daiuso*, meaning devil.

By September of 1551, Francis left Yamaguchi, sojourned briefly in Bungo, and then left Japan, to which he never returned. Father Cosme de Torres was left in charge of the Japanese mission. Spending the first months of 1552 back in Goa, Francis resolved to evangelize China, setting out in April. By September, he had reached an island off the coast of the country, near present-day Hong Kong. However, falling ill in November, he on died December 2. His body was returned for burial in Goa. He was canonized a saint, together with Ignatius Loyola, in 1622.

SIGNIFICANCE

Evangelizing in Japan from 1549 to 1552, Francis Xavier and two Jesuit colleagues established Roman Catholic communities on the islands of Kyūshū and southern Honshū. After initial difficulties of social acceptance, they converted several thousand followers among the lower classes and attracted a handful of admirers among the provincial nobility. From this nucleus, Christianity grew and took root in southern Japan during the second half of the sixteenth century and the first half of the seventeenth, a period in Japan known as the Christian Century.

Ports in southern Japan were generally where foreign traders, including the Portuguese, Spanish, Dutch, and Chinese, concentrated. The growth of Christianity occurred because no central state or national religious opposition existed in the country to thwart it. Moreover, it offered promising commercial, strategic, and cultural ties in regional power centers. Jesuits opened numerous secondary schools (*colégios*) noted as centers of Western learning.

The national consolidation of Japanese state, military, religious, and cultural power beginning in 1600 with the rise of the Tokugawa shogunate reversed the favorable conditions for foreign religious, commercial, and strategic activities. During the 1620's, Christian missionaries and their converts were executed in the tens of thousands, their churches and property were confiscated, and the Japanese were forbidden any contact with foreigners. The novelist Shūsaku Endō recalled this persecution in his work appearing in 1966, *Chimmoku* (*Silence*, 1969). Until the reopening of Japan in the late nineteenth century, Christianity survived in a rudimentary form in southern Japan as a hidden sect. In 1913, the Jesuits opened Sophia University in Japan. A statue of St. Francis Xavier stands prominently on the campus.

—*Edward A. Riedinger*

FURTHER READING

Fernandes, Naresh. "Tomb Raider: Looking for St. Francis Xavier." *Transition* 84 (2000): 4-19. An Indian of Portuguese descent retraces steps of missionary in Asia, recounting how devotees have distributed relics of Xavier's body to shrines in various parts of world.

Gowen, Herbert H. *Five Foreigners in Japan*. Freeport, N.Y.: Books for Libraries Press, 1967. Includes a chapter on Xavier.

Moran, Joseph Francis. *The Japanese and the Jesuits: Alessandro Valignano in Sixteenth-Century Japan*. London: Routledge, 1993. Examines earliest activities of Jesuits in Japan through the record of an Italian Jesuit.

O'Neill, Charles E., and Joaquín Ma. Dominguez, comps. *Diccionario histórico de la compañía de Jesús: biográfico-temático*. Rome: Institum Historicum, 2001. The most complete compilation of Jesuit biographies; includes an article on Xavier. In Spanish.

Ross, Andrew C. *A Vision Betrayed: The Jesuits in Japan and China, 1542-1742*. Maryknoll, N.Y.: Orbis Books, 1994. A missionary Catholic interpretation of the pioneer work of the Jesuits in East Asia.

Schurhammer, Georg. *Francis Xavier: His Life, His Times*. 4 vols. Rome: Jesuit Historical Institute, 1973-1982. The authoritative Jesuit biography of Xavier.

SEE ALSO: 1457-1480's: Spread of Jōdo Shinshū Buddhism; 1467-1477: Ōnin War; 1477-1600: Japan's "Age of the Country at War"; Mar. 5, 1488: Composition of the *Renga* Masterpiece *Minase sangin hyakuin*; Beginning 1513: Kanō School Flourishes; 1514-1598: Portuguese Reach China; 1532-1536: Temmon Hokke Rebellion; 1550's-1567: Japanese Pirates Pillage the Chinese Coast; 1550-1593: Japanese Wars of Unification; Sept., 1553: First Battle of Kawanakajima; June 12, 1560: Battle of Okehazama; 1568: Oda Nobunaga Seizes Kyōto; 1583-1610: Matteo Ricci Travels to Beijing; 1587: Toyotomi Hideyoshi Hosts a Ten-Day Tea Ceremony; 1590: Odawara Campaign; 1592-1599: Japan Invades Korea; 1594-1595: Taikō Kenchi Survey; Oct., 1596-Feb., 1597: *San Felipe* Incident; Oct. 21, 1600: Battle of Sekigahara.

RELATED ARTICLES in *Great Lives from History: The Renaissance & Early Modern Era, 1454-1600:* Hōjō Ujimasa; Hosokawa Gracia; Oda Nobunaga; Ōgimachi; Oichi; Sesshū; Toyotomi Hideyoshi; Saint Francis Xavier.

1549-1570's
LA PLÉIADE PROMOTES FRENCH POETRY

A group of ambitious young French poets, commonly known as La Pléiade, strove to elevate French poetry to the level of its venerated Greek, Latin, and Italian predecessors, thus creating a national literature that would correspond to and illustrate France's prominent position in early modern Europe.

LOCALE: Touraine region and Paris, France
CATEGORY: Literature

KEY FIGURES
Pierre de Ronsard (1524-1585), French poet and leader of La Pléiade
Joachim du Bellay (1522-1560), foremost theoretician and second most influential poet of the movement
Pontus de Tyard (c. 1522-1605), French poet and theorist
Antoine de Baïf (1532-1589), French poet
Jacques Peletier du Mans (1517-1582), French poet and translator of Horace

SUMMARY OF EVENT
In 1546, Joachim du Bellay met Jacques Peletier du Mans, translator of Horace's *Ars poetica* (c. 17 B.C.E.; *The Art of Poetry*, 1567), ardent advocate of the potential of the French language, and an acquaintance of Pierre de Ronsard. At the time, Ronsard and his friend Antoine de Baïf were students of the Hellenist Jean Dorat. In 1547, Dorat was appointed to the Collège de Coqueret in Paris, and Ronsard, Baïf, and du Bellay followed him there to study Greco-Latin and Italian culture with him. These ambitious poets called themselves the "Brigade"—a name that Ronsard would change into "Pléiade" in the mid-1550's—and, following Italy's example, they set out to create a national French literature that would rival and eventually surpass its illustrious predecessors.

The publication of Thomas Sébillet's *Art poétique françoys* (1548; French poetic art) triggered a violent reaction by the Brigade. Sébillet's treatise expressed many of the group's convictions but advocated the imitation of French models, particularly those from the author's own school of poetry, which was headed by the late Clément Marot (1496-1544). The Brigade's answer, du Bellay's *La Défense et illustration de la langue française* (1549; *The Defense and Illustration of the French Language*, 1939), dismissed all previous literary productions in the vernacular as inferior, with the exception of Guillaume de Lorris and Jean de Meung's *Le Roman de la rose* (thirteenth century; *The Romance of the Rose*, partial transla-

tion c. 1370, complete translation 1900). Du Bellay was particularly dismissive of French medieval genres, of the verbal acrobatics of the fifteenth and early sixteenth century "great rhetorical" school (*les Grands Rhétoriqueurs*), and the merely amusing "superficial" style of Clément Marot and his disciples.

This sweeping and exaggerated condemnation of Sébillet's poetics was necessary from a political point of view, since the Brigade tried to present itself as the true beginning of French letters, adopting Petrarchism and Neoplatonism as its main guiding principles. Sébillet answered the Brigade rather violently in his preface to his 1549 edition of Euripides' *Iphigenia ē en Aulidi* (405 B.C.E.; *Iphigenia in Aulis*, 1782), an illustration of his poetic principles, to which du Bellay responded in turn in the preface to the 1550 second edition of *L'Olive* (first edition 1549; the olive), a work meant to put into practice the Pléiade's theories. The dispute was continued by Barthélémy Aneau's *Quintil horatian* (1550), which responded to du Bellay by quoting and refuting all the major points of the later's treatise in an attempt to rehabilitate Sébillet. Other significant treatises to follow were Pontus de Tyard's *Solitaire Premier* (1552; first recluse), Peletier's *Art poétique* (1555; poetic art), and Ronsard's *Abrégé de l'art poétique français* (1565; résumé of French poetic art).

Although there was some fluctuation within the group, as well as conflicting opinions in certain areas, the Pléiade's main goal was to establish lyrical poetry as a genre independent from rhetoric. Sébillet's treatise was in fact the first one to be devoted to poetry, which, up to then, had been considered a subcategory of rhetoric, a second rhetorical art (*art de seconde rhétorique*). The Pléiade asserted that the characteristics of lyrical poetry would confer a sublime status to the genre and, by extension, to the poet. The latter would henceforth be clearly superior to his predecessor, the orator, a mere craftsperson who mechanically applied rules to his "artificial" (or unnatural) creations. The major consequence of poetry's newly sublime status would be the inevitable elevation of French culture, which, in turn, was meant to complete the prestigious transfer of power and learning (*translatio imperii et studii*) from Italy to the new supreme nation, France. This ambitious undertaking inevitably hinged on a redefinition of the nature of poetry that was developed with the help of three key concepts: imitation, invention, and inspiration.

Imitation was probably the single most important and most complex of these concepts. It derived from the Pléiade's admiration for their Greek, Roman, and Italian forebears. Several major problems presented themselves, however, especially the question of how to create a unique and original national identity by following foreign models. This issue was exacerbated by the well-known Platonic principle that all imitation is intrinsically inferior to the original.

The Pléiade endeavored to refute fundamental theoretical objections to the practice of imitation in several ways. The goal, du Bellay stated, was not to copy admired models mechanically but to create an "ancient *renewed* poetry." In his *Defense and Illustration of the French Language*, the poet had already used the metaphors of graft and digestion to describe an "intelligent" form of imitation that could lead to something new. Both metaphors were meant to suggest the organic appropriation and transformation of ancient and foreign poetic practice into something novel and inherently French. In fact, du Bellay's treatise was itself a case study, modeled closely after Sperone Speroni's *Il dialogo delle lingue* (1542; the dialogue of languages).

Drawing on the sixteenth century understanding of Aristotelian thought, the Pléiade claimed that poetic imitation, as opposed to historiography, should show what is likely or possible, not what is real or true. Poetry would thus depict particular cases and situations that would allow the reader a glimpse of universal truths. In this idea of the Pléiade, that poetry should create rather than capture truth, can be found the kernel of a modern understanding of invention. Invention, the first element of the traditional

Baïf   J. du Bellay   Remy Belleau

J. Daurat   Jodelle   P. Ronsard

Members of the French literary group, La Pléiade. (Frederick Ungar Publishing Co.)

1540's

DU BELLAY'S SONNET TO THE ENEMY OF GOOD LETTERS

At the conclusion of his Defence and Illustration of the French Language, *Joachim du Bellay produced a sonnet meant to contrast himself and other members of the Pléiade with those whose lives are driven by greed rather than nobler poetic sentiments.*

To the Ambitious and Greedy, Enemy of Good Letters
Serf of largess, and slave of greed
Not e'en of self hast thou control;
I such a master choose, my soul
Grows free to suit its will and need.
Chance, weather, rules by men decreed
Engrip of all that's thine the whole.
We pay the hungry judge no toll,
From spites of Time and the Sisters freed.
For worthiness of choice compare
Safety and danger, ease and care;
For honour—deathless life is mine.
A name unclouded fears no doom.
'Tis death's, the name obscur'd that's thine:
And so you both shall share one tomb.

Source: From The Defence and Illustration of the French Language, *by Joachim du Bellay. Translated by Gladys M. Turquet (London: J. M. Dent & Sons, 1939), p. 108.*

model of rhetoric, derived from the Latin *invenire*, meaning "to find," and it almost exclusively designated the poet's task of finding extant in reality appropriate subjects for his writing. With the theories of the Pléiade, however, a more recognizably modern concept of invention as original, imaginative creation, rather than mere discovery of something in the world, began to appear.

To explain how original, imaginative creation was possible, the Pléiade employed their third key concept: inspiration, or divine furor. Tyard's *Solitaire Premier* furnished a detailed explanation of this Neoplatonic idea, which involved the infusion of divine powers into selected souls. These souls, thus empowered, were able to create lyrical poetry, to experience the revelation of a higher truth, and ultimately to achieve salvation. Infused by divine inspiration, which revealed both divine and natural secrets to him, the poet was able to take advantage of the powerfully allegorical images of ancient mythology and to exploit them in a Christian context, embracing a syncretism typical of Renaissance thought.

The divine nature of poetic inspiration irrefutably demonstrated the sublime status of poetry and its creators

in human society. This privileged status also had its price, however. The poet had to prepare his soul for the reception of the divine furor by cleansing it of all vice. He also owed it to his calling to be well versed in classical mythology and to perfect his technique to supplement his inspiration. This, as the Pléiade saw it, was precisely the difference between themselves and the condemned "versifiers" of earlier French poetry: Earlier craftspeople lacked the supreme qualification of a true poet, divine furor. They had perfected their technique, not as a means to an end (to be worthy of and to express their inspiration) but as an end in itself, having seen poetry as entirely a matter of technique.

The elitist attitude of the Pléiade—their belief that they were the first French poets, and the only ones then writing, to be blessed with divine inspiration—inevitably led to highly erudite poetry. This erudition necessitated the inclusion of a detailed commentary in the 1553 second edition of Ronsard's *Les Amours* (first edition 1552; loves). Officially responding to public criticism, the Pléiade poets later showed their versatility by turning away from Petrarchism and obscure classical allusions to adopt a much simpler and allegedly more natural style, imitating poets like Ovid and Catullus. As if to underscore his mastery of various techniques, Ronsard returned to Petrarchism toward the end of his career.

SIGNIFICANCE

The Pléiade had a considerable impact in several respects. Its promotion of the vernacular boosted national self-confidence and supported a fledgling French cultural nationalism. Such cultural nationalism was an integral component of the nation-building process in early modern Europe, as national identity gradually replaced the former supranational religious identity of Catholicism as the primary register of self-understanding. The quasi-sacred character of poetry also helped assert the autonomy of literature and of the poet at a time when artists depended almost exclusively on patronage, which usually affected the quality and the character of their creations. The redefinition of the poet as an extraordinary *persona*, blessed with divine inspiration which must then be developed and realized through labor (refining technique and studying ancient and Italian models), can also be seen as a precursor of later bourgeois ethics. Finally, the Pléiade's poetics laid the groundwork for modern literary aesthetics that informed nineteenth and twentieth century poets and critics such as Charles-Augustin Sainte-Beuve, Victor Hugo, Charles Baudelaire, and Paul Valéry, who freely expressed their admiration for and admitted their debt to the Pléiade. Modern literature would be quite different without these Renaissance "avant-garde" poets' contribution.

—Bernd Renner

FURTHER READING

Castor, Grahame. *Pléiade Poetics: A Study of Sixteenth Century Thought and Terminology.* Cambridge, England: Cambridge University Press, 1964. Groundbreaking and still the authoritative study in English on the movement as a whole; analyzes its aesthetics from a Renaissance point of view.

Conley, Tom. *The Graphic Unconscious in Early Modern French Writing.* New York: Cambridge University Press, 1992. Innovative approach stressing the visual impact and the role of psychoanalysis in Renaissance literature; chapters on Marot and Ronsard.

Greene, Thomas M. *The Light in Troy: Imitation and Discovery in Renaissance Poetry.* New Haven, Conn.: Yale University Press, 1982. Essential study of the concept of imitation.

Hampton, Timothy. *Literature and Nation in the Sixteenth Century: Inventing Renaissance France.* Ithaca, N.Y.: Cornell University Press, 2001. Chapter on du Bellay and the lyric invention of national character as part of a study of literary nationhood.

Langer, Ullrich. *Invention, Death, and Self-Definitions in the Poetry of Pierre de Ronsard.* Saratoga, Calif.: ANMA Libri, 1986. In-depth study of Ronsard's poetry.

Ronsard, Pierre de. *Selected Poems.* Translated by Malcolm Quainton and Elizabeth Vinestock. London: Penguin, 2002. Bilingual edition with an informative basic introduction covering Ronsard's life, career, and technique.

SEE ALSO: Early 16th cent.: Fuzuli Writes Poetry in Three Languages; c. 1589-1613: Shakespeare Writes His Dramas.

RELATED ARTICLES in *Great Lives from History: The Renaissance & Early Modern Era, 1454-1600:* Joachim du Bellay; Pierre de Ronsard.

Mid-16th century
DEVELOPMENT OF THE CARACOLE MANEUVER

The invention of wheel lock pistols spurred the development of a new cavalry tactic called the caracole, which attempted to reestablish the primacy of cavalry on the battlefield. The maneuver involved tight, rotating formations of soldiers using pistols on horseback, but it proved less than adequate in battle and was thus superseded by the end of the sixteenth century.

LOCALE: Dreux, southwest of Paris near Chartres (now in France)

CATEGORY: Wars, uprisings, and civil unrest

KEY FIGURES

Anne, duke of Montmorency (1493-1567), constable of France

Louis I of Bourbon (1530-1569), prince of Condé

SUMMARY OF EVENT

One significant feature of warfare during the Renaissance was the declining importance of cavalry on the battlefield. During the Middle Ages, feudal knights and heavily armored men-at-arms dominated the battlefield. A charge of close-packed horsemen could be stopped only by obstacles, well-disciplined infantry armed with pikes, or effective use of projectile weapons. During the fourteenth century both disciplined pike forces, such as the Swiss, and effective archers or crossbowmen were able to inflict terrible defeats on armies composed primarily of mounted men-at-arms.

The introduction of gunpowder changed this balance slowly, as early handheld guns were cumbersome, inaccurate, and hard to use on the battlefield. In the fifteenth century, though, the introduction of the harquebus (also called arquebus) began to change this equation. The harquebus was fired by lowering a slow-burning match into a gunpowder-filled pan. This ignited the main charge in the breech, which in turn fired the harquebus. This type of mechanism was called a matchlock. Soldiers wielding a harquebus could inflict serious damage, but they were especially vulnerable to cavalry charges because the long process of reloading required both hands and thus left gunners unable to defend themselves. A matchlock was reasonably easy to use on foot, but the smoldering matches they required often frightened the horses, so they were inconvenient weapons for mounted use.

During the fifteenth century, Spanish captains began to create a new tactical system that combined the firepower of the harquebus with the protection of pikes. Dense formations of pikemen, if well disciplined, provided defensive bulwarks behind which harquebusiers could safely fire and reload. Units that combined pike and harquebus were capable of defeating most cavalry charges; at the same time, the increasing lethality of handheld firearms forced horsemen to wear armor that came to be progressively heavier. As a result, armies in the field reduced the numbers of mounted men-at-arms. By the beginning of the sixteenth century many mounted men were wearing less armor and looking for better ways to incorporate firearms into their tactics so as to restore their potency on the battlefield.

The invention of the wheel lock presented this opportunity. Invented around the year 1515, the wheel lock featured a steel wheel mounted on a spring and facing a hammer that held iron pyrite. After the spring was wound, pulling the trigger released the wheel to spin against the pyrite. Like a modern cigarette lighter, the spinning of the wheel against the pyrite would strike sparks that would then ignite the gunpowder. Since no prelit smoldering match was necessary, a gunner could load the piece, wind up the spring, and carry it into action ready to fire. The drawback was that wheel locks were complex to make—they required a clockmaker's precision to work properly—and thus expensive. As a result, they were common weapons among the wealthy only, such as knights or military entrepreneurs, and far too expensive for the common foot soldier.

The increasing complexity of Renaissance warfare led to an increase in military entrepreneurs—mercenaries whose occupation was warfare. One particularly fertile area for recruiting such mercenaries was the cluster of small states and kingdoms that made up what is today Germany. These states were too small to need large numbers of homegrown men-at-arms, so these surplus soldiers sought their fortunes elsewhere. Such men were called reiters—German for "riders." The name first came into use in the 1540's, the same time that wheel lock pistols were introduced in large numbers. Armed with

The values—and limitations—of the caracole maneuver were witnessed at the Battle of Dreux in 1562. (Frederick Ungar Publishing Co.)

wheel locks and lighter armor, reiters were easier and cheaper to recruit, and they were faster on the battlefield than the more ponderous heavy cavalry.

To make themselves more effective, they began to charge with their wheel locks rather than to depend on sword or lance. By the mid-1500's this tactic was codified as the caracole. In the caracole, reiters would mass and charge in columns. At the last possible moment, the first rank of the column would wheel and fire their pistols into the enemy formation. Then as the second rank followed suit, the first rank would trot toward the rear and reload or unholster and prepare a second pistol. Using this technique, rank after rank could continuously pour fire into a pike formation until it lost cohesion, and then use their swords to finish off the infantry.

Although the caracole returned some potency to mounted formations, it rarely proved decisive. The short barrels of pistols ensured that they were lethal at close range only, unlike harquebus fire, which remained deadly at longer ranges. Against knights using only lance or sword, the caracole could disorganize formations while the reiters' lighter armor allowed them enough mobility to avoid a countercharge, but the caracole also minimized the fire to small—and thus less devastating—volleys. This dissipated the effects of each volley and made reiter formations much less deadly.

Contemporary critics compared the caracole with a stately court dance, for the slow and deliberate pace of the caracole, with its constant flow of horsemen riding back to the end of the column while reloading, resembled a dance more than a battle-winning tactic. Instead of overwhelming an enemy, a caracole-style attack was likely to result in a desultory—and irritating, but not particularly deadly—fire on the enemy. During the Thirty Years' War, the Swedish cavalry under Gustavus II Adolphus would return to the sharp impact delivered by massed cavalry charges. To do this, Gustavus's cavalry learned to fire a volley and then charge in with swords before the enemy could reload or reform. This Swedish innovation restored shock power to cavalry and once again made the charge a battle-winning tactic.

An instructive example of the value—and limitations—of the caracole can be found in the Battle of Dreux in 1562, which was the first major battle in France's sixteenth century Wars of Religion. The Huguenot (French Protestant) forces under Louis I of Bourbon, the prince of Condé, unexpectedly bumped into a French Catholic army under the overall command of the duke de Montmorency. Both forces had been strengthened by contingents of mercenaries; the Huguenots deployed a number of reiter companies while the Catholics fielded a large force of Swiss infantry.

In the opening phases of the battle, attacks by Huguenot reiters swept away the Catholic light and medium cavalry forces, but then the reiters became dispersed during pursuit. Subsequent attacks on the well-formed Swiss formations in Montmorency's center failed to dislodge them. The Swiss pikemen were supported by a number of harquebusiers, and before long attrition and exhaustion depleted the attacking Huguenot forces. Once the Huguenot units began to lose cohesion, the Catholics began to counterattack and advance. The cavalry that had pursued the broken Catholic cavalry—including many reiters—were reformed and returned to the field to put up a spirited defense that slowed the Catholic advance. Nightfall ended the battle in a virtual draw. During the day's seesaw fighting, the attacks of the reiters had broken or disordered several cavalry formations but had not been powerful enough to shatter the Swiss. Thus, the caracole had played a role in the battle, but it by no means decided the battle's outcome.

SIGNIFICANCE

During the middle of the sixteenth century, innovative cavalrymen, including military entrepreneurs like the reiters, attempted to incorporate the new technology of wheel lock firearms into their battlefield tactics. The result was the caracole maneuver. While in the short term the caracole did reestablish some value to cavalry action in the battle line, it was not in itself a decisive tactic. Not until the reforms of Gustavus II Adolphus combined the massed cavalry charge with a pistol volley by the entire unit did cavalry once again become a battle-winning arm.

—*Kevin B. Reid*

FURTHER READING

Arnold, Thomas T. *Renaissance at War.* London: Cassell, 2001. Arnold provides in this work a good overview of military developments during the Renaissance.

Eltis, David. *The Military Revolution in Sixteenth Century Europe.* New York: Barnes & Noble Books, 1998. Eltis provides a clear and concise description of the changes that occurred in warfare during the Renaissance, such as the increasing importance of infantry firepower and the declining significance of cavalry forces.

Hall, Bert S. *Weapons and Warfare in Renaissance Europe.* Baltimore: Johns Hopkins University Press, 1997. This is a very thorough and accessible history of the development of gunpowder weapons. The work looks at both the technologies of the new weapons and

1540's

the changes in tactics heralded by these technological innovations.

Oman, Sir Charles William Chadwick. *A History of the Art of War in the Sixteenth Century.* Mechanicsburg, Pa.: Greenhill Books, 1999. This is a reprint of Oman's 1937 classic, a work upon which most other studies of Renaissance warfare are based. It also features an excellent description of the Battle of Dreux.

SEE ALSO: 16th cent.: Proliferation of Firearms; June 28, 1522-Dec. 27, 1522: Siege and Fall of Rhodes; 1550's: Tartaglia Publishes *The New Science*; Mar., 1562-May 2, 1598: French Wars of Religion.
RELATED ARTICLES in *Great Lives from History: The Renaissance & Early Modern Era, 1454-1600:* Oda Nobunaga; Süleyman the Magnificent; Niccolò Fontana Tartaglia.

1550's
TARTAGLIA PUBLISHES *THE NEW SCIENCE*

Tartaglia's treatise on physics, specifically his theories on bodies in motion, gave rise to a generation of scientific investigation into the science that came to be known as ballistics. His observation-based theories helped pry sixteenth century physics away from Aristotelean thinking, which was entrenched in the Church-supported schools and universities, and toward an empirical, experimentally based physics approaching the modern scientific method.

LOCALE: Republic of Venice (now Venice, Italy)
CATEGORIES: Physics; science and technology

KEY FIGURES
Niccolò Fontana Tartaglia (c. 1500-1557), Italian mathematician
Gerolamo Cardano (Jerome Cardan; 1501-1576), Italian mathematician and astrologer
Giovanni Battista Benedetti (1530-1590), Italian mathematician and physicist

SUMMARY OF EVENT
The influence of the Greek philosopher Aristotle's theory of motion and of other scientific concepts, left over from the study of the physical world in classical Greece, was pervasive throughout the Middle Ages. Attempts to devise new theories of motion took the form of commentaries on the works of Aristotle rather than being based on observation and description of the physical world. The mathematics used in these descriptions could be found in the geometry of the *Elements*, by the Alexandrian geometer Euclid (c. 330-c. 270 B.C.E.). Then, work in Italy in the middle of the sixteenth century led to a reevaluation of the basis for mathematical models of motion in the physical world.

Aristotle (384-322 B.C.E.) had devoted a certain number of the works that circulated under his name to questions having to do with physics, although they were usually addressed from the standpoint of what might be called philosophy instead of mathematics or science. His concern was primarily to understand how motion and change were possible, in resisting the arguments of many of his contemporaries, who denied that possibility. By contrast, the tradition associated with the Greek mathematician Archimedes (c. 287-212 B.C.E.) started from the reality of certain physical processes and then tried to analyze them in terms of the mathematics known at the time, especially the geometry of Euclid. Both approaches to the study of motion continued through the Middle Ages, although the Aristotelean ideas received a larger share of attention and blessing from the Church. Those who studied questions of motion in the universities of Western Europe could be guaranteed a fair dose of Aristotelean doctrine.

It is therefore not surprising that the originator of the most lasting revolution in the study of motion outside the tradition of Aristotle was not the product of a university. Niccolò Fontana Tartaglia came from a family unable to bear the cost of formal education, so he was largely self-educated. That did not mean that he was unfamiliar with the extensive classical literature surrounding issues of motion, but he had no particular predisposition in favor of the Aristotelean view. Throughout the early part of the sixteenth century, various treatises, from both classical and medieval times, appeared in Italy, and Tartaglia was involved in bringing the work of Archimedes before the public. Tartaglia's approach to the science of mechanics, which included the laws of motion, was based partly on his independence from tradition and partly on the need to try to resolve questions of pressing interest to those who had resources with which to support scholars.

Tartaglia's *La nova scientia* (1537; *The New Science*, partial translation in *Mechanics in Sixteenth-Century*

Italy: Selections from Tartaglia, 1969) first appeared in Latin in 1537 and then appeared in the vernacular within fifteen years afterward. In it, Tartaglia addressed one of the most compelling practical problems of the time: the study of the behavior of projectiles in motion, which came to be known as ballistics. These questions were key to understanding the operations of siege weapons, cannon, and firearms, or guns.

There had been plenty of practical discussion of gunnery previously, but not much of it had aspired to the dignity of a science. Tartaglia did not see any reason why the methods of mathematics could not be used to find solutions for the problems of gunnery, of which the most notable was the relationship between the angle at which a projectile was launched and the trajectory it followed. This was not an idle matter, with city walls to be bombarded in sieges, but it also could be fit into a mathematical framework. In Aristotelean accounts of motion, the fundamental curves were the straight line and the circle, so it had been assumed that the motion of a projectile could be analyzed as a mixture of those two. Just as the Aristotelean version of mechanics had been built into the system for planetary motion developed by the Greek astronomer Ptolemy (c. 100-c. 178), only to be replaced in 1543 by the system developed by the Polish astronomer Nicolaus Copernicus, so the Aristotelean theory of motion as applied to projectiles was rejected by Tartaglia, who recognized that circles and straight lines were not the best constructs for analyzing motion.

Tartaglia's mathematical treatment of the path of a projectile arose from empirical observation. He observed that even if the projectile started off in a straight line, it began to curve and followed that curve for the rest of its flight. The curve was clearly not a circular arc, which left Tartaglia with the problem of determining what angle would produce the maximum range. Even though there was an error in Tartaglia's mathematical analysis, he did obtain the correct value, namely, 45 degrees as the angle of inclination. Tartaglia did not have a theoretical model that explained the deviations from a straight line, but his empirical approach allowed the application of mathematics to this practical problem.

Gerolamo Cardano, a professor of mathematics in Milan and a rival of Tartaglia, held views on motion that were similar to those of Tartaglia. Unlike Tartaglia, however, Cardano was the product of the Italian university system and did not express his ideas as explicit deviations from Aristotle. Cardano asserted that if two spheres of different sizes were released at the same time, they would reach the ground at the same time. His mathematical argument for this theory was unconvincing, however, and Tartaglia—incensed over Cardano's intellectual theft—impugned both his character and his mathematical competence. History, however, has recognized Tartaglia's achievement and credits him as the father of ballistics.

The third member of the school of northern Italians who created the new science of ballistics was Giovanni Battista Benedetti, who claimed to have been a student of Tartaglia. He shared with Tartaglia the lack of a university education and in 1553 published a work on mechanics, *De resolutione*, that included a letter of dedication in which he asserted the "law of equal times of fall" that had been presented less clearly and argued for less effectively by Cardano. This law asserts that the time of descent for a body depends on the vertical distance traveled rather than the distance covered in other directions. The fact that the letter of dedication was to a priest is typical of the extent to which Tartaglia and Benedetti managed to stay on good terms with the Church in presenting notions contrary to the teachings of Aristotle. It is interesting to note

Niccolò Fontana Tartaglia's La nova scientia *(1537) is considered the first scientific work in ballistics.* (Hulton|Archive by Getty Images)

that Cardano, by contrast, did spend some time in prison at the behest of the Inquisition. Perhaps his efforts to give an Aristotelean flavor to his novelties in the theory of motion were regarded with more alarm by the Church than the more practical speculations of Tartaglia and Benedetti.

SIGNIFICANCE

The appearance of Tartaglia's work and its influence on the school that included Cardano and Benedetti indicates a change from the intellectual and mathematical traditions of the past. Even though Tartaglia was familiar with the works of Euclid, he had a stronger interest in trying to predict the motion of projectiles than in trying to fit his observations into the geometry that Euclid presents. In particular, the idea that motion requires more than lines and circles for its analysis helped to remove the Aristotelean qualitative discussions from the center of the stage in favor of mathematical models.

As for the influence of Tartaglia's work on the generations ahead, the outstanding example is certainly Galileo. When Galileo wrote about the two new sciences in *Discorsie dimostrazioni matematiche intorno à due nuove scienze* (1638; *Dialogue Concerning Two New Sciences*, 1665), he was echoing the title of Tartaglia's work. In fact, Galileo in many ways was trying to perfect the ideas roughly sketched out by Tartaglia, Cardano, and Benedetti, by fitting them into a full world system. It was perhaps the attempt to make a world system out of his calculations that caused Galileo to follow Cardano into the clutches of an Inquisition reluctant to allow quite so much of Aristotelean physics to be abandoned. It is also clear that political protection was an important consideration for research into the motion of projectiles, with safety coming to those whose mathematical models helped their patrons to remain the victors.

—*Thomas Drucker*

FURTHER READING

Clagett, Marshall. *Archimedes in the Middle Ages*. Madison: University of Wisconsin Press, 1964. Traces the mathematical stream from antiquity to the period in which Tartaglia started to work.

DiCanzio, Albert. *Galileo: His Science and His Significance for the Future of Man*. Portsmouth, N.H.: ADASI, 1996. Brief sketches of the figures leading up to Galileo's theory of motion, including Tartaglia and Benedetti.

Drake, Stillman. *Galileo at Work*. Chicago: University of Chicago Press, 1978. Indicates how Galileo would have come across the works of Benedetti and Tartaglia.

Drake, Stillman, and I. E. Drabkin, eds. *Mechanics in Sixteenth-Century Italy*. Madison: University of Wisconsin Press, 1969. The only book-length collection in English on this revolution in mechanics, with extensive translations from Tartaglia and Benedetti and an excellent essay by Drake.

Field, J. V. *The Invention of Infinity: Mathematics and Art in the Renaissance*. New York: Oxford University Press, 1997. Investigates how practical considerations entered into theoretical mathematics during the sixteenth century.

Swetz, Frank, et al., eds. *Learn from the Masters*. Washington, D.C.: Mathematical Association of America, 1995. Includes an essay by Swetz on Tartaglia's modeling the flight of a cannonball with more mathematical details than are available elsewhere.

SEE ALSO: 1462: Regiomontanus Completes the *Epitome* of Ptolemy's *Almagest*; c. 1478-1519: Leonardo da Vinci Compiles His Notebooks; Beginning 1490: Development of the Camera Obscura; c. 1510: Invention of the Watch; 1530's-1540's: Paracelsus Presents His Theory of Disease; 1543: Copernicus Publishes *De Revolutionibus*; 1543: Vesalius Publishes *On the Fabric of the Human Body*; 1572-1574: Tycho Brahe Observes a Supernova; 1580's-1590's: Galileo Conducts His Early Experiments; 1582: Gregory XIII Reforms the Calendar; 1583-1600: Bruno's Theory of the Infinite Universe; 1600: William Gilbert Publishes *De Magnete*.

RELATED ARTICLES in *Great Lives from History: The Renaissance & Early Modern Era, 1454-1600:* Gerolamo Cardano; Niccolò Fontana Tartaglia.

1550's-1567
JAPANESE PIRATES PILLAGE THE CHINESE COAST

Political instability in Japan during the mid-sixteenth century allowed pirates known as wakō *to raid coastal East Asia and even make incursions inland. These attacks caused major economic instability in Korea and northern China but abated when official trade in the region increased.*

LOCALE: Japan, China, Korea, and Southeast Asia
CATEGORIES: Wars, uprisings, and civil unrest; trade and commerce; economics; diplomacy and international relations

KEY FIGURES

Ashikaga Yoshimitsu (1358-1408), shogun, r. 1368-1394
Oda Nobunaga (1534-1582), the first unifier of Japan, r. 1573-1582
Toyotomi Hideyoshi (1537-1598), military leader who completed the unification of Japan

SUMMARY OF EVENT

For four hundred years, pirates sailing from bases in Japan and surrounding areas caused havoc all over East Asia. These pirates were referred to as *wakō* in Japanese, *wokou* in Chinese, and *waeku* in Korean. Each is a different pronunciation of the same Chinese characters: The first translates roughly as "dwarf" and was a way of referring to Japan in ancient times; the second character merely means bandit. Some historians believe that the word *wakō* was derived from an ancient Korean term used to describe the Japanese armies active in the Korean peninsula from the fifth century. Most scholars believe that Japanese pirates were active in East Asia from the thirteenth century, and their social and economic impact in the region cannot be overstated.

It was in Korea that Japanese pirates first began to make their presence known. While China was a major victim of the activities of the *wakō*, their primary target had always been Korea. The late fourteenth century, because of political instability in Japan and the military weakness of the rulers of China and Korea, saw a dramatic rise in *wakō* raids, and the economic impact of these raids on Korea was dramatic. The Japanese raiders targeted rice used to pay taxes, and they were so effective at taking official convoys that a halt was called to the transport of rice by sea. The Japanese pirates also took Korean coins—so many that shortages caused a reversion to the barter system. Entire coastal districts were abandoned, and maritime activities such as fishing, whaling, and salt production were given up as well. The economic damage wrought by the *wakō* on the Korean peninsula was tremendous, a testament to the ruthlessness, and effectiveness, of the Japanese raiders. It was only with the consolidation of central power in Korea under the Yi Dynasty in the 1390's that Korean forces were able to take decisive steps to drive the *wakō* from Korean waters.

The *wakō* were also a serious problem in northern China from the fourteenth century. In the 1350's, Japanese pirates conducted a number of daring raids along the Shandong Peninsula. These incursions continued unabated until a sizable group of *wakō* were defeated by Chinese forces in 1363. Nevertheless, Japanese raids continued to cause significant economic disruption in a time in which a new Chinese dynasty, the Ming (1368-1644), was attempting to consolidate national political and economic authority. As a countermeasure against Japanese raids, the new authorities built forts along the northern Chinese coast, but to little avail.

More effective in hampering the *wakō* were the efforts of the Japanese leader Ashikaga Yoshimitsu to restore official trading relations with China. Yoshimitsu was so anxious to gain access to the lucrative China trade that he was willing to accept a largely symbolic tributary status in relation to the Chinese court. With China trade in his sights, he convinced his major vassals to take action against the pirates who took shelter in their domains. While these measures proved effective in the short term, Yoshimitsu's successors grew increasingly weak, as did the power—and indeed, the desire—of Japanese authorities to limit *wakō* raids on the Chinese and Korean coasts.

All these developments led to something of a renaissance for Japanese piracy in the fifteenth and sixteenth centuries, a period of Japanese history known as the Sengoku Jidai, or Warring States period, for the total breakdown in central authority and the rise to power of a number of regional daimyo (warlords). The lack of central control left the *wakō* free to increase in their activities. While in earlier times, the pirates referred to as *wakō* were mostly Japanese sailors, by the sixteenth century, their ethnic makeup had changed considerably. Koreans and Chinese joined the Japanese raiders, along with sailors from Southeast Asia. Some scholars argue that they counted Portuguese adventurers among their numbers.

1550's

By the mid-sixteenth century, the *wakō* were mostly Chinese bandits, and their attention had shifted from purely maritime raiding to focused attacks on inland centers such as Nanjing and Suzhou. Other cities were targeted by the *wakō* as well.

In an effort to stop this revival of piracy, the Chinese authorities placed a ban on trade at ports such as Ningbo in an effort to diminish maritime traffic. This move merely inspired some enterprising *wakō* to fill the economic void through smuggling and other illicit activities. The situation became so serious that a ban on trade was lifted in 1567, which provided an impetus for legitimate commercial voyages under government protection. During this time, the warlord Oda Nobunaga was beginning to exercise more central political authority in Japan, including a control over the shogunal and imperial political institutions at Kyōto. A string of victories in the 1570's gave Nobunaga more maritime control, and he used his influence to encourage trade rather than to support piracy.

While efforts to foster legitimate trading between China and Japan sapped the strength and influence of the *wakō*, it was not until 1587, when Nobunaga's successor Toyotomi Hideyoshi issued an edict prohibiting piracy, that the activities of the *wakō* were curtailed to a great degree. Many crews had sailed from Japan's Inland Sea and Hideyoshi's conquest of the island of Kyūshū in 1587 gave him regional influence and allowed the anti-piracy edicts to be effectively enforced. Nevertheless, by this time Japanese piracy had transformed into a truly international phenomenon. Most of the "Japanese" pirates raiding in Korea, China, and Southeast Asia were foreign-born and based abroad.

SIGNIFICANCE

As the regulatory net tightened and central power increased in Japan, first under the warlord Hideyoshi and then under the shoguns of the Tokugawa family in the seventeenth century, many *wakō* began to engage in legitimate trade in places such as the Philippines or what is now Indonesia. This caused a final decline in Japanese piracy in East Asia. In addition, measures taken by the Western powers in the Far East caused a decline in the activities of the *wakō*. So serious was the *wakō* threat in South Asia in the late sixteenth century that the Portuguese authorities at the port of Macao issued laws banning Japanese from carrying weapons. The Spanish, try-

ing to protect their imperial presence in the region took similar measures.

A final blow to the activities of the *wakō* came as a result of the Tokugawa shogunate's decision to restrict foreign trade to a select number of ports and to ban Japanese from sailing abroad. Nevertheless, in the sixteenth and early seventeenth centuries, the *wakō*, both as pirates and as traders, did much to increase the presence of the Japanese in Southeast Asia and had a great economic impact across the region.

—*Matthew Penney*

FURTHER READING

Masuda, Wataru. *Japan and China: Mutual Representations in the Modern Era*. Translated by Joshua Fogel. New York: St. Martin's Press, 2000. Includes a chapter on the impact of Japanese pirates in Ming China.

Sansom, George. *A History of Japan, 1334-1615*. 3 vols. Stanford, Calif.: Stanford University Press, 1961. Despite its age, Sansom's history of premodern Japan is still the most authoritative on the subject in English. Includes coverage of the *wakō* and puts their raids into historical perspective.

Turnbull, Stephen. *Samurai Warfare*. London: Arms and Armour Press, 1996. The best English-language history of the Japanese wars of unification. Contains details concerning Japanese naval tactics and piracy.

SEE ALSO: 1457-1480's: Spread of Jōdo Shinshū Buddhism; 1467-1477: Ōnin War; 1477-1600: Japan's "Age of the Country at War"; Mar. 5, 1488: Composition of the *Renga* Masterpiece *Minase sangin hyakuin*; Beginning 1513: Kanō School Flourishes; 1532-1536: Temmon Hokke Rebellion; 1549-1552: Father Xavier Introduces Christianity to Japan; 1550-1593: Japanese Wars of Unification; Sept., 1553: First Battle of Kawanakajima; June 12, 1560: Battle of Okehazama; 1568: Oda Nobunaga Seizes Kyōto; 1587: Toyotomi Hideyoshi Hosts a Ten-Day Tea Ceremony; 1590: Odawara Campaign; 1592-1599: Japan Invades Korea; 1594-1595: Taikō Kenchi Survey; Oct., 1596-Feb., 1597: *San Felipe* Incident; Oct. 21, 1600: Battle of Sekigahara.

RELATED ARTICLES in *Great Lives from History: The Renaissance & Early Modern Era, 1454-1600:* Hōjō Ujimasa; Hosokawa Gracia; Oda Nobunaga; Ōgimachi; Oichi; Sesshū; Toyotomi Hideyoshi.

1550's-c. 1600
EDUCATIONAL REFORMS IN EUROPE

During the second half of the sixteenth century, a new level of education called the Latin school formed in Europe, falling between elementary school and the university. At the same time, the university turned away from Scholasticism toward Humanism and studia humanitatis, or the humanities and liberal arts. Humanist reformers believed individuals from all social classes could be more pious and could best know God through a liberal arts education.

LOCALE: Western Europe

CATEGORIES: Cultural and intellectual history; education; organizations and institutions; social reform

KEY FIGURES
Desiderius Erasmus (1466?-1536), Dutch Humanist scholar who inspired educational reform

Martin Luther (1483-1546), German religious and educational reformer

Philipp Melanchthon (1497-1560), German philosopher and educational reformer who put Luther's ideas into practice

Saint Ignatius of Loyola (1491-1556), founder of the Jesuit order

Juan Luis Vives (1492-1540), Spanish Humanist and educator

SUMMARY OF EVENT
During the fifteenth century and the first half of the sixteenth, European educators reacted against the Scholastic Aristotelianism that had dominated the thought of the Middle Ages. Many intellectuals and students alike—especially where the influence of the Protestant Reformation was dominant—considered universities to be outdated institutions bound by the power of the Catholic Church.

The expansion of the Humanistic school (also known as the Latin school, *gymnasium*, or grammar school) lent force to this gradual decline of the old universities.

The Humanists were not bound by the direct influence of state or church, which undoubtedly facilitated their ability to abandon the entrenched medieval curriculum and move toward the *studia humanitatis*—what we would now call the humanities. Students of the Latin schools were between the ages of twelve and eighteen; a university's faculty of arts normally accepted students between the ages of thirteen and seventeen as a prelude to

entering other faculties. The Humanistic school's ideology centered on the formation of men (at this time only men were generally allowed entry into the university) free to occupy positions of responsibility in society or to continue to higher studies.

Among the best known of the Latin schools were the Sélestat or Schlettstadt in Alsace, founded in 1452. Its name is linked to Humanists such as Jakob Wimpfeling, Beatus Rhenanus, Desiderius Erasmus, and Philipp Melanchthon. These scholars—and others unrelated to Sélestat, such as Rodolphus Agricola (Roelof Huysman), John Calvin, and Huldrych Zwingli—were central to the development of education in central and northern Europe, united since Martin Luther to the Protestant Reformation and its medieval model of teaching. Among them, Melanchthon stands out for shaping the core curriculum in Saxony, Würtemberg, Nuremberg, Königsberg, Tübingen, Heidelberg, Leipzig, and other German states and cities.

In response to the new tide of Humanism, the universities adjusted by gradually adopting the Humanistic curriculum and abandoning the medieval model. In Italian universities, this substitution occurred earlier than in other European regions. In Germany (notably Heidelberg, Erfurt, Rostock, and Colmar), the majority of universities embraced Humanism and separated themselves from the teachings of Luther. The substitution did not occur in the university where Luther taught, at Wittemberg (founded in 1502); there, the Reformation and Humanistic approaches merged. Oxford, Cambridge, Uppsala, and newly created universities such as Harvard in North America also adopted the Humanistic curriculum. In Paris, the deep-seated medieval curriculum was successfully transitioned into the Humanist mold in the second quarter of the sixteenth century, precisely at the moment when Ignatius of Loyola, founder of the Society of Jesus (Jesuits), completed his studies there.

The Catholic Counter-Reformation, emerging from the Council of Trent (1545-1563), dedicated much of its energy to education with the aim of spreading Catholic doctrine to secular students. In the southern regions of Europe and in the Spanish Americas, where the influence of the Catholic Church was particularly strong, Humanism and Scholasticism merged, the universities in Salamanca, Louvain, and most of South America being prime examples.

Among the new orders of the Catholic Church, the Jesuit order played a major role in education. Within a few years of its founding in 1534, its centers throughout Europe multiplied: Fifty Jesuit boarding schools appeared in Europe between 1552 and 1559. Students of all social classes were admitted, even if those from the upper classes were preferred (boarding schools of Rome, Turin, Padua, and Parma were dedicated specifically to the aristocracy). The Jesuits focused on secondary education: Students were between the ages of ten and sixteen. To enroll in one of their schools, students had to be able to read and write in Latin, as instruction was conducted in this language. The curriculum was essentially the *studia humanitatis*, but the new humanities were synthesized with the Scholastic medieval tradition, thus preserving an avenue for traditional church teachings. At the elementary level, the Jesuits used Donatus's *Ars minor* (fourth century; morphology) to teach Latin grammar and Juan Luis Vives's *Colloquiasive Linguae Latinae exercitatio* (1538; *Tudor School-boy Life*, 1970) as lecture books; with these works the preparatory phase of the Humanistic curriculum was complete.

At the conclusion of this stage, the Humanistic curriculum really began: grammar, rhetoric, poetry, history,

and moral philosophy—the latter through reading original texts on the topic. One or more authors were generally studied for each subject. Current subjects such as geography, mathematics, cosmology, and manners were not taught directly as separate courses but instead were integrated into the lessons for the core subjects listed above.

The most important authors of the curriculum were Cicero, Vergil, and Julius Caesar, whose works were memorized to acquire style and clarity of expression. Others were Horace, Ovid, Plautus, Statius, Seneca, Juvenal, Sallust, Livy, Tacitus, Curtius, Justinus, Valerius Maximus, Pomponius Mela, and Solinus. The grammar manual for the advanced level (syntax) was Guarino of Verona's *Regulae*. Later, *De institutione grammatica* (1572), by the Portuguese Jesuit Manuel Álvares, became widely used. The subjects that formed the nucleus of the *studia humanitatis* were completed by Greek, logic, and, in some cases, Hebrew. The authors studied in Greek were Ptolemy, Isocrates, Sophocles, Aristophanes, Plato, and Aristotle. The manuals were *Institutiones in linguam graecam* (1530) and *Meditationes graecanicae in artem grammaticam* (1531), by Nicolas Cley-

A sixteenth century schoolroom in Europe. (Frederick Ungar Publishing Co.)

naerts (Clenardus). In logic, Aristotle's *Organon* (335-323 B.C.E.) was taught, probably using an epitome (summary). Humanistic logic was normally addressed through two textbooks: *De inventione dialectica* (1479), by Agricola, and *Dialectica* (1532), by Johann Kayser (Caesarius).

During the sixteenth century, the idea of the generalization of education—at least for the elementary studies of reading, writing, and arithmetic—became widespread and rooted. In many places (such as Italy, the Low Countries, and especially England), municipal authorities established free schools for those students lacking economic resources. The majority of students attending the Latin schools, however, remained young men of the nobility, families of high civil servants, professionals, and crafts people or citizens connected with trade and commerce—those, in other words, with a relatively high level of income. Coeducation (boys and girls learning together) was rare and limited to independent and vernacular schools.

Girls who received instruction tended to do so at home or through private lessons. They were also able to get an education as laywomen in convents, which, after the Council of Trent, toughened their rules for admission. In general, it was believed that the education of women should be limited to religious texts and to those authors most representative in the vernacular. Through them, one could learn elementary arithmetic. The primary aim was to create honest wives and mothers, and it was widely held that only those women with responsibilities to the state should receive a Humanistic education.

SIGNIFICANCE

The development and expansion of the Humanistic schools and the type of education imparted there—the *studia humanitatis*—had an enormous impact on the history of Western education. The system of study that had developed during the Middle Ages through two institutions—on one hand the monastic or cathedral school and, on the other, the university—was reshaped as three. By the second half of the sixteenth century, yet another type of school developed, the vernacular *abbaco* school, a four-year secondary school for boys starting at age ten or eleven, where business arithmetic was taught. Such developments would, a century later, lead Johannes Amos

Comenius (1592-1670) to propose his system of educational reforms.

The efforts carried out in Protestant Europe as well as those of the Catholic Counter-Reformation (particularly by the Jesuits) demonstrated the potential of general education. Finally, the progressive universities' adaptation of Humanism and the Humanistic curricula in their faculties of arts formed the basis for the liberal arts that dominate today's Western schools and universities. It could be said that the educational reforms of the sixteenth century were antecedent to the current structure of primary, secondary, and university education.

—*Mariano Madrid Castro*

FURTHER READING

Black, Robert. *Humanism and Education in Medieval and Renaissance Italy.* New York: Cambridge University Press, 2001. Focuses on teaching practices in the classroom.

Bushnell, Rebecca W. *A Culture of Teaching: Early Modern Humanism in Theory and Practice.* Ithaca, N.Y.: Cornell University Press, 1996. Discusses the Italian origins of Humanism and educational development in Anglo-Saxon countries.

Grafton, Anthony, and Lisa Jardine. *From Humanism to the Humanities: Education and the Liberal Arts in Fifteenth- and Sixteenth-Century Europe.* Cambridge, Mass.: Harvard University Press, 1986. Explores Humanism in its practical and theoretical dimensions and discusses specifically the Humanistic education of girls and women.

Grendler, Paul F. *Schooling in Renaissance Italy: Literacy and Learning, 1300-1600.* Baltimore: Johns Hopkins University Press, 1989. The author examines education in Italy, focusing on the pre-university level. Rich in statistics.

SEE ALSO: 1499-1517: Erasmus Advances Humanism in England; Oct. 31, 1517: Luther Posts His Ninety-five Theses; 1545-1563: Council of Trent.
RELATED ARTICLES in *Great Lives from History: The Renaissance & Early Modern Era, 1454-1600:* Desiderius Erasmus; Saint Ignatius of Loyola; Martin Luther; John Calvin; Philipp Melanchthon; Huldrych Zwingli.

1550's

1550-1571
MONGOLS RAID BEIJING

Mongols from the north and northwest of China raided the capital at Beijing for more than two decades, demanding trade privileges. The conflict ceased when a peace treaty was agreed between Altan, the Mongol leader or khan, and the Longqing emperor.

LOCALE: Beijing, China, and its vicinity
CATEGORIES: Wars, uprisings, and civil unrest; diplomacy and international relations; trade and commerce

KEY FIGURES

Jiajing (reign name, also Chia-ching; personal name Zhu Houzong, Chu Hou-tsung; posthumous name Sudi, Su-ti; temple name Shizong, Shih-tsung; 1507-1567), Ming emperor of China, r. 1522-1567
Longqing (reign name, also Lung-ch'ing; personal name Zhu Zaihou, Chu Tsai-hou; posthumous name Zhuangdi, Chuang-ti; temple name Muzong, Mu-tsung; 1537-1572), Ming emperor of China, r. 1567-1572
Altan (1507-1582), Mongol khan, r. 1543-1582
Darayisun (fl. mid-sixteenth century), leader of the eastern Mongols
Qiu Luan (Ch'iu-Luan; 1505-1552), the Chinese commandant at Datong, Shanxi Province
Wang Chonggu (Wang Ch'ung-ku; 1515-1589), the Datong governor-general who initiated the peace treaty between China and Mongolia

SUMMARY OF EVENT

After the eviction of the Mongolian government from Chinese soil at the end of the Yuan Dynasty (1279-1368), these so-called northern barbarians remained a constant threat to the Chinese. Along the border between Mongolia and China, the Ming government established military garrisons as a defense mechanism, the most important of which were the garrisons at Datong and Xuanfu in the northern part of Shanxi Province. However, the soldiers stationed there were not well prepared for warfare, and the commanders were not loyal to the point that they would sacrifice their lives for the Ming court.

Toward the end of the fifteenth century, the most powerful and influential leader among the various Mongolian tribes was Batu Mongke, who created the Mongolian confederation and ruled for thirty-two years. One of his grandsons, Altan, who after his father's death inherited the land north of Shanxi, was an ambitious and power-hungry man who launched military campaigns against other Mongolian tribes, such as the Oyrats in the West. To gather supplies for his army, Altan led his troops to raid northern China, taking cotton, grains, and metal. From 1530 to the 1540's, Mongolia was devastated by repeated smallpox epidemics. The decade after this was filled with periods of severe drought and famine in southern Mongolia. To gather the resources for his military campaigns and to provide relief to his people after the natural disasters, Altan had no choice but to look southward to China.

The Ming ruler Shizong, the Jiajing emperor, was not an efficient leader. During the early part of his reign, he was more concerned with securing an heir, for whom he appealed to the Daoist Shao Yuanzhi for prayers. After he had had several sons, the emperor turned his attention to acquiring the elixir of immortality, leaving the welfare of the country to his subjects. Jiajing was also prejudiced against the Mongols, who, to him, were barbarians and could not be trusted.

Between the years 1541 and 1545, rain was scanty in northern China. As a result, famine broke out in both Mongolia and the northern Chinese provinces. Altan, in an effort to relieve his people, requested trading privileges with China but was ignored. In 1547, Altan even suggested an alliance with the Ming court to fight against the eastern Mongols under Darayisun's rule. The Jiaging emperor ordered divinations of the results of future campaigns against the Mongols; when these divinations proved to be in favor of the Ming, he ignored Altan, who then turned to Darayisun against the Chinese.

In July, 1550, the Mongols approached the Chinese garrison at Datong, where they received a bribe from the commandant Qiu Luan to go east. Qiu, fully aware of his men's inability to ward off their enemies, persuaded the Mongols to go somewhere else. On September 26, the Mongols arrived at Gubei Pass, 40 miles (about 64 kilometers) northeast of Beijing. They then moved on to Tongzhou, northern terminal of the Grand Canal, where they camped for the night of September 30. On October 1, the Mongols besieged the city of Beijing and looted the suburbs.

Most of the resident troops in the Beijing capital were assigned construction projects and were not fit to fight. When reinforcements arrived, they were met with no provisions and starved. The Ming minister of war could do nothing except to wait for the Mongols to withdraw. They did so several days later, happily with the looted goods intact. In 1551, Altan requested trading privileges again, especially the establishment of horse fairs. The Chinese agreed to two horse fairs annually and hence the raiding stopped for six months. Yet when the Mongols suggested trading cattle and sheep for beans and grains, the Chinese not only denied this request but also stopped the horse fairs altogether. Thereupon the Mongols resumed their constant raiding. Between 1550 and 1566, the Mongols raided China every year.

The Jiajing emperor took advice from his subjects not only to consolidate the Great Wall but also to build an eastern wall to protect the southern suburbs in Beijing. At the same time, for his own safety he established a palace army, or *nei wu fu*, which comprised eunuchs. None of these measures proved to be of any effect to curb the Mongols' raids.

In 1556, a major earthquake took place in Shaanxi and Shanxi Provinces, where revenues were not collected for years after. In the capital, the main audience palaces were burned down in 1557 and needed to be rebuilt. Burdened by the incessant encounters with the Mongols, the Ming national treasury was severely depleted over the years. Often, there was not enough money to sustain the border garrisons. In 1557, a garrison near Datong was abandoned for almost a year. During the twenty-one-year campaign with the Mongols (1550-1571), the Ming army won only once, in 1560.

In 1571, an opportunity for peace opened for the Chinese. Altan's grandson defected to Wang Chonggu, the governor-general at Datong. Instead of treating him as a hostage, Wang respected him as a royal guest. For the release of his grandson, Wang proposed a negotiation with Altan in which the latter would commit to a solemn oath not to attack China again. Later a settlement was reached between Altan and the Longqing emperor, who unlike his father, the Jiajing emperor, had long ago wished to put an end to the hostility between the two nations. The peace treaty consisted of five main provisions:

(1) Trade markets would be held on the frontiers. Horse fairs would be resumed.

(2) The Mongols were allowed to bring five hundred horses as annual tributes and receive Chinese products in return.

(3) Altan was granted the title of *shunyiwang*, or prince of obedience and righteousness.

(4) Altan was to return some of the important defectors to the Ming court.

(5) Altan would have lesser tribes as his subordinates.

SIGNIFICANCE

The Jiajing emperor, Shizong, can be held responsible for the Mongols' raids. Between the years 1539 and 1550, he did not attend court but left his business to the grand secretary and eunuchs. He devoted most of his time to the pursuit of immortality. In 1550, following the Daoist's advice, the emperor ordered young virgins from the ages of eight to fifteen to be summoned to court to help him in his search for immortality. Shizong also ordered his subjects to search for the magic herb *ningzhi*, which was rumored to give miraculous effects. The reason he refused to trade with the Mongols was his fear of abetting the Chinese defectors living in Mongolian territories. By giving in to the Mongols, the Ming court would also be helping these defectors to erode Ming rule.

In reality, the trade treaty actually benefited both nations. The Chinese needed a great number of horses for their garrisons and armies, while the Mongols could use cotton, silk, grain, metal, and other daily goods. Sheep, cattle, and furs had been tribute items from Mongolia for years in the Ming court. "Tribute" here is a euphemism: These items were being exchanged for goods desired by the Mongols, and as a rule, all the cost of the tributes was assumed by the Chinese. Seen from this point of view, the peace treaty of 1571 was a covenant between the two nations that sanctioned and regularized trade. From 1571 until the end of the Ming Dynasty in 1644, contact and harmony were maintained between the two neighboring countries.

—Fatima Wu

FURTHER READING

Cameron, Nigel, and Brian Brake. *Peking: A Tale of Three Cities*. Tokyo: Weatherhill, 1965. Discusses the sociopolitical issues of Beijing in three historical eras: from the ancient period to the Mongol rule, from the Ming to the Qing Dynasty, and from the Republic to the People's Republic.

Mote, Fredrick W. *Imperial China, 900-1800*. Cambridge, Mass.: Harvard University Press, 1999. Part 3, "China and the Mongol World," and Part 4, "The Restoration of Native Rule Under the Ming," provide a history of the Mongol presence in China.

Twitchett, Denis, and Frederick W. Mote, eds. *The Ming Dynasty, 1368-1644, Part 2*. Vol. 8 in *The Cambridge History of China*. New York: Cambridge University Press, 1998. Excellent coverage of Ming administration and government. Chapter 4, "Ming and Inner Asia," examines the relationship between China and Mongolia.

SEE ALSO: 16th cent.: China's Population Boom; 1521-1567: Reign of Jiajing; Jan. 23, 1556: Earthquake in China Kills Thousands; 1567-1572: Reign of Longqing; 1573-1620: Reign of Wanli.

RELATED ARTICLES in *Great Lives from History: The Renaissance & Early Modern Era, 1454-1600:* Wang Yangming; Xiaozong; Zhengde.

1550-1593
JAPANESE WARS OF UNIFICATION

After nearly a century of civil war and decentralization of authority in Japan, three successive generals—Oda Nobunaga, Toyotomi Hideyoshi, and Tokugawa Ieyasu—defeated rival warlords and formed the basis of a new system of social and political order that lasted until the nineteenth century.

LOCALE: Japan

CATEGORIES: Wars, uprisings, and civil unrest; expansion and land acquisition; government and politics

KEY FIGURES

Oda Nobunaga (1534-1582), ruler of Owari Province and the first unifier of Japan, r. 1573-1582

Toyotomi Hideyoshi (Kinoshita Hideyoshi; 1537-1598), military leader who completed the unification of Japan, r. 1590-1598

Tokugawa Ieyasu (Matsudaira Takechiyo, later Matsudaira Motoyasu; 1543-1616), shogun and founder of the Tokugawa shogunate, r. 1603-1605

Akechi Mitsuhide (1526-1582), one of Nobunaga's generals

SUMMARY OF EVENT

From the end of the Ōnin War of 1467-1477 until the mid-sixteenth century, Japan was in the midst of what has come to be known as the Sengoku Jidai or Warring States period. The feudal order of the Ashikaga shoguns had been replaced by a state of constant warfare as local strongmen known as *sengoku daimyō* vied with one another for territorial control. By the 1550's, a number of these regional warlords had increased their power to the point where they began to aim for national hegemony. Oda Nobunaga, the ruler of the province of Owari (near modern Nagoya in southern Honshū's Aichi Prefecture), displayed a military genius and ruthlessness that made him stand out from his peers as the leading candidate in the drive toward national reunification.

Oda Nobunaga inherited control of part of Owari Province on the death of his father in 1551. After first consolidating his control over his father's holdings, Nobunaga in 1555 moved against Hikogoro, a member of another branch of the Oda family in Owari. Nobunaga defeated Hikogoro in battle and continued his campaign, eventually bringing all of Owari under his sway by 1560.

The actions of the ambitious young general in Owari attracted the attention of Imagawa Yoshimoto of neighboring Mikawa. Imagawa sought to attack Nobunaga before the upstart could expand his power further and led a force of twenty-five thousand troops into Owari in June of 1560. Contemporary accounts report that Nobunaga could raise a force of only three thousand to defend his territory. However, on June 12, Nobunaga seized an opportune moment during a fierce storm to take Imagawa unawares and soundly routed the larger army. Imagawa was killed during the panic, and Nobunaga found himself in a strong strategic position on the south coast of the main Japanese island.

In 1561, one of the important Imagawa vassals, Matsudaira Takechiyo, who shortly thereafter changed his name to Tokugawa Ieyasu, allied himself with Nobunaga. Around the same time, a young officer in Nobunaga's service named Kinoshita Hideyoshi (better known by his later name Toyotomi Hideyoshi) was beginning to distinguish himself.

By the late 1560's, Nobunaga had subjugated other territories around Owari. By 1568, Nobunaga's power in central Japan was secured to the point where he was able to march into Kyōto and install a candidate of his choice into the office of shogun. The position had long since been reduced to a figurehead, but Nobunaga rightly concluded that control over the shogunate would be useful in giving his campaign of expansion more legitimacy.

In 1570, Nobunaga and his ally Tokugawa Ieyasu challenged the powerful warlords Asai Nagamasa and Asakura Yoshikage to the north of Kyōto. After a number of initial setbacks, Nobunaga defeated their combined forces in the Battle of Anegawa. The victory was only temporary, however, and Nobunaga's situation became increasingly grim as he also found himself pitted against an uprising of Pure Land Buddhist followers known as the Ikkō Ikki as well as the forces of Takeda Shingen, a powerful Eastern daimyo who had allied himself with Asai and Asakura.

Partly through his own ingenuity and partly because of help from his generals, Toyotomi Hideyoshi and Tokugawa Ieyasu, Nobunaga gradually began to gain the upper hand. After being defeated by Shingen at the Battle of Mikatagahara in 1573, Nobunaga rallied and in 1573 eliminated both Asai and Asakura. In the following year, after a series of brutal attacks, Nobunaga broke the Ikkō Ikki fortress of Nagashima, and the movement's vitality was sapped. In 1575, he employed firearms to great effect with a victory over Takeda Shingen's son Katsuyori in the Battle of Nagashino.

In 1576, Nobunaga relocated his headquarters to Azuchi Castle to the north of Kyōto and began to concentrate his military efforts against the Mōri, a powerful family in Western Japan. Hideyoshi proved to be a key figure in this fight, and by 1580 the Mōri had been significantly weakened. In 1580, Nobunaga also secured the surrender of the Ōsaka Honganji, the last powerful stronghold of Pure Land Buddhism, and effectively eliminated it as a military player.

In 1582, however, Nobunaga was betrayed by Akechi Mitsuhide, one of his generals who was preparing to lead an expedition against the Mōri. Nobunaga killed himself at Honnoji, a Buddhist temple in Kyōto, to avoid capture, and the balance of power in Japan was inexorably altered. Hideyoshi quickly established himself as Nobunaga's chief successor by eliminating Akechi at the Battle of Yamazaki.

Hideyoshi initially found himself in conflict with Tokugawa Ieyasu, but the two quickly realized that an alliance was more beneficial. Ieyasu continued to consolidate his holdings in the east, while Hideyoshi, after having gained the court title of *kampaku* (imperial regent) in 1585, began to concentrate his efforts on subduing the southern Japanese island of Kyūshū. In 1588, Hideyoshi used the prestige of his new court title to secure the allegiance of all of the daimyo in central Japan. In that year, he also promulgated his famous "sword hunt" edict, which helped to preserve order by disarming the peasant class. He and Ieyasu then combined their forces to war against the Hōjō family in the Kantō region of the east and eventually laid siege to their fortress at Odawara, which

was surrendered in 1590. Hideyoshi granted Ieyasu lordship over the Kantō region after the fighting had ended.

With the victory over Odawara, Hideyoshi had come to exercise a military power almost unprecedented in Japanese history. In 1592, he chose to direct this power abroad with an invasion of Korea. Because of long supply lines, disease, and fierce resistance in the Korean peninsula, the fighting there was a stalemate. In 1593, Chinese forces intervened and Hideyoshi's representatives began peace negotiations. His authority in Japan, however, seemed unshakable, and after nearly fifty years of campaigns that had been begun by Oda Nobunaga, the Japanese wars of unification had effectively come to an end.

SIGNIFICANCE

By 1593, Hideyoshi's most productive and energetic years were behind him. Some scholars theorize that he may have suffered from mental illness between this time and his death in 1598. Tokugawa Ieyasu, who had prevented this dissipation of his military might by declining to participate in Hideyoshi's Korean adventure emerged as Hideyoshi's successor after defeating a coalition of rivals in the Battle of Sekigahara in 1600. In 1603, Tokugawa Ieyasu was given the title of shogun by the emperor. This marks the beginning of the Tokugawa shogunate, which continued to rule Japan until the nineteenth century. The system of feudal alliances and territorial holdings that originated during the time of Nobunaga and Hideyoshi was further developed under Ieyasu and given a legal legitimacy that lasted as long as the rule of his successors.

Despite the destruction wrought during these wars of unification, the period between 1550 and 1593 was also a period of significant economic growth. As early as 1569, Nobunaga ordered the destruction of toll barriers to provide an impetus to the development of commerce. Nobunaga and Hideyoshi also aggressively pursued trade with Western powers such as Spain and Portugal, resulting in an increased role for Japan in the burgeoning global economy.

In addition, Nobunaga and Hideyoshi were both recognized as great patrons of the arts as well as great generals, and the period is considered something of a cultural renaissance in the history of Japan. New styles of art incorporating Western influences were perfected, and the quality of domestic craft in areas such as architecture continued to advance.

—*Matthew Penney*

1550's

FURTHER READING

Sansom, George. *A History of Japan, 1334-1615*. 3 vols. Stanford, Calif.: Stanford University Press, 1961. Despite its age, Sansom's history of premodern Japan is still the most authoritative on the subject in English. Includes detailed coverage of the wars of unification.

Sato, Hiroaki. *Legends of the Samurai*. New York: The Overlook Press, 1995. This work contains accounts of the careers of Nobunaga, Hideyoshi, and Ieyasu as well as details about their battles.

Turnbull, Stephen. *Samurai Warfare*. London: Arms and Armour Press, 1996. The best English language history of the Japanese wars of unification.

SEE ALSO: 1457-1480's: Spread of Jōdo Shinshū Buddhism; 1467-1477: Ōnin War; 1477-1600: Japan's "Age of the Country at War"; Mar. 5, 1488: Composition of the *Renga* Masterpiece *Minase sangin hyakuin*; Beginning 1513: Kanō School Flourishes; 1532-1536: Temmon Hokke Rebellion; 1549-1552: Father Xavier Introduces Christianity to Japan; 1550's-1567: Japanese Pirates Pillage the Chinese Coast; Sept., 1553: First Battle of Kawanakajima; June 12, 1560: Battle of Okehazama; 1568: Oda Nobunaga Seizes Kyōto; 1587: Toyotomi Hideyoshi Hosts a Ten-Day Tea Ceremony; 1590: Odawara Campaign; 1592-1599: Japan Invades Korea; 1594-1595: Taikō Kenchi Survey; Oct., 1596-Feb., 1597: *San Felipe* Incident; Oct. 21, 1600: Battle of Sekigahara.

RELATED ARTICLES in *Great Lives from History: The Renaissance & Early Modern Era, 1454-1600:* Hōjō Ujimasa; Hosokawa Gracia; Oda Nobunaga; Ōgimachi; Oichi; Sesshū; Toyotomi Hideyoshi.

January-May, 1551
THE STOGLAV CONVENES

The Stoglav, or Council of One Hundred Chapters, an assembly of Russian clergymen, was convened by the czarist government to combat the vestiges of pagan practices in Russia, to strengthen the church against heretical movements, to increase clerical and administrative discipline, and to bring the church under the jurisdiction of the secular authorities.

LOCALE: Moscow, Russia
CATEGORIES: Religion; government and politics; organizations and institutions

KEY FIGURES
Ivan the Terrible (1530-1584), grand prince of Moscow, r. 1533-1547, and czar of Russia, r. 1547-1584
Macarius (c. 1482-1564), metropolitan of Moscow and of all Russia, r. 1542-1564
Sylvester (d. 1566), Kremlin priest
Saint Joseph of Volokolamsk (Ivan Sanin; 1439-1515), Russian Orthodox abbot and monastic reformer

SUMMARY OF EVENT
The Stoglav, or Council of One Hundred Chapters, was a church council held in Moscow in January and February, 1551 (although the work of the council was not fully completed until May of that year). The council is named after the collection of documents it published, which were compiled into one hundred chapters. It was summoned by Czar Ivan the Terrible, who was assisted in ecclesiastical matters by Metropolitan Macarius—the head of the Russian Church—and his protégé, Sylvester, a priest in the Annunciation Cathedral of the Kremlin, where the czars were crowned and where the metropolitan often officiated at liturgies in the presence of the czar.

In the late fifteenth and early sixteenth centuries, the grand princes of Moscow had completed the "gathering of the Russian lands" by taking direct political control of the important commercial and cultural centers of Novgorod (1478) and Pskov (1510) on the northwestern frontier of Russia. Religious control was not yet so centralized, however. While it was always under the nominal authority of the metropolitan, who was based first in Vladimir and then in Moscow, the Russian Orthodox Church throughout the medieval period had been divided up among dioceses and archdioceses, which were often largely autonomous and maintained their own administrative structures and liturgical practices. Thus, to absorb these areas religiously as well as politically, Moscow needed to establish a uniform ecclesiastical administration and uniform liturgical practices for all Russian dioceses. Moreover, Novgorod and Pskov had experienced heresies in the fourteenth and fifteenth centuries, and the Novgorodian lands still had large pagan populations. The Orthodox Church, then, needed both to establish a strong internal administration and to combat external pagan and heretical practices.

The czar convened the Stoglav to accomplish these tasks. It was charged with combating pagan practices in Russia, strengthening the church against heretical movements, reforming the internal life of the church (especially the educational and moral discipline of the clergy), and bringing ecclesiastics under the jurisdiction of secular authorities. The reforms were presented in the form of questions from the throne, apparently drawn up by Sylvester. The members of the council understandably supported the czar's goals. Thus they forbade folk musicians and dancers from performing at weddings (seen as a pagan practice), forbade *skomorokhi* (popular musicians or troubadours) from performing, and condemned various pagan rituals performed between Christmas and Epiphany, and between Easter and St. Peter's Day.

The council standardized church rituals and liturgies, increased the authority of the episcopate (to ensure that the standardized liturgies were carried out), and increased the discipline and educational level of the clergy. Clerical reform was achieved in part through the election by the clergy in each town or district of priests' elders, who oversaw liturgical, disciplinary, and financial matters at the local level. Monasteries, which had been granted immunity from czarist courts, were brought under the jurisdiction of the episcopal courts, further strengthening the bishops. Seminaries and religious schools were envisioned, but this aspect of the reform was not realized. However, the church was given control over scribes and icon painters so that the words and images used to teach theological principles would be controlled and standardized.

The members of the council did not accept all of the czar's reforms, though. His efforts to secularize church lands and subjugate the clergy and other church people to the regular law courts were rejected. Most of the members of the council were Josephites (also called Possessors), followers of Saint Joseph of Volokolamsk. One of the most important figures in the church in the late fifteenth and early sixteenth centuries, Joseph had articulately and forcefully supported the possession of land by

---

MUSCOVITE RUSSIA AND ORTHODOX SUPREMACY

The Council of One Hundred Chapters, or Stoglav, convened during a time in Russian history that saw the strengthening of the Russian Orthodox Church. The excerpt here tells of the church's rise to supremacy at a time when the Muscovy state also was reigning supreme. The Russian Church increased its power and influence during an era marked by the fall of many other Eastern Orthodox Churches.

Religion occupied a central position in Muscovite Russia and reflected the principal aspects and problems of Muscovite development: the growth and consolidation of the state; ritualism and conservatism; parochialism and the belonging to a larger world; ignorant, self-satisfied pride and the recognition of the need for reform. . . . [T]he expansion and strengthening of the Muscovite state found a parallel in the evolution of the Church in Muscovy. The Church councils of 1547, 1549, 1551, and 1554 strove to improve ecclesiastical organization and practices and eliminate various abuses. In 1547 twenty-two Russians were canonized, and in 1549 seventeen more. The resulting consolidated national pantheon of saints represented a religious counterpart to the political unification. The Hundred-Chapter Council of 1551 [the Stoglav] dealt, as its name indicates, with many matters in the life of the Church. . . .

The rising stature of the Russian Church at a time when many other Orthodox Churches, including the patriarchate of Constantinople itself, fell under the sway of the Moslem [Muslim] Turks increased Muscovite confidence and pride. References to the holy Russian land, to Holy Russia, date from the second half of the sixteenth century.

Source: A History of Russia, by Nicholas V. Riasanovsky, 2d ed. (New York: Oxford University Press, 1969), pp. 218-219.

---

the church (especially by the monasteries), and his followers dominated the church into the 1570's, when he was canonized (1578). Far from accepting the czar's proposal to secularize church lands, then, the members of the council proclaimed church lands inviolable. They also declared that ecclesiastics were subject only to church courts, but in actuality members of the clergy accused of murder and certain forms of theft were tried in the czarist courts. In return for the czar conceding these points to the council, the church agreed to limit the number of new monastic settlements (*slobody*), thus limiting the growth of ecclesiastical landholdings.

SIGNIFICANCE

Pagan practices continued into the nineteenth or even the twentieth centuries, despite their condemnation by the Stoglav (and numerous other councils). Letters from bishops later in the sixteenth and early seventeenth centuries indicate that clerical discipline was not fully achieved, although there was some improvement. How-

1550's

ever, the council did succeed in strengthening episcopal power and allowed the church to maintain a large degree of autonomy from the czar. A council called in 1594 in effect reissued the decisions of the Stoglav, however, demonstrating that the same problems persisted in the church and had not been dealt with effectively by the first council.

Whatever its level of effectiveness, the Stoglav was, with the Nomocanon (the code of canon law of the Orthodox churches), the fundamental source of the Russian Church's administrative and legal norms up to the end of the Muscovite period, when Peter the Great (r. 1682-1725) finally succeeded in bringing the church under secular control and destroying its autonomy. The fact that Ivan the Terrible could not carry out his entire body of reform, specifically his failure to secularize church lands and to bring ecclesiastics under the control of secular courts, also shows that the traditional view of czarist autocracy is overstated. In fact, the czar did not autocratically control the church at that time, and it was only with Peter that truly autocratic control over the church, and over broader Russian society, was fully achieved.

—*Michael C. Paul*

FURTHER READING

Bushkovitch, Paul. *Religion and Society in Russia: The Sixteenth and Seventeenth Centuries.* New York: Oxford University Press, 1992. A study of the changing religious views of Russian society and the church's changing focus from a miracle-based, liturgical church to a more ethics-based church, including the part played by the Stoglav in that transformation.

Kollmann, Jack E. "Stoglav and Parish Priests." *Russian History/Histoire russe* 7 (1980): 65-91. The impact of the Stoglav on the morality and educational level of parish priests.

Martin, Janet. *Medieval Russia, 980-1584.* New York: Cambridge University Press, 1995. The definitive work on medieval Russia, with a good overview of the Russian Orthodox Church, including the Stoglav.

Platonov, Sergei F. *Ivan the Terrible.* Edited and translated by Joseph L. Wieczynski. Gulf Breeze, Fla.: Academic International Press, 1974. Study of Ivan the Terrible's reign, including discussion of the Stoglav and the role it played in his reign.

Vernadsky, George, and Ralph T. Fisher, Jr., eds. *A Source Book for Russian History from Early Times to 1917.* Vol. 1. New Haven, Conn.: Yale University Press, 1972. Translations of primary source material on Russian history, including excerpts of the Stoglav.

Weickhardt, George G. "The Canon Law of Rus', 1100-1551." *Russian History/Histoire russe* 28, nos. 1-4 (2001): 411-46. Discusses the development of canon law in Russia during the medieval period, including the Stoglav's impact on ecclesiastical law.

SEE ALSO: 1478: Muscovite Conquest of Novgorod; 1480-1502: Destruction of the Golden Horde; After 1480: Ivan the Great Organizes the "Third Rome"; Jan. 16, 1547: Coronation of Ivan the Terrible; 1589: Russian Patriarchate Is Established.

RELATED ARTICLE in *Great Lives from History: The Renaissance & Early Modern Era, 1454-1600:* Ivan the Terrible.

1552

LAS CASAS PUBLISHES *THE TEARS OF THE INDIANS*

Bartolomé de Las Casas exposed and criticized the cruelties of the Spanish conquistadores toward the indigenous peoples of the New World, describing the human price of the Spanish conquest, in a work that was widely distributed during his time.

LOCALE: Spanish Americas

CATEGORIES: Cultural and intellectual history; colonization

KEY FIGURE

Bartolomé de Las Casas (1474-1566), Dominican priest

SUMMARY OF EVENT

The Dominican priest Bartolomé de Las Casas arrived in the West Indies during 1502, ten years after Christopher Columbus's first voyage to the Americas. Las Casas became a constant critic of Spanish cruelties toward indigenous peoples, writing several books on the subject, in-cluding *Brevísima relación de la destruyción de las Indias* (1552; *The Tears of the Indians*, 1656; also known as *A Brief Account of the Devastation of the Indies*). While the reports of Las Casas did little to stop the cruelty of the conquest, they did help influence papal declarations that the indigenous were to be regarded as human beings and not as beasts. Las Casas and other priests also found the indigenous peoples to be eligible for conversion to Christianity.

The writings of Las Casas were part of a broader debate in Spain over the treatment of the indigenous by the Spanish during the sixteenth century. The Spanish crown was very legalistic, and very concerned that its policy concerning the indigenous pass muster with the Church's moral dictates. A debate raged beginning about the year 1500 over whether the indigenous peoples of the New World possessed souls and could be regarded as human by European standards. The Church, after lengthy de-

Spanish troops destroy idols of the Aztecs after the Spanish conquest of the Aztec Empire in 1521. Bartolomé de Las Casas decried such desecration and mistreatment in his work, The Tears of the Indians *(1552).* (Hulton|Archive by Getty Images)

1550's

623

AGAINST THE SLAUGHTER OF THE INDIGENOUS

Dominican priest Bartolomé de Las Casas wrote a candid account of the mistreatment of the indigenous peoples of the Americas by the Spanish conquistadores and explorers.

This infinite multitude of people [the American Indians] was . . . without fraud, without subtilty or malice . . . toward the Spaniards whom they serve, patient, meek and peaceful. . . .

To these quiet Lambs . . . came the Spaniards like most c(r)uel Tygres, Wolves and Lions, enrag'd with a sharp and tedious hunger; for these forty years past, minding nothing else but the slaughter of these unfortunate wretches, whom with divers kinds of torments neither seen nor heard of before, they have so cruelly and inhumanely butchered, that of three millions of people which Hispaniola [the Americas] it self did contain, there are left remaining alive scarce three hundred persons.

Source: Quoted in *A History of World Societies*, edited by John P. McKay et al., 5th ed. (Boston: Houghton Mifflin, 2000), p. 516.

---

bate, agreed with Las Casas that the indigenous did indeed possess souls, and that these souls were fit to receive Christianity.

Once that question had been settled, European kings, popes, and savants wrestled with the question of how their nations could "discover" and then "own" lands that were obviously already occupied by the peoples of the Americas. Around 1550, the Spanish king and Holy Roman Emperor, Charles V, initiated a debate over these questions in which Las Casas argued for indigenous rights and Spanish theologian, Juan Ginés de Sepúlveda, argued against.

Another Spanish theologian, Francisco de Vitoria, had already written in 1532 that "the aborigines in question were true owners, before the Spanish came among them, both from the public and the private point of view." Vitoria wrote in *De Indis et de juri belli relectiones* (1557; English translation, 1917) that "The aborigines undoubtedly had true dominion in both public and private matters . . . neither their princes nor private persons could be despoiled of their property on the ground of their not being true owners." Spain could not, therefore, simply assert ownership of lands occupied by indigenous peoples; title by discovery could be justified only if the land was without an owner. In Vitoria's opinion, Spain could legally acquire title to indigenous peoples' land in the New World by conquest resulting from a "just" war, unless the indigenous surrendered their title by "free and voluntary choice." A "just war" was precisely defined. War was not to be undertaken on a whim or solely to dispossess the original inhabitants.

In the Americas, the conquistadores generally ignored the dictates of Spanish theologians. *The Tears of the Indians* and other books by Las Casas are filled with graphic details describing the horrors of the Spanish conquest. Las Casas wrote, for example, of how the Spaniards disemboweled indigenous men, women, and children.

Unlike the conquistadores, Las Casas did not want gold. He wanted, instead, to convert American Indians to Christianity. While he was not averse to Spanish exploration and Catholic conversion, the state and Church conundrum on which the conquest was built, Las Casas bitterly opposed the brutality with which both were carried out. Las Casas protested the brutal aspects of the conquest, but never doubted the religious virtue of the Spanish religious mission.

In Mexico, Las Casas speculated that the Aztec Empire had been the most densely populated area on earth before Cortés's conquest and European diseases depopulated it. He wrote that

The Spanish found pleasure in inventing all kinds of odd cruelties, the more cruel the better, with which to spill human blood. They built a long gibbet, low enough for the toes to touch the ground and prevent strangling, and hanged thirteen [indigenous] at a time in honour of Christ Our Savior and the twelve Apostles. When the indigenous were thus alive and hanging, the Spaniards tested their strength and their blades against them, ripping chests open with one blow and exposing entrails, and there were those who did worse. Then straw was wrapped around their torn bodies and they were burned alive. One man caught two children about two years old, pierced their throats with a dagger, then hurled them down a precipice.

Las Casas also described one conquistador pastime that was indicative of their sadistic disregard for human life. It was called "dogging"—the hunting and maiming of indigenous people by canines specifically trained to relish the taste of human flesh. The use of dogs occurred so frequently during the conquest that a scholarly book described this aspect of the conquest alone. Some of the dogs were kept as pets by the conquistadores. Vasco Núñez de Balboa's favorite was named Leoncito, or "Little Lion," a cross between a greyhound and a mastiff. On one occasion, Balboa ordered forty individuals "dogged" at once. "Just as the Spanish soldiers seem to have particularly enjoyed testing the sharpness of their yard-long blades on the bodies of indigenous children, so their dogs seemed to find the soft bodies of infants especially tasty," wrote scholar David E. Stannard in his 1992 book.

Las Casas also severely criticized the practice of "commending" the indigenous to *encomenderos*, a condition of virtual slavery, but was rebuffed by Spanish authorities. Las Casas, the first priest ordained in the New World and son of a veteran of Columbus's first voyage, called down a formal curse on the main agent of the bloody terror that eliminated indigenous people from Cuba, Pánfilo de Narváez. Las Casas wrote that one of the gentle Tainos, who had been offered baptism as he was about to be burned at the stake, refused it because he thought it might take him to heaven, where he might meet even more Christians.

In writing of the Spanish conquest of the Caribbean, Las Casas stated that the Spanish viewed the indigenous "not like beasts, for that would have been tolerable, but look upon them as if they had been but the dung and filth of the earth." Las Casas pointed out in another work, *Historia de las Indias* (wr. 1527-1561, pb. 1875-1876; partial translation, *History of the Indies*, 1971), that the Spanish

> have so cruelly and inhumanely butchered [the indigenous peoples], that of three million people which Hispaniola itself did contain, there are remaining alive scarce three hundred people.

SIGNIFICANCE

Like few other Spaniards, Las Casas understood the human dimensions of the Spanish conquest of the Americas. The Caribs, Arawaks, and other indigenous peoples whom Columbus met during his earliest voyages were not the simple, autonomous savages he often imagined them to be. As in many other areas of the New World, the places that Columbus visited were thickly populated. The island chain including Cuba, Hispaniola, Puerto Rico, and the Bahamas was home to roughly four million people in 1492. The indigenous people of the islands had evolved a class-stratified society, with a caste of chiefs (Tainos) at the top. Indigenous economies had developed an intricate seaborne trade between the islands.

While modern historians calculate that Hispaniola's original population was 250,000 (not the three million that Las Casas estimated), the priest's testimony is nevertheless a searing tale of conquest and death for the Taino people.

—*Bruce E. Johansen*

FURTHER READING

González-Casanovas, Roberto J. *Imperial Histories from Alfonso X to Inca Garcilaso: Revisionist Myths of Reconquest and Conquest*. Potomac, Md.: Scripta Humanistica, 1997. Examines the political and ideological functions of official historiographies of Spanish conquest in America and reconquest in Iberia. Reads Las Casas's critiques of colonialism alongside the pro-colonial writings of his contemporaries.

Hodgkins, Christopher. *Reforming Empire: Protestant Colonialism and Conscience in British Literature*. Columbia: University of Missouri Press, 2002. Study of the ways in which Protestantism became a major discourse for both justifying and condemning the early modern English colonial project. Includes a study of English representations of Spanish conquistadors and the relationship between Las Casas's descriptions of Spanish conquest and Milton's portrayals of satanic Spaniards.

Keegan, William F., ed. *Earliest Hispanic/Native American Interactions in the Caribbean*. New York: Garland, 1991. A scholarly collection of articles about both Spanish and Native American institutions, including the *encomienda* system.

Keen, Benjamin. *Essays in the Intellectual History of Colonial Latin America*. Boulder, Colo.: Westview Press, 1998. This collection includes an essay surveying 460 years of Las Casas scholarship, and another essay evaluating his legacy.

Las Casas, Bartolomé de. *The Devastation of the Indies*. Translated by Herma Briffault. New York: Seabury Press, 1974. A fine translation, but not the earliest in English, of the Spanish missionary's most famous work.

_____. *History of the Indies*. Translated and edited by Andree Collard. New York: Harper & Row, 1971. This ably edited translation provides an excellent introduction to the famous history written by Las Casas. Offers a vivid description of indigenous-Spanish conflicts.

Lupher, David A. *Romans in a New World: Classical Models in Sixteenth Century Spanish America*. Ann Arbor: University of Michigan Press, 2003. Study of the influence of Roman models of empire upon the Spanish imperial project. Discusses competing attitudes of Las Casas and Sepúlveda.

Remesal, Antonio de. *Bartolomé de Las Casas, 1474-1566, in the Pages of Father Antonio de Remesal*. Translated and annotated by Felix Jay. Lewiston, N.Y.: E. Mellen Press, 2002. Translation and com-

1550's

mentary upon a life of Las Casas written sixty years after his death.

Stannard, David E. *American Holocaust: Columbus and the Conquest of the New World.* New York: Oxford University Press, 1992. This scholarly work provides a revisionist perspective on the legacy of the Spanish conquest of the New World.

Varner, John Greer, and Jeanette Johnson Varner. *Dogs of the Conquest.* Norman: University of Oklahoma Press, 1983. A history of the harsh treatment of the indigenous peoples of the Americas.

SEE ALSO: Oct. 12, 1492: Columbus Lands in the Americas; June 7, 1494: Treaty of Tordesillas; 1495-1510: West Indian Uprisings; 1500-1530's: Portugal Begins to Colonize Brazil; 1502-1520: Reign of Montezuma

II; Beginning 1519: Smallpox Kills Thousands of Indigenous Americans; Apr., 1519-Aug., 1521: Cortés Conquers Aztecs in Mexico; Aug., 1523: Franciscan Missionaries Arrive in Mexico; 1527-1547: Maya Resist Spanish Incursions in Yucatán; 1537: Pope Paul III Declares Rights of New World Peoples; Feb. 23, 1540-Oct., 1542: Coronado's Southwest Expedition; 1542-1543: The New Laws of Spain; 1545-1548: Silver Is Discovered in Spanish America; 1552: Las Casas Publishes *The Tears of the Indians.*

RELATED ARTICLES in *Great Lives from History: The Renaissance & Early Modern Era, 1454-1600:* José de Acosta; Charles V; Christopher Columbus; Guacanagarí; Francisco Jiménez de Cisneros; Bartolomé de Las Casas; Paul III; Philip II.

1552
STRUGGLE FOR THE STRAIT OF HORMUZ

The Ottomans sought to displace the Portuguese from the entrance to the Persian Gulf, a key point for Middle Eastern trade. Three engagements by the Ottomans failed, however, and the Arabian Sea remained in Portuguese control until the coming of the Dutch in the seventeenth century.

LOCALE: Strait of Hormuz, Persian Gulf, Gulf of Oman, and Arabian Sea

CATEGORIES: Wars, uprisings, and civil unrest; expansion and land acquisition; trade and commerce

KEY FIGURES

Pirī Reis (d. 1554?), admiral of the Turkish fleet of the Indies and a cartographer

Murad Reis (fl. 1553), admiral of the Turkish fleet of the Indies

Seydi Ali Reis (d. 1562), admiral of the Turkish fleet of the Indies, military leader, and scholar

Dom Afonso de Noronha (fl. 1552), Portuguese governor of India, 1550-1554

Dom Fernando de Meneses (fl. 1554), commander of the Portuguese fleet in 1554

SUMMARY OF EVENT

Having secured a headquarters for the Portuguese Empire of the East (Estado da India) at Goa in 1510, Governor Afonso de Albuquerque moved to secure the strategic emporia cities of trade across the Indian Ocean for the

Portuguese in an attempt to control trade and effect a monopoly.

The fortress of Hormuz was one of these strategic emporia, or key points (*pontos chaves*), as it stood on the strait that led into the Persian Gulf. Control of the Kingdom of Hormuz after the fortress had surrendered to Albuquerque's fleet in 1515 was not difficult, and its rulers either readily accommodated the Portuguese or were assassinated, as happened to Turan Shah at the beginning of the 1520's. Turan Shah's removal allowed younger, more pliant members of the royal family, such as Muḥammad Shah, to take their places.

The situation was complicated, however, by Ottoman designs on the Indian Ocean and its customs revenues beginning around 1515, as letters in the Topkapi archives show. Campaigns of the mid-1530's yielded the Ottomans two Iraqs: *Iraq-l Ajem* (Persian Iraq) and *Iraq-l Arab* (Arabian Iraq). The Ottomans had entered Basra in 1546. Amicable overtures were then made to the Portuguese by an Arab merchant sent to the governor of Hormuz, Manuel de Lima, but the merchant's attempted intervention was ineffective, as Portugal was determined to control trade routes to Basra.

In 1550, the Arabs of Katif (Al-Qaṭif) yielded their Persian Gulf fortress to the Ottomans. With some of the local Arab chieftains now seeking the intervention of the Portuguese, Dom Afonso de Noronha, the Portuguese governor of India, sent a force of twelve hundred men and seven galleys to move against the Ottoman Turks, calling upon the ruler of Hormuz to supply an additional three thousand men. The Ottoman garrison in Katif surrendered after eight days, and Noronha was diverted from moving against Basra only because the *beylerbey* of Basra managed to sow misinformation in Noronha's camp.

From the mid-1540's, the Ottomans had worked on building up their Red Sea fleet. The son of Vasco da Gama had been sent to sail up the Red Sea and attack the Ottoman naval base at Suez in 1541, but the mission failed. Heightened tension in the area again broke out during the governorships of Dom João de Castro (1545-1548) and Afonso de Noronha. Command of the Ottoman fleet was given to Pırı Reis, appointed in 1547 to the post of admiral of the newly created Indian Ocean fleet. Pırı Reis's first step in early 1548 was to retake Aden, which had lapsed into the hands of local sheikhs since the Ottomans first occupied it in 1538. The sheikhs, however, had invited the Portuguese in 1547 to ally with them.

A Portuguese expeditionary force under Dom João de Castro's son, which was sent to preempt the Ottomans, failed, in part because of a lack of initiative shown by the Portuguese representative already in Aden. After Basra came under direct Ottoman control, the Ottomans could launch annual expeditions against the Portuguese into the Indian Ocean. It was in this period that distant Islamic potentates in the Indian Ocean world—in Sumatra, for example—allied with the Sublime Porte (the Ottoman government) and pooled their resources to resist the Portuguese.

The buildup in tensions between the Ottomans and the Portuguese served as a backdrop to the events of 1552. Pırı Reis set sail from Suez with twenty-five galleys, four galleons, and one other ship carrying 850 soldiers. His forces captured the Portuguese fort at Maskat and proceeded to Hormuz. The Turks managed to take the city, but they then withdrew to the neighboring island of Qeshm. There are various theories about why the Turks disengaged, including that Reis came to appreciate the superior strength of the Portuguese, the Ottomans started to run short of munitions, and, having been informed that the richest merchants of Hormuz resided on Qeshm, Pırı Reis preferred to move off and seek loot. Pırı Reis's political enemies sought to impute that he had been bribed. In any event, full with plunder—which Portuguese chroniclers assess at "more than a million of gold"—Pırı Reis sailed for Basra.

Meanwhile, Goa had also heard of the impending Ottoman threat, so Afonso de Noronha decided to sail to Hormuz with more than eighty ships. It was heard in Diu, a Portuguese territory in India, that the Ottoman fleet had sailed to Basra, so the Portuguese sent another force led by Noronha's nephew.

On the arrival of Pırı Reis in Basra, the *beylerbey* of that province sent the sultan a report to the Porte, which was apparently critical of Pırı Reis. Pırı Reis sailed back to Suez without the imperial fleet. Despite his notability as a geographer, cartographer, and expert seaman, he was arrested and later beheaded for his failure to take Hormuz.

SIGNIFICANCE

The struggles for the Strait of Hormuz in 1552 did not mean the end of Ottoman attempts to gain control of the Persian Gulf. The Ottomans were faced with the predicament of having a small fleet positioned at Basra that was cut off from the main body of the Ottoman navy in the Red Sea. Thus, attempts were made by the new *kapudan* (admiral), Murad Reis, to sail the fleet through the strait, but this attempt, too, failed because of the intervention of the Portuguese who inflicted considerable damage to the fleet.

His successor as admiral, Seydi Ali Reis (no relation), the well-known Turkish geographer with a few naval successes to his credit, was then enlisted to fulfil the same regrouping exercise as his predecessor. Working from good intelligence, the Portuguese took the initiative under commander Dom Fernando de Meneses and engaged the Turks in 1554 in a naval battle near Khawr Fakkān, on the coast of Oman. In an account of his fortunes, Seydi Ali Reis relates that although the first encounter went well for the Ottomans, a second one made them suffer heavy losses. Forced to abandon ship and to return to the Ottoman domains over land after an extended sojourn in Gujarat, Sind, Afghanistan, and Central Asia, Seydi Ali Reis died in 1562.

Thereafter, despite sporadic engagements, the status quo remained. The island of Bahrain continued to serve as a buffer, although Ottoman control was strengthened on the northwestern shores of the Persian Gulf, where the *beylerbeylik* of Lahsa had just been created. Ottoman naval activity in the Indian Ocean remained limited to single, short-lived battles.

—*Stefan C. A. Halikowski Smith*

FURTHER READING

Brumitt, Palmira J. *Ottoman Seapower and Levantine Diplomacy in the Age of Discovery.* Albany: State

University of New York Press, 1994. Attempts to confront the Ottoman "economic mind" of the sixteenth century, and demonstrates that the Ottoman Empire was not purely a reactionary entity intent on territorial conquest. Chapter 6 details the commercial rationale for Ottoman expansion into the Indian Ocean.

Salih, Ozbaran. "The Ottoman Turks and the Portuguese in the Persian Gulf, 1534-81." *Journal of Asian History* 6 (1972). A definitive account of the circumstances leading up to the struggle for Hormuz between 1552 and 1554, with a focus on the role of Bahrain in the larger picture.

_____. "Two Letters of Dom Álvaro de Noronha from Hormuz. Turkish Activities Along the Coast of Arabia, 1550-1552." In *The Ottoman Response to European Expansion*. Istanbul, Turkey: Isis Press, 1994. A reproduction of and comment on two letters written by Dom Álvaro de Noronha in 1550 and 1552 that report on Turkish movements along the coast of Arabia and into the Persian Gulf and the Portuguese reaction to these movements.

Serjeant, R. B. *The Portuguese Off the South Arabian Coast*. Oxford, England: Oxford University Press,

1963. A sourcebook of South Arabian notices of Portuguese incursions into their world. There is a worthwhile introduction detailing the political divisions within the Islamic world.

Seydi Ali Reis. *Mirat ul-Memalik: The Travels and Adventures of the Turkish Admiral Sidi Alī Reis in India, Afghanistan, Central Asia, and Persia, During the Years 1553-1556*. Translated, with notes, by A. Vambéry. 1899. Reprint. Lahore, Pakistan: 1975. A sensibly abridged edition of the original, published in 1557, this account enjoys the privilege of being first-hand. It illustrates the Ottoman's policy in Muslim Asia and starts with a recap of events under Pırı Reis.

SEE ALSO: 1489: ʿĀdil Shah Dynasty Founded; c. 1490: Fragmentation of the Bahmani Sultanate; 1509-1565: Vijayanagar Wars; 1565: Spain Seizes the Philippines; 1587-1629: Reign of ʿAbbās the Great.

RELATED ARTICLES in *Great Lives from History: The Renaissance & Early Modern Era, 1454-1600*: Afonso de Albuquerque; Barbarossa; Pêro da Covilhã; Vasco da Gama; John II; Manuel I; Süleyman the Magnificent.

1553
SERVETUS DESCRIBES THE CIRCULATORY SYSTEM

Servetus was the first person to publish his findings on how blood circulates from the heart, through the lungs, and then back to the heart, and how breathing has a function other than the cooling of the blood. His theories and discoveries marked major breakthroughs in the history of medicine and human anatomy and physiology and differed dramatically from the Aristotelian thought of his day.

LOCALE: France
CATEGORIES: Health and medicine; science and technology; biology

KEY FIGURES
Michael Servetus (1511-1553), Spanish physician and church reformer
John Calvin (1509-1564), French Protestant theologian of the Reformation
William Harvey (1578-1657), English physician, first to establish firmly the function of the heart and describe the circulation of blood
Symphorien Champier (c. 1472-1539), French

physician and founder of the medical faculty at Lyon, France
Johann Guenther von Andernach (c. 1505-1574), a translator of Galen and a professor of medicine

SUMMARY OF EVENT
Michael Servetus was convicted of heresy, condemned to death, and burned at the stake along with his books on October 27, 1553. Born Miguel Serveto in Villanueva de Sixena, Spain), in 1511, he received an education in law and mathematics. Later, he occupied himself with geography and astronomy and developed a strong interest in biblical studies before undertaking work as an editor of medical works.

As a literary assistant influenced by Symphorien Champier, founder of the medical faculty at Lyon, Servetus quickly distinguished himself in the field of medicine. He later returned to Paris in 1536 to study medicine. As part of his studies, Servetus took part in anatomical dissections, which was key to his later insights. His proficiency in anatomy was praised by the professor of anatomy, Johann Guenther von Andernach, who said that Servetus was second to none in his knowledge of Galen.

During the Renaissance, the study of medicine relied on, primarily, the interpretation of the Greek and Latin texts of such figures as the Greek physician Hippocrates (c. 460-c. 377 B.C.E.) and the Roman physician Galen (129-c. 199). Although Servetus supported the medical views of Champier, a well-known Galenist, and while he expressed an acceptance of Galenism, his scholarly reflection allowed him to question strict Galenic ideas regarding the functions of the arterial and venous systems, and, in particular, the movement of blood from the left to the right side of the heart through pores in the septum.

Servetus formulated his concept of pulmonary circulation for the first time in 1546, contradicting Galen's misconceptions involving the functions of the lungs, and he accepted theories declaring the existence of pores in the septum separating right and left ventricles. Servetus stated that blood could only pass from the right ventricle to the left by means of the pulmonary artery and the lungs. This significant discovery in human physiology was incorporated into a manuscript of Servetus's, one on theological ideas called *Christianismi restitutio* (1553; partial translation, 1953), which was his final work. In the hope that his treatise would bring about a return to Christianity in its original form, Servetus sought but failed to find a willing publisher, primarily because his work incorporated heretical religious views involving the Trinity and opposition to the sacrament of infant baptism. Servetus, however, secretly agreed to print the manuscript in 1553 at his expense. A draft of the work was sent in 1546 to the Reformer of Geneva, John Calvin, who became Servetus's main enemy. The book was criticized vehemently from the moment of its release and its theories and claims led to Servetus's execution.

Undeniably, the small section of Servetus's ill-fated treatise that contained a detailed description of the pulmonary circulatory system constituted a significant anatomical breakthrough. Not only did Servetus describe the circulation of blood in the heart and the lungs accurately, his work heralded the declaration of the existence of general blood circulation, which was to be fully described seventy-five years later by the English physician William Harvey.

Servetus's description of pulmonary circulation, however, was not an exercise in human anatomy alone. In addition, the work was theological. Servetus discussed the Holy Spirit, but he also argued, controversially, that there was a physiological basis to the principle of life.

Michael Servetus. (Hulton|Archive by Getty Images)

The principle of life was traditionally believed to be manifested in the form of a soul or vital spirit. Aristotle and Galen believed the heart to be the source of what was called animal heat, that blood circulated to warm the body, and that respiration's function was to cool the blood. Galenic thought, however, acknowledged that the vital spirit circulated in blood and originated in the liver. Servetus calculated that the soul of a human being was instilled during the first respiration at birth; the infant's first breath started the circulation of blood.

Servetus argued also for the existence of a "triple spirit" in humans: natural (specifically located in the liver and in the veins), vital (situated in the heart and arteries), and animal (seated in the brain and in the nerves). To explain how these parts of the spirit were joined together, Servetus reasoned that the vivifying factor resided in blood, which, because it constituted a moving component, connected all parts of the body. His idea was similar to the Hebrew conception that the soul resides in blood and originates from the "breath of lives." This conformed in large measure with Galen's teaching regarding the pneuma, that is, the soul or spirit.

1550's

629

Because Servetus had extensive knowledge of anatomical dissection, he could observe firsthand and thus describe the course of blood in the heart and the lungs precisely. Although he maintained Galenic thoughts on the origin of blood in the liver, Servetus amended Galen's claims that blood passes through orifices in the middle partition of the heart; Servetus had observed that in the heart, the primary movement of blood from right to left did not occur by way of the heart partition because it lacked orifices. This septum was not, according to Servetus, permeable to blood. Instead, he postulated that blood passed from the right ventricle to the left by means of a complex device, or communication joining the pulmonary artery with the pulmonary vein through a system of vessels by way of the lungs. Consequently, he figured that blood passed through the lungs to aerate, that is, to supply blood with oxygen through respiration; it was obvious to him that respiration was a physiological phenomenon. Yet he considered it also to be an aspect of divine process. Servetus's ideas were influenced by two significant foundations of Renaissance thought: the Bible and Galenism.

SIGNIFICANCE

The consequences of Servetus's discovery of the pulmonary circulation of blood are wide-ranging, and few figures in medicine can compare in stature and significance. In his final work, *Christianismi restitutio*, Servetus's description of the pulmonary circulation system linked oxygen, the air humans breath, with life.

He showed that there were capillaries in the lungs and in the brain that join the veins with the arteries and perform special functions. This discovery was a critical one.

—*Karen R. Sorsby*

FURTHER READING

Bainton, Roland H. *Hunted Heretic: The Life and Death of Michael Servetus, 1511-1553*. Boston: Beacon Press, 1960. A landmark study on the career and heresy trial of Servetus, and the theological debates with Calvin.

_____. "Michael Servetus and the Pulmonary Transit." *Bulletin of the History of Medicine* 7 (1938): 1-7. A short but helpful discussion of the major medical discovery made by Servetus. This article is especially useful for those interested in Servetus as a physician.

Cunningham, Andrew. *The Anatomical Renaissance: The Resurrection of the Anatomical Projects of the Ancients*. Brookfield, Vt.: Ashgate, 1997. This important study of the history of anatomy emphasizes work that addressed Galenic anatomy and the importance of ancient science to Renaissance thinkers generally.

Goldstone, Lawrence, and Nancy Goldstone. *Out of the Flames: The Remarkable Story of a Fearless Scholar, a Fatal Heresy, and One of the Rarest Books in the World*. New York: Broadway Books, 2002. Examines the life, death, and writings of Servetus. Useful for detailing the growth of literacy, Renaissance scholastic doctrine, and theological inquiry.

Hillar, Marian, and Claire S. Allen. *Michael Servetus: Intellectual Giant, Humanist, and Martyr*. New York: University Press of America, 2002. An authoritative analysis of Servetus as a scholar, inquisitive experimenter, philosopher, and Christian reformer.

O'Malley, Charles Donald. *Michael Servetus: A Translation of His Geographical, Medical, and Astrological Writings, with Introductions and Notes*. Philadelphia: American Philosophical Society, 1953. Provides useful translations of Servetus's nontheological works, including selections from *Christianismi restitutio*.

SEE ALSO: c. 1478-1519: Leonardo da Vinci Compiles His Notebooks; 1530's-1540's: Paracelsus Presents His Theory of Disease; 1543: Vesalius Publishes *On the Fabric of the Human Body*.
RELATED ARTICLES in *Great Lives from History: The Renaissance & Early Modern Era, 1454-1600:* Georgius Agricola; Martin Bucer; John Calvin; Andrea Cesalpino; Charles V; Desiderius Erasmus; Girolamo Fracastoro; Balthasar Hubmaier; Menno Simons; Nostradamus; Paracelsus; Michael Servetus; Andreas Vesalius; Huldrych Zwingli.

July, 1553
CORONATION OF MARY TUDOR

Mary Tudor's accession to the English throne resulted in a five-year return to Catholicism for the English nation. It was a turbulent period characterized by foreign influence over English political life and violence in the name of Catholic orthodoxy.

LOCALE: London, England
CATEGORIES: Government and politics; religion

KEY FIGURES

Mary I (1516-1558), queen of England, r. 1553-1558
Reginald Pole (1500-1558), papal legate, 1556-1558, and archbishop of Canterbury, 1556-1558
Thomas Cranmer (1489-1556), archbishop of Canterbury, 1533-1556
Philip II (1527-1598), king of Spain, r. 1556-1598, and husband of Queen Mary I
Lady Jane Grey (1537-1554), queen of England, r. 1553
Sir Thomas Wyatt the Younger (c. 1521-1554), rebel leader
John Knox (c. 1514-1572), Scottish religious reformer and founder of Presbyterianism

SUMMARY OF EVENT

The accession of Mary Tudor to the throne of England in 1553 and the subsequent implementation of reactionary, pro-Catholic policies that were advanced during the five years of her reign confused English political and religious life. Many prominent leaders, including Archbishop Thomas Cranmer and bishops Nicholas Ridley and Hugh Latimer, were arrested and executed on charges of heresy. Others, such as the prominent Scottish religious reformer John Knox, went into exile on the Continent and were influenced by Protestant reformers John Calvin, Theodore Beza, and others.

Foreign policy was tied to religious policy, and English hostility toward Mary, her Spanish husband, Philip II, and the Catholic cause increased with each passing year of the reign. The nation tolerated this government by the daughter of Henry VIII because of its respect for the succession plan that had been enacted by law.

Mary Tudor was the daughter of Henry VIII and Catherine of Aragon. Until the early 1530's, her position as heir to the throne was secured. With Henry VIII's annulment of his marriage to Catherine, however, and the subsequent Act of Succession (1534), Mary Tudor was declared illegitimate. Thus, she had no claim to the throne until Henry VIII would later sanction it by another Act of Succession and state in his will that she would succeed her younger half brother, Edward VI, were he to die without an heir. Even though Mary was adamant in her refusal to abandon Catholicism, she survived the brief reign of her half brother.

In 1550, an unsuccessful plan was developed so that Mary could escape England for Habsburg protection on the Continent. On July 6, 1553, Edward VI died and Mary Tudor's claim to the throne was challenged by the devout Protestant, Lady Jane Grey (who was manipulated by her husband, Guildford Dudley), by members of the Privy Council, and by others. Lady Jane Grey was declared queen of England on July 9, 1553, because she was the granddaughter of Henry VIII's younger sister, Mary. The coalition that rallied to Lady Jane Grey's support was focused on retaining the power that they had enjoyed under Edward VI. Within nine days, their effort failed, after army troops who supported Mary Tudor's claim of succession scattered Northumberland's few forces. Mary initially spared Lady Jane Grey's life, but in January, 1554, another attempt to deny the throne to Mary emerged in Kent under the leadership of Sir Thomas Wyatt the Younger, who was outraged at the prospect of Mary Tudor's announced intention to marry King Philip II of Spain.

Wyatt joined in a larger conspiracy to restore Protestantism, but that effort failed. Wyatt's Rebellion, however, acquired support that had to be suppressed. The initial action to defeat Wyatt failed when most of the opposing troops deserted to his cause. Wyatt then marched on London but was confronted by a city that stood by Mary. His army was dispersed, and Wyatt was arrested and executed.

In November, 1554, relations were restored between England and the Roman Catholic Church. In the same year, Mary married Philip II and began her efforts to restore the Catholic Church in England. She eliminated the religious changes that had been introduced during the reigns of Henry VIII and Edward VI. Parliament supported her policies with the exception of returning the lands that had been taken from the monasteries. She returned the monastic lands that were still under royal control.

In 1554, Mary I's cousin, Cardinal Reginald Pole, returned to England to assist her in the restoration of Catholicism. Their plans were affected by the election of Paul IV as pope in 1555; he was Pole's enemy and he pursued anti-Spanish policies. Paul IV went so far to direct Pole to return to Rome to stand trial for heresy; Pole resisted and remained in England. From 1554 to 1558, the Marian regime conducted its reign of terror and became involved in unsuccessful foreign ventures that caused a further decline in Mary I's popularity.

Her marriage to Philip was a childless one, and Mary's acceptance of Philip's control over English foreign policy was disastrous. At his request, England went to war with France and, in a most unlikely situation, the Papacy in 1557. While achieving some initial success, the war was a failure, with England losing Calais in 1558, its last outpost on the Continent.

In 1558, Mary I thought she was pregnant; her initial excitement was short-lived, however, after she found out that she was not pregnant but instead had a serious stomach ailment, from which she died on November 17, 1558. Her cousin and ally, Pole, died of natural causes within a few hours. With their deaths, the effort to reintroduce Roman Catholicism in England also died. As specified in the Act of Succession of 1544, the last of the Tudors, Elizabeth I, became queen. Within five years Elizabeth restored a moderate form of Protestantism through a series of measures referred to as the Elizabethan Settlement (1559).

SIGNIFICANCE

Mary Tudor failed to reestablish Catholicism in England as the national religion. While her supporters were successful in suppressing two attempts to deny her the throne and most English tolerated her accession, Mary Tudor was a fundamentally reactionary monarch who did not demonstrate an affection for her people or possess the intelligence and stamina to pursue effective domestic and foreign policies that would develop confidence in a Catholic monarch.

Regardless of her innate qualities, she was at a decided disadvantage in her relationship with Parliament. Many members of Parliament had worked with her father, Henry VIII, and supported the country's break with Rome, and others had been involved in the government of her brother, Edward VI, which was clearly sympathetic to Protestantism.

The use of violence during Mary's reign, including more than three hundred executions in the name of religious uniformity, resulted in her being called Bloody Mary and a decline in support for her government. Her most noteworthy achievement was her failure to take serious action against her Protestant half sister, Elizabeth, who would succeed her in 1558.

—*William T. Walker*

FURTHER READING

Erickson, Carolly. *Bloody Mary: The Life of Mary Tudor.* New York: Quill, 1993. A balanced, well-researched, and well-written biography of Mary by one of the most prolific biographers of the Tudor and Stuart period. Erickson's interpretation presents a portrait of a troubled and easily persuaded monarch.

Loach, Jennifer. *Parliament and the Crown in the Reign of Mary Tudor.* Oxford, England: Clarendon Press, 1994. An important study of the relationship between Mary's court and her parliaments.

Loades, David M. *Mary Tudor: A Life.* Oxford, England: Basil Blackwell, 1989. Loades's academic biography is based on extensive primary material and is considered the current standard work. It is a balanced and readable work that is fully documented.

Prescott, H. F. M. *Mary Tudor: The Spanish Tudor.* London: Phoenix, 2003. Prescott's sympathetic biography portrays Mary as a monarch who was overwhelmed by the complexities of her time.

Ridley, Jasper Godwin. *Bloody Mary's Martyrs: The Story of England's Terror.* New York: Carroll and Graf, 2001. Ridley advances the traditional hostile interpretation of Mary in which she was a tyrant who murdered loyal subjects and failed to recognize the formidable hold that the acceptance of Protestantism had on England.

Tittler, Robert. *The Reign of Mary I.* 2d ed. New York: Longman, 1991. Tittler's history of Mary's reign provides valuable insight into the major historical forces that dominated the 1550's, and the impact of those forces on the major personalities of Mary's time.

SEE ALSO: Beginning 1485: The Tudors Rule England; Jan. 25-Feb. 7, 1554: Wyatt's Rebellion; Jan., 1563: Thirty-nine Articles of the Church of England; Nov. 9, 1569: Rebellion of the Northern Earls.

RELATED ARTICLES in *Great Lives from History: The Renaissance & Early Modern Era, 1454-1600:* Anne Boleyn; John Calvin; Catherine of Aragon; Charles V; Clement VII; Thomas Cranmer; Edward VI; Elizabeth I; Lady Jane Grey; Henry VIII; John Knox; Hugh Latimer; Martin Luther; Mary I; Philip II; Nicholas Ridley; First duke of Somerset; The Tudor Family.

September, 1553
FIRST BATTLE OF KAWANAKAJIMA

The Battle of Kawanakajima in 1553 was the first in a series of five battles fought between the warlords Takeda Shingen and Uesugi Kenshin. Although ultimately indecisive, the battles at Kawanakajima were considered archetypal clashes of Japan's Warring States period.

LOCALE: Kawanakajima, Shinano Province (now Matsushiro City, Nagano Prefecture), Japan
CATEGORY: Wars, uprisings, and civil unrest

KEY FIGURES

Takeda Shingen (Takeda Harunobu; 1521-1573), daimyo of Kai
Uesugi Kenshin (Nagao Kagetora; 1530-1578), daimyo of Echigo
Murakami Yoshikiyo (1503-1573), warrior chieftain from Shinano

SUMMARY OF EVENT

The alluvial plain known as Kawanakajima (meaning "island between the rivers") is located in what was during the sixteenth century northern Shinano Province (now Nagano Prefecture), at the confluence of the Chikuma and Saigawa Rivers. As one of the strategic approaches to the north, the plain of Kawanakajima is reported to have been a battlefield as early as the twelfth century. Starting in 1553, it was the point where the ambitions of two major daimyo (warlords) Takeda Harunobu, later known as Takeda Shingen, and Nagao Kagetora, later known as Uesugi Kenshin, clashed violently.

Takeda Shingen came from a long line of *shugo* (military governors) who had ruled mountainous Kai Province (now Yamanashi Prefecture) in eastern Japan since the thirteenth century. In 1541, he had ousted his father Takeda Nobutora (1494-1574) and had assumed the headship of the Takeda family himself. Landlocked Kai Province had traditionally been considered a somewhat backward area famous for thoroughbred horses and fierce warriors. Shingen appears to have been eager to use these natural assets for military expansion, for he waited scarcely a year after the expulsion of his father to invade neighboring Shinano Province (now Nagano Prefecture) in 1542. The greater part of Shinano Province came under the control of the Shingen before the decade was over. However, his steady northward advance toward the Sea of Japan was checked when he was about to cross the border into Echigo Province (now Niigata Prefecture).

Echigo had long been the domain of the prominent Uesugi family, but the real power was in the hands of the Nagao house. Nagao Kagetora succeeded to the position of family head and *shugo-dai* (deputy governor) in 1549. Although another twelve years would pass before he formally assumed the family name of his erstwhile superiors, the Uesugi, and the Buddhist name Kenshin, he had already made a name for himself as a powerful daimyo. His position as de facto ruler of Echigo would have been seriously compromised by an invasion of the Takeda forces into that province. In this strategic context, the Kawanakajima Plain was of utmost importance, since the mountain passes on its northern side led straight to Kenshin's headquarters at Kasugayama. Kenshin thus had ample reason to try to prevent enemy forces from occupying the Kawanakajima Plain.

Guarding the southern access to Kawanakajima were several fortresses belonging to Murakami Yoshikiyo, one of several *kokujin* (provincial barons) in Shinano. Takeda Shingen's campaigns in that province in the late 1540's had reduced other barons, such as the Suwa and the Ogasawara, to relative insignificance. However, the Murakami forces had defeated Shingen's army in 1548 at Uedahara, some 20 miles (32 kilometers) up the Chikuma River from Kawanakajima.

Murakami Yoshikiyo thus emerged by the early 1550's as the main opponent to Takeda Shingen's advance into northern Shinano, and by default as a buffer between Shingen to the south and Uesugi Kenshin to the north. In 1550, Takeda Shingen renewed his attack on the Murakami by besieging Koishi Castle on the Chikuma River only to be beaten back once again. The castle was finally taken in the summer of 1551, thus opening up the way north along the Chikuma valley.

To the north and down river from Koishi lay Katsurao Castle, the Murakami stronghold guarding the southern access to Kawanakajima. After the fall of Koishi, it was only a matter of time until the Takeda forces would overrun Katsurao as well. Yet Shingen took almost two years before finally pressing on northward, taking Katsurao Castle in May of 1553. It was this Takeda victory that prompted the defeated Murakami Yoshikiyo to flee north into Echigo and seek the assistance of Uesugi Kenshin.

The promptness of Kenshin's response suggests that he was well aware of the strategic implications of a Takeda presence around Kawanakajima. Control of this area would have given the Takeda forces easy access to several routes into Echigo, while an adequate defense of all passes and river valleys against hostile forces presented severe logistical problems. Kenshin consequently chose to forestall a further Takeda advance by deploying his forces at the first sign of trouble. As several castles higher up in the mountains were still in Murakami hands but under the threat of a Takeda attack, time was of critical importance.

As the Takeda army was slowly advancing on the right bank of the Chikuma River toward Kawanakajima, Uesugi Kenshin and his troops, including, according to some accounts, Murakami Yoshikiyo, moved southward on the opposite side. The opposing forces met for the first time at the ford of Hachiman, just south of Kawanakajima, on June 3, 1553. The skirmish resulted in a reported victory for the Uesugi, who appear to have disengaged from the enemy and continued their push southward. Having attacked but failed to recapture Katsurao Castle, Murakami proceeded southwest into the mountains to reoccupy some of the fortresses lost to the Takeda earlier.

Takeda Shingen, evidently unwilling to risk a pitched battle in unfamiliar terrain, had withdrawn to safer ground for the summer but was back in the area by early fall. In September his force recaptured the Murakami castles in the mountains, killing the entire garrisons of two of them. Murakami Yoshikiyo was once again forced to flee northward, with the Takeda forces in hot pursuit. The sources relate that in the process of this pursuit, the Takeda encountered and fought the main body of the Uesugi forces at a place called Fuse on the Kawanakajima Plain. It is this encounter that is commonly referred to as the First Battle of Kawanakajima. No precise date for this battle has been established, but circumstantial evidence points to the end of September of 1553 as the most likely time frame. Fuse marks the northernmost point reached by the Takeda forces during that campaign. After suffering a defeat there, Shingen withdrew southward, but the Uesugi vanguard caught up with the Takeda again at Hachiman on October 8, obtaining yet another victory in the process.

The Takeda forces managed an orderly retreat southward along the left bank of the river, fighting the pursuing Uesugi army. After scorched-earth tactics left several castles along the Chikuma River in ruins, both forces retreated before the advance of winter in November. Uesugi Kenshin appeared to have achieved his objective. He had denied the Takeda a foothold in northern Shinano. The Takeda forces, having suffered three defeats in their first series of encounters with the Uesugi,

would not be back in the area until two years later. Shingen evidently preferred to secure territories farther west before confronting Kenshin once again in 1555.

SIGNIFICANCE

The 1553 Takeda campaign into northern Shinano set the stage for a bitter conflict between Shingen and Kenshin. Ever since the dust settled on Kawanakajima, the series of battles fought there between 1553 and 1564 have been described, analyzed, and romanticized by a succession of writers. The contestants, Takeda Shingen and Uesugi Kenshin, loom exceptionally large in the history of the Warring States period partially because of their exploits at Kawanakajima. Although there was no clear winner, or perhaps for that very reason, the repeated clashes of their armies on ostensibly the same battlefield occupied a prominent place in later chronicles.

Most of what historians know about the battles fought at Kawanakajima comes from a multitude of *gunki* (war tales) written well after the sixteenth century. Mixing fact and fiction, combining detached analysis with personal memoirs, and condemning upheaval and disorder while making heroes out of those responsible for it, these semiliterary works have obvious limitations as historical sources. Comparisons of the various accounts make apparent that the various chroniclers could not agree on such facts as the number of battles fought or the years (let alone the dates) when they occurred. There remains considerable doubt about the intensity of fighting at Kawanakajima. Furthermore, it should also be noted that the battles occurred in the general vicinity of Kawanakajima but were not all fought on the same battlefield. At the same time, one cannot help but agree with the view shared by all later chroniclers: that the Battles of Kawanakajima were an epic struggle epitomizing the Warring States period as few other conflicts do.

—*Ronald K. Frank*

FURTHER READING

Hall, John W., et al., eds. *The Cambridge History of Japan. Volume 4: Sengoku and Edo.* Cambridge, England: Cambridge University Press, 1991. Contains the most comprehensive, up-to-date account of the Sengoku period available in English.

Hall, John W., Nagahara Keiji, and Kozo Yamamura. *Japan Before Tokugawa: Political Consolidation and Economic Growth, 1500 to 1650.* Princeton, N.J.: Princeton University Press, 1981. A collection of scholarly essays on sixteenth century Japan.

Lamers, Jeroen. *Japonius Tyrannus: The Japanese War-*

lord Oda Nobunaga Reconsidered. Leiden: Hotei, 2000. A detailed scholarly account with ample quotations from primary sources.

Turnbull, Stephen. *Kawanakajima, 1553-1564*. Oxford, England: Osprey, 2003. Though not a scholarly work and not without inconsistencies, this is the only work available in English devoted exclusively to the topic.

_____. *War in Japan, 1467-1615*. Oxford, England: Osprey, 2002. From the same series as the preceding book, this volume provides an analysis of samurai warfare in the Warring States period with brief accounts of major battles.

SEE ALSO: 1457-1480's: Spread of Jōdo Shinshū Buddhism; 1467-1477: Ōnin War; 1477-1600: Japan's "Age of the Country at War"; Mar. 5, 1488: Composition of the *Renga* Masterpiece *Minase sangin hyakuin*; Beginning 1513: Kanō School Flourishes; 1532-1536: Temmon Hokke Rebellion; 1549-1552: Father Xavier Introduces Christianity to Japan; 1550's-1567: Japanese Pirates Pillage the Chinese Coast; 1550-1593: Japanese Wars of Unification; June 12, 1560: Battle of Okehazama; 1568: Oda Nobunaga Seizes Kyōto; 1587: Toyotomi Hideyoshi Hosts a Ten-Day Tea Ceremony; 1590: Odawara Campaign; 1592-1599: Japan Invades Korea; 1594-1595: Taikō Kenchi Survey; Oct., 1596-Feb., 1597: *San Felipe* Incident; Oct. 21, 1600: Battle of Sekigahara.

RELATED ARTICLES in *Great Lives from History: The Renaissance & Early Modern Era, 1454-1600:* Hōjō Ujimasa; Hosokawa Gracia; Oda Nobunaga; Ōgimachi; Oichi; Sesshū; Toyotomi Hideyoshi.

January 25-February 7, 1554
WYATT'S REBELLION

Wyatt led a rebellion that attempted to prevent the Catholic queen Mary I's marriage to Philip of Spain and to place Princess Elizabeth, Mary's Protestant half sister, on the English throne. The rebellion failed, however, leading to Mary's reign, England's five-year return to Catholicism, and the persecution of Protestants.

LOCALE: Maidstone, Rochester, Kent; London, England

CATEGORIES: Government and politics; wars, uprisings, and civil unrest; religion

KEY FIGURES

Sir Thomas Wyatt the Younger (c. 1521-1554), rebel leader

Elizabeth I (1533-1603), queen of England, r. 1558-1603

Mary I (1516-1558), queen of England, r. 1553-1558

Stephen Gardiner (c. 1493-1555), bishop of Winchester, 1531-1555, and Lord Chancellor, 1553-1555

Edward Courtenay (c. 1527-1556), earl of Devon

Lady Jane Grey (1537-1554), queen of England, r. 1553

Henry Grey (c. 1517-1554), duke of Suffolk, conspirator

SUMMARY OF EVENT

Queen Mary I was unmarried when she succeeded King Edward VI in July, 1553. With the suppression of the nine-day reign of Lady Jane Grey, Mary's marriage was of pressing importance. Parliament urged her to marry "within the realm" to prevent rule by a foreign prince, preferably to Edward Courtenay, whose Plantagenet blood gave him a claim to the throne. Mary's harsh rebuff of their request forced the hand of many who had supported her previously. They had to decide whether to accept her decision to marry Philip of Spain and with it rule by a foreign prince and loss of preferment to his Spanish entourage, or rebel.

A small group of conspirators met November 26 to decide a course of action. Their precise numbers are not known, but the conspirators included men of standing in their counties and who had held office in previous reigns. Although they all wished to thwart Mary's proposed marriage, the group never agreed on their ultimate objective. Some preferred merely a show of force to coerce her into marrying Courtenay, and others proposed deposing her in favor of Princess Elizabeth; one went so far as to call for Mary's assassination.

By Christmas, they had decided on four simultaneous uprisings to take place on Palm Sunday (March 18, 1554). The main rebellion was to take place in Devon, led by Sir Peter Carew. Henry Grey, the duke of Suffolk and Lady Jane Grey's father, would raise Leicestershire, while Sir James Croft would lead on the Welsh borders, and Sir Thomas Wyatt would lead in Kent. After securing their counties, the four were to converge on London.

Rumors of the plot soon circulated at Court, however, and on January 2, the Queen's Council summoned Carew to answer unspecified questions. He ignored the summons, but it was one of several incidents that forced the conspirators to act precipitously. On January 18, Simon Renard, the imperial ambassador, told the queen what he knew or suspected. Mary then acted decisively, promptly ordered members of the royal household to take a special oath acknowledging Philip as king, and wrote a letter inviting Elizabeth to come to Court for her "safety." Three days later, Bishop Stephen Gardiner, the Lord Chancellor, got details of the plot from his former protégé, Courtenay.

Three events on January 25 set the course of the rebellion. Upon receiving a summons to appear before the council, Suffolk bolted from the capital for Leicestershire; Wyatt raised his standard at Maidstone, proclaiming the realm to be in danger; and in the west, after failing to get much response to his claim of the threat of imminent Spanish invasion, Carew took ship for France. The inept Suffolk soon found that his name no longer carried weight in his home county. Only his two brothers and a few others answered his call to "rescue" the queen. Disguised, he attempted to flee to Denmark but was soon apprehended and returned to London. Croft urged Elizabeth to flee to her castle at Donnington, but never took up arms, leaving only Wyatt to carry out the rebellion.

After proclaiming the realm in danger, Wyatt raised a force of about two thousand and moved to Rochester, where, on January 28, he met an army of about one thousand that was raised from the Yeoman of the Guard and the London-trained bands, the "whitecoats," and was led by the eighty-year-old duke of Norfolk. The rebels won the first battle after most of the London whitecoats and some of the guard defected, leaving the others to drop their weapons, conceal their uniforms, and flee to safety.

Had Wyatt acted promptly to follow up his victory, he might have found the gates of London open to him, but by January 31, initial despair turned to hope as Mary's forces begged for the chance to redeem themselves, and the queen proved that she had the Tudor family's courage under fire. Rejecting advice to flee to safety, the next day she left for the Guildhall, where she gave a stirring speech proclaiming that she would marry Philip only with her council's consent. She also pledged that she would not forget that she was already married to her realm.

When Wyatt reached Southwork on February 3 with a force of about three thousand, he found the bridge stoutly defended. Meanwhile, the council tried to allay fears by conducting business as usual and by keeping the courts at Westminster open, even though lawyers wore armor under their robes.

After three days of indecision, Wyatt made up his mind. On February 6, he marched up river, crossing at Kingston, and turned toward London, hoping to surprise the city the next day. At St. James's Park the rebels split, the smaller force attacking Whitehall, where once more the queen's guard turned and ran, but the gentlemen pensioners rallied. Meanwhile, the bulk of Wyatt's forces reached Ludgate, where they found the gates firmly barred, and after a brief skirmish, all was over and Wyatt surrendered. Had he attacked the queen at Whitehall with his main force, the results might have been very different.

The aftermath of the rebellion was as important as the rebellion itself. With Wyatt safely in the Tower, the council turned to Elizabeth, whose pleas of illness were put aside, and she was brought to Whitehall for questioning. She refused to admit complicity, and, fortunately for her, none of the conspirators would implicate her. The most that could be proved against her was that the plotters had urged her to flee, but she had committed nothing to paper and her verbal replies were consistently noncommittal. After repeated questioning, she was sent to the Tower to await her fate. Although one recent scholar thinks that Elizabeth was as guilty as Mary suspected, and Wyatt may have confessed as much under torture, at his execution he defended her innocence. In the end, when a London jury surprisingly acquitted English diplomat Sir Nicholas Throckmorton, who was thought by many to be the real instigator and leader of the rebellion and who had gone on record against the reinstitution of Catholicism, Mary decided not to put Elizabeth on trial and the affair was closed.

SIGNIFICANCE

The rebellion, which lasted just eighteen days, consisted of three small engagements with a combined loss of between sixty and seventy lives. Only one of the four proposed uprisings took place, but even so, Mary and her council were clearly shaken. Four days after Wyatt surrendered, Bishop Gardiner preached his Lenten sermon at court, calling for swift and harsh retribution. The executions began the next day. Lady Jane Grey's earlier exploits as a pawn attempting to prevent Mary from becoming queen were to be punished, and she and her husband, Lord Guildford Dudley, were first in line for execution. Suffolk, Wyatt, and a few other leaders soon followed. In the end about five hundred rebels were tried and convicted, but only between seventy and one hundred were actually executed. The others were released and pardoned. Even Carew, convicted in absentia, was back in Mary's service by the end of the reign.

If Mary had been shaken, so had Elizabeth, who had gone so far as to select the method of her execution if she could not appeal to Mary's sense of family loyalty. After months in the Tower, she was released to spend the remaining four years of Mary's reign under house arrest, knowing that Mary was surrounded by some who continued to urge her to execute Elizabeth for her own safety.

Mary, who always thought that the rebels' goals were religious rather than political, learned nothing from the episode and went on to marry Philip. Although the conspirators' fears of rule by a foreign prince proved to be unfounded, Mary's marriage was unpopular and she sacrificed the good will she had earned by her victories over Lady Jane Grey and Wyatt.

—Robert C. Braddock

FURTHER READING

Loades, David. *Elizabeth I.* New York: Hambledon and London, 2003. An interpretive biography by a leading authority on the rebellion.

_____. *The Reign of Mary Tudor.* 2d ed. New York: Longman, 1991. A detailed political history.

_____. *Two Tudor Conspiracies.* Cambridge, England: Cambridge University Press, 1965. Still the standard account of the rebellion.

Starkey, David. *Elizabeth: The Struggle for the Throne.* New York: HarperCollins, 2001. Most complete account of Elizabeth's life before 1558. Maintains that Elizabeth was an active participant in the conspiracy.

SEE ALSO: Oct., 1536-June, 1537: Pilgrimage of Grace; July, 1553: Coronation of Mary Tudor; 1558-1603: Reign of Elizabeth I; Nov. 9, 1569: Rebellion of the Northern Earls; Feb. 25, 1570: Pius V Excommunicates Elizabeth I; Apr., 1587-c. 1600: Anglo-Spanish War.

RELATED ARTICLES in *Great Lives from History: The Renaissance & Early Modern Era, 1454-1600:* Edward VI; Elizabeth I; Stephen Gardiner; Lady Jane Grey; Mary I; Philip II.

1555-1556
CHARLES V ABDICATES

Charles V's abdication as Holy Roman Emperor led to the division of his lands between his son Philip and his brother Ferdinand, separating the Spanish and German territories and laying the foundation for the political and cultural greatness of Spain.

LOCALE: Brussels (now in Belgium) and the Spanish Netherlands (now the Netherlands)

CATEGORIES: Government and politics; expansion and land acquisition

KEY FIGURES

Charles V (1500-1558), Holy Roman Emperor, r. 1519-1556, and king of Spain as Charles I, r. 1516-1556

Philip II (1527-1598), king of Spain, r. 1556-1598, and son of Charles

Ferdinand I (1503-1564), Holy Roman Emperor, r. 1558-1564, and brother of Charles

Duke of Alva (Fernando Álvarez de Toledo; 1507-1582), Spanish general

SUMMARY OF EVENT

Charles V, the Holy Roman Emperor who also ruled Spain as Charles I, had inherited the largest empire of his day. From his mother, he inherited his claim to the Span-

ish throne and to Spain's overseas empire and its territories in Italy. From his father, he inherited the Low Countries and the Habsburg lands in central Europe.

Charles encountered enormous problems in attempting to rule such an extensive and diverse area. He fought the Turks in central Europe and in the Mediterranean, repressed rebellion in the Low Countries, tried to suppress the Protestant Reformation in the German principalities, worked to protect his developing empire in the New World, and fended off attempts by the kings of France to break the encirclement of France by Habsburg territories.

Charles also had constant money problems. The accumulated pressures of these responsibilities adversely affected his health. He was frequently incapacitated for long periods of time and became discouraged over his inability to accomplish his religious and political objectives in the German states and in the Low Countries.

When Charles V left Germany in 1553, he had in all probability already decided to lay down at least some of the burden that he had been carrying for thirty-four years. He was disgusted with, and defeated by, the German situation. Privately he drew up a document that criticized both the Catholic and the Protestant princes of Germany.

1550's

He believed that the secular princes were untrustworthy, while the bishops lacked the vigor and concern needed to make the necessary reforms in the Roman Catholic Church.

His brother Ferdinand persuaded Charles to carry the imperial title a little longer. Although he recognized the necessity for compromise, Charles earnestly warned Ferdinand against granting doctrinal concessions at the Diet of Augsburg, which convened in 1555.

He was only fifty-four years old, but Charles was worn out and ill from carrying the immense burdens of his vast empire. He had determined to abdicate without duress or compulsion and devote himself to religion in preparation for his death. Charles gave three reasons for his abdication: First, he wanted to retire; second, he believed he was unfit to fulfill his duties; and third, he was suffering from ill health. The difficulty was to decide what arrangement should be followed in disposing of territories within the Holy Roman Empire. Even before Charles's election in 1519, it was realized that one person alone could not govern both Spain and Germany, and Charles had been advised to allow Ferdinand to seek the imperial throne. Charles had indignantly rejected the suggestion then, but now the earlier counsel had become acceptable.

Charles apparently considered having his son Philip elected to the imperial throne, but Philip was Spanish in temperament and education; he was not familiar with German affairs, and he was more uncompromising than his father on religious issues.

At Brussels on October 25, 1555, Charles solemnly abdicated rule of the Netherlands and turned the nation over to Philip. On that occasion, he acted in a public ceremony and delivered a speech calling attention to his illness and his military setbacks, and reviewing his long years of rule. The Netherlands had always been the territory closest to his heart, and many nobles wept during his speech.

On January 16, 1556, he abdicated the rule of Spain and all Spanish-held lands to Philip. On that occasion, he acted in a private ceremony. Ferdinand was already designated "king of the Romans," a title that normally carried with it the connotation of heir apparent to the imperial throne. On September 12, 1556, Charles sent to Ferdinand an emissary carrying his letter of abdication. For some time, Ferdinand ruled as regent of the empire, but in February of 1558, the electors formally accepted the abdication and elected Ferdinand emperor.

Almost immediately Charles left Brussels for Spain, never again to visit his former territories. He settled at a monastery near Yuste in Castile, and although he lived in regal style and paid close attention to political affairs, his major interests were now religious. Charles did assume some minor political responsibilities at the request of Philip but refused most. Weakened by gout and diabetes, Charles contracted malaria and died on September 21, 1558.

The division of the Habsburg Empire left Ferdinand with formal authority in Germany, but with real power limited largely to the hereditary Habsburg lands centered in Austria. He also had undefined interests in northern Italy. Philip, now Philip II of Spain, could also lay claim to the Netherlands, vast Spanish possessions overseas, and most of Italy except the Papal States. The French invaded the Italian peninsula in 1557, but they were defeated by Philip's general, Fernando Álvarez de Toledo, the duke of Alva. In 1559, the Treaty of Cateau-Cambrésis was signed, and the dominance of Spain in European affairs over the next century dates from the signing of this treaty.

Charles V's death in 1558 was followed by mournful processions, including a solemn funeral ceremony with this elaborate vehicle-drawn vessel in Charles's honor in Brussels. (Frederick Ungar Publishing Co.)

The German and Spanish branches of the Habsburg family maintained somewhat loose connections, although there was never any doubt that they would form a united front if the interests of either were seriously threatened. Nevertheless, Ferdinand's settlement of the religious problem in Germany, the Peace of Augsburg, became possible because the German problem could now be considered by itself, without reference to the rest of Europe.

Philip also was left to pursue a policy that was thoroughly Spanish. On ascending the throne, he was faced with two major problems: bankruptcy, largely caused by Charles's military expenditures in Italy and Germany; and the spread of what was believed to be heresy in Spain. Philip gave strong support to the Inquisition, which succeeded in eliminating almost all traces of heterodoxy from Spanish society. Yet the king was less successful with his financial problems. He remained burdened with debt for the remainder of his reign, and the economic problems of Spain became acute after his death.

Philip's devotion to the Roman Catholic Church was the major factor in what was perhaps the chief disaster of his reign: the loss of half the Netherlands through rebellion. Heavy taxation and other grievances were contributing factors, but the issue that aroused permanent opposition was Philip's attempt in 1559 to reorganize the Roman Catholic Church in the Netherlands by introducing the Inquisition to quell Protestantism, which flourished in great variety in the relaxed atmosphere of the heterogeneous towns of the Netherlands.

Armed revolt broke out in 1566, with the Catholics joining the Protestants to resist curtailment of their historic liberties. The duke of Alva instituted a reign of terror that stiffened resistance still further. Prince William the Silent, a Protestant, took over leadership of the rebellion, which by 1575 had succeeded in detaching the northern provinces (roughly the area of what is now the Netherlands) from Spanish control. Philip held on to the southern provinces (comprising the area of modern Belgium) but was forced to concede the temporary independence of the northern territory. The northern provinces later gained permanent independence during the Thirty Years' War.

SIGNIFICANCE

For the remainder of the sixteenth century, the emperors in Germany accepted a position less exalted than Charles V had conceived. With the religious issue temporarily settled, their major problem was dealing with the Turks, to whom they were forced to pay tribute for the safety of their eastern frontiers. After the Turkish fleet was defeated at the Battle of Lepanto in 1571, there was temporary respite from this threat.

—*James F. Hitchcock, updated by Robert D. Talbott*

FURTHER READING

Blockmans, Wim. *Emperor Charles V, 1500-1558*. Translated by Isola van den Hoven-Vardon. London: Arnold, 2002. Blockmans attempts to survey the scope of the vast territory and diverse culture of the Holy Roman Empire by analyzing the relationship between Charles as an individual and the complex, rigid yet unstable power structures within which he governed.

Brandi, Karl. *The Emperor Charles V: The Growth and Destiny of a Man and of a World-Empire*. Translated by C. V. Wedgwood. London: Jonathan Cape, 1968. Written by the foremost authority on Charles V, this biography has become the standard account. According to Brandi, Charles was chiefly responsible for developing the dynastic theory of the Habsburgs.

Fernandez Alvarez, Manuel. *Charles V: Elected Emperor and Hereditary Ruler*. Translated by J. A. Lalaguna. London: Thames and Hudson, 1975. A readable, interesting biography with a useful chapter on Charles's retreat at Yuste.

Hughes, Michael. *Early Modern Germany, 1477-1806*. Philadelphia: University of Pennsylvania Press, 1992. Hughes presents a concise overview of Germany and the changes that took place on the eve of the Protestant Reformation.

Kamen, Henry. *Philip of Spain*. New Haven, Conn.: Yale University Press, 1997. A massive and detailed biography of Philip, documenting almost every aspect of his life, but somewhat light on his legacy and influence on future events.

Lynch, John. *Spain, 1516-1598: From Nation-State to World Empire*. Cambridge, Mass.: Blackwell, 1991. One of the foremost historians of Spain, Lynch provides a definitive history of Spain under Charles V and Philip II. Explores the conflicting demands that his roles as king of Spain and Holy Roman Emperor placed on Charles.

Maltby, William. *The Reign of Charles V*. New York: Palgrave, 2002. This monograph balances a biography of Charles with broad analysis of his foreign and domestic policies and their historical consequences.

Parker, Geoffrey. *The Grand Strategy of Philip II*. New Haven, Conn.: Yale University Press, 1998. Contests the traditional view of Philip as conducting his empire by reacting to events as they occurred without any

1550's

grand plan to guide him. Uses correspondence and other historical documents to delineate a "strategic culture" informing Philip's decisions and his reign.

_____. *Philip II*. 4th ed. Chicago: Open Court, 2002. A good overview of Philip's reign, this edition is updated with a new bibliographic essay.

Rodriguez-Salgado, M. J. *The Changing Face of Empire: Charles V, Philip II, and Habsburg Authority, 1551-1559*. New York: Cambridge University Press, 1988. The author focuses on the 1550's, a period of transition when Charles experienced physical, mental, and political collapse and Philip received control of a portion of the vast Habsburg Empire.

Tracy, James D. *Emperor Charles V, Impresario of War: Campaign Strategy, International Finance, and Domestic Politics*. New York: Cambridge University Press, 2002. Examination of the financial and political consequences of Charles V's military campaigns. Discusses Charles as a field commander of his armies, as well as the international financial community that loaned Charles the money to pay for battles and thereby gained control over parts of his lands. Also

discusses the local governments within the empire that learned to exploit Charles's need for money.

SEE ALSO: Oct. 19, 1469: Marriage of Ferdinand and Isabella; Aug. 17, 1477: Foundation of the Habsburg Dynasty; 1482-1492: Maximilian I Takes Control of the Low Countries; Jan. 23, 1516: Charles I Ascends the Throne of Spain; June 28, 1519: Charles V Is Elected Holy Roman Emperor; 1521-1559: Valois-Habsburg Wars; May 6, 1527-Feb., 1528: Sack of Rome; Feb. 27, 1531: Formation of the Schmalkaldic League; Sept. 25, 1555: Peace of Augsburg; 1568-1648: Dutch Wars of Independence; July 26, 1581: The United Provinces Declare Independence from Spain.

RELATED ARTICLES in *Great Lives from History: The Renaissance & Early Modern Era, 1454-1600:* Duke of Alva; Ferdinand II and Isabella I; Francis I; Henry II; Saint Ignatius of Loyola; Martin Luther; Margaret of Austria; Margaret of Parma; Mary of Hungary; Mary I; Maximilian I; Mehmed II; Mehmed III; Paul III; Philip II; Süleyman the Magnificent; William the Silent.

September 25, 1555
PEACE OF AUGSBURG

The Peace of Augsburg brought an end to the first religious war of the Reformation era between Catholics and Lutherans and laid the foundation for the spread of Lutheranism in Northern Europe.

LOCALE: Augsburg (now in Germany)
CATEGORIES: Religion; diplomacy and international relations; wars, uprisings, and civil unrest

KEY FIGURES
Philip the Magnanimous (1504-1567), leader of the Schmalkaldic League and a leading Lutheran prince
Charles V (1500-1558), Holy Roman Emperor, r. 1519-1556, and king of Spain as Charles I, r. 1516-1556
Philipp Melanchthon (1497-1560), Lutheran theologian
Ferdinand I (1503-1564), Holy Roman Emperor, r. 1558-1564, and brother of Charles
August (1526-1586), elector of Saxony, a leading Lutheran prince
Joachim II (1505-1571), elector of Brandenburg and a leading Lutheran prince

Maximilian II (1527-1576), Holy Roman Emperor, r. 1564-1576, and son of Ferdinand I
Rudolf II (1552-1612), Holy Roman Emperor, r. 1576-1612, and son of Maximilian II
Frederick III (1515-1576), elector of the Palatinate and a leading Calvinist prince

SUMMARY OF EVENT
The Truce of Passau, which ended the Wars of the Schmalkaldic League in August of 1552, specified the speedy summoning of a diet to settle religious issues on a basis more favorable to the Lutherans than the Augsburg Interim of 1548. Charles V, the Holy Roman Emperor and chief advocate of the Catholic position in Germany, wrote to his brother Archduke Ferdinand that, because of illness and problems in the Netherlands, he would not attend the diet.

Ferdinand was given full authority, although he was not to act in the name of the emperor, but in his own name as "king of the Romans," heir designate to the imperial throne. It is generally believed that Charles recognized the need for some kind of accommodation with the Lutherans, but could not bring himself to grant it.

The diet called for in 1552 did not meet until 1555 because the emperor was loath to make concessions, Ferdinand was engaged in a war with the Turks in his Hungarian kingdom, and the military truce agreed on at Passau in 1552 was slow in being accepted by the German princes.

The Diet of Augsburg, one of the most important in German history, finally convened in February, 1555, with Ferdinand presiding. Most of the major princes were represented by delegates. Some of the leading Lutherans, including Philip the Magnanimous of Hesse, the elector August of Saxony, and the elector Joachim of Brandenburg, held a separate meeting at Naumburg. August was the brother of Maurice, the duke of Saxony, who had successfully gained control of the Saxon electoral dignity but had been killed in battle against the Turks in 1553. Joachim even proposed accepting the Interim of 1548 as a basis for a religious settlement, but eventually they determined to adhere to Philipp Melanchthon's Augsburg Confession (1530), a foundational Lutheran document that summarizes Luther's teachings, and to oppose any religious settlement by majority vote. On this basis, parity and perpetual peace were established between the "members of the old faith" and the "members of the Augsburg Confession," and a compromise settlement could be adopted.

The parties to the Peace of Augsburg were the Catholics and the Lutherans, those Protestants who had accepted the Augsburg Confession drawn up by Melanchthon at the Diet of Augsburg of 1530 in an unsuccessful attempt to achieve theological agreement with the Catholics. Sacramentarians (the Zwinglians and the Calvinists) and sectarians (the Anabaptists) were not included in the peace, at least in part because they had no political support in 1555. Both the Catholics and the Lutherans accepted this compromise peace only reluctantly, because in 1555 neither could impose its own version of eternal truth on the other. Each expected that, in the future, religious unity would be restored. Toleration of religious differences was seen as a practical necessity, not a desirable good.

PROVISIONS OF THE PEACE OF AUGSBURG

On September 25, 1555, Holy Roman Emperor Ferdinand I issued the Peace of Augsburg, embodying the decrees of the 1530 Diet of Augsburg, which had been summoned by Holy Roman Emperor Charles V. The diet, however, attempted unsuccessfully to achieve theological agreement between the Lutherans of the empire's German states and the Catholics. The principal provisions of the Peace of Augsburg are as follows:

- Catholic and Lutheran parties were to maintain perpetual peace.
- The Lutheran princes, imperial knights, and imperial cities were to enjoy security equal to that of the Catholics.
- Each secular principality was to have the right to choose either Catholicism or Lutheranism as its official religion, but the practice of all other faiths was prohibited.
- Each ecclesiastical principality would revert to Church control if its prince adopted a non-Catholic faith.
- The imperial cities were to maintain the religious parity in effect at the time of the 1552 Truce of Passau, which temporarily halted the religious schism.
- Church lands were to belong legally to the confession actually in possession at the time of the Truce of Passau.
- All persons would have the right to emigrate from a territory espousing a religion different from their own.

In the years to come, German lawyers evolved the principle *cuius regio, eius religio* (literally, whose rule, his the religion) to summarize the most important provision of the document, that which gave the ruler of each territory the right to determine its official religion. In some principalities, this decision was reached autocratically by the ruler, in others by the ruler in conjunction with his provincial diet. In many principalities, a practical, though unofficial, toleration prevailed.

SIGNIFICANCE

When he succeeded his brother as Holy Roman Emperor in 1556, Ferdinand respected his secret promise to the Lutherans, largely out of a desire for peace. In 1555, the Lutherans claimed the overwhelming majority of the population of the empire and most of its secular princes. The Catholicism of the imperial house and the presence of three archbishops among the seven electors, however, gave the Catholics approximately equal strength.

Ferdinand's son Maximilian II described himself as "neither a Papist nor a Lutheran but a Christian," but remained formally a Catholic at his father's wish. During his reign as emperor from 1564 to 1576, and that of his son Rudolf II from 1576 to 1612, religious toleration continued to be practiced by the imperial court. During

An engraving of Lutheran theologian Philipp Melanchthon. (Metropolitan Museum of Art, New York)

the later sixteenth century, however, Catholicism began to revive. Rudolf gave full encouragement to the Jesuits in their missionary and educational activities, as did some other princes, notably the dukes of Bavaria. In both Catholic and Lutheran territories where tolerance had previously existed, religious uniformity was now imposed. By the end of the sixteenth century, the Protestants were probably still in the majority but their status had diminished. Most of southern and western Germany was then firmly Catholic, while northern and eastern Germany became entirely Protestant.

The easygoing policies of the emperors after 1555 permitted many ecclesiastical principalities and a significant amount of Church property to pass from Catholic to Protestant hands during the later sixteenth century, in violation of the terms of the Peace of Augsburg. As the strength of the Catholic party revived during these same years, this situation became less and less acceptable to them.

The religious and political situation in Germany was further complicated by the spread of the Reformed Church (Zwinglianism and Calvinism), although it was

illegal. In 1559, Elector Frederick III of the Palatinate, a Calvinist, came to power in that important territory, giving the Reformed Church its first significant political support. Except for a short break under Frederick's son Ludwig from 1576 to 1583, it remained the official religion of the Palatinate until 1685. Bitter quarrels broke out across Germany between the Lutherans and Calvinists. In 1580, the Lutherans, at the insistence of August of Saxony, issued the Formula of Concord, which defined their own position with respect to the Calvinists.

As the seventeenth century dawned, the provisions of the Peace of Augsburg were less satisfactory than they had appeared fifty years earlier. The problems of the control of ecclesiastical principalities and properties, and the spread of the Reformed Church were difficulties that had to be settled by force in the Thirty Years' War.

—*James F. Hitchcock, updated by William C. Schrader*

FURTHER READING

Bobbitt, Philip. *The Shield of Achilles: War, Peace, and the Course of History.* New York: Knopf, 2002. Discusses the Peace of Augsburg, explains its effects upon history, and compares it to other major peace treaties and agreements. Includes bibliographic references and index.

Evans, Malcolm D. *Religious Liberty and International Law in Europe.* New York: Cambridge University Press, 1997. Traces the principles of religious liberty in international law back to the Peace of Augsburg. Includes bibliographic references and index.

Evans, R. J. W. *Rudolf II and His World: A Study in Intellectual History, 1576-1612.* London: Thames and Hudson, 1997. A reprinted work with corrections. Especially important for the policies of the emperors Maximilian II and Rudolf II.

Grimm, Harold J. *The Reformation Era, 1500-1650.* 2d ed. New York: Macmillan, 1973. An excellent, balanced account of the entire Reformation period, including the Catholic weakness in 1555 and subsequent revival.

Holborn, Hajo. *The Reformation.* Vol. 1 in *A History of Modern Germany.* 1959. Reprint. Princeton, N.J.: Princeton University Press, 1982. Still the best overall history of Germany in English for this period, and a standard source.

Janssen, Johannes. *History of the German People at the Close of the Middle Ages.* Vols. 6-8. Translated by A. M. Christie. 1903. Reprint. New York: AMS Press, 1966. Provides a detailed, pro-Catholic account of the Diet of Augsburg and the application of the peace.

Lindberg, Carter. *The European Reformations.* Cambridge, Mass.: Blackwell, 1996. A convenient up-to-date survey of the entire Reformation era.

Ranke, Leopold von. *History of the Reformation in Germany.* Translated by Sarah Austin. Reprint. New York: Frederick Ungar, 1966. A classic German source written from a pro-Protestant perspective, balancing Janssen's work.

SEE ALSO: Oct. 31, 1517: Luther Posts His Ninety-five Theses; 1523: Gustav I Vasa Becomes King of Sweden; Feb. 27, 1531: Formation of the Schmalkaldic League; Mar., 1536: Calvin Publishes *Institutes of the Christian Religion*; 1555-1556: Charles V Abdicates; 1576-1612: Reign of Rudolf II.

RELATED ARTICLES in *Great Lives from History: The Renaissance & Early Modern Era, 1454-1600:* Martin Bucer; John Calvin; Charles V; Frederick III; Gustav I Vasa; Balthasar Hubmaier; Martin Luther; Maximilian I; Maximilian II; Philipp Melanchthon; Menno Simons; Philip the Magnanimous; Rudolf II; Huldrych Zwingli.

1556-1605
REIGN OF AKBAR

The reign of the Mughal emperor Akbar marked one of the most renowned eras in India's history, not only for its economic, political, and military accomplishments but also for its religious and artistic developments. Akbar's imperial government became the model for subsequent rulers of India, including the colonial British, until the nineteenth century.

LOCALE: India
CATEGORY: Government and politics

KEY FIGURES
Akbar (1542-1605), Mughal emperor of India, r. 1556-1605
Bairam Khan (fl. sixteenth century), Akbar's adviser and regent, 1556-1560
Padmini (fl. sixteenth century), Akbar's wife
Salim (1569-1627), Akbar's son and successor, who ruled as Jahāngīr, r. 1605-1627

SUMMARY OF EVENT
Akbar, nicknamed Akbar the Great, was one of India's most famous emperors, and his reign, from his accession in 1556 to his death in 1605, is considered to be a golden age in Indian civilization. He was born in 1542 in northwest India, when his father Humāyūn was fleeing India, driven from the Mughal throne by Shēr Shāh Sūr, an Afghan noble and future emperor of Delhi.

Akbar's childhood was largely spent in Kandahar, Afghanistan. The Mughals were descended from the conqueror Genghis Khan (r. 1206-1227), a distant ancestor of Bābur, the first Mughal Indian emperor and Akbar's grandfather. Akbar's mother was Hamida, a Persian. As a young child he loved to hunt, and he mastered the military skills deemed necessary for someone of his noble birth. However, he was never was able to read or to write, possibly due to dyslexia, but whatever the cause of his illiteracy, it was not because he lacked intelligence.

When Humāyūn invaded India from Afghanistan in 1554 to regain his throne, Akbar accompanied his father. Within a year, Humāyūn had restored his Indian empire, but he died the following year. Akbar was thirteen years old when crowned as the new Mughal ruler in the Punjab, where he was serving as governor.

His accession was challenged, initially most seriously by Hemu, a Hindu who took the title of raja. After seizing the city of Delhi, Hemu headed for the Punjab. Many of Akbar's advisers urged the young emperor to flee to Kabul in Afghanistan, but his regent, Bairam Khan, urged him to resist Hemu's army. On November 5, 1556, the opposing forces met at Panipat, the earlier site of Bābur's victory over the Lodī Delhi sultans in 1527, which had resulted in the establishment of Mughal rule in India. Although Hemu had fifteen hundred war elephants, Bairam Khan was victorious. Hemu was beheaded, and the Mughals were once again in control of Delhi. Bairam Kahn remained regent until 1560, when Akbar dismissed him at the instigation of one of Akbar's nurses, Maham Anaga, who intended that her son would become the new power behind the throne. However, he soon abused his position, and was executed in 1562. Akbar's personal rule began with the deaths of the two khans.

In that same year, Akbar married Padmini, daughter of the Rājput raja Bihari Mal of Amber. Padmini's family were Hindus who had been allies of Humāyūn, and with the marriage, the family became the maharajas of Jaipur.

The marriage was politically advantageous and gained support from many Hindu Rājputs. Hindu loyalty and the formidable Rājput military prowess strengthened the non-Indian Muslim Mughal Dynasty but, reciprocally, the Hindu Rājputs gained access to imperial power and prestige.

In 1564, Akbar abolished the *jizya*, or non-Muslim poll tax, gaining wide support throughout India's majority Hindu community. Marriage alliances did not resolve all the challenges faced by Akbar. Rana Udai Singh, the ruler of the Sisodia Dynasty, proved a resourceful opponent of Akbar's rule. In October, 1567, the emperor led the siege of Rana Udai Singh's fortress of Chitar. When it finally succumbed in February of 1568, between twenty thousand and thirty thousand civilians were massacred.

Miniature painting of Akbar's court in a pavilion. (Hulton Archive by Getty Images)

By 1570, as result of his bloody victory at Chitar, Akbar had successfully ended the major Rājput resistance.

Campaigns against other foes continued. Gujarat, south and west of Delhi, was invaded in 1572, and Amahabad and Surat were captured, giving Akbar control of the Arabian Sea. It was Bengal's turn in the east in 1574. Within two years, the entire region was absorbed into the expanding Mughal Empire. In the northwest, Afghanistan's Kabul fell to Akbar in 1581, Orissa was taken over in 1592, and Baluchistan in 1595. Akbar's rule extended over all of northern and central India, and in territory was larger than the great Mauryan Empire of around 300 B.C.E.

The population of Akbar's empire, divided into twelve provinces, is estimated to have been one hundred million. The government bureaucracy or administration was made up of thirty-three ranks, with administrators responsible for providing cavalry for the imperial army, the number depending on their rank. The higher ranks were made up of Muslim soldiers born outside India (generally in Persia and Afghanistan). Native-born Indians made up the rest. About 15 percent of the higher ranks were Hindus, mostly Rājputs. Most of the population was peasant farmers, who were required to pay one-third of their annual crop as taxes, which was not considered excessive in comparison to past and future practices.

Government officials received grants of land. Because the land grants would revert to the emperor upon the death or removal of any official, there was little incentive to invest in long-range improvements; thus immediate conspicuous consumption was the rule. Palaces, slaves, dancing girls, and jewels were the "rewards" for the elite.

Like all the Mughal emperors, Akbar was a Muslim, but his own religious practices and beliefs were tolerant and eclectic. Although he was Sunni Muslim, Akbar found solace from a Sufi, Sheikh Salim, after his twin sons died shortly after birth and while he and his wife were still childless. Orthodox Muslims considered Sufism a heresy. Akbar's policy of toleration was not just political: He was sincerely interested in the various religions of his subjects, and he presided over debates between Muslims and Hindus, Sunnis and Sufis, Jains, Sikhs, and Parsis, and even Christians (the Portuguese, led by explorer Vasco da Gama, first arrived in India in 1498). All undoubtedly hoped to convert Akbar to their faith, but his beliefs combined what he believed was best for his subjects and what salved his own conscience.

Akbar came to see himself as God's earthly representative, and he claimed to have taken on divine qualities, establishing a religion called the Divine Faith (*Din-i-Ilahi*). *Allahu Akbar!* (God is Great!) was the traditional Muslim invocation, but for many at court it could also be interpreted as "Akbar is God." Orthodox Muslims thus saw Akbar as a heretic or worse, and there were Muslim rebellions against his rule, notably in 1581 by his half brother, Mirza Muhammad Hakim, all of which failed, in part because of Akbar's military and administrative reforms but also because he had support from the non-Muslim community.

Persian culture was a major influence at Akbar's court, and Persian was the court's official language. Akbar was also attracted to Hindu culture. The blended aspects of the various Indian cultures became known as "Mughlai," a combination of Mughal and Rājput, or Perso-Islamic and Rājput-Hindu cultural styles. Akbar encouraged the development and translation of Hindu literary texts, and the painting of the era, both portraits and miniatures, exhibits a marvelous synthesis of Hindu and Islamic cultures.

The Mughal capital had been the city of Āgra, but after the birth of Akbar's son and heir Salim in Sikri in 1569, the emperor chose Sikri as the site of his new capital, which was renamed Fatehpur Sikri (city of victory), an extravagant mélange of various Indian styles, both Persian and Hindu, notable for its red sandstone palace. Pollution and a shortage of water, though, forced the abandonment of the city in 1585.

SIGNIFICANCE

Generational rivalry was customary among the Mughals. Toward the end of Akbar's life his son and heir Salim challenged his rule. In 1601, Salim declared himself emperor, or *padishah*. Akbar resisted Salim's ambitions, but on October 17, 1605, Akbar died, probably poisoned by Salim, who as the new emperor took the name Jahāngīr (world seizer).

Akbar perhaps was the greatest of the Mughal emperors and his reign the most glorious. His diplomacy and military victories gave the Mughals control of most of India. His administrative reforms formed the basis for future Mughal rule and were adopted later by the British

when they ruled India. The artistic achievements of the era rank among the greatest in Indian history, and Akbar's tolerant religious policies stand as a beacon of enlightenment in a frequently intolerant world.

—*Eugene Larson*

FURTHER READING

Burn, Richard, ed. *The Mughal Period*. Vol. 4 in *The Cambridge History of India*. London: Cambridge University Press, 1922. The standard multivolume history of India; this volume includes a comprehensive discussion of Akbar and his reign.

Eraly, Abraham. *The Last Spring: The Lives of the Great Mughals*. New Delhi, India: Viking, 1997. A readable account of the Mughal emperors, including Akbar.

Habib, Irfan, ed. *Akbar and His India*. New York: Oxford University Press, 1997. Articles on the history of India during the time of Akbar.

Khan, Iqtidar Alam. *Akbar and His Age*. New Delhi, India: Northern Book Centre, 1999. A collection of articles that were presented at an international seminar on Akbar.

Streusand, Douglas E. *The Formation of the Mughal Empire*. New York: Oxford University Press, 1999. An excellent study of the early Mughal Empire, with an emphasis upon Akbar.

Wolpert, Stanley. *A New History of India*. New York: Oxford University Press, 2000. This easily available and widely used text includes an entire chapter about Akbar.

SEE ALSO: 1451-1526: Lodī Kings Dominate Northern India; Early 16th cent.: Devotional Bhakti Traditions Emerge; Apr. 21, 1526: First Battle of Panipat; Mar. 17, 1527: Battle of Khānua; Dec. 30, 1530: Humāyūn Inherits the Throne in India; Feb. 23, 1568: Fall of Chitor; Mar. 3, 1575: Mongol Conquest of Bengal; 1578: First Dalai Lama Becomes Buddhist Spiritual Leader.
RELATED ARTICLES in *Great Lives from History: The Renaissance & Early Modern Era, 1454-1600:* Akbar; Bābur; Vasco da Gama; Humāyūn; Ibrāhīm Lodī; Krishnadevaraya.

1550's

January 23, 1556
EARTHQUAKE IN CHINA KILLS THOUSANDS

One of the biggest earthquakes in human history occurred in 1556 in Shaanxi Province, China, killing thousands of people. This natural disaster had a pivotal influence on the decline of the Ming Dynasty.

LOCALE: Huaxian County, Shaanxi Province, China
CATEGORIES: Environment; natural disasters

SUMMARY OF EVENT

On January 23, 1556, one of the most devastating earthquakes in recorded human history occurred in China. Translated into the Chinese lunar calendar, the date of disaster fell on the twelfth day of the twelfth month in the thirty-fourth year of the Jiajing (Chia-Ching) emperor's reign (1522-1567) during the Ming Dynasty (1368-1644).

Although the epicenter of this violent earthquake was situated at Huaxian, Weinan, Huayin, Tongguan, and Puzhou counties in Shaanxi Province, its destruction extended to the neighboring provinces of Shanxi, Henan, Gansu, Hebei, Shandong, Anhui, Hubei, and Hunan. The magnitude of the tremor was 8 on the Richter scale and above XI on the twelve-grade seismic intensity scale used in China. The total epicentral area covered approximately 108,100 square miles (280,000 square kilometers), while the total disaster area reached 347,500 square miles (900,000 square kilometers), including 185 counties. The total area across which the quake was felt is estimated to have been approximately 772,200 square miles (2 million square kilometers).

According to the *Ming shilu* (true records of Ming), a historical record of the Ming Dynasty, the number of casualties that could be named and found was 820,000, while countless others went unidentified or missing. Because the quake occurred at midnight, most people were crushed to death in bed and had no chance to escape. Heavy rumbling sounds were heard as if mountains were rolling. Landmasses sank or were uplifted; cracks and fissures opened to form gullies; water rose from underground through the fissures. In the epicentral regions of Huaxian, Weinan, and Huayin, city walls, temples, storehouses, offices, and civilian homes collapsed totally.

No single wall was left standing in Huaxian, where even the topography was affected: Mountains and plains moved, and the course of the Wei River, whose lower basin cut into Huaxian, was changed after the land shifted, placing under water many areas formerly on dry land. In Weinan County, all peaks of Mount Wuzhi fell, while

land fissures as deep as 230-330 feet (70-100 meters) were formed. Underground water was also redirected in its course. Some wells and springs dried up, while victims drowned in flooded gullies and fissures. Trees fell, were displaced, or were broken. Landslides occurred while in some places well water boiled. Sixty percent of the inhabitants of Huaxian—tens of thousands of people—were killed or injured. Details of the destruction were recorded in official or semiofficial historical chronicles, local records, and inscriptions on stone walls and artifacts found in the affected areas.

Aftershocks of this earthquake were as numerous as they were destructive. A few days after the main shocks, dozens of aftershocks happened daily for a month. In the counties of Weinan, Chaoyi and Huayin, aftershocks lasted as long as four years. A strong aftershock affected Huaxian county two years later, resulting in significant damage.

SIGNIFICANCE

The Wei River Valley, located in the southern end of the great Hebei fault, has been the scene of seismic activity throughout Chinese history. According to historical records, between the years 1177 B.C.E. and 1976 C.E., there were thirty-six earthquakes of magnitude of 5 to 8 in the province of Shaanxi. The great loss of lives in the 1556 earthquake and its aftermath was the result of two factors: the construction of the dwellings and the dense population at the epicenter. From different sources, the total number of lost human lives exceeded 830,000, making this earthquake the most devastating natural disaster in Chinese history.

Shaanxi Province is situated at the northwestern part of China, with the Mongolian nomads in the north. Shaanxi is dry and cold, with snow falling from September to April in some places. Its northern region is mountainous, and the soil is sandy and ill suited to agriculture. The silk and cotton trade failed to prosper in this impoverished land. During the Ming reign, Shaanxi natives depended on merchants from other provinces for their daily goods. These merchants not only monopolized the market but also practiced usury, charging their clients high rates for their loans. The province was never an attractive place for government officials, who sought transfers rather than stay to help the people.

Politically, the Ming Dynasty at the beginning of the sixteenth century witnessed a time of turmoil and decline. Corruption festered in court as the emperors neglected their duties. To keep foreign powers—such as the Japanese, the Mongols, and the Manchus—at bay, the Ming court spent a fortune in defense during a time when national treasury was low. As a result, heavy taxation on an already decrepit peasant population was the only recourse. Starvation became a common phenomenon among the poor, who, having been rejected by the rich and the nobility, turned to violence to survive.

Major droughts hit Shaanxi in 1504 and again in 1528; the latter year was the most serious drought of the whole Ming period. Following the droughts, widespread famine and epidemics took place and the common people suffered. The Jiajing emperor neglected the country in his pursuit of Daoist immortality. Thus, by the time the earthquake of 1556 hit Shaanxi, it acted as a catalyst to the rapid deterioration of the Ming Dynasty.

In 1569, a revolt of bandits was reported in Shaanxi, and this revolt eventually spread to the Sichuan region. During the reign of the Ming emperor Wanli (1573-1620), famines occurred so frequently that the hungry were forced to revolt. The price of rice rose so high that the poor had no means to feed themselves. Famine revisited the province in 1627, during the reign of Tianqi (r. 1621-1627), when the people murdered the magistrate of Chengxian, who demanded the payment of taxes despite the national crisis. In 1628, an hungry and angry mob in Shaanxi grew to the size of six thousand. These rebels were joined by soldiers, miners, destitute people, foreign bandits from across the border, and the Mohammadans, a Muslim group who resided along the border among the Shaanxi, Gansu, and Sichuan Provinces. Li Zicheng (Li Tzu-ch'eng, 1606-1645), one of the rebels responsible for bringing down the Ming Empire, was rumored to be a Mohammedan from Shaanxi.

By 1632, there were twenty-four divisions of rebels in Shaanxi and thirty-eight in Henan and Shanxi. The approximate number of rebels in 1635 was 600,000. These rebels held three main strategic points, the northern part of Shaanxi being the first and the most important. The area was surrounded by a chain of mountains with deep streams and winding paths over a stretch of several hundred miles. It would have been extremely difficult for a nonnative force, let alone government forces, to attack this difficult terrain. The rebellious mob in northern Shaanxi supported themselves and their families by hiding and growing crops that they shared with the local peasants. By the same token, in Hanzhong, the southern part of Shaanxi, hungry men from the neighboring provinces came to volunteer as rebels. Hanzhong too, was

surrounded by mountains and marshes hundreds of miles in radius; in this area alone, the total number of rebels reached 100,000 by 1637. It was these hungry bandits in Shaanxi who later joined forces with those of Li Zicheng and Zhang Xianzhong (Chang Hsien-chung, 1606-1647), two arch-rebels who brought an end to the Ming Dynasty in the year 1644. The province of Shaanxi played an important role in this downfall, and the rebellions there certainly were exacerbated by the earthquake of 1556 and its aftermath.

—*Fatima Wu*

FURTHER READING

Chan, Albert. *The Glory and Fall of the Ming Dynasty.* Norman: University of Oklahoma Press, 1982. The author talks about Shaanxi's role in the fall of the Ming Dynasty in the chapter titled "End of a Great Empire."

Gere, James M., and Haresh C. Shah, ed. *The 1976 Tangshan, China Earthquake.* Stanford, Calif.: Earthquake Engineering Research Institute, 1980. Appendix B in this book presents an important document on the Chinese seismic intensity scale. The maximum grade is XII, and each grade is accompanied by characteristic types of damage.

Gu, Gongxu, et al., eds. *Catalogue of Chinese Earthquakes, 1831 B.C.-1969 A.D.* Beijing: Science Press, 1989. Details the damage in each area affected. There are catalogs for both strong earthquakes and provincial earthquakes.

Tang, Xiren. *A General History of Earthquake Studies in China.* Beijing: Science Press, 1988. The value of this book lies in its extensive research on ancient earthquake records from 1177 B.C.E. to 1976 C.E.

Teng, T. L., and W. H. K. Lee, eds. *Chinese Geophysics.* Washington, D.C.: American Geophysical Union, 1978. A collection of essays on Chinese earthquakes by international scholars. The Shaanxi 1556 earthquake is discussed by Japanese professor Syun'itiro Omote in his article "Earthquake Damage and Earthquake Prediction in China."

1550's

Summer, 1556
IVAN THE TERRIBLE ANNEXES ASTRAKHAN

With the defeat and annexation of the Khanate of Astrakhan, Russia under Ivan the Terrible enjoyed control over the entire course of the Volga River. The victory opened the way for the subordination of neighboring Muslim khanates and non-Russian steppe peoples, expansion into Siberia, and trade with Persia and Central Asia. It also allowed Ivan to portray himself as the true successor to the khans of the Golden Horde.

LOCALE: Khanate of Astrakhan, around the mouth of the Volga River (now in Russia and Kazakhstan)

CATEGORIES: Wars, uprisings, and civil unrest; expansion and land acquisition

KEY FIGURES

Ivan the Terrible (1530-1584), grand prince of Moscow, r. 1533-1547, and czar of Russia, r. 1547-1584

Derbysh (fl. 1554-1556), khan of Astrakhan, r. 1554-1556

Ismāʿīl (d. 1563), khan of the Nogai Tatars, r. 1554-1555, 1556-1563

Ivan Sheremetev (fl. 1556), general and commander of Muscovite forces in the 1556 campaign

SUMMARY OF EVENT

Located at the extreme southern end of the Volga River, north of the Caspian Sea, the territories comprising the Khanate of Astrakhan became part of the Golden Horde in the wake of the Mongol invasion of Kievan Rus (1237-1241). Achieving political independence in 1466 as the Golden Horde crumbled from internal political dissension, the khanate emerged as one of three sophisticated, well-organized Muslim successor states, the others being the Khanate of Crimea (1430)—which quickly became a vassal of the Ottoman Empire—and the Khanate of Kazan (1436). These three khanates proved a tremendous problem for the Russian Muscovite state and its rulers from the Danilovich branch of the Rurik Dynasty. They blocked Muscovy's southern and eastward expansion, and they periodically raided Russian territory, devastating the lands and taking thousands of Russians as slaves.

Prior to the mid-sixteenth century, Muscovite rulers relied on a combination of defensive military force and diplomacy to keep the Golden Horde successor states at bay. This changed, however, with Czar Ivan the Terrible, the first of the Rurik Muscovite princes officially to be crowned czar of Russia. Ivan went on the offensive against the Khanate of Kazan. In a series of campaigns commenc-

ing in 1545 and ending in 1552, Russian military forces subdued Kazan, annexing it to Russia and establishing Russian control over the entire central Volga region.

Following his dramatic victory at Kazan, Ivan soon turned his attention southward. In spring, 1554, the czar ordered to the Khanate of Astrakhan a military force more than thirty thousand strong, commanded by Prince Yuri Ivanovich Pronsky-Shemyakin and Prince Alexander Vyazemsky. Traveling primarily by boat down the Volga River, Russian forces seized Perevolok, the portage between the Don and Volga Rivers, on June 29 and reached the city of Astrakhan on July 2. Encountering no resistance—Astrakhan's defenders having fled upon learning of the Russian approach—the Russians seized the city but discovered, to their dismay, that Khan Yamgurchey and his family had escaped.

Although Prince Vyazemsky's forces ultimately captured Yamgurchey's wives and children, the khan himself managed to make his way to Azov before being murdered by Nogai Tatars. Whatever his eventual fate, the khan's entire khanate was at Moscow's mercy once its capital city had been captured. Rather than annex the khanate immediately, however, Ivan placed in power a new khan, Derbysh, who pledged loyalty to the czar and signed a treaty providing that the khanate pay Moscow an annual tribute of 120,000 kopecks and 3,000 fish, that Muscovite fishermen be allowed to fish the Volga from Kazan to the Caspian Sea without payment, and that Ivan and his successors enjoy the exclusive right to select all future khans.

Derbysh's loyalty to Ivan the Terrible proved short lived. During 1555 and early 1556, Derbysh allied himself with Khan Devlet Giray of Crimea, one of Muscovy's most ferocious enemies, and with the Ottoman Empire. With Ottoman military support, Derbysh murdered those members of the Astrakhan elite known to be loyal to Ivan and attacked Russian forces in the city, killing 192 of 500 men and chasing the survivors to the Don-Volga portage. Muscovite forces in the region and their steppe ally, Khan Ismāʿīl of the Nogai Tatars, responded by moving against Astrakhan. Like Yamgurchey before him, Derbysh fled from the approaching Russian army. Left undefended, Astrakhan once again fell to the Muscovites in the summer of 1556.

After fortifying the city, the Russian commander, General Ivan Sheremetev, and his forces proceeded down the Volga toward the Caspian Sea. Discovering that

Derbysh had set up camp some 13 miles (21 kilometers) west of the river, the Muscovites launched a successful night attack that inflicted heavy casualties but did not destroy the khan's forces. The khan counterattacked the next day and drove the Russians back to the Volga. Immediately thereafter, Derbysh contacted Sheremetev, to whom he explained that he had broken his oath to Ivan under duress. He then begged the czar's mercy, pledging to return to Astrakhan and to serve Ivan loyally.

Apparently, Derbysh's professions to Sheremetev were nothing but an attempt to buy time. Without waiting to learn of Ivan's response, Derbysh joined forces with the Yusufs, a Nogai Tatar clan who were in rebellion against Khan Ismāʿīl, Ivan's ally. This alliance, however, dissolved almost as quickly as it was formed: The Yusuf clan and its forces made peace with Ismāʿīl, offered to surrender to Muscovite forces, and promised to serve the czar as Ismāʿīl served him. Sheremetev immediately accepted the Yusuf offer of surrender and agreed to provide them with boats to cross the Volga so they could return to Nogai territory.

The defection of the Yusuf clan sealed the fate of both Derbysh and the Khanate of Astrakhan. Before returning home, Yusuf forces attacked their recent ally, forcing Derbysh to flee to Azov and permanent exile. In the process, they captured cannon dispatched by the khan of Crimea and turned them over to Sheremetev. Upon discovering the fate of Derbysh, the common people of Astrakhan, who had fled at the approach of Muscovite forces, petitioned Sheremetev, begging to be allowed to swear an oath of allegiance to the czar and to return to the city. Claiming that they were simple folk who had been forced to follow Derbysh against their will, they asked that the czar not punish them and agreed to pay tribute. Although he agreed to these requests, Ivan also decided to annex Astrakhan outright, making it a part of the growing Russian empire.

SIGNIFICANCE

Learning of the Muscovite conquest of Astrakhan, the Bashkirs, a non-Russian people living in the steppe east of the Volga, voluntarily declared their association with Muscow, while the khans of the Nogai Horde and the Sibir Khanate, along with the princes of Pyatigorsk and Kabardia, declared themselves vassals of the czar. Additionally, Ivan decided to undertake an assault against the Crimean Khanate, the third of the three troublesome Golden Horde successor states. In preparation, he ordered the construction of a fleet on the Don and Dnieper Rivers, which was to transport *streltsy* (musketeers) for the campaign. Ultimately, however, Ivan abandoned his plan when he became convinced that he could not build up sufficient forces. The Crimean Tatars would thus remain a problem for Russia and her rulers until 1783, when Empress Catherine the Great (r. 1762-1796) finally annexed their territories.

Most historians agree that the reign of Czar Ivan the Terrible marked the real birth of the Russian Empire as a Eurasian, multinational state. In this regard, Ivan's conquest of the Khanate of Astrakhan represented a critical development. Along with the 1552 defeat of the Kazan Khanate, the annexation of Astrakhan gave Muscovy control over the entire course of the Volga River. Furthermore, it allowed Moscow to subordinate the neighboring Muslim Khanate of Sibir and non-

Russian military forces subdued Kazan and its people (seen here submitting to Ivan the Terrible), annexed the khanate of Kazan to Russia, and established Russian control over the entire central Volga region. (R. S. Peale and J. A. Hill)

Russian steppe peoples including the Nogai Tatars and the Bashkirs, as well as to establish regular trade, via the Caspian Sea, with Persia and Central Asia. Finally, the defeat of Astrakhan allowed Ivan and those who succeeded him on the Russian throne to portray themselves as the legitimate successors to the khans of the Golden Horde, that portion of the Mongol Empire to which the territories of Kievan Rus had belonged from 1241 to 1480.

—Bruce J. DeHart

FURTHER READING

Hosking, Geoffrey. *Russia and the Russians: A History.* Cambridge, Mass.: Harvard University Press, 2001. Includes a chapter on Muscovy's expansion during the reign of Ivan IV that emphasizes the significance of the annexations of Kazan and Astrakhan.

Kappeler, Andreas. *The Russian Empire: A Multiethnic History.* Translated by Alfred Clayton. New York: Longman, 2001. Traces the history of the Russian Empire from a multiethnic perspective. Chapter 2, which deals with the acquisition of the territories of

the Golden Horde includes an entire section on the conquest of the Khanates of Kazan and Astrakhan and its significance.

Soloviev, Sergei. *The Reign of Ivan the Terrible: Kazan, Astrakhan, Livonia, the Oprichnina, and the Polotsk Campaign.* Vol. 10 in *History of Russia from Ancient Times,* edited and translated by Anthony L. H. Rhinelander. Gulf Breeze, Fla.: Academic International Press, 1995. Originally published in the nineteenth century, Soloviev's volume remains the best secondary account of Ivan's capture of Astrakhan.

SEE ALSO: 1462: Regiomontanus Completes the *Epitome* of Ptolemy's *Almagest*; 1480-1502: Destruction of the Golden Horde; After 1480: Ivan the Great Organizes the "Third Rome"; 1499-c. 1600: Russo-Polish Wars; Jan. 16, 1547: Coronation of Ivan the Terrible; 1581-1597: Cossacks Seize Sibir; 1584-1613: Russia's Time of Troubles.

RELATED ARTICLE in *Great Lives from History: The Renaissance & Early Modern Era, 1454-1600:* Ivan the Terrible.

1557-1582
LIVONIAN WAR

The Livonian War brought an end to the Livonian Confederation, left Russia in defeat and confusion, and established Sweden and Poland as the major powers in the Baltic Sea region.

LOCALE: Livonia (now in Latvia and Estonia)

CATEGORIES: Expansion and land acquisition; wars, uprisings, and civil unrest; diplomacy and international relations

KEY FIGURES

Ivan the Terrible (1530-1584), czar of Russia, r. 1547-1584

Wilhelm von Fürstenberg (d. 1568), master of the Livonian Order, 1557-1559

Gotthard Kettler (1517-1587), master of the Livonian Order, 1559-1562, and duke of Courland, r. 1562-1587

Sigismund II Augustus (1520-1572), king of Poland-Lithuania, r. 1548-1572

Stephen Báthory (1533-1586), king of Poland-Lithuania, r. 1575-1586

John III (1537-1592), king of Sweden, r. 1568-1592

SUMMARY OF EVENT

In the mid-1550's, the lands along the eastern coast of the Baltic Sea were governed by the Livonian Confederation, which represented German-speaking nobles, bishops, abbots, and burghers who had established themselves as rulers during the Crusades of the thirteenth century. The most important member of the Confederation was the Livonian Order, a military order that was finding it difficult to recruit Roman Catholic knights now that northern Germany was Protestant. The order lacked the funds to modernize its army and was unable to interest distant popes in its problems; nevertheless, it was able to defend Livonia effectively until Ivan the Terrible consolidated power in Moscow. Ivan's expansion south at the expense of the Tatars, Russia's traditional enemy, increased both his military strength and his imperial ambition.

Even so, Ivan probably did not want war with Livonia at this time. Without question, he wanted money, and he also sought to lay the foundation for later claims on the Baltic coastlands, as his demands that the Livonian Confederation pay tribute and three hundred years of back taxes confirm. The Confederation could have paid such an amount, though not easily, but its members were reluctant to contribute to arming a tyrant who would undoubtedly discover new claims on their modest wealth in the future and then might well declare war. The Confederation's diplomats delayed, obfuscated, and prayed for divine deliverance. They also sought more earthly support from King Sigismund II Augustus of Poland-Lithuania, agreeing to accept Polish suzerainty in the 1557 Treaty of Poswol. The treaty, however, did nothing except perhaps frighten Ivan into thinking that he had to strike quickly before his enemies could perfect their alliance. He soon attacked.

The Livonian Confederation was not ready for war. Its members were so fearful of one another they had even fought one another briefly, and there was strong disagreement about what policies should be followed. Master of the Livionian Order Wilhelm von Fürstenberg attempted to defend the Confederation, but to no avail. The other members of the Confederation refused to accept Fürstenberg's leadership, and it seems that his tactics in any case were ineffective. As a result, Ivan's forces captured the strategic castle at Narva in May, 1558. Suddenly all of Livonia lay open to Russian armies.

Ivan sent new armies into the country, capturing Dorpat easily in July, then occupying one fortress after another. Master Fürstenberg, and his successor, Gotthard Kettler, managed to replace aging and ineffective officers with younger and more daring warriors and to hire mercenaries. However, Fürstenberg was captured at Fellin with much of the order's military supplies in the late winter of 1560, and Kettler's field army was destroyed in battle at Ermes in the summer of 1560.

Livonian appeals for help to the Holy Roman Empire, Denmark, Sweden, and Poland-Lithuania had gone largely in vain until this time, but the monarchs of those countries now asked their national assemblies to endorse intervention. Little help came from Germany, except in the form of permission to recruit mercenary soldiers and strongly worded declarations of solidarity. Most Livonians submitted to Sigismund II Augustus in 1561 with the Treaty of Vilnius, and soon afterward, Lithuanian troops occupied the lands south of the Western Dvina River. Sigismund eventually granted some of these territories to Kettler and his officials, thus creating a duchy on the model of Prussia (where the Teutonic Knights had ruled until 1525, when the military order was secularized and the last grand master became duke of Prussia).

Meanwhile, the king of Denmark, rather than defending Livonia, attempted to use the situation in Livonia to strengthen Danish security. The king purchased the diocese of Oesel-Wiek for his troublesome younger brother, Magnus of Holstein, thus eliminating him as a danger to the Danish crown. He hoped that a marriage alliance between Magnus and Ivan the Terrible's niece would result in central Livonia's becoming a coastal buffer state that would protect Denmark from future Russian encroachments. The Swedish king, Erik XIV, likewise sent garrisons to help defend the fortresses along the Gulf of Finland, lest that region become a base for Russian attacks on Finnish possessions, but he did no more to aid the Livonian Confederation.

Ivan's actions in the ensuing years cannot be explained to universal satisfaction. His armies could probably have conquered all of Livonia, but only at the cost of a general war he did not want. Therefore, he tried more subtle approaches. From 1561 to 1570, he was largely inactive against the Swedes. One reason was that he needed to deal with the Crimean Tatars, who were encouraged by the Poles to attack Russia's southern frontiers while the Poles pinned down Ivan's forces around Smolensk. Another reason was his willingness to allow the Swedes and the Danes to destroy one another in their war of 1563-1570, in which the Poles assisted the Danes. Yet another was the defection of his most capable commander, Prince Andrey Mikhaylovich Kurbski, to Lithuania in 1564, after which Ivan ordered his secret police, the Oprichnina, to root out all other potential traitors.

Ivan had hoped to divide his enemies. This seemed likely when Swedish king Erik XIV's younger brother, John, married Sigismund II Augustus's daughter Katrina. John appeared ready to establish an independent state in Finland. Ivan demanded that the princess be sent to him, her fate unclear, in order further to destabilize the situation. John found himself in prison from 1563 until a rebellion among the Swedish nobles removed the unstable Erik in 1568 and made him King John III. Quickly, Ivan sent two "traitors," Johann Taube and Eilert Kruse, to persuade the city of Revel (Tallinn) to surrender, and then he besieged the city. When the siege failed, the two nobles chose not to return to Moscow and an inevitable beheading but instead became proponents of war to the death against Russia.

Next, Ivan employed a version of the compromise that had worked so well for Poland in Prussia: He sought to rule through a puppet and chose Magnus of Holstein. However, the czar's paranoia made it impossible for him to allow Magnus sufficient authority to build a substantial party among the Livonians, and Ivan's fervent Orthodox beliefs made Roman Catholics and Protestants fear-

1550's

ful. More important, the stories of Ivan's misrule at home made potential subjects reluctant to trust him. Although western propaganda has to be discounted, there is no doubt that the czar was by now periodically mentally ill and that he did not hesitate to destroy entire families of prominent nobles and communities in retaliation for real or imagined crimes. Meanwhile, atrocities committed by Ivan's Tatars cost him the early welcome that he had received from the native Livonians. Moreover, as the villagers fled westward to safer districts, they found that the Germans viewed them less as allies or subjects than as potential traitors. For the coalescing Estonian and Latvian peoples, this was a truly terrible war.

Ivan's forces managed to occupy almost all of Estonia, but the situation quickly unraveled once the Polish state recovered stability under Stephen Báthory and John III dispatched Swedish armies across the sea. In 1578, a Polish-Swedish army crushed the czar's army at Wenden in central Livonia. Stephen Báthory consolidated his position there and in Riga; meanwhile, Swedish mercenaries under Pontus de la Gardie cleared Russian forces from most of Estonia and in 1581 captured Narva. In the summer of 1582, as Stephen Báthory's army was camped outside Pskov, the czar offered to surrender the remaining forts in Livonia in return for a ten-year truce. The Swedes, unable to continue the war alone, made peace in 1583.

SIGNIFICANCE

The Livonian War ended with Ivan the Terrible ill and confused. The czar had lost all his gains, his state was bankrupt, and a period of Russian decline was in the offing. At the same time, Sweden and Poland eyed one another warily over their newly acquired territories, while their national assemblies protested the war taxes. Many German-speaking nobles of Livonia had survived but had relocated from ancestral estates to safer lands; many others had died, and their lands had been given to mercenary commanders in place of their salaries, which were long in arrears. The various peoples native to the region, many of whom had spent years fleeing one army after another, had lost many of their regional identities; they were becoming more homogeneous linguistically and

culturally. The losses in population were staggering. Furthermore, economic costs and the imposition of a crushing serfdom—mainly to prevent the surviving peasants from leaving the estates—resulted in an intellectual and cultural stagnation that had profound effects upon the future.

—William L. Urban

FURTHER READING

Kirby, David. *Northern Europe in the Early Modern Period: The Baltic World, 1492-1772*. New York: Longman, 1990. Solid overview of the war.

Kirchner, Walther. *The Rise of the Baltic Question*. Westport, Conn.: Greenwood, 1954. A seminal study of the reasons for the war.

Kruse, Elert, Heinrich Tisenhausen, et al. *"The Chronicle of Balthasar Russow," "A Forthright Rebuttal," and "Errors and Mistakes of Balthasar Russow."* Translated by Jerry C. Smith, Juergen Eichhoff, and William L. Urban. Madison, Wis.: Baltic Studies Center, 1988. A contemporary chronicle that is often cited for its lively anecdotes and insights.

O'Connor, Kevin. *The History of the Baltic States*. Westport, Conn.: Greenwood Press, 2003. Survey history concentrating on the modern era.

Urban, William L. *The Livonian Crusade*. 2d ed. Chicago: Lithuanian Research and Studies Center, 2003. Shows the conflict as the culmination of long-developing trends.

SEE ALSO: 1480-1502: Destruction of the Golden Horde; After 1480: Ivan the Great Organizes the "Third Rome"; 1499-c. 1600: Russo-Polish Wars; Jan. 16, 1547: Coronation of Ivan the Terrible; Summer, 1556: Ivan the Terrible Annexes Astrakhan; Nov., 1575: Stephen Báthory Becomes King of Poland; 1581-1597: Cossacks Seize Sibir; 1584-1613: Russia's Time of Troubles; Beginning 1497: Danish-Swedish Wars.

RELATED ARTICLES in *Great Lives from History: The Renaissance & Early Modern Era, 1454-1600*: Ivan the Terrible; Sigismund II Augustus; Stephen Báthory.

1558-1593
Burmese-Laotian Wars

Burmese and Laotian plans for expansion brought the two kingdoms into conflict. Laos managed to shake off Burmese dominance through alliances with the Siamese, who were under constant attack from the Burmese, and declare independence from Burma in 1593. Siam would come to dominate the region, however, as Laos and Burma began a period of decline.

Locale: Central and northern Siam (now Thailand), northeastern Burma (now Myanmar), and southern Laos

Categories: Expansion and land acquisition; wars, uprisings, and civil unrest; diplomacy and international relations

Key Figures

Setthathirat I (1534-1571), king of Chiang Mai, r. 1545-1551, and king of Lan Xang, r. 1547-1571

Bayinnaung (1515-1581), king of the Toungoo Dynasty of Burma, r. 1551-1581

Mekhuti (fl. 1551-1565), king of Chiang Mai, r. 1551-1565

Vorawongse I (Maha Oupahat; d. 1579), brother of Setthathirat, vice-king of Laos, r. 1547-1575, and Burmese-sponsored king of Lan Xang, r. 1575-1579

Sen Soulinthara (1511-1582), father-in-law of Setthathirat, regent of Lan Xang, r. 1571-1572, and king of Lan Xang, r. 1572-1575 and 1580-1582

Nokeo Koumane (d. 1596), son of Setthathirat and king of Lan Xang, r. 1571-1572 and 1591-1596

Summary of Event

Burma (now Myanmar) was an expanding power in mainland Southeast Asia in the sixteenth century, ruled by the Toungoo Dynasty, named after the original location of the capital. The second ruler of the Toungoo Dynasty, Tabinshwehti (r. 1531-1546), defeated the kingdom of Pegu in southern Burma in 1535 and had plans to conquer Siam (central Thailand). A rival Burmese prince leading a rebellion assassinated Tabinshwehti, who was by this time the king of unified Burma, in 1550. Tabinshwehti's brother-in-law, the military leader Bayinnaung, put down the rebellion. Bayinnaung then had himself crowned king and took up the goal of expansion.

The Laotian kingdom of Lan Xang, also, was expanding its reach. The mother of the Lao king Photisarath (d. 1547) was a princess of the kingdom of Lan Na, located in what is now northern Thailand, which had a cap-ital city at Chiang Mai. In 1545, the king of Chiang Mai was assassinated, leaving the kingdom without an heir to the throne. Photisarath claimed the vacant throne and sent a force of soldiers to claim the Crown, which he accepted in the name of his eldest son, Setthathirat (also known as Jetthadiraja and Setthavong). The new king settled in Chiang Mai, but after he died in a hunting accident in 1547, Setthathirat returned to Lan Xang to be crowned.

It was difficult for Setthathirat to maintain his position in Chiang Mai from the old Laotian capital of Luang Pra-bang or from the growing city of Vientiane (Viangchan), which had been established by his father. The Siamese attacked Chiang Mai, but were beaten back by Laotian forces. Setthathirat did not want to return to Chiang Mai, so, in 1551, he agreed to recognize Mekhuti, a prince of Shan ethnicity elected by local leaders, as the new king of Chiang Mai.

Bayinnaung had been conquering the Shan territories of what is now northern Myanmar (Burma), and the absence of Setthathirat encouraged him to attempt to take Chiang Mai too. Bayinnaung arrived at Chiang Mai in 1556. Mekhuti offered little resistance and swore allegiance to Bayinnaung, promising to pay tribute to the Burmese king. After Bayinnaung's return to Burma, though, the Laotian forces of Setthathirat reinvaded in 1558 and defeated Mekhuti. The Burmese returned and placed Mekhuti back on the throne of Chiang Mai. Bayinnaung proclaimed that Setthathirat was no longer the king of Lan Xang, prompting Setthathirat to form an alliance against Burma with the Shan states. In turn, Bayinnaung sent his army into the Shan states, depriving Setthathirat of allies.

To counter the threat from Burma, Setthathirat sought close relations with the Siamese. who were also under pressure from Bayinnaung's military. Setthathirat concluded an alliance with the Siamese kingdom of Ayut-thaya, under King Chakrapat, in 1560. Bayinnaung's occupation of Chiang Mai, however, gave the Burmese king an excellent strategic location for launching a full-scale invasion of Siamese lands in 1563.

Mekhuti attempted to express his independence from Burma by refusing to help in the invasion of Siamese lands and by trying to prevent Burmese supply boats from leaving Chiang Mai. The Burmese then sent soldiers, under the command of Bayinnaung's son, to unseat Mekhuti. In the meantime, Bayinnaung enjoyed a string of victories against Siam and, after laying siege to Ayutthaya, he received the surrender of Chakrapat early in 1564. Chakrapat apparently became a Buddhist monk, which was common for royalty leaving public life, and his son, Mahin, took over as ruler under Burmese domination. According to some accounts, Chakrapat was placed by Bayinnaung in a monastery in Burma. A Siamese prince of the city of Phitsanulok served as regional deputy of Burma and helped keep watch over Mahin.

While the war with the Siamese was under way, the Burmese subdued Chiang Mai, and Mekhuti fled to Vientiane. Setthathirat had made Vientiane, located along the Mekhong River, the new capital of the Laotian kingdom, believing Vientiane was a better location than Luang Prabang strategically. The Burmese forces, having for the time finished with the Siamese, set out in boats to Vientiane. The city fell to the invaders in 1565, but Setthathirat managed to escape. The Burmese seized Setthathirat's brother, his queen, and Mekhuti, though, and took them back to Burma as prisoners. An aging princess of the old royal family of Chiang Mai was placed in charge there under the guidance of Burmese guards.

With the departure of the Burmese, Setthathirat returned to Vientiane. Mahin, the Siamese ruler at Ayutthaya, was eager to throw off Burma's control, so he contacted Setthathirat for help against their mutual enemy. Together, they attacked the central Siamese city of Phitsanulok in 1566, which was allied with Burma. However, Bayinnaung sent defenders and the Lao and Siamese were forced to give up the effort for the time. The following year, though, Chakrapat managed to leave his monastery and join his son's revolt. The Siamese again assaulted and laid siege to Phitsanulok.

Bayinnaung sent forces to help his ally at Phitsanulok, and Setthathirat marched from the north to help the Siamese. The Laotians and Siamese were pushed back by the combined strength of Phitsanulok and the Burmese. In late 1568, Bayinnaung undertook a second massive invasion of Siam. He relieved Phitsanulok and then marched to Ayutthaya. After a siege of several months, the Siamese capital fell. Both Chakrapat and Mahin died—Chakrapat during the siege and Mahin while on his way to Burma as a captive. The ruler of Phitsanulok, Thammaracha (r. 1569-1590), became the new Burmese sponsored-king of Ayutthaya in 1569.

After the fall of Ayutthaya, Bayinnaung again attacked Vientiane. The Laotians managed to defend Vientiane, forcing the Burmese army to give up; the Burmese returned home in the spring of 1570. Laos was not free of the Burmese for long, however, because Setthathirat died the following year, giving Bayinnaung an excuse to again intervene. Setthathirat's brother Vorawongse, who had been appointed vice-king years earlier, had been a prisoner in Burma since the invasion of 1564. From 1571 to 1572, Setthathirat's young son Nokeo Koumane was recognized as king under the regency of his maternal grandfather, Sen Soulinthara, but Sen Soulinthara would soon declare himself king. As a result, the Burmese invaded once again, took Sen Soulinthara prisoner, and placed Vorawongse onto the throne.

The Laotians refused to accept Vorawongse as their legitimate ruler. He accidentally drowned while fleeing from a revolt in 1579, leaving the throne of Lan Xang empty once more. The aging Bayinnaung reinstated Sen Soulinthara as king of Lan Xang. Both rulers soon died, though. After a period of nearly one decade with no definitive king, Nokeo Koumane, Setthathirat's son, who had been a prisoner in Burma for years, took back the throne in 1591. Two years later, Nokeo Koumane declared Laotian independence from Burma.

SIGNIFICANCE

Setthathirat is considered a national hero in Laos because he resisted Burmese domination. The Burmese-Laotian Wars marked the high point of Burmese expansion. At the end of this era, both Burma and Laos went into a period of decline, and Siam began its rise to regional dominance.

—*Carl L. Bankston III*

FURTHER READING

Coedés, George. *The Making of Southeast Asia*. Translated by H. M. Wright. London: Routledge, Kegan & Paul, 1966. A classic introduction to early Southeast Asian history that examines the Siamese-Cambodian wars of the sixteenth century.

Hall, D. G. E. *A History of South-East Asia*. 4th ed. New York: St. Martin's Press, 1981. A standard, comprehensive history of the region. Chapter 15, "Burma and the T'ai Kingdoms in the Sixteenth Century," examines events related to the Burmese-Laotian Wars.

Stuart-Fox, Martin. *A History of Laos*. New York: Cambridge University Press. Although concerned mainly with the history of modern Laos, the book's first chapter provides an excellent introduction to the events of the Lan Xang period.

_____. *The Lao Kingdom of Lan-Xang: Rise and Decline*. Bangkok, Thailand: White Lotus Press, 1998.

Written by an Australian historian recognized as one of the foremost contemporary scholars on Laos, this work tells the story of the Laotian kingdom that flourished from the fourteenth to the eighteenth centuries. It includes the history of the Burmese invasions.

SEE ALSO: 1450's-1529: Thai Wars; 1454: China Subdues Burma; 1469-1481: Reign of the Ava King

Thihathura; c. 1488-1594: Khmer-Thai Wars; 1505-1515: Portuguese Viceroys Establish Overseas Trade Empire; 1527-1599: Burmese Civil Wars; c. 1580-c. 1600: Siamese-Cambodian Wars.

RELATED ARTICLES in *Great Lives from History: The Renaissance & Early Modern Era, 1454-1600:* Afonso de Albuquerque; Tomé Pires; Saint Francis Xavier.

1558-1603
REIGN OF ELIZABETH I

Anglicanism, or the Church of England, came to prominence during the reign of Elizabeth I, a reign also marked by a major peak in cultural accomplishments, especially in literature, the establishment of the nation as a world naval and trade power, and the beginnings of the largest colonial empire in world history.

LOCALE: London, England
CATEGORY: Government and politics

KEY FIGURES
Elizabeth I (1533-1603), queen of England, r. 1558-1603
Henry VIII (1491-1547), king of England, r. 1509-1547
Mary I (1516-1558), queen of England, r. 1553-1558
William Cecil (1520-1598), Lord Burghley, secretary of state, Lord Treasurer, and chief adviser to Elizabeth I

SUMMARY OF EVENT
Two significant reigns preceded the reign of Elizabeth I. Her father, Henry VIII, separated the church in England from the Roman Catholic Church. The Act of Supremacy in 1534 made the monarch the Supreme Head of the Church of England, but made no doctrinal changes; some were made, however, under Henry's son, King Edward VI. The second important reign was that of Queen Mary I, a Catholic who took the throne in 1553 and promptly realigned England with the Catholic Church in Rome. She earned the moniker Bloody Mary for the persecution of those who would not conform to the change. After her death, the stage was set for another ecclesiastical and doctrinal upheaval, this time beginning in 1558, when the Protestant Elizabeth I replaced her half sister as monarch.

Conditions in England at the time of Elizabeth's ascension were far from ideal. Mary had joined her husband, King Philip II of Spain, in a war against France.

English losses in that war included heavy debt, decline in trade, and a shortage of qualified military leadership. The nation was divided socially between those favoring Catholicism and those aligning with the Protestant Reformation and Protestantism.

Elizabeth was the daughter of Henry VIII's second wife, Anne Boleyn, whom the king later had beheaded for failing to produce a male heir and for reputed adultery and sorcery. Still, Elizabeth admired her father and tried to emulate his style of leadership. She followed the Tudor family pattern of ambition and power but often subordinated these traits to her duties as queen. Elizabeth rejected a marriage proposal, with conflicting political ramifications, from her former brother-in-law, Philip II of Spain. In spite of numerous other proposals, Elizabeth remained single and became known as the Virgin Queen. She later encouraged the poet Edmund Spenser to describe her as the bride of her people in his work *The Faerie Queene* (1590-1609).

The first major project of Elizabeth's reign was to sort out and settle the ecclesiastical confusion of her realm. Her basic goal was an independent national church in which all of her subjects would feel comfortable. With the help of her major adviser, William Cecil, the Elizabethan Settlement was initiated in 1559. The settlement was a compromise involving two acts of Parliament. The first, a new Act of Supremacy, made Elizabeth the Supreme Governor of the church rather than the Supreme Head as Henry VIII had been. Clergy and government officials, but not laity, were required to swear allegiance to the Supreme Governor. The second act, the Act of Uniformity, required all to attend church on Sundays and holy days. It also mandated that church services would follow the second, and more Protestant, Book of Common Prayer, adopted in 1552. The first was adapted in 1549 and written mostly by church reformer Thomas Cranmer.

1550's

The Elizabethan Settlement was strengthened in 1563 by the Treason Act, which made the expression of support for a return to papal jurisdiction punishable by death. In the same year the Thirty-nine Articles of Religion established Protestant doctrines but also retained much Roman Catholic ritualism. Elizabeth's goal of an independent national church had been attained, with all content except extreme Protestants (the later Puritans) and extreme Roman Catholics.

With a more tolerant religious attitude, England became the home of religious refugees from less-tolerant parts of Europe. Many of these immigrants were skilled artisans who had a major effect on English industrial development, both by improving established trades and by introducing new ones.

Elizabeth sought to increase foreign trade, as recent military losses, such as at Calais in France in 1558, weakened existing trade. New trading companies were established, many of which were granted monopolies. In 1600, the British East India Company was chartered and controlled the colonization of India. These changes caused negative social changes, with a population shift from rural areas to urban centers.

The new prosperity paved the way for a cultural flowering, centered in London and marked by literary highlights. Poet Edmund Spenser led the way with his *Shepheard's Calendar* in 1579 and later with *Faerie Queene*. English drama came into its own, first with the works of Christopher Marlowe and then William Shakespeare. Although often chaotic and lacking in unity, Marlowe's plays did have originality and sometimes produced majestic effects, and they paved the way for Shakespeare.

Shakespeare's plays, beginning in the last years of Elizabeth's reign, are the most famous in English literature. They were performed in various theaters— including the first playhouse built for public performances, The Theatre—in or near London before the building of the Globe Theatre in 1599. The most significant period for Shakespeare, from 1593 to 1601, includes his best-known romantic comedies, such as *The Merchant of Venice* and *A Midsummer Night's Dream*.

Among the historical works of this period is *Actes and Monuments of These Later and Perillous Dayss* by John Foxe, the English version of which was published in London in 1563. Better known as *Foxe's Book of Martyrs*, this work tells the story of persecution and martyrdom throughout Church history, including the acts carried out under Queen Mary I.

For the future glory of England, the most significant

Elizabeth I being carried to Parliament. (R. S. Peale and J. A. Hill)

event of Elizabeth's reign was the English defeat of the Spanish Armada in 1588. To gain control of England following Elizabeth's rejection of his marriage proposal, King Philip II of Spain planned an invasion. His armada of more than 130 ships, 7,000 sailors, and 17,000 soldiers was thought to be invincible, especially after a planned addition of 17,000 soldiers in the Netherlands. Inexperienced leadership, slow speed, lack of firepower, and weather conditions soon removed the armada's invincible status.

After its initial encounter with the smaller, faster, and more maneuverable English ships, the armada pulled into the French port at Calais rather than the Dutch port at Flushing to pick up the additional soldiers. With a favorable wind, the English floated fireships into the port, forcing the disorganized Spanish ships back out into the English Channel, where they were battered by superior English firepower. One by one the great Spanish vessels sank beneath the waters of the Channel. The surviving and heavily damaged ships sought to travel home by sailing around Scotland and Ireland, where the "the Protestant wind," socalled by the English, damaged and sunk even more ships.

With this victory, England became the greatest naval power in the world. Sir Walter Ralegh, a favorite of Elizabeth, was a focal point in this victory. Although he built the *Ark Royal*, a huge ship that led the fleet against the Spanish, Ralegh himself was part of the coastal defenses and could only watch the English victory. However, in the aftermath he led privateers in capturing many Spanish ships that were bringing treasure from the New World.

Another of Elizabeth's favorites was Francis Drake, a true hero of the Spanish defeat. Drake also became a privateer, whose effectiveness earned him the nickname El Draque (the Dragon) by the Spanish. Drake had previously led the first English circumnavigation of the world (1577-1580). In doing so, he claimed part of what is now called the California coast for Elizabeth, although his exact place of landing is in dispute.

SIGNIFICANCE

The Elizabethan Settlement became the foundation for Anglican churches around the world, including the Episcopal Church in the United States and many African churches. The literary works of Spenser, Shakespeare, and others are among the world's best-known literary works.

Naval superiority after the defeat of the Spanish Armada made England the Mistress of the Seas, a title re-

Elizabeth I in the later years of her long reign. (R. S. Peale and J. A. Hill)

tained for three and a half centuries. Being an island nation, this was vital, both in protecting the nation and in helping it build a vast colonial empire.

—*Glenn L. Swygart*

FURTHER READING

Bucholz, Robert, and Newton Key. *Early Modern England: 1485-1714, A Narrative History.* Malden, Mass.: Blackwell, 2004. A detailed study of both the Tudor and Stuart monarchies of England. Chapters 4 and 5 provide in-depth analyses of the reign of Elizabeth I and chapter 6 summarizes the conditions in England at the time of her death in 1603.

Davies, Norman. *The Isles: A History.* New York: Oxford University Press, 1999. More of a cultural history of the British Isles, includes many references to the time of Elizabeth I. Color illustrations include a painting of the defeat of the Spanish Armada.

Guy, John, ed. *The Reign of Elizabeth I: Court and Culture in the Last Decade.* New York: Cambridge University Press, 1995. A collection of papers presented at a workshop in 1991. Topics cover royal patronage, ecclesiastical policy, social conditions, the cult of Elizabeth, and literature.

1550's

Levin, Carole. *"The Heart and Stomach of a King": Elizabeth I and the Politics of Sex and Power*. Philadelphia: University of Pennsylvania Press, 1994. A prize-winning study of Elizabeth I, which looks at the issues of women in power. Some illustrations.

Loades, David. *Elizabeth I*. New York: Hambledon and London, 2003. An interpretive biography of Elizabeth and her reign.

Walker, Julia M. *The Elizabeth Icon, 1603-2003*. New York: Palgrave Macmillian, 2004. A good analysis of the impact of Elizabeth on public opinion, literature, art, and history in general.

SEE ALSO: Beginning 1485: The Tudors Rule England; 16th century: Worldwide Inflation; Jan. 25-Feb. 7, 1554: Wyatt's Rebellion; May, 1559-Aug., 1561: Scottish Reformation; Apr. or May, 1560: Publication of the Geneva Bible; Jan., 1563: Thirty-nine Articles of the Church of England; Jan. 20, 1564: Peace of Troyes; Nov. 9, 1569: Rebellion of the Northern Earls; Feb. 25, 1570: Pius V Excommunicates Elizabeth I; 1576: James Burbage Builds The Theatre; July 26, 1581: The United Provinces Declare Independence from Spain; Apr., 1587-c. 1600: Anglo-Spanish War; Apr., 1587-c. 1600: Anglo-Spanish War; July 31-Aug. 8, 1588: Defeat of the Spanish Armada; c. 1589-1613: Shakespeare Writes His Dramas; Dec., 1598-May, 1599: The Globe Theatre Is Built; Dec. 31, 1600: Elizabeth I Charters the East India Company.

RELATED ARTICLES in *Great Lives from History: The Renaissance & Early Modern Era, 1454-1600:* William Cecil; Thomas Cranmer; Sir Francis Drake; Elizabeth I; Henry VIII; Christopher Marlowe; Mary I; Bernardino de Mendoza; Thomas Morley; Philip II; Sir Walter Ralegh; William Shakespeare; Edmund Spenser.

January 1-8, 1558
FRANCE REGAINS CALAIS FROM ENGLAND

François, duke of Guise, defeated the English to take possession of the northern French city of Calais, returning it to French hands for the first time in more than two hundred years. With the loss of Calais, England lost its last French territory.

LOCALE: Calais, France
CATEGORIES: Government and politics; expansion and land acquisition; wars, uprisings, and civil unrest

KEY FIGURES
Mary I (1516-1558), queen of England, r. 1553-1558
François, duke of Guise (1519-1563), second duke of Guise, 1550-1563, French Catholic general and statesman
Elizabeth I (1533-1603), queen of England, r. 1558-1603
Henry II (1519-1559), king of France, r. 1547-1559
Catherine de Médicis (1519-1589), queen of France, r. 1547-1559, and regent of France, r. 1560-1563

SUMMARY OF EVENT
In August, 1346, Edward III of England began a yearlong siege against the French seaport of Calais that ended with its capture in August, 1347. The acquisition of this seaport was part of Edward's broader campaign to defend his claim to the French province of Guienne (later called

Aquitaine), a campaign that marked the beginning of the Hundred Years' War between England and France (1337-1453). During this long war, various French territories shifted ownership back and forth several times, but by 1453, England had lost nearly all of its possessions in France, even Bordeaux, the capital of Aquitaine. On August 29, 1475, England signed the Peace of Picquigny and forfeited any future claims to Aquitaine or to the throne of France, but it was able to retain Calais. Despite the treaty, however, the English continued their attempts to acquire territory in France during the ensuing decades.

In the sixteenth century, during the early Tudor reign, Henry VIII once again attempted to gain French lands. Henry's 1512 campaign to recapture Aquitaine was a failure, but in 1544, he successfully took Boulogne. After the Treaty of Boulogne was signed on March 24, 1550, however, Henry was paid a ransom by the French king, Francis I, for the return of Boulogne; once again, Calais was the sole English remnant on French soil.

Calais spent more than two hundred years in English hands, but the French finally recaptured the port during the reign of Mary I, the Catholic daughter of Henry VIII and Catherine of Aragon. Having married her cousin, the future Philip II of Spain, in July, 1554, Mary was drawn into supporting her husband's Spanish Habsburg war against France. On June 7, 1557, she declared war against Henry II of France. In August, Philip was victorious at Saint-Quentin, and the acquisition of more French territory seemed imminent. However, Henry II and his military general, François de Lorraine, duke of Guise, were strategizing the final routing of the English from France.

The duke of Guise, one of the chief leaders of the Catholic party and the best soldier in France, arrived in secret with his army at Calais on New Year's Eve, 1557. Although Henry VIII had fortified Calais in 1539, it was now undermanned, underequipped, and undermaintained. Requests from Calais to Mary and her council for funds to repair the area and for more staffing had not seemed urgent. The English took their ownership of Calais for granted, since it was considered impregnable and, with their aversion to winter campaigns, did not foresee any imminent danger.

After a surprise eight-day attack from land and sea, the duke of Guise and his twenty-seven thousand troops captured the Calais Castle area from its eight-hundred-man garrison. By the end of the month, the entire 120-mile (193-kilometer) outlying area was securely in French hands. Ironically, Mary and her council were in the final process of sending help to Calais when the news reached them that it had fallen to the French: They were late by only a matter of days. In a humiliating defeat for the English, Mary signed away Calais in the Tapestry Room of Saint James's Place. According to a secondhand report from John Foxe, the chronicler of Mary's persecution of Protestant reformers, Mary had said that if they opened up her body they would find "Calais" lying in her heart.

Negotiations were still under way when Mary died in November of 1558. They ended on April 2, 1559, with the Treaty of Cateau-Cambrésis. Elizabeth I, the Protestant daughter of Henry VIII who had succeeded her half sister Mary, sought to regain Calais through the continuing negotiations. The terms of the treaty—primarily between the French and the Spanish—dictated that Henry II would restore Calais to England in eight years or pay 500,000 crowns. However, this term of the treaty was provisional: It would take effect only if Eliza-

French troops, led by François de Lorraine, duke of Guise, retake the northern French city of Calais from England, which had occupied the city since 1347. England thereby lost its last territory in France. (Hulton|Archive by Getty Images)

beth were to forgo territorial aggression both against France and against Scotland, whose queen, Mary, Queen of Scots, was the niece of the duke of Guise.

Despite the treaty and suspicious that the French would never return the city, Elizabeth continued to seek the return of Calais in a variety of ways. Its loss was seen as the result of Mary's ill-advised embrace of Catholic Spain, and Elizabeth wanted to restore the honor and glory of England as well as her father's legacy of ownership of Calais. In September, 1562, she signed the Treaty of Hampton Court with the French Huguenot leader, Louis I of Bourbon, prince of Condé. Elizabeth offered Bourbon troops and money for his planned uprising against the Catholic ruling party. She was given the port of Le Havre as a pledge for the return of Calais. However, the duke of Guise defeated the Huguenots at the Battle of Dreux in December of 1562, ending this attempt to regain Calais.

In April, 1564, according to the Peace of Troyes between Elizabeth and French regent Catherine de Médicis, the English not only had to restore Le Havre to France but also had to forfeit any claim either to Calais or to the promised payment for it. Always undaunted, Elizabeth—in her 1579-1581 discussions with Catherine about marriage to one of her sons, the duke of Alençon—made the return of Calais one of the points of the (unsuccessful) negotiations. Later, in 1596, when Philip II briefly captured Calais, Elizabeth offered France's Henry IV assistance in exchange for Calais, but her assistance was refused.

The loss of Calais in 1558, despite Elizabeth's myriad efforts over a period of almost forty years, proved to be a permanent loss for the English. It meant that—for the first time since 1066, when William the Conqueror ruled territory on both sides of the English Channel—the English had no foothold on the European continent.

SIGNIFICANCE

The recapture of Calais was a stunning blow to English pride and a patriotic triumph for the French. No matter how much territory had been won or lost in France during centuries of fighting, Calais had remained an English possession, much to the continued rancor of the French. For more than two centuries, England had possessed this area, only 26 miles (42 kilometers) southwest of Dover, which had been its gateway to the continent, its chief economic center for exporting raw wool, and a symbol of English rights to other French territories. On the French side, however, since its capture in 1347, Calais had become a cause. Forty years after its loss, the French poet Eustache Deschamps had penned a refrain taken up by the people that captured the feelings of the nation: "No peace until they give back Calais."

The loss of Calais by England and its return to France ended an era in English-French relations. Elizabeth implicitly recognized this shift in her later negotiations. She consistently requested Calais in exchange for something else, rather than asserting an inherent English right to possess the city. England ceased to be a continental power and instead continued the maritime expansion that it had begun under Henry VIII. France, after centuries of incursions and of foreign rule over various parts of the country, concentrated on becoming geographically whole and on dealing with its growing civil wars of religion. Centuries of English-French entanglement over

territorial disputes and claims to each other's thrones had finally come to an end.

—*Marsha Daigle-Williamson*

FURTHER READING

Dunne, Jane. *Elizabeth and Mary: Cousins, Rivals, Queens*. New York: Alfred A. Knopf, 2004. Relations between England, France, and Scotland during the reigns of Elizabeth and Mary, Queen of Scots, the niece of the duke of Guise.

Guy, John. *Tudor England*. New York: Oxford University Press, 1988. Tudor relations with France; some details of the battle at Calais; extensive footnotes and bibliography.

Knecht, Robert J. *Catherine de' Medici*. New York: Longman, 1998. French side of relations with England before and after the loss of Calais; bibliography, maps, genealogical tables, and index.

Prescott, H. F. M. *Mary Tudor*. New York: Macmillan, 1953. Chronological life of Mary I, with a very detailed, day-by-day account of the fall of Calais in chapter 21 and its aftermath in chapter 22.

Weir, Alison. *The Life of Elizabeth I*. New York: Ballantine Books, 1998. Account of the Elizabethan era, including ongoing attempts to regain Calais; genealogical tables, portraits of key figures, and extensive bibliography.

SEE ALSO: Aug. 29, 1475: Peace of Picquigny; June 5-24, 1520: Field of Cloth of Gold; Dec. 18, 1534: Act of Supremacy; 1544-1628: Anglo-French Wars; July, 1553: Coronation of Mary Tudor; 1555-1556: Charles V Abdicates; 1558-1603: Reign of Elizabeth I; Apr. 3, 1559: Treaty of Cateau-Cambrésis; Mar., 1562-May 2, 1598: French Wars of Religion; Jan. 20, 1564: Peace of Troyes; Apr., 1587-c. 1600: Anglo-Spanish War; Aug. 2, 1589: Henry IV Ascends the Throne of France.

RELATED ARTICLES in *Great Lives from History: The Renaissance & Early Modern Era, 1454-1600:* Catherine de Médicis; Elizabeth I; Francis I; Henry II; Henry IV; Henry VIII; Mary, Queen of Scots; Mary I; Philip II.

1559-1561
SÜLEYMAN'S SONS WAGE CIVIL WAR

Two of Süleyman's sons, Selim II and Bayezid, fought a violent civil war to decide who would become the next sultan of the Ottoman Empire. The often ineffective, cruel, and deadly practice of primogeniture—the crowning of the eldest son as monarch and the execution of his brothers—ended in the empire in the early seventeenth century.

LOCALE: Ottoman Empire

CATEGORIES: Government and politics; wars, uprisings, and civil unrest

KEY FIGURES

Süleyman the Magnificent (1494/1495-1566), Ottoman sultan, r. 1520-1566

Selim II (1524-1574), Ottoman sultan, r. 1566-1574, and son of Süleyman and Roxelana

Bayezid (1526-1561), son of Süleyman and Roxelana

Mustafa (1521?-1553), son of Süleyman and Gulbehar

Roxelana (Hürrem Sultana; c. 1510-1558), Selim's and Bayezid's mother

SUMMARY OF EVENT

From the mid-1400's until the early 1700's, succession to the Ottoman throne commonly was decided on the battlefield. When the reigning sultan died, all of his sons were eligible to succeed him. The son with the most powerful army would be installed as the new sultan. The other sons were then killed by strangulation.

Authorities on Muslim law, called *ʿulama*, approved the practice as the only effective way of preventing civil wars. Although the violent contest between brothers was not supposed to occur before the death of the reigning sultan, preparations usually began as soon as an aging sultan appeared to be in poor health.

In 1553, Süleyman the Magnificent, about sixty years old, had been suffering from gout and other chronic conditions. That year, when he ordered his troops to march against Persia, he stayed at home rather than lead the troops personally. This displeased the army. The grand vizier, Rustem, was appointed commander in chief of the campaign. Since Rustem was the son-in-law of Roxelana (also called Hürrem Sultana), Rustem had good reason to hope that one of her sons would be the next sultan. The major obstacle was Süleyman's favorite son, Mustafa, whose mother was one of Roxelana's rivals. After arriving in Persia, Rustem wrote Süleyman an explosive letter, warning that many leaders of the professional army corps, the Janissaries, wanted a young sultan as their commander and that Mustafa, who was popular with the army, had encouraged this sentiment.

Alarmed by the letter, Süleyman decided to go to Persia and assume personal command of the army. Even though Mustafa had been his favorite son, he decided that he could not risk the possibility that the ambitious young man might try to seize power or lead an armed revolt. After the empire's chief religious scholar, Ebussuûd Efendi, agreed that Mustafa's death was justified, Süleyman ordered his son to appear at court. As soon as he was in his father's presence, palace executioners strangled him with a bowstring. The body was then exposed to the soldiers as a warning against disloyalty. A few of Mustafa's allies among the Janissaries revolted, but Süleyman's loyal troops easily suppressed the uprisings.

With Mustafa dead, Roxelana's two sons, Selim and Bayezid, became the only two serious contenders for the succession. The older of the two, Selim, was described as obese, incompetent, and unpopular. The younger Bayezid was handsome, talented, and popular. Roxelana, nevertheless, preferred Selim and was determined that he would succeed his father as sultan. Most of the Janissaries preferred Bayezid because he would make a better commander, although Selim also had supporters in the army. Both brothers understood clearly that only one of them would become sultan and that the other would be killed. Since they despised each other, Süleyman kept them apart, appointing them governors of provinces that were widely separated.

In 1558, Roxelana unexpectedly died, and Süleyman was devastated. Increasingly ill, he appeared to have lost interest in political affairs, as he spent most of his days in mourning, praying, and fasting. Observing his health and behavior, Selim and Bayezid expected a soon-approaching struggle for succession. With Roxelana's restraining influence gone, the two brothers frantically attempted to make additional alliances and gather resources for a violent fight to the death. Both men had learned how to use bribes and promises of political appointment.

In the summer of 1559, civil war broke out in Anatolia. Despite Bayezid's advantage in popularity, Selim surprisingly managed to gather a more formidable military force and win a number of significant battles. Süleyman was extremely angry with both sons for fighting a war before his demise. He therefore prepared his troops to march into Anatolia to stop the fighting. Each of the sons wrote him a personal letter assuring him of undivided loyalty. Bayezid's letter, however, was intercepted and destroyed by one of Selim's agents. Bayezid, thinking the letter had been received, became alarmed when he did not get a reply. He knew that his popularity among the Janissaries might have aroused his father's suspicions. He had seen his father deal with Mustafa and others suspected of disloyalty. Bayezid soon received an impersonal and succinct order to appear at his father's court.

Frightened for his life, Bayezid fled to the Persian capital in desperation, where he requested Shah Ṭahmāsp I to grant him, his wife, and four of his sons political asylum. The request was quickly granted. The shah apparently thought that the royal family might somehow be useful in their continuing struggles with the Ottoman Empire. Because Süleyman interpreted Bayezid's flight as clear proof of treason, he unequivocally supported Selim for the succession.

Süleyman demanded that the shah's government either extradite Bayezid or execute him as a traitor. The Persian government first replied that this was impossible because of the principles of Muslim hospitality. After a long series of diplomatic exchanges, however, the Persians indicated that they might turn over Bayezid in exchange for territory in Mesopotamia. Initially, Süleyman refused, threatened to invade Persia if necessary, but then offered to pay 400,000 pieces of gold in exchange for the prince. Shah Ṭahmāsp accepted the offer.

The Persians escorted the unfortunate Bayezid to the frontier town of Tabrīz. On September 25, 1561, they turned him over to a small Turkish delegation that included the sultan's chief executioner. Knowing his fate, Bayezid asked for permission to kiss his wife and children one last time. A spokesperson for the delegation replied that there was no time and that they must attend to the business at hand. The executioner placed a bowstring around Bayezid's neck and strangled him. The executioner then strangled his four sons. Another son, a three-year-old, had been left behind with a nurse in the Mesopotamian city of Basra. This young child was soon found and executed, too. Süleyman reportedly gave thanks to Allah for ensuring a peaceful succession for Selim.

SIGNIFICANCE

In the contest between Bayezid and Selim, most historians believe that the less competent of the two brothers succeeded to the throne. Selim II, frequently called "Selim the Drunk," was the first of the disinterested Ottoman sultans. Addicted to alcohol and sexual pleasures,

he spent most of his time in his harem, and he was unable to impose his authority over the Janissaries. It was during his reign that the Ottomans suffered their first significant defeat, the naval Battle of Lepanto in 1571. It is impossible to know, of course, whether Bayezid would have been more successful as a ruler and military commander.

Succession in monarchical governments, the practice of primogeniture (automatically giving the crown to the eldest son), had the advantage of minimizing the threat of civil war, but, frequently, it could lead to the accession of an incompetent or otherwise ineffective monarch. Although this early Ottoman practice often produced a strong leader, violent civil war with great loss of life and property could also ensue.

In the early seventeenth century, the Ottoman rulers stopped the murderous competition for the throne. Rather than being put to death, the brothers of a new sultan would be imprisoned for life. Potential successors to the throne would no longer be appointed military governors of provinces as preparation for the fight over succession. Although the reform prevented civil war, it often produced weak and indolent rulers, considered one of the reasons for the gradual decline of the empire.

—Thomas Tandy Lewis

FURTHER READING

Bridge, Antony. *Suleiman the Magnificent: Scourge of Heaven*. New York: Franklin Watts, 1983. An interesting narrative account that includes a great deal of information about the human dimension of Süleyman and his times.

Goodwin, Jason. *Lords of the Horizons: A History of the Ottoman Empire*. New York: Henry Holt, 1998. A well-written history of the empire.

Lamb, Harold. *Suleiman the Magnificent: Sultan of the East*. Garden City: Doubleday, 1951. A readable work of historical fiction, with factual material based on sound research but conjectures of probable dialogue and thoughts of the subjects.

Merriman, Roger. *Suleiman the Magnificent, 1520-1566*. Cambridge, Mass.: Harvard University Press, 1944. Although somewhat dated, this biography is still recognized as a dependable and interesting sourcebook.

Rogers, J. M., and R. M. Ward. *Süleyman the Magnificent*. New York: Tabard Press, 1988. An excellent summary of his life, with an abundance of beautiful illustrations and a helpful glossary.

SEE ALSO: 1512-1520: Reign of Selim I; 1520-1566: Reign of Süleyman; 1534-1535: Ottomans Claim

Sovereignty over Mesopotamia; 1566-1574: Reign of Selim II; Oct. 7, 1571: Battle of Lepanto; 1574-1595: Reign of Murad III; 1589: Second Janissary Revolt in Constantinople.

RELATED ARTICLES in *Great Lives from History: The Renaissance & Early Modern Era, 1454-1600:* İbrahim Paşa; Süleyman the Magnificent.

April 3, 1559
TREATY OF CATEAU-CAMBRÉSIS

The Treaty of Cateau-Cambrésis ended decades of war between France and Spain and made Spain the preeminent power in the much-contested Italian peninsula. The treaty was sealed by a dynastic marriage between Spain's King Philip II and Elizabeth of Valois, the daughter of King Henry II of France.

LOCALE: Le Cateau, France
CATEGORIES: Diplomacy and international relations; wars, uprisings, and civil unrest; expansion and land acquisition

KEY FIGURES

Philip II (1527-1598), king of Spain, r. 1556-1598
Henry II (1519-1559), king of France, r. 1547-1559
Elizabeth I (1533-1603), queen of England, r. 1558-1603
Fernando Álvarez de Toledo (1507-1582), duke of
   Alva, Spanish commander of imperial forces in
   Italy, 1552-1559, and viceroy of Naples, 1556-1559
Lamoraal van Egmond (1522-1568), prince of Gavre,
   Flemish general and statesman
William the Silent (1533-1584), prince of Orange,
   r. 1544-1584, and count of Nassau, r. 1559-1584
Elizabeth of Valois (1545-1568), daughter of Henry II
   and queen of Spain, r. 1559-1568

SUMMARY OF EVENT

France and Spain were at war for much of the sixteenth century, a turbulent era that also saw the split of the universal Roman Church as a result of the Protestant Reformation. Europe's two great states—led by the Habsburg dynasty in Spain and the Valois of France—were confessionally united in their adherence to the Catholic faith, but they were divided in a power struggle over the Italian peninsula, which served as their unfortunate battleground. The Valois-Habsburg wars began with French king Charles VIII's invasion of Italy in 1494, and they continued, despite several temporary or abortive truces, for sixty-five years. The wars were disastrous for the Italian states, especially for Rome, which was sacked by the marauding troops of Holy Roman Emperor Charles V

(Charles I of Spain) in 1527. A lasting peace between the two powers finally came with the signing of the Treaty of Cateau-Cambrésis in 1559.

By the late 1550's, both the French and the Spanish sides were exhausted, almost bankrupt, and ready to negotiate a peace. Spain held the upper hand, and France was prepared to give up its claims in Italy. French king Henry II, however, stubbornly refused to cede Calais, a town in northern France that was also claimed by England. The situation was complicated by Spain's relationship to England through the marriage between the Spanish king, Philip II, and Queen Mary I of England. This relationship made it difficult if not impossible for Spain to cede Calais to England's sworn enemy. However, Mary's death in November of 1558 opened the possibility of negotiation.

Peace talks began in February of 1559. Representatives of Henry II, Philip II, and Elizabeth I, the new queen of England, met at the château of Le Cateau-Cambrésis in the north of France. Philip was represented by the Spanish general Fernando Álvarez de Toledo, duke of Alva, and by two noblemen from the Netherlands, the prince of Orange, William the Silent, and Count Lamoraal van Egmond. These three men would later find themselves at bloody odds in the bitter struggle over Spanish possession of the Netherlands, with the duke of Alva responsible for the execution of Egmond in 1568—events immortalized in Johann Wolfgang von Goethe's play *Egmont* (pb. 1788, pr. 1789; English translation, 1837).

After several difficult months of negotiations, which often seemed destined to fail, the Treaty of Cateau-Cambrésis was officially signed on April 3, 1559. In actuality, there were two treaties: one between England and France, signed on April 2, and one between France and Spain, signed on April 3. The difficult issue of Calais was resolved in favor of the French, who won control of the town for eight years. (Eight years later, France would refuse to give it up.) France also won permanent possession of three bishoprics in northeastern France—Metz, Toul, and Verdun—which played a key role in the bor-

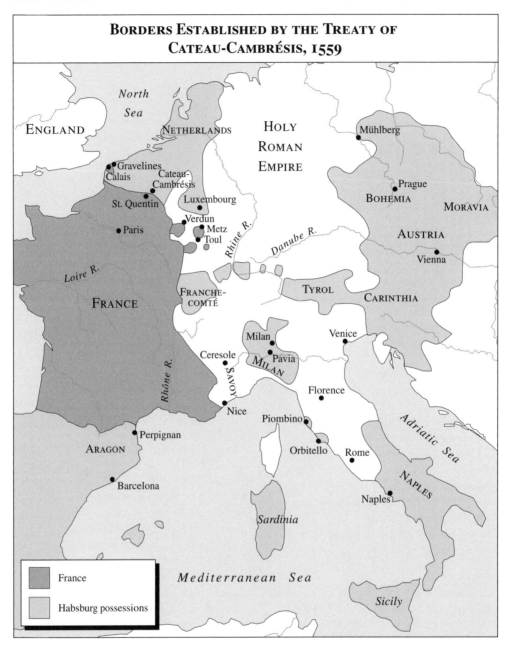

BORDERS ESTABLISHED BY THE TREATY OF CATEAU-CAMBRÉSIS, 1559

der area between France and the Holy Roman Empire.

The Spanish gains were even more significant. Without surrendering any territory himself, Philip II won formal recognition of Spanish possessions in the Low Countries and in Italy, including Naples and Milan. With a few minor exceptions, France agreed to withdraw entirely from the Piedmont region (the rich northwestern area of Italy that shares a border with France). The treaty in effect gave Spain control of Italy, with holdings in Sic-

ily and Sardinia, Naples, and Milan. Florence and Sienna were also beholden to Spain, leaving the Republic of Venice alone as an independent Italian state.

The Treaty of Cateau-Cambrésis also resolved the fate of Savoy, the contested Alpine region of eastern France. The duchy of Savoy had been taken over by the French and its duke, Carlo III, deposed in 1544. The Treaty of Cateau-Cambrésis restored to power the expelled duke's son, Emmanuel Filibert, and it also made provision for the restored duke of Savoy to marry Margaret, the sister of the French king.

A marriage between Philip II of Spain and Elizabeth of Valois, the daughter of Henry II of France, sealed the Treaty of Cateau-Cambrésis. The wedding took place shortly after the negotiations had been concluded, in a ceremony at the cathedral of Notre Dame in Paris. Philip's representative, the duke of Alva, stood in for the Spanish king, who was in Flanders at the time. This marriage made Elizabeth of Valois the queen of Spain; she would die in childbirth in 1568.

Celebrating the peace and the dynastic marriage with a jousting tournament, King Henry II of France suffered a fatal lance wound to the eye and died on July 10, 1559. He was succeeded by his son Francis II, fifteen years old at the time, whose short reign (1559-1560) would leave France embroiled in civil wars for the next four decades. Philip II lived on to the end of the century, and on May 2, 1598, he ratified the terms of the Treaty of Cateau-Cambrésis with the Treaty of Vervins. Philip II died later that year, passing the throne to his son, Philip III, whose ineffectual rule through his favorite, the duke of Lerma, would leave Spain in tatters.

SIGNIFICANCE

The Treaty of Cateau-Cambrésis, which brought peace to the continent by resolving hostilities between the great clashing dynasties of the Habsburgs and Valois, was one of the most important treaties in European history. Its great success was in leaving both parties satisfied, and its territorial settlements remained in place until the even more decisive Peace of Westphalia ended the Thirty Years' War in 1648.

In addition to ending the wars in Italy and solidifying the Spanish presence there, the Treaty of Cateau-Cambrésis marked a shift in the Spanish Empire away from the continental focus of Philip II's father, Holy Roman Emperor Charles V, and toward a more Atlantic-focused empire based on Spain's holdings in the Americas. France, on the other hand, turned inward, as it was

French king Henry II is wounded in a joust the year of the treaty between France and Spain, which ended decades of war between the two countries. (Frederick Ungar Publishing Co.)

embroiled in the terrible Wars of Religion that ravaged the country until the Edict of Nantes was signed by Henry IV in 1598.

—Amanda Wunder

FURTHER READING

Baumgartner, Frederic J. *Henry II: King of France, 1547-1559.* Durham, N.C.: Duke University Press, 1988. A political biography of Henry II and his brief reign. Maps; some illustrations.

Kamen, Henry. *Empire: How Spain Became a World Power, 1492-1763.* New York: HarperCollins, 2003. Survey of Spain's rise and fall as a global imperial power.

Koenigsberger, H. G., George L. Mosse, and G. Q. Bowler. *Europe in the Sixteenth Century.* 2d ed. London: Longman, 1989. A general introduction to Europe in the sixteenth century. With recommended readings on various topics. Maps, genealogical charts, chronology.

Levin, Carole. *"The Heart and Stomach of a King": Elizabeth I and the Politics of Sex and Power.* Philadelphia: University of Pennsylvania Press, 1994. Prize-winning study of Elizabeth I, focusing on the special problems and issues that confronted a woman in power. Some illustrations.

Mattingly, Garrett. *Renaissance Diplomacy.* New York: Dover, 1988. Classic study of diplomatic history from the fifteenth to the seventeenth centuries. Chapters on sixteenth century diplomacy focus on Franco-Spanish relations.

Parker, Geoffrey. *The Grand Strategy of Philip II.* New Haven, Conn.: Yale University Press, 1998. Biography of the Spanish king that seeks to discover whether or not Philip II had a grand strategy with which he governed his global empire. Illustrations; extensive chronology of events.

SEE ALSO: July 16, 1465-Apr., 1559: French-Burgundian and French-Austrian Wars; Aug. 17, 1477: Foundation of the Habsburg Dynasty; Sept., 1494-Oct., 1495: Charles VIII of France Invades Italy; September 22, 1504: Treaty of Blois; 1508: Formation of the League of Cambrai; Aug. 18, 1516: Concordat of Bologna; 1521-1559: Valois-Habsburg Wars; May 6, 1527-Feb., 1528: Sack of Rome; July, 1553: Coronation of Mary Tudor; Jan. 1-8, 1558: France Regains Calais from England; Mar., 1562-May 2, 1598: French Wars of Religion; Apr. 13, 1598: Edict of Nantes; May 2, 1598: Treaty of Vervins.

RELATED ARTICLES in *Great Lives from History: The Renaissance & Early Modern Era, 1454-1600:* Charles V; Charles VIII; Elizabeth I; Henry II; Henry IV; Mary I; Philip II; William the Silent.

May, 1559-August, 1561
SCOTTISH REFORMATION

The Scottish Reformation solidified the hold of Protestantism on Britain and established the Presbyterian Kirk as the national church of Scotland.

LOCALE: Scotland

CATEGORIES: Religion; organizations and institutions; social reform

KEY FIGURES

John Knox (c. 1514-1572), leader of Scottish Protestant reformers

Mary of Guise (1515-1560), queen regent of Scotland, r. 1554-1560

John Calvin (1509-1564), Protestant reformer and mentor of John Knox

Archibald Campbell (1530-1573), fifth earl of Argyll, 1558-1573, later Lord High Chancellor of Scotland, 1572-1573

John Erskine of Dun (1509-1591), superintendent of the Reformed Church of Scotland for Angus and Mearns, 1560-1589

James Stewart (c. 1531-1570), earl of Moray, 1544-1570, half brother and primary minister of Mary, Queen of Scots, 1561-1565, later regent of Scotland, r. 1567-1570

Mary Stuart (1542-1587), queen of Scotland, r. 1542-1567

Elizabeth I (1533-1603), queen of England, r. 1558-1603

SUMMARY OF EVENT

The Scottish Reformation transformed the nature and character of politics, society, and worship in Scotland. This transformation was not without its antecedents. Since the 1530's, the need for religious reformation had been apparent among leaders in the kirk (church). Initially the call for change came from within the kirk, but by 1540, Protestant preachers such as George Wishart were calling for separation from the Roman Catholic Church and a faith that was based on the Bible. John Knox, who would later be the chief catalyst of the Reformation in Scotland, converted to Protestantism in 1543. Still, the number of Scottish Protestants was small. To the majority of Scots, the kirk seemed distant, and they were apathetic toward religious matters.

Church reform was also hindered by political instability. In 1542, James V was murdered, and his infant daughter, Mary, Queen of Scots, ascended to the throne. In 1554, Mary of Guise became regent of Scotland, replacing the earl of Arran. Mary of Guise realized that Scottish independence was threatened by Protestant England. To strengthen her authority, she renewed Scotland's traditional alliance with France. Her overtures toward the French and her increasing intolerance toward Protestants frightened several leading Scottish nobles, including Archibald Campbell, James Stewart, and John Erskine of Dun. In 1557, these nobles founded the Lords of the Congregation, whose dual aim was to reform the kirk and to extricate Scotland from the influence of Catholic France.

Many other nobles and important clergy sided with the queen regent and the Catholic Church, however. In April, 1558, Mary of Guise succeeded in allying Scotland and France through the marriage of Mary, Queen of Scots to the French dauphin, Francis. In November, the Scottish parliament agreed that Francis would become king of Scotland through marriage. With French support secured, the regent began to move against the Lords of the Congregation in 1559. Simultaneously, the Lords of the Congregation tried to form an alliance with the English and their new Protestant queen, Elizabeth I. They also helped John Knox to return to Scotland from Geneva in May, 1559.

Knox had been in Geneva since 1554. While in the Swiss city, he had come under the influence of John Calvin. Calvin helped Knox to develop most of his theology. Knox modeled his style of worship, his emphasis on the Bible, and his Presbyterian style of church government on what he had seen in Calvin's Geneva. What separated Knox from Calvin was his doctrine of "righteous rebellion." Calvin believed that Protestants could disobey an unjust (usually Catholic) ruler, but Knox argued that it was the duty of righteous subjects actively and, if necessary, violently to depose an evil monarch. To allow an ungodly ruler to stay in power would invite God's judgment on the nation.

The Lords of the Congregation were uneasy about Knox's resistance theory, but they understood that the

Scottish Protestants needed a leader. When Knox returned to Scotland in 1559, his preaching and that of other Protestants sparked armed rebellions. For instance, at Perth, in eastern Scotland, a Knox sermon incited a riot that destroyed Catholic images and altars. Armed conflict was limited and revolved around the capital in Edinburgh. Between May and October, Protestant ministers were appointed to positions in several leading towns, including St. Andrews, Ayr, Dundee, and Perth. Knox became the minister of Saint Giles's Cathedral in Edinburgh. Despite these successes, however, Protestants remained a minority, and Mary of Guise still had French troops at her disposal. Also, in several locales the addition of a Protestant minister did not signal the deposition of his Catholic counterpart. Often, both priest and minister served the same congregation.

In October, the Lords of the Congregation suspended the queen regent, but this legal move lacked political force. The necessary force to neutralize Mary was provided by Elizabeth I and an English army in March, 1560, when they besieged Leith in southern Scotland. In June, Mary died, and French support for Catholics in Scotland began to wane. The French and English signed the Treaty of Leith in July, in which both armies agreed to withdraw from Scottish territory. Viewed as God's hand at work by the reformers, this treaty removed effective political resistance to Protestantism. On August 1, the Reformation Parliament convened in Edinburgh. This group of one hundred Scottish lairds (nobles) outlawed the Mass, abolished the pope's jurisdiction in Scotland, and ratified the Scots Confession. What the Parliament did not do was depose Catholic office holders or provide for the upkeep of a Protestant clergy. The thorny issue of how to finance the reformed kirk was left up to the first General Assembly of the new kirk in December, 1560.

In the same month, Francis I died, ensuring that a French monarch would not sit on the Scottish throne. The period between the General Assembly of December, 1560, and the return of Mary, Queen of Scots to Scotland in August, 1561, was crucial to the foundation of a reformed kirk. The political obstacles for Protestantism were gone, but the kirk lacked cohesion. During this time, Knox and other reformers drew up the *First Book of Discipline* (1560). This document defined the doctrine of the new kirk. Whereas the Reformation Parliament had negated the old faith, the *First Book of Discipline* defined the new kirk without condemning the Catholic Church. This document was only a preliminary step in formulating the doctrine of the new kirk, but it was to provide a starting point for future statements of faith.

1550's

SIGNIFICANCE

From August, 1561, until Mary, Queen of Scots, was deposed in 1567, the reformed kirk was severely tested. Mary was a Catholic but did not have enough support in Scotland to reverse the Reformation. Knox disliked Mary strongly, and she had no love for him. Their "interviews" usually consisted of Knox's condemnation of Mary's Catholicism and Mary's refusal to change. Eventually, Knox called for Mary's assassination as an unrighteous ruler. Mary would have withstood Knox's attacks if she had been able to gain the support of the Scottish nobility, but they rejected her authority because of her close ties with France and her attempt to marry the son of Philip II of Spain. Her foreign allies and her scandalous private life made Mary increasing unpopular. Her unpopularity combined with civil strife between Catholics and Protestants eventually led to Mary's downfall and her exile in England.

By 1603, the reformed kirk had solidified its position in Scotland. During the forty-two years between 1561 and 1603, the crucial issues left hanging by the Reformation Parliament and the *First Book of Discipline* were largely resolved. The Protestant clergy was financed, the system of kirk government became Presbyterian, and the authority of the kirk in ecclesiastical matters was established. These positive consequences were not the only fruit of the Reformation. Knox's idea of "righteous rebellion" was expanded by later thinkers such as Andrew Melville, George Buchanan, and Samuel Rutherford. The idea that the righteous should resist an unrighteous ruler created strife between the kirk and the king. Mary's son, James VI, was able to dominate the kirk and keep order. This tension, however, boiled over in 1637, when James's son, Charles I, attempted to impose a new liturgy in Scotland. The resulting wars between Charles and his Scottish subjects destabilized Charles's government and pushed England into civil war.

—*John McDonnell Hintermaier*

FURTHER READING

Cameron, Nigel M. de S., David F. Wright, Donald Lachman, and Donald Meek, eds. *Dictionary of Scottish Church History and Theology*. Downers Grove, Ill.: InterVarsity Press, 1993. An extensive survey of Scottish church history from its beginnings to the late twentieth century. Contains a large section on the Reformation.

Cowan, Ian B. *The Scottish Reformation: Church and Society in Sixteenth-Century Scotland*. New York: St. Martin's Press, 1982. A study of the Scottish church and its relationship to society before, during, and after the Reformation.

Donaldson, Gordon. *The Scottish Reformation*. Cambridge, England: Cambridge University Press, 1960. An older but still insightful work written by the preeminent Scottish historian of the second half of the twentieth century.

Dunn, Jane. *Elizabeth and Mary: Cousins, Rivals, Queens*. New York: Alfred A. Knopf, 2004. Study of the rivalry and political intrigue between Elizabeth I and Mary, Queen of Scots, attempting to portray the private emotions behind their public acts. Includes photographic plates, illustrations, bibliographic references, index.

Graham, Roderick. *John Knox: Democrat*. London: R. Hale, 2001. Comprehensive if laudatory biography that seeks to defend Knox from modern charges of misogyny. Includes illustrations, bibliographic references, and index.

Guy, John. *Queen of Scots: The True Life of Mary Stuart*. Boston: Houghton Mifflin, 2004. Exhaustive reexamination of Mary's life and rule, attempting to rejuvenate her reputation somewhat by blaming her fall on the plots and intrigues of those around her. Reads correspondence usually used to condemn Mary in a different way to show how it may actually enhance history's judgment of her. Includes photographic plates, illustrations, maps, bibliographic references, and index.

Kellar, Clare. *Scotland, England, and the Reformation, 1534-61*. New York: Oxford University Press, 2003. Argues that, contrary to the general belief, the Scottish and English Reformations were thoroughly intertwined. Includes bibliographic references and index.

Kirk, James. *Continuity and Change in the Reformation Kirk*. Edinburgh: T. & T. Clark, 1989. Representative of the changing interpretation of the Reformation, this study emphasizes the similarities that existed between the pre- and post-Reformation kirk.

Kyle, Richard G. *The Mind of John Knox*. Lawrence, Kans.: Coronado Press, 1984. An intellectual historian examines Knox's thought on the kirk, politics, and theology drawn from his writings.

Marshall, Rosalind K. *John Knox*. Edinburgh: Birlinn, 2000. A portrait both of Knox and of the Scotland in which he lived, this study seeks to separate myth from reality to capture the complexities of his life and career. Includes illustrations, map, bibliographic references, and index.

Merriman, Marcus. *The Rough Wooings: Mary Queen of Scots, 1542-1551*. East Linton, East Lothian, Scotland: Tuckwell, 2000. Study of Mary's childhood and her early efforts to preserve Scottish autonomy from England by marrying France's Francis I.

Wormald, Jenny. *Court, Kirk, and Community: Scotland 1470-1625.* Toronto: University of Toronto Press, 1981. A broad treatment of Scottish history that argues that the Reformation was neither inevitable nor complete.

SEE ALSO: Aug. 22, 1513-July 6, 1560: Anglo-Scottish Wars; Oct. 31, 1517: Luther Posts His Ninety-five Theses; Dec. 18, 1534: Act of Supremacy; July, 1535-

Mar., 1540: Henry VIII Dissolves the Monasteries; Oct., 1536-June, 1537: Pilgrimage of Grace; May, 1539: Six Articles of Henry VIII; Feb. 27, 1545: Battle of Ancrum Moor; July, 1553: Coronation of Mary Tudor; 1558-1603: Reign of Elizabeth I; Jan., 1563: Thirty-nine Articles of the Church of England; July 29, 1567: James VI Becomes King of Scotland; Feb. 25, 1570: Pius V Excommunicates Elizabeth I.

RELATED ARTICLES in *Great Lives from History: The Renaissance & Early Modern Era, 1454-1600:* John Calvin; Elizabeth I; John Knox; Mary, Queen of Scots; Mary of Guise; Philip II.

c. 1560's
INVENTION OF THE "LEAD" PENCIL

The lead pencil, which made writing, drawing, and other forms of marking easier and more permanent, readable, and otherwise discernible, was invented after a large graphite deposit was unearthed in rural England.

LOCALE: Seatoller Fell near Keswick, northwest England

CATEGORIES: Science and technology; cultural and intellectual history; communications; inventions

KEY FIGURES
Conrad Gesner (1516-1565), German-Swiss physician and naturalist often credited with the invention of the pencil
Andrea Cesalpino (1525-1603), Italian physiologist and botanist who wrote about a writing substance called "Borrowdale lead"
Elizabeth I (1533-1603), queen of England, r. 1558-1603, who brought Germans to Cumberland to mine various ores

SUMMARY OF EVENT
Before the advent of the lead, or graphite, pencil, writing without ink was accomplished either with a metallic lead stylus—hence the term "lead" applied to the similar-looking graphite pencil—or with a pencil brush made of animal hairs. The lead stylus left a faint, hard-to-read impression, and the pencil brush made a dry and much darker impression, giving it the qualities that characterize contemporary pencils. The brush's impression wore out quickly, though, limiting its practicality and usefulness.

The word "pencil" is derived from the Latin *penicillus,* a variant form of the Latin word *penis,* meaning

tail. The *penicillus* was made by pushing small bundles of fine animal hair, usually from the tail of the animal, into a hollow cylinder.

Pencils were developed not because their inventors set out to create a form that resembled the brushes used by the Romans, but rather because graphite deposits in England provided a raw material that was effective for writing. These instruments, once created, looked enough like the Roman writing instruments that they were named for them, which lead to the misnomer "lead" in lead pencil.

The material from which the earliest pencils were made has been variously called *wadd, wadt, kellow, killow, Borrowdale lead,* and *black lead.* Legend relates that shepherds in the English county of Cumberland, in what is generally referred to as the Lake District, first came upon the mineral when a large tree was uprooted by a storm, exposing the graphite, or plumbago, beneath it.

People in the area did not know how to classify the substance, which they had never before encountered. The substance was not malleable like most metals. It certainly could not be classified as a stone because it was not hard. People began to use pieces of it wrapped in paper, string, or vines for both writing and drawing. Indeed, the term "graphite," by which the substance is known today, is derived from the Greek word for writing, *graphein,* although the substance was not named graphite until late in the eighteenth century. As late as the nineteenth century, in some parts of England, pencils were still referred to as *vines,* indicating the material in which graphite was once wrapped.

Those who used the new mineral valued it because it was much easier than a quill pen to write with. Also, the mineral left a dark, readable impression, yet it could also be rubbed out easily.

In 1565, Queen Elizabeth I imported workers from Germany to Cumberland County to mine the county's minerals, including plumbago or graphite in the Borrowdale mines. Numerous uses were found for what was called *wadd*, which was generally used by wrapping cylindrical pieces of graphite in string or vines so that people writing or drawing with it would not soil their fingers. These pieces of *wadd* wrapped in this way were the earliest, primitive pencils.

In 1565, Swiss-German physiologist and naturalist Conrad Gesner, who is often credited with inventing the pencil, published his most significant book, *De rerum fossilium, lapidum, et gemmarum maximè, figuris et similitudinibus liber* (on the shapes and resemblances of fossils, stones, and gems). In it, he wrote about, among other things, the amazing substance that had been found in Cumberland County and about its uses in writing and, more particularly, in drawing. He did take credit for inventing the pencil, however, but some later scholars have attributed its invention to him.

The Italian botanist Andrea Cesalpino wrote about the substance in *De metallicis libri tres* (1602; three books on metals), calling it "Borrowdale lead" after the area where it was mined. He claimed that a similar substance found in Germany was called bismuth. Cesalpino compared Borrowdale lead to molybdenum, saying that it felt slippery and stained the hands of those who touched it. He also noted that artists used thin sticks of the substance, inserted into small tubes, but not in the wooden "tubes," or casings, that distinguish modern pencils.

The earliest wooden casings appeared in the early seventeenth century. People grew frustrated using *wadd* the way it had been devised earlier, so they came up with ways to stabilize the *wadd* by gluing it to wood in which a groove had been carved and then by placing a corresponding piece of wood on top and either gluing it to the lower piece or binding it tightly with string or metal. This earlier sort of pencil required frequent sharpening, but writers and artists, who had grown used to sharpening quills for writing and drawing, had no difficulty trimming the points of pencils as necessary.

According to legend, an unidentified Keswick joiner working in the late sixteenth and early seventeenth centuries was a pioneer in encasing rods of *wadd* in wood. He manufactured and sold such pencils, some of them bought by people who gave them as valued gifts to their friends. By 1662, pencil making was recognized by the carpenters' guild of Nuremberg, Germany, as an area of

Miners were brought to England from Germany to dig for the mineral later called graphite, a newfound substance used for writing and drawing. Graphite was appealing because it left a dark and readable—yet erasable—impression. (R. S. Peale and J. A. Hill)

specialization. Pencil makers soon became members of the carpenters' guild. Such recognition was essential to marketing their product.

The earliest pencils were made from plumbago, also know as lead, or from similar substances, usually mixed with clay to stabilize them. As pencils came to be encased in wooden cylinders, the cylinders were painted, generally in yellow, with lead-based paints. Modern pencils, however, contain no lead, either in the substance encased in the wooden cylinder or in the paint used to decorate it. Modern pencils do not differ much from earlier kinds. Wood, often cedar, is grooved lengthwise and laid flat. The writing compound is then placed in the groove, after which another strip of wood is placed on the lower strip and glued in place.

SIGNIFICANCE

The development of the pencil lent a flexibility to writing that had never been seen. Before the time of the pencil, writing was a tedious process that involved using a metallic stylus, whose marks were almost too light to read, or sharpening goose quills that often became dull. Also, writing with ink was permanent, whereas marks made by pencils could be expunged easily.

Pencils were well developed by the early nineteenth century when John Thoreau (1787-1859), father of Henry David Thoreau, became one of the earliest pencil manufacturers in the United States. Henry worked in his father's pencil factory and also traveled with his father to other cities marketing their product.

Heated political debate occurred when pencil manufacturers had to decide whether to put erasers on the ends of their pencils. Some outraged purists argued that to do so would encourage sloppiness because, with erasers, people would write carelessly and then expunge what they had written.

—*R. Baird Shuman*

FURTHER READING

Atkin, William K., Raneiro Corbelletti, and Vincent R. Fiore. *Pencil Techniques in Modern Design*. New York: Reinhold, 1953. The authors consider some of the more important uses of the pencil historically and delve briefly into its early development.

Basalla, George. *The Evolution of Technology*. New York: Cambridge University Press, 1988. In this overall view of how various technologies have evolved, Basalla gives passing attention to the invention of the pencil as a new technology in the sixteenth century.

Ecenbarger, William. "What's Portable, Chewable, Doesn't Leak, and Is Recommended by Ann Landers?" *Philadelphia Inquirer Magazine* (June 16, 1985): 14-19. A popular essay on the pencil that offers some insights into its history and development.

Lefebure, Molly. *Cumberland Heritage*. London: Arrow Books, 1974. The author writes about the area in which the great graphite deposits were first found around Seatoller Fell and of how they led to the early manufacture of pencils.

Petroski, Henry. *The Pencil: A History of Design and Circumstance*. New York: Alfred A. Knopf, 2003. Originally published in 1989, this is the quintessential book on the history of the pencil. Well written and exhaustive, it is essential (and highly pleasurable) reading for anyone seriously interested not only in the invention of the pencil but also in the history of writing technology, communications, and design.

Ritter, Steve. "What's That Stuff? Pencils and Pencil Lead." *Science & Technology* 79, no. 42 (October 15, 2001). A brief, easy-to-read article on the composition of the lead pencil and the history of the lead pencil in general.

SEE ALSO: c. 1478-1519: Leonardo da Vinci Compiles His Notebooks; c. 1510: Invention of the Watch; 1517: Fracastoro Develops His Theory of Fossils.

RELATED ARTICLES in *Great Lives from History: The Renaissance & Early Modern Era, 1454-1600:* Andrea Cesalpino; Conrad Gesner.

April or May, 1560
PUBLICATION OF THE GENEVA BIBLE

The Geneva Bible was a masterpiece of Humanist and Reformation scholarship, the people's Bible of late seventeenth century England and the Bible that shaped the literary imaginations of Edmund Spenser, William Shakespeare, and John Milton.

LOCALE: Geneva, Switzerland

CATEGORIES: Religion; literature; cultural and intellectual history

KEY FIGURES

William Whittingham (c. 1524-1579), general editor of the Geneva Bible

John Calvin (1509-1564), Genevan Reformer and biblical commentator

Theodore Beza (1519-1605), New Testament scholar and first rector of the Geneva academy

Henry VIII (1491-1547), king of England, r. 1509-1547

Edward VI (1537-1553), king of England, r. 1547-1553

Mary I (1516-1558), queen of England, r. 1553-1558

Elizabeth I (1533-1603), queen of England, r. 1558-1603

SUMMARY OF EVENT

The Geneva Bible is a symbol of the religious and cultural transformation of England in the sixteenth century. In England, as on the European continent, the critical philology of Renaissance Humanism, the spread of the printing press, and the Reformation doctrine of *sola Scriptura* (religious truth contained in Scripture alone)

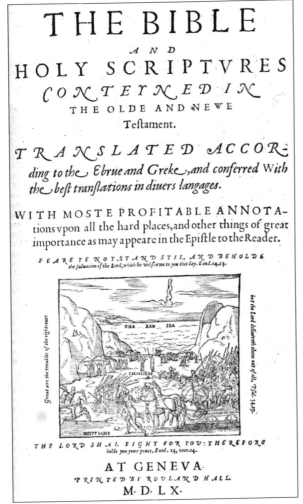

Facsimile of the title page of the Geneva Bible (1560). (University of Wisconsin Press)

all fed demand for new vernacular translations of the Bible. In the 1520's, William Tyndale completed a translation of the New Testament into English and began work on the historical books of the Old Testament. Initially, Henry VIII prohibited the printing of Tyndale's translations in England, with the result that the first printed edition of the New Testament in English was published in the German city of Worms. The king's subsequent break with Rome soon opened the door to a Bible revolution, however.

Following the 1534 Act of Supremacy, Henry VIII's chief minister, Thomas Cromwell, and archbishop of Canterbury Thomas Cranmer legalized and promoted biblical translations. In 1535, Miles Coverdale produced the first English translation of the entire Bible; in 1537,

Tyndale's associate John Rogers produced a second complete edition (under the name Thomas Matthew); and in 1539, Coverdale published a revision of this so-called Matthew's Bible, which became known, because of its unwieldy size, as the Great Bible. Finally, in 1541, Henry VIII decreed that there be an English Bible in each parish church. During the brief reign of Edward VI, the government reaffirmed this decree and removed nearly all restrictions on English translations of the Bible. A veritable profusion of new editions of the Tyndale and Coverdale translations greeted the publication of the Book of Common Prayer in English in 1549.

With the accession of the Roman Catholic queen Mary I in July of 1553, the Bible revolution of the reigns of Henry VIII and Edward VI confronted the Counter-Reformation. The publication of translations ceased and English Bibles were removed from parish churches. Increasing Protestant resistance soon led to increasing numbers of arrests and eventually the execution of more than three hundred Protestant church leaders, including Thomas Cranmer and John Rogers, the compiler of Matthew's Bible.

Faced with mounting persecution, a group of gifted Protestant biblical scholars from Oxford and Cambridge—led by William Whittingham and including the Hebraist Anthony Gilby—joined the Scottish Reformer John Knox in the Swiss city of Geneva. Here they found John Calvin at work on his Old and New Testament commentaries and overseeing a revision of the French Bible. Here, too, they found Theodore Beza, perhaps the preeminent Protestant scholar of the Greek New Testament at that time. In 1559, the establishment of the Geneva Academy, with Beza as its first rector, secured the city's position as a European center of biblical scholarship and translation.

Already, in 1557, Whittingham had finished a revision of the John Rogers edition of Tyndale's New Testament. The same year, there appeared a translation of Psalms—sometimes attributed to Gilby—for English exile congregations to use in worship. The death of Mary I in November, 1558, and the willingness of her successor, Elizabeth I, once again to allow translations encouraged efforts to create a standard household Bible for Protestant England. With the support of Calvin and Beza and with financial help from the wealthy merchant John Bodley (whose son Thomas would later found Oxford's Bodleian Library), Whittingham, Gilby, and a small group of "godly and learned brethren" remained in Geneva and completed their translation of the entire Bible. Sometime between April 10, 1560, the date of the preface, and May 30, 1560, the date Whittingham left

Geneva to return to England, the printer Rowland Hall, another Marian exile, published the first complete English Geneva Bible.

Whittingham's work was aptly named: One of its great achievements was to have enriched the English experience of reading Scripture with the Genevan Reformation of the Bible. The Geneva Bible's five maps and the twenty-six woodcut illustrations are the work's most obvious debts to its French predecessors. Like the French Geneva Bibles, the Bible that Whittingham produced used a roman font for greater clarity, divided the text into verses, and used italics where English syntax required the interpolation of words into the translation. Also like the French Geneva Bibles, the Bible that Whittingham and his colleagues produced enveloped the text with book and chapter summaries (or "arguments"), page headings, alternative literal translations, and a variety of historical and textual notes.

This elaborate textual apparatus allowed Whittingham and his colleagues to provide a more faithful translation of Old Testament Hebrew, even as they strove to make the text more accessible to the nonspecialist reader. Indeed, the Geneva Bible provided the first translation of the poetic and prophetic books of the Old Testament directly into English (and not, as in Coverdale's Bible, through the intermediary of the Latin Vulgate). The elaborate apparatus also allowed the Geneva Bible to extend significantly the scope of concordances. Most important, the apparatus had an edifying function. It encouraged readers to move back and forth between the literal sense and the theological meaning of the text. In effect, it made them active participants in a community of interpretation.

Although the Geneva Bible would ultimately prove far more popular than its predecessors, it was met with initial resistance. While John Bodley received a patent to print the Geneva Bible in England, that patent was subject to the approval of the archbishop of Canterbury, Matthew Parker. Parker, however, was already busy commissioning a Bishops' Bible intended to serve a moderate Elizabethan religious settlement. Thus, from 1560 to 1575, the Geneva Bible was printed only in Geneva and the accepted English Bible remained the parish church's large folio volume of either the older Great Bible or the new Bishops' Bible.

SIGNIFICANCE

With the death of Matthew Parker in 1575, the primary obstacle to publication of the Geneva Bible in England was eliminated. Handy and relatively inexpensive quarto editions of the Geneva Bible began to be printed in Lon-

don. Over the next ten years alone, there were twenty editions of the Geneva Bible. In all between 1560 and 1611, a Geneva Bible that never received formal authorization would go through more than 120 editions, compared with a mere 7 editions for the Great Bible and 22 editions of the Bishops' Bible. In sum, Whittingham and his associates had succeeded in creating a family Bible that popularized and secured the Reformation in England. It was from this "people's Bible," literary scholars generally agree, that Edmund Spenser, William Shakespeare, John Bunyan, and John Milton drew the majority of their Scriptural references.

Across its many editions, the Geneva Bible would undergo significant changes. In 1576, for example, Laurence Tomson revised Whittingham's New Testament according to Beza's 1565 critical edition of the Greek text. From 1599, many editions also contained a new translation of Revelation based on the work of the Huguenot François du Jon (Franciscus Junius). With these textual changes came changes in the Geneva Bible's famous notes. Annotations that in 1560 had been largely exegetical and only generally Protestant spoke more and more the particular language of Reformed theology and Presbyterian church polity. As a consequence, the Geneva Bible, while still cited in sermons or scholarship by establishment figures like Parker, gradually became more closely associated with the Puritan movement and a culture of religious dissent. Moreover, the fact that the notes borrowed from Beza a willingness to justify armed resistance to tyrannical authority placed the Geneva Bible on the side of a culture of political dissent as well. When, in 1604, King James I commissioned a new translation of the Bible, he expressly condemned the Geneva Bible's notes as "seditious, and savouring too much of dangerous, and traitorous conceits."

In 1611, the Authorized Version was published, and in 1616, Archbishop William Laud prohibited the publication of the Geneva Bible in England. Nevertheless, for a generation, editions published in Amsterdam continued to hold their own with the Authorized Version. In 1620, the Geneva Bible accompanied the Pilgrims on the Mayflower. In 1643, during the English Civil War, Oliver Cromwell drew on the Geneva Bible for the *Soldiers' Pocket Bible* that he supplied to the New Model Army. The Geneva Bible lived on even in the translation that came to replace it. The King James Version owed nearly 20 percent of its text and such memorable phrases as "through a glass darkly" to that great achievement of the Marian exiles.

—*Charles R. Sullivan*

1560's

FURTHER READING

Berry, Lloyd E. Introduction to *The Geneva Bible: A Facsimile of the 1560 Edition*, edited by Lloyd E. Berry. Madison: University of Wisconsin Press, 1969. An important essay on the Geneva Bible by the editor of its modern facsimile reprint.

Daniell, David. *The Bible in English: Its History and Influence*. New Haven, Conn.: Yale University Press, 2003. Ambitious survey of the religious, cultural, and linguistic effects of over three thousand English translations of the Bible, from its first appearance in England in the fourth century to American English versions in the twenty-first.

Pelikan, Jaroslav. *The Reformation of the Bible, the Bible of the Reformation*. New Haven, Conn.: Yale University Press, 1996. Explores the mutual influence of the Bible upon the Reformation and of the intellectual, political, and cultural forces of the Reformation upon the Bible.

Price, David, and Charles C. Ryrie. *Let It Go Among Our People: An Illustrated History of the English Bible from John Wyclif to the King James Version*. Cambridge: The Lutterworth Press, 2004. Illustrated history of the translation and production of the Bible in English, written to commemorate the 400th anniversary of the commission of the King James Bible.

SEE ALSO: 1456: Publication of Gutenberg's Mazarin Bible; Oct. 31, 1517: Luther Posts His Ninety-five Theses; Dec. 18, 1534: Act of Supremacy; Mar., 1536: Calvin Publishes *Institutes of the Christian Religion*; May, 1539: Six Articles of Henry VIII; Jan. 28, 1547-July 6, 1553: Reign of Edward VI; July, 1553: Coronation of Mary Tudor; 1558-1603: Reign of Elizabeth I; May, 1559-Aug., 1561: Scottish Reformation; Jan., 1563: Thirty-nine Articles of the Church of England; Feb. 25, 1570: Pius V Excommunicates Elizabeth I.

RELATED ARTICLES in *Great Lives from History: The Renaissance & Early Modern Era, 1454-1600:* John Calvin; Miles Coverdale; Thomas Cranmer; Thomas Cromwell; Elizabeth I; Henry VIII; John Knox; Mary I; Matthew Parker; William Shakespeare; Edmund Spenser; William Tyndale.

June 12, 1560
BATTLE OF OKEHAZAMA

In the Battle of Okehazama, Japan's future dictator Oda Nobunaga defeated the numerically superior force of Imagawa Yoshimoto, one of the most powerful regional warlords of sixteenth century Japan. This event is commonly considered the first step in Nobunaga's rise to national prominence.

LOCALE: Dengakuhazama, Owari Province (now Toyoake City, Aichi Prefecture), Japan

CATEGORY: Wars, uprisings, and civil unrest

KEY FIGURES

Imagawa Yoshimoto (1519-1560), daimyo of Suruga, Tōtōmi, and Mikawa

Oda Nobunaga (1534-1582), warrior chieftain from Owari, eventual military dictator of Japan, r. 1573-1582, first of the Three Unifiers of Japan

Tokugawa Ieyasu (Matsudaira Takechiyo, later Matsudaira Motoyasu; 1543-1616), warrior from Mikawa, third of the Three Unifiers of Japan and founder of the Tokugawa shogunate, r. 1603-1605

SUMMARY OF EVENT

In the spring of 1560, Imagawa Yoshimoto, lord of Suruga, Tōtōmi, and Mikawa Provinces (modern Shizuoka and Aichi Prefectures), made the fateful decision to expand his domain westward along the Tōkaidō, the main overland route linking eastern Japan to Kyōto, the seat of the courts of both emperor and shogun. After almost a century of civil wars in Japan, it appeared as if the Imagawa clan was uniquely positioned to succeed in the quest of occupying the capital. If the ruler of a large, prosperous, and well-organized domain were to control Kyōto, the prestige and authority of the center could effectively be linked with the very real power that had developed on the periphery and perhaps put an end to the era now known as the Sengoku Jidai, or Warring States period.

Yoshimoto knew that he was not without competitors. The year before, Nagao Kagetora of Echigo Province (present-day Niigata Prefecture), who would later take the name Uesugi Kenshin, had visited the capital with an entourage of five thousand, paying his respects to Emperor Ōgimachi (r. 1557-1586) and Shogun Ashikaga Yoshiteru (r. 1547-1565), who had just returned to Kyōto after nine years of exile. Mōri Motonari, a daimyo (war-lord) from far western Japan, was about to pay the considerable costs of the emperor's enthronement ceremonies, which had been postponed for years for lack of funds. Yoshimoto, who had proudly stated in his 1553 law code that he had pacified his domain without any endorsement from the center, was nevertheless aware of the considerable prestige that the imperial and shogunal courts still conveyed. Closer to the capital than any other domain of comparable size, strategically located on the main overland road in Eastern Japan, and facing only considerably smaller domains to the west, Imagawa appeared ideally poised for a successful march on Kyōto.

One of those smaller domains was that of Oda Nobunaga in Owari Province (present-day Aichi Prefecture), who as *shugo-dai* (vice governor) of Owari had clashed with Imagawa Yoshimoto when trying to expand eastward into Mikawa. The Matsudaira family, whose domain was in Mikawa, found themselves torn between aligning themselves with the Imagawa and supporting the Oda clan. Matsudaira Motoyasu, heir of the clan's chieftain, spent his childhood years as a hostage first of the Oda and then of the Imagawa. He saw his first action in 1558 at the age of fifteen, fighting on behalf of the Imagawa against the Oda in western Mikawa. Oda Nobunaga had been trying to consolidate his hold over Owari Province and in 1559 had also gone to the capital for an audience with the shogun, who, according to one source, promoted him to *shugo* (military governor) of Owari. Yet Nobunaga's control of his home province remained tenuous at best, and his forces were no match for the vastly superior war machine of the Imagawa.

Imagawa Yoshimoto's move westward into Owari and beyond was designed to deal once for all with the Oda and other small daimyo blocking his path to the capital. The Imagawa forces, numbering about twenty-five thousand, set out in the fifth month (according to the lunar calendar) of the year Eiroku 3, or in June of 1560. Leaving his son Ujizane (1538-1614) in charge in the domain capital of Sumpu (Shizuoka), Yoshimoto held his first campaign council on June 11 at Kutsukake in Owari, whence he ordered three vanguard units to attack the Oda forts at Narumi, Washizu, and Marume.

At dawn on June 12, Matsudaira Motoyasu commenced his attack on Marume. The fort was soon taken, and its commander Sakuma Morishige perished in battle. Washizu suffered the same fate soon thereafter. This victory effectively eliminated the eastern defenses of the Oda, and Yoshimoto, following Matsudaira Motoyasu's unit in the direction of Okehazama, decided to rest the main force of his army at nearby Dengakuhazama Gorge.

Nobunaga had received a warning about the impending attack and during the night of June 11 had held a council at his headquarters at Kiyosu Castle. He persuaded his men to take the fight to the enemy against seemingly impossible odds. One chronicle reports that the main force set out from Kiyosu with only six horsemen and two hundred foot soldiers as the smoke from Marume and Washizu was already visible to the east. Nobunaga collected three hundred more men from two of his remaining forts and attacked the enemy at Ōtaka Castle, killing no fewer than fifty enemy fighters on horseback.

Having gathered approximately two thousand more men, Nobunaga made his way toward the Imagawa forces. The enemy was in control of Narumi, Marune, and Washizu, but Nobunaga soon received word that the main Imagawa army was resting at Dengakuhazama, with Yoshitomo reportedly celebrating the auspicious start of his campaign and viewing the heads of the vanquished defenders of the castles taken earlier. According to later chroniclers, it was Yanada Masatsuna who pointed out to Nobunaga the futility of trying to engage the enemy contingents at Narumi, since they could easily be reinforced by other Imagawa troops. Instead, he suggested tricking the Imagawa forces at Narumi into believing that the Oda army was camped nearby by hoisting battle flags visible from the fort. In reality, Nobunaga and his men would quietly move around the Imagawa main force toward Dengakuhazama and stage a surprise attack there while the enemy was resting. Facing a force ten to twelve times more numerous than his own, Nobunaga saw the advantages of this stratagem.

As it happened, a thunderstorm accompanied by a torrential downpour helped Nobunaga to conceal his movements from the Imagawa forces. As the storm let up, his men had taken position on the wooded hills surrounding Dengakuhazama Gorge. Nobunaga gave the order to attack. The Imagawa forces were caught by complete surprise. Not ready for battle, confined to a very small space, and literally being forced to fight an uphill battle against an enemy of unknown strength, their ranks quickly disintegrated. Imagawa Yoshimoto was apparently killed before he could put up much of a fight. Later chroniclers stated that he initially assumed a quarrel had broken out among his own men and showed surprise at being surrounded by Oda warriors. Upon learning of the fate of their commander, the survivors of the Imagawa army took to flight. Nobunaga had achieved a truly stunning victory, with only very moderate losses.

In the aftermath of the battle that would enter the history books as the Battle of Okehazama, after a nearby village, Matsudaira Motoyasu—the erstwhile hostage of Nobunaga and now hostage and field commander of the slain Yoshimoto—decided to return to his home province of Mikawa. There he occupied his ancestral castle at Okazaki, resolving to stand his ground against both the Oda in the west and the Imagawa in the east.

Nobunaga would spend the better part of the 1560's consolidating his hold over Owari. He forged a lasting alliance with Matsudaira Motoyasu, who had changed his name to Ieyasu soon after Okehazama, and his surname to Tokugawa later in the decade. Eventually Nobunaga would accomplish what Imagawa Yoshimoto had attempted. In 1568, he entered the capital at Kyōto and installed Ashikaga Yoshiaki as shogun. Once in control of the capital, Nobunaga proceeded to unify Japan by naked military force, supported by the emperor's endorsement of his actions.

SIGNIFICANCE

Although of minor importance from the point of view of strictly military history, the Battle of Okehazama was a crucial turning point in the career of both Oda Nobunaga and Tokugawa Ieyasu, who, along with Toyotomi Hideyoshi, proved to be the pivotal figures in the process of Japan's reunification in the late sixteenth century. Nobunaga's victory allowed him to create an independent power base in Owari from which he would launch his successful quest for the capital and national prominence. His quest to unify Japan would ultimately be brought to fruition by Tokugawa Ieyasu with the founding of the Tokugawa shogunate in 1603.

—*Ronald K. Frank*

FURTHER READING

Hall, John W., et al., eds. *The Cambridge History of Japan. Volume 4: Sengoku and Edo*. Cambridge, England: Cambridge University Press, 1991. Contains the most comprehensive, up-to-date account of the Sengoku period available in English.

Hall, John W., Nagahara Keiji, and Kozo Yamamura. *Japan Before Tokugawa: Political Consolidation and Economic Growth, 1500 to 1650*. Princeton, N.J.: Princeton University Press, 1981. A collection of scholarly essays on sixteenth century Japan.

Lamers, Jeroen. *Japonius Tyrannus. The Japanese Warlord Oda Nobunaga Reconsidered*. Leiden: Hotei, 2000. A detailed scholarly account with ample quotations from primary sources.

Turnbull, Stephen. *War in Japan, 1467-1615*. Oxford, England: Osprey, 2002. Though not a scholarly work, this book contains a well-researched brief account of the Battle of Okehazama.

March, 1562-May 2, 1598
FRENCH WARS OF RELIGION

This series of eight civil wars, fought intermittently over a thirty-six-year period between French Catholics and Protestants, ended only when Henry IV issued the 1598 Edict of Nantes, which established limited religious toleration in France.

LOCALE: France
CATEGORIES: Wars, uprisings, and civil unrest; religion; government and politics

KEY FIGURES

Francis II (1544-1560), king of France, r. 1559-1560
Charles IX (1550-1574), king of France, r. 1560-1574
François de Lorraine (1519-1563), second duke of Guise, 1550-1563, opposed to Protestantism
Henry I of Lorraine (1550-1588), third duke of Guise, 1563-1588, leader of the anti-Huguenot movement and head of the Catholic League
Henry III (1551-1589), last Valois king of France, r. 1574-1589
Henry IV (1553-1610), first Bourbon king of France, r. 1589-1610
Catherine de Médicis (1519-1589), queen of France, r. 1547-1559, regent, r. 1560-1563, and queen mother, 1563-1589
Philip II (1527-1598), king of Spain, r. 1556-1598

SUMMARY OF EVENT

In the early 1560's, France came apart in a series of civil conflicts. Eight different wars were fought over a thirty-six-year period in which intervals of violence alternated with tenuous periods of peace. The key political players in these wars included the last Valois monarchs—Francis II, Charles IX, Henry III, and their mother, Catherine de Médicis—and their chief rivals, the Guise, Bourbon, and Montmorency families. The wars resulted in the founding of a new French dynasty, as the Protestant Bourbons' leader, Henry of Navarre, ascended the throne as King Henry IV in 1589.

The French Wars of Religion were fought between Protestants seeking to bring the Reformation to France and Catholics defending the Roman Church. By the mid-1550's, John Calvin was sending missionaries into France and converting a large following to the Protestant faith. About 10 percent of the French population, or around 1,250,000 people, adopted the reformed religion and were called Huguenots. Most of the Huguenot population lived in three great regions in central and south-

western France: Aquitaine, Languedoc, and Dauphiné. Huguenot strongholds included the important towns of La Rochelle, Montauban, and Nîmes. Around 1570, the largest of these towns was La Rochelle, with approximately twenty thousand inhabitants. Most of France, however, remained Catholic, and few individuals of the time could envision more than one accepted religion. Many French people worried that God would punish the realm if two religions were allowed to coexist, and they developed a violent hatred of people of differing faiths.

The wars of religion were also fought for political reasons. They occurred during a time when the French monarchy was very weak. The politically ambitious Catherine de Médicis was a widow by 1559. She greatly influenced all of her sons while they sat on the throne, and she even served as queen regent during the first years of Charles IX's reign. Because weak boy-kings occupied the throne, political factions vied for leverage over the Valois court. Even though Catherine tried to maintain peace in the realm, she never succeeded in either diminishing the influence of the factions or settling the country's religious differences. The Catholic Guise family, the Protestant Bourbon family, and the Catholic but more politically and religiously moderate (*politique*) Montmorency family each tried to dominate Catherine and her weak sons.

The spark that ignited the wars occurred in March of 1562, when the powerful François de Lorraine, duke of Guise, and his troops came upon a group of unarmed Huguenots worshiping in a barn in the small Champagne village of Vassy. Violence erupted and several hundred

MAJOR BATTLES OF THE FRENCH WARS OF RELIGION

October 26, 1562	Battle of Rouen
December 19, 1562	Battle of Dreux
1563	Siege of Orléans
November 10, 1567	Battle of Saint-Denis
March 13, 1569	Battle of Jarnac
October 3, 1569	Battle of Moncontour
June 15, 1570	Battle of Arnay-le-Duc
1573	Siege of La Rochelle
October 20, 1587	Battle of Courtras
March 14, 1590	Battle of Ivry
June, 1595	Battle of Fontaine-Française

people were killed or wounded, prompting the Huguenots to call the event a massacre. One month later, Huguenot leaders began raising troops to defend the Protestant population, and the first military engagements between Protestant and Catholic forces occurred in July of 1562.

The wars of religion were noted for the violence they engendered. Key military engagements included the 1563 Siege of Orléans, the 1573 Siege of La Rochelle, the 1587 Battle of Courtras, the 1590 Battle of Ivry, and the 1595 Battle of Fontaine-Française. The wars were also marked by horrible massacres. The St. Bartholomew's Day Massacre in 1572 was particularly infamous: The Protestant leadership came to Paris as part of Catherine de Médicis's attempt to balance rival court factions, but a massacre ensued in which most of the Huguenot leadership was killed. This led to similar massacres of Huguenots throughout the French provinces and a serious weakening of the Protestant movement.

The Catholic League dominated the last phase of the wars. It consisted of zealous Catholics who wanted to keep the Protestant Henry of Navarre from ever sitting on the throne. The very popular Henry I of Lorraine, duke of Guise, headed the league until his assassination in 1588, and Philip II of Spain supported the league with money and troops. By the time Henry III was murdered in 1589, most of the towns in France had succumbed to the league.

By the early 1590's, France was war-weary, the economy was severely depressed, and the population had been decimated by famine and disease. Henry of Navarre became Henry IV in 1589 and emerged as the only person forceful enough to solve France's problems. In 1593, he abjured his Protestantism and became a Catholic king. Paris accepted him, and soon thereafter other key towns capitulated as well. Over the next five years, Henry besieged towns and bribed key nobles and League leaders. He offered generous terms to the vanquished willing to accept him as king. Henry was forced to go to war with

Violence and torture by French Protestant Huguenots against Catholics. (Frederick Ungar Publishing Co.)

Spain in 1595 to drive the Spanish supporters of the Catholic League out of France.

The religious wars officially ended in 1598 with the Treaty of Vervins. In that year, Henry also issued the Edict of Nantes to settle the religious conflict that had plagued France for so long. The edict mandated limited toleration of Huguenots by allowing them to practice their faith in more than two hundred towns in France.

SIGNIFICANCE

The French Wars of Religion reveal how fundamentally important religion was in the lives of sixteenth century people, who often derived their personal identities primarily from their religious faith. The organization of Protestant churches and the strengthening of the Catholic Church in the sixteenth century were also preludes to the political reorganization in the European states that occurred in the next century.

The wars additionally stimulated political thought. Huguenot writers, for example, stressed the limited nature of monarchy. They developed resistance theories to argue that people did not have to obey a king who was a tyrant. Conversely, other political thinkers stressed the divine nature of monarchy and argued that kings did not need the consent of their subjects to rule. Their rule was absolute and constrained only by rules of succession and divine law.

Political theory in France mirrored political actuality. Most of France proved willing to give up some of its autonomy to Henry IV to end the wars. This strengthened the power and authority of the king and laid the foundations of absolutism in France. It took a strong ruler to issue and enforce the Edict of Nantes. Some historians believe the edict was a great document of religious toleration. Even so, it established a state within a state—a separate Protestant infrastructure within the larger Catholic nation—which in part explains the revocation of the edict in 1685. More recent historians stress that the toleration established in 1598 was very limited and was probably meant only to give Protestants time to reconvert to Catholicism.

—*Stephanie Annette Finley-Croswhite*

FURTHER READING

Finley-Croswhite, S. Annette. *Henry IV and the Towns: The Pursuit of Legitimacy in French Urban Society, 1589-1610.* New York: Cambridge University Press,

Protestant Huguenots are shot and killed by Catholic militia while trying to escape from a meeting house. (Hulton|Archive by Getty Images)

1999. Explores how Henry IV won the support of his urban subjects during and after the wars of religion.

Greengrass, Mark. *France in the Age of Henri IV: The Struggle for Stability.* 2d ed. New York: Longman, 1995. A general survey of Henry's reign with emphasis on how he ended the wars of religion and returned stability to France.

Holt, Mack P. *The French Wars of Religion, 1562-1629.* New York: Cambridge University Press, 1995. A comprehensive examination of the religious wars designed for undergraduates and graduates. Holt questions the idea that the Edict of Nantes was designed to offer religious toleration to Huguenot France in chapter 6.

Knecht, R. J. *The French Wars of Religion, 1559-1598.* 2d ed. New York: Longman, 1996. Knecht offers excellent background on the spread of Protestantism in

France in chapter 1. The book also contains key document excerpts.

Parrow, Kathleen. *From Defense to Resistance: Justification of Violence During the French Wars of Religion.* Transactions of the American Philosophical Society 83, part 6. Philadelphia: American Philosophical Society, 1993. A short work that examines the legal theories sixteenth century writers used to justify violence in their society. The research is based largely on political pamphlets published during the period of the wars.

Racaut, Luc. *Hatred in Print: Catholic Propaganda and Protestant Identity During the French Wars of Religion.* Burlington, Vt.: Ashgate, 2002. Rare study of the pro-Catholic pamphleteers in France. Analyzes the strategies, production, and impact of pro-Catholic propaganda of the period. Includes bibliographic references and index.

Sutherland, N. M. *Henry IV of France and the Politics of Religion, 1572-1596.* 2 vols. Bristol, Avon, England: Elm Bank, 2002. Extremely detailed account of the role of religion in France's monarchy and political sphere during the late sixteenth century. Each chapter discusses a specific political event or issue from the point of view of the conflict between Protestants and Catholics. Includes illustrations, map, bibliographic references, and index.

Wolfe, Michael. *The Conversion of Henri IV: Politics, Power, and Religious Belief in Early Modern France.* Cambridge, Mass.: Harvard University Press, 1993. Wolfe examines the controversies and ramifications surrounding Henry IV's 1593 decision to abjure his Protestant faith and reconvert to Catholicism.

SEE ALSO: Oct. 31, 1517: Luther Posts His Ninety-five Theses; Mid-16th cent.: Development of the Caracole Maneuver; Aug. 24-25, 1572: St. Bartholomew's Day Massacre; July 7, 1585-Dec. 23, 1588: War of the Three Henrys; Aug. 2, 1589: Henry IV Ascends the Throne of France; Apr. 13, 1598: Edict of Nantes; May 2, 1598: Treaty of Vervins.

RELATED ARTICLES in *Great Lives from History: The Renaissance & Early Modern Era, 1454-1600:* Catherine de Médicis; Henry III; Henry IV; Philip II.

1563-1584
CONSTRUCTION OF THE ESCORIAL

One of the most significant complexes built in the sixteenth century, the Escorial embodied the values of Catholic reform espoused by the devout King Philip II, a major promoter of the Counter-Reformation.

LOCALE: El Escorial, northwest of Madrid, Spain
CATEGORIES: Architecture; religion

KEY FIGURES
Philip II (1527-1598), king of Spain, r. 1556-1598
Juan Bautista de Toledo (c. 1515-1567), Spanish architect
Juan de Herrera (c. 1530-1597), Spanish architect

SUMMARY OF EVENT

The Escorial, one of the largest and most important architectural complexes constructed in the sixteenth century, was built at the direction of King Philip II of Spain between 1563 and 1584. A unique, multifunctional foundation, it included a royal pantheon, church, monastery, palace, library, college, and hospital. Its main purpose was to serve as a Habsburg funerary monument. To that end, the Escorial's monastery housed an order of Hieronymite monks dedicated to offering perpetual prayers for the souls of the royal family.

Built during the period of the Counter-Reformation, the zealous Catholic reform movement of the sixteenth century, the Escorial has been interpreted as a politically calculated symbol of the power of the Spanish monarchy and its commitment to combating the spread of Protestantism. Contemporaries hailed it as the "eighth wonder of the world."

The Spanish architect Juan Bautista de Toledo began designing the Escorial in 1559 after Philip II named him royal architect. Known for his classicizing style, Toledo had been Michelangelo's assistant in Rome from 1546 to 1548, when the Renaissance master was at work on St. Peter's Basilica. Several different sources have been suggested for Toledo's plan for the Escorial, a design in the form of blocks produced between 1559 and 1563. These sources include the ancient Roman Palace of Diocletian (295-305), the Hospital Tavera in Toledo, begun in 1541, and Spanish medieval palace-monasteries.

According to tradition, the Escorial's plan, designed as a grid, symbolically refers to the martyrdom of Saint Lawrence, purportedly burned alive on a flaming gridiron. The complex is dedicated to the saint, in fulfillment of a vow made by Philip II, when, on the saint's feast day, August 10, 1557, Spanish troops destroyed a French church during the Battle of Saint-Quentin.

In 1567, Toledo died. It seems that by 1570, Juan de Herrera, named Toledo's assistant in 1563, was in charge of construction until the Escorial's completion in 1584. Whereas the Escorial's general layout can be attributed to Toledo, Herrera was responsible for the buildings' elevations. He introduced several innovations, adding an imperial staircase and changing the basilica's design significantly. Today, Herrera is regarded as the sole author of the complex, but it is difficult to separate his work from that of his predecessor. In addition, a number of Italian architects designed or consulted at the Escorial, including, most important, Francesco Paciotto.

The myth that Herrera was the Escorial's sole designer can, in fact, be traced to the architect himself. In 1589, he published a series of eleven engravings of the Escorial's plans, elevations, and sections with accompanying text promoting this very notion. In all fairness, though, Herrera presided over most of the construction and was responsible for its coherent style, combining sober classicism with Flemish-style roofs and spires.

The Escorial's main entrance, located on the west façade, illustrates Herrera's stylistic synthesis. It takes the form of an ecclesiastical temple front, uniting two levels of classical orders, a triangular pediment, and a high-pitched Flemish pavilion. This entrance leads to the most important structures of the complex—the library, basilica, and royal pantheon. The monastery and the adjacent royal apartments can be found on the Escorial's south side, while the college, additional royal apartments, and suites for courtiers and visiting dignitaries are located to the north.

The basilica, built between 1557 and 1586, is a core building of the Escorial. It functions as both palace chapel and monastic church. Scholars have detected the influence of several Italian Renaissance architects here, in-

El Escorial, which took twenty-one years to construct. (R. S. Peale and J. A. Hill)

cluding Leon Battista Alberti. The basilica's plan, a centralized configuration of a Greek cross within a square, reflects Michelangelo's design for St. Peter's. The cupola, which rests on a high drum, is traceable to Donato Bramante's design for St. Peter's from 1506 to 1514. It is the first such dome in Spanish architecture. The church's interior is sober and solemn, unified by the use of granite and articulated by majestic Doric pilasters. The lavish main altarpiece, executed in colored jaspers and gilded bronze, relieves the severe classicism of the interior. Sculptures of the royal family, by Pompeo Leoni, flank the altar, kneeling in perpetual adoration. The royal burial vaults are located below.

In addition to presiding over most of the construction of the Escorial, Herrera also oversaw its decoration, a massive undertaking that involved creating, acquiring, and arranging thousands of paintings, sculptures, altars, reliquaries, tapestries, pieces of furniture, and other decorative objects. Several Spanish artists were involved, including court painters Juan Fernández de Navarette and Alonso Sánchez Coello, among others. The vast majority of artists at work decorating the Escorial, though, were Italian, reflecting King Philip II's taste in painting. Key painters included Romulo Cincinnato, Luca Cambiaso,

Federico Zuccari, and Pellegrino Tibaldi, who worked in the dry, didactic style of the Counter-Reformation. The king demanded that all artists comply with Inquisition guidelines for sacred imagery, rejecting works that were not strictly orthodox, such as El Greco's painting of *The Martyrdom of Saint Maurice* (c. 1580), which he had removed from the basilica. Philip II intended that the carefully planned decoration, like the architecture itself, give visual form to his Catholic faith. The Escorial also served as a showcase for the royal art collection, one of the greatest in Europe, which included works by such Italian and Flemish luminaries as Titian, Hieronymous Bosch, and Rogier van der Weyden.

Architectural historians have offered various explanations to account for the genesis of Herrera's restrained classicism, called "plain style." According to some, it represented a Christianized form of classicism. Another has detected the influence of Saint Augustine (354-430), who advocated aesthetic harmony, consonance, unity, and reason. Herrera's style might also reflect the ideals of the medieval philosopher Raymond Lull (1235-1316), particularly in its penchant for abstraction and rational geometry. Architectural historians waver about whether to classify Herrera's architecture as an example of Renaissance or mannerist style. More significantly, its sobriety, chastity, and gravity perfectly manifested Philip II's religiosity as well as the ideology of the Spanish Counter-Reformation.

After its completion in 1584, the Escorial underwent various renovations through the centuries. Most important, during the reign of Philip III (r. 1598-1621), the Pantheon of the Kings was built to the designs of Giovanni Battista Crescenzi (1617-1618). The underground octagonal chamber is richly coloristic, its lavish use of marbles, colored jasper, and gilt bronze an example of the Spanish Baroque. In the 1650's, the court artist Diego Rodríguez de Silva Velázquez supervised a redecoration, commissioning new paintings by Spanish artists. From 1692 to 1694, Luca Giordano frescoed the monastery with scenes from the life of Saint Lawrence. In the 1780's and 1790's, the architect Juan de Villanueva constructed additional service buildings and auxiliary residences. In the same century, Kings Charles IV and Ferdinand VII commissioned new fresco decorations. The Escorial underwent major restoration in the 1950's, in preparation for the fourth centennial of 1963, in which extensive termite damage was repaired.

SIGNIFICANCE

The Escorial was one of the largest and most significant architectural complexes built in the sixteenth century. It was Philip II's most important artistic commission. Contemporaries described it as a new Temple of Jerusalem, likening the king to Solomon. Its sober and severe style embodied the values of Catholic reform espoused by the devout Philip, a major promoter of the Counter-Reformation.

Juan de Herrera's major contribution was his "plain style," which established classicism as the preferred architectural language throughout Spain. The numerous workers who labored at the construction site spread the style, when, after the Escorial's completion in 1584 they traveled to other building sites, bringing with them Herrera's sober classicism. Herrera's influence is visible in Spanish ecclesiastical architecture in particular, but can be observed even in the Americas, especially in the Cathedrals of Mexico City and Puebla, Mexico.

—*Charlene Villaseñor Black*

FURTHER READING

Kubler, George. *Building the Escorial*. Princeton, N.J.: Princeton University Press, 1982. The definitive study of the building of the Escorial. Reproduces numerous period documents.

Mulcahy, Rosemarie. *The Decoration of the Royal Basilica of El Escorial*. New York: Cambridge University Press, 1994. The major study of the basilica's decoration and ornamentation.

Taylor, René. "Architecture and Magic: Considerations on the Idea of the Escorial." In *Essays in the History of Architecture Presented to Rudolf Wittkower*, edited by Douglas Fraser, Howard Hibbard, and Milton J. Lewine. London: Phaidon, 1967. An important early study of the iconography and meaning of the building.

Wilkinson Zerner, Catherine. *Juan de Herrera: Architect to Philip II of Spain*. New Haven, Conn.: Yale University Press, 1993. The definitive study of the architect and his work.

SEE ALSO: 1462: Founding of the Platonic Academy; c. 1500: Netherlandish School of Painting; 1577: Ram Dās Founds Amritsar.

RELATED ARTICLES in *Great Lives from History: The Renaissance & Early Modern Era, 1454-1600:* Leon Battista Alberti; Donato Bramante; El Greco; Juan de Herrera; Michelangelo; Philip II.

January, 1563
THIRTY-NINE ARTICLES OF THE CHURCH OF ENGLAND

The Thirty-nine Articles of Religion, which revisited and revised the Forty-two Articles of 1553 that addressed the Protestant makeup of the Church of England, permanently reestablished Protestant institutions in England by Queen Elizabeth I and her religious advisers.

LOCALE: London, England
CATEGORIES: Religion; government and politics

KEY FIGURES

Elizabeth I (1533-1603), queen of England, r. 1558-1603
Matthew Parker (1504-1575), archbishop of Canterbury, 1559-1575
Thomas Cranmer (1489-1556), archbishop of Canterbury, 1533-1556
Edward VI (1537-1553), king of England, r. 1547-1553
Mary I (1516-1558), queen of England, r. 1553-1558

SUMMARY OF EVENT

Elizabeth I became queen of England on November 17, 1558, upon the death of her half sister, Queen Mary I. Even though both had been declared illegitimate during the lifetime of their father, King Henry VIII, there was little opposition to Elizabeth's succession. She was the logical candidate, and there was no other possible claimant except her Roman Catholic cousin, Mary, Queen of Scots.

As expected, Elizabeth, the daughter of Henry VIII's second queen, Anne Boleyn, restored the English Protestantism in which she had been raised, reversing the Catholic restoration under Mary I that had occurred from 1553 to 1558. Within the first month of her reign, Elizabeth ordered several parts of the Mass translated into English and also forbade the elevation of the bread and wine for the adoration of the congregation. Attacks on symbols of Catholicism were largely ignored by the new government.

Anticipating these changes, only one of the bishops, all of whom had been appointed during Mary's reign, agreed reluctantly to crown Elizabeth. Early in 1559, Parliament began to reenact some of the ecclesiastical legislation of Henry VIII. Papal taxes were once again to be paid to the Crown and certain Church lands were seized, despite strong opposition by the bishops in the House of Lords.

When Parliament subsequently took up a bill to define the doctrine of the English Church, the bishops and the lower clergy in convocation denied that such matters were subject to parliamentary control. They also reaffirmed certain Catholic doctrines, especially the real presence of Christ in the Eucharist.

On March 22, Parliament passed a bill restoring to Elizabeth the title Supreme Head of the Church of Christ in England, which had been borne by Henry VIII and Edward VI. Instead of signing it, Elizabeth recessed Parliament because she had reservations about the title Supreme Head.

On May 8, a reconvened Parliament passed a new Act of Supremacy in which the queen's title was the somewhat more modest Supreme Governor of the Church in England. An oath to that effect was to be taken, as in the days of Henry VIII, by all clergy, all agents of the Crown and public officials, and all graduates of the universities or the law courts.

A second bill, which passed the House of Lords by only three votes, abolished the Mass in England officially, substituting a communion service that was to be celebrated regularly. These new Elizabethan bills together revived most of the ecclesiastical legislation of King Henry VIII's reign. In addition, the Act of Uniformity prescribed that the second edition of the Book of Common Prayer (1552), most of which had been translated from the Latin by Thomas Cranmer, but with significant omissions and additions to make it Protestant as well as Catholic, was to be the official liturgy of the Church of England. Not a single bishop took the Oath of Supremacy, reversing the situation at the time of Henry VIII. All the bishops were thus deprived of their offices, to be replaced by men of Protestant sympathies, many of whom had been in exile on the Continent during Mary's reign and had close contacts with Protestant leaders. As in the days of Henry VIII, the great majority of the parish clergy took the oath and remained in office; the great majority of the laity to whom it was proffered also took the oath.

During the next several years, the business of reforming the English Church to reflect its Protestant focus proceeded with general success. A substantial number of laypersons, including some of the nobility, constituted a self-conscious Catholic minority called recusants because of their refusal to take the oath; but the majority of the nation conformed quietly to the third major reversal of religious practice they had been asked to undergo in thirty-five years. The earlier reversals were Henry VIII's reform of 1534 and Mary's return to Catholicism in 1553. The most vocal discontent was expressed by Protestants, who already were coming to be known as Puritans. They were disappointed that Elizabeth retained Catholic remnants as bishops, ritual services, and sacraments.

Early in 1563, a convocation was summoned under the presidency of Matthew Parker, archbishop of Canterbury, to deal with disciplinary problems in the Church, including the low level of morality and lack of learning among many parish clergy, and also to define an official and comprehensive doctrine for the Church. The last non-Catholic attempt to accomplish this task had been Edward VI's Forty-two Articles of Religion, which had been enacted in June, 1553, shortly before the young king's death and the restoration of Catholicism under Mary. During 1562, the Forty-two Articles, which addressed measures to be adopted by the Church of England that ran counter to Catholicism, were revised by Parker. In their new form as the Thirty-nine Articles of Religion, they were submitted to the convocation early in January, 1563. By the end of the month, all the bishops had accepted them, and they became the official doctrine of the Church of England.

The new articles recognized two sacraments—baptism and holy communion—that were said not to confer grace on the recipient but merely to strengthen his or her faith. The physical presence of Christ in the communion was denied, although its actual meaning was left somewhat ambiguous. The idea of holy communion as a reenactment of Christ's sacrifice on the cross was also denied.

In accordance with the Protestant pattern, the articles affirmed that anything not in Scripture could not be a matter of importance for belief, thus in effect rejecting the Catholic affirmation of the importance of tradition. The question of salvation was also defined in Protestant terms. People are saved by faith alone and solely by God's action, not by any merit of their own. The doctrine of predestination was specifically upheld.

Diversity of ceremonies among the various national churches was also upheld, as was the use of English in official worship. A married priesthood was permitted, although Elizabeth was somewhat uncomfortable with the idea and snubbed Archbishop Parker's wife.

By Act of Parliament in 1571, the Thirty-nine Articles were to be subscribed to by all those required to take the Oath of Supremacy. Elizabeth had rejected a similar bill in 1566, declaring that matters of belief were within her prerogative and not within the scope of Parliament.

SIGNIFICANCE

The legislation of the early years of Elizabeth's forty-five-year reign gave a distinctly Protestant bias to the Church of England, which it had not had under her father and had only briefly under her half brother. In effect, the Thirty-nine Articles completed the establishment of the Anglican Church in England.

Committed Protestants, many of whom occupied high positions in the Church, in time became increasingly frustrated at the obvious unwillingness of the queen to move beyond the Elizabethan Settlement of 1559, which established Elizabeth as the Supreme Governor of the church and required the Oath of Allegiance and also established the Act of Uniformity. In various ways, the Puritans attempted to make unauthorized changes in the church that led to many suspensions from office, imprisonments, and even a few executions. Several times Puritans in the House of Commons attempted to legislate liturgical or organizational reforms, but Elizabeth successfully resisted each time.

By the end of Elizabeth's reign in 1603, the Puritans were temporarily exhausted, but the issues left unsolved by the Elizabethan Settlement would become major crises in the Civil War period from 1640 to 1649.

—*James F. Hitchcock, updated by Clifton W. Potter, Jr.*

FURTHER READING

Brigden, Susan. *London and the Reformation.* New York: Oxford University Press, 1990. A work that is essential to an understanding of the forces that shaped Elizabethan religious opinion.

Doran, Susan. *Queen Elizabeth I.* New York: New York University Press, 2003. Portrays Elizabeth as a flawed but brilliant manipulator who used this ability to protect her country and to steer it safely through a host of dangers. Includes illustrations, map, bibliographic references, index.

Dunn, Jane. *Elizabeth and Mary: Cousins, Rivals, Queens.* New York: Alfred A. Knopf, 2004. Study of the rivalry and political intrigue between Elizabeth I and Mary, Queen of Scots, attempting to portray the private emotions behind their public acts. Includes photographic plates, illustrations, bibliographic references, index.

Haigh, Christopher, ed. *The Reign of Elizabeth I.* Athens: University of Georgia Press, 1985. An excellent collection of revisionist essays on Elizabeth I and her era.

Hughes, Philip. *The Reformation in England.* Vol. 3. Rev. ed. Reprint. Brookfield, Vt.: Ashgate, 1993. Although biased by current standards, this work is still the most thorough study available on the English reformation.

Levin, Carole. *The Heart and Stomach of a King: Elizabeth I and the Politics of Sex and Power.* Philadelphia:

University of Pennsylvania Press, 1994. One of the new interpretations of Elizabeth I, this work focuses on the succession and the queen as a religious figure. A host of other topics are also covered that are essential to an understanding of Elizabeth I.

MacCulloch, Diarmaid. *The Later Reformation in England, 1547-1603.* 2d ed. New York: Palgrave, 2001. Study of the major events of the Reformation in England after Henry VIII's death, together with a discussion of the reception and understanding of those events by the English people. Includes bibliographic references and index.

Marshall, Peter. *Reformation England, 1480-1642.* New York: Oxford University Press, 2003. Extremely detailed, meticulously supported argument that the English Reformation should be understood to begin in the late fifteenth century and to last well into the seventeenth century. Grapples with and explicates the specific meanings of Protestantism and Catholicism to the major players and to laypeople during the Renaissance. Includes bibliographic references and index.

Meyer, Carl S. *Elizabeth I and the Religious Settlement of 1558.* St. Louis, Mo.: Concordia, 1960. Earlier scholarship tended to see the English Church under Edward VI and Elizabeth I as essentially Calvinistic in theology, but Meyer tends to find Lutheran influences equally important, if not more so.

Ridley, Jasper G. *Elizabeth I: The Shrewdness of Virtue.* New York: Viking Press, 1988. Ridley's biography of the "Virgin Queen" is one of the best because the author fully analyzes the personality of the queen.

Shagan, Ethan H. *Popular Politics and the English Reformation.* New York: Cambridge University Press, 2003. Study of the way in which ordinary English subjects interpreted and reacted to Protestantism. Argues that religious history cannot be understood independently of political history, because commoners no less than royals understood religion and politics as utterly intertwined. Includes bibliographic references and index.

Trimble, William Raleigh. *The Catholic Laity in Elizabethan England.* Cambridge, Mass.: Harvard University Press, 1964. An exhaustive recent study of the subject.

SEE ALSO: 1531-1540: Cromwell Reforms British Government; Dec. 18, 1534: Act of Supremacy; July, 1535-Mar., 1540: Henry VIII Dissolves the Monasteries; Oct., 1536-June, 1537: Pilgrimage of Grace; May, 1539: Six Articles of Henry VIII; July, 1553: Coronation of Mary Tudor; 1558-1603: Reign of Elizabeth I; Nov. 9, 1569: Rebellion of the Northern Earls; Feb. 25, 1570: Pius V Excommunicates Elizabeth I.

RELATED ARTICLES in *Great Lives from History: The Renaissance & Early Modern Era, 1454-1600:* Thomas Cranmer; Edward VI; Elizabeth I; Mary I; Matthew Parker.

January 20, 1564
PEACE OF TROYES

The Peace of Troyes effectively put an end to the five-hundred-year presence of the English in France. It also freed England to pursue prosperous trade routes and to recover financially from the costly wars it had been fighting in France.

LOCALE: Calais

CATEGORIES: Diplomacy and international relations; wars, uprisings, and civil unrest; expansion and land acquisition

KEY FIGURES

Elizabeth I (1533-1603), queen of England, r. 1558-1603

William Cecil (1520-1598), first minister of Queen Elizabeth

Catherine de Médicis (1519-1589), queen of France, r. 1547-1589

Sir Nicholas Throckmorton (1515-1571), ambassador to France

Sir Thomas Smith (1513-1577), scholar and diplomat

SUMMARY OF EVENT

Hostilities between England and France over English possession of French lands began in 1152, when Henry Plantagenet, count of Anjou, married Eleanor of Aquitaine. Two years later, when Henry assumed the English throne as Henry II, he possessed both Anjou and Aquitaine. That situation pleased neither the French nor the English since France could interfere with England's lucrative wool trade with the Low Countries and Henry was a vassal to the French king, while the French naturally resented an English presence on their shores.

For the next four hundred years, there were several small wars between the French and the English, and a number of treaties were made and broken, including the Treaty of Calais (1360), the Treaty of Arras (1435), and the earlier Peace of Troyes (1420), which followed King Henry V's victory at Agincourt.

Elizabeth, who became queen in 1558, was not entirely secure on her throne since the problem of succession loomed over her head, and Mary, Queen of Scots, and her Catholic followers were still quite powerful. As queen of Scotland, Mary was also important because there were attempts to link Scotland and France against the British. Spain and France, Catholic countries, were always possible threats, especially since Elizabeth was willing to aid the Protestants, the Huguenots, in France. That aid, in the form of finances and personnel, was expensive and stretched England's resources.

According to the terms of the Treaty of Cateau-Cambrésis (1559), England was to assume control of Calais within eight years of the treaty, but one of the treaty's caveats called for the English to refrain from hostile actions against the French. Elizabeth, however, was unwilling to abandon her claims to Calais, so she not only created a secret network of spies in France but also undertook military action. She also helped the French Huguenots, whose cause was nearly failing. In her efforts, she also had the sympathetic support of King Philip II of Spain, who wanted to see his sometime-ally England regain Calais. His help was contingent on his marriage to Elizabeth, who turned down his offer.

Elizabeth's forces attacked Le Havre and occupied the city, but her troops were unable to hold it against the French. Her forces, without adequate supplies and suffering from a debilitating plague, were forced to surrender. Aware of the situation at Le Havre, she dispatched reinforcements across the Channel, but by the time they arrived, the city had already surrendered to French troops. Elizabeth's quest to regain a foothold in France, which her predecessors had maintained for hundreds of years, was futile. A new treaty, which would actually benefit both countries and enable each to save face, was the only feasible course of action. Although Elizabeth continued to refer to the original Troyes treaty, which called for England to regain control of Calais in 1567, she was not in a position to enforce her claims. The protracted hostilities between the two countries had proved to be prohibitively expensive, and it was in their best interests to cease the hostilities that were making them both

susceptible to military attacks from other enemies. (It is worth remembering that at the Council of Trent in 1563, Spain and France were called on to recover England by the sword and that Mary, Queen of Scots, was supported by the French.) In response to Elizabeth's claims, France pointed out that England had in fact broken the original treaty that prohibited English aggression.

Elizabeth appointed Sir Thomas Smith and Sir Nicholas Throckmorton as her English emissaries, acting under William Cecil's guidance, and they conducted the negotiations. There is some question about Throckmorton's effectiveness because he and Cecil were enemies, but the treaty was finally drafted. Because of English pride, the treaty was couched in language ("verbal subterfuge," according to J. B. Black) that softened England's humiliation at the hands of its traditional enemies. England renounced the claim to Calais in the Peace of Troyes treaty on January 20, 1564, in exchange for 220,000 crowns, much less than Elizabeth had first demanded. Given their history of involvement in France, the English suffered a blow to their prestige; but they also gained from the treaty. The money was welcome in England, which was strapped for cash, and it also meant a cessation of the costly wars against the French.

After the treaty was signed in London, Catherine de Médicis (the French king's mother), King Charles IX of France, Smith, and Throckmorton traveled to the Cathedral of Troyes to celebrate the peace treaty. The politically ambitious and astute Catherine de Médicis then accompanied her son on a triumphal tour to several other French cities to celebrate the victory that did much to solidify Charles's position as king.

SIGNIFICANCE

The immediate result of the treaty was an end to the costly hostilities between the two countries. It also meant that England's flourishing wool trade with the Low Countries could continue with a minimum of French intervention, important because the wars with France had left England with limited resources in staffing, ships, finances, and munitions. Although England had defensive capability, it lacked offensive power, and because Elizabeth's foreign policy was devoted to preventing hostile countries from establishing power bases on the English Channel, the treaty effectively removed France as a possible hostile force, at least for the next few years.

Elizabeth also continued to help the Huguenot cause in France, where she had earlier offered the Protestant prince of Condé, Louis I of Bourbon, six thousand troops and 30,000 pounds.

The Peace of Troyes Treaty was consistent with Elizabeth's foreign policy of cautious isolationism. It may have been a blow to English nationalism, but in the long run, it was beneficial because it helped Elizabeth form a more stable and central government. By the end of the 1560's, Elizabeth had passed some important tests: She had freed herself from foreign wars and defeated Catholic rebels at home, thereby shaping her regime and establishing herself as the queen. During her reign, England flourished not only in terms of exploration but also in cultural terms, including literature and the arts.

—*Thomas L. Erskine*

FURTHER READING

Black, J. B. *The Reign of Elizabeth 1558-1603*. 2d ed. Oxford, England: Clarendon Press, 1959. Chapter 2 contains the most thorough treatment of the peace treaty. Black explores the events leading to the treaty and traces its effects on the development of England as an international power.

Loades, David. *Elizabeth I*. New York: Hambledon and London, 2003. Loades claims that the events leading to the treaty and its aftermath left Elizabeth with "a lasting distaste for continental adventures" and increased Cecil's influence at court.

MacCaffrey, Wallace. *The Shaping of the Elizabethan Regime*. Princeton, N.J.: Princeton University Press,

1968. Sees the treaty as marking the return of diplomatic civility between the two countries and as freeing Elizabeth to turn her attention to domestic affairs.

Mahoney, Irene. *Madame Catherine*. New York: Coward, McCann & Geoghegan, 1975. Important for its coverage of the events that necessitated the treaty between France and England. Mahoney also discusses how the treaty enhanced the prestige and credibility of the French king, Catherine de Médicis' son.

Read, Conyers. *Mr. Secretary: Cecil and Queen Elizabeth*. New York: Alfred A. Knopf, 1961. Stresses Cecil's role in the negotiations leading to the Peace of Troyes treaty. Read also provides information about Elizabeth's envoys, Sir Thomas Smith and Sir Nicholas Throckmorton, who negotiated with the French.

SEE ALSO: 1544-1628: Anglo-French Wars; 1558-1603: Reign of Elizabeth I; Jan. 1-8, 1558: France Regains Calais from England; Apr. 3, 1559: Treaty of Cateau-Cambrésis; Mar., 1562-May 2, 1598: French Wars of Religion; Feb. 25, 1570: Pius V Excommunicates Elizabeth I; Apr., 1587-c. 1600: Anglo-Spanish War; May 2, 1598: Treaty of Vervins.

RELATED ARTICLES in *Great Lives from History: The Renaissance & Early Modern Era, 1454-1600:* Catherine de Médicis; William Cecil; Elizabeth I; Henry II; Louis XI; Mary I.

June, 1564
TINTORETTO PAINTS FOR THE SCUOLA DI SAN ROCCO

Completed in 1587, Tintoretto's three monumental pictorial cycles in the Scuola di San Rocco illustrate the Passion of Christ, the life of the Virgin and various biblical scenes that involved a complex iconography. Beyond exemplifying the artist's mature painting style, these paintings represent one of the most complex pictorial cycles ever completed.

LOCALE: Scuola di San Rocco, Venice (now in Italy)
CATEGORY: Art

KEY FIGURE
Tintoretto (Jacopo Robusti; c. 1518-1594), painter in charge of the decoration of the Scuola di San Rocco

SUMMARY OF EVENT
Established only in 1478, the Scuola di San Rocco was the last born of the great *scuole*, brotherhoods or confra-

ternities, of Venice. In only a few decades, however, it became one of the most important institutions of charity in the city. Its main building, a grandiose structure, was completed in 1560, and only then were its interior decorations undertaken. Jacopo Robusti, known as Tintoretto, was the Venetian painter who undertook this task, and he presented his first painting for the building in June of 1564. In the course of three distinct painting campaigns (1564-1567, 1576-1581, and 1582-1587), he decorated the main halls—respectively, the Albergo Hall (Sala dell'Albergo), the Upper Hall (Sala Superiore), and the Lower Hall (Sala Terrena). Including more than sixty canvases, often very large, the three pictorial cycles are unprecedented in both their iconographic complexity and their artistic creativity. Indeed, they mark a high point not only of Tintoretto's career but also of Renaissance art.

In art literature, there is a famous anecdote about the awarding of the commission to decorate the Albergo Hall to Tintoretto. According to the famous art biographer Giorgio Vasari in *Le vite de' più eccellenti architetti, pittori, et scultori italiani, da cimabue insino a' tempi nostri* (1550, 2d ed. 1568; *Lives of the Most Eminent Painters, Sculptors, and Architects*, 1855-1885), Tintoretto won the commission over his competitors by installing the large painting representing *Saint Roch in Glory* on the ceiling of the Albergo Hall. The other artists participating in the competition—including Giuseppe Salviati, Paolo Veronese, Federico Zuccari, and Andrea Schiavone—simply submitted their finished sketches, as required by the rules of the competition. Surviving documents corroborate this story: The competition was announced on May 31 and annulled on June 29, 1564, the month in which the Scuola accepted Tintoretto's painting as a donation.

In spite of the fact that the painter donated the painting, the decision to award him the commission was a matter of great debate among the members of the confraternity. Aside from the artist's breach of the terms of the competition, they were probably more preoccupied by the controversial reputation of Tintoretto, who was known for his daring compositions and furious brushwork. These were properties that imbued his paintings with a distinctive energy but were also unconventional and were therefore criticized. Tintoretto most likely won the commission for two reasons: Titian, the Venetian painter who rivaled Michelangelo in fame, was not available; conversely, the confraternity included many members of Tintoretto's guild, the cloth dyers (*tintori*).

In 1565, Tintoretto completed the enormous (536-by-1,124-centimeter) *Crucifixion* and laid to rest all lingering doubts about his artistic merit. This powerful painting captures the beholder's heart and mind at first sight. Although the modern viewer first marvels at the painter's ability to create a deep space for a scene populated by numerous figures often admirably depicted in very difficult and unusual poses (such as the soldiers playing dice or the man digging with a shovel), Tintoretto's achievement lies in the successful rendering of the intense pathos of the event. The mood of the scene is dominated by the stark contrast between the peaceful Christ rising over the group of the Marys at the foot of the Cross and the dozens of detached onlookers, participants and men busy preparing and hoisting the crosses of the two thieves. The compositional solutions and interplay of lighting effects, together with figural postures that guide the beholder's eye and emotional response, form an eloquent testimony to Tintoretto's artistic genius.

Covering a similar amount of space, on the opposite wall the painter completed three scenes of the Passion of Christ. Like the *Crucifixion*, Tintoretto's three paintings of *Christ Before Pilate*, *Ecce Homo*, and *Way to Calvary* also propose daring compositions, radical spatial divisions, and dramatic use of highlights and illumination effects. They too are scenes charged with an intense pathos that invites a pious response from the faithful beholder.

Before the completion of the Albergo Hall (1567), Tintoretto became a member of the confraternity. In 1575, he began the cycle decorating the Upper Hall, again by donating the ceiling's largest painting, *The Brazen Serpent*, which was in place by August, 1576. Subsequently, he proposed to the confraternity that he produce all of the decorations that the Scuola requested, in exchange for the expense of his materials and a yearly provision of one hundred ducats to provide for his retirement. The confraternity officially accepted Tintoretto's proposal on December 2, 1577.

For the Upper Hall, the artist painted thirty-three paintings that explore themes and connections between the Old and the New Testaments, such as *The Fall of the Manna* and *The Last Supper*. The themes chosen concern sacrifice and redemption, the sacraments of Baptism and Eucharist, and divine cleansing and feeding. The latter was a theme particularly dear to the Scuola because of its charitable mission. However, more than the subject, the influence of the confraternity's values is best seen in Tintoretto's emphasis on the sanctity of poverty, articulated in the various appearances of the Holy Family. An innovative aspect of Tintoretto's interpretation of a pictorial cycle is the fact that, rather than appear side by side, works addressing the same theme are visually separated; if this solution forgoes the canonical continuity between paintings in a narrative cycle or those addressing a related subject, it succeeds in providing each painting with a separate identity.

After completing the paintings for the Upper Hall in 1581 and despite the many commissions that Tintoretto had accepted in these years (including very large paintings for the Ducal Palace), he started working on the cycle of the Lower Hall in 1582. The last payment for the painting materials dates from August 12, 1587, when the artist was seventy-eight years old—he would die on May 31, 1594. The cycle of the Lower Hall focuses on the life of the Virgin and the infancy of Christ, including the *Annunciation*, *Adoration of the Magi*, *Flight into Egypt*, *Massacre of the Innocents*, and *Assumption of the Virgin*.

The canvases suggest two trends in Tintoretto's stylistic progression in the later stages of his career. The painter becomes particularly interested in the landscape element while reducing the size of the figures with respect to the pictorial field available. This is readily evident in the *Flight into Egypt*, in which the Holy Family is relegated to the lower left, occupying about one-sixth of the canvas; the rest features vegetation and a distant view of a landscape populated by peasants at work set under the pinkish sky of a setting sun. The active role assigned by the artist to the flora reappears even more forcefully in two scenes, the subject of which has been debated by scholars. Placed on opposite sides of the altar, each of these two paintings features a woman (representing either saints or Ecclesia and Sinagoga) reading by a stream and set in luxuriant vegetation while offering an expansive landscape and sky, elements that create a poetic mood of great intensity.

SIGNIFICANCE

Tintoretto's paintings for the Scuola di San Rocco constitute one of the largest pictorial cycles ever created. From the perspective of Renaissance art, these paintings not only document the stylistic evolution of one of the period's most important painters but also epitomize many of the contributions of the Venetian tradition to the discourse and development of painting. Tintoretto offered many exemplary interpretations of dramatic highlights and compositional solutions that both problematize and expand on the established notions of perspectival space, natural light, and narrative temporality. While exemplifying Mannerist elegance, his elongated figures display the artist's famous brushwork and its mimetic potential. In his accomplished search for the pictorial elements that define pathos and mood in a painting, Tintoretto helped establish the goals pursued by artists for the next century.

—*Renzo Baldasso*

FURTHER READING

Nichols, Tom. *Tintoretto: Tradition and Identity*. London: Reaction Books, 1999. This monograph on Tintoretto dedicates two substantial chapters to the artist's work at the Scuola di San Rocco, paying particular attention to issues of patronage and to the cultural context.

Romanelli, Giandomenico. *Tintoretto: La Scuola Grande di San Rocco*. Milan: Electa, 1994. The most complete monographic study of Tintoretto's work at San Rocco. The volume is accompanied by a full bibliography and more than two hundred color plates illustrating the artist's paintings in all their glorious details. In Italian.

Rosand, David. *Painting in Sixteenth-Century Venice: Titian, Veronese, Tintoretto*. Rev. ed. New York: Cambridge University Press, 1997. In this selective introduction to Venetian Renaissance painting, the author offers insightful formal analyses. Particularly commendable are the pages on Tintoretto's paintings in the Albergo Hall.

Tietze, Hans. *Tintoretto: The Paintings and Drawings with Three Hundred Illustrations*. New York: Phaidon, 1948. Although old, a very good study of Tintoretto.

Valcanover, Francesco. *Jacopo Tintoretto and the Scuola Grande of San Rocco*. Venice: Edizioni Storti, 1991. A concise volume that explores each painting separately, indicating its subject while offering some insightful artistic comments. Includes many color illustrations and a brief introduction to the building and the brotherhood's history.

SEE ALSO: 1469-1492: Rule of Lorenzo de' Medici; 1477-1482: Work Begins on the Sistine Chapel; c. 1478-1519: Leonardo da Vinci Compiles His Notebooks; 1495-1497: Leonardo da Vinci Paints *The Last Supper*; c. 1500: Netherlandish School of Painting; c. 1500: Revival of Classical Themes in Art; 1508-1520: Raphael Paints His Frescoes; 1508-1512 and 1534-1541: Michelangelo Paints the Sistine Chapel; Nov. 3, 1522-Nov. 17, 1530: Correggio Paints the *Assumption of the Virgin*; 1532: Holbein Settles in London; Dec. 23, 1534-1540: Parmigianino Paints *Madonna with the Long Neck*; 1563-1584: Construction of the Escorial.

RELATED ARTICLES in *Great Lives from History: The Renaissance & Early Modern Era, 1454-1600:* The Carracci Family; Jacopo Sansovino; Tintoretto; Marietta Robusti Tintoretto; Titian; Giorgio Vasari; Paolo Veronese.

1560's

1565
SPAIN SEIZES THE PHILIPPINES

Spain's seizure of the Philippines opened a lucrative spice trade route between the Mexican city of Acapulco and the Filipino city of Manila, which flourished for more than two centuries. Spain also used the route to spread the Christian faith to non-Christian peoples around the world.

LOCALE: The Philippines, Spain, Mexico, and the Pacific basin

CATEGORIES: Expansion and land acquisition; trade and commerce; wars, uprisings, and civil unrest; colonization

KEY FIGURES

Miguel López de Legazpi (c. 1510-1572), leader of the first successful expedition to establish a Spanish settlement in the Far East

Andrés de Urdaneta (1498-1568), Catholic friar and cosmographer, charged with the navigation of Legazpi's ships

Ferdinand Magellan (c. 1480-1521), explorer who led the first expedition to circle the globe

Charles V (1500-1558), king of Spain as Charles I, r. 1516-1556, at the beginning of Spain's explorations to the Far East

Philip II (1527-1598), son of Charles V and king of Spain, r. 1556-1598, when the Philippines was colonized

Alexander VI (Rodrigo de Borja y Doms; 1431-1503), Roman Catholic pope, 1492-1503

John II (1455-1495), king of Portugal, r. 1481-1495, and Spain's rival for conquests in the Far East

SUMMARY OF EVENT

In the late fifteenth century, Spain and Portugal were great rivals for sovereignty over the uncharted seas. To keep peace between the wrangling sovereigns of the two Catholic nations, Pope Alexander VI issued a bull in 1493 that drew an imaginary dividing line across the globe from north to south. The pope reserved all lands and seas east of the dividing line to Spain and those west of the line to Portugal. In 1494, by the Treaty of Tordesillas, the two nations moved the line of demarcation to 370 leagues west of the Cape Verde Islands.

The rivalry between Spain and Portugal arose out of the geography of the known world of the period. Traders used three primary overland routes for the movement of their trade goods to and from the Far East. The northern

trade route started in northern China and passed through Constantinople on its way to the Mediterranean. The central route went from the Malay Peninsula to the Mediterranean by way of Constantinople. The southern route also started on the Malay Peninsula, traced its way to the Red Sea, and continued on to Cairo, Egypt. Constantinople was a stop on two of three trade routes; whoever controlled Constantinople was poised to control the very lucrative spice trade. The Ottoman Turks had captured Constantinople in 1453 and had closed the northern and central land trade routes. By treaty, the Turks had allowed Venice control of the southern trade route. Venice had monopolized the coveted Asian spice trade.

Spices were highly desired by the Europeans who needed them, not only for improving their bland food but also for preserving their meat supply. Spices, especially peppercorns, were more valuable than silver or gold; peppercorns were used as payment for land, traded for livestock, and collected for dowries. Spain and Portugal, cut off from the southern trade route, vied with each other to be the first to find another way to the Far East and the lucrative spice trade—a sea route.

A sea route from Europe to the Far East seemed impossible. The large land mass of the American continent, discovered by Christopher Columbus, was thought to block all sea voyages from Europe to the Far East. In 1513, Vasco Núñez de Balboa discovered the large body of water on the far side of the North and South American continents, which became known as the Pacific Ocean. Then, the race was on to see who would be first to discover a sea route from Europe across the Atlantic Ocean, around or through the Americas, to the Pacific Ocean, and on to the Spice Islands in the Far East. Spain had the advantage, having established New Spain (Mexico) on North America's western coast, in the wake of Balboa's discovery.

During this period, Ferdinand Magellan, a young Portuguese explorer, had tried to persuade King John II of Portugal to authorize an expedition that would sail west across the Atlantic to reach the Far East. Angered by King John's refusal to authorize such an expedition, Magellan approached King Charles I of Spain, and won Charles's support. Magellan's expedition left Spain in 1520. Three years later, one of Magellan's ships, the *Victoria*, returned to Spain from the Far East by way of the Pacific Ocean.

Charles, now convinced that the Spice Islands could

be reached by sailing west, authorized four successive expeditions. All the expeditions failed. Only one, led by Ruy Lópes de Villalobos in 1542, managed to leave behind a Spanish presence in what later became known as Mindinao, Philippine Islands. Tiring of his fruitless efforts to establish Spanish colonies in the Far East, King Charles abdicated to his son, Philip II, in 1556.

Philip authorized still another expedition to the Far East and the islands later known as the Philippines. He appointed Father Andrés de Urdaneta navigator and cosmographer. He appointed Miguel López de Legazpi, a relative of Urdaneta, leader of the expedition. Urdaneta at first refused to accompany the expedition, feeling that, according to the tenets of the 1529 Treaty of Zaragoza, the Philippines lay in Portugal's sphere of influence rather than Spain's. The Treaty of Zaragoza drew an imaginary line, north to south, at 297½ leagues east of the Moluccas (Spice Islands). All lands east belonged to Portugal's sphere of influence; all to the west belonged to Spain's. Urdaneta believed the Philippines to be east of the line and, therefore, reserved for Portugal's exploration.

Mexico's *audiencia* (supreme court) under the reign of Spain's Philip II, did not contradict Urdaneta. They simply sent sealed orders with the expedition to be opened when Legazpi's ships had left La Navidad and reached the open seas of the Pacific Ocean. The *audiencia*'s order directed Legazpi and Urdaneta to lay claim to the Philippines and discover a return route from the Philippines to Mexico to use for the trading of spices and for spreading the Catholic faith. Legazpi and Urdaneta eased their disappointment in King Philip's flouting of the Treaty of Zaragoza by considering their claim to the Philippines in the name of Spain a service to God and the Catholic Church.

Legazpi's expedition consisted of two galleons, the *San Pedro* and the *San Pablo*, and two tenders, the *San Juan de Letran* and the *San Lucas*. Legazpi, Urdaneta, four Augustinian missionaries, and 380 men left La Navidad, on the Mexican coast, on November 21, 1564, and reached Cebu, in the archipelago of the Philippines, in February of 1565.

Legazpi, after exploring nearby islands, chose Cebu for the establishment of the Spanish settlement and took possession of the island in the name of Spain. The natives that he and his men encountered on Cebu were hostile. Later, Legazpi discovered that Portuguese sailors had landed there in earlier years and passed themselves off as Spaniards. They had looted native villages, burned fields, and turned the people of Cebu against Spaniards.

When Legazpi attempted to make friends with Tupas, chieftain of the island of Cebu, Legazpi's overtures of friendship were met with opposition. Tupas and his people torched their own villages and fled to the mountains rather than submit to Legazpi and his Spanish rule.

Legazpi's own men caused many of Legazpi's problems. They robbed graves and took jewelry, gold, silver, and other valuables, buried with Cebu's dead. The natives reciprocated by attacking the unfinished settlement, harassing the Spanish soldiers, and making off with food supplies. Legazpi put a stop to his men's despicable behavior, and finally succeeded in winning the trust of Tupas and his people. After this peaceful alliance was formed, Legazpi and his men were able to complete the first permanent Spanish settlement, known as San Miguel.

To establish the return route to Mexico (as instructed by Philip II's sealed orders), Legazpi sent Urdaneta back to Mexico to report the establishment of a Spanish settlement in the Philippines. Urdaneta left Cebu on the *San Pedro* on June 1, 1565, sailed northwest across the Pacific toward the California coast, and then south along the Mexican coast to La Navidad and Acapulco.

SIGNIFICANCE

Urdaneta's return trip to Mexico fulfilled King Philip's sealed orders. For the next two centuries, Manila galleons, engaged in the spice trade, sailed between Acapulco, Mexico, and Manila, Philippines, along Urdaneta's navigational route.

—Barbara C. Stanley

FURTHER READING

Abueva, Jose V., ed. *The Making of the Filipino Nation and Republic: From Barangays, Tribes, Sultanates, and Colony.* Quezon City: University of the Philippines Press, 1998. Comprehensive history of the Philippines from prehistory to the present. Includes bibliographic references and index.

Agoncillo, Teodoro. "Spanish Foundations." In *A Short History of the Philippines.* New York: New American Library, 1969. An early chapter of this short, well-written history, is a highly readable chronology of Spain's conquest of the Philippines.

Arcilla, Jose S. "The Coming of the Spaniards." In *An Introduction to Philippine History.* Manila: Ateneo Publications Office, Ateneo de Manila University, 1971. This work is an overview rather than a detailed chronology. Its discussion of early Filipino history is informative and colorful.

1560's

Headley, John M. "Spain's Asian Presence, 1565-1590: Structures and Aspirations." *Hispanic American Historical Review* 75 (1995): 623-657. Although written in an unnecessarily flowery style, this article offers valuable historical context and is worth reading for those with some knowledge of Spain's presence in Asia.

One Hundred Events That Shaped the Philippines. Mandaluyong City, Philippines: National Centennial Commission and Adarna Book Services, 1999. A close analysis of the historical consequences of one hundred specific events in Filipino history, from prehistory through the Third Republic. Includes illustrations, maps, and bibliographic references.

Parker, Geoffrey. *The Grand Strategy of Philip II.* New Haven, Conn.: Yale University Press, 1998. Contests the traditional view of Philip as conducting his empire by reacting to events as they occurred without any grand plan to guide him. Uses correspondence and other historical documents to delineate a "strategic culture" informing Philip's decisions and his reign.

Includes illustrations, maps, bibliographic references, and index.

Phelan, John Leddy. *The Hispanization of the Philippines: Spanish Aims and Filipino Responses, 1565-1700.* Madison: University of Wisconsin Press, 1959. An annotated, well-indexed discussion of Spanish influences in the history of the Philippines.

SEE ALSO: 1490's: Decline of the Silk Road; Oct. 12, 1492: Columbus Lands in the Americas; June 7, 1494: Treaty of Tordesillas; 1500-1530's: Portugal Begins to Colonize Brazil; 1511-c. 1515: Melaka Falls to the Portuguese; 1542-1543: The New Laws of Spain; 1552: Struggle for the Strait of Hormuz; Dec. 31, 1600: Elizabeth I Charters the East India Company.

RELATED ARTICLES in *Great Lives from History: The Renaissance & Early Modern Era, 1454-1600:* Alexander VI; Vasco Nuñez de Balboa; Charles V; Christopher Columbus; John II; Miguel López de Legazpi; Ferdinand Magellan; Philip II.

May 18-September 8, 1565
SIEGE OF MALTA

The failure of the Turks to seize the island of Malta from the Knights Hospitaller, Christian warriors, crippled the Ottoman naval advance across the Mediterranean.

LOCALE: Island of Malta

CATEGORIES: Expansion and land acquisition; wars, uprisings, and civil unrest

KEY FIGURES

Süleyman the Magnificent (1494/1495-1566), Ottoman sultan, r. 1520-1566

Jean Parisot de La Valette (1494-1568), grand master of the Knights of St. John, 1557-1568

Mustafa Paşa (fl. early sixteenth century), Turkish general

Piali Paşa (fl. sixteenth century), Turkish admiral

Dragut Rais (1485-1565), Turkish corsair

SUMMARY OF EVENT

Like members of the other military orders created in the Kingdom of Jerusalem after the First Crusade (1095-1099), the Knights of the Hospital of St. John of Jerusalem, or the Knights Hospitaller, were soldier-monks, fighters under monastic vows. Though organized to provide charitable services to Christian pilgrims, they soon joined other orders as the backbone of the Crusader kingdom's military resources, guarding its fortresses in the Holy Land.

With the final destruction of that kingdom in 1291, the orders sought new roles and rationales. Better focused than the Templars, who were disbanded by 1312, the Hospitallers seized the Byzantine island of Rhodes in 1310 for their fortress-base and continued with their mandate as protectors against Islamic powers in the eastern Mediterranean.

Within a century, their enemy had become the new Ottoman Turkish sultanate, which completed its conquest of old Byzantine lands with the taking of Constantinople in 1453 by Sultan Mehmed II. In 1480, the year before his death, Mehmed attempted to capture Rhodes but failed. Forty years later, the new sultan, Süleyman the Magnificent, considered it a priority to remove the Hospitallers because he saw them as a threat to his sea-lanes. After a long and bitter siege in 1522, the order was forced to capitulate, though its survivors were allowed an honorable departure.

In 1530, the Hospitallers reluctantly accepted from the Holy Roman Emperor, Charles V, the archipelago of Malta, together with the north African fortress of Tripoli, because they had been looking for a new base. Fortifying the main island of Malta itself, the Hospitallers supported the policies of Charles V in opposing the Turkish conquest of north Africa, thereby assuming a central role in this latest phase of Christian-Muslim struggle.

The election of Jean Parisot de La Valette as the new grand master in 1557 revitalized Hospitaller efficiency and energy. Determined in his last years of his reign to complete what he had left unfinished in 1522, the aging sultan prepared a massive expedition against the Christians.

The episode's protagonists themselves symbolized the Christian-Muslim struggle over the Mediterranean. Born in about the same year, the grand master and the sultan were both seventy years old: Süleyman, plagued by gout, was made more determined by his ailments; La Valette, in remarkably robust health for his age, was a superlative leader. A Provençal by birth, La Valette had joined the order when he was twenty and was a survivor of the 1522 siege of Rhodes. Captured by Turkish corsairs at age forty-seven in 1541, he served a year's term as a galley slave before release in a prisoner exchange. He rose rapidly through all the important Hospitaller commands, demonstrating both military and administrative talent.

Süleyman assigned three talented but individualistic commanders against La Valette, and their differences undermined the project from the start. Mustafa Paşa was as old as both the sultan and the grand master, perhaps older. Born of a family claiming descent from the Prophet's standard-bearer, Mustafa was an experienced general whose fanatic hatred of Christians made him a brutal foe. He had incurred disgrace during the siege of Rhodes in 1522, but he had reestablished himself in subsequent military service to the sultan; now he had his chance for belated vindication against the Hospitallers.

Mustafa's cocommander was Piali Paşa, the sultan's chief admiral. Born of Christian parents, raised a Muslim, and known as a distinguished naval warrior, he had served Süleyman in the conquest of the north African coast, culminating in the seizure of Djerba in 1558. Married to the sultan's granddaughter, he was about forty-five at this time.

The third Turkish commander was to be the corsair admiral Dragut Rais, trained by the brilliant Ottoman military leader Khayr al-Dīn (d. 1546), better known as Barbarossa. Four years in captivity and as a galley slave (from 1540 to 1544) hardened Dragut's hatred of Christians. After Barbarossa's death in 1546, Dragut had succeeded him in ravaging Christian coasts and humiliating the Genoese admiral Andrea Doria (1466-1560). Peerless in strategic skill and in knowledge of Mediterranean geography, Dragut knew Malta particularly well, having raided it no less than seven times between 1540 and 1565. On one occasion, in 1551, after ravaging the neighboring island of Gozo and enslaving most of its population, Dragut crossed over to Tripoli, forcing its surrender and disgracing its governor: La Valette. Joined by Piali Paşa in 1560, Dragut had foiled La Valette's efforts to recover Tripoli and also had seized the island of Djerba. By now Dragut and La Valette were quintessential adversaries.

Though aware of Süleyman's intentions, La Valette had been counting on another month's grace when Mustafa and Piali unexpectedly appeared off the coasts of Malta on the night of May 18, 1565. He had about seven hundred knights only and about eighty-five hundred mercenaries and levies from the local population (who generally supported the knights). The huge Turkish force from Constantinople, in striking contrast, had about thirty thousand men and nearly two hundred ships. Landing unopposed, the two Turkish commanders intended a quick seizure of the fortresses around Grand Harbour and the order's headquarters on the island's east side. However, the knights bravely fought off initial attacks. Mustafa and Piali impetuously decided to concentrate on the fortress of St. Elmo, which commanded the entrance to the Grand Harbour, and mounted a massive artillery attack. They had anxiously anticipated Christian relief, and had attacked without waiting for Dragut's advice.

Dragut arrived at the end of May with additional forces from Tripoli. He was too late to reverse the strategic mistakes of Mustafa and Piali, so he set about perfecting the siege of the crucial fortress. Desperate for the promised reinforcements, La Valette knew that holding St. Elmo was an essential stalling operation. After superhuman resistance for more than one month, the defenders fought virtually to the last man when the final Turkish assault was launched on June 23. The victory cost the Turks more than six thousand men—including Dragut, who was fatally wounded by a stray shot. Uluch ʿAlī, a renegade Muslim corsair, hardly compensated for the loss of Dragut.

A small Spanish relief force of more than six hundred men arrived by June 29 and, thanks to Turkish negligence, reached the beleaguered knights one week later. Meanwhile, continuing with their mistaken strategy, the

Turks attacked the two settled peninsulas within the Grand Harbour—Senglea and Birgu—each with important fortresses at their tips. The war of attrition now became prolonged siege operations, pressed by the Turks and resisted by the Christians with equal bitterness. Another Turkish commander, this time Hassem Barbarossa, son of the great Barbarossa, son-in-law of Dragut, and governor of Algiers, arrived to join the first Turkish assault on one fortress on July 15. That assault failed, and the fighting dragged on.

On August 7, a renewed assault nearly succeeded but was beaten back by La Valette's dogged leadership and the devastation of the Turkish camp by knights from the inland fortress of Mdina. Two weeks later, a Turkish siege tower directed against the walls was destroyed. To be sure, the desperate defenders were reduced to barely six hundred fighting men, but on September 7 and 8, the viceroy of Sicily arrived with a relief force that eventually totaled sixteen thousand. The Turks panicked and began a disordered retreat; Mustafa's efforts to reverse this failed, and on September 11, the shattered Turkish forces departed for Constantinople.

Mustafa and Piali evaded the sultan's rage: The former faded into obscurity, while the latter commanded again in the annexation of Chios (1566) and the conquest of Cyprus (1570), and Uluch ʿAlī fought heroically again at the Battle of Lepanto (1571). Meanwhile, vowing to lead another attack on Malta, Süleyman died campaigning in Hungary in 1566. Heaped with honors, La Valette survived two years more, during which he began building Malta's new capital behind the St. Elmo fortress, naming it Valetta, after himself. The Knights Hospitaller continued to rule Malta until expelled by Napoléon I (1769-1821) in 1798 and transferred to Rome (they are still there, and the order continues with its charitable activities). Under British rule, Malta heroically resisted another blistering attack, this time from the German bombing in World War II; it became an independent republic in 1974.

SIGNIFICANCE

If the Turks' failure to seize Malta did not immediately end their dominant presence in the central Mediterranean, it did signal its waning (furthered by the verdict of Lepanto), and it guaranteed the future of Spanish power in the region. It also thrilled Christian Europe with the example of epic heroism set by the defenders of Malta, in what has been seen as a climactic episode in the broader history of the Crusades.

—John W. Barker

FURTHER READING

Bradford, Ernle. *The Great Siege*. New York: Harcourt, Brace & World, 1962. A lively "popular" account, if sometimes a little insecure on details.

_____. *The Shield and the Sword: The Knights of St. John, Jerusalem, Rhodes, and Malta*. New York: E. P. Dutton, 1973. A broader account of the Hospitallers' entire history and a vivid treatment for the general reader.

Goodwin, Stefan. *Malta, Mediterranean Bridge*. Westport, Conn.: Bergin & Garvey, 2002. Good overview of the island's history and its culture and society.

Nicholson, Helen. *The Knights Hospitaller*. Woodbridge: Boydell, 2001. Concise scholarly overview, with an excellent bibliography.

Pickles, Tim. *Malta, 1565: Last Battle of the Crusades*. Wellingborough: Osprey, 1998. Part of the Campaign series. A detailed account of the battle, richly illustrated and with a "war-gaming" epilogue.

Seward, Desmond. *The Monks of War: The Military Religious Orders*. 2d ed. London: Penguin Books, 1995. A popular and reliable study of the Hospitallers as warrior-monks.

Sire, H. J. A. *The Knights of Malta*. New Haven, Conn.: Yale University Press, 1994. Another comprehensive history, though heavily weighted toward the later centuries.

SEE ALSO: 1520-1566: Reign of Süleyman; June 28, 1522-Dec. 27, 1522: Siege and Fall of Rhodes; 1536: Turkish Capitulations Begin; Oct. 20-27, 1541: Holy Roman Empire Attacks Ottomans in Algiers; 1552: Struggle for the Strait of Hormuz; July, 1570-Aug., 1571: Siege of Famagusta and Fall of Cyprus; Oct. 7, 1571: Battle of Lepanto.

RELATED ARTICLES in *Great Lives from History: The Renaissance & Early Modern Era, 1454-1600:* Barbarossa; Bayezid II; Charles V; Süleyman the Magnificent.

September, 1565
ST. AUGUSTINE IS FOUNDED

The first permanent European settlement in North America began with a failed quest to convert the indigenous peoples of Florida to Christianity. After fighting French Protestant settlers and the Florida Indians who supported them, the Spanish abandoned that settlement. The founding of St. Augustine, however, led to Spanish domination of Florida that would last for more than two centuries.

LOCALE: Village of Seloy (now in Florida)
CATEGORIES: Exploration and discovery; colonization; expansion and land acquisition

KEY FIGURES

Pedro Menéndez de Avilés (1519-1574), explorer who founded St. Augustine, Florida
Doña Antonia (fl. sixteenth century), Calusa Indian whom Menéndez "married"
Chief Carlos (d. 1567), cacique of the Calusa
René de Laudonnière (d. 1582), French Huguenot who settled Fort Caroline

SUMMARY OF EVENT

In September, 1565, the Saturiba inhabitants of the village of Seloy welcomed the Spaniards who had sailed into the inlet's shallow harbor by kissing them on their hands. Pedro Menéndez de Avilés stepped onto shore to the blare of trumpets and the echo of gunpowder. As banners were raised, Menéndez named the village San Agustín (St. Augustine) and claimed it for Spain and its king, Philip II.

Many countries saw the merit in gaining a foothold along the prized eastern coastline of North America. Spain, however, believed that the vast empire belonged to it because Spanish explorer Juan Ponce de León had taken possession of Florida for the Crown in 1513. In addition, Philip II wished to protect the many unexplored waterways of Florida, thinking that one of them might be a passage to the East.

In 1564, however, French Huguenot René de Laudonnière established the settlement of Fort Caroline on the St. Johns River. When the news reached Philip, he contracted the services of Menéndez for a period of three years. Philip named Menéndez *adelantado* (contractual conqueror and governor) of Florida and commissioned him to conquer and settle the land.

Menéndez, a native of Asturias, was an experienced seaman and leader. Although at one time he had been convicted and jailed for smuggling, Menéndez could boast of skills as a privateer, businessman, and captain-general of the Spanish fleet in 1555-1556, which had won him favor with the king. For Menéndez, the assignment took on many meanings. His only son, Don Juan Menéndez, had been shipwrecked along the coast, and he hoped to find him. He also wished to rid the land of heretic French Protestants, to convert the indigenous peoples to Catholicism, and to gain position and wealth.

After his successful landing at St. Augustine, Menéndez quickly launched an attack on the Huguenots (French followers of Protestant reformer John Calvin), who had settled at Fort Caroline. Menéndez marched 40 miles north through the rain to the fort with a force of five hundred harquebusiers. Eager to be rid of the French, the indigenous Saturibas aided the Spanish by leading the way. The soldiers met with little resistance, because most men of fighting age had struck out in pursuit of two ships from Menéndez's fleet. The women and children were spared and sent to Puerto Rico, but a reported 130 men were killed. In a letter to the king, Menéndez justified the killing by saying that the men were from the "evil Lutheran sect."

Menéndez renamed the fort San Mateo and, leaving a small garrison of soldiers to guard it, returned to St. Augustine. There, he learned that the French who had left Fort Caroline had been shipwrecked. Menéndez intercepted the survivors at a broad inlet 18 miles south of St. Augustine. The French offered to surrender, provided their lives would be spared. Menéndez agreed to the surrender, only to kill all but a few Catholics, adolescents, and some musicians and tradesmen. The site of the massacre retained the name Matanzas (slaughters). Again, Menéndez explained his action by claiming that it was a necessary strike against heresy.

Although Menéndez contended that both the indigenous and Protestant beliefs had the same Satanic roots, he believed that he could convert the indigenous in the area if he eliminated the French and kept the two cultures from becoming enmeshed. Conversion was one of his intentions when he visited the Calusa settlement in southwestern Florida in 1566. Menéndez also wished to find his son and establish a Spanish settlement in the same area to protect the coastal shipping lanes from the French, the English, and the Calusas, who were noted for their plundering of Spanish shipwrecks.

The cacique, Chief Carlos (also known as Escambaba

or Escambaha), eagerly formed a friendship with Menéndez, hoping to arrange a political alliance with Spain. Carlos's power was precarious, and he needed an ally to thwart his cousin and rival, Don Felipe. To cement his relationship, Carlos demanded that Menéndez take his middle-aged sister, called Doña Antonia by the Spaniards, to be his wife. Menéndez did not wish to offend the Calusas, and although he already had a wife, he acquiesced. The Calusas were not an agricultural people but rather survived through fishing and trading. The Calusa had a highly sophisticated culture, with art that included carved wooden figures and painted wooden masks. Scavengers of wrecked Spanish ships, they recovered gold, silver, and copper, then developed hammering and embossing techniques.

Menéndez did not succeed in converting the indigenous nor in settling Calusa lands. He did make peace,

A sixteenth century street-life scene of St. Augustine, the oldest continuously populated city in what is now the United States. (Hulton|Archive by Getty Images)

however, between Carlos and the Tequestas, who were blood relations. In a series of plots and counterplots, Menéndez's captain, Francisco de Reinoso, murdered Carlos, placing Don Felipe in power. The Calusas nevertheless retaliated, and the Spanish abandoned their fort. The Calusas retained their power in southwestern Florida, and although they decreased in numbers over the centuries, it is believed that they still occupied the area in the mid-nineteenth century as part of the Seminole and Miccosukee tribes.

Menéndez's initial goal was to establish two or three fortified and populated settlements within three years. The first winter was harsh. Few supply ships came into port to provide the residents with food, and the palm thatch huts of St. Augustine barely kept out the elements. Those who took the advice of the indigenous to drink boiled sassafras tea survived. Despite all the hardships, within a year and a half Menéndez had established five forts along the east coast and two garrisons on the west coast.

Before long, however, the French rallied against the Spanish, allying again with the indigenous. The Saturiba had changed their allegiance after being assaulted by the Spanish soldiers and condemned by missionaries for their religious beliefs and practices. In 1568, they joined the French privateer Dominique de Gourgues in destroying Fort San Mateo. In retaliation for the earlier massacre of his fellow countrymen, de Gourgues hanged the remaining Spaniards from the same trees, it is said, that the Spaniards had used for hanging the French. The French destroyed all the Spanish garrisons except Santa Elena and St. Augustine.

Although Florida was a key element in protecting Caribbean interests, its lack of precious gems was a detriment. Unable to get funding from the Crown to reclaim lost settlements, and given the added office of the governorship of Cuba, Menéndez's leadership began to wane. Menéndez could not comprehend the turnaround of the indigenous, and he condemned them as warlike and having bad dispositions. He recommended that the entire population of Florida Indians be sold into slavery in the Caribbean. The Spanish government opposed the move, however.

SIGNIFICANCE

Menéndez died in 1574 in Spain, but not without a legacy: By founding St. Augustine and other forts, he has been credited with establishing a Spanish

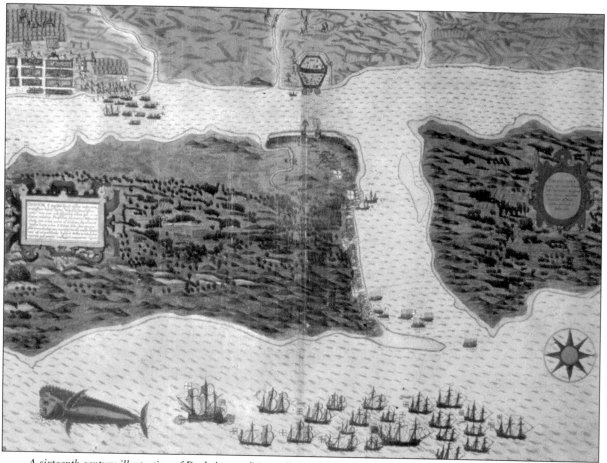

A sixteenth century illustration of Drake's expedition, off the coast of St. Augustine. (Hulton|Archive by Getty Images)

dominance in Florida that lasted for more than two centuries.

In 1576, Orista Indians forced Santa Elena to be abandoned, and, in 1587, it was dismantled. St. Augustine remained a Spanish colony, except for a twenty-one-year British occupation, for more than 250 years, until Spain ratified the Adams-Onís Treaty (1819), ceding Florida to the United States.

—*Marilyn Elizabeth Perry*

FURTHER READING

Bushnell, Amy. *The King's Coffer: Proprietors of the Spanish Florida Treasury, 1565-1702.* Gainesville: University Press of Florida, 1981. Uses correspondence to piece together the economic, social, and cultural histories of the early days of St. Augustine.

Deagan, Kathleen A., ed. *America's Ancient City: Spanish St. Augustine, 1565-1763.* New York: Garland, 1991. Selected writings by noted Florida historians on different aspects of the first period of Spanish occupation in Florida, through investigation of documents, archaeological findings, and cartography.

Gallay, Alan, ed. *Voices of the Old South: Eyewitness Accounts, 1528-1861.* Athens: University of Georgia Press, 1994. Menéndez's account of his travels in Florida is one of many first-person narratives reproduced in this anthology of antebellum primary sources.

Glete, Jan. *War and the State in Early Modern Europe: Spain, the Dutch Republic, and Sweden as Fiscal-Military States, 1500-1660.* New York: Routledge, 2002. An account of the development of Spain into an empire founded upon military power and economic exploitation of foreign territories. Provides the larger context for Menéndez's life and career.

Larsen, Clark Spencer, ed. *Bioarchaeology of Spanish Florida: The Impact of Colonialism.* Gainesville: University Press of Florida, 2001. Anthology detailing the effects of St. Augustine upon all aspects of indigenous life in Florida, from diet to disease to everyday behavior.

Lyon, Eugene, ed. *Pedro Menéndez de Avilés*. New York: Garland, 1995. Volume 24 in the Spanish Borderlands Sourcebooks series, this work explores Menéndez's legacy with illustrations and maps.

Mancall, Peter C., and James Merrell, eds. *American Encounters: Natives and Newcomers from European Contact to Indian Removal, 1500-1850*. New York: Routledge, 1999. Republished academic essays, mostly from scholarly journals, describing first-contact encounters throughout North America.

Milanich, Jerald, and Samuel Proctor, eds. *Tacachale: Essays on the Indians of Florida and Southeastern Georgia During the Historic Period*. Gainesville: University Press of Florida, 1978. A thoroughly researched collection depicting the interaction of indigenous and European cultures at the time of conquest.

Waterbury, Jean Parker, ed. *The Oldest City: St. Augustine, Saga of Survival*. St. Augustine, Fla.: St. Augustine Historical Society, 1983. A detailed chronology of St. Augustine, with each chapter written by a Florida historian knowledgeable in a particular period.

Weber, David J. *The Spanish Frontier in North America*. New Haven, Conn.: Yale University Press, 1992. A well-researched narration of the Spanish colonization of North America and its impact on the peoples, institutions, and lives of the explorers, the colonists, and the indigenous.

SEE ALSO: Oct. 12, 1492: Columbus Lands in the Americas; 1493-1521: Ponce de León's Voyages; 1528-1536: Narváez's and Cabeza de Vaca's Expeditions; May 28, 1539-Sept. 10, 1543: De Soto's North American Expedition; Feb. 23, 1540-Oct., 1542: Coronado's Southwest Expedition; 1542-1543: The New Laws of Spain; July 4, 1584-1590: Lost Colony of Roanoke; Jan., 1598-Feb., 1599: Oñate's New Mexico Expedition.

RELATED ARTICLES in *Great Lives from History: The Renaissance & Early Modern Era, 1454-1600:* Christopher Columbus; Pedro Menéndez de Avilés; Philip II; Juan Ponce de León; Hernando de Soto; Tascalusa.

1566-1574
REIGN OF SELIM II

Selim's reign marks the beginning of the decline of the Ottoman Empire and of a succession of incompetent sultans who left the details of governing to their chief ministers.

LOCALE: Constantinople, Ottoman Empire (now Istanbul, Turkey)
CATEGORY: Government and politics

KEY FIGURES
Selim II (1524-1574), Ottoman sultan, r. 1566-1574
Süleyman the Magnificent (1494/1495-1566), Ottoman sultan and father of Selim, r. 1520-1566
Mehmed Paşa Sokollu (1505-1579), Ottoman grand vizier under Selim
Roxelana (Hürrem Sultana; c. 1510-1558), mother of Selim, made possible his sultanship
Murad III (1546-1595), son of Selim and sultan, r. 1574-1595

SUMMARY OF EVENT
In 1566, at the age of forty-two, Selim II became sultan of what was then the greatest empire in the world. Selim in-

herited the Ottoman Empire from his father, Süleyman the Magnificent, who reigned during the peak of the Ottoman Empire's golden age. Süleyman was one of a succession of highly competent and administratively involved sultans who always accompanied his troops into major battles. He died in his tent, at the age of seventy-two, as his forces faced those of the Holy Roman Emperor Maximilian II. Süleyman's death was kept secret for three weeks, so that Selim had enough time to reach Constantinople and be proclaimed sultan.

Selim's selection from the pool of possible heirs had little to do with his native talents and even less to do with preparation for leadership. For more than two centuries, Ottoman leaders had trained favored heirs in military and administrative affairs. It was not by accident that a relatively obscure Turkish tribe was able to conquer a large empire and rule it efficiently.

Selim's selection to rule the empire can be attributed to his dynamic mother Roxelana, who was Süleyman's favorite concubine. Roxelana, of Slavic descent, lived her life with the singular goal of obtaining the throne for Selim. To achieve this end, she intrigued to convince

Süleyman to order the murder of his sons Mustafa and Bayezid, born to other harem women. Both of these sons were well accomplished in combat and administration. Roxelana died in 1558, five years after the murder of Mustafa, who was strangled with the traditional silk cord (to avoid spilling royal blood) while visiting Süleyman's tent for dinner.

Due to his fair complexion and blond hair, Selim was known at the beginning of his reign as "yellow Selim." He was well educated, spoke eloquently, and composed both poetry and music. Unlike his murdered step brothers, however, he had no military training and little experience in government. Much of his early life was spent in the harem of the Topkapi Palace. He was the first sultan without training from his predecessor. His only political experience came later in life, when he was a rather inept governor of several remote Anatolian provinces. At the time of Süleyman's death, Selim was serving as governor of Kütahya in western Turkey.

Selim's lack of training was exceeded only by his lack of interest in governing. His first official act was to banish his father's harem and establish his own new harem of 150 ladies-in-waiting. He then plunged into the pleasures of harem life and soon established a reputation for multiple orgies. He also descended into the depths of chronic alcoholism, earning infamy in Islamic history as "Selim the drunkard," notorious for his alcohol-induced rages. He became the first sultan to never have accompanied his troops into battle. Instead, his life became devoted to daily pleasures.

By default, Ottoman policy was set by the sultan's ministers. Selim was fortunate to be served by the talented Mehmed Paşa Sokollu, who was the last grand vizier (prime minister) to wield considerable power in Constantinople. Selim inherited Sokollu from Süleyman. Under Sokollu's guidance, early in 1568, the Ottomans were able to end their conflict with the Holy Roman Empire. At the same time, they established friendly relations between the Turks and their rivals, the Ṣafavid rulers of Iran. In 1570, Sokollu established peaceful relations with Russia, but only after he failed to take Astrakhan and after he lost a fleet in a storm. Expeditions to Tunis and Yemen to put down rebellious leaders were successful. Hence, the first years of Selim's reign were relatively peaceful and stable. The stability was upset in 1571, however, by Selim's decision to expand the empire by taking Cyprus.

The invasion of Cyprus was the one instance where Selim overruled Sokollu, who feared the invasion could forge an anti-Ottoman alliance and result in major war-

Ottoman sultan Selim II at a military camp, with tents and armed soldiers, during the time of the Ottomans' war with Russia (1568-1571). (Hulton|Archive by Getty Images)

fare. Detractors pointed to Selim's desire to gain free access to his favorite Cypriot wine, which was stocked in great abundance, as one factor behind his sudden political interest. Though the invasion was successful, it caused Pope Pius V to summon an alliance of Spain, Germany, and the major northern Italian states (the Holy League) to repel Ottoman expansion. This led to a fleet of more than two hundred Holy League ships, which faced nearly three hundred Turkish ships at the Battle of Lepanto in 1571. Although commanded by the capable admiral Kilic Ali, the Turks lost 90 percent of their ships and also lost control of Tunis.

Though Lepanto was a serious humiliation, it was by no means the end of the world for the Ottomans. Sokollu rapidly built a larger and more modern fleet, while the Holy League failed to follow up its victory, preferring in-

1560's

stead to engage in divisive quarrels. Tunis was retaken in 1574, and the Turks were able to keep control of Cyprus. The Mediterranean was still very much in Ottoman control.

Selim died December 12, 1574, while Sokollu was planning an attack on Venice using his newly constructed fleet. After drinking a vintage bottle of his favorite Cypriot wine, Selim retired to his Turkish bath, slipped on the marble floor, and fractured his skull.

SIGNIFICANCE

Selim's short, dramatic reign did not include any major catastrophes. Even the defeat at Lepanto had largely symbolic value. Ships and seamen were easily replaceable. What was significant, however, was that Selim was the first of a number of self-indulgent sultans, lacking both the capacity and will to rule effectively. Selim's son and successor Murad III had his father's love of alcohol and an addiction to opium. Murad had a love of painting and clock making, but little interest in ruling.

After Selim's reign there were no grand viziers of Sokollu's caliber to rescue the empire administratively, which complicated matters for the sultans who followed. Viziers and members of the divan (ruling council) became increasingly corrupt. Decisions were often influenced by harem infighting, palace intrigues, and military revolts. The Turkish expression "the fish rots from the head down," aptly describes the effects of Selim's reign. The Ottoman Empire had peaked and would decline after Selim, until it became known by the nineteenth century as the "sick man of Europe."

Although historians point to the reign of Selim as the beginning of Turkish decline, they do not blame him specifically for its decline. Süleyman the Magnificent, during the last years of his reign, also preferred to leave decision making to his grand vizier and engaged in lavish spending. Moreover, Ottoman control of the Mediterranean did not, by Selim's reign, mean world economic hegemony. Real wealth and power were increasingly based on transoceanic trade. Finally, systemic flaws in palace life and the ways potential imperial successors were raised functioned largely to produce sultans with manifest personality disorders.

—Irwin Halfond

FURTHER READING

Barber, Noel. *Subjects of the Sultan: Culture and Daily Life in the Ottoman Empire*. New York: I. B. Tauris, 2000. A detailed presentation of everyday life in Ottoman Turkey.

Freely, John. *Inside the Seraglio: The Private Lives of the Sultans in Istanbul*. New York: Penguin, 2001. A study of life at Topkapi and other palaces, and the private lives of the sultans. Contains a bibliography, an index, and maps.

Goodwin, Jason. *Lords of the Horizon: A History of the Ottoman Empire*. New York: Henry Holt, 1999. Aspects of political and social life in the Ottoman Empire in an enjoyable, popular history. Contains a chronology, glossary, bibliography, and an index.

Imber, Colin. *The Ottoman Empire, 1300-1650: The Structure of Power*. New York: Palgrave Macmillan, 2004. A scholarly study of the expansion of the Ottoman Empire and the political structures created to rule it. Glossary, bibliography, index, and maps.

Inalcik, Halil. *The Ottoman Empire: The Classical Age, 1300-1600*. London: Phoenix Press, 2001. An excellent and detailed analysis of the rise of the Ottoman Empire as a world power by a leading Turkish scholar. Includes a glossary of terms, a bibliography, and an index.

Shaw, Stanford J. *Empire of the Gazis: The Rise and Decline of the Ottoman Empire, 1280-1808*. Vol. 1 in *History of the Ottoman Empire and Modern Turkey*. New York: Cambridge University Press, 1983. A reliable treatment of the empire of the sultans. Contains maps, an index, and a bibliography.

SEE ALSO: 1454-1481: Rise of the Ottoman Empire; Beginning 1504: Decline of the Ḥafṣid Dynasty; 1512-1520: Reign of Selim I; 1559-1561: Süleyman's Sons Wage Civil War; c. 1568-1571: Ottoman-Russian War; July, 1570-Aug., 1571: Siege of Famagusta and Fall of Cyprus; Oct. 7, 1571: Battle of Lepanto; 1574-1595: Reign of Murad III.

RELATED ARTICLES in *Great Lives from History: The Renaissance & Early Modern Era, 1454-1600:* Bayezid II; İbrahim Paşa; Maximilian II; Pius V; Süleyman the Magnificent.

July 22, 1566
PIUS V EXPELS THE PROSTITUTES FROM ROME

Pope Pius V's edict expelling the prostitutes from Rome was part of his wide-ranging reform program that sought to improve the disciplinary life of both the clergy and laity and to regenerate the city morally in the face of Protestant criticism.

LOCALE: Rome, Italy
CATEGORIES: Religion; social reform

KEY FIGURE
Pius V (Antonio Ghislieri; 1504-1572), Roman
     Catholic pope, 1566-1572

SUMMARY OF EVENT
During the early sixteenth century, the number of prostitutes within Rome had made the city an object of derision by Protestant and Catholic reformers alike. As the city's population had grown, so had the number of ambassadors, envoys, and businessmen who visited the Christian capital—and so had the number of prostitutes. Many of the Roman prostitutes were famous and were even able to rent houses from some of the best Roman families. Such were the conditions in Rome when Pius V became pope in 1566.

Although his reign lasted only six years, until 1572, Pius V was one of the most important popes of the Counter-Reformation. Born in 1504 of peasant parents in Alessandria in northern Italy, Antonio Ghislieri entered the Dominican order at the age of fourteen and assumed the religious name Michele. He went to Bologna for higher studies, lectured in philosophy and theology at Pavia, and was nominated commissar of the Inquisition there. He served as subprovincial (*diffinitor*) of Lombardy and was appointed to the post of Inquisitor in Como in northern Italy in 1550. His success in these positions attracted the attention of the papacy, and in 1551, Julius III appointed him commissar general of the Roman Inquisition, a position that Pope Paul IV reconfirmed in 1556.

In 1556, Ghislieri was consecrated bishop of Sutri and Nepi, in 1557, he was elevated to the cardinalate, and in 1558, he was named Grand Inquisitor of the Roman church for life. Although Ghislieri fell out of favor with Pope Pius IV (1559-1565), upon the latter's death the majority of cardinals elected him to the papacy. Despite his reluctance to accept the position, in 1566, Ghislieri assumed the pontificate under the name Pius V.

Pius had become famous for his austerity, devout piety, and strenuous asceticism. As pope, he continued to wear his friar's habit under pontifical robes. He moreover sported a long white beard and walked barefoot and bareheaded in penitential processions. He attended inquisitorial sessions personally and was determined to prevent the penetration of Protestantism into the Italian peninsula.

As a fiery reformer, Pius had a new palace for the Inquisition built at Rome, he established the Congregation of the Index to tighten control over what was printed through the Index of Prohibited Books, and he strongly enforced the decrees of the Council of Trent (1545-1563), Catholicism's response to the Protestant Reformation. Pius also introduced a monastic austerity into the papal residence and sought to regenerate a moral revival within the city of Rome. He had a clear program of moral and disciplinary reform for both the clergy and the laity. Shortly after becoming pope, he issued edicts against moral offenses, blasphemy, and concubinage for the city of Rome. These were followed throughout early 1566 with renewed decrees concerning the profanation of Sundays and festivals, simony, sodomy, dress, luxury, begging, and gossiping.

As a reformer, one of Pius's most notable attempts to cleanse Rome of immorality was his edict against prostitution. While previous popes, such as Leo X, Clement VII, and Paul IV, had legislated against prostitution, many Roman prostitutes (*cortegiane*) had gained a celebrated and privileged status. As part of the reforming trend of the Counter-Reformation, all of the popes tried to eliminate prostitution within Rome, as the city had become, in the view of many of the Protestant Reformers, the Babylon of Christendom. As a precursor to Pius's decree, in June of 1566, the Roman police had already driven prostitutes out of some of the quarters of the city.

On July 22, 1566, the feast of St. Mary Magdalene (the patron saint of prostitutes), Pius ordered that the most notorious prostitutes leave Rome within six days and evacuate the Papal States within a circumscribed period of time if they refused either to marry or to enter a convent. This was the first of his edicts against prostitution, and as a result, twenty-four of the most famous Roman courtesans fled the city. Two weeks later, Pius promulgated a new edict that resulted in the expulsion of thirty-seven more Roman prostitutes from the city.

The Roman populace fiercely protested these measures. As more prostitutes received their notices of ex-

REGULATING PROSTITUTION

Pope Pius V's expulsion of prostitutes from Rome was part of a long history of church and secular regulations placed on prostitutes. The daily life of a prostitute was marked by contradiction: They were condemned and scorned by society, church, and state, but they also were tolerated because of their earnings, which were appropriated through government taxation and by those who provided a place for the woman and her client to "do business."

- As an independent agent in sixteenth- and seventeenth-century Venice, the prostitute gave over a fifth of her earnings to those who supplied the bed, linens, and food. Should she try for more [money], men were quick to punish. In Rome there was the supposed justice of the *trentuno* to punish prostitutes thought to have cheated or robbed a client: the threat of gang-rape by thirty-one men.
- Pope Pius V taxed the women's earnings even after he had officially banned them from the town [Rome], insisting that the tax would cut down the numbers of women in the trade. The tax went for streets and for bridges.
- The appearance of syphilis in epidemic proportions, coupled with the religious enthusiasms of the sixteenth century, made it temporarily impossible for any women to work as prostitutes. As the virus spread from Italy to the west and north of Europe, townsmen identified women as the sole carriers. Secular and religious authorities tried to protect men by forbidding all contact.
- A sixteenth-century Spanish Catholic churchman described the function of the brothel: "It is like the stable or latrine for the house. Because just as the city keeps itself clean by providing a separate place where filth and dung are gathered, etc., so . . . acts the brothel: where the filth and ugliness of the flesh are gathered like the garbage and dung of the city."

Source: Excerpted from *A History of Their Own: Women in Europe from Prehistory to the Present*, edited by Bonnie S. Anderson and Judith P. Zinsser, vol. 1 (New York: Harper & Row, 1989), pp. 363 *passim.*

pulsion, many who did not have the means to leave the city fled for security to the quarter of the city named the Trastevere. Many inhabitants of the Trastevere complained about the appearance of the prostitutes in their quarter, and some allegedly claimed that they would rather burn down the quarter than live near prostitutes.

Not only were the prostitutes dislocated physically, but many of them were also in difficult economic straits. While some of the wealthier ones had items such as clothes and shoes that they could sell for hard currency, under Pius's reform legislation, all trade between Jews and Christians was now prohibited in Rome. Jewish merchants had traditionally filled an economic role in the city by buying small items in exchange for hard currency. Now, however, some prostitutes were forced to leave the city with many possessions but little or no money.

Other prostitutes, however, were in debt, and business

owners who had loaned items to them on credit were afraid that they would be deprived of their income. Business owners were not the only Romans to protest Pius's decrees; customs officials likewise complained that the expulsion of prostitutes would lead to a decrease in the importation of taxable goods. Property owners claimed that Pius's actions had precipitated a drastic drop in rents; others feared the possible depopulation of the city.

Thus Pius's decrees transformed a large sector of the Roman economy into a black market overnight and sent shock waves throughout Rome and beyond. The city council of Rome first sent a deputation to Pius to encourage him to rescind the decree; when it met with refusal, the council presented him a written complaint. The ambassadors of Spain and Portugal also appealed the decree, but with no success.

Pius remained intransigent on the issue, and by August 10, many of the most notorious prostitutes had left Rome or had been converted to other activities. However, news soon reached Rome that many of the expelled prostitutes had met death at the hands of highwaymen outside the city. The refugees had provided easy targets for highway robbers, and Pius was once again asked to reconsider the issue. Pius's stance softened somewhat, and he assigned prostitutes to a segregated quarter of Rome, which they were forbidden to leave either day or night under the penalty of public flogging. Furthermore, they could remain within the quarter only on condition that they end their public disorder.

Pius arranged for special sermons to be delivered to prostitutes in their quarter every Sunday afternoon, and in September of 1566, he mandated that incorrigible prostitutes be expelled from the city altogether. In 1567, Pius persuaded several elderly women to attempt to convert the prostitutes to a moral way of life. He had prostitutes who illegally left the quarter whipped and had, by 1569, walls and gates erected around the prostitutes' quarter to separate it physically from Rome.

SIGNIFICANCE

As a reforming pope, Pius attempted to cleanse the Church and began to eradicate immorality within his own city. Although his edict concerning prostitution within Rome met with limited success, the austere and devout manner of life that Pius displayed within the papal residence became a hallmark of the papacy and endures to this day.

In a larger historical context, the reforms of Pius V characterized the Counter-Reformation, the effort of the Church to correct corruption that it had earlier tolerated both within its own institutionalized practices and in society at large. This movement was prompted to a significant degree by the Reformation, a largely northern European movement by clerics (notably Martin Luther in 1517 as well as Huldrych Zwingli, John Calvin, John Knox, and others) protesting Roman Catholic corruption and what they perceived to be the Church's consequent deviation from its Christian mission. The result was the division of Christendom into Protestant and Catholic camps and the concomitant dissolution of the Catholic Church's political influence over the next two centuries. Pius V's reforms formed part of the Catholic counter-reformatory response in an attempt to maintain the Church's universal authority over European Christendom. That attempt would eventually fail, but Pius's reforms would result in his canonization by Pope Clement XI in 1712.

—*A. G. Traver*

FURTHER READING

Dickens, A. G. *The Counter Reformation*. New York: W. W. Norton, 1968. A brief and useful survey of the Counter-Reformation.

Jones, Martin D. W. *The Counter Reformation: Religion and Society in Early Modern Europe*. Cambridge, England: Cambridge University Press, 1995. A scholarly survey of the Catholic Church's response to Protestantism.

Larivaille, Paul. *La Vie quotidienne des courtisanes en Italie au temps de la Renaissance: Rome et Venise, XVe et XVIe siècles*. Paris: Hachette, 1975. A rare and useful survey of prostitution during the Renaissance. In French.

Lemaître, Nicole. *Saint Pie V*. Paris: Fayard, 1994. An important biography of the reforming pope Pius V. In French.

Mullet, Michael A. *The Catholic Reformation*. London: Routledge, 1999. A scholarly and important reassessment of the Counter-Reformation.

Pastor, Ludwig von. *The History of the Popes from the Close of the Middle Ages*. 3d ed. Vols. 17-18, edited by Ralph Francis Kerr. St. Louis, Mo.: Herder, 1951-1952. Still the standard history of the Renaissance and Reformation popes.

1567
PALESTRINA PUBLISHES THE *POPE MARCELLUS MASS*

Palestrina's composition contributed to the decision to retain art music for Catholic rites and the general acceptance of polyphonic sacred music in the Counter-Reformation.

LOCALE: Rome, Papal States (now in Italy)
CATEGORIES: Music; religion

KEY FIGURES
Giovanni Pierluigi da Palestrina (c. 1525-1594),
    Italian composer
Marcellus II (Marcello Cervini; 1501-1555), Roman
    Catholic pope, 1555
Pius IV (Giovanni Angelo de' Medici; 1499-1565),
    Roman Catholic pope, 1559-1565
Gregory XIII (Ugo Buoncompagni; 1502-1585),
    Roman Catholic pope, 1572-1585

SUMMARY OF EVENT
Giovanni Pierluigi da Palestrina, known in his lifetime by the town of his supposed birth, received his musical training in Rome. Aside from his initial employment in Palestrina, virtually his entire career was spent in Rome.

Palestrina held varying positions at several of Rome's major churches, including Santa Maria Maggiore, San Giovanni in Laterano, and the Vatican Basilica of San Pietro, where he led the important Cappella Giulia and served in the Capella Sistina. He also did much supplemental freelance work for such patrons as the Este family and the Gonzaga duke of Mantua. Financial differences prevented him from accepting a post at the Habsburg court of Vienna in 1568. Problems of low pay, declining health, and family deaths plagued him. After his first wife's demise in 1580, he briefly planned to enter the priesthood, but instead he married a wealthy widow, renewing his musical productivity amid new prosperity. By the time of his death, in February, 1594, he was perhaps the most revered composer in Europe.

Palestrina was a devout and dedicated adherent of the Catholic Counter-Reformation. This is not to say that he ignored the secular market. Even though he expressed regret for setting profane words to music, he published three books of Italian madrigals between 1555 and 1586, plus a volume of "spiritual madrigals" in 1594; individual items also appeared in anthologies. Despite their conservative style, Palestrina's madrigals were an important contribution to sixteenth century musical history.

Nevertheless, Palestrina was primarily a composer of Latin liturgical music for use in the Roman rite. He published five collections of motets and four other volumes of short sacred works. Of his mass settings (ultimately totaling 104), seven books were published in his lifetime and six more after his death. In both categories, individual works also appeared in anthologies, while reprintings of his own publications preserved Palestrina's fame for generations.

The most famous of Palestrina's settings of the Mass Ordinary is that known as the *Missa Papae Marcelli* (*Pope Marcellus Mass*), which appeared in his *Missarum liber secundus* (1567; second book of masses). Composed in the early 1560's for six vocal parts, the mass's style falls between the elaborate contrapuntalism of some of his more elaborately polyphonic masses and the spectacular antiphonal effects of those for opposing choirs. It is notable for its essentially homophonic, chordal clarity, as well as a magnificently lucid projection of the sacral words. (As one tribute to its popularity, if a left-handed one, some two decades after Palestrina's death one of his pupils, Francesco Soriano, adapted this mass to the more spacious scoring of twelve voices in two choirs.)

In a publication of 1607, musician and theorist Agostino Agazzari claimed that this mass setting "saved" polyphonic music for the Church at the culmination of the Council of Trent (1545-1563). In their redefinition of Roman Catholic Christianity, the council fathers expressed age-old clerical concerns that the growing complexities and intellectualism of polyphonic music obscured the words they were supposed to convey. They also deplored the use of popular song tunes as germinal or allusive material in mass settings—Palestrina himself was not free of that practice. Such concerns were heightened at a time when new Protestant musical movements were emphasizing maximum verbal clarity, as well as a shift from Latin to vernacular languages and increased congregational participation.

Agazzari's claim was elaborated in 1828 by Palestrina's first modern biographer, Giuseppe Baini. Baini asserted that, at a crucial point when the council was considering the abolition of polyphonic music and a return to plainchant, Palestrina was commissioned to compose a demonstration piece to prove that polyphonic music could indeed be "pure" and straightforwardly functional. The demonstration was a success, the story has it, and polyphony was "saved" for the Church. The name given this mass was a tribute to the earlier Pope Marcellus, whose pioneering commitment to reform was cut short by death only twenty-two days after his election, but who had urged his musicians (Palestrina then among them) to reduce florid elements in favor of projecting the words. Agazzari's claim and Baini's account achieved wide acceptance, and they were ultimately embodied in an opera, the lavishly idolatrous and hopelessly fictionalized *Palestrina* (pr. 1917), by Hans Pfitzner (1869-1949).

Though this legend still survives in some writing, modern scholarship has deflated it. The truth is more complicated but does not entirely omit Palestrina's role. Between September, 1562, and November, 1563, sessions of the council discussed abuses and "scandalous noises" corrupting liturgical celebration, ranging from misconduct by those attending rites to the artistic excesses of musicians. One faction advocated the abolition of any kind of newly composed music, while opponents insisted that the beauties and power of polyphonic music should never be abandoned.

Some advocates sponsored musical demonstrations. One cardinal had German composer Jacobus de Kerle (1531?-1591) compose a set of prayers for the council in an austere polyphonic style. Other composers, such as Orlando di Lasso (1532-1594) in Munich, are said to have written demonstration mass settings of "purified" character. Such efforts perhaps influenced the decision made in December, 1563, that Latin must remain the liturgical language and that music would be retained by the Church if properly purified of all profane elements.

Reform-minded Pope Pius IV issued a decree in August, 1564, designed to implement the council's decisions. A commission was created and charged with liturgical reform. Among its members was the great Cardinal Carlo Borromeo, who joined Cardinal Vitellozzo Vitelli in championing the retention of polyphonic music. Borromeo commissioned the music-director of his own Milan cathedral, Vincenzo Ruffo (1508-1587), to compose a mass setting that would demonstrate the feasibility of clarity and verbal comprehensibility. This seems to have been one of some three masses that were performed by the pontifical choir on April 28, 1565, at the residence of Vitelli, with very positive results.

It has been suggested that one or more of Palestrina's masses was included in this performance (specifically the *Pope Marcellus Mass*, according to Baini), but there is no explicit evidence on that point. One contemporary quoted Palestrina himself as claiming that masses he had composed overcame Pius IV's doubts about the viability of polyphonic music, but without detail or corroboration. On stylistic bases, Knud Jeppesen has argued that the *Pope Marcellus Mass* "can be assigned to the years 1562-1563, and that it was indeed written in connection with the Council of Trent." It need not have been the only influential mass setting, however, nor was Palestrina the only composer active in vindicating music for the Church.

CHURCH MUSIC AND THE COUNCIL OF TRENT

Palestrina composed music at a time when the Council of Trent was addressing the music of Catholic Church services. The council's decree was clear only on two things: that music should be pure and nonsecular and that other concerns should be settled at the local level. The first paragraph below comes from a petition presented by representatives of Holy Roman Emperor Ferdinand I in 1562. The second paragraph presents a local-level interpretation of the council's decrees by Cardinal Giulio della Rovere in 1576.

Services are currently performed, prayers are said, and psalms are sung laughably, negligently, irreverently, and so first as to be unintelligible even to the performers. The church hierarchy ought therefore to consider how to correct this so that what is said or sung will be pronounced correctly, distinctly, slowly, and with respectful gravity. Since many faults have crept into the church's songs and prayers, service books should be reviewed and corrected so that nothing is read, sung, offered in prayer, or presented to the people that does not appear in scripture or is not proper according to the Church Fathers or accepted church histories. If lengthy prayers and songs provoke inconsiderate haste in performing the service, that tedious longwindedness should be cut back. Better five psalms sung in peace and joy than the entire psalter in sadness and anxiety.

A chapel master should be appointed, moreover, who would obey the laws laid down by the Council of Trent for church musicians, namely, not to mix in anything indecent or impure in their songs; but let him remember his presence in the church, where angelic harmonies echo the praises of Christ the Lord and of his Virgin Mother. Therefore, whenever it can be done smoothly, he should be a man most skillful in the art of music, and he should adorn the divine praises with rhythm and vocal harmony in such a way that the words do not get entangled or confused, but let them be uttered distinctly, so that they may be clearly understood by everyone.

Source: Quoted in "The Council of Trent Revisited," by Craig A. Monson. *Journal of the American Musicological Society* 55, no. 1 (Spring, 2002), pp. 25-26, 32.

Palestrina's employer at the conclusion of the council was not the pope but the Seminario Romano, run by the new Jesuit order (founded 1534). The Jesuits were enthusiastic supporters of the reform movement, liturgical and otherwise. Palestrina was deeply involved in more ways than one. Pope Gregory XIII commissioned Palestrina and another musician to revise the chant repertoire, a task that became controversial and was brought to fulfillment by others after his death. Above all, however, Palestrina's Latin liturgical music became a prime model for lucid, seamless webbing of voice parts in the last, glorious phase of polyphonic writing.

SIGNIFICANCE

Palestrina and his disciples temporarily continued the "Roman" school of sober, refined, and gorgeously proportioned *a cappella* polyphony. The years after his death, however, saw the gradual replacement of High Renaissance polyphonic compositions with the new musical language of monodic homophony, tonality, and the integration of instruments into choral writing. Nevertheless, Palestrina did play a role in preserving art music in the Roman Catholic Church. His reputation as a contrapuntal master long survived him, preserved in textbooks and tradition, even while his music was studied less for performance than for instruction. Labeled Prince of Music or Father of Music, he was almost the sole composer before Johann Sebastian Bach (1685-1750) and George Frideric Handel (1685-1759) still considered worthy of notice. The revival at the beginning of the twenty-first century of earlier musical literature redefined him to be among the supreme figures of his time. His music is beloved by choral singers, and the *Pope Marcellus Mass* is by far the most popular of his masses, whether or not it was part of the pontifical choir's historic performance in 1565.

—John W. Barker

FURTHER READING

Fellerer, G. K. "Church Music and the Council of Trent." *Musical Quarterly* 39 (1953): 576-594. Discussion of the interaction between Church doctrine and liturgical composition.

Jeppesen, Knud. *The Style of Palestrina and the Dissonance.* Introduction by Edward J. Dent. Corr. ed. New York: Dover, 1970. This work, examining the distinctive style of Palestrina and its evolution, provides evidence for dating the composition of the *Pope Marcellus Mass* to the final years of the Council of Trent.

Leichentritt, Hugo. "The Reform of Trent and Its Effect on Music." *Musical Quarterly* 30 (1944): 319-328. Looks at the importance placed upon music by the reformers of the Trent Council, and the practical effects of the council upon contemporary Church composers.

Lockwood, Lewis, et al. "Palestrina." In *The New Grove Dictionary of Music and Musicians*, edited by Stanley Sadie. 2d ed. Vol. 18. New York: Macmillan & Grove, 2001. This basic overview essay includes biographical information about Palestrina, as well as an evaluation of his career and a bibliography of further reading.

Owens, Jessie Ann. *Composers at Work: The Craft of Musical Composition, 1450-1600.* New York: Oxford University Press, 1997. Interesting exploration of compositional methods, with a section on Palestrina himself.

Palestrina, Giovanni Pierluigi da. *Missa Papae Marcelli.* Edited by Lewis Lockwood. New York: Norton, 1975. Useful edition, with invaluable background material, source texts, and analytical essays by Lockwood and Knud Jeppesen.

Pyne, Zoë Kendrick. *Giovanni Pierluigi da Palestrina: His Life and Times.* London: Lane-Bodley Head, 1922. Dated but still useful short biography.

Reese, Gustave. *Music in the Renaissance.* 2d rev. ed. New York: Norton, 1959. Magisterial classic, with sections on the Council of Trent, Palestrina, and his contemporaries or followers.

SEE ALSO: 1545-1563: Council of Trent; 1575: Tallis and Byrd Publish *Cantiones Sacrae*; 1588-1602: Rise of the English Madrigal; 1590's: Birth of Opera; Oct. 31, 1597: John Dowland Publishes *Ayres*.

RELATED ARTICLES in *Great Lives from History: The Renaissance & Early Modern Era, 1454-1600:* William Byrd; Giovanni Gabrieli; Gregory XIII; Thomas Morley; Saint Philip Neri; Orlando di Lasso; Giovanni Pierluigi da Palestrina.

1567-1572
REIGN OF LONGQING

Although lasting only five and one-half years, the short reign of the Longqing emperor (Muzong) produced landmark domestic and foreign policy changes that resulted in governmental reforms, an economic boom, and peace with the Mongols.

LOCALE: China
CATEGORY: Government and politics

KEY FIGURES

Longqing (reign name, also Lung-ch'ing; personal name Zhu Zaihou, Chu Tsai-hou; posthumous name Zhuangdi, Chuang-ti; temple name Muzong, Mu-tsung; 1537-1572), Ming emperor of China, r. 1567-1572

Jiajing (reign name, also Chia-ching; personal name Zhu Houzong, Chu Hou-tsung; posthumous name Sudi, Su-ti; temple name Shizong, Shih-tsung; 1507-1567), Ming emperor of China, r. 1522-1567, father of the Longqing emperor

Zhang Juzheng (Chang Chü-cheng; 1525-1582), senior grand secretary under Longqing and Wanli

Altan (1507-1582), Mongol khan, r. 1543-1582

Qi Jiguang (Ch'i Chi-kuang; 1528-1587), Ming engineer, general, patriot, and national hero

Tan Lun (1520-1577), Ming general and minister of defense under Longqing

SUMMARY OF EVENT

In 1537, Zhu Zaihou. who would become the Longqing emperor, was born to the Jiajing emperor (Shizong) and the concubine Kang, later Empress Du. Although Zhu Zaihou was the third son to be born, he became the eldest living son when both the first and second sons died in childhood. However, his father had favored his first two sons and despised and neglected Zhu Zaihou. There was little contact between them, and Zhu Zaihou never expected to become emperor. Jiajing preferred a fourth son, born one month after Zhu Zaihou, for his successor. Nevertheless, after Jiajing died from poisoning in 1567, his posthumous edict (equivalent to his will) confirmed Zhu Zaihou's succession. Inexperienced in state affairs, Zhu Zaihou ascended the throne as the Longqing emperor, with the temple name Muzong, or "Reverent Ancestor."

In his accession edict, Longqing promised significant, radical changes from the policies and style of government under his father. To implement these new domestic policies and reforms and to help him govern, Longqing would depend on the extraordinary Zhang Juzheng, his former tutor and now a grand secretary of the cabinet.

First, they expelled the corrupt Daoist authorities from the court and discontinued his father's extravagant support of Daoist temples and activities. Then they set about to eradicate government corruption by requiring performance evaluations and ratings at all levels, from the grand secretaries down to the provincial magistrates. Many of Jiajing's opponents were released from jail or given special amnesties. "Imperial estates" or lands seized by imperial relatives and friends were returned to the original owners. General tax remission provided relief, especially for the farmers, who had been especially burdened by Jiajing's stifling taxes.

Jiajing had also ignored the needs of the military, who did not receive adequate compensation and rations. Both the frontier military colonies and interior regiments had dwindled seriously from deaths and desertions. In the autumn of 1569, Zhang Juzheng organized an imperial review of the troops, an extravagant spectacle that had occurred only once before in Ming rule. The parade of trained soldiers in new uniforms delighted the cheering crowds and improved military morale.

In the area of commerce and foreign trade, the Longqing reign changed long-standing Ming practices. The Ming had banned individuals from participating in maritime trade. In reaction to this restriction, Chinese merchants had often organized armed rebellions and encouraged Japanese piracy in China's coastal areas. In the first year of his reign, 1567, Longqing lifted the ban against individuals carrying on foreign trade, permitted private business in Japan and Southeast Asian countries, and eased restrictions on domestic commerce. This was a significant change of policy that curtailed coastal piracy and led to economic growth and prosperity.

During Longqing's reign there were also momentous developments in dealing with the insurgent Mongols. During his father's reign, there were mounting threats from the north. Altan, a seventeenth-generation descendant of Genghis Khan and the chieftain of the Tumed tribe, had united the Mongols in the northeast and was invading China at will. In one month in 1542, the Mongol troops burned dwellings, killed livestock, and massacred approximately 200,000 people. In 1550, Altan's troops broke through a vulnerable, poorly built part of the Great

1560's

Wall, assaulted the town of Gubeikou, near Beijing proper, and forced the Ming army to surrender. The invaders then advanced to the gates of the capital. They looted and burned several towns in the suburbs of Beijing for three days before withdrawing via Gubeikou.

Recognizing the need to tighten frontier defenses against the resurgent Mongols, Longqing's senior grand secretary, Zhang Juzheng, initiated a major renovation of the Great Wall, especially in the four areas crucial to the defense of Beijing: Jizhou, Baoding, Liaodong, and Changping. Tan Lun and Qi Jiguang, two generals famous for defeating Japanese pirates pillaging China's coastal areas, were appointed to plan and direct the large-scale reconstruction.

Tan Lun had been the prefecture magistrate of Taizhou, Zhejiang Province, and later governor of Fujiang. When he became emperor, Longqing appointed Tan Lun to be minister of defense. A national hero, Qi Jiguang was also an outstanding military strategist, civil engineer, and author of books on warfare, including a work in which he describes much of the reconstruction of the Great Wall, especially the new idea of watchtowers, to be implemented by him and Tan Lun. Qi Jiguang observed that despite earlier Ming improvements, the old Great Wall was built too low and thin, with no connected terraces, no shelter for soldiers, and no storage facilities for supplies and arms. Their plan was to widen and reinforce the walls and build and strategically place about three thousand watchtowers that would resemble high fences. Each tower would have three stories or levels, with apertures on all four sides, and would hide thirty to fifty men, as well as arms and supplies. Cannons could be fired from the lower level. The reconstruction work began in the 1568 and continued after Longqing's reign.

In the meantime, the Ming and Mongol leaders had made peace. In 1571, Longqing and Altan concluded a peace treaty that recognized Mongolian control of Turkestan and Tibet. Placing himself under Ming rule, Altan was granted the official Ming title of *shunyiwang*, or prince of obedience and righteousness.

Unfortunately, although he was a sincere ruler and reformer, Longqing's relentless pursuit of pleasure in the inner quarters of his palaces eventually led to total mental and physical exhaustion. After several months of illness, Longqing died in July, 1572. He was buried in the Zhaoling mausoleum of the Ming tombs, about 31 miles (50 kilometers) from Beijing. His young son Zhu Yijun (Chu I-chün, temple name Shenzong or Shen-tsung; 1563-1620) succeeded him as the emperor Wanli, who would rule from 1572 to 1620.

SIGNIFICANCE

When he ascended the throne, Longqing had no preparation or training to be emperor. To his credit, he supported and trusted his remarkable administrators and cabinet to help govern. Also, Longqing was an earnest leader intent on reform: eliminating political corruption on all levels of government, providing tax relief, removing restrictions on trade and commerce, reviving the military, and improving frontier defenses.

The large-scale renovation of the Great Wall continued into the Wanli reign and resulted in a superior defense structure. The best-preserved and strongest parts of the Great Wall at Beijing are the areas developed by Longqing's generals, Tan Lun and Qi Jiguang.

Longqing's peace treaty with Altan in 1571 ended several centuries of war between China and the Mongols. At peace with the Ming, Altan then directed military efforts against Tibet. Ironically, he eventually converted to a reformed sect of Tibetan Buddhism.

After Longqing's death, Zhang Juzheng became the chief grand secretary under Wanli and was able to continue his constructive fiscal programs for a decade, with an armed peace on the borders.

—*Alice Myers*

FURTHER READING

Elverskog, Johan. *The Jewel Translucent Sutra: Altan Khan and the Mongols in the Sixteenth Century*. Boston: Brill, 2003. Critical history of Altan's reign, including the 1550 siege of Beijing and the 1571 peace treaty with Longqing. Includes illustrations, a bibliography, and an index.

Mote, Fredrick W. *Imperial China, 900-1800*. Cambridge, Mass.: Harvard University Press, 1999. This comprehensive work includes an informative section, "The Brief Reign of Emperor Longqing, 1567-1572." Detailed notes, appendix, and bibliography.

Paludan, Ann. *Chronicle of the Chinese Emperors: The Reign-by-Reign Record of the Rulers of Imperial China*. London: Thames and Hudson, 1998. Accounts of the Chinese emperors, including Longqing's reign. Includes 368 illustrations and a bibliography.

Qiao, Yun. *Defense Structures: Ancient Chinese Architecture*. New York: Springer, 2001. A complete study of the history, design, and construction techniques of the Great Wall, including extensive information, maps, and sketches of the Ming Dynasty Great Wall.

Waldron, Arthur. *The Great Wall of China: From History to Myth*. Cambridge, England: Cambridge University Press, 2003. The chapter "The Heyday of Wall-Building" describes the important fortification work and details of construction during Longqing's reign. Extensive bibliography.

SEE ALSO: 16th cent.: China's Population Boom; 16th cent.: Single-Whip Reform; 1505-1521: Reign of Zhengde and Liu Jin; 1514-1598: Portuguese Reach

China; 1521-1567: Reign of Jiajing; 1550's-1567: Japanese Pirates Pillage the Chinese Coast; 1550-1571: Mongols Raid Beijing; Jan. 23, 1556: Earthquake in China Kills Thousands; 1573-1620: Reign of Wanli; 1592-1599: Japan Invades Korea.

RELATED ARTICLES in *Great Lives from History: The Renaissance & Early Modern Era, 1454-1600:* Wang Yangming; Xiaozong; Zhengde.

July 29, 1567
JAMES VI BECOMES KING OF SCOTLAND

James was a Protestant who often compromised with clergy on issues of who should control matters of faith, but he later insisted on his divine right to rule state and church. He was committed to Scottish Church reform, thus gaining the favor of the English queen, who named him her successor as king of England, assuring the two nations' continuing religious autonomy from the Catholic Church.

LOCALE: Church of the Holy Rood, Stirling, Scotland
CATEGORY: Government and politics

KEY FIGURES
James VI (1566-1625), king of Scotland as James VI, r. 1567-1625, and king of England as James I, r. 1603-1625
Mary Stuart (1542-1587), queen of Scotland, r. 1542-1567
Lord Darnley (1545-1567), Henry Stewart, second cousin and second husband to Mary, Queen of Scots
James Hepburn (1535?-1578), fourth earl of Bothwell, third husband to Mary, Queen of Scots
Elizabeth I (1533-1603), queen of England, r. 1558-1603

SUMMARY OF EVENT
James Stewart became James VI, king of Scotland, in 1567 when he was just a toddler. On July 29, 1567, just days after his mother abdicated the throne, James was crowned king at the Church of the Holy Rood in Stirling. The events that led up to the young king's coronation profoundly affected James's future as monarch of both Scotland and England.

Much of James's young life was marked by violence and scandal. When Mary was still pregnant, James's father, Lord Darnley, stabbed to death his mother's Italian secretary, David Rizzio. Mary's husband was led to murder Rizzio most likely because Rizzio was becoming one

of Mary's favorites, while Darnley was losing his wife's affections. Feeling angry and resentful, Darnley murdered Rizzio in front of the queen. James may have been traumatized by this act of violence early in his life, as he later developed an intense fear of weapons and went about in padded clothing to protect himself from possible attacks.

On February 10, 1567, when James was just eight months old, Darnley was killed in an explosion at his lodgings. On examination of his body, it appeared that Darnley had been strangled, and James's mother was a suspect in the murder. Though she may have loved Darnley at some point, it is probable that she married the Protestant after the 1561 death of her first husband (Francis II) to strengthen her claim to England's throne. Since both she and Darnley were descendants of Henry VII, they thought they would have a better claim on the English monarchy than that of England's queen, Elizabeth I.

Whatever the reason for her marriage to Darnley, Mary permitted him to be king consort only, a partner with no royal power, and soon grew to dislike him strongly. She had called Darnley back from Glasgow and arranged for him to stay in the house in the countryside where he died. The young queen looked even more suspect when, soon after her husband's death, she married the man who was thought to be Darnley's murderer.

James Hepburn, fourth earl of Bothwell, was put on trial for Darnley's murder, but he was acquitted. Soon after, he abducted and married Mary on May 15, 1567. This union with Bothwell upset Scottish nobles, since even though they were not fond of Darnley, Bothwell seemed worse. They revolted against their monarch, forcing her to choose between her husband and her country.

In June of 1567, Scottish nobles who disapproved of Mary's marriage to Bothwell gathered and then confronted the couple at Carberry Hill. The Protestant rebels

1560's

agreed to submit themselves to their queen if she promised to abandon Bothwell, but Mary would not leave her husband. Even those who supported her at Carberry Hill believed they would be defeated and so deserted her. With the rebels clearly in control by this point, the queen was forced to give up. Though she agreed to surrender, Mary made the rebels promise to allow Bothwell to flee unharmed. Bothwell managed to escape to Denmark; the couple never again saw each other. Mary was taken to Edinburgh and held captive in Lochleven Castle, where she miscarried Bothwell's twins. Mary abdicated the throne officially in July, and a few days later her son, just over one year old, was crowned king of Scotland.

Once Mary gave up the throne, James never again saw his mother. During the time Mary was on the run from Scottish noblemen as well as in prison, the child-king was educated by Protestants in spite of his Catholic baptism. Under the guidance of one of his tutors, Peter Young, the young king was taught to embrace Calvinist theology and abhor Catholicism. He was well-read and proved to be an intelligent young man, though he was beginning at this early age to develop some of the less attractive habits for which he would be remembered, including his bad manners and his high opinion of himself. Because James was still too young at this point to rule the country, a succession of four regents took charge of politics in Scotland. The earl of Moray was the first. The three regents who followed—the earl of Lennox (James's grandfather and Darnley's father), the earl of Mar, and the earl of Morton—all treated James as a pawn in their own struggles for power.

On May 13, 1568, Mary escaped from Lochleven Castle. Her forces clashed with Protestant forces led by the earl of Moray, Mary's half brother and regent at the time. After a short battle, Mary's men retreated and the former queen fled to England. She headed south, expecting to be saved by her cousin, Elizabeth I, but was much surprised when on May 19 the queen of England arrested her in Carlisle.

Although many of the rumors about plans to kill Elizabeth and replace her with Mary may have been fabricated by Mary's enemies, Elizabeth's anxieties about the imprisoned queen grew in the following years. Elizabeth eventually signed the warrant for Mary's death, alleging that the former queen was involved in the Babington plot of 1586, which sought to murder her. Mary presented herself as a Catholic martyr by wearing red at her execution at Fotheringhay Castle in Northamptonshire, England, on February 8, 1587.

About this time, James had reached his majority and began his rule as king of Scotland, a country that had become predominantly Protestant and would remain so under James. James's Protestant sympathies would later make him a good candidate for the Crown of England, which Elizabeth would bestow on him as she was on her deathbed in 1603.

SIGNIFICANCE

Just before James became king of Scotland, the struggle over religion was fierce. As battle lines were being drawn between Protestants and Catholics, the Catholic Mary was seen as a threat to Protestants and James appeared to be the answer to their problems. By removing their Catholic queen and replacing her with her infant son, Protestant nobles could raise the child-king as a Protestant, thus ensuring the success of their religion.

This plan worked, as James later would reduce the power of Catholics in Scotland and secure that country as a Protestant nation. Although Catholicism had already been replaced officially by Protestantism in Scotland when James was crowned, the king had to make an effort to quiet the Catholics who remained in the country and reduce the influence of Catholics on the Continent.

The Protestant James shared his religion with Queen Elizabeth I, and so the Scottish ruler was able to maintain a good relationship with the English monarch even after his mother's attacks on Elizabeth and even after Elizabeth had his mother executed. James's alliance with the queen allowed him both to advance the Protestant cause in Scotland and to advance his own chances to succeed Elizabeth. When Elizabeth died in 1603, James reaped the benefits of their relationship.

—*Stephannie S. Gearhart*

FURTHER READING

Fraser, Antonia. *Mary, Queen of Scots*. 1969. Reprint. New York: Dell, 1993. Fraser's biography of Mary is generally sympathetic with Mary in her struggles with her lovers and her enemies.

Guy, John. *Queen of Scots: The True Life of Mary Stuart*. Boston: Houghton Mifflin, 2004. This biography claims she was not helpless, emotional, and prone to poor decision making as is generally believed. Rather, she was intelligent and politically savvy, a match for her cousin, Elizabeth I, and for the Scottish nobles who were trying to oust her.

Lockyer, Roger. *James VI and I*. London: Longman, 1998. This biography of James discusses mostly his kingship of England, examining his philosophy of kingship as well as others' opinions about his reign.

Weir, Alison. *Mary, Queen of Scots, and the Murder of Lord Darnley*. New York: Random House, 2003. Weir argues that Mary was innocent of Lord Darnley's murder, arguing that the evidence against Mary is weak and was put together by rebellious Scottish nobles.

Willson, David Harris. *King James VI and I*. New York: Oxford University Press, 1956. Willson's biography of James gives readers a good sense of the king as a leader of Scotland and of England. This book is a good starting point for studying James.

SEE ALSO: Aug. 22, 1513-July 6, 1560: Anglo-Scottish Wars; Mar., 1536: Calvin Publishes *Institutes of the Christian Religion*; Feb. 27, 1545: Battle of Ancrum Moor; May, 1559-Aug., 1561: Scottish Reformation; Feb. 25, 1570: Pius V Excommunicates Elizabeth I.
RELATED ARTICLES in *Great Lives from History: The Renaissance & Early Modern Era, 1454-1600*: George Buchanan; John Calvin; Elizabeth I; John Knox; Mary, Queen of Scots; First Earl of Salisbury.

1568
ODA NOBUNAGA SEIZES KYŌTO

In 1568, Oda Nobunaga, a warlord in central Japan, marched on Kyōto and established control there, a major step in his drive to establish the central authority lacking during the preceding century of Japanese civil wars. Nobunaga's capital at Kyōto laid the foundation for Japanese unification.

LOCALE: Kyōto, Japan, and environs
CATEGORIES: Expansion and land acquisition; wars, uprisings, and civil unrest; government and politics

KEY FIGURES

Oda Nobunaga (1534-1582), warlord of Owari Province and first unifier of Japan, r. 1573-1582
Tokugawa Ieyasu (Matsudaira Takechiyo, later Matsudaira Motoyasu; 1543-1616), military leader who completed the unification of Japan
Akechi Mitsuhide (1526-1582), one of Nobunaga's generals
Ashikaga Yoshiaki (1537-1597), shogun, r. 1568-1573

SUMMARY OF EVENT

In the 1550's, Oda Nobunaga was the ruler of a small corner of the province of Owari, a domain to the south of Kyōto in central Japan. In 1560, Nobunaga was attacked by the warlord Imagawa Yoshimoto of neighboring Mikawa Province. Nobunaga was outnumbered by nearly ten to one, but he managed to surprise Imagawa's forces during at Okehazama and defeated him. With the Battle of Okehazama, Nobunaga ceased to be simply a local force in Owari and became a major regional force. Following a strategic alliance with former Imagawa vassal Matsudaira Motoyasu (better known by his later name, Tokugawa Ieyasu) to protect his eastern flank, Nobunaga shifted his attention to the north. In 1561,

Nobunaga's forces attacked the domain of Mino, and by 1567, he had driven out local strongman Saitō Tatsuoki and captured his castle at modern Gifu.

The conquest of Mino Province made Nobunaga a major force in central Japan. Like Owari, Mino was a very prosperous and populous domain, two factors that supported Nobunaga's plans for further military expansion. Moreover, Nobunaga instituted a number of significant economic reforms, such as the introduction of duty-free markets, that gave impetus to trade in the region and also played into Nobunaga's strategy: military expansion supported by a strong economic base.

By 1568, Nobunaga's gains had brought him into a position of prominence. Ashikaga Yoshiaki, one of the claimants to the position of shogun—now a largely ornamental office but one Nobunaga sought to control for the legitimacy it conferred—asked the warlord for aid in settling a succession dispute. Nobunaga brought his forces to Kyōto and installed Yoshiaki as shogun. Because of complex issues of succession, Nobunaga was unable to claim the office of shogun himself. However, he saw great potential in the symbolic power of the shogunal institution and sought to control it by dominating Yoshiaki. Nobunaga issued a number of regulations that stripped Yoshiaki of all decision-making power and placed him squarely under the control of the warlord from Owari.

Despite the fact that he was now securely in control of the titular head of the old regime, Nobunaga did not rest. Throughout 1569, he continued to make further territorial gains in central Japan. He enjoyed considerable success in the south, and it was only during his march north that he was seriously challenged. In 1570, Nobunaga invaded the domain of Echizen to the north of Kyōto. The local warlord, Asakura Yoshikage, called on neighbor

Asai Nagamasa for aid, and when their combined forces closed in from two different directions, Nobunaga was forced to withdraw. Nobunaga quickly rallied, however, and called on his ally Tokugawa Ieyasu for aid. The pair beat back the combined armies of Asai and Asakura at the Battle of Anegawa (1570), but the victory was short-lived. Asai and Asakura regrouped quickly and marched on Kyōto. Nobunaga confronted them to the north of the city and beat back their armies again. In 1571, he also razed the nearby Enryakuji, a temple complex on Mount Hiei, home of the Jōdo Shinshū (Pure Land) Buddhists, which had a long history of interfering in the political affairs of the capital, because the monks there had offered aid to his enemies.

In 1572 Nobunaga found himself unable to strike a decisive blow against Asai and Asakura and was beset by a religious uprising known as the Ikkō Ikki which had even made its impact felt in Owari, his home province. Nobunaga's grip on Kyōto—indeed his entire power base in central Japan—-was becoming increasingly tenuous. The situation became progressively worse when his enemies made overtures toward Takeda Shingen, the most powerful of the warlords of eastern Japan. In 1573, Shingen defeated Nobunaga and Ieyasu at the Battle of Mikatagahara and marched into Ieyasu's territory. Later that year, the Shogun Yoshiaki, who had long sought an opportunity to transform his symbolic authority into real political power, rebelled against Nobunaga.

Despite these setbacks, however, a string of victories restored Nobunaga's fortunes. Shingen died before he was able to follow up his victories in the south, and Nobunaga was able to send forces to Kyōto, burning part of the city and sending Yoshiaki into exile. Nobunaga followed up by attacking Asai and Asakura in the north. This time he not only defeated his rivals but also killed them and claimed their domains. Nobunaga's hegemony in central Japan looked more secure than ever.

This situation was not to last, however, and in 1574, Nobunaga found himself bested by new problems. The Ikkō Ikki staged a rebellion in Echizen, Asakura's old province, and it slipped from Nobunaga's control. Takeda Shingen's old armies, now led by his son Katsuyori, now threatened Nobunaga in the east. In 1575, Nobunaga again restored his fortunes, employing firearms and a new tactic of having his men divide into three ranks so that they could provide constant fire, to defeat the Takeda forces at the Battle of Nagashino. He also put down the religious rebellion in Echizen with such violence that the province was once again brought under his total control.

SIGNIFICANCE

The power base that Nobunaga built in central Japan and the prestige that he gained by exerting his control over the shogunate and the imperial court in Kyōto continued to have significant ramifications after the warlord's death. Akechi Mitsuhide, Nobunaga's assassin, died after his forces were crushed by the army of Toyotomi Hideyoshi. After Akechi's death, Hideyoshi set about establishing himself as Nobunaga's successor, continuing the slain warlord's drive toward national unification. Despite the fact that he faced stiff resistance from Nobunaga's other supporters, such as Tokugawa Ieyasu, Hideyoshi managed to gain control of the political and military apparatus that Nobunaga had established in the regions around Kyōto.

In addition, the economic reforms that Nobunaga introduced provided his successors with the sound economic base that he needed, not only to consolidate his position but also to support campaigns to the far east and west of the Kyōto heartland. Hideyoshi, operating from a base of operations near Kyōto, brought the southern island of Kyūshū under his control in 1587 and succeeded in subjugating the Hōjō, the most powerful warrior family in the east, in 1590. Scattered pockets of resistance aside, these gains brought Hideyoshi what Nobunaga had pursued for his entire career: hegemony over the other warlords and the creation of a central political authority.

Hideyoshi died in 1598, and Tokugawa Ieyasu, after besting a rival coalition in combat at the Battle of Sekigahara in 1600, went on to build upon the foundations of political control established by Nobunaga and strengthened by Hideyoshi. The result in 1603 was the full political unification of Japan under the Tokugawa shogunate, which continued to rule Japan until the imperial restoration of the 1860's.

—*Matthew Penney*

FURTHER READING

Sansom, George. *A History of Japan, 1334-1615*. 3 vols. Stanford, Calif.: Stanford University Press, 1961. Despite its age, Sansom's history of premodern Japan is still the most authoritative on the subject in English. Includes detailed coverage of Nobunaga's life and his seizure of power in Kyōto.

Sato, Hiroaki. *Legends of the Samurai*. New York: The Overlook Press, 1995. This work contains accounts of the career of Nobunaga and his contemporaries. It also contains translations of Japanese sources.

Turnbull, Stephen. *The Samurai Sourcebook*. London: Arms and Armour Press, 1998. Offers encyclopedic coverage of the important figures in the history of the samurai as well as details of Nobunaga's most famous battles and campaigns.

_____. *Samurai Warfare*. London: Arms and Armour Press, 1996. The best English-language history of the Japanese wars of unification with particular attention paid to Nobunaga's career and his campaigns against Asai and Asakura.

SEE ALSO: 1457-1480's: Spread of Jōdo Shinshū Buddhism; 1467-1477: Ōnin War; 1477-1600: Japan's "Age of the Country at War"; Mar. 5, 1488: Composition of the *Renga* Masterpiece *Minase sangin hyakuin*; Beginning 1513: Kanō School Flourishes; 1532-1536:

Temmon Hokke Rebellion; 1549-1552: Father Xavier Introduces Christianity to Japan; 1550's-1567: Japanese Pirates Pillage the Chinese Coast; 1550-1593: Japanese Wars of Unification; Sept., 1553: First Battle of Kawanakajima; June 12, 1560: Battle of Okehazama; 1587: Toyotomi Hideyoshi Hosts a Ten-Day Tea Ceremony; 1590: Odawara Campaign; 1592-1599: Japan Invades Korea; 1594-1595: Taikō Kenchi Survey; Oct., 1596-Feb., 1597: *San Felipe* Incident; Oct. 21, 1600: Battle of Sekigahara.

RELATED ARTICLES in *Great Lives from History: The Renaissance & Early Modern Era, 1454-1600:* Hōjō Ujimasa; Hosokawa Gracia; Oda Nobunaga; Ōgimachi; Oichi; Sesshū; Toyotomi Hideyoshi.

c. 1568-1571
OTTOMAN-RUSSIAN WAR

The Ottoman Empire launched a failed attack against a Russian army that was attempting to secure a passage to the Black Sea. However, with the military support of the Tatars, long-time enemies of the Russians, the Ottomans were able to temporarily halt the Russian move southward and also secure the Ottoman's eastern borders against Russian invasion for more than two hundred years.

LOCALE: Don steppe region between the Don and Volga Rivers and Black and Caspian Seas

CATEGORIES: Wars, uprisings, and civil unrest; diplomacy and international relations; expansion and land acquisition

KEY FIGURES

Ivan the Terrible (Ivan IV; 1530-1584), czar of Russia, r. 1547-1584, and leader of the Rurik Dynasty

Mehmed Paşa Sokollu (1505-1579), Ottoman grand vizier, 1565-1579, general, and leader of the invasion of Russia

Devlet I Giray (d. 1577), khan, r. 1551-1577, and leader of the Crimean Tatars

Selim II (1524-1574), Ottoman sultan, r. 1566-1574

SUMMARY OF EVENT

The reign of Sultan Süleyman the Magnificent (r. 1520-1566) had seen the Ottoman Empire expand into Eastern Europe, the Caucasus Mountains, and the Russian steppes. After Süleyman's conquests, the Turks found themselves threatened by the military powers of Austria,

Persia, and Russia at their borders. To combat this, the Turks formed alliances with buffer states, providing the Ottoman Empire with breathing space from their enemies. To protect them from the Russians, the Turks brokered alliances with the Tatars in the Crimean Peninsula and southern Russia, and with Kazan in the region between the Caspian and Black Seas. These alliances allowed the Ottomans to focus their military strength in eastern Europe and Persia.

The aggressive reign of Ivan the Terrible in Russia made the Ottomans' north border less secure. Ivan sought to eliminate the threats to his capital, Moscow, and open new avenues of conquest and trade. He set his sights on three khanates, or kingdoms, that were successors to the former Golden Horde: Kazan, Astrakhan, and the Crimea. Ivan's first attack on Kazan drew a response from the Tatars in Crimea. After defeating the Tatar invasion, Ivan renewed his attack and defeated the Kazan rulers in 1552, sweeping to the Caspian Sea. From there, he took Astrakhan in 1556 and granted it a degree of independence. The leaders of Astrakhan, though, sought to renew their alliance with the Tatars and Ottomans, forcing Ivan to retake the city and extend his control as far south as the Terek River at the northern reaches of the Caucasus Mountains. From the Terek, the Russians could move south into the Caucasus and threaten the Ottomans, or east into Central Asia to conquer the Muslims allied with the Ottomans. Ivan's move south also threatened the Tatars in the Crimea.

Around 1568, the Turkish general, Grand Vizier

Mehmed Paşa Sokollu, came up with a daring plan to sweep the Russians back across the steppes. Instead of crossing the dangerous Caucasus Mountains, he would take an Ottoman army across the Black Sea and up the Don River to where it flowed closest to the Volga River. The Ottomans hoped to build a canal between the Don and Volga, connecting both rivers and allowing the Turks to float their ships into the Caspian Sea.

Mehmed was depending on the Ottomans' allies, particularly the Tatars, to provide support for the advance. The Tatars were old enemies of the Russians, who wanted the Crimea because of its many warm-water ports in the Black Sea and its close proximity to the Bosporus Strait, controlled by the Ottomans.

The Ottoman navy was able to transport its troops across the Black Sea and onto the Don River. While the navy conducted a blockade of the Russian port of Azov, the Ottoman army under Mehmed moved swiftly forward into the Volga region and toward Astrakhan. The Turks began building the canal but never finished. The Ottoman army reached Astrakhan and laid siege to the city, but the Russian commander outmaneuvered the Ottomans, escaped from Astrakhan and attacked the Turks who were building the canal. The Russian attack on the rear only worsened the supply troubles for the Ottoman army. Unable to continue the battle or defeat the Russian army before them, the Ottomans were forced to retreat, their invasion plans ruined and the Russians secure in the Volga River region.

After Mehmed's failed attack, the Ottomans realized they could not mount an offensive into the endless steppes of Russia. Instead, they would come to rely on their Tatar allies to continue the war even as the Turks negotiated peace. In 1570, the Ottomans signed a peace agreement with the Russians that officially ended the war. The conflict continued, however, as the Ottomans financed a proxy war against the Russians by providing troops and guns to the Tatars in the Crimea, trying to convince the Tatar khan to attack to the north.

The Tatars did move against the Russians two years later. On April 5, 1571, Tatar khan Devlet I Giray began to attack northward from the Crimea. He had been prodded by Ottoman sultan Selim II and had the support of the Ottoman Janissaries and cannon. The Tatar khan caught Ivan and his army out of position and swept into the city of Tula, just south of Moscow. The Tatars captured and burned Tula to the ground and continued to the north. On May 24, the Tatars pushed aside the Russian armies that were formed to defend Moscow, captured the city, and burned it to the ground as Ivan retreated to the city of

Vologda, a fair distance from his capital. The Tatars did not remain in the city. Instead, their invasion became a massive raid in which they took captive 100,000 Russians who were then sold into slavery. Their trek back to the Crimea was marked by destruction of the countryside and towns, leaving a burned path from Moscow to the Black Sea.

The Tatars' military victories were followed by a diplomatic offensive. The Tatar khan sent ambassadors to Moscow, and on June 15, 1571, they demanded that the Russians surrender their conquests of Kazan and Astrakhan. The Tatars ridiculed Ivan for fleeing Moscow and for the incompetence of the Russian military in preventing the destruction of the capital city. Ivan delayed his reply, at first agreeing to surrender Astrakhan but refusing to turn over Kazan, which was closer to Moscow. Ivan had delayed just as the Russians were involved in fighting in the north against Lithuania and Poland for control of the Balkans. Once those wars were complete, he believed he could redirect his military toward the Tatars.

The khan and his main ally, the Ottomans, however, sought immediate advantage. Selim II feared that the Russians might move east against the Turk provinces of Moldavia and Transylvania. Only if the Tatars permanently weakened the Russians and controlled the Volga River region would the Ottomans be safe from Russian attack.

On July 26, 1572, the Tatars moved north again. The Russians had been forewarned of the possibility of a Tatar invasion and had their armies prepared to meet the enemy from the south. At the village of Molodi near Moscow, the Tatars were defeated. The Tatar leader had been captured by the Russians and most of the Tatar army had been wiped out. The Tatar khan was forced to flee back to the Crimea, never again to launch a meaningful attack against the Russians through the remainder of Ivan's reign. The war between the Tatars and Russians did, however, divert Ivan from attacking the Ottomans. While the Tatars attacked toward Moscow, the Ottomans were able to acquire greater control over their provinces of Moldavia and Walachia.

SIGNIFICANCE

The advance of the Russian military into the Caucasus region was a threat to the northern borders of the Ottoman Empire. The advance sparked the brief Ottoman-Russian War, which saw a Turkish army advance into the Don steppe to halt the Russian movement south. Even though the initial attack failed to reach the Caspian, which had been the attack's objective, it did temporarily stop the

Russian southward movement. The Ottomans were able to strengthen their alliance with the Tatars in the Crimean Peninsula and build new alliances on Russia's western borders, serving to block Russia and prevent its advance to the south and west.

—*Douglas Clouatre*

FURTHER READING

Imber, Colin. *The Ottoman Empire, 1300-1650.* New York: Palgrave Macmillan, 2004. This brief work examines the Ottoman Turks as they battled the Byzantine Empire, conquered Constantinople, then built their own empire by sweeping into eastern Europe. The book focuses mainly on the rise of the Ottomans, leaving out the empire's subsequent decline and fall.

Kinross, Lord. *The Ottoman Centuries.* New York: Quill, 1992. A sweeping story of the Ottoman Empire, this book describes the various sultans, their contributions to the Ottoman system, and their roles in the rise or fall of the empire. It also describes the social system and its evolution.

Martin, Janet. *Medieval Russia.* New York: Cambridge University Press, 1996. This wide-ranging book describes the Russian struggle to establish a state and the leaders of the Rurik Dynasty, including Ivan the Great and Ivan the Terrible. It discusses how the Ruriks fought and destroyed the Golden Horde, which had ruled the Russian people for centuries.

Payne, Robert, and Nikita Romanoff. *Ivan the Terrible.* New York: Thomas Crowell, 1975. An in-depth work on the rule of Ivan the Terrible, this book describes the internal turmoil faced by the Russian ruler and the external threats from his neighbors. It also details his battles with the Lithuanians to the north and the Ottomans and their Tatar allies to the south.

SEE ALSO: 1480-1502: Destruction of the Golden Horde; 1499-c. 1600: Russo-Polish Wars; 1520-1566: Reign of Süleyman; 1593-1606: Ottoman-Austrian War; 1594-1600: King Michael's Uprising.

RELATED ARTICLES in *Great Lives from History: The Renaissance & Early Modern Era, 1454-1600:* Ivan the Great; Ivan the Terrible; Süleyman the Magnificent.

1568-1648
DUTCH WARS OF INDEPENDENCE

Riots by Calvinists in the Low Countries and the brutal policies of the region's Spanish Habsburg rulers led to the Eighty Years' War and the formation of the Dutch Republic and Flanders. Independence from Spain situated the Netherlands as an economic and cultural power and led to the downfall of Spain as a major dynastic power in Europe.

LOCALE: Low Countries (now Belgium, the Netherlands, and Luxembourg)

CATEGORIES: Wars, uprisings, and civil unrest; government and politics; diplomacy and international relations

KEY FIGURES

William the Silent (1533-1584), prince of Orange and stadholder of the Netherlands

Maurice of Nassau (1567-1625), prince of Orange and stadholder of the Netherlands, son of William

Philip II (1527-1598), king of Spain, r. 1556-1598

Margaret of Parma (1522-1586), governor of the Netherlands

Duke of Alva (Fernando Álvarez de Toledo; 1507-1582), governor of the Netherlands

Alessandro Farnese (1545-1592), duke of Parma and governor of the Netherlands

SUMMARY OF EVENT

The marriage of Maximilian I of Austria and Mary of Burgundy attached the Netherlands, territories encompassing present-day Belgium, the Netherlands, and Luxembourg, to the Habsburg family's domains. Crowned Holy Roman Emperor in 1493, Maximilian expanded Habsburg holdings further by marriage, treaty, and conquest. His grandson and heir, Charles V, ruled a vast empire that included Austria, Hungary, the Holy Roman Empire, the Netherlands, Spain, and large parts of Italy and the New World.

From the late Middle Ages onward, the economic situation of the Low Countries was very favorable. Textile manufacturing grew rapidly. Throughout the fifteenth century, Antwerp rose as the region's main port. Culturally, the Netherlands produced some of Europe's

"Beggars" before the Council of Blood, a tribunal that hunted down moderate Catholics, Protestants, and all others labeled heretics. (R. S. Peale and J. A. Hill)

greatest art. Beginning with the Antwerp firm of book-binder Christophe Plantin, printing flourished, too. However, by the middle of the sixteenth century, multiple crises emerged, accompanied by bad harvests and a trade embargo by Protestant England, the leading source of raw wool for the Netherlands. Spawned by humanist and reformist thinkers such as Desiderius Erasmus, Martin Luther, and John Calvin, Humanism and Protestantism became popular. To the Habsburgs, criticizing the Catholic Church also meant rejecting the established political order. These were heretical challenges that had to be exterminated.

Charles V's son and heir, Philip II, tried to impose absolute authority on the seventeen historically self-governing provinces of the Netherlands. Ruling from distant Spain from 1556 to 1598, he sent Spanish troops to the Low Countries and ignored the independent thinking of local townspeople and nobles and their long established parliament, the States-General. Those disagreeing were hunted down as enemies of the state. Unrest and opposition grew under the eight-year governorship of

Philip's sister, Margaret of Parma, who tried to moderate her brother's fanatical intolerance. Believing they would get a sympathetic hearing, some nobles turned to her, but her adviser, Antoine Perrenot de Granvelle, contemptuously dismissed them as "beggars" and refused to consider petitions that questioned actions taken against heretics.

Granvelle was recalled by Philip II in 1564 at the insistence of the leading Dutch noble, Prince William the Silent. Much discord had developed within the ranks of the ruling elite, however. Concluding an alliance in Breda in 1566, Dutch aristocrats, proudly calling themselves Geuzen (beggars), defied the governor. Meanwhile, fueled by high grain prices, riots marred towns in Flanders, Holland, and Zeeland. Opposing idolatry, radical purist Protestants, known as Iconoclasts, destroyed decorations in hundreds of churches. Offended proponents of the church showed equal intolerance.

In 1567, Philip II replaced Margaret with a new and extremely intolerant Spanish governor, the duke of Alva. Fresh Spanish troops were sent to crush the rebellion, which had already subsided. Provocatively, Alva established the Council of Blood, first called the Council of Troubles, a sham tribunal that treacherously hunted down moderate Catholics, Protestants, and all others labeled heretics. Perhaps thousands were executed. In 1568, Alva had the moderate Catholic counts of Egmont and Hoorn beheaded in Brussels. For the king's critics, this execution was the last straw.

A friend of the executed counts and a moderate Protestant, Prince William the Silent, gathered Calvinist forces and led the fight against Spanish domination. His attempt to occupy Brabant in 1568 sparked the conflict called the Eighty Years' War. In the North Sea, a rebel fleet, known as the Water Geuzen, or Sea Beggars, took coastal towns, beginning with Brill and Flushing in April of 1572. Racked by failure, Alva was replaced in November of 1573. Under a new commander, the Spaniards besieged Leiden for a year but were forced to withdraw when William ordered the dikes breached in 1574. Throughout most of 1576, the Pacification of Ghent ensured an armistice. However, the era's worst atrocity thwarted all peace efforts: In November, 1576, unpaid Spanish troops mutinied in Antwerp, inflicting three days of wanton violence and plunder on the wealthy port city and murdering some seven thousand of its inhabitants.

Italian nobleman Alessandro Farnese, duke of Parma, replaced the new commander. Farnese's diplomacy, intelligence, and imagination won the loyalty of many in the southern parts of the Netherlands. Seeking out friends while pursuing enemies relentlessly, he turned the tide in favor of Spain. On January 6, 1579, the southern provinces of Artois, Hainault, Namur, Luxembourg, and Limburg founded the pro-Spanish Union of Arras, which condemned the uprising against the king. On January 23, 1579, seven northern Calvinist provinces (Friesland, Gelderland, Groningen, Holland, Overijssel, Utrecht, and Zeeland) formed a protective alliance called the Union of Utrecht. This union, which provided the constitutional basis for the Dutch political system through 1795, provided a republican form of government, presided over by the House of Orange, whose leaders, begin-

ning with William the Silent, served as stadholders (presidents). Standing between the two unions, Brabant and Flanders became war zones. In 1581, the States-General condemned Philip's violations of his subjects' rights. As a result, he was no longer recognized as the sovereign. The Union of Utrecht (also known as the United Provinces of the Netherlands or the Dutch Republic) declared its independence, and with it died any hope of preserving a unified greater Netherlands. Seeking the support of France, the arch-enemy of the Habsburgs, William offered rule over the Netherlands to the duke of Anjou in 1580. Infuriated, Philip denounced William as a traitor and set a high price on his head.

Events continued to turn in Spain's favor. A fanatical Catholic assassinated William in Delft in 1584. The next year, Farnese reconquered Antwerp and Ghent. In retaliation, the Dutch closed the River Scheldt to shipping, thereby halting Antwerp's development for two centu-

---

THE SPANIARDS' "ENEMY OF THE HUMAN RACE"

Prince William the Silent led the fight against Spanish domination of the provinces of the Netherlands. The Eighty Years' War began in 1568 after William attempted to occupy and then secure the province of Brabant from Spanish rule. The first extract below comes from a proclamation by Spanish King Philip II (1580), which made William an outlaw. The second extract comes from William's "Apology," a response to Philip's accusations delivered to the States General of the Netherlands (1581).

Philip: [F]or his evil doings as chief disturber of the public peace and as a public pest, we outlaw him forever and forbid all our subjects to associate with him or communicate with him in public or in secret. We declare him an enemy of the human race. . . .

William: My enemies object that I have "established liberty of conscience." I confess that the glow of fires in which so many poor Christians have been tormented is not an agreeable sight to me, although it may rejoice the eyes of the duke of Alva and the Spaniards; and that it has been my opinion that persecutions should cease in the Netherlands. . . .

When later I became their [the Spaniards'] opponent and enemy in the interest of your freedom, I do not see what hypocrisy they could discover in me, unless they call it hypocrisy to wage open war, take cities, chase them out of the country, and inflict upon them, without disguise, all the harm that the law of war permits. . . .

Might it please God that my perpetual exile, or even my death, should bring you a true deliverance from all the evils and calamities to which the Spaniards are preparing for you and which I have so often seen them considering in council and devising in detail! How agreeable to me would be such a banishment! how sweet death itself. . . !

Source: Excerpted from *Readings in European History*, by James Harvey Robinson, abridged ed. (Boston: Athenaeum Press, 1906), pp. 325, 327-328.

1560's

ries. Amid epidemics, wars, and famines, the migration of more than 100,000 artisans, merchants, intellectuals, artists, and others from the Spanish Netherlands to the north between 1540 and 1630 led to rapid decline in the south, where support for the rebellion waned.

In 1596, two years before his death, Philip II ceded the Netherlands to his nephew, Austrian archduke Albert VII. Spanish troops and officials remained, however, and Catholicism was reintroduced forcibly. Meanwhile, Maurice of Nassau, son of William the Silent, consolidated his hold in the north. His victory at the Battle of Nieuwpoort in 1600 forced the Spaniards to completely withdraw from the Dutch Republic. However, the last Dutch base in the southern provinces, the fortified port of Ostend, was lost to the Spanish in 1604 after a three-year siege. Reaching into Spain's home waters, Dutch admiral Jacob van Heemskerk defeated the Spanish off Gibraltar in 1607.

The Eighty Years' War was interrupted by a truce from 1608 to 1621. During this brief period, Dutch maritime trade flourished. Amsterdam became Europe's most important merchant city, the Dutch founded New Amsterdam, later known as New York, and their East Indies and West Indies companies, founded in 1602 and 1621 respectively, acquired possessions in Indonesia and the Americas. New conflicts broke out, however, between provinces, between local assemblies and the House of Orange, and between competing Protestant sects.

The end of the Eighty Years' War coincided with the last phase of the wider Thirty Years' War. Dutch victories once again pushed back the republic's opponents. Spain finally recognized the Dutch Republic in the Treaty of Munster (1648), part of the Peace of Westphalia. The partition of the Low Countries was confirmed.

The Peace of Utrecht (1713) granted the Spanish Netherlands to the Austrian Habsburgs, who ruled the area until 1794. Following brief periods of French revolutionary and Dutch royal rule, the southern (Austrian) Netherlands emerged as Belgium in 1830.

SIGNIFICANCE

The repressive policies of King Philip II of Spain provoked a rebellion of the seven northern provinces of the Low Countries, which had been part of the vast empire of the Habsburg family since the time of Philip's great-grandfather, Maximilian I. A long, bloody, and destructive war followed, which separated the Protestant Dutch Republic (now called the Netherlands) from the Catholic Spanish Netherlands (now called Belgium). This conflict solidified religious divisions in the region,

reduced the power of the faltering Holy Roman Empire, laid out the territorial frontier between present-day Belgium and the Netherlands, and seriously disrupted the textile-based economies of Flanders and Antwerp, which had dominated northern Europe since late medieval times.

Despite its limited area and population, the Netherlands emerged as a major seagoing trading power for several decades. Belgium would eventually develop into continental Europe's first industrialized economy, but only after numerous invasions stemming from dynastic conflicts.

—Randall Fegley

FURTHER READING

Blom, J. C. H., and E. Lamberts. *History of the Low Countries.* Translated by James C. Kennedy. New York: Berghahn Books, 1999. An excellent history of the region, including the Dutch Wars of Independence.

Darby, Graham, ed. *The Origins and Development of the Dutch Revolt.* New York: Routledge, 2001. Anthology examines the causes and consequences of the sixteenth century Dutch rebellion.

Israel, Jonathan. *The Dutch Republic.* Oxford, England: Clarendon Press, 1998. A detailed history of the Netherlands from 1477 to 1806.

Koenigsberger, H. G. *Monarchies, States Generals, and Parliaments: The Netherlands in the Fifteenth and Sixteenth Centuries.* New York: Cambridge University Press, 2001. History of the States-General of the Netherlands, its internal and external strife, and its division into the Dutch Republic and the Spanish Netherlands.

Rady, Martyn. *From Revolt to Independence: The Netherlands, 1550-1650.* London: Hodder & Stoughton, 1990. A short but detailed textbook on the Wars of Independence.

Schama, Simon. *The Embarrassment of Riches: An Interpretation of Dutch Culture in the Golden Age.* New York: Vintage, 1997. An insightful, already classic look at the history and culture of the Netherlands from the Dutch Wars of Independence to the 1700's.

Swart, K. W. *William of Orange and the Revolt of the Netherlands, 1572-84.* Translated by J. C. Grayson. Edited by R. P. Fagel, M. E. H. N. Mout, and H. F. K. van Nierop. Burlington, Vt.: Ashgate, 2003. A major and authoritative biography, with introductory essays and commentary by noted scholars of William's reign.

See also: Aug. 17, 1477: Foundation of the Habsburg Dynasty; c. 1500: Netherlandish School of Painting; 1531-1585: Antwerp Becomes the Commercial Capital of Europe; 1555-1556: Charles V Abdicates; July 26, 1581: The United Provinces Declare Independence from Spain.

Related articles in *Great Lives from History: The Renaissance & Early Modern Era, 1454-1600:* Duke of Alva; John Calvin; Charles V; Elizabeth I; Alessandro Farnese; Kenau Hasselaer; Martin Luther; Margaret of Austria; Margaret of Parma; Johan van Oldenbarnevelt; Philip II; William the Silent.

February 23, 1568
Fall of Chitor

The siege of Chitor formed a part of Emperor Akbar's project of securing the capital city of Mewar along with its powerful fort. Chitor's fall facilitated the Mughal conquest of a prosperous coastline province in western India, leading to the empire's further expansion.

Locale: Chitor, northwest India

Categories: Wars, uprisings, and civil unrest; government and politics; expansion and land acquisition

Key Figures

Akbar (1542-1605), Mughal emperor of India, r. 1556-1605

Rana Udai Singh (d. 1572), Rājput ruler of Sisodia Dynasty, r. 1541-1572

Khan-i Jahan (d. 1578), governor of Bengal

Jaimal Rathor of Badnor (1507-1568), commander of Chitor

Patta Sisodia of Amet (d. 1568), one of the leaders of the Chitor garrison

Asaf Khan (fl. after 1568), Mughal administrator of Chitor

Abu-l-Fazl ʿAllāmī (1551-1602), Akbar's court historian

Summary of Event

Chitorgarh, or the fortress of Chitor (variation of the Sanskrit Chitrapura), the capital city of Mewar, was strategically situated between the headquarters of the Mughal rulers in Delhi or Āgra and the prosperous coastal region of Gujarat. Emperor Akbar's imperial project of unification of Hindustan (India) under a central command called for securing the intractable chieftaincy of Mewar ruled by the *ranas* (chiefs) of the formidable Sisodia Dynasty (royal section of the Guhilot clan dating back to the seventh century).

Chitor's fortress (along with the town of Chitor), probably the greatest of its kind in contemporary Hindu-

stan, stands on a 3-mile-long ridge on the bank of the River Gambhiri, 500 feet above the surrounding plain, and about 1,850 feet above sea level. It has a circumference at the base extending a little more than 8 miles. The main entranceway zigzags up the hillside through seven gates (*pol*).

According to contemporary historian Abu-l-Fazl ʿAllāmī, Akbar's operations against Chitor began on or about September 19, 1567, to teach the "audacious and immoderate" Rana Udai Singh a lesson for displaying hospitality toward an offending fugitive Mughal chief of Malwa (situated to the north of Ajmer) and, especially, for an incident involving the *rana*'s son at the nearby town of Dholpur.

In the early days of September, 1567, Akbar had set up a hunting camp in Dholpur to gather the loyal local chiefs to help him put down the rebellion of the sons of the Mughal noble Muhammad Sultan Mirza of Mordabad as rebellious fugitives. The emperor was attended on by Udai Singh's son Sakat Singh (it is not known why he was at Akbar's camp), whose help Akbar, reportedly jokingly, solicited in bringing his father Udai Singh to submission. When the young man fled upon hearing Akbar's request, the enraged emperor contemplated attacking the Rājput stronghold of Chitor. A number of his trusted men, who had received fiefs in Malwa, were dispatched to Malwa to crush the rebellion of the Mirzas.

According to ʿAllāmī, the Mughal army occupied three forts and Akbar himself advanced with a small force toward the target city. Akbar's party halted in the vicinity of Fort Gagrun near the town of Kotah. The Mughal strategy was to entice Rana Udai Singh into a pitched battle. However, the *rana* decided against giving battle and withdrew into the Girwa Valley in the Aravalli hills, leaving the fortress under the command of a number of chiefs, notably Jaimal Rathor of Badnor and Patta Sisodia of Amet, with a garrison of five thousand to eight thousand Rājputs and with enough provisions for several years. Udai Singh also carried out a scorched-earth policy, destroying crops in the surrounding areas of Chitor.

On October 20, 1567, Akbar set up a 10-mile-long camp outside Chitor to the northeast of the ridge and began a siege. After a careful reconnaissance, lines were constructed that surrounded the fort, establishing many batteries in the course of one month. Asaf Khan was dispatched to take Rampur and Khan-i Jahan to apprehend the fugitive *rana*, though to little effect. Following completion of the siegeworks, Akbar attempted to storm Chitorgarh but failed. According to the Rājput folklore, the Mughal forces were successfully repulsed by the courageous queen of the *rana* and the besiegers' camp was broken up. Nevertheless, the Mughals persisted with grim determination.

Akbar decided on a siege by sap and mine process. Accordingly, two mines and a wide trench (*sabat*, wide enough so that ten men could walk side by side and high enough for a mounted elephant to pass) were dug and a 40-pound mortar was cast in the camp. The news of the gun persuaded the defending garrison to open negotiations, but, despite the Rājput offer of surrender and a hefty *peshkash* (tribute) to the Mughals, negotiations failed. Akbar, however, remained obdurate because he was bent on capturing the *rana* before accepting any offer.

Intense fighting resumed on both sides. Despite heavy casualties, the besiegers brought two mines to the foot of the fort and exploded two charges on December 17, 1567. The first caused a large breach through which two hundred cavalrymen galloped, but about forty Rājputs were immolated when the second mine exploded. On February 23, 1568, the Mughal army entered the fort gate and engaged the defending garrison in a pitched battle in which Patta Sisodia and Jaimal Rathor were killed.

ʿAllāmī reported that Akbar shot a man, later identified as Jaimal, who had been seen supervising the repair of the Mughal breach. His death broke the morale of the garrison. The surviving garrison in the fort, some eight thousand men, proceeded to immolate the women inside through the ritual of *jauhar* and then, after donning their saffron robes and partaking of the last *bira* (an aromatic leaf laced with shell-lime and pieces of areca nuts), flung themselves at the enemy.

Akbar then ordered an assault of the fort with three hundred elephants in the charge, and Patta was trampled to death. Some forty thousand peasants, allegedly participants in Chitor's defense by working for the garrison, were killed or taken prisoner. In ʿAllāmī's reckoning, some thirty thousand soldiers perished in the battle. Remarkably enough, about one thousand expert marksmen from Kalpi, who were among the defending garrison, managed to escape from the besieged fort along with their families.

On February 28, Akbar left Chitor for a pilgrimage to the shrine of Khwaja Muin-ud-din Chishti in Ajmer, appointing Asaf Khan the new administrator of Chitor. It is also on record that the Mughal emperor had stone statues sculpted of his two valiant adversaries, Jaimal and Patta, and placed them at the gates of his palace at Āgra.

SIGNIFICANCE

The conquest and fall of Chitor demonstrated the superiority of a Mughal military that combined mounted archers, effective artillery, and infantry with firearms. The sack of the fort facilitated Emperor Akbar's control of the principalities of Rājasthān, thus marking a significant stage in the formation of the Mughal Empire.

—*Narasingha P. Sil*

FURTHER READING

Abu-l-Fazl ʿAllāmī. *The Akbar Näma of Abu-l-Fazl.* Translated by H. Beveridge. 3 vols. Delhi, India: Ess Ess, 1977. A detailed eyewitness account by Akbar's court historian, manifestly pro-Mughal yet the most valuable source on the fall of Chitor.

Mehta, Balwant S., and Jodh S. Mehta. *Chittorgarh: The Cradle of Chivalry and Culture.* Udaipur: Rajasthan Itihas Parishad, 1966. An excellent short introduction to the fort's history and environs.

Roy, Dwijendralal. *Mevar Patan: Or, Fall of Mevar.* Translated by Dilip K. Roy. 2d ed. Mumbai: Bharatiya Vidya Bhavan, 1970. An entertaining historical play written during the nationalist movement in India in the nineteenth century celebrating Rājput patriotism against Mughal imperialism.

Shastri, Pandit Sobhalal, comp. *Chittorgarh.* Udaipur, India: State Printing Press, 1928. A brief but very helpful historical and topographical guide for visitors to Chitor.

Smith, Vincent A. *Akbar the Great Mogul, 1542-1605.* 3d rev. ed. New Delhi, India: S. Chand, 1966. Concise, critical, and very well written. Long reputed in India as a standard biography of Akbar.

Stratton, J. P. *Chitor and the Mewar Family.* Ajmer: Scottish Mission Industries, 1909. A relatively short narrative of the siege of Chitor.

Streusand, Douglas E. *The Formation of the Mughal Empire.* New York: Oxford University Press, 1999. A well-researched, succinct account of the siege of Chitor.

Tod, James. *Annals and Antiquities of Rajasthan: Or, The Central and Western Rajpoot States on India.* Reprint. New Delhi, India: K. M. N., 1971. A classic and elegiac history of Rājputana.

SEE ALSO: 1459: Rāo Jodha Founds Jodhpur; Mar. 17, 1527: Battle of Khānua; Dec. 30, 1530: Humāyūn Inherits the Throne in India; 1556-1605: Reign of Akbar; Mar. 3, 1575: Mughal Conquest of Bengal; 1580-1587: Rebellions in Bihar and Bengal; Feb., 1586: Annexation of Kashmir.

RELATED ARTICLES in *Great Lives from History: The Renaissance & Early Modern Era, 1454-1600:* Akbar; Bābur; Humāyūn; Ibrāhīm Lodī; Krishnadevaraya.

1569
MERCATOR PUBLISHES HIS WORLD MAP

Mercator's world map provided a representation of the surface of the earth called the Mercator projection, which allowed navigators into modern times to plot a course of travel along lines that follow a constant and single compass bearing and that appear on a map as straight and equally spaced instead of curved.

LOCALE: Duisberg, duchy of Cleves (now in Germany)
CATEGORIES: Geography; science and technology

KEY FIGURES

Gerardus Mercator (1512-1594), cosmographer, mapmaker, printer, engraver, letterer, and maker of scientific instruments
Reiner Gemma Frisius (1508-1555), astronomer and mathematician who worked with Mercator
Abraham Ortelius (1527-1598), cosmographer, book and map dealer in Antwerp, who is known for his world atlas

SUMMARY OF EVENT

How can one represent a curving three-dimensional space such as Earth on a two-dimensional surface without distorting the image? This problem may appear astonishingly simple in the age of digital technologies, but it was more than a simple aesthetic dilemma for Renaissance artists, geographers, and mathematicians. For cartographers such as Gerardus Mercator, the question of projecting an accurate image of the world onto the two-dimensional surface of a map or nautical chart had been a preoccupation since the great second century Alexandrian geographer Ptolemy first attempted to depict Earth on a map.

At the heart of this problem of representation lies two functions of a map: It is both a representation of space that gives shape and form to a space one imagines and also a tool that can be used to navigate and travel within the space represented.

The publication of Mercator's world map in Duisberg in 1569 was an event whose significance would be felt long after the cartographer's death. Mercator's career as a cartographer began in Louvain, where he worked alongside one of the greatest astronomers of the Low Countries, Reiner Gemma Frisius. In Frisius's workshop, the two worked to produce terrestrial and celestial globes (1537). Also, Mercator developed his skills as an engraver and as a maker of astronomical instruments.

The sixteenth century, which followed the century that included the discoveries of Christopher Columbus and other world explorers, witnessed extraordinary accomplishments in the production and technology of mapmaking. The rediscovery and new editions of Ptolemy's *Geographike hyphegesis* and the first published accounts of exploration narratives of the New World prompted cartographers such as Mercator, Frisius, Oronce Finé in France, and Sebastian Münster in Germany to produce increasingly accurate national atlases, topographical maps, nautical charts, and world maps. The new technologies of print culture (the printing press as well as woodcut and copper plate engraving) that accompanied this effervescence in map production allowed mapmakers and authors to quickly reproduce illustrated texts in significant quantities and to disseminate them to the public at a more reasonable cost. Also, print technology was of particular interest to sixteenth century cartographers because it allowed them to incorporate the most recent data from territorial surveys and the exploration of the Americas into their maps and to update their charts for accuracy.

Mercator's first world map, *Orbis imago* (1538), depicted the image of the world in the form of two mirrored hearts. In the language of cartography, any representation of a round body, like the earth, onto a flat surface is called a map projection. Mercator's first world map used

A condensed version of Mercator's 1569 wall map of the world, Nova descriptio, *as produced several years later by his son, Rumold Mercator.* (Corbis)

a double cordiform projection, a representation of the world shaped like a heart that had already been used by the French cartographer Oronce Finé in 1531. Although Mercator's map resembled Finé's earlier cordiform projections, it actually bore greater resemblance to Frisius's terrestrial globe.

An important innovation in Mercator's world map was his use of the names "North America" and "South America" (*Americae pars septemtrionalis* and *Americae pars meridionalis*), the first time these words had been used on a map. Although Mercator's first map innovatively projected the spherical form of the earth onto the flat surface of the map, it was extremely difficult to interpret and its capacity to function as a navigational tool was hampered by the tremendous distortion that occurred around the poles.

Beginning in 1540, Mercator set out to produce a lightweight globe that could be used by navigators at sea. The concept behind the production of this globe and also his world map of 1569 was to reduce the distortion in the higher latitudes near the poles and to allow navigators to follow lines of constant and straight compass direction, known as rhumb lines. Unlike his fellow cartographer, Abraham Ortelius, whose atlas *Theatrum orbis terrarum* (1570) attempted to represent more realistic images of

the shape of the world and its territories, Mercator was less interested in producing an accurate graphic image of the earth than producing a map that would facilitate navigation.

Published in August of 1569 and dedicated to Duke Wilhelm of Cleves, Mercator's second world map, *Nova et aucta orbis terrae descriptio ad usum navigantium emendate accomodata* (also known as *Nova descriptio*; new and more accurate description of the world properly adapted for the use of navigators), was a wall-map produced from copper plate engravings. Measuring 51.5 by 82 inches (131 by 208 centimeters) over 18 separate sheets, this was the largest map Mercator had ever produced, and it included incredible detail, extensive commentary in legends, and place-names lettered in italics.

Because calculus had yet to be invented, there has been much conjecture about how Mercator developed his new projection in view of the complicated mathematics involved in its production. It is generally accepted that Mercator developed the projection by experimenting with the spacing of meridians and parallels on his 1541 globe. In the *Nova descriptio*, the meridians (great circles on the surface of the earth that pass through the poles) were represented as perpendicular to the equator. Mercator then augmented the parallels of latitude progressively from the equator to the poles to attenuate the distortion of lands situated close to the higher latitudes.

With his map, Mercator was able to straighten the lines that are naturally curved and to produce networks of straight lines of latitude and longitude, or graticule. His map facilitated ease in navigation, yet as a graphic representation of the world, the continents of North America, Europe, and Asia appeared as enormous masses that occupied nearly half of the northern hemisphere, and the southern continents of South America and Africa appeared as diminutive land masses to the south. The effect of this distortion was that Greenland appeared equivalent in size to China. Although to the modern eye, the image of the world appears even more distorted than in other sixteenth century map projections and somehow less navigable, Mercator's invention of the conformal map projection would nevertheless prove to be the most reliable and accurate guide that navigators would use through the present day.

SIGNIFICANCE

Four maps from Mercator's eighteen-sheet world map of 1569 appeared in Abraham Ortelius's atlas published between 1570 and 1612. Bernard van den Putte also published the entire map in a full-size woodcut edition in 1574. The projection was effectively launched in 1599 when an English cartographer, Edward Wright of Cambridge, published a table of the divisions of meridians based on Mercator's map. Wright's *Certaine Errors in Navigation* (1599) allowed Mercator's innovative projection to be disseminated to cartographers in the centuries that followed.

Although there was no single map projection in the sixteenth century favored or universally adopted by cartographers as the correct projection of the earth, Mercator's world map of 1569 came to be preferred by navigators from the eighteenth century through the twenty-first century. Virtually all nautical charts use Mercator's projection to plot steady compass courses along rhumb lines. Yet, despite the practical advantages and historical significance of Mercator's map projection, it continues to spark controversy. As recently as the 1970's, the distortion and larger size given to the continents in the northern hemisphere on Mercator's map prompted the publication of a map projection in Germany by Arno Peters, called the Peters projection, which attempted to correct Mercator's distortion of the relative size of continents.

—*Elisabeth Hodges*

FURTHER READING

Broc, Numa. *La Géographie de la Renaissance, 1420-1620*. Paris: Editions du C.T.H.S., 1986. A history of the development and technology of geography in the Renaissance.

Crane, Nicholas. *Mercator: The Man Who Mapped the Planet*. New York: H. Holt, 2003. A biographical overview of Mercator's life and contributions to the scientific development of cartography in the sixteenth century.

Karrow, Robert W., Jr. *Mapmakers of the Sixteenth Century and Their Maps: Biographies of the Cartographers of Abraham Ortelius, 1570*. Chicago: Speculum Orbis Press, 1993. A detailed catalog of maps and biographies of sixteenth century mapmakers who contributed to the production of Ortelius's atlas.

Mercator, Gerhard. *The Mercator Atlas of Europe: Facsimile of the Maps by Gerardus Mercator Contained in the "Atlas of Europe," Circa 1570-1572*. Edited by Marcel Watelet. Translated by Simon Knight. Pleasant Hill, Oreg.: Walking Tree Press, 1998. A facsimile edition of Mercator's original maps of Europe, with commentary.

Osley, A. S. *Mercator: A Monograph on the Lettering of Maps, etc., in the Sixteenth Century Netherlands, with a Facsimile and Translation of His Treatise on the Italic Hand and a Translation of Ghim's "Vita Mercatoris."* London: Faber & Faber, 1969. This volume contains an overview of Mercator's important contributions to cartography, a facsimile and translation of Mercator's treatise on italic lettering, and a translation of the only contemporary biography of Mercator by Walter Ghim.

Snyder, John Parr, *Flattening the Earth: Two Thousand Years of Map Projections*. Chicago: University of Chicago Press, 1993. A history of map projection from ancient Greece through the twentieth century.

Wilford, John Noble. *The Mapmakers*. Rev. ed. New York: Alfred A. Knopf, 2000. A history of mapmaking from antiquity to the present that explains the importance of Mercator's projection method.

SEE ALSO: 1490-1492: Martin Behaim Builds the First World Globe.
RELATED ARTICLES in *Great Lives from History: The Renaissance & Early Modern Era, 1454-1600:* John Cabot; Sebastian Cabot; Charles V; John Dee; Gerardus Mercator.

1560's

November 9, 1569
REBELLION OF THE NORTHERN EARLS

The failed Rebellion of the Northern Earls was the only significant attempt at returning Protestant England to Roman Catholicism by dethroning Queen Elizabeth I, a Protestant, and supporting the enthronement of Mary, Queen of Scots, a Catholic.

LOCALE: York and Durham, northern England
CATEGORIES: Government and politics; religion; wars, uprisings, and civil unrest

KEY FIGURES

Elizabeth I (1533-1603), Protestant queen of England, r. 1558-1603
Mary Stuart (1542-1587), queen of Scotland, r. 1542-1567, Elizabeth's half sister and claimant to English throne
William Cecil (1520-1598), secretary of state and chief adviser to Elizabeth I
Thomas Percy (1528-1572), seventh earl of Northumberland
Charles Neville (1543-1601), sixth earl of Westmoreland
Richard Norton (1502-1588), Catholic rebel
Walter Devereux (1539-1576), earl of Essex

SUMMARY OF EVENT

The Rebellion of the Northern Earls was prompted by a desire to replace Queen Elizabeth I, who supported the Protestant cause, with Mary, Queen of Scots, a Catholic, and to return England to the Roman Catholic fold. Elizabeth, who had narrowly escaped death in 1562 when she contracted smallpox, had been urged to name a successor to her throne to avert civil war. An Act of Succession called for the crown to go to the Suffolk line and the Grey family, Protestants in faith, but Parliament contained several Catholics who considered Mary to be the legitimate heir to the English throne. Mary was King Henry VIII's daughter by his first wife, Queen Catherine of Aragon, a Spaniard and a Roman Catholic; Elizabeth was his daughter by Anne Boleyn, for whom Henry had divorced Catherine in defiance of the Catholic Church. Elizabeth was therefore born as the Anglican offspring of England's first Protestant king. In 1568, Mary, who had been deposed as queen, came to northern England, which was still a hotbed of Catholicism and where Catholic Mass was still being celebrated openly in churches.

In response to Mary's presence in the north, Elizabeth reduced the influence of some Catholic families in that region, among them the Percies and the Nevilles, who were in Northumberland and Westmoreland. None of the northern earls were members of the Privy Council, and Elizabeth had removed the earl of Northumberland as warden of the Middle March, an influential post. When their roles at court and in the north were reduced substantially, they were naturally concerned and apprehensive about their futures.

Some of the dissident Catholics proposed a plan whereby Mary would marry Thomas Howard, the fourth duke of Norfolk, and then take the crown from Elizabeth. William Cecil, Elizabeth's chief secretary of state, was afraid that there would be an insurrection. Concerned about rumors about the plot, the duke of Norfolk, who was weak and timid, returned to his country estate but then returned to London and was then sent to the Tower of London. He urged the northern earls (the earl of Westmoreland, Charles Neville, was his brother-in-law) to abort any planned rebellion. Christopher Neville, the uncle of the earl of Westmoreland, and Richard Norton had proposed using the duke of Alva's Spanish troops to overthrow Elizabeth and put Mary on the throne.

Cecil suspected that the earls of Westmoreland and Northumberland were implicated in the Neville/Norton plot, and the earls went before the Northern Council, where Thomas Radcliffe, the earl of Sussex and an opponent of Cecil, presided. Although they convinced Sussex that there was, in fact, no plot, Elizabeth wanted to bring them before the Privy Council at court. Meanwhile, she had Mary moved from Tutbury to Coventry to keep her away from the earls.

Elizabeth forced the hand of the insurrectionists, who did not have enough lead time to secure Spanish help or determine the amount of support among the other Catholic northern earls. To some extent, the rebellion depended on assistance from Lancashire and Cheshire, but that did not materialize, and help from the Cumbrians arrived too late. In fact, there was not as much support for their cause as they had anticipated. Nevertheless, on November 9, at the sound of church bells pealing backward, the revolt began. Westmoreland and Northumberland (Thomas Percy) led their troops to Durham, which they occupied. When they entered the cathedral there, Norton entered with a crucifix, and the rebels then ripped the English Bible and the Book of Common Prayer, symbols of the Anglican faith. They celebrated their victory with a Catholic

Mass at the cathedral on November 30, 1569. They next moved south and succeeded in restoring Catholic worship at churches in Staindrop, Darlington, Richmond, and Ripon. When they arrived at Bramham Moor, they had four thousand foot soldiers and seventeen hundred soldiers on horseback.

They had planned to then invade York, the episcopal city, but Walter Devereux, the earl of Essex, had raised a formidable force against them, so they turned instead to Raby Castle and then to Barnard Castle. Sir George Bowes and his brother defended Barnard Castle for eleven days before surrendering. When they arrived at Clifford Moor, the rebel force was greatly diminished, and some of the earl of Westmoreland's troops deserted. The depleted forces faced Essex and his soliders and another army led by the earl of Warwick on December 13, 1569. The rebels retreated to Raby first and then to Naworth Castle, where they disbanded. Many of the rebels were killed or captured as they attempted to flee, most of them to Scotland. Four of the most prominent of the leaders were jailed at York Castle and later hanged, beheaded, and quartered; their heads were then mounted at the four city gates. Three thousand Cumbrians under the command of Leonard Dacre were late to the fray and were defeated at Gelt's Bridge by Lord Hundson's troops. The rebellion was over, but intrigues and schemes continued to plague Elizabeth.

The penalty for rebellion or treason was severe. The earl of Northumberland was captured by the Scots, then ransomed and given to Elizabeth, who had him hanged and beheaded in York in 1572. His head was affixed to a pole over Micklegate Bar for two years. Westmoreland was only a bit more fortunate. Hidden for a while at Fernyhurst Castle, he was betrayed by a kinsman but escaped to Flanders, where he died a pauper in 1601. Richard Norton also escaped to Flanders, where he joined Westmoreland in poverty. His brother Thomas and his son Christopher were hanged and quartered. Even some of the less notable rebels were punished severely. The earl of Essex and Bowes executed sixty-six of them at Durham, and others were killed at York and London. An estimated 750 rebels were executed. The lands of the prominent rebels (Northumberland, Westmoreland, Norton, and Swinburne) were forfeited and awarded to Elizabeth's supporters.

SIGNIFICANCE

The Rebellion of the Northern Earls reflects what was a chaotic situation in England regarding not only the question of who should rule but also what should be the state religion. Mary, for many the legitimate queen, was a devout Catholic; Elizabeth, the reigning monarch, was committed to Protestantism. That there was a rebellion, however short-lived, indicates that there were substantial numbers of Roman Catholics intent on returning England to Catholicism. That the rebellion did not succeed indicates that for many Catholics, the state was more important than religion.

Moreover, the rebellious northern earls were attempting to cling to a past that elevated local autonomy over a centralized government, and many of their colleagues saw the winds of change and either remained neutral in the conflict or gave lukewarm support to Elizabeth. After the failure of the revolt, there were no other significant attempts to reinstitute Catholicism in England. The Anglican Church continues its ties to the monarchy to this day.

—*Thomas L. Erskine*

FURTHER READING

Hume, Martin A. S. *The Great Lord Burghly: A Study in Elizabethan Statecraft*. London: James Nisbet, 1893. Focuses on Cecil's handling of the rebellion and finds that Norfolk's hesitation and cowardice contributed to the failure of the revolt.

Kinney, Arthur F., ed. *Elizabethan Backgrounds: Historical Documents of the Age of Elizabeth*. Hamden, Conn.: Archon, 1975. A concise four-page summary of the events leading to the revolt and to Elizabeth's proclamation about the rebellion. Kinney provides information about the involvement of Norfolk's sister Jane, Lady Westmoreland, who shamed the rebels into action.

Loades, David. *Tudor Government*. Oxford, England: 1997. Loades attributes the failure of the rebellion to changing times, asserting that even in the conservative north the "days had passed when a great nobleman could raise a private army to trouble the king."

MacCaffrey, Wallace. *The Shaping of the Elizabethan Regime*. Princeton, N.J.: Princeton University Press, 1968. The most extensive coverage of the revolt. MacCaffrey sees the revolt and the Ridolfi plot as the "testing-time of the regime" and provides a thorough discussion of events leading to the revolt and the revolt's aftermath.

Read, Conyers. *Mr. Secretary Cecil and Queen Elizabeth*. New York: Alfred A. Knopf, 1961. Explores the relationship between Norfolk, whom Read sees as a tool of the conspirators, and Cecil, who managed to maintain communication with the rebellious earls and with the queen. Norfolk became irritated at Cecil's domination of English foreign policy.

SEE ALSO: July, 1553: Coronation of Mary Tudor; Jan. 25-Feb. 7, 1554: Wyatt's Rebellion; 1558-1603:

Reign of Elizabeth I; Jan., 1563: Thirty-nine Articles of the Church of England; Feb. 25, 1570: Pius V Excommunicates Elizabeth I.

RELATED ARTICLES in *Great Lives from History: The Renaissance & Early Modern Era, 1454-1600:* William Cecil; Elizabeth I; Mary, Queen of Scots; Mary I.

February 25, 1570
PIUS V EXCOMMUNICATES ELIZABETH I

Elizabeth's excommunication by Pope Pius V did little for the position of the Catholic Church in England and instead instilled even deeper anti-Catholic resentment as the English stood by their queen. Elizabeth's excommunication consolidated her position as the undisputed leader of European Protestants.

LOCALE: Rome, Papal States (now in Italy)
CATEGORIES: Religion; organizations and institutions; government and politics

KEY FIGURES
Elizabeth I (1533-1603), queen of England, r. 1558-1603
Pius V (Antonio Ghislieri; 1504-1572), Roman Catholic pope, 1566-1572
Pius IV (Giovanni Angelo de' Medici; 1499-1565), Roman Catholic pope, 1559-1565
Philip II (1527-1598), king of Spain, r. 1556-1598, brother-in-law of Elizabeth I
Ferdinand I (1503-1564), Holy Roman Emperor, 1558-1564, uncle of Philip
Gregory XIII (Ugo Buoncompagni; 1502-1585), Roman Catholic pope, 1572-1585
Mary Stuart (1542-1587), queen of Scotland, r. 1542-1567, cousin of Elizabeth I

SUMMARY OF EVENT
Elizabeth I's preference for a modified form of Roman Catholic worship during the early years of her reign created problems for some English Catholics. In general, their lives were not in danger, although known recusants in areas where the magistrates were unsympathetic to Catholicism were often subject to fines and imprisonment for failing in the minimum attendance required at Church of England services. Occasionally, laypeople who concealed priests were charged with treason and executed.

A lack of priests compounded the problems of English Catholics. The majority of the clergy adhered to the Elizabethan Settlement of 1559; those who did not were

deprived of their livings and compelled to retire or enter secular life. Although the Catholic laity were not subject to the death penalty for the practice of their faith, the clergy were. Celebration of the Mass and the hearing of confession were legal grounds for execution, although these stringent regulations were rarely enforced.

In the decades following Elizabeth's accession, recusants who did not go so far as to assert their principles boldly were sometimes troubled by the proper attitude they were required to assume toward the queen. Most Catholics were reluctant on principle, and for the sake of expediency, to repudiate their loyalty to Elizabeth. At the same time they regarded her as a heretic; thus, according to the dogma of the Roman Catholic Church, her regal authority was suspect.

As early as 1561, Pope Pius IV considered excommunicating Elizabeth as a heretic because of the religious changes the queen had made since her accession. He was dissuaded from doing so by Philip II of Spain, the widower of Queen Mary I, Elizabeth's half sister and predecessor. Philip argued that the sentence of excommunication implied deposition and was consequently unenforceable. Besides, Philip hoped to marry Elizabeth, and such a marriage would have been impossible if she were a declared heretic.

At the request of the pope, the matter was discussed at the Council of Trent. According to canon law, there was little doubt that Elizabeth had rendered herself subject to excommunication, and a group of English Catholic refugees on the Continent presented the council with a petition demanding such action on the grounds that failure to act would further mislead the English nation.

The Habsburg rulers, Philip II and his uncle, Ferdinand I, the Holy Roman Emperor, again played major roles in preventing the council from acting, with the same arguments Philip had used two years earlier. Ferdinand pointed out that many German princes deserved excommunication as much as Elizabeth did, but to pronounce sentence against all of them would invite chaos. Like Philip, the emperor was optimistic about securing a marriage between Elizabeth and a prince of his own imperial house.

Pope Pius IV died late in 1565 and was succeeded by Pius V, a former head of the Inquisition. Pius V saw an opportunity to proceed against Elizabeth in 1569, when she confined her cousin Mary, Queen of Scots, who had fled to Elizabeth for protection. Soon suspected of involvement in Catholic intrigues, Mary was placed under house arrest and appeared to Catholics to be a martyr for the religion that Philip II had sworn to defend. After 1569, when English vessels began regularly to prey on Spanish treasure ships sailing from the New World, Philip's patience was tried further.

On February 5, 1570, the case against Elizabeth was formally opened in Rome. She was charged with assuming authority over the English Church, depriving and imprisoning bishops, denying the authority of the Papacy, and encouraging heresy. English exiles were summoned as witnesses, and the bull of excommunication, *Regnans in Excelsis*, was issued by the pope on February 25, 1570. Despite worsening relations with England, Philip and Ferdinand protested strongly, but the pope remained adamant.

There was, however, a legal flaw in the process of excommunication, since no advance warning of the sentence had been given to the queen. Moreover, the bull declared her deposed as a ruler as well as excommunicated, and canon law provided the former sentence only if a ruler did not seek relief from excommunication within a year. English Catholics, placed by the bull in the difficult position of having to repudiate their loyalty to Queen Elizabeth and risk charges of treason, seized on these flaws to reaffirm their allegiance to her.

The bull had little effect in England except to deepen anti-Catholic feeling and thus strengthen Elizabeth's position with the nation. The year before the condemnation, there had been a feudal uprising in the north, the Rebellion of the Northern Earls, which had strong Catholic overtones, but it had been crushed and some of the participants executed. The Catholic faction no longer had any hope of armed rebellion, as Pius's decree envisioned.

Actually, there were few English Catholics who seriously desired revolt or the overthrow of the queen. Although their situation was perplexing, it was not hopeless, but they realized that any suspicion of political disloyalty would lead to harsher measures.

The pope attempted to persuade Philip to institute a blockade against England, but Philip declined, claiming that France would not cooperate. In general, the papal bull also had a negligible effect in terms of international affairs. The Roman Catholic nations continued their diplomatic and economic relations with England without regard to the sentence against Elizabeth.

The spiritual condition of English Catholics began to improve about 1575, with the arrival of the first seminary priests, Englishmen trained at the English College, established in 1568 at Douai in France. Although there were never more than a few dozen seminary priests working in England at one time, they enjoyed considerable success reconciling lapsed Catholics to the Church and establishing pockets of firm recusancy, centers to which priests could regularly come in safety. While they encouraged Catholic laity not to participate in Anglican worship, for the most part they did not encourage disobedience to the queen in other matters.

PIUS V'S BULL EXCOMMUNICATING ELIZABETH

[T]he number of the ungodly has so much grown in power that there is no place left in the world which they have not tried to corrupt with their most wicked doctrines; and among others, Elizabeth, the pretended queen of England and the servant of crime, has assisted in this, with whom as in a sanctuary the most pernicious of all have found refuge. This very woman, having seized the crown and monstrously usurped the place of supreme head of the Church in all England together with the chief authority and jurisdiction belonging to it, has once again reduced this same kingdom—which had already been restored to the Catholic faith and to good fruits—to a miserable ruin.

We, seeing impieties and crimes multiplied one upon another the persecution of the faithful and afflictions of religion daily growing more severe under the guidance and by the activity of the said Elizabeth—and recognising that her mind is so fixed and set that she has not only despised the pious prayers and admonitions with which Catholic princes have tried to cure and convert her but has not even permitted the nuncios sent to her in this matter by this See to cross into England, are compelled by necessity to take up against her the weapons of justice.... Therefore, ... we do out of the fullness of our apostolic power declare the foresaid Elizabeth to be a heretic and favourer of heretics, and her adherents in the matters aforesaid to have incurred the sentence of excommunication and to be cut off from the unity of the body of Christ.

Source: Adapted from "Pope Pius V's Bull Against Elizabeth (1570)." Tudorhistory.org/primary/papalbull.html. Accessed September 27, 2004.

In 1580, the Jesuits also began to send missionaries to England. Two of them, Robert Parsons and Edmund Campion, obtained from Pope Gregory XIII a declaration that stated that as long as Elizabeth's deposition was unenforceable, English Catholics were not bound by the decree. As a result, Gregory was able to partially mitigate the work of his predecessor without repudiating it. Henceforth, virtually all priests captured and charged with treason insisted that they acknowledged Elizabeth as their ruler in all matters of state.

Elizabeth's government pursued alternately strict and lax policies toward English Catholics, according to internal affairs such as Puritan agitation and Catholic plots. Most wealthy Catholics were forced to pay large fines, while their poorer brethren were often left alone. The prohibition against the mass, however, continued to be enforced rigorously.

On several occasions Catholics, especially from among the nobility, were involved in plots against Elizabeth. The missionary priests, with few exceptions, remained aloof from such schemes. In 1586, one such plot led to the execution of Mary, Queen of Scots, whom the plotters hoped to place on the throne of England.

The Papacy knew of several of these plots and encouraged them. Gradually, relations between Spain and England deteriorated to the point of intense and bitter rivalry. Philip II increasingly came to regard himself as the champion of the Roman Catholic Church in Europe; he determined to punish Elizabeth for her heresy and set his own daughter on the English throne. Finally, in 1588, Philip launched the reputedly invincible Armada against England. Attacked by Sir John Hawkins and Sir Francis Drake, and wrecked by storms off the British coasts, the Armada failed to defeat England.

SIGNIFICANCE

The excommunication of Elizabeth I in 1570 proved a pivotal event in the history of England and of Europe. Not only was the loyalty and devotion of the English people to their sovereign reaffirmed by this event but also Elizabeth came to be regarded as the leader of the Protestant cause. Thus, Pope Pius V unwittingly provided Protestants with a living symbol of resistance to Roman Catholicism.

—James F. Hitchcock,
updated by Clifton W. Potter, Jr.

FURTHER READING

Brigden, Susan. *London and the Reformation.* New York: Oxford University Press, 1990. An essential work for understanding the forces that shaped Elizabethan religious opinion.

Doran, Susan. *Queen Elizabeth I.* New York: New York University Press, 2003. Portrays Elizabeth as a flawed but brilliant manipulator who used this ability to protect her country and to steer it safely through a host of dangers. Includes illustrations, map, bibliographic references, index.

Haigh, Christopher, ed. *The Reign of Elizabeth I.* Athens: University of Georgia Press, 1985. An excellent collection of revisionist essays concerning the Elizabethan Age.

Haynes, Alan. *Invisible Power: The Elizabethan Secret Service, 1570-1603.* New York: St. Martin's Press, 1992. Haynes provides a fascinating examination of those responsible for the security of England.

Hughes, Philip. *The Reformation in England.* Vol. 3. Rev. ed. Reprint. Brookfield, Vt.: Ashgate, 1993. The most thorough study available on the English Reformation.

MacCaffrey, Wallace T. *Queen Elizabeth and the Making of Policy, 1572-1588.* Princeton, N.J.: Princeton University Press, 1981. McCaffrey presents a thorough examination of the queen's role in making foreign policy.

MacCulloch, Diarmaid. *The Later Reformation in England, 1547-1603.* 2d ed. New York: Palgrave, 2001. Study of the major events of the Reformation in England after Henry VIII's death, together with a discussion of the reception and understanding of those events by the English people. Includes bibliographic references and index.

Marshall, Peter. *Reformation England, 1480-1642.* New York: Oxford University Press, 2003. Extremely detailed, meticulously supported argument that the English Reformation should be understood to begin in the late fifteenth century and to last well into the seventeenth century. Explicates the specific meanings of Protestantism and Catholicism to the major players and to laypeople during the Renaissance. Includes bibliographic references and index.

Parker, Geoffrey. *The Grand Strategy of Philip II.* New Haven, Conn.: Yale University Press, 1998. Contests the traditional view of Philip as conducting his empire by reacting to events as they occurred without any grand plan to guide him. Uses correspondence and other historical documents to delineate a "strategic culture" informing Philip's decisions and his reign. Includes illustrations, maps, bibliographic references, and index.

Rendina, Claudio. *The Popes: Histories and Secrets.*

Translated by Paul D. McCusker. Santa Ana, Calif.: Seven Locks Press, 2002. Massive, comprehensive study of the biographies, historical significance, personal experiences, political and religious milieus, and controversies surrounding each of the popes from Saint Peter to John Paul II. Includes bibliographic references and index.

Ridley, Jasper G. *Elizabeth I: The Shrewdness of Virtue.* New York: Viking Press, 1988. Among the more up-to-date biographies, this work is one of the best because the author fully analyzes the personality of the queen.

Shagan, Ethan H. *Popular Politics and the English Reformation.* New York: Cambridge University Press, 2003. Study of the way in which ordinary English subjects interpreted and reacted to Protestantism. Argues that religious history cannot be understood independently of political history, because commoners no less than royals understood religion and politics as utterly intertwined. Includes bibliographic references and index.

Trimble, William Raleigh. *The Catholic Laity in Elizabethan England.* Cambridge, Mass.: Harvard University Press, 1964. An exhaustive study of the Catholic population in England during the time of Elizabeth I.

Wright, A. D. *The Early Modern Papacy: From the Council of Trent to the French Revolution, 1564-1789.* New York: Longman, 2000. Examination of both the scope and the limitations of the powers of the popes after the Council of Trent. Emphasizes the multiple, potentially conflicting obligations of the popes to the city of Rome, the Italian church, the transnational Catholic church, the Papal States, and other specific religious and political entities.

SEE ALSO: Oct. 31, 1517: Luther Posts His Ninety-five Theses; Apr.-May, 1521: Luther Appears Before the Diet of Worms; Mar., 1536: Calvin Publishes *Institutes of the Christian Religion*; 1545-1563: Council of Trent; Jan. 25-Feb. 7, 1554: Wyatt's Rebellion; 1558-1603: Reign of Elizabeth I; Jan., 1563: Thirty-nine Articles of the Church of England; Nov. 9, 1569: Rebellion of the Northern Earls; Apr., 1587-c. 1600: Anglo-Spanish War; July 31-Aug. 8, 1588: Defeat of the Spanish Armada.

RELATED ARTICLES in *Great Lives from History: The Renaissance & Early Modern Era, 1454-1600:* Martin Bucer; John Calvin; Elizabeth I; Gregory XIII; Martin Luther; Philip II; Pius V; Mary, Queen of Scots.

July, 1570-August, 1571
SIEGE OF FAMAGUSTA AND FALL OF CYPRUS

After an eleven-month siege, Venetian defenders surrendered to the Ottoman Turks and were then treacherously slaughtered. The massacre led directly to the Battle of Lepanto, in which the assembled sea power of Spain and the Italian states crushed the Ottoman fleet.

LOCALE: Island of Cyprus
CATEGORIES: Wars, uprisings, and civil unrest; expansion and land acquisition; diplomacy and international relations

KEY FIGURES

Marcantonio Bragadin (d. 1571), Venetian commander
Astorre Baglioni (d. 1570), Venetian commander
Niccolò Dandolo (d. 1570), Venetian governor
Lala Mustafa Paşa (fl. mid-sixteenth century), Turkish general
Piali Paşa (fl. mid-sixteenth century), Turkish admiral

SUMMARY OF EVENT

A byproduct of the Crusades, the Kingdom of Cyprus lasted nearly three centuries under the Lusignan Dynasty, creating a lively fusion of French, Greek, and polyglot Levantine elements. It built a lucrative economy around production of wine, salt, and refined sugar, while its strategic location in the eastern Mediterranean made it enormously important commercially. Accordingly, the island attracted the attention of two rival commercial powers, Genoa and Venice, each eager for concessions in the vibrant port of Famagusta on the island's eastern coast.

In 1376, the Genoese seized the city, holding it until 1464. The Lusignan regime recovered Famagusta with help from the Venetians, who were by then already crucial investors and entrepreneurs in the Cypriot economy. In 1468, the last Lusignan king, James II, married Caterina Cornaro (or Corner), a member of a Venetian family long deeply involved in Cypriot affairs. Caterina gave birth to a son in 1473, several months after the death of her husband. Maintaining Caterina as their puppet, especially after the death of her son (1474), the Venetians became virtual rulers of Cyprus. In 1489, they dispensed with even the pretense of Caterina's reign: She was made to abdicate her throne and sent back to Venice, while Cyprus was officially incorporated into Venice's maritime empire.

As the last great acquisition of that empire, however, Cyprus was governed less well than other parts of Venice's efficient dominion. Tradition has perhaps exaggerated Venetian failures, but undoubtedly corruption was unusually rife, and the local Greek population was alienated by the oppressive, moribund, and unreformed feudal institutions that Venice installed on the island. Meanwhile, the Ottomans' rapid rise to dominate the Levant by the early sixteenth century guaranteed that Cyprus would, sooner or later, become a Turkish target.

Several times during the 1560's, delegations representing the disaffected Greek Cypriots appealed to the sultan in Istanbul as a preferable ruler to come and seize their island from the Venetians. Certainly the Porte was smarting from the Turkish failure in 1565 to conquer Malta. The new sultan, Selim II "the Sot," was supposedly incited against Cyprus by his Jewish (and rabidly anti-Venetian) favorite, Joseph Nasi, who promised Selim not only rich loot but also freer access to his favorite Cypriot wines. Joined by another favorite, the general Lala Mustafa Paşa, Nasi persuaded Selim to direct an expedition against the island.

The Venetian regime on the island, in serious disarray, had not maintained its defenses consistently. The head of the civil administration in Nicosia, *luogotenente* Niccolò Dandolo, was notably incompetent, though the military commander based in Famagusta, Marcantonio Bragadin, and an additional general newly sent by Venice, the Perugian-born Astorre Baglioni, were both highly able men. Due to Dandolo's dithering, only minimal opposition was mounted when the Turkish expeditionary force reached Cyprus on July 1, 1570.

The Turks, under the command of Lala Mustafa and Admiral Piali Paşa (one of the failed commanders against Malta), coasted the southern shore, raiding Limassol and then disembarking at Larnaca. From the outset, the opponents displayed wildly different attitudes toward the island's Greek population. Fearing an uprising, the Venetians had massacred several hundred Greeks in one area suspected of disloyalty. Mustafa, on the other hand, immediately instituted a policy of promising the locals rewards for support, as well as a milder, less burdensome government once the Ottomans were victorious.

Joined on July 22 by massive reinforcements from the mainland, Mustafa moved on Nicosia, where his menace had been underestimated and defenses were inadequate. Nevertheless, the city held out against a siege of forty-five days, falling only when Mustafa had been strengthened by still more reinforcements. The final, successful assault was mounted on September 9. Dandolo was summarily beheaded as the bloodthirsty Turks swarmed through the city and plundered its enormous wealth. Once-mighty Kyrenia, now hopelessly indefensible, surrendered without a fight. This left the Turks one final and truly formidable obstacle to complete control of the island: Famagusta. Though its defenders numbered barely 8,000, against Mustafa's forces of some 200,000, the city had massive and updated fortifications, and it had in Bragadin and Baglioni two superlative and deeply respected commanders.

Lala Mustafa and Piali united at Famagusta on September 17, 1570, to invest the city. Conflicts between besiegers and besieged became regular and robust, and they lasted into winter. The Venetian commanders believed that they could preserve Famagusta and, with it, Venetian control of the island. Back in Venice, however, there was more pessimism, and an allied effort at naval relief of Cyprus proved an embarrassing failure. Two enterprising brothers, Marco and Marcantonio Querini, did reach Famagusta in late January, 1570, with a force of fifteen hundred men, bolstering both the resources and the spirits of the defenders. By spring, however, there was renewed concern about food supplies, and Bragadin accordingly expelled numerous militarily useless civilians. The Turks constructed a massive network of trenches around the walls, to allow freer access to them, and a series of ten siege towers was set near the walls, from which the defenders could be targeted. A massive bombardment was begun on May 15. Only prodigious feats of bravery and determination beat back repeated Turkish assaults.

The defenders still hoped for a massive relief, if not by direct reinforcement, then by naval disruption of the Turks on a wide front. Indeed, in Rome on May 25, 1571, the Holy League was established, by which Pope Pius V, King Philip II of Spain, and the Venetian Republic agreed to mount a massive fleet against Turkish naval might. The Venetians hoped that one result of the alliance would be relief of Famagusta and recovery of Cyprus.

It was too late for Famagusta, however. While the league's naval preparations dragged on, the beleaguered defenders approached desperation. By July, food supplies were all but exhausted. A series of Turkish assaults in the last days of the month drastically depleted manpower. The two commanders concluded that diminished ammunition and food could no longer sustain resistance. On August 1, 1571, they proposed capitulation, and Lala Mustafa agreed to remarkably generous terms, by which all Italians and any allies could depart in full honor and safety. Arrangements to implement these terms were begun, not without some violence in the streets, but with displays of mutual respect between leaders. The two Venetian generals, with appropriate retinue, were to call upon Lala Mustafa on the evening of August 5 for a formal ceremony of surrender.

Then something went terribly wrong. After initial courtesies, Lala Mustafa fell into one of his characteristic violent moods. He began insulting the Venetian generals, accusing them of atrocities against Turkish prisoners and violations of the surrender terms. His rage mounting, he ordered the arrest and execution of the whole delegation. Baglioni and the others were beheaded, though Bragadin, mutilated facially, was kept apart. This spectacle quickly escalated still further, as the fury of the Turkish troops began to mirror that of their leader. They proceeded to massacre and pillage the city.

Bragadin had been spared for even worse horrors. Imprisoned for nearly two weeks while his wounds festered, the half-dead commander refused to accept conversion to Islam. After an appalling round of public abuse, he was tied to a stake in the main square and flayed alive, before he was finally killed. His body was divided and his skin, tanned and stuffed with straw, was paraded around the city in symbolic degradation. This skin (plus his head) was taken back to Istanbul as part of the loot. Almost a decade later, a Venetian survivor of the siege was able to make off with the skin, bringing it to Bragadin's family. It was deposited in an urn as part of a memorial erected among the tombs of the doges in Venice's Church of Saints Giovanni and Paolo—one of its few monuments to a nondoge, reverencing him as a civic martyr to the republic's honor.

SIGNIFICANCE

Too late for Bragadin and the defenders of Famagusta, Venice had some measure of revenge two months later. The struggling armada of the Holy League finally confronted the full Turkish fleet at Lepanto, off the Gulf of Corinth, on October 7, 1571, and smashed it in one of the spectacular naval battles of history. Selim readily ordered the building of a new Turkish fleet, under the supervision of Piali Paşa. Lepanto ultimately, if not decisively, spelled the end of the Turkish menace in the Mediterranean sea lanes.

Though Turkish naval power was now on the wane, the Ottoman Empire had acquired a valuable new province, guaranteeing security to its situation in the Levant. Cyprus itself, long with ambiguous ties to the Hellenic world, was now infused with a new Turkish population. It remained in Turkish hands until 1878, when it came under British administration. In the twentieth century, the island became an independent republic (1960), but the tensions between Turkish and Greek portions of the population remained, each fearing annexation by the other's nation of origin. In 1974, Turkey did indeed invade Cyprus, dividing the island into Turkish and Greek sections, although the division was not formally recognized by the international community. This division has lasted into the early twenty-first century.

—*John W. Barker*

FURTHER READING

Arbel, Benjamin. *Cyprus, the Franks, and Venice, Thirteenth-Sixteenth Centuries.* Burlington, Vt: Ashgate/ Variorum, 2000. A collection of the author's articles (nine in English, four in French, one in Italian), this constitutes a rare and insightful treatment of the island under the Venetians.

Bicheno, Hugh. *Crescent and Cross: The Battle of Lepanto, 1571.* London: Cassell, 2003. A concise account of the fall of Cyprus appears on pages 182-193 and on 204-208, in the broader context of international war with the Ottomans.

Edbury, Peter W. *The Kingdom of Cyprus and the Crusades, 1191-1374.* New York: Cambridge University Press, 1991. The best study of the island's Lusignan era.

Kinross, J. P. D. B. *The Ottoman Centuries: The Rise and Fall of the Turkish Empire.* New York: William Morrow, 1977. Good general account of Ottoman history for the general reader, including pages on the conquest of Cyprus.

Norwich, John Julius. *A History of Venice.* New York: Alfred A. Knopf, 1982. Excellent general history with the Cyprus episode generously treated in context.

Rodgers, William L. *Naval Warfare Under Oars, Fourth to Sixteenth Centuries.* Annapolis, Md.: U.S. Naval Institute, 1939. Classic study of naval tactics with almost one hundred pages devoted to Cyprus and Lepanto.

Setton, Kenneth M. *The Sixteenth Century.* Vol. 4 in *The Papacy and the Levant, 1204-1571.* Philadelphia: American Philosophical Society, 1984. Covers the fall of Cyprus, closely following the sources, in the context of contemporaneous diplomacy.

1570's

SEE ALSO: 1463-1479: Ottoman-Venetian War; June 28, 1522-Dec. 27, 1522: Siege and Fall of Rhodes; Sept. 27-28, 1538: Battle of Préveza; Oct. 20-27, 1541: Holy Roman Empire Attacks Ottomans in Algiers; 1552: Struggle for the Strait of Hormuz; May 18-Sept. 8, 1565: Siege of Malta; 1566-1574: Reign of Selim II; Oct. 7, 1571: Battle of Lepanto.
RELATED ARTICLES in *Great Lives from History: The Renaissance & Early Modern Era, 1454-1600:* Philip II; Pius V.

October 7, 1571
BATTLE OF LEPANTO

The Battle of Lepanto brought the forces of the Holy League and the Turkish fleet together in a major naval confrontation that marked the last great galley battle fought between Mediterranean Christendom and Islam.

LOCALE: Gulf of Corinth, between Thessaly and Morea (now in Greece)
CATEGORY: Wars, uprisings, and civil unrest

KEY FIGURES
Philip II (1527-1598), king of Spain, r. 1556-1598
Selim II (1524-1574), Ottoman sultan, r. 1566-1574
Don Juan de Austria (1547-1578), half brother of King Philip II and commander of the fleet of the Holy League
Ali Paşa (d. 1571), commander of the Turkish fleet
Augustino Barbarizo (fl. mid-sixteenth century), leader of the Venetian fleet
Andrea Doria (1540-1606), admiral of the Genoese squadron of the Holy League
Marco Antonio Colonna (d. 1584), commander of papal forces
Uluch ʿAlī (fl. mid-sixteenth century), Algerian corsair who commanded the Turkish left squadron
Mahomet Sirocco (fl. mid-sixteenth century), Egyptian commander of the Turkish right squadron
Pius V (Antonio Ghislieri; 1504-1572), Roman Catholic pope, 1566-1572

SUMMARY OF EVENT
A key episode in the protracted conflict between Christians and Muslims for control of the Mediterranean, the Battle of Lepanto was one of the greatest sea engagements in fifteen centuries. In the years following the fall of Constantinople to the Ottoman Empire in 1453, Egypt, Mesopotamia, North Africa, much of the Balkans, and about two-thirds of the Mediterranean coast came under Turkish domination. Turkish sea power was virtually unchallenged, and it threatened a disunited Europe.

In the face of the dominant Ottoman navy, King Philip II of Spain was conscious of his exposed coastline and his vulnerable imperial holdings in North Africa, Naples, and Sicily. He sought an alliance with the Republic of Venice against the Ottoman Empire. Venice traditionally had sought an accommodation with the Turks to profit from the Levant trade. Sultan Selim II's attack on Venetian Cyprus in 1570, however, persuaded the Venetians to join Spain and the crusading Counter-Reformation pope Pius V in a Holy League. Their goal was to destroy the Turkish fleet, protect Christian Europe, defeat Islam, and drive a wedge between the European and African parts of the Turkish empire.

Don Juan de Austria, Philip's illegitimate half brother, was chosen for the delicate task of commanding the Christian fleet, which was united in name only. Don Juan had already distinguished himself in combat against the Moriscos (Moors, or Muslims) in Granada. Though only twenty-four years old, he was aggressive, capable, forceful, and well able to blend his makeshift fleet into an effective fighting force. He had to unify Augustino Barbarizo's Venetians; their arch rivals, the Genoese, commanded by Andrea Doria; and Marco Antonio Colonna's papal fleet.

All together, Don Juan commanded more than two hundred galleys (historical accounts vary as to precise numbers). The long shallow-draft galley was the basic Mediterranean warship, dependent upon human oarsmen for its mobility and maneuverability. The typical galley used at Lepanto had a displacement of about 170 tons. It was about 150 feet (46 meters) long and carried a crew of 225. While it was new and still clean, its oarsmen could move the ship at 7 knots for a few minutes before becoming totally exhausted. Galleys carried ten days' provisions. Ship life was bleak for the warriors but miserable for the galley slaves; permanently imprisoned at their positions and living in constant filth, they generally died in chains.

The general tactics employed at sea were similar to

those used in land battles: An attacking ship would ram an enemy and then hold the stricken vessel close with grappling lines while its infantry went aboard for hand-to-hand combat. The harquebus, an early type of musket, was the Western infantryman's weapon of choice. Most ships mounted a large gun on their bows that fired a thirty-pound shot, the beginning of the use of artillery in naval warfare. Several smaller guns were mounted beside the big gun, and some galleys had a few side-firing guns as well.

The early sixteenth century experimented with naval gunships, and Don Juan had six galleasses at Lepanto. Each displaced seven hundred tons and carried a crew of

seven hundred, half of whom were rowers. These oar-powered gunnery ships mounted heavy broadside batteries able to fire 326 pounds of shot compared with the 90 pounds discharged by a galley. The large ships were unwieldy and had to be towed into position, but they proved the feasibility of heavy broadside batteries for future naval warfare. Although there is some disagreement about their decisiveness at Lepanto, modern scholars believe the galleasses were effective at breaking the line of Turkish ships and caused considerable casualties.

The Christian fleet put to sea on September 16, 1571. It was a troubled and divided fleet, beset by disputes and bitter dissension. The various admirals, meeting in council, were still undecided about a plan. The Venetians advocated a bold attack on the Turkish supply base. Doria, head of the Genoese, feared to risk the entire Christian fleet in a single battle and urged caution. Don Juan was for searching out and engaging the Ottoman fleet. On October 6, a ship from Crete brought the news that the Turks had taken the fortress of Famagusta on Cyprus and killed its Venetian defenders. The allies were horror-stricken and a new unity, forged by the bad news, spurred them to sail at once and attack the Turkish fleet.

After an attack on Crete, Ali Paşa, the commander of the Turkish ships, had anchored near Lepanto, 80 miles (129 kilometers) up the Gulf of Corinth. With him was Uluch ʿAlī, a corsair from Algeria, and Mahomet Sirocco, an able sailor who knew the shallow waters nearby. Paşa's combined fleet numbered nearly three hundred galleys, rowed by captured Christian galley slaves.

At dawn on October 7, the two most powerful forces that had ever met at sea sighted each other and moved ponderously into attack formation. Don Juan put his galleasses to the front and deployed seventy galleys in crescent formation to form his center. Fifty more galleys were positioned on each side of the center to guard their respective flanks. Thirty ships were held in reserve half a mile away. The Turks also formed a crescent with one hundred ships at the center, fifty-five on the right, and an assault force of ninety-five on the left flank. Forty galleys were in reserve. Don Juan's forces, with the wind to their backs, advanced.

Ponderously the centers of both forces closed, and thereafter, maneuver counted for lit-

An engraving of the Christian fleet's defeat of the Muslim Ottomans at the Battle of Lepanto, one of the greatest sea engagements in fifteen hundred years. (F. R. Niglutsch)

tle. A confusing and terrible melee erupted. Fierce hand-to-hand fighting surged from one deck to another. In three hours of desperate battle, galleys continually broke through the opposing line and attacked from the rear. Boarding assaults, ramming, and cannon fire raged continually in disorderly fashion. The two opposing flagships, the *Real* and the *Sultana*, closed in decisive combat and both commanders took part in the assault. Ali Paşa died in the battle. At least one woman, Maria la Bailadora, disguised as a man, fought aboard the *Real*.

A crisis was narrowly averted on the Christians' left flank when a galleass held the Turks in check while the Venetian commander maneuvered boldly in dangerously shallow water to gain the advantage of position. Don Juan's force slowly gained the upper hand, as his veteran infantry gained the advantage at close quarters. The Turkish center was routed, and the whole Turkish line collapsed.

The Turks were soundly beaten. Only forty of their ships returned to Constantinople. More than one hundred were captured; the remainder were burned and sunk. Twenty-five thousand Turks were killed and five thousand taken prisoner. Fifteen thousand Christians were freed from slavery at a cost of seventeen ships and eight thousand Christian dead.

An iron shield, inscribed with the words "Christ has won the victory; it is He who reigns and governs," given to Don John of Austria, the commander of the fleet of the Holy League, after the Christian victory at the Battle of Lepanto. (Frederick Ungar Publishing Co.)

SIGNIFICANCE

According to tradition, Lepanto was a decisive battle that eliminated the threat of the Turks in the Mediterranean and marked the beginning of Ottoman decline. Yet, the Ottomans' defeat did not prevent their conquest of Cyprus, and the Christian alliance crumbled after the battle. Sultan Selim II quickly rebuilt his fleet and used it to retake Tunis from the Spanish in 1574. Philip II of Spain remained on the offensive until a truce in 1580 allowed the two powers to disengage. Nevertheless, the battle was one of the greatest sea battles in history and one of the worst Ottoman defeats. A great psychological victory, destroying the myth of Turkish invincibility, it was celebrated throughout Europe.

—Paul A. Whelan, updated by Douglas Clark Baxter

FURTHER READING

Beeching, Jack. *The Galleys of Lepanto*. New York: Charles Scribner's Sons, 1983. Vivid narrative providing the larger geopolitical background as well as an exciting history of the battle.

Bicheno, Hugh. *Crescent and Cross: The Battle of Lepanto, 1571*. London: Cassell, 2003. Voluminous study of both the battle itself and the long-term political and military history leading up to it. Includes illustrations, maps, bibliographic references, and index.

Fregosi, Paul. *Jihad in the West: Muslim Conquests from the Seventh to the Twenty-First Centuries*. Amherst, N.Y.: Prometheus Books, 1998. The Battle of Lepanto is one of the conflicts discussed in this study of Islamic wars in the West. Includes photographic plates, map, bibliographic references, and index.

Guilmartin, John Francis, Jr. *Gunpowder and Galleys: Changing Technology and Mediterranean Warfare at Sea in the Sixteenth Century*. Rev. ed. Annapolis, Md.: Naval Institute Press, 2003. Sophisticated analysis of galleys and their place in naval warfare.

Hanson, Victor Davis. *Carnage and Culture: Landmark Battles in the Rise of Western Power*. New York: Anchor, 2002. Discusses the link between the early development of global capitalism and the Battle of Lepanto. Includes illustrations, maps, bibliographic references, and index.

Hess, Andrew C. "The Battle of Lepanto and Its Place in Mediterranean History." *Past and Present* 57 (November, 1972): 53-73. Scholarly revisionism that questions the battle's traditional significance.

Paulson, Michael G., and Tamara Alvarez-Detrell. *Lepanto: Fact, Fiction, and Fantasy.* Lanham, Md.: University Press of America, 1986. First two chapters concisely summarize the battle and its place in literature, art, and popular culture.

Petrie, Charles. *Don John of Austria.* New York: W. W. Norton, 1967. Standard biography of the victor of Lepanto.

Rodgers, William L. *Naval Warfare Under Oars, Fourth to Sixteenth Centuries.* Annapolis, Md.: U.S. Naval Institute, 1939. Classic study of naval tactics with almost one hundred pages devoted to Cyprus and Lepanto.

Williams, Ann. "Mediterranean Conflict." In *Süleyman the Magnificent and His Age: The Ottoman Empire in the Early Modern World*, edited by Metin Kunt and

Christine Woodhead. New York: Longman, 1995. Good overview of the Ottoman struggle from 1453 to 1580 with Venice and Spain.

SEE ALSO: 1463-1479: Ottoman-Venetian War; 1478-1482: Albanian-Turkish Wars End; 16th cent.: Evolution of the Galleon; June 28, 1522-Dec. 27, 1522: Siege and Fall of Rhodes; 1552: Struggle for the Strait of Hormuz; 1559-1561: Süleyman's Sons Wage Civil War; Apr. 3, 1559: Treaty of Cateau-Cambrésis; May 18-Sept. 8, 1565: Siege of Malta; 1566-1574: Reign of Selim II; July, 1570-Aug., 1571: Siege of Famagusta and Fall of Cyprus; July 31-Aug. 8, 1588: Defeat of the Spanish Armada; 1593-1606: Ottoman-Austrian War.

RELATED ARTICLES in *Great Lives from History: The Renaissance & Early Modern Era, 1454-1600:* Philip II; Pius V.

1572-1574
TYCHO BRAHE OBSERVES A SUPERNOVA

Brahe's observation of a supernova led him to develop new, precise instruments for observing and measuring the locations and movements of celestial bodies. Johannes Kepler used Brahe's work to help demonstrate his radical theory that planets, including Earth, moved in ellipses around the sun.

LOCALE: Herrevad Abbey, near Copenhagen, Denmark

CATEGORIES: Astronomy; science and technology; physics

KEY FIGURES
Tycho Brahe (1546-1601), Danish astronomer
Frederick II (1534-1588), king of Denmark, r. 1559-1588
Johannes Kepler (1571-1630), mathematician and astronomer

SUMMARY OF EVENT
Tyge Brahe was born in Scandia, Denmark. His parents were Otto Brahe, a Danish nobleman, and Beate Bille, whose family included leading politicians and churchmen. Although Tycho was named Tyge at birth, he adopted the Latinized version of that name, Tycho, when he was about fifteen years old, and is generally known to astronomers as Tycho. His sister Sophie, the youngest of

ten children and also an astronomer, was born when Tycho was a teenager.

In 1559, at age thirteen, Tycho enrolled at the University of Copenhagen to study rhetoric and philosophy, but he quickly developed an interest in astronomy. He observed an eclipse on August 21, 1560, and was particularly impressed by how precisely it was predicted. He soon became interested the methods used to measure the position and the motion of objects in the sky.

In 1562, Brahe was sent to the University of Leipzig to study law, a field he found difficult. So instead, Brahe moved to the study astronomy with Bartholomaeus Scultetus (Bartholomew Schultz). By August of 1563, Brahe began to record his observations, including the conjunction of Jupiter and Saturn, but he found that neither the astronomical data tables based on the work of Nicolaus Copernicus and of Ptolemy gave the correct date for this event. Brahe thought he could do better, so he was determined to make more-precise observations that could be used to develop better tables. Schultz taught Brahe how to make extremely accurate observations of the positions of stars and planets. Brahe knew that accurate observations required high-quality measuring instruments, so he began to acquire them during his stay in Leipzig. He also constructed his first astronomical instrument, the Jacob Stave, during this period.

In 1570, Brahe returned to Denmark, where he lived with his uncle, Steen Bille, who had founded the first paper mill and glassworks in Denmark. Brahe worked in the alchemy lab that Bille had established at Herreved Abbey. Bille was the only relative of Brahe who approved of his interest in astronomy, but Brahe devoted most of his efforts to alchemy until November of 1572, when he observed an unusual object in the sky.

On November 11, 1572, as Brahe was leaving Bille's alchemy lab, he noticed that a new star, one that he would call Stella Nova, had appeared in the constellation Cassiopeia, an experience that changed Brahe's life. Brahe did not believe his eyes, so he called upon others to view the new star and to reassure him that it was really there. The new star, brighter than the planet Venus and observable during daylight hours, was visible for eighteen months. The object Brahe and the others had seen is known now as a supernova, a rare astronomical event defined as a stellar explosion that expels a star's outer layers and fills the surrounding space with a cloud of gas and dust.

After Brahe's observation, astronomers and philosophers began to ask, Where, exactly, was this new star located? Tradition had always taught that Earth was the center of creation, and that the objects in the sky were located on spheres that rotated around Earth. The stars were located on the outermost sphere, and both Aristotelian and Christian philosophy taught that the sphere of the stars had remained unchanged since the day of creation. In this view, it was not possible for a new star to appear in the perfect and unchanging sky.

The planets and the moon were known to move relative to the stars, so it was thought that this supernova was located either in Earth's atmosphere or on one of the inner spheres, where the planets and the moon were located. If so, then the supernova would move relative to the stars, as did the planets and the moon.

Two leading astronomers, Michael Maestlin in Tübingen and Thomas Digges in England, tried to detect movement in the new star by lining it up with known fixed stars, using stretched threads to measure the separation. They saw no movement. Brahe, however, knew he could make more accurate measurements by using instruments that were built to precise standards and were much larger than those traditionally employed. Brahe had just finished building a new sextant, which had huge arms, 5.5 feet long. In addition, Brahe had developed a table of data allowing him to correct for the tiny errors in his sextant. Using this new sextant, Brahe determined that the new star did not move relative to the fixed stars. Thus, the new star was on the eighth, or outermost, sphere, a sphere that was not changing.

Brahe published a detailed account of his methods and results the next year. His book *De nova et nullius aevi memoria prius visa stella* (1573; better known as *De nova stella*; partial English translation in *A Source Book in Astronomy*, 1929) made him famous among astronomers throughout Europe. Other young noblemen asked Brahe to teach a course on astronomy, but he refused. He changed his mind only when the king asked him to teach. In September of 1574, Brahe began lecturing on astronomy at the University of Copenhagen.

In the spring of 1775, Brahe began a trip around Europe, visiting astronomers in many cities, including Frankfurt, Basel, and Venice. During his travels, Brahe de-

An illustration of Tycho Brahe's system of planetary motion. (Hulton|Archive by Getty Images)

cided to move to Basel. However, King Frederick II of Denmark did not want Brahe, recognized as the best astronomer in Denmark, to leave the country. So, the king offered Brahe the island of Ven (also known as Hven or Hveen), a 3-mile-long island on the sound between Denmark and Sweden and just off the coast of the storied castle of Shakespeare's Hamlet at Elsinore. The king agreed to pay for the building of an observatory and a house on Ven, and the island's inhabitants were to become Brahe's subjects.

Brahe's observatory, which was called Uraniborg, was equipped with instruments that allowed him to determine, much more precisely than had previously been possible, the positions of the stars and the planets. Brahe made astronomical observations during a twenty-year-period at Uraniborg, and he recorded each of these measure-

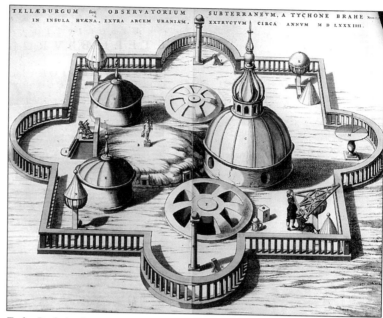

Tycho Brahe's observatory at Uraniborg was located on the island of Ven, off the coast between Denmark and Sweden. (Hulton|Archive by Getty Images)

ments meticulously. Brahe obtained particularly detailed measurements of the positions of Mars, which were so precise that they demonstrated that the orbit of Mars was not a circle but was actually an ellipse.

A new king, Christian IV, came to power in Denmark in 1588 and chose not to support Brahe's astronomical efforts. Brahe moved to Prague shortly thereafter and was joined by a new assistant, Johannes Kepler. Upon Brahe's death, all of his astronomical measurements were given to Kepler, who used them to develop his three laws of planetary motion.

SIGNIFICANCE

Brahe's observation of the supernova was significant for several reasons. First, it revived Brahe's interest in astronomy after he had spent several years working on alchemy. Second, Brahe's demonstration that this new star was truly a star overturned prevailing religious dogma, which stated that the heavens were perfect and unchanging.

Third, Brahe's observations and *De nova stella* brought his work to the attention of the king of Denmark, who gave him the island of Ven and the income generated by its inhabitants to build and equip the Uraniborg Observatory. It was at this observatory that he obtained twenty years of critical astronomical measurements. As a result of the king's support, also, Brahe was able to purchase or build the most precise instruments available to

measure the positions of the stars and the planets, long before the invention of the telescope.

Finally, Brahe's precise measurements of the positions of the planets in the sky provided the foundation for Kepler's laws of planetary motion, which in turn were used by Isaac Newton to demonstrate the validity of his law of gravity over the astronomical distance scale.

—*George J. Flynn*

FURTHER READING

Chapman, Allan. *Astronomical Instruments and Their Users: Tycho Brahe to William Lassell.* Brookfield, Vt.: Variorum, 1996. A study that examines the tools of astronomy, their uses, and their users. Includes illustrations, bibliographical references, and an index.

Christianson, John Robert. *On Tycho's Island: Tycho Brahe, Science, and Culture in the Sixteenth Century.* New York: Cambridge University Press, 1999. A 451-page account of the life of Brahe, including his contributions to astronomy and to the administration of science, explaining how Brahe managed to assemble a team of workers skilled in science, technology, and the arts, which foreshadowed the large research groups important in modern science.

Ferguson, Kitty. *The Nobleman and His Housedog: Tycho Brahe and Johannes Kepler, the Strange Partnership That Revolutionized Science.* London: Headline, 2002. A 372-page biographical account of the lives of Brahe and Johannes Kepler and their contributions to the understanding of planetary motion.

Gow, Mary. *Tycho Brahe: Astronomer.* Berkeley Heights, N.J.: Enslow, 2002. A brief biography of Brahe, part of the Great Minds of Science series. Intended for students in Grades 6 through 10.

Shapley, Harlow, and Helen E. Howarth. *A Source Book in Astronomy.* New York: McGraw-Hill, 1929. Contains a partial translation of Brahe's famous work, *De nova stella.*

Thoren, Victor E., with John R. Christianson. *The Lord of Uraniborg: A Biography of Tycho Brahe.* New York: Cambridge University Press, 1990. A massive and comprehensive biography that attempts to reevaluate and reinterpret nearly every aspect of Brahe's career and contribution to science. Includes illustrations, bibliographic references, index.

SEE ALSO: 1462: Regiomontanus Completes the *Epitome* of Ptolemy's *Almagest*; c. 1478-1519: Leonardo da Vinci Compiles His Notebooks; 1543: Copernicus Publishes *De Revolutionibus*; 1580's-1590's: Galileo Conducts His Early Experiments; 1600: William Gilbert Publishes *De Magnete*.

RELATED ARTICLES in *Great Lives from History: The Renaissance & Early Modern Era, 1454-1600:* Sophie Brahe; Tycho Brahe; Giordano Bruno; Nicolaus Copernicus; William Gilbert; John Napier; Georg von Peuerbach; Rheticus.

August 24-25, 1572
ST. BARTHOLOMEW'S DAY MASSACRE

With King Charles IX's approval, France's Catholic nobles murdered several Huguenot leaders and thousands of other Protestants in an attempt to eliminate Protestantism in the nation once and for all. Instead, the massacre renewed the civil wars of religion, severely undermined the crown's authority, and created profound social disorder throughout France.

LOCALE: Paris, France

CATEGORIES: Wars, uprisings, and civil unrest; government and politics; religion

KEY FIGURES

Charles IX (1550-1574), king of France, r. 1560-1574

Catherine de Médicis (1519-1589), queen of France, r. 1547-1559, regent, r. 1560-1563, and queen mother, 1563-1589

Henry I of Lorraine (1550-1588), third duke of Guise, 1563-1588, and Catholic leader

Henry of Navarre (1553-1610), Huguenot leader, king of Navarre as Henry III, r. 1572-1589, later king of France as Henry IV, r. 1589-1610

Gaspard II de Coligny (1519-1572), lord of Châtillon, admiral of France, 1552, and Huguenot leader

François (1554-1584), duke of Alençon, 1566-1574, duke of Anjou, 1574-1584, and brother of King Charles IX

Louis I of Bourbon, prince of Condé (1530-1569), Huguenot leader

Henry I of Bourbon (1552-1588), prince of Condé, son of Louis I of Bourbon

Claude Marcel (c. 1520-1590), former Catholic mayor of Paris

Jeanne d'Albret (1528-1572), queen of Navarre, r. 1562-1572, and mother of Henry of Navarre

Marguerite of Valois (1553-1615), queen consort of Navarre, r. 1572-1615, wife of Henry of Navarre, 1572-1599, and daughter of Catherine de Médicis

Henry III (1551-1589), king of France, r. 1574-1589

Philip II (1527-1598), king of Spain, r. 1556-1598

SUMMARY OF EVENT

In 1562, a series of civil wars between Huguenot and Catholic forces broke out in France. These wars, known as the French Wars of Religion, were to last, with intermittent periods of calm, until the 1598 Treaty of Vervins and Henry IV's Edict of Nantes, which together created a peace and established limited freedom of religion in the country. The immediate causes of the wars were the 1559 decision by Queen Catherine de Médicis to persecute and execute leading Protestants and the 1562 massacre by troops of the Guise family of numerous Protestants in the French provincial city of Vassy.

After several years of intense fighting, the 1568 Treaty of Longjumeau put a temporary end to the civil war. Both sides, however, continued their intrigues, and war broke out again in September, 1568. Charles IX adopted a strong anti-Huguenot policy out of fear that the

An engraving of the St. Bartholomew's Day Massacre, when Huguenot leaders and thousands of other Protestants were killed by French Catholic nobles in Paris. (Frederick Ungar Publishing Co.)

Huguenots might ally with Dutch Protestant rebels, who had revolted against the Spanish occupation of the Netherlands, and provoke a Spanish attack on France. This fear of a possible Spanish invasion of France played a decisive role in August, 1572, when the king approved what came to be known as the St. Bartholomew's Day Massacre. Meanwhile, at Jarnac on March 13, 1569, Catholic forces won a decisive victory in which the Huguenot leader, Louis I of Bourbon, prince of Condé, was captured and later assassinated. Admiral Gaspard II de Coligny then became leader of the Huguenots. When Coligny's forces marched on Paris in June, Charles made peace.

Religious tolerance was nominally established once again by the Treaty of St. Germain, and certain towns were given to the Huguenots as strongholds. The most important provision of this treaty was a marriage alliance between Marguerite of Valois, the sister of Charles IX, and Henry of Navarre, the leading Huguenot prince and son of Antoine de Bourbon. Henry was in the line of suc-

cession to the French throne. Suspicious of Catherine de Médicis and Charles IX in spite of this treaty, Coligny, Henry of Navarre, and his mother Jeanne d'Albret hesitated to come to court. Their fears were perfectly reasonable, because Catherine de Médicis and Charles IX had already approved several political assassinations, and their promises therefore seemed meaningless. Coligny, however, finally arrived at the royal court in September of 1571, and he was well received.

Coligny persuaded Jeanne d'Albret to accept the marriage proposal, and the marriage of Marguerite of Valois and Henry of Navarre was planned for August 18, 1572. Jeanne d'Albret joined the court in March, 1572, but when she died shortly afterward, her fellow Huguenots suspected that she had been poisoned. This may well have been the case. Mistakenly believing that Catherine de Médicis and Charles IX would not risk killing them since to do so would ensure a resumption of the civil war, Coligny and Henry of Navarre (who had entered Paris in July, 1572, with an entourage of Huguenot nobles) did not realize that they were walking into a carefully pre-pared trap.

During the early summer of 1572, Huguenot forces had confirmed Charles IX's worst fears by supporting a Dutch uprising against the Spanish occupation of their homeland. Charles IX believed that King Philip II of Spain now had an excuse for invading France if that was his plan. What exactly transpired next is not entirely clear, but historians generally agree that sometime before the wedding of Marguerite and Henry, Catherine de Médicis decided to have her Catholic forces assassinate Coligny and other leading Huguenots. The presence of so many Protestants at the royal court gave her a unique opportunity to reduce Protestant influence in France with a single stroke. The Guises hired an assassin named Maurevert to kill Admiral Coligny.

On August 22, four days after the wedding, Maurevert shot Coligny. Coligny, however, survived the attack. The complicity of the Guises was quickly established, and the Huguenots demanded justice from King Charles IX. It has never been determined whether Charles IX approved the failed assassination of Coligny. However, it is known that, faced with the ruin of her plans, Catherine de Médicis and her advisers now urged Charles IX to ap-prove another murder attempt on Coligny for the good of the kingdom. Plans of a fictitious Huguenot conspiracy were shown to the king.

Charles gave in to their arguments. It was reported that he ran from the room shouting: "Kill them all, so that none will return to reproach me!" By thus approving the mass murder of his own subjects, King Charles IX guar-anteed a resumption of the French civil wars and his own place in history as a monarch who had committed crimes against humanity. With the help of her son François, duke of Alençon (better known by his later title, duke of Anjou), Catherine drew up a list of prominent Huguenots who were to be slain and made arrangements with Claude Marcel, a former mayor of Paris, to recruit thugs and common criminals for the indiscriminate slaughter of all the Protestants who had remained in the city after the wedding. Early on the morning of August 24, Coligny was stabbed to death in his room, and his body was muti-lated. Henry of Navarre and Henry I of Bourbon, prince of Condé, were forced to recant their religious beliefs un-der threat of death.

Dozens of Huguenot nobles were killed in the court-yard of the Louvre. Criminals led by the duke of Alençon and Henry I of Lorraine, duke of Guise, then went through the city systematically attacking and slaying prominent Huguenots. These gangs then began killing Protestants all over Paris. Pregnant women and even chil-dren were tortured and murdered. Peter Ramus, the lead-ing French philosopher of the era, was killed, and the En-glish ambassador to France barely escaped with his life. King Charles IX accepted full responsibility for this butchery, and he ordered his troops to carry out similar massacres in provincial cities. He claimed that Hugue-nots had plotted against his throne. However, only the most fanatical supporters of Catherine de Médicis and the Guises believed this lie.

SIGNIFICANCE

It has been impossible to determine the precise number of people murdered during the St. Bartholomew's Day Massacre. Contemporaries spoke of between 2,000 and 100,000 victims. An extremely conservative estimate is that at least 7,000 French Protestants were killed as a re-sult of the criminal activity ordered by King Charles IX.

News of the massacre quickly spread throughout Eu-rope. In Rome, Pope Gregory XIII had a solemn thanksgiving sung. Many French Catholics, however, were revolted by the killings. Protestants throughout Eu-rope were appalled by this state-sponsored terrorism. The eminent French Protestant writer Theodore Beza, who was then living in Geneva, eloquently summarized the general Protestant reaction by writing that those re-sponsible for this massacre would be "held in perpetual execration." Both Catholic and Protestant historians have agreed with Beza's judgment.

Much to the displeasure of Catherine de Médicis and Charles IX, the massacre of St. Bartholomew's Day did not produce the effect they had expected. The civil war quickly resumed, and it did not end for another twenty-five years. Having approved the political assassinations, Charles IX launched a cycle of violence that would end in the assassinations of his two successors: Henry III in 1589 and Henry IV in 1610.

—*James F. Hitchcock, revised by Edmund J. Campion*

FURTHER READING

Conner, Philip. *Huguenot Heartland: Montauban and Southern French Calvinism During the Wars of Reli-gion.* Burlington, Vt.: Ashgate, 2002. Study of the Wars of Religion, especially of the differences be-tween the experiences of southern and northern France during the wars. Focuses on the southern town of Montauban as a case study of the larger religious, cultural, and political upheavals. Includes maps, bib-liographic references, and index.

England, Sylvia L. *The Massacre of Saint Bartholomew.*

London: John Long, 1938. In this reliable history, the author argues that almost the entire blame for the massacre lies with Catherine de Médicis.

Frieda, Leonie. *Catherine de Medici*. London: Weidenfeld & Nicolson, 2003. Extensively researched, well-written attempt to rejuvenate Catherine's reputation and produce a balanced evaluation of her place in history. Includes illustrations, bibliographic references, index.

Garrisson, Janine. *A History of Sixteenth-Century France, 1483-1598*. Translated by Richard Rex. London: Macmillan, 1995. This well-researched book examines the social and political disorder that ended in the St. Bartholomew's Day Massacre.

Holt, Mack P. *The French Wars of Religion, 1562-1629*. New York: Cambridge University Press, 1995. A well-written account of the French religious civil wars. Includes bibliography and index.

Kingdon, Robert M. *Myths About the St. Bartholomew's Day Massacres, 1572-1576*. Cambridge, Mass.: Harvard University Press, 1988. Although the title of this book was poorly chosen, Robert Kingdon provides useful descriptions of Catholic and Protestant reactions to this massacre.

Love, Ronald S. *Blood and Religion: The Conscience of Henri IV, 1553-1593*. Ithaca, N.Y.: McGill-Queen's University Press, 2001. An assessment of Henry of Navarre's early career and later reign against the background of civil war and religious strife. Concludes with a discussion of Henry's perception of the conflicting requirements of his crown and his soul, and his 1593 conversion to Catholicism. Includes photographic plates, illustrations, bibliographic references, and index.

Mentzer, Raymond A., Jr. *Blood and Belief: Family Survival and Confessional Identity Among Provincial Huguenot Nobility*. West Lafayette, Ind.: Purdue University Press, 1994. Presents reactions to the St. Bartholomew's Day Massacre from the point of view of provincial Huguenot noble families.

Racaut, Luc. *Hatred in Print: Catholic Propaganda and Protestant Identity During the French Wars of Religion*. Burlington, Vt.: Ashgate, 2002. Rare study of the pro-Catholic pamphleteers in France. Analyzes the strategies, production, and impact of pro-Catholic propaganda of the period. Includes bibliographic references and index.

Sutherland, N. M. *Henry IV of France and the Politics of Religion, 1572-1596*. 2 vols. Bristol, Avon, England: Elm Bank, 2002. Extremely detailed account of the role of religion in France's monarchy and political sphere during the late sixteenth century. Each chapter discusses a specific political event or issue from the point of view of the conflict between Protestants and Catholics. Includes illustrations, map, bibliographic references, and index.

Williamson, Hugh R. *Catherine de' Medici*. New York: Viking Press, 1973. Contains an objective analysis of Catherine's amoral approach to the use and abuse of political power.

Wood, James B. *The King's Army: Warfare, Soldiers, and Society During the Wars of Religion in France, 1562-1576*. New York: Cambridge University Press, 1996. An in-depth look at the internal military campaigns of Charles IX and Henry III. Includes bibliographical references and an index.

SEE ALSO: Oct. 31, 1517: Luther Posts His Ninety-five Theses; Mid-16th cent.: Development of the Caracole Maneuver; Mar., 1562-May 2, 1598: French Wars of Religion; 1568-1648: Dutch Wars of Independence; July 7, 1585-Dec. 23, 1588: War of the Three Henrys; Aug. 2, 1589: Henry IV Ascends the Throne of France; Apr. 13, 1598: Edict of Nantes; May 2, 1598: Treaty of Vervins.

RELATED ARTICLES in *Great Lives from History: The Renaissance & Early Modern Era, 1454-1600:* Catherine de Médicis; Gregory XIII; Henry II; Henry III; Henry IV; Philip II; William the Silent.

1573-1620
REIGN OF WANLI

The reign of Wanli witnessed the rapid deterioration of the imperial government and marked a turning point in the history of the Ming Dynasty.

LOCALE: China
CATEGORY: Government and politics

KEY FIGURES

Wanli (reign name, also Wan-li; personal name Zhu Yijun, Chu I-chün; posthumous name Xandi, Hsien-ti; temple name Shenzong, Shen-tsung; 1563-1620), emperor of the Ming dynasty, r. 1368-1644)

Zhang Juzheng (Chang Chü-cheng; 1525-1582), chief grand secretary under Wanli and his predecessor, Longqing

Feng Bao (Feng Pao; fl. late sixteenth and early seventeenth centuries), director of the eunuchs under Wanli

SUMMARY OF EVENT

Wanli (whose temple name, Shenzong, means "Divine Progenitor") ascended the imperial throne at the age of ten and inherited an empire ridden with crises and challenges. Externally, with its frontier defenses deteriorating—despite efforts under Wanli's father Longqing to bolster the Great Wall with new construction—the empire was faced with the renewed danger of Mongol raids in the northern frontier and by Japanese pirates in the southeastern coastal regions. Domestically, the imperial governmental system had become inefficient, plagued with inertia (in the wake of Longqing's inattentiveness and irresponsibility), bureaucratic corruption, and rampant factionalism as well as financial difficulties. These problems worsened during Wanli's reign, except for the early part of Wanli's reign, from 1573 to 1582, when Zhang Juzheng, grand secretary under Longqing and now Wanli, was in charge of state affairs.

In his early years of reign, Wanli lived in the shadow of Zhang Juzheng, whose office combined the roles of head of the civil administration with imperial tutor. The young emperor pursued his education diligently under Zhang's rigorous supervision. He also depended on Zhang for administrating state affairs. He showed great respect for Zhang, calling him "Mr. Zhang" rather than by his familiar name. Zhang Juzheng was a competent, prudent, and pragmatic statesman. The decade of his administration represented, as modern scholars generally admit, an excellent phase in late Ming history.

Zhang adopted an austerity program to reduce expenditures, especially by suspending or curbing unnecessary and unimportant court expenses and eunuch procurement missions. He initiated the reform of taxation known as the single-whip system, under which all the various labor service levies, surcharges, and miscellaneous requisitions were combined into a single payment of silver bullion. This method significantly simplified the tax-paying procedure and reduced abuses in tax collections, hence increasing state revenues. Zhang also set in motion a nationwide review of local accounts, with the purpose of checking corruption of local officials. In addition, he took measures to strengthen administrative discipline and curb factionalism. The implementation of these policies was successful: State revenues increased and governmental efficiency was enhanced.

In conducting state affairs, Zhang Juzheng enlisted and enjoyed the strong backing of the emperor's mother and the close cooperation of the eunuch director Feng Bao. Unlike most other eunuch officials during the Ming Dynasty, who were unscrupulous and corrupt, Feng was believed to be conscientious. He commanded enormous respect from the young emperor, who treated Feng as his "big companion."

During these early years, Wanli, intelligent and perceptive, showed signs of a wise ruler: He was concerned with the welfare of the populace and with the frontier defenses, he held regular audiences with his officials, and he was ready to endorse policy proposals potentially beneficial to the state. However, these years were also ones of frequent frustration for the young emperor. Although an absolute ruler in theory, his power and activities were in practice circumscribed even with regard to his personal life. For example, he was once forced by his mother to kneel on the ground for failing to finish his assigned readings; he was criticized for getting drunk and for practicing archery, horse riding, and even calligraphy too often. Such experiences were to shape Wanli's behavior and performance in later years.

The death of Zhang Juzheng in 1582 ushered in a new phase of Wanli's reign, during which the imperial rule began to decline rapidly and irrevocably. Immediately after Zhang's death, he was accused by his erstwhile political enemies, those who suffered during his administration, of being corrupt: taking bribes, living in luxury, and deceiving the emperor. Without bothering to inquire whether these charges were true, Wanli angrily and vengefully denounced Zhang Juzheng, not only depriving him of his titles of honor, confiscating his family property, and persecuting his sons, but also annulling the programs initiated and implemented by Zhang. The emperor particularly felt insulted by what he believed to be Zhang's "hypocrisy": Zhang had cut back court expenses and urged the emperor to live a frugal life, whereas he himself had lived luxuriously. The emperor also vented his spite upon the eunuch head Feng Bao and ordered his arrest based on the accusation that he had been corrupt (accumulating personal wealth).

An adult now and full of pride, Wanli was ready to pursue his life and to exercise his imperial power as he desired. He became greedy and fond of accumulating personal wealth. Among his money-making techniques was dispatching eunuchs to the provinces to collect taxes and to supervise mining and other local administrative operations. This practice often led to conflict between eunuchs and local officials. Wanli was also eager to assume direct control of state affairs. When he attempted to do so, however, the emperor found himself in confrontation with his civil officials, who severely undermined his power. For example, the emperor's own appointees to official positions were often met with disagreement or opposition from incumbent civil officials, especially those of the censorial branch of the government. He was also criticized by them for his so-called negligence.

Wanli encountered the strongest opposition over the issue of succession. He attempted to raise the rank of his third son, borne by his favorite concubine Lady Zheng, to that of heir apparent. Yet this attempt caused such a great uproar among the bureaucrats, who unyieldingly defended the conventional principle of primogeniture, that the emperor had to give up his attempt. After a long delay and under enormous pressure from his advisers, Wanli finally installed his eldest son as heir apparent.

As the ultimate ruler, Wanli did have the power to punish those officials who disobeyed him—and indeed he often did so by demoting them or having them beaten—but many officials, for seeking personal fame or driven by moral consideration, proved recalcitrant and ready to run the risk of being punished. Deeply frustrated and helpless, Wanli adopted the strategy of inaction and passivity. He chose to isolate himself from his officials, avoiding meeting them and ignoring their remonstrances. Eventually, he suspended all public audiences and retreated into the deep recesses of the imperial palace, indulging in personal pleasures with his favorite women.

Wanli's negligence of state affairs exacerbated the persistent problem of partisan struggles or factionalism, as evidenced by the rise and activities of the Donglin Faction. This faction primarily included those retired scholar-officials who were known for their adherence to Confucian ethics. Members of this faction were especially inclined to conduct moral evaluations of the officials at the central government, with the proclaimed goal of removing officials whose moral character was allegedly deficient. These evaluations led to frequent changes in bureaucratic personnel, accompanied by so many accusations and counteraccusations that eventually the bureaucracy became paralyzed. By the end of Wanli's reign, the political structure of the Ming Dynasty was in crisis.

The deterioration of government during Wanli's reign heralded the demise of the Ming Dynasty. During this politically unstable era, however, Chinese economy, society, and culture continued to develop. The pace of commercialization and urbanization accelerated. Merchants prospered. Urban and popular culture flourished. Brilliant fiction, often reflecting the life of urban people, emerged as the dominant form of literature. Moreover, China's contact with the outside world accelerated as Jesuit missionaries arrived from Europe and American crops were spread to China.

SIGNIFICANCE

The political deterioration during the reign of Wanli illustrates some fundamental defects and contradictions inherent within the Ming governmental structure. The emperor was acknowledged as the ultimate ruler. In reality, however, his power was often compromised by his officials, who intended to reduce the emperor to the status of a nominal or ritual figurehead, while reserving substantial power for themselves.

Political stability and governmental efficiency under the Ming system depended upon the availability of extremely competent and conscientious monarchs or administrators such as Zhang Juzheng and, to a lesser extent, Feng Bao. Because such figures were not always available, there was no guarantee that government would operate efficiently and honestly. The reign of Wanli illustrates that this monarchal system, dependent on the chance that individuals in power would ruler wisely and well, was an unreliable and ineffective form of government.

—*Yunqiu Zhang*

FURTHER READING

Brook, Timothy. *The Confusion of Pleasure: Commerce and Culture in Ming China.* Berkeley: University of

California Press, 1998. An account of the impact of commercialization on social and cultural life during Ming Dynasty.

Cass, Victoria Baldwin. *Dangerous Women: Warriors, Grannies, and Geishas of the Ming.* Lanham, Md.: Rowman and Littlefield, 1999. Contains valuable information about official attitudes toward women and women's situation in Ming times.

Huang, Ray. *1587, a Year of no Significance: The Ming Dynasty in Decline.* New Haven, Conn.: Yale University Press, 1981. A highly readable and interesting description of the major events and the working of the government during Wanli's reign.

_____. *Taxation and Governmental Finance in Sixteenth-Century China.* Beijing: Shenghuo, Dushu, Xinzhi Sanlian Press, 2001. An analysis of the financial institutions of Ming China.

Mote, Frederick W., and Denis Twitchett, eds. *The Ming Dynasty, 1368-1644, Part 1.* Vol. 7 in *The Cambridge History of China.* Cambridge, England: Cambridge University Press, 1988. An account of the political history of the Ming dynasty, including chapters on Wanli's reign.

Twitchett, Denis, and Frederick W. Mote, eds. *The Ming Dynasty, 1368-1644, Part 2.* Vol. 8 in *The Cambridge History of China.* New York: Cambridge University Press, 1998. Addresses the Ming Dynasty's governmental structure, fiscal and legal systems, socioeconomic situations, and intellectual trends.

Zhu, Dongyun. *Biography of Zhang Juzheng.* Shanghai: Shanghai Press, 1989. An detailed examination of Zhang Juzheng's reform programs and his relations with Wanli.

SEE ALSO: 16th cent.: China's Population Boom; 16th cent.: Single-Whip Reform; 1505-1521: Reign of Zhengde and Liu Jin; 1514-1598: Portuguese Reach China; 1521-1567: Reign of Jiajing; 1550's-1567: Japanese Pirates Pillage the Chinese Coast; 1550-1571: Mongols Raid Beijing; Jan. 23, 1556: Earthquake in China Kills Thousands; 1567-1572: Reign of Longqing; 1592-1599: Japan Invades Korea.

RELATED ARTICLES in *Great Lives from History: The Renaissance & Early Modern Era, 1454-1600:* Tomé Pires; Matteo Ricci; Wang Yangming; Xiaozong; Zhengde.

1574-1595
REIGN OF MURAD III

Murad III inherited an Ottoman Empire that had lived through its golden age and, despite continued territorial expansion, had started its decline. Murad was isolated from his subjects, lost control of the elite Janissary corps and his government, and left the empire in near ruins.

LOCALE: Ottoman Empire
CATEGORY: Government and politics

KEY FIGURES
Murad III (1546-1595), Ottoman sultan, r. 1574-1595
Baffo (c. 1547-1603), Murad's wife
Süleyman the Magnificent (1494/1495-1566), Ottoman sultan, r. 1520-1566, father of Selim and grandfather of Murad
Selim II (1524-1574), Ottoman sultan, r. 1566-1574, father of Murad
Mehmed Paşa Sokollu (1505-1579), Ottoman grand vizier under Selim and Murad
Mehmed III (1566-1603), Ottoman sultan, r. 1595-1603, son of Murad

SUMMARY OF EVENT
The Ottoman Empire was at its height during much of the fifteenth and early sixteenth centuries and especially thrived under the leadership of Murad III's grandfather Süleyman the Magnificent. Süleyman struggled to undo the injustices his father Selim I had imposed upon his subjects and to repair the inefficient, ineffective, and declining government that came out of Selim's despotic rule.

Early in his regime, Süleyman, also known as "the lawgiver," enacted laws that assured individual rights that had been seriously compromised during Selim's reign. In his forty-six years as sultan, the empire flourished and expanded. Murad III's father, Sultan Selim II, depended greatly on the advice of Grand Vizier Mehmed Paşa Sokollu. Murad retained Sokollu as an adviser, but from 1570, the so-called sultanate of the women, composed of members of the harem who had educated Selim, had begun to wield considerable influence.

Murad, also raised and educated in the harem, trusted the harem more than he did Sokollu. Although Sokollu was a brilliant strategist, Murad frequently ignored his grand vizier in favor of the harem. The women, and petty politicians (*agas*), assumed increasing influence over Murad's sultanate. After the grand vizier was murdered by an assassin in 1579, they quickly filled the power vacuum caused by his death.

Before he assumed office as sultan, Murad had served as governor of Manisa in Anatolia, his birthplace. In 1574, after rising to power and ordering the execution of his five brothers, who were possible rivals for the office he inherited through his father's death, Murad set about expanding the Ottoman Empire through military engagement. In 1578, he waged war against Iran, which had been racked by social and political problems. This act of aggression, through which the Ottoman Empire annexed Azerbaijan, Tiflis, Hamadan, and Nahävand, resulted in a long-term conflict between the Ottoman Empire and Iran, which continued intermittently for more than sixty years, ending finally in 1639.

Murad invaded areas east of Constantinople and, by 1590, had conquered the whole of the Caucasus, a geographical region east of the Black Sea bordered by Turkey, Russia, and Iran. This conquest, begun in 1461 under Mehmed II, had continued sporadically through the intervening years.

Simultaneous with Murad's assault on Iran was his battle in Morocco, where, in 1578, his forces took Fez (now called Fès) from the Portuguese, thereby extending the Ottoman Empire into northwest Africa. Spurred by this victory and by the initial success of his forces in Iran, in 1593, Murad broke the peace that had existed between the Ottoman Empire and the Habsburg Empire to the north. He began a war with Austria that continued on and off until 1606. This conflict united the rulers of Moldavia, Walachia, and Transylvania to ally against Ottoman rule. As a result they sided with the Habsburgs against Murad's attempts to grasp power in Austria. The three had previously allied themselves with the Ottoman Empire.

Around the time of Sokollu's death, England's queen Elizabeth I, under pressure to form a strong alliance with a Mediterranean nation because of the threat Spain posed to the British Empire, initiated diplomatic relations with Murad's administration. The economy of the Ottoman Empire was severely burdened by expansionism, financed by heavy taxation imposed on the entire populace. Murad managed to maintain excellent diplomatic

Sultan Murad III. (Hulton|Archive by Getty Images)

relations with Queen Elizabeth through her ambassador to Turkey, Sir Edward Barton. Elizabeth very much needed a Mediterranean ally against Spain. Murad answered this need.

Without Sokollu, Murad began to impose his own policies. In 1581, he reached an accord with the French, demanding that all ships of foreign registry—except for British vessels—had to display the French flag in Ottoman harbors.

Murad's expansionism led to escalating taxes and an economic inflation caused largely by South America flooding the Spanish market with cheap silver. The silver was then sold to the Ottomans for coinage that was essentially without value. In 1589, when these worthless coins were used to pay the Janissary corps, the empire's elite guard that had traditionally supported the sultan, the corps rebelled in Istanbul. As a result, several government officials accused of distributing the coins were executed and the Janissary corps began to disintegrate, which substantially weakened Murad's control of his government.

The Janissary corps had generally been composed of male youths who were part of the child levy (*devshirme*), which decreed that a given number of male children be conscripted into the service of the sultan. This child levy, which occurred every three to seven years, affected male youths between eight and twenty years of age in Turkish, Balkan, and Anatolian Christian villages. Those selected for the child levy were taken to Istanbul, where the most outstanding were groomed to be government administrators. Group members received extensive training in the sultan's palace. Those not singled out for such training were sent to Turkish villages to learn the Turkish language if they did not already know it and to be schooled in Turkish traditions. This group of youths made up the Janissary corps. Throughout the 1580's, the Janissary corps weakened considerably. Many parents resisted participating in the child levy, so new recruits were drawn from anywhere they could be found. By the end of the decade, the Janissary corps was no longer an elite group but was essentially a band of hard-to-control youth. The revolt of 1589 was staged by an undisciplined group of the corps.

Murad's regime lost additional favor through the activities of his wife, Baffo, who was politically active. Murad's mother, Nur Banu, and Baffo were at odds with each other, each striving strenuously to undercut the other. Their contentious relationship continued until Nur Banu's death in 1583. She was thoroughly corrupt and was known to sell her influence, arranging for people to be appointed to high administrative posts in return for bribes. Not only did this practice cast a dark shadow over the sultanate but it also permitted incompetents to gain control within the administration.

In later life, Murad became increasingly self-indulgent. He gorged himself on unhealthy foods, all washed down by quantities of wine, an overindulgence that had killed his father. In 1594, Murad's kidneys began to fail, and in the first month of 1595, he suffered an epileptic seizure and succumbed to it almost immediately. Thus, what had been a corrupt reign that involved land grabs, bribery, and military involvements in Iran and Austria had ended, temporarily: The corruption would continue for years after the sultan's death.

By the time Murad died in 1595, corruption was so widespread that some thought the government was beyond repair. The sultanate was given to Murad's son, Mehmed III, whose first official act was to order the execution of his nineteen younger brothers.

SIGNIFICANCE

The reign of Murad III marks the beginning of the long decline of the Ottoman Empire. Murad III showed little concern for the people he governed, and he became increasingly isolated from his subjects, as weak administrators often do. He was blind to the corrupt practices of his wife, which contributed to the failure of his regime. After he lost control of the Janissary corps, he then failed to preside over a moribund administration. Murad's avarice impelled him to make land grabs, sometimes on several fronts simultaneously. Although he experienced some immediate successes in his expansion efforts, they failed miserably in the long term and led his empire and that of succeeding sultans to the brink of disaster.

—*R. Baird Shuman*

FURTHER READING

Barber, Noel. *Subjects of the Sultan: Culture and Daily Life in the Ottoman Empire*. New York: I. B. Tauris, 2000. A detailed presentation of everyday life in Ottoman Turkey.

_____. *The Sultans*. New York: Simon and Schuster, 1973. A lively and thorough presentation of the lives of the sultans.

Goodwin, Godfrey. *The Janissaries*. London: Saqi, 1997. The best source in print about the Janissaries.

_____. *Ottoman Turkey*. London: Scorpion, 1977. A thorough consideration of politics in Ottoman Turkey.

Somel, Selcuk Aksin. *Historical Dictionary of the Ottoman Empire*. Lanham, Md.: Scarecrow Press, 2003. Provides a brief but comprehensive overview of the reign of Murad III.

SEE ALSO: 1454-1481: Rise of the Ottoman Empire; 1520-1566: Reign of Süleyman; 1545-1548: Silver Is Discovered in Spanish America; 1559-1561: Süleyman's Sons Wage Civil War; 1566-1574: Reign of Selim II; 1578-1590: The Battle for Tabrīz; 1589: Second Janissary Revolt in Constantinople; 1593-1606: Ottoman-Austrian War.

RELATED ARTICLES in *Great Lives from History: The Renaissance & Early Modern Era, 1454-1600:* Elizabeth I; İbrahim Paşa; Mehmed III; Süleyman the Magnificent.

Mid-1570's
POWHATAN CONFEDERACY IS FOUNDED

Powhatan forged a political alliance between Native American tribes in the Virginia region to defend against encroaching European settlers.

LOCALE: Eastern Virginia (now in the United States)
CATEGORIES: Diplomacy and international relations; government and politics; expansion and land acquisition

KEY FIGURES

Powhatan (Wahunsenacawh; c. 1550-1618), leader of the Powhatan Confederacy

Iopassus (fl. late sixteenth-early seventeenth centuries), Powhatan's brother and king of the Potomacs

Kekataugh (fl. late sixteenth-early seventeenth centuries), Powhatan's brother and ruler of the village of Pamunkey

Opechancanough (c. 1544-1644), Powhatan's brother, chief of the Pamunkey Indians, and a Powhatan successor

Opitchapam (fl. late sixteenth-early seventeenth centuries), Powhatan's brother and successor

Pocahontas (Matoaka; c. 1596-1617), daughter of Powhatan

William Strachey (1572-1621), English writer who described the Virginia Indians during his 1610-1611 stay

SUMMARY OF EVENT

Powhatan was one of the names of the leader of the Powhatan Confederacy in eastern Virginia. It was also the name given to a group of tribes of Virginia Indians, the name of an Indian village, and the throne name of a chief. Although historians have consistently referred to the chief of the Powhatan Indians and the ruler of the Powhatan Confederacy as Powhatan, his birth name was Wahunsenacawh. This discrepancy was caused by the English, who either did not know his birth name or found it more convenient to call him Powhatan, because he had so many names. At its largest, the Powhatan Confederacy extended north to Alexandria along the Potomac River, south to the Neuse River in North Carolina, west along Virginia's fall line, and east to the Atlantic Ocean.

It has been suggested that Powhatan's father may have come to Virginia from the south. This contention is supported by the fact that Powhatan succeeded his father as chieftain, a practice in opposition to the matriarchal sys-

tem of succession practiced by the Algonquians of eastern Virginia. Whatever the case, it was Powhatan's father who, in the mid-1570's, founded what came to be known as the Powhatan Confederacy, which during his lifetime consisted of six tribes: the Arrohattoc (Arrohateck), Appomattoc (Appomattox), Mattaponi, Pamunkey, Youghtanund, and Powhatan. Upon his father's death, Powhatan inherited control over those tribes.

Powhatan soon began incorporating more tribes into the confederacy, which expanded dramatically under his reign. At its height, the Powhatan Confederacy included twenty-nine tribes. In addition to the original six, it encompassed the Accohannock, Accomac, Chesapeake, Chickahominy, Chiskiack, Cuttatawomen, Kecoughtan, Moraughtacund (Morattico), Nandtaughtacund, Nansemond, Onawmanient, Opiscopank (Piscataway), Paspahegh, Piankatank, Pissaseck, Patawomeck (Potomac), Quiyoughcohannock, Rappahannock (Tappahannock), Sekakawon (Secacawoni), Warraskoyack, Weanoc (Weyanock), Werowocomoco, and Wiccocomico (Wiccomico).

Relatively little is known of Powhatan's career before English settlers encountered him around 1607, since the confederacy itself kept no written records. Most historians agree, however, that Powhatan forged his confederacy through a combination of treachery, force, and terror. Powhatan allegedly attacked the Piankatank tribe at night and slaughtered all the captives he took. When Powhatan invaded the Kecoughtan, he killed all who resisted and distributed the captives throughout his domain. He was reputed to have slaughtered the entire Chesapeake tribe because an oracle had divined that Powhatan would be overthrown by a force from the east. He then transplanted his own people to the area formerly occupied by the Chesapeake.

Powhatan consolidated his power by conferring chiefdoms on his relatives, by his own multiple marriages with the daughters of chieftains, and by the intermarriage of his family with the sons and daughters of locally powerful chiefs. The four known brothers of Powhatan all became chiefs: Opitchapam succeeded his brother as ruler of the Confederacy, Opechancanough was chief of the Pamunkey Indians and a later successor to the confederacy's throne, Kekataugh ruled the village of Pamunkey, and Iopassus was king of the Potomacs. William Strachey, an English writer who lived in Virginia in the early 1600's, suggested that Powhatan's

747

twelve marriages increased his authority among Virginia's native tribes. A thirteenth wife has been attributed to Powhatan—Oholasc, the regent of the Tappahannocks.

There is no accurate listing of the number of children fathered by Powhatan. At the time of the English arrival in 1607, it was estimated that Powhatan had twenty living sons and twelve living daughters. The better-known Powhatan offspring included Taux-Powhatan, his eldest son and the ruler of the Powhatans; Na-mon-tack, who was presented to King James I; Pocahontas; Cleopatre; Tohahcoope, chief of the Tappahannocks; Nantaquaus, described by John Smith as the manliest, comeliest, and boldest spirit in a "savage"; Matachanna; and Pochins, chief of the Kecoughtan.

An idealized rendering of Powhatan leading a council of tribal chiefs and others in eastern Virginia at the time of the first contact with the English. The council regulated matters of concern to the whole Confederacy. (Library of Congress)

The village was the administrative unit of the Powhatan Confederacy, with power invested in a cockarouse, the weroance or war-leader, the tribal council, and the priest of each village. Each village was expected to pay four-fifths of its rude wealth in tribute to Powhatan. There is dispute about the exact number of villages in the confederacy. Strachey counted 34 villages; historians have estimated anywhere from 30 to 128 villages. Population is similarly difficult to determine, but the confederacy probably had between nine thousand and fifteen thousand inhabitants.

The cockarouse was the highest elected civil magistrate of a given village and a member of the tribal council, over which he or she presided. Cockarouses were chosen based on their experience and wisdom. Cockarouses exercised authority only during times of peace, however. They received the first fruits of the harvest, and they were in charge of all public and private concerns of their respective villages. Each cockarouse was also a delegate to Powhatan's council and held the office for life on condition of good behavior. Although elective, the position of cockarouse might be hereditary in the female line. Women could be cockarouses.

Powhatan appointed the weroance. The weroance was a member of Powhatan's council, the leader in hunting and fishing expeditions, and in charge of all military affairs. The weroance exercised the power of life and death over the members of his tribe, collected the tribute due Powhatan, declared war, maintained a crude ceremonial state, and presided over the village council in the absence of the cockarouse.

The tribal council regulated matters of concern to the whole Confederacy. It governed in accordance with a sense of right and wrong, with custom, with fashion, with public opinion, and with a sense of honor. It is difficult to determine whether the tribe or the village was the basic political unit of the Powhatan Confederacy, because they were frequently one and the same. Historians generally agree that a king or queen ruled over a tribe. Usually, the king was a weroance. Strachey mentions one queen, Opossunoquonuske of the Mussasran, who was also a weroance. This is probably an exception, because Oholasc was a queen but her son was the weroance.

The highest political authority resided with Powhatan and his council (Matchacomoco). The council was composed of cockarouses, weroances, and the priests of all the subject and allied tribes. The council shared the supreme authority over the Powhatan Confederacy with Powhatan. It was convened by the people and held open meetings. Powhatan presided over this advisory body to declare war or peace, conduct foreign relations, and manage domestic affairs. A unanimous vote of the council was required to implement decisions, but the personal authority of Powhatan greatly affected council policy.

SIGNIFICANCE

In 1607, a group of English colonists founded Jamestown in eastern Virginia. Thus, Powhatan and his confederacy formed the primary basis for the English understanding of America's native inhabitants in the early seventeenth century. By the same token, it was primarily through the inhabitants of Jamestown that Powhatan entered the pages of Western history.

Powhatan's original capital, Werowocomoco, was about 10 miles (16 kilometers) from Jamestown. In 1608, Werowocomoco was abandoned for Orapax on the Chickahominy River to keep Powhatan geographically distant from the English. Powhatan apparently used his retreat to the interior and the new threat of the English presence to increase his control over the tribes of the confederacy. The English, for their part, courted Powhatan as the most powerful American Indian in the vicinity. They gave him gifts and even a royal crown in 1609. Five years later, Powhatan's daughter, Pocahontas, married an Englishman named John Rolfe after converting to Christianity.

From the time of Pocahontas's marriage, relations between the Powhatan Confederacy and the Jamestown settlement steadily improved. After the deaths of Pocahontas (1617) and Powhatan (1618), however, Powhatan's successors (particularly his brother Opechancanough) viewed the English as intruders and sought to remove the English from ancestral native lands. From 1622 until 1676, Native American rebellions occurred intermittently until the eastern Virginia tribes were either defeated or fled westward, leaving the English in firm control of the lands of the Powhatan Confederacy.

—*William A. Paquette*

FURTHER READING

Barbour, Philip L. *Pocahontas and Her World*. Boston: Houghton Mifflin, 1970. A good synthesis of seventeenth century accounts of Jamestown's founding, including much information on Powhatan.

Beverly, Robert. *The History and Present State of Virginia*. Reprint. Indianapolis: Bobbs-Merrill, 1971. A study of Indian life and customs in the seventeenth century, first published in 1705.

Bial, Raymond. *The Powhatan*. New York: Benchmark Books, 2002. An informative study of the Powhatan geared toward younger readers. Includes illustrations, map, bibliographic references, and index.

Gleach, Frederic W. *Powhatan's World and Colonial Virginia: A Conflict of Cultures*. Lincoln: University of Nebraska Press, 1997. Study of the encounters between the Powhatan Confederacy and the English, arguing that the two cultures civilized each other. Includes maps, bibliographic references, and index.

McCary, Ben C. *Indians in Seventeenth Century Virginia*. Williamsburg: Virginia 350th Anniversary Celebration Corporation, 1957. Reviews the history of seventeenth century Native Americans in Virginia.

Mossiker, Frances. *Pocahontas: The Life and the Legend*. Reprint. New York: Da Capo Press, 1996. Biography attempting to extricate Pocahontas from the cloud of myth and ideology in which she has become surrounded. Includes illustrations, bibliographic references, and index.

Rountree, Helen C. *Pocahontas's People: The Powhatan Indians of Virginia Through Four Centuries*. Norman: University of Oklahoma Press, 1990. Written by an ethnohistorian and anthropologist, this is one of the best studies of Jamestown and the settlement's relationship to the Powhatan Confederacy.

_____. *The Powhatan Indians of Virginia: Their Traditional Culture*. Norman: University of Oklahoma Press, 1989. A comprehensive study of all aspects of life among the Powhatan Confederacy tribes.

Rountree, Helen C., and E. Randolph Turner, III. *Before and After Jamestown: Virginia's Powhatans and Their Predecessors*. Gainesville: University of Florida Press, 2002. Detailed account of the history, customs, and culture of the Powhatans.

Smith, John. *The General History of Virginia, New England, and the Summer Isles*. Reprint. Philadelphia: Kimber and Conrad, 1812. An account of life in Virginia by the first Englishman to meet Chief Powhatan.

Strachey, William. *The Historie of Travell into Virginia Britania, 1612*. Edited by Louis Wright and Virginia Freund. Reprint. Nendeln, Liechtenstein: Kraus Reprint, 1967. A contemporaneous account of Virginia's Native Americans.

SEE ALSO: Oct. 12, 1492: Columbus Lands in the Americas; June 24, 1497-May, 1498: Cabot's Voyages; Early 16th cent.: Rise of the Fur Trade; 16th cent.: Decline of Moundville; 16th cent.: Iroquois Confederacy Is Established; Beginning 1519: Smallpox Kills Thousands of Indigenous Americans; Apr. 20, 1534-July, 1543: Cartier and Roberval Search for a Northwest Passage; Sept., 1565: St. Augustine Is Founded;

June 7, 1576-July, 1578: Frobisher's Voyages; July 4, 1584-1590: Lost Colony of Roanoke.

RELATED ARTICLE in *Great Lives from History: The Renaissance & Early Modern Era, 1454-1600:* Pemisapan.

1575
TALLIS AND BYRD PUBLISH *CANTIONES SACRAE*

Tallis and Byrd's motets utilized the sophisticated compositional techniques of Continental European composers, which helped to define England as a full and equal participant in the blossoming of Renaissance musical art at a time when England was distancing itself from the religious authority of the Catholic Church in Rome.

LOCALE: London, England
CATEGORIES: Music; religion

KEY FIGURES
Thomas Tallis (c. 1505-1585), English composer
William Byrd (1543-1623), English composer
Elizabeth I (1533-1603), queen of England, r. 1558-1603
Thomas Vautrollier (d. 1587), French-born publisher and bookseller

SUMMARY OF EVENT
A great deal of music by major composers in European countries outside England had been printed by 1575, so England had fallen behind. A notable exception was the *XX Songes* of 1530, the first printed collection of English music, both secular and religious and including music in English, with pieces by John Taverner and others. There were other modest publications of Protestant religious music, but nothing on the scale of music publishing on the Continent. Also, the use of the vernacular rather than Latin in these early efforts reflected a more local rather than international audience.

All this would change in 1575, when Queen Elizabeth I granted a monopoly on music publishing (including printing and selling music and lined music paper) to Thomas Tallis and William Byrd, who both served as organists and composers for the Chapel Royal. Tallis, who was Byrd's teacher and was forty years older, already had served in the courts of Henry VIII, Edward VI, and the Counter-Reformationist Mary I. Tallis had been trained in a monastic environment and had also written music to

be used for the Sarum rite, or liturgy, the English variant of the Catholic liturgy that became the basis for Anglican practice. He had survived the rapid shifts in religious and political orientation, adapting his music to fit the changing needs of the court, and was well-respected.

Byrd, who rose to prominence under the guidance of Tallis, was beginning a long and successful career in the court. Although Byrd was a recusant, one who followed Catholic practice privately in an officially Protestant state, this was offset by his musical brilliance and his loyal service to Elizabeth. Byrd followed the innovations of his Continental contemporaries and was especially adept at the use of imitation, a musical technique in which different voices would be interwoven in long sequences based on the shared melodic patterns displaced by time and pitch, resulting in very active but tightly constructed compositions.

For their first publication, the two composers planned a very ambitious collection of choral pieces written for a minimum of five voices. To print the volume, they chose Thomas Vautrollier, a refugee from France who fled the persecutions of Protestant Huguenots. Vautrollier brought with him a valuable music font. The publication's text was in Latin, which was generally required at the time for international readability and academic integrity. Interestingly, Latin was used to announce the importance of English music and intellectual culture in the volume's opening verses. The queen was fond of Latin motets, which were still performed in various devotional contexts. The motets served as the unifying musical genre of the thirty-four pieces in their famous 1575 collection *Cantiones, quae ab argumento sacrae vocantur*, better known as *Cantiones sacrae*.

Although there was some subdivision and merging of the musical works to arrive at the proper sum, the two composers each officially contributed seventeen compositions to the collection, in honor of the seventeen years of Elizabeth's reign at the time of publication. The pieces were organized by mode and utilized many kinds of religious texts, including hymns, psalms, prayers, and biblical quotations.

Some of Tallis's contributions had been written during the reigns of previous monarchs, including "Suscipe Quaeso," a seven-voice piece Tallis wrote twenty years earlier, probably for a service attended by Queen Mary and her husband, Philip II of Spain. Tallis's older motets included five that utilized the very traditional cantus firmus (firm voice) technique. In this practice of great antiquity, a preexisting melody, usually a sacred chant or "plainsong" melody, precedes the composition and is then included within it as an unchanging element in the musical texture. In this tradition, the cantus firmus influences the compositional structure of the newly composed elements, which must be consonant with the original melody.

A wide range of sophisticated compositional techniques were used in *Cantiones sacrae*, including the use of cancrizans, or retrograde, another practice inherited from medieval musicians. One of Byrd's motets, "Diliges Dominum," a piece in eight voices, utilizes this

technique, even though its surface harmonies are very simple. A reversal of melodic direction takes place in the middle of the motet, so that if sung from end to beginning, the same music would result.

The more modern-sounding motets in *Cantiones sacrae* were influenced by the work of Alfonso Ferrabosco the Elder, an Italian musician who was present at Elizabeth's court during this period. Ferrabosco was especially well-known for his composition of madrigals, secular pieces inspired by a fusion of poetry and music. Byrd's pieces, in particular, share Ferrabosco's tendency to explore the expressive potential of a text, an ideal of the madrigal style that reflected the humanistic tendencies of the Renaissance.

In spite of their landmark artistic achievement in publishing *Cantiones sacrae*, the two composers overestimated the commercial demand for their printed music and underestimated the cost of the production, to the point that they were soon forced to request more funds from Queen Elizabeth. Even their monopoly on music printing, possibly intended to encourage their prosperity, was of limited financial benefit, especially to Tallis, who lived just ten more years and was unable to publish more of his works. Tallis willed his half of the monopoly to Byrd's son, and Byrd published, along with other works, additional volumes of *Cantiones sacrae* in 1589 and 1591.

SIGNIFICANCE

Although it was not financially profitable, the publication of *Cantiones sacrae* was politically and culturally significant. The retention of Latin texts in the music reflected an element of cultural continuity within the English Reformation, which at this time was more conservative than its German counterpart. Because it served both as a kind of retrospective for the older Tallis and as a relatively early collection of pieces by Byrd, a broad range of Renaissance musical styles was included in the 1575 publication.

Subsequent generations of English musicians have been inspired by *Cantiones sacrae*, and some of its pieces later appeared with English texts, becoming part of the standard Anglican repertoire. Today, the music is performed internationally in concert settings, usually in the original Latin. Because the project was supervised by the composers, the quality of printing and notational accuracy of *Cantiones sacrae* also made it a valuable document for musicologists, who have used it to deci-

Musicians of the sixteenth century. (Hulton|Archive by Getty Images)

pher musical pieces not well-preserved or well-notated.

Although the musical excellence of this single collection is generally accepted, the exclusive patent under which it was produced silenced other voices in the two decades after its publication. Whether because of a lack of foresight or because of a deliberate attempt at political suppression on the part of the queen, a monopoly of twenty-one years could not have been beneficial to the development of English music, even with the optimistic introductory verses of the first *Cantiones sacrae.*

—John Myers

FURTHER READING

Brown, Allen, and Richard Tubet, eds. *Byrd Studies.* New York: Cambridge University Press, 1992. Detailed information and research concerning the structure and context of Byrd's music, including his contributions to *Cantiones sacrae.*

Harley, John. *William Byrd: Gentleman of the Chapel Royal.* Aldershot, England: Scolar Press, 1997. Organized into two sections, covering biographical narrative and musical analysis. Illustrated, with an extensive bibliography, appendices, tables, and indexes.

Kerman, Joseph. *The Masses and Motets of William Byrd.* Berkeley: University of California Press, 1981. A complete exploration of Byrd's sacred compositions, highlighting the unique aspects of various pieces and the evolution of his style. Includes a bibliography, tables, musical examples, detailed footnotes, an index of Byrd's works, and an index of names.

Morehen, John, ed. *English Choral Practice, 1400-1650.* New York: Cambridge University Press, 1995. Detailed studies of the performance practice of the time period, including reference to the contrast between English and Latin pronunciation and other issues affecting music interpretation. Includes a chapter on Byrd, Tallis, and Ferrabosco.

Smith, Jeremy L. *Thomas East and Music Publishing in Renaissance England.* New York: Oxford University Press, 2003. Includes relevant information about the emergence of a music publishing industry during this period, including the effects of Byrd's monopoly, and covers social context as well. Illustrated, with a bibliography, appendices, and an index.

SEE ALSO: 1567: Palestrina Publishes the *Pope Marcellus Mass*; 1588-1602: Rise of the English Madrigal; Oct. 31, 1597: John Dowland Publishes *Ayres.***RELATED ARTICLES** in *Great Lives from History: The Renaissance & Early Modern Era, 1454-1600:* William Byrd; John Dowland; Elizabeth I; Andrea Gabrieli; Giovanni Gabrieli; Josquin des Prez; Orlando di Lasso; Luca Marenzio; Thomas Morley; Giovanni Pierluigi da Palestrina; Thomas Tallis.

March 3, 1575
MUGHAL CONQUEST OF BENGAL

The conquest of the independent Indian state of Bengal by Mughal forces ensured the continued growth and economic prosperity of the flourishing Mughal Empire.

LOCALE: Bengal (now in Bangladesh and West Bengal, India)

CATEGORIES: Wars, uprisings, and civil unrest; expansion and land acquisition; diplomacy and international relations

KEY FIGURES

Akbar (1542-1605), Mughal emperor of India, r. 1556-1605

Daud Khan Karrani (d. 1576), last independent Afghan sultan of Bengal, r. 1573-1576

Munim Khan (d. 1575), governor of Jaunpur and general under Akbar

SUMMARY OF EVENT

Bengal, which recognized Mughal emperor Akbar's government before 1572, also sent regular tribute to Akbar. Akbar's relatively stable rule of Bengal ended, however, with the death of Sultan Sulaiman Karrani in 1573 and the accession of his youngest son, Daud Khan, who had ordered a reading of the *khuṭba* (an Islamic sermon), naming him ruler. Also, Daud Khan besieged Zamaniya, a frontier stronghold of Akbar. He was adequately equipped to do so, given his 140,000 infantry, 40,000 cavalry, 20,000 pieces of artillery, 3,600 elephants, and hundreds of war boats.

Akbar attempted to deal with Daud remotely because he was then occupied with the Rājputs and Gujaratis. Munim Khan, governor of Jaunpur, was ordered to march against Daud. Munim did so, meeting him at Patna, but instead of battling, they made peace. Munim met his old friend Ludi Khan, Daud's prime minister, and began negotiations. They came to a generous peace agreement; unfortunately, neither Daud nor Akbar was happy with the terms. Daud killed Ludi and confiscated his property. Akbar, however, realized that it would not be advantageous to lose a valuable governor and general in his new empire, so Munim was given a second chance and again was ordered to attack Daud's forces.

Following the above directive, Munim Khan laid siege to Patna, where Daud had taken shelter. Munim realized that Daud's forces offered a fairly strong defense, and he appealed to Akbar for reinforcements. In 1574, Akbar marched against Daud, reinforced by the generals Todar Mall and Man Singh. Akbar attacked Hajipur, the supply source of the forces at Patna, which was on the opposite bank of the Ganges River. Hajipur was captured easily, and it was only a slightly greater feat when Akbar subdued Patna shortly thereafter. Akbar decided that his work was done, appointed Munim governor of Bihar and Bengal, left General Todar Mall to assist Munim, and then returned to Āgra, instructing Munim to continue the onslaught against Daud with an army of twenty thousand.

Munim continued to advance toward Bengal, capturing what was then its capital, Tanda, on September 25, 1574, and also controlling Satgaon, an important port and cultural center. Daud retired feebly into Orissa, but Munim and Todar followed him. Daud prepared for battle by digging trenches in Hajipur and building a defensive wall. By this time, his armies had been reduced significantly and had few reserves on which to draw, whereas the Mughal forces remained strong and had plenty of relief soldiers.

The armies met at Tukaroi on March 3, 1575, the beginning of the Bengali summer, well before the monsoon period and after the pleasant winter. Tukaroi was a river village that formed the border between Orissa and West Bengal. Initially, it seemed that victory would belong to Daud. Munim Khan had to retreat but was pursued by Gujar Khan; several officers in the Mughal army were killed. Ultimately, however, Daud was defeated and fled Tukaroi for refuge at the fort of Katak.

Katak was easy to locate. The Mughal forces laid siege to the fort soon after, and Daud surrendered on April 12, 1575, signing the Treaty of Katak. The terms of the treaty required Daud Khan to cede both Bengal and Bihar to the Mughals, but it did allow him to keep the far-less-lucrative Orissa.

For six months, Munim Khan attempted to create a moderately tepid regime in Bengal and Bihar, and Daud remained under control in Orissa. However, once Munim Khan was killed by plague in October, 1575, Daud redoubled his rebellion and fomented conflict in Bengal, Bihar, and Orissa. Daud reconquered the lands as far as Teliagarhi, which was then the northwestern limit of Bengal and an important pass for travel. Thus Daud again was the lord of western and northern Bengal

When word reached Akbar, he appointed Husain Quli Beg governor of Bengal, titled him Khan-i Jahan, and ordered him to attack Daud. Khan-i Jahan, supported by Todar Mall, advanced on Tanda, Daud's capital. Geography worked in Daud's favor, as he was able to block their route through the narrow Rajmahal pass between the Ganges on the northwest and the hills on the southeast. Khan-i Jahan first met Daud's forces at Teliagarhi and was victorious, taking possession of the pass and using it to enable continued mobility. Daud and the other Karranis, however, continued to resist the Mughals from Orissa. Khan-i Jahan promptly marched toward Rajmahal. Daud's forces fought the Mughals at Rajmahal on July 12, 1576. Finally, Daud was captured and executed, resulting in triumph for the Mughals but disorganization for the rebels. The victory also ensured there would be no resistance to the Mughals' consolidation of power.

SIGNIFICANCE

Bengal's prosperity, one of the richest regions of India because of its agriculture, helped to fund Mughal expansion. In addition, by 1580, the Portuguese had established a settlement in the region under Akbar's approval, and so, in addition to agrarian productivity, Bengal offered economic and political gain through trade with the Europeans.

It was clear that the possession of Bengal was integral to the growth and prosperity of the Mughal Empire, so quelling rebellions, whether they were the products of Karrani resistance to Mughal overlords or jealous factionalism within the Mughal Empire, was essential to the continued central strength of Akbar's empire. Bengali remoteness and relative discontent under Mughal rule, however, made the region an excellent bridgehead of the British Empire in India, leading to the establishment of British East India Company rule beginning in 1757.

—*Monica Piotter*

FURTHER READING

Eaton, Richard M. *The Rise of Islam and the Bengal Frontier, 1204-1706.* Berkeley: University of California Press, 1996. Part of the Comparative Studies on Muslim Societies series, this work identifies Bengal as a "frontier" for the spread of Islam into India, and as a frontier of ideas and nationhood.

Gommans, Jos. *Mughal Warfare: Indian Frontiers and Highroads to Empire, 1500-1700*. New York: Routledge, 2003. Offers a superb overview of the Mughal Empire's military methods of conquest, concentrating particularly on Akbar, whose reign afforded the greatest expansion.

Sarkar, Jadunath. *The History of Bengal*. Delhi, India: B. R., 2003. Part of a multivolume history of Bengal, volume 2 examines Bengal under Islamic rule prior to the British takeover. Sarkar includes a discussion of the tumultuous transfer of power from Daud Khan to Mughal rule.

SEE ALSO: 1540-1545: Shēr Shāh Sūr Becomes Emperor of Delhi; 1556-1605: Reign of Akbar; Feb. 23, 1568: Fall of Chitor; 1580-1587: Rebellions in Bihar and Bengal; Feb., 1586: Annexation of Kashmir.

RELATED ARTICLE in *Great Lives from History: The Renaissance & Early Modern Era, 1454-1600:* Akbar.

November, 1575
STEPHEN BÁTHORY BECOMES KING OF POLAND

Stephen Báthory was one of the most eminent kings of Poland. He established new tribunal systems, reformed the taxes and army, led three victorious military operations against Muscovy, regained Polotsk, and strengthened Polish rule over Livonia.

LOCALE: Polish-Lithuanian Commonwealth and its fiefs (now Poland, Lithuania, Ukraine, Belarus, part of Russia, Latvia, and Estonia)

CATEGORY: Government and politics

KEY FIGURES

Stephen Báthory (1533-1586), prince of Transylvania, r. 1571-1575, and king of Poland, r. 1575-1586

Anna Báthory (1523-1596), Báthory's wife from 1576 and queen of Poland

Ivan the Terrible (1530-1584), the first czar of Russia, r. 1547-1584

Jan Zamoyski (1542-1605), Polish chancellor, 1578-1605, and grand hetman, 1581-1602

Samuel Zborowski (d. 1584), banished Polish magnate

SUMMARY OF EVENT

In 1575, the Polish-Lithuanian Commonwealth found itself in a difficult situation. For several months, the first elected king of Poland, Henry of Valois, was absent from Poland. He had fled in June of 1574, having learned about the death of his brother, Charles IX, king of France. Henry decided to claim the French crown. Perhaps he planned to secure both crowns, but he did not intend to stay in Poland. After a long dispute, the Polish gentry proclaimed an interregnum. Another election was organized. The Convocation Seym was assigned on October 3, 1575, in Warsaw. The election was to take place on November 7.

The most important candidates were the emperor Maximilian II Habsburg, a rather indefinite Piast proposed by the gentry, and John III, king of Sweden (r. 1568-1592). The candidacy of Stephen Báthory, the *voivode* (prince) of Transylvania, was at first condemned. The pro-Habsburg party—mostly the senators, with the support of the primate—had proclaimed the emperor Maximilian king of Poland. Three days later the anti-Habsburg gentry elected the princess Anna and assigned Báthory as her husband. Both parties considered their choices the only valid ones. Báthory managed to reach Krakōw sooner. On May 1, 1576, he married Anna (then fifty-three years old; the marriage was a ceremonial and political union) and was crowned both king of Poland and great duke of Lithuania. The emperor Maximilian died the same year, in October. Báthory then became the only elected king.

Before Maximilian's death, the inhabitants of Danzig had already refused to be subordinated to Báthory. The king therefore undertook a war, and soon he defeated the city's divisions at the Vistual River port of Tczew (1577). Despite his military superiority, Báthory did not subordinate the town absolutely. He obtained the contributions necessary for the planned Muscovite war, but the town retained some autonomy. Báthory was forced to agree to a truce by the gentry, who were afraid of his energy and foresaw an absolute regime. In fact, the king was seeking to strengthen his power. He was trying to balance both the gentry and the magnates but was often in conflict with both. "Sum rex vester non fictus neque pictus" ("I am your vested king, not a fictitious or painted one"), he said at the Diet in Torun in 1576.

As he had been confirmed by oath (the *pacta*

conventa) before his coronation, Stephen decided to regain Livonia, which was held by Ivan the Terrible. Intending to gain the support of the gentry, he relinquished part of his judicial power and established the Supreme Court of Appeals in 1578 for the Crown and in 1581 for Lithuania. Such a move set a precedent in Europe. Báthory could now create elite peasant infantry troops (the so-called Piechota Wybraniecka), reform the cavalry and secure tax revenues for his army, which as a result obtained better weapons, including firearms. Having formed an army of almost fifty thousand men, Stephen started his campaign.

In the summer of 1579, the military operation began. The first expedition of the Polish-Lithuanian army retook the Russian-held principality of Polotsk, which had been lost during Sigismund August's reign. To retake Livonia, Báthory again had to secure tax revenues. The next year, after a ten-day siege, he took the Russian fortress of Wielkie Luki. With Ivan still refusing to return Livonia, Báthory in 1580 led a third expedition and reached Pskov. Despite the several months' siege, Báthory managed merely to damage the walls, but the stronghold, perhaps the most powerful one in all the Grand Duchy of Muscovy, remained unconquered. However, Báthory's forces were prevailing and the king managed to impose a truce. Concluded at Yam Zapolski in 1582, this peace directed that Russia return Livonia to Poland. Báthory's forces were to withdraw from the captured Russian lands.

During the war with Muscovy, Jan Zamoyski—who in 1578 had been appointed grand chancellor of the Crown and thus one of the greatest dignitaries of the realm—was a distinguished strategist. In 1581, he became grand hetman (the supreme military commander). Keeping close to Báthory, he multiplied his fortune, rising from a representative of the middle gentry to become a great magnate. As a Humanist and lawyer educated in Paris, Rome, and Padua, he was responsible for the majority of Báthory's decisions. Today historians argue about his role, sometimes accusing him of political errors, especially of a too concessive policy against Danzig. The fact is that he was Báthory's most important policy adviser both at home and abroad and one of the most eminent statesmen of his time.

Báthory often confirmed his intention not to be a "painted" king, or king in name only. The case of Samuel Zborowski may be called in evidence. This man, who had mortally wounded a Polish noble, was banished by Poland's previous king Henry of Valois; the incident had taken place during Henry's coronation. Zborowski, hop-

ing for the protection of his magnate family, soon returned from Transylvania, where he had been active as Báthory's partisan. He had participated in the Muscovite war and then returned to Poland. There, with all his family, he took some steps against Báthory, provoking him with intrigues and threats. Finally Báthory, invoking the saying "A rabid dog, once killed, does not bite more," permitted Zamoyski to capture and execute Zborowski. The decapitation of Zborowski took place in on May 26, 1584. This case—like the beheading in 1578 of Ivan Podkova, the hospodar-imposter of Moldavia—provoked several protests from the gentry, who called Báthory "the Hungarian tyrant."

The most important of Báthory's political campaigns was a planned war against Ottoman Turkey, which held sway over a part of the Hungarian state. Báthory's homeland, Transylvania, was also subject to Turkish power. Báthory tried to persuade the gentry to secure new taxes for this campaign and strove to form an anti-Turkish league. Simultaneously, he planned a new expedition against Muscovy. However, the disappointment of the gentry with Báthory's domestic policy was growing steadily, and discord in the Seym increased. The exasperated king's health declined. Hoping for a recovery, he left for his beloved Grodno (now in Belarus), where he had commenced rebuilding the castle. There, he died on December 12, 1586. His sudden death caused several rumors about whether he had been poisoned. However, Báthory's death was the result of uremia.

SIGNIFICANCE

The ten years of Báthory's rule were spent mostly in wars and military plans. Despite the panegyrics of Reinhold Heidenstein, the king's biographer and chronicler of the Muscovite war, several historians have revealed weaknesses in Heidenstein's account. Certainly Báthory, busy with wars, did not accomplish internal reforms and rather ignored the gentry, who defended their "golden liberty." On the other hand, the king was an excellent commander and strategist to whom the Polish army owed its modern shape. His military campaigns also led to economic progress and improvements in the nation's infrastructure: The king ordered the building of pontoon bridges, mints, and military hospitals.

Báthory's wars demonstrated the military power of the Commonwealth. In the opinion of some historians, this power was almost exclusively Báthory's achievement, and the Commonwealth, orphaned by him, plunged again into political chaos. The rule of Báthory, who supported the Counter-Reformation but at the same time respected religious toleration, was contrasted by the posterity with that of his successor.

Certainly Báthory's legend was remembered best after the third partition of Poland in 1795, especially under Russian rule, when Báthory's fight with Muscovy was particularly admired. The monumental painting by Jan Matejko (1838-1893) titled "Báthory at Pskov" is evidence of that latter-day veneration.

—*Elwira Buszewicz*

FURTHER READING

Butterwick, Richard, ed. *The Polish-Lithuanian Monarchy in European Context, c. 1500-1795.* New York: Palgrave, 2001. A collection of essays by various historians and scholars that together cast light on the phenomenon of the Polish-Lithuanian state. The essay by Jerzy Lukowski, "The Szlachta and the Monarchy: Reflections on the Struggle *inter maiestatem ac libertatem,*" is especially instructive as to the tensions between the gentry and Báthory.

Halecki, Oscar. *Borderlands of Western Civilization: A History of Central-Western Europe.* Edited by Andrew L. Simon. New York: Ronald Press, 1953. Examines the history of the Jagiellonian state from a political perspective in a large cultural and international context. The reader is guided through a labyrinth of sociopolitical dependencies and complications.

Jasienica, Paweł. *The Commonwealth of Both Nations: The Silver Age.* Translated by Alexander T. Jordan.

New York: Hippocrene Books, 1987. Vivid historical narrative enriched with numerous anecdotes showing the great Polish-Lithuanian state under the rule of the elective kings.

Köpeczi, Béla, ed. *History of Transylvania.* Translated by Péter Szaffkó et al. Translation edited by Bennett Kovrig. 3 vols. Boulder, Colo.: Social Science Monographs, 2001-2002. Volume 1, "From the Beginnings to 1606," provides excellent coverage of Báthory's early career. Includes bibliographical references and indexes.

Payne, Robert, and Nikita Romanoff. *Ivan the Terrible.* New York: Crowell, 1975. Based on the source biography of the first czar of Russia, who was Báthory's military enemy. The author relates the amazing facts of his life and career, including crimes and massacres with which he was associated. The minimal historical analysis in deference to biography makes this lengthy (five-hundred-page) work well suited to nonspecialists.

SEE ALSO: Oct. 19, 1466: Second Peace of Thorn; c. 1500: Rise of Sarmatism in Poland; 1543: Copernicus Publishes *De Revolutionibus.*

RELATED ARTICLES in *Great Lives from History: The Renaissance & Early Modern Era, 1454-1600:* Elizabeth Báthory; Henry III; Ivan the Terrible; Mary of Hungary; Maximilian II; Sigismund I, the Old; Sigismund II Augustus; Stephen Báthory; Vlad III the Impaler.

1576
JAMES BURBAGE BUILDS THE THEATRE

Historians generally agree that The Theatre was the first public playhouse in London built for theatrical performances. It presented William Shakespeare's plays and gave great impetus to professional actors, including those performing with England's well-known acting companies, the King's Men especially.

LOCALE: Shoreditch, northeast of London, England

CATEGORIES: Theater; architecture; cultural and intellectual history

KEY FIGURES

James Burbage (c. 1530-1597), builder of The Theatre

Richard Burbage (c.1567-1619), Shakespearean actor and head of the Lord Chamberlain's Men

Philip Henslowe (c. 1550-1616), producer and head of the Lord Admiral's Men

William Kemp (d. 1603), comic Shakespearean actor

Christopher Marlowe (1564-1593), playwright working for Henslowe

William Shakespeare (1564-1616), playwright and shareholder in the Lord Chamberlain's Men

SUMMARY OF EVENT

In early sixteenth century England, medieval religious plays were performed less frequently and secular professional theater began to take shape. The ultimate glory and heritage of this new professional theater would be the work of William Shakespeare. As great a writer as Shakespeare was, however, he may well have been lost to his-

The famous "de Witt sketch" (1596) of the interior of the Old Swan Theatre, Bankside, London.(University of Pennsylvania)

Important student playwrights such as Christopher Marlowe and Thomas Kyd (1558-1594), known as the University Wits, began to compose a powerful body of secular drama.

Actors and theatrical producers who were not players of the king's interludes sought out likely public spaces in which to present the works of the University Wits. Among such spaces were the entry yards of the various London inns as well as certain sports arenas, not unlike modern football stadiums, where bull and bear baiting took place. In the center of the arenas and in the inn yards, the actors would erect a stage surrounded by an audience. There is evidence that a performance hall of some type, called The Red Lion, had been erected for professional productions by 1567, but neither of these places gave the emerging acting companies absolute control over scheduling, physical layout, or, most important, audience entrance fees.

The lack of an actual theater building did not, however, retard the growth of professional acting. Companies of professionals organized and were sufficiently successful to be recognized and licensed as corporate entities by Parliament in 1572. This licensing act required that the companies exist only under the patronage of a court noble. Chief among these professional theatrical troupes were the Lord Howard-sponsored group and the company sponsored by the earl of Leicester; both companies were locked in stern competition for control of the theater market. On the surface, it appeared that the Howard's Men, headed by the producer Philip Henslowe and the actor Edward Alleyn (1556-1626), had the upper hand because it had the plays of such University Wits as Christopher Marlowe. Leicester's Men, however, had as members the great actor Richard Burbage and the comedian William Kemp.

Leicester's Men also had the services of Richard Burbage's father, James, who, although not a major acting talent, was a part-time builder and was willing to risk his fortune in the construction of a permanent theater for the company. To avoid control by London's government, James Burbage elected to place his new building in Shoreditch, a suburb just northeast of London proper. To

tory were it not for the success of the acting company called the King's Men, which had the talent and the physical facilities to present Shakespeare's work successfully. Furthermore, Shakespeare's renown was greatly enhanced because the first public theater building in England provided the company a place to work. This building, The Theatre, was built in 1576 by James Burbage.

Except for entertainers and clowns maintained by the king and the more powerful nobles, there were few professional actors in England during the Middle Ages, and the existing dramatic literature was devoted to religious subjects. During the early sixteenth century, there emerged a growing number of individuals who sought to earn their living as professional actors. Some of them were hired by the king to perform short works known as interludes. In addition to the interludes, there appeared a body of secular plays produced at English universities. The universities encouraged these plays as a means of learning history, the classics, and the English language.

make clear the building's function, Burbage called it, simply, The Theatre.

The artistic and financial impact of James Burbage's innovative structure was immediate and profound. Indeed, so good was the income from The Theatre that Burbage was able to build, within a year, a second playhouse in Shoreditch, called The Curtain. So dominant had James Burbage's operations become that, from time to time, he rented out The Curtain for use by his chief competitors, the Lord Howard's Men.

The exact physical configuration of The Theatre is not known, but since the company also performed at The Curtain, as did other troupes, there must have been some similarities between all Elizabethan playhouses. Some evidence is extant, including the ground plan of the Rose Theatre, which was uncovered in excavations in 1989, the 1596 sketch by Dutch student Johannes de Witt of the Swan Theatre, various stage directions, and written allusions to the theater's physical structure in the plays. From this evidence, one can see that the playhouses either were round, polygonal, or square, and were laid out so that the audience surrounded, on three or even four sides, the raised stage or playing area.

The Theatre was three stories in height. The ground floor comprised a large arena in which a sizable stage was placed, surrounded on three sides by a standing audience, known as groundlings, who paid the lowest admission price. The second floor comprised a balcony in which a seated audience of ladies and gentlemen surrounded groundlings and the stage. Balcony seats were much more expensive. Other very expensive seats, or stools, were provided on the stage or playing area itself. A third floor featured a small peaked house for the musicians.

The success of professional theater in general and the two leading companies in particular is evident in a further development. In 1593-1594, a great plague ravished London, forcing the closure of all theaters and performance areas. When the actors could again perform, two companies were considered superior: the company of Philip Henslowe and Edward Alleyn, which was under the new patronage of the powerful Lord Admiral, and the Burbage family's company, with the great actor Richard Burbage and other actors and playwrights such as William Kemp and William Shakespeare. This group was under the patronage of the highest noble in the land, the Lord Chamberlain, and was still performing in The Theatre. In 1599, however, James Burbage's lease on the ground on which The Theatre stood expired, and because of complicated legal issues, the Lord Chamberlain's Men tore down The Theatre and floated the salvaged materials across the Thames River to a section of London known as Bankside, where the company built the most famous Elizabethan playhouse of all time out of the remains of The Theatre: the Globe Theatre.

Not to be outdone, the Lord Admiral's Men also built a theater in Bankside, called the Fortune Theatre. After several decades of competition, the Lord Chamberlain's Men was most successful. In 1603, it was renamed the King's Men by King James I and was often invited to perform at his court. The recompense there was extremely high, and the publicity furthered attendance at The Globe.

SIGNIFICANCE

Although there is some evidence that a playhouse of some sort may have existed prior to The Theatre, most scholars agree that The Theatre was the first public playhouse in England built exclusively for professional theater. Once The Theatre was in operation, the Lord Chamberlain's Men gained the upper hand in competition with the Lord Admiral's Men for royal favor.

Moreover, the financial and artistic base provided by The Theatre allowed for the performance of such important Shakespearean plays as *The Comedy of Errors*, *Love's Labour's Lost*, *The Merchant of Venice*, and *Romeo and Juliet*. It was, for instance, from one of the two upper stories in The Theatre that Juliet's famous balcony scene was staged.

—*August W. Staub*

FURTHER READING

Barry, Herbert, ed. *The First Public Playhouse: The Theatre in Shoreditch, 1576-1598*. Toronto: University of Toronto Press, 1979. Collection of essays on various issues concerning the building and use of The Theatre.

Brockett, Oscar, and Franklin J. Hildy. *History of the Theatre*. 9th ed. Boston: Allyn and Bacon, 2002. The fundamental general reference work in theater history.

Hildy, Franklin J., ed. *New Issues in the Reconstruction of Shakespeare's Theatre*. New York: Peter Lang, 1990. A collection of essays by experts on the general design of Elizabethan theaters.

SEE ALSO: 1558-1603: Reign of Elizabeth I; Dec., 1598-May, 1599: The Globe Theatre Is Built.

RELATED ARTICLES in *Great Lives from History: The Renaissance & Early Modern Era, 1454-1600:* Christopher Marlowe; William Shakespeare.

1576-1612
REIGN OF RUDOLF II

Rudolf, who reigned as Holy Roman Emperor during a pivotal period in European history, established a court in Prague that was notable for its intellectual, artistic, and cultural brilliance. The emperor's poor mental health and his lack of attention to politics and religion would cause his downfall.

LOCALE: Holy Roman Empire, mainly Vienna, Habsburg domains (now in Austria) and Prague, Bohemia (now in the Czech Republic)
CATEGORY: Government and politics

KEY FIGURES

Rudolf II (1552-1612), Holy Roman Emperor, r. 1576-1612

Maximilian II (1527-1576), Holy Roman Emperor, r. 1564-1576

Matthias (1557-1619), younger brother of Rudolf II and later Holy Roman Emperor, r. 1612-1619

Tycho Brahe (1546-1601), Danish mathematician, astronomer, and chief astrologer at Rudolf's court

Johannes Kepler (1571-1630), German mathematician and astronomer who succeeded Brahe as Rudolf's chief astrologer

István Bocskay (1557-1606), leader of the Hungarian Revolt of 1604-1606 and prince of Transylvania, r. 1605-1606

SUMMARY OF EVENT

On January 16, 1556, Holy Roman Emperor Charles V abdicated his throne and officially put into place the division of the vast Habsburg holdings between two branches of the family. Charles's son, Philip II, became king of Spain, while Charles's younger brother, Ferdinand I, was elected Holy Roman Emperor (r. 1558-1564). Ferdinand I was succeeded as emperor by his son Maximilian II, whose eldest son and heir was Archduke Rudolf (born July 18, 1552).

From 1564 to 1571, at the insistence of his mother, Maria of Spain (1526-1603), Rudolf was reared at the strict Catholic court of his uncle, Philip II, but the pious and deadly serious atmosphere in Madrid so repelled Rudolf that, after he returned to Austria, the young archduke demonstrated a more liberal attitude in religious affairs, even if many Protestants in the empire still had reservations about his acceptance. His father, who had feared that his son's experience in Spain might turn him into a Catholic like his uncle, was delighted at this turn of events and had his heir crowned king of Hungary (1572), and king of Bohemia (1575). After his father's death on October 12, 1576, the archduke was elected Holy Roman Emperor under the title of Rudolf II.

It was not long before Rudolf began to exhibit signs of the mental instability that would plague him for the rest of his life. This may well have been inherited from his mother and great-grandmother (Joan the Mad, queen of Castile), and was certainly exacerbated by the pressures of imperial responsibility. It is possible that the emperor suffered from severe depression, which would have caused him to withdraw completely from public affairs for lengthy periods of time. Rudolf appeared incapable of making decisions, and many of the processes of government were slowed or even halted during his reign.

He would often express fear over plots against his life and occasionally endured severe nervous breakdowns. During such bouts—which occurred with increasing frequency over time—his childhood friend, Wolfgang von Rumpf, who served as chief minister, directed day-to-day matters of state. In 1600, Rudolf allegedly attempted suicide by slashing himself with broken glass. That same year, he turned against von Rumpf, accusing the minister of conspiracy and then dismissing him from office.

The state of the empire then deteriorated rapidly. Also neglected was the matter of ensuring imperial succession. While Rudolf was the father of illegitimate children, his only legitimate heir was his younger brother, Matthias, whom he detested heartily. Though the emperor was engaged for many years to a cousin, Isabella of Spain (daughter of his uncle, Philip II), he kept putting off a wedding date until it was too late.

Rudolf grew tired of the hustle and bustle of Vienna and in 1583 abandoned the city for good to set up his court and seat of administration in Prague, the capital of Bohemia. It was in Prague that, for the next twenty or so years, his court flourished intellectually and became one of the liveliest and avant-garde courts of the time. To be certain, the emperor himself set much of the tone; his eccentricities were legendary. He had a private zoo with animals from all corners of the globe and amassed a vast personal collection of objects such as artwork, antiques, weapons, and clocks.

Among the outstanding members of the intelligentsia at the Rudolfine Court were the scientists Tycho Brahe and Johannes Kepler. It was in Prague that Brahe was able to complete his astronomical observations, chart the heavens, and draw calculations of planetary movement, which he called the "Rudolfine Tables." Brahe's chief disciple and assistant, Kepler, was able to draw on the vast store of his master's notebooks and the tables to determine laws of planetary motion that confirmed the Copernican theory of the universe. Prague also became a haven for individuals like the Welsh occultist John Dee and for the "nonscientific" areas of astrology and Hermetism. Even Brahe and Kepler made their living as imperial astrologers rather than as mathematicians and astronomers in the traditional sense. Famed fine arts practitioners were at Rudolf's court, also, including mannerist and other painters, sculptors, and antiquaries from throughout Europe.

The one area of foreign affairs that demanded Rudolf's attention was the formidable status of the Ottoman Empire, still strong even after the death of its sultan, Süleyman the Magnificent. Border clashes with Ottoman armies degenerated into all-out war, which raged for fifteen years.

The imperial forces on the border were notoriously undisciplined and often looted and pillaged and turned the Hungarian population on the frontiers against them. In 1604, a charismatic Transylvanian noblemen named István Bocskay transferred his allegiance to Ottoman sultan Ahmed I and launched a revolt that Archduke Matthias (acting for the moribund Rudolf) could end only by negotiating with Bocskay—who became prince of Transylvania.

From that point on, Matthias had steadily advanced his cause and amassed greater and greater power at Rudolf's expense. Archduke Matthias already had been named overlord of Lower Austria and was, by contrast to his imperial sibling, a model of action. He already had ingratiated himself with the Austrian nobility and estates through his energetic suppression of peasant uprisings in 1597. In 1609, Matthias was powerful enough to force his brother to renounce the Crown of Hungary in his favor. To maintain the support of the Bohemian estates, Rudolf was forced to grant extensive liberties to his Protestant subjects through his Letter of Majesty of 1609.

Two years later, however, the Habsburg family named Matthias its head, and the triumphant archduke marched to Prague, leading an army, to compel his brother to abdicate as king of Bohemia and hand that role to him, too. Though Rudolf II retained the title of emperor, he lived for less than two months after the humiliation by Matthias. Nearly secluded, in an alcoholic daze, and sometimes babbling incoherently, he died on January 20, 1612.

SIGNIFICANCE

Rudolf's reign, despite its faults and failures, would glow as a milestone of cultural vitality and artistic and scientific achievement. The depredations of the seventeenth century would make this period of comparative peace and toleration appear like a golden age to the generations that followed, and the age survived through the Thirty Years' War.

Rudolf's weakness, however, contributed materially to the coming of this conflict. Forced to cede rights, privileges, and power to the Protestant nobility to counteract the machinations of Archduke Matthias, he created a significant Protestant bloc, especially in Bohemia. Matthias, whose own position was never that secure, in turn enlarged and reinforced these concessions to such an extent that his eventual successor, the fervently Catholic Ferdinand II (r. 1619-1637), was determined to break the Bohemian Protestants and ignite a conflict that would engulf most of Central Europe.

—*Raymond Pierre Hylton*

FURTHER READING

Christianson, John Robert. *On Tycho's Island: Tycho Brahe and His Assistants*. New York: Cambridge University Press, 2000. Describes the network that Brahe built around himself. Includes a biographical sketch of Kepler.

Evans, R. J. W. *Rudolf II and His World: A Study in Intellectual History, 1576-1612*. Oxford, England: Clarendon Press, 1973. The most extensive study to date on the subject. Stresses the dualistic nature of the emperor and what he achieved for Bohemia.

Fichtner, Paula Sutter. *The Hapsburg Monarchy, 1490-1848*. New York: Palgrave, 2003. Stresses Rudolf's inept governance as a cause for conflict and imperial decline.

Fučíková, Eliška, Lubomír Konecny, and Jaroslava Hausenblasová, eds. *Rudolf II and Prague: The Court and the City*. New York: Thames and Hudson, 1997. Addresses Rudolfine architectural and artistic influences on Bohemia's capital.

Hughes, Michael. *Early Modern Germany, 1477-1806*. Philadelphia: University of Pennsylvania Press, 1992. Rudolf is depicted in a somewhat negative and even dismissive fashion.

Koenigsberger, H. C., George L. Mosse, and G. Q. Bowler. *Europe in the Sixteenth Century*. New York: Longmans, 1989. Provides excellent background but disappointingly little insight into Rudolf's complex personality.

SEE ALSO: Aug. 17, 1477: Foundation of the Habsburg Dynasty; 1555-1556: Charles V Abdicates; 1593-1606: Ottoman-Austrian War.
RELATED ARTICLES in *Great Lives from History: The*

Renaissance & Early Modern Era, 1454-1600: Elizabeth Báthory; Tycho Brahe; Matthias I Corvinus; Maximilian II; Mehmed III; Philip II; Rudolf II; Süleyman the Magnificent.

1570's

June 7, 1576-July, 1578
FROBISHER'S VOYAGES

England's failed attempt to discover the fabled Northwest Passage to the Indies led to contact with the Inuit and launched a gold rush in northeastern Canada that was also a failure.

LOCALE: Northeast coast of North America (now southeastern Baffin Island, Canada)
CATEGORIES: Exploration and discovery; trade and commerce

KEY FIGURES

Sir Martin Frobisher (c. 1535-1594), British privateer and explorer, later knighted as a naval hero, 1588
Michael Lok (1532?-1615?), merchant, financier, and governor of the Cathay Company
Arnaq (d. 1577), Inuit woman who was captured during the second Frobisher voyage
Kalicho (d. 1577), Inuit man who, along with Arnaq and her child, was kidnapped by Frobisher
George Best (d. 1584), official chronicler of the three expeditions who published one of the earliest written accounts of the Inuit
John White (fl. 1585-1593), Elizabethan artist known for his watercolor paintings of the American Indians of the Virginia Colony
Charles Francis Hall (1821-1871), U.S. explorer who rediscovered the Frobisher sites and collected Inuit oral histories

SUMMARY OF EVENT

On June 7, 1576, Martin Frobisher set off from Deptford, England, in search of a Northwest Passage to India and the Far East. This former privateer headed a flotilla consisting of a pinnace and two small ships, the *Gabriel* and the *Michael*. The pinnace sank off the coast of Greenland, and the *Michael* turned back toward England after losing sight of the *Gabriel* in stormy seas The captain of the *Michael* incorrectly reported that Frobisher was lost at sea. On August 11, 1576, however, the *Gabriel*, with its party of nineteen, sailed into a large bay along southeastern Baffin Island. They sailed 150 miles (241 kilo-

meters) along the coast, finding neither an outlet nor a dead end. Thinking that he had found a northern sea route to the Indies, Frobisher named the waterway Frobisher Straits. This body of water is now known as Frobisher Bay.

The group had its first encounter with Inuit natives eight days later, when Frobisher, his sailing master Christopher Hall, and several others landed on a small island near the mouth of the bay. While they were scanning the area from a small hill, a party of Inuit in kayaks landed on the beach and attempted to prevent the intruders from returning to their boat. The sailors rushed back to the boat landing, barely reaching the *Gabriel* ahead of the Inuit. This and several other incidents suggest that the Inuit had had prior experience with European sailors, probably Portuguese fishermen.

The next day, Frobisher led a small party ashore and engaged in some friendly trade. This was followed by a visit to the ship by a group of Inuit. A day later, on August 21, 1576, five sailors took the ship's boat ashore to continue the contacts. It remains uncertain what transpired, but the sailors were apparently taken captive. Frobisher attempted various strategies to recover his men, but without the ship's boat, the crew of the *Gabriel* was unable to go ashore to rescue them. The crew attempted to sink one of the Inuit's *umiaks* (large skin boats) and take hostages to exchange for the sailors, but the Inuit remained wary and out of range of the ship's ordnance. Frobisher then lured a lone kayaker to the ship by holding out a bell. When the Inuit came alongside the *Gabriel*, he was, according to George Best, official chronicler of the expedition, "plucked . . . boat and al[l] . . . out of the sea." The unfortunate man was reported to be so upset by his capture that "he bit his tong[ue] in twayne [in half] within his mouth."

Unable to rescue the missing sailors, Frobisher set sail for England with his Inuit captive and an unusual black rock as tokens. The captive died soon after his arrival in London, but the black rock set in motion a series of events which, in retrospect, can only be considered a comic disaster.

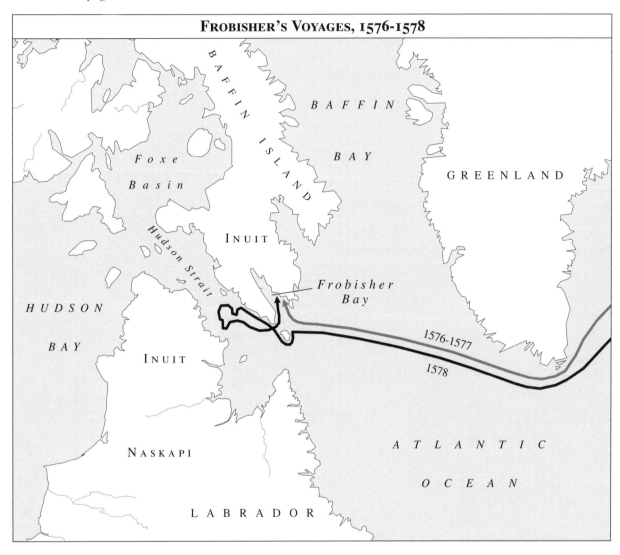

FROBISHER'S VOYAGES, 1576-1578

The rock, which seemed unusually heavy and appeared to sparkle, was presented to Michael Lok, the merchant who had financed the voyage. Lok came to believe it contained gold. At least two assayers assured Lok that the rock was ordinary, but he refused to be dissuaded. He continued to consult assayers until one finally assured him that the rock contained considerable quantities of gold. The Cathay Company, quickly formed by Lok and Frobisher to mine the gold, succeeded in attracting numerous investors, including Queen Elizabeth I.

Frobisher sailed from Blackwell on May 25, 1577, with three ships, the *Michael*, the *Gabriel*, and his flagship, the *Ayde*, which had been loaned by the queen. They entered Frobisher Bay on July 19, 1577, and remained there for five weeks. There were two goals of this second

expedition: to mine as much gold as possible and to recover the five men lost the previous year.

The 30 miners included among the ships' 120 passengers and crew succeeded in loading approximately 180 tons of ore in the allotted time. The second goal proved more troublesome. After a fruitless search of the southern margin of the bay, Frobisher and his sailing master went ashore and attempted to capture two natives. The Inuit escaped and managed to wound Frobisher with an arrow to his buttocks. A small skirmish, in which three Inuit were captured, ensued. This event is the subject of a highly detailed painting by Elizabethan artist John White, who may have witnessed the incident. The trio, a man named Kalicho, a woman, Arnaq, and her infant son, Nutaaq, were transported back to England, where they caused a sensation. The three, who died within months of their capture, are the subjects of several drawings by White. Their Asiatic features reinforced the belief that Frobisher had found a northern water route to the Far East.

Numerous delays in obtaining assays of the ore meant that Frobisher sailed a third time before any results were known or profits could be realized. In fact, the subscribers were forced to increase their investments to outfit the fifteen ships that sailed from England on May 31, 1578. Frobisher planned to leave one hundred men to mine gold throughout the winter, but the sinking of the ship that carried most of the building materials caused him to abandon that idea. Thick ice and bad weather forced Frobisher into what is now known as the Hudson Strait, and he concluded that this, and not Frobisher Bay (or "Strait," as he still believed it to be), was the true Northwest Passage. It was not until the end of July that the party reached its mining site at the mouth of Frobisher Bay. Although the group had no further encounters with North American Indians, they built a small house that they left stocked with small trade items and freshly baked bread. The bread was intended as a means to educate the Inuit in the ways of civilization. The expedition returned to England with 1,225 tons of worthless ore.

SIGNIFICANCE

In the wake of the discovery of the ore's true worth, the Cathay Company was declared insolvent, and Lok spent part of 1581 in debtors' prison. Frobisher, though somewhat disgraced, went on to distinguish himself in naval battle and was knighted in 1588 for heroism against the Spanish Armada. The search for an Arctic route to Asia continued for another few years but then was largely abandoned until the early years of the nineteenth century. The Inuit were spared further attempts at colonization until those later years.

In 1861, U.S. journalist and explorer Charles Francis Hall visited southeastern Baffin Island and made the first systematic ethnographic observations of the Inuit living there. He collected detailed oral histories and was astonished to discover that these included extremely accurate references to the Frobisher expeditions nearly three hundred years earlier. According to his informants, many years earlier two ships had come to the area. The following year, three ships arrived; the next year, there were many ships. The five men that Frobisher lost on the first voyage were said to have built a ship with a mast and attempted to sail away. They were blown back to shore and later, all died. With the aid of his Inuit informants, Hall

visited the site of Frobisher's mines and collected a number of artifacts. Thus, Frobisher's expeditions shaped in some small but lasting way the culture and history of the Inuit people, and they certainly affected their dealings with later explorers such as Hall.

—*Pamela R. Stern*

FURTHER READING

Fitzhugh, William W., and Jacqueline S. Olin, eds. *Archeology of the Frobisher Voyages*. Washington, D.C.: Smithsonian Institution Press, 1993. Combines historical documents, oral histories, and archeological evidence to provide a full account of the Frobisher expeditions. Numerous black-and-white photographs and maps.

Francis, Daniel. *Discovery of the North: The Exploration of Canada's Arctic*. Edmonton, Alta.: Hurtig, 1985. Chapter 1 contains a thorough description of the Frobisher voyages.

Hall, Charles Francis. *Life with the Esquimaux*. 1865. Reprint. Rutland, Vt.: C. E. Tuttle, 1970. Hall's observations and oral histories of the Baffin Island Inuit.

Halton, P. H. "John White's Drawings of Eskimos." *The Beaver* 41 (Summer, 1961): 16-20. Reproduction and discussion of several of White's lesser-known works.

McDermott, James. *Martin Frobisher: Elizabethan Privateer*. New Haven, Conn.: Yale University Press, 2001. Extremely thorough biography, the product of thirty years of research, provides virtually all known details of Frobisher's life and attempts imaginatively to fill in the undocumented gaps. Includes photographic plates, illustrations, bibliographic references, and index.

McGhee, Robert. *The Arctic Voyages of Martin Frobisher: An Elizabethan Adventure*. Seattle: University of Washington Press, 2001. Study utilizes archaeological evidence and Inuit oral history as well as the written records left behind by Frobisher and his men to develop a complete picture of his three voyages.

Oswalt, Wendell H. *Eskimos and Explorers*. Novato, Calif.: Chandler and Sharp, 1979. Chapter 2 presents a thoughtful discussion of contacts between Inuit and the Elizabethan-era British.

Payne, Edward John. *Voyages of the Elizabethan Seamen: Selected Narratives from the "Principal Navagations" of Hakluyt*. Oxford, England: Clarendon Press, 1907. Contains George Best's sixteenth century accounts of the three Frobisher voyages, with the spellings modernized.

Symons, Thomas H. B., ed. *Meta Incognita, a Discourse of Discovery: Martin Frobisher's Arctic Expeditions, 1576-1578.* 2 vols. Hull, Que.: Canadian Museum of Civilization, 1999. In-depth report of the findings of the Meta Incognita Project, which excavated, studied, and preserved archaeological sites related to Frobisher's expeditions. Includes illustrations, maps, and bibliographic references.

SEE ALSO: Oct. 12, 1492: Columbus Lands in the Americas; June 24, 1497-May, 1498: Cabot's Voyages; Early 16th cent.: Rise of the Fur Trade; Apr. 20, 1534-July, 1543: Cartier and Roberval Search for a Northwest Passage; 1545-1548: Silver Is Discovered in Spanish America; June 17, 1579: Drake Lands in Northern California; July 4, 1584-1590: Lost Colony of Roanoke; July 31-Aug. 8, 1588: Defeat of the Spanish Armada; Dec. 31, 1600: Elizabeth I Charters the East India Company.

RELATED ARTICLES in *Great Lives from History: The Renaissance & Early Modern Era, 1454-1600:* Elizabeth I; Sir Martin Frobisher.

1577
RAM DĀS FOUNDS AMRITSAR

Ram Dās, the fourth in the line of ten Sikh gurus, founded the holy city of Amritsar and inspired its development into what is still the center of Sikh pilgrimage, education, culture, and commerce.

LOCALE: Amritsar, Punjab, northwestern India
CATEGORIES: Religion; architecture; cultural and intellectual history; organizations and institutions

KEY FIGURES
Amar Dās (1479-1574), third Sikh guru, 1552-1574
Ram Dās (1534-1581), fourth Sikh guru, 1574-1581
Arjan (1563-1606), fifth Sikh guru, 1581-1606

SUMMARY OF EVENT
Sikhism, which incorporates elements of Hinduism and Islam, was founded as a separate religion by Nānak (1469-1539), who subsequently took the name Guru Nānak. A series of gurus, or leaders, continued the Sikh tradition. In its early years, Sikhism was helped by a tolerant attitude on the part of the Mughal emperor Akbar (r. 1556-1605), who was sympathetic to all religions in the region.

It was in this relatively benign religious atmosphere that Guru Ram Dās was born in 1534 in Lahore. He was appointed as the fourth Sikh guru by the third guru, Amar Dās. Ram Dās, whose name means "slave of God" or "God's servant," was Amar Dās's son-in-law, but historians agree that he was appointed guru on merit because of his selfless service to Amar Dās rather than because of his family connection. Ram Dās began his work as guru after the death of Amar Dās in 1574.

Verifiable details of his seven-year period as guru are scarce. Tradition says that Amar Dās wanted to establish a new place of pilgrimage, so he sent Ram Dās to locate a suitable site. Ram Dās founded the new city, which was to become the holy city of Amritsar, at the site that had been granted to his wife by Akbar. Another tradition states that Ram Dās purchased the land from the villagers of Tung, although this may have been at the request of Akbar as part of his land grant. Another tradition attributes the move away from the pilgrimage center of Goindwal, the home of Amar Dās in northwest India, to the hostility of the Amar Dās's sons. According to some accounts, Amar Dās suggested the founding of a new center because he feared conflict between Ram Dās and his own descendants.

Yet another story says that before Ram Dās became the fourth guru, he was passing through the area where the new city would eventually be built and heard a story that a pond nearby had magical healing properties. The pond was said to have cured leprosy. Sikh historians would claim that this natural pond was where Ram Chandra, a hero in the ancient Indian epic *Rāmāyana* (c. 500 B.C.E.; *The Ramayana*, 1870-1889), was healed of wounds sustained in battle. When Ram Dās visited the site, the legend goes, he was so impressed by its beauty that he decided to create it as a new site of pilgrimage. Even before becoming guru, he would visit the site once every month and swim in the pond. Another story relates how he told his followers that the location would become a large pilgrimage site and would constitute an enlightened and emancipated society.

After Ram Dās became the fourth guru, he set about constructing the new city, which was about 25 miles north of Goindwal, in the Majha area between two rivers. The exact year in which the city was founded is disputed.

Some historians date it to 1577, but others favor an earlier date, 1573, before the death of Amar Dās.

Ram Dās's first task was to recruit labor from nearby villages and construct a tank at the site, to be filled with water from a local stream. He also encouraged his disciples to take part in the work. Construction of the pool was supervised by a Sikh saint. Building on the local belief that the water in the area possessed healing properties, the tank, or pool, came to be regarded as sacred, and was called Amrita Saras (pool of nectar). When the tank was completed in 1581, Ram Dās composed poetry in honor of the occasion. He assured his followers that those who bathed in the tank and meditated on the name of God would have their sins washed away.

Because building the tank was a large project, many houses were constructed in the area to house workers, disciples, and visitors. The city was first called Guru ka Chak (village of the guru), and later Ram Dās Pura (city of Ram Dās). Unlike the established site of Goindwal, Ram Dās Pura was not on the main road between Delhi and Lahore, but it was favorably situated for the development of trade between India and Afghanistan. Ram Dās Pura quickly increased its population and prospered. Many merchants, bankers, businessmen of all types, craftsmen, and workers traveled long distances to settle there, and a market called Guru-ka-Bazar was established. Wells were dug to provide drinking water. Ram Dās encouraged this economic development, urging his followers to raise capital so they could start their own businesses. Ram Dās is applauded in later Sikh literature for his work in building up the economy of the new town. The site emerged as a religious center, and the tank of water was visited by Sikh pilgrims.

Guru Ram Dās died in September of 1581, at Goindwal, at the age of forty-seven. Before his death, he appointed his youngest son, Arjan, as the fifth Sikh guru. It was Arjan who changed the name of the city from Ram Dās Pura to Amritsar. Arjan continued the work of his father by renovating and enlarging the tank and building a golden temple in the center of the pool. The golden temple, called Harimandir, is the spiritual center for the Sikh religion.

Significance

Although Guru Ram Dās did not live to see the full flowering of his work, the city he founded quickly became, and remains, the most important center of the Sikh religion. The fact that its name, Amritsar, refers to the pool of nectar that was constructed under his guidance is testimony to the enduring value of his contribution. When the golden temple was built by Guru Arjan, it became the holiest of all Sikh sites. Amritsar has been referred to as the Vatican of Sikhism, a sacred city of the developing Sikh Empire.

In later centuries, the Sikhs were periodically driven out of Amritsar by Muslim armies because Muslim leaders were alarmed at the number of converts from Islam to Sikhism. On a number of occasions, the sacred pool was drained and filled in, and the golden temple destroyed. Both the pool of nectar and the golden temple, however, were rebuilt by determined Sikhs. It is said that even when Amritsar was under Muslim occupation, Sikhs would risk capture and death to bathe in the sacred water.

Today, Amritsar is a flourishing city on the border of India and Pakistan. It also is one of India's foremost tourist destinations. A park called Ram Bagh was created in a new part of the town as a tribute to Ram Dās.

—*Bryan Aubrey*

FURTHER READING

Banerjee, Anil Chandra. *The Sikh Gurus and the Sikh Religion*. New Delhi, India: Munshiram Manoharlal, 1983. Explores the salient features of the lives and teachings of the ten Sikh gurus.

Johar, Surinder Singh. *The Sikh Gurus and Their Shrines*. Delhi, India: Vivek, 1976. Includes chapters on the ten Sikh gurus and their associated shrines. Also contains an account of Sikh beliefs and the role of the guru in Sikhism.

Kaur, Madanjit. *The Golden Temple: Past and Present*. Amritsar, India: Guru Nānak Dev University Press, 1983. A history of the golden temple, including its foundation, ceremonial practices, architecture, and ancillary shrines.

Khalsa, Gurudharm Singh. *Guru Ram Dās in Sikh Tradition*. New Delhi, India: Harman, 1997. A composite portrait of Ram Dās as it has appeared over the course of four centuries. Ram Dās is viewed through the eyes of his disciples and Sikh poets, teachers, and historians.

McLeod, Hew. *Sikhism*. New York: Penguin, 1997. Explores how Sikhism emerged from the Hindu background of the times, how a number of separate sects split off, and how far the ideals of sexual equality have been observed in practice.

Singh, Parm Bakhshish. "Devinder Kumar Verma." In *Golden Temple*, edited by R. K. Ghai and Gurshan Singh. Patiala, India: Punjabi University Publication Bureau, 1999. A German-language chapter in a volume that contains thirty-six articles relating to the variegated aspects of the golden temple.

SEE ALSO: 1451-1526: Lodī Kings Dominate Northern India; c. 1490: Fragmentation of the Bahmani Sultanate; Early 16th cent.: Devotional Bhakti Traditions Emerge; 1556-1605: Reign of Akbar.

RELATED ARTICLES in *Great Lives from History: The Renaissance & Early Modern Era, 1454-1600:* Akbar; Nānak.

1578
FIRST DALAI LAMA BECOMES BUDDHIST SPIRITUAL LEADER

Buddhism continued to metamorphose ideologically and gain political power in Tibet until 1578, when the Mongol leader Altan created the designation of Dalai Lama, ushering in a single Buddhist spiritual and political leadership that remained in place until Chinese domination in the mid-twentieth century.

LOCALE: Tibet (now an autonomous region in China)
CATEGORY: Religion

KEY FIGURES

Altan (1507-1582), Mongol khan, r. 1543-1582, who converted to Buddhism

Sonam Gyatso (Bsod-nams-rgya-mtsho; 1543-1588), abbot of Drepung monastery and third Dalai Lama, 1578-1588

Lozang Gyatso (Ngag-dbang-rgya-mtsho; 1617-1682), fifth Dalai Lama, who unified Tibet under Gelug order

SUMMARY OF EVENT

Buddhism was founded in the late sixth century B.C.E. by the prince Siddhartha, who later adopted the name Buddha. Buddhism is a religion of thinking and living, whose followers seek nirvana, or enlightenment, in various forms. Buddhism rejects ascetic religion that emphasizes suffering as well as an Epicurean pleasure-seeking way of life. In contrast, it favors a balanced mental and emotional life, a middle way that is devoid of extremes of thought, emotion, and action.

Buddhism divided into two forms—Māhāyana and Theravāda—around the first century. Māhāyana is found in East Asia and Tibet, whereas Theravāda is based in India and Sri Lanka. Māhāyana, using texts known as sutras, believes in multiple possible manifestations of the Buddha and argues that there is no distinction between self and other. It emphasizes also the importance of bodhisattvas, followers who have reached Enlightenment and use their enlightened power to help others find Enlightenment. All schools of Tibetan Buddhism are subsets of the Māhāyana tradition. Theravāda Buddhism focuses on the Pali (perfected saint) canon of ancient Indian Buddhism, believing that only through perfecting oneself, as would a Buddhist monk but not a layperson, can one attain enlightenment.

Between the seventh and thirteenth centuries, Buddhism was both persecuted and revered in Tibetan political circles. Śākya Buddhism gained temporal power in 1247, when the Mongolians conquered Tibet and gave secular authority to the Śākya master. In 1254, Chogyal Phagpa converted Mongol emperor Kublai Khan, who made Buddhism a state religion in Mongolia and made Chogyal Phagpa the first religious and secular leader of Tibet.

Scholar Lama Tsong Khapa founded the Ganden monastery near Lhasa in 1409, a place that would become a center of the Gelug (virtuous ones) form of Buddhism. The central teachings of the Gelug school are those of the Lamrim (stages of the path), whereby one gains profound insight into the doctrine of emptiness, universal compassion, and liberation (key components of the Gelug school) by following a step-by-step path of understanding. Gelug Buddhists would govern Tibet until the mid-twentieth century. The Mongols had remained in control of Tibet, and became convinced that Gelug Buddhism was more than adequate as a replacement for Śākya as a state school of Buddhism.

In 1577, the Mongol ruler Altan invited the Gelug abbot of the Drepung monastery, the master Sonam Gyatso, to his court. Sonam Gyatso, an erudite scholar, established the Namgyal monastery and became well known as the leader of Gelug Buddhism. Altan invited Sonam Gyatso to Koko Nor (Qinghai) in 1569, but it appears that Sonam Gyatso was too busy to actually travel there. He again was invited in 1577, and accepted, both because his schedule permitted and because Altan had risen to power. They met in the summer of 1578. Sonam Gyatso's clearly advanced scholarship, his compelling speech, and his quiet wisdom convinced Altan of the merits of Gelug Buddhism. Altan attempted to spread the word to the remainder of the Mongols, asking many of his attendants to witness the greatness of Sonam Gyatso; many embraced Buddhism after contact with the Gelug master.

Sonam Gyatso had complimented Altan after his conversion by calling him King of the Turning Wheel and Wisdom, a reference to the eight "spokes" of Buddhism, often depicted in illustrations of a wheel. Altan in turn addressed Sonam Gyatso as All Knowing Vajra-Holder, the Dalai Lama, thus awarding Sonam Gyatso in 1578 the title *ta-le*, the Mongolian term close in meaning to the Tibetan *rgya-mtsho* (ocean of wisdom), anglicized as "dalai." The Gelug monks then awarded the title posthumously to Sonam Gyatso's two predecessors, Gedun Truppa and Gedun Gyatso, making Sonam Gyatso the third Dalai Lama.

By this exchange of titles, Altan and Sonam Gyatso reestablished the priest/patron relationship, not unlike the relationship between the Papacy and the states of Europe in the medieval period. A Mongol historian in the following century suggested that Altan believed himself to be a reincarnation of Kublai Khan.

Altan worked to incorporate Buddhism into law because of Gelug Buddhism's extensive ethical emphasis. In 1586, the Erdene Zuu temple in Karakorum was established as the Mongolian center of Gelug. Sonam Gyatso worked to convert more Mongols to Buddhism, ended shamanistic customs such as a version of wife-sacrifice not unlike sati, and helped to spread Gelug influence into eastern Tibet. When he left Altan's court, he appointed Yonten Gyatso as his representative at Hohhot to ensure the strength of congresses between Tibet and Mongolia.

Sonam Gyatso continued to evangelize Buddhism. In 1580, he founded the Champaling monastery in Kham, and erected the Sandalwood Temple in Amdo. He taught Buddhism to the son and successor of Altan, and so convinced him that his devotion to Sonam Gyatso and to Buddhism were as strong as his father's. Sonam Gyatso eschewed the lengthy scholarly writing of his predecessors so that he could become a Buddhist missionary in Mongolia. Sonam Gyatso died in 1588 while returning to Tibet from Mongolia.

Altan's grandson, Yonten Gyatso, succeeded Sonam as the fourth Dalai Lama, the only non-Tibetan Dalai Lama. Mongol leaders who had no authority to do so recognized young Yonten as a reincarnation of Sonam. The fifth Dalai Lama, Lozang Gyatso, allied with Mongol leader Gushri Khan to unify Tibet under the Gelug order, thus returning unity to Tibetan Buddhism. In 1642, Gushri recognized Lozung as temporal and spiritual leader of Tibet. Lozang instituted new rules for the Gelug order pertaining to monastic organization, studies, ritu-

als, and behavior, which remain in effect into the twenty-first century. Lozang was able to establish a relationship with the Qing Dynasty's emperor, effecting a patron/priest symbiosis between Chinese emperors and Dalai Lamas.

SIGNIFICANCE

Until the Chinese conquest of Tibet in the twentieth century, the Dalai Lama remained both the spiritual and political leader of Tibet. The Tibetan people have differed in their interpretations of Buddha's way of life since the introduction of Indian Buddhism to Tibet, but they were largely united as Buddhists, and the government was united under the Gelug school. The Dalai Lama and Tibetan leadership, even in exile, continue to be revered by the Tibetan Buddhists, and Buddhism shows no signs of relinquishing its intellectual and cultural base in Tibet.

—*Monica Piotter*

FURTHER READING

Ling, T. O. *A Dictionary of Buddhism: A Guide to Thought and Tradition*. New York: Charles Scribner's Sons, 1972. This is a superb reference work on Buddhism in general. It offers a dictionary of terms, concepts, historical figures, myths, and countries relevant to the history of Buddhism.

Mills, Martin A. *Identity, Ritual, and State in Tibetan Buddhism: The Foundations of Authority in Gelukpa Monasticism*. Richmond, Surrey, England: Curzon Press, 2003. A thorough study of the aspects of Gelug Buddhism that enabled it to persist as a political tool and a religious ideology. Ideal for readers with some knowledge of Tibetan Buddhism.

Newman, Bruce. *A Beginner's Guide to Tibetan Buddhism*. Ithaca, N.Y.: Snow Lion, 2004. Directed toward practitioners by a practitioner, this work is more accessible than Powers's book and full of interesting stories about the author's journey through Tibetan Buddhism.

Powers, John. *Introduction to Tibetan Buddhism*. Ithaca, N.Y.: Snow Lion, 1995. Quite possibly the clearest and most thorough introductory text in English. Powers explains both the history and tradition of Tibetan Buddhism.

SEE ALSO: 1451-1526: Lodī Kings Dominate Northern India; 1467: End of King Parākramabāhu VI's Reign; 1469-1481: Reign of the Ava King Thihathura; Early 16th cent.: Devotional Bhakti Traditions Emerge; Apr. 21, 1526: First Battle of Panipat; 1556-1605: Reign of Akbar.

1578-1590
THE BATTLE FOR TABRĪZ

Since the era of Sultan Selim I, Tabrīz repeatedly had been conquered and lost by the Ottomans. The seesawing battles between the Ottomans and the Persians, two long-time Muslim adversaries who fought over territory, power, and religion, continued with the Ottoman occupation of Tabrīz in 1585 and a treaty in 1590. The region's borders were not fixed until the nineteenth century.

LOCALE: Tabrīz, northwest Persia (now Iran), in Azerbaijan Province

CATEGORIES: Wars, uprisings, and civil unrest; diplomacy and international relations; expansion and land acquisition

KEY FIGURES

ʿAbbās the Great (1571-1629), fifth Ṣafavid shah, r. 1587-1629

Hamza Mirza (1564-1587), Persian crown prince and son of Shah Muḥammad Khudabanda

Muḥammad Khudabanda (d. 1596), fourth Ṣafavid shah, r. 1578-1587, who was forced to abdicate

Murad III (1546-1595), Ottoman sultan, r. 1574-1595

Özdemiroğlu Osman Paşa (1526/1527-1585), Ottoman grand vizier and commander who conquered Tabrīz

Ṭahmāsp I (1514-1576), second Ṣafavid shah, r. 1524-1576

SUMMARY OF EVENT

In 1578, Ottoman sultan Murad III decided to attack Persia despite his own court being a hotbed of feuds involving palace slaves and two harem factions. The intrigues, major internal turmoil, and civil war relating to the succession to the Ṣafavid Persian throne, and the intermittent dissidence and double-dealing of various Kizilbash tribes, provided Murad with the opportunity to engage in what he mistakenly thought would be the permanent conquest of the Caucasus, the land between the Black and Caspian Seas, which Persia controlled.

By this time, his Ottoman Empire was in decline, and unfriendly European powers were always threatening. The hostility of the Ottomans toward their eastern neighbors, the Ṣafavid Persians, had to do not only with the contested power of two empires but also with the actions of the Ṣafavid Dynasty's founder, Ismāʿīl I (r. 1501-1524). Ismāʿīl I had overseen his nation's transition to Shiism, which orthodox Sunni Ottomans considered to be heretical. Since the Ottoman heads of state appropriated the title of "caliph," indicating that they were successors to the Prophet Muḥammad and thus the spiritual leaders of Islam, they were therefore unwilling to countenance any possible challenge to their position.

Following an earlier round of fighting and the Ottoman conquest and loss of the territory in and around Tabrīz, Süleyman's Ottomans had been compelled to return much of it to the Persians under the 1555 Peace of Amasya. In 1578, however, Murad was encouraged by the perennial strife for succession in the Persian Empire in which the Kizilbash feudal lords fought each other and the shah over the matter. These tribal people of Turkmen origin became especially troublesome during the rule of Shah Muḥammad Khudabanda, a mild-mannered ascetic. The Kizilbash were trying to persuade him to choose a weak successor while, to ensure the success of their own schemes, they became involved in the execution of most Ṣafavid princes (paradoxically, ʿAbbās, who later became the strong Shah ʿAbbās I, was to be one of the exceptions). Accordingly, Ottoman grand vizier Mehmed Paşa Sokollu was unable to persuade Murad to abide by the 1555 treaty signed by Süleyman.

Thus, in the summer of 1578, the Ottoman commander in chief Lala Mustafa Paşa assembled a large army of crack Janissary infantrymen and feudal *sipahi* cavalrymen at Trebizond (Trabzon) on the south shore of the Black Sea.

Advancing with the main army from Erzurum that summer, Ozdemiroglu Osman Paşa scored two victories—the first in August, 1578, at Childir, north of Kars, and the second a month later near the Alazan River. The decisive breakthrough remained elusive, however. That winter, while the main army was withdrawn to Erzurum, Osman Paşa remained behind to defend the conquered territory. It was now the Persians' turn, under Crown Prince Hamza Mirza, to counterattack. The shah's son fought valiantly, and Osman was forced to retreat to Derbend on the Caspian Sea. It was not until reinforcements reached him that the Ottoman general was finally able to defeat the Persians in the spring of 1583, dislodging them from Shirvan and Daghistan on the western shore of the Caspian. Osman continued his advance, and by 1585, he had reached Tabrīz. He seized its citadel and occupied the town. Prince Hamza Mirza failed to recapture the city and was assassinated.

Throughout the campaign, the long lines of communication and the problems of resupply, all under the harassment of hostile tribesmen, had slowed the advancing Ottoman army. Shah Khudabanda, for his part, was deserted by some important feudatories. Conditions were not ideal on either side, and the war dragged on even after the fall of Tabrīz.

A humiliating treaty in 1590 forced the Ṣafavids to concede all Azeri land to the Ottomans. The new shah, ʿAbbās the Great, however, reorganized the army with more firearms and artillery, which the Persians had been reluctant to adopt widely. Also, the Turks were too distracted by rival European powers to want to press their earlier victory at Tabrīz.

Thus, by 1603, ʿAbbās had retrieved the city, thereby denying the Ottomans the ability to establish a permanent presence in the Caucasus. It was not until the nineteenth century that the borders between the two formerly hostile great powers were fixed. Through much of their feuding there was an impasse, with the Ottomans unable to control conquered Persian territory and the Persians unable to militarily defeat the Ottomans.

SIGNIFICANCE

Murad III's victory provided only temporary relief from the empire's increasing financial difficulties. By this time, the Ottomans were squeezed by decreasing revenues from diminishing war booty, and corruption and bribery plagued the government. Also, military recruitment increasingly targeted Muslim-born populations, because the earlier *devshirme*—the recruitment of Christian boys from the Balkans—was sharply reduced after the Janissary corps began to allow its members to marry and to enlist their relatives and friends, many of them no-shows. These conditions led to a breakdown of discipline and military effectiveness.

There also was growing administrative atrophy, increasing anarchy, misrule by incompetent sultans, high inflation, and the fragmentation of the empire into hostile communities. Thus, Tabrīz, because of its geographical location and because it was in the middle of ongoing disputes between the two empires, was to change hands several more times, as in the centuries before.

—*Peter B. Heller*

FURTHER READING

Cicek, Kemal, ed. *The Great Ottoman-Turkish Civilisation.* Vol. 1. Ankara, Turkey: Yeni Turkiye, 2000. This illustrated volume focuses on the politics of the strategically important Caucasus. The chapter by Mustafa Budak, "The Caucasus and the Ottoman Empire (sixteenth to 20th Centuries)," is especially helpful.

Cook, Michael A., ed. *A History of the Ottoman Empire to 1730.* New York: Cambridge University Press, 1976. Provides a good account of the Persian-Ottoman wars of 1578-1590. The chapter by V. J. Parry, "The Successors of Sulaiman, 1566-1617," is especially useful. Maps, bibliographical notes, index.

Goodwin, Godfrey. *The Janissaries.* London: Saqi, 1997. Discusses how the Ottoman Empire's elite infantry corps became involved in public policy making and war strategy and tactics. Genealogy, glossary, bibliography, illustrations, index.

Inalcik, Halil. *The Ottoman Empire: The Classical Age, 1300-1600.* Translated by Norman Itzkowitz and Colin Imber. New Rochelle, N.Y.: Orpheus, 1989. Highlights the role played by the Persian campaign in the Ottomans' ascent as a world power from 1529 to 1596.

Jackson, Peter, ed. *The Cambridge History of Iran.* New York: Cambridge University Press, 1986. Volume 6 includes a good account of the 1578-1590 battles. Plates, maps, table, bibliographies, index.

Morgan, David. *Medieval Persia, 1040-1797.* New York: Longman, 1988. Examines how Persia dealt with one of its traditional enemies, the Ottoman Empire. Map, genealogy, glossary, bibliographical survey, index.

Savory, Roger M. *Iran Under the Ṣafavids.* New York: Cambridge University Press, 1980. A masterful study of Persia and Ṣafavid rule. Map, illustrations, index.

SEE ALSO: 1512-1520: Reign of Selim I; 1534-1535: Ottomans Claim Sovereignty over Mesopotamia; 1574-1595: Reign of Murad III; 1589: Second Janissary Revolt in Constantinople; 1593-1606: Ottoman-Austrian War.

RELATED ARTICLE in *Great Lives from History: The Renaissance & Early Modern Era, 1454-1600:* Süleyman the Magnificent.

August 4, 1578
BATTLE OF KSAR EL-KEBIR

At Ksar el-Kebir, Moroccan forces won an important victory over an invading Portuguese army, decisively ending a century and a half of conflict between the two countries.

LOCALE: Wādī al-Makhāzin riverbank, near Ksar el-Kebir, Morocco

CATEGORIES: Diplomacy and international relations; wars, uprisings, and civil unrest

KEY FIGURES

Sebastian (1554-1578), king of Portugal, r. 1557-1578

'Abd al-Malik (d. 1578), sultan of Morocco, r. 1576-1578

Muḥammad al-Mutawakkil (d. 1578), sultan of Morocco, r. 1574-1576, and pretender, 1576-1578

Aḥmad al-Manṣūr (1549-1603), sultan of Morocco, r. 1578-1603

SUMMARY OF EVENT

The Battle of Ksar el-Kebir represented the culmination of a century and a half of sporadic conflict between Portugal and Morocco. The battle is also known, variously, as the Battle of Wādī al-Makhāzin (in Morocco), the Battle of Alcazar (a European corruption of el-Kebir), and the Battle of the Three Kings.

The ongoing conflict between Morocco and the Portugal was originally initiated by Portuguese attacks along the Moroccan coast. Portugal's motives were economic, strategic, and religious. After 1520, the war turned in Morocco's favor because of the rise of a new dynasty, the Sa'dīs, and their adoption of gunpowder-based weapons. By the time Sebastian assumed the throne in Portugal, his country was left with only a few coastal fortresses.

Sebastian was full of romantic notions, chief of which was to lead a crusade across North Africa to wipe out Islam and recapture the Holy Land. In 1576, a dynastic struggle within the Sa'dīan family provided him with the opportunity for which he had been waiting. The sultan, Muḥammad al-Mutawakkil, was overthrown by his uncle, 'Abd al-Malik, and al-Mutawakkil appealed to Sebastian for help regaining his throne. Seizing on the legitimate excuse to go to war, Sebastian quickly assembled an army.

Sebastian's invasion force was composed of around twenty thousand troops, including two thousand to three thousand German mercenaries, about the same number of Spanish troops on loan from Sebastian's uncle,

Philip II of Spain, six hundred Italian mercenaries paid for by the pope, several units of Portuguese nobles and gentlemen-volunteers who hoped to be rewarded by the king, and a large mass of hastily levied and poorly trained troops drawn from the lower segments of Portuguese society. The army was heavily weighted in favor of infantry, with al-Mutawakkil providing perhaps a thousand cavalry from among his followers. In the train of Sebastian's army was a huge number of noncombatants, including priests, servants, camp followers, and many families of the soldiers.

Opposing these twenty thousand Europeans, according to modern estimates, was a Moroccan army of around seventy thousand. The majority of al-Malik's force consisted of tribal cavalry armed with lances and swords, although the most effective units were composed of Andalusian, renegade, and Turkish infantry and cavalry musketeers equipped with matchlock harquebuses.

The Portuguese expedition landed at Arzila in early July, 1578, but it remained there for nineteen days, giving al-Malik time to assemble his forces. Sebastian, in fact, does not appear to have accepted good advice or to have made good decisions throughout the expedition. After almost three weeks, he finally set off with the objective of taking the port of Larache, 20 miles (32 kilometers) to the south. He was intercepted on the way by the Moroccan army at a point near the meeting of the Wādī al-Makhāzin and Lixus Rivers.

Both rivers were tidal and could be crossed only at low tide; Sebastian's force became trapped in a cul-de-sac between them. The Moroccans deployed in a crescent shape, with cavalry on either side and infantry in the center. The Portuguese units were in small rectangles around a large hollow square. The Moroccan force mounted the attack and surrounded the Portuguese early in the battle. Mounted Moroccan harquebusiers rode up to the enemy, discharged their weapons point blank, then rode off to reload. On the Portuguese side, the front ranks of gentlemen-volunteers in the center, supported by Germans on the right and Spanish and Italians on the left, proved their mettle. At one point they attacked and severely mauled the Andalusian musketeers who held the Moroccan center.

The battle is reported to have lasted from three to six hours. Several tactical and strategic factors proved decisive in the Moroccan victory. The frontline attack by the Portuguese was so successful, it opened a fatal gap on the left between the Spanish and Italian formations and the less capable Portuguese units behind them, who were charged with protecting the side of the square. Moroccan cavalry poured into this breech. On a more general level, the disproportion between infantry and cavalry gave the Moroccans a decided advantage in mobility and limited the offensive capability of the Portuguese.

The third and perhaps decisive consideration was that of size. Unless al-Malik's army fell apart—and this was a real possibility given that more than half of it was made up of tribesmen who could easily lose heart and desert if the battle began going badly—the Moroccans would eventually grind down the Portuguese. Once the Moroccan cavalry broke into the Portuguese square, it could attack from front and rear. The Spanish and Italian units never made it back to the larger square and were obliterated. The Germans and a unit of Portuguese cavalry held out until the Moroccans released a new wave of reserve horsemen who overran the field.

The battle was fought at high tide, making retreat impossible. Muḥammad al-Mutawakkil, along with a number of soldiers, attempted to swim to safety but drowned. Many others, including Sebastian, died on the battlefield. Some modern estimates put the number of dead on each side at about seven thousand to eight thousand, but others insist that the kill ratio was closer to two-to-one in favor of the Moroccans. The number of prisoners taken has been estimated to be at least fourteen thousand and perhaps many more, considering the many noncombatants in the Portuguese train. Nobles and higher-ranking Portuguese were ransomed by their families, while the rest were enslaved. On the Moroccan side, ʿAbd al-Malik died during the battle as well, apparently from natural causes. His death was kept secret from all but a few, however, for fear that such news might lead to large-scale desertions. Following the battle, al-Malik was replaced as sultan by his brother Aḥmad, who took the title al-Manṣūr, "the Victorious," in celebration.

SIGNIFICANCE

The defeat at Ksar el-Kebir was a great blow to Portuguese prestige, both in Europe and in the Indian Ocean area where the Portuguese maintained an empire. As Sebastian was childless (he had not bothered even to marry), the crown passed temporarily to one uncle, a churchman, then to another, Philip II of Spain. As a result, Portugal disappeared as an independent state from 1580 to 1640.

For Morocco, the battle brought wealth in the form of battlefield plunder and ransom money along with considerable prestige. The reign of Aḥmad al-Manṣūr is considered a glorious period in Moroccan history, during which the state reached its pinnacle of power. On the international scene, the Battle of Ksar el-Kebir helped draw to a close the larger conflict between Christian and Muslim forces that had raged across the Mediterranean for most of the sixteenth century.

—*Richard L. Smith*

FURTHER READING

Bovill, E. W. *The Battle of Alcazar: An Account of the Defeat of Don Sebastian of Portugal at el-Ksar el-Kebir.* London: Batchworth Press, 1952. Still the most complete account in English, even if minor facts have since been revised and some matters of interpretation reconsidered.

Cook, Weston F. *The Hundred Years War for Morocco: Gunpowder and the Military Revolution in the Early Modern Muslim World.* Boulder, Colo.: Westview Press, 1994. A thorough study of the rise of Morocco under the Saʿdīan dynasty, culminating in a chapter devoted to the battle of Ksar el-Kebir.

El Fasi, M. "Morocco." In *Africa from the Sixteenth to the Eighteenth Century,* edited by B. A. Ogot. Vol 5 in *General History of Africa.* Berkeley: University of California Press, 1992. Includes a lengthy section on the battle and its consequences from the Moroccan perspective; has a useful map.

Yahya, Dahiru. *Morocco in the Sixteenth Century: Problems and Patterns in African Foreign Policy.* Atlantic Highlands, N.J.: Humanities Press, 1981. Puts the battle in the larger context of Moroccan history and the geopolitical situation of the western Mediterranean during the late sixteenth century.

SEE ALSO: 1481-1482: Founding of Elmina; c. 1485: Portuguese Establish a Foothold in Africa; Jan., 1498: Portuguese Reach the Swahili Coast; 16th cent.: Proliferation of Firearms; 1505-1515: Portuguese Viceroys Establish Overseas Trade Empire; 1510-1578: Saʿdī Sharifs Come to Power in Morocco; 1580-1581: Spain Annexes Portugal; 1591: Fall of the Songhai Empire.

RELATED ARTICLE in *Great Lives from History: The Renaissance & Early Modern Era, 1454-1600:* Sebastian.

June 17, 1579
DRAKE LANDS IN NORTHERN CALIFORNIA

Francis Drake arrived in Northern California and claimed the land for England. Drake's was the first English land claim in North America.

LOCALE: California coast, probably near San Francisco Bay

CATEGORIES: Exploration and discovery; expansion and land acquisition

KEY FIGURES

Francis Drake (c. 1540-1596), English privateer, explorer, and later vice admiral

Elizabeth I (1533-1603), queen of England, r. 1558-1603

Francis Fletcher (fl. 1577-1580), chaplain and chronicler of the Drake voyage

Martin Frobisher (c. 1535-1594), Drake's rival in exploration, who attempted to discover the Northwest Passage in 1576

Philip II (1527-1598), king of Spain, r. 1556-1598, and king consort of England, r. 1554-1558

SUMMARY OF EVENT

On November 15, 1577, Francis Drake, commanding five ships, set sail from Plymouth, England, obeying Elizabeth I's order to "encompass the world." Before the voyage was completed, the sole surviving flagship, the *Pelican*, later renamed the *Golden Hind*, had circumnavigated the globe. Rounding the Strait of Magellan, Drake navigated up the western coast of South America to Peru, plundering Spanish ships and settlements along the way. Heavy with Spanish gold, silver, trade route maps, and occasionally human captives, his ship cruised up the North American coast past Mexico and California, going as far north as Oregon. Inclement weather forced him back south to what is today Marin County, California.

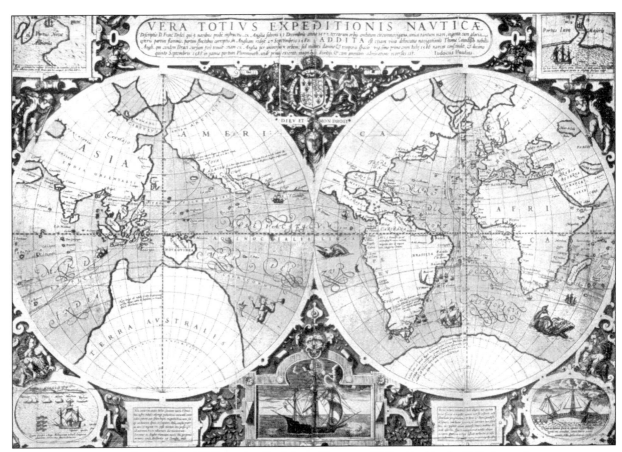

A map from the late 1500's tracing Drake's world voyage. (Hulton|Archive by Getty Images)

There he anchored for repairs before setting sail across the Pacific Ocean. Drake, who eight years later was to play an important role in England's defeat of the Spanish Armada, reached as far as the Pelew Islands (Palau) before returning home to Plymouth, England, in 1580 by way of Ternate (in the Moluccas), Java, the Cape of Good Hope, and Sierra Leone.

For the significance of Drake's 1579 excursion to California to become clear, the political situation in England must be understood. Thirty-five years earlier, Prince Philip of Spain had become king consort of England by marrying Queen Mary I. When his reign ended upon Mary's death in 1558, he attempted to maintain his powerful position by marrying the new monarch, Mary's sister Elizabeth I. After Elizabeth rejected his marriage proposal, Philip canceled all commerce, including trade treaties, between England and the Spanish colonies. Thus, finding new English trade routes in the South Pacific became paramount for England's economic survival. Discovery of the Northwest Passage, formerly thought of as a possible route from the Atlantic to the Pacific, seemed the most expedient way to accomplish this goal.

In 1576-1578, Martin Frobisher explored northeastern Canada seeking the Atlantic entrance to the Northwest Passage. Drake's voyage was, in part, an attempt to discover the passage from its Pacific end. It was in making this attempt that Drake found "a faire and good baye" in California. It was popularly believed at that time that the west coast of North America ran in a northeasterly direction until the passage was reached. After reaching at least 40° north latitude (possibly as far as 48° north latitude), Drake concluded that the passage did not exist, or, if it did, that it would be unnavigable. Backtracking to approximately 38° north latitude, the *Golden Hind* dropped anchor on June 17, 1579.

The exact location of Drake's anchorage remains controversial. It was not far from modern-day San Francisco, and it is likely that it was the unsheltered bay known as Drake's Bay, behind the hook on the end of the Point Reyes Peninsula. Scholars continue to argue, placing Drake's landing at various points around San Francisco, including Drake's Bay, San Francisco Bay, Bodega Bay, Drake's Estero, Bolinas Lagoon, and Tomales Bay. However, a geographical feature chronicled in the journal of Drake's chaplain, Francis Fletcher, may provide evidence that Drake's Bay was in fact the original landfall site. Fletcher recorded that, because of its similarity to England's white banks and cliffs, Drake renamed the country New Albion (New England). A line of white

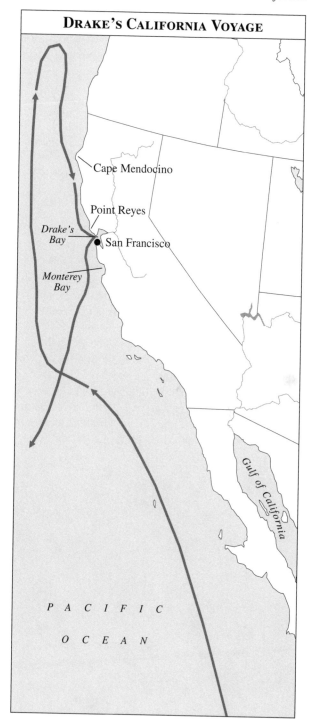

DRAKE'S CALIFORNIA VOYAGE

Cape Mendocino

Point Reyes

Drake's Bay

San Francisco

Monterey Bay

Gulf of California

PACIFIC OCEAN

diatomaceous shale cliffs stretches for miles across from Drake's Bay. Although not as striking as the English chalk cliffs, these are the only white cliffs now in the area.

On shore, Drake erected a commemorative metal plaque, rediscovered in 1936 by a group of picnickers at Greenbrae Hill overlooking Point San Quentin, which reads:

> Be it known unto all men by these presents, June 17, 1579, by the Grace of God in the name of Her Majesty Queen Elizabeth of England and Her successors for ever, I take possession of this Kingdom, whose king and people freely resign their right and title in the whole land unto Her Majesty's keeping, now named by me and to be known unto all men as Nova Albion.
>
> —*Francis Drake*

The rediscovery of this commemorative brass plate at Greenbrae Hill fueled the controversy over Drake's actual landfall site and added credence to the claim that San Francisco Bay was the anchorage location. A comparison of modern charts to explorer Jodocus Hondius's 1589 commemorative Drake and Cavendish World Map supports this claim. In addition, the chaplin Fletcher's description of "Barbarie Conies" and "Deere" in the area better reflects the ecology of Greenbrae than that of Point Reyes. Significantly, if Drake anchored in San Francisco Bay, he would have been the first European at this geographical site, antedating Gaspar de Portolá's land expedition by 190 years. The inhospitable coastline, prevalent fog, and narrow entrance long prevented earlier explorers such as Juan Rodríguez Cabrillo, who had charted the entire coast of California by 1542, from finding the Golden Gate.

Anthropologists have determined from fragments of speech recalled by one of Drake's crew that the people encountered by Drake were Coast Miwoks who lived in the area now occupied by Marin and Sonoma Counties, north of San Francisco. The native people left no record of their first impressions of Drake and his crew, but according to Fletcher, they were happy upon the arrival of the British, referred to Drake as "Hich," or king, gave over their land voluntarily, and were saddened when the British left.

Drake's crew spent six weeks coping with a cold, foggy summer in California and repairing the leaking *Golden Hind* before setting sail on July 23. They stopped briefly at the Farallon Islands to replenish supplies before riding the northeast trade winds across the Pacific Ocean bound for the Moluccas (Spice Islands).

SIGNIFICANCE

It was not until Francis Drake returned to England in 1580 that the true significance of the California expedition began to develop: The Spanish ambassador to Elizabeth's court, Don Bernardin de Mendoza, pronounced the goods that Drake brought home Spanish property and demanded their return to the Spanish crown. In the document that was to become England's central expansion doctrine for the next three centuries, Elizabeth claimed that since the Spaniards had prohibited commerce with the British, England had been forced to take its own exploratory steps. Because Protestant England was not under Rome's jurisdiction, she continued, it need not honor Spain's papal title to the New World. England was suddenly a colonial power in its own right, in a position to explore and claim land in the Americas. By 1609, the Virginia Charter extended to the Pacific Ocean and included Drake's Nova Albion.

Until Drake claimed possession of the Miwoks' coastal lands, there was no English interest in North America. Indeed, until Drake's action, no non-European was ruled by an English sovereign. That situation quickly

Sir Francis Drake meeting the leader of a tribe of indigenous peoples in California. (Hulton|Archive by Getty Images)

changed in the wake of the colonial doctrine declared by Elizabeth to the Spanish ambassador. Sir Walter Ralegh's Roanoke Colony was founded just six years later, in 1584, and the permanent Virginia settlement came twenty-three years after that. Thus, Drake not only established the first nominal protectorate colony of the British Commonwealth of Nations but also motivated his monarch to enunciate and follow the policy that was to lead to the creation of that commonwealth. This milestone marked the beginning of Great Britain's worldwide system of empire, which acknowledged local authority but maintained jurisdiction under the British crown.

—*M. Casey Diana*

FURTHER READING

Bawlf, Samuel. *The Secret Voyage of Sir Francis Drake, 1577-1580.* Vancouver, B.C.: Douglas & McIntyre, 2003. Reveals evidence that Drake's secret mission on his circumnavigation of the globe was to explore the Pacific Northwest in an attempt to seek out the North-west Passage. Beyond this new information, the book provides a multifaceted portrayal of Drake himself, reconciling his religious convictions with his ruthless acts of piracy. Includes illustrations, maps, bibliographic references, index.

Coote, Stephen. *Drake: The Life and Legend of an Elizabethan Hero.* New York: Simon & Schuster, 2003. Biography combines novelistic dramatization of Drake's life with important analysis of the way his legend became a national symbol through which England understood itself and its global actions. Includes illustrations, maps, bibliographic references, and index.

Drake, Sir Francis. *The World Encompassed by Sir Francis Drake.* Reprint. Cleveland: World, 1966. Offset edition of the Huntington Library copy of the first edition (London, 1628). Recounts the complete circumnavigation, including the six weeks spent in Marin County. Based on the Fletcher's journal.

Dudley, Wade G. *Drake: For God, Queen, and Plunder.* Washington, D.C.: Brassey's, 2003. This entry in Brassey's "Military Profiles" series examines Drake's naval career and his role in the defeat of the Spanish Armada. Includes photographic plates, illustrations, maps, bibliographic references, and index.

Jenkins, Dorothy G. "Opening of the Golden Gate." In *Geologic Guidebook of the San Francisco Bay Counties: History, Landscape, Geology, Fossils, Minerals, Industry, and Routes to Travel.* San Francisco: California Division of Mines, 1951. Detailed natural history of San Francisco Bay counties. Illustrations include Drake's brass plate.

Kelleher, Brian T. *Drake's Bay: Unraveling California's Great Maritime Mystery.* Cupertino, Calif.: Kelleher & Associates, 1997. Extremely technical and detailed discussion of where Drake claimed to have landed in California, where he most likely actually landed, and the reasons for the discrepancy. Includes illustrations, maps, bibliographic references, index.

Kelsey, Harry. "Did Francis Drake Really Visit California?" *Western Historical Quarterly* 21, no. 4 (1990): 444-462. A scholarly article that discusses the uncertainties and contradictions inherent in nearly every aspect of accounts of Drake's voyage.

Power, Robert H. *Francis Drake and San Francisco Bay: A Beginning of the British Empire.* Davis: University of California Press, 1974. Short, scholarly work that posits San Francisco Bay as Drake's landfall site. Emphasizes the influence that the Coast Miwok people had on British expansion policies.

Williams, Neville. *Francis Drake.* London: Weidenfeld & Nicolson, 1973. Readable account of Drake's life and the historical forces that shaped it. Many illustrations, no index.

SEE ALSO: June 7, 1494: Treaty of Tordesillas; 1519-1522: Magellan Expedition Circumnavigates the Globe; Apr. 20, 1534-July, 1543: Cartier and Roberval Search for a Northwest Passage; June 27, 1542-c. 1600: Spain Explores Alta California; July, 1553: Coronation of Mary Tudor; 1558-1603: Reign of Elizabeth I; Feb. 25, 1570: Pius V Excommunicates Elizabeth I; June 7, 1576-July, 1578: Frobisher's Voyages; July 4, 1584-1590: Lost Colony of Roanoke; Sept. 14, 1585-July 27, 1586: Drake's Expedition to the West Indies; Dec. 31, 1600: Elizabeth I Charters the East India Company.

RELATED ARTICLES in *Great Lives from History: The Renaissance & Early Modern Era, 1454-1600:* Sir Francis Drake; Elizabeth I; Sir Martin Frobisher; Mary I; Philip II; Sir Walter Ralegh.

1580's-1590's
GALILEO CONDUCTS HIS EARLY EXPERIMENTS

Galileo's scientific experiments, the uses he made of them, and the concepts he developed led directly to reexaminations of the traditional Aristotelian view of nature and laid the foundation for Newtonian mechanics.

LOCALE: Florence, Pisa, and Padua (now in Italy)
CATEGORIES: Science and technology; physics

KEY FIGURES

Galileo (1564-1642), Italian mathematician and astronomer
Vincenzo Galilei (c. 1520-1591), Galileo's father, Florentine patrician, and musician
Guidobaldo Marchese del Monte (1545-1607), scientist, engineer, wealthy aristocrat, and Galileo's patron
Santorio Santorio (1561-1636), innovative medical doctor and a member of Galileo's learned circle
Vincenzio Viviani (1622-1703), Galileo's pupil and first biographer
Paolo Sarpi (1552-1623), highly educated and influential monk and a member of Galileo's learned circle

SUMMARY OF EVENT

Galileo was one of a number of scientists who questioned the Aristotelian view of the workings of nature and turned to experiment to find answers. His frequent discussions with friends and colleagues have led some to believe that many of his findings should be credited to a group effort. As important as his colleagues were, however, probably no one influenced Galileo's scientific life more than did his musician father, Vincenzo Galilei.

During 1588 and 1589, Galileo was at his father's home in Florence and most likely worked with him on a problem that involved physics and music. It was commonly believed that the pitch of a plucked string depended directly on both the length and the tension of the string. Doubling the tension should raise the pitch one octave. Using strings of various lengths and under different tensions, the elder Galilei showed that the pitch did depend on the length of the string, but it depended on the square root of the tension. Questioning what was commonly accepted and appealing to experimentation became hallmarks of Galileo's scientific career.

In 1581, Galileo enrolled at the University of Pisa to study medicine, but he soon changed to the study of mathematics. According to Vincenzio Viviani, a student of Galileo's and his first biographer, during Galileo's own student days in 1583, while standing in the cathedral of Pisa, he happened to notice the chandelier swing with the air currents from an open window. He was amazed to note that the period with which the chandelier swung back and forth remained the same regardless of whether the chandelier swung in a smaller arc or a larger arc. He probably timed the period with his heartbeat.

Galileo later stated that the pendulum is isochronous, that is, that the period of the swing is the same, regardless of amplitude, no matter how large. He was in error on this point, for the pendulum is nearly isochronous only if the arc of the pendulum swing is small. (Grandfather clocks make use of such an isochronous pendulum to regulate their movement.) One of Galileo's friends, a physician named Santorio Santorio, began using a short pendulum to time the pulse of patients in 1602. Galileo completed four years of studies at the University of Pisa but left without a degree in 1585. He returned to his father's home, taught private students, and occasionally gave public lectures. Galileo admired the work of Archimedes greatly. He reconstructed Archimedes' method of weighing an object in air and then weighing it in water to determine the object's density and, therefore, the purity of the precious metal used. In doing so, Galileo devised a more accurate balance. He described it in a small booklet called *La bilancetta* (c. 1586; the little balance). His balance had a vertical support for the pivot of a horizontal arm. The item to be weighed was suspended from one side of the arm, and a counterweight was suspended from the other side of the arm. The counterweight was moved along the arm until balance was achieved, and then its weight and distance from the pivot allowed the weight of the item to be computed. Galileo's simple, but brilliant, improvement consisted of winding a fine wire around the counterweight arm so that the counterweight's position could be very accurately located by counting the number of turns of wire from an index mark to the counterweight's position. If the fineness of the wire "bedazzled the eye," making it difficult to count turns, Galileo suggested running a lightly held, sharp stiletto along the turns and counting the clicks as the stiletto passed from turn to turn.

At the recommendation of Galileo's friend and patron, Guidobaldo Marchese del Monte, Galileo was appointed to the chair of mathematics at the University of Pisa in 1589. Some of Galileo's lecture notes from 1589 to 1592 were gathered into a collection referred to as *De motu* (c. 1590; *On Motion*, 1960). In it, Galileo still used the Aristotelian concepts of natural and forced motions, but he proved Aristotle wrong on several points. He introduced the new concepts of infinitesimal forces and "neutral motion," a precursor to the modern concept of inertia. He reported on his experiments with bodies falling in various media, and by casting the problem in terms of relative densities, he was able to avoid some of Aristotle's errors.

Around 1590, according to Viviani, Galileo dropped a large cannon ball and a musket ball from the Leaning Tower of Pisa simultaneously. The two hit the ground at nearly the same time, contrary to Aristotle's prediction. While others before Galileo had done the same experiment and reached the same conclusion, Galileo's public demonstration assured not only that his experiment was memorable but also that it countered false tradition.

After his father died in 1591, the financial responsibility for his brother and sisters fell to Galileo. Guidobaldo helped him obtain a better position at the University of Padua in 1592. Notes from his lectures from 1593 to 1600 were compiled for the collection *Le meccaniche* (c. 1600; *On Mechanics*, 1960), considered the best work on simple machines up to that time. One of its gems is a clever proof based on balances: for a body on an inclined plane, the component of the weight acting down the plane is proportional to the sine of the angle of incline of the plane (to use modern terms).

In Aristotelian theory, heat and cold were fundamental properties that simply *were*. Until Galileo's time it seems that people believed hot and cold could not, or should not, be measured. As early as 1592, Galileo built a crude thermometer by fusing a long glass tube "as fine as wheat straw" to a hollow glass egg. If the egg were warmed by cupping it in the hand and then inverted with the end of the tube in water, water would be drawn into the tube as the air in the egg cooled. If the egg was warmed or cooled, the water in the tube would fall or rise. Santorio marked a scale on the tube, making it a proper thermometer. While useful, this type of thermometer had the serious defect of depending not just on the temperature but also on atmospheric pressure.

Guidobaldo concentrated on practical applications of science and influenced Galileo to do the same. Galileo studied and taught about fortifications, and in 1597, he invented and began to manufacture a "military compass" that could be used to measure the elevation angle of cannon. It was engraved with tables and scales to show such things as the proper charge of powder for the cannon or the number of soldiers required for various formations.

The flight of a cannon ball is far too swift for the eye to determine its trajectory, but evidence found in Galileo's notes, and in those of his intellectual companions, Guidobaldo and Paolo Sarpi, shows that around 1592, Galileo and Guidobaldo proved that the trajectory was a parabola. Their marvelously simple method was to cover a small brass ball with ink, fasten a sheet of paper to a board, and hold the board nearly upright. Then the ball was launched upward against the paper and allowed to trace out its path. They quickly recognized the inked curve as a parabola. The ascending and descending arcs of the trajectory were the same, contrary to Aristotle's claim.

SIGNIFICANCE

When Galileo recognized that the trajectory of a projectile was a parabola, he would have known by the parabola's mathematical properties that the distance the projectile fell increased as the square of the time elapsed. Thus, he had all of the elements of "the law of the fall"

Galileo looking at the night sky through an early telescope. (Hulton|Archive by Getty Images)

1580's

but did not publish these results until many years later when he could present them as part of a coherent system.

Galileo was a true Renaissance figure. He was a good artist, wrote poetry, and played the lute and the organ. He was a hands-on scientist who performed experiments and constructed his own instruments. He was the only scientist of his time to gain international recognition in mathematics, physics, and astronomy. This enabled him to bring mathematics to physics and (eventually) bring physics to astronomy. In so doing, he helped place modern science firmly on course.

Ideally, science has a dual role: It approaches questions theoretically by soundly predicting the outcome of "events," and then it proves those predictions through sound experiment and observation. Galileo's experiments, backed by mathematical models and proofs, paved the way for Isaac Newton's formulation of the three laws of motion.

—Charles W. Rogers

FURTHER READING

Galileo. *On Motion, and On Mechanics*. Madison: University of Wisconsin Press, 1960. Translated and introduced by I. E. Drabkin and Stillman Drake. A translation of and introductions and notes to Galileo's *De motu* and *Le meccaniche*. Also includes illustrations. Part of the Medieval Science series.

Drake, Stillman. *Galileo Studies: Personality, Tradition, and Revolution*. Ann Arbor: University of Michigan Press, 1970. An excellent look at Galileo and his character and his influence on science.

Machamer, Peter, ed. *The Cambridge Companion to Galileo*. New York: Cambridge University Press, 1998. Twelve historians examine in depth Galileo's place in the history of science. Suitable for all readers.

Sharratt, Michael. *Galileo: Decisive Innovator*. Cambridge, Mass.: Blackwell, 1994. Examines Galileo's ability as a scientific innovator who explored the natural world through varying means.

Sobel, Dava. *Galileo's Daughter: A Historical Memoir of Science, Faith, and Love*. New York: Penguin Books, 2000. An annotated compilation of letters written to Galileo by his daughter, Virginia, who took the convent name Sister Maria Celeste. It provides a warm look at Galileo the individual.

SEE ALSO: 1462: Regiomontanus Completes the *Epitome* of Ptolemy's *Almagest*; c. 1478-1519: Leonardo da Vinci Compiles His Notebooks; 1543: Copernicus Publishes *De Revolutionibus*; 1572-1574: Tycho Brahe Observes a Supernova; 1600: William Gilbert Publishes *De Magnete*.

RELATED ARTICLES in *Great Lives from History: The Renaissance & Early Modern Era, 1454-1600:* Sophie Brahe; Tycho Brahe; Giordano Bruno; Nicolaus Copernicus; William Gilbert; Leonardo da Vinci; John Napier; Georg von Peuerbach; Rheticus; Simon Stevin.

1580-1581
SPAIN ANNEXES PORTUGAL

Spanish king Philip II took advantage of a Portuguese crisis of succession to annex Portugal within the Spanish Empire, adding the Portuguese spice empire to Spain's already extensive imperial holdings and suppressing Portugal's sovereignty for sixty years.

LOCALE: Madrid, Spain, and Lisbon, Portugal
CATEGORY: Expansion and land acquisition

KEY FIGURES

Philip II (1527-1598), king of Spain, r. 1556-1598, king of Portugal, r. 1581-1598
John III (1502-1557), king of Portugal, r. 1521-1557
Sebastian (1554-1578), king of Portugal, r. 1557-1578
Henry (1512-1580), king of Portugal, r. 1578-1580
António (1531-1595), prior of Crato

Cristóbal de Moura (c. 1528-1613), Portuguese agent of Philip II
Cardinal Antoine Perrenot de Granvelle (1517-1586), chief adviser of Philip II

SUMMARY OF EVENT

Succession to the throne of Portugal was placed in doubt by the accession of King Sebastian following the death of John III in 1557. Only three years of age at the time of his coronation, Sebastian remained physically weak throughout his life. He never married and had no direct heir. In 1578, he launched an ill-conceived and poorly planned invasion of Morocco, a self-styled crusade against the Moors, and many Portuguese nobles joined his venture. In August, 1578, the Moors trapped Sebastian's forces and killed him, while most of the Portuguese nobility were captured and held for ransom. The throne passed to Henry, brother of John III and Sebastian's great-uncle. This succession did not resolve the dynastic crisis, however, for the new monarch was sixty-seven years old and also had no heir. He was a weak ruler, moreover, and various claimants began conspiring to succeed him.

The strongest claim was put forward by Philip II of Spain—a grandson of Manuel I of Portugal, who had reigned before John III. Spain needed spices from Portugal's East Indian empire, but Portuguese merchants needed Spanish gold and silver, as did the Portuguese aristocrats being held for ransom by the Moors; a merger of the two economies seemed to be mutually desirable. Henry was sympathetic to Philip but dared not name him as heir because of popular support for António of the Order of the Knights of Malta, prior of Crato, an illegitimate nephew of John III, and also a grandson of Manuel I. António was a vigorous contender and a staunch upholder of Portugal's independence from Spain. A third claimant was Catherine, a granddaughter of Manuel I, but she had little support.

Henry died in 1580 without naming an heir, and a council of regency was appointed to govern until a successor could be chosen. Philip of Spain had anticipated these events, however, and through Cardinal Antoine Perrenot de Granvelle, his chief adviser and a strong proponent for the annexation of Portugal, Philip selected Cristóbal de Moura, a pro-Spanish native of Portugal, to plead his case in Lisbon. Backed by Spanish gold, Moura persuaded the regency council to name Philip heir to the Portuguese throne.

Philip then had to contend with the Portuguese army, led by the popular António. Philip sent the duke of Alva and twenty thousand troops, who defeated the Portuguese forces. The entire country was occupied within four months. In April, 1581, before a Portuguese Cortes (parliament) in the town of Tomár, Philip was formally recognized as king of Portugal. As Moura had promised earlier, Portuguese rights were respected, and Philip's interference in the internal affairs of his new kingdom remained minimal.

SIGNIFICANCE

Portugal under Philip II essentially remained intact, with changes occurring only in the head of its government. At Tomár, Philip had promised to maintain all the laws of the kingdom, never to hold a Portuguese Cortes outside Portugal, and not to allow any foreign assembly to legis-

late for Portugal. All official positions were filled by Portuguese natives, and the viceroy of Portugal, who governed in Philip's absence, was also Portuguese. Colonial trade continued in Portuguese vessels, Spanish taxation was not introduced into the country, and customs frontiers between the two countries were abolished. Thus, Spain gained a kingdom without Portugal losing either its national identity or its economic and political institutional structures. Portugal remained a self-contained Spanish kingdom for sixty years.

—*José M. Sánchez*

FURTHER READING

Birmingham, David. *A Concise History of Portugal.* 2d ed. New York: Cambridge University Press, 2003. A good and accessible overview that includes discussion of Sebastian and Philip. Also includes bibliographical references.

Bovill, E. W. *The Battle of Alcazar.* London: Batchworth Press, 1952. This narrative of the battle in which Sebastian was killed and his nobility captured also covers the international implications of the annexation.

Davies, R. Trevor. *The Golden Century of Spain, 1501-1621.* Reprint. Westport, Conn.: Greenwood Press, 1984. This survey includes a useful chapter on the acquisition of Portugal.

Elliott, John H. *Imperial Spain, 1469-1716.* Reprint. New York: Penguin, 1990. A portion of this work on imperial Spain is devoted to the Portuguese succession. Asserts that one of the few periods when the government of Philip II was solvent was during the annexation of Portugal.

Kamen, Henry. *Philip of Spain.* New Haven, Conn.: Yale University Press, 1997. A massive and detailed biography of Philip, documenting almost every aspect of his life, but somewhat light on his legacy and influence on future events. Includes photographic plates, illustrations, maps, bibliographic references, and index.

Livermore, Harold V. *A New History of Portugal.* 2d ed. New York: Cambridge University Press, 1976. One of the best and most detailed histories of Portugal in English. Includes photographic plates, illustrations, and index.

Lynch, John. *Spain, 1516-1598: From Nation-State to World Empire.* Cambridge, Mass.: Blackwell, 1991. Emphasizes the support given to Philip by Portuguese mercantile interests who stood to profit from a merger of the economies. Includes a brief but useful bibliography and tables of economic facts.

1580's

Merriman, Roger B. *The Prudent King.* Vol. 4 in *The Rise of the Spanish Empire in the Old World and in the New.* Reprint. New York: Cooper Square, 1962. This volume, the last section of Professor Merriman's classic study of sixteenth century Spain, contains a judicious evaluation of Philip and a complete narrative of the annexation of Portugal, though some scholars have criticized inaccuracies in his economic evaluations.

Nowell, Charles E. *A History of Portugal.* New York: Van Nostrand, 1952. Along with Livermore, the other top English-language history of Portugal. Includes illustrations, maps, and bibliography.

Parker, Geoffrey. *The Grand Strategy of Philip II.* New Haven, Conn.: Yale University Press, 1998. Contests the traditional view of Philip as conducting his empire by reacting to events as they occurred without any grand plan to guide him. Uses correspondence and other historical documents to delineate a "strategic culture" informing Philip's decisions and his reign. Includes illustrations, maps, bibliographic references, and index.

_____. *Philip II.* 4th ed. Chicago: Open Court, 2002. A good overview of Philip's reign, this edition is updated with a new bibliographic essay. Also includes map, portraits, genealogical table, bibliography, and index.

Walsh, William Thomas. *Philip II.* London: Sheed and Ward, 1937. Reprint. New York: McMullen Books, 1953. A laudatory, pro-Catholic work written with masterful style.

Williams, Patrick. *Philip II.* New York: Palgrave, 2001. Biography that attempts to capture the complexities of Philip's public and private lives and of the evolution of both his private persona and his royal career over time. Includes maps, bibliographic references, and index.

SEE ALSO: 1505-1515: Portuguese Viceroys Establish Overseas Trade Empire; 1563-1584: Construction of the Escorial; Aug. 4, 1578: Battle of Ksar el-Kebir.

RELATED ARTICLES in *Great Lives from History: The Renaissance & Early Modern Era, 1454-1600:* John III; Manuel I; Philip II; Sebastian.

1580-1587
REBELLIONS IN BIHAR AND BENGAL

The Mughal governor of Bengal set limits on the Bengali army, including pay, which incited rebellions. Rebellions also ensued after Mughal emperor Akbar was accused of abandoning Islam.

LOCALE: Bengal and Bihar, India
CATEGORIES: Wars, uprisings, and civil unrest; expansion and land acquisition

KEY FIGURES; GOVERNMENT AND POLITICS
Akbar (1542-1605), Mughal emperor of India, r. 1556-1605
Muzaffar Khan (fl. late sixteenth century), governor of Bengal, 1578-1580
Mirza Muhammad Hakim (d. 1585), governor of Kabul and Akbar's half brother

SUMMARY OF EVENT
On March 3, 1575, Munim Khan defeated Daud Khan Karrani at the Battle of Tukaroi, laying the foundations for Mughal rule in Bengal. However, Daud and the other Karranis continued to resist the Mughals for a number of years from Orissa, to the southwest of Bengal. In July of 1576, at Rajmahal, the Mughals conquered Bengal a second time under the leadership of Man Singh. This time, however, they executed Daud, thereby ensuring that he would not resist their consolidation of power. There were other obstacles, however, as Afghan chiefs continued to resist Mughal expansion and fight among themselves.

One of the great strengths of Mughal emperor Akbar was his ability to work with subject kings, governors, and other rulers to develop a strong network of power. Under Akbar, Bengal was made a *suba* (governed dominion). Muzaffar Khan became *subadar* (governor) on December 19, 1578. Akbar's half brother, Mirza Muhammad Hakim, governed Kabul as an independent ruler.

The lack of central control of the northeast opened the door for the rebellions. The *suba* administration was introduced at the end of 1586 to establish control over the rebellions. Because Bengal demonstrated the need for a structured and uniform administration, the *subadar* path of succession was well-delineated in Bengal. If the *subadar* of Bengal died, the highest imperial officer at Monghyr would succeed him. If this officer did not exist, then the governor of Bihar would take over the rule of

Bengal, because of the proximity of the provinces. In addition to a *subadar*, Bengal had a *diwan*, with extensive powers over the provincial exchequer, and a *bakshi*, who controlled military finance. This prevented the *subadar* from becoming too autocratic within the province, and it removed the possibility of rebellion against central authority.

The *suba* also had a *waqai-navis*, a news reporter and liaison who communicated the actions of the governors to Akbar, acting as a watchdog for viceregal affairs. These officers were all appointed by Akbar in 1587 but developed true power within the empire under Jahāngīr's reign, a few decades later. As part of the *suba* system, the *subadar* was required to send a form of tribute called *peshkash* to Akbar on a regular basis. This defined Bengal's relationship with the central court as one of a subject dominion.

Yet, when Bengal was conquered by the Mughals in 1576, there was no such system in place. The Afghans continued to battle with one another and, in reality, Bengal looked less like an extension of Mughal rule than a continuation of embattled disputes among rival chieftains in a divided principality. In 1580, however, centralized authority completely vanished when the Mughal chiefs' united front gave way to competing interests. Muzaffar Khan, Akbar's governor in Bengal, had put in place many strict policies in the region, limiting the actions of the Bengali army. Muzaffar Khan reduced the pay of troops, enforced the branding of army horses to prevent fraud and theft, and revoked the unauthorized alienation of land.

When Mirza Muhammad Hakim declared himself independent in Kabul, rebels within the Bengali army attached themselves to his cause quickly, in part because of sympathy with Mirza Hakim. Many rebels, though, simply wished to consolidate their forces against Muzaffar Khan, and Mirza Hakim's rebellion provided a convenient excuse. Others sought the strength in numbers that a rebel coalition would provide between supporters of Mirza Hakim and disgruntled Bengali and Bihari army officers.

The chief religious judge (mullah) in Jaunpur called for loyal Muslims to rise against Akbar, too, fearing that Akbar was a threat to orthodox Islam. These fears were not wholly unsubstantiated, as Akbar had great tolerance for other religions. He also had developed a hybrid religion called Din-i-Ilahi (Divine Faith), which combined Islamic principles with Hinduism and Jainism and borrowed also from the Parsis, Sikhs, and Christians whom Akbar frequently invited to discuss their faiths. Several

of the rebels answered this call and joined the revolt out of religious loyalty, and a belief that Akbar had wholly abandoned Islam.

Whatever their reasons, the rebellion took hold in Bengal and Bihar. They defeated Muzaffar Khan and his loyalists, and Bengal and Bihar were declared to be under the control and protection of Mirza Hakim. Loyal Mughal troops regained Bihar easily, but Bengal and Orissa proved more difficult. As Mirza Hakim was preoccupied by Akbar's invasion of Kabul in 1581, the Afghans returned to their factionalized fighting and took de facto control of the region.

After defeating Mirza Hakim, Akbar turned to conquering Bengal for a third time. He sent a new governor to Bengal, who in turn won a partial victory, but parts of the region remained under the Afghans. The next *subadar* continued gradually to regain territory, but still, the Afghan rulers maintained power. In June, 1584, however, the Mughals had a major victory, as Kutlu Khan of Orissa, who had taken over parts of Bengal and Orissa, was defeated.

In 1586, the last Afghans finally accepted Mughal overlords in their territories, and what rebels remained were crushed in 1587. This allowed for the institution of the *subadar* system in Bengal. Wazir Khan was the first *subadar*, but he died in 1587 shortly after his tenure began. He was followed by Sayyid Khan, who held the post from 1587 to 1594.

SIGNIFICANCE

Because of Bengal's riches, especially its agriculture, the Mughals had a vested interest in the region. Possessing Bengal was integral to the growth and prosperity of the Mughal Empire, so quelling rebellions, regardless of the cause, was essential to the continued central strength of Akbar's empire. The defeat of the Afghans and the rebels demonstrated the real end of the Karranis in Bengal and ensured that Mughal supremacy in the region would be maintained.

—*Monica Piotter*

FURTHER READING

Eaton, Richard M. *The Rise of Islam and the Bengal Frontier, 1204-1706.* Berkeley: University of California Press, 1996. Part of the Comparative Studies on Muslim Societies series, this work identifies Bengal as a "frontier" for the spread of Islam into India and as a frontier of ideas and nationhood.

Raychaudhuri, Tapan. *Bengal Under Akbar and Jahāngīr: An Introductory Study in Social History.* Delhi,

India: Munshiram Manoharlal, 1969. Raychaudhuri's work remains valuable as a study of social life of ordinary Bengalis from 1574 to 1627, as he discusses the social structures, culture, gender relations—the daily lives—of Bengalis. He examines some possible reasons for the actions of Bengalis during this period, and also discusses administrative structures, expanding the idea of Bengali exceptionalism.

Sarkar, Jadunath. *The History of Bengal.* Vol. 2. Delhi, India: B. R., 2003. Part of a multivolume history of Bengal, this volume examines Bengal under Islamic rule prior to the British takeover. Sarkar includes a discussion of the tumultuous transfer of power from the Afghan sultan Daud Khan to Mughal rule.

SEE ALSO: 1459: Rāo Jodha Founds Jodhpur; Mar. 17, 1527: Battle of Khānua; Dec. 30, 1530: Humāyūn Inherits the Throne in India; 1556-1605: Reign of Akbar; Feb. 23, 1568: Fall of Chitor; Mar. 3, 1575: Mughal Conquest of Bengal; Feb., 1586: Annexation of Kashmir.

RELATED ARTICLE in *Great Lives from History: The Renaissance & Early Modern Era, 1454-1600:* Akbar.

1580-1595
MONTAIGNE PUBLISHES HIS *ESSAYS*

Montaigne created a new genre of Western world literature when he published the first personal, or familiar, essays.

LOCALE: Château de Montaigne, near Bourdeux, France
CATEGORIES: Cultural and intellectual history; literature

KEY FIGURES

Michel Eyquem de Montaigne (1533-1592), moral philosopher and originator of the personal essay
Marie le Jars de Gournay (1565-1645), adoptive daughter, pupil, friend, and editor of Montaigne
Étienne de La Boétie (1530-1563), a humanist and friend of Montaigne
Françoise de La Chassaigne (1544-1627), wife of Montaigne

SUMMARY OF EVENT

Of the four major modern genres of Western literature—poetry, fiction, drama, essay—only the essay is a creation or invention of modern times. Poetry, fiction, and the drama are inherited from ancient Greece, but the literary essay, the personal or familiar essay, is the creation of the French Renaissance and of the gifted thinker, philosopher, and writer Michel Eyquem de Montaigne.

Montaigne was born Michel Eyquem at his father's Château de Montaigne; being the eldest son he inherited the title Montaigne and the château on his father's death in 1568 and styled himself Montaigne thereafter. Like his father, he was counselor of the Bordeaux parlement (1557-1570), and he was elected twice as mayor of Bordeaux (1581 and 1583). Nevertheless, he spent much of his life in isolation, in reading, and in meditation in his tower library at his château. The major result of this reading and meditation is *Essais* (1580-1595; *The Essays,* 1603).

An engraved portrait of Michel Eyquem de Montaigne. (Hulton Archive by Getty Images)

Montaigne's father reared young Montaigne with classical Latin as his native language and the classics as his teachers. He learned French as a "foreign" language. He was essentially a solitary. Montaigne, however, was devoted to his father, and he had one close friend who died young, Étienne de La Boétie, in whose honor he wrote the memorable essay "On Friendship." He did not have a close relationship with his wife Françoise de La Chassaigne. It is known that his children, except for one daughter, died in infancy, and he was not close to the surviving daughter either. Toward the end of his life, however, he developed a close friendship with Marie le Jars de Gournay, his adoptive daughter, pupil, and later editor of the posthumous publication in 1595 of a complete edition of *The Essays*. He seems otherwise to have lived a lonely and not particularly happy life.

As a consequence of his solitary meditation, reading, and introspection, however, he came upon an appropriate vehicle for trying to understand himself and all humanity—a new literary technique and genre—the personal essay. It took him some five or six years of writing and rewriting to invent the essay genre as a vehicle to say what he wanted to say. The earliest essays, those written roughly between 1572 and 1574, are short and relatively impersonal. A major turning point is to be seen in the composition in 1576 of "Apology for Raymond Sebond," his longest and most skeptical writing. After that, a self-portrait clearly becomes his central theme.

In 1580, the first edition of *The Essays* appeared, published by Montaigne at Bordeaux in two books. He continued rewriting and adding to the essays but mainly during 1582 when there was a second Bordeaux edition. A third edition also appeared in 1587 in Paris. In 1588, Montaigne published a fourth edition of *The Essays* in Paris, containing a completely new third book plus more than six hundred additions to books one and two. The essays in the third book are even longer and more personal than the earlier ones. This was the last edition Montaigne actually saw through publication. He continued, how-

---

MONTAIGNE'S "OF REPENTANCE"

Montaigne developed the genre of the personal essay, which reflected his belief in the literary and intellectual significance of the self. Here, Montaigne outlines the thoughts that led him to form the new genre, and, in contradiction to this essay's title, he does not apologize for his creation.

- Others form man; I describe him, and portray a particular, very ill-made one, who, if I had to fashion him anew, should indeed be very different from what he is. But now it is done.
- I cannot fix my object; it is befogged, and reels with a natural intoxication. I seize it at this point, as it is at the moment when I beguile myself with it. I do not portray the thing in itself. I portray the passage; not a passing from one age to another, or, as they put it, from seven years to seven years, but from day to day, from minute to minute. I must adapt my history to the moment.
- I am holding up to view a humble and lustreless life, that is all one. Moral philosophy, in any degree, may apply to an ordinary and secluded life as well as to one of richer stuff; every man carries within him the entire form of the human constitution.
- Authors communicate themselves to the world by some special and extrinsic mark; I am the first to do so by my general being, as Michel de Montaigne, not as a grammarian or a poet or a lawyer. If the world finds faults with me for speaking too much of myself, I find fault with the world for not even thinking of itself.
- When a man of ordinary conversation writes uncommon things, it means that his talent lies in the place from which he borrows them, and not in himself. A learned man is not learned at all things; but the accomplished man is accomplished in all things, even in ignorance.

Source: From *Essais*, excerpted in *The Norton Anthology of World Masterpieces*, edited by Maynard Mack, vol. 1 (New York: W. W. Norton, 1980), pp. 1329-1331, *passim*.

---

ever, to revise and edit using one of his own copies of the 1588 edition, and in the year of his death, 1592, he was preparing a "final" edition for the press. This editing is in the form of Montaigne's marginal additions to what is sometimes called the "Bordeaux copy" of 1588; further, this editing is extensive, being about one quarter of the total length of the whole work. Montaigne died on September 13, 1592. In 1593, a fifth edition appeared posthumously in Lyons; a sixth edition also appeared there in 1595.

Marie le Jars de Gournay incorporated Montaigne's edited material into the first complete edition of *The Essays*, which also was published posthumously in 1595, this time in Paris. One would then consider this to be the seventh edition. (It should be noted that there are other legitimate ways of designating edition numbers, because, as usual, it is often arbitrary to distinguish between actual editions and printings or reprintings. The numbering of editions here is standard and conservative.) *The Essays* of Montaigne were first translated into English by John Florio and published in London in 1603 with the title *The Essayes*.

The French word *essai* has its root in the Latin *exagium:* to weigh. In sixteenth century French, *essai* meant attempt, practice, prelude, sample. The term *essaier* meant to experience, to expose, to feel, to make an attempt, to taste, to test, to undertake, to weigh. The English word *assay* in both its archaic (trial, attempt) and its current (try, attempt) meanings is close to the French meanings and suggests much about Montaigne's methodology. His use of the word *essais* for his writings is more an indication of his technique than it is a name for a literary genre.

In the essays, Montaigne tried to look at all sides of a topic or question, positive as well as negative. After encountering his work, readers may not know exactly what something is, but they are aware of what it might be, what it could be, what it ought to be, what it is trying to be, or something in between. In other words, he created the essay as literature. It is not history, philosophy, religion, a social science, or science. It is literature. It is exploratory. It is as close to the combination of the thought, the emotion, and the feeling of total humanity as one can get.

The topics of the essays vary not only in subject but also in length and in treatment. Some are long, some are short. Some are lists, some are highly and intricately developed. Many have overlapping and interlinking topics of exploration. For example, in book 1 he explores, among other topics, sadness, idleness, fear, friendship, moderation, and solitude. In book 2, again among many others, he explores drunkenness, books, cruelty, virtue, anger, and war. In book 3, among others, he explores repentance, diversion, discussion, vanity, physiognomy, and experience. Through reading these and other of Montaigne's essays, readers come to know him better than actual acquaintances and come to know themselves better than they could without his aid. Montaigne knows that the only thing one can really know is himself or herself. In his essays, he comes to know himself, and readers come to know themselves.

SIGNIFICANCE

Montaigne created and set the standard for the personal informal essay, a form of writing not seen before Montaigne. Like Homer with fiction, Sappho with lyric poetry, Aeschylus, Euripides, and Sophocles with drama, Montaigne had invented and perfected what was to become one of the four literary genres of Western world literature. He and his essays are not likely to be surpassed. Throughout *The Essays*, Montaigne portrays himself as a very ordinary, simple, unimportant person. Ironically, he comes through as anything but ordinary, simple, or unimportant. He reveals the human soul in all its complexity within a very real and complicated body; he reveals the same about himself and about each reader who reads him.

—Douglas J. McMillan

FURTHER READING

Coleman, Dorothy Gabe. *Montaigne's "Essais."* London: Allen & Unwin, 1987. A study of how to read Montaigne, how to understand the intellectual, philosophical, and classical literary backgrounds, and how to follow Montaigne through the ages.

Friedrich, Hugo. *Montaigne.* Translated by Dawn Eng. Edited by Philippe Desan. Rev. ed. Berkeley: University of California Press, 1991. Although originally written in 1949, this work is still considered by many to be the most authoritative total study of Montaigne. It has stood the test of time.

Hartie, Ann. *Michel de Montaigne: Accidental Philosopher.* New York: Cambridge University Press, 2003. This study of Montaigne's work seeks to counter the perception that his achievements were primarily literary rather than philosophical. Argues for the philosophical originality and importance of his ideas. Includes bibliographic references and index.

Henry, Patrick, ed. *Approaches to Teaching Montaigne's "Essays."* Approaches to Teaching World Literature 48. New York: Modern Language Association of America, 1994. Comprehensive information on editions, texts, and reference works plus twenty essays on various approaches to Montaigne and his essays.

Hoffman, George. *Montaigne's Career.* New York: Oxford University Press, 1998. This study of the relationship between politics and writing in the sixteenth century charts Montaigne's various occupations and sources of income to determine the influence of financial and practical considerations on his writings and his thought. Includes bibliographic references and index.

Leschemelle, Pierre. *Montaigne: Or, The Anguished Soul.* Translated by William J. Beck. Currents in Comparative Romance Languages and Literatures 29. New York: Peter Lang, 1994. A psychological analysis of Montaigne through his own essays.

Levine, Alan. *Sensual Philosophy: Toleration, Skepticism, and Montaigne's Politics of the Self.* Lanham,

Md.: Lexington Books, 2001. Based on the presumption that until now practitioners of various disciplines (literary criticism, political science, philosophy, history) have each studied and appropriated only fragments of Montaigne's work, this study aims to be the first to synthesize his model of the self, his attitudes toward Native Americans, his skepticism, and his arguments in favor of tolerance into a single comprehensive model of Montaigne's thought showing how each piece relates to the whole. Includes bibliographic references and index.

March, Dudley M. *Montaigne Among the Moderns: Receptions of the "Essais."* Providence, R.I.: Berghahn Books, 1994. A study of the influence of the essays from the time of composition through such writers as Ralph Waldo Emerson, Friedrich Nietzsche, Walter Pater, and Virginia Woolf and up to the 1990's.

Montaigne, Michel de. *The Essays of Michel de Montaigne.* Translated and edited by M. A. Screech. London: Allen Lane/Penguin Press, 1991. One among

many attempts to translate the essays into English adequately. Helpful introductions, annotations, and appendices.

O'Neill, John. *Essaying Montaigne: A Study of the Renaissance Institution of Writing and Reading.* 2d ed. Liverpool, England: Liverpool University Press, 2001. Examines Montaigne's practice of writing, its cultural context, and his personal understanding of what it meant to write. Also discusses the reception of Montaigne's work, both by his contemporaries and by successive generations up to the present. Includes bibliographic references and index.

SEE ALSO: 1494: Sebastian Brant Publishes *The Ship of Fools*; 1499-1517: Erasmus Advances Humanism in England; 1516: Sir Thomas More Publishes *Utopia*.

RELATED ARTICLES in *Great Lives from History: The Renaissance & Early Modern Era, 1454-1600:* Desiderius Erasmus; Michel Eyquem de Montaigne; Sir Thomas More; François Rabelais.

c. 1580-c. 1600
SIAMESE-CAMBODIAN WARS

Conflict between the Siamese and Cambodians led to the conquest of the Cambodian capital at the end of the sixteenth century, leading to Siam's political domination of Cambodia.

LOCALE: Siam (now Thailand) and Cambodia
CATEGORIES: Expansion and land acquisition; wars, uprisings, and civil unrest; diplomacy and international relations

KEY FIGURES
Naresuan (1555-1605), king of Siam, r. 1590-1605
Chetta I (Satha I; d. 1596), king of Cambodia, r. 1576-1594
Barom Reachea IV (d. 1618), brother of Chetta, king of Cambodia and a vassal of Siam, r. 1603-1618

SUMMARY OF EVENT
Before the rise of major Thai (Siamese) kingdoms in mainland Southeast Asia, the Cambodians (also known as the Khmer) were culturally and politically dominant in modern Cambodia, in much of modern Thailand, and in parts of southern Vietnam. During the 1200's, powerful Thai principalities (kingdoms) began to challenge the Cambodians, and the kings of the rising power of the

Thai kingdoms, Ayutthaya, continued to struggle against powerful neighbors throughout the kingdom's history. In 1431, the Siamese of Ayutthaya attacked and sacked the Cambodian capital at Angkor. Rival forces of the kingdom of Burma (now called Myanmar) exerted continual pressure on Ayutthaya too. In 1569, the Burmese king Bayinnaung conquered Ayutthaya and its surrounding territory.

The weakness of the Siamese enabled the Cambodians once again to stage several invasions of central Thailand. In 1570, 1575, and 1578, Cambodia invaded Ayutthaya, expecting that the kingdom that had been subjected to Burmese rule would be an easy source of loot. The Siamese, however, succeeded in repelling the Cambodian forces, but the invasions inflicted great hardship on the local population.

Naresuan was the most active Siamese defender. The Burmese had appointed Naresuan as governor of the Siamese province of Phitsanulok in 1571. However, Naresuan declared himself independent of Burma in 1584 and, through continual fighting, managed to reestablish the independence of Ayutthaya.

About 1580, the Cambodians reopened the war against the Siamese from the east. In that year, the Cambodian king Chetta I raised an army and captured the Siamese city of Phet Buri. The following year, Chetta's forces again pushed into the eastern part of Siam and took large numbers of captives.

Chetta had helped to encourage European involvement in Southeast Asian affairs. He surrounded himself with Spanish and Portuguese bodyguards, who were soldiers of fortune. He also maintained contact with the Spanish authorities who had recently established themselves in Manila, the Philippines.

For a time, Naresuan was too preoccupied with his struggles against the Burmese to give much attention to the Cambodians. The Siamese and Cambodians even paused in their rivalry for a brief alliance. In 1586, during yet another invasion of Siamese territory, Chetta sent forces under the command of his brother Barom Reachea IV to help Naresuan defeat Burmese troops who had invaded the northern Thai kingdom of Chiang Mai. The alliance was short-lived. The Cambodian king's brother apparently treated Naresuan in a manner that the Siamese prince considered disrespectful. Naresuan expressed his anger by cutting off the heads of some prisoners and then putting the heads on stakes close to Barom Reachea's boat. The mutual insults propelled Siam and Cambodia into war. When Burma invaded Siam again the next year, Chetta took advantage of the occasion to stage an invasion from the other side. After defeating the Burmese, Naresuan returned his attention to the Cambodian enemy. The Siamese prince recaptured his lands from Chetta's forces and then drove into Cambodia. Naresuan captured Battambang and Pursat in Cambodia and then advanced to Lavek, the Cambodian capital at that time. Lack of supplies, however, forced the Siamese to return home.

Burma's puppet king of Siam, Maha Thammaracha (r. 1569-1590), died in 1590, and Naresuan became the new king of the Siamese kingdom of Ayutthaya. Naresuan had been planning to attack Cambodia in 1592, when the Burmese made another effort to retake Siam. After defeating Burma, Naresuan focused again to the east. In 1593, he raised an army said to consist of between fifty thousand and one hundred thousand troops. This time, the march into Cambodia was a series of victories for the Siamese. Naresuan's forces faced almost no resistance when they took the Cambodian strongholds of Battambang and Pursat. Barom Reachea, with whom Naresuan had quarreled during the brief alliance, brought a force of thirty thousand soldiers to Boribun but fled before putting up a fight, and Boribun too fell. As Naresuan advanced on the Cambodian capital at

Lavek, he met Siamese troops moving in from the north.

The fight for the Cambodian capital was much more difficult than were earlier battles, and both sides suffered heavy casualties. Chetta appealed for help from the Spanish at Manila, but the Europeans did not arrive in time to help him. Finally, in July of 1594, the Siamese managed to take the city. According to Thai legend but disputed by modern historians, Naresuan ordered Chetta executed so that he could bathe his feet in the blood of the Cambodian king. Historians, instead, argue that Chetta had escaped and made his way to Luang Prabang in Laos, where he died two years later.

The Siamese took Barom Reachea prisoner and held him for several years. The Kingdom of Cambodia fell into civil war in the last few years of the sixteenth century, with several changes of rulers. In 1597, the Spanish, who had arrived too late to help Chetta, nevertheless placed one of Chetta's sons on the throne. The Cambodian royal family asked Naresuan to return Barom Reachea as the new Cambodian ruler and, in return, promised allegiance to Siam. In 1603, Siamese soldiers enabled Barom Reachea to seize the throne and rule for the next decade and a half as the vassal of Siam.

SIGNIFICANCE

The Siamese-Cambodian Wars of the sixteenth century changed the balance of power in mainland Southeast Asia decisively. Cambodia, which had dominated the region when the Siamese kingdoms began to appear in the thirteenth century, had been in decline for centuries, but Cambodia was still a state to be reckoned with when Chetta I came to the throne.

From Naresuan's conquest of Lavek until the French claimed Cambodia in the nineteenth century, Cambodia was a vassal state of Siam, which was later renamed Thailand. Although the Siamese continued to fight against the Burmese, Cambodia never again represented a serious threat either to the kingdom centered in Ayutthaya or to the succeeding Siamese state ruled from Bangkok. Naresuan became a Thai national hero and a symbol of Thai independence because of his victories against both the Burmese and the Cambodians.

—*Carl L. Bankston III*

FURTHER READING

Chandler, David. *A History of Cambodia*. 3d ed. Boulder, Colo.: Westview Press, 2000. One of the best general histories of Cambodia, this edition updates earlier editions and traces events in Cambodia from the first century through the late twentieth century.

Coedés, George. *The Making of Southeast Asia.* Translated by H. M. Wright. London: Routledge, Kegan & Paul, 1966. A classic introduction to early Southeast Asian history that examines the Siamese-Cambodian wars of the sixteenth century.

Hall. D. G. E. *A History of South-East Asia.* 4th ed. New York: St. Martin's Press, 1981. A standard, comprehensive history of the region.

Wood, W. A. R. *A History of Siam.* 1924. Reprint. Bangkok, Thailand: Wachrin, 1994. Often based as much on legend as on fact, this often-cited work is one of the first English language works to attempt a scholarly understanding of Siamese history.

Wyatt, David K. *Thailand: A Short History.* New Haven, Conn.: Yale University Press, 1986. Provides an introduction to Thai history, including coverage of the Ayutthaya period.

SEE ALSO: 1450's-1529: Thai Wars; 1454: China Subdues Burma; 1469-1481: Reign of the Ava King Thihathura; c. 1488-1594: Khmer-Thai Wars; 1527-1599: Burmese Civil Wars; 1548-1600: Siamese-Burmese Wars; 1558-1593: Burmese-Laotian Wars; 1565: Spain Seizes the Philippines.

RELATED ARTICLES in *Great Lives from History: The Renaissance & Early Modern Era, 1454-1600:* Afonso de Albuquerque; Tomé Pires; Saint Francis Xavier.

1580's

1581-1597
COSSACKS SEIZE SIBIR

Prompted by the untapped riches of Siberian furs and the desire to secure Russia's eastern frontiers against raids by nomadic tribesmen, Russian forces under the Cossack leader Yermak invaded and conquered the Khanate of Sibir.

LOCALE: Lower Volga, Urals, and Western Siberia (now in Russia and Kazakhstan)

CATEGORIES: Expansion and land acquisition; wars, uprisings, and civil unrest

KEY FIGURES

Yermak Timofeyevich (d. 1584/1585), Cossack leader hired to lead expedition against the Khanate of Sibir

Kuchum (d. after 1598), Tatar ruler of Sibir, r. 1556-1598

Ivan the Terrible (Ivan IV; 1530-1584), grand prince of Moscow, r. 1533-1547, and czar of Russia, r. 1547-1584

Boris Godunov (c. 1551-1605), czar of Russia, r. 1598-1605

SUMMARY OF EVENT

The Cossacks have long been associated with romantic images of proud and independent horsemen living on the open steppe, the vast grasslands on the southern and eastern frontiers of Russia. Many had fled the constraints of serfdom to pursue an uncertain life on the fringes of society, learning customs and skills from the very Tatar tribesmen who were their sworn enemies. Even the word

"Cossack" comes from a Tatar term meaning "independent fighter." As the Russian czars expanded their domain and created a strong, centralized government, the Cossacks represented a force of lawlessness that had to be brought to heel. At the same time, however, their ferocious bravery and skill as mounted fighters made them a potentially valuable resource.

This ambiguity colored the attitude of Czar Ivan the Terrible toward Yermak Timofeyevich, a Cossack leader, or ataman, who alternated between banditry and mercenary service. Yermak was hired by the Stroganovs, a family of wealthy merchants, to protect them from raiding tribes from the east, beyond the Ural Mountains. Although Czar Ivan had forbidden his leading families to succor "bandits," as he frequently described the Cossacks, he granted permission for Yermak to lead an expedition to make war on the khan of the Siberian Tatars and to take his lands for the Russian crown.

In 1581, the expedition set out with 540 experienced warriors armed with primitive firearms, as well as swords and bows. They were led by five subordinate atamans of fierce reputation: Ivan Koltso, Bogdan Bryazga, Matvei Meshcheryak, Nikitin Pan, and Yakov Mikhailov. They went by water up the Kama and Chusovaya Rivers through the Ural Mountains, portaging several times before they finally abandoned their boats and trekked overland to the river Tagil. There they camped for some time and built new boats.

Shortly after their departure from their encampment,

787

they were ambushed by the Voguls, a tribe tributary to the khan. After repelling the attack, the Cossacks pursued the Voguls back to their settlement of Chingi-tura, near modern Tyumen. They seized the settlement, captured the khan's tax collector, and sent him back to his master with gifts and promises of their peaceful intent. However, the khan distrusted their embassy and set up a second ambush for them at the river Tobol.

After losing a fair portion of his force, Yermak decided it would be prudent to return to European Russia to resupply before winter. However, his scouts soon returned with news that there was no easy way home. Yermak was now committed to storming the Tatar capital, Sibir (a name ultimately extended to the entirety of Russia's Asian conquests and anglicized as Siberia). The Cossacks were in desperate straits, but the khan commanded a divided force, in which a Tatar elite led levies of warriors from the various tributary peoples. The tribal levies soon broke and ran, having no desire to die for the khan. After a long and pitched battle, the Tatars themselves finally fled, enabling the Cossacks to seize Sibir and shelter for the winter. In doing so, they also took over the Tatars' tribute payments.

Yermak sent messengers back to Moscow to report his success, but by this time Czar Ivan's mood had changed. He was fully ready to slay the Cossacks as bandits, and only their rich bundles of furs saved their lives. Taking the furs, Ivan agreed to send reinforcements to consolidate Yermak's hold on the area.

In Sibir, the Cossacks spent a long and painful winter struggling with constant pressure from the Tatars, who ambushed their foraging missions. Only the capture of the Tatar prince Mahmet-kul, whom they held as a hostage against further raids, brought them any security. During that brief period of relative peace, the Cossacks also defeated a tribe known as the Ostyaks by stealing the idol they worshiped.

When Czar Ivan's reinforcements arrived in the spring, they proved ill-prepared and more of a burden than an asset. Many of them died of disease, and the Cossacks suffered major setbacks, including the loss of several of their leaders. Yermak himself was shot through the eye during a battle, then drowned when his heavy armor pulled him to the bottom of the river he was trying to cross to escape. However, it was later said that his ghost continued to haunt and fight the Tatars long afterward.

Although deprived of their charismatic leader, the Cossacks continued the fight, and better-prepared reinforcements enabled them to establish a large measure of control over western Siberia. Khan Kuchum was not en-

tirely displaced, however. He continued to resist the czar's rule in the region, primarily by organizing guerrilla attacks against the Russian forces. Finally, in 1598, he was captured by the Russians, along with most of his family and household retainers. Czar Boris Godunov, himself of Tatar descent, offered Kuchum clemency if he would submit to Russian rule. Kuchum refused, however, and went into exile with the Nogai Horde. The Nogais killed him soon thereafter.

The lucrative fur trade drove further exploration into Siberia, and the possibility of attaining the status of a free Cossack by living successfully in that wild land drew many dissatisfied people. Within fifty years, the Cossacks had reached the Pacific Ocean and even visited Japan. The activities of these hardy explorers were often marked by rapacious brutality alongside noble acts of self-sacrifice, further cementing their ambiguous images. The Cossacks' expeditions eastward led them to become organized into well-defined hosts with privileges that distinguished them from the ordinary peasantry. At the same time, however, much of the original freedom of the Cossacks eroded, and this was difficult for some of the more wild spirits among them to accept.

SIGNIFICANCE

The Cossack expeditions into Siberia were critical in transforming Russia from a relatively modest nation in the deciduous forests of Eastern Europe into the world's largest country in terms of land mass. The conquest of Siberia gave Russia an enormous frontier region to which the dissatisfied could go to seek their fortunes. In addition, Russian leaders found Siberia a useful place of exile for criminals and political malcontents, a practice that would reach its ultimate expression in the GULAG system of Soviet dictator Joseph Stalin, himself a survivor of several periods of Siberian exile as a revolutionary.

The expeditions also began a transformation of the Cossacks from lawless bandits to the staunchest defenders of the autocracy. Their legendary skills as mounted warriors were an integral part of their way of life, and in return for the special privileges that enabled that lifestyle, they were required to render military service to the czars. The freedom-loving Cossacks were never brought completely under control, however, and they were responsible for two major, bloody rebellions against the Russian aristocracy, one led by Stepan Timofeyevich Razin (1667-1671), and one led by Emelyan Pugachev (1773-1775). In both cases, the Cossack leaders stirred up the Russian peasantry and led brutal attacks on government officials and members of the nobility. In re-

THE RENAISSANCE & EARLY MODERN ERA

sponse to the second rebellion, Empress Catherine the Great withdrew many Cossack privileges, including the right to choose their own leader.

The last great expression of Cossack military horsemanship may be seen in Semyon Budyonny's Mounted Army of the 1918-1920 Russian Civil War, as portrayed in Isaak Babel's novel *Red Cavalry*. The Cossacks, however, had no place in Soviet society, and their culture was systematically destroyed in Stalin's drive to collectivization, although post-Soviet Russia has seen some efforts at a Cossack revival.

—*Leigh Husband Kimmel*

FURTHER READING

Payne, Robert, and Nikita Romanoff. *Ivan the Terrible*. Lanham, Md.: Cooper Square Press, 2002. Biography of the czar who sent Yermak to conquer Siberia; gives an idea of the politics behind the decision.

Seaton, Albert. *The Horsemen of the Steppes: The Story of the Cossacks*. New York: Hippocrene Books, 1985. Study of the origins of the Cossacks from the collision of Tatar and Russian, including the Cossack expeditions into Siberia.

Ure, John. *The Cossacks: An Illustrated History*. New York: Penguin, 2002. Accessible history of the Cossacks, their explorations and their rebellions.

SEE ALSO: 1480-1502: Destruction of the Golden Horde; After 1480: Ivan the Great Organizes the "Third Rome"; 1499-c. 1600: Russo-Polish Wars; Jan. 16, 1547: Coronation of Ivan the Terrible; 1556-1605: Reign of Akbar; July 21, 1582: Battle of the Tobol River.

RELATED ARTICLES in *Great Lives from History: The Renaissance & Early Modern Era, 1454-1600:* Boris Godunov; Ivan the Terrible.

July 26, 1581
THE UNITED PROVINCES DECLARE INDEPENDENCE FROM SPAIN

The United Provinces of the Netherlands launched a successful armed revolt against Spain, declared its independence, and assured the triumph of Protestantism in the northern Netherlands.

LOCALE: The Netherlands
CATEGORIES: Government and politics; wars, uprisings, and civil unrest; religion

KEY FIGURES

William the Silent (1533-1584), prince of Orange and count of Nassau
Duke of Alva (Fernando Álvarez de Toledo; 1507-1582), military governor of the Netherlands, 1567-1573
Alessandro Farnese (1545-1592), duke of Parma and governor of the Netherlands, 1578-1592
Cardinal Antoine Perrenot de Granvelle (1517-1586), president of the Council of State, 1559-1563
Margaret of Parma (1522-1586), regent of the Netherlands, 1559-1567
Maurice of Nassau (1567-1625), son of William the Silent, who led the Dutch to victory
Philip II (1527-1598), king of Spain, r. 1556-1598, whose policies of repression provoked the Dutch Revolt

SUMMARY OF EVENT

In 1556, Philip II ascended the throne of Spain after promising Charles V, his father, that he would efface Protestantism in the Spanish empire. The effort to accomplish this design coincided with Philip's desire to subject the Netherlands to a rigorous central government congruent with the manner in which he ruled Spain. The success of this ambition meant stripping the Netherlander nobles of their autonomy, imposing heavy taxation, and employing the Inquisition to destroy Protestantism. Since the king regarded religious uniformity as essential to the health of his empire, he suppressed nonconformity vigorously.

Philip's program for the Low Countries entailed installing Spanish officials in the Church and in the state and using troops to enforce their authority. The imposed changes provoked resistance from all who saw them as threats to their rights, and, at first, Protestant and Catholic nobles joined in opposing Spanish policy. Political and economic issues incited the opposition, but religion soon became a powerful influence that encouraged armed rebellion.

In 1559, Philip made Margaret of Parma regent of the Netherlands and Cardinal Antoine Perrenot de Granvelle president of the Council of State, and he ordered them to impose political union and religious uniformity. The

THE UNITED PROVINCES IN 1581

United Provinces

Archbishopric of Liège

North

Sea

GRONINGEN
• Groningen

FRIESLAND

DRENTHE

HOLLAND

Haarlem
• •Amsterdam

OVERYSSEL

Leiden
•

The Hague •

GELDERLAND

Rotterdam •

UTRECHT

ZEELAND

Rhine River

Breda •

BRABANT

Bruges •

•Antwerp

Spanish Inquisition was to accomplish the religious objective.

Spanish absolutism led some nobles to protest royal policy and to ask for toleration of religious diversity, but Philip responded with a declaration that he would enforce the decrees of the Council of Trent (1563) against alleged heretics. This inflamed Calvinists into action, and some sympathetic Catholics approved of the resistance. Persecution made the Protestants more zealous and increased conversions to their cause. Pastors of the Reformed Church evangelized boldly and urged the populace to defy Spain, and segments from all social classes joined the opposition. Philip reacted to riots by sending Fernando Álvarez de Toledo, the duke of Alva, to restore order by placing the country under military occupation and by systematic repression of dissenters (1567-1573). The initial success of Alva's policy led England to aid the

rebels, and Dutch pirates sailed from English ports and captured several coastal towns and blockaded others. Alva ordered the destruction of all Protestant literature and copies of the Scriptures, and he decreed death by decapitation for male heretics and burial alive for females. About eighteen hundred Protestants perished in three months. A shortage of men and money, however, prevented Alva from smashing the rebels, and Philip recalled him in 1573.

Early in the struggle against Spain, William the Silent became the leader of the Dutch rebels. Although reared in Roman Catholicism and once in the employ of Charles V, William became a Calvinist. Unlike most religious leaders of that era, however, he favored freedom of belief for everyone. Since Spanish forces were poorly financed, William urged the rebels to withhold taxes, and he became a reluctant leader of a war for independence. He defined his goal as being "to restore the entire fatherland in its old liberty and prosperity out of the clutches of the Spanish vultures." He had no desire to impose the Reformed faith on Dutch Catholics. The official condemnation of William accused him of advocating "liberty of conscience—which we hold to be nothing else but veritable confusion in religion." Philip II put a price on William's head, and a bounty hunter murdered him in 1584.

The early collaboration of the Catholics and Protestants did not endure. The barbarities of the Inquisition and the intolerance of many Calvinists allowed the Spaniards to exploit disagreements about religion. Alessandro Farnese, who became governor of the Netherlands in 1578, enticed the Walloons, Catholic noblemen in the southern provinces, to support Spain in return for a promise to respect their traditional liberties. Spanish-Walloon cooperation enabled Farnese to take Flanders and Brabant, and final victory was within reach when Philip II withdrew forces for war against France. The Scheldt River became the dividing line, and the seven provinces north of that river declared independence in 1581 as the United Provinces of the Netherlands. After 1590, Spain made no further energetic moves against the Dutch Republic, but formal recognition of its independence did not occur until 1648, in the Peace of Westphalia.

Once he was in firm control of the southern provinces, Farnese methodically destroyed the remnants of Protestantism there. In the Dutch republic, contrary to the hopes of William the Silent, the Calvinists who led the revolt after his death harshly suppressed Catholicism.

When the Dutch declared they had deposed Philip as their king, they made William the Silent temporary head of state until they could choose a new governor. William obtained French aid against Spain, and his son Maurice of Nassau succeeded him at the age of seventeen, while a Council of State directed the new nation. The provinces of Holland and Zeeland dominated the government and the representative body known as the States General. When French aid faltered, the Dutch appealed to Queen Elizabeth I of England in 1585. Unfortunately, the forces she sent under Robert Dudley, earl of Leicester, performed poorly, and the earl was an incompetent leader who returned to England in 1587. Young Maurice of Nassau then led the Dutch in expelling the Spaniards from the northern provinces. In 1598, King Henry IV of France, together with Elizabeth I, allied with the United Provinces, thereby extending formal recognition to the Dutch state. By 1609, Spain admitted it could not defeat the Dutch and therefore signed a truce with

them. Independence had been secured in everything but name.

The United Provinces consisted of Holland, Zeeland, Utrecht, Friesland, Groningen, Gelderland, and Overyssel, an ethnically homogeneous state, but one with a history of provincialism. Soon after securing their independence, the Dutch resumed their traditional ways, and assemblies in the provinces exerted decisive influence on the States General. The long war against Spain had strengthened the commercial economy, especially in Holland and Zeeland, as refugees from the south had brought their skills and money to invest. Successful seamanship enabled the Dutch to compete effectively with the Portuguese and Spaniards in overseas trade and colony planting. The Dutch East India Company, for example, was one of history's most profitable enterprises.

SIGNIFICANCE

It is a mistake to regard the Dutch struggle against Spain as a war of religion because political and economic factors were the first causes for resistance. Calvinism, nevertheless, provided a zeal for the defense of the Reformed faith, which infused the rebels with dynamic energy that sustained them throughout the war. Although the Dutch Reformed Church was the national religion, the republic soon relaxed the rigors of its posture toward other faiths, and the Netherlands became, perhaps, the freest, most tolerant nation in Europe, a political and economic success that made it the envy of other countries. Art and education flourished as consequences of prosperity, and, while many other nations experienced the demands of authoritarian government, genuine republicanism prevailed in the Netherlands.

—James Edward McGoldrick

FURTHER READING

Darby, Graham, ed. *The Origins and Development of the Dutch Revolt*. New York: Routledge, 2001. Anthology of scholarship on the causes and consequences Dutch rebellion against Spanish rule. Includes illustrations, maps, bibliographic references, and index.

Geyl, Pieter. *The Revolt of the Netherlands*. 2d ed. Reprint. London: Cassell, 1988. This thorough study emphasizes political and economic factors that provoked the revolt.

Koenigsberger, H. G. *Monarchies, States Generals, and Parliaments: The Netherlands in the Fifteenth and Sixteenth Centuries*. New York: Cambridge University Press, 2001. History of the States General of the Netherlands, its internal and external strife, and its di-

1580's

vision into the United Provinces and the Spanish Netherlands. Includes illustrations, maps, bibliographic refernces, index.

Motley, John Lothrop. *The Rise of the Dutch Republic*. 3 vols. 1855. Reprint. New York: E. P. Dutton, 1950. This reprint of the 1906 edition contains the most thorough study of the subject ever written; this classic of research and writing exaggerates the role of religion as a cause for the war against Spain.

Parker, Geoffrey. *The Dutch Revolt*. Rev. ed. New York: Penguin Books, 1985. An excellent narrative history with copious notes and a full bibliography.

Rowen, Herbert H., ed. *The Low Countries in Early Modern Times*. New York: Walker, 1972. A carefully selected and edited collection of primary documents from the period.

Swart, K. W. *William of Orange and the Revolt of the Netherlands, 1572-1584*. Translated by J. C. Grayson. Edited by R. P. Fagel, M. E. H. N. Mout, and H. F. K. van Nierop. Burlington, Vt.: Ashgate, 2003. A major and authoritative biography, with introductory essays and commentary by noted scholars of William's reign. Includes illustrations, maps, bibliographic references, and index.

Wedgwood, C. V. *William the Silent*. Reprint. New York: W. W. Norton, 1968. First published in 1944, this work present a vivid life of the Dutch hero written by a master biographer.

Wilson, Charles. *The Dutch Republic and the Civilization of the Seventeenth Century*. New York: McGraw-Hill, 1968. A readable account of the Netherlands' development in economics, politics, law, science, philosophy, and the arts made possible by the successful war for independence.

SEE ALSO: Aug. 17, 1477: Foundation of the Habsburg Dynasty; 1482-1492: Maximilian I Takes Control of the Low Countries; c. 1500: Netherlandish School of Painting; 16th century: Worldwide Inflation; Jan. 23, 1516: Charles I Ascends the Throne of Spain; June 28, 1519: Charles V Is Elected Holy Roman Emperor; 1531-1585: Antwerp Becomes the Commercial Capital of Europe; 1555-1556: Charles V Abdicates; 1558-1603: Reign of Elizabeth I; 1568-1648: Dutch Wars of Independence; July 31-Aug. 8, 1588: Defeat of the Spanish Armada.

RELATED ARTICLES in *Great Lives from History: The Renaissance & Early Modern Era, 1454-1600:* Duke of Alva; Charles V; Elizabeth I; Alessandro Farnese; Henry IV; Kenau Hasselaer; Earl of Leicester; Margaret of Austria; Margaret of Parma; Maximilian I; Johan van Oldenbarnevelt; Philip II; William the Silent.

1582
GREGORY XIII REFORMS THE CALENDAR

Pope Gregory XIII and his calendar reform commission were mandated to calculate the proper date of Easter, thus reaffirming the import of Catholicism in a Western Europe challenged by Protestantism. The reformed calendar, adopted as a human construct and not as a necessary truth, also acknowledged the imperfection of human knowledge.

LOCALE: Rome, Papal States (now in Italy)
CATEGORIES: Cultural and intellectual history; religion; science and technology; astronomy

KEY FIGURES
Gregory XIII (Ugo Buoncompagni; 1502-1585), Roman Catholic pope, 1572-1585, who commissioned and implemented the reform of the Julian calendar
Aloysius Lilius (1510-1576), author of a now-lost calendar reform proposal used as the basis for Gregory's calendar

Christopher Clavius (1537-1612), professor of mathematics, supported Lilius's reform proposal
Nicolaus Copernicus (1473-1543), astronomer and author of a treatise that addressed calendar reform

SUMMARY OF EVENT

The calendar in common use during the Renaissance in Europe was noticeably out of harmony with the true length of both the tropical year (the time it takes the earth to complete the seasonal cycle) and the sidereal year (the time it takes the earth to return to the exact point with respect to a fixed star in its orbit). This calendar, instituted by Julius Caesar in 46, counted an average of 365.25 days per tropical year (365 plus 1 every fourth or leap year). Since the true tropical year is only 365.2422 days long— or 11 minutes, 12 seconds shorter than that projected by the Julian calendar—the Julian dates had been falling behind the those of the sun.

That Julius's calendar was seriously flawed had been known for many centuries. Its deficiencies were of particular concern to the Christian Church, which depended on both the solar and lunar calendars for the celebration of Easter, its principal ecclesiastical feast. At the Council of Nicaea in 325, Easter had been established as the first Sunday after the first full moon after the vernal equinox; the vernal equinox was then assumed to fall on March 21. With each passing century, the date of the vernal equinox moved up about three quarters of a day (falling on March 11 by 1582), whereas the lunar calendar was mismatched with respect to the moon's real cycles by about four days in 1582. The simultaneous dependence on two faulty calendars caused the date of Easter to fall on inappropriate days (with respect to the Nicene Council's original intentions) because of the large discrepancy between the conventional date of March 21 for the vernal equinox used for the calculations and the real vernal equinox. Earlier attempts at calendar reform had foundered because of a lack of consensus on the part of scientists and the lack of interest on the part of heads of state.

Pope Gregory XIII took up the cause as a consequence of the final session of the Council of Trent (1563), during which Pope Pius IV (1559-1565) had given the mandate to reform the breviary. In Gregory's eyes, reforming the breviary implicitly required the revision of the solar and lunar calendars so that moveable feasts such as Easter could be calculated properly. Soon after his election, Gregory established a papal commission, composed mainly of clerics, to address the problem both scientifically and theologically. Important members included the Jesuit mathematician and astronomer, Christopher Clavius, and the sixteenth century Spanish historian, Pedro Chacón, both of whom authored important documents during and after the deliberations. Other members were the Dominican mathematician and cosmographer, Ignazio Danti (1537-1586), and scholar-cardinal, Gugliemo Sirleto (1514-1585), president of the commission, who was instrumental in pressing for a final consensus.

Aloysius Lilius's proposal was accepted by the commission. His solution was simple and easy to implement, and it was relatively accurate. Although the original goal of the commission had been to devise an error-free calendar that reflected the motions of the true tropical year—as opposed to hypothetical figures based on mean values, as had always been done—this idealistic goal was eventually abandoned. The astronomical data then available was recognized as being too inaccurate and, furthermore, there was no universally accepted model of planetary motion within which to locate that data. Nicolaus Coper-

nicus's monumental book *De revolutionibus orbium coelestium* (1543; *On the Revolutions of the Heavenly Spheres*, 1952; better known as *De revolutionibus*), which theorized that the earth revolved around the sun, was mined for its updated astronomical data, but his theory of planetary motion was considered one of the least appealing of the many competing models of the universe then in circulation.

Lilius's solution to the calendar problem sidestepped such existential questions and made no claims to total accuracy. By canceling the leap year on century years not divisible by 400, he eliminated three days every 400 years, resulting in an average year length of 365.2425. This calendar would take three thousand years to run a day ahead. With similar logic, the lunar calendar was to be reduced by one day every 300 years for seven such periods and then again one day was to be dropped after 400 years. These two reforms, applied to a year that began correctly, would guarantee an appropriate date for Easter for millennia.

Although Lilius died before the commission had made any official decisions, his manuscript served as the basis for Gregory's reform after a shortened version written by Chacón (known as the "Compendium") was sent to Catholic rulers for approval in 1578. Despite some concerns, criticisms, and counterproposals, the papal bull *Inter Gravissimas* was signed February 24, 1582. The new calendar was to go into effect that year. To compensate for the ten-day drift that had occurred since the time of the Council of Nicaea (325), Gregory suppressed ten days in the month of October so that October 15 followed October 4 in 1582. Some Catholic countries that abided by the reform chose to distribute the lost days in other ways.

The papal bull generated much controversy among both Catholics and Protestants. Clavius, commonly dubbed the "Euclid of the sixteenth century," was charged by Gregory to defend the new calendar and its Easter reckoning, which he did in a number of publications. In 1603, he published a lengthy definitive explanation of the reform entitled *Romani calendarii a Gregorio XIII P. M. restituti explicatio*. By then, all Catholic and some Protestant nations were following the Gregorian calendar, whereas most Protestant nations did not. It was not until the mid-eighteenth century that all major European powers were on Gregorian time, England being among the last to convert in 1752. The Eastern Orthodox Church enacted its own calendar reform in 1923.

SIGNIFICANCE

Pope Gregory XIII's momentous reform of the calendar was less scientific triumph than affirmation of Catholic tradition. Enacted on the heels of the final decrees of the Council of Trent, the Gregorian calendar commission adopted as its point of departure the original theological principles for the calculation of Easter put forward by the Council of Nicaea in 325. Sponsored by the Emperor Constantine to resolve doctrinal differences among the various Christian communities, this first ecumenical council was the spiritual predecessor of the Council of Trent and the origin of a unified Catholic doctrine. Linking calendar reform to the Nicene Council's original intentions thus amounted to reinforcing the historical relevance of the Catholic Church in a period when it was under intense pressure from Protestant factions.

The reform commission's ecclesiastical motivation, moreover, allowed it to push for reform expeditiously. Following Lilius's lead, the commission's recognition of humanity's imperfect ability to collect astronomical data and the incompleteness of its understanding of God's universe was an important milestone in the reform process: It made it permissible to back a simple, easy-to-implement calendar adjustment that was self-consciously a human construct rather than a perfect map or true reflection of celestial motion. Nevertheless, the reform that was adopted was remarkably accurate, given that the data available had been collected without the benefit of a telescope.

—*Maia Wellington Gahtan*

FURTHER READING

Archer, Peter. *The Christian Calendar and the Gregorian Reform.* New York: 1942. An overview of the theological and astronomical principles behind the calculation of the dates of Christian feast days, Easter in particular, and the effect this had on Gregory XIII's plans for calendar reform.

Coyne, G. V., M. A. Hoskin, and O. Pederson, eds. *Gregorian Reform of the Calendar: Proceedings of the Vatican Conference to Commemorate Its Four-Hundredth Anniversary, 1582-1982.* Vatican City: Specola Vaticana, 1983. A collection of essays on the scientific, technical, theological, and historical issues and outcomes surrounding Gregory's calendar reform, published by the Vatican in commemoration of the event. The most important book on this subject to date.

Duncan, David Ewig. *Calendar: Humanities Epic Struggle to Determine a True and Accurate Year.* New York: Avon Books, 1998. A lively and well-written general introduction to the calendar as a subject, with several chapters devoted to Gregory's reform.

Richards, E. G. *Mapping Time: The Calendar and Its History.* New York: Oxford University Press, 1998. A historical and comparative analysis of calendars used throughout the world, including a special section on the history of determining the date of Easter.

Swerdlow, J. "The Origin of the Gregorian Civil Calendar." *Journal for the History of Astronomy* 5 (1974). A succinct discussion of the issues facing the Gregorian calendar commission.

SEE ALSO: 1462: Regiomontanus Completes the *Epitome* of Ptolemy's *Almagest;* c. 1478-1519: Leonardo da Vinci Compiles His Notebooks; c. 1510: Invention of the Watch; 1543: Copernicus Publishes *De Revolutionibus;* 1545-1563: Council of Trent; 1572-1574: Tycho Brahe Observes a Supernova; 1580's-1590's: Galileo Conducts His Early Experiments; 1600: William Gilbert Publishes *De Magnete.*

RELATED ARTICLES in *Great Lives from History: The Renaissance & Early Modern Era, 1454-1600:* Nicolaus Copernicus; Gregory XIII; Pius IV.

July 21, 1582
BATTLE OF THE TOBOL RIVER

Russian mercenary captain Yermak Timofeyevich and his Cossacks, armed with firearms, faced Tatar khan Kuchum, whose forces had only bows. Yermak's defeat of Kuchum was the key battle in the Russian annexation of Siberia, because it allowed the Cossacks to seize the Tatars' capital before winter.

LOCALE: Tobol River, western Siberia (now in Russia)
CATEGORIES: Wars, uprisings, and civil unrest; expansion and land acquisition

KEY FIGURES

Yermak Timofeyevich (d. 1584/1585), Russian Cossack adventurer and mercenary captain
Kuchum (d. after 1598), Tatar khan of Sibir, r. 1556-1598
Ivan the Terrible (1530-1584), grand prince of Moscow, r. 1533-1584, and first Russian czar, r. 1547-1584

SUMMARY OF EVENT

In the fifteenth century, the Uzbek (Tatar) khans established themselves in the region between the headwaters of the Tobol River and the Tura River in western Siberia, forming the khanate of Sibir. These Turkic Mongols had split from the larger khanate of Kazan, which was the rump of the once-mighty Golden Horde.

In the mid-sixteenth century, Ivan the Terrible instituted his campaign of centralization and expansion of the Russian Empire. With the conquest of Kazan (1552) and Astrakhan (1556), Ivan brought the Russians well south and east of the Urals and to the doorstep of the Sibir khanate. In 1555, Yadigar, the khan of Sibir, submitted to Ivan as vassal and ally, arranging an annual tribute to Moscow. In 1563, the Shaybanid Uzbek warlord Kuchum fought and defeated Yadigar. Kuchum took the title of khan for himself and, like Yadigar, recognized Ivan's sovereignty. In 1571, however, he renounced and suspended his people's payment of tribute to Moscow. Kuchum had the Russian embassy who was sent to retrieve the tribute in 1572 murdered, clearly dissolving the vassalage relationship.

Through the 1570's, Russians and Tatars skirmished along the borderlands, while Russian blockhouses popped up in Tatar territory as points for trade and defense. In 1574, Ivan charged the Stroganov family with the defense of the vague and ill-defined eastern Ural border region. They were to utilize their own resources and reap whatever benefits they could—especially from the lucrative trade in furs. Ivan specifically charged them

with building defensive strongholds in Kuchum's territory, along the Tobol, Ob, and Irtysh Rivers. Around 1579, the Stroganovs hired the Cossack ataman (military leader) Yermak Timofeyevich. His army of Cossacks, Lithuanians, and Muscovite adventurers protected Russian interests and prevented further westward expansion by the Tatars into the Urals region, especially the disputed protectorate of Ostiak.

For his part, Kuchum had replaced the initially hostile Voghul and Ostiak tribal leaders with allies. Muscovite encroachment in search of silver, iron, and rich pastures led to brutal violence on both sides as Kuchum sought to protect his vassals. When one of these Voghul leaders, Begbely Agtakov, raided Stroganov holdings in the Kama River region, the Stroganovs struck back at the heart of the khanate.

Yermak's campaign is described in several chronicles, but at times these descriptions conflict, especially on important points of chronology. In addition, Yermak's fame as a popular hero spawned later embellishments on the story, some of which are clearly fictional, some of which are quite plausible. Of the various accounts extant, the Esipov Chronicle (1636) seems to provide the most trustworthy version of events.

According to that chronicle, on September 1, 1581, Yermak and 840 men—including 300 Livonian prisoners of war—gathered on the banks of the Kama River near Kankor. Well armed with guns, ammunition, and food, they set out on a journey to Sibir to confront Kuchum. They wintered in the Ural foothills and followed the Tura River into Siberia the following spring. Kuchum had ample warning of their approach and organized a formidable defense of Tatar warriors and a peasant levy of Votiaks and Voghuls under the command of his nephew Mahmet-kul. In May, 1582, a small Tatar force fought Yermak near the mouth of the Tobol River, but Russian harquebusiers easily defeated the bow-wielding horsemen.

Further along the river, at Babasany, Mahmet-kul set a trap for Yermak. On July 21, Tatar skirmishers drew the Russians on, but Yermak sensed the trap, and he sent a small flotilla of unmanned decoy boats into its teeth. Meanwhile, his men circled behind their enemies and struck mercilessly from their rear. With the river now suddenly at their backs instead of before them, Kuchum's men had no place to which to fall back. Moreover, the peasant fighters they had levied had neither the desire nor the necessary experience to weather Yermak's attack, and their Tatar commanders could not keep them in line. Kuchum's army was scattered.

In late October, Yermak confronted Kuchum himself at a palisade hastily erected by Kuchum's men at Chyu-vashevo, at the confluence of the Tobol and Irtysh Rivers. Yermak's victory there left open the way to the Tatar capital, Sibir (also known as Isker or Kashlyk), which Kuchum abandoned and Yermak seized on October 26. The city provided badly needed supplies of food, but the Russians required more men, ammunition, and weaponry, including artillery.

Yermak sent word both of his victories and of his needs to Moscow with Ivan Koltso. In May, 1583, Ivan the Terrible complied, adding numerous fur coats and two sets of beautifully wrought and decorated armor for Yermak. Meanwhile, according to the Esipov Chronicle,

> Yermak with his company displayed his valour through all the Siberian land, stepping out freely and fearing no man, for the fear of God was on all those living there, like a two-edged sword going before the face of the Russian army, mowing down and destroying and spreading terror. He took many strongholds and encampments on the River Irtysh, and on the great Ob they captured the stronghold of Nazim with its prince and with all its wealth.

SIGNIFICANCE

Reinforcements of Russian guardsmen, or *streltsy*, did arrive in November, 1584, under the leadership of S. D. Bolkhovsky, but they brought little food with them, and the whole lot suffered terribly in the following famine-struck winter. Despite heavy losses, Yermak remained in Siberia the following spring and summer. Kuchum, seeking once again to trap the Russians, let it be known that a rich caravan was moving through the area from Bukhara. Yermak moved to intercept it but was ambushed on August 6 along the Irtysh—some say Vagai—River and lost his life. One story has it that his force was spending the night on a river island, and the watch sought shelter in a summer rainstorm. The Tatars took advantage and attacked the camp. Yermak donned his new armor and drowned in the swollen river.

The loss of their leader prompted the Russian expedition to retreat to the Urals, and soon Kuchum was back in control of Sibir. Russians quickly returned under Ivan Mansurov, however, and Tiumen, the first Russian settlement in Siberia, appeared in 1586. The following year, Tobol'sk was built to serve as a center for Russian administration in the region. Kuchum continued to oppose the growing flood of Russians eastward, but was finally forced into exile in 1598 with the Nogai Horde, which saw to his execution shortly afterward.

In the short run, Yermak's campaign in Siberia was a failure: The Russians, despite their superiority in arms, fell prey to Tatar tactics and tenacity and abandoned the lands through which they had traveled. Their leader was dead, his story left as grist for the word mills of dozens of poets and story-tellers. In the longer run, however, the Russians were not to be denied their eastward expansion, and the expedition may be seen as an initial probing of the region. It uncovered many of the Tatars' weaknesses and undermined Kuchum's hold on the region: He was left to fight both Russians and predatory Tatars.

—*Joseph P. Byrne*

FURTHER READING

Armstrong, Terence E., ed. *Yermak's Campaign in Siberia: A Selection of Documents*. Translated by Tatiana Minorsky and David Wileman. London: Hakluyt Society, 1975. All of the major primary documentation from chronicles and Russian imperial letters for the campaign is included.

Bobrick, Benson. *East of the Sun: The Epic Conquest and Tragic History of Siberia*. New York: Poseidon Press, 1992. Very useful account of the campaign and subsequent history of the region under Russian control.

_____. *Fearful Majesty: The Life and Reign of Ivan the Terrible*. New York: G. P. Putnam's Sons, 1987. Sets the campaign and its results within the framework of Ivan's policies and plans for Russia.

Forsyth, James. *A History of the Peoples of Siberia: Russia's North Asian Colony, 1581-1990*. New York: Cambridge University Press, 1994. Comprehensive work on Siberian history that focuses on ethnicity as a factor in the initial conquest and its aftermath.

Vernadsky, George. *Russia at the Dawn of the Modern Age*. New Haven, Conn.: Yale University Press, 1959. Classic text on the situation surrounding the Siberian campaign.

SEE ALSO: 1480-1502: Destruction of the Golden Horde; After 1480: Ivan the Great Organizes the "Third Rome"; 1499-c. 1600: Russo-Polish Wars; Jan. 16, 1547: Coronation of Ivan the Terrible; 1556-1605: Reign of Akbar; 1581-1597: Cossacks Seize Sibir.

RELATED ARTICLE in *Great Lives from History: The Renaissance & Early Modern Era, 1454-1600:* Ivan the Terrible.

1583-1600
BRUNO'S THEORY OF THE INFINITE UNIVERSE

Giordano Bruno's books and papers described an endless, eternal universe governed by intrinsic laws that produced innumerable worlds. This model, both in its infinitude and its implicit displacement of Earth from the center of the cosmos, challenged the Catholic view of the world and ultimately led to Bruno's execution by the Inquisition.

LOCALE: England, France, Germany, and Italy
CATEGORIES: Astronomy; religion; cultural and intellectual history

KEY FIGURES

Giordano Bruno (1548-1600), Dominican priest, philosopher, and speculative cosmologist
Clement VIII (1536-1605), Roman Catholic pope, 1592-1605

SUMMARY OF EVENT

Giordano Bruno entered a Dominican monastery in Naples, Italy, in 1565. He was ordained priest in 1572 and earned a doctor of theology degree in 1575. Despite his Catholic background, however, Bruno developed a cosmological model antithetical to the teachings of the Church. He posited an unprecedented, systematic explanation of universal nature, which he published from 1583 to 1591. The Inquisition, Roman Catholic church courts in Europe designed to root out heresy, at that time under Clement VIII, declared Bruno a heretic and had him imprisoned in 1592. He refused to recant his position in prison and was finally burned at the stake on February 19, 1600.

From 1232, the Roman Catholic Church had used Inquisition courts to prosecute those who questioned its teachings, whether in matters of religion or science. The Church believed that religion and science, as forms or bodies of knowledge, worked together to reveal God's ways. In Bruno's lifetime, the Church feared challenges to its authority from the Protestant Reformation, an effort to return to the original teachings of Jesus Christ. The Reformation stressed the individual in matters of faith and revolted against medieval religious attitudes. The Reformation both compounded and was fueled by Renaissance cultural trends that emphasized human ability, potential, and versatility. These trends hastened the growth of science, in which direct observation of physical nature became more important than biblical testi-

mony and the claims of ancient and medieval writers and philosophers. Bruno's radical open-mindedness, knowledge of several fields, generalized curiosity, and soaring imagination typified both Reformation and Renaissance culture.

Already in 1575, the Dominican Order, whose members often served as judges on the Inquisition courts, had begun to suspect Bruno of censurable offenses. The order's priests believed he contested the Catholic Church's interpretative control over the Bible and enforcement of orthodoxy upon believers, as well as the full sufficiency of traditional knowledge, biblical or secular, to answer life's vast and final questions. In 1576, Bruno was excommunicated from the Catholic Church. The order charged him with doctrinal errors. Further, it charged him with denying the Church's view of the universe as a perfect spherical shape in which the planets and other celestial bodies, including the Sun, revolved around the Earth, thought to be the center of all things, a privileged place created by God solely for human beings.

Bruno rejected the closed, immutable model of the universe developed by the Church fathers and medieval theologians who had drawn upon the Bible, the Greek philosopher Aristotle (384-322 B.C.E.), and the Greco-Egyptian astronomer Ptolemy (c. 100-c. 178). He favored the views of several early Greek philosophers who described an open-ended, dynamic universe, including Anaximander (c. 610-547 B.C.E.), Anaxagoras (c. 500-c. 428 B.C.E.), and Heraclitus of Ephesus (c. 540-c. 480 B.C.E.). In addition, he was influenced by Lucretius (c. 98-55 B.C.E.), a Roman philosopher, whose poem *De rerum natura* (c. 60 B.C.E.; *On The Nature of Things*, 1682) had described a universe made up of atoms that had evolved out of a chaos of all possible laws and would forever remain in a state of change or flux governed by those natural laws. Bruno had also been influenced by Nicholas of Cusa (1401-1464), a Roman Catholic cardinal. In his book, *De docta ignorantia* (1440; *Of Learned Ignorance*, 1954), he depicted an eternal, limitless universe which represented a manifestation of God and in which the stars were other worlds.

Bruno, moreover, had access to new knowledge that his predecessors had not had. It provided him with new points of departure for philosophic and scientific speculation. In particular, Bruno had learned from Nicolaus Copernicus (1473-1543), the Polish astronomer who, in his treatise, *De revolutionibus orbium coelestium* (1543;

On the Revolutions of the Celestial Spheres, 1939; better known as *De revolutionibus*), had described the Sun as the center of all things, with Earth revolving around it.

For nearly sixteen years after his excommunication in 1575, having escaped from the Church's control, Bruno lived as an itinerant philosopher, teacher, and writer. He traveled throughout Europe in search of the freedom of thought and expression as well as the economic security necessary to develop, synthesize, and publish his ideas. He remained, however, a marked man, singled out as an object of suspicion.

In 1583, having arrived in England, Bruno started to write important cosmological works, including *La cena de le cereni* (1584; *The Ash Wednesday Supper*, 1975), *De la causa, principio et uno* (1584; on cause, prime origin, and the one), *De l'infinito et mondi* (1584; *On the Infinite Universe and Worlds*, 1950). After returning to the continent, prior to his arrest by the Inquisition, he published *De monade, numero et figura liber consequens quinque de minimo magno et mensura* (1591; on the monad, number, and form in one book: being a sequel to the five books on the great minimum and on measurement) and *De innumerabilibus immenso et infigurabili: sue de universo et mundis libri octo* (1591; on the innumerable, the immense, the formless: on the universe and worlds in eight books).

In these works, Bruno formulated a theory of everything, which linked physical nature on the smallest scale, the *minima*, with physical nature on the largest scale, the *maxima*. He described a boundless, eternal, all-pervading, interacting unity of space, time, matter, and energy or inherent momentum within matter. God united diverse natural phenomena. Settling Copernicus's work into what he regarded as the correct framework, Bruno argued that there was no margin, limit, center, surface, or absolute up or down in the universe; it extended infinitely in all directions. The universe contained numberless stars or suns around which revolve worlds or planets, likely inhabited by other intelligent beings shaped by physical conditions of their worlds. The universe contained finite bodies whose motion or rest could only be determined by comparing one body with another, and it would appear generally the same to an observer on any heavenly body.

Bruno thought the universe itself was immovable, but everything in it, its matter and energy, was in a state of continual motion and change that was irregular in rate and scale depending on local variables. Nevertheless, he believed that despite this incessant motion and change, physical nature—particles, bodies of matter, and energy—

followed laws or rules that made change or complexity possible. Universally valid constants, the result of God's universal intellect, underlay seen and unseen regularities of nature. Moreover, Bruno believed that after matter and energy formed bodies with particular shapes, living and non-living, there occurred a process of redistribution of matter and energy through decay or destruction which resulted in new or continuous creation or evolution. He apparently thought that after long periods of time the values of the universal constants changed and thus the outcomes changed, producing new patterns, systems, and differences without end.

SIGNIFICANCE

Bruno's cosmology—pioneering, comprehensive, and strikingly modern—might well place him among the founders of modern cosmology. In his time, however, it was the ultimate reason for his condemnation. He thought that a far greater diversity of life, of living forms and behavior of those forms, existed than any one expression of religion, including the Roman Catholic, or any one branch of science or knowledge could account for, explain, or describe. His cosmology, as well as his own life and death, indicated that all uniformity of thought, all censorship, must be rejected, that more and more wonderful questions and mysteries awaited discovery. The sheer scope of the universe was such that it must always remain imperfectly known, endlessly open.

Bruno influenced a number of important philosophers, scientists, and writers, including Baruch Spinoza (1632-1677), Gottfried Wilhelm Leibniz (1646-1716), Pierre Simon Laplace (1749-1827), Georg Wilhelm Friedrich Hegel (1770-1831), Samuel Taylor Coleridge (1772-1834), and Friedrich Wilhelm Joseph Schelling (1775-1854). Scholars continue to reveal Bruno's influence, since he was one of the first to set human action against its true background: the infinite.

—*Timothy C. Miller*

FURTHER READING

Gatti, Hilary. *Giordano Bruno and Renaissance Science*. Ithaca, N.Y.: Cornell University Press, 1998. Traces Bruno's contributions to the scientific thought and practice of the sixteenth and seventeenth century, including ways he used non-mathematical forms of inquiry and fostered changes in mental approach to problems.

Mendoza, Ramon G. *The Acentric Labyrinth: Giordano Bruno's Prelude to Contemporary Cosmology*. Rockport, Mass.: Element Books, 1995. An authoritative, comprehensive, and multifaceted study of Bruno's cosmological thought in the context of his own time and in the context of the twentieth century.

Singer, Dorothea Waley. *Giordano Bruno—His Life and Thought: With Annotated Translation of His Work, "On the Infinite Universe and Worlds."* Reprint. New York: Greenwood Press, 1968. Essential translation of Bruno's work combined with a superb introduction to it as well as to his diverse intellectual and literary abilities.

White, Michael. *The Pope and the Heretic*. New York: William Morrow, 2002. A narrative, biographical account of Bruno's confrontation of the Roman Catholic Inquisition, exploring his originality, insistent and en-thusiastic personality, and courage in the face of execution.

SEE ALSO: 1462: Regiomontanus Completes the *Epitome* of Ptolemy's *Almagest*; c. 1478-1519: Leonardo da Vinci Compiles His Notebooks; 1543: Copernicus Publishes *De Revolutionibus*; 1572-1574: Tycho Brahe Observes a Supernova; 1580's-1590's: Galileo Conducts His Early Experiments; 1582: Gregory XIII Reforms the Calendar; 1600: William Gilbert Publishes *De Magnete*.

RELATED ARTICLE in *Great Lives from History: The Renaissance & Early Modern Era, 1454-1600:* Giordano Bruno.

1583-1610
MATTEO RICCI TRAVELS TO BEIJING

Matteo Ricci established a successful missionary enterprise in Ming China as a result of Christian adaptation and assimilation of Chinese culture.

LOCALE: China
CATEGORIES: Exploration and discovery; religion

KEY FIGURES

Matteo Ricci (Li Madou, Li Ma-tou; 1552-1610), Jesuit scholar and missionary

Xu Guangqi (Hsü Kuang-ch'i, Paul Hsü; 1562-1633), Ricci's Chinese friend and collaborator, later a grand secretary at the Ming court

Li Zhizao (Li Chih-tsao, Leo Lee; 1565-1630), director of the Board of Public Works

Michele Ruggieri (1543-1607), Ricci's fellow Jesuit in Rome, Goa, and Kwantung

Alessandro Valignano (1539-1606), vicar-general of the Jesuit order in the Indies, including the Far East

Wanli (reign name, also Wan-li; personal name Zhu Yijun, Chu I-chün; posthumous name Zhu Yijun, Chu I-chün; temple name Shenzong, Shen-tsung; 1563-1620), the thirteenth Ming emperor, r. 1573-1620

Saint Francis Xavier (Francisco de Yasu y Javier; 1506-1552), Jesuit missionary in the Far East

SUMMARY OF EVENT

Matteo Ricci's China mission was part of the Jesuit evangelical enterprise in the Far East begun by Saint Francis Xavier, one of the first members of the Society of Jesus and its greatest missionary. Although Xavier's mission in the Far East was confined to Japan, he had seen the importance of a mission to the Middle Kingdom (China). His Chinese project failed to materialize because of his untimely death in 1552, but he shrewdly recognized the need for adaptation and assimilation of local cultures. He was also the first European to appreciate the importance of science and technology in making an impact on Asiatic societies.

The man who heeded Xavier's admonition and planned an effective method of penetrating China was the Italian Jesuit lawyer Alessandro Valignano, vicar-general of the Jesuit order in the Indies including the Far East, who visited Macao in 1577. He discarded traditional missionary exertions for conquest of soul and conversion of heathens and instead devised a strategy similar to that of Xavier for transforming China from within. He thus enjoined missionaries to learn the language, culture, and customs of the Chinese. He summoned two Italian priests, Michele Ruggieri and Matteo Ricci, to implement this policy and thus realize Xavier's dream.

Born in the papal state of Macerata in 1552, Matteo traveled to Rome in 1568 to study law and mathematics at the University of Rome but decided to enter the Sant' Andrea Jesuit novitiate in 1571. Nine months later, he took his vows and worked for a brief period in a Jesuit college in Florence. He returned to Rome in 1573 to study rhetoric, philosophy, and mathematics at the Collegio Romano. He opted for a missionary career, however, and was sent to Portugal in 1577, and from there to Goa, India, in 1578. At Goa, he studied theology at the College of St. Paul, where he also taught. He was ordained a priest at Cochin in July, 1580. In 1582, he was summoned to Macao, where Ruggieri had gone in 1579. The two missionaries settled at Kwantung (Chao-ch'ing) in 1583.

Their initial aim was not to win converts but to make Christianity accepted and respected in Chinese society. With a view to making themselves at home with the Chinese, they donned the garb of Buddhist *bonze* (monks), used the Buddhist title *ho-shang*, studied Chinese, learned Chinese culture, and became familiar with Confucianism. On realizing the people's respect for the educated, they deliberately presented themselves as scholars and scientists to their Chinese friends, with whom they also often discussed religion. Ricci established himself as a learned scholar of Chinese culture, maker of a world map, teacher of mathematics and astronomy, and only lastly as a Catholic missionary. Ruggieri wrote a book of catechism in Latin, which was translated into Chinese by Ricci and a Chinese scholar under the title *Tianzhu shiyi* (wr. 1579-1584, pb. 1603; *The True Meaning of the Lord in Heaven*, 1985).

After spending fifteen years at Kwantung and five years in Kiangsi (Nanchang) and Nanjing, and having befriended many influential Chinese scholars and mandarins, Ricci went to Beijing in 1601, seeking an imperial *imprimatur* to strengthen the cause of the missionaries. To this end, Ruggieri, whose expertise in Chinese was far from adequate and who had gotten himself into trouble with the Chinese, had been dispatched by Valignano to Europe in 1588 to solicit an embassy from the pope. Ruggieri's papal mission came to naught and he never returned to China, having retired to Salerno in Naples.

Ricci's stay in Beijing was eased by the tributes he had brought for the Wanli emperor: paintings of the Madonna, the Blessed Mother with the infant Jesus and John the Baptist, a Roman breviary, a reliquary in the form of a cross, a spinet, two clocks, and a mappamundi. He soon obtained from the emperor a job of looking after the clocks in exchange for lodging and a small stipend. For the rest of his short life, Ricci never ventured outside Beijing. In collaboration with his closest friend, Xu Guangqi, he translated several mathematical books, brought out new editions of his mappamundi, and, during the last two years of his life (1608-1610), wrote a history of his China mission, *Della entrata della Compagnia di Giesù e Christianità nella Cina* (1609; history of the expedition of the Company of Jesus to China). His proselytizing work was slow in Beijing—there being no mass conversions—but his scholarly output was enormous. Utterly fatigued and exhausted by overwork, Ricci died

on May 11, 1610. He was buried in Beijing, but on April 22 the next year, his body was taken outside the city walls to Chala and buried there on November 1. The funerary inscriptions composed for him by the governor of Beijing described the missionary as one who "loved righteousness and wrote books."

SIGNIFICANCE

Ricci's missionary strategy was predicated on Valignano's prescription of "patience, prudence, and a measured approach." His method of pacific penetration, cultural adaptation, and accommodation won for him friends and admirers, among whom were many dignitaries such as Xu Guangqi, who would become a grand secretary after Ricci's death, and Li Zhizhao, director of the Board of Public Works. The latter collaborated closely with Ricci in writing numerous scientific essays.

Realizing that Confucian culture was too entrenched to be displaced by Christianity and convinced of the efficacy of Confucian ethical principles, Ricci became a convert to the ideas of the classical master before trying to convert the Chinese to Christianity. He sincerely believed that Confucian principles of filial piety, reciprocity, and personal virtue could and must be accommodated in the universal church of Christ. Ricci interpreted references to *shangdi* (lord-on-high) and *tian* (loosely meaning heaven) in the Confucian classics as proof that the Chinese did worship God in ancient times. It was only during the regime of the Ming that the original Confucian teachings were subverted by the Neo-Confucians such as Cheng Zhu (Ch'eng Chu), who debunked the idea of a personal God but emphasized *Li* as the Supreme Ultimate that created the universe with whom human beings could become one.

Moreover, he was aware that the Chinese, who prized moral principles above everything else, could never be persuaded to accept Christianity merely as a faith-system promising a rewarding afterlife. Therefore, it was imperative that Christian teachings be presented as ethical principles like Confucianism. In his *De amicitia jiaoyoulun* (1595; treatise on friendship), Ricci articulated the conjunction between the Confucian Three Bonds and Five Cardinal Relations and Christianity. He saw that the Confucian *jen* (humanity) had been largely forgotten or debased in the Ming period. As a corrective and also to improve upon the universal appeal of Confucian morality, he equated the Christian principle of love of God with the Confucian canon of love for humanity. Although he was an avid admirer of Confucius (as could be seen in essays such as "The Twenty-five Words," 1605, and "The

Ten Paradoxes," 1608), Ricci never deviated from the quintessential Christian doctrines. He indeed was a creative syncretist who envisioned an amalgam of the best in the West and the best of the East—Christian love and Confucian *jen*.

—*Narasingha P. Sil*

FURTHER READING

Boxer, Charles R. "Jesuits at the Court of Peking." *History Today*, September, 1957: 582-590. A straightforward account written in popular style by an eminent scholar.

Criveller, Gianni. *Preaching Christ in Late Ming China: The Jesuits' Presentation of Christ from Matteo Ricci to Giulio Aleni*. Taipei, Taiwan: Taipei Ricci Institute, 1997. Study of Ricci's missionary work in China, his understanding of Christianity, and his transmission of that understanding to the Chinese. Includes bibliographic references.

Cronin, Vincent. *The Wise Man from the West*. Reprint. London: Harvill Press, 1999. Covers Ricci's early years in Rome, his ordination in India, his disheartening bid for acceptance among the Ming Dynasty elite, his subsequent successes as a scholar in astronomy and mathematics, his many converts to Christianity, and his role in bringing the reclusive China into the modern world.

Dunne, George. *Generation of Giants*. Notre Dame, Ind.: University of Notre Dame Press, 1962. Well-written account. Pages 23 through 108 will be of particular interest to readers interested in Ricci.

Gallagher, Louis J. *China in the Sixteenth Century: The Journals of Matteo Ricci, 1583-1610*. New York: Random House, 1953. An English translation of the Latin version of Ricci's diary by the Belgian Jesuit Nicolas Trigault published in Augsburg in 1615.

Gernet, Jacques. *A History of Chinese Civilization*. Translated by J. R. Foster and Charles Hartman. New York: Cambridge University Press, 1996. Examines the historical evolution of the Chinese world from early nomadic antiquity through the unification of China during the medieval area, the great upsurge of Buddhism, and the Mandarin and Mongol influence leading to Ricci's arrival. Also discusses Ricci's and other Catholic missionaries' influence and places Ricci and his work in historical perspective.

Harris, George L. "The Mission of Matteo Ricci, S.J.: A Case Study of an Effort at Guided Culture Change in China in the Sixteenth Century." *Monumenta Serica* 25 (1966): 1-168. A long article attempting a comprehensive study of Ricci's China mission.

Marsden, George. "Matteo Ricci and the Prodigal Culture." In *A Catholic Modernity? Charles Taylor's Mirianist Award Lecture*, edited by James L. Heft. New York: Oxford University Press, 1999. A discussion of Ricci in response to a lecture on the relationship between Catholicism and modernity. Includes bibliographic references and index.

Spence, Jonathan D. *The Search for Modern China*. Reprint. New York: W. W. Norton, 2001. Written in an informative, but not overly scholarly style. Covers Chinese history beginning with the sixteenth century Ming Dynasty, when Ricci made his influential mark on China. Contains more than two hundred illustrations, including maps.

Young, John D. *East-West Synthesis: Matteo Ricci and Confucianism*. Hong Kong: The University Press, 1980. Succinct and brilliant analysis of Ricci's intellectual alignment of Confucian and Christian morality.

SEE ALSO: 1514-1598: Portuguese Reach China; Aug. 15, 1534: Founding of the Jesuit Order; 1583-1610: Matteo Ricci Travels to Beijing.

RELATED ARTICLES in *Great Lives from History: The Renaissance & Early Modern Era, 1454-1600:* Gregory XIII; Matteo Ricci.

1584-1613
RUSSIA'S TIME OF TROUBLES

The death of Russian czar Ivan the Terrible ushered in a thirty-year period of dynastic confusion, foreign invasion, natural disasters, and social revolt that would end in 1613 with the establishment of the Romanov Dynasty.

LOCALE: Russia

CATEGORIES: Government and politics; wars, uprisings, and civil unrest; natural disasters

KEY FIGURES

Ivan the Terrible (1530-1584), grand prince of Moscow, r. 1533-1547, and czar of Russia, r. 1547-1584

Prince Dmitry Ivanovich (d. 1591), murdered son of Ivan IV

Fyodor I (1557-1598), czar of Russia, r. 1584-1598

Boris Godunov (c. 1551-1605), czar of Russia, r. 1598-1605

Vasily Shuysky (1552-1612), czar of Russia, r. 1606-1610

Michael Romanov (1596-1645), czar of Russia as Michael, r. 1613-1645

Grigory Otrepyev (d. 1606), the first False Dmitry, 1605-1606

Sigismund III Vasa (1566-1632), king of Poland, r. 1587-1632

Ivan Bolotnikov (d. 1610), leader of a peasant-Cossack rebellion

SUMMARY OF EVENT

The death of Czar Ivan the Terrible in 1584 inaugurated a period in Russian history known to historians as the Time of Troubles. The troubles included dynastic confusion, with five major and with many minor pretenders contesting for the throne of Russia. During the period, the boyars (the old Russian aristocracy) attempted to force the various pretenders to return the property and political rights the boyars had surrendered during Ivan's reign. The troubles of this period also included widespread famine and epidemic diseases, which together killed many hundreds of thousands of Russians. The hard times prodded many peasants and Cossacks to attempt to overthrow the oppressive social, political, and religious system established by previous Russian rulers. Attempting to take advantage of Russian weakness, moreover, the Polish and Swedish kings invaded the Russian empire during the period, further exacerbating the troubles and adding to the misery of the Russian people. The troubles finally abated with the establishment of the Romanov Dynasty in 1613.

Ivan the Terrible died in 1584, leaving two heirs, Fyodor and Dmitry. By most reports, Fyodor suffered from weak-mindedness, while Dmitry was only a child. The most powerful aristocrat in Russia, Boris Godunov, dominated the incompetent Fyodor and made him czar. Evidence suggests that Godunov was responsible for the murder of the younger Dmitry. Godunov arranged for his daughter to marry Fyodor, and he ruled Russia from behind the throne for the remainder of Fyodor's life. Fyodor died childless in 1598, leaving Russia without a legitimate heir to the throne. The Rurik Dynasty, which had ruled in Russia for more than seven hundred years, was over. Godunov arranged a convention of delegates from all regions of the empire and all social classes of Russian society, which elected him czar in 1598.

By most reports, Godunov reigned benignly and successfully for three years, despite the opposition of many of the boyars, who opposed him because he refused to restore the ancient privileges that Ivan the Terrible had taken from them. In 1601, the Russians experienced the first of three successive years of drought and famine, accompanied by a devastating disease (probably cholera) that decimated the population in both the cities and the countryside. More than 100,000 died in Moscow alone. Russians ate dogs, cats, tree bark, and grass (and, some reports say, each other) in their desperation. In the countryside, bands of brigands and robbers added to the plight of the people. The rumor spread—aided by the boyars—that God was punishing the Russian people with these calamities because they allowed a false czar to rule the country.

In 1604, an adventurer named Grigory Otrepyev began to gather a large following among the suffering Russian people by claiming that he was Ivan the Terrible's son Dmitry and had escaped the attempt by Godunov to murder him. Many Boyars supported this first False Dmitry, hoping to depose Godunov and regain their lost privileges. The Russian people flocked to his banner, believing him to be the true czar who would remove God's curse from them. King Sigismund III Vasa of Poland supported Otrepyev with money and troops, hoping thereby to profit territorially from the confusion in Russia. For the next year, civil war added to the woes of the Russian people.

SIGNIFICANCE

Boris Godunov died in 1605, just as his forces seemed to be winning the civil war. The first False Dmitry, confirmed (apparently under duress) by the mother of the real Dmitry as her true son, became czar. He immediately married a Polish noblewoman and elevated many Catholic Poles to high positions in the Russian court, government, and army. The boyars rebelled against Otrepyev, and civil war once more tortured the land, this time with large contingents of Polish troops occupying much of western Russia and claiming it for Sigismund III Vasa.

Despite the Polish army, the boyars defeated Otrepyev's forces and captured him in 1606. The boyars executed the pretender, burned his corpse, and shot his ashes toward Poland from a huge cannon as a warning to Sigismund. The boyars then elected one of their leaders, Vasily Shuysky, as the new czar. Shuysky signed a document prepared by the boyars restoring the privileges they had lost during the reign of Ivan the Terrible. Shuysky and the boyars did nothing to alleviate the plight of the Russian people and soon faced a huge peasant rebellion led by a Don Cossack named Ivan Bolotnikov. Bolotnikov and his followers wanted to overthrow the entire Russian social system dominated by nobles and leaders of the Russian Orthodox Church.

As Bolotnikov's army approached Moscow, another adventurer appeared in Poland claiming to be Dmitry. The true identity of this second False Dmitry remains unknown, but Sigismund supported him with money and troops, and the real Dmitry's mother and the Polish wife of Otrepyev, the first pretender, identified him as the legitimate czar. The second pretender failed to capture Moscow but set up a court in the nearby town of Tushino and proceeded to collect taxes and decree laws as though he were the czar. With his throne challenged from two directions, Shuysky concluded an agreement with the king of Sweden ceding much of northern Russia to the Swedes in return for their help against Bolotnikov, the second False Dmitry, and the Poles. Many of Shuysky's boyar supporters abandoned him when he concluded the alliance with the Swedes. The boyars signed a pact with Sigismund whereby his son Władysław would become czar in place of Shuysky. In return for their support, the boyars gained Sigismund's assurance that their privileges would be preserved and that Polish troops would aid in expelling the Swedes and suppressing the peasant rebellion.

In 1610, Russia had three major pretenders to the throne and a host of minor pretenders in the armies of Bolotnikov and other peasant and Cossack leaders. Civil war and anarchy raged throughout the empire, threatening everyone's life and property. The Swedes occupied most of northwestern Russia, while the Poles held most of the west and southwest. The Time of Troubles seems an appropriate description of the agonies suffered by the Russian people.

In the summer of 1610, the nonaristocratic landowning gentry of Russia began raising a national army with the help of minor functionaries of the Russian Orthodox Church. Their goals included the restoration of order, the expulsion of foreign armies, and the establishment of a stable monarchy. The boyars aided the cause of these nationalists by forcing Shuysky to abdicate, thus removing one pretender to the throne. Władysław's forces captured and executed Bolotnikov shortly thereafter, and the peasant-Cossack rebellion began to collapse. In December of 1610, one of the second False Dmitry's followers murdered him, eliminating another obstacle to a unified crown. Over the next two years, the nationalist armies defeated the Poles and Swedes, whereupon the gentry convened a new national assembly, which chose Michael Romanov as the new czar, establishing a dynasty that lasted until 1917. With Czar Michael's coronation on July 24, 1613, the Time of Troubles ended.

—Paul Madden

FURTHER READING

Avrich, Peter. *Russian Rebels, 1600-1800*. New York: Macmillan, 1972. Account of four major rebellions in Russia, including that of Bolotnikov. Avrich outlines the continuity of goals and heroes between Bolotnikov's rebellion during the Time of Troubles and subsequent rebellions.

Dunning, Chester S. L. *Russia's First Civil War: The Time of Troubles and the Founding of the Romanov Dynasty*. University Park: Pennsylvania State University Press, 2001. Massive volume covering the Time of Troubles. Provides post-Marxist analysis of the civil uprisings, claiming that they were struggles between factions of equal rank, rather than initial attempts by serfs to win their freedom. Includes illustrations, maps, bibliographic references, and index.

Pavlov, Andrei, and Maureen Perrie. *Ivan the Terrible*. London: Pearson/Longman, 2003. Major reassessment of Ivan's reign seeks to do away with the stereotypes of Cold War-era historians and achieve a balanced and accurate appraisal of Ivan as neither an evil genius nor a wise and benevolent statesman. Argues that Ivan's campaign of terror was motivated not merely by personal sadism but by a belief in the divine

1580's

right of the monarch to punish treason on earth in a manner as extreme as the punishments of Hell. Includes maps, genealogical tables, bibliographic references, index.

Payne, Robert, and Nikita Romanoff. *Ivan the Terrible.* New York: Caps, 1975. An account of the antecedents of the Time of Troubles written for a popular audience. Recounts Godunov's rise to prominence and Ivan's suppression of the boyars.

Perrie, Maureen. *Pretenders and Popular Monarchism in Early Modern Russia: The False Tsars of the Time of Troubles.* New York: Cambridge University Press, 1995. Study of the claims of the imposters to the throne during the Time of Troubles, and the reactions of the populace to their claims. Includes illustrations, maps, bibliographic references, and index.

Platonov, Sergei Feodorovich. *Boris Godunov, Tsar of Russia.* Gulf Breeze, Fla.: Academic International Press, 1973. Sympathetic account of the life and times of Godunov written by Russia's leading authority on the subject. Follows Godunov's career from his elevation to aristocratic rank under Ivan the Terrible to his death in 1605.

_____. *The Time of Troubles: A Historical Study of the Internal Crisis and Social Struggle in Sixteenth- and Seventeenth-Century Muscovy.* Translated by James Alexander. Lawrence: University Press of Kansas,

1970. The first book-length treatment of the subject in English. Written for a scholarly audience, based almost entirely on primary sources.

Shulman, Sol. *Kings of the Kremlin: Russia and Its Leaders from Ivan the Terrible to Boris Yeltsin.* London: Brassey's, 2002. Ivan IV is the first of the major Russian leaders profiled in this history of the Kremlin. Includes photographic plates, illustrations, bibliographic references, and index.

Vernadsky, G. *The Tsardom of Moscow, 1547-1682.* Vol. 5 in *A History of Russia.* New Haven, Conn.: Yale University Press, 1959. General history of Russia from the beginning of Ivan IV's reign to the death of Czar Alexis in 1683. Includes an excellent account of the Time of Troubles. Written for a scholarly audience.

SEE ALSO: After 1480: Ivan the Great Organizes the "Third Rome"; 1499-c. 1600: Russo-Polish Wars; Jan. 16, 1547: Coronation of Ivan the Terrible; Summer, 1556: Ivan the Terrible Annexes Astrakhan; c. 1568-1571: Ottoman-Russian War; 1581-1597: Cossacks Seize Sibir; 1589: Russian Patriarchate Is Established.

RELATED ARTICLES in *Great Lives from History: The Renaissance & Early Modern Era, 1454-1600:* Boris Godunov; Ivan the Terrible.

July 4, 1584-1590
LOST COLONY OF ROANOKE

The first British attempt to colonize North America ended in mystery after the first colony's settlers disappeared. The colonists had been plagued by a lack of supplies, an inability to obtain food from the land, internal conflict, little interest in local custom, and a preoccupation with gold.

LOCALE: Roanoke Island, Virginia
CATEGORIES: Exploration and discovery; expansion and land acquisition; colonization

KEY FIGURES
Philip Amadas (b. 1565?) and
Arthur Barlowe (1550?-1620?), captains of the 1584 expedition
Richard Grenville (1542-1591), commander of the 1585 expedition
Ralph Lane (1530?-1603), governor of the 1585 colony

Pemisapan (Wingina; d. 1586), chief of the Roanoc tribe
Sir Walter Ralegh (c. 1552-1618), sponsor of the expeditions
Thomas Harriot (1560-1621), astronomer, mathematician, and scientist
John White (fl. 1585-1593), artist and governor of the 1587 colony

SUMMARY OF EVENT
During the reign of Queen Elizabeth I, England experienced prosperity, and mariners were interested in establishing colonies in the Americas. On March 25, 1584, Elizabeth issued to mariner Walter Ralegh a charter to discover and occupy lands in North America that were not held by Christians. In April, two ships, captained by Philip Amadas and Arthur Barlowe, left England on a re-

connaissance expedition and on July 4 arrived off the coast of the Outer Banks.

On the third day after their arrival, the two English captains had their first encounter with a member of the Roanoc tribe. He was Granganimeo, brother of the chief, Wingina (Pemisapan). After delivering a welcoming speech to the captains, he was taken aboard their ships for a tour and given presents.

For several days, Granganimeo and other members of his tribe visited the English on their ships and received more gifts. These meetings led to a period of extended trade between the two groups. Granganimeo and his family dined with the English on their ships. After developing a trusting relationship, Captain Barlowe and seven sailors went to the Roanoc's village, where they received a cheerful and friendly welcome. Barlowe described his hosts as kind and loving. After six weeks of exploration and trade, the English carried back favorable reports and two Roanocs, Manteo and Wanchese. Staying at Ralegh's estate, Manteo and Wanchese learned English from Thomas Harriot.

On January 6, 1585, when Ralegh was knighted by the queen, he called the land Virginia in her honor and made plans for a permanent settlement. The second expedition of approximately six hundred men left Plymouth, England, on April 9, with seven ships under the command of Richard Grenville. With Manteo and Wanchese, they arrived at Ocracoke Inlet on June 26. Ralph Lane served as governor. They reached Roanoke Island, constructed Fort Ralegh, and built small houses.

Early Roanoke colonist Thomas Harriot, an astronomer, mathematician, and scientist, recorded detailed observations of the Roanoc tribe and its land. (Hulton|Archive by Getty Images)

After two months of careful exploration, Grenville returned to England with detailed maps. Left with 107 men, Lane spent nearly a year organizing numerous exploratory expeditions that gathered information about the country, its resources, and the American Indians. John White painted many pictures of the surroundings and the inhabitants. Harriot made a lengthy report on the area.

Having arrived too late to plant crops, Lane expected a shipment of supplies from Grenville to arrive before winter. Winter passed with no supplies, however. In addition, Lane's colony was plagued by internal rivalries, a preoccupation with gold, and a pathetic inability to find food in an abundant region. Efforts to grow sugarcane, wheat, oranges, and lemons failed. Therefore, Lane established a close relationship with Wingina and his people. Harriot learned about local products, including grass silk, worm silk, flax, and hemp. The Roanocs constructed fish weirs for the English, taught them the medicinal properties of local herbs, and demonstrated how to extract flour from chestnuts.

In return, the colonists demonstrated such advanced goods as iron weapons of war, the compass, and spring clocks. Because the workings of such items exceeded the comprehension and technologies of the American Indians, they thought they were the works of gods rather than of humans.

Lane's men had little interest in learning the ways of the Roanocs. They were more interested in the hints of pearl fisheries farther to the north and of gold to the west.

In March, 1586, Lane dispatched an expedition north to find the pearl fisheries, while he took another group to look for gold in the western mountains. Each evening, they stopped at a different indigenous village. They stopped at Choanoke on the Chowan River, where Chief Menatonon of the Chawonoac Kingdom lived. Impressed with the chief's knowledge of the surrounding area and wanting to learn more, Lane took the chief as prisoner on his expedition. To ensure Menatonon's cooperation, Lane took the chief's son, Skiko, prisoner and sent him to Roanoke Island. Menatonon was then released, and Lane took a group of thirty men to sail up the Roanoke River looking for gold.

Lane assumed that members of the Moratuck and Mangoak tribes would provide him with the necessary supplies along the way. The indigenous were forewarned that the English were conquerors; therefore, Lane found their villages abandoned and stripped clean. With little food, Lane and his men decided to return to Roanoke Island. On the way back, they were attacked by American Indians who were dispersed by Lane's men.

When they reached Roanoke Island in April, Grenville had not arrived, and Wingina, who had changed his name to Pemisapan, had heard of Lane's activities. After his initial request for the release of Skiko was denied, Menatonon sent a large delegation to Lane seeking his son's release in exchange for his loyalty to the English crown.

This shattered Pemisapan's hopes for a unified action against Lane. With the support of Wanchese, he united the different tribes, including the Chanoacs, Moratucks, and Mangoaks, in a conspiracy to destroy the conquerors. Instead, Lane, Harriot, and some soldiers made a preventive attack on Pemisapan's village and killed him and other tribe members.

In June, Francis Drake checked on the colonists. Turning down an offer of supplies, Lane persuaded Drake to take his colony and Manteo back to England. They left in such a rush that Lane left behind an exploratory party.

Immediately afterward, Grenville arrived with the anticipated supplies. Finding the colony gone, he left fifteen men with supplies for two years, but they would not be heard from again. Had Lane waited a little longer, he would have succeeded in establishing England's first permanent American colony. Instead, he demonstrated that the land was hospitable for the English.

Ralegh sent another expedition to Roanoke in May, 1587, under the command of John White. This group of 110 was to pick up the men left by Lane and Grenville and to establish the city of Raleigh on the Chesapeake Bay. However, the pilot, Simon Fernandez, refused to take them farther than Roanoke Island. When White's party reached Fort Ralegh, they learned from the evidence at the site and from friendly indigenous peoples that the men left by Grenville had been murdered by indigenous from the mainland. The houses left by Lane were repaired and new ones were built. Manteo, who had returned with White, was baptized and made Lord of Roanoke.

Like the Lane colony, the White colony discovered it had arrived too late to plant crops. Having inadequate supplies and receiving little help from the American Indians, White was encouraged to return home for supplies. He left his daughter and newborn granddaughter, Virginia Dare, the first child born of English parents in North America, with the colonists and set sail. Because England was involved in a war with Spain, White could not return to Roanoke Island immediately. After Spain was defeated, White set sail for Roanoke in 1590.

SIGNIFICANCE

Upon arriving, he found no one, only a stake in the ground with the word "Croatoan" written or carved on it. White assumed his colony had migrated southward to Croatoan Island, south of Cape Hatteras and the birthplace of Manteo. The following day, White set sail for Croatoan Island. A storm developed that pushed his ship into the North Atlantic and did such severe damage that he had to return to England for repairs.

By this time, Ralegh and England had lost interest in building colonies and were concentrating on raiding Spanish vessels directly from England. It was not until the expeditions of the first decade of the 1600's, and the 1607 founding of the Jamestown Colony, that the English expressed the desire to return to North America as settlers.

—Bill Manikas

FURTHER READING

Hunter, John L. *Backgrounds and Preparations for the Roanoke Voyages, 1584-1590*. Raleigh: North Carolina Department of Cultural Resources, 1986. Includes chapters on the personnel, ships, food and supplies, and financing of the expeditions.

Loades, David. *England's Maritime Empire: Seapower, Commerce, and Policy, 1490-1690*. New York: Longman, 2000. Study of the development of England into a colonial power. Places the settlement of Virginia within the larger context of England's imperial project.

Miller, Lee. *Roanoke: Solving the Mystery of the Lost Colony*. New York: Penguin Books, 2002. An iconoclastic work that takes a radically different view, arguing that Lane was paranoid and becoming mentally ill and that Pemisapan's plot was nonexistent.

Miller, Shannon. *Invested with Meaning: The Ralegh Circle in the New World*. Philadelphia: University of Pennsylvania Press, 1998. Study of the failed New World colonies attempted by Ralegh and his circle. Explains the links between these projects and changes in England's economy and social structure.

Quinn, David B. *The Lost Colonists, Their Fortune and Probable Fate*. Raleigh: North Carolina Department of Cultural Resources, 1984. The first five chapters describe the setting, the relations with American Indians, and the problems among the colonists.

Rountree, Helen C., and E. Randolph Turner, III. *Before and After Jamestown: Virginia's Powhatans and Their Predecessors*. Gainesville: University of Florida Press, 2002. In the absence of substantial material on the Outer Banks Algonkians, this detailed account of a similar, neighboring society is highly useful.

Sinclair, Andrew. *Sir Walter Raleigh and the Age of Discovery*. New York: Penguin Books, 1984. The first three chapters explain the interest and attempts by the queen and Raleigh to establish colonies in the New World.

Stick, David. *Roanoke Island: The Beginnings of English America*. Chapel Hill: University of North Carolina Press, 1983. A detailed description of each expedition and the geography, the indigenous peoples, and principals involved.

Trevelyan, Raleigh. *Sir Walter Raleigh*. New York: H. Holt, 2004. Exhaustive biography of Ralegh, written by a direct descendant.

SEE ALSO: Oct. 12, 1492: Columbus Lands in the Americas; 1493-1521: Ponce de León's Voyages; May 28, 1539-Sept. 10, 1543: De Soto's North American Expedition; Sept., 1565: St. Augustine Is Founded; Mid-1570's: Powhatan Confederacy Is Founded; Sept. 14, 1585-July 27, 1586: Drake's Expedition to the West Indies.

RELATED ARTICLES in *Great Lives from History: The Renaissance & Early Modern Era, 1454-1600*: Sir Francis Drake; Elizabeth I; Sir Richard Grenville; Pedro Menéndez de Avilés; Pemisapan; Sir Walter Ralegh; Hernando de Soto; Tascalusa.

July 7, 1585-December 23, 1588
WAR OF THE THREE HENRYS

The War of the Three Henrys represented an important turning point in the broader French Wars of Religion. When it was over, the royal authority of King Henry III had been thoroughly questioned, the powerful leader of the Catholic League was dead, and the Protestant Henry of Navarre was positioned to become the next king of France.

LOCALE: France

CATEGORIES: Wars, uprisings, and civil unrest; religion; government and politics

KEY FIGURES

Henry III (1551-1589), the last Valois king of France, r. 1574-1589

Henry I of Lorraine, duke of Guise (1550-1588), third duke of Guise, 1563-1588, and leader of the Catholic League, 1585-1588

Henry of Navarre (1553-1610), king of Navarre as Henry III, r. 1572-1589, and king of France as Henry IV, r. 1589-1610

Catherine de Médicis (1519-1589), queen of France, r. 1547-1559, regent, r. 1560-1563, and queen mother, 1563-1589

François (1554-1584), duke of Alençon, 1566-1574, duke of Anjou, 1574-1584, and youngest son of Henry II and Catherine de Médicis

Philip II (1527-1598), king of Spain, r. 1556-1598, who gave financial and military support to the Catholic League

SUMMARY OF EVENT

France fought a series of religious civil wars between 1562 and 1598. Arguably the climactic war of the series was the War of the Three Henrys (1585-1588), which inaugurated the conflict known as the War of the Catholic League (1585-1598). The War of the Three Henrys was fought between the factions and armies of three political leaders: Henry III, king of France; Henry I of Lorraine, duke of Guise, head of a Catholic alliance of nobles and cities called the Catholic League; and Henry of Navarre, head of the Protestants in France, who were known as the Huguenots. The War of the Three Henrys brought France into the bloodiest and most extreme period of collective violence experienced during the religious wars. Both Henry I of Lorraine and Henry III lost their lives in 1588-1589, while Henry of Navarre emerged victorious as King Henry IV.

Circumstances leading to the War of the Three Henrys became critical in June of 1584, when Henry III's youngest brother, François, duke of Anjou, died unexpectedly with no heir. The last Valois king, Henry III was also childless, and a crisis of succession ensued. Succession questions in France were dictated by the Salic Law, which failed to recognize inheritance through females. This meant that if a French king died without a son, the throne passed to the king's closest surviving male relative. In 1584, the Salic Law made a Protestant, King Henry of Navarre, the presumptive heir to the throne. Even so, most French men and women refused to recognize a Protestant as a possible king of Catholic France.

After Anjou's death, an alliance of Catholics committed to keeping Henry of Navarre from the throne took shape. The Catholic League was made up of Catholic nobles and urban elites who used their influence throughout cities and towns to convince the Catholic masses that Henry of Navarre was an evil heretic. They preached that France could expect God's punishment if Navarre ascended the throne. The very popular Henry, duke of Guise, quickly assumed the leadership of the Catholic League and represented himself as the defender of Catholicism. In December of 1584, he signed a secret agreement, the Treaty of Joinville, with Spain's King Philip II. Philip pledged to give Guise financial and military support.

The three Henrys knew one another well but could not have been more different. Henry III was Queen Catherine de Médicis's most intelligent and dedicated son. Even so, his enemies attacked him for his alleged homosexuality and accused him of extravagance and corruption. Henry was extremely religious and often participated as a penitent in religious processions. The sight of the king in penitent garb shocked many French men and women, who rejected him without his symbols of sovereignty.

The king's persona contrasted sharply with the other two Henrys. Henry of Guise was considered the most handsome man in France. He was called "the Scarred" (*le Balafré*) because of a sabre wound on his cheek that gave him a virile appearance. Henry of Navarre was a superb

The assassination of the duke of Guise, leader of the Catholic League, by guards of the French king, Henry III, ended the War of the Three Henrys. (R. S. Peale and J. A. Hill)

military leader famous for his courage in battle and infamous for his pursuit of women. His one failing in the eyes of the French was his Protestant faith. Guise was strong in northern France, while Navarre's support came from the south.

In March of 1585, the Catholic League issued a manifesto rejecting Navarre as heir to the throne and recognizing his aged cousin, the cardinal of Bourbon, as Henry III's successor. Henry III tried to manipulate the League and put himself at its head at the urging of his mother, Catherine de Médicis. On July 7, 1585, Henry III signed the Treaty of Nemours. The treaty revoked all edicts of pacification granted formerly to the French Protestants and forbade the practice of Protestantism. The Huguenots were ordered to abjure their faith or be exiled. With the Treaty of Nemours, the wars of religion resumed, as Guise and his league forces tried to enforce the treaty throughout France.

Henry III and Henry of Guise made poor allies, just as their French Catholic followers seldom agreed on the proper course of action. In 1587, the king tried to discredit Guise by sending him with inadequate forces to battle German supporters of Henry of Navarre. Guise succeeded, however, and his popularity rose. Afterward, Henry III feared Guise might depose him and forbade the duke to enter Paris. Hoping to make a show of strength in May of 1588, the king ordered five thousand Swiss troops to stand ready near Paris to defend his royal power. The king's plan backfired, however, as Paris had always enjoyed an exemption from billeting troops. The Swiss guards only angered the populace, who turned against Henry III.

The Parisians took to the streets and put up barricades. A group of radical league leaders in the city known as the Sixteen, along with Guise's supporters and clients, incited Paris's inhabitants to violence. A Spanish ambassador suggested Guise occupy Paris to divert attention from the sailing of the Spanish Armada. Guise arrived on May 9 as a Catholic hero. Several days later, on May 12, 1588, the king ordered his troops into Paris, and the populace revolted. On this Day of the Barricades, Henry III's authority was no longer recognized, and he fled Paris. The monarchy had reached a new low.

Henry III's revenge came several months later at a meeting of the States-General in Blois. The meeting was dominated by zealous leaguers, and the king felt threatened. He wrongly believed his problems would end if he could do away with Guise. On December 23, 1588, he ordered Guise to his chamber in the château and had him murdered by his guards. Queen Catherine de Médicis

was supposedly in a nearby room and heard the misdeed. Guise's brother, Louis II of Lorraine, the archbishop of Reims, was also arrested and killed the next day.

SIGNIFICANCE

The assassination of the duke of Guise effectively ended the War of the Three Henrys, but the War of the Catholic League continued until 1598. Guise's murder had serious consequences. It radicalized the league throughout France and caused many urban centers to declare their loyalties for the league. Catholic theorists also began to call Henry III a tyrant and advocated rebellion. Violence engulfed the country. In April of 1589, Henry III was forced into an alliance with Henry of Navarre, and the two began an armed attack on Paris. The alliance ended in August with Henry III's death. A Catholic extremist, Jacques Clément, stabbed the king, who died on August 2, 1589.

Henry of Navarre became King Henry IV, the first Bourbon king of France, but he continued to fight for his throne for many years. Navarre owed a great debt to Henry III and not just because the last Valois king named Navarre his successor. By killing Guise, Henry III had done away with Navarre's chief rival while taking all the blame for the assassination upon himself. With Guise dead, the Catholic League no longer had a charismatic leader. When the cardinal of Bourbon died in 1590, the league was left without a French heir to the throne as well.

Henry IV reconverted to Catholicism in 1593 and won over most of Catholic France in 1594-1595. He made peace with the Catholic League and Spain in 1598 and attempted to settle France's religious conflicts by granting Protestants limited religious freedom in the Edict of Nantes. Yet, Protestants living inside France continued to be the focus of problems for years to come. Extreme measures were once more taken against the Protestants in the succeeding reigns of Louis XIII (r. 1610-1643) and Louis XIV (r. 1643-1715), demonstrating the difficulty of eliminating religious anxiety and intolerance by royal decree.

—Stephanie Annette Finley-Croswhite

FURTHER READING

Baumgartner, Frederic J. *France in the Sixteenth Century.* New York: St. Martin's Press, 1995. Offers a detailed history of the sixteenth century for advanced undergraduates. The Guise family and the Catholic League are considered in chapter 14.

Bell, David A. "Unmasking a King: The Political Uses

1580's

of Popular Literature Under the French Catholic League, 1588-1589." *Sixteenth Century Journal* 20 (1998): 371-386. Provides a detailed account of Henry III's erratic behavior and how his enemies used it to undermine his authority and prestige.

Carroll, Stuart. "The Guise Affinity and Popular Protest During the Wars of Religion." *French History* 9 (June, 1995): 125-152. Carroll reconstructs the duke of Guise's circle of supporters to explain how members of this "affinity" promoted popular protest during the Wars of Religion.

Conner, Philip. *Huguenot Heartland: Montauban and Southern French Calvinism During the Wars of Religion*. Burlington, Vt.: Ashgate, 2002. Study of the Wars of Religion, especially of the differences between the experiences of Southern and Northern France during the wars. Focuses on the southern town of Montauban as a case study of the larger religious, cultural, and political upheavals. Includes maps, bibliographic references, and index.

Finley-Croswhite, S. Annette. *Henry IV and the Towns: The Pursuit of Legitimacy in French Urban Society, 1589-1610*. New York: Cambridge University Press, 1999. Study of Henry's labors to win support from his new subjects, focusing on his courtship of the urban population and the consolidation of his claims to legitimate sovereignty. Includes illustrations, maps, bibliographic references, and index.

Frieda, Leonie. *Catherine de Medici*. London: Weidenfeld & Nicolson, 2003. Extensively researched, well-written attempt to rejuvenate Catherine's reputation and produce a balanced evaluation of her place in history. Includes illustrations, bibliographic references, index.

Holt, Mack P. *The French Wars of Religion, 1562-1629*. New York: Cambridge University Press, 1995. A comprehensive examination of the religious wars designed for undergraduates and general readers. Holt discusses Henry of Guise and the Catholic League in chapter 5.

Love, Ronald S. *Blood and Religion: The Conscience of Henri IV, 1553-1593*. Ithaca, N.Y.: McGill-Queen's University Press, 2001. An assessment of Henry IV's reign against the background of civil war and religious strife. Concludes with a discussion of Henry's perception of the conflicting requirements of his crown and his soul, and his 1593 conversion to Catholicism. Includes photographic plates, illustrations, bibliographic references, and index.

Racaut, Luc. *Hatred in Print: Catholic Propaganda and Protestant Identity During the French Wars of Religion*. Burlington, Vt.: Ashgate, 2002. Rare study of the pro-Catholic pamphleteers in France. Analyzes the strategies, production, and impact of pro-Catholic propaganda of the period. Includes bibliographic references and index.

Roelker, Nancy Lyman. *The Paris of Henry of Navarre as Seen by Pierre de l'Estoile: Selections from His Mémoires-Journaux*. Cambridge, Mass.: Harvard University Press, 1958. The author provides translated excerpts from the journal of a sixteenth century man. The entries for 1588 cover Henry of Guise's triumphs and death.

Salmon, J. H. M. *Society in Crisis: France in the Sixteenth Century*. New York: Cambridge University Press, 1975. A prominent scholar offers advanced readers an in-depth investigation of the religious wars to 1598.

Sutherland, N. M. "Henri III, the Guises, and the Huguenots." In *From Valois to Bourbon Dynasty: State and Society in Early Modern France*, edited by Keith Cameron. Exeter, Devon, England: University of Exeter, 1989. Sutherland provides information on Henry, the duke of Guise, and his impact on Huguenot history.

_____. *Henry IV of France and the Politics of Religion, 1572-1596*. 2 vols. Bristol, Avon, England: Elm Bank, 2002. Extremely detailed account of the role of religion in France's monarchy and political sphere during the late sixteenth century. Each chapter discusses a specific political event or issue from the point of view of the conflict between Protestants and Catholics. Includes illustrations, map, bibliographic references, and index.

Wood, James B. *The King's Army: Warfare, Soldiers, and Society During the Wars of Religion in France, 1562-1576*. New York: Cambridge University Press, 1996. An in-depth look at the military campaigns of Charles IX and Henry III. Includes bibliographical references and an index.

SEE ALSO: Oct. 31, 1517: Luther Posts His Ninety-five Theses; Mid-16th cent.: Development of the Caracole Maneuver; Mar., 1562-May 2, 1598: French Wars of Religion; 1568-1648: Dutch Wars of Independence; Aug. 24-25, 1572: St. Bartholomew's Day Massacre; July 31-Aug. 8, 1588: Defeat of the Spanish Armada; Aug. 2, 1589: Henry IV Ascends the Throne of France; Apr. 13, 1598: Edict of Nantes; May 2, 1598: Treaty of Vervins.

RELATED ARTICLES in *Great Lives from History: The Renaissance & Early Modern Era, 1454-1600:* Catherine de Médicis; Henry III; Henry IV; Philip II.

September 14, 1585-July 27, 1586
DRAKE'S EXPEDITION TO THE WEST INDIES

Drake's expedition, which began in Spain and continued to the West Indies to plunder Spanish settlements there, initiated the Anglo-Spanish naval war and culminated in the English victory over the Spanish Armada in 1588.

LOCALE: Spain, the West Indies, South America, southeastern and eastern North America

CATEGORIES: Diplomacy and international relations; exploration and discovery; wars, uprisings, and civil unrest

KEY FIGURES

Sir Francis Drake (c. 1540-1596), English sea captain and admiral of the expedition

Elizabeth I (1533-1603), queen of England, r. 1558-1603

Philip II (1527-1598), king of Spain, r. 1556-1598

Sir Martin Frobisher (c. 1535-1594), English sea captain and vice admiral of the expedition

Christopher Carleill (1551?-1593), commander of English ground forces that were part of the expedition

SUMMARY OF EVENT

Relations between England and Spain during the reigns of Elizabeth I and Philip II were deteriorating because of tensions that resulted from several key factors, including colonial and commercial rivalry, English support for the Dutch Wars of Independence (1568-1648) against Philip II and Spain, Spanish involvement in plots to assassinate Elizabeth I, Spanish intervention in the French Wars of Religion (1562-1598), and Protestant-Catholic antagonism generated by the Protestant Reformation.

Parallel with these tensions was Drake's participation in several key Spanish-English conflicts, including a raid in the Caribbean (1567-1569), which had ended in disaster when the Spanish fleet surprised the English at San Juan de Ulúa, a small island off Veracruz, Mexico. Also, from 1571 to 1573, Drake explored Panama and captured a mule train of Spanish silver, and while completing his circumnavigation of the globe between 1577 and 1580, Drake conducted raids on lightly defended Spanish settlements in South America and Central America. Next came smuggling and raids on Spanish shipping by the English and their attacks on Spain and its colonial possessions.

The immediate cause for the 1585-1586 expedition to the West Indies was the seizure by the Spanish of English grain ships in Spanish ports in June of 1585. In July,

1585, Elizabeth I and the English government issued orders for Drake to take a fleet to Spain to procure release of the ships and also permitted English reprisals against Spanish shipping. Elizabeth I, government officials, prominent nobles, and merchants contributed funds for the raising of the fleet in the hopes of procuring money for the government and for individual profit. Elizabeth I supplied £20,000, one half of the entire £40,000 cost of the expedition. A delay in sailing, however, was caused by the need to provision the fleet of twenty-three or twenty-five ships (the sources differ) and eight pinnaces with a crew of between sixteen hundred and nineteen hundred, with experienced sea captain and explorer Martin Frobisher as vice admiral under Drake and Christopher Carleill commander of the approximately five hundred to seven hundred troops.

Leaving the port of Plymouth on September 14, 1585, the fleet made its way toward Spain, encountering a group of French ships carrying salt. Drake confiscated the newest ship, renaming it the *Drake*. From September 27 until October 11, 1585, Drake's fleet was in Vigo Bay in northwestern Spain while he discussed the seized ships with Spanish officials. The English perpetrated some minor plunder and learned that the seized ships had been released, which should have precluded additional activities by Drake's fleet.

After Drake purchased supplies, his fleet sailed away on its "unofficial" mission—plundering Spanish settlements—while the Spanish officials scrambled to alert Spanish colonies in the Caribbean that Drake might be headed their way. Drake's prolonged stay at Vigo Bay had aroused curiosity—was he trying to humiliate the Spanish or was he lying in wait for the Spanish treasure fleet? Ironically, the treasure fleet reached the Spanish ports safely while Drake tarried at Vigo Bay.

Drake's fleet raided the Canary Islands and Cape Verde Islands from October 24 through November 29, 1585, burning settlements and netting supplies, including confiscated church bells, which could be melted and refashioned for military use. Drake set sail for the West Indies when, several days into the Atlantic passage, a serious illness, thought by some scholars to be a form of bubonic plague, decimated the crew, leaving several hundred dead in its wake. Upon reaching the island of Dominica in the West Indies on December 18, 1585, the crew rested, buried some of their dead, and obtained supplies and water.

1580's

The fleet's next destination was Santo Domingo on the southern side of Hispaniola. They arrived there on December 31, 1585. Many citizens had fled with their valuables, and the Spanish had made ill-planned attempts to prepare defenses. Following his accustomed tactic of assaulting a settlement, Drake landed Carleill and about one thousand men at night a short distance from the city and prepared the fleet to fire on the city in support of the land attack. On January 1, 1586, Drake launched his two-pronged attack, and by midday he had overcome Spanish resistance. Drake's demands for a ransom to spare the city were rebuffed, and his men began plundering the town, taking money, brass cannon, and church bells. To apply pressure on the Spanish to grant his ransom request, Drake ordered the burning of portions of the settlement, which caused the Spanish to agree to pay 25,000 ducats by January 30, 1586. Before leaving, Drake exchanged three of his older vessels for three newer Spanish ships and also requisitioned a Spanish ship, which he renamed *New Year's Gift*.

The assault was a substantial psychological and financial blow to Philip II, exposing the defenseless state of Spanish colonies and causing the reassignment of resources designated for use in Europe to the Caribbean and the Americas.

After leaving Santo Domingo, the fleet sailed for Cartagena, along the northern coast of South America. Spurred by warnings received from Santo Domingo, local officials had taken precautions—women, children, and valuables were removed from the city; barricades were erected; trenches were dug; a huge chain was stretched across the harbor; and galleys were positioned in the harbor. On February 9, 1586, Drake tauntingly sailed his fleet in front of the city and into the outer harbor. Repeating the tactics successful at Santo Domingo—a night landing of troops and a ground assault supported by fire from his fleet—Drake was in control of the city by morning, as gaps in the defenses and the poor morale of the defenders contributed to the city's swift collapse. Drake's exorbitant ransom demand of 500,000 gold ducats was rejected by the Spanish, who offered 25,000 gold ducats instead.

Negotiations became protracted when Drake insulted the Spanish officials after he discovered a letter in which Philip II had called Drake a pirate. As he had done at Santo Domingo, Drake burned parts of the city to force compliance with his ransom demands; the Spanish agreed to pay 110,000 ducats, beginning March 10, 1586. The king's bullion was used for the ransom, and wealthy individuals and Franciscan friars paid separate ransoms. In addition to this loot, Drake's men removed brass cannon from the town and galleys and plundered valuables from individuals and churches in the city. Disputes developed among the English over the accounting of ransom and plunder, and many of the crew openly expressed a desire to return to England.

The fleet left for Cuba on March 31, 1586, but returned to Cartagena several days later to repair a badly leaking ship, redistribute plunder and cargo between ships, and bake biscuits in preparation for the return voyage to England. On April 14, 1586, the fleet resumed its journey to Cuba. The Havana settlement was not attacked because of its strong fortifications, so Drake sailed for Florida, arriving at St. Augustine on May 27, 1586. In an attack launched the following day, Drake destroyed the fort and burned the settlement and crops. The plunder of the town yielded food, cannon, and a treasure chest containing 6,000 ducats. Santa Elena, a settlement north of St. Augustine, was spared attack because of dangerous shoals.

The last stop for the fleet was Sir Walter Ralegh's Roanoke Colony in June, along the Outer Banks of what is now North Carolina. Governor Ralph Lane revealed the serious state of the colonists because hoped-for supplies had not arrived. Generously, Drake offered supplies and one ship to transport the colonists to England, but these plans changed because a storm of three days' duration dispersed Drake's fleet and the ship promised the colonists had sailed for England. Modifying his original offer, Drake transported the 105 colonists to England, arriving at Portsmouth on July 27, 1586, just five days after the ship that had left earlier during the storm.

SIGNIFICANCE

The hoped-for financial gain did not materialize because the booty did not cover the £40,000 investment in the expedition. Also, the sailors and soldiers had to wait for their pay. On another level, however, the expedition had been a tremendous success; English and European Protestants were exultant over the damage inflicted on Catholic Spain's pride and resources, and Drake would be sent in 1587 to raid Cádiz to disrupt preparations for the Spanish Armada.

The voyage also expanded English knowledge of the Americas and helped stimulate interest in further colonization. Philip II was forced to expend greater resources to defend Spanish settlements in the Americas, which diverted funds that had been earmarked for the Spanish Armada against England and for stopping the Dutch Wars of Independence.

—Mark C. Herman

FURTHER READING

Dudley, Wade G. *Drake: For God, Queen, and Plunder*. Washington, D.C.: Brassey's, 2003. Monograph on Drake's naval exploits that paints a picture of Elizabethan privateering and the naval battles between England and Spain in Drake's time.

Keeler, Mary Frear, ed. *Sir Francis Drake's West Indian Voyage, 1585-86*. London: Hakluyt Society, 1981. An extensive edition of primary documents with an introduction, analysis, and a glossary of the major personnel.

Kelsey, Harry. *Sir Francis Drake: The Queen's Pirate*. New Haven, Conn.: Yale University Press, 1998. An excellent scholarly analysis of Drake's career, based on archival research and supported by excellent maps.

Parker, Geoffrey. *The Grand Strategy of Philip II*. New Haven, Conn.: Yale University Press, 1996. This study puts Drake's voyage within the context of the Anglo-Spanish conflict by analyzing Philip's response to the English actions.

Sugden, John. *Sir Francis Drake*. New York: Touchstone Books, 1992. A readable scholarly biography with several chapters on the voyage.

SEE ALSO: 1495-1510: West Indian Uprisings; 1500-1530's: Portugal Begins to Colonize Brazil; 1558-1603: Reign of Elizabeth I; June 17, 1579: Drake Lands in Northern California; July 4, 1584-1590: Lost Colony of Roanoke; July 31-Aug. 8, 1588: Defeat of the Spanish Armada.

RELATED ARTICLES in *Great Lives from History: The Renaissance & Early Modern Era, 1454-1600:* Thomas Cavendish; Sir Francis Drake; Elizabeth I; Sir Martin Frobisher; Sir Richard Grenville; Philip II; Sir Walter Ralegh.

1580's

February, 1586
ANNEXATION OF KASHMIR

After many failed attempts during the reigns of Bābur and Humāyūn, the Mughals under Akbar succeeded in wholly subjugating Kashmir as a province of the Mughal Empire.

LOCALE: Kashmir (now a disputed region between India and Pakistan)

CATEGORIES: Expansion and land acquisition; wars, uprisings, and civil unrest; government and politics

KEY FIGURES

Akbar (1542-1605), Mughal emperor of India, r. 1556-1605

Bhagwan Das (d. 1589), Mughal general and governor, 1574-1589

Yūsuf Shah Chak (fl. 1579-1586), ruler of Kashmir, r. 1579-1586

SUMMARY OF EVENT

Emperor Humāyūn's general Mirza Haidar recognized that a country entrenched in sectarian conflicts could offer little resistance to invasion. Despite Humāyūn's relative incompetence, which nearly put down the invasion, Mirza Haidar continued with plans to seize Kashmir using a very small force. He ruled Kashmir for the next ten years as governor under Humāyūn. After Mirza Haidar's death, however, the Mughals lost control of Kashmir be-

cause of other priorities. Kashmir again returned to its fighting factions.

In 1578, Akbar sent a message to ʿAlī Shah of Kashmir, demanding his allegiance, but the demand was not met. Not until January, 1580, did Akbar find a pretext for invading Kashmir. ʿAlī Shah's son Yūsuf Shah Chak had succeeded his father's tenuous existence as ruler of Kashmir. Lohar Chak, however, had usurped the throne, so Yūsuf went to Akbar, pleading for assistance to regain his throne. Akbar ordered his officers to support Yūsuf and sent him into the Punjab, but Kashmiri nobles promised Yūsuf their allegiance and support only if he returned to Kashmir alone. They knew that an invasion by Akbar's army would mean that Kashmir would become a possession of the Mughal Empire. On November 8, 1580, Yūsuf regained the throne without Akbar's assistance, removing Akbar's "right" to invade Kashmir under the premise of assisting a rightful ruler against a usurper.

In 1585, shortly after the arrival of the first Englishmen at Akbar's court, conflict occurred between Kashmir and the Mughal Empire. Yūsuf politely had refused to perform homage to Akbar and sent a message to him saying as much through his envoys. This impudence, combined with Akbar's increased arrogance from recent contact with Europeans and recollections of his offers to aid Yūsuf five years before, sparked Akbar's interest in Kashmir. He decided to enforce obedience and sent an army on the last day of 1585 to Kashmir, officially headed by Mirza Shah Rukh but in reality led by Bhagwan Das.

The force marched from Attock into Kashmir, while another marched into Swat and Bajaur under the leadership of Zain Khan to ensure submission of the Yusufzai tribe. This second force, however, was made up of amateur soldiers and was led by two individuals without military experience (Raja Birbal, a jester, and Hakim Abu'l Fath, a physician). Since they were both favored by Akbar, though, Zain Khan was intimidated and allowed them to override his judgment. Because of Birbal's and Fath's inexperience, the army took a difficult route through the passes of Swat and fell victim to the Yusufzai in the Malandarai Pass. Eight thousand men, about half of the forces involved, perished, including Birbal. Zain Khan and Fath survived and led the forces back to camp on February 24, 1586. Akbar blamed Fath for insubordination to Zain Khan, but it is more likely that the responsibility truly lay with Akbar for appointing a jester and a doctor to lead an army. An experienced general was sent to attempt to regain some Mughal dignity and to successfully establish posts throughout Yusufzai territory.

Bhagwan Das had advanced into Kashmir around the same time. Yūsuf Shah realized that it was possible that Bhagwan Das might reach the city of Srinagar in spite of obstacles such as cold weather and hunger. Out of fear, Yūsuf offered to do homage to Akbar. On February 22, 1586, Yūsuf surrendered on the well-understood terms that Akbar required personal submission and a promise of monetary tribute, and, having done so, Yūsuf would then be permitted to return to Kashmir as a vassal ruling under the emperor. Bhagwan Das was relieved because his army was suffering from cold and rain, and he welcomed Yūsuf's submission. Akbar was less pleased, however, so he ratified the surrender treaty, made Yūsuf a state prisoner, and prepared another army to complete the subjugation of Kashmir. Since Akbar had overruled Bhagwan Das, thus destroying his honor as a commander, Bhagwan Das was sent to Kabul and attempted suicide along the way.

Despite the counsel of his advisers, stubborn Akbar persevered in his plans to ready another army, which, in July, 1586, invaded Kashmir, entering Srinagar on October 15. The *khutba*, an Islamic sermon read at Friday services and for special occassions, was recited in the name of Akbar, confirming his supremacy, and Kashmir was formally annexed. Resistance continued under Yūsuf's

son, who managed to evade capture. His son also surrendered to Akbar, however, in August, 1589.

In May, 1589, Akbar visited Kashmir, inquiring into sources of revenue, with the attention to economics characteristic of his reign. Akbar's inquiries, however, caused trouble. Mirza Yūsuf Khan, the newest governor of Kashmir, reported to Akbar that the assessment that he had proposed was far too high, but Akbar maintained justification of his demand. Mughal officers in Kashmir were convinced that the higher rate would leave very little for them and for their troops, and so they rebelled with the governor's cousin, Yadgar, as their leader. Yadgar caused the *khutba* to be read in his own name, assuming the royal title. Akbar sent out a force to put down the rebellion, and Yadgar was captured and killed.

Akbar entered Srinagar on October 14, 1592, and Mirza Yūsuf Khan resigned in protest, stating that he would be unable to govern Kashmir properly under the revenue administration. The province became imperial land and was assigned to the financial officer of the Punjab, but because it was something of a geographical confusion for the Mughals, it was assigned to the *suba* (province) of Kabul.

SIGNIFICANCE

Akbar's conquest of Kashmir completed the year in which his power reached its apex, adding its submission to the total subjection of Orissa, the Sind, Kathiawar, and Gujarat. Akbar's long acquaintance with the factionalized, divided nature of Kashmir influenced his decision to pursue religious unification through his Din-i-Ilahi (Divine Faith), so as to strengthen the power of the Mughal Empire through greater religious tolerance and cultural unity.

Completing his conquest of northern India allowed him to turn his eye to the Deccan. The relative stability under subjugation enjoyed by Kashmir during Akbar's reign was destroyed under Jahāngīr, Akbar's son, who was more interested in preserving an idealized, unilateral paradise that privileged Sunni Islam than in facilitating a truly harmonious and tolerant province.

—Monica Piotter

FURTHER READING

'Allāmī, Abu-l-Fazl. *The Akbar Nāma of Abu-l-Fazl.* Translated by Henry Beveridge. 3 vols. Delhi, India: Ess Ess, 1977. A detailed eyewitness account by Akbar's court historian, manifestly pro-Mughal yet valuable nevertheless. Best for readers with some familiarity with Mughal history.

Gommans, Jos. *Mughal Warfare: Indian Frontiers and Highroads to Empire, 1500-1700*. New York: Routledge, 2003. This work provides an overview of the military expansion, including the technological and strategic advantages, that allowed the Mughals to enlarge their territory, as Akbar did by annexing Kashmir.

Habib, Irfan, ed. *Akbar and His India*. New York: Oxford University Press, 1997. A good collection of essays on topics relating to Akbar and his reign as emperor, particularly with respect to the beliefs and ideas that led him to his political, administrative, and military actions.

Richards, John F. *The Mughal Empire: New Cambridge History of India*. New York: Cambridge University Press, 1996. A superb overview of India's Mughal emperors, from Bābur to ʿĀlamgīr, with special attention to Akbar's reign.

Streusand, Douglas E. *The Formation of the Mughal Empire*. New York: Oxford University Press, 1999. A study of Mughal political, economic, and military institutions in the early years, with emphasis on Akbar's political and administrative innovations. Examines the cultural and religious context as well, especially important for studies of Kashmir.

SEE ALSO: 1451-1526: Lodī Kings Dominate Northern India; Early 16th cent.: Devotional Bhakti Traditions Emerge; Apr. 21, 1526: First Battle of Panipat; Dec. 30, 1530: Humāyūn Inherits the Throne in India; Feb. 23, 1568: Fall of Chitor; Mar. 3, 1575: Mughal Conquest of Bengal.

RELATED ARTICLES in *Great Lives from History: The Renaissance & Early Modern Era, 1454-1600:* Akbar; Bābur; Humāyūn; Ibrāhīm Lodī; Krishnadevaraya.

1580's

1587

TOYOTOMI HIDEYOSHI HOSTS A TEN-DAY TEA CEREMONY

In 1587, the forces of Japanese warlord Toyotomi Hideyoshi subjugated the southern island of Kyūshū. To celebrate the victory and make a display of wealth that would announce his claim to central authority, Hideyoshi and tea master Sen no Rikyū organized an ostentatious tea ceremony in Kyōto.

LOCALE: Kitano Tenmangu Shirine, Kyōto, Japan
CATEGORIES: Cultural and intellectual history; government and politics

KEY FIGURES

Toyotomi Hideyoshi (1537-1598), military leader who completed the unification of Japan, r. 1590-1598
Sen no Rikyū (1522-1591), tea master
Go-Yozei (1572-1617), emperor of Japan, r. 1586-1611

SUMMARY OF EVENT

Toyotomi Hideyoshi was born in Owari Province in 1537. Hideyoshi was of humble birth and moved through the ranks of the forces of local warlord Oda Nobunaga on talent and ambition alone. In 1560, Nobunaga launched a series of stunning military victories over neighboring rulers, and by the late 1560's he had established himself as the leading warlord in central Japan. Hideyoshi distinguished himself during these campaigns and continued to be one of Nobunaga's most important followers through the 1570's. In 1582, Nobunaga was assassinated

by another of his supporters, Akechi Mitsuhide. Wasting no time, Hideyoshi attacked and defeated Akechi at the Battle of Yamazaki and established himself as Nobunaga's successor in the drive to unify all of Japan under a central power. In 1585, Hideyoshi was appointed *kampaku*, the most important post in the largely symbolic imperial court.

In 1587, Hideyoshi decided to extend his power from his base in central Japan and invaded the southern island of Kyūshū. He subjugated the Shimazu, the most powerful family on the island, and reorganized landholdings there. Hideyoshi's victory in Kyūshū increased his power and prestige greatly. It also removed one of the most serious potential barriers to his unification of the country. To celebrate his great victory, Hideyoshi, upon returning to Kyōto, hosted what was to become the most famous tea party of its time. The festivities were held outdoors at the Kitano Tenmangu shrine in northern Kyōto.

Sen no Rikyū, a friend and companion of Hideyoshi, was the founder of the Sen school of tea preparation. His family had long been associated with the practice of the tea ceremony in Kyōto. In his youth, Sen no Rikyū had studied the preparation of tea under a number of different masters and also had studied Zen Buddhism. He gained some prominence in Kyōto and was called upon to perform the tea ceremony for Oda Nobunaga. He performed the same function for Hideyoshi and was awarded with land for his services. Considered a true connoisseur, both of the art of tea and of the implements that were used in the ceremony, he was placed in charge of the Kitano tea ceremony.

The festivities, while celebrating elite culture, were not exclusive and involved those from all walks of life. Hideyoshi was passionately interested in the tea ceremony and the rituals and implements surrounding it. In the past, he had held tea celebrations on a large scale, but the gathering that he organized at Kitano outdid them all. The festivities were of such a great scale that they were held not only on the grounds of the shrine itself but in the nearby Kitano Matsubara area as well. Period documents report that more than one thousand brewed tea there and that many more came to observe the festivities. The event was of such great contemporary significance that tea connoisseurs came from as far as northern Kyūshū to participate. Contemporary sources report that Hideyoshi himself served tea to 803 people.

While Hideyoshi had a genuine interest in the tea ceremony and the artwork traditionally associated with it, the tea ceremony that he held at Kitano had far more than an artistic significance. The audacious display of wealth was calculated to increase Hideyoshi's prestige and to intimidate both the imperial court and his rivals. The emperor Go-Yozei, who had ascended to the throne during the previous year, was in attendance and was reportedly awed by what he witnessed. In the past, Hideyoshi had been sure to display his wealth and authority before the emperor in an effort to impress the titular ruler, but the Kitano festivities outdid all earlier efforts. For the Kitano tea ceremony, Hideyoshi had a tea house built from solid gold. While this flew completely in the face of the aesthetic values of the tea ceremony, which stress austerity as an aesthetic virtue, it awed visitors, including the emperor, as a supreme symbol of the warlord's power and wealth. In the end, few measures could have done as much to increase Hideyoshi's reputation, both as a cultivated individual and as a major power in the country.

SIGNIFICANCE

While it is difficult for scholars to talk about direct consequences of the Kitano tea ceremony in the 1580's and 1590's, its symbolic value for Hideyoshi is evident. He overawed important figures such as emperor Go-Yozei with his display of wealth and entrenched his political power.

In addition, as a result of the Kitano tea ceremony, the prestige and aura of connoisseurship associated with the tea ceremony in Japan received a significant boost. It had long been considered one of the most important accomplishments of high-born men, but the developments that took place under the patronage of Hideyoshi and the auspices of Sen no Rikyū are considered to be particularly significant. The Kitano tea ceremony represented the high point in the relationship between Hideyoshi and the tea master.

After the conclusion of the ten-day festival, there was a rapid worsening of their relations. In 1591, Hideyoshi ordered Sen no Rikyū to commit suicide. Scholars are at odds as to the nature of Sen no Rikyū's infraction. Some argue that surviving evidence points to the fact that Hideyoshi and Sen no Rikyū had a falling out over the erection of a

---

CALLING ALL TO TEA

Toyotomi Hideyoshi announced a tea ceremony to celebrate his subjugation of the island of Kyūshū. The ceremony served also to display his wealth, prestige, power, and control over the performance of rituals.

1. Lord [Hideyoshi] will hold a large Tea [ceremony] in the forest of Kitano [shrine] and display all his famous utensils in order to show them to the suki experts and amateurs.

2. All Tea practitioners, regardless of whether they are warrior attendants, townsmen or peasants, or people of lower status should bring a kettle, a tsurube, and a bowl, and even if they have no tea, they should all come even though they may only serve kogashi (powdered roast rice and parched salt).

3. As for the zasshiki, as long as they are in the forest, two-mat arrangements are appropriate. However, *wabi* [poor] people may simply spread out straw mats or rice-hull bags [to accommodate their guests] where they please.

4. Not only Japanese, but Chinese and Koreans with an interest in Tea must participate.

5. So that even those who come from far away can see it, the Lord will keep his collection on display until the tenth.

6. All *wabi* people who, despite this order, refuse to participate, will no longer be allowed to serve Tea, let alone kogashi. The same applies to their disciples.

7. Lord Hideyoshi will serve Tea to all *wabi* people, regardless from how far they came.

Source: Quoted in "An Anthropological Perspective on the Japanese Tea Ceremony," by Herbert Plutschow. *Anthropoetics* 5, no. 1 (1999), p. 9. Subscription-based online journal. http://www.humnet.ucla.edu/humnet/anthropoetics/. Accessed September 30, 2004.

A sixteenth century tea ceremony on a street in Japan, with musical entertainment. Toyotomi Hideyoshi's ten-day tea ceremony clearly was much grander, and meant to be ostentatious. (Hulton|Archive by Getty Images)

FURTHER READING

Berry, Mary Elizabeth. *Hideyoshi.* Cambridge, Mass.: Harvard University Press, 1982. The best single-volume treatment of Hideyoshi's career in English. Contains details on his support of the arts and the Kitano tea ceremony.

Graham, Patricia Jane. *Tea of the Sages: The Art of Sencha.* Honolulu: University of Hawaii Press, 1999. An excellent history of the tea ceremony in Japan and its cultural and philosophical underpinnings.

Hirota, Dennis. *Wind in the Pines: Classical Writings of the Way of Tea as a Buddhist Path.* Fremont, Calif.: Asian Humanities Press, 1995. An introduction to the philosophy of the tea ceremony and a collection of related original sources from the Buddhist tradition.

Okakura, Kakuzo. *The Book of Tea.* Reprint. Tokyo: Kodansha International, 1989. Written in English by a connoisseur of the traditional arts, this work is still the best introduction to the tea cermoney in English more than a century since its first publication.

Sansom, George. *A History of Japan, 1334-1615.* 3 vols. Stanford, Calif.: Stanford University Press, 1961. Despite its age, Sansom's history of premodern Japan still offers the most authoritative coverage of the subject in English. Includes detailed coverage of Hideyoshi's time in power and the cultural background of his age.

statue of Sen no Rikyū at the Daitokuji, a Zen temple complex in Kyōto. There is also some evidence suggesting that Hideyoshi was angered by the great sums of money the tea master had begun to charge for his services and for the tea kettles and other implements that were used in the ceremony. In any case, it is clear that the type of prestige that Hideyoshi won, not only through military conquest but also though ostentatious displays of wealth like the Kitano tea ceremony, gave him leave to take such arbitrary action. It is believed that Hideyoshi regretted this course of action after Sen no Rikyū's death.

During the Edo period of Japanese history (1603-1863), the drinking of tea proliferated among all social classes. Today it remains a cornerstone of Japanese culture. Most Japanese drink tea at all sorts of social occasions, and mastery of the tea ceremony is considered a significant cultural accomplishment. The Kitano Shrine in Kyōto still holds an annual tea festival in commemoration of Hideyoshi's late sixteenth century extravaganza.

—*Matthew Penney*

1580's

1587-1629
REIGN OF ʿABBĀS THE GREAT

Under ʿAbbās the Great, Ṣafavid Persia reached its height of political unity, economic prosperity, and cultural advancement. The Ṣafavid golden age was made possible by military, administrative, and economic transformations made by ʿAbbās before 1600.

LOCALE: Iran and much of present-day Iraq
CATEGORY: Government and politics

KEY FIGURES

ʿAbbās the Great (1571-1629), shah of Persia, r. 1587-1629
Sir Anthony Sherley (1565?-1636), and
Sir Robert Sherley (1581?-1628), English adventurers
Ismāʿīl I (1487-1524), first Ṣafavid shah, r. 1501-1524

SUMMARY OF EVENT

At the age of sixteen, ʿAbbās the Great took advantage of animosity between his nearly blind father and support from several leading nobles to seize the throne and become shah. The main force intended to use the young ʿAbbās as a puppet ruler. Family intrigues were an integral part of the Ṣafavid Dynasty and Persian palace life long before and long after ʿAbbās's reign, the problem being that there was no clear system of inheritance.

Brothers of the shah plotted against brothers, and son against son, as nobles allied to various factions. ʿAbbās's own life nearly ended at the age of five when his uncle, Shah Ismāʿīl II (r. 1576-1577), ordered the execution of his brothers and their male children. Ismāʿīl's own untimely death prevented the murders.

During his first few years in power, ʿAbbās solved the problem of intrigues by the nobles by manipulating factions that threatened the independent decision making of the throne. In attempting to govern his kingdom, however, ʿAbbās faced difficulties far exceeding the efforts by leading nobles to control him. ʿAbbās's father and uncle had been inept rulers. The Ottoman Turks to the west and Uzbek tribesmen to the northeast had occupied considerable portions of territories once ruled by Persia. His own Turkmen supporters, which formed the bulk of the Persian cavalry, were engaging in intertribal quarrels, leading to a state of near anarchy.

To unify the disintegrating Ṣafavid Empire, ʿAbbās had to move one step at a time. In 1590, he concluded a humiliating treaty with the Ottoman Turks to buy time, first to subdue Turkmen rebellions in 1592 by ravaging

the Black Sea province of Gilan and then to concentrate his forces on the Uzbeks. He regained Mashhad, and in 1597, he decimated Uzbek forces in a major battle near Herāt. By 1598, the Uzbek khan had died and Persia's eastern borders were secured. It was now time to confront the Ottoman Turks. However, ʿAbbās's armies were made up largely of Kizilbash ("red heads"), men from the seven Turkish tribes that helped the Ṣafavids first come to power. They were given to the army by provincial landholders as a form of local taxation and were unpaid, ill trained, poorly equipped, and highly unreliable. The Kizilbash tended to act as a power of their own.

To prepare to fight the Turks, ʿAbbās created the *ghulām* system. *Ghulāms* were personal slaves of the shah trained for becoming either administrators, if they were bright, or professional soldiers of a new standing army. Most of the *ghulāms* were non-Persians and came from Armenian, Circassian, and Georgian populations under Ṣafavid rule. They were converted to Shīʿite Islam and were immune from Persian tribal politics. Other foreigners were encouraged to help forge an army capable of battling the Turks and to help construct a more efficient administration. Two English brothers, Sir Anthony Sherley and Sir Robert Sherley, would have a significant role in modernizing the standing Persian army, bureaucracy, and diplomatic corps.

The Sherleys came to Persia in 1598 with the intention of serving as mercenaries. Robert was accomplished in military strategy and the use of artillery. Accompanying him was a group of cannon founders capable of constructing a native Persian cannon industry. Anthony was well connected and talented in diplomacy. He would be sent to Italy, Spain, and England to forge cooperation against the Turks. *Ghulāms* were trained in the use of muskets and artillery. Infantry were recruited from the Persian peasantry. Though the new army was far smaller than the old, it was far more modern and cohesive, and was also considerably more expensive to maintain. The new army was to be paid from funds of the royal treasury. Increased royal revenues, however, were obtained by confiscating the lands of the Kizilbash tribal chiefs. Several tribes were moved to other locales to weaken their power.

Finally, in preparation for war, ʿAbbās moved the capital from Qazvīn in 1598 to the more defensible central Persian city of Eṣfahān. From Eṣfahān, ʿAbbās could communicate with the whole country and with trading outlets on the Persian Gulf. A relatively smooth-running central administration was constructed, too. New provinces were created and put under the administration of royal governors, many of whom were *ghulāms*.

ʿAbbās also made Eşfahān one of the most beautiful cities in the world. The magnificence of the capital and the court, and the lavish patronage given to philosophers, scientists, and artists, were intended to symbolize the dawning of a new glorious age for the Şafavids. He united the nation by forcing the people to convert to Shiism, a process started nearly one century earlier by the first Şafavid shah, Ismāʿīl I, and by establishing Farsi as the national language. All these changes were designed to concentrate power in the hands of ʿAbbās.

It was expensive, however, to build a new capital city and prepare for a war against the Ottomans. To obtain new revenues from taxes, ʿAbbās hoped to launch a commercial transformation. European merchants were invited to Persia by the granting of special privileges and immunities. Whole communities of Armenian merchants were moved to Eşfahān to help with the growth of the silk trade with India. The silk trade itself was made a royal monopoly. Additional revenues were reinvested and turned into

construction projects, including highways, bridges, and even merchant lodges. Infrastructure investment, designed to create increased future revenues, indicates both far-sightedness and considerable optimism about the outcome of the planned war with the Ottomans.

ʿAbbās also was a skilled politician, well liked by his subjects. He maintained the loyalty of his people, projected the image of a benevolent ruler, attended Christmas Mass with his Christian subjects, and acted humbly in public while often wearing simple clothes. He demanded honesty from public officials and dealt harshly with officials who were corrupt. He showed an active love of painting, music, and poetry.

SIGNIFICANCE

The war against Turkey started in 1603, and an initial success was the retaking of Tabrīz, given to the Ottomans by ʿAbbās at the beginning of his reign. By 1623, victory over the Ottomans was complete, and ʿAbbās would rule a unified state that included modern-day Iran and most of Iraq.

Not resting on his accomplishments, ʿAbbās was able to use Robert Sherley to help get naval aid from the British East India Company to remove, in 1622, Portuguese control of the strategically located island of Hormuz. The new center of trade on Hormuz was named after the shah. By defeating the Portuguese, ʿAbbās became master of the Persian Gulf. The Persian economy would be heavily integrated into world trade with England and the Netherlands.

Even though the empire forged by ʿAbbās the Great was magnificent, it was also short-lived because of inept successors. Paranoid about his own family, ʿAbbās had his oldest son executed and two other sons blinded, rendering them unfit to rule and leaving a poorly trained grandson to become shah.

The empire was fragmented after a renewed push by the Ottomans from the west and the Mughals from the east following ʿAbbās's death. In 1722, the Ghilzai Afghans seized Eşfahān, marking the end of Şafavid rule.

—*Irwin Halfond*

FURTHER READING

Canby, Sheila. *The Golden Age of Persian Art: 1501-1722*. New York: Harry N. Abrams, 2000. A scholarly and beautifully illustrated study of the arts and crafts of Şafavid Persia.

Melville, Charles, ed. *Şafavid Persia: The History and Politics of an Islamic Society*. New York: St. Martin's Press, 1996. Scholarly articles on the Şafavids, in-

Persian shah ʿAbbās the Great. (Hulton|Archive by Getty Images)

1580's

cluding a forty-page chapter on ʿAbbās the Great. Index and footnotes.

Monshi, Eskandar. *History of Shah ʿAbbās the Great.* Boulder, Colo.: Westview Press, 1978. The only major study of ʿAbbās, this work is valuable as a reference but difficult to read. Index, glossary, and bibliography.

Savory, Roger. *Iran Under the Ṣafavids.* New York: Cambridge University Press, 1980. Provides an excellent general context and account of the reign of ʿAbbās and other Ṣafavids. Includes bibliography, references, and index.

SEE ALSO: 1469-1508: Ak Koyunlu Dynasty Controls Iraq and Northern Iran; 1501-1524: Reign of Ismāʿīl I; Dec. 2, 1510: Battle of Merv Establishes the Shaybānīd Dynasty; 1512-1520: Reign of Selim I; 1534-1535: Ottomans Claim Sovereignty over Mesopotamia; 1552: Struggle for the Strait of Hormuz; 1578-1590: The Battle for Tabrīz; 1598: Astrakhanid Dynasty Is Established.

RELATED ARTICLES in *Great Lives from History: The Renaissance & Early Modern Era, 1454-1600:* Bayezid II; Süleyman the Magnificent.

April, 1587-c. 1600
ANGLO-SPANISH WAR

England's war against Spain thwarted Spanish hegemony in western Europe, ensured England's survival as a Protestant nation, greatly weakened Spain, and paved the way for creation of a British empire.

LOCALE: English and Spanish Empires

CATEGORIES: Wars, uprisings, and civil unrest; diplomacy and international relations; expansion and land acquisition; religion

KEY FIGURES

Sir Francis Drake (c. 1540-1596), English sea captain
Elizabeth I (1533-1603), English queen, r. 1558-1603
Philip II (1527-1598), Spanish king, r. 1556-1598
Sir John Norris (c. 1547-1597), English military commander
Robert Devereux (1566-1601), earl of Essex and English military commander
Alessandro Farnese (1545-1592), duke of Parma and Spanish military commander
Sir John Hawkins (1532-1595), English sea captain

SUMMARY OF EVENT

The hostilities between England and Spain during the late sixteenth century were both colonial and commercial in nature, as well as being couched in the broader context of the European wars of religion during the Reformation and Counter-Reformation. The English feared threats to their trade in the Netherlands and the Spanish bid for hegemony in western Europe. They knew that such hegemony would be devastating for any European Protestant nation. For their part, the Spanish were both intensely nationalistic and devoutly Catholic and saw it as their right and duty to exercise such control.

Several events in 1584 brought the tensions between England and Spain to a head, triggering an overt military conflict. In June, the duke of Anjou, heir to the French throne, died, opening the path for greater Spanish influence in France, as Philip II subsidized the French Catholic League via the Treaty of Joinville. The next month, William the Silent, the Protestant leader of the Dutch Revolt against Spain, was assassinated, creating a leadership vacuum in the Netherlands. These events resulted in the English and Dutch signing the Treaty of Nonsuch in August, 1585, which provided for the English commitment of troops under Sir John Norris and later Robert Dudley, earl of Leicester, to aid the Dutch. This was an extraordinary measure, given England's lack of military resources compared to the continental powers.

In addition to waging a land war in the Netherlands alongside the Dutch, the English used their traditional maritime strategy. From September, 1585, to July, 1586, Sir Francis Drake conducted naval raids on Spain, the Canaries, the Cape Verde Islands, the West Indies, and Florida. Drake's attacks damaged Spanish prestige and caused Philip II to shift resources to the Americas. In April, 1587, Drake raided Cádiz, and in this famous "singeing of the beard of the king of Spain," he destroyed supplies destined for the Spanish Armada and captured the ship *San Lorenzo*. Perhaps the most spectacular and pivotal campaign of the entire conflict was Philip II's attempt in May-July, 1588, to gain control of the English Channel with the Spanish Armada and to escort Italian troops under Alessandro Farnese, duke of Parma, onto

English soil to conduct a full-scale invasion. The failure of the Armada and the successful Anglo-Dutch defense of Bergen-op-Zoom were significant setbacks for Spain.

In April-July, 1589, the English launched a two-pronged land and sea attack on the Iberian Peninsula. They sought to capture the remnants of the Armada, to capture the Spanish treasure fleet, and to restore the Portuguese pretender Don Antonio to the Portuguese throne. Sir John Norris, commander of the troops, and Sir Francis Drake raided Coruña and Lisbon seeking to create a popular uprising on behalf of Don Antonio. No such uprising occurred, however, and the only benefit the English gained in this campaign was the seizure of sixty grain ships from the Baltic, which strained their relations with the Hanseatic League and northern European countries.

Shortly after the return of England's fleet, however, dramatic events in France created a huge shift in power. The assassinations of both Henry I of Lorraine, duke of Guise, and King Henry III (r. 1574-1589) brought the Protestant Henry of Navarre to the throne as King Henry IV (r. 1589-1610). Henry IV opposed Spanish influence in France. As a result of Henry's ascension to the throne, Philip II sent troops to France in 1590 to support his demand that his oldest daughter become queen of France. Philip's troops seized towns in Brittany, and the duke of Parma moved troops from the Netherlands to France to relieve the siege of Paris. What had been sporadic ad hoc aid from England now had to become regular and substantial if France's Protestant king was to survive.

In 1591, England launched another naval assault focused on the Azores and interdiction of the treasure fleet. The English were overwhelmed by superior numbers, however. Lord Thomas Howard broke off the assault as hopeless, but Sir Richard Grenville refused to give up and died in battle. The English also committed their ground forces to aid their allies: seven thousand to assist the Dutch, three thousand to Brittany, and four thousand under Robert Devereux, earl of Essex, to relieve Rouen in April, 1592.

In another dramatic reversal, Henry IV converted to Catholicism on July 10, 1593, changing the dynamics of the French war and the positions of both Spain and England. At Brest, Sir John Norris led four thousand troops alongside a fleet of eight ships under the command of Sir Martin Frobisher to defend the town from Spanish forces. They managed to relieve the pressure on France during the critical period from 1593 to 1594 when Henry IV was consolidating his power. This relief of Brest, combined with the Dutch's gaining control of im-

portant rivers and Henry IV's breaking the power of the Catholic League, marked a significant ebbing of Spanish power. Spain did, however, capture Calais, thereby forging an Anglo-French "offensive and defensive alliance" in 1596 which was expanded to a Triple Alliance with the inclusion of the Dutch in 1597.

The English, attempting to repeat the success of Drake's West Indies raid of 1585-1586, unleashed Drake once more on the Indies alongside Sir John Hawkins, this time with disastrous results. The Spanish were prepared for the attack, the two English admirals had major disagreements, and both died before the end of the expedition. In June-July, 1596, the Cádiz Expedition was launched under the command of Charles, Lord Howard, and the earl of Essex to stop preparation of another Spanish Armada. Cádiz was seized and sacked, but the expedition failed to capture a Spanish merchant fleet in the harbor or to recover any significant treasure. This failure, in addition to Essex's knighting of too many soldiers, angered Elizabeth I. A Spanish Armada was sent out in October, 1596, but it was dispersed by storms before it got very far. Another Armada in October, 1597, met the same fate.

The Treaty of Vervins of May, 1598, between Spain and France ended Spanish involvement in the French Wars of Religion; this treaty coupled with the death of Philip II in September, 1598, brought Philip III (r. 1598-1621) to the throne and initiated the final phase of the Anglo-Spanish War. The Spanish Armada of 1599 broke off its approach to England to meet the threat of a Dutch fleet on the Azores and Canaries, and no later Armada was assembled to attack England. Spain's involvement in the Tyrone Rebellion in Ireland was the last significant episode of the conflict. The thirty-five hundred Spanish troops assisting the Irish at Kinsale surrendered to English forces on January 2, 1602. The death of Elizabeth I on March 24, 1603, and the accession of James VI of Scotland as James I of England (r. 1603-1625) brought about a cessation in hostilities and led to the Treaty of London (August, 1604), which allowed English trade with the Netherlands and promised that English merchants in Spain would not be subject to the Spanish Inquisition. The treaty was silent, however, on the issue of English trade with the West Indies.

SIGNIFICANCE

Scholars have noted that English military intervention on the continent resembles subsequent actions against Louis XIV of France, Napoleon I, Kaiser Wilhelm II, and Adolf Hitler. It therefore stands as both a factual and a symbolic beginning of England's influence as a true world power in Europe. The end of the Anglo-Spanish War brought considerable advantages to England and its new king, James I. Relations between England and Scotland were greatly improved, because the same monarch ruled both countries. The Irish rebellion had been subdued. The huge financial burden of continuing the war, which increased the importance of Parliament as a source of funding, was brought to an end, although considerable debt remained. England's sale of patents of monopoly and draining of revenue from church property had raised necessary funds but had created resentment toward the government. Moreover, although there had been no successful Spanish invasion of England and Spain's bid for dominance in western Europe had been stopped, the English still maintained a significant fear of Spanish influence.

On Spain's part, the empire's "golden age" was over; its merchant fleet was largely destroyed, and much of its trade with its colonial possessions had been usurped by others, primarily the English and Dutch. English privateering and naval activity greatly expanded England's reach in the Mediterranean, the Caribbean, the Atlantic, and Asian trade routes, and they led to the first serious attempts at colonization in North America, first at Roanoke and then at Jamestown. The chartering of the East India Company (1600) also helped pave the way for the formation of an empire. The Dutch were able to pursue greater commercial and colonial opportunities, while France was able to recover from the Wars of Religion (1562-1598). The preservation of England as a Protestant nation led to a strong connection between patriotism and an anti-Spanish, anti-Catholic attitude.

—*Mark C. Herman*

FURTHER READING

Cruickshank, C. G. *Elizabeth's Army.* 2d ed. Oxford, England: Oxford University Press, 1966. A major study of the composition and structure of the Elizabethan ground forces with a concise treatment of the 1596 campaign against Spain.

Kamen, Henry. *Philip of Spain.* New Haven, Conn.: Yale University Press, 1997. This biography contains a strong focus on Philip II's wars, especially the Anglo-Spanish War.

Parker, Geoffrey. *The Grand Strategy of Philip II.* New Haven, Conn.: Yale University Press, 1998. A major work of analysis of Philip's military undertakings, and his leadership.

Wernham, R. B. *After the Armada: Elizabethan England and the Struggle for Western Europe, 1588-1595.* Oxford, England: Oxford University Press, 1984. This detailed study focuses on the continental aspect, which the author asserts has been overlooked in favor of the naval actions.

_____. *Before the Armada: The Emergence of the English Nation, 1485-1588.* New York: Harcourt, Brace, and World, 1966. A survey which places the Anglo-Spanish War within the context of the Tudor Dynasty and explains the context for the beginning of the struggle.

_____. *The Return of the Armadas: The Last Years of the Elizabethan War Against Spain, 1585-1603.* New York: Oxford University Press, 1994. This narrative examines the policy of Elizabeth I and her ministers and the events of the final stage of the Anglo-Spanish War.

SEE ALSO: 1558-1603: Reign of Elizabeth I; Mar., 1562-May 2, 1598: French Wars of Religion; 1580-1581: Spain Annexes Portugal; July 26, 1581: The United Provinces Declare Independence from Spain; July 7, 1585-Dec. 23, 1588: War of the Three Henrys; Sept. 14, 1585-July 27, 1586: Drake's Expedition to the West Indies; July 31-Aug. 8, 1588: Defeat of the Spanish Armada; 1597-Sept., 1601: Tyrone Rebellion.

RELATED ARTICLES in *Great Lives from History: The Renaissance & Early Modern Era, 1454-1600:* Sir Francis Drake; Elizabeth I; Alessandro Farnese; Sir Martin Frobisher; Henry III; Henry IV; Philip II.

1588-1602
RISE OF THE ENGLISH MADRIGAL

The influence of the Italian madrigal in England reached its height in the 1590's, largely because of the compositions and publications of Thomas Morley, who composed some of the most famous and enduring English madrigals.

LOCALE: England
CATEGORY: Music

KEY FIGURES

Thomas Morley (1557/1558-1602), English musician, composer, and publisher

Thomas Weelkes (1576?-1623), English musician, composer, and organist at Chichester Cathedral

John Wilbye (1574-1638), privately employed musician and composer in Bury St. Edmunds, England

George Kirbye (d. 1634), privately employed musician and composer to Sir Robert Jermyn

SUMMARY OF EVENT

From the 1560's until the end of the sixteenth century, Italian musical forms enjoyed an ever-increasing level of popularity and influence in Elizabethan England. In particular, examples of the Italian madrigal—and of its related forms, the ballett and canzonet—were more frequently translated and performed in England in the late 1580's and 1590's than ever before, and this fascination with Italian music led to a flowering of the English madrigal throughout the 1590's. Thomas Morley, who was extremely active both as a composer and as a publisher of music during this period, was a driving force behind the development and popularity of English madrigalism.

The Italian madrigal is a specific genre of vocal music, popular during the sixteenth and early seventeenth centuries, typically written for four to six parts, usually (especially in its sixteenth century versions) polyphonic—that is, consisting of more than one musical line, in which each line, or part, is relatively independent. Madrigals are typically elaborate compositions that employ a number of musical devices, such as chromaticism and word painting, and because of the complexity of the vocal line, madrigal singing tends to be virtuosic. The leading exponents of the madrigal in sixteenth century Italy were Andrea Gabrieli, Orlando di Lasso, Giovanni Pierluigi da Palestrina, Luca Marenzio, Don Carlo Gesualdo, and Claudio Monteverdi.

The royal court of Elizabeth had been familiar with the Italian madrigal as early as the 1560's, when the Italian composer Alfonso Ferrabosco the Elder was in residence there (although there is evidence that madrigals made their way into the court as early as the 1520's). In 1588, the English musician Nicholas Yonge published *Musica Transalpina*, a collection of Italian madrigals translated into English, effectively introducing madrigals to a wider audience and making them available to an English-speaking public. The collection was well received, and only two years later, Thomas Watson published *First Sett of Italian Madrigalls Englished* (1590), another collection of madrigals devoted to the works of the well-known Italian composer Luca Marenzio.

By far the most prolific disseminator of madrigal collections in the 1590's was the composer Thomas Morley, who published no fewer than five collections of madrigal music within a period of five years, including *Canzonets to Three Voyces* (1593), *Madrigalls to Foure Voyces* (1594), *Canzonets to Two Voices* (1595), *First Book of Ballets to Five Voices* (1595), and *Canzonets to Five and Sixe Voices* (1597). Canzonets and balletts are also Italian-derived forms of music that are closely related to the madrigal, and it has even been suggested that Morley (like other Elizabethans) did not make a rigid distinction between the three forms in his work. At any rate, Morley's canzonet and ballett collections included pieces easily recognizable as conventional madrigals. Morley's *A Plaine and Easie Introduction to Practicall Musicke* (1597), by far the most popular English treatise on musical performance and composition throughout the seventeenth century, also contained several original madrigal compositions by Morley. It is in this work, moreover, that Morley offers a comprehensive definition of the madrigal, especially in relation to other contemporary musical forms, such as the motet and the canzonet.

Morley's contribution to the madrigal tradition in England was significantly aided by the fact that, in addition to being a prolific composer in the Italian genres, he was extremely active as a music publisher during a period in which publication was strictly restricted by the royal court. In 1598, Morley was granted a patent to publish printed music, after the monopoly originally belonging to William Byrd expired in 1596. In addition to allowing him to publish standard English books of metrical psalms and ruled paper, Morley's patent allowed him to publish a large number of part books (that is, ensemble or polyphonic music, such as madrigals, in which each part appears in a separate book), including works of his own composition as well as works by contemporary English musicians. For example, *The Triumphes of Oriana*, published by Morley in 1601, contained twenty-nine madrigals, each written by a different composer (including one by Morley himself).

Although some of Morley's adaptations of Italian musical forms betray the influence of an older, English tradition of polyphonic church music (which he undoubtedly learned, at least in large part, from the English composer William Byrd), most of Morley's English madrigals tend to have a lighter musical texture and do not place as much importance on the poetic vocal text. This tendency has occasionally prompted scholars to term Morley's work the "light" approach to the madrigal. Other contemporary English composers, dubbed as exemplars of the "serious" approach to the madrigal, preferred a weightier musical texture, in which the poetic text was chiefly important in determining the shape or features of the musical line. The best examples of this approach include George Kirbye's *First Set of English Madrigals to Four, Five, and Six Voices* (1597), Thomas Weelkes's *Madrigals to Three, Four, Five, and Six Voices* (1597) and *Ballets and Madrigals to Five Voices* (1598), and John Wilbye's *First Set of Madrigals to Three, Four, Five, and Six Parts* (1598). Both of these approaches to the madrigal were well received in Elizabethan England, although the madrigal as a whole had already started to wane by the beginning of the seventeenth century, replaced in terms of popularity by the lute song.

SIGNIFICANCE

Although little credence is now given to the traditional idea that English music in the sixteenth and early seventeenth centuries did not have much of a history outside Italian influences, the fact remains that the introduction of the Italian madrigal to England spurred one of the most creative and richest periods of English music composition in the Renaissance. The astonishing output of collections of madrigals and related forms in the 1590's, best represented by the compositional and publishing efforts of Thomas Morley, gave impetus to the business of music publishing in England and consolidated a commercial market for printed music. In addition, the development and popularity of the madrigal in England—as a musical form that combines poetic text with complex, polyphonic harmony—helped to shape contemporary debates over the relationship between music and language. It is probably no coincidence that the great dramatist William Shakespeare, for example, included a song by Morley in one of his many works that deal with the relationship of music to poetry.

—Joseph M. Ortiz

FURTHER READING

Jacobson, David Christopher. "Thomas Morley and the Italian Madrigal Tradition: A New Perspective." *Journal of Musicology* 14 (1996): 80-91. Discusses Morley's understanding of the different genres of the Italian music he was adapting, paying special attention to the discussion of music in Morley's *A Plaine and Easie Introduction to Practicall Musicke*. The article addresses modern scholarly debates over the Renaissance classification of madrigals, balletts, and canzonets.

Kerman, Joseph. *The Elizabethan Madrigal*. New York: American Musicological Society, 1962. The classic book-length study of the madrigal tradition in Renaissance England, focusing on the late sixteenth and early seventeenth centuries and treating at length the influence of the Italian sources. Morley's contributions to the genre are discussed at length. Illustrations, several musical examples.

Perkins, Leeman L. *Music in the Age of the Renaissance*. New York: Norton, 1999. Includes a section on the Italian madrigal tradition in England and English madrigals, most of which is centered on a discussion of Morley's composition and publication of madrigals and canzonets. Bibliography, illustrations, musical examples (including a lengthy excerpt from Morley's "April Is in My Mistress' Face").

SEE ALSO: 1567: Palestrina Publishes the *Pope Marcellus Mass*; 1575: Tallis and Byrd Publish *Cantiones Sacrae*; 1590's: Birth of Opera.

RELATED ARTICLES in *Great Lives from History: The Renaissance & Early Modern Era, 1454-1600:* William Byrd; John Dowland; Andrea Gabrieli; Giovanni Gabrieli; Josquin des Prez; Orlando di Lasso; Luca Marenzio; Claudio Monteverdi; Thomas Morley; Giovanni Pierluigi da Palestrina; Thomas Tallis.

July 31-August 8, 1588
DEFEAT OF THE SPANISH ARMADA

The defeat of the Spanish Armada by the English eliminated Spain's threat to the English navy, prevented Spanish conquest of the Republic of the Netherlands, limited Spanish involvement in the French religious wars, and set the stage for the global acceptance of Protestantism.

LOCALE: English Channel
CATEGORY: Wars, uprisings, and civil unrest

KEY FIGURES

Lord Charles Howard of Effingham (1536-1624), commander of the English fleet
Alonzo Pérez de Guzmán (1550-1615), duke of Medina-Sidonia, commander of the Spanish Armada
Elizabeth I (1533-1603), queen of England, r. 1558-1603
Philip II (1527-1598), king of Spain, r. 1556-1598
Alessandro Farnese (1545-1592), duke of Parma, commander of the Spanish army of Flanders
Sir John Hawkins (1532-1595), comptroller of the English navy
Sir Francis Drake (c. 1540-1596), English squadron commander

SUMMARY OF EVENT

The enterprise of the Spanish Armada was part of Spanish king Philip II's strategy to defeat the Republic of the Netherlands, which had begun to rebel against Spanish rule in 1568. England's queen Elizabeth I feared the expansion of Spanish power in the French religious wars (1562-1594) and sought to divert it by supporting the Dutch revolution.

At the inception of the Netherlands' revolt, Elizabeth I seized the Spanish pay fleet for its famed army of Flanders and sent Sir John Hawkins and Sir Francis Drake to raid coastal cities in the Spanish Indies. Finally, Philip II decided to take action against the English and reviewed several plans in 1586. Alessandro Farnese, duke of Parma and commander of the army of Flanders in the Netherlands, proposed a secret, quick channel crossing by his troops. Spain's foremost admiral, the marquis de Santa Cruz, believed a self-sufficient army and navy should sail from Spain prepared for an eight-month campaign; he requested 150 galleons and 320 auxiliary supply ships to carry the soldiers, munitions, and supplies. The cost of the Santa Cruz plan seemed prohibitive while the Parma plan seemed extremely risky.

Exactly who bears the responsibility for Philip's belief that he could combine the two plans into a cost-efficient strategy remains a subject of historical debate. Philip's chief adviser, Juan de Zúñiga, is blamed by some, but the basis of "the enterprise" lay in Parma's original belief that he could get his troop barges into the channel. Since Parma did not have a deep-water port, a rendezvous with the Armada was nearly impossible because of the Dutch coastal guard. Parma's preparation for the crossing is another issue hotly debated. Some argue he made only token progress in barge building while others say he was ready and blame his failure to go to sea on faulty communications.

The fleet to escort Parma's army across the channel assembled in Lisbon and consisted of approximately 30,000 men on 120 vessels with 43 armed ships weighing more than 350 tons. The legend that the Spanish fleet was larger in number and in the size of its ships is mythical. In terms of front-line warships, the two fleets were about equal in number and size. One reason for the myth about ship size was John Hawkins's "race-built" galleons produced after 1577. They did not have the large forecastles for carrying troops to grapple and board. This allowed space for more cannons and partly accounts for the greater damage inflicted by English gunnery at close range. The comparison in the firepower of the two fleets has long been contested, but all authors acknowledge the huge advantage the English had in being able to replenish their ships with shot and powder from shore. Drake's daring assault on Cádiz in 1587 delayed the Armada for one year. His destruction of tons of barrel staves, essential for ships' supplies, contributed to the hellish return voyage of the Armada.

Admiral Santa Cruz died three months before the Armada set sail, and Philip II appointed the duke of Medina-Sidonia, Alonzo Pérez de Guzmán, as his replacement. As captain general in western Andalusia, the duke helped outfit the annual American fleets, but he begged not to take the Armada command because of his lack of experience at sea. His own humility was grist for later scapegoat seekers. In Lisbon, he found preparations in total disarray; the fact that the fleet set sail in 1588 was a testament to his managerial and organizational skill.

The Armada entered the English Channel on July 29 and prepared to fight the English fleet on July 31 by creating a crescent formation with the strongest ships on the wings so they could encircle any English stragglers and board them with their superior number of soldiers. Led by Lord Charles Howard, the English met the Spanish with a double-line formation intent on turning back the Spanish fleet. The English, however, could not break the Spanish formation as they stood off, using their superiority in long-range cannons and munitions but inflicting little damage. Howard had let the Spanish fleet through his line. The English fell behind, gained the wind, and forced repeated engagements but could not stop the Armada's inexorable advance to an illusory union with Parma. As the Spanish fire reply slowed because of their lack of munitions, the English began to sail closer and to inflict greater damage. The Armada dropped anchor near Calais Roads on August 6 to await Parma's barges from Sluys. Medina-Sidonia thought Parma was capable of leaving the shallows of Sluys, but his barges would have to exit one at a time, making them easy targets for the Dutch fly boats. Parma communicated with Philip, but not with Medina-Sidonia.

On the night of August 7-8, the English sent eight fire ships into the Spanish fleet, scattering their ships. When the double-loaded cannons exploded, many Spanish captains believed these were "hellburners," ships packed full of powder and shot, which could devastate a closely formed fleet. On the morning of August 8, Medina-Sidonia struck his sails and offered battle to an enemy now three times his size. As the Battle of Gravelines ensued, Spanish ships slowly returned to their courageous admiral. The crescent re-formed under a ferocious pounding. The English ran out of powder, and the winds shifted to Spanish advantage. With no word from Parma, little ammunition, and a badly damaged fleet, Medina-Sidonia decided to sail north and return as many ships and men as possible to fight another day.

After all the channel battles, the Armada had lost only three ships to English gunfire, but the damage to others proved fatal during two weeks of severe storms on the return voyage. Lack of water and food led several ships to seek harbor in Ireland. The English executed all the Spaniards they could find, but the Irish helped hundreds of others to escape to Scotland. All the ships that followed Medina-Sidonia's course returned to Spain. Two-

An engraving depicting English war ships among the scattering armada of Spanish ships, which had been anchored before the arrival of the English. (Hulton|Archive by Getty Images)

thirds of the fleet was saved, but only half was fit for future service. Half the men had perished. Many crewmen died in Spanish ports because it was impossible to requisition sufficient supplies for the thousands of starving and sick survivors.

SIGNIFICANCE

The defeat of the Armada did not crush Spain and usher in British naval supremacy (that would occur one hundred years after the defeat). Philip II began a crash naval construction program and sent two more Armadas against England; the last in 1597 had 136 ships and was considerably superior to the British fleet. The war with England that officially began with the Armada ended in a stalemate in 1604.

Yet the defeat of the Armada was a psychological lift for international Protestantism. Spain had had a series of unbroken military victories since the 1540's. The Republic of the Netherlands was saved and its independence eventually recognized by Spain in 1648. Hope was given to the French Huguenots, whose leader, Henry of Bourbon, would ascend the throne after converting to Catholicism in 1593. The war with England diverted Spanish resources from the Netherlands and France when Spanish power may otherwise have been overwhelming in those regions.

—*Daniel A. Crews*

FURTHER READING

Coote, Stephen. *Drake: The Life and Legend of an Elizabethan Hero.* New York: Simon & Schuster, 2003. Biography combines novelistic dramatization of Drake's life with important analysis of the way his legend became a national symbol through which England understood itself and its global actions. Includes illustrations, maps, bibliographic references, and index.

Doran, Susan. *Queen Elizabeth I.* New York: New York University Press, 2003. Portrays Elizabeth as a flawed but brilliant manipulator who used this ability to protect her country and to steer it safely through a host of dangers. Includes illustrations, map, bibliographic references, index.

Dudley, Wade G. *Drake: For God, Queen, and Plunder.* Washington, D.C.: Brassey's, 2003. This entry in Brassey's "Military Profiles" series examines Drake's naval career, including his role in the defeat of the Spanish Armada. Includes photographic plates, illustrations, maps, bibliographic references, and index.

Fernández-Armesto, Felipe. *The Spanish Armada: The*

An engraved illustration of twelve ships of the Spanish Armada called the "twelve apostles." (Hulton|Archive by Getty Images)

Experience of War in 1588. New York: Oxford University Press, 1988. Good analysis of the variety of plans offered to Philip. The author defends Philip's decision and views the battle as having little significance for the outcome of the Anglo-Spanish War.

Martin, Colin, and Geoffrey Parker. *The Spanish Armada.* New York: W. W. Norton, 1988. Martin and Parker use recent underwater archaeology of Armada wrecks to speculate that Spanish cannon carriages made reloading nearly impossible during battle, thus explaining the greater damage inflicted upon Spanish ships.

Mattingly, Garrett. *The Armada.* Reprint. Boston: Houghton Mifflin, 1987. This Pulitzer Prize-winning account is the beginning of modern Armada scholarship. It is particularly strong on the context of international relations and Spanish diplomacy.

Pierson, Peter. *Commander of the Armada: The Seventh Duke of Medina Sidonia.* New Haven, Conn.: Yale University Press, 1989. The first biography of the Armada commander develops the duke's character and career before and after the disaster. The appendices and diagrams provide a highly accurate account of Spanish fighting tactics.

Rodriguez-Salgado, M. J. *Armada, 1588-1988: An Inter-*

national Exhibition to Commemorate the Spanish Armada—The Official Catalogue. London: Penguin Books in association with the National Maritime Museum, 1988. This catalog of the British National Maritime Museum's Armada Exhibition in 1988 includes 430 illustrations and pictures of artifacts, maps, leaders, rival armies and navies, invasion plans and defense measures, and ship life in the sixteenth century along with informative text.

Williams, Patrick. *Armada*. Charleston, S.C.: Tempus, 2000. Monograph on the English defeat of the Armada. Details the causes of the attempted invasion, the battle itself, and its aftermath. Includes illustrations, maps, bibliographic references, and index.

SEE ALSO: 16th cent.: Evolution of the Galleon; Mar., 1562-May 2, 1598: French Wars of Religion; July 26, 1581: The United Provinces Declare Independence from Spain; July 7, 1585-Dec. 23, 1588: War of the Three Henrys; Sept. 14, 1585-July 27, 1586: Drake's Expedition to the West Indies; Apr., 1587-c. 1600: Anglo-Spanish War.

RELATED ARTICLES in *Great Lives from History: The Renaissance & Early Modern Era, 1454-1600:* William Cecil; Sir Francis Drake; Earl of Leicester; Elizabeth I; Alessandro Farnese; Sir Martin Frobisher; Henry IV; Philip II; First Earl of Salisbury; William the Silent.

1589
RUSSIAN PATRIARCHATE IS ESTABLISHED

The Russian Orthodox Church, headed by the Russian Patriarchate, officially lost its subordinate status to Constantinople and became a fully independent branch of Eastern Orthodoxy.

LOCALE: Moscow, Russia
CATEGORIES: Religion; organizations and institutions

KEY FIGURES

Jeremias II (c. 1530-1595), patriarch of
    Constantinople, 1572-1579, 1580-1584, 1586-1595
Jove (d. 1607), first patriarch of the Russian Church
Fyodor I (1557-1598), son of Ivan the Terrible and
    czar of Russia, r. 1584-1598
Boris Godunov (c. 1551-1605), brother-in-law and
    regent of Fyodor and later czar of Russia, r. 1598-
    1605
Isidore of Kiev (c. 1385-1463), patriarch of Kiev and
    all Russia, 1436-1441, and later Greek patriarch of
    Constantinople, 1459-1463

SUMMARY OF EVENT

The establishment of an independent Russian patriarchate in 1589 was the logical result of the growth of the Russian state throughout the sixteenth century, and it could not have occurred without that political development. Long before Moscow emerged as the political center of northeast Russia, however, the Eastern Orthodox Church directed the spiritual and cultural life of the nation. Until the middle of the fifteenth century, Russian Christians recognized the patriarch of Constantinople, the capital of the Byzantine Empire, as the ultimate source of authority within Christendom. To enforce that authority within the Russian states, Constantinople would appoint a metropolitan of Greek descent to govern the local Russian archbishops and bishops.

By the early part of the fifteenth century, the Byzantine Empire was locked in a struggle for its very existence against the Ottoman Turks. Hoping to obtain support from the West, the Greeks convened the Council of Florence, and the Greek clergy signed an agreement with Rome in 1439, recognizing papal supremacy in exchange for Western assistance against the Turks. Isidore of Kiev, the Greek-born Russian metropolitan, participated in the council's deliberations. Upon his return to Moscow in 1441, he preached in its favor and even read a prayer for the pope. Grand prince Vasily II ordered Isidore arrested. In 1448, a council of Russian bishops condemned the union of Eastern and Western churches and chose the Russian-born Archbishop Iona to replace Isidore as metropolitan of the Russian Church. This action signaled an end to the dependence of the Russian Church on the Byzantine Church. The fall of Constantinople to the Turks in 1453 led to the belief among Russians that their country was the successor empire to the Byzantines and the new leader of the Christian world.

When Ivan the Terrible was crowned czar in 1547, then, although Russia was still nominally subordinate to the patriarch of Constantinople, the Russian Church as a practical matter had been autocephalous—independent of external patriarchal authority—since 1448. However, its highest ranking official was still merely a metropolitan, that is, the subordinate representative of a patriarch. In the absence of a Russian patriarchate, the metropolitan of Russia assumed the functions but not the divine office of an autonomous spiritual leader.

The task of solving this anomalous situation fell to Ivan's son and successor, Fyodor I, and more properly to his regent, Boris Godunov. Following lengthy negotiations during a visit to Moscow, Patriarch Jeremias II of Constantinople agreed to help in raising the Russian Church to the level of a patriarchate. Jeremias was invited to stay in Moscow and to exercise his duties from there. Although he declined to do so, he did consecrate Jove, the metropolitan of the Russian Church, as the first Russian patriarch. At last, the Muscovite Church had won recognition as an independent and equal member of the Orthodox Church.

SIGNIFICANCE

Russia had hoped to be "ranked" number three in the established order of preference within the Orthodox Church but instead became number five, after Constantinople, Alexandria, Antioch, and Jerusalem. The Russian Orthodox Church, however, went on to become the single largest autocephalous Orthodox Church in the world. Its relative power and even its ability to exist varied greatly throughout its later history, primarily as a result of the struggle of the Church at various times either to seize political power from the state or to retain religious power coveted by the state. In the seventeenth century, Patriarch Nikon pursued policies meant to guide Russia toward becoming a theocratic state. In the eighteenth century, Czar Peter the Great abolished the patriarchate to establish a state-run Church. Throughout the twentieth century, the Church's fate was in constant flux in the Communist Soviet Union, as it was at times vilified as a religious institution and at times embraced as an authentically Russian institution. Patriarchal elections, for example, were forbidden in 1927 but were reestablished by Joseph Stalin in 1943.

The existence or nonexistence of a Russian patriarch, then, has since 1589 been a consistent indication of the status of the Russian Orthodox Church in relation to the Russian state. Moreover, the power and respect accorded to the patriarch, either by the state or despite the will of the state, have colored both the religious and the political histories of the Russian people.

—Edward P. Keleher, updated by Donald L. Layton

FURTHER READING

Fennell, John. *A History of the Russian Church to 1448.* New York: Longman, 1995. An overview of the Russian Church's medieval history. Provides important historical background for the founding of the Patriarchate. Includes map, bibliographic references, and index.

Florinsky, Michael T. *Russia: A History and an Interpretation.* Vol. 1. New York: Macmillan, 1955. An older study that continues to be the best general survey of Russia prior to the Soviet period. Volume 1 presents a good overview of the history of the Russian Church in medieval and early modern times.

Kivelson, Valerie A., and Robert H. Greene, eds. *Orthodox Russia: Belief and Practice Under the Tsars.* University Park: Pennsylvania State University Press, 2003. Anthology of essays by noted scholars on the history of the Russian Orthodox Church. Includes illustrations, maps, bibliographic references, and index.

Pospielovsky, Dmitry V. *The Orthodox Church in the History of Russia.* Crestwood, N.Y.: St. Vladimir's Seminary Press, 1998. A survey of the history of the Russian Orthodox Church meant to introduce undergraduates to the subject. Includes bibliographic references and index.

Treadgold, D. W. *Russia, 1472-1917.* Vol. 1 in *The West in Russia and China: Religious and Secular Thought in Modern Times.* Cambridge, England: Cambridge University Press, 1973. In comparison to the work of other scholars, Treadgold offers a contrasting view of the role and development of the Orthodox Church in Russia and the secularization of Russian society.

Vernadsky, G. *The Tsardom of Moscow, 1547-1682.* Vol. 5 in *A History of Russia.* New Haven, Conn.: Yale University Press, 1959. A useful general history of Russia from the beginning of Ivan IV's reign to the death of Czar Alexis in 1683. Provides useful political context for controversies within the Russian Church.

SEE ALSO: 1478: Muscovite Conquest of Novgorod; 1480-1502: Destruction of the Golden Horde; After 1480: Ivan the Great Organizes the "Third Rome"; Jan. 16, 1547: Coronation of Ivan the Terrible; Jan.-May, 1551: The Stoglav Convenes.

RELATED ARTICLES in *Great Lives from History: The Renaissance & Early Modern Era, 1454-1600:* Boris Godunov; Ivan the Terrible.

1589
SECOND JANISSARY REVOLT IN CONSTANTINOPLE

The revolt of the Ottoman Empire's elite and highly respected Janissary military corps, angered at being paid in debased currency, reflected the declining power of the empire and its sultans.

LOCALE: Constantinople, Ottoman Empire (now Istanbul, Turkey)

CATEGORIES: Wars, uprisings, and civil unrest; government and politics

KEY FIGURES
Murad III (1546-1595), Ottoman sultan, r. 1574-1595
Selim II (1524-1574), Ottoman sultan, r. 1566-1574, father of Murad

SUMMARY OF EVENT
The once-proud Janissary corps, the Ottoman Empire's elite military organization made up of slaves, those captured in battle, and Christian youth recruited from throughout the empire and southern Europe, declined significantly during the 1580's, largely because Sultan Murad III failed to gain the corps' respect. Murad's father, Sultan Selim II, an inconsequential ruler, had a regime in which bribery flourished and political offices could be bought for a price. Because the sultan was the designated commander of the Janissaries, their effectiveness depended on the sultan's ability to gain and command the respect of his troops.

Selim II had not met this criterion, and his son, Murad III, fell short even more significantly. The Janissaries, top infantry troops supplied with firearms rather than the lances, bows, and swords of the cavalry, were essential to his expansionist visions. Lacking their confidence in him, he had to command through fear of harsh punishment rather than through genuine respect. The Janissaries, however, turned into an undisciplined and uncontrollable group within Selim's chaotic ruling environment.

The Janissary corps, in addition to being made up of slaves, also included young men brought to Constantinople under the child levy laws of the time. The child levy, also called *devshirme*, decreed that every three to seven years one male child was to be taken, or recruited, from each non-Muslim family in Turkish, Balkan, and Anatolian villages and transported to Constantinople to serve the sultan.

These youth were trained intensively in the sultan's palace, where their conversion to Islam was required. The most promising of them remained in the palace to serve the sultan as slaves, but as privileged slaves. Those who were not retained for the palace were sent to Turkish villages to learn the Turkish language and traditions and for physical fitness. It is from this second group that the Janissary corps had traditionally been formed.

The corps had been established by Murad I in the last half of the fourteenth century as an elite and respected military force under the direct command of the sultan. Its members had long been forbidden to marry. Selim's father, Süleyman the Magnificent, however, relaxed that ban in the sixteenth century.

Janissary service was considered a privilege. Unwavering and unquestioning loyalty to the sultan was demanded, but the benefits were alluring. Janissaries received a regular salary and were considered part of the Ottoman Empire's ruling class. Those who performed well as military commanders were often made viziers or, in some rare cases, grand viziers. Upon retirement, Janissaries who had performed well could be sent into the provinces, where they led comfortable and secure lives as provincial administrators.

Under Selim and Murad, Janissaries were permitted to work outside the corps during their off hours to earn extra money, which, unlike earlier Janissaries, gave them a tie to the community. Being able to work outside the corps for money, and being allowed to marry and have families, led to drastic changes in the nature of the corps.

When Murad became sultan, many of his subjects resisted the child levy. Desperate to fill the ranks, those responsible for enforcing the levy drew recruits from wherever they could find them, even from the Muslim population. The rule excluding Muslims from becoming members (according to the religious tradition, Muslims could not be enslaved) had to be relaxed to fill the need. What was once viewed as a privilege was now considered compulsory and, therefore, something to be avoided. The Janissary corps became quite unlike the elite military corps it had been before the end of the sixteenth century.

There were, at minimum, two salient factors that led to widespread discontent throughout the empire, including the corps. The government's spending excesses necessitated higher taxes, which strained the populace. During the mid-1580's, inflation overtook the Ottoman Empire because of an influx of cheap silver to Spain from South America. The Ottomans, who bought this silver from Spain and made coins that had little value, used the coins to pay the Janissaries. In essence, however, the Janissaries had not been paid. A corps already demoralized by high taxation, inflation, and administrative chaos grew restive. In 1589, Janissaries revolted, storming their way into the Seraglio, the meeting place of the divan, or imperial council. They demanded punishment for those responsible for the empire's declining state of affairs.

Murad, knowing how dependent he was on the Janissaries to implement his land-grabs, responded to their demands by ordering the executions of the chief treasurer, the *beylerbey* of Rumelia (Europe), and the master of the mint. This temporary palliative, along with payment to the Janissaries in a more stable currency, did not offer a permanent solution to the deep-seated problems within the Janissary corps, but it did contain the immediate problem.

SIGNIFICANCE

The 1589 revolt of the Janissaries—who, despite their loyalty to the sultan, did hold political power within the empire—reflects the decline of a once-powerful empire and an all-powerful sultan. Murad had to meet the demands of what were *his* Janissaries in a military culture that epitomized the Ottoman ideal of subservience and absolute loyalty to the sultan.

The revolt also reflects the increased power of the Janissaries, who, after 1589, began to demand higher wages because of inflation. The corps also became more and more undisciplined as the revolts multiplied into the next century. The Janissary corps was officially dissolved in 1826 and replaced by an army fashioned like the armies of other European countries.

—R. Baird Shuman

FURTHER READING

Barber, Noel. *The Sultans*. New York: Simon and Schuster, 1973. Barber's highly readable account of the Ottoman sultans is an essential resource.

Faroqhi, Suraiya. *Subjects of the Sultan: Culture and Daily Life in the Ottoman Empire*. New York: I. B. Tauris, 2000. A lively account of everyday life and culture in the Ottoman Empire.

Goodwin, Godfrey. *The Janissaries*. London: Saqi, 1997. A complete and comprehensive resource on the Janissaries.

Itzkowitz, Norman. *Ottoman Empire and Islamic Tradition*. New York: Alfred A. Knopf, 1972. The author provides considerable detail about the formation and activities of the Janissary corps.

Kinross, John P. *The Ottoman Centuries: The Rise and Fall of the Ottoman Empire*. New York: William Morrow, 1977. In addition to a general history of the empire, this work also contains a compelling overview of the Janissary movement.

Somel, Selcuk Aksin. *Historical Dictionary of the Ottoman Empire*. Lanham, Md.: Scarecrow Press, 2003. A brief but comprehensive overview of the reign of Murad III.

SEE ALSO: 1454-1481: Rise of the Ottoman Empire; 1512-1520: Reign of Selim I; Aug. 29, 1526: Battle of Mohács; 1534-1535: Ottomans Claim Sovereignty over Mesopotamia; 1559-1561: Süleyman's Sons Wage Civil War; 1574-1595: Reign of Murad III.

RELATED ARTICLES in *Great Lives from History: The Renaissance & Early Modern Era, 1454-1600:* Barbarossa; Mehmed III; Süleyman the Magnificent.

1580's

c. 1589-1613
SHAKESPEARE WRITES HIS DRAMAS

Shakespeare produced a body of dramatic work that helped define theatrical convention in Elizabethan England and that has been appropriated by countless schools of dramatic performance and literary criticism ever since.

LOCALE: London, England
CATEGORIES: Theater; literature

KEY FIGURES

William Shakespeare (1564-1616), English actor, poet, and playwright
Ben Jonson (1573-1637), English poet, playwright, and critic
Christopher Marlowe (1564-1593), English playwright
John Fletcher (1579-1625), English playwright
Thomas Kyd (1558-1594), English playwright
John Heminge (c. 1556-1630), actor and cocompiler and editor of the first edition of Shakespeare's plays
Henry Condell (d. 1627), actor and cocompiler and editor of the first edition of Shakespeare's plays
Robert Greene (1558-1592), English playwright
John Lyly (c. 1554-1606), English playwright

SUMMARY OF EVENT

English playwright William Shakespeare wrote thirty-nine plays between approximately 1589 and 1613. These plays, which have been broadly categorized as histories, comedies, tragedies, and romances, are widely considered to be the finest dramatic work in the English language. This judgment is especially noteworthy, because Shakespeare worked at a time when the theater as a formal literary institution in England, and especially as an arena for individual expression or accomplishment, was still a relatively novel phenomenon.

In the sixth century, the Catholic Church exerted its influence to close down the decadent theater of the late Roman Empire. An official, institutionalized form of theater did not exist in Western Europe for four centuries thereafter. Ironically, it was the Catholic Church that also sponsored the beginnings of a new dramatic form within the church liturgy in the tenth century. Semidramatic and dramatic representations of the events of Easter evolved by the end of the twelfth century into complex and lengthy dramas dealing with other festivals in the liturgical calendar.

In the early fourteenth century, drama moved out of the churches and into the streets. Various town craft guilds began to present cycles of plays depicting biblical stories, from accounts of the Creation and the Garden of Eden to the ascension of Christ; these plays were known as Corpus Christi plays because they were associated with the midsummer feast of Corpus Christi. Saints' plays, focusing on the lives of the saints, and morality plays, which presented allegorical renditions of humanity's spiritual journey through life, were also widely current in England. Morality plays were performed by wandering troupes of actors, contained stock characters and low comedy, and were intended to entertain as well as to instruct.

These plays survived into the late sixteenth century and had an appreciable influence on William Shakespeare. Shakespeare probably saw Corpus Christi plays as a youth. In the early sixteenth century, teachers and schoolboys began to produce plays that were based on Roman comedy but adapted to English customs and mores. Tragedies based on classical models, particularly those of Roman playwright Seneca the Younger (4 B.C.E.-65 C.E.), began to appear in the mid-sixteenth century.

An engraving of William Shakespeare done from the Chandos portrait. (Library of Congress)

Shakespeare Writes His Dramas

The most influential Renaissance play-wrights to precede Shakespeare were Robert Greene, who opened up for Shakespeare the work of Greek romance; John Lyly, known for his elaborate, courtly language and a sensitive portrayal of the psychology of love; Thomas Kyd, whose play *The Spanish Tragedy* (pr. c. 1585-1589) was probably the most frequently performed play in the sixteenth century; and Christopher Marlowe, whose "mighty lines," tragic seriousness, and spirit of aspiration heavily influenced subsequent dramatists.

When Shakespeare arrived in London in the late 1580's, the city proper and its suburbs had a population of approximately 200,000 inhabitants, making it the largest city in Europe. The city stretched along the north bank of the Thames River from the old Tower of London on the east to St. Paul's Cathedral and the Fleet Ditch on the west. Visitors approaching London from the south bank of the Thames (the Bankside) crossed London Bridge to enter the city. London authorities frowned on large public gatherings because they believed such gatherings made both crime and spread of the bubonic plague more likely. Consequently, public theaters were constructed in the suburbs to escape the stringent regulations imposed by the Lord Mayor and council of aldermen.

London's first public theater, known as The Theatre, was built in Finsbury Fields by James Burbage in 1576. The Curtain was built the following year, and the Rose, the first playhouse on the Bankside, was built about ten years later. Richard and Cuthbert Burbage, sons of James, dismantled The Theatre in 1599 because of trouble about the lease of the land. They rebuilt the theater on the Bankside and renamed it the Globe Theatre. These public theaters held about two to three thousand people.

Smaller private theaters, based on the great halls of Tudor houses, flourished in the city proper during the 1580's and again in 1598-1599. The prices charged at these theaters were higher, the accommodations were more comfortable, and the audiences were more elite than at the larger venues. The plays written for these select audiences tended to be more satirical and were oriented to courtly values.

By the time Shakespeare arrived in London, then, the flimsy mobile scaffolds of traveling acting troupes had been replaced by permanent structures, and the theater

---

HAMLET ON THE PURPOSE OF PLAYING

In Hamlet, Prince of Denmark*, Shakespeare's title character stages a play for his uncle, Claudius, which is meant to remind Claudius of the crime he has committed and to make him react in a way that will confirm his guilt. In this speech, Hamlet explains the purpose of drama to performers.*

Suit the action to the word, the word to the action, with this special observance, that you o'erstep not the modesty of nature: for any thing so o'er done is from the purpose of playing, whose end, both at the first and now, was and is, to hold as 'twere the mirror up to nature; to show virtue her own feature, scorn her own image, and the very age and body of the time his form and pressure.

Source: From *The Tragedy of Hamlet, Prince of Denmark*, by William Shakespeare: act 3, scene 2, ll. 17-24. In *The Riverside Shakespeare* (Boston: Houghton Mifflin, 1974), pp. 1161-1162.

1580's

---

was a thriving enterprise. It was not, however, altogether a respectable one. Gentlemen poets were perfectly acceptable in polite society, but commoners, particularly ones like Shakespeare, who did not have the benefit of a university education, were highly suspect. Shakespeare was one of the first men to earn a fortune with his pen, and even then, it was as a theatrical producer rather than as a playwright that he earned the bulk of his income.

Shakespeare apparently coveted respectability and earned it long before he died. He began to purchase property in the 1590's and was established in the rank and title of gentleman in 1596. His rapid rise in the world came through his association with the Burbages. By 1594, Shakespeare was a partner in, as well as actor and primary playwright for, the Lord Chamberlain's Men. This company was dominated by James Burbage, the owner of The Theatre; Cuthbert Burbage, manager of the company; and Richard Burbage, the principal actor of the troupe. Upon the death of Queen Elizabeth, the troupe became known as the King's Men, to honor the accession of King James to the English throne.

Shakespeare began writing plays around 1589. He was the author of two historical tetralogies. The first tetralogy comprised *Henry VI, Part I* (wr. 1589-1590, pr. 1592), *Henry VI, Part II* (pr. c. 1590-1591), *Henry VI, Part III* (pr. c. 1590-1591), and *Richard III* (pr. c. 1592-1593). *Richard II* (pr. c. 1595-1596), *Henry IV, Part I* (pr. c. 1597-1598), *Henry IV, Part II* (pr. 1598), and *Henry V* (pr. c. 1598-1599) constituted the second tetralogy. The history plays are concerned with the consequences of civil strife and with questions about the nature of kingship and the relationship between humanity, morality, depth of character, and the ability to rule well. Characteristically, Shakespeare presents paradoxes, dilemmas, and questions rather than answers. His comedies—from joyous early ones, such as *A Midsummer Night's Dream* (pr. c. 1595-1596) to darker ones, such as *Measure for Measure* (pr. 1604)—are wonderfully complex, entertaining, and perplexing. Shakespeare never ceases to examine the nature of human life and the mysteries of sexual attraction and romantic love.

The tragedies are generally taken to be Shakespeare's most profound and compelling works. *Romeo and Juliet* (pr. c. 1595-1596), *Othello, the Moor of Venice* (pr. 1604), *Hamlet, Prince of Denmark* (pr. c. 1600-1601), *Macbeth* (pr. 1606), *King Lear* (pr. c. 1605-1606), and *Antony and Cleopatra* (pr. c. 1606-1607) are all intensely engaging, disturbing, and enriching works that probe the darker mysteries of human life and the human heart with unrelenting eloquence and honesty. Their greatness triumphantly survives translation and transposition, compelling attention in virtually every culture in the world. Finally, in the romances, such as *The Tempest* (pr. 1611) and *The Winter's Tale* (pr. c. 1610-1611), Shakespeare returns to the great themes of the tragedies with a more hopeful and quiet mind.

Shakespeare died without ever having bothered to publish his plays. Apparently, he had little concern for their ultimate fate or for his own enduring fame. Fortunately, John Heminge and Henry Condell, actors in the King's Men, gathered copies of thirty-six plays, half of which had already been printed in individual quarto editions, and published the First Folio edition of Shakespeare's dramatic works in 1623. Only *Pericles, Prince of Tyre* (pr. c. 1607-1608), *Two Noble Kinsmen* (pr. c. 1612-1613, with John Fletcher), and *Henry VIII* (pr. 1613, with Fletcher) were missing from the first edition. The fact that Shakespeare did not oversee the production of the Folio, as Ben Jonson had overseen the publication of his own *The Workes of Benjamin Jonson* (1616), means that neither the Folio texts nor any surviving quartos or playbook copies of particular plays can be said to be definitive. Although there are numerous discrepancies among the surviving copies of the plays, however, textual critics and editors are in general agreement about the most accurate versions.

SIGNIFICANCE

In *The Western Canon: The Books and School of the Ages* (1994), critic Harold Bloom summarized the genius of Shakespeare, acknowledging that he "perceived more than any other, and had an almost effortless mastery of

language, far surpassing everyone." Shakespeare's greatest originality was arguably in the representation of human character and personality and their mutability. His characters live beyond the bounds of his plays: Bottom, Shylock, Falstaff, Hamlet, Lear.

Part of what made Shakespeare a unique author, besides his extraordinary facility with language, was what nineteenth century poet John Keats called "negative capability," that is, Shakespeare's ability to see into characters' lives with an extraordinary self-effacing sympathy. It is as if Shakespeare overhears his characters rather than making them speak. Even his minor characters are individuals with distinct and consistent voices that seem real.

Shakespeare is fascinating, in part, because he is the least aggressive and self-conscious of the greatest artists. Audiences and readers know what Hamlet thinks, or Antony, or Prospero, but they are never sure of Shakespeare; he has the generosity and largeness and indifference of nature. Michelangelo said in one of his letters: "the ultimate artist has no idea." Shakespeare seems to have been such an artist. Truly, as his contemporary Ben Jonson said, "He was not of an age, but for all time."

—*Hal Holladay*

FURTHER READING

Andrews, John F., ed. *William Shakespeare: His World, His Work, His Influence*. 3 vols. New York: Charles Scribner's Sons, 1985. A comprehensive general reference work that contains sixty essays on the historical and cultural context of Shakespeare's work, career, and influence on his own time and on future generations.

Bloom, Harold. *The Western Canon: The Books and School of the Ages*. New York: Harcourt Brace, 1994. A humanist defense of the canon and canonicity, in which Shakespeare figures prominently. Includes index.

_____, ed. *Elizabethan Drama*. Philadelphia: Chelsea House, 2004. Anthology of essays that place Shakespeare and his plays in their cultural context, evaluating both his originality and his indebtedness to tradition. Includes bibliographic references and index.

Cavell, Stanley. *Disowning Knowledge in Seven Plays of Shakespeare*. New York: Cambridge University Press, 2003. An updated edition of one of the greatest works of Shakespeare criticism. Cavell delves into the philosophy of self and other in Shakespearean tragedy. His reading of *King Lear* is unparalleled. Includes bibliographic references and index.

De Grazia, Margreta, and Stanley Wells, eds. *The Cambridge Companion to Shakespeare*. New York: Cambridge University Press, 2001. Anthology of commissioned essays on the life and work of the Bard. Includes a survey of Shakespeare criticism in the seventeenth through the nineteenth centuries, a survey of performances from 1660 to 1900, an overview of Shakespeare on film, an essay on genre, and an exploration of Shakespeare's reading habits, among others. With illustrations, bibliographic references, and index.

Evans, G. Blakemore, with J. J. M. Tobin, eds. *The Riverside Shakespeare*. 2d ed. Boston: Houghton Mifflin, 1997. An excellent edition of the complete works of Shakespeare with thorough annotation, full critical introductions, and a wealth of ancillary material.

Greenblatt, Stephen. *Renaissance Self-Fashioning: From More to Shakespeare*. Chicago: University of Chicago Press, 1980. A pioneering work in new historicism that continues to serve as one of the most important contributions in the field and one of the most rewarding for readers.

Kahn, Coppèlia. *Man's Estate: Masculine Identity in Shakespeare*. Berkeley: University of California Press, 1981. Written by a distinguished feminist critic, this work provides a study of masculinity in Shakespeare's plays.

Loomba, Anita. *Gender, Race, Renaissance Drama*. Manchester, England: Manchester University Press, 1989. Loomba analyzes race as it affects drama of the Renaissance period and discusses the uses of Shakespeare in colonialist and postcolonialist contexts.

McDonald, Russ, ed. *Shakespeare: An Anthology of Criticism and Theory, 1945-2000*. Malden, Mass.: Blackwell, 2004. Collects approximately fifty of the most influential essays and book chapters on Shakespeare from the second half of the twentieth century. Organized on the basis of the school of criticism represented in fourteen sections, such as "New Criticism," "Psychoanalytic Readings," and "Race and Postcolonialism." Includes illustrations, bibliographic references, and index.

Wells, Stanley. *Shakespeare: A Life in Drama*. New York: W. W. Norton, 1996. A noted Shakespearean scholar offers a critical introduction to Shakespeare's literary achievements as a playwright, grouping the plays together to analyze comparable themes and characters.

_____. *Shakespeare: For All Time*. New York: Oxford University Press, 2003. Survey of Shakespeare reception and criticism, from the Renaissance through the twentieth century. Includes illustrations, bibliographic references, and index.

SEE ALSO: 1558-1603: Reign of Elizabeth I; 1576: James Burbage Builds The Theatre; 1590's: Birth of Opera; Dec., 1598-May, 1599: The Globe Theatre Is Built.

RELATED ARTICLES in *Great Lives from History: The Renaissance & Early Modern Era, 1454-1600:* Francis Beaumont and John Fletcher; George Chapman; Christopher Marlowe; Thomas Nashe; William Shakespeare.

August 2, 1589
HENRY IV ASCENDS THE THRONE OF FRANCE

In the wake of Henry III's assassination, Henry of Navarre became King Henry IV of France. The first French monarch of the House of Bourbon and a Protestant, Henry found his subjects at best distrustful and at worst openly rebellious. Once he converted to Catholicism, however, he was able to end the French Wars of Religion, to establish a limited degree of religious toleration, and to restore somewhat the power and authority of the French monarchy.

LOCALE: St. Cloud, France
CATEGORIES: Government and politics; religion

KEY FIGURES
Henry IV (1553-1610), king of Navarre as Henry III, r. 1572-1589, and king of France, r. 1589-1610

Henry I of Lorraine (1550-1588), third duke of Guise, 1563-1588, and leader of the Catholic League, 1585-1588

Charles de Lorraine (1554-1611), duke of Mayenne, younger brother of Henry I of Lorraine and leader of the Catholic League, 1589-1595

Henry III (1551-1589), king of France, r. 1574-1589

Maximilien de Béthune (1560-1641), marquis of Rosny, Henry IV's principal minister, later duke of Sully, 1606-1641

Jeanne d'Albret (1528-1572), queen of Navarre, r. 1562-1572, and Protestant mother of Henry IV

Philip II (1527-1598), king of Spain, r. 1556-1598

François Ravaillac (1578-1610), assassin of Henry IV

François de Lorraine (1519-1563), duke of Aumale,
1547-1563, second duke of Guise, 1550-1563,
prince of Joinville, 1552-1563

SUMMARY OF EVENT

The rise of Protestantism in Europe set in motion a period of religious warfare between Protestants and Catholics. By the mid-1550's, John Calvin's Protestant missionary efforts had produced approximately 1,250,000 converts in France, called Huguenots, but this figure represented no more than 10 percent of the French population. Most French men and women remained staunchly Catholic.

People living during the sixteenth century could not envision a country with more than one religion and believed in the idea of "one faith, one law, one king." War broke out in 1562, when the Catholic François de Lorraine, duke of Guise murdered a group of Huguenots at Vassy. Protestant retaliation ensued. There were eight religious wars altogether, and their history was marked by extreme religious intolerance and great atrocities. During the St. Bartholomew's Day Massacre of 1572, for example, most of the Protestant leadership in France lost their lives in a night of violent slaughter. The religious wars lasted thirty-six years until 1598, and they brought Henry of Navarre to the throne of France as King Henry IV.

The wars were both political and religious in origin. Politically, the last Valois kings, Francis II (r. 1559-1560), Charles IX (r. 1560-1574), and Henry III (r. 1574-1589), were weak and manipulated by their mother, Catherine de Médicis (1519-1589). Noble families such as the conservative Catholic Guises, the more moderate Catholic Montmorencys, and the Protestant Bourbons vied for control of each Valois king and engulfed court life in factional politics. Yet, the wars were also directly tied to religion, as fiery priests and evangelists went from town to town stirring the emotions of urban populations. Many people believed God's Last Judgment was imminent, and outbreaks of collective violence associated with religious anxiety overwhelmed French society. Catholics killed Protestants as Protestants slew Catholics, each believing they needed to annihilate the other before Christ would return.

The last phase of the religious wars was dominated by the Catholic League (1585-1598), an association of zealous nobles, churchmen, and urban elites intent on preventing the Protestant Henry of Navarre from inheriting the French throne. The Guise family headed the Catholic League with support from the Spanish king, Philip II. In 1588, during the War of the Three Henrys, Henry I of Lorraine, duke of Guise, entered Paris against Henry III's wishes, and the king retaliated by bringing Swiss soldiers into the city. On May 12, 1588, the Day of the Barricades, the Parisian population drove the king's troops out of Paris, and the king fled. Extreme Catholic zealots known as the Sixteen then controlled the capital in alliance with the Guise faction.

Henry III struck back at the duke of Guise several months later at a meeting of the States-General at Blois. Guise was murdered on December 23, 1588, by Henry's royal guard. News of the duke's murder radicalized the Catholic League, and League leaders quickly took control of most of the important urban centers in France, including Rouen, Amiens, Lyons, Orléans, Dijon, Reims, Toulouse, and Marseilles. The slain duke's younger brother, Charles de Lorraine, duke of Mayenne, took over as League chief.

Henry III next allied with Henry of Navarre to try to recapture Paris, but the king never regained his authority, and League propaganda promoted the idea of tyrannicide. On August 1, 1589, a Dominican monk named Jacques Clément drove a dagger into Henry III. The childless king died the next day at his camp at St. Cloud outside Paris. Before expiring, he recognized his Protestant cousin, Henry of Navarre, as king of France.

Henry IV was reared a Protestant by his devout mother, Jeanne d'Albret. He had become the leader of the Protestant party after the St. Bartholomew's Day Massacre. At Henry's ascension, *politiques*, or individuals who put matters of state above religious issues, urged him to become Catholic, but Henry was in no position to turn his back on his Protestant supporters. He delayed talk of conversion but promised to protect Catholicism. Between 1590 and 1593, Henry won many battles against Catholic insurgents, including the Battle of Ivry (1590), in which he defeated the duke of Mayenne's army. In 1593, he felt secure enough to adopt Catholicism, and he abjured his Protestant faith on July 25, 1593, at a ceremony held at the cathedral of Saint-Denis near Paris.

Henry never uttered the famous words "Paris is worth a mass," but the aphorism reflects his pragmatism and keen sense of timing. His conversion caused war-weary French men and women to flock to the king's side at the very moment the Catholic League was becoming more dependent on Spain and a Spanish heir to the French throne. Henry represented himself as a forgiving conqueror and bought off many League nobles and urban elites with cash gifts. He was formally crowned at Chartres on February 17, 1594, and Paris capitulated the next month on March 22, 1594. Between 1593 and 1595, most of urban France left the Catholic League.

Henry ended the war against the League and Spain in 1598 with the Treaty of Vervins. To settle internal religious issues, on April 13, 1598, the Bourbon king issued the Edict of Nantes, granting limited religious toleration to Huguenots in France. The liberty to exercise the reformed religion publicly was conceded to the Huguenots in approximately two hundred fortified towns throughout France. It is often said the document created "a state within a state." Actually, the right to practice the reformed faith was tied to the will of the king. Although Henry declared the edict "irrevocable," his grandson, Louis XIV, rescinded it in 1685.

SIGNIFICANCE

After 1598, Henry IV and his minister, Maximilien de Béthune, marquis of Rosny, set about returning order and stability to France. Rosny (better known by his later title, duke of Sully) was an administrative genius who worked vigorously to reduce government corruption, oversee taxation, and build roads and canals. Henry possessed a dynamic personality and took his role as "father" of his people seriously. He exerted stronger control over the patron-client system, which in turn tied him to the nobility and French towns through reciprocal bonds of expectation and obligation. He placed men he could trust in key positions throughout the country and relied on their advice to oversee the realm. Even so, Henry faced minor revolts during his reign, and the sincerity of his abjuration was questioned. In the spring of 1610, Henry was preparing for what was perceived as an anti-Catholic war in Germany and Italy, and this led a fanatical Catholic named François Ravaillac to stalk him. On May 14, 1610, Ravaillac assaulted Henry IV's carriage on a street in Paris and stabbed the king in the jugular vein, ending his life.

Henry IV strengthened the position of the French crown through his personal rule, but one must be careful in crediting him with founding an absolute monarchy. Henry IV never used the word "absolutism," nor did he think in modern terms of centralization. He wanted his kingship recognized throughout France, and he promised a return to peace and order. In so doing, he took a more authoritative stance in dealing with nobles, towns, law courts, and provincial assemblies and brought new power and prestige to the Crown after decades of weak kingship. Nevertheless, Henry did not impose his will universally throughout France. His rule was based on negotiating power through key "client" subjects, and he

successfully put himself at the head of several noble clienteles. The conclusion of the religious wars led to the development of a stronger monarchy in France. Yet Henry never envisioned "absolutism" as a systematic plan. His personal rule was predicated on the fact that he wanted to prevent Catholic League resurgence and secure the future for his dynasty.

—*Stephanie Annette Finley-Croswhite*

FURTHER READING

Buisseret, David. *Henry IV.* London: George Allen & Unwin, 1984. A solid biography of the first Bourbon monarch; particularly useful for those interested in Henry IV's role as a military leader.

Conner, Philip. *Huguenot Heartland: Montauban and Southern French Calvinism During the Wars of Religion.* Burlington, Vt.: Ashgate, 2002. Study of the Wars of Religion, especially of the differences between the experiences of southern and northern France during the wars. Focuses on the southern town of Montauban as a case study of the larger religious, cultural, and political upheavals. Includes maps, bibliographic references, and index.

Finley-Croswhite, S. Annette. *Henry IV and the Towns: The Pursuit of Legitimacy in French Urban Society, 1589-1610.* New York: Cambridge University Press, 1999. Study of Henry's labors to win support from his subjects, focusing on his courtship of the urban population and the consolidation of his claims to legitimate sovereignty. Includes illustrations, maps, bibliographic references, and index.

Greengrass, Mark. *France in the Age of Henry IV: The Struggle for Stability.* London: Longman, 1984. This entry in the Longman's Studies in Modern History series provides a general survey of Henry IV's reign with an emphasis on the king's attempts to reestablish order after the religious wars.

Holt, Mack P. *The French Wars of Religion, 1562-1629.* New York: Cambridge University Press, 1995. A thorough survey written by a noted authority who argues that the French civil wars were primarily fought over religious issues. The work includes a chronological table of events and a section of brief biographies of key figures.

Love, Ronald S. *Blood and Religion: The Conscience of Henri IV, 1553-1593.* Ithaca, N.Y.: McGill-Queen's University Press, 2001. An assessment of Henry's reign against the background of civil war and religious strife. Concludes with a discussion of Henry's perception of the conflicting requirements of his

1580's

crown and his soul, and his 1593 conversion to Catholicism. Includes photographic plates, illustrations, bibliographic references, and index.

Mousnier, Roland. *The Assassination of Henry IV: The Tyrannicide Problem and the Consolidation of the French Absolute Monarchy in the Early Seventeenth Century.* Translated by Joan Spencer. New York: Charles Scribner's Sons, 1973. A profile of Henry IV's assassin with emphasis on the political ramifications of the king's murder.

Racaut, Luc. *Hatred in Print: Catholic Propaganda and Protestant Identity During the French Wars of Religion.* Burlington, Vt.: Ashgate, 2002. Rare study of the pro-Catholic pamphleteers in France. Analyzes the strategies, production, and impact of pro-Catholic propaganda of the period. Includes bibliographic references and index.

Sutherland, N. M. *Henry IV of France and the Politics of Religion, 1572-1596.* 2 vols. Bristol, Avon, England: Elm Bank, 2002. Extremely detailed account of the role of religion in France's monarchy and political sphere during the late sixteenth century. Each chapter discusses a specific political event or issue from the point of view of the conflict between Protestants and Catholics. Includes illustrations, map, bibliographic references, and index.

Wolfe, Michael. *The Conversion of Henry IV: Politics, Power, and Religious Belief in Early Modern France.* Cambridge, Mass.: Harvard University Press, 1993. An in-depth analysis of the complicated dynamics surrounding Henry IV's conversion to Catholicism in 1593.

SEE ALSO: Oct. 31, 1517: Luther Posts His Ninety-five Theses; Mid-16th cent.: Development of the Caracole Maneuver; Mar., 1562-May 2, 1598: French Wars of Religion; 1568-1648: Dutch Wars of Independence; Aug. 24-25, 1572: St. Bartholomew's Day Massacre; July 7, 1585-Dec. 23, 1588: War of the Three Henrys; Apr. 13, 1598: Edict of Nantes; May 2, 1598: Treaty of Vervins.

RELATED ARTICLES in *Great Lives from History: The Renaissance & Early Modern Era, 1454-1600:* Catherine de Médicis; Henry III; Henry IV; Philip II.

1590's
BIRTH OF OPERA

Set to music and the singing voice, the melodrama Dafne *became the first opera. The Florentine Camerata, an informal academy of Humanist intellectuals and musicians, sought to revive and reconstruct the dramas of Greek and Roman antiquity because of their inherent ethical and moral powers.*

LOCALE: Florence, Italy
CATEGORIES: Music; literature; theater

KEY FIGURES

Jacopo Corsi (1561-1602), Florentine noble and composer-musician
Jacopo Peri (1561-1633), Italian composer
Ottavio Rinuccini (1562-1621), Italian poet and librettist
Giovanni Bardi (1534-1612), count di Vernio, Italian scholar and music patron
Vincenzo Galilei (c. 1520-1591), Italian composer and theorist
Giulio Caccini (c. 1545-1618), Italian singer and composer

SUMMARY OF EVENT

Between 1594 and 1598, the Florentine composers Jacopo Corsi and Jacopo Peri set Ottavio Rinuccini's pastoral play *Dafne* (c. 1590) to music. Although many dramatic works in sixteenth-century Italy contained musical numbers, *Dafne* was the first to be entirely sung. It has earned the distinction as the first opera, if opera is taken to mean a drama whose text is sung throughout.

The first opera's musicological origins were complex, growing out of many precedents in late medieval and Renaissance culture, including, among others, musical intermissions between the acts of plays called *intermedi*, courtly entertainments, liturgical dramas, and the Italian tradition of solo singing. Most closely associated with the provenance of opera, however, were the deliberations of the Florentine Camerata, a private, informal, loosely structured group of aristocratic Humanists and composers founded by Giovanni Bardi around 1580. This unofficial academy met around Bardi, a scion of a wealthy family of bankers and a patron of artists and intellectuals, to ruminate over various aspects of antiquity, including drama and music.

Like other Humanists of the Renaissance, the Camerata revered the culture of Greek and Roman antiquity, emphasized classical rhetorical theory, and hoped to reform modern culture on ancient examples. Convening throughout the last third of the sixteenth century, the Camerata moved deliberately and did not consciously set out to create a new musical form; the discussions and writings that eventuated in the first opera gestated over at least two decades and began as investigations of ancient theater. Early on, Vincenzo Galilei, a musician and one of the group's aesthetic theorists and the father of the famed mathematician and astronomer Galileo (1564-1642), read the letters of Girolamo Mei (1519-1594), a Florentine philologist and historian of Greek music living in Rome. Mei's research into Greek music led Galilei to conclude that Greek drama was sung rather than spoken, a dubious thesis that stimulated Galilei to speculate on the idiosyncrasies of Greek music.

In his *Dialogo della musica antica e della moderna* (1581; *Dialogue on Ancient and Modern Music*, 2003), Galilei argued that Greek music had an almost magical characteristic that modern music lacked. Music of the Greeks had the power to produce ethical effects in audiences, moving hearers to courage, virtue, sorrow, joy, or any other morally beneficial state of mind. Although only a few indecipherable fragments of ancient musical scores survived as evidence for the way Greek music sounded or how composers infused into them ethical components, many classical authors wrote about music, including Plato (c. 427 B.C.E.-347 B.C.E.) in his *Timaeus* (1793). Galilei combed these references for clues about ancient methods of composition but found it difficult to translate literary allusions into actual musical techniques.

In the end, Galilei calculated that Greek music differed from modern compositions in two fundamental ways. He asserted that it was not polyphonic (that is, it was not sung in several melodically independent parts simultaneously, as was fashionable in sixteenth century madrigals and motets) but was monophonic (sung to a single melodic line). Furthermore, he reasoned that Greek music gained its moral power from its seamless union of poetry and music, a unity in which music was subordinated to text; for ethical effects to take hold, it was imperative that the words be distinctly understood, which was impossible in counterpoint. To re-create morally powerful music, Galilei proposed that composers abandon polyphony and replace it with solo singing.

The Camerata was a diverse and opinionated collection of independent, contentious spirits, and Galilei's

theories were not the last word in musical matters. Thus, it is not clear if Galilei's ideas actually steered the Camerata in the direction of innovation. By about the late 1580's, though, several of its members had worked out a new of kind of singing that seemed to fit the design suggested in Galilei's *Dialogue on Ancient and Modern Music*. Sung by a single voice and accompanied by a single instrument sounding slow moving and undistracting chords, it conveyed the meaning of the text in a vivid way and seemed an ideal musical mechanism to replicate theatrical monologue and dialogue. This species of monody (solo singing) was to become the musical vehicle of dramatic narrative and was a direct manifestation of the Humanists' insistence on clear, expressive rhetoric upon communication in the most direct and cogent manner.

With further refinement, this strikingly expressive singing was brought to its preoperatic pinnacle in the *stile rappresentativo* (Latin for theatrical style), which was related closely to the *stile recitativo* (a dramatic recitative) of Giulio Caccini and Jacopo Peri. Rhythmically flexible and matching the natural inflections of speech, the recitativo (as noted above) was more than mere speech and less than full-on melodic song. Although rivals within the Camerata, Caccini and Peri shared the view that the *recitativo* was the way to resuscitate the authentic performance practice of Greek drama, for it made rapid musical narration possible, moving dramatic action forward and heightening the emotional and ethical content of key aspects of the libretto. Inasmuch as the *recitativo* coupled poetic meter to musical rhythm to duplicate the natural cadence of speech, it forged, also, a unity of poetry and music.

While the *recitativo* developed privately and contentiously (both Caccini and Peri claimed exclusive credit for its genesis and disliked one another intensely), Bardi accepted a position in Rome in 1592, and the Camerata reconstituted itself under the auspices of Jacopo Corsi, at whose palace it met. Like Bardi, Corsi was heavily involved in producing musical extravaganzas for the entertainment of the ruling Medici family and for the glorification of the family's public image. The gradual process of evolution toward fully realized opera culminated at Corsi's palazzo. In 1594, Peri, Corsi, and the poet Ottavio Rinuccini began a pastorale called *Dafne*. Taking its subject from innocuous love stories in bucolic settings, the pastorale usually had a simple plot with a happy ending and was, along with tragedy and comedy, one of the three most important classes of Italian drama in the sixteenth century. Ironically, for all the desire the Florentine

Humanists had for the restoration of the Greek stage, Rinuccini took his inspiration from the rendition of Apollo and the python in *Metamorphoses* by the Roman poet Ovid (43 B.C.E.-17 C.E.) rather than from Greek tragedy.

Completed in 1598, *Dafne* far transcended its traditional theatrical materials and literary conventions. Peri, the principal composer, added narrative recitatives in the *recitativo* and other numbers, and thereby set the whole play to music, giving birth to opera. Unpublished, most of it has been lost. Originally performed at Corsi's residence with Peri singing Apollo and performed later at the Medici court and at several other locations, *Dafne* was such a success that it encouraged Peri and Rinuccini to cooperate on another opera in 1600. *Euridice* premiered at the Palazzo Pitti, attendant on the wedding of Maria de' Medici (1573-1642) and King Henry IV (r. 1589-1610) of France. There soon followed a version of the same opera by Peri's nemesis, Caccini, whose own *Euridice* (1602) derived its poetry also from Rinuccini, the librettist for all three inaugural operas.

The first operas, then, owed their existence to Renaissance Humanism's adoration of all things ancient. Not only were the opera's plots rephrased, venerable classical myths (which would remain the staple of opera libretti for almost two centuries), their distinctive musical innovation, the dramatic recitative, was conceived not as something new but rather as a reflection of how Bardi's group imagined that Greek musico-dramatic declamation must have sounded.

SIGNIFICANCE

Less than a decade after the debut of *Dafne* and the two *Euridici*, opera spread to Mantua. The *Orpheo* (1607) of Claudio Monteverdi (1567-1643) owed much to its Florentine predecessors, but it far surpassed them in musical complexity and dramatic interest. In Rome, too, opera flourished. After 1623 it was nourished by the patronage of Pope Urban VIII (1568-1644) and his Barberini kin.

Within forty years of *Daphne*, about twenty-five operas appeared in Florence, Mantua, and Rome, as court entertainments, mostly, presented to fairly small aristocratic audiences and designed in large measure to magnify the image of patrons who were politically powerful. When opera arrived in republican Venice, however, it became more socially inclusive and commercialized. In 1637, musical entrepreneurs (the first impresarios) financed the production of *Andromeda* by Francesco Manelli (1594-1667), rented a hall, sold tickets to the public, and made enough money to continue its performance.

Other enterprising businessmen saw the benefits of expanding the audience. Between 1637 and 1650, fifty new operas, many of them staged and costumed with great and elaborate spectacle, competed for the Venetian public's attention. Thereafter, as opera drifted away from its socially elitist and intellectually esoteric origins, it became what it remains to this day, the profitable high end of Italian popular culture.

—David Allen Duncan

FURTHER READING

Carter, Tim. *Jacopo Peri, 1561-1633: His Life and Works*. New York: Garland, 1989. The first modern, full-length study of Peri and his operatic and nonoperatic compositions.

_____. *Music, Patronage, and Printing in Late Renaissance Florence*. Aldershot, England: Ashgate, 2000. Twenty-five scholarly essays reevaluate the complex web of influences among musicians, patrons, and businessmen in Florentine musical culture.

Galilei, Vincenzo. *Dialogue on Ancient and Modern Music*. Translated by Claude V. Palisca. New Haven, Conn.: Yale University Press, 2003. A complete translation of Galilei's influential work. Includes an introduction and notes by the translator, illustrations, a bibliography, and an index.

Katz, Ruth. *Divining the Powers of Music: Aesthetic Theory and the Origins of Opera*. New York: Pendragon Press, 1986. Analyzes the ancient philosophical underpinning of opera, and is especially strong on Mei's role as a historical musicologist.

Parker, Roger, ed. *The Oxford Illustrated History of Opera*. New York: Oxford University Press, 2001. Contains rare illustrations and a lucid text for general readers.

Sonneck, O. G. "Dafne, the First Opera: A Chronological Study." *Sammelband der Internationalen Musik-Gesellschaft* 15 (1913/1914): 102-110. A still-valuable resource for the study of opera and its flowering. Examines the birth of opera chronologically, setting the stage for readers.

Sternfeld, Frederick William. *The Birth of Opera*. Oxford, England: Clarendon Press, 1995. Describes technical problems associated with the singing of drama and analyzes the popularity of the Orpheus myth as an operatic subject.

Walker, D. P. "Musical Humanism in the Sixteenth and Early Seventeenth Centuries." *Music Review* 2 (1941): 1-14, 111-121, 220-227, 288-308; and *Music Review* 3 (1942): 55-71. A two-part classic study of Humanism's influence on Renaissance musical thought.

SEE ALSO: 1567: Palestrina Publishes the *Pope Marcellus Mass*; 1575: Tallis and Byrd Publish *Cantiones Sacrae*; Oct. 31, 1597: John Dowland Publishes *Ayres*; 1599: Castrati Sing in the Sistine Chapel Choir.

RELATED ARTICLES in *Great Lives from History: The Renaissance & Early Modern Era, 1454-1600:* William Byrd; John Dowland; Elizabeth I; Andrea Gabrieli; Giovanni Gabrieli; Orlando di Lasso; Luca Marenzio; Cosimo I de' Medici; Lorenzo de' Medici; Thomas Morley; Giovanni Pierluigi da Palestrina; Thomas Tallis.

1590
ODAWARA CAMPAIGN

In 1590, Japanese warlord Toyotomi Hideyoshi completed his plan for national unification by laying siege to Odawara Castle, the headquarters of the Hōjō family. When Odawara fell, it gave Hideyoshi control of the strategic Kantō region and helped persuade the lords of northern Japan to submit to his authority.

LOCALE: Odawara, Kantō region of Japan
CATEGORIES: Wars, uprisings, and civil unrest; expansion and land acquisition; government and politics

KEY FIGURES
Hōjō Ujimasa (1538-1590), shogun, r. 1560-1590
Hōjō Ujiano (1562-1591), Ujimasa's son
Tokugawa Ieyasu (Matsudaira Takechiyo, later Matsudaira Motoyasu; 1543-1616), shogun, r. 1603-1605
Toyotomi Hideyoshi (1537-1598), military leader under whom Japan achieved unification, r. 1590-1598

SUMMARY OF EVENT
After the assassination of the powerful warlord Oda Nobunaga in 1582, Toyotomi Hideyoshi, one of his trusted generals, sought to carry on his efforts to unify Japan's disparate domains under a new central authority. Hideyoshi, a man of humble birth, had risen through the ranks through a combination of ambition and tactical skill. In the mid-1580's, Hideyoshi consolidated his position as Nobunaga's successor and then began a fervent campaign of expansion. In 1587, he moved armies to the southern island of Kyūshū and brought it under his authority. He not only managed to maintain control of the areas that Nobunaga had subjugated but also added to them.

With the subjugation of the warlords of Kyūshū, particularly the Shimazu family, who had posed a significant threat to Hideyoshi's hegemony, the main forces of opposition lay in the east. The Hōjō family, based in the Kantō

Plain in eastern Japan, were a major threat to Hideyoshi. The Hōjō, sometimes referred to as the Go-Hōjō or "later Hōjō" were not related to the Hōjō regents who had wielded power from behind the scenes during the Minamoto shogunate in the thirteenth century. Rather, they had been founded by a warlord named Hōjō Soun (1432-1519), whose ascendancy in one of the wealthiest parts of the country is considered by scholars to be a sign of the beginning of a century-long period of civil war known as the Sengoku Jidai, or Warring States period. In Hideyoshi's day, the Hōjō were led by Ujimasa and his son Ujiano, able rulers who were prepared to resist Hideyoshi. Not only were they militarily powerful, but they also were connected by marriage to the powerful warlord Tokugawa Ieyasu, who had been an important ally of Nobunaga and had maintained an uneasy alliance with Hideyoshi after the warlord's death. Hideyoshi initially tried to get the Hōjō to submit to his authority through diplomatic overtures and negotiation, but when it became clear that the Hōjō were less than willing to negotiate and that Ieyasu would support him in a proposed military campaign, Hideyoshi decided to launch an attack instead.

Odawara is in what is now Kanagawa Prefecture. Before the establishment of the center of Tokugawa rule at Edo, the fortress at Odawara was considered the key to the control of the Kantō region. The Kantō Plain is one of the most fertile parts of Japan. It is also strategically important as a gateway to the eastern part of the country. The fortress at Odawara was considered invincible, but Hideyoshi decided on a strategy that focused more on intimidation than on direct military confrontation. The Hōjō, confident that their castle would not fall, decided on a similar strategy, choosing to pull all of their forces within the fortress's defenses and not to harass Hideyoshi during his approach. There are reports that Hideyoshi's forces numbered as many as 200,000 men gathered from all over Japan. The same sources indicate that the Hōjō and their allies could muster only 50,000. In addition, Hideyoshi's forces, in possession of guns and cannons, had superior armaments. Sources also report that many of the troops on the Hōjō side were peasants who had been pressed into participating in the defense of the castle.

The campaign, as it developed, was not a stressful one for Hideyoshi. In addition to allowing the men to bring their wives or concubines to the battlefield, he provided for their entertainment by organizing tea ceremonies and dramatic performances. The military camp was transformed into something of an extravagant outing. These measures proved particularly frustrating to the Hōjō forces, who felt confined and faced shortages of provisions. While there was sporadic fighting, the main damage done by Hideyoshi was psychological.

The victory at Odawara came about more as a result of Hideyoshi's ingenuity as a showman and organizer than as a result of military skill. Hideyoshi began construction of a new fortress on a mountain near Odawara, a measure that persuaded many on the Hōjō side that victory was impossible. Hideyoshi's men first built a series of walls and fences, which gave the impression that the castle had been erected in a single day. The impact on the morale of Hōjō's men was tremendous.

After a siege of one hundred days, the fortress at Odawara, previously considered to be impregnable, was surrendered. Hideyoshi ordered the suicide of Hōjō Ujimasa as well as his brother and son, sparing those who had fought for them. With this, the Hōjō family were all but eradicated, and Hideyoshi's victory in the east was complete. By 1591, Hideyoshi's armies quelled the small pockets of resistance that remained, and the entire country was brought under his control.

SIGNIFICANCE

The fall of Odawara not only brought the Kantō region under Hideyoshi's power but also proved to be the decisive step in the unification of the entire country under his authority. It was not necessary for Hideyoshi to conquer every region of Japan physically; he simply needed to secure the allegiance of the local power holders. The warlords of northern Japan had considered the Hōjō domains and their fortress at Odawara to form a buffer between Hideyoshi's power base in central Japan and their own lands. With the surrender of the Hōjō, powerful northern leaders such as Date Masamune in the Tohoku region had little choice but to submit to Hideyoshi to avoid the invasion of their domains.

After the fall of the Hōjō, Hideyoshi decided to award their lands to Tokugawa Ieyasu. This was not done out of a desire to reward Ieyasu for his loyalty or for his role in the campaign, but rather to remove him from central Japan, where he was a major force. In exchange for his ancestral lands and hard-fought gains to the south of Kyōto, Ieyasu received some of the best agricultural land in the country. After Hideyoshi's death, Ieyasu was able to rely on his power base in the Kantō region and assembled a fighting coalition with which to challenge his rivals. This led to the Battle of Sekigahara in 1600, which resulted in a victory for Ieyasu. In 1603, Ieyasu solidified his political authority by taking over the office of shogun, marking the beginning of the Tokugawa shogunate, which would survive for more than two and a half centuries. The Kantō region, won as a result of the Siege of Odawara, became the center of power of the new shogunate. The city of Edo, built up near Odawara and renamed Tokyo after the fall of the Tokugawa and restoration of imperial rule in the 1860's, has continued to be the center of Japanese political and economic life.

—*Matthew Penney*

FURTHER READING

Berry, Mary Elizabeth. *Hideyoshi*. Cambridge, Mass.: Harvard University Press, 1982. The best single volume treatment of Hideyoshi's career in English. Contains details of his support of the arts and the Kitano tea ceremony.

Sansom, George. *A History of Japan, 1334-1615*. 3 vols. Stanford, Calif.: Stanford University Press, 1961. Despite its age, Sansom's history of premodern Japan is still the most authoritative on the subject in English. Includes detailed coverage of the wars of Hideyoshi's lifetime, including the Odawara campaign.

Sato, Hiroaki. *Legends of the Samurai*. New York: The Overlook Press, 1995. This work contains accounts of the career of Hideyoshi as well as original sources that provide details of his campaigns.

Turnbull, Stephen. *The Samurai Sourcebook*. London: Arms and Armour Press, 1998. Offers encyclopaedic coverage of the important figures in the history of the samurai as well as aspects of their military culture including coverage of the siege of Odawara.

_____. *Samurai Warfare*. London: Arms and Armour Press, 1996. The best English language history of the Japanese wars of unification with coverage of Hideyoshi's Odawara campaign.

tion of the *Renga* Masterpiece *Minase sangin hyakuin*; Beginning 1513: Kanō School Flourishes; 1532-1536: Temmon Hokke Rebellion; 1549-1552: Father Xavier Introduces Christianity to Japan; 1550's-1567: Japanese Pirates Pillage the Chinese Coast; 1550-1593: Japanese Wars of Unification; Sept., 1553: First Battle of Kawanakajima; June 12, 1560: Battle of Okehazama; 1568: Oda Nobunaga Seizes Kyōto; 1587:

Toyotomi Hideyoshi Hosts a Ten-Day Tea Ceremony; 1592-1599: Japan Invades Korea; 1594-1595: Taikō Kenchi Survey; Oct., 1596-Feb., 1597: *San Felipe* Incident; Oct. 21, 1600: Battle of Sekigahara.

RELATED ARTICLES in *Great Lives from History: The Renaissance & Early Modern Era, 1454-1600:* Hōjō Ujimasa; Hosokawa Gracia; Oda Nobunaga; Ōgimachi; Oichi; Sesshū; Toyotomi Hideyoshi.

1591
FALL OF THE SONGHAI EMPIRE

Despite having reached its cultural apex, the Songhai Empire experienced political infighting and divisions within its society that set the stage for its downfall. Songhai was invaded by Morocco, ending the last empire of the Sahel region.

LOCALE: Songhai Empire, west-central Sudan (now principally in Mali), West Africa
CATEGORIES: Expansion and land acquisition; wars, uprisings, and civil unrest; government and politics

KEY FIGURES
Askia Ishak II (d. 1591), Songhai king, r. 1588-1591
Aḥmad al-Manṣūr (1549-1603), ruler of Morocco, r. 1578-1603
Djūdar Pasha (fl. 1591), Moroccan general
Mahmūd ibn Zarqun Pasha (d. 1594), Moroccan general

SUMMARY OF EVENT
By the mid-sixteenth century, the Songhai Empire had reached the zenith of its political and cultural development, especially under king Askia Daud (r. 1549-1582). Askia Daud had briefly restored the empire to the position it had held under its greatest ruler, Mohammed I Askia (r. 1493-1528). The Songhai government and society balanced both native Sudanese and Islamic influences and structures, and the Askia Dynasty ruled over a varied group of peoples in relative peace and security. Songhai controlled natural salt supplies to the north and some of the region's gold sources to the south, as well as the upper Niger River routes down which much of the gold and salt flowed. It also controlled the southern end of the trans-Saharan caravan routes, which ran northward from Timbuktu and Walata through Teghazza and Zagora to Tlemcen and other major cities of the southwestern Mediterranean littoral. In addition to salt and

gold, slaves captured in battles or raids traveled northward to the Moroccan and Algerian ports and bazaars.

In the 1540's, Moroccan sultan Muhammad I al-Shaykh claimed the salt mines around Teghazzi, which lay at the northern tip of Songhai territory. In return, Songhai Askia Ishak I (r. 1539-1549) sent a detachment of Sudanese cavalry on a raid into the Dar'a Valley in southern Morocco. Near the end of his own long reign, Askia Daud negotiated an agreement with the new Moroccan caliph, Aḥmad al-Manṣūr, which made many trade concessions to the Moroccans but left the salt mines in Songhai hands. Al-Manṣūr had gained the Sa'dī throne of Morocco after winning the Battle of Wādī al-Makhāzin (also known as the Battle of Ksar el-Kebir) against the Spanish and Portuguese (August, 1578). The former ruler, his brother, died during the battle.

Once he became Morocco's ruler, al-Manṣūr fought unsuccessfully to force the Portuguese out of the North African ports of Ceuta, El Jadida (formerly Mazagan), and Tangier. He saw himself as the hero of western Islam and mixed general political expansionism with a fiery compulsion to destroy Islam's enemies and unite her peoples under his rule as caliph. He saw the Muslim Songhai Empire as threatened on two fronts: the Turkish movements through the Maghreb to the east and the potential Portuguese expansion inland from the Atlantic coast. Both threatened to siphon off the lucrative trade that otherwise trundled northward through Teghazza. Morocco, al-Manṣūr thought, would be better able to defend the region from these threats to its trade. Moroccan control of Timbuktu would also mean Moroccan control of the upper Niger River and much of the trade that sailed down its reaches.

Under the guise of keeping the peace, Moroccan troops occupied oases of Tūwāt and Gurāra, which al-Manṣūr expected to use as jumping-off and supply points

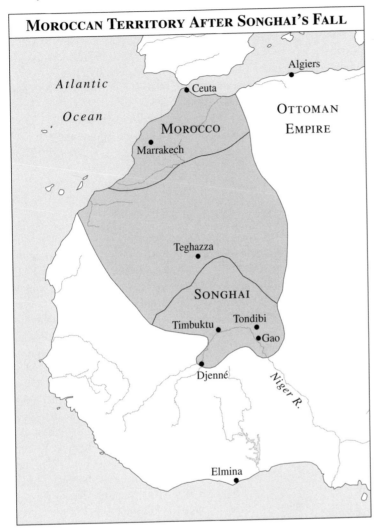

MOROCCAN TERRITORY AFTER SONGHAI'S FALL

Atlantic

Ocean

Algiers

Ceuta

OTTOMAN

EMPIRE

MOROCCO

Marrakech

Teghazza

SONGHAI

Timbuktu   Tondibi

        Gao

Djenné

Niger R.

Elmina

Manşūr knew that biding his time meant further preparation for war.

It was generally the eldest son of the preceding ruler that succeeded to the Songhai throne. He was acclaimed by the court and placed on the traditional throne in the capital of their homeland, Kûkya. However, the selection of Muhammad IV Bano (r. 1586-1588) was disputed by several of his brothers, the leader among whom was the chief administrator of the major western province of Kurmina. Their disaffection led to a brief civil war in 1588 that polarized much of the Songhai society, alienating many from the government at Gao, the Empire's official capital.

For many in the west, when the time came, government from Morocco was considered preferable to government from Gao. In addition, there were economic problems: Civil war had stopped the flow of booty from raiding in surrounding ethnic homelands, and the loss of Teghazza meant the loss of salt revenues. Portuguese coastal trade was draining the flow of goods away from the interior state. Socially, the Songhai minority ruled over a patchwork of ethnic territories, and there was a growing split between the urbanized Islamic leadership, with its Moroccan-trained, Arabic-speaking clerics and judges, and the people of the villages, who retained much of their traditional systems of belief and ritual. The polity worked in large part because the Songhai central government allowed the tribal territories to maintain their own local administration under a broad umbrella.

On October 30, 1590, a Moroccan army led by Djūdar Pasha filed out of Marrakech. It moved south, traversing the Atlas Mountains and meeting the great Sahara at Ktawa. Two months later, the men began a forced march that lasted an additional two months; they reached the banks of the Niger River on March 1, 1591. By March 12, they had reached Tondibi, only 35 miles (56 kilometers) from Gao itself. Their advance had been largely unopposed to that point, but at Tondibi, Emperor Askia Ishak II would stand and fight. Much of Djūdar's infantry was armed with early muskets called harquebuses, while the thirty thousand freemen and captives who fought as infantry for Songhai carried spears and shot only arrows.

for an invasion force. In 1583, he intervened along the Songhai border to aid the king of Borno, May Idrīs Alaōma, who feared Turkish encroachment southwestward through the Fezzān. The Borno king's fears allowed al-Manşūr to maintain reinforced garrisons right at the Songhai throat. In 1585, he boldly seized the salt mines of Teghazza. The native Tuareg people who worked the mines refused to work for the invaders, however, and migrated south to Teghazza al-Ghizlān (Taoudeni). This left Teghazza terribly undermanned and created a rival source of salt in the region. The Moroccan caliph considered mounting his invasion in 1586, but he had too many critics at home: It would, after all, be an assault on another Islamic state, and it was risky. In 1586, however, there was a change in Songhai rulership that would eventually reduce Moroccan risks considerably, and al-

Their leather or copper shields were no match for the Moroccans' projectiles. Askia Ishak's ten thousand cavalrymen were the country's noble elite, and their iron breastplates afforded them rather better protection; the Moroccan Berber cavalry, however, was second to none in all of Africa. Ishak's force was the largest in the western Sudan but proved unable to withstand the withering fire of the northerners. The battle was long but decisive: Ishak's army was shattered.

Djūdar Pasha quickly seized the deserted Gao and halted. Ishak wanted a formal truce and offered himself as a hostage. Djūdar was tempted, since his army needed rest badly, but al-Manṣūr wanted conquest, not peace, and replaced him with Morocco's second general, Mahmūd ibn Zarqun Pasha. Zarqun took over the campaign and conquered the Songhai homeland, driving Ishak out and trapping and killing his appointed successor, Askia Muhammad-Gao. From 1592 to 1594, Zarqun campaigned in Dendi, chasing down the remaining Songhai guerrillas. He slaughtered or exiled the political, cultural, and religious leadership of the empire and the intelligentsia in Timbuktu. The resistance led by Askia Nuh (r. 1592-1599) managed to kill Zarqun at Bandiagara in 1594, and al-Manṣūr replaced him with Manṣūr ibn ʿAbd al-Raḥmān Pasha. Al-Raḥmān completed the pacification of Dendi and installed several loyal governments among the people. Elsewhere, the reappointed Djūdar struggled against very tough opposition by the Bambora, Fulbe, and Manden peoples.

SIGNIFICANCE

Once administrations that gave allegiance to Moroccan pashas had replaced all Songhai institutions, the Moroccans left matters largely as they had been. They purposefully controlled Timbuktu but left the patchwork of ethnic, tribal, clan, and even town administrations to their own devices. In many of these, the traditional warrior ethic and religious animism replaced Islamic social structures, if only for a time. The area was also opened up to new immigration: The Moroccans sent Guish, Haha, Maʾkil and Djusham peoples—some of whom had proven troublesome to the Saʿdīs—to the south, while the lack of a strong, effective central authority opened up border regions to encroachments from neighboring Tuareg and

Fulbe people. Under Moroccan rule, the region became an economic backwater stripped of its cultural base.

For a while, the road from the Darʾa Valley to Teghazza became a major internal trade route for the Moroccans, but as major international routes shifted to the east and west, it lost its importance. The seventeenth century saw ecological and economic disasters reduce what had been an empire to a depressed and depopulated Moroccan colony. Moroccan and European slavers plied their trade with no regulation or compunction, as one ethnic enclave blithely turned on its neighbors. By dividing and conquering its enemies and stripping away the area's cultural and religious leadership, Morocco had severely retarded any type of progress in the western Sudan. It was an unmitigated disaster that further weakened central Africa, eventually leaving it helpless in the face of European imperialism.

—*Joseph P. Byrne*

FURTHER READING

Hunwick, John O. *Timbuktu and the Songhay Empire.* Boston: Brill, 1999. Discussion of the city under the later Songhai rulers and the impact of the conquest can be found in chapters 20 to 25.

Ogot, B. A., ed. *Africa from the Sixteenth to the Eighteenth Century.* Vol. 5 in *The UNESCO General History of Africa.* Berkeley, Calif.: James Curry, 1999. Contains a very strong chapter on the fall of the Songhai.

Yahya, Dahiru. *Morocco in the Sixteenth Century: Problems and Patterns in African Foreign Policy.* New York: Longman, 1981. Chapter 7 on the Sudanese campaign and rule discusses the Songhai fall from the perspective of Moroccan expansionism.

SEE ALSO: 1460-1600: Rise of the Akan Kingdoms; c. 1464-1591: Songhai Empire Dominates the Western Sudan; 1481-1482: Founding of Elmina; 1493-1528: Reign of Mohammed I Askia; 16th century: Trans-Saharan Trade Enriches Akan Kingdoms; 1510-1578: Saʿdī Sharifs Come to Power in Morocco.

RELATED ARTICLES in *Great Lives from History: The Renaissance & Early Modern Era, 1454-1600:* Askia Daud; Muhammed I Askia; Sonni ʿAlī.

1592
PUBLICATION OF WU CHENGEN'S *THE JOURNEY TO THE WEST*

Since its publication, The Journey to the West, *or* Monkey, *has remained one of the most popular classic novels in China, influencing Chinese literary writing, serving as a source for other genres, and offering religious and political inspiration.*

LOCALE: China
CATEGORY: Literature

KEY FIGURE

Wu Chengen (Wu Ch'eng-en; c. 1500-c. 1582), author of *The Journey to the West,* or *Monkey*

SUMMARY OF EVENT

Xiyou ji (pb. 1592; also known as *Hsi-yu chi*; partial translation as *Monkey,* 1942; *The Journey to the West,* 1977-1983) was written by Wu Chengen, a native of Shanyang district (present-day Huaian county) in Jiangsu Province. Wu was born into a family of shopkeepers with literary credentials. His great-grandfather and grandfather both had served as local officials in charge of educational affairs. Although Wu's father worked as a businessman for his livelihood, he was well read and familiar with classics of Confucianism and other schools of thought. Under the influence of his father, the young Wu cultivated a keen interest in literature, particularly in the literary tales of the Tang and Song Dynasties, and was able to write elegant poems and essays.

Despite his literary talent, however, Wu failed the civil service examinations, the primary legitimate channel for an official career. Only in his mid-forties, in 1544, was he selected as *sui gong sheng* (a "tribute student"). In his sixties, Wu served as a minor official (assistant for a county magistrate). Having stayed about one and one-half years in this position, he was falsely charged with misconduct in collecting grain taxes. After being rehabilitated, Wu retired and relied on conducting small business and selling his literary works for a living.

Wu Chengen lived during the middle of the Ming Dynasty (1368-1644), when signs of dynastic decline were already visible, including inefficiency and corruption of the emperors and government bureaucrats. Many emperors, indolent and dissolute, chose to confine themselves to the imperial palaces, seeking personal pleasures and immortality (by taking "golden elixirs" made by Daoist priests) while neglecting state affairs. Bureaucrats were preoccupied with factional bickering, power struggles, and accumulating personal wealth. Nevertheless, the time when Wu lived was one of remarkable economic, social, and intellectual developments: acceleration of commercialization, rapid growth of urban population, increasing syncretization of the Three Teachings (Confucianism, Buddhism, and Daoism), and emergence of novels, long and short, as the main form of literature.

The Journey to the West is based on the pilgrimage of the Buddhist monk Xuanzang (c. 602-664) during the Tang Dynasty (618-907). Xuanzang traveled from China to India between 629 and 645 in quest of Buddhist scriptures and returned with 657 texts of Buddhist scripture, translating the most important of them into Chinese. He became perhaps the best-known and most revered Buddhist monk in Chinese history, and his hazardous yet successful journey became part of the permanent legacy of Chinese Buddhist lore. His journey also became, over nearly a millennium, a favorite subject of popular legends and various literary works, including poetic tales and dramas. It was based on these literary antecedents about Xuanzang that Wu Chengen completed his hundred-chapter novel. It is set in a mythic world populated by deities, animal spirits, and monsters.

The Tang Monk (the protagonist representing Xuanzang) is accompanied in his journey by three animal-figured disciples with supernatural powers: Monkey (Sun Wukong), Pig (Zhu Bajie), and Sha Monk. The journey is full of dangers and difficulties such as desolate mountains and deep waters infested with ferocious beasts and demons. After having successfully undergone eighty-one ordeals, the companions successfully arrive in the West, where they acquire Buddhist scriptures and carry them home.

In stark contrast to the historical Xuanzang, who was believed to be intelligent and courageous, the character Tang Monk is dull, cowardly, ineffectual, muddle-headed, and even ignorant, often confusing right and wrong and confounding evil and good. He is totally dependent on his three disciples, especially Monkey, who is really the novel's central character.

Powerful, resourceful, heroic, optimistic, and above all committed and trustworthy, Monkey serves as Tang Monk's protector and guide, subduing bloodthirsty beasts. The first seven chapters depict Monkey before he is recruited as Tang Monk's companion. He is portrayed as an independent and freedom-loving, yet rebellious figure who defies the authority of powerful deities from the Dragon King and the King of the Underworld to the most powerful Jade Emperor. Monkey creates turmoil in the Heavenly Palace by disrupting the Peach Festival and stealing the elixirs of immortality. He believes that right of kingship should not be hereditary but instead should be conferred only on the wisest and ablest.

A quite different but fascinating character in the novel is Pig (Zhu Bajie). Possessed of impressive magic powers and often fighting bravely, Pig makes significant contributions to the success of the journey. On the other hand, however, he occasionally wavers, sometimes appearing selfish, lazy, gossipy, and womanizing. Despite these defects, Pig is a humorous and intriguing figure.

Despite its ability to entertain, *The Journey to the West* is not a work simply for fun or, as Hu Shi argued, a book of profound nonsense. It is a work with serious political and religious meanings. The world described in the novel is a reflection of the political and social realities of the author's time. In exposing the dark side of that world— particularly the corruption of those who held power— Wu was able to satirize the political problems of his real world. Some modern scholars insist that the most satirical descriptions in the novel were reserved for the emperor Jiajing (Chia-Ching, r. 1522-1567), who was notoriously corrupt and irresponsible. Some Chinese scholars believe that the novel reflects the peasants' struggle (represented by the rebellious acts of Monkey) against the existing political order (represented by the Jade Emperor and his subordinates), while Monkey's subjugation by and submission to Tathagata (*rulai*, the highest Buddhist deity) embodies the limitations and failure of this struggle.

Pervaded by religious themes and rhetoric, *The Journey to the West* also can be understood as religious allegory. In the novel, China's two main religions, Buddhism and Daoism, peacefully coexist and their deities work together—a sign of religious reconciliation or syncretism. Monkey, for example, gains his immortality and magic powers through Daoist self-cultivation, yet he also follows the guide of the bodhisattva Kun-yin when he becomes one of Tang Monk's companions. Self-cultivation, aiming at longevity or immortality, is stressed, and Daoist and Buddhist training (particularly purifying and stilling the mind) is highly recommended as the way to achieve self-cultivation. Another major religious theme of the novel concerns atonement: All the pilgrims—Tang Monk, his three disciples, and even the dragon-horse— have been condemned for certain misdeeds. The westward journey may represent a process of seeking salvation, and the pilgrims are forced to endure preordained ordeals both as a test of their sincerity and to accumulate sufficient good deeds to atone for their crimes. In this regard, the journey is a success for all the pilgrims.

SIGNIFICANCE

For approximately four hundred years, *The Journey to the West* has been widely circulated among Chinese of all walks of life and has been one of their favorite literary works. People not only have found the novel entertaining but also have drawn literary, artistic, moral, religious, and even political inspiration from it. The novel has provided subjects for artistic works from plays to paintings to films. It has played a significant role in education and moral cultivation (of children especially), with its praise for justice and good and its condemnation of injustice and evil. Today, Monkey is familiar to schoolchildren as a symbol of good and the White-Bone Spirit as a symbol of evil, and the story stands as a familiar metaphor for the triumph of good over evil. The religious syncretism endorsed in the novel highlights a Chinese cultural tradition of religious tolerance and love of harmony. Political figures have drawn from the novel significant lessons for their careers and their causes. Mao Zedong, for example, often called on his followers to emulate Monkey's vigilance, his toughness toward enemies, his optimism in times of adversity, and his courage in carrying out the revolutionary struggle.

—*Yunqiu Zhang*

FURTHER READING

Dudbridge, Glen. *The His-yu Chi: A Study of Antecedents to the Sixteenth-Century Chinese Novel.* Cambridge, England: Cambridge University Press, 1970. A comprehensive examination of *The Journey to the West*'s textual history.

Jianxi Academy of Social Sciences, ed. *Study of the Journey to the West.* Nanjing: Jiangsu Ancient Works Press, 1982. A collection of scholarly articles on the novel.

Liu Yinbai. *Materials for the Study of "The Journey to the West."* Shanghai: Shanghai Ancient Works Press, 1990. Contains rich information about the author and literary antecedents of the novel.

Qu, Xiaoqiang. *Unsettled Questions in "The Journey to the West."* Chengdu: Sichuan People's Press, 1994. Interpretations of various issues concerning the novel.

Su, Xing. *Biography of Wu Chengen.* Tianjin: Baihua Literature and Art Press, 1980. An account of Wu's family background, life, and career.

Yu, Anthony C., trans. and ed. *The Journey to the West.* Chicago: University of Chicago Press, 1977. The four-volume unabridged English version of the novel.

Zhou Wenzhi. *Penetrating "The Journey to the West."* Kunming: Yunnan People's Press, 1999. An interpretation of the novel using theories of Daoism and Buddhism as well as Chinese medicine.

SEE ALSO: 1457-1480's: Spread of Jōdo Shinshū Buddhism; 1567-1572: Reign of Longqing; 1573-1620: Reign of Wanli; 1578: First Dalai Lama Becomes Buddhist Spiritual Leader.

RELATED ARTICLES in *Great Lives from History: The Renaissance & Early Modern Era, 1454-1600:* Wang Yangming; Xiaozong.

1592-1599
JAPAN INVADES KOREA

In 1592, the Japanese warlord Toyotomi Hideyoshi ordered the invasion of Korea. His troops wreaked havoc on the country and were driven back only with the help of Chinese forces. The Japanese did not leave Korea until after Hideyoshi died in 1598.

LOCALE: Korea

CATEGORIES: Wars, uprisings, and civil unrest; diplomacy and international relations

KEY FIGURES

Toyotomi Hideyoshi (1537-1598), military leader who unified Japan, r. 1590-1598

Katō Kiyomasa (1562-1611), one of Hideyoshi's principal commanders during the invasion of Korea

Konishi Yukinaga (1556?-1600), another of Hideysoshi's commanders

Sŏnjo (1552-1608), king of Korea, r. 1567-1608

Yi Sun-sin (1545-1598), the admiral who led Korea's naval resistance against the invasion

SUMMARY OF EVENT

On the morning of May 23, 1592, the vanguard of a Japanese invasion force of more than 150,000 men landed on the southern coast of Korea. The invasion had been ordered by Toyotomi Hideyoshi, the military leader who was the de facto ruler of Japan. Having unified Japan on the battlefield, he believed he could conquer the rest of the world, starting with China. Moreover, launching a military campaign abroad afforded him a good opportunity to send his vassals, the daimyo (feudal barons or warlords) he had subjected, out of the way. Although they had pledged loyalty, they still commanded strong armies; sending them on a foreign campaign would strain their resources and prevent them from challenging his authority. He issued an ultimatum to the Korean king, Sŏnjo, to grant passage to the Japanese for their invasion of China, and when this ultimatum was rejected, he or-

dered the invasion of Korea. Hideyoshi himself never left Japan; instead, he sent an army composed of his liege barons, each heading his own division.

Although the Koreans had been warned of the invasions, they were caught completely off guard. Severe factional fighting among the Confucian literati who ran the government and staffed the bureaucracy meant that a planned upgrading of the garrisons and the army had not taken place. After the Japanese had landed near Pusan and taken its fortresses, they met with very little resistance on their march to the capital, Seoul. The Japanese troops were battle-hardened through their experience in the wars of unification, and they possessed superior tactics, arms, and discipline. Moreover, they were equipped with firearms, introduced to Japan by the Portuguese in 1542. The Korean commanders and troops sent out to meet this invasion force simply were not up to the task and either were annihilated or ran away. As a result, in barely three weeks the Japanese reached Seoul, which fell without any resistance; Sŏnjo had fled with his court and ministers a few days earlier.

Not everything went well for the Japanese, however. After the initial walkover, resistance soon sprang up in the south, harassing the rear guard. At sea, the Koreans soon established supremacy thanks to the leadership of admiral Yi Sun-sin. His "turtle ships" caused the enemy all kinds of trouble: The decks of these flat-bottomed ships were completely covered in spikes hidden by straw, making them almost impossible to enter. They were effective both because of their firepower and because they could ram enemy vessels. Yi Sun-sin also used his knowledge of the many islands, inlets, and tidal systems to track down and destroy enemy vessels, thereby cutting off the main supply routes of the Japanese.

After regrouping in Seoul, the Japanese pushed farther north. A short distance beyond Seoul they split into two groups, one led by Konishi Yukinaga, pushing for

Pyongyang, which fell on July 23, and one led by Katō Kiyomasa, which ventured into the northeast provinces. While Katō subjugated the northeast, imposing Japanese taxation and registration systems on the population, Konishi did not venture farther than Pyongyang. The fleeing Korean court, which had gone as far as the Yalu River, had appealed to the Chinese Ming Dynasty, the suzerain state of Chŏson Korea, to intervene. After Chinese envoys had ascertained the gravity of the situation, a force of about three thousand soldiers was dispatched. The first Chinese soldiers crossed the Yalu on the same day that Pyongyang was taken. When this initial contingent proved too small to trouble the Pyongyang garrison, the Chinese initiated negotiations to bid for time until a larger force arrived. This larger force drove Konishi out of Pyongyang on February 8, 1593, forcing all the Japanese to retreat to Seoul. After a few months, Hideyoshi's armies reached a truce with the Chinese emissary, evacuated Seoul, and dug in around Pusan in the southeast of the peninsula.

This marked the end of the first phase of the war. The Ming, as Korea's suzerain, took it on themselves to negotiate with Hideyoshi and obtain full withdrawal; the Koreans were left out of these negotiations. Unfortunately, there was very little common ground in the worldviews of Hideyoshi and the Ming court. Hideyoshi demanded a treaty on an equal basis, to be sealed by a marriage between a daughter of the Chinese emperor and the Japanese emperor, and also expected to get the southern part of Korea. For the Chinese, the only possible form of foreign diplomacy was the submission of a "barbarian" foreign country to the Ming emperor, to be formalized by tribute missions from Japan and the investiture of Hideyoshi as king of Japan by the Chinese emperor. Konishi, as Hideyoshi's main representative, knew that his master's terms could never be met and did not relay the demands to the Ming court. After considerable subterfuge on the part of Konishi and his Chinese counterparts, a Chinese mission of investiture was finally sent to Japan in late 1596. Only after the ceremony of investiture was over did Hideyoshi learn that he had been misled and that none of his demands had been met. He flew into a rage and ordered the immediate resumption of the war.

This second phase of the war was fought mainly in the southern half of the country. The Japanese fell back on a few forts they had built in the southeast and successfully repelled the combined Chinese-Korean armies that tried to dislodge them. The Japanese commanders had had enough, however, and it was only Hideyoshi's will that kept them in Korea. When news that Hideyoshi had died on September 18, 1598, finally reached them, they started to organize the retreat back to Japan. Fighting continued until the very last Japanese left the peninsula on Christmas, 1598. For the Koreans, the war ended only when the Chinese emperor officially proclaimed its end in the spring of 1599, at the same time absolving King Sŏnjo of any culpability in the invasions.

SIGNIFICANCE

Hideyoshi's invasions inflicted a terrible toll on the Korean people. It is impossible to estimate the exact loss of lives, but certainly it amounted to tens of thousands, as the grisly reports of severed noses sent back to Japan as proof of military success attest. Whole swaths of the countryside had been laid to waste, giving rise to famine and disease. The capital had been razed, and innumerable cultural treasures were destroyed or shipped back to Japan. Yet although it took decades for Korea to repair the damage, ironically the effect of the wars was arguably greater on China and Japan.

For Ming China, the economic burden of the Korean campaigns was one of the contributing factors to its decline and finally its demise in 1644. For Hideyoshi, too, the failure of his grandiose conquest undoubtedly weakened his leadership and interfered with his plans to secure a stable succession of leadership. Instead, power shifted to Tokugawa Ieyasu, who founded the Tokugawa shogunate when he became shogun in 1603.

King Sŏnjo, on the other hand, continued to reign until 1608 and secured the survival of the Chŏson Dynasty, which lasted until 1910. He even oversaw the resumption of normal diplomatic relations with Japan, formalized in a treaty the year after he died. Also, through these wars Korea achieved an important cultural impact on Japan. The artisans forcibly taken back to Japan contributed greatly to the development of Japanese crafts, especially pottery, while looted Neo-Confucian books and even some abducted scholars may have had an impact on the development of Neo-Confucianism in Tokugawa Japan.

—*Sem Vermeersch*

FURTHER READING

Elisonas, Jurgis. "War and Peace: The Background of Japanese Aggression in Korea." In *Early Modern Japan*. Vol. 4 in *Cambridge History of Japan*, edited by John W. Hall. Cambridge, England: Cambridge University Press, 1991. Still the best overview of the development of the invasions and the political context.

Ledyard, Gari. "Confucianism and War: The Korean Security Crisis of 1598." *The Journal of Korean Studies* 6 (1988-1989): 81-119. Though this study deals only with the last phase of the war, it is important for treating the ideological dimension of the Korea-China partnership.

Park, Yune-hee. *Admiral Yi Sun-sin and His Turtleboat Armada.* Seoul: Sinsaeng, 1973. Though dated, still the only English-language study of Yi Sun-sin's exploits.

Yi Sun-sin. *Nanjung ilgi: War Diary of Admiral Yi Sun-sin.* Translated by Ha Tae-hung. Seoul: Yonsei University Press, 1977. Yi Sun-sin's war diaries are among the most important sources for the naval campaigns.

_____. *Imjin changch'o: Admiral Yi Sun-sin's Memorials to Court.* Seoul: Yonsei University Press, 1981. Supplements his diaries, parts of which are missing.

Yu Song-nyong. *The Book of Corrections: Reflections on the National Crisis During the Japanese Invasions of Korea, 1592-1598.* Translated by Choi Byonghyon. Berkeley: Institute of East Asian Studies, 2002. An attempt by King Sŏnjo's prime minister to come to terms with the war's causes and effects.

SEE ALSO: 1457-1480's: Spread of Jōdo Shinshū Buddhism; 1467-1477: Ōnin War; 1477-1600: Japan's "Age of the Country at War"; Mar. 5, 1488: Composition of the *Renga* Masterpiece *Minase sangin hyakuin*; Beginning 1513: Kanō School Flourishes; 1532-1536: Temmon Hokke Rebellion; 1549-1552: Father Xavier Introduces Christianity to Japan; 1550's-1567: Japanese Pirates Pillage the Chinese Coast; 1550-1593: Japanese Wars of Unification; Sept., 1553: First Battle of Kawanakajima; June 12, 1560: Battle of Okehazama; 1568: Oda Nobunaga Seizes Kyōto; 1587: Toyotomi Hideyoshi Hosts a Ten-Day Tea Ceremony; 1590: Odawara Campaign; 1594-1595: Taikō Kenchi Survey; Oct., 1596-Feb., 1597: *San Felipe* Incident; Oct. 21, 1600: Battle of Sekigahara.

RELATED ARTICLES in *Great Lives from History: The Renaissance & Early Modern Era, 1454-1600:* Hōjō Ujimasa; Hosokawa Gracia; Oda Nobunaga; Ōgimachi; Oichi; Sesshū; Toyotomi Hideyoshi.

1593-1606
OTTOMAN-AUSTRIAN WAR

The Habsburg Dynasty in Austria failed to keep the advancing Ottoman Empire from Transylvania and Hungary. The Ottoman Turks remained a threat to the Austrian capital and regained dominance of the Balkan region.

LOCALE: Danube River Valley

CATEGORIES: Wars, uprisings, and civil unrest; diplomacy and international relations; expansion and land acquisition

KEY FIGURES

Gabriel Bethlen (1580-1629), leader of the resistance to Austrian rule in Transylvania

Mehmed III (1566-1603), Ottoman sultan, r. 1595-1603, during part of the Ottoman-Austrian War

SUMMARY OF EVENT

The late sixteenth and early seventeenth centuries saw the Habsburg and the Ottoman empires fighting for control of the Danube River Valley and the Balkan region. Under Sultan Süleyman the Magnificent, the Ottomans laid siege to the Habsburg capital, Vienna (1463-1479), but they were forced to retreat. The Turkish army had remained in the Danube River Valley, however, threatening the Austrian capital. The proximity of the Ottomans to

Vienna provoked another war between the two countries, which began in 1593.

Initially, the Austrians utilized irregular forces to harass the Ottoman positions along their border. The Ottomans responded with attacks of their own against the Austrians. In 1593, these skirmishes broke out into full-scale war, which continued for some thirteen years.

The war started badly for the Ottomans. In June of 1593, the Austrians defeated the Ottoman army, pushing the Turks back from the territory now known as Croatia. Smaller battles had the Austrians driving the Ottomans farther away from Vienna.

In addition to the Austrian army, the Ottomans also faced attacks from their Christian citizens in other parts of the Balkans. In the eastern portion of the Ottoman Empire sat the newly conquered territories of Walachia and Moldavia. Both were important buffers because of their proximity to the expanding Russian Empire. The Walachians rebelled under their king, Michael the Brave. The Austrians provided military and political support for the revolt, and Walachia soon wrenched control of its territory from the Turks. Battling in their front and the rear, the Ottomans were soon overwhelmed. In October of 1595, the Turks were nearly wiped out by the Walachians. Thousands of Ottoman soldiers drowned while attempting to cross the Danube during their retreat. The Turks were saved through Polish intervention.

With the army reeling and threatening to be pushed back from the Danube region, the Ottoman sultan, Mehmed III, took personal control of the army. Mehmed was a weak leader who was under the influence of his mother, Safiye Sultan. His weakness and uncertainty were magnified by his first act as sultan: He ordered the murder of his nineteen brothers so they would not challenge his authority.

With the sultan present, the army led a counterattack against the Austrians in 1596. In October, Mehmed pushed the Turks to the fortress of Erlau near Transylvania. The brief siege and battle saw the Austrians defeated and the Ottomans sweep north to regain the initiative in the war. Erlau was an important capture because it stood over the Austrian supply lines into Transylvania and Walachia. It also placed the Austrian army on the defensive just as winter was starting.

The Ottomans did not allow bad weather to stop their advance, however, and two weeks after Erlau they were able to smash the Austrian army in another battle. Fought on the Hungarian plain, the battle stretched for three days. The Austrians had the initial advantage, pushing the Ottoman forces back and causing Mehmed III to panic and order a retreat. On the third day of battle the Ottomans were rescued in a dramatic cavalry charge by an Italian Muslim general. This sudden attack on the Austrian flank spread confusion through the ranks, and the army collapsed. Thirty thousand Austrian troops perished during a wild rush across a nearby river, and the Ottomans controlled the battlefield. Only the start of winter weather, which blocked the mountain passes in the area, prevented a total Austrian collapse.

The victories of the fall of 1596 did not continue into the following year. Mehmed returned to Constantinople to handle the empire's political problems, including a growing revolt. Without his leadership the Ottoman army facing the Austrians began to drift. Control ebbed and flowed across the region as Turks would capture forts, then surrender them when the Austrians counterattacked.

Between 1597 and 1601, the Ottomans were on the defensive, having been attacked at their front and rear. In 1598, the Austrian army split the Ottomans and drove them back from their border. An even worse defeat came with a renewed revolt in Walachia. The Walachian army stormed into nearby Transylvania, seized control of it from the Turks, and appeared on the verge of declaring independence and an alliance with the Austrians.

Walachia also moved east and south, taking control of its sister province Moldavia.

The Ottoman army was unable to counter these attacks because the political leadership was paralyzed with internal problems, revolts in the countryside, and threats to the empire's other border areas. Political instability became worse with the death of Mehmed III and the assumption of the throne by his son. Ahmed I was only thirteen when he became sultan, and he depended on his advisers to run the country.

Ahmed delegated control over the war to his tutor, Lala Mehmed Paşa, who was a Bosnian familiar with the territory where the Ottomans and Austrians were battling. Starting in the summer of 1604, Paşa launched an offensive against the Austrians in Hungary. In September, he recaptured Pest, the capital of Hungary, and placed the Ottoman army within one hundred miles of Vienna.

The Austrians also faced problems with revolts in their newly captured territories. The Catholic Habsburgs initiated a series of purges, attempting to drive Protestant believers from the empire. By 1605, the Austrians faced a full-scale religious revolt in territories such as Transylvania and Walachia. Both territories had been taken recently from the Ottomans. The rebel leader Gabriel Bethlen raised an army and battled the Austrians in Transylvania. He received considerable military support from the Ottomans, who took advantage of the revolt to attack the Austrians in Hungary also.

Paşa attacked in Hungary and Bosnia, sweeping into key cities and threatening the Austrian hold in both regions. Paşa also used raids within Austria to bring the war to the Habsburgs and hasten their desire for peace.

The Austrians mishandled the region to such an extent that their former ally in the east, Transylvanian prince István Bocskay (r. 1605-1606), signed an agreement with the Ottomans to fight the Austrians in return for a degree of independence. Facing two military forces, the Austrians were forced to retreat from Transylvania and seek the quickest way out of the war. The treaty was signed in 1606, in the town of Sitva-Torok. Both sides gained from the treaty: The Austrians would stop paying tribute to the Ottomans, and the sultan would recognize the Habsburg leader as equal to him. At the same time, Austria would recognize Ottoman control of the areas of Transylvania and Walachia and that the Habsburg armies would have little success at seizing those territories by force. The Ottomans secured their control by signing an agreement with Gabriel Bethlen, who ruled the eastern portion of the European empire while recognizing that the Ottomans were the dominant power.

SIGNIFICANCE

The Ottoman-Austrian War of the late sixteenth-early seventeenth century was a seesaw battle that established Ottoman dominance of the Balkan region. The Austrians attempted to capture the province of Transylvania while aiding the province of Walachia in its attempts to break away from Turkish rule. The Austrians were initially successful, but the Ottomans were able to regain control of the eastern European regions and seat their own rulers. This solidified the Ottomans' eastern border in Europe and allowed the empire to remain a threat to western Europe and Austria.

—*Douglas Clouatre*

FURTHER READING

Barber, Noel. *The Sultans*. New York: Simon and Schuster, 1973. This work focuses on the Ottoman sultans and the rise and fall of the empire. It examines the major trends and leaders in Ottoman politics and explains how the declining quality of the empire's leadership led to its collapse.

Coles, Paul. *The Ottoman Impact on Europe*. New York: Harcourt Brace, 1968. This work examines how Ottoman control of the Balkan area and conflicts with Austria, Russia, and Britain shaped Europe, its culture, and its politics.

Goffman, Daniel. *The Ottoman Empire and Early Modern Europe*. New York: Cambridge University Press, 2002. This work examines the relationship between the Muslim Ottomans and the Christians in eastern and western Europe. Also describes the conflicts, both political and military, and how they affected both regions.

Imber, Colin. *The Ottoman Empire, 1300-1650*. New York: Palgrave Macmillan, 2004. This brief work examines the Ottoman Turks as they battled the Byzantine Empire, conquered Constantinople, and then built their own empire by sweeping into eastern Europe. The book focuses mainly on the rise of the Ottomans, leaving out the empire's decline and fall.

Kinross, Lord. *The Ottoman Centuries*. New York: Quill, 1992. A sweeping story of the Ottoman Empire, this book describes the various sultans, their contributions to the Ottoman system, and their roles in the rise or fall of the empire. It also describes the social system and how it evolved during the empire.

SEE ALSO: 1454-1481: Rise of the Ottoman Empire; 1463-1479: Ottoman-Venetian War; Aug. 17, 1477: Foundation of the Habsburg Dynasty; 1478-1482: Albanian-Turkish Wars End; 1514: Hungarian Peasants' Revolt; 1534-1535: Ottomans Claim Sovereignty over Mesopotamia; 1574-1595: Reign of Murad III; 1576-1612: Reign of Rudolf II; 1578-1590: The Battle for Tabrīz; 1594-1600: King Michael's Uprising.

RELATED ARTICLES in *Great Lives from History: The Renaissance & Early Modern Era, 1454-1600:* Mehmed II; Mehmed III; Rudolf II; Süleyman the Magnificent.

1594-1595
TAIKŌ KENCHI SURVEY

The Taikō Kenchi, a nationwide government survey of farmland in Japan, was ordered by Japan's de facto ruler Toyotomi Hideyoshi. Growing out of earlier regional surveys, its definitive findings helped establish the Tokugawa system of agricultural organization and national taxation.

LOCALE: Japan
CATEGORIES: Agriculture; economics

KEY FIGURES

Toyotomi Hideyoshi (1537-1598), military ruler of Japan, r. 1590-1598
Toyotomi Hidetsugu (1568-1595), Hideyoshi's heir until Hideyoshi caused his death in 1595

Oda Nobunaga (1534-1582), Hideyoshi's military mentor and one of the three unifiers of Japan, r. 1573-1582
Asano Nagamasa (1546-1610), an aide of Hideyoshi who participated in the land surveys and became an important adviser to the Tokugawa shogunate
Ishida Mitsunari (1563-1600), an aide of Hideyoshi who played an important role in the survey in Hitachi Province
Natsuka Masaie (d. 1600), an aide of Hideyoshi and a skilled administrator

SUMMARY OF EVENT

The Taikō Kenchi, a nationwide survey (*kenchi*) of land in Japan, was conducted under the mandate of the *taikō*

Toyotomi Hideyoshi, the de facto military ruler of Japan. In 1591, Hideyoshi took the title of *taikō*, created to refer to the father of the *kampaku*, or chief imperial adviser, when Hideyoshi awarded the position of *kampaku* to his adopted son Hidetsugu. As Hideyoshi's forces conquered territory in a series of campaigns from 1570 to 1590, his regime was faced with the need for a uniform administrative system. One of the most basic tasks required was a land survey, to determine the exact amount of land Hideyoshi held, the estimated crop (especially rice) yields, and the potential taxes that could be levied on the rice produced.

Feudal rulers of some domains had earlier surveyed land under their control, but varying methods and measurements were used in these scattered surveys. After 1582 until his death in 1598, Hideyoshi conducted a series of uniform land surveys as territories came under his control. Earlier domain surveys were revised to conform to uniform standards and methods. In general, each farming village, together with its surrounding fields, was surveyed as a unit, so tax officials had figures for each village as a whole as well as for individual farms. Distinctions were made between rice paddies and fields growing vegetables, and the number of dwellings was also recorded. Farmers in possession of fields and crops were listed and were held responsible for paying taxes on crop yields. These farmers and their descendants were expected to remain on this land and provide the authorities with tax payments every year.

The surface area and projected crop yield were recorded for each field. The basic units of surface measurement were the *bu* (3.95 square yards, or about 3.3 square meters), the *se* (119 square yards, equal to about 100 square meters or 1 acre), the *tan* (0.245 acre, or about 0.1 hectare), and the *chō* (2.45 acres, or about 1 hectare). Fields were also ranked by arability and apparent fertility into four grades: high, medium, low, and very low. The average yield of a rice paddy was stated in terms of the number of *kyōmasu*, "measuring boxes" full of rice grains, based on the standard measures used in the Kyōto area. Farm taxes were paid in the form of percentages of harvested rice crops, and this local information gave government officials a way to make sure the proper amounts of rice were paid. Bulk rice levies collected were measured in *koku*, a grain measure of approximately 180 liters. Official stipends and salaries were often denominated in *koku* of rice, certificates for which could later be brokered and converted into cash.

The survey information was recorded in *kenchichō*, "survey ledgers." Two copies of these ledgers were prepared for each village, containing both individual farm survey information and total figures for the village as a whole. These copies were jointly examined and verified by a government official and a designated representative of all the farmers in the village. One copy was kept in the village and the other went to the central government's tax and accounting officials. Although these ledgers did not always contain totally accurate information regarding the number of farmers required to pay taxes at the time, they do provide important information about rural populations for historians today.

Hideyoshi took a personal interest in the land survey. In 1573, he defeated forces led by the Asai family, and his overlord Oda Nobunaga rewarded him with the Asai domain in what is now northern Shiga Prefecture, making him a feudal lord for the first time. Hideyoshi conducted a thoroughgoing survey of this new territory, and after gaining control of most of Harima Province (present-day Hyōgo Prefecture) in 1580, he had an extensive land survey carried out there as well.

After Nobunaga's death in 1582, Hideyoshi became a national warlord in his own right. A series of campaigns resulted in his de facto rule over the entire country by 1590. Starting in the Kyōto area in 1582, Hideyoshi ordered regional land surveys in each territory he conquered, including modern-day Fukui Prefecture (1583), Shikoku and the Kii Peninsula (1585), Kyūshū (1587), and the Kantō and Tohoku regions (1590). Hideyoshi's surveys were conducted mainly under the supervision of three of his leading generals: Asano Nagamasa, Ishida Mitsunari, and Natsuka Masaie.

Much of the land in Japan had thus been surveyed by the time Hideyoshi consolidated control of the country in 1590, but he had a new and more comprehensive nationwide survey planned and implemented. Most of the consolidated survey took place in 1594-1595, and it was known at the time as the Taikō Kenchi, or "Land Survey of the Taikō, Hideyoshi." This term later also came to refer loosely to all the land surveys conducted by Hideyoshi throughout his career. The later, consolidated survey was also called the *koku-naoshi*, or "*koku* revision," because it involved recalculation of the number of *koku* of rice produced and it revised estimates of the number of *koku* to be taken as taxes.

Ishida Mitsunari, a leading military figure and civil administrator under Hideyoshi's command, was instrumental in planning and conducting the consolidated land survey. In 1594-1595, Ishida was in charge of a model survey of territory in Hitachi Province (modern Ibaraki Prefecture), in the Kantō region. The Tokugawa Mito domain in this area subsequently became a model of enlightened administration and efficient farming, which may be partly attributable to the groundwork established by Ishida's survey.

SIGNIFICANCE

Many of the administrative practices and procedures in the following Tokugawa era (1603-1868) were introduced by Hideyoshi. The land survey system is a prime example of this. Prior to Hideyoshi's time, a considerable amount of land in Japan was in the actual or nominal possession of religious institutions, and the crops were used to support a particular Buddhist temple or Shinto shrine. In recurring times of civil disorder and social upheaval, some government officials appointed to administer regional areas came to regard their positions as permanent, and they took possession of large amounts of land as their own property. Hideyoshi's land surveys dramatically changed this ownership system.

By Hideyoshi's time, the Ashikaga shogunate and the Imperial Court had little real authority to grant or assign land to anyone. The last Ashikaga shogun was deposed by Oda Nobunaga in 1573, the same year that Oda made Hideyoshi a domain lord. The warfare carried on by Oda, and then Hideyoshi, cleared the land titles of many large holdings by eliminating the owners, such as the Asai family. These holdings were then given to victorious generals. The nationwide Taikō Kenchi survey system legitimized the taxation rights of Hideyoshi's new central government, identified local farmers, village by village, made them responsible for their own land, essentially bound them to that land, and put them under the authority of assigned village leaders. This nationwide land survey process became the basis for the entire Tokugawa system of taxation and of social control at the local level.

—*Michael McCaskey*

FURTHER READING

Berry, Mary Elizabeth. *Hideyoshi*. Cambridge, Mass.: Harvard University Press, 1989. This is the definitive biography of Toyotomi Hideyoshi in English, written by a leading American authority on Japanese history in the late sixteenth and early seventeenth centuries, and based on original sources.

Hall, John W., Nagahara Keiji, and Kozo Yamamura. *Japan Before Tokugawa: Political Consolidation and Economic Growth, 1500 to 1650*. Princeton, N.J.: Princeton University Press, 1981. A standard authoritative work on pre-Tokugawa Japan, from the combined perspectives of Japanese and American scholars.

Hall, John W., and Toyoda Takeshi. *Japan in the Muromachi Age*. Ithaca, N.Y.: East Asia Program, Cornell University, 2001. A revision of an authoritative work combining Japanese and American scholarly perspectives.

Lamers, Jeroen. *Japonius Tyrannus: The Japanese Warlord, Oda Nobunaga Reconsidered*. Leiden: Hotei, 2000. A highly readable and substantial biography of Oda, Hideyoshi's mentor, who was the source of many of the ideas Hideyoshi later implemented on a national scale.

Totman, Conrad D. *Pre-Industrial Korea and Japan in Environmental Perspective*. Boston: Brill, 2004. A detailed institutional study from economic and ecological perspectives by a leading authority on life in Japan during the late sixteenth century and the subsequent Tokugawa era.

1594-1600
KING MICHAEL'S UPRISING

Michael the Brave's uprising put an end to the harsh political and economic domination of the Ottoman Empire. The final goal was to unite three principalities, Walachia, Moldavia, and Transylvania, in an anti-Ottoman block, and ultimately to preserve their autonomous status as states under Ottoman suzerainty.

LOCALE: Transylvania, Walachia, Moldavia, Hungary, Austria, Poland, and the Ottoman Empire

CATEGORIES: Wars, uprisings, and civil unrest; expansion and land acquisition; diplomacy and international relations; government and politics

KEY FIGURES

Michael the Brave (1558-1601), prince of Walachia, r. 1593-1600, and prince of Transylvania, r. 1599-1600

Rudolf II (1552-1612), Holy Roman Emperor, r. 1576-1612

Jan Zamoyski (1542-1605), Polish chancellor, 1578-1605, and grand hetman, 1581-1602

Sigismund Báthory (1572-1613), prince of Transylvania, r. 1588-1598

SUMMARY OF EVENT

At the end of the sixteenth century, the Habsburg monarchy, Poland, and the Ottoman Empire clashed in a conflict designed to win control over the Romanian principalities. The intention of the Habsburgs was to recover first Transylvania and then the other two autonomous principalities, Walachia and Moldavia (or Moldova). Their plans for political expansion in this region were opposed by Poland's aspirations for expansion toward the Black Sea.

During the last decades of the sixteenth century, the political and economic situation of Walachia had worsened mainly as a result of the increasing financial and material demands of the Ottomans. Walachian princes were often deposed, leading to political instability. The right of the estates to elect their own prince was drastically diminished, with appointments being made by the Ottomans in Constantinople. The throne was in fact bought for huge, borrowed sums whose repayment caused mounting financial pressures. A great number of Levantine creditors, connected to the interests of the Ottomans, settled in the Walachian principality, where they acquired real estate. Many of them succeeded in penetrating government offices. This development triggered a

xenophobic reaction among the autochthonous boyars and ultimately prompted a movement to end this unbearable situation. At the beginning of Michael the Brave's reign in 1593, therefore, Walachia was on the brink of rebellion.

The external political context of the uprising was dominated by the efforts of the Papacy to form an anti-Ottoman alliance comprising Austria and the Italian dukedoms of Ferrara, Tuscany, and Mantua. Poland and England, however, were reluctant to join. Austria played the leading role in the coalition, and in February, 1594, Sigismund Báthory, prince of Transylvania, joined the anti-Ottoman coalition by signing a treaty with Emperor Rudolf II. His role was to attract Moldavia and Walachia into the anti-Ottoman coalition. Thus, in August, 1594, the prince of Moldavia, Aaron the Tyrant (also known as Aron the Terrible), signed a treaty of alliance with Rudolf and recognized the suzerainty of Sigismund Báthory in Moldavia. In September, Michael the Brave entered an alliance with Sigismund. In this way, the three principalities formed an anti-Ottoman political bloc that prepared for the war.

Michael the Brave started the uprising on October 13, 1594, by slaughtering the Levantine creditors and an Ottoman military unit in Bucharest. He then attacked and destroyed Ottoman towns and strongholds situated near the Danube. At the same time, Aaron the Tyrant launched a similar attack against the Ottoman garrison of Tighina (Bender). Under these conditions, the Ottomans halted their war against the Habsburgs in Austria to suppress the rebellion of the principalities. In April, 1595, Sigismund Báthory arrested Aaron the Tyrant and replaced him with Ştefan Răzvan.

In May, a delegation of boyars representing the estates of Walachia signed a treaty in Alba Iulia that recognized Sigismund as ruler of Walachia, which was to be governed by a council of twelve boyars. Michael was limited to the role of a lieutenant of Sigismund Báthory. The prince of Moldavia signed a similar treaty in June. Through these political maneuvers, Sigismund became the suzerain of the other two principalities. His political ambitions were limited, however, by the aspirations of the Habsburgs, who considered Sigismund their vassal. However, Poland's aspirations to acquire Moldavia were thwarted, and in the summer the chancellor Jan Zamoyski invaded the principality, putting Ieremia Movilă (or Moghila) on the throne.

855

Michael the Brave, prince of Walachia and prince of Transylvania. (Hulton|Archive by Getty Images)

Also in the summer of 1595, the Ottomans decided to suppress the rebellion and to transform the principalities into Ottoman provinces. The main battle took place on August 23 at Călugăreni. Michael's army was overwhelmed and forced to withdraw to the north, where he waited for reinforcements from Transylvania. In September, the Ottomans occupied the country and began to transform the churches into mosques. Starting in October, the united forces of the three principalities won victories and forced the Ottoman army to retreat beyond the Danube. Despite this success, the anti-Ottoman alliance of the three principalities dissolved later that fall, when Poland signed a treaty with the Ottomans recognizing its influence in Moldavia through the reign of its puppet, Ieremia Movilă.

In 1596, Michael successfully resisted the attacks of the Ottoman forces and repelled an expedition of Crimean Tatars, although Sigismund and the Habsburgs were defeated at Timișoara, Eger, and Mezőkerezstes. Although victorious in Hungary, the Ottomans decided to make peace with the Austrians, and at the end of 1596, they recognized Michael as prince of Walachia. In January of 1597, he entered direct negotiations with Emperor Rudolf II, who promised him subsidies for four thousand soldiers. In December, 1597, Sigismund Báthory signed a treaty through which Transylvania was relinquished to Rudolf II, and in April, 1598, he departed the principality. In June, Rudolf became the suzerain of Walachia and recognized Michael's rule and his family's hereditary rights to the throne. Very soon, however, Sigismund Báthory again abdicated (March, 1599) in favor of his cousin, Cardinal Andrew Báthory, who represented the interests of Poland. The Ottomans recognized Andrew as prince of Transylvania and allowed Poland to pursue its own policy in Transylvania and Walachia, anticipating in this way a war between Poland and Austria.

The changes in the political situation in Transylvania created a dangerous situation for Michael, whose throne was threatened from the north. Indeed, Andrew Báthory expressed his intention to oust Michael and give the throne of Walachia to Simion Movilă, the brother of the prince of Moldavia. In June, 1599, Michael announced to the Habsburgs his intention of overthrowing Andrew Báthory and requested their help. A Walachian army crossed the Carpathian Mountains and defeated the army of Andrew on October 28 at Șelimbăr. In May, 1600, Michael conquered Moldavia. Nevertheless, the Transylvanian nobility rebelled and defeated him in September at Mirăslău. A Polish army led by Chancellor Jan Zamoyski marched into Walachia, defeated Michael, and gave the throne to Simion Movilă. In this way, in a very short time, Michael the Brave managed to unite the three principalities under a unique political authority during the course of the anti-Ottoman war.

SIGNIFICANCE

Michael the Brave's uprising against the Ottomans began in a favorable international context although it was provoked by the aggravation of the Ottoman domination. The three principalities Walachia, Moldavia, and Transylvania were first united politically by Sigismund Báthory to resist the Ottoman threat. Michael nourished the same intentions through 1598-1599 and, at least for a short time, was able to realize this plan.

The main achievement of the uprising consisted of the relaxation of the Ottoman demands and in the preservation of Walachia, Moldavia, and Transylvania as autonomous states. In the nineteenth century this achievement and Michael's victories against the Ottomans won him the status of a national hero as the first unifier of what is today Romania.

—Cosmin Popa-Gorjanu

FURTHER READING

Andreescu, Ştefan. "Some Reflections on Michael the Brave's Denominational Policy." In *Ethnicity and Religion in Central and Eastern Europe*, edited by Maria Craciun and Ovidiu Ghitta. Cluj, Romania: Cluj University Press, 1995. This article deals with the policy toward the Catholic and Protestant churches.

_____. *Studii cu privire la Mihai Viteazu, 1593-1601*. Vol. 3 in *Restitutio Daciae*. Bucharest: Editura Albatros, 1997. For the serious scholar, this is the most comprehensive study of the reign of Michael the Brave. Available only in Romanian.

Prodan, David. *Supplex Libellus Valachorum: Or, The Political Struggle of the Romanians in Transylvania During the Eighteenth Century*. Bucharest, Romania: Publishing House of the Academy, 1971. One chapter of this work deals with the rule of Michael the Brave in Transylvania in 1599-1600 and with his attitude toward the Transylvanian estates and the Romanian population from the principality.

SEE ALSO: Apr. 14, 1457-July 2, 1504: Reign of Stephen the Great; Nov., 1575: Stephen Báthory Becomes King of Poland; 1576-1612: Reign of Rudolf II; 1593-1606: Ottoman-Austrian War.

RELATED ARTICLES in *Great Lives from History: The Renaissance & Early Modern Era, 1454-1600:* Elizabeth Báthory; Rudolf II; Stephen Báthory; Vlad III the Impaler.

1596
RALEGH ARRIVES IN GUIANA

Ralegh's attempt to discover the fabled gold-rich land of El Dorado fueled Britain's imperial ambitions for conquest and colonial expansion. His enormously popular geographical and topographical survey, The Discoverie of the Large, Rich, and Bewtiful Empyre of Guiana (1596), *functioned as an advertisement for the spread of English imperialism and increased colonization in South America.*

LOCALE: Guiana (now in Venezuela)

CATEGORIES: Expansion and land acquisition; trade and commerce; colonization; exploration and discovery

KEY FIGURES

Sir Walter Ralegh (c. 1552-1618), English explorer, privateer, and poet

Elizabeth I (1533-1603), queen of England, r. 1558-1603

James I (1566-1625), king of England, r. 1603-1625

SUMMARY OF EVENT

Although his attempt to discover the fabled land of El Dorado (The Golden Land) failed dismally, Sir Walter Ralegh, the world-famous poet, adventurer, and explorer, nevertheless greatly fueled Britain's imperial ambitions for conquest and colonial expansion.

Ralegh took up the project of finding the legendary land of El Dorado, which he was certain was abundant in gold, in an attempt to regain his favored position in the court of English queen Elizabeth I. The ambitious courtier, who earlier gained the queen's attention by covering a muddy puddle with his colorful cloak for her to pass, had fallen out of favor by secretly marrying maid of honor Elizabeth Throckmorton in 1592. The queen, who forbade her courtiers from marrying to keep their attention focused on her, learned of the marriage and imprisoned Ralegh and his wife in the Tower of London.

Before his fall from grace, the dashing, brilliant, and powerful Ralegh's adventures had made him one of the queen's favorites. He had sailed the seas as an explorer and adventurer, gone to the West Indies on a mission to attack Spanish ships laden with gold, and diplayed significant talent as a poet, elevating this contradictory and complex Elizabethan figure greatly in the queen's eyes. Moreover, as a fervent Protestant, Ralegh saw Catholic Spain as England's greatest enemy. His ship, the *Ark Royal*, was the flagship of the English fleet during the enormously successful campaign against the Spanish Armada (1588) and made him one of the best-known men in England. His exploratory attempts to find and mine gold in North America resulted in the discovery of Virginia, which Ralegh named for Elizabeth, the Virgin Queen.

Upon his release from the Tower of London, Ralegh planned his expedition to find the legendary golden city. Since the discovery of Virginia had gained him such recognition, Ralegh felt sure a similar conquest, this time the attainment of South American El Dorado and all of its fabled riches, would place him firmly once again in the queen's favor and diminish the popularity of the queen's new favorite, the earl of Essex. Thus, in 1595, Ralegh led an expedition of one hundred men under royal commission into the Amazon basin in the company of adventurer Laurence Kemys to find El Dorado.

According to legend, the city was situated on a 200-league (600-mile or 966-kilometer) saltwater lake near the mouth of the Orinoco River in Guiana, in what is today called Venezuela. Spanish documents and stories told by South American Indians told of the city's existence, claiming that it was composed of gold. The legend originated with the Chibcha people of Colombia, who claimed that the area was so rich in gold that every year they covered a man in gold (the city's name literally translates as "the gilded man"). Earlier, the Spanish conquistador Francisco Pizarro and many other explorers, including Francisco Vásquez de Coronado, had attempted to find this land of legends whose supposed location kept shifting as, one after another, the explorers failed to find it.

In 1596, Ralegh's expedition penetrated 300 miles (483 kilometers) up the Orinoco River into the heart of Spain's colonial empire, eventually arriving at the port of Morequito, Guiana. There Ralegh met the king of Arromaia, who was supposedly 110 years old. With patriotic fervor, Ralegh later described the British Empire's role as one of rescuer of the native people from the oppressive Spanish and wrote of his attempts to persuade the native *Casiqui* to worship and serve Queen Elizabeth. However, although Ralegh's expedition claimed to find "*El Madre del oro*" (the mother of gold) and did locate some gold-flecked pieces of quartz, they failed to discover gold in any significant quantities.

After he returned to England, dejected but with a head full of adventure tales, Ralegh wrote the enormously popular geographical and topographical survey, *The Discoverie of the Large, Rich, and Bewtiful Empyre of Guiana* (1596). In this book, Ralegh paints the lands of the Amazon and its people in a highly colorful, dramatic light and suggests that amazing riches lie there just for the taking. The book was quickly translated into German, Dutch, and Latin, an amazing accomplishment in the Renaissance. Thus, although Ralegh failed to discover gold in South America, he succeeded brilliantly as a writer describing his adventures in the New World. Also, through his dreamy, eloquent prose, Ralegh indirectly urged imperial expansion by advocating the colonization of Guiana and other colonies. The account of his expedition acted as a form of alluring advertising, which implanted the grow-rich-quick fantasy of El Dorado in English minds and made them even more eager to colonize the Americas.

SIGNIFICANCE

Ralegh's hopes to regain favor at court were shattered upon the death of Elizabeth and the accession of James I in 1603. He was sentenced to death for plotting against the new king, who commuted his sentence to life in prison in the Tower of London, where he remained imprisoned this time for twelve years. In the tower, he wrote his famous *The History of the World* (1614).

In 1616, Ralegh convinced James I that Guiana's native chiefs had ceded their country to England, and he gained the king's permission for a second expedition in search of gold. Ralegh failed disastrously. The king, who wanted peace, had ordered him not to attack Spain in any capacity on pain of his life. However, his officer Laurence Kemys, while searching for El Dorado, attacked the Spanish settlement of St. Thomas and burned it to the ground. Spain demanded that Ralegh suffer severe punishment, and his attempt to escape to France failed. King James accordingly reinstated Ralegh's original death sentence, and the adventurer was beheaded on October 29, 1618.

Sir Walter Ralegh's attempt to discover the fabled gold-rich land of El Dorado fueled England's imperial ambitions for further conquest and increased colonial expansion. Although the 1596 exploratory expedition failed, Ralegh's subsequent enormously popular geographical and topographical survey fired the imaginations of his readers, leading to increased colonization of South America and other colonies.

—*M. Casey Diana*

FURTHER READING

Aronson, Marc. *Sir Walter Ralegh and the Quest for El Dorado*. New York: Houghton Mifflin, 2000. Details Ralegh's life during the tumultuous Elizabethan era, providing a cultural context for the poet, soldier, and explorer in his quest for El Dorado. Provides maps and prints.

Hyland, Paul. *Ralegh's Last Journey: A Tale of Madness, Vanity, and Treachery*. New York: HarperCollins, 2003. Concentrates on the last five months of Sir Walter Ralegh's eventful life: his final voyage to Guinea, return home, attempted escape to France in a false beard, and ultimate beheading.

Lacey, Robert. *Phoenix: Sir Walter Ralegh*. London: Phoenix Press, 2001. In seven sections that cover 50 chapters, Lacey charts Ralegh's multifaceted life and nature from poet to solider, adventurer, scientist, statesman, lover, and family man. Pays particular attention to how Ralegh paved the way for expanded colonization in the Americas.

Naipaul, V. S. *The Loss of El Dorado: A Colonial History*. New York: Vintage, 2003. A 2001 Nobel Prize winner who brought Walter Ralegh severely to task in his prize acceptance speech, Naipaul illustrates the drastic results of English colonialism brought about by such men as Ralegh in the Orinoco region, which includes Naipaul's own home, Trinidad.

Ralegh, Sir Walter. *The Discoverie of the Large, Rich, and Bewtiful Empyre of Guiana*. 1596. Reprint. Edited by Neil L. Whitehead. Norman: University of Okla-

homa Press, 1998. Ralegh's transcribed original 1596 text of his expedition to Guiana. Provides a 100-page critical introduction highlighting the historical, geographical, and political aspects of Ralegh's adventure.

SEE ALSO: Oct. 12, 1492: Columbus Lands in the Americas; Feb. 23, 1540-Oct., 1542: Coronado's Southwest Expedition; 1545-1548: Silver Is Discovered in Spanish America; 1558-1603: Reign of Elizabeth I; Apr., 1587-c. 1600: Anglo-Spanish War; July 31-Aug. 8, 1588: Defeat of the Spanish Armada.

RELATED ARTICLES in *Great Lives from History: The Renaissance & Early Modern Era, 1454-1600:* Francisco Vásquez de Coronado; Elizabeth I; Philip II; Francisco Pizarro; Sir Walter Ralegh.

October, 1596-February, 1597
SAN FELIPE INCIDENT

Toyotomi Hideyoshi's confiscation of the Spanish galleon San Felipe *marked the beginning of a long period of Japanese isolationism and persecution of Catholic missionaries.*

LOCALE: Nagasaki, Kyōto, and Shikoku Island, Japan
CATEGORY: Diplomacy and international relations

KEY FIGURES

Oda Nobunaga (1534-1582), dictator of central Japan who welcomed the first Christians, r. 1573-1582

Toyotomi Hideyoshi (1537-1598), successor of Nobunaga who conquered and unified Japan, r. 1590-1598

Tokugawa Ieyasu (Matsudaira Takechiyo, later Matsudaira Motoyasu; 1543-1616), shogun, r. 1603-1605, and founder of the Tokugawa shogunate

Masuda Nagamori (1545?-1615), a lieutenant of Hideyoshi who met the crew of the *San Felipe* when they arrived in Japan

Francisco de Olandia (fl. late sixteenth century), captain of the *San Felipe*

SUMMARY OF EVENT

Before the arrival of the Spanish galleon *San Felipe* in 1596, the ruling Japanese Lords, Oda Nobunaga and his successor Toyotomi Hideyoshi, had for the most part befriended the Catholic missionaries in Japan. The first Catholics to arrive in Japan in 1549 were the Jesuits, a Portuguese order. They inaugurated what is now known

as the Christian Century in Japan (1549-1650). Nobunaga hoped to unify all the regions of Japan under his control and believed the Jesuits would serve as allies against the Buddhists, who opposed him. He also believed his relationship with the missionaries would facilitate trade with the Portuguese.

Succeeding Nobunaga in 1582 as the de facto military ruler of Japan, Hideyoshi followed the latter's policy and showed favor to the missionaries. In July of 1587, however, Hideyoshi issued the first edict against Christianity, banning all foreign missionaries from Japan. The ruler apparently realized that the Jesuits had acquired too much territorial power. The Jesuits had converted a number of influential regional lords (or daimyo) and had thus gained control over their lands. For instance, the area of Nagasaki was essentially controlled by the Jesuits. In the edict, Hideyoshi stated that the foreign missionaries were politically subversive and a threat to the national security of Japan.

Shortly thereafter, however, Hideyoshi changed his mind and ignored the ban. The ruler himself was seen wearing Portuguese attire and carrying a rosary. He probably knew that it was not an appropriate time to persecute the Jesuits, since he needed the military aid of the Portuguese to win a forthcoming war in Korea. Thus, the Jesuits resumed their activities and successfully continued their conversions.

Hoping to emulate the success of the Portuguese Jesuits, the Franciscans, a Spanish Catholic order, arrived in

Japan in 1593. Hideyoshi welcomed the Spaniards and even donated land for the missionaries. Some historians estimate that, by the time the *San Felipe* arrived in 1597, as many as 300,000 Japanese, including high-ranking advisers and generals, had already converted to Catholicism. Hideyoshi's main motive for aiding the Spanish Franciscans was to attract Spanish trade, just as the Jesuits had served to attract Portuguese merchants. Since their arrival, the Franciscans and the Jesuits clashed with the Jesuits over power and jurisdiction of territories.

In October of 1596, on its way from the Philippines to Mexico, the Spanish galleon *San Felipe* was blown off course by a typhoon and became stranded on the coast of Shikoku Island. The local daimyo held the ship, detained its crew, and requested guidance from Hideyoshi's lieutenant Masuda Nagamori. The daimyo informed Nagamori that the ship was carrying heavy arms and a rich cargo, as well as many Franciscan missionaries on board. Nagamori then went to the site and met the officers of the ship, who had become upset at the possibility that their cargo could be confiscated. According to the Jesuit account, the captain of the ship, Francisco de Olandia, attempted to prevent the confiscation of the cargo by boasting about the power of the Spanish Empire and its plan for world conquest. Olandia supposedly pointed out that the Franciscans had been sent by the Spanish as precursors to a subsequent Spanish military conquest. The Spanish plan was to first conquer Japan by converting the Japanese into Christians. Then, the Spanish were to send military troops to take the islands of Japan just as they had done in Peru, Mexico, and the Philippine Islands.

The Spanish Franciscans' version of the incident, however, was different. According to the Franciscans, Olandia's story was a Jesuit fabrication to have the Franciscans removed from Japan. In the end, the quarrel between the Catholic orders only exacerbated the situation, resulting in Hideyoshi's mistrust of all Franciscans, and subsequently of all Jesuits as well. In December, when Hideyoshi's anti-Christian advisers informed him of Captain Olandia's account of the Spanish Empire's scheme to invade Japan, the ruler became furious. This was probably not a good time to try Hideyoshi's patience. He had just been struck by a series of unfortunate events: his recent defeat in Korea, the destruction of his new palace in Kyōto during a series of earthquakes, and the deterioration of his personal health. With this background, Hideyoshi's advisers managed to persuade him that the *San Felipe* incident presented proof that a "martial Catholic church" in Japan was a threat to national security.

Hideyoshi issued arrest warrants for all Franciscans in Japan. He then ordered their execution by crucifixion in Nagasaki. He justified these death sentences as just punishment for breaking the ban on Christianity of 1587, a ban that he had not enforced.

The initial list of the condemned numbered 160, but the officer in charge felt compassion for the large number of Japanese Christians involved and cut the list to 24. The final list included 6 European Franciscans, 10 Japanese Franciscans, 3 Japanese Jesuits—who were probably included by mistake—and 4 Japanese laymen who worked as aids to the missionaries. Hideyoshi sought to make an example of the condemned and gave them an excruciating sentence. In the beginning of January, in the middle of winter, the Christians had their ears and noses cut—rituals of humiliation—and were paraded for a distance of 600 miles (966 kilometers), for an entire month, making stops in the towns between Kyōto and Nagasaki.

Catholic accounts portray the event as the triumph of the Christian faith in pagan lands. They describe the martyrs' journey as the way to the Calvary. They recount tales of how during their long journey the martyrs never stopped preaching and singing hymns. They also depict all the martyrs as displaying such remarkable joy, courage, and undying faith that even the pagan witnesses of the apotheosis were convinced of the truthfulness of the Christian faith. By the time the Christians reached Nagasaki, more Japanese laymen had been added to the list. It is believed that these two volunteered to die as martyrs.

The crucifixion took place in Mount Tateyama on February 5. Catholic sources recall the martyrs' singing, praying, and preaching the Christian gospel from their crosses until the very end. The martyrs became known as the Twenty-six Martyrs of Nagasaki. Two months after their execution, Hideyoshi ordered all Jesuits to leave the country. The Twenty-six Martyrs of Japan were canonized in 1862 by Pope Pius IX.

SIGNIFICANCE

The *San Felipe* affair and the crucifixion of the Twenty-six Martyrs in 1597 mark an important point in the history of Japan because they established another stage of Japan's self-imposed isolationist policy, also known as the Sakoku policy. The anti-Christian aspect of the Sakoku policy was completed with the martyrdom. It also represents the first time Europeans were put to death for preaching Christianity in Japan. In the history of the Catholic Church, it marks the end of open missionary works of the Catholic missionaries, closing the first half of the Christian Century.

During the second half of the Christian Century (1597-1650), the rulers of Japan formed a clear ideological structure aimed at the eradication of Christianity and mobilized the common Japanese people to join the persecution of Christians. At the beginning of this period, an estimated 150,000 Japanese were practicing Christianity underground.

In 1614, Hideyoshi's successor, Tokugawa Ieyasu, passed an edict that suppressed all Christian activity. It demanded that all foreign missionaries be deported and all churches be destroyed. As a result, there were crucifixions, decapitations, burnings, and hangings. The excruciating torments imposed on Christians drove many Japanese converts, and even a number of missionaries, to apotheosize their faith. Others, including about three thousand Japanese (between 1597 and 1650), refused to do so and were sentenced to death. Still, Christianity was not eradicated completely. When Japan reemerged from its isolationist policy in the 1850's, a French Catholic priest discovered a secret group of Christians that lived in the mountains and practiced an indigenous form of archaic Catholicism that dated back to the time of the *San Felipe* incident.

—*Christina H. Lee*

FURTHER READING

Ellison, George. "Hideyoshi and the Sectarians." *Deus Destroyed: The Image of Christianity in Early Modern Japan*. Cambridge, Mass.: Harvard University Press, 1973. The chapter presents a well-balanced revision of "the rise and fall" of the Christian Century (1549-1639) in Japan. Its discussion on the Jesuit/Franciscan antagonism is particularly enlightening.

Nelson, John. "Myths, Missions, and Mistrust: The Fate of Christianity in 16th and 17th Century Japan." *History and Anthropology* 13, no. 2 (2002): 93-111. Article points out the strategic blunders of the missionaries in Japan that contributed to the decision of the Japanese Lords to persecute Catholicism.

Ross, Andrew C. "The Christian Century in Japan, 1549-1650." *A Vision Betrayed: The Jesuits in Japan and China 1542-1742*. New York: Orbis, 2000. Survey of the Jesuit missions in Japan and of their underlying philosophy.

Whelan, Christal. *The Beginning of Heaven and Earth: The Sacred Book of Japan's Hidden Christians*. Honolulu: University of Hawaii Press, 1996. Provides an anthropological perspective on the Christian missionaries' interactions from the sixteenth century through modern times.

SEE ALSO: 1457-1480's: Spread of Jōdo Shinshū Buddhism; 1467-1477: Ōnin War; 1477-1600: Japan's "Age of the Country at War"; Mar. 5, 1488: Composition of the *Renga* Masterpiece *Minase sangin hyakuin*; Beginning 1513: Kanō School Flourishes; 1532-1536: Temmon Hokke Rebellion; 1549-1552: Father Xavier Introduces Christianity to Japan; 1550's-1567: Japanese Pirates Pillage the Chinese Coast; 1550-1593: Japanese Wars of Unification; Sept., 1553: First Battle of Kawanakajima; June 12, 1560: Battle of Okehazama; 1568: Oda Nobunaga Seizes Kyōto; 1587: Toyotomi Hideyoshi Hosts a Ten-Day Tea Ceremony; 1590: Odawara Campaign; 1592-1599: Japan Invades Korea; 1594-1595: Taikō Kenchi Survey; Oct. 21, 1600: Battle of Sekigahara.

RELATED ARTICLES in *Great Lives from History: The Renaissance & Early Modern Era, 1454-1600:* Hōjō Ujimasa; Hosokawa Gracia; Oda Nobunaga; Ōgimachi; Oichi; Sesshū; Toyotomi Hideyoshi.

1597-September, 1601
TYRONE REBELLION

As part of the Nine Years' War (1594-1603), the earl of Tyrone, Hugh O'Neill, led an Irish rebellion against England which came to be viewed by the Irish as a war of liberation. Defeat of O'Neill's Irish forces and Spanish allies at the Battle of Kinsale cemented Irish submission to English sovereignty.

LOCALE: Ireland

CATEGORIES: Wars, uprisings, and civil unrest; government and politics

KEY FIGURES

Hugh O'Neill (1540?-1616), third baron of Dunganon and second earl of Tyrone

Charles Blount (c. 1562-1606), eighth baron Mountjoy, lord deputy of Ireland, 1600, and later earl of Devonshire, 1603-1606

Robert Devereux (1566-1601), second earl of Essex, 1576-1599, earl marshal of England, 1597-1599, lord lieutenant and governor of Ireland, 1599

Elizabeth I (1533-1603), queen of England, r. 1558-1603

James I (1566-1625), king of Scotland as James VI, r. 1567-1625, and king of Great Britain, r. 1603-1625

Sir William Fitzwilliam (1526-1599), lord deputy of Ireland, 1572-1575, 1588-1594, and governor of Fotheringhay Castle, 1575-1588, who oversaw the execution of Mary, Queen of Scots

Sir John Perrot (c. 1527-1592), president of Munster, 1570-1573, and Lord Deputy of Ireland, 1584-1588

SUMMARY OF EVENT

Sixteenth century Irish society was composed of vast feudal lordships and smaller dissident clans who warred with their rivals and with the English. The English Council in Dublin backed one or another of the powerful Anglo-Norman earls during these struggles. These Irish leaders with English backing were given the title Lord Deputy, to distinguish them from the English viceroys who governed Ireland under the title Lord Lieutenant. The lord deputies received inconsistent support from the English government and were usually recalled in disgrace. This was true of both of the English governors who preceded the Tyrone Rebellion. Sir John Perrot was actually charged with treason on trumped-up charges and died in the Tower of London. Sir William Fitzwilliam, one of his successors, was also charged with graft and corruption.

In the late sixteenth century, Hugh O'Neill, earl of Tyrone, became the leader of a rebellion that attracted the support of Spain and had some successes, but even Tyrone was not able to defeat the English. English policy toward Ireland oscillated between schemes for pacification and halfhearted military campaigns.

The 1579 rebellion of Gerald Fitzgerald, earl of Desmond (c. 1538-1583) had facilitated the plantation of Munster. As a traitor to the queen, Desmond had his property confiscated, and these attainted lands were parceled out to loyal Englishmen and Irish lords, who were expected to plant colonies. The English planters were supposed to entice English tenants to resettle in Ireland and then serve as models of English civility to their Gaelic neighbors. Some of the planters rented the land back to Irish tenants and remained safely in England; others resettled in Ireland and clamored for England to protect them from their hostile neighbors. Although each

Hugh O'Neill, earl of Tyrone. (Hulton|Archive by Getty Images)

of the lord deputies had troops at his disposal, England resisted expending the resources necessary to subjugate warring and rebellious factions and maintain peace.

Irish historians refer to the uprisings and retaliations at the close of the sixteenth century as the Nine Years' War. These historians date the rebellion from June, 1594, when Hugh Roe O'Donnell and Hugh Maguire attacked the fortress at Enniskillen. In its early stages, the war consisted of guerrilla skirmishes, offensives, and counteroffensives. During this time, the earl of Tyrone—a consummate politician as well as an experienced military leader—used the English to fight against his traditional enemies and so consolidate his own power. Once his power was consolidated around 1597, Tyrone took charge of the rebellion, and it is this portion of the Nine Years' War that is properly referred to as the Tyrone Rebellion. Tyrone promoted himself as the leader of Catholic Ireland and used this position to negotiate foreign assistance and military intervention from Catholic Spain. Under Tyrone's command, the Irish dealt the English a decisive defeat at the Battle of Yellow Ford on August 14, 1598.

Tyrone's victory at the Battle of Yellow Ford shocked England. It was a pitched battle, not a guerrilla attack. The English forces numbered 4,200 and were led by the English marshal, Sir Henry Bagenal. About 830 men were killed, including Bagenal himself; 400 were wounded and another 300 deserted to the Irish side. Tyrone was in fact the brother-in-law of Sir Henry, who was named English marshal in succession to his father. His father had rejected Tyrone's suit for his daughter's hand. Mabel Bagenal then eloped with the earl, a man twice her age but reputed to be charming as well as shrewd.

Tyrone had borne a grudge against the elder Bagenal, due to the marshal's refusal to grant him Mabel's substantial dowry and her share of the family inheritance. English and Irish landowners, aware that the Battle of Yellow Ford was partly a settlement of that grudge, sympathized with Tyrone. Alarmed by Tyrone's victory, the English council in Dublin seems to have feared an attack on the pale (the Anglo-Irish settlement around Dublin). Tyrone's decisive victory inspired more people to join the rebellion. He did send forces south to Munster and Limerick and successfully laid waste to the English plantations there, symbols of the defeat of the earlier Desmond Rebellion. The resident English planters fled to the urban coastal centers of Cork, Youghal, and Waterford, where they petitioned the queen for support.

The spreading rebellion and Tyrone's triumphs prompted a determined English retaliation. A new army was sent to Ireland under the leadership of Robert Devereux, earl of Essex, who was credited with triumphing over the Spanish at Cádiz in 1596. Essex, an English military hero and talented general, was appointed Lord Lieutenant of Ireland: the queen's lieutenant and governor in her name. In March, 1599, a huge army of 17,300 troops began to arrive in Ireland. Essex had boasted that he would defeat Tyrone in the field. After touring Munster and establishing his troops in various garrisons, he turned north, where he met Tyrone at the head of a much larger force on the Monaghan Pale border. The two men rode their horses into the middle of a river and held a private conference.

No one knows what transpired at the conference between Essex and Tyrone, but it was later rumored that Tyrone had offered Ireland to Essex. The result was another truce, one which seemed to benefit the insurgents. Shortly after this meeting with Tyrone, Essex returned to England without permission and set in motion the events that led to his own rebellion and execution in 1601. However, even with this respite, Tyrone was unable to unify Ireland against the crown because key Irish landowners, such as the earl of Ormond, remained loyal to the queen. Many Irish believed in deference to royalty, and indeed, Ireland would later support the king, not the Parliament, in the English Civil War of the next century.

Though Tyrone could not unify his country behind him, his bid for support from Spain was successful. On September 21, 1601, a Spanish force of 3,400 landed at Kinsale. Charles Blount, Lord Mountjoy, the newly appointed lord deputy of Ireland, hurried south from Dublin hoping to engage the Spanish force before Tyrone arrived. Mountjoy besieged the Spanish troops, holding them at Kinsale for two months. When Tyrone finally arrived at Kinsale, Mountjoy found himself sandwiched between the Spanish in the town and the approaching Irish army, but his experienced troops won the day, scattering the Irish troops and surrounding the Spanish.

SIGNIFICANCE

Tyrone retreated to Ulster, where he held out for the next year, but he finally surrendered on March 30, 1603. Queen Elizabeth I had died six days earlier, but Tyrone was unaware of her death at the time of his surrender. Kneeling before the English lord deputy, he renounced all dependence upon foreign rulers, the title of the O'Neill, and his overlordship rights over the chiefs in Ulster. The English could have broken up his lordship and divided it among those who had remained loyal to the crown, repeating their actions toward Desmond. However, Tyrone, always the astute politician, negotiated a royal pardon from James I and a patent for nearly all the lands he had held before the rebellion, with the exception of those needed to support two new garrisons.

Thus, in the wake of his rebellion, Tyrone's authority in Ireland was ironically confirmed rather than rescinded by the English crown. James's concessions, in fact, conferred local authority upon the earl under the auspices of the English sovereign. James perhaps hoped in this manner to avoid another costly war in the future. The English crown had spent more than two million pounds on the Tyrone Rebellion, and Tyrone himself was rumored to have spent five hundred pounds a day at the height of the war. Subjugating the Irish was very costly to the English, and it remained so into the next century, when minor rebellions followed in 1603 and 1609 and a major revolt again occurred in 1641. The latter revolt would lead to the Cromwellian conquest.

Hugh O'Neill, earl of Tyrone, identified himself as the sponsor of Roman Catholicism in Ireland and used religious allegiances to bring together Gaelic lords, Anglo-Norman nobles, and members of the clans. His rebellion established a pattern that would be repeated in British history. O'Neill became a romantic figure in Irish history and a model for future Irish heroes.

—*Jean R. Brink*

FURTHER READING

Boyce, D. George, and Alan O'Day, eds. *The Making of Modern Irish History: Revisionism and the Revisionist Controversy.* London: Routledge, 1996. Important discussion of approaches to revisionist national history. Discusses and reevaluates the traditional assumption that Ireland was intentionally victimized under British rule.

Canny, Nicholas. *Making Ireland British, 1580-1650.* New York: Oxford University Press, 2003. Skillful analysis by a leading Irish historian.

Cunningham, Bernadette. *The World of Geoffrey Keating: History, Myth, and Religion in Seventeenth-Century Ireland.* Dublin: Four Courts Press, 2000. Examines the aftermath of the Nine Years' War.

Lennon, Colm. *Sixteenth-Century Ireland: The Incomplete Conquest.* New York: St. Martin's Press, 1995. Overview of the revolt in Ulster and rise of Hugh O'Neill as part of the colonial enterprise.

Morgan, Hiram. *Tyrone's Rebellion: The Outbreak of the Nine Years War in Tudor Ireland.* Woodbridge, Suffolk, England: Boydell & Brewer, 1993. Important recent study on the rebellion by a prominent Irish historian.

Morgan, Hiram. *Political Ideology in Ireland, 1541-1641.* Dublin: Four Courts Press, 1999. Collection of essays commenting on the past and present politics of writing Irish history. Supplies a useful bibliography as well as evaluation of current scholarship.

SEE ALSO: 1489: Yorkshire Rebellion; Dec. 1, 1494: Poynings' Law; 1497: Cornish Rebellion; Aug. 22, 1513-July 6, 1560: Anglo-Scottish Wars; Dec. 18, 1534: Act of Supremacy; 1536 and 1543: Acts of Union Between England and Wales; Oct., 1536-June, 1537: Pilgrimage of Grace; 1549: Kett's Rebellion; Jan. 25-Feb. 7, 1554: Wyatt's Rebellion; 1558-1603: Reign of Elizabeth I; Nov. 9, 1569: Rebellion of the Northern Earls; Feb. 25, 1570: Pius V Excommunicates Elizabeth I.
RELATED ARTICLE in *Great Lives from History: The Renaissance & Early Modern Era, 1454-1600:* Elizabeth I.

October 31, 1597
JOHN DOWLAND PUBLISHES *AYRES*

Dowland's The First Booke of Songs or Ayres, *designed for polyphonic music, established the popularity of the ayre, which was composed for the voice primarily and played principally with the lute. The ayres, printed in a distinct table-layout format, flourished as a musical subgenre in which England excelled for a quarter century.*

LOCALE: London, England
CATEGORY: Music

KEY FIGURES
John Dowland (1562/1563-1626), English composer and lutenist
Peter Short (d. 1603), publisher of Dowland's works
Thomas Morley (1557/1558-1602), English composer and musician

SUMMARY OF EVENT
In the first half of the sixteenth century, music publishing was widespread on the European continent, particularly in Venice, Nuremberg, Antwerp, and Paris, but it was almost nonexistent in England until the 1570's. Some religious books with collections of metrical psalms were printed, however.

Queen Elizabeth I attempted to promote the publication of musical works by granting printing monopolies in 1559 to John Day for psalm books and in 1575 to Thomas Tallis and William Byrd for polyphonic music. Tallis was replaced by Thomas East, who published Byrd's *Psalmes, Sonets, and Songs of Sadness and Pietie* (1588) before the monopoly expired in 1596. In the absence of a monopoly, Peter Short published four works in 1597: Thomas Morley's *A Plaine and Easie Introduction to Practicall Musicke* and his *Canzonets to Five and Six Voices*, Anthony Holborne's *Cittarn Schoole*, and John Dowland's *The First Booke of Songs or Ayres*. Dowland's book and Morley's *Canzonets to Five and Six Voices*, which Short listed in the Stationers' Register on October 31, 1597, were the first two English books of polyphonic vocal music with a tablature part.

Dowland published his ayres in part because he was disappointed about not obtaining an appointment as lutenist in Elizabeth I's court; he had twice appealed for the post, the second time in 1597. (It was not until 1612 that he obtained a position as lutenist in King James I's English court.) When he traveled to Paris in 1580 as an aide to Sir Henry Cobham, the British ambassador to France, he converted to Catholicism, by his own admission, and he later attributed his failure to secure a court appointment to his being what he termed an "obstinate papist." There is some doubt about Dowland's claim, since Elizabeth protected William Byrd, a Catholic musician, and even granted him and Thomas Tallis exclusive rights to print music and music paper in 1575.

If his Catholicism was a problem, it might have been because of his brief involvement with British Catholics living in Florence, who were plotting against Elizabeth. Diana Poulton suggested that the real reason for his not being appointed was financial, since the post Dowland sought was vacant for several years, thereby saving the court a substantial amount of money. By publishing *Ayres*, which the work is known as collectively, Dowland may well have thought that he could enhance his chances of securing the appointment.

Sixteenth century Tudor brass musicians performing in church. (Hulton|Archive by Getty Images)

MOVING THE SOUL, MIND, AND BODY

Thomas Lodge (1558-1625), an English poet and writer, summed up John Dowland's musical achievements in the following dedication, written in 1621.

Musicke . . . ravisheth the minde much more by melody, than either Bacchus by the taste of Wine, or Venus, by the itching pleasures of Lust. This makes me admire Doctor Dowland, an ornament of Oxford . . . whose Musicall consent (by reason of the aeriall nature thereof) being put in motion, moveth the body, and by purified aire, inciteth the aeriall spirit of the soule, and motion of the body: by affect, it attempteth both the sence and soule together; by signification, it acteth on the minde: to conclude, by the very motion of the subtill [subtle] aire, it pierceth vehemently and by contemplation sucketh swetly; by comfortable qualitie it infuseth a wondrous delight; by the nature thereof both spirituall and materiall, it ravisheth the whole unto it selfe, and maketh a man to be wholly Musiques, and for her cause onely his: Thus much in memory of his excellence.

Source: From *John Dowland, Complete Lute Works.* Excerpted in "John Dowland's Lute Music—The Background," by Jos Smeets. Classical Composers Database. http:/www.classical-composers.org. Accessed September 27, 2004. Orthography modernized by the editors.

Ayres was very popular and was reprinted at least four times by 1613. In *The First Booke of Songs or Ayres*, Dowland established the melancholy tone that characterized his entire corpus. Death and sleep are recurrent themes in the songs, which are strophic rather than influenced by the madrigal, which found its way into *The Second Booke of Songs or Ayres* (1600) and *The Third and Last Booke of Songs or Ayres* (1603). The ayre, which was a popular musical form from approximately 1596 to 1622, according to Daniel Fischlin, was a kind of subgenre of the lyric poem that provided a transition between the Tudor lyric and the later metaphysical lyric.

The principal musical instrument in *Ayres* was the seven-course lute. Solo lute music was included in the *Ayres*, but most of the compositions were designed for the lute and one voice. Others were written for lute, voice, and other instruments, such as the bass or viol. The format of *Ayres* was unusual because it was designed in a table layout. Before 1597, polyphonic music was published in quarto part-books, each of which printed all the parts in the collection for a particular instrument or voice range. *Ayres* was printed in folio, designed to be put on a small table and opened to the music to be played, so that the players who were around the table could all read their music. Peter Holman explained that the cantus and the lute tablature were underlaid on the left-hand page, and

the other three vocal parts were grouped on the three sides of the facing right-hand page.

Dowland, who had degrees in music from both Oxford and Cambridge Universities and who had been trained in Continental Europe, used his extensive experience abroad and even borrowed and adapted the work of lutenist Gregorio Howet and singer-instrumentalist Alessandro Orologio for his *Ayres*. Though his book did not bring him his desired position at Elizabeth I's court, it did win him a post in 1598 with King Christian IV of Denmark and Norway, where he was paid handsomely. During one of his leaves of absence from the Danish court, he published his best-known work, *Lachrimae: Or, Seaven Teares* (1604), a melancholy volume of consort music that featured the dance music for the pavan and the galliard. He also published *The Second Booke of Songs or Ayres* (1600) and *The Third and Last Booke of Songs or Ayres* (1603). His position as the best lutenist of his time was established, and after he returned to England in 1606, he continued to write music and music instructions. Most of his best work, however, was written in the early part of his career. After his court appointment in 1612, his duties took time away from his composition.

SIGNIFICANCE

Testaments to John Dowland's significance as a composer appear in many artistic arenas. In contemporary poetry, Richard Barnfield coupled his name with that of Edmund Spenser, and he was included with English musicians who compared favorably with the Greek musicians of antiquity. Lines from Dowland's ayres are also included in the plays of John Webster, John Fletcher, and Ben Jonson.

Dowland did, however, suffer at the hands of English composer, organist, and music historian Charles Burney, who, in his *General History of Music* (1767-1789), complained that Dowland had not studied composition regularly at an early period of his life, an unfounded charge considering Dowland's university degrees and study in Europe. Unfortunately, Dowland's reputation suffered subsequently, and though his music was hardly forgotten, it was not rediscovered until the 1900's.

Dowland's work resurfaced in the twentieth century, when Desmond Dupré and Julian Bream performed his music in concerts and recordings. Poulton wrote in 1974 that almost all of Dowland's output was available in print, and several performers have made recordings of his songs. Anthony Rooley and the Consort of Musicke have recorded all of *The First Booke of Songs or Ayres* on a L'Oiseau disc, and famed English singer Alfred Deller (1912-1979) recorded Dowland's songs for Harmonia Mundi of France. There are also several allusions to Dowland's works in the science fiction of Philip K. Dick.

Peter Holman made an interesting comparison of Dowland to Sir Edward William Elgar (1857-1934), another British composer, who was born three hundred years after Dowland. Both were initially recognized abroad rather than at home; were denied advancement by the establishment; found it difficult to enjoy their fame and fortune; were melancholic, complex people; and lost their inspiration once they received the recognition they sought.

—*Thomas L. Erskine*

FURTHER READING

Fischlin, Daniel. *In Small Proportions: A Poetics of the English Ayre 1596-1622*. Detroit, Mich.: Wayne State University Press, 1998. Fischlin examines the themes and the metrics of the poetry in the ayres, and he devotes one chapter to Dowland's *The First Booke of Songs or Ayres*. He focuses on the lyrics, written by Fulke Greville (1554-1628) and perhaps Sir Henry

Lee (1533-1611), and discusses probable reasons for their inclusion, noting that Dowland selected lyrics most compatible with his own sensibility.

Holman, Peter. *Dowland: Lachrimae (1604)*. New York: Cambridge University Press, 1999. Though his focus is on Dowland's *Lachrimae*, Holman provides helpful information about music publishing prior to 1597, contemporary musical instruments, and the table-layout format Dowland used in his *Ayres*.

Poulton, Diana. *John Dowland*. Berkeley: University of California Press, 1982. A most thorough scholarly biography of Dowland, Poulton's book covers Dowland's works, his patrons and friends, and his posthumous reputation. Poulton, who has performed Dowland's ayres, includes an index of Dowland's works, an extensive bibliography, and an essay on fretting and tuning the lute.

SEE ALSO: 1567: Palestrina Publishes the *Pope Marcellus Mass*; 1575: Tallis and Byrd Publish *Cantiones Sacrae*; 1590's: Birth of Opera.

RELATED ARTICLES in *Great Lives from History: The Renaissance & Early Modern Era, 1454-1600:* William Byrd; John Dowland; Elizabeth I; Andrea Gabrieli; Giovanni Gabrieli; Orlando di Lasso; Luca Marenzio; Thomas Morley; Giovanni Pierluigi da Palestrina; Thomas Tallis.

1598

ASTRAKHANID DYNASTY IS ESTABLISHED

The Turko-Mongol Astrakhanid Dynasty was formed after infighting over succession engulfed the khanate of the Uzbek Shaybānīd Dynasty. The Astrakhanid Dynasty would endure until the end of the eighteenth century.

LOCALE: Transoxiana (now in Uzbekistan and Turkmenistan)

CATEGORIES: Government and politics; expansion and land acquisition

KEY FIGURES

Bāqī Muḥammad Bahādur (d. 1605), first Uzbek khan of the Astrakhanids, r. 1598-1605

ʿAbd Allāh II ibn Iskandar Shaybānī (1532/1533-1598), Uzbek khan of the Shaybānīds, r. 1557-1598

Pir Muḥammad II Shaybānī (d. 1598), Uzbek khan of the Shaybānīds, r. 1598

ʿAbd al-Maʾmūn ibn ʿAbd Allāh Shaybānī (d. 1598), Uzbek khan of the Shaybānīds, r. 1598

SUMMARY OF EVENT

In the early sixteenth century, Turko-Mongol Uzbeks, led by members of the Shaybānīd house, established themselves in Transoxiana, the region in west Asia that includes what are now Uzbekistan and Turkmenistan. In doing so, the Uzbeks replaced the region's last ruling descendants of the Turkic military leader and conqueror Tamerlane (1336-1405).

During the sixteenth century, the Shaybānīds pursued aggressive policies against their neighbors, especially the Ṣafavid Persians to their south. They developed a high level of commercial activity in the area and fostered a vibrant Islamic culture, especially in urban areas such as Samarqand and Bukhara, which served as dual capitals. Khan ʿAbd Allāh II was responsible for much Uzbek success, uniting leadership of the khanate. Ruling from Bukhara, he transformed the city into a religious and commercial center.

His policies against the Ṣafavids backfired in the early 1590's, however, when a Persian army led by Shah ʿAbbās the Great defeated his forces in a major engagement near Herāt. The Persians regained Khorāsān rapidly, and the Uzbeks lost their leader in 1598.

In 1556, the western Uzbek khanate that was centered on Astrakhan was annexed by the Russian czar Ivan the Terrible as part of his policy of expansion southward and eastward. Like the Shaybānīd Uzbeks, the Astrakhanids were descendants of Mongol conqueror and ruler Genghis Khan (r. 1206-1227). Yār Muḥammad, one of the Uzbek princes scattered by the Russian advances, his son Bāqī Muḥammad Bahādur, and their followers migrated to the territory controlled from Samarqand by Iskandar (r. 1561-1583). Iskander was ʿAbd Allāh II's father and ruled simultaneously from Bukhara. Iskandar cemented the new alliance with the marriage of his daughter—ʿAbd Allāh's sister—to Bāqī (also known as Jani). She gave birth to three sons who, under their father's leadership, assumed important roles in the clan and the khanate in the 1590's. Dynasties are often named for the father of the first ruler, so the Astrakhanid ruling families, the Tuqay-Timurids, are often referred to as Janids.

After ʿAbd Allāh's death, the Uzbek khanate suffered from a dearth of possible successors. ʿAbd Allāh's only legitimate son, ʿAbd al-Maʾmūn ibn ʿAbd Allāh Shaybānī, had been ruling as khan from Balkh. In 1590, ʿAbd Allāh broke with tradition and announced ʿAbd al-Maʾmūn his successor at an Uzbek assembly of the clan sultans (*quriltay*). In 1598, ʿAbd al-Maʾmūn assumed the seat of power in Bukhara quickly. Unfortunately, he began liquidating enemies, family members, and other claimants to his position. After only a few months he was killed, perhaps assassinated by his own shocked followers. This left Jani and his sons in a key position.

One of Jani's sons, Din Muḥammad, had provided important leadership in ʿAbd Allāh's campaigns in Khorāsān and already had a powerful following. Just after ʿAbd Allāh's death he proclaimed a khanate in Khorāsān that would rival the last Shaybānīd khanate. Soon, he lost his life in battle against the Persians near Herāt. ʿAbd al-Maʾmūn's place was taken by Pir Muḥammad II, a Shaybānīd whose ancestors had ruled from Samarqand prior to Iskandar's installation in 1561. At Bukhara, Bāqī challenged and defeated Pir Muḥammad.

In 1599, a *quriltay* decided that leadership of the khanate should go to Bāqī, who in turn installed his son Bāqī in Bukhara and his son Wali Muḥammad in Balkh. They were deemed acceptable leaders by the Uzbeks because they were, from their mother's side of the family, Shaybānīds. The two ruled together until Bāqī's death in 1605, when Wali took control also of Bukhara. Wali died in 1608 and was succeeded by his nephew Sayyid Imām Qulī Bahādur, the son of Din Muḥammad.

SIGNIFICANCE

Life in the Uzbek khanate of Bukhara continued, for the most part, unaltered by the dynastic change. The Toqay-Timurids had lived among the Uzbeks and within their cultural universe for four decades before assuming power. Nonetheless, the clan leaders still regarded the Janids as foreigners, and their cooperation was never a certain thing. ʿAbd Allāh had abolished the appanage system of clan territoriality, and the sultans had long chafed under this blow to their power. Now they could exert it even more directly.

Culturally, the Janids were more like the Timurids than the Shaybānīds, and they continued to develop the regional roles of Bukhara and Balkh as centers of Islamic Sufism and long-distance trade. As with the sultans, the newcomers had to rely on the well-established Naqshbandīyah dervishes for their support, and this clerical party gained even more influence over Bukharan leadership.

Bukhara's fame grew as its Sunni Muslim educational institutions (madrasas) earned it the name Bukhara i-Sharīf (Bukhara the noble). The omnipresent power of Muslim clergy in Bukhara and its urban dependencies would continue into the twentieth century.

In large part because of Din Muḥammad's failed attempt at establishing his own khanate in Khorāsān, the Janids would remain firmly anchored in Central Asia and out of the shadow of the Ṣafavids.

—*Joseph P. Byrne*

FURTHER READING

Allworth, Edward A. *The Modern Uzbeks, from the Fourteenth Century to the Present: A Cultural History.* Stanford, Calif.: Hoover Institute, 1990. Covers the background of the dynastic change and especially its implications for Uzbek foreign policy in the region.

Burton, Audrey. *The Bukharans: A Dynastic, Diplomatic, and Commercial History, 1550-1702.* New York: St. Martin's Press, 1997. This massive study traces the period of Uzbek domination of Bukhara under the later Shaybānīds and the early Janids. Focused on politics and commerce rather than culture or ethics, it is a good complement to broad regional and cultural studies.

Grousset, René. *The Empire of the Steppes: A History of Central Asia.* Translated by Naomi Walford. New Brunswick, N.J.: Rutgers University Press, 1970. Well-organized and comprehensive work that covers the Shaybānīd era and its transition.

Kalter, Johannes, and Margareta Pavaloi. *Uzbekistan: Heir to the Silk Road.* New York: W. W. Norton, 1997. With text in Russian and English, this elaborately illustrated book links the region of the end of the twentieth century to its Uzbek past, with special attention given to sixteenth and seventeenth century arts, crafts, and architecture.

Soucek, Svat. *The History of Inner Asia.* New York: Cambridge University Press, 2000. Chapter 11, "The Shaybānīds," provides a useful overview of the dynasty.

SEE ALSO: c. 1462: Kazak Empire Is Established; 1507: End of the Timurid Dynasty; Dec. 2, 1510: Battle of Merv Establishes the Shaybānīd Dynasty; 1512-1520: Reign of Selim I; Summer, 1556: Ivan the Terrible Annexes Astrakhan; July 21, 1582: Battle of the Tobol River; 1587-1629: Reign of ʿAbbās the Great.

RELATED ARTICLES in *Great Lives from History: The Renaissance & Early Modern Era, 1454-1600:* Ivan the Great; Ivan the Terrible.

January, 1598-February, 1599
OÑATE'S NEW MEXICO EXPEDITION

North American Pueblo Indians rose up against early Spanish efforts to colonize their homeland. In a Spanish expedition flawed from the start, mistranslations and misunderstandings led to the revolt, which ended with the enslavement, torture, and slaughter of countless Puebloans and their pacification for nearly a century.

LOCALE: Acoma Pueblo, southwestern North America (now in New Mexico)

CATEGORIES: Wars, uprisings, and civil unrest; colonization; expansion and land acquisition; exploration and discovery

KEY FIGURES

Juan de Oñate (1550-1630), expedition leader

Luis de Velasco (1534-1617), Spanish official who granted the contract to colonize New Mexico

Alonso Martínez (fl. sixteenth century), father commissary of the expedition's Franciscan contingent

Vicente Zaldívar Mendoza (1565-1625?), nephew of Oñate and his principal lieutenant

Juan de Zaldívar (d. 1599), Vicente's brother, who was killed at Acoma

SUMMARY OF EVENT

Spanish intrusion into New Mexico began in the sixteenth century, after early explorers had reported that there were cities of great wealth there. The legend of these golden Seven Cities of Cíbola grew until Francisco Vásquez de Coronado explored the territory between 1540 and 1542. After two years of fruitless searching, the disillusioned Coronado returned to Mexico, concluding that New Mexico was a barren land that would never yield much wealth and that any attempt to colonize would require constant financial support from the Spanish crown. Thus, New Mexico was protected for a time against any further large-scale Spanish invasion.

Eventually, however, rumors again arose of a fabulous mineral wealth in the territory. Economic opportunism, along with Franciscan desire to establish missions there, prompted Viceroy Luis de Velasco to award a contract for the colonization of New Mexico to Juan de Oñate, a wealthy mine owner from Zacatecas. Oñate's contract, issued on September 21, 1595, gave him the powers of a dictator, with the title of governor and captain general of New Mexico. He would be the highest judicial officer in the territory, with the right to award patronage to those who accompanied him.

Oñate's intentions from the start, however, were counter to the spirit of the Law of 1573. This law had been enacted by King Philip II, who, concerned about some of the early conquistadores's abuse of indigenous populations, intended to set guidelines for future exploration of the New World. The Law of 1573 replaced the idea of conquest with that of pacification, stating that American Indians were to be given the opportunity to become Christians and vassals of the king, with the same rights to property, freedom, and dignity enjoyed by all subjects of the Crown. Oñate, however, had insisted on the right to allot sections of the land and its indigenous residents to himself and his people and to levy tribute upon those whom he did not claim in servitude.

By January, 1598, Oñate had assembled an expedition of more than four hundred people, including settlers, soldiers, and seven Franciscan friars and two lay brothers led by Fray Alonso Martínez, the father commissary. Eighty-three ox carts carried supplies, and a herd of animals provided meat. After crossing the Rio Grande at El Paso del Norte, Oñate took formal possession of New Mexico for the Crown and made his first demand for supplies from the Puebloans, loading eighty pack animals with grain from Teypana pueblo. The expedition then traveled across the Jornada del Muerto (the Journey of Death), ninety miles of waterless desert, which they crossed with no casualties.

At one of the first pueblos he came to, Oñate discovered two Mexican Indians who had lived among the Puebloans for many years, and they became his interpreters. Proceeding up the Rio Grande Valley, Oñate visited the pueblos at Tiguex, San Felipe, and Santo Domingo. Although many Puebloans fled in terror before the invaders, those who remained received Oñate and his men hospitably. On July 7, 1598, Oñate met in council with Pueblo leaders at Santo Domingo pueblo. Declaring that he had come to protect the Puebloans and save their souls, Oñate demanded that they swear allegiance and vassalage to their new rulers, the Spanish king and the Catholic Church. Oñate explained the advantages to be gained if the Puebloans voluntarily submitted to the two majesties, while also informing them that disobedience of the law would result in severe punishment.

At this point, serious misunderstanding undoubtedly occurred on both sides. One of Oñate's soldiers translated his Castilian into a Mexican Indian language understood by the two interpreters, who then translated the message into a Pueblo tongue. It is highly unlikely that this double translation communicated a complete understanding of the complex structure of vassalage to the Puebloans. Nevertheless, the Pueblo leaders, always courteous in council, indicated their acceptance.

On the other hand, Oñate completely misunderstood the system of government in the pueblos. He thought he was dealing with Pueblo chiefs who had authority to speak for all the people, when no such system of chieftainship existed. In all probability, the representatives from each pueblo were either war captains, delegates chosen by a council of elders to attend this one meeting,

or leaders of small factions promoting peaceful coexistence with the Spaniards. In any case, what occurred was the acceptance of something that was little understood by a few people who had no authority to speak for anyone but themselves. Oñate, however, thought that he had achieved an agreement from all the Puebloans to render obedience and vassalage to Crown and Church.

Oñate next turned his attention to establishing permanent quarters for his colony. Requiring the Puebloans to vacate the pueblo of Ohke, he changed its name to San Juan de los Caballeros and moved his people in. When they needed more space, the Spaniards occupied the larger pueblo of Yunque, which they renamed San Gabriel. The Spaniards, having arrived too late in the year to plant crops, demanded food, blankets, skins, and firewood from the Puebloans, as their own supplies dwindled.

That autumn, Oñate traveled north up the Rio Grande Valley, convening councils with Pueblo leaders and administering the oath of vassalage as he went. The Franciscans accompanied him, building churches and establishing missions. Oñate then explored westward, looking for wealth to satisfy the demands of his colonists and to recoup his own fortune. In October, he reached Acoma pueblo, where, after the usual ceremony of swearing allegiance to king and church, the inhabitants were asked to give generously of their food, robes, and blankets. Oñate continued on to the Zuñi and Hopi pueblos. In early December, Juan de Zaldívar and thirty soldiers, following Oñate, arrived at Acoma and demanded provisions, ignoring pleas from the indigenous people that they had nothing left to spare. When the Spaniards insisted, the Puebloans attacked, killing Zaldívar and twelve of his men.

Oñate vowed to avenge this serious blow to Spanish authority. At San Juan, planning the punishment of Acoma, he consulted the Franciscans. They agreed this was a just war under Spanish law, because the Puebloans, having sworn obedience and vassalage to the Spanish crown, were now royal subjects who were guilty of treason. On January 21, 1599, Juan's brother, Vicente Zaldívar Mendoza, and his forces reached Acoma, where they found the Puebloans ready to defend themselves. Fighting with arrows and stones, the Puebloans were no match for the Spanish, who were armed with guns. After two days of bitter fighting, Acoma was defeated, with more than eight hundred dead. The pueblo was destroyed, and some five hundred men, women, and children were captured. Those who did not surrender immediately were dragged from their hiding places and killed.

On February 12, Oñate himself decreed the punishment of the captives: All men more than twenty-five years of age had one foot cut off and served twenty years in slavery, all men between the ages of twelve and twenty-five years and all women over twelve years of age served twenty years in slavery, the old men and women were given to the Querechos (Plains Apaches) as slaves, and the children less than twelve years of age were given to Fray Martínez and to Vicente Zaldívar Mendoza. Two Hopi men who were visiting Acoma when the battle began had their right hands cut off and were sent back to the Hopi as an object lesson to those pueblos.

SIGNIFICANCE

From the beginning, it was obvious that Oñate's own intentions with regard to the colonization of New Mexico conflicted with the spirit of the Law of 1573. Instead of cooperating with the indigenous people and giving them the opportunity to convert to Christianity, as the Law mandated, and to accept the Spanish king as their ruler, he eventually punished them for rebelling against their own abuse.

To discourage future rebellions, the Spaniards carried out the sentences of mutilation in public at several different pueblos. Evidently, this was as effective as Oñate had planned; it would be eighty years before the Puebloans dared to organize another rebellion against Spanish rule.

—*LouAnn Faris Culley*

FURTHER READING

Fergusson, Erna. *New Mexico: A Pageant of Three Peoples*. Albuquerque: University of New Mexico Press, 1973. Relies greatly on a work published in 1610 by Gaspar de Villagrá, a member of Oñate's expedition.

Hendricks, Rick. "Juan de Oñate, Diego de Vargas, and Hispanic Beginnings in New Mexico." In *New Mexican Lives: Profiles and Historical Stories*, edited by Richard W. Etulain. Albuquerque: University of New Mexico Press, 2002. A chapter on Oñate's expedition and its legacy.

John, Elizabeth A. *Storms Brewed in Other Men's Worlds*. College Station: Texas A&M Press, 1975. The most complete and detailed account of the expedition. Explains Oñate's eventual fall from official favor.

Minge, Ward Alan. *Acoma: Pueblo in the Sky*. Albuquerque: University of New Mexico Press, 1976. A less detailed account of the expedition than John's, above, but includes the transcript of Oñate's sentence upon the Acoma survivors.

Sando, Joe S. *The Pueblo Indians*. San Francisco, Calif.: Indian Historian Press, 1976. Summarizes the facts of the expedition and explains the Spanish system of *encomienda*—a way of exacting labor from the Puebloans.

Simmons, Marc. *The Last Conquistador: Juan de Oñate and the Settling of the Far Southwest*. Norman: University of Oklahoma Press, 1991. Biography of Oñate and study of his expedition and interactions with American Indians.

Snow, David H. *New Mexico's First Colonists: The 1597-1600 Enlistments for New Mexico Under Juan de Oñate, Adelante and Gobernador*. Albuquerque: Hispanic Genealogical Research Center of New Mexico, 1998. Provides a list of and commentary upon the members of the Oñate expedition. Includes maps and a portrait.

SEE ALSO: Oct. 12, 1492: Columbus Lands in the Americas; 1493-1521: Ponce de León's Voyages; Apr., 1519-Aug., 1521: Cortés Conquers Aztecs in Mexico; Aug., 1523: Franciscan Missionaries Arrive in Mexico; 1528-1536: Narváez's and Cabeza de Vaca's Expeditions; May 28, 1539-Sept. 10, 1543: De Soto's North American Expedition; Feb. 23, 1540-Oct., 1542: Coronado's Southwest Expedition; 1542-1543: The New Laws of Spain.

RELATED ARTICLES in *Great Lives from History: The Renaissance & Early Modern Era, 1454-1600:* Álvar Núñez Cabeza de Vaca; Francisco Vásquez de Coronado; Pedro Menéndez de Avilés; Philip II; Juan Ponce de León; Hernando de Soto.

1590's

April 13, 1598
EDICT OF NANTES

The Edict of Nantes granted limited religious rights to French Protestants, or Huguenots, finally ending the French Wars of Religion, which had begun in 1562.

LOCALE: Nantes, Brittany, France
CATEGORIES: Laws, acts, and legal history; religion; wars, uprisings, and civil unrest

KEY FIGURES

Henry IV (1553-1610), king of France, r. 1589-1610
Philippe-Émmanuel de Lorraine (1558-1602), duke of Mercoeur, Catholic general, and governor of Brittany, 1582-1602
Philip II (1527-1598), king of Spain, r. 1556-1598
François Ravaillac (1578-1610), French schoolmaster who assassinated Henry IV
Henry III (1551-1589), king of France, r. 1574-1589

SUMMARY OF EVENT

The full significance of the 1598 Edict of Nantes, by which King Henry IV granted freedom of religion to French Protestants, can be understood only if one recalls the nearly four decades of violent civil war between French Catholics and Protestant Huguenots that preceded it. This civil strife began in 1562, when Catherine de Médicis, the queen regent, and the powerful Guise family started persecuting and executing French Protestants. Quite naturally, the Huguenots fiercely resisted Catholic violence. Despite attempts to destroy Huguenot opposition, such as the St. Bartholomew's Day Massacre of August, 1572, in which at least seven thousand Huguenots were killed by royal forces, French kings came to realize that force alone would never unite their kingdom. Henry IV had himself experienced religious persecution during the first evening of the St. Bartholomew's Day Massacre, when he was forced under threat of death to convert from Protestantism to Catholicism. Upon his return to his kingdom of Navarre in southern France, he quickly recanted this forced conversion.

After the assassination of King Henry III, Henry IV, who was then still a Huguenot, was the next in line for the French throne. His assumption of political power was fiercely resisted by a coalition called the Catholic League, and Henry IV's forces had to win several important battles in provincial cities, most notably Ivry (1590), before his successful entrance into Paris in 1594. For political reasons, Henry reconverted to Catholicism in 1593 in an attempt to consolidate his support from both French

Catholics and Protestants. By his coronation in 1594, most of his subjects gave their support to Henry IV because of their belief that he would restore peace to France.

In January, 1595, a new war broke out, begun by King Philip II of Spain, who feared that a unified France would endanger his control over the Netherlands. Virtually all the fighting took place on French soil. Henry IV had the support of almost the entire French nation with the exception of the Catholic Philippe-Émmanuel de Lorraine, duke of Mercoeur, who made Brittany into a pro-Spanish stronghold. Henry appealed to French nationalism by branding as traitors those who had sided with the enemy. This argument proved persuasive with his subjects, who were no longer willing to support the Catholic League. In its initial stages, however, this war went badly for Henry.

In March of 1597, Amiens fell to the Spanish; it was retaken by the French in September. After this decisive victory, the war with the Spanish soon ended. Henry had regained the military advantage in the country, and Philip II's many imperial campaigns had become far too costly, effectively bankrupting his nation. Moreover, by successfully retaking Amiens, Henry IV also consolidated his political power with both Catholic and Protestant subjects. Those who opposed his policies were inevitably viewed as traitors whose loyalty was not to France. The Treaty of Vervins was signed the following year.

In June of 1597, a Huguenot assembly met in Chatellerault and demanded that certain towns be given to it as sureties, as provided for in the truces of the later phases of the religious wars. The assembly sent a delegation to the king to press for a settlement. Henry IV was in an especially strong position. He had effectively destroyed Catholic opposition, because no Catholic leader could oppose the now-Catholic king of France without his patriotism being called into question. Huguenot leaders, moreover, understood the practical reasons for the king's conversion to Catholicism, and they realized that the only alternative to Henry IV would be a member of the Catholic League, which had persecuted the Huguenots cruelly. It was in the self-interest of both Catholic and Huguenot leaders to come up with a solution which would bring a final ending to the French civil war.

The delegates from the Huguenot assembly met with Henry IV in Nantes, where in March, 1598, he had made peace with the duke of Mercoeur. He spent some time in earnest negotiations with the Huguenots, and on April

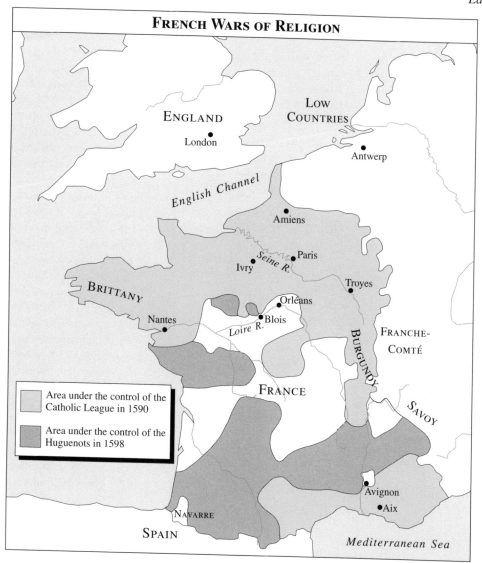

FRENCH WARS OF RELIGION

- Area under the control of the Catholic League in 1590
- Area under the control of the Huguenots in 1598

ENGLAND
London

LOW COUNTRIES
Antwerp

English Channel

Amiens

Paris
Ivry *Seine R.*

Troyes

BRITTANY

Orléans
Nantes Blois
Loire R.

BURGUNDY

FRANCHE-COMTÉ

SAVOY

FRANCE

Avignon
Aix

NAVARRE

SPAIN

Mediterranean Sea

1590's

13, he promulgated the Edict of Nantes, embodying the results of these negotiations. The published documents contained ninety-five articles. There were also fifty-six secret articles, and on April 30, an additional twenty-three secret articles were accepted.

The Edict of Nantes granted Huguenots the right to dwell anywhere in France without harassment and without being required to answer for their beliefs. The higher nobility were permitted to hold Protestant services on any of their domains for the benefit of any Protestants. The lesser nobility were permitted to have services only for themselves, their families, and their servants. Those cities previously designated as cities of Huguenot worship in the 1577 Edict of Poitiers were now permanently

authorized to hold Protestant services, and in addition one town in each district was designated as a place of free worship.

Henry IV's clear intention was to eliminate religious conflicts in France so that the economy could function normally and he could consolidate his own power throughout his kingdom. He granted to Huguenots the same basic rights enjoyed by his Catholic subjects. The universities and charitable institutions were to be open to all French subjects without respect to religion. Protestants were permitted to open schools in all towns where free worship was allowed. They were also to have their own cemeteries. All civil offices were to be open to Protestants. The edict further provided that within each

THE EDICT OF NANTES

The Edict of Nantes is a prime example of early attempts in Europe to provide limited freedom of religion, a profound feat in a Europe dominated by Catholic monarchs and Catholicism and featuring incessant wars between Catholics and Protestants. The edict, excerpted here, put an end to the thirty-six-year French Wars of Religion.

[W]e have permitted, and herewith permit, those of the said religion called Reformed [Protestant] to live and abide in all the cities and places of this our kingdom and countries of our sway, without being annoyed, molested, or compelled to do anything in the matter of religion contrary to their consciences. . . .

We very expressly forbid to all those of the said religion its exercise, either in respect to ministry, regulation, discipline, or the public instruction of children, or otherwise, in this kingdom and the lands of our dominion, otherwise than in the places permitted and granted by the present edict.

It is forbidden as well to perform any function of the said religion in our court or retinue. . . .

We also forbid all our subjects, of whatever quality and condition, from carrying off by force or persuasion, against the will of their parents, the children of the said religion, in order to cause them to be baptized or confirmed in the Catholic Apostolic and Roman Church; and the same is forbidden to those of the said religion called Reformed, upon penalty of being punished with special severity. . . .

We ordain that there shall be no difference or distinction made in respect to the said religion, in receiving subjects to be instructed in the universities, colleges, and schools; and in receiving the sick and poor into hospitals, retreats, and public charities.

Source: From *The Great Documents of Western Civilization*, edited by Milton Viorst (New York: Bantam Books, Matrix Editions, 1967), pp. 105, 106.

macy and threats, Henry IV imposed his will throughout France. The edict reduced but certainly did not eliminate religious hatred and intolerance in France. It allowed the kingdom to begin to heal after four decades of violent civil wars. In addition to his sympathy for the plight of Protestants, Henry believed that if Huguenots enjoyed the same rights as other French subjects, they would cooperate with his government to restore political unity and economic growth in France.

A great tragedy in French history was the assassination of King Henry IV by a Catholic schoolmaster named François Ravaillac on May 14, 1610. It has been generally assumed that Ravaillac hated Protestants and killed Henry IV because of his opposition to the king's policy of religious tolerance. Henry IV understood that his Edict of Nantes was a workable solution to the religious problems of France. It is unfortunate that he was succeeded by two kings, Louis XIII (r. 1610-1643) and Louis XIV (r. 1643-1715), who had little concern for the destructive impact of religious intolerance on national unity and economic growth. In 1629, Louis XIII authorized the brutal siege of La Rochelle, a Protestant stronghold, and Louis XIV revoked the Edict of Nantes in 1685. Both actions had disastrous effects on the French economy.

—*James F. Hitchcock, revised by Edmund J. Campion*

parlement (a regional court whose responsibility was to register and interpret royal edicts), a chamber was to be set up, including a substantial minority of Protestant judges who alone could deal with violations of this edict. By secret agreement, the king promised to continue his financial support of the Huguenot clergy. He also permitted the Huguenots to retain for eight years all the towns that they still retained from the civil wars. This concession was renewed as late as 1615.

SIGNIFICANCE

Despite opposition from Catholic bishops and certain members of regional *parlements*, Henry IV succeeded in implementing the Edict of Nantes in conformity with his policies. He pointed out to Catholic bishops and judges that he was now a Catholic, and he further added that any opposition to his Edict of Nantes would be viewed as treason. By means of an effective combination of diplo-

FURTHER READING

Buisseret, David. *Henry IV.* London: Allen & Unwin, 1984. A well-documented biography of Henry IV that describes both his military successes and his political effectiveness.

Finley-Croswhite, S. Annette. *Henry IV and the Towns: The Pursuit of Legitimacy in French Urban Society, 1589-1610.* New York: Cambridge University Press, 1999. Study of Henry's labors to win support from his subjects, focusing on his courtship of the urban population and the consolidation of his claims to legitimate sovereignty. Includes illustrations, maps, bibliographic references, and index.

Garrisson, Janine. *A History of Sixteenth-Century France, 1483-1598.* Translated by Richard Rex. London: Macmillan, 1995. A very reliable history of sixteenth century France which explains the significance of the Edict of Nantes in relation to the French civil wars.

Greengrass, Mark. *France in the Age of Henri IV.* 2d ed. London: Longman, 1995. Contains an excellent study of political, economic, and administrative changes during the reign of Henry IV.

Holt, Mack P. *The French Wars of Religion, 1562-1629.* New York: Cambridge University Press, 1995. A comprehensive examination of the religious wars, designed for undergraduates and general readers. The work includes a chronological table of events and a section of brief biographies of key figures.

Horowitz, Maryanne Cline. "French Free-Thinkers in the First Decades of the Edict of Nantes." In *Early Modern Skepticism and the Origins of Toleration,* edited by Alan Levine. Lanham, Md.: Lexington Books, 1999. Analyzes the intellectual reception of the edict and its consequences for a culture of religious toleration in France.

Love, Ronald S. *Blood and Religion: The Conscience of Henri IV, 1553-1593.* Ithaca, N.Y.: McGill-Queen's University Press, 2001. An assessment of Henry's reign against the background of civil war and religious strife. Concludes with a discussion of Henry's perception of the conflicting requirements of his crown and his soul, and his 1593 conversion to Catholicism. Includes photographic plates, illustrations, bibliographic references, and index.

Major, J. Russell. *From Renaissance Monarchy to Absolute Monarchy: French Kings, Nobles, and Estates.* Baltimore: Johns Hopkins University Press, 1994. The long chapter on Henry IV (pages 130-180) examines his extraordinary administrative skill in dealing with social and economic problems.

Mentzer, Raymond A., Jr. *Blood and Belief: Family Survival and Confessional Identity Among Provincial Huguenot Nobility.* West Lafayette, Ind.: Purdue University Press, 1994. Thoroughly examines reactions by provincial Huguenots to the policy of tolerance implemented by Henry IV.

Sutherland, N. M. *Henry IV of France and the Politics of Religion, 1572-1596.* 2 vols. Bristol, Avon, England: Elm Bank, 2002. Extremely detailed account of the role of religion in France's monarchy and political sphere during the late sixteenth century. Each chapter discusses a specific political event or issue from the point of view of the conflict between Protestants and Catholics. Includes illustrations, map, bibliographic references, and index.

Whelan, Ruth, and Carol Baxter, eds. *Toleration and Religious Identity: The Edict of Nantes and Its Implications in France, Britain, and Ireland.* Portland, Oreg.: Four Courts, 2003. Anthology of essays tracing the history leading up to the Edict of Nantes and examining its consequences in Britain and on the Continent. Includes illustrations, bibliographic references, and index.

SEE ALSO: Oct. 31, 1517: Luther Posts His Ninety-five Theses; Mid-16th cent.: Development of the Caracole Maneuver; Mar., 1562-May 2, 1598: French Wars of Religion; Aug. 24-25, 1572: St. Bartholomew's Day Massacre; July 7, 1585-Dec. 23, 1588: War of the Three Henrys; Aug. 2, 1589: Henry IV Ascends the Throne of France; May 2, 1598: Treaty of Vervins.

RELATED ARTICLES in *Great Lives from History: The Renaissance & Early Modern Era, 1454-1600:* Catherine de Médicis; Henry III; Henry IV; Philip II.

May 2, 1598
TREATY OF VERVINS

The Treaty of Vervins ended the war between France and Spain and reinforced the 1559 Treaty of Cateau-Cambrésis. It is considered a victory more for France than for Spain.

LOCALE: Vervins, France
CATEGORIES: Diplomacy and international relations; wars, uprisings, and civil unrest

KEY FIGURES

Henry IV (1553-1610), king of France, r. 1589-1610

Albert VII (1559-1621), cardinal and archduke of Austria, cardinal and archbishop of Toledo, 1577-1599, viceroy of Portugal, 1585-1595, governor of Spanish Netherlands, 1595-1621, and Spanish negotiator at Vervins

Pomponne de Bellièvre (1529-1607), Henry IV's chancellor, 1599-1607, and French negotiator at Vervins

Alessandro de' Medici (1535-1605), archbishop of Florence, 1574-1605, cardinal of Florence, 1583-1605, papal legate, and negotiator at Vervins, later Pope Leo XI, 1605

Philippe-Émmanuel de Lorraine (1558-1602), duke of Mercoeur, Catholic League general, governor of Brittany, 1582-1602

Charles Emmanuel I (1562-1630), duke of Savoy, r. 1580-1630, an ally of Philip II

Clement VIII (1536-1605), Roman Catholic pope, 1592-1605

Philip II (1527-1598), king of Spain, r. 1556-1598

Elizabeth I (1533-1603), queen of England, r. 1558-1603

Robert Cecil (1563-1612), English secretary of state, 1596-1608

SUMMARY OF EVENT

Between 1562 and 1598, Catholics and Protestants in France fought eight religious civil wars. The last phase of these wars was known as the War of the Catholic League. The Catholic League was an extremely zealous religious-political organization given military and financial aid by the devoutly Catholic king of Spain, Philip II.

In 1589, Henry of Navarre became King Henry IV of France. The Catholic League refused to recognize him, because he was a Protestant, so Henry fought the League to defend his crown. Philip II wanted his daughter, the Infanta Isabella, made queen of France, but Catholic

League moderates were suspicious of Spain and denounced the plan. The Infanta issue weakened the League and strengthened Henry's legitimacy as the true king of France.

In 1593, Henry converted to Catholicism, undermining the ideological foundations of the Catholic League. By the end of 1594, he had destroyed most Catholic League resistance in France and rallied many former enemies to his side. Spanish forces remained in parts of southern France, however, and controlled the province of Brittany. This prompted Henry to declare war on Spain on January 17, 1595. Henry incited anti-Spanish sentiment by portraying Philip as an unscrupulous would-be usurper of the French throne.

The war with Spain was focused on France's northeastern frontier, where Philip enjoyed solid support. The province of Picardy had been a major Catholic League stronghold in the early 1590's. Although Picardy capitulated in 1594, pro-Spanish interests remained strong in the province. Philip II also maintained an army of sixty thousand in nearby Flanders.

Spanish influence in northern France caused England's Elizabeth I to offer Henry IV aid. Sealing an alliance between England and France in May of 1596, Elizabeth extended Henry a loan and sent two thousand English soldiers to France to fight Spain. The Dutch United Provinces joined the English-French alliance shortly thereafter, but the alliance did not immediately halt Spanish advances. Spain held the French towns of Doullens and Calais and enjoyed a major success on March 11, 1597, when Spanish troops disguised as peasants took the capital city of Picardy, Amiens.

Henry was dancing when he heard the news of the fall of Amiens. He supposedly uttered the statement, "That's enough of being king of France, it's time to be king of Navarre." Henry mustered his forces and soon raised an army of twenty-three thousand, even though the *parlement* of Paris hesitated in backing him with necessary finances and many Protestants refused to send troops to help him retake Amiens. Losing Amiens was devastating to Henry because he had been using the city as a munitions depot. When the Spanish captured the city, they also secured a fortune in powder, guns, and cannon. After a bitter six-month siege, Henry recaptured Picardy's capital city on September 25, 1597.

Henry's success in Picardy gave him the resolve to end the Catholic League war in Brittany, the last League stronghold. Although Philippe-Émmanuel de Lorraine, duke of Mercoeur, enjoyed a splendid court in the provincial capital at Nantes, his strong ties with the Spanish alienated many of his supporters, who were prepared to accept Henry as king by 1598. Henry marched a large army into Brittany in February of 1598, and the war with the Catholic League came to an end. Mercoeur gave up his ambition to create an independent state in Brittany and capitulated in March of 1598.

Once Amiens was regained, Henry began making peace overtures toward Spain. The papacy supported his effort. Pope Clement VIII hoped to end the hostility between the Catholic countries of France and Spain. He felt the dispute diminished Catholic power in Europe and benefited Protestant influence. Clement had already made peace with Henry and granted him papal absolution in September of 1595. Philip, for his part, was severely overextended both financially and militarily. He needed to settle matters in France. In 1596, after years of war with the northern Protestant provinces in the Netherlands, he had declared the Spanish crown bankrupt and had begun reducing Spain's international financial commitments.

By 1598, Philip II was "withered and feeble," and many of his own advisers perceived the war with France as too costly to continue. Philip's cousin and brother-in-law (and soon to be son-in-law), Archduke Albert VII of Austria, strongly advocated peace with France. Thus, peace talks began, and Rome acted as mediator through the papal legate, Alessandro de' Medici. England's secretary of state, Robert Cecil, tried to sabotage the peace settlement, but Pomponne de Bellièvre, representing France, and Archduke Albert, representing Spain, hammered out an accord. The agreement was signed at Vervins, near the border of the Spanish Netherlands, on May 2, 1598.

The provisions of the Treaty of Vervins reinforced the Treaty of Cateau-Cambrésis of 1559, so that all towns captured during the war were returned. France lost Cambrai to Spain but regained Ardres, Blavet, Calais, Doullens, Metz, Toul, Verdun, and several other urban centers. France also agreed to papal arbitration over French claims to the principality of Saluzzo, seized by the Spanish ally Charles Emmanuel I, duke of Savoy in 1588. Henry IV swore to observe the Treaty of Vervins at a ceremony held in Paris on June 21, 1598. Two days later, at the Hôtel de Ville, symbols of war were burned in a magnificent ceremony meant to herald the advent of peace. On July 12, 1598, Albert VII participated in a similar ceremony in Brussels.

Clement tried to make headway with Spain over Saluzzo but to no avail. In 1599, Henry suggested ceding the duchy of Bresse to France in place of Saluzzo. The duke of Savoy proved recalcitrant, and France went to war with Savoy in 1600. The Peace of Lyons, signed on January 17, 1601, relinquished French claims to Saluzzo. Henry accepted the territories of Bresse, Bugey, and Gex instead. While the Treaty of Vervins was considered a French victory, the subsequent Peace of Lyons proved a disappointment, since Saluzzo was more highly valued than Bresse, Bugey, and Gex, and its forfeiture weakened France's diplomatic power in Italy. Saluzzo dominated a key pass between France and Italy, and without it, French military support of key northern Italian allies became more difficult to deliver.

SIGNIFICANCE

After Vervins, Philip II decided to loosen his commitments in the southern Catholic Netherlands while continuing his war against the northern Protestant United Provinces. He married his daughter, Isabella, to Archduke Albert and ceded the ten southern provinces to them on May 6, 1598. Philip did not renounce Spain's hereditary rights to the territory, however, and the southern provinces did not become independent. The southern provinces accepted this arrangement, while the Dutch United Provinces in the north continued their resistance to Spanish domination.

The Treaty of Vervins brought financial relief to both France and Spain. Philip returned his army to the Netherlands, preventing more useless expenditures in France. Henry began concentrating on internal reform after years of warfare. The treaty solved little, however, since France violated its terms almost immediately and offered help to the United Provinces. Spain was soon bankrupt again and could not maintain its position as the maker of European diplomacy. Philip had involved Spain in too many ruinous wars and died disillusioned on September 13, 1598. The Treaty of Vervins was only one of many accords involving the Habsburgs that revealed the eclipse of Spain's imperial power. If the sixteenth century belonged to the Spanish, the seventeenth century would belong to the French.

—*Stephanie Annette Finley-Croswhite*

FURTHER READING

Carter, Charles Howard. *The Secret Diplomacy of the Habsburgs, 1598-1625.* New York: Columbia University Press, 1964. Exploring early modern diplomacy, the author examines the Treaty of Vervins as one of several peace settlements negotiated by the European powers with the Habsburgs.

Darby, Graham, ed. *The Origins and Development of the Dutch Revolt*. New York: Routledge, 2001. Anthology of scholarship on the causes and consequences of Dutch rebellion against Spanish rule. Includes illustrations, maps, bibliographic references, and index.

Elliott, J. H. *Europe Divided, 1559-1598*. 2d ed. Malden, Mass.: Blackwell, 2000. Study of the political divisions, intrigues, and strife of the second half of the sixteenth century. Includes genealogical tables, maps, bibliographic references, and index.

Greengrass, Mark. *France in the Age of Henri IV: The Struggle for Stability*. London: Longman, 1984. Chapter 8 contains a concise discussion of the complications of the Treaty of Vervins with regard to the principality of Saluzzo.

Jensen, De Lamar. *Diplomacy and Dogmatism: Bernardino de Mendoza and the French Catholic League*. Cambridge, Mass.: Harvard University Press, 1964. One of the first books available in English in which Spanish policy in France during the French religious wars is examined in depth.

Kamen, Henry. *Golden Age Spain*. Atlantic Highlands, N.J.: Humanities Press, 1988. A survey of Spanish history from 1470 to 1714. The short book contains a good bibliography with emphasis given to works published in English.

_____. "The Habsburg Lands: Iberia." In *Handbook of European History, 1400-1600: Late Middle Ages, Renaissance, and Reformation*, edited by Thomas Brady, Jr., Heiko Oberman, and James Tracy. Boston: E. J. Brill, 1994. Reviews major themes in Spanish history and historiography. Excellent bibliography.

Lynch, John. *Spain, 1516-1598: From Nation State to World Empire*. Cambridge, Mass.: Basil Blackwell, 1991. A new edition of Lynch's 1964 work, *Spain Under the Habsburgs*, revised with new research. Discussion of the Treaty of Vervins is found in chapter 10.

Parker, Geoffrey. *The Grand Strategy of Philip II*. New Haven, Conn.: Yale University Press, 1998. Contests the traditional view of Philip as conducting his empire by reacting to events as they occurred without any grand plan to guide him. Uses correspondence and other historical documents to delineate a "strategic culture" informing Philip's decisions and his reign. Includes illustrations, maps, bibliographic references, and index.

_____. *Philip II*. 4th ed. Chicago: Open Court, 2002. A good overview of Philip's reign, this edition is updated with a new bibliographic essay. Also includes map, portraits, genealogical table, bibliography, and index.

Wernham, R. B. *The Return of the Armadas: The Last Years of the Elizabethan War Against Spain, 1595-1603*. New York: Oxford University Press, 1994. This study of the later Anglo-Spanish Wars discusses the Peace of Vervins and its consequences for the English. Includes illustrations, bibliographic references, and index.

SEE ALSO: July 16, 1465-Apr., 1559: French-Burgundian and French-Austrian Wars; Aug. 17, 1477: Foundation of the Habsburg Dynasty; 1482-1492: Maximilian I Takes Control of the Low Countries; September 22, 1504: Treaty of Blois; June 28, 1519: Charles V Is Elected Holy Roman Emperor; 1544-1628: Anglo-French Wars; Apr. 3, 1559: Treaty of Cateau-Cambrésis; Mar., 1562-May 2, 1598: French Wars of Religion; July 26, 1581: The United Provinces Declare Independence from Spain; July 7, 1585-Dec. 23, 1588: War of the Three Henrys; Apr., 1587-c. 1600: Anglo-Spanish War; Aug. 2, 1589: Henry IV Ascends the Throne of France.

RELATED ARTICLES in *Great Lives from History: The Renaissance & Early Modern Era, 1454-1600:* Elizabeth I; Henry IV; Philip II; First Earl of Salisbury.

December, 1598-May, 1599
THE GLOBE THEATRE IS BUILT

The building of the Globe Theatre marks the flowering of the Elizabethan amphitheater, a design first established and perfected in 1576 by a London-area playhouse, The Theatre. The Globe gave William Shakespeare an apt and secure home for his mature work, launching an extraordinary period in English literature.

LOCALE: Bankside, London, England

CATEGORIES: Theater; architecture; cultural and intellectual history

KEY FIGURES

James Burbage (c. 1530-1597), builder of The Theatre
Cuthbert Burbage (c. 1566-1636), company manager
Richard Burbage (c. 1567-1619), principal actor
William Shakespeare (1564-1616), playwright

SUMMARY OF EVENT

In 1599, London was at the center of a long period of expansion. Its population had doubled in the previous fifty years and had continued to grow. By 1650, London would be the largest city in the world. This confident, prosperous capital was hungry for news and entertainment. Every day, several thousand people crossed the Thames to the liberty of Bankside. Located just outside the city limits, Bankside was free to host the more scandalous forms of entertainment. The area was packed with brothels, animal-baiting pits, and theaters. Audiences from all social classes crowded through the noise and dirt to hear the latest plays. With the arrival of the Globe Theatre, Bankside offered Londoners the best drama in the world, drama that served also as a kind of theater for reportage, in which the plays presented and discussed news of the day. With a fresh play opening on Bankside almost daily, there was always something that spoke to the moment.

In 1594, James Burbage brought the Lord Chamberlain's Men, an acting company that included William Shakespeare, to The Theatre, which was built in 1576. The company's landlord, Giles Allen, refused to extend their lease beyond April of 1597. Meanwhile, Philip Henslowe's Rose Theatre (established in 1587) and Francis Langley's Swan Theatre (established in 1595) brought London's theater district to Bankside. In 1596, Burbage purchased a hall in Blackfriars, planning a more exclusive theater, but local residents refused permission. James died in February, 1597, and for two years follow-

ing, his sons, Cuthbert and Richard Burbage, negotiated with Allen for a new lease. They rented other theaters to survive and were in need of a solution to the lease problem.

In December of 1598, after Allen's final refusal, the Burbages took decisive action. First, the brothers agreed on an unprecedented step: Five members of the company could become part owners of their new theater. John Heminge, William Kemp, Augustine Phillips, Thomas Pope, and William Shakespeare would each buy a 10 percent share. Sure of their finances, the Burbages secured a plot in Bankside from Sir Nicholas Brend at a good price. The lease would be signed February 21, 1599, with the partnership agreement, but the company took possession on Christmas Day, 1598.

Three days after Christmas came the second, and most striking, part of the plan. Hiring the master carpenter Peter Street, and with the aid of about ten others, the Burbages trespassed onto Giles Allen's Shoreditch estate, broke out the main timbers of The Theatre, and transported them across the Thames River to their new site. Here, Street reassembled the precisely cut, interlocking beams of The Theatre to form a playhouse skeleton. It would have been several months into the New Year, 1599, before the Globe was finally furnished and completed around this framework. On May 16, the structure was referred to as *de novo edificata*, literally "newly built."

The name chosen for the rebuilt playhouse showed a company intent on offering astonishment and wonder. The term *globe* was relatively new in 1599, in currency since about 1550 and given force with Sir Francis Drake's circumnavigation of the globe between 1577 and 1580. The term reflected the outward-looking ambition of the age, and it promised, in the form of a new theater, to bring the entire, expanded world of the late Renaissance before an audience. The motto for the theater's flag was *totus mundus agit histrionem*, or "everybody acts." The theater wanted to reflect human life in its entirety, both in content and in form, and the Globe was no exception; it reflected a true microcosm of the world. William Shakespeare would make good on both claims, exploring the full intensity of human experience and conjuring up exotic locations from Venice to Troy.

The exact floor plan of the Globe is not known, but it resembled its rivals structurally. A lime-plastered wall, perhaps 80 to 100 feet in width, with three levels of gal-

The Globe Theatre in a detail from Claes Jansz Visscher's panoramic view of London, Londinum Florentisima Britanniae Urbs *(c. 1625). (The Folger Shakespeare Library)*

a roof of thatch. The years since James Burbage built The Theatre in 1576 had brought refinements, yet the Globe was still built around the same basic plan. Recent gimmicks, including a mechanical throne for the descent of gods, were eschewed. The design relied on the skill of poet and player to bring the theater's empty space alive, and the poet and player would prove astonishingly apt to the task.

Although Shakespeare's genius was independent of the Globe, the space did give him remarkable freedom to study and reflect, and it did provide stability. Here, he reached further than anyone before or since. The reverberation of his words against the wood and plaster transformed the Globe into a great symbol of the universe and humanity's condition within it. On September 21, 1599, at about two in the afternoon, Thomas Platter recorded that he and his friends went across the Thames to this house with the thatched roof. They saw *Julius Caesar* aptly performed. The next year it would be *Hamlet*, and humankind would have a new self-image. From 1599 until 1613, the Globe would hear all of Shakespeare's finest plays, including *Macbeth* and *King Lear*.

leries, encircled a yard open to the sky. Into the yard projected a platform stage both deep and broad. Two doors opened onto the stage from the actors' tiring house, set into the gallery wall; a shallow discovery space was available between them. An upper stage ran over the doors for scenes held "above"—as on the battlements of a castle, for example. A "hell" trapdoor in the main stage allowed for entrances from the depths, or supplied a grave for Ophelia. A painted roof, or "heavens," spangled with stars and signs of the zodiac, was supported on two mighty columns that rose from the stage, and it protected valuable costumes from the rain. A penny bought only standing room in the exposed yard. More well-to-do customers paid to sit in the galleries. Lords could buy special rooms nearest the stage, or they could occupy the upper stage if it was not in use.

The Globe was Bankside's new theater. Richly painted and more splendid than either the Rose or the Swan, it was nonetheless a spare theatrical machine, with

SIGNIFICANCE

The Globe was not the first theater of its kind. Rather, it marks a tradition at maturity: the frame of the first Elizabethan amphitheater refitted in line with twenty years of experience. The unique financial arrangement—players sharing ownership of the theater—gave the company creative control, brought much-needed stability, and focused the talent. Though built on the cheap and in a hurry, the Globe was made to order for the Lord Chamberlain's Men, later to become the King's Men, and was delivered into their hands.

The Globe's layout had no legacy until attempts at reconstruction began in the 1790's. Puritans closed the theaters in 1642, marking the effective end of the particular design and leaving its details in mystery, but for its life span the Globe proved vital. It could accommodate all social levels and up to three thousand people. It became London's political forum, the place where controversial views could be argued in play. Under the afternoon sun, citizens shared common pleasures and anxieties and emerged perhaps a little more human. Although not their first choice of venue, the company nonetheless was won over by the theater's success. The amphitheater's human scale bred a new kind of drama. When the Globe burned to the ground in 1613, a victim of its cheap thatch, it was rebuilt more magnificently than before, and with a tiled roof.

—*Marc Sidwell*

FURTHER READING

Gurr, Andrew. *Playgoing in Shakespeare's London.* 2d ed. New York: Cambridge University Press, 1996. Comprehensive survey of the Globe's and other theaters' audiences of the period. Appendix lists references to playgoing from the period.

_____. *The Shakespearean Stage, 1574-1642.* 3d ed. New York: Cambridge University Press, 1992. Excellent overview of the theater, placing it in context.

Kermode, Frank. *Shakespeare's Language.* London: Penguin, 2001. Primarily a study of Shakespeare's plays, but Kermode stresses Shakespeare's move to the Globe as a watershed in his writing.

Mulryne, J. R., and M. Shewring, eds. *Shakespeare's Globe Rebuilt.* Cambridge, England: Mulryne & Shewring, 1997. Collection of essays on London's reconstruction of the Globe. Thorough discussions of likely decorative schemes and construction techniques used for the original.

Thomson, Peter. *Shakespeare's Theatre.* 2d ed. London: Routledge, 1992. Speculative in places but full of suggestive details. Also provides a broad picture of the Globe and its players. A good starting point.

SEE ALSO: 1576: James Burbage Builds The Theatre; c. 1589-1613: Shakespeare Writes His Dramas.

RELATED ARTICLES in *Great Lives from History: The Renaissance & Early Modern Era, 1454-1600:* Christopher Marlowe; William Shakespeare.

1599
CASTRATI SING IN THE SISTINE CHAPEL CHOIR

Papal registers identified two castrati, or eunuchs, as new singers in the choir of the Sistine Chapel, marking what many consider the first documented, official acknowledgment of castrati in Church choirs.

LOCALE: Italy
CATEGORIES: Music; cultural and intellectual history; religion; health and medicine

KEY FIGURES

Clement VIII (Ippolito Aldobrandini; 1536-1605), Roman Catholic pope, 1592-1605, who sanctioned the first castrati into the Sistine Chapel choir

Sixtus V (1521-1590), Roman Catholic pope, 1585-1590, who issued a bull that outlined the character and duties of the choir of St. Peter's Basilica

SUMMARY OF EVENT

The identification of femininity with sexuality and carnal temptation prompted early Christian thinkers to exclude women from formal worship and ceremonies, leaving Christian liturgy a mostly male province for centuries. With the expansion of polyphonic music and its need for a broad vocal range, certain boys were castrated so that their prepubescent, feminine voices could be preserved and even enhanced. The papal court in Rome became the pioneering force in this direction, though castrato singing soon was extended into the sensational new idiom of opera.

The historical record is unclear as to when castrati were first acknowledged as Church choristers. Though documented as a falsettist (or countertenor), Padre Soto, who began singing at the Vatican in the early 1560's, was a castrato, and, likewise, castrato Giacomo Spagnoletto was hired for the Sistine Choir in 1588. According to composer and music historian Anthony Milner, Pope Sixtus V issued a bull in 1589 that reorganized the choir at St. Peter's Basilica, considered Christianity's primary cathedral. In the bull, Sixtus set forth the makeup of the choir, including four eunuchs. The bull has never been challenged.

In 1599, however, papal registers (the Sistine Diary) explicitly identify two new singers, Pietro Paolo Folignato and Girolamo Rossini, as castrati. Pope Clement VIII found their voices preferable, because of their "natural" sweetness, to the shrill straining of the falsettists. With papal recognition, castrato singers quickly took over soprano parts in choirs, restricting falsettists to contralto functions only; within a century even the contralto parts were given to castrati.

The discovery of the musical range of castrated boys was apparently a by-product of the age-old creation of eunuchs for employment in certain court traditions. Such was true of the Chinese imperial court and of courts in ancient Mesopotamia, culminating in Persia. This created troupes of court functionaries used in palace harems, representing no sexual threat to the sovereign. From Persia, such practices worked their way into the Roman world by the late third century and continued for a millennium in the Byzantine court. The Romans and Byzantines were concerned less with the sexual implications for palace life and more with the nourishing of a cadre of officials whose loyalty would not be compromised by family and hereditary self-interests.

Early Christian society by no means felt abhorrence for eunuchs, who were able to rise to important ranks not only in government but also in the Church and in the military. Indeed, some Christian theologians believed the wound of castration to be a symbolic counterpart to the pious suffering of martyrs and the Savior. Deliberate castration as an act of religious fervor was common to some early religious cults and even found some endorsement by the early Christian Church. The early Church father Origen (c. 185-c. 254) and, later, Saint Benedict (c. 480-c. 547), pioneer of Western monasticism, are said to have made themselves eunuchs because of such fervor.

Musical effects of castration depended both on the degree of the operation and on its timing. It involved not the total excision of the male genitalia, as in some court practices, but the removal of the testicles (scrotum with testes) only. The operation had to be performed before the onset of puberty, when the juvenile voice would normally "break" to the lower male ranges. (The "ideal" age later became those boys eight to ten years old.) Assuming the boy already had a pleasing voice, the operation would prevent the descent and expansion of the larynx that is normal in male development, preserving for it instead the range of a soprano (or high alto) that would flourish in some female voices naturally. By hindering the development of testosterone, castration resulted in hormonal processes causing bodily development partly along female lines, but with some exaggerations. Castratos often became unusually tall and burly; above all, enlargement of the thorax gave them expanded lung capacity. Thus, a boy who started with a good voice grew into a singer who combined female tonal range with exceptional masculine strength of projection. Such singers produced sounds of unearthly beauty and compelling power.

It is not clear exactly when the consequences of castration were understood, but they certainly were known by Roman times, and they fitted the misogynist mentality of early Christian thought. The exclusion of women from Christian liturgical worship was founded in part on the oft-quoted dictum of Saint Paul, *mulier taceat in ecclesia*. The full wording and context of his dictum show that it extended Hebrew attitudes about the subjection of wives to husbands, even in religious matters.

> Let your women keep silence in the churches: for it is not permitted unto them to speak; but they are commanded to be under obedience, as also saith the law. And if they will learn any thing, let them ask their husbands at home: for it is a shame for women to speak in the church.

The prohibition was really against speaking (indeed, against asking questions) rather than against singing. Still, the dictum justified the male monopoly in Church affairs.

The role of eunuchs in Church singing seems to have been limited and perhaps sporadic in the west, but it flourished in the East Roman and Byzantine traditions of Constantinople (now Istanbul, Turkey). A liturgical chorister who was also a eunuch was first identified around the late fourth and early fifth centuries. How extensively or consistently eunuchs were used in Byzantine worship remains unsettled, though it is becoming clear that through the centuries eunuchs had a larger place than previously thought. There is clear evidence of their importance by the twelfth century. Ecclesiastical scholar Theodore Balsamon (who, it is said, was also a eunuch) wrote of the extensive use of eunuchs. It is also known that a Byzantine eunuch named Manuel had traveled to distant Smolensk (now in western Russia) in 1137 and had sung there, and Odo of Deuil, while stopping at Constantinople in 1147 during the Second Crusade, admired the singing eunuchs (along with their hand-clapping and graceful movements) mingling with "manly" male choristers.

The Byzantine use of castrati had little influence in Western Europe, where the employment of eunuchs in court functions likewise found little currency. The normal ranges of the male voice sufficed for singing Latin plainchant in formal worship (nuns, too, sang the plainchant, but while isolated in their convents). When a wider range was needed, especially for special feast celebrations, the voices of children, especially boys, could be used. In addition, "normal" masculine ranges were extended by the cultivation of falsetto singing by adult males.

The steady evolution of polyphonic music, from the eleventh century onward, encouraged greater experimentation with vocal ranges. By the fifteenth century, these experiments had led to the development of elaborate and complex writing in four or more parts, often straining falsetto capacities in the upper ranges. Still, the male falsettist remained a necessary part of any liturgical choir or ensemble into the final golden age of sixteenth century polyphony. Carefully trained boys would take the highest part or parts in larger church choirs regularly, though they lacked the stability of adult singers.

A sixteenth century school of outstanding falsetto singing developed in Spain, and a number of Spanish falsettists found employment in the papal choir of the Vatican's Sistine Chapel. The phenomenal range and strength of these Spanish singers raised suspicions that their talents might have been enhanced surgically. Castration as a medical strategy was unusual but not unknown in European medicine, and either by accident or design it may have been discovered to enhance the potentials of talented choirboys. The great composer Orlando di Lasso had six acknowledged castrati, of Spanish origins, in his Munich chapel during the mid-sixteenth century. By the end of the century, the famous Spanish singers in Rome were identified as falsettists to cloak anatomical changes.

SIGNIFICANCE

Having triumphed in church singing, the castrati almost immediately found new and better employment, and they turned the castration of choirboys for art and profit into a widespread practice. In the early years of the sixteenth century, the bold new idiom of opera was coming into being, and brilliant singing was at a new premium. Again, the papal court set a precedent by forbidding the participation of female singers in dramatic presentations, opening the field to castrati. Beyond that, however, the combination of commanding physical presence with vocal power made the castrato the preferred singer in not just male roles but also roles as heroic male leads (such as those given to tenors in later years).

Castrati were drawn into the new world of theaters and opera houses—although reluctantly at first—to become by the eighteenth century the commanding stars and celebrities of the musical world; their popularity faded only in the early years of the 1800's. Their role in church singing remained paramount in Italy, however, and lasted at the Vatican until the death in 1922 of its last castrati, Alessandro Moreschi.

—*John W. Barker*

FURTHER READING

Barbier, Patrick. *The World of the Castrati: The History of an Extraordinary Operatic Phenomenon.* London: Souvenir Press, 1996. Excellent overview of the castrati in their operatic heyday.

Bergeron, Katherine. "The Castrato as History." *Cambridge Opera Journal* 8, no. 2 (1996): 167-184. Examines castrati as lost figures, part of an unrecoverable history.

Heriot, Angus. *The Castrati in Opera.* London: Secker & Warburg, 1956. Classic, if flawed, predecessor to Barbier, with more emphasis on individual singers' careers.

Milner, Anthony. "The Sacred Capons." *Musical Times* 114, no. 1561 (1973): 250-252. A brief but detailed examination of the uncertain history of castrati and eunuchs in choirs of the Church.

Rosselli, John. "The Castrati as a Professional Group and a Social Phenomenon, 1550-1850," *Acta Musicologica* 60 (1988): 143-179. Also in a revised abridgment in Rosselli's *Singers of Italian Opera: The History of a Profession.* New York: Cambridge University Press, 1992. An important study of the profession in economic and religious contexts.

Taylor, Gary. *Castration: An Abbreviated History of Western Manhood.* New York: Routledge, 2002. Wide-ranging contemplation of the practice, including the musical dimensions.

Tougher, Shaun F. "Byzantine Eunuchs: An Overview, with Special Reference to Their Creation and Origin." In *Women, Men, and Eunuchs: Gender in Byzantium,* edited by Liz James. New York: Routledge, 1997. Good introduction to a still-understudied topic.

SEE ALSO: 1590's: Birth of Opera.
RELATED ARTICLE in *Great Lives from History: The Renaissance & Early Modern Era, 1454-1600:* Sixtus V.

1600
WILLIAM GILBERT PUBLISHES *DE MAGNETE*

Gilbert, physician to Queen Elizabeth I, published the first great work of English science, De magnete, *in which he presented his investigations into magnetic bodies and electrical attraction, opening up the study of electricity and magnetism and setting an example of experimental methods in science.*

LOCALE: London, England
CATEGORIES: Science and technology; astronomy

KEY FIGURES
William Gilbert (1544-1603), English physician, scientist, and philosopher
Edward Wright (1558-1615), Cambridge cartographer and Gilbert's collaborator
Elizabeth I (1533-1603), queen of England, r. 1558-1603
Francis Bacon (1561-1626), English philosopher and statesman

SUMMARY OF EVENT
William Gilbert of Colchester in County Essex, northeast of London, was trained in medicine at Cambridge University, completing his master of arts degree in 1564 and his doctor of medicine degree in 1569. He became a prominent physician in London, eventually serving as president of the Royal College of Physicians and royal physician to Queen Elizabeth I by 1600.

His most significant contribution came from nearly two decades of research on magnetism and electricity, encouraged by Elizabeth, who provided him with an annual pension for his philosophical studies. His research culminated in the one work published during his lifetime, *De magnete, magneticisque corporibus, et de magno magnete tellure* (1600; *A New Natural Philosophy of the Magnet, Magnetic Bodies, and the Great Terrestrial Magnet,* 1893), better known as *De magnete.*

De magnete was the first great book of English science, emerging during the scientific revolution. The work marks the transition from Renaissance naturalism to experimental science and was the first comprehensive treatment of magnetism since the *Epistola de magnete* (1269; *Epistle of Peter Peregrinus of Maricourt to Sygerus of Foncaucourt, Soldier, Concerning the Magnet,* 1902) of Peter Peregrinus. Its strong emphasis on observation and experiment (about fifty experiments are described) probably grew out of Gilbert's collaboration with practical navigators and cartographers, especially

the Cambridge mathematician, Edward Wright, England's leading cartographer and expert on the compass. Wright not only provided practical information but also wrote the introductory address and chapter 12 of book 4 on magnetic declination (variation from true north). He also contributed to book 5 on magnetic dip (vertical inclination of the magnetic needle) and its relation to latitude, as well as designing an instrument for measuring dip.

The first of the six books in *De magnete* discusses the history of magnetism, refuting legends about the lodestone (naturally occurring magnetic stones) and describing its properties. Characteristically, Gilbert denied the Aristotelian concept of pure elements, and, in particular, elemental earth, to establish and advance his principle that Earth is a giant lodestone. He argued that this principle explains the phenomena of terrestrial magnetism. In so doing, he rejected the accepted view that the compass is attracted to the poles of the celestial sphere about which the stars and planets revolve. He described ways to demonstrate the behavior of the lodestone, marking his own experiments and discoveries with asterisks of varying size to indicate their relative importance. In the last five books, Gilbert discussed five magnetic movements, which he called coition, direction, variation, dip, and revolution.

Before proceeding with magnetic motions, Gilbert describes in book 2, chapter 2, his experiments on the amber effect to distinguish between magnetism and electricity, thus opening up a new field of study and naming it after the Greek word *electron* (meaning "amber"). He showed that some thirty different materials, including glass, hard sealing wax, and several semiprecious gems, have an attractive effect when rubbed. He called these materials "electrics" and distinguished them from "nonelectrics," which do not exhibit an amber effect. He also described the working of the first electroscope, or *versorium*, by pivoting a metal needle on a post so that it would be deflected when a rubbed electric was brought near. He used an animate or formal cause to describe magnetism in which magnetic materials shared in the basic magnetic form or "soul" of Earth. By contrast, electric attraction is explained as a material cause in which electrics, when rubbed, emit "effluvia," a kind of vapor that attaches to matter and pulls it inward.

In his study of magnetic phenomena, Gilbert assumed that every magnet is surrounded by an invisible "orb of virtue" (*orbis virtutis*) that affects any other magnetic material placed within its orb of virtue. He produced lathe-turned spherical lodestones, which he called *terrellae* (little earths), as laboratory models for the study of terrestrial magnetism. He preferred the word "coition" for magnetic attraction to emphasize that it was a mutual action between two magnetic bodies, each coming within the orb of virtue of the other. The direction or orientation of a magnetic compass is described in book 3 as the alignment of a compass needle with the earth's magnetic orb of virtue rather than the celestial poles. To support this idea, he gave numerous demonstrations with a *terrella*, using small compass needles (*versoria*) to identify its poles as analogous with the earth's north and south poles.

In book 4, Gilbert turned to variations in the orientation of the compass, the well-known declination of the magnetic needle from true north. He demonstrated a similar declination with a *terrella* by making a gouge on its surface analogous to the Atlantic Ocean and showing how such deviations from a smooth sphere affected the compass direction. He also discussed the possibility of using declination to determine longitude at sea. In book 5, he discussed the magnetic dip (inclination from the horizontal). Again using a *terrella*, he showed that there is no dip at the equator but there is increasing dip as the magnetic needle moves toward either pole. This led to the suggestion of using dip to measure latitude when the skies are clouded.

The last book of *De magnete*, book 6, discusses magnetic rotation, based on a suggestion in Peregrinus's letter on magnetism that a spherical lodestone perfectly aligned with the celestial poles would rotate once every 24 hours. Gilbert floated a *terrella* on a cork raft and observed the *terrella*'s tendency to rotate into magnetic alignment. He suggests that magnetic rotation causes a daily rotation of the earth on its axis. Although he neither accepts nor rejects the heliocentric theory of the earth's annual revolution around the sun, he does support Copernican ideas by denying the solid celestial spheres and their daily revolution, suggesting that the fixed stars are spread through space. He also suggests that the tides result from magnetism of the earth and moon. These extensions of magnetic philosophy were not as strongly supported by experiment and were the source of later criticisms of Gilbert's work.

SIGNIFICANCE

De magnete not only initiated the study of magnetism and electricity but also rejected natural philosophy and its support of new views of the world, including a me-

chanical explanation for the daily rotation of the earth. Its strong emphasis on experimental methods preempted ideas later developed by Francis Bacon. Ironically, the book was criticized by Bacon for its attempt to develop an entire philosophy based on magnetism and for the concept of a moving earth. The book was especially valuable for providing a modern understanding of terrestrial magnetism and the basis and terminology for later studies of electricity.

Most of Gilbert's contemporaries, both in England and on the Continent, praised *De magnete* both for its content and for its new experimental methods. A second edition was published in 1628 and a third in 1633; it was widely distributed and it strongly influenced the emerging scientific revolution. Galileo Galilei (1564-1642) was greatly impressed and turned his attention to magnetic studies. Johannes Kepler (1571-1630) tried to incorporate Gilbert's magnetic theory into an explanation of planetary motions in the Copernican system. Although the theory of the magnetic movement of the planets was later rejected, it provided a good explanation until the concept of gravitation could be further developed.

—*Joseph L. Spradley*

FURTHER READING

Gilbert, William. *De magnete.* New York: Dover, 1958. This reprint of P. Fleury Mottelay's 1893 translation of *De magnete* includes a brief biographical memoir by the translator (containing some inaccuracies).

Margolis, Howard. *It Started with Copernicus.* New York: McGraw-Hill, 2002. This book discusses the work of Gilbert along with that of Simon Stevin, Kepler, and Galileo, in the context of the development of Copernican heliocentric theory.

Pumfrey, Stephen. "William Gilbert." In *Cambridge Scientific Minds,* edited by Peter Harman and Simon Mitton. New York: Cambridge University Press, 2002. The first chapter in a book about Cambridge scientists that provides a good discussion of the context and contributions of Gilbert's work.

Roller, Duane H. D. *The "De Magnete" of William Gilbert.* Amsterdam: Menno Hertzberger, 1959. This is probably the best single source on William Gilbert and his work.

Rossi, Paolo. *The Birth of Modern Science.* Malden, Mass.: Blackwell, 2001. Chapter 9, "Magnetic Philosophy," begins with a discussion of Gilbert's work and explores the development of Gilbert's ideas by other scientists in the seventeenth century.

Verschuur, Gerrit L. *Hidden Attraction: The History and*

Battle of Sekigahara

Mystery of Magnetism. New York: Oxford University Press, 1993. Chapter 3, "On the Magnetical Philosophy," is devoted to the work of William Gilbert.

SEE ALSO: 1462: Regiomontanus Completes the *Epitome* of Ptolemy's *Almagest*; c. 1478-1519: Leonardo da Vinci Compiles His Notebooks; 1543: Copernicus Publishes *De Revolutionibus*; 1572-1574: Tycho Brahe Observes a Supernova; 1580's-1590's: Galileo

Conducts His Early Experiments; 1582: Gregory XIII Reforms the Calendar; 1583-1600: Bruno's Theory of the Infinite Universe.

RELATED ARTICLES in *Great Lives from History: The Renaissance & Early Modern Era, 1454-1600:* Francis Bacon; Sophia Brahe; Tycho Brahe; Giordano Bruno; Nicolaus Copernicus; Elizabeth I; Girolamo Fracastoro; William Gilbert; Leonard da Vinci; Paracelsus; Rheticus; Simon Stevin.

October 21, 1600
BATTLE OF SEKIGAHARA

The Battle of Sekigahara marked the last major conflict in the Japanese wars of unification. Tokugawa Ieyasu defeated an alliance of rival warlords and assumed uncontested control of Japan. As shogun, he outlawed private armies to ensure domestic peace and tranquillity, and he imposed a policy of enforced isolation that lasted until American warships opened Japan to international trade in 1846.

LOCALE: A small post station in Mino Province (now southwest of Gifu), Japan
CATEGORIES: Wars, uprisings, and civil unrest; government and politics; expansion and land acquisition

KEY FIGURES

Kobayakawa Hideaki (1577-1602), military commander
Tokugawa Ieyasu (Matsudaira Takechiyo, later Matsudaira Motoyasu; 1543-1616), military dictator of Japan, r. 1603-1605
Ishida Mitsunari (1563-1600), aide to Hideyoshi
Toyotomi Hideyoshi (1537-1598), military ruler of Japan, r. 1590-1598

SUMMARY OF EVENT

In Japanese society, local warlords known as daimyo owned and administered districts or provinces. Although in theory the emperor was supreme, only the daimyo could raise taxes, so during Japan's medieval era most emperors were weak and held only titular power. Real political power rested with the daimyo, and throughout the era a number of highly influential daimyo fought one another to expand their holdings or to gain preeminence. The highest rank a daimyo could attain was that of sho-

gun. Although the literal translation of the Japanese word *shōgun* is "barbarian-quelling generalissimo," in reality, the position was that of military dictator.

In 1185, the first shogunate, or administration of a shogun, was established. For the next five centuries numerous daimyo struggled for supremacy. The conflicts of the sixteenth century were particularly vigorous and bloody. Japanese historians refer to this period as Sengoku Jidai, the Age of the Country at War, or the Warring States period. During the later years of this century, one particularly successful general was Toyotomi Hideyoshi. By 1585, Hideyoshi had defeated rivals and administered the nation for the emperor as *kampaku* (chancellor of the emperor) through his control over a coalition of dependant daimyo. Hideyoshi was the first leader to unify Japan under one man's authority.

When Hideyoshi died in 1598, however, his six-year-old son was too young to come to power, so the coalition of subordinate daimyo dissolved into two rival alliances. The primary leaders of these alliances had been important subordinates of Hideyoshi. Ishida Mitsunari had been a civil administrator more than a general, and by virtue of his schemes and political manipulations he came to command what became known as the Western Army. Many of the daimyo in the Western Army were less inclined to support Mitsunari than they were eager to oppose Tokugawa Ieyasu. Ieyasu had been one of Hideyoshi's generals and was also the richest daimyo in Japan. His wealth made him both the target of much resentment and a natural leader. Many assumed that when Hideyoshi died, Ieyasu would be his successor by default. The forces of the daimyo that supported Ieyasu soon came to be called the Eastern Army.

In 1600, Ieyasu's leading opponents attempted to isolate him politically. In response, Ieyasu mobilized his forces and began the decisive campaign. Mitsunari's strategy was to divert Ieyasu with attacks on Ieyasu's eastern lands. With Ieyasu thus distracted, Mitsunari's Western Army would concentrate and overwhelm Ieyasu. On the day of battle, the Western Army numbered about 80,000 soldiers. In response to Mitsunari's gambit, Ieyasu diverted some of his troops to screen the eastern attack while he rapidly moved approximately 88,000 men to confront Mitsunari's Western Army. Surprised, Mitsunari retreated to the small crossroad village named Sekigahara. There he planned to ambush Ieyasu. Mitsunari deployed his forces in a long, L-shaped array. About 34,000 troops were deployed in the lower bar of the L in blocking positions athwart the road that ran through Sekigahara. The shaft of the L lay along the sides of two mountains, Matsuo and Nangu. Upon and behind these heights, Mitsunari stationed nearly 48,000 soldiers. These troops were held far enough above the valley floor to be screened from view. Mitsunari's plan was that Ieyasu's forces would attack along the valley floor without seeing these forces, and at the opportune moment Mitsunari would order the contingents on Matsuo and Nangu to charge down the mountains to surround and destroy Ieyasu's army.

What Mitsunari did not realize was that his own arrogant personality and lack of diplomatic skill had alienated many of the ostensibly anti-Ieyasu daimyo. Mitsunari had, for example, relegated his most experienced battlefield commander to a virtual exile in Ōsaka, where the man was locked into a largely ceremonial position. Thus Mitsunari removed a rival, while also depriving the Western Army of its most talented battle leader. Ieyasu benefited from such slights, and before the battle began, he secretly convinced many of the disaffected daimyo in the Western Army to defect. These daimyo agreed to not switch sides until battle was joined.

The battle began early on the morning of October 21, 1600. The weather was foul, with a heavy fog masking Ieyasu's approach. Around 8:00 A.M. the fog burned off, and Ieyasu's men attacked headlong into Mitsunari's position. The fighting was heavy and bitter throughout the morning. Both sides fielded large numbers of harquebusiers, but the mist and light rain dampened the gunpowder and minimized the impact of fire. A hastily erected fence acted as a shield for some of Mitsunari's gunners and helped to anchor his position. Throughout the morning, Ieyasu's men attacked a force that comprised less than half of the Western Army, much as Mitsunari had planned. Although Ieyasu's forces were

more numerous at the point of contact, Mitsunari's defensive position and the valor of his men allowed them to resist effectively.

Having held Ieyasu's men in place, Mitsunari ordered the forces from the two mountainsides to move out from cover and attack. The crucial force for this attack was the contingent led by Kobayakawa Hideaki, as his force was the pivot connecting Mitsunari's contingent with the other forces deployed along the length of Mount Nangu. Because Hideaki was between these forces and Mitsunari, the other daimyo deployed along the mountain could not see the signal to attack. Hideaki had secretly agreed to aid Ieyasu, and at about noon, he ordered his men to attack Mitsunari's position. Mitsunari loyalists arrayed behind Hideaki were unaware of Mitsunari's commands to attack and were thus thrown into confusion by Hideaki's attack on Mitsunari.

Mitsunari's men, who had been holding off Ieyasu's forces since dawn, were suddenly confronted on two sides. Exhausted by the long morning's fight and demoralized by the treacherous attack, Mitsunari's forces began to disintegrate. Hideaki's contingent was not the only group of turncoats. Five other daimyo switched sides during the battle, bringing about 23,000 men to Ieyasu's assistance. Once Mitsunari saw what was happening, he abandoned his forces and fled from the battlefield.

Mitsunari's plan had failed because of treachery, but his rapid departure from the battle rendered impossible any rally of the remaining loyalist contingents. Ieyasu's victory shattered the Western Army, and many of its daimyo rapidly shifted their loyalties to him. Mitsunari was ultimately captured and executed. Although Ieyasu would require another sixteen years to secure undisputed rule of Japan, the victory at Sekigahara removed the only effective and unified force that could have opposed his campaign to be named shogun.

SIGNIFICANCE

Ieyasu's victory at Sekigahara made possible his rise to the position of shogun. As the military dictator of Japan, he was able to carry through a number of reforms that had begun under Hideyoshi. These reforms included destroying privately owned fortifications, outlawing the ownership of arms by anyone other than samurai, and ossifying the social classes. These laws essentially ended the private armies of the daimyo and turned the samurai class into government administrators.

Ieyasu also outlawed foreign trade and, as a result, isolated Japan from developments elsewhere. These reforms profoundly changed Japanese life. In addition,

1590's

Ieyasu's success allowed him to found a dynasty of sho-guns that came to be known as the Tokugawa shogunate. Ieyasu's descendants would rule Japan until 1868, a future that would have been impossible without the clear-cut victory at Sekigahara.

—*Kevin B. Reid*

FURTHER READING

Bryant, Anthony. *Sekigahara, 1600: The Final Struggle for Power*. London: Osprey Books, 1996. This is an excellent study of the battle and the political maneuverings that created the two alliances.

Turnbull, Stephen. *The Samurai: A Military History*. New York: Macmillan, 1977. Turnbull is a tremen-dously well-respected scholar of the samurai. This book is an excellent study of the development of the samurai and their ethos. It is a particularly valuable work for its battle studies.

_____. *Samurai: The World of the Warrior*. London: Osprey Books, 2003. An excellent and accessible book, this work is suitable for a wide variety of ages.

_____. *Samurai Warfare*. London: Arms and Armour Press, 1996. Another very fine effort by Turnbull, this

work is an excellent overview of the nuts and bolts of how samurai forces were organized, equipped, and led, and how they fought.

SEE ALSO: 1457-1480's: Spread of Jōdo Shinshū Bud-dhism; 1467-1477: Ōnin War; 1477-1600: Japan's "Age of the Country at War"; Mar. 5, 1488: Composi-tion of the *Renga* Masterpiece *Minase sangin hyakuin*; Beginning 1513: Kanō School Flourishes; 1532-1536: Temmon Hokke Rebellion; 1549-1552: Father Xavier Introduces Christianity to Japan; 1550's-1567: Japa-nese Pirates Pillage the Chinese Coast; 1550-1593: Japanese Wars of Unification; Sept., 1553: First Bat-tle of Kawanakajima; June 12, 1560: Battle of Oke-hazama; 1568: Oda Nobunaga Seizes Kyōto; 1587: Toyotomi Hideyoshi Hosts a Ten-Day Tea Ceremony; 1590: Odawara Campaign; 1592-1599: Japan Invades Korea; 1594-1595: Taikō Kenchi Survey; Oct., 1596-Feb., 1597: *San Felipe* Incident.

RELATED ARTICLES in *Great Lives from History: The Renaissance & Early Modern Era, 1454-1600:* Hōjō Ujimasa; Hosokawa Gracia; Oda Nobunaga; Ōgi-machi; Oichi; Sesshū; Toyotomi Hideyoshi.

December 31, 1600
ELIZABETH I CHARTERS THE EAST INDIA COMPANY

Elizabeth I, hoping to steal Spain's status as the primary world power and to quell the Dutch monopoly on the spice trade, signed a charter that gave English merchants exclusive rights to trade in the East Indies. The conglomerate of merchant companies became the East India Company, which focused on trade in India after Elizabeth's death and which eventually enabled the British Empire in India.

LOCALE: London, England

CATEGORIES: Trade and commerce; economics; exploration and discovery; laws, acts, and legal history; expansion and land acquisition; organizations and institutions

KEY FIGURES

Elizabeth I (1533-1603), queen of England, r. 1558-1603

Sir Thomas Smythe (1558?-1623), first governor of the East India Company

Sir James Lancaster (c. 1554-1618), general of the fleet of the East India Company

SUMMARY OF EVENT

On December 31 1600, Elizabeth I of England signed a charter granting the organization called Governor and Company of Merchants of London Trading to the East Indies, later known as the British East India Company, exclusive trade rights in the east for the next fifteen years. In other words, only the English affiliated with the East India Company were permitted to trade in a region rang-ing from the Cape of Good Hope to the Straits of Magel-lan. This monopoly could be extended to the charter members' heirs and employees, and there was no limit on potential renewals of the charter upon its expiration.

The petitioning group comprised 219 men, including George de Clifford, third earl of Cumberland, and Sir John Hart. They had formed their coalition in September of 1599 and then lobbied for a charter. Many were mem-bers of the Levant or Muscovy Companies, or both, and the East India charter was not dissimilar from the former two monopolies. The approximately fifty merchants who were involved in Levant trade recognized the declining value of their merchandise; for example, by 1599, pepper had dropped to one-quarter of its previous value. Several traders also had experience with the voyages to North America, so the East India Company was a group not of new, untrained explorers and merchants but of seasoned and worldly merchants who wanted to expand trade within a new, more ambitious, and wider sphere.

Elizabeth specified in the charter that the control of the company would rest in the hands of one governor and a council of twenty-four individuals. This group would control the voyages, the manners of shipping, and the process by which the goods retrieved from the voyages were sold. The first governor was Sir Thomas Smythe, the founder of the Virginia Colony in North America and member of the London Haberdashers' and Skinners' companies. Many council members also were involved in the Virginia voyages. Elizabeth did not name a deputy governor, but she stated that one could be selected through assembly. Governors, deputy governors, and members of the council would be elected to one-year terms, following the tenure of those whom Elizabeth empowered in the charter. The members of this governing body were entrusted with the responsibility of making laws that would limit the conduct of its members in trade with Asia. Essentially, Elizabeth structured the company in such a way that it would maintain itself without needing her constant involvement.

A number of factors motivated Elizabeth to charter the East India Company. Having defeated the Spanish Armada in 1588, Elizabeth was eager to destroy the reputation the Spanish had as the primary and dominant European empire. Additionally, she hoped to eliminate the Dutch monopoly on the East Indian spice trade. The focus of the company, however, later turned from Indonesia to India after the Dutch massacred the English in Ambon, Indonesia, in 1623, reportedly because of a history of treachery by the English. Nevertheless, in 1600, Elizabeth hoped that by superseding Spanish and Dutch interests, she could continue the development of England as a grand empire.

Even before she commenced rule, Elizabeth had exhibited a keen interest in the foreign world. Her delight at the reports and acquisitions of Sir Francis Drake and

An ambassador for Queen Elizabeth I standing before India's emperor, seeking privileges to charter the East India Company for the English. (Hulton|Archive by Getty Images)

other explorers was encouragement enough to explore the East Indies, viewed as idyllic by the Elizabethans.

The company's first voyage left six weeks after its charter, in February, 1601. Fleet general James Lancaster set sail with four ships and five hundred men for Indonesia, carrying a letter from Elizabeth to Sumatran sultan Ala'ud'din Riayat Syah. The letter signified her interest in and support for the East India Company. Lancaster's journey was long and arduous; by the time he and his ships reached the Cape of Good Hope, only four hundred of the five hundred men remained. They reached Sumatra, delivered Elizabeth's letter, and were received with joy by the sultan, who plied them with a liquor so strong that Lancaster's men later expressed they would have preferred to dilute it with water. Eventually, in 1602, they landed at Bantam, where they set up a post with merchants.

This first voyage of the East India Company was not lucrative; in fact, shareholders lost money. Lancaster's voyage, and the twelve ventures for the first ten years of the company's chartered existence, was not a venture in which all shareholders were required to participate. The ships would return with their cargo, the cargo would be auctioned, and the shareholders would be paid. Lancaster did not return until 1605, after Elizabeth's death in 1603. He brought with him a letter from Sultan Alaʾudʾdin Riayat Syah, but it was read by Elizabeth's successor, King James I of England (r. 1603-1625). The company reached India by 1608, landing at the port of Surat in Gujarat, where it would establish a factory. By 1615, it had become clear that this independent organization functioned poorly, often failing to reward the shareholders. The East India Company then became a true joint-stock company, which paved the way for similar ventures.

SIGNIFICANCE

The British East India Company originally was established to develop English interests in the Indonesian spice trade, but the English elected to leave the Spice Islands to the Dutch and to concentrate their ventures on the Indian subcontinent after the Ambon Massacre of 1623. From that time forward, the English developed an empire in India that would become the "jewel in the crown" of the British Empire.

Centers of power developed during the seventeenth century in Surat as well as Calcutta, Bombay, and Madras. In 1698, a rival company, the English Company Trading to the East Indies, was created, but it merged with the Governor and Company of Merchants Trading into the East Indies in 1702 to form the United Company of Merchants of England Trading to the East Indies.

The East India Company successfully fought local resistance in Bengal in 1757 at the Battle of Plassey, which established British supremacy over the French and British domination of India. The company soon established tea cultivation in Assam, Vietnam, as well, and instituted a center in Canton to trade tea and silver.

The trade monopoly begun by Elizabeth ended in 1813, and thus the company's power declined. Yet it was not until after the Sepoy Mutiny of 1857, often considered the first rebellion against English colonial rule in India, that the East India Company started to dissolve, despite eloquent attempts by political philosopher John Stuart Mill to keep it intact as the center of British power in India. By this time, the East India Company controlled an area from Gujarat to Hong Kong, a region with one-fifth of the world's population. England had become, as Elizabeth had dreamed, an empire on which the sun never set.

—*Monica Piotter*

CHARTERING THE BRITISH EAST INDIA COMPANY

The British East India Company was officially sanctioned in 1600 when England's queen Elizabeth I issued a charter granting a company of merchants full and exclusive trade rights. Here, Elizabeth outlines the company's mandate to not only trade but also to govern.

To all our officers, ministers, and subjects, and to all other people, as well within this our realm of England as elsewhere, under our obedience and jurisdiction, or otherwise, unto whom these our Letters Patents shall be seen, showed, or read, greeting. Whereas our most dear and loving Cousin, George, Earl of Cumberland, and our well-beloved subjects, Sir John Hart, of London, and others . . . have of our certain knowledge been petitioners unto us, for our Royal assent and licence to be granted unto them, that they, at their own adventures, costs, and charges, as well for the honour of this our realm of England, as for the increase of our navigation, and advancement of trade of merchandize, within our said realms and the dominions of the same, might adventure and set forth one or more voyages, with convenient number of ships and pinnaces, by way of traffic and merchandize to the East Indies, in the countries and parts of Asia and Africa and to as many of the islands, ports and cities, towns and places, thereabouts, as where trade and traffic may by all likelihood be discovered, established or had; divers of which countries, and many of the islands, cities and ports, thereof, have long since been discovered by others of our subjects, albeit not frequented in trade of merchandize.

Know ye, therefore, that we . . . do give and grant unto our said loving subjects before in these presents expressly named, that they and every of them from henceforth be, and shall be one body corporate and politick, in deed and in name. . . .

Source: Excerpted from "Charter Granted by Queen Elizabeth to the East India Company, 31 December 1600." Project South Asia, South Dakota State University. http://projectsouthasia.sdstate.edu/docs. Accessed September 27, 2004.

FURTHER READING

Andrews, Kenneth R. *Trade, Plunder, and Settlement: Maritime Enterprise and the Genesis of the British Empire, 1480-1630.* Cambridge, England: Cambridge University Press, 1984. Andrews develops a history of British trade, exploration, and colonization.

Bowen, H. V., Margarette Lincoln, and Nigel Rigby. *The Worlds of the East India Company.* Rochester, N.Y.: Boydell & Brewer, 2003. A collection that deals with multiple aspects of the company's history, including culture, politics, art, and trade. This edition covers the company from its origins to the end of its existence as an agent of territorial expansion in India.

Chaudhuri, K. N. *The English East India Company: The Study of an Early Joint-Stock Company, 1600-1640.* London: Frank Cass, 1965. A superb study of the company from its origins to its period of neglect during the English Civil Wars. Describes the ways in which the charter was modified and carried out.

Farrington, Anthony. *Trading Places: The East India Company and Asia, 1600-1834.* London: British Library, 2002. Farrington's short discussion is a very good general overview of the company's involvement in Asia after 1600.

Scott, William R. *The Constitution and Finance of English, Scottish, and Irish Joint Stock Companies to 1720.* London, 1912. This three-volume set, while out of date, remains the best study of the structure and finance of British joint-stock companies.

SEE ALSO: Late 15th cent.: Mombasa, Malindi, and Kilwa Reach Their Height; Aug., 1487-Dec., 1488: Dias Rounds the Cape of Good Hope; 1490's: Decline of the Silk Road; Jan., 1498: Portuguese Reach the Swahili Coast; 16th cent.: Evolution of the Galleon; 16th century: Worldwide Inflation; 1511-c. 1515: Melaka Falls to the Portuguese; 1519-1522: Magellan Expedition Circumnavigates the Globe; Apr. 20, 1534-July, 1543: Cartier and Roberval Search for a Northwest Passage; 1536: Turkish Capitulations Begin; 1558-1603: Reign of Elizabeth I; 1565: Spain Seizes the Philippines.

RELATED ARTICLE in *Great Lives from History: The Renaissance & Early Modern Era, 1454-1600:* Elizabeth I.

Appendices

Time Line

The time line below includes the events and developments covered in the essays in this publication (appearing in small capital letters) as well as more than 250 other important events and developments. Each event is tagged by general region or regions, rather than by smaller nations or principalities, which changed significantly over the millennium covered in this publication; by this means, the time line can be used to consider general trends in the same region over time. However, because many events, although occurring in one or two regions, nevertheless had a global or cross-regional impact, they have been left in strict chronological order to facilitate a better understanding of simultaneous events and their occasional interaction. The abbreviation "c." is used below to stand for both "circa" (when it precedes the date) and "century" or "centuries" (when it follows the date).

Date	Region	Event
Mid-15th c.	Middle East	FOUNDATION OF THE SAUD DYNASTY
1450's-1471	South Asia	CHAMPA CIVIL WARS
1450's-1529	South Asia	THAI WARS
1451-1526	South Asia	LODĪ KINGS DOMINATE NORTHERN INDIA
1454	East Asia	CHINA SUBDUES BURMA
1454	Europe	Sultan Mehmed II grants Venice trading privileges
1454-1466	Europe	Thirteen Years' War
1454-1481	Middle East	RISE OF THE OTTOMAN EMPIRE
Apr. 9, 1454	Europe	PEACE OF LODI
1455-1485	Europe	WARS OF THE ROSES
1456	South Asia	Battle of Kamphaeng Phet
1456	Africa	Ca'da Mosto, working for Portugal, discovers the Cape Verde Islands
1456	Europe	János Hunyadi prevents the Ottomans from conquering Belgrade
1456	Europe	PUBLICATION OF GUTENBERG'S MAZARIN BIBLE
1456	Europe	Treaty of Iazhelbitsy
1457-1480's	East Asia	SPREAD OF JŌDO SHINSHŪ BUDDHISM
Feb. 11, 1457	East Asia	RESTORATION OF ZHENGTONG
Apr. 14, 1457-July 2, 1504	Europe	REIGN OF STEPHEN THE GREAT
1458	South Asia	Ban La Tra Nguyet usurps the throne of Champa
1458-1490	Europe	HUNGARIAN RENAISSANCE
1459	South Asia	RĀO JODHA FOUNDS JODHPUR
1459	Europe	Serbia becomes a province of the Ottoman Empire
Early 1460's	Europe	LABOR SHORTAGES ALTER EUROPE'S SOCIAL STRUCTURE
c. 1460	Europe	Ottomans take control of Greece
1460-1600	Africa	RISE OF THE AKAN KINGDOMS
July 10, 1460	Europe	Battle of Northampton
Dec. 30, 1460	Europe	Richard, duke of York, is killed in the Battle of Wakefield
1461	Middle East	Ottomans conquer Trebizond
1461	Europe	Vlad III the Impaler attacks the Ottoman Empire and captures Vidin
Mar. 29, 1461	Europe	Battle of Towton
1462	Central Asia	Astrakhan splits from the Golden Horde
1462	Europe	FOUNDING OF THE PLATONIC ACADEMY
c. 1462	Central Asia	KAZAK EMPIRE IS ESTABLISHED
1462	Europe	REGIOMONTANUS COMPLETES THE *EPITOME* OF PTOLEMY'S *ALMAGEST*
1462	Europe	Vlad III the Impaler is dethroned
Beginning 1462	Europe	Hungary's Matthias I Corvinus organizes a standing army of mercenaries known as the Black Army

DATE	REGION	EVENT
Beginning 1462	Europe and Central Asia	Russian Colonial Wars
Sept., 1462	Europe	Battle of Puck
1463	South Asia	Battle of Doi Ba
1463	Europe	Ottomans expand into southern and central Bosnia
1463	Americas	Topa Inca becomes commander of the Incan army
1463-1464	Europe	Treaty of Wiener Neustadt
1463-1479	Europe and Middle East	OTTOMAN-VENETIAN WAR
Fall, 1463	Europe	Prussian League's navy destroys the Teutonic Knights' fleet
Sept. 12, 1463	Europe	Venice and Hungary form an alliance against the Ottoman Empire
1464	Europe	French nobles form the League of the Public Weal under Charles the Bold
1464	Europe	Ottomans begin their conquest of Albania
c. 1464-1591	Africa	SONGHAI EMPIRE DOMINATES THE WESTERN SUDAN
1465	Europe	Stephen the Great of Moldavia captures the Hungarian fortress at Kiliya
1465-Aug., 1467	Europe	Castilian Civil War
1465-1487	East Asia	REIGN OF XIANZONG
July 16, 1465-Apr., 1559	Europe	FRENCH-BURGUNDIAN AND FRENCH-AUSTRIAN WARS
c. 1466-1473	Africa	Siege of Djenné
Oct. 19, 1466	Europe	SECOND PEACE OF THORN
1467	South Asia	END OF KING PARĀAKRAMABĀHU VI'S REIGN
1467	Europe	Charles the Bold becomes Duke of Burgundy
1467-1477	East Asia	ŌNIN WAR
Nov., 1467	Europe	Matthias I Corvinus of Hungary invades Moldavia
Nov. 11, 1467	Middle East	Ak Koyunlu army destroys Kara Koyunlu army, ending the Kara Koyunlu Dynasty
Dec. 14, 1467	Europe	Battle of Baia ends the Hungarian invasion of Moldavia
1468	Europe	Ficino completes his Italian translations of Plato's dialogues
1468	Central Asia	Khan Abū'l-Khayr dies in battle with Girei's forces
1468	Europe	Pact of Los Toros de Guisando between Isabella of Castille and Henry IV
1468	Africa	Sonni ʿAlī captures Timbuktu and massacres its Muslim inhabitants
c. 1468-1478	Europe	Bohemian-Hungarian War
1469	Middle East	Abū Saʿīd dies in the Battle of Karabakh
1469	Europe and Africa	Fernão Gomes purchases exclusive rights to explore Africa's west coast from Afonso V of Portugal
1469-1481	South Asia	REIGN OF THE AVA KING THIHATHURA
1469-1492	Europe	RULE OF LORENZO DE' MEDICI
1469-1508	Middle East	AK KOYUNLU DYNASTY CONTROLS IRAQ AND NORTHERN IRAN
Oct. 19, 1469	Europe	MARRIAGE OF FERDINAND AND ISABELLA
1470's	Middle East	Mehmed II founds eight major Muslim colleges (*madrasas*)
1470	Europe	Frederick III and Matthias I Corvinus meet in Vienna, quarrel, and renounce their friendship
1470	Europe	Novgorod becomes a vassal state of Poland
1470	Europe	Richard Neville, earl of Warwick, invades England; King Edward IV flees to Bruges
June, 1470	Europe	Ottomans attack Negroponte
Nov. 28, 1470	South Asia	Vietnam declares war on Champa
1471	Europe	Stephen the Great refuses to pay a tribute to the Ottoman Empire
1471-1493	Americas	REIGN OF TOPA INCA
Apr. 14, 1471	Europe	Battle of Barnet: Edward IV defeats Warwick and reclaims the English throne

Date	Region	Event
May 4, 1471	Europe	Battle of Tewkesbury
Mar. 18-22, 1471	South Asia	BATTLE OF VIJAYA
July 14, 1471	Europe	Battle of Shelon River
1472	Middle East	Mamlūk army drives Ak Koyunlu out of northern Syria
1472	Europe	Marriage of Ivan the Great and Sophia Palaeologus
c. 1472	Africa	Portuguese explorers reach the mouth of the Niger River
1472	Europe	Siege of Beauvais
Summer, 1472	Middle East	Venetian fleet under Pietro Mocenigo raids Izmir and Antalya
c. 1473	East Asia	ASHIKAGA YOSHIMASA BUILDS THE SILVER PAVILION
1473	Europe	JAKOB II FUGGER BECOMES A MERCHANT
1473	Middle East	Ottomans defeat the Ak Koyunlu at Tercan
c. 1473-1478	Europe	Hugo van der Goes paints the *Portinari Altarpiece*
1473-1600	Europe	WITCH-HUNTS AND WITCH TRIALS
Aug. 11, 1473	Middle East	Battle of Başkent
1474	East Asia	GREAT WALL OF CHINA IS BUILT
1474	Europe	Treaty of London: Charles the Bold and England's Edward IV make plans to conquer and divide France
1474-1479	Europe	CASTILIAN WAR OF SUCCESSION
Late 15th c.	Africa	MOMBASA, MALINDI, AND KILWA REACH THEIR HEIGHT
Late 15th-mid-16th c.	Africa	Nomadic preachers bring Islamic Sufi mysticism to the western Sudan
1475	Europe	Crimean Khante submits to Ottoman authority
1475	South Asia	Yawnghwe submits to Avan authority
Jan. 10, 1475	Europe	Battle of Podul Inalt
July 4, 1475	Europe	Edward IV arrives in France to lead his invasion force
Aug. 29, 1475	Europe	PEACE OF PICQUIGNY
1476	Europe and Central Asia	Ivan the Great refuses to pay tributes to the Golden Horde
Mar. 1, 1476	Europe	Battle of Toro
Mar. 2, 1476	Europe	Battle of Granson
June 22, 1476	Europe	Battle of Morat
July 26-Aug. 10, 1476	Europe	Mehmed II invades Moldavia
Dec. 24, 1476	Europe	Assassination of Galeazzo Maria Sforza
1477-1482	Europe	WORK BEGINS ON THE SISTINE CHAPEL
1477-1600	East Asia	JAPAN'S "AGE OF THE COUNTRY AT WAR"
Jan. 5, 1477	Europe	Charles the Bold dies in the Battle of Nancy
June 12, 1477-Aug. 17, 1487	Europe	HUNGARIAN WAR WITH THE HOLY ROMAN EMPIRE
Aug. 17, 1477	Europe	FOUNDATION OF THE HABSBURG DYNASTY
Dec. 1, 1477	Europe	Hungary signs a peace treaty with the Holy Roman Empire
1478	Europe	MUSCOVITE CONQUEST OF NOVGOROD
1478-1482	Europe	ALBANIAN-TURKISH WARS END
c. 1478-1519	Europe	LEONARDO DA VINCI COMPILES HIS NOTEBOOKS
Apr. 26, 1478	Europe	PAZZI CONSPIRACY
Nov. 1, 1478	Europe	ESTABLISHMENT OF THE SPANISH INQUISITION
1479	Europe	Hungary defeats the Ottomans at the Battle of Kenyérmező
1479	Europe	Ottomans occupy the Ionian Isles
1479-1481	Middle East	Gentile Bellini paints a portrait of Sultan Mehmed II
1480	Europe	Ottomans seize Otranto
1480-1502	Europe	DESTRUCTION OF THE GOLDEN HORDE
After 1480	Europe	IVAN THE GREAT ORGANIZES THE "THIRD ROME"
1481	Europe	Aragon retakes Otranto
1481-1482	Africa	FOUNDING OF ELMINA
1481-1499	Europe	LUDOVICO SFORZA RULES MILAN
1481-1512	Middle East	REIGN OF BAYEZID II AND OTTOMAN CIVIL WARS

DATE	REGION	EVENT
Jan., 1481	Europe	Battle of Győr
May, 1481	Europe	Hungary signs a truce with the Holy Roman Empire
June, 1481	Middle East	Battle of Yenişehir
c. 1482	Africa	Portuguese explorers reach the mouth of the Congo River
1482-1484	Europe	War of Ferrara
1482-1492	Europe	MAXIMILIAN I TAKES CONTROL OF THE LOW COUNTRIES
Mar., 1482	Europe	Hungary invades Austria
1483	Europe	Ottomans annex Herzegovina
1483-1485	Europe	RICHARD III RULES ENGLAND
1484	Middle East	Construction of the mosque and complex at Nasriyya is completed
c. 1484	Europe	Sandro Botticelli paints the *Birth of Venus*
Mar. 11, 1484	Europe	Battle of Leitzersdorf
July, 1484	Europe	Ottomans capture Kiliya and Cetatea Albş
Nov., 1484	Europe	Frederick III, fleeing Vienna, resettles in Linz
1485	Europe	Muscovy annexes Tver'
c. 1485	Africa	PORTUGUESE ESTABLISH A FOOTHOLD IN AFRICA
1485	Europe	William Caxton publishes Sir Thomas Malory's *Le Morte d'Arthur*
Beginning 1485	Europe	THE TUDORS RULE ENGLAND
Jan. 29-June 1, 1485	Europe	Siege of Vienna
May, 1485-Apr. 13, 1517	Africa and Middle East	MAMLŪK-OTTOMAN WARS
Aug. 22, 1485	Europe	Battle of Bosworth Field
1486	Europe	The *Decretum majus* is proclaimed, protecting the individual rights of Hungarian subjects
c. 1486	Europe	Krämer and Sprenger publish the *Malleus maleficarum*
c. 1486	East Asia	Sesshū paints his Long Landscape Scroll
1486-1487	Europe	PICO DELLA MIRANDOLA WRITES *ORATION ON THE DIGNITY OF MAN*
Feb. 9, 1486	Middle East	First Battle of Adana
Mar. 15, 1486	Middle East	Second Battle of Adana
1487	Europe	Siege of Wiener Neustadt
1487	Europe	Torquemada becomes Grand Inquisitor of Spain
Aug., 1487-Dec., 1488	Africa	DIAS ROUNDS THE CAPE OF GOOD HOPE
1488	East Asia	Japanese Ikko take control of Kaga Province
1488-1505	East Asia	REIGN OF XIAOZONG
c. 1488-1594	South Asia	KHMER-THAI WARS
Mar. 5, 1488	East Asia	COMPOSITION OF THE *RENGA* MASTERPIECE *MINASE SANGIN HYAKUIN*
Aug. 16, 1488	Middle East	Battle of Aga-Cayiri
1489	South Asia	'ĀDIL SHAH DYNASTY FOUNDED
1489	Europe	Poland signs a peace treaty with the Ottoman Empire, and Moldavia resumes paying tribute to the sultan
1489	Europe	YORKSHIRE REBELLION
1489-1517	South Asia	Sultan Sikandar Lodī rules Delhi
1490's	Europe	ALDUS MANUTIUS FOUNDS THE ALDINE PRESS
1490's	Central Asia	DECLINE OF THE SILK ROAD
Beginning 1490	Europe	DEVELOPMENT OF THE CAMERA OBSCURA
c. 1490	South Asia	FRAGMENTATION OF THE BAHMANI SULTANATE
c. 1490	Europe	The Medici family become patrons of Michelangelo
1490	Europe	Moldavia invades Poland
c. 1490	Central Asia	Uzbeks gain control of Turkistan
1490-1492	Europe	MARTIN BEHAIM BUILDS THE FIRST WORLD GLOBE
1491	Europe	Greek is first taught at Oxford University
1491	Europe	Treaty of Pressburg
1491-1545	Africa	CHRISTIANITY IS ESTABLISHED IN THE KINGDOM OF KONGO
1492	Americas	FALL OF GRANADA

DATE	REGION	EVENT
1492	Europe	JEWS ARE EXPELLED FROM SPAIN
July, 1492	Europe	Peace of Kadzand
Oct. 12, 1492	Americas	COLUMBUS LANDS IN THE AMERICAS
1493	South Asia	Battle of Tungabhadra River
1493-1521	Americas	PONCE DE LEÓN'S VOYAGES
1493-1525	Americas	REIGN OF HUAYNA CAPAC
1493-1528	Africa	REIGN OF MOHAMMED I ASKIA
Aug. 19, 1493-Jan. 12, 1519	Europe	REIGN OF MAXIMILIAN I
1494	Europe	Ludovico Sforza receives the official title of duke of Milan
1494	Europe	SEBASTIAN BRANT PUBLISHES *THE SHIP OF FOOLS*
June 7, 1494	Europe and Americas	TREATY OF TORDESILLAS
Sept., 1494-Oct., 1495	Europe	CHARLES VIII OF FRANCE INVADES ITALY
Sept., 1494-Apr., 1559	Europe	The Italian Wars
Dec. 1, 1494	Europe	POYNINGS' LAW
Beginning c. 1495	Europe	REFORM OF THE SPANISH CHURCH
1495-1497	Europe	LEONARDO DA VINCI PAINTS *THE LAST SUPPER*
1495-1510	Americas	WEST INDIAN UPRISINGS
1496	Americas	Bartolomé Columbus founds Santo Domingo, capital of the first Spanish colony in the New World
1496	Europe	Philip, Duke of Burgundy, marries Joan of Castille
1496	Europe	Posthumous publication of the complete works of Pico della Mirandola
1496	Europe	Regiomontanus's *Epitome* of Ptolemy's *Almagest* is published
1497	Europe	CORNISH REBELLION
1497	Europe	Ivan the Great passes the *Sudebnik*, a code of common law
1497-1503	Americas	Amerigo Vespucci's voyages
Beginning 1497	Europe	DANISH-SWEDISH WARS
June 24, 1497-May, 1498	Americas	CABOT'S VOYAGES
Aug., 1497	Europe	Poland invades Moldavia
Oct. 26, 1497	Europe	Battle of Codrii Cosminului
1498	Europe	Moldavia invades Poland
1498	Europe	Ottomans annex Moldavia
1498	South Asia	Vasco da Gama reaches India
Jan., 1498	Africa	PORTUGUESE REACH THE SWAHILI COAST
1499	Europe	Amerigo Vespucci becomes the first navigator to determine longitude using lunar distances
1499	Europe	LOUIS XII OF FRANCE SEIZES MILAN
1499-1517	Europe	ERASMUS ADVANCES HUMANISM IN ENGLAND
1499-c. 1600	Europe	RUSSO-POLISH WARS
Beginning c. 1500	World	COFFEE, CACAO, TOBACCO, AND SUGAR ARE SOLD WORLDWIDE
1500	Europe	Aldus publishes Erasmus's *Adagia*
c. 1500	Europe	NETHERLANDISH SCHOOL OF PAINTING
c. 1500	Europe	REVIVAL OF CLASSICAL THEMES IN ART
c. 1500	Europe	RISE OF SARMATISM IN POLAND
1500	Europe	ROMAN JUBILEE
1500-1530's	Americas	PORTUGAL BEGINS TO COLONIZE BRAZIL
Early 16th c.	Americas	ATHAPASKANS ARRIVE IN THE SOUTHWEST
Early 16th c.	South Asia	DEVOTIONAL BHAKTI TRADITIONS EMERGE
Early 16th c.	Middle East	FUZULI WRITES POETRY IN THREE LANGUAGES
Early 16th c.	Americas	RISE OF THE FUR TRADE
16th c.	East Asia	CHINA'S POPULATION BOOM
16th c.	Americas	DECLINE OF MOUNDVILLE
16th c.	Europe	EVOLUTION OF THE GALLEON

DATE	REGION	EVENT
16th c.	Americas	IROQUOIS CONFEDERACY IS ESTABLISHED
16th c.	World	PROLIFERATION OF FIREARMS
16th c.	East Asia	RISE OF THE *SHENSHI*
16th c.	East Asia	SINGLE-WHIP REFORM
16th c.	Africa	TRANS-SAHARAN TRADE ENRICHES AKAN KINGDOMS
16th c.	World	WORLDWIDE INFLATION
1501-1504	Europe	Michelangelo sculpts his *David*
1501-1507	Central Asia	Shaybānī-Timurid War
1501-1524	Middle East	REIGN OF ISMĀ'ĪL I
1502	Middle East	Battle of Nakhichevan
1502	Africa and Americas	BEGINNING OF THE TRANSATLANTIC SLAVE TRADE
1502	Europe	Muslims are expelled from Spain
1502	Africa	Portugal occupies Kilwa
1502-1520	Americas	REIGN OF MONTEZUMA II
c. 1503	Europe	Leonardo da Vinci begins painting the *Mona Lisa*
1503	South Asia	Ramathibodi II of Ayutthaya oversees construction of an immense and priceless statue of the Buddha
1503-1513	Europe	Papacy of Julius II, the "Warrior Pope"
June, 1503	Central Asia	Battle of Akhsi
1504	Middle East	Ismā'īl seizes Baghdad
Beginning 1504	Africa	DECLINE OF THE ḤAFṢID DYNASTY
Sept. 22, 1504	Europe	TREATY OF BLOIS
Nov. 26, 1504	Europe	JOAN THE MAD BECOMES QUEEN OF CASTILE
1505	South Asia	Earthquake destroys Āgra
1505	Africa	Portuguese sack and burn Mombasa
1505-1506	Central Asia	Siege of Khiva
1505-1515	South Asia	PORTUGUESE VICEROYS ESTABLISH OVERSEAS TRADE EMPIRE
1505-1521	East Asia	REIGN OF ZHENGDE AND LIU JIN
1506	Europe	Charles Habsburg becomes ruler of the Low Countries and the Franche-Comté
1506-1543	Africa	Afonso I rules Kongo
1507	Central Asia	END OF THE TIMURID DYNASTY
1508	Europe	FORMATION OF THE LEAGUE OF CAMBRAI
1508-1520	Europe	RAPHAEL PAINTS HIS FRESCOES
1508-1512 and 1534-1541	Europe	MICHELANGELO PAINTS THE SISTINE CHAPEL
1508-1572	Americas	Spanish conquest of the Americas
1509-1565	South Asia	VIJAYANAGAR WARS
May 14, 1509	Europe	Battle of Agnadello
c. 1510	Europe	INVENTION OF THE WATCH
1510	Europe	Muscovy annexes Pskov
1510-1578	Africa	SA'DĪ SHARIFS COME TO POWER IN MOROCCO
Nov. 25, 1510	South Asia	Portugal captures Goa
Dec. 2, 1510	Central Asia	BATTLE OF MERV ESTABLISHES THE SHAYBĀNĪD DYNASTY
1511	Central Asia	Bābur seizes Samarqand and Bukhara
1511-c. 1515	South Asia	MELAKA FALLS TO THE PORTUGUESE
1512	Europe	Spain annexes Navarre
1512	Americas	Spain's Law of Burgos is passed, establishing the *encomienda* system in the Americas
1512-1520	Middle East	REIGN OF SELIM I
Apr. 11, 1512	Europe	BATTLE OF RAVENNA
Dec. 12, 1512	Central Asia	Battle of Ghazdivan
Beginning 1513	East Asia	KANŌ SCHOOL FLOURISHES
July-Dec., 1513	Europe	MACHIAVELLI WRITES *THE PRINCE*

DATE	REGION	EVENT
Aug. 16, 1513	Europe	Battle of the Spurs
Aug. 22, 1513-July 6, 1560	Europe	ANGLO-SCOTTISH WARS
Sept. 9, 1513	Europe	Battle of Flodden
Sept. 29, 1513	Americas	BALBOA REACHES THE PACIFIC OCEAN
1514	Europe	HUNGARIAN PEASANTS' REVOLT
1514	Europe	Muscovy annexes Smolensk
1514-1555	Middle East	Turko-Persian Wars
1514-1598	East Asia	PORTUGUESE REACH CHINA
Aug. 23, 1514	Middle East	Battle of Chāldirān
1515	South Asia	Battle of Lampang
1515	Europe	Emperor Maximilian I, Vladislav II of Hungary, and Sigismund I, the Old, meet in Vienna and arrange marriages that will expand the Habsburg empire
1515-1529	Europe	WOLSEY SERVES AS LORD CHANCELLOR AND CARDINAL
Sept. 13-14, 1515	Europe	BATTLE OF MARIGNANO
1516	Europe	Ludovico Ariosto publishes *Orlando furioso*
1516	Europe	SIR THOMAS MORE PUBLISHES *UTOPIA*
c. 1516-1576	Europe	Titian paints his masterpieces
Jan. 23, 1516	Europe	CHARLES I ASCENDS THE THRONE OF SPAIN
Aug. 18, 1516	Europe	CONCORDAT OF BOLOGNA
Aug. 24, 1516	Middle East	Mamlūk sultan Qānṣawh dies at the Battle of Marj Dabiq
1517	Europe	FRACASTORO DEVELOPS HIS THEORY OF FOSSILS
1517	Africa	Ottomans conquer Egypt
1517	East Asia	Portugal reaches Canton
Oct. 31, 1517	Europe	LUTHER POSTS HIS NINETY-FIVE THESES
1518	East Asia	Siege of Arai
Beginning 1519	Americas	SMALLPOX KILLS THOUSANDS OF INDIGENOUS AMERICANS
1519-1522	World	MAGELLAN EXPEDITION CIRCUMNAVIGATES THE GLOBE
Jan., 1519	America	Balboa is executed for treason
Apr., 1519-Aug., 1521	Americas	CORTÉS CONQUERS AZTECS IN MEXICO
June 28, 1519	Europe	CHARLES V IS ELECTED HOLY ROMAN EMPEROR
Nov. 8, 1519	Americas	Meeting of Montezuma II and Cortés
1520-1522	Europe	COMUNERO REVOLT
1520-1560	Europe	Western Europe experiences a temporary decrease in witch trials
1520-1566	Middle East	REIGN OF SÜLEYMAN
June 5-24, 1520	Europe	FIELD OF CLOTH OF GOLD
1521	Europe	Muscovy annexes Ryazan'
1521	East Asia	Portuguese are banned from all Chinese ports
1521-1559	Europe	VALOIS-HABSBURG WARS
1521-1567	East Asia	REIGN OF JIAJING
Apr.-May, 1521	Europe	LUTHER APPEARS BEFORE THE DIET OF WORMS
1522	Europe	Battle of Bicocca
June 28, 1522-Dec. 27, 1522	Europe	SIEGE AND FALL OF RHODES
Nov. 3, 1522-Nov. 17, 1530	Europe	CORREGGIO PAINTS THE *ASSUMPTION OF THE VIRGIN*
1523	Europe	GUSTAV I VASA BECOMES KING OF SWEDEN
1523	South Asia	Krishnadevaraya annexes parts of Bijāpur to Vijayanagar
1523	Europe	England enters the Valois-Habsburg conflict on the side of the Habsburgs
Spring, 1523	East Asia	ŌUCHI FAMILY MONOPOLIZES TRADE WITH CHINA
Aug., 1523	Americas	FRANCISCAN MISSIONARIES ARRIVE IN MEXICO
1524-1529	South Asia	Bābur conquers northern India
June, 1524-July, 1526	Europe	GERMAN PEASANTS' WAR
1525-1532	Americas	HUÁSCAR AND ATAHUALPA SHARE INCA RULE

DATE	REGION	EVENT
1525-1600	Africa	OTTOMAN-RULED EGYPT SENDS EXPEDITIONS SOUTH AND EAST
Feb., 1525	Europe	BATTLE OF PAVIA
1526	Central Asia	Kazak Empire is divided into three territories
1526-1530	South Asia	Reign of Bābur
1526-1547	Europe	HUNGARIAN CIVIL WARS
Beginning 1526	Europe and Middle East	Austro-Turkish Wars
Apr. 21, 1526	South Asia	FIRST BATTLE OF PANIPAT
Aug. 29, 1526	Europe	BATTLE OF MOHÁCS
1527	South Asia	Sack of Ava by the Maw Shans
1527-1543	Africa	ETHIOPIA'S EARLY SOLOMONIC PERIOD ENDS
1527-1547	Americas	MAYA RESIST SPANISH INCURSIONS IN YUCATÁN
1527-1554	Africa	Saʿdī-Wattasid Wars
1527-1561	Americas	Las Casas writes his *History of the Indies*
1527-1599	South Asia	BURMESE CIVIL WARS
Mar. 17, 1527	South Asia	BATTLE OF KHĀNUA
May 6, 1527-Feb., 1528	Europe	SACK OF ROME
1528	Africa	Askia Mūsā overthrows Mohammed I Askia
1528	Europe	CASTIGLIONE'S *BOOK OF THE COURTIER* IS PUBLISHED
1528-1536	Americas	NARVÁEZ'S AND CABEZA DE VACA'S EXPEDITIONS
1529	Europe	Peace of Cambrai
1529	Africa	Portuguese sack and burn a rebuilt Mombasa
1529-1574	Africa	NORTH AFRICA RECOGNIZES OTTOMAN SUZERAINTY
Mar. 7, 1529	Africa	BATTLE OF SHIMBRA-KURE
Apr. 22, 1529	Europe and South Asia	Treaty of Zaragoza confirms Portugal's claim to the Spice Islands
Sept. 27-Oct. 16, 1529	Europe	SIEGE OF VIENNA
1530's-1540's	Europe	PARACELSUS PRESENTS HIS THEORY OF DISEASE
1530	East Asia; South Asia	China recognizes Ayutthaya
Dec. 30, 1530	South Asia	HUMĀYŪN INHERITS THE THRONE IN INDIA
1531	East Asia	Hosokawa Takakuni dies in a coup
1531	South Asia	Ottoman navy helps Sultan Bahādur of Gujarat to repel Portuguese attempting to capture Diu
1531-1540	Europe	CROMWELL REFORMS BRITISH GOVERNMENT
1531-1585	Europe	ANTWERP BECOMES THE COMMERCIAL CAPITAL OF EUROPE
Feb. 27, 1531	Europe	FORMATION OF THE SCHMALKALDIC LEAGUE
1532	Europe	Charles V's *Lex Carolina* makes witchcraft a criminal offense in the Holy Roman Empire
1532	Europe	HOLBEIN SETTLES IN LONDON
1532	Europe	Machiavelli's *The Prince* is published, five years after his death
1532-1536	East Asia	TEMMON HOKKE REBELLION
1532-1537	Americas	PIZARRO CONQUERS THE INCAS IN PERU
1532-1552	Europe	François Rabelais writes *Gargantua and Pantagruel*
1533	Europe	Catherine de Médicis marries Henry, duke of Orléans
1534	Africa	Barbarossa captures Tunis
1534-1535	Middle East	OTTOMANS CLAIM SOVEREIGNTY OVER MESOPOTAMIA
Apr. 20, 1534-July, 1543	Americas	CARTIER AND ROBERVAL SEARCH FOR A NORTHWEST PASSAGE
Aug. 15, 1534	Europe	FOUNDING OF THE JESUIT ORDER
Dec. 18, 1534	Europe	ACT OF SUPREMACY
Dec. 23, 1534-1540	Europe	PARMIGIANINO PAINTS *MADONNA WITH THE LONG NECK*
1535	Africa	Charles V recaptures Tunis from the Ottomans
July, 1535-Mar., 1540	Europe	HENRY VIII DISSOLVES THE MONASTERIES
1536	Americas	Establishment of the Colegio de Santa Cruz in Tlatelolco Tenochtítlan
1536	Europe	France captures Turin

DATE	REGION	EVENT
1536	Middle East	TURKISH CAPITULATIONS BEGIN
1536 and 1543	Europe	ACTS OF UNION BETWEEN ENGLAND AND WALES
Mar., 1536	Europe	CALVIN PUBLISHES *INSTITUTES OF THE CHRISTIAN RELIGION*
May 19, 1536	Europe	Anne Boleyn is executed
Oct., 1536-June, 1537	Europe	PILGRIMAGE OF GRACE
1537	Europe	The *Bishops' Book* is published in England
1537	Europe and Americas	POPE PAUL III DECLARES RIGHTS OF NEW WORLD PEOPLES
c. 1538	Central Asia	Aq Nazak Khan reunifies Kazak Empire
1538	Europe	Charles V and Francis I meet at Nice and reaffirm the Peace of Cambrai
1538	Europe	Moldavia becomes a vassal state of the Ottoman Empire
Sept. 27-28, 1538	Middle East	BATTLE OF PRÉVEZA
1539	South Asia	JIAJING THREATENS VIETNAM
May, 1539	Europe	SIX ARTICLES OF HENRY VIII
May 28, 1539-Sept. 10, 1543	Americas	DE SOTO'S NORTH AMERICAN EXPEDITION
June, 1539	South Asia	Battle of Chausa
1540	Americas	Orrellana navigates the Amazon River
1540-1545	South Asia	SHĒR SHĀH SŪR BECOMES EMPEROR OF DELHI
Feb. 23, 1540-Oct., 1542	Americas	CORONADO'S SOUTHWEST EXPEDITION
Oct. 20-27, 1541	Africa	HOLY ROMAN EMPIRE ATTACKS OTTOMANS IN ALGIERS
1542	Europe	Francis I allies with the Ottomans against the Habsburgs; the Ottoman fleet uses the French harbor of Toulon as a base to raid the coast of Western Europe
1542	South Asia	Muslims massacre Hindus at Raisin
1542	Africa	Saʿdīs capture the Portuguese fort at Agadir
1542-1543	Europe and Americas	THE NEW LAWS OF SPAIN
Feb. 13, 1542	Europe	Catherine Howard is executed
June 27, 1542-c. 1600	Americas	SPAIN EXPLORES ALTA CALIFORNIA
July 15, 1542-1559	Europe	PAUL III ESTABLISHES THE *INDEX OF PROHIBITED BOOKS*
1543	Europe	COPERNICUS PUBLISHES *DE REVOLUTIONIBUS*
1543	Europe	VESALIUS PUBLISHES *ON THE FABRIC OF THE HUMAN BODY*
Autumn, 1543	East Asia	EUROPEANS BEGIN TRADE WITH JAPAN
1544	Europe	Coronation of Mary, Queen of Scots
1544-1628	Europe	ANGLO-FRENCH WARS
Apr. 14, 1544	Europe	Battle of Cerisolles
July 19, 1544-Sept. 14, 1544	Europe	English Siege of Boulogne
Sept., 1544	Europe	Peace of Crépy
1545-1548	Americas	SILVER IS DISCOVERED IN SPANISH AMERICA
1545-1563	Europe	COUNCIL OF TRENT
Feb. 27, 1545	Europe	BATTLE OF ANCRUM MOOR
1546	Europe	FRACASTORO DISCOVERS THAT CONTAGION SPREADS DISEASE
1546	South Asia	Vijayanagar signs a treaty of nonaggression with the Portuguese
June, 1546-June, 1547	Europe	Schmalkaldic War
Jan. 16, 1547	Europe	CORONATION OF IVAN THE TERRIBLE
Jan. 28, 1547-July 6, 1553	Europe	REIGN OF EDWARD VI
Apr. 24, 1547	Europe	Battle of Mülberg
Sept. 10, 1547	Europe	Battle of Pinkie
1548-1600	South Asia	SIAMESE-BURMESE WARS
1549	East Asia	Battle of Kajiki Castle: First use of firearms in Japanese warfare
1549	Europe	French Siege of Boulogne
1549	Europe	KETT'S REBELLION
1549-1552	East Asia	FATHER XAVIER INTRODUCES CHRISTIANITY TO JAPAN
1549-1570's	Europe	LA PLÉIADE PROMOTES FRENCH POETRY

DATE	REGION	EVENT
Mid-16th c.	Europe	DEVELOPMENT OF THE CARACOLE MANEUVER
1550's	Europe	Sofonisba Anguissola develops her style of mannerist painting
1550's	Europe	TARTAGLIA PUBLISHES *THE NEW SCIENCE*
1550's-1587	East Asia	JAPANESE PIRATES PILLAGE THE CHINESE COAST
1550's-c. 1600	Europe	EDUCATIONAL REFORMS IN EUROPE
1550-1571	East Asia	MONGOLS RAID BEIJING
1550-1593	East Asia	JAPANESE WARS OF UNIFICATION
Jan.-May, 1551	Europe	THE STOGLAV CONVENES
c. 1552	Europe	France captures the Three Bishoprics of Lorraine
1552	Europe and Americas	LAS CASAS PUBLISHES *THE TEARS OF THE INDIANS*
1552	Middle East	STRUGGLE FOR THE STRAIT OF HORMUZ
1552-1555	Central Asia	Kazak Empire repels invasions from Mongolia and Kobdo
1553	Europe	SERVETUS DESCRIBES THE CIRCULATORY SYSTEM
July, 1553	Europe	CORONATION OF MARY TUDOR
July 10-19, 1553	Europe	Lady Jane Grey is queen of England for nine days
Sept., 1553	East Asia	FIRST BATTLE OF KAWANAKAJIMA
Oct. 27, 1553	Europe	Servetus is burned as a heretic
1554	Africa	The last Wattasid is killed; Marrakech becomes the capital of Saʿdīan Morocco
Jan. 25-Feb. 7, 1554	Europe	WYATT'S REBELLION
1555-1556	Europe	CHARLES V ABDICATES
Sept. 25, 1555	Europe	PEACE OF AUGSBURG
1556-1605	South Asia	REIGN OF AKBAR
Jan. 23, 1556	East Asia	EARTHQUAKE IN CHINA KILLS THOUSANDS
Summer, 1556	Europe and Central Asia	IVAN THE TERRIBLE ANNEXES ASTRAKHAN
1557-1574	Africa	Reign of Abdallah al-Ghālib in Morocco
1557-1582	Europe	LIVONIAN WAR
Aug. 10, 1557	Europe	Battle of Saint-Quentin
1558-1593	South Asia	BURMESE-LAOTIAN WARS
1558-1603	Europe	REIGN OF ELIZABETH I
Jan. 1-8, 1558	Europe	FRANCE REGAINS CALAIS FROM ENGLAND
July 13, 1558	Europe	Battle of Gravelines
1559-1561	Middle East	SÜLEYMAN'S SONS WAGE CIVIL WAR
Apr. 3, 1559	Europe	TREATY OF CATEAU-CAMBRÉSIS
May, 1559-Aug., 1561	Europe	SCOTTISH REFORMATION
c. 1560's	Europe	INVENTION OF THE "LEAD" PENCIL
Apr. or May, 1560	Europe	PUBLICATION OF THE GENEVA BIBLE
June 12, 1560	East Asia	BATTLE OF OKEHAZAMA
1562-1565	Americas	French Huguenots attempt to colonize South Carolina and Florida, but the Spanish drive them away
Mar., 1562-May 2, 1598	Europe	FRENCH WARS OF RELIGION
1563	East Asia	Jesuit missionary Luis Frois settles in Japan
1563-1584	Europe	CONSTRUCTION OF THE ESCORIAL
Jan., 1563	Europe	THIRTY-NINE ARTICLES OF THE CHURCH OF ENGLAND
Jan. 20, 1564	Europe	PEACE OF TROYES
June, 1564	Europe	TINTORETTO PAINTS FOR THE SCUOLA DI SAN ROCCO
1565	South Asia	SPAIN SEIZES THE PHILIPPINES
Jan., 1565	South Asia	Battle of Talikota
May 18-Sept. 8, 1565	Europe	SIEGE OF MALTA
Sept., 1565	Americas	ST. AUGUSTINE IS FOUNDED
1566-1574	Middle East	REIGN OF SELIM II
July 22, 1566	Europe	PIUS V EXPELS THE PROSTITUTES FROM ROME

DATE	REGION	EVENT
1567	Europe	PALESTRINA PUBLISHES THE *POPE MARCELLUS MASS*
1567-1572	East Asia	REIGN OF LONGQING
July 29, 1567	Europe	JAMES VI BECOMES KING OF SCOTLAND
1568	Europe	Battle of Langside: Supporters of Mary, Queen of Scots are defeated, and Mary flees to England, where Elizabeth I imprisons her
1568	Americas	Jesuits found the first missionary school for North American Indians at Havana
1568	East Asia	ODA NOBUNAGA SEIZES KYŌTO
c. 1568-1571	Europe and Central Asia	OTTOMAN-RUSSIAN WAR
1568-1648	Europe	DUTCH WARS OF INDEPENDENCE
Feb. 23, 1568	South Asia	FALL OF CHITOR
1569	Europe	MERCATOR PUBLISHES HIS WORLD MAP
1569	East Asia	Siege of Odawara
Nov. 9, 1569	Europe	REBELLION OF THE NORTHERN EARLS
Feb. 25, 1570	Europe	PIUS V EXCOMMUNICATES ELIZABETH I
July, 1570-Aug., 1571	Middle East	SIEGE OF FAMAGUSTA AND FALL OF CYPRUS
c. 1571-1603	Africa	Bornu-Kanem Empire reaches the height of its power, using firearms purchased from the Ottoman Turks
Oct. 7, 1571	Europe	BATTLE OF LEPANTO
1572-1574	Europe	TYCHO BRAHE OBSERVES A SUPERNOVA
1572-1589	Europe	Siege of La Rochelle
Aug. 24-25, 1572	Europe	ST. BARTHOLOMEW'S DAY MASSACRE
1573-1582	East Asia	Oda Nobunaga deposes the shogun and unifies half of Japan under his rule
1573-1620	East Asia	REIGN OF WANLI
1574-1595	Middle East	REIGN OF MURAD III
c. 1574-1600	East Asia	Japan's Azuchi-Momoyama Period
Mid-1570's	Americas	POWHATAN CONFEDERACY IS FOUNDED
1575	Europe	Diana Mantuana moves to Rome and receives papal permission to print and sell her engravings, becoming the first sanctioned woman engraver.
1575	Europe	Saint Philip Neri founds the Institute of the Oratory in Rome
1575	Europe	TALLIS AND BYRD PUBLISH *CANTIONES SACRAE*
1575-1680	Africa	Portuguese take control of the Angolan coast
Mar. 3, 1575	South Asia	MONGOL CONQUEST OF BENGAL
June 28, 1575	East Asia	Battle of Nagashino
Nov., 1575	Europe	STEPHEN BÁTHORY BECOMES KING OF POLAND
1576	Europe	JAMES BURBAGE BUILDS THE THEATRE
1576-1612	Europe	REIGN OF RUDOLF II
June 7, 1576-July, 1578	Americas	FROBISHER'S VOYAGES
1577	South Asia	RAM DĀS FOUNDS AMRITSAR
1578	East Asia	Battle of Mimigawa
1578	Central Asia	FIRST DALAI LAMA BECOMES BUDDHIST SPIRITUAL LEADER
1578	Europe	Joseph of Volokolamsk is canonized
1578	Europe	Raphael Holinshed publishes his *Chronicles of England, Scotland, and Ireland*
1578-1590	Middle East	THE BATTLE FOR TABRĪZ
1578-1603	Africa	Reign of Aḥmad al-Manṣūr
Aug. 4, 1578	Africa	BATTLE OF KSAR EL-KEBIR
June 17, 1579	Americas	DRAKE LANDS IN NORTHERN CALIFORNIA
1580's-1590's	Europe	GALILEO CONDUCTS HIS EARLY EXPERIMENTS
1580	Europe	Formula of Concord

DATE	REGION	EVENT
1580	East Asia	Surrender of the Ōsaka Honganji, the last major military stronghold of Pure Land Buddhism
1580-1581	Europe	SPAIN ANNEXES PORTUGAL
1580-1587	South Asia	REBELLIONS IN BIHAR AND BENGAL
1580-1595	Europe	MONTAIGNE PUBLISHES HIS *ESSAYS*
c. 1580-c. 1600	South Asia	SIAMESE-CAMBODIAN WARS
1581	Central Asia	Kabul falls to Akbar
1581-1597	Central Asia	COSSACKS SEIZE SIBIR
July 26, 1581	Europe	THE UNITED PROVINCES DECLARE INDEPENDENCE FROM SPAIN
1582	Europe	GREGORY XIII REFORMS THE CALENDAR
1582	East Asia	Battle of Yamakazi
1582	East Asia	Oda Nobunaga commits suicide
1582-1598	East Asia	Toyotomi Hideyoshi completes the unification of Japan
Summer, 1582	Europe	Sir Philip Sidney writes *Astrophel and Stella*
July 21, 1582	Central Asia	BATTLE OF THE TOBOL RIVER
1583-1600	Europe	BRUNO'S THEORY OF THE INFINITE UNIVERSE
1583-1610	East Asia	MATTEO RICCI TRAVELS TO BEIJING
1584	Europe	Assassination of William of Orange
1584	Europe	Lavinia Fontina becomes the first woman publicly commissioned to produce a painting
1584-1585	Europe	Siege of Antwerp
1584-1613	Europe and Central Asia	RUSSIA'S TIME OF TROUBLES
July 4, 1584-1590	Americas	LOST COLONY OF ROANOKE
July 7, 1585-Dec. 23, 1588	Europe	WAR OF THE THREE HENRYS
Sept. 14, 1585-July 27, 1586	Americas	DRAKE'S EXPEDITION TO THE WEST INDIES
c. 1586-1593	Europe	Christopher Marlowe writes his dramas
Feb., 1586	South Asia	ANNEXATION OF KASHMIR
1587	East Asia	TOYOTOMI HIDEYOSHI HOSTS A TEN-DAY TEA CEREMONY
1587	East Asia	Toyotomi Hideyoshi issues an edict prohibiting piracy
1587-1629	Middle East	REIGN OF ʿABBĀS THE GREAT
Feb. 8, 1587	Europe	Execution of Mary, Queen of Scots
Apr., 1587-c. 1600	Europe	ANGLO-SPANISH WAR
Oct. 20, 1587	Europe	Battle of Courtras
1588-1602	Europe	RISE OF THE ENGLISH MADRIGAL
July 31-Aug. 8, 1588	Europe	DEFEAT OF THE SPANISH ARMADA
Dec. 23, 1588	Europe	Assassination of the third duke of Guise
1589	Europe	RUSSIAN PATRIARCHATE IS ESTABLISHED
1589	Middle East	SECOND JANISSARY REVOLT IN CONSTANTINOPLE
c. 1589-1613	Europe	SHAKESPEARE WRITES HIS DRAMAS
Aug. 2, 1589	Europe	HENRY IV ASCENDS THE THRONE OF FRANCE
1590's	Europe	BIRTH OF OPERA
1590	Europe	Edmund Spenser publishes *The Faerie Queene*
1590	East Asia	ODAWARA CAMPAIGN
Beginning 1590	Europe	Russo-Swedish Wars
Mar. 14, 1590	Europe	Battle of Ivry
1591	Africa	FALL OF THE SONGHAI EMPIRE
Beginning 1591	South Asia	Mogul conquest of the Deccan
After 1591	Africa	The Hausa states become a center of trans-Saharan trade in the wake of Songhai's fall
1592	Africa	Mombasa falls to Portugal and Malindi
1592	East Asia	PUBLICATION OF WU CHENGEN'S *THE JOURNEY TO THE WEST*
July 8, 1592-July 10, 1592	East Asia	Battle of the Yellow Sea
1592-1599	East Asia	JAPAN INVADES KOREA

DATE	REGION	EVENT
1593-1606	Europe and Middle East	OTTOMAN-AUSTRIAN WAR
1594-1595	East Asia	TAIKŌ KENCHI SURVEY
1594-1600	Europe	KING MICHAEL'S UPRISING
c. 1595	Europe	Zacharias Janssen produces the first compound microscope
1596	Americas	RALEGH ARRIVES IN GUIANA
Oct., 1596-Feb., 1597	East Asia	*SAN FELIPE* INCIDENT
1597-Sept., 1601	Europe	TYRONE REBELLION
Oct. 31, 1597	Europe	JOHN DOWLAND PUBLISHES *AYRES*
1598	Central Asia	ASTRAKHANID DYNASTY IS ESTABLISHED
1598	Americas	Tepic Indian miners revolt against the Spanish
Jan., 1598-Feb., 1599	Americas	OÑATE'S NEW MEXICO EXPEDITION
Apr. 13, 1598	Europe	EDICT OF NANTES
May 2, 1598	Europe	TREATY OF VERVINS
Aug. 14, 1598	Europe	Battle of Yellow Ford
Dec., 1598-May, 1599	Europe	THE GLOBE THEATRE IS BUILT
1599	Europe	CASTRATI SING IN THE SISTINE CHAPEL CHOIR
c. 1600	Americas	Spain imports sheep into the American Southwest
1600	Europe	WILLIAM GILBERT PUBLISHES *DE MAGNETE*
Oct. 21, 1600	East Asia	BATTLE OF SEKIGAHARA
Dec. 31, 1600	Europe and South Asia	ELIZABETH I CHARTERS THE EAST INDIA COMPANY

GLOSSARY

Abbey: A church, such as a monastery or nunnery, that is also a self-sufficient residence for holy men or women.

Abbott (*fem.*, abbess): The leader of a monastery or other church inhabited by people in religious seclusion.

Altarpiece: A painting that hangs in the space behind a church altar.

Annex: To absorb the territory of one political entity within another political entity.

Anti-pope: A person claiming to be the legitimate Roman Catholic pope, despite his failure to be chosen in accordance with Roman Catholic canon law.

Anti-Semitism: Hatred or persecution of Jewish people based on religion or ethnicity.

Appanage: A grant of noble title and rights of taxation over a parcel of land, such as a county, duchy, or earldom, made to the child or vassal of a ruler.

Archbishop: A bishop who, in addition to directly governing his own diocese, exercises administrative authority over the bishops of several other dioceses.

Archdeacon: A cleric who functions as assistant to a bishop.

Archdiocese: The diocese directly and solely governed by an archbishop. The archdiocese and the dioceses of the other bishops under his jurisdiction together form the archbishop's ecclesiastical province.

Archduke: A duke or prince whose territory enjoys full national sovereignty.

Assize: A civil or criminal court, especially one that sits only periodically or one that travels within its jurisdiction to sit at different places at different times.

Auto-da-fé: The public pronouncement of a sentence by a religious court of the Inquisition, followed by the public execution of that sentence by secular authorities.

Barbary: The coast of North Africa. The term "Barbary" was strongly associated with the pirates who operated in that region during the Renaissance and who preyed upon Mediterranean merchant ships.

Baron: A title of nobility. In England and Japan, barons are the lowest rank of the nobility, but in continental Europe the rank attached to the title varies in different countries.

Benefice: Land awarded in return for service rendered; the award may take the form of a secular feudal title or an ecclesiastical title granted to an individual, or it may be given to an entire church or religious or secular order.

Bey: The governor of a province of the Ottoman Empire.

Bishop: The highest-ranking priest within a diocese, responsible for the administration and guidance of all other clergy within that diocese.

Boyar: A Russian noble ranking just below the ruling prince; in the Renaissance, the boyars of Muscovy (and later of Russia) formed a council that advised and sometimes exerted significant influence over the grand prince (later the czar) in both foreign and domestic affairs.

Bull: *See* Papal bull.

Bushido: The code of conduct of the Japanese warrior class, stressing martial prowess, honor and fearlessness in battle, and unwavering loyalty to one's lord.

Byzantine Empire: An empire that succeeded Rome after Rome's fall as the major Christian power in eastern and central Europe.

Caliph: Islamic ruler claiming both spiritual and secular authority as the successor of the Prophet Muḥammad.

Camera obscura: A device, consisting of a closed box or room with a small hole in one wall, that projects images of objects outside the chamber onto the opposite wall.

Canon law: The laws governing a church, especially the Roman Catholic Church.

Caravel: A small and maneuverable full-rigged sailing ship, useful for exploring new territories but without sufficient cargo capacity to be an effective merchant vessel.

Cardinal: A high official in the Roman Catholic Church, second only to the pope. Cardinals are appointed by the pope, and the college of cardinals is the body that elects a new pope.

Carrack: A large, bulky, full-rigged sailing ship, able to carry much cargo, but lacking maneuverability.

Cathedral: A church that functions as the administrative center of a diocese and as the home church of its bishop.

Catholicism: A branch of Christianity organized in a strict hierarchy and subscribing to a complex body of religious dogma, including belief in transubstantiation, in papal infallibility, and in justification by faith in combination with good works. The two Catholic

Churches are the Roman Catholic Church and the Eastern Orthodox Church.

Chamberlain: The chief officer governing the household affairs of a royal or noble family.

Chancellor: The secretary of a king or noble.

Chancery: A court of equity in England, headed by the lord high chancellor, whose job was to hear petitions for the redress of wrongs done by the common law courts or to bypass those courts altogether and provide more just judgments than were available at common law.

Chivalry: A set of values and practices that evolved to define the ideal of knighthood in the Middle Ages, centered around courtly grace, skill in battle, honor, and devoted loyalty to the lord and lady one serves.

City-state: A sovereign state composed of a single city and its surrounding territory.

Classicism: The aesthetic and stylistic principles characteristic of ancient Greek and Roman art, and of those later artists who imitated the ancients. The major features of Renaissance classicism are harmony and balance: The composition of a work of art or the design of a building is meant to be balanced and harmonious, and the representation of a given object, especially the human body, is meant to strike a balance between the conflicting demands of realism (the body should look like a real body) and idealism (the body should be ideally beautiful).

Clergy: All ordained or otherwise recognized members of a church, from minor initiates up to and including the church leader.

Cleric: Any member of the clergy.

Colony: A territory taken and occupied by citizens of a different, usually distant, nation and often also inhabited by indigenous peoples who previously controlled the territory.

Commodity: Any good that circulates as an article of exchange in a money economy.

Commoner: Anyone who is not a member of the clergy, who is not a member of a noble family, and who is not a member of a royal family.

Communion: The consumption of consecrated bread and wine in a Christian sacrament symbolizing or enacting spiritual union with Christ.

Condottiere: The leader of a mercenary band or army.

Conquistador: A Renaissance-era Spanish explorer and conqueror, especially of the Americas.

Consort: A spouse; when used in conjunction with a royal title, consort becomes the title of a royal spouse, such as queen consort, prince consort, and so forth.

Contrapuntal: Characterized by the juxtaposition of independent melodies to form a harmonious compositional whole; polyphonic.

Corsair: A pirate or a privateer, especially one operating on the Barbary Coast.

Count: A title of nobility; in continental Western Europe, a count is equivalent in rank to an English earl.

Counter-Reformation: A movement within the Catholic Church in the sixteenth and seventeenth centuries, designed both to defeat the external threat of the Protestant Reformation and to institute reforms to respond to some of the internal issues that gave rise to Protestantism in the first place.

Court: The group of officials, councillors, and hangers-on assembled at the official residence of a monarch or other ruler. Especially in the Renaissance, European courts contained a mixture of those who wielded real power, those who served the ruler or the ministers, an entourage of people who merely desired to be near power, and practitioners of the arts who enjoyed the patronage of their ruler.

Courtier: A member of a ruler's entourage at court.

Create: To grant someone a title that did not previously exist: Thomas Howard was created earl of Suffolk in 1603.

Crusade: One of a series of medieval holy wars fought by Christian armies against Islamic forces to take control of the Holy Land. In the Renaissance, several popes and other Christian leaders desired to engage in further crusades, but their plans were never realized.

Curate: A cleric who functions as assistant to a rector or parish priest.

Czar: A Russian or other Slavic emperor. The word "czar" is derived from the Roman title caesar and is meant to suggest a ruler of equal stature to the emperors of imperial Rome.

Daimyo: A Japanese feudal lord. Daimyos first arose around the tenth century, but in the fourteenth and fifteenth centuries, a new group called the *shugo daimyō*, or military governors, developed. These were appointed by the shogun to govern large areas, but they owned only a small portion of the territory they governed. Around the mid-fifteenth century, the shugo daimyo were replaced by the *sengoku daimyō*, who generally controlled a smaller area, but whose entire territories belonged directly to them or to their vassals.

Deacon: A member of the clergy ranking just below priest in the Roman Catholic, Anglican, and Eastern

Orthodox Churches. In Roman Catholicism, the deacon is the middle rank of the three major orders, falling between priest and subdeacon in the hierarchy.

Diocese: The basic administrative and territorial unit of the Church; each diocese is governed by a bishop.

Dispensation: Official papal exemption from canon law.

Doge: Title given to the ruler of the Republic of Venice.

Dogma: The body of beliefs and doctrines formally held and sanctioned by a church.

Dowager: A widow who retains the noble or royal title or the property she derived from her husband.

Duke (*fem.*, duchess): A title of nobility or of rulership. In continental Europe, dukes often reigned as sovereigns over autonomous or semi-autonomous territories called duchies. In England, duke was the highest rank of the nobility, but it did not signify sovereign control of a territory.

Dynasty: A line of rulers who succeed one another based on their familial relationships.

Earl: A title of British nobility ranking below marquess and above viscount.

Early modern period: A value-neutral designation for the Renaissance, the term "early modern" is meant to emphasize the beginning development of the economic, technological, and social structures that would make possible the Industrial Revolution. It implicitly locates the Renaissance as the period of transition between feudalism and capitalism.

Eastern Orthodox Church: A group of self-governing Catholic churches that split off from the Roman Catholic Church in 1054. While the patriarch, or leader, of each branch of Orthodoxy is ranked hierarchically in relation to the others, each branch is essentially self-governing, and the relationship between the various branches is that of a loose federation.

Ecclesiastical: Of or relating to a church.

Emir: General title given to Islamic military commanders, rulers, and governors.

Empire: A large realm, ruled by an emperor or empress, that consists of previously distinct political units joined together under the ruler's central authority. In the Renaissance, some empires, such as the Spanish, were primarily colonial, whereas others, such as the Songhai and the Russian Empires, were primarily the result of annexing immediately adjacent territories.

Encomienda: A legal system instituted in Spain's American colonies wherein the Crown granted control over a specific number of American Indians to a conquistador or other colonizer. The recipient of the grant was given the right to exact a tribute from the Indians, and this tribute was generally paid in the form of forced labor. The recipient also gained de facto control of the land occupied by the Indians, although the land was not technically included in the grant.

Excommunicate: To formally censure and ostracize someone from a church.

Feudalism: A political and economic system characterized by a strict social hierarchy based upon each person's relationship to land. At the top is a monarch or other ruler who is the ultimate owner of all land in the country. The monarch grants lands to nobles, who in turn assign parcels to lower nobles and to serfs. The serfs must work the land and give any surplus beyond what they need to subsist to their lords, while the lords owe allegiance, including military support, to superior nobles and to their monarch.

Flank: The side of a military formation.

Folio: A book consisting of pieces of paper folded in half and bound together. The folio is a larger format than the quarto, and it was the format used for collections of plays such as Shakespeare's.

Fresco: A painting created on plaster spread directly on a wall.

Friar: A member of one of the mendicant orders of the clergy; that is, a holy man who has taken vows against owning property and who begs for sustenance.

Full-rigged: Utilizing both square and lateen (triangular) sails.

Galleon: A large, often full-rigged sailing ship used for both warfare and commerce.

Galley: A long ship driven primarily by oars and often rowed by slaves.

Gold Coast: Coastal area of West Africa, corresponding roughly with the coast of modern-day Ghana.

Golden Horde: A nation that began as the western portion of Genghis Kahn's Mongol Empire and later became autonomous. The Golden Horde dominated Russia in the late Middle Ages and early Renaissance.

Gout: A disease in which the blood is contaminated with excess amounts of uric acid and the joints become inflamed. Gout was associated with wealth in the medieval and early modern periods, because it was thought to be caused by a diet dominated by foods then available only to the rich.

Governor: The proxy representative of an emperor or central government who rules over a colony or an imperial territory; viceroy.

Grand duke: The ruler of a sovereign territory called a grand duchy; an archduke.

Grand prince: The ruler of a Russian city-state.

Groundlings: The poorer audience members at an Elizabethan play who stood in the pit near the stage.

Hadith: The collected traditions of Islam, detailing the words and deeds of Muḥammad; after the Qurʾān, one of the most important sources of Islamic law and belief.

Hagiography: Biography or study of the saints.

Halberd: A weapon in which both a pike and a battle axe are mounted on the same six-foot shaft.

Harquebus: An early, heavy matchlock firearm, often fired from a support.

Hegemony: Dominance; military hegemony in a region consists of reliable control of that region and the ability to defeat any potential invaders or insurgents.

Heresy: Making a statement or holding a belief that contradicts established church dogma. In the Renaissance, heresy against the Roman Catholic Church constituted a serious crime subject to punishments up to and including death.

Heretic: Someone judged to have committed heresy.

House: A royal or noble family.

Humanism: A Renaissance intellectual and artistic movement emphasizing individualism, secularism, rational critical thought, and an embrace of classicism in art and literature. adj.: Humanist.

Humanistic: Relating to a broad concern with the values or tenets associated with Humanism; "humanistic" applies to more general and less systematic beliefs and practices than does "Humanist."

Imam: An Islamic religious and political leader.

Indigenous: Native to a particular region.

Individualism: The belief that the individual is the most important unit of society, and that society and social structures should protect the interests of each of its individual members.

Indulgence: In Roman Catholicism, remission of punishment either on Earth or in Purgatory, granted for a sin that has already been confessed and forgiven and whose eternal punishment in Hell has therefore already been remitted. Indulgences were granted in exchange either for an act of penance or for money.

Infidel: One who does not believe in a particular religion.

Inquisition: A Roman Catholic court of religious inquiry charged with discovering and punishing heresy.

Invest: Formally to place someone in office, especially a religious office such as a bishopric.

Ivory Coast: Coastal area of West Africa, corresponding roughly with the coast of the modern-day Republic of Côte d'Ivoire.

Janissary: An elite soldier of the Ottoman Empire.

Jihad: Islamic holy war.

Khan: Title given to Tatar, Turkish, Chinese, and Mongolian rulers, warlords, and tribal leaders.

King: The ruler of a kingdom. In the Renaissance, most kingdoms were still essentially feudal in their political structures; that is, all nobles were vassals of the king (either directly, or indirectly as vassals of superior nobles), and the king ruled by virtue of the combined political and military support of these vassals.

Lateen-rigged: Utilizing triangular sails.

Latitude: The distance between a given point on Earth and the earth's equator, expressed in angular degrees.

Legate: *See* Papal legate.

Liturgy: Any public rite or ceremony of the Church.

Longitude: The distance between a given point on Earth and a line (called the prime meridian) that extends from the North Pole to the South Pole, expressed in angular degrees.

Lord: In a feudal society, a person who grants land rights to a vassal in return for service.

Lord deputy: In Ireland, a governor who functions as the indirect representative of the English crown, subordinate to the lord lieutenant.

Lord lieutenant: The direct representative of the English crown in Ireland, equivalent to a viceroy.

Lord protector: *See* Protector.

Madrigal: An a cappella, polyphonic, secular song; the form flourished in and is distinctive of the sixteenth and seventeenth centuries.

Mamlūk: (1) A soldier in an Islamic army of slaves. (2) A dynasty of sultans that employed such slave armies to rule Egypt and Syria from the mid-thirteenth to early sixteenth centuries.

Mannerism: A late-Renaissance artistic movement that developed in reaction to High Renaissance classicism. Mannerism was characterized by stylistic techniques designed to express the point of view of the artist, rather than techniques that effaced the artist to represent beautiful ideal forms realistically. Mannerists were also interested in representing liminal objects and experiences—infinite space, miraculous revelation, motion captured in the static image—that challenged the type of realism characteristic of Renaissance classicism.

March: A border territory, especially one that is or was originally used as a defensive boundary against invasion.

Margrave: A title of European nobility equivalent in rank to an English marquess.

Marquess: An English noble ranking between an earl and a duke (originally the earl of a march).

Mass: The Roman Catholic liturgy performed in conjunction with the taking of Communion.

Matchlock: A firing mechanism employed in early firearms. The gun is fired by applying a slow-burning match directly to a gunpowder charge through a hole in the weapon's breech.

Mendicant: A member of any religious order that takes vows against owning property and begs for the order's daily subsistence needs.

Mercantilism: An economic system characterized by centralized governmental control of trade, manufacturing, and agriculture, through which the government seeks to accumulate wealth and strengthen the national economy. Mercantilism arose in several European Renaissance countries to stabilize their economies during the decline of feudalism.

Mercenary: A soldier who fights for wages, especially one hired by a foreign government.

Metropolitan: In Eastern Orthodoxy, the equivalent of an archbishop.

Minister: In a secular context, a minister in the Renaissance was an adviser to a monarch or other head of state. In a religious context, minister is the Protestant title given to a cleric with the same rank or function as a Catholic priest.

Mission: A colonial ministry whose task is to convert indigenous people to Christianity.

Missionary: An agent of the Church commissioned to travel to a colony or other distant location to gain converts.

Modern: Characterized by the economic, technological, and social structures of industrial capitalism and the nation-state.

Monastery: A home for monks or other persons living in accordance with religious vows. *See also* nunnery

Monk: A man who has taken religious vows of self-privation, and who lives in seclusion or semiseclusion from the material world.

Monopoly: Control by one person, group, or government over a raw material, commodity, or trade route.

Motet: A sacred, polyphonic, choral song, usually performed a cappella.

Movable type: A set of individual letters or characters used for printing that can be placed in any sequence to form words and can be reused and reordered to form new words. Moveable type is the basis of the printing press, although it was invented several centuries before the press itself.

Mysticism: The belief that personal, subjective experience can transcend its limitations and result in direct, objective knowledge of God, truth, or reality.

Nation-state: A modern, sovereign nation, ruled by a centralized government, which enjoys an absolute legal monopoly on violence within its borders.

Nativity: A representation of the birth of Jesus Christ.

Naturalism: An artistic style emphasizing the realistic portrayal of an object as it appears in nature.

Neo-Confucianism: A philosophical and spiritual movement involving the resurgence and reinterpretation of the teachings of the Chinese sage Confucius.

Neopaganism: A Renaissance artistic movement in which pagan images and themes from antiquity were reintroduced into painting. Such motifs often existed alongside orthodox Christian themes and images.

Netherlandish school: A school of painting that combined Renaissance Humanist sensibilities and concerns with an inherited gothic tradition very different from the classical tradition that shaped the Italian Humanists. Notable for the representation of light and a distinctive approach to symbolism.

Noble: In a feudal society, any member of the landed aristocracy, who derive their titles and lands from lord/vassal relationships.

Nun: A woman who has taken religious vows of self-privation, and who lives in seclusion or semiseclusion from the material world.

Nunnery: A home for nuns or other persons living in accordance with religious vows.

Oyer and terminer: A commission authorizing a judge or panel of judges sitting at the assizes to hear a specific case or complaint.

Palette: The set of colors or tones commonly used by a given artist or artistic school.

Papal bull: A formal order or decree issued by the pope.

Papal legate: An emissary or ambassador of the papacy.

Papal nuncio: A papal legate sent as a permanent envoy to a particular government and residing at the seat of that government.

Papal States: A sovereign Italian city-state, based in Rome, ruled by the pope and serving as the spiritual seat of his papacy.

Parish: The portion of a diocese under the care of a single pastor or priest.

Parliament: An assembly of representatives, usually a mix of nobles, clergy, and commoners, that functions as a legislative body serving under the sovereignty of a monarch.

Paşa: The highest title of rank or honor in the Ottoman Empire. In the Renaissance, the title generally attached to governors of foreign territories and to viziers of the domestic government.

Patriarch: The head of one of the self-governing branches of the Eastern Orthodox Church.

Patron: A person who financially or materially supports an artist, composer, poet, or other creator.

Peasant: The lowest rank of commoner, who works the land in order to subsist.

Perspective: A system for mapping the three-dimensional world onto a two-dimensional surface in a mathematically precise fashion. In perfect or "true" perspective, the size of any image varies as the inverse of the square of its (represented) distance from the observer. In other words, if a tree that is 10 feet away is painted 1 inch tall, a tree of the same height that is 20 feet away will be painted 1/4 inch tall, and a tree of the same height that is 30 feet away will be painted 1/9 inch tall.

Pietà: An image of the Virgin Mary mourning over the body of Jesus Christ.

Pike: A heavy spear with an extremely long shaft.

Polyphonic: Characterized by the juxtaposition of independent melodies to form a harmonious compositional whole; contrapuntal.

Pope: The spiritual leader of the Roman Catholic Church and temporal ruler of the Papal States.

Pre-Columbian: Relating to events in the Americas before the arrival of Christopher Columbus.

Prelate: Any superior cleric holding an office that has jurisdiction over lower clerics. Prelates include bishops, abbots, archdeacons, and administrative church officials such as provosts or deans.

Pretender: Someone who falsely claims to be a rightful ruler. Since the "right" of a ruler in the Renaissance was often asserted and defended by force, a pretender who succeeded in overthrowing a sitting monarch was no longer a pretender.

Priest: A holy man sanctified and authorized to perform the central rites and ceremonies of a religion. In Roman Catholicism, the title "priest" attaches to clerics who rank between bishop and deacon in the religious hierarchy.

Primate: A bishop who exercises authority over several ecclesiastical provinces. A primate is more powerful than an archbishop, who governs the dioceses within a single province.

Prior (*fem.*, prioress): A cleric in a position of monastic authority. Originally a generic term, the precise rank and duties of a prior vary widely between orders and denominations, but he is often either the leader of a small monastery or the highest-ranking assistant to an abbot.

Privateer: A pirate or pirate ship commissioned or licensed by a government to raid the ships of other nations.

Protector: Title sometimes given to a regent, signifying that he is both the protector of the young monarch and the protector of the realm during the monarch's youth.

Protestantism: A branch of Christianity, incorporating many different churches, that rejects the doctrine of papal infallibility and that believes in justification by faith alone and in a priesthood of all believers who read the Bible for themselves rather than having it interpreted to them by the clergy.

Quarto: A book printed on pages the size of a quarter sheet of paper each. Renaissance quartos were best suited to publishing individual plays or short collections of poetry, as opposed to the larger folio editions of collected works.

Quattrocento: Fifteenth century conventions of Italian art and literature, especially those techniques considered to mark the beginning of the Early Renaissance and to lay the foundation for the High Renaissance.

Queen mother: A former queen who is the mother of the current ruler.

Rector: A religious leader. In some Protestant churches, the leader of a parish; in the Roman Catholic Church, the head of a church that has no pastor or a cleric who shares duties with a pastor.

Reformation: The Protestant movements that swept through Europe during the Renaissance, ending Catholicism's position as the sole form of Christianity.

Regent: One who temporarily governs in place of a monarch or other ruler who is too young or infirm to govern for him- or herself.

Renaissance: A general term for the resurgence of cultural production in a given area, the Renaissance also refers to the specific flourishing of art and culture during the transition from medieval to modern political, economic, and social structures in Western Europe in the fifteenth and sixteenth centuries.

Republic: A political unit not ruled by a monarch, especially one governed by a group of representatives chosen by and responsible to its citizens. In Renaissance republics, the citizenry was still a small subsection of the populace.

Ronin: A masterless samurai. Because serving one's master well was the central value of the samurai code of bushido, ronin were usually considered dishonorable, either because they had failed their lord or because they had willfully rejected the code.

Sack: The plundering of a captured city or territory.

Samurai: A member of the Japanese warrior caste, especially a warrior who serves a daimyo and who subscribes to a strict code of conduct called bushido.

Schism: A split or division within a formerly unified entity, especially a formal split within a church or other religious institution.

Secular: Nonreligious, either in content or in context. Thus, secular can be a simple antonym for religious, but it can also refer to members of the clergy who live and act in the public sphere rather than spending their lives in religious seclusion in a monastery or abbey.

See: The seat of power of a high-ranking cleric, such as a bishop, archbishop, or pope.

Serf: A peasant bound to the land through a feudal contract. Serfs were given a parcel of land to live and work on, but any surplus they produced was owed to their landlord as rent, tax, or tribute.

Sharia: Islamic holy law.

Shia, Shī'ite: Members of the branch of Islam that believes that Ali and the imams are the only rightful successors of Muḥammad and that the last imam will someday return.

Shogun: Japanese military ruler.

Siege: A military operation in which a city or other territory is cut off from the outside world in order to compel its surrender when food and other supplies are exhausted.

Silk Road: A land-based trading route between China and the West, the Silk Road was largely superceded by the discovery of sea routes between the West and the East.

Square-rigged: Utilizing square or rectangular sails.

Stadholder: A provincial governor of the Netherlands. The stadholders were initially viceroys of Burgundy and of the Habsburgs, but after the Dutch Revolt, the offices became elective.

State: An autonomous, self-governing, sovereign political unit.

Succession: The passing of sovereign authority from one person or group to another person or group, or the rules governing that process.

Sultan: The political or secular ruler of an Islamic state.

Sunni: Members of the orthodox branch of Islam that considers the first four caliphs to be rightful successors of Muḥammad.

Syncretism: The combination or coexistence of radically different artistic forms, styles, technologies, cultures, beliefs, or practices.

Temporal: Dealing with the physical, material world; not spiritual.

Tribute: A regular, periodic payment by one sovereign nation to a more powerful one in return for protection or for allowing the tributary to remain sovereign.

Triptych: A set of three paintings meant to be displayed together and usually painted on three attached panels. Triptychs were commonly used as altarpieces.

Trompe l'oeil: A painting technique in which the eye is momentarily fooled into believing the painted object is a real object.

Vassal: In a feudal society, a person who gives loyalty and service to a lord in return for land.

Vicar: A cleric who represents another cleric, especially one who serves as a substitute or agent for a parish priest or a prelate.

Viceroy: A representative of an emperor or other monarch that serves as governor of a colony or province in the name of that monarch.

Viscount: A title of British nobility ranking below earl and above baron.

Vizier: Title given to high officials of Muslim nations. In the Ottoman Empire beginning around 1453, the viziers were specifically ministers to the sultan. The chief minister was known as the grand vizier, and members of the council that assisted and filled in for the grand vizier were called dome viziers. Use of the title was later expanded to include other important domestic officials, as well as provincial governors.

Wheel lock: The next evolution of the firearm after the matchlock, the wheel lock consisted of a wheel that would produce sparks from a flint when it turned, thereby eliminating the need for a match to fire the gun.

Workshop: In Renaissance Europe, a group of young artists that both aided a master in creating his works and studied the master's technique, producing works of their own in imitation of the master's style. The workshop system of apprenticeship has lead to problems of attribution for art historians, because workshop paintings were often unsigned, and apprentices' styles often resembled those of each other, as well as those of their masters.

—Andy Perry

BIBLIOGRAPHY

CONTENTS

GENERAL STUDIES AND REFERENCE WORKS

Bergin, Thomas G., and Jennifer Speake, eds. *Encyclopedia of the Renaissance and the Reformation.* Rev. ed. New York: Facts on File, 2004.

Brotton, Jerry. *The Renaissance Bazaar: From the Silk Road to Michelangelo.* New York: Oxford University Press, 2002.

Burckhardt, Jacob. *The Civilization of the Renaissance in Italy.* Introduction by Peter Gay, afterword by Hajo Holborn. New York: Modern Library, 2002.

Cameron, Euan, ed. *Early Modern Europe: An Oxford History.* New York: Oxford University Press, 1999.

Campbell, Gordon. *The Oxford Dictionary of the Renaissance.* New York: Oxford University Press, 2003.

Carney, Jo Eldridge, ed. *Renaissance and Reformation, 1500-1620: A Biographical Dictionary.* Westport, Conn.: Greenwood Press, 2000.

Dewald, Jonathan, ed. *Europe, 1450-1789: Encyclopedia of the Early Modern World.* 6 vols. New York: Charles Scribner's Sons, 2004.

Drees, Clayton J., ed. *The Late Medieval Age of Crisis and Renewal, 1330-1500: A Biographical Dictionary.* Westport, Conn.: Greenwood Press, 2000.

Grendler, Paul F. *The Renaissance: An Encyclopedia for Students.* 4 vols. New York: Charles Scribner's Sons, 2004.

———, ed. *Encyclopedia of the Renaissance.* 6 vols. New York: Charles Scribner's Sons, 1999.

Hale, J. R. *Renaissance Europe, 1480-1520.* 2d ed. London: Blackwell, 2000.

Halecki, Oscar. *Borderlands of Western Civilization: A History of Central-Western Europe.* 2d ed. Edited by Andrew L. Simon. Safety Harbor, Fla.: Simon Publications, 2000.

Hillerbrand, Hans J. *The Oxford Encyclopedia of the Reformation.* 4 vols. New York: Oxford University Press, 1996.

Hinds, Kathryn. *Life in the Renaissance.* 4 vols. Tarrytown, N.Y.: Marshall Cavendish, 2004.

Lindberg, Carter. *The European Reformations.* Cambridge, Mass.: Blackwell, 1996.

Pettegree, Andrew. *Europe in the Sixteenth Century*. Malden, Mass.: Blackwell, 2002.

Rachum, Ilan. *The Illustrated Encyclopedia of the Renaissance*. New York: Henry Holt, 1996.

Renaissance Europe, 1300-1600. Vol. 1 in *Arts and Humanities Through the Eras*. Detroit: Gale, 2004.

Rundle, David, ed. *The Hutchinson Encyclopedia of the Renaissance*. Boulder, Colo.: Westview Press, 1999.

Saari, Peggy, and Aaron Saari, eds. *Renaissance & Reformation: Almanac*. 2 vols. Detroit: UXL, 2002.

_____. *Renaissance & Reformation: Biographies*. 2 vols. Detroit: UXL, 2002.

_____. *Renaissance & Reformation: Primary Sources*. Detroit: UXL, 2002.

Taylor, Larissa J., ed. *Great Events from History: The Renaissance & Early Modern Era, 1454-1600*. Pasadena, Calif.: Salem Press, 2005.

_____. *Great Lives from History: The Renaissance & Early Modern Era, 1454-1600*. Pasadena, Calif.: Salem Press, 2005.

Thackeray, Frank W., and John E. Findling, eds. *Events That Changed the World Through the Sixteenth Century*. Westport, Conn.: Greenwood Press, 2001.

Winks, Robin W., and Lee Palmer Wandel. *Europe in a Wider World, 1350-1650*. New York: Oxford University Press, 2003.

AFRICA

Abun-Nasr, Jamil. *A History of the Maghrib*. New York: Cambridge University Press, 1987.

Anquandah, James. *Rediscovering Ghana's Past*. Harlow, Essex, England: Longman, 1982.

Brooks, Lester. *Great Civilizations of Ancient Africa*. New York: Four Winds Press, 1971.

Chambers, Catherine. *Looking Back: West African States Before Colonialism*. London: Evans Brothers, 1999.

Clancy-Smith, Julia. *North Africa, Islam, and the Mediterranean*. London: Cass, 2001.

DeCorse, Christopher R. *An Archaeology of Elmina: Americans and Europeans on the Gold Coast, 1400-1900*. Washington, D.C.: Smithsonian Institution Press, 2001.

Fage, J. D. *A History of Africa*. 4th ed. New York: Routledge, 2001.

Falola, Toyin. *The History of Nigeria*. Westport, Conn.: Greenwood Press, 1999.

_____, ed. *African History Before 1885*. Vol. 1 in *Africa*. Durham, N.C.: Carolina Academic Press, 2000.

Freeman-Grenville, G. S. P. *The Swahili Coast, Second to Nineteenth Centuries: Islam, Christianity, and Commerce in Eastern Africa*. London: Variorum Reprints, 1988.

Henze, Paul B. *Layers of Time: A History of Ethiopia*. New York: Palgrave, 2000.

Holt, P. M., and M. W. Daly. *A History of the Sudan*. London: Longman, 1988.

Hunwick, John O. *Timbuktu and the Songhay Empire*. Boston: Brill, 1999.

Kusimba, Chapurukha M. *The Rise and Fall of Swahili States*. Walnut Creek, Calif.: AltaMira Press, 1999.

Northrup, David. *Africa's Discovery of Europe, 1450-1550*. New York: Oxford University Press, 2002.

Ogot, B. A., ed. *African from the Sixteenth to the Eighteenth Century*. Vol. 5 in *General History of Africa*. Berkeley: University of California Press, 1999.

Oliver, Roland, and Anthony Atmore. *The African Middle Ages, 1400-1800*. New York: Cambridge University Press, 1981.

Page, Willie F. *Encyclopedia of African History and Culture*. 3 vols. New York: Facts on File, 2001.

Petry, Carl F., ed. *Islamic Egypt, 640-1517*. Vol. 1 in *The Cambridge History of Egypt*. New York: Cambridge University Press, 1998.

Roese, Peter M., and D. M. Bondarenko. *A Popular History of Benin: The Rise and Fall of a Mighty Forest Kingdom*. New York: Peter Lang, 2004.

Saad, Elias. *A Social History of Timbuktu: The Role of Muslim Scholars and Notables, 1400-1900*. New York: Cambridge University Press, 1983.

Wilks, Ivor. *Forests of Gold: Essays on the Akan and the Kingdom of Asante*. Athens: Ohio University Press, 1993.

Wolf, John. *The Barbary Coast and Algiers Under the Turks*. New York: Norton, 1979.

Yahya, Dahiru. *Morocco in the Sixteenth Century: Problems and Patterns in African Foreign Policy*. Atlantic Highlands, N.J.: Humanities Press, 1981.

THE AMERICAS

Bakewell, P. J. *A History of Latin America: c. 1450 to the Present*. 2d ed. Malden, Mass.: Blackwell, 2004.

Beardsell, Peter. *Europe and Latin America: Returning the Gaze*. New York: Manchester University Press, 2000.

Bolton, Herbert E. *The Spanish Borderlands: A Chronicle of Old Florida and the Southwest*. Reprint. Albuquerque: University of New Mexico Press, 1996.

Brown, Ian W., ed. *Bottle Creek: A Pensacola Culture Site in South Alabama*. Tuscaloosa: University of Alabama Press, 2003.

Brundage, Burr C. *A Rain of Darts: The Mexica Aztecs.* Austin: University of Texas Press, 1973.

Clendinnen, Inga. *Ambivalent Conquests: Maya and Spaniard in Yucatán, 1517-1570.* 2d ed. New York: Cambridge University Press, 2003.

D'Altroy, Terence N. *The Incas.* Malden, Mass.: Blackwell, 2002.

Deagan, Kathleen A., ed. *America's Ancient City, Spanish St. Augustine: 1565-1763.* New York: Garland, 1991.

Diffie, Bailey W. *A History of Colonial Brazil, 1500-1792.* Malabar, Fla.: Robert E. Krieger, 1987.

Farriss, Nancy M. *Maya Society Under Colonial Rule: The Collective Enterprise of Survival.* Princeton, N.J.: Princeton University Press, 1984.

Fergusson, Erna. *New Mexico: A Pageant of Three Peoples.* Albuquerque: University of New Mexico Press, 1973.

Francis, R. Douglas, Richard Jones, and Donald B. Smith. *Origins: Canadian History to Confederation.* 5th ed. Scarborough, Ont.: Nelson Canada, 2004.

Hemming, John. *The Conquest of the Incas.* New York: Harcourt Brace Jovanovich, 1970.

Leon-Portilla, Miguel, ed. *The Broken Spears: The Aztec Account of the Conquest of Mexico.* Boston: Beacon Press, 1992.

Longhena, Maria. *Ancient Mexico: The History and Culture of the Maya, Aztecs, and Other Pre-Columbian Peoples.* New York: Stewart, Tabori & Chang, 1998.

McInnis, Edgar, with Michael Horn. *Canada: A Political and Social History.* 4th ed. Toronto: Holt, Rinehart, and Winston of Canada, 1982.

Miller, Lee. *Roanoke: Solving the Mystery of the Lost Colony.* New York: Penguin Books, 2002.

Naipaul, V. S. *The Loss of El Dorado: A Colonial History.* New York: Vintage, 2003.

Prescott, William H. *History of the Conquest of Peru.* London: Phoenix Press, 2002.

Rountree, Helen C. *Pocahontas' People: The Powhatan Indians of Virginia Through Four Centuries.* Norman: University of Oklahoma Press, 1990.

Sauer, Carl O. *Sixteenth Century North America: The Land and the Peoples as Seen by the Europeans.* Berkeley: University of California Press, 1971.

Stannard, David E. *American Holocaust: Columbus and the Conquest of the New World.* New York: Oxford University Press, 1992.

Stick, David. *Roanoke Island: The Beginnings of English America.* Chapel Hill: University of North Carolina Press, 1983.

Townsend, Richard F. *The Aztecs.* Rev. ed. New York: Thames and Hudson, 2000.

ART AND ARCHITECTURE

Asher, Catherine B. *Architecture of Mughal India.* New York: Cambridge University Press, 1992.

Bambach, Carmen, Hugo Chapman, Martin Clayton, and George Goldner. *Correggio and Parmigianino: Master Draftsmen of the Renaissance.* London: British Museum Press, 2000.

Barnhart, Richard M., et al. *The Jade Studio: Masterpieces of Ming and Qing Painting and Calligraphy from the Wong Nan-p'ing Collection.* New Haven, Conn.: Yale University Art Gallery, 1994.

Barral i Altet, Xavier, ed. *Art and Architecture of Spain.* Boston: Little, Brown, 1998.

Baxandall, Michael. *Painting and Experience in Fifteenth-Century Italy: A Primer in the History of Pictorial Style.* 2d ed. New York: Oxford University Press, 1988.

Beach, Milo Cleveland. *Mughal and Rajput Painting.* New York: Cambridge University Press, 1992.

Beck, James. *Italian Renaissance Painting.* 2d ed. Cologne, Germany: Könemann, 1999.

Benevolo, Leonardo. *The Architecture of the Renaissance.* 2 vols. Reprint. New York: Routledge, 2002.

Blair, Sheila A. S., and Jonathan Bloom. *The Art and Architecture of Islam, 1250-1800.* New Haven, Conn.: Yale University Press, 1994.

Blunt, Anthony. *Art and Architecture in France, 1500-1700.* 5th ed. Revised by Richard Beresford. New Haven, Conn.: Yale University Press, 1999.

Borchert, Till, ed. *The Age of Van Eyck: The Mediterranean World and Early Netherlandish Painting, 1430-1530.* New York: Thames & Hudson, 2002.

Bosch, Hieronymus, et al. *Hieronymus Bosch: The Complete Paintings and Drawings.* Translated by Ted Alkins. New York: Harry N. Abrams, 2001.

Boucher, Bruce. *Andrea Palladio: The Architect in His Time.* Rev. and updated ed. New York: Abbeville Press, 1998.

Buck, Stephanie, and Jochen Sander. *Hans Holbein the Younger: Painter at the Court of Henry VIII.* London: Thames & Hudson, 2004.

Butterfield, Andrew. *The Sculptures of Andrea del Verrocchio.* New Haven, Conn.: Yale University Press, 1997.

Campbell, L. *The Fifteenth Century Netherlandish Schools.* London: National Gallery Publications, 1998.

Canby, Sheila R. *The Golden Age of Persian Art: 1501-1722*. New York: Harry N. Abrams, 2000.

Chang, Joseph, and Qianshen Ba. *In Pursuit of Heavenly Harmony: Paintings and Calligraphy by Bada Shanren from the Estate of Wang Fangyu and Sum Wai*. Washington, D.C.: Freer Gallery of Art, Smithsonian Institution, 2003.

Christensen, Carl C. *Art and the Reformation in Germany*. Athens: Ohio University Press, 1979.

Davies, David, ed. *El Greco*. New Haven, Conn.: Yale University Press, 2003.

De Vecchi, Pierluigi. *Raphael*. New York: Abbeville Press, 2002.

Gardner, Helen, et al. *Gardner's Art Through the Ages*. 11th ed. Fort Worth, Tex.: Harcourt College, 2001.

Garlake, Peter. *Early Art and Architecture of Africa*. Oxford, England: Oxford University Press, 2002.

Gill, Anton. *Il Gigante: Michelangelo, Florence, and the David, 1492-1504*. New York: T. Dunne Books, 2003.

Grafton, Anthony. *Leon Battista Alberti: Master Builder of the Italian Renaissance*. New York: Harvard University Press, 2002.

Hall, Marcia. *Michelangelo: The Frescoes of the Sistine Chapel*. New York: Abrams, 2002.

Hartt, Frederick, and David G. Wilkins. *History of Italian Renaissance Art: Painting, Sculpture, Architecture*. 5th ed. New York: H. N. Abrams, 2003.

Hopkins, Andrew. *Italian Architecture: From Michelangelo to Borromini*. New York: Thames & Hudson, 2002.

Howard, Deborah, and Sarah Quill. *The Architectural History of Venice*. Rev. and enlarged ed. with new photographs. New Haven, Conn.: Yale University Press, 2002.

Humphrey, Peter, ed. *The Cambridge Companion to Giovanni Bellini*. New York: Cambridge University Press, 2004.

Janson, H. W., and Anthony F. Janson *History of Art*. 6th ed. 2 vols. New York: Harry N. Abrams, 2001.

Kanter, Laurence B., Hilliard T. Goldfarb, and James Hankins. *Botticelli's Witness: Changing Style in a Changing Florence*. Boston: Isabella Stewart Gardner Museum, 1997.

Krischel, Roland. *Jacopo Tintoretto, 1519-1594*. Translated by Anthea Bell. Köln, Germany: Könemann, 2000.

Lavin, Marilyn Aronberg. *Piero della Francesca*. New York: Phaidon, 2002.

Lotz, Wolfgang. *Architecture in Italy, 1500-1600*. Translated by Marty Hottinger. Introduction by Deborah

Howard. New Haven, Conn.: Yale University Press, 1995.

Marani, Pietro C. *Leonardo da Vinci: The Complete Paintings*. New York: Harry N. Abrams, 2000.

Markschies, Alexander. *Icons of Renaissance Architecture*. New York: Prestel, 2003.

Meilman, Patricia, ed. *The Cambridge Companion to Titian*. New York: Cambridge University Press, 2004.

Mitchell, George. *Architecture and Art of Southern India: Vijanagara and the Successor States*. New York: Cambridge University Press, 1995.

Morse, Anne Nishimura. *Japanese Art in the Museum of Fine Arts, Boston*. Boston: Museum of Fine Arts, 1998.

Mowry, Robert D. *China's Renaissance in Bronze: The Robert H. Clague Collection of Later Chinese Bronzes, 1100-1900*. Phoenix, Ariz.: Phoenix Art Museum, 1993.

Pächt, Otto. *Venetian Painting in the Fifteenth Century: Jacopo, Gentile, and Giovanni Bellini, and Andrea Mantegna*. Edited by Margareta Vyoral-Tschapka and Michael Pächt. Translated by Fiona Elliott. London: Harvey Miller, 2003.

Phillips, Quitman E. *The Practices of Painting in Japan, 1475-1500*. Stanford, Calif.: Stanford University Press, 2000.

Phillips, Tom, ed. *Africa: The Art of a Continent*. New York: Prestel, 1995.

Price, David Hotchkiss. *Albrecht Dürer's Renaissance: Humanism, Reformation, and the Art of Faith*. Ann Arbor: University of Michigan Press, 2003.

Richter, Gottfried. *The Isenheim Altar: Suffering and Salvation in the Art of Grünewald*. Translated by Donald Maclean. Edinburgh, Scotland: Floris Books, 1998.

Roberts-Jones, Philippe, and Françoise Roberts-Jones. *Pieter Bruegel*. New York: Harry N. Abrams, 2002.

Rosand, David. *Painting in Sixteenth-Century Venice: Titian, Veronese, Tintoretto*. Rev. ed. New York: Cambridge University Press, 1997.

Sadao, Tsuneko S., and Stephanie Wada. *Discovering the Arts of Japan: A Historical Overview*. New York: Kodansha International, 2003.

Snyder, James. *Northern Renaissance Art: Painting, Sculpture, the Graphic Arts from 1350 to 1575*. New York: Harry N. Abrams, 1985.

Tatton-Brown, Tim, and Richard Mortimer, eds. *Westminster Abbey: The Lady Chapel of Henry VII*. Rochester, N.Y.: Boydell Press, 2003.

Visonà, Monica Blackmun, et al. *A History of Art in Africa*. New York: Harry N. Abrams, 2001.

Wittkower, Rudolf, Joseph Connors, and Jennifer Montagu. *Art and Architecture in Italy, 1600-1750.* 6th ed. New Haven, Conn.: Yale University Press, 1999.

BRITISH ISLES

Alford, Stephen. *Kingship and Politics in the Reign of Edward VI.* New York: Cambridge University Press, 2002.

Bevan, Bryan. *Henry VII: The First Tudor King.* London: Rubicon Press, 2000.

Black, Jeremy. *A New History of Wales.* Stroud, Gloucestershire, England: Sutton, 2000.

Brigden, Susan. *London and the Reformation.* New York: Oxford University Press, 1990.

Bucholz, Robert, and Newton Key. *Early Modern England: 1485-1714, A Narrative History.* Oxford, England: Blackwell, 2004.

Canny, Nicholas. *Making Ireland British, 1580-1650.* Oxford, England: Oxford University Press, 2003.

Doran, Susan. *England and Europe in the Sixteenth Century.* New York: St. Martin's Press, 1999.

_____. *Queen Elizabeth I.* New York: New York University Press, 2003.

Duffy, Sean. *An Illustrated History of Ireland.* New York: McGraw-Hill, 2002.

Gill, Louise. *Richard III and Buckingham's Rebellion.* Stroud, Gloucestershire, England: Sutton, 1999.

Graves, Michael A. R. *Henry VIII: A Study in Kingship.* London: Pearson Longman, 2003.

Haynes, Alan. *The Gunpowder Plot: Faith in Rebellion.* Stroud, Gloucestershire, England: Sutton, 1994.

Hicks, Michael. *English Political Culture in the Fifteenth Century.* New York: Routledge, 2002.

_____. *The Wars of the Roses, 1455-1485.* New York: Routledge, 2004.

Loades, David. *Chronicles of the Tudor Queens.* Stroud, Gloucestershire, England: Sutton, 2002.

Ridley, Jasper. *A Brief History of the Tudor Age.* New York: Carroll & Graf, 2002.

Shagan, Ethan H. *Popular Politics and the English Reformation.* New York: Cambridge University Press, 2003.

Smith, Lacey Baldwin. *This Realm of England, 1399 to 1688.* Vol. 2 in *A History of England*, edited by Lacey Baldwin Smith. 7th ed. Lexington, Mass.: D. C. Heath, 1996.

Solt, Leo F. *Church and State in Early Modern England, 1509-1640.* New York: Oxford University Press, 1990.

Starkey, David. *Six Wives: The Queens of Henry VIII.* New York: HarperCollins, 2003.

CENTRAL ASIA

Allworth, Edward A. *The Modern Uzbeks: From the Fourteenth Century to the Present: A Cultural History.* Stanford, Calif.: The Hoover Institute, 1990.

Burton, Audrey. *The Bukharans: A Dynastic, Diplomatic, and Commercial History, 1550-1702.* New York: St. Martin's Press, 1997.

Franck, Irene M., and David M. Brownstone. *The Silk Road: A History.* New York: Facts on File, 1986.

Grousset, René. *The Empire of the Steppes: A History of Central Asia.* Translated by Naomi Walford. New Brunswick, N.J.: Rutgers University Press, 1970.

Kalter, Johannes, and Margareta Pavaloi. *Uzbekistan: Heir to the Silk Road.* New York: W. W. Norton, 1997.

McCauley, Martin. *Afghanistan and Central Asia: A Short History.* Boston: Pearson Longman, 2002.

CHINA

Chan, Albert. *The Glory and Fall of the Ming Dynasty.* Norman: University of Oklahoma Press, 1982.

Dreyer, Edward L. *Early Ming China: A Political History, 1355-1435.* Stanford, Calif.: Stanford University Press, 1982.

Ebrey, Patricia Buckley. *The Cambridge Illustrated History of China.* New York: Cambridge University Press, 1996.

Fairbank, John King, and Merle Goldman. *China: A New History.* Enlarged ed. Cambridge, Mass.: Harvard University Press, 1998.

Franck, Irene M., and David M. Brownstone. *The Silk Road: A History.* New York: Facts on File, 1986.

Gernet, Jacques. *A History of Chinese Civilization.* New York: Cambridge University Press, 1990.

Hook, Brian, and Denis Twitchett, eds. *The Cambridge Encyclopedia of China.* 2d ed. Cambridge, England: Cambridge University Press, 1991.

Huang, Ray. *1587, A Year of No Significance: The Ming Dynasty in Decline.* New Haven, Conn.: Yale University Press, 1981.

Hucker, Charles O. *The Ming Dynasty: Its Origins and Evolving Institutions.* Ann Arbor: Center for Chinese Studies, the University of Michigan, 1978.

Lach, Donald. *Asia in the Making of Europe.* 3 vols. Chicago: University of Chicago Press, 1965-1993.

Mote, Frederick W. *Imperial China, 900-1800.* Cambridge, Mass.: Harvard University Press, 1999.

Paludan, Ann. *Chronicle of the Chinese Emperors. The Reign-by-Reign Record of the Rulers of Imperial China.* London: Thames and Hudson, 1998.

Ricci, Matteo. *China in the Sixteenth Century: The Journals of Matteo Ricci, 1583-1610.* Translated by Louis J. Gallagher, foreword by Richard J. Cushing, Archbishop of Boston. New York: Random House, 1953.

Spence, Jonathan D. *The Search for Modern China.* 2d ed. New York: W. W. Norton, 1999.

Twitchett, Denis, and Frederick W. Mote, eds. *The Ming Dynasty, 1368-1644.* Vol 7 in *The Cambridge History of China.* Cambridge, England: Cambridge University Press, 1998.

Zhu, Dongyun. *Biography of Zhang Juzheng.* Shanghai: Shanghai Press, 1989.

EAST CENTRAL EUROPE

Lendvai, Paul. *The Hungarians: A Thousand Years of Victory in Defeat.* Translated by Ann Major. Princeton, N.J.: Princeton University Press, 2003.

Sadoveanu, Mihail. *The Life of Stephen the Great.* Vol. 3 in *Classics of Romanian Literature.* New York: Columbia University Press, 1991.

Sedlar, Jean W. *East Central Europe in the Middle Ages, 1000-1500.* Vol. 3 in *A History of East Central Europe.* Seattle: University of Washington Press, 1994.

Engel, Pál. *The Realm of St. Stephen: A History of Medieval Hungary, 895-1526.* New York: I. B. Tauris, 2001.

Sugar, Peter F. *Southeastern Europe Under Ottoman Rule, 1354-1804.* Vol. 5 in *A History of East Central Europe.* Seattle: University of Washington Press, 1977.

Sugar, Peter F., Peter Hanak, and Tibor Frank, eds. *A History of Hungary.* Bloomington: Indiana University Press, 1994.

Varga, Domokos G. *Hungary in Greatness and Decline: The Fourteenth and Fifteenth Centuries.* Translated by Martha S. Liptaks. Budapest: Corvina Kiadó, 1982.

EDUCATION AND SCHOLARSHIP. *See also* PHILOSOPHY

Bejczy, István. *Erasmus and the Middle Ages: The Historical Consciousness of a Christian Humanist.* Boston: Brill, 2001.

Black, Robert. *Humanism and Education in Medieval and Renaissance Italy.* New York: Cambridge University Press, 2001.

Bushnell, Rebecca W. *A Culture of Teaching: Early Modern Humanism in Theory and Practice.* Ithaca, N.Y.: Cornell University Press, 1996.

Grafton, Anthony. *Joseph Scaliger: A Study in the History of Classical Scholarship.* 2 vols. New York: Oxford University Press, 1983-1994.

Grafton, Anthony, and Lisa Jardine. *From Humanism to the Humanities.* Cambridge, Mass.: Harvard University Press, 1986.

Grendler, Paul F. *Schooling in Renaissance Italy: Literacy and Learning, 1300-1600.* Baltimore: Johns Hopkins University Press, 1989.

Kallendorf, Craig W., ed. and trans. *Humanist Educational Treatises.* Cambridge, Mass.: Harvard University Press, 2002.

Morris, Jan, ed. *The Oxford Book of Oxford.* Oxford, England: Oxford University Press, 1978.

Pfeiffer, Rudolf. *History of Classical Scholarship from 1300 to 1850.* New York: Oxford University Press, 1976.

Schoeck, R. J. *Erasmus of Europe: The Making of a Humanist, 1467-1500.* 2 vols. Savage, Md.: Barnes & Noble Books, 1990.

EXPLORATION

Adorno, Rolena, and Patrick Charles Pautz. *Alvar Nuñez Cabeza de Vaca: His Account, His Life, and the Expedition of Pánfilo de Narváez.* 3 vols. Lincoln: University of Nebraska Press, 1993.

Arciniegas, Germán. *Why America? Five Hundred Years of a Name: The Life and Times of Amerigo Vespucci.* Translated by Harriet de Onís. 2d ed. Bogotá, Colombia: Villegas Editores, 2002.

Aronson, Marc. *Sir Walter Ralegh and the Quest for El Dorado.* New York: Houghton Mifflin, 2000.

Bawlf, Samuel. *The Secret Voyage of Sir Francis Drake, 1577-1580.* Vancouver, B.C.: Douglas & McIntyre, 2003.

Bergreen, Laurence. *Over the Edge of the World: Magellan's Terrifying Circumnavigation of the Globe.* New York: William Morrow, 2003.

Cieza de León, Pedro de. *The Discovery and Conquest of Peru: Chronicles of the New World Encounter.* Edited and translated by Alexandra Parma Cook and Noble David Cook. Durham, N.C.: Duke University Press, 1998.

Cortés, Hernán. *Letters from Mexico.* Translated and edited by A. R. Pagden. New York: Grossman, 1971.

Coulter, Tony. *Jacques Cartier, Samuel de Champlain, and the Explorers of Canada.* New York: Chelsea House, 1993.

Cuyvers, Luc. *Into the Rising Sun: Vasco da Gama and the Search for the Sea Route to the East.* New York: TV Books, 1999.

Firstbrook, Peter. *The Voyage of the Matthew: John Cabot and the Discovery of North America.* London: BBC Books, 1997.

Flint, Richard, and Shirley Cushing Flint, eds. *The Coronado Expedition: From the Distance of 460 Years.* Albuquerque: University of New Mexico Press, 2003.

Fuson, Robert H. *Juan Ponce de Léon and the Spanish Discovery of Puerto Rico and Florida.* Blacksburg, Va.: McDonald & Woodward, 2000.

Hudson, Charles. *Knights of Spain, Warriors of the Sun: Hernando de Soto and the South's Ancient Chiefdoms.* Athens: University of Georgia Press, 1997.

Lehane, Brendan. *The Northwest Passage.* Alexandria, Va.: Time-Life Books, 1981.

McDermott, James. *Martin Frobisher: Elizabethan Privateer.* New Haven, Conn.: Yale University Press, 2001.

Morison, Samuel Eliot. *The Great Explorers: The European Discovery of America.* New York: Oxford University Press, 1978.

_____. *Admiral of the Ocean Sea: A Life of Christopher Columbus.* Rev. ed. New York: Book-of-the-Month Club, 1992.

Parry, J. H. *The Discovery of South America.* New York: Taplinger, 1979.

Winius, George D., ed. *Portugal, the Pathfinder: Journeys from the Medieval Toward the Modern World, 1300-ca. 1600.* Madison, Wis.: Hispanic Seminary of Medieval Studies, 1995.

Wright, Louis B. *West and by North: North America Seen Through the Eyes of Its Seafaring Discoverers.* New York: Delacorte Press, 1971.

FRANCE

Baumgartner, Frederic. *France in the Sixteenth Century.* New York: St. Martin's Press, 1995.

Garrisson, Janine. *A History of Sixteenth-Century France, 1483-1598.* Translated by Richard Rex. London: Macmillan, 1995.

Heller, Henry. *Iron and Blood: Civil Wars in Sixteenth Century France.* Montreal, Que.: McGill-Queen's University Press, 1991.

Holt, Mack P. *The French Wars of Religion, 1562-1629.* Cambridge, England: Cambridge University Press, 1995.

_____. *Renaissance and Reformation France.* Oxford, England: Oxford University Press, 2002.

Knecht, R. J. *Catherine de' Medici.* New York: Longman, 1998.

_____. *French Renaissance Monarchy: Francis I and Henry II.* 2d ed. New York: Longman, 1996.

Love, Ronald S. *Blood and Religion: The Conscience of Henri IV, 1553-1593.* Ithaca, N.Y.: McGill-Queen's University Press, 2001.

Mentzer, Raymond A., and Andrew Spicer, eds. *Society and Culture in the Huguenot World, 1559-1685.* New York: Cambridge University Press, 2002.

Potter, David. *A History of France, 1460-1560: The Emergence of a Nation State.* Basingstoke, Hampshire, England: Macmillan, 1995.

Vaughan, Richard. *Charles the Bold: The Last Valois Duke of Burgundy.* New ed. Rochester, N.Y.: Boydell & Brewer, 2004.

HOLY ROMAN EMPIRE, GERMANY, AND AUSTRIA

Blockmans, Wim. *Emperor Charles V, 1500-1558.* Translated by Isola van den Hoven-Vardon. London: Arnold, 2002.

Brook-Shepherd, Gordon. *The Austrians: A Thousand Year Odyssey.* New York: Carroll & Graf, 1996.

Detwiler, Donald S. *Germany: A Short History.* Carbondale: Southern Illinois University Press, 1976.

Fichtner, Paula Sutter. *Ferdinand I of Austria: The Politics of Dynasticism in the Age of the Reformation.* New York: Columbia University Press, 1982.

_____. *The Habsburg Monarchy, 1490-1848: Attributes of Empire.* New York: Palgrave Macmillan, 2003.

Fulbrook, Mary. *A Concise History of Germany.* 2d ed. New York: Cambridge University Press, 2004.

Hsia, R. Po-chin. *The German People and the Reformation.* Ithaca, N.Y.: Cornell University Press, 1988.

Hughes, Michael. *Early Modern Germany, 1477-1806.* Philadelphia: University of Pennsylvania Press, 1992.

Maehl, William H. *Germany in Western Civilization.* Tuscaloosa: University of Alabama Press, 1979.

Maltby, William. *The Reign of Charles V.* New York: Palgrave, 2002.

Okey, Robin. *The Habsburg Monarchy: From Enlightenment to Eclipse.* New York: St. Martin's Press, 2000.

Scribner, R. W., and C. Scott Dixon. *The German Reformation.* 2d ed. New York: Palgrave Macmillan, 2003.

Stayer, James M. *The German Peasants' War and the Anabaptist Community of Goods.* Montreal, Que.: McGill-Queen's University Press, 1991.

INDIA

Ahmad, Aziz. *Studies in Islamic Culture in the Indian Environment.* Oxford, England: Oxford University Press, 1999.

Bābur. *The Bāburnāma.* Edited and translated by Wheeler M. Thackston. Introduction by Salman Rushdie. New York: Modern Library, 2002.

Chandra, Satish. *Essays on Medieval Indian History.* New Delhi, India: Oxford University Press, 2003.

Eraly, Abraham. *The Last Spring: The Lives of the Great Mughals.* New Delhi, India: Viking, 1997.

Erskine, William. *A History of India Under the Two First Sovereigns of the House of Taimur, Baber and Humayun.* New York: Barnes and Nobles, 1972.

Foltz, Richard C. *Mughal India and Central Asia.* New York: Oxford University Press, 2001.

Jayapalan, N. *Medieval History of India.* Delhi, India: Atlantic, 2001.

Karashima, Noboru. *Towards a New Formation: South Indian Society Under Vijayanagar Rule.* Oxford, England: Oxford University Press, 1997.

Keay, John. *A History of India.* New York: Atlantic Monthly Press, 2000.

Khan, Iqtidar Alam. *Akbar and His Age.* New Delhi, India: Northern Book Centre, 1999.

Pearson, M. N. *The Portuguese in India.* New York: Cambridge University Press, 1987.

Richards, John F. *The Mughal Empire.* New York: Cambridge University Press, 1993.

Sarkar, Jadunath. *The Muslim Period, 1200 A.D.-1757 A.D.* Vol.2 in *The History of Bengal.* Delhi, India: B. R. Publishing, 2003.

Shastry, B. S. *Goa-Kanara Portuguese Relations, 1498-1763.* Edited by Charles J. Borges. New Delhi, India: Concept, 2000.

Stein, Burton. *Vijayanagara.* New York: Cambridge University Press, 1989.

Streusand, Douglas E. *The Formation of the Mughal Empire.* Paperback ed. Delhi, India: Oxford University Press, 1999.

Wolpert, Stanley. *A New History of India.* New York: Oxford University Press, 2000.

Ziad, Zeenut, ed. *The Magnificent Mughals.* New York: Oxford University Press, 2002.

INVENTION AND TECHNOLOGY. *See also* SCIENCE

Basalla, George. *The Evolution of Technology.* New York: Cambridge University Press, 1988.

Dohrn-van Rossum, Gerhard. *History of the Hour: Clocks and Modern Temporal Orders.* Translated by Thomas Dunlap. Chicago: University of Chicago Press, 1996.

Hammond, John H. *The Camera Obscura.* Bristol, England: Adam Hilger, 1981.

Lane, Frederic Chapin. *Venetian Ships and Shipbuilders of the Renaissance.* Baltimore: Johns Hopkins University Press, 1992.

Misa, Thomas J. *Leonardo to the Internet: Technology and Culture from the Renaissance to the Present.* Baltimore: Johns Hopkins University Press, 2004.

Petroski, Henry. *The Pencil: A History of Design and Circumstance.* New York: Alfred A. Knopf, 2003.

Wheatley, Joseph. *Historic Sail: The Glory of the Sailing Ship from the Thirteenth to the Nineteenth Century.* London: Greenhill Books, 2000.

ITALY

Abulafia, David, ed. *The French Descent into Renaissance Italy, 1494-1495: Antecedents and Effects.* Brookfield, Vt.: Ashgate, 1995.

Arbel, Benjamin. *Cyprus, the Franks, and Venice, Thirteenth-Sixteenth Centuries.* Burlington, Vt.: Ashgate, 2000.

Cohen, Elizabeth S., and Thomas V. Cohen. *Daily Life in Renaissance Italy.* Westport, Conn.: Greenwood Press, 2002.

Connell, William J., ed. *Society and Individual in Renaissance Florence.* Berkeley: University of California Press, 2002.

Fletcher, Stella, and Christine Shaw, eds. *The World of Savonarola: Italian Elites and Perceptions of Crisis.* Burlington, Vt.: Ashgate, 2000.

Greenblatt, Miriam. *Lorenzo de Medici and Renaissance Italy.* New York: Benchmark Books, 2003.

Hays, Denys, and John Law. *Italy in the Age of the Renaissance, 1380-1530.* New York: Longman, 1989.

Martines, Lauro. *Power and Imagination: City States in Renaissance Italy.* New York: Alfred A. Knopf, 1979.

Morris, Jan. *The Venetian Empire.* London: Penguin Books, 1990.

Najemy, John M., ed. *Italy in the Age of the Renaissance, 1300-1500.* New York: Oxford University Press, 2004.

Norwich, John Julius (Lord). *A History of Venice.* New York: Alfred A. Knopf, 1982.

Pyle, Cynthia M. *Milan and Lombardy in the Renaissance: Essays in Cultural History.* Rome: La Fenice, 1997.

Rowland, Ingrid D. *The Culture of the High Renaissance: Ancients and Moderns in Sixteenth Century Rome.* New York: Cambridge University Press, 1998.

Stinger, Charles L. *The Renaissance in Rome.* 1st paperback ed. with a new preface by the author. Bloomington: Indiana University Press, 1998.

JAPAN

Beasley, W. G. *The Japanese Experience: A Short History of Japan.* Berkeley: University of California Press, 1999.

Berry, Mary E. *The Culture of Civil War in Kyoto.* Berkeley: University of California Press, 1994.

_____. *Hideyoshi.* Cambridge, Mass.: Harvard University Press, 1990.

Bowring, Richard, and Peter Kornicki. *The Cambridge Encyclopedia of Japan.* New York: Cambridge University Press, 1993.

Bryant, Anthony. *Sekigahara, 1600: The Final Struggle for Power.* London: Osprey Books, 1996.

Hall, John W., et al., eds. *Sengoku and Edo.* Vol. 4 in *The Cambridge History of Japan.* Cambridge, England: Cambridge University Press, 1991.

Hall, John W., and Toyoda Takeshi. *Japan in the Muromachi Age.* Cornell East Asia Series 109. Ithaca, N.Y.: East Asia Program, Cornell University, 2000.

Hall, John W., Nagahara Keiji, and Kozo Yamamura, eds. *Japan Before Tokugawa: Political Consolidation and Economic Growth, 1500 to 1650.* Princeton, N.J.: Princeton University Press, 1981.

Henshall, Kenneth G. *A History of Japan: From Stone Age to Superpower.* New York: St. Martin's Press, 1999.

Kang, Etsuko Hae-jin. *Diplomacy and Ideology in Japanese-Korean Relations: From the Fifteenth to the Eighteenth Century.* New York: St. Martin's Press, 1997.

Kitagawa, Joseph. *Religion in Japanese History.* New York: Columbia University Press, 1990.

Lach, Donald. *Asia in the Making of Europe.* 3 vols. Chicago: University of Chicago Press, 1965-1993.

McMullin, Neil. *Buddhism and the State in Sixteenth-Century Japan.* Princeton, N.J.: Princeton University Press, 1984.

Murdoch, James. *A History of Japan During the Century of Early Foreign Intercourse, 1542-1651.* Vol. 2 in *A History of Japan.* Reprint. New York: Routledge, 1996.

Okakura, Kakuzo. *The Book of Tea.* Tokyo: Kodansha International, 1989.

Souyri, Pierre. *The World Turned Upside Down: Medieval Japanese Society.* Translated by Käthe Roth. New York: Columbia University Press, 2001.

Yu Song-nyong. *The Book of Corrections: Reflections on the National Crisis During the Japanese Invasions of Korea, 1592-1598.* Translated by Choi Byonghyon. Berkeley, Calif.: Institute of East Asian Studies, 2002.

JEWISH STUDIES

Bonfil, Roberto. *Jewish Life in Renaissance Italy.* Translated by Anthony Oldcorn. Berkeley: University of California Press, 1994.

_____. *The World of the Renaissance Jew: The Life and Thought of Abraham ben Mordecai Farissol.* Cincinnati, Ohio: Hebrew Union College Press, 1981.

Brooks, Andrée Aelion. *The Woman Who Defied Kings: The Life and Times of Doña Gracia Nasi, a Jewish Leader During the Renaissance.* St. Paul, Minn.: Paragon House, 2002.

Edwards, John, ed. and trans. *The Jews in Western Europe, 1400-1600.* New York: Manchester University Press, 1995.

Katz, Israel J., and M. Mitchell Serels, eds. *Studies on the History of Portuguese Jews from Their Expulsion in 1497 Through Their Dispersion.* New York: Sepher-Hermon Press, 2000.

Meyerson, Mark D. *A Jewish Renaissance in Fifteenth Century Spain.* Princeton, N.J.: Princeton University Press, 2004.

Netanyahu, Benzion. *The Origins of the Inquisition in Fifteenth Century Spain.* New York: Random House, 1995.

Paris, Erna. *The End of Days: A Story of Tolerance, Tyranny, and the Expulsion of the Jews from Spain.* Amherst, N.Y.: Prometheus Books, 1995.

Roth, Norman. *Conversos, Inquisition, and the Expulsion of the Jews from Spain.* Madison: University of Wisconsin Press, 2002.

Ruderman, David B. *Essential Papers on Jewish Culture in Renaissance and Baroque Italy.* New York: New York University Press, 1992.

Sapir Abulafia, Anna. *Christians and Jews in the Twelfth Century Renaissance.* London: Routledge, 1995.

Shulvass, Moses A. *The Jews in the World of the Renaissance.* Translated by Elvin I. Kose. Leiden, the Netherlands: Brill, 1973.

KOREA

Kang, Etsuko Hae-jin. *Diplomacy and Ideology in Japanese-Korean Relations: From the Fifteenth to the Eighteenth Century.* New York: St. Martin's Press, 1997.

Park, Yune-hee. *Admiral Yi Sun-sin and His Turtleboat Armada.* Seoul, Korea: Sinsaeng, 1973.

Yu Song-nyong. *The Book of Corrections: Reflections on the National Crisis During the Japanese Invasions of Korea, 1592-1598.* Translated by Choi Byonghyon. Berkeley, Calif.: Institute of East Asian Studies, 2002.

LAW

Grewe, Wilhelm G. *The Epochs of International Law.* Translated and revised by Michael Byers. New York: Walter de Gruyter, 2000.

Janin, Hunt. *Medieval Justice: Cases and Laws in France, England, and Germany, 500-1500.* Jefferson, N.C.: McFarland, 2004.

Maitland, Frederic W., and Francis C. Montague. *A Sketch of English Legal History.* Edited by James F. Colby. Reprint. Union, N.J.: The Lawbook Exchange, 1998.

Meron, Theodor. *War Crimes Law Comes of Age: Essays.* New York: Oxford University Press, 1998.

Witte, John, Jr. *From Sacrament to Contract: Marriage, Religion, and Law in the Western Tradition.* Louisville, Ky.: Westminster John Knox Press, 1997.

_____. *Law and Protestanism: The Legal Teachings of the Lutheran Reformation.* Foreword by Martin E. Marty. New York: Cambridge University Press, 2002.

LITERATURE

Andrews, Walter, Najaat Black, and Mehmet Kalpakli. *Ottoman Lyric Poetry: An Anthology.* Austin: University of Texas Press, 1997.

Beecher, Donald, Massimo Ciavolella, and Roberto Fedi, eds. *Ariosto Today: Contemporary Perspectives.* Bloomington: University of Indiana Press, 1985.

Berger, Harry. *The Absence of Grace: Sprezzatura and Suspicion in Two Renaissance Courtesy Books.* Stanford, Calif.: Stanford University Press, 2000.

Brand, C. P. *Ludovico Ariosto: A Preface to the Orlando Furioso.* Edinburgh, Scotland: Edinburgh University Press, 1974.

Burke, Peter. *The Fortunes of the Courtier: The European Reception of Castligione's "Cortegiano."* University Park: Pennsylvania State University Press, 1996.

Camões, Luis de, et al. *Epic and Lyric.* Edited by L. C. Taylor. Translated by Keith Bosley. Manchester, England: Carcanet, 1990.

Dudbridge, Glen. *The His-yu Chi: A Study of Antecedents to the Sixteenth-Century Chinese Novel.* Cambridge, England: Cambridge University Press, 1970.

Field, P. J. C. *The Life and Times of Sir Thomas Malory.* Rochester, N.Y.: D. S. Brewer, 1999.

Freeman, Michael. *François Villon in His Works: The Villian's Tale.* Amsterdam: Rodopi, 2000.

Günsberg, Maggie. *The Epic Rhetoric of Tasso: Theory and Practice.* Oxford, England: European Humanities Research Centre, Modern Humanities Research Association, 1998.

Hadfield, Andrew, ed. *The Cambridge Companion to Spenser.* New York: Cambridge University Press, 2001.

Hale, Thomas A. *Scribe, Griot, and Novelist: Narrative Interpreters of the Songhay Empire.* Gainesville: University of Florida Press, 1990.

Hampton, Timothy. *Literature and the Nation in the Sixteenth Century: Inventing Renaissance France.* Ithaca, N.Y.: Cornell University Press, 2001.

Horton, H. Mack. *Song in an Age of Discord: The Journal of Sōchō and Poetic Life in Late Medieval Japan.* Stanford, Calif.: Stanford University Press, 2002.

Irele, F. Abiola, and Simon Gikandi, eds. *The Cambridge History of African and Caribbean Literature.* 2 vols. New York: Cambridge University Press, 2004.

Jaikishandas, Sadani, trans. *Rosary of Hymns (Selected Poems) of Surdas.* New Delhi: Wiley Eastern, 1991.

Keene, Donald. *Seeds of the Heart: Japanese Literature from the Earliest Times to the Late Sixteenth Century.* New York: Henry Holt, 1993.

Klein, Lisa M. *The Exemplary Sidney and the Elizabethan Sonneteer.* Newark: University of Delaware Press, 1998.

Lewis, Bernard. *Music of a Distant Drum: Classical Arabic, Persian, Turkish, and Hebrew Poems.* Princeton University Press, 2001.

Looney, Dennis. *Compromising the Classics: Romance Epic Narrative in the Italian Renaissance.* Detroit: Wayne State University Press, 1996.

McGinn, Donald J. *Thomas Nashe.* Boston: Twayne, 1981.

Malio, Nouhou, et al. *The Epic of Askia Mohammed.* Translated, edited, and annotated by Thomas A. Hale. Bloomington: Indiana University Press, 1996.

Maurreu, Pierre. *The Image of Ivan the Terrible in Russian Folklore*. New York: Cambridge University Press, 1987.

Monteiro, George. *The Presence of Camões: Influences on the Literature of England, America, and Southern Africa*. Lexington: University Press of Kentucky, 1996.

Parente, James A., Jr., Richard Erich Schade, and George C. Schoolfield. *Literary Culture in the Holy Roman Empire, 1555-1720*. Chapel Hill: University of North Carolina Press, 1991.

Parkin, John. *Interpretations of Rabelais*. Lewiston, N.Y.: E. Mellen Press, 2002.

Qu, Xiaoqiang. *Unsettled Questions in "The Journey to the West."* Chengdu, China: Sichuan People's Press, 1994.

Rebhom, Wayne A. *Courtly Performances: Masking and Festivity in Castiglione's "Book of the Courtier."* Detroit: Wayne State University Press, 1978.

Ronsard, Pierre de. *Selected Poems*. Translated and edited by Malcolm Quainton and Elizabeth Vinestock. London: Penguin Classics, 2002.

Sagarra, Eda, and Peter Skrine. *A Companion to German Literature: From 1500 to the Present*. Malden, Mass.: Blackwell, 1997.

Taylor, Jane H. M. *The Poetry of François Villon: Text and Context*. New York: Cambridge University Press, 2001.

Willett, Laura, ed. and trans. *Poetry and Language in Sixteenth-Century France: Du Bellay, Ronsard, Sébillet*. Toronto: Centre for Reformation and Renaissance Studies, 2004.

Zegura, Elizabeth Chesney, ed. *The Rabelais Encyclopedia*. Westport, Conn.: Greenwood Press, 2004.

MALTA

Bradford, Ernle. *The Shield and the Sword: The Knights of St. John, Jerusalem, Rhodes, and Malta*. New York: E. P. Dutton, 1973.

Goodwin, Stefan. *Malta, Mediterranean Bridge*. Westport, Conn.: Bergin & Garvey, 2002.

MATHEMATICS

Burton, David M. *The History of Mathematics: An Introduction*. 5th ed. Boston: McGraw-Hill, 2003.

Field, J. V. *The Invention of Infinity: Mathematics and Art in the Renaissance*. Oxford, England: Oxford University Press, 1997.

Gladstone-Millar, Lynne. *John Napier: Logarithm John*. Edinburgh: National Museums of Scotland, 2003.

Hay, Cynthia, ed. *Mathematics from Manuscript to Print*. New York: Oxford University Press, 1988.

Neal, Katherine. *From Discrete to Continuous: The Broadening of Number Concepts in Early Modern England*. Boston: Kluwer Academic, 2002.

MEDICINE AND DISEASE

Arrizabalaga, Jon, John Henderson, and Roger French. *The Great Pox: The French Disease in Renaissance Europe*. New Haven, Conn.: Yale University Press, 1997.

Cantor, David, ed. *Reinventing Hippocrates*. Burlington, Vt.: Ashgate, 2002.

Carlino, Andrea. *Books of the Body: Anatomical Ritual and Renaissance Learning*. Translated by John Tedeschi and Anne C. Tedeschi. Chicago: University of Chicago Press, 1999.

Debus, Allen G. *The Chemical Philosophy: Paracelsian Science and Medicine in the Sixteenth and Seventeenth Centuries*. Mineola, N.Y.: Dover Publications, 2002.

Eustachi, Bartolomeo. *A Little Treatise on the Teeth: The First Authoritative Book on Dentistry (1563)*. Edited and introduced by David A. Chernin and Gerald Shklar. Canton, Mass.: Science History Publications, 1999.

Fenn, Elizabeth. *Pox Americana*. New York: Hill and Wang, 2001.

Fracastoro, Girolamo. *Fracastoro's "Syphilis": Introduction, Text, Translations, and Notes with a Computer-Generated Word Index*. Edited by Geoffrey Eatough. Liverpool, Lancashire, England: F. Cairns, 1984.

French, Roger. *Ancients and Moderns in the Medical Sciences: From Hippocrates to Harvey*. Brookfield, Vt.: Ashgate, 2000.

Friedman, Meyer, and Gerald W. Friedland. *Medicine's Ten Greatest Discoveries*. New Haven, Conn.: Yale University Press, 2000.

Furdell, Elizabeth Lane. *Publishing and Medicine in Early Modern England*. Rochester, N.Y.: University of Rochester Press, 2002.

Grell, Ole Peter, and Andrew Cunningham, eds. *Medicine and the Reformation*. New York: Routledge, 1993.

Harrison, Mark. *Disease and the Modern World: 1500 to the Present Day*. Malden, Mass.: Polity Press, 2004.

Huppert, George. *After the Black Death: A Social History of Early Modern Europe*. Bloomington: Indiana University Press, 1998.

McConchie, Roderick W. *Lexicography and Physicke: The Record Of Sixteenth-Century English Medical Terminology.* New York: Oxford University Press, 1997.

Paracelsus. *Four Treatises Together with Selected Writings.* Birmingham, Ala.: Classics of Medicine Library, 1988.

Persaud, T. V. N. *A History of Anatomy: The Post-Vesalian Era.* Springfield, Ill.: Charles C Thomas, 1997.

Sawday, Jonathan. *The Body Emblazoned: Dissection and the Human Body in Renaissance Culture.* New York: Routledge, 1995.

Stillwell, John Maxson. *Paracelsus: His Personality and Influence as Physician, Chemist and Reformer.* Belle-Fourche, S.D.: Kessinger, 1997.

Wear, A., R. K. French, and I. M. Lonie, eds. *The Medical Renaissance of the Sixteenth Century.* New York: Cambridge University Press, 1985.

MIDDLE EAST. *See also* **OTTOMAN EMPIRE**

Al-Rasheed, Madawi. *A History of Saudi Arabia.* New York: Cambridge University Press, 2002.

Fisher, Sydney Nettleton, and William Ochsenwald. *The Middle East: A History.* 6th ed. Boston: McGraw-Hill, 2004.

Jackson, Peter, ed. *The Timurid and Safavid Periods.* Vol. 6 in *The Cambridge History of Iran.* New York: Cambridge University Press, 1986.

Melville, Charles, ed. *Safavid Persia: The History and Politics of an Islamic Society.* New York: St. Martin's Press, 1996.

Peterson, J. E. *Historical Dictionary of Saudi Arabia.* Asian Historical Dictionaries 14. Washington, D.C.: Scarecrow Press, 1993.

MUGHAL EMPIRE. *See* **INDIA**

MUSIC

Apel, Willi. *The History of Keyboard Music to 1700.* Translated by Hans Tischler. Bloomington: Indiana University Press, 1972.

Arnold, Alison, ed. *South Asia, The Indian Subcontinent.* Vol. 5 in *Garland Encyclopedia of World Music.* New York: Garland, 2000.

Brown, Howard Mayer, and Louise K. Stein. *Music in the Renaissance.* 2d ed. Upper Saddle River, N.J.: Prentice Hall, 1999.

Cho, Gene J. *The Discovery of Musical Equal Temperament in China and Europe in the Sixteenth Century.*

Studies in the History and Interpretation of Music 93. Lewiston, N.Y.: E. Mellen Press, 2003.

Danielson, Virginia, Scott Marcus, and Dwight Reynolds, eds. *The Middle East.* Vol. 6 in *Garland Encyclopedia of World Music.* New York: Garland, 2002.

Fenlon, Iain. *Music and Culture in Late Renaissance Italy.* New York: Oxford University Press, 2002.

Hanning, Barbara Russano. *Concise History of Western Music.* 2d ed. New York: Norton, 2002.

Harley, John. *William Byrd: Gentleman of the Chapel Royal.* Brookfield, Vt.: Ashgate, 1997.

Keister, Jay. *Shaped by Japanese Music: Nagauta Shamisen in Tokyo.* New York: Routledge, 2004.

Meconi, Honey. *Pierre de la Rue and Musical Life at the Habsburg-Burgundian Court: Beginnings.* New York: Oxford University Press, 2003.

Nettle, Bruno, and Ruth M. Stone, eds. *The Garland Encyclopedia of World Music.* New York: Garland, 1998- .

Ongaro, Giulio. *Music of the Renaissance.* Westport, Conn.: Greenwood Press, 2003.

Owens, Jessie Ann. *Composers at Work: The Craft of Musical Composition, 1450-1600.* Oxford, England: Oxford University Press, 1997.

Parker, Roger, ed. *The Oxford Illustrated History of Opera.* Oxford, England: Oxford University Press, 2001.

Perkins, Leeman L. *Music in the Age of the Renaissance.* New York: Norton, 1999.

Poulton, Diana. *John Dowland.* Rev. ed. Berkeley: University of California Press, 1982.

Sadie, Stanley, ed. *The New Grove Dictionary of Music and Musicians.* 2d ed. 29 vols. New York: Grove, 2001.

Stone, Ruth M., ed. *Africa.* Vol. 1 in *Garland Encyclopedia of World Music.* New York: Garland, 1998.

Whitwell, David. *Aesthetics of Music in Sixteenth Century Italy, France, and Spain.* Northridge, Calif.: Winds, 1996.

THE NETHERLANDS AND BELGIUM

Blom, J. C. H., and Emil Lamberts. *History of the Low Countries.* Translated by James C. Kennedy. New York: Berghahn Books, 1999.

Darby, Graham, ed. *The Origins and Development of the Dutch Revolt.* New York: Routledge, 2001.

Israel, Jonathan. *Dutch Republic: Its Rise, Greatness, and Fall, 1477-1806.* Oxford, England: Clarendon, 1995.

Nicholas, David. *Medieval Flanders.* London: Longman, 1992.

Rady, Martyn. *From Revolt to Independence: The Netherlands, 1550-1650.* London: Hodder & Stoughton, 1990.

Rowen, Herbert H., ed. *The Low Countries in Early Modern Times.* New York: Walker, 1972.

Schama, Simon. *The Embarrassment of Riches: An Interpretation of Dutch Culture in the Golden Age.* New York: Vintage, 1997.

Swart, K. W. *William of Orange and the Revolt of the Netherlands, 1572-84.* Translated by J. C. Grayson, edited by R. P. Fagel, M. E. H. N. Mout, and H. F. K. van Nierop. Burlington, Vt.: Ashgate, 2003.

OTTOMAN EMPIRE. *See also* **MIDDLE EAST**

Ahmed, S. Z. *The Zenith of an Empire: The Glory of the Suleiman the Magnificent and the Law Giver.* New York: Weatherhill, 2001.

Bicheno, Hugh. *Crescent and Cross: The Battle of Lepanto, 1571.* London: Cassell, 2003.

Bridge, Antony. *Suleiman the Magnificent, Scourge of Heaven.* New York: Franklin Watts, 1983.

Brumitt, Palmira. *Ottoman Seapower and Levantine Diplomacy in the Age of Discovery.* Albany: State University of New York Press, 1994.

Faroqhi, Suraiya. *Subjects of the Sultan: Culture and Daily Life in the Ottoman Empire.* New York: I. B. Tauris, 2000.

Goffman, Daniel. *The Ottoman Empire and Early Modern Europe.* London: Cambridge University Press, 2002.

Imber, Colin. *The Ottoman Empire, 1300-1650.* New York: Palgrave Macmillan, 2004.

McCarthy, Justin. *The Ottoman Turks: An Introductory History to 1923.* New York: Longman, 1997.

Somel, Selcuk Aksin. *Historical Dictionary of the Ottoman Empire.* Lanham, Md.: Scarecrow Press, 2003.

Turnbull, Stephen. *The Ottoman Empire, 1326-1699.* New York: Routledge, 2004.

THE PAPACY

Chamberlin, E. R. *The Bad Popes.* Stroud, Gloucestershire, England: Sutton, 2003.

Collins, Michael. *The Fisherman's Net: The Influence of the Papacy on History.* Chester Springs, Pa.: Dufour Editions, 2003.

Coppa, Frank J., ed. *Great Popes Through History: An Encyclopedia.* Westport, Conn.: Greenwood Press, 2002.

Maxwell-Stuart, P. G. *Chronicles of the Popes.* London: Thames & Hudson, 1997.

Rendina, Claudio. *The Popes: Histories and Secrets.* Translated by Paul D. McCusker. Santa Ana, Calif.: Seven Locks Press, 2002.

Setton, Kenneth M. *The Papacy and the Levant, 1204-1571.* 4 vols. Philadelphia: The American Philosophical Society, 1984.

Shaw, Christine. *Julius II: The Warrior Pope.* London: Blackwell, 1997.

Wright, A. D. *The Early Modern Papacy: From the Council of Trent to the French Revolution, 1564-1789.* New York: Longman, 2000.

PHILOSOPHY

Berthrong, John H. *Transformations of the Confucian Way.* Boulder, Colo.: Westview Press, 1998.

Bellitto, Christopher M., Thomas M. Izbicki, and Gerald Christianson, eds. *Introducing Nicholas of Cusa: A Guide to a Renaissance Man.* New York: Paulist Press, 2004.

Cophenhaver, Brian P., and Charles B. Schmitt. *Renaissance Philosphy.* New York: Oxford University Press, 1992.

Feng, Yu-lan. *The Period of Classical Learning.* Vol. 2 in *A History of Chinese Philosophy.* Translated by Derk Bodde. Princeton, N.J.: Princeton University Press, 1983.

French, Peter A., Howard K. Wettstein, and Bruce Silver, eds. *Renaissance and Early Modern Philosophy.* Malden, Mass.: Blackwell, 2002.

Gatti, Hilary, ed. *Giordano Bruno: Philosopher of the Renaissance.* Aldershot, Hampshire, England: Ashgate, 2002.

Gaukroger, Stephen. *Francis Bacon and the Transformation of Early-Modern Philosophy.* New York: Cambridge University Press, 2001.

Hartie, Ann. *Michel de Montaigne: Accidental Philosopher.* New York: Cambridge University Press, 2003.

Ivanhoe, Philip J. *Ethics in the Confucian Tradition: The Thought of Mengzi and Wang Yangming.* 2d ed. Indianapolis, Ind.: Hackett, 2002.

Kristeller, Paul Oskar. *Renaissance Thought and Its Sources.* New York: Columbia University Press, 1979.

McConica, James, Anthony Quinton, Anthony Kenny, and Peter Burke. *Renaissance Thinkers.* New York: Oxford University Press, 1993.

Raffini, Christine. *Marsilio Ficino, Pietro Bembo, Baldassare Castiglione: Philosophical, Aesthetic, and Political Approaches in Renaissance Platonism.* New York: P. Lang, 1998.

Yamaki, Kazuhiko, ed. *Nicholas of Cusa: A Medieval Thinker for the Modern Age.* Richmond, Surrey, England: Curzon Press, 2002.

POLAND

Jasienica, Pawel. *Jagiellonian Poland.* Translated by Alexander Jordan. Miami, Fla.: American Institute of Polish Culture, 1978.

Lukowski, Jerzy, and Hubert Zawadzki. *A Concise History of Poland.* New York: Cambridge University Press, 2001.

Tazbir, Janusz. *Poland: A Rampart of Christian Europe.* Warsaw, Poland: Interpress, 1987.

POLITICAL SCIENCE

Elton, Geoffrey R. *The Tudor Constitution, Documents, and Commentary.* 2d ed. Cambridge, England: Cambridge University Press, 1982.

Fernández-Santamaría, J. A. *The State, War, and Peace: Spanish Political Thought in the Renaissance, 1516-1559.* Cambridge, England: Cambridge University Press, 1977.

Kelly, Donald R. *François Hotman: A Revolutionary's Ordeal.* Princeton, N.J.: Princeton University Press, 1972.

Mattingly, Garrett. *Renaissance Diplomacy.* New York: Dover Publications, 1988.

Myers, A. R. *Parliaments and Estates in Europe to 1789.* New York: Harcourt Brace Jovanovich, 1975.

O'Donovan, Oliver, and Joan Lockwood O'Donovan, eds. *From Irenaeus to Grotius: A Sourcebook in Christian Political Thought, 100-1625.* Grand Rapids, Mich.: William B. Eerdmans, 1999.

Pocock, J. G. A. *The Machiavellian Moment: Florentine Political Thought and the Atlantic Republican Tradition.* 2d ed. Princeton, N.J.: Princeton University Press, 2003.

Richardson, Glenn. *Renaissance Monarchy: The Reigns of Henry VIII, Francis I, and Charles V.* New York: Oxford University Press, 2002.

Skinner, Quentin. *Machiavelli: A Very Short Introduction.* Rev. ed. New York: Oxford University Press, 2000.

_____. *The Foundations of Modern Political Thought.* 2 vols. Cambridge, England: Cambridge University Press, 1978.

Tuck, Richard. *Philosophy and Government, 1572-1651.* New York: Cambridge University Press, 1993.

Viroli, Maurizio. *Machiavelli.* New York: Oxford University Press, 1998.

PORTUGAL

Anderson, James M. *The History of Portugal.* Westport, Conn.: Greenwood Press, 2000.

Birmingham, David. *A Concise History of Portugal.* Cambridge, England: Cambridge University Press, 2003.

Diffie, Bailey, and George D. Winius. *Foundations of the Portuguese Empire, 1415-1580.* Minneapolis: University of Minnesota Press, 1977.

Gomes, Rita Costa. *The Making of a Court Society: Kings and Nobles in Late Medieval Portugal.* Translated by Alison Aiken. New York: Cambridge University Press, 2003.

Hanson, Carl. *Atlantic Emporium: Portugal and the Wider World, 1147-1497.* New Orleans: University Press of the South, 2001.

Marques, Antonio Henrique R. de Oliveira. *History of Portugal.* 2d ed. New York: Columbia University Press, 1976.

Russell-Wood, A. J. R. *The Portuguese Empire, 1415-1808: A World on the Move.* Reprint. Baltimore: Johns Hopkins University Press, 1998.

Subrahmanyan, S. *The Portuguese Empire in Asia.* London: Oxford University Press, 1993.

Wheeler, Douglas L. *Historical Dictionary of Portugal.* Lanham, Md.: Scarecrow Press, 2002.

PRINTING AND THE BIBLE

Bennett, Adelaide Louise. *Medieval Mastery: Book Illumination from Charlemagne to Charles the Bold, 800-1475.* Turnhout, Belgium: Brepols, 2002.

Daniell, David. *The Bible in English: Its History and Influence.* New Haven, Conn.: Yale University Press, 2003.

_____. *William Tyndale: A Biography.* New Haven, Conn.: Yale University Press, 2001.

Edwards, Mark U. *Printing, Propaganda, and Martin Luther.* Berkeley: University of California Press, 1994.

Febvre, Lucien, and Henri-Jean Martin. *The Coming of the Book: The Impact of Printing, 1450-1800.* Translated by David Gerard, edited by Geoffrey Nowell-Smith and David Wooter. London: Foundations of History Library. 1997.

Lowry, Martin. *The World of Aldus Manutius: Business and Scholarship in Renaissance Venice.* Ithaca, N.Y.: Cornell University Press, 1979.

McGrath, Alister E. *In the Beginning: The Story of the King James Bible and How It Changed a Nation, a Language, and a Culture.* New York: Anchor Books, 2002.

Man, John. *Gutenberg: How One Man Remade the World with Words.* New York: John Wiley & Sons, 2002.

Moynahan, Brian. *God's Bestseller: William Tyndale, Thomas More, and the Writing of the English Bible— A Story of Martyrdom and Betrayal.* New York: St. Martin's Press, 2003.

Rhodes, Neil, and Jonathan Sawday, eds. *The Renaissance Computer: Knowledge Technology in the First Age of Print.* New York: Routledge, 2000.

RELIGION AND THEOLOGY

Atkinson, James. *Martin Luther and the Birth of Protestantism.* Reprint. Atlanta: John Knox Press, 1981.

Brecht, Martin. *Luther: His Road to the Reformation, 1483-1521.* Translated by James L. Schaff. Philadelphia: Fortress Press, 1985.

Burnett, Amy Nelson. *The Yoke of Christ: Martin Bucer and the Christian Discipline.* Kirksville: Northeast Missouri State University, 1994.

Cottret, Bernard. *Calvin: A Biography.* Translated by M. Wallace McDonald. Grand Rapids, Mich.: W. B. Eerdmans, 2000.

Criveller, Gianni. *Preaching Christ in Late Ming China: Jesuits' Presentation of Christ from Matteo Ricci to Giulio Aleni.* Taipei, Taiwan, Republic of China: Taipei Ricci Institute, 1997.

Davidson, Nicholas S. *The Counter Reformation.* Oxford, England: Blackwell, 1987.

Dobbins, James C. *Jodo Shinshu: Shin Buddhism in Medieval Japan.* Honolulu: University of Hawaii Press, 2002.

Donnelly, John Patrick. *Ignatius of Loyola: Founder of the Jesuits.* New York: Longman, 2004.

Estep, William R. *The Anabaptist Story: An Introduction to Sixteenth-Century Anabaptism.* 3d rev. and enlarged ed. Grand Rapids, Mich.: William B. Eerdmans, 1996.

Fine, Lawrence. *Physician of the Soul, Healer of the Cosmos: Isaac Luria and His Kabbalistic Fellowship.* Stanford, Calif.: Stanford University Press, 2003.

Fisher, John. *English Works of John Fisher, Bishop of Rochester, 1469-1535: Sermons and Other Writings, 1520 to 1535.* Edited by Cecilia A. Hatt. New York: Oxford University Press, 2002.

Gordon, Bruce. *The Swiss Reformation.* New York: Manchester University Press, 2002.

Hillar, Marian, and Claire S. Allen. *Michael Servetus: Intellectual Giant, Humanist, and Martyr.* New York: University Press of America, 2002.

Howells, Edward. *John of the Cross and Teresa of Avila: Mystical Knowing and Selfhood.* New York: Crossroad, 2002.

Jedin, Hubert. *The Medieval and Reformation Church: An Abridgment of "History of the Church."* Vol. 5. New York: Crossroad, 1993.

Jelsma, Auke. *Frontiers of the Reformation: Dissidence and Orthodoxy in Sixteenth-Century Europe.* Brookfield, Vt.: Ashgate, 1998.

Kottman, Karl A., ed. *Catholic Millenarianism: From Savonarola to the Abbé Grégoire.* Vol. 2 in *Millenarianism and Messianism in Early Modern European Culture.* Boston: Kluwer, 2001.

Lonsdale, David. *Eyes to See, Ears to Hear: An Introduction to Ignatian Spirituality.* Rev. ed. Maryknoll, N.Y.: Orbis Books, 2000.

Luebke, David M., ed. *The Counter-Reformation: The Essential Readings.* Malden, Mass.: Blackwell, 1999.

McKim, Donald K., ed. *The Cambridge Companion to Martin Luther.* New York: Cambridge University Press, 2003.

McLeod, W. H. *Guru Nānak and the Sikh Religion.* Reprinted in *Sikhs and Sikhism.* New York: Oxford University Press, 2004.

Marshall, Rosalind K. *John Knox.* Edinburgh, Scotland: Birlinn, 2000.

Marty, Martin. *Martin Luther.* New York: Viking Penguin, 2004.

Naphy, William G. *Calvin and the Consolidation of the Genevan Reformation.* 1994. Reprint. Louisville, Ky.: Westminster John Knox Press, 2003.

Newman, Bruce. *A Beginner's Guide to Tibetan Buddhism.* Ithaca, N.Y.: Snow Lion, 2004.

Null, Ashley. *Thomas Cranmer's Doctrine of Repentance: Renewing the Power to Love.* New York: Oxford University Press, 2000.

Olin, John C. *Catholic Reform from Cardinal Ximenes to the Council of Trent.* New York: Fordham University Press, 1990.

Ozment, Stephen B. *Protestants: The Birth of a Revolution.* New York: Doubleday, 1992.

Prebish, Charles S. *Historical Dictionary of Buddhism.* Metuchen, N.J.: Scarecrow Press, 1993.

Reardon, Bernard M. G. *Religious Thought in the Reformation.* 2d ed. New York: Longman, 1995.

Ritters, Ronald K. *The Reformation of the Keys: Confession, Conscience, and Authority in Sixteenth Century Germany.* Cambridge, Mass.: Harvard University Press, 2004.

Schaff, Philip. *The Swiss Reformation.* Vol. 8 in *History of the Christian Church.* 3d ed. Peabody, Mass.: Hendrickson, 1996.

Seebohm, Frederic. *The Oxford Reformers: John Colet, Erasmus, and Thomas More.* Reprint. New York: AMS Press, 1971.

Wengert, Timothy J., ed. *Harvesting Martin Luther's Reflections on Theology, Ethics, and the Church.* Grand Rapids, Mich.: W. B. Eerdmans, 2004.

Wilcox, Donald J. *In Search of God and Self: Renaissance and Reformation Thought.* Boston: Houghton Mifflin, 1975.

Wright, A. D. *The Counter-Reformation: Catholic Europe and the Non-Christian World.* New York: St. Martin's Press, 1982.

Wright, D. F., ed. *Martin Bucer: Reforming Church and Community.* New York: Cambridge University Press, 2002.

RUSSIA

Bobrick, Benson. *Fearful Majesty: The Life and Reign of Ivan the Terrible.* New York: G. P. Putnam's Sons, 1987.

Bushkovitch, Paul. *Religion and Society in Russia: The Sixteenth and Seventeenth Centuries.* Oxford, England: Oxford University Press, 1992.

Crummey, R. O. *The Formation of Muscovy, 1304-1613.* New York: Longman, 1987.

Dunning, Chester S. L. *Russia's First Civil War: The Time of Troubles and the Founding of the Romanov Dynasty.* University Park: Pennsylvania State University Press, 2001.

Forsyth, James. *A History of the Peoples of Siberia: Russia's North Asian Colony, 1581-1990.* New York: Cambridge University Press, 1994.

Hosking, Geoffrey. *Russia and the Russians: A History.* Cambridge, Mass.: Harvard University Press, 2001.

Hunczak, Taras, ed. *Russian Imperialism from Ivan the Great to the Revolution.* Reprint. Lanham, Md.: University Press of America, 2000.

Kappeler, Andreas. *The Russian Empire: A Multiethnic History.* Translated by Alfred Clayton. New York: Longman, 2001.

Riasanovksy, Nicholas V. *A History of Russia.* 6th ed. New York: Oxford University Press, 1999.

Ure, John. *The Cossacks: An Illustrated History.* New York: Penguin, 2002.

Zernov, N. *Moscow, the Third Rome.* Reprint. New York: AMS Press, 1971.

SCIENCE. *See also* INVENTION AND TECHNOLOGY

Christianson, John Robert. *On Tycho's Island: Tycho Brahe, Science, and Culture in the Sixteenth Century.* New York: Cambridge University Press, 1999.

Crane, Nicholas. *Mercator: The Man Who Mapped the Planet.* New York: H. Holt, 2003.

Crombie, A. C. *Science in the Later Middle Ages and Early Modern Times.* Vol. 2 in *Augustine to Galileo.* 2d rev. and enlarged ed. Cambridge, Mass.: Harvard University Press, 1979.

Dear, Peter Robert. *Revolutionizing the Sciences: European Knowledge and Its Ambitions, 1500-1700.* Princeton, N.J.: Princeton University Press, 2001.

Duncan, David Ewig. *Calendar: Humanity's Epic Struggle to Determine a True and Accurate Year.* New York: Avon Books, 1998.

Faul, Henry. *It Began with a Stone.* New York: John Wiley & Sons, 1983.

Ferguson, Kitty. *Tycho and Kepler: The Unlikely Partnership That Forever Changed Our Understanding of the Heavens.* New York: Walker, 2002.

Gatti, Hilary. *Giordano Bruno and Renaissance Science.* Ithaca, N.Y.: Cornell University Press, 1998.

Gross, John. *Mapmaker's Art: An Illustrated History of Cartography.* Chicago: Rand McNally, 1995.

Henry, John. *Knowledge Is Power: How Magic, the Government, and an Apocalyptic Vision Inspired Francis Bacon to Create Modern Science.* Cambridge, England: Icon, 2004.

Jacob, James R. *The Scientific Revolution: Aspirations and Achievements, 1500-1700.* Atlantic Highlands, N.J.: Humanities Press, 1998.

Machamer, Peter, ed. *The Cambridge Companion to Galileo.* New York: Cambridge University Press, 1998.

Margolis, Howard. *It Started with Copernicus.* New York: McGraw-Hill, 2002.

Oldroyd, D. R. *Sciences of the Earth: Studies in the History of Mineralogy and Geology.* Variorum Collected Studies Series CS 628. Brookfield, Vt.: Ashgate, 1998.

Selin, Helaine, ed. *Encyclopedia of the History of Science, Technology, and Medicine in Non-Western Cultures.* Boston: Kluwer Academic, 1997.

Silver, Brian L. *The Ascent of Science.* New York: Oxford University Press, 1998.

White, Michael. *Leonardo: The First Scientist.* New York: St. Martin's Press, 2000.

SOUTHEAST ASIA

Andaya, Barbara Watson, and Leonard Y. *A History of Malaysia.* 2d ed. Honolulu: University of Hawaii Press, 2001.

Aung-Thwin, Michael A. *Myth and History in the Historiography of Early Burma: Paradigms, Primary Sources, and Prejudices.* Monographs in International Studies, Southeast Asia Series 102. Athens: Ohio University Center for International Studies, 1998.

Chandler, David. *A History of Cambodia.* 3d ed. Boulder, Colo.: Westview Press, 2000.

Chapuis, Oscar. *A History of Vietnam.* Westport, Conn.: Greenwood Press, 1995.

Hall, D. G. E. *A History of South-East Asia.* 4th ed. New York: St. Martin's Press, 1981.

Lieberman, Victor. *Integration in the Mainland.* Vol. 1 in *Southeast Asia in Global Context, c. 800-1830.* New York: Cambridge University Press, 2003.

Stuart-Fox, Martin. *A History of Laos.* New York: Cambridge University Press, 1997.

Wyatt, David K. *Thailand: A Short History.* 2d ed. New Haven, Conn.: Yale University Press, 2003.

SPAIN

Anderson, James M. *Daily Life During the Spanish Inquisition.* Westport, Conn.: Greenwood Press, 2002.

Edwards, John. *The Spain of the Catholic Monarchs, 1474-1520.* Oxford, England: Blackwell, 2000.

_____. *The Spanish Inquisition.* Stroud, Gloucestershire, England: Tempus, 1999.

Kamen, Henry. *Empire: How Spain Became a World Power, 1492-1763.* New York: HarperCollins, 2003.

_____. *Spain, 1469-1714: A Society of Conflict.* 2d ed. New York: Longman, 1991.

_____. *The Spanish Inquisition: A Historical Revision.* New Haven, Conn.: Yale University Press, 1998.

Lynch, John. *Spain 1516-1598: From Nation State to World Empire.* Oxford, England: Blackwell, 1991.

Parker, Geoffrey. *Philip II.* 4th ed. Chicago: Open Court, 2002.

Payne, Stanley G. *A History of Spain and Portugal.* 2 vols. Madison: University of Wisconsin Press, 1973.

Read, Jan. *The Moors in Spain and Portugal.* London: Faber & Faber, 1974.

Ruiz, Teofilo F. *Spanish Society, 1400-1600.* New York: Longman, 2001.

Weissberger, Barbara F. *Isabel Rules: Constructing Queenship, Wielding Power.* Minneapolis: University of Minnesota Press, 2004.

Woodward, Geoffrey. *Spain in the Reigns of Isabella and Ferdinand, 1474-1516.* London: Hodder & Stoughton, 1997.

THEATER

Andrews, Richard. *Scripts and Scenarios: The Performance of Comedy in Renaissance Italy.* New York : Cambridge University Press, 1993.

Banham, Martin, ed. *A History of Theatre in Africa.* New York: Cambridge University Press, 2004.

Bloom, Harold, ed. *Elizabethan Drama.* Philadelphia: Chelsea House, 2004.

Bowers, Faubion. *Japanese Theatre.* 1952. Reprint. Westport, Conn.: Greenwood Press, 1976.

Brandon, James R., ed. *The Cambridge Guide to Asian Theatre.* New York: Cambridge University Press, 1997.

Brandt, George W., ed. *German and Dutch Theatre, 1600-1848.* New York: Cambridge University Press, 1993.

Brereton, Geoffrey. *French Comic Drama from the Sixteenth to the Eighteenth Century.* London: Methuen, 1977.

Brockett, Oscar, and Franklin J. Hildy. *History of the Theatre.* 9th ed. Boston: Allyn and Bacon, 2003.

De Grazia, Margreta, and Stanley Wells, eds. *The Cambridge Companion to Shakespeare.* New York: Cambridge University Press, 2001.

Di Maria, Salvatore. *The Italian Tragedy in the Renaissance: Cultural Realities and Theatrical Innovations.* Lewisburg, Pa.: Bucknell University Press, 2002.

Fei, Faye Chunfang, ed. and trans. *Chinese Theories of Theater and Performance from Confucius to the Present.* Ann Arbor: University of Michigan Press, 1999.

Gurr, Andrew. *The Shakespearean Stage, 1574-1642.* 3d ed. New York: Cambridge University Press, 1992.

Henke, Robert. *Performance and Literature in the Commedia Dell'arte.* New York: Cambridge University Press, 2002.

Hochman, Stanley, ed. *McGraw-Hill Encyclopedia of World Drama: An International Reference Work in Five Volumes.* 2d ed. New York: McGraw-Hill, 1984.

Jondorf, Gillian. *French Renaissance Tragedy: The Dramatic Word.* New York: Cambridge University Press, 1990.

Kerr, David. *African Popular Theatre: From Pre-Colonial Times to the Present Day.* Portsmouth, N.H.: Heinemann, 1995.

Leach, Robert, and Victor Borovsky. *A History of Russian Theatre.* New York: Cambridge University Press, 1999.

Leiter, Samuel L., ed. *A Kabuki Reader: History and Performance.* Armonk, N.Y.: M. E. Sharpe, 2002.

Lunney, Ruth. *Marlowe and the Popular Tradition: Innovation in the English Drama Before 1595.* New York: Manchester University Press, 2002.

Mackerras, Colin, ed. *Chinese Theater: From Its Origins to the Present Day.* Honolulu: University of Hawaii Press, 1988.

Olsen, Kirstin. *All Things Shakespeare: An Encyclopedia of Shakespeare's World.* 2 vols. Westport, Conn.: Greenwood Press, 2002.

Oz, Avraham, ed. *Marlowe.* New York: Palgrave Macmillan, 2003.

Rollyson, Carl, ed. *Critical Survey of Drama.* 2d rev. ed. 8 vols. Pasadena, Calif.: Salem Press, 2003.

Rosenblum, Joseph. *Shakespeare.* Pasadena, Calif.: Salem Press, 1998.

Wells, Stanley. *Shakespeare: A Life in Drama.* New York: W. W. Norton, 1996.

TRADE AND COMMERCE

Andrews, Kenneth R. *Trade, Plunder, and Settlement: Maritime Enterprise and the Genesis of the British Empire, 1480-1630.* New York: Cambridge University Press, 1984.

Bakewell, P. J. *Silver Mining and Society in Colonial Mexico: Zacatecas, 1546-1700.* New York: Cambridge University Press, 2002.

Blackburn, Robin. *The Making of New World Slavery: From the Baroque to the Modern, 1492-1800.* London: Verso, 1997.

Bovill, E. W., and Robin Hallet. *The Golden Trade of the Moors.* 2d rev. ed. 1958. Reprint. Princeton, N.J.: Markus Weiner, 1999.

Bowen, H. V., Margarette Lincoln, and Nigel Rigby. *The Worlds of the East India Company.* Rochester, N.Y.: D. S. Brewer, 2002.

Brook, Timothy. *The Confusion of Pleasure: Commerce and Culture in Ming China.* Berkeley: University of California Press, 1998.

Brown, Jennifer S. H. *Strangers in Blood: Fur Trade Company Families in Indian Country.* Norman: University of Oklahoma Press, 1996.

Farrington, Anthony. *Trading Places: The East India Company and Asia, 1600-1834.* London: British Library, 2002.

Fisher, David Hackett. *The Great Wave: Price Revolutions and the Rhythm of History.* New York: Oxford University Press, 1996.

Foster, Nelson, and Linda S. Cordell, eds. *Chilies to Chocolate: Foods the Americas Gave to the World.* Tucson: University of Arizona Press, 1992.

Hicks, Michael. *Bastard Feudalism.* New York: Longman, 1995.

Klein, Herbert S. *The Atlantic Slave Trade.* New York: Cambridge University Press, 1999.

Loades, David. *England's Maritime Empire: Seapower, Commerce, and Policy, 1490-1690.* New York: Longman, 2000.

Marks, Robert B. *Tigers, Rice, Silk, and Silt: Environment and Economy in Late Imperial South China.* Cambridge, England: Cambridge University Press, 1998.

Middleton, John. *African Merchants of the Indian Ocean: Swahili of the East African Coast.* Long Grove, Ill.: Waveland Press, 2004.

Reese, Ted. *Soft Gold: A History of the Fur Trade in the Great Lakes Region and Its Impact on Native American Culture.* Bowie, Md.: Heritage Books, 2001.

Stein, Stanley J., and Barbara Stein. *Silver, Trade, and War: Spain and America in the Making of Early Modern Europe.* Baltimore: Johns Hopkins University Press, 2003.

Thomas, Hugh. *The Slave Trade: The Story of the Atlantic Slave Trade, 1440-1870.* New York: Simon & Schuster, 1997.

Wallenstein, Immanuel. *The Modern World-System: Capitalist Agriculture and the Origins of the European World-Economy in the Sixteenth Century.* New York: Academic Press, 1974.

TURKEY. *See* OTTOMAN EMPIRE

WARFARE

Arnold, Thomas F. *The Renaissance at War.* London: Cassell, 2001.

Chase, Kenneth. *Firearms: A Global History to 1700.* New York: Cambridge University Press, 2003.

Eltis, David. *The Military Revolution in Sixteenth Century Europe.* New York: Barnes & Noble Books, 1998.

Fernández-Armesto, Felipe. *The Spanish Armada: The Experience of War in 1588.* New York: Oxford University Press, 1988.

Fissel, Mark Charles. *English Warfare, 1511-1642.* New York: Routledge, 2001.

Gommans, Jos. *Mughal Warfare: Indian Frontiers and High Roads to Empire, 1500-1700.* New York: Routledge, 2002.

Graff, David A., and Robin Higham, eds. *A Military History of China*. Boulder, Colo.: Westview Press, 2002.

Guilmartin, John Frances. *Gunpowder and Galleys: Changing Technology and Mediterranean Warfare at Sea in the Sixteenth Century*. Rev. ed. Annapolis, Md.: United States Naval Institute Press, 2004.

Hall, Bert. *Weapons and Warfare in Renaissance Europe*. Baltimore: Johns Hopkins University Press, 1997.

Norris, John. *Artillery: A History*. Stroud, Gloucestershire, England: Sutton, 2000.

Parker, Geoffrey. *The Cambridge Illustrated History of Warfare*. Cambridge, England: Cambridge University Press, 2000.

Perrin, Noel. *Giving Up the Gun: Japan's Reversion to the Sword, 1543-1879*. Boston: David R. Godine, 1979.

Powell, John, ed. *Magill's Guide to Military History*. 5 vols. Pasadena, Calif.: Salem Press, 2001.

_____. *Weapons and Warfare*. 2 vols. Pasadena, Calif.: Salem Press, 2002.

Turnbull, Stephen R. *Samurai: The World of the Warrior*. London: Osprey Books, 2003.

Williams, Patrick. *Armada*. Charleston, S.C.: Tempus, 2000.

WOMEN'S STUDIES

Beilen, Elaine. *Redeeming Eve: Women Writers of the English Renaissance*. Princeton, N.J.: Princeton University Press, 1987.

Blade, Melinda K. *Education of Italian Renaissance Women*. Rev. and corrected. Woman and History 21. Mesquite, Tex.: Ide, 1983.

Capp, B. S. *When Gossips Meet: Women, Family, and Neighbourhood in Early Modern England*. New York: Oxford University Press, 2003.

Cass, Victoria Baldwin. *Dangerous Women: Warriors, Grannies, and Geishas of the Ming*. Lanham, Md.: Rowan & Littlefield, 1999.

Cohn, Samuel Kline. *Women in the Streets: Essays on Sex and Power in Renaissance Italy*. Baltimore: John Hopkins University Press, 1996.

Conn, Marie A. *Noble Daughters: Unheralded Women in Western Christianity, Thirteenth to Eighteenth Centuries*. Contributions to the Study of Religion 60. Westport, Conn.: Greenwood Press, 2000.

Harris, Barbara J. *English Aristocratic Women, 1450-1550: Marriage and Family, Property and Careers*. New York: Oxford University Press, 2002.

Jensen, Sharon L. *The Monstrous Regiment of Women: Female Rulers in Early Modern Europe*. New York: Palgrave Macmillan, 2002.

King, Margaret L., and Albert Rabil, Jr., eds. and trans. *Her Immaculate Hand: Selected Works by and About the Women Humanists of Quattrocento Italy*. Asheville, N.C.: Pegasus Press, 2000.

Levin, Carole, et al. *Extraordinary Women of the Medieval and Renaissance World: A Biographical Dictionary*. Westport, Conn.: Greenwood Press, 2000.

Maclean, Ian. *The Renaissance Notion of Woman: A Study in the Fortunes of Scholasticism and Medical Science in Europe Intellectual Life*. New York: Cambridge University Press, 1980.

Meek, Christine, and Catherine Lawless, eds. *Studies on Medieval and Early Modern Women: Pawns or Players?* Portland, Oreg.: Four Courts, 2003.

Mikesell, Margaret, and Adele Seeff, eds. *Culture and Change: Attending to Early Modern Women*. Newark: University of Delaware Press, 2003.

Musacchio, Jacqueline Marie. *The Art and Ritual of Childbirth in Renaissance Italy*. New Haven, Conn.: Yale University Press, 1999.

Nader, Helen, ed. *Power and Gender in Renaissance Spain: Eight Women of the Mendoza Family, 1450-1650*. Urbana: University of Illinois Press, 2004.

Peters, Christine. *Women in Early Modern Britain, 1450-1640*. New York: Palgrave Macmillan, 2004.

Pitkin, Hanna Fenichel. *Fortune Is a Woman: Gender and Politics in the Thought of Niccolò Machiavelli*. Berkeley: University of California Press, 1984.

Sim, Alison. *The Tudor Housewife*. Stroud, Gloucestershire, England: Sutton, 1998.

Van Kirk, Sylvia. *Many Tender Ties: Women in Fur-Trade Society*. Norman: University of Oklahoma Press, 1983.

Wheeler, Elizabeth Darracott. *Ten Remarkable Women of the Tudor Courts and Their Influence in Founding the New World, 1530-1630*. Lewiston, N.Y.: E. Mellen Press, 2000.

Wiesner, Merry E. *Working Women in Renaissance Germany*. New Brunswick, N.J.: Rutgers University Press, 1986.

Zahl, Paul F. M. *Five Women of the English Reformation*. Grand Rapids, Mich.: William B. Eerdmans, 2001.

—Rebecca Kuzins

ELECTRONIC RESOURCES

FREE WEB SITES

The sites listed below were visited by the editors of Salem Press in February, 2005. Because URLs frequently change or are moved, the accuracy of the Web addresses cannot be guaranteed; however, long-standing sites—such as those of university departments, national organizations, and government agencies—generally maintain links when sites move or upgrade their offerings.

GENERAL

The Catholic Encyclopedia
http://www.newadvent.org/cathen/
The electronic version of this reference book contains more than 11,000 alphabetically arranged articles exploring the entire range of Catholic interests. The article about the Reformation provides an excellent overview of the ideas and purposes of the Protestant reformers, written from a Catholic perspective. The encyclopedia also contains articles about the Renaissance and the Counter Reformation, a list of popes and biographical information about each pope, and numerous biographies of important Renaissance figures, such as Luther, Loyola, Erasmus, Gutenberg, and Sir Thomas More.

The Centre for Reformation and Renaissance Studies
http://www.crrs.ca/library/webresources/
webresources.htm#web
This page of the Centre for Reformation and Renaissance Studies's Web site contains numerous links to Web resources, electronic databases, and online texts. The links provide information about theologians, authors, and philosophers. There are also links to sites about women in history and the history of the book.

Development of Western Civilization: World History, the Renaissance
http://history.evansville.net/renaissa.html
This page about the Renaissance is part of a Web site that Nancy Mautz, a professor at the University of Evansville, designed for her course in Western Civilization. The page contains links about people, places, events, art, architecture, literature, drama, music, dance, and daily life.

Eyewitness to the Middle Ages and the Renaissance
http://www.eyewitnesstohistory.com/mefrm.htm
This site includes first-person accounts of historical events, such as the Black Death of 1348, the Spanish massacre of the French in Florida in 1565, and crime and punishment in Elizabethan England.

History World International
http://history-world.org
This recently revised site contains a wealth of information about history from the Neolithic period to the present. Users can access "Contents A-Z" for a list of pages with information about the Americas, art and architecture, Asia and the Middle East, Europe, science, world religions, and other general topics. The "Europe" section includes pages about the Renaissance, a history of England, and French history before the French Revolution, while the World Religions section contains pages about the Reformation and Counter Reformation.

The Islamic World to 1600
http://www.ucalgary.ca/applied_history/tutor/islam/
The Applied History Research Group at the University of Calgary has produced several excellent multimedia tutorials, including this one about the Islamic world from the seventh to the seventeenth centuries. There is information about Muslim beliefs and practices, the Mongol invasions, and the Islamic empires of Asia, Africa, and Europe.

Renaissance: What Inspired This Age of Balance and Order?
http://www.learner.org/exhibits/renaissance/
A collection of multimedia resources for teachers, including information about Renaissance Florence, exploration and trade, printing and thinking, architecture, painting, and music. The site was created by Annenberg/CPB, a satellite television channel available to schools, colleges, and public television stations.

Virtual Renaissance: A Journey Through Time

http://www.twingroves.district96.k12.il.us/
    Renaissance/VirtualRen.html

This is an extremely comprehensive site created by students and teachers at Twin Groves Junior High School in Buffalo Grove, Illinois. The site combines information about real people, such as Shakespeare and Queen Elizabeth I, and real places, like the University of Padua and the Globe Theatre, with fictionalized characters who discuss various aspects of Renaissance life and history. Information can be accessed by characters, locations, and chronologies. The information about Renaissance inventions and technology is especially useful.

WebChron: Web Chronology Project

http://campus.northpark.edu/history/webchron/

The Web Chronology Project was created by the History Department of North Park University. It includes a series of hyperlinked time lines for use in history classes. The site includes chronologies of developments in Islam, Christianity, and Judaism, and time lines for art, music, literature, and speculative thought in the Western tradition.

AFRICA

Civilizations in Africa

http://www.wsu.edu/~dee/CIVAFRCA/
    CIVAFRCA.HTM

Created and maintained by Washington State University, this site includes discussions of various African civilizations and a glossary of African terms and concepts. There is also an annotated resource list of Africa and African Studies Web links. Some of the other sections contain information about African history and art.

Internet African History Sourcebook

http://www.fordham.edu/halsall/africa/
    africasbook.html

One of the "sourcebook" products of Fordham University, maintained by Paul Halsall. This site provides information on the many civilizations who have resided on the African continent from prehistoric times to the present day.

THE AMERICAS

Ancient Aztec, Olmec and Mesoamerica by History Link 101

http://historylink101.com/1/aztec/ancient_aztec.htm

This page is part of History Link 101, a Web site containing information about various aspects of world history. This portion of the site features Web links, pictures, and maps about history, art, and daily life of the Aztecs, Olmecs and other Mesoamericans.

Ancient Mayan by History Link 101

http://historylink101.com/1/mayan/ancient_mayan.htm

Like all of History Link 101's Web pages, the Ancient Mayan site provides a series of Web links, pictures, and maps about history, art, and daily life of the Mayans.

Canada's First Nations

http://www.ucalgary.ca/applied_history/tutor/
    firstnations/

Created by the University of Calgary and Red Deer College, this site offers a multimedia tutorial on the history of Canada's First Nations people from antiquity to the nineteenth century. The site contains information about native life and culture, and the social, economic, and political impact of European contact.

Internet Resources on Native Americans

http://www.wsu.edu:8080/~dee/NAINRES.HTM

This site provides a comprehensive series of links to Web sites about the nations, history, art, literature, and texts of Native Americans in the United States. There is also information about the indigenous peoples of Mexico, and Central and South America. The site was created by Richard Hooker of Washington State University.

ART AND ARCHITECTURE

Art History Resources on the Web

http://witcombe.sbc.edu/ARTHLinks.html

Chris Witcombe, a professor of art history at Sweet Briar College in Virginia, has compiled this extensive list of Web sites about art history. Two sections of the site specifically deal with fifteenth- and sixteenth-century Renaissance art. There also are links to sites about Asian art and to sites for art museums and galleries throughout the world.

Asian Historical Architecture

http://www.orientalarchitecture.com/

With links to more than 450 Web sites, Asian Historical Architecture makes it possible to look at thousands of photographs of Asian architecture.

Metropolitan Museum of Art: Time line of Art History

http://www.metmuseum.org/toah/splash.htm

This site describes itself as "a chronological, geographical, and thematic exploration of the history of art from around the world, as illustrated especially by the Metropolitan Museum of Art's collection." Each time line page contains photographs of art, a chart of time periods, a map of the region, an overview, and a list of key events. There are also numerous pages devoted to special topics, including European Art in the Renaissance, African Art, Asian Art, and Islamic Art.

Palladio's Italian Villas

http://www.boglewood.com/palladio/

The work and life of architect Andrea Palladio is explored in this easy-to-use Web site. The site contains biographical information about Palladio, placing his life and buildings within the context of fifteenth-century Venice. There also are photographs of five of Palladio's villas located in and around Venice, a bibliography, and a political time line about the Republic of Venice.

Renaissance and Baroque Architecture: Architectural History 102

http://www.lib.virginia.edu/dic/colls/arh102/

This collection of images is a project of the University of Virginia Library Digital Image Center. The site contains photographs of art and architecture in Italy and other European countries during the fifteenth through seventeenth centuries.

World Art Treasures

http://www.bergerfoundation.ch/

A collection of more than 100,000 slides compiled by art historian Jacques-Edouard Berger. The site includes slides and information about Italian Renaissance gardens, Botticelli, and Caravaggio, as well as information about the art of Egypt, India, China, Japan, and other Asian countries.

ASIA

Center for Chinese Studies Library, Berkeley

http://www.lib.berkeley.edu/CCSL/

In addition to including the Center's catalog and bibliography, this site lists numerous links to other sites that focus on Chinese history.

Internet East Asian History Sourcebook

http://www.fordham.edu/halsall/eastasia/eastasiasbook.html

One of the highly-regarded "sourcebook" projects of Fordham University, maintained by Paul Halsall. Through this site, it is possible to find historical and cultural information on China, Japan, and Korea. The site also features information about European exploration of East Asia and the activities of the East India Company.

Internet Indian History Sourcebook

http://www.fordham.edu/halsall/india/indiasbook.html

Maintained by Paul Halsall, this site is one of Fordham University's "sourcebook" products. Like its counterparts, this site contains an exceptional amount of historical and cultural information, including sections about the Mughal Empire, the Delhi Sultanate, and Sikhism.

EXPLORATION

The Age of Exploration Curriculum Guide

http://www.mariner.org/age/index.html

This collection of materials about exploration from ancient times through 1768 was compiled by The Mariners' Museum in Newport News, Virginia. The site provides information on Portuguese exploration and navigation, Christopher Columbus, Francis Drake, Jacques Cartier, and other explorers.

Conquistadors

http://www.pbs.org/conquistadors/

Conquistadors supplements a series of programs shown on the Public Broadcasting Service. The site follows the paths of conquistadors Hernán Cortés in Aztecan Mexico, Francisco Pizarro in the Incan Empire, Cabeza de Vaca in Texas, and Francisco de Orellano along the Amazon River.

The European Voyages of Exploration: The Fifteenth and Sixteenth Centuries

http://www.ucalgary.ca/applied_history/tutor/eurvoya/

Another multimedia tutorial created by the University of Calgary, this site focuses on Spanish and Portuguese explorations and conquests in the Americas, the Atlantic, the Caribbean, Asia, and Africa. The site contains maps, material about the political, economic, and cultural circumstances that led to exploration, and articles about Columbus, slavery, and navigation.

1492: An Ongoing Voyage

http://www.loc.gov/exhibits/1492/

The Library of Congress has placed portions of its exhibition, "1492: An Ongoing Voyage," on the Web. In addition to providing information about Columbus and his voyage, the site describes the people who lived in the Americas before the voyage, and the Europeans and Africans who came to the Americas in the sixteenth and seventeenth centuries.

Spain, the United States, and the American Frontier: Historias Paralelas

http://international.loc.gov/intldl/eshtml/

A joint project of the Library of Congress and the National Library of Spain, this site documents the history of Spanish expansion in North America from the different perspectives of the United States and Spain. Material is presented in both English and Spanish, and includes texts, manuscripts, letters, maps, photographs, and early edition books.

Virtual Museum of New France

http://www.civilization.ca/vmnf/vmnfe.asp

A project of the Canadian Museum of Civilization, the site focuses on French exploration and settlement of North America. It includes biographies of explorers, maps, glossaries, and information about the education of children in New France.

GREAT BRITAIN
Tudor History

http://www.tudorhistory.org

A comprehensive exploration of British history from 1485-1603, with information on Tudor monarchs, the wives of Henry VIII, life in Tudor England, electronic texts and documents, chronologies, glossaries, and genealogical trees.

LITERATURE
The Cambridge History of English and American Literature : An Encyclopedia in Eighteen Volumes

http://www.bartleby.com/cambridge/

Among the many pages contained within this comprehensive literary encyclopedia are sections featuring essays and literary criticism about prose fiction, poetry, drama, and other literature of Renaissance and Reformation England.

CERES: Cambridge English Renaissance Electronic Service

http://www.english.cam.ac.uk/ceres/

Developed in 1996 by the Faculty of English at the University of Cambridge, this site features online resources for the study of Renaissance English literature. It includes dozens of links to Web sites and databases, including online anthologies, literary journals, and information about authors.

Luminarium: Anthology of Renaissance English Literature (1485-1603)

http://www.luminarium.org/medlit

Created by Anniina Jokinen in 1996 and continually updated since, this site includes the literature of Sir Thomas More, Philip Sidney, Edmund Spenser, Christopher Marlowe, Thomas Nashe and William Shakespeare. A collection of essays and articles concerning the literature of this period are also included, as are links to related sites concerning English literature and history.

Literary Resources: Renaissance

http://andromeda.rutgers.edu/~jlynch/Lit/ren.html

This in one of the pages in *Literary Resources on the Net*, a Web site designed by Jack Lynch, Associate Professor of English Literature at Rutgers University. The site contains an extensive list of links to Web resources about literature, drama, poetry, and ballads. In addition, there are numerous links to specific authors, with an especially good collection of links regarding Shakespeare.

Voice of the Shuttle: Literatures (Other Than English)

http://vos.ucsb.edu/browse.asp?id=2719

This site is a page from *Voice of the Shuttle*, an extraordinarily comprehensive collection of Web resources about the humanities compiled by professors at the University of California, Santa Barbara. The page links to a wide assortment of sites about world literature in general, as well as to more specific sites about literature in Arabic, Chinese, French, German, Italian, Japanese, Persian, Spanish, and other languages.

Voice of the Shuttle: Renaissance & Seventeenth Century

http://vos.ucsb.edu/browse.asp?id=2749

Another page from the excellent *Voice of the Shuttle*,

this site contains links to English-language essays, literary criticism, and examples of prose, poetry, and drama from a long list of authors.

THE MIDDLE EAST
Encyclopedia of the Orient
http://lexicorient.com/e.o/

This ready-reference online encyclopedia covers all of the countries of North Africa and the Middle East. The articles are geared toward the high-school and undergraduate student who needs quick and concise information on the people and places of this often neglected region of the world.

Internet Islamic History Sourcebook
http://www.fordham.edu/halsall/islam/islamsbook.html
This site is one of the "sourcebook" products of Fordham University and is maintained by Paul Halsall. Many links to original documents are included as well as links to other online resources.

Internet Jewish History Sourcebook
http://www.fordham.edu/halsall/jewish/
  jewishsbook.html
One of Fordham University's "sourcebook" products that is maintained by Paul Halsall. As with the other sourcebook sites, this one includes a wealth of relevant information as well as links to other Web resources.

MUSIC
Essentials of Music
http://www.essentialsofmusic.com/

Built around Sony's Essential Classics music series, the site includes an overview of Renaissance music from 1450-1600 and biographies of five Renaissance composers. It also contains about 200 musical excerpts from the Classics music series in RealPlayer format. The site was created by Sony Classical Music and W. W. Norton & Company.

A Guide to Medieval and Renaissance Instruments
http://www.s-hamilton.k12.ia.us/antiqua/instrumt.html
More than thirty musical instruments are described at this site, including the bagpipe, dulcimer, harpsichord, hurdy-gurdy, lute, recorder, and viol. History, pictures, alternate names, and sound-wave clips are provided for each instrument.

The Internet Renaissance Band
http://www.csupomona.edu/~jcclark/emusic/
Curtis Clark, a musician and teacher at California State Polytechnic University, Pomona, created this collection of early music "midi" files. "Midi," or musical instrument digital interface, is a technology that enables people to listen to music with most Web browsers. The site features an alphabetized list of Renaissance composers, each with midi files of his music. There are similar listings and midi files for medieval music and European carols.

PHILOSOPHY
EpistemeLinks.com
http://www.epistemelinks.com

EpistemeLinks.com contains about 16,000 cataloged links to philosophy Web sites. It contains pages describing the philosophy of specific historical eras, including a page about Renaissance Philosophy with links to information about Erasmus, Machiavelli, Bruno and other philosophers.

Internet Encyclopedia of Philosophy
http://www.utm.edu/research/iep/
The site features a collection of articles by philosophy professors, including articles about the Renaissance, Humanism, Erasmus, and Francis Bacon. An alphabetical list of article subjects helps users readily find information.

POLITICAL SCIENCE AND GOVERNMENT
Medici: Godfathers of the Renaissance
http://www.pbs.org/empires/medici/
This site is a companion to the Public Broadcasting Service's series of the same name. The site describes Renaissance developments in art, architecture, politics, religion, and science. It also features an interactive tour of Florence, Italy, a bibliography, and a list of Web links.

Niccolo Machiavelli: The Prince
http://www.the-prince-by-machiavelli.com/
Dedicated to Machiavelli and his treatise, "The Prince," the site contains a full English translation of the treatise, a bibliography, and a brief biography of Machiavelli.

PRIMARY SOURCES
EuroDocs: Primary Historical Documents from Western Europe
http://library.byu.edu/~rdh/eurodocs/homepage.html

This collection of transcripts, facsimiles, and translations was compiled by Richard Hacken, European Studies Bibliographer at Brigham Young University. The site includes numerous documents from the Middle Ages and the Renaissance, including government records of the plague and public health in Europe, manuscripts from the Vatican Library, and information about European life in the fifteenth through eighteenth centuries.

Internet Archive of Texts and Documents
http://history.hanover.edu/texts.html

The History Department of Hanover College has compiled this collection of links to primary and secondary sources on the World Wide Web. The site includes links to texts and documents from the Protestant and Catholic Reformations.

RELIGION
About.com: European History, The Reformation
http://europeanhistory.about.com/od/reformation/

Created by About.com, this site contains links to articles and resources about the Reformation, including texts, chronologies, a bibliography, and a glossary of Medieval and Reformation church terms.

Project Wittenberg
http://www.iclnet.org/pub/resources/text/wittenberg/wittenberg-home.html

The creators of this site describe it as the first step towards an electronic library of Lutheranism. It contains works by and about Martin Luther, information about other prominent theologians, and numerous texts, including commentaries, hymns, and theological treatises.

SCIENCE AND TECHNOLOGY
About.com: European History, Science and Technology
http://europeanhistory.about.com/od/scienceandtechnology/

This site, one of About.com's European history Web pages, contains information about the effect of the printing press, the Jesuits and the sciences, the introduction of the Gregorian calendar, and the scientific revolution of the sixteenth through eighteenth centuries.

Art of Renaissance Science: Galileo and Perspective
http://www.mcm.edu/academic/galileo/ars/arshtml/intro.html

This site, written by Professor Joseph W. Dauben of the City University of New York, explores Galileo, mathematics, and connections between art and science in the Renaissance.

Eric Weisstein's World of Science
http://scienceworld.wolfram.com/

This online reference source has been compiled by a research scientist and former professor of astronomy. It contains comprehensive encyclopedias of astronomy, chemistry, mathematics, and physics, as well as a brief biographies and pictures of noteworthy scientists.

The Galileo Project
http://es.rice.edu/ES/humsoc/Galileo/

Created and maintained by Rice University, this site provides information about the life and work of Galileo and the science of his time. The site includes a searchable database of 600 prominent scientists from the sixteenth and seventeenth centuries, as well as a time line of Galileo's life, maps, glossary, bibliography, and list of Web links.

Paracelsus, Five Hundred Years: Three American Exhibits
http://www.nlm.nih.gov/exhibition/paracelsus/paracelsus_1.html

This site was a companion to the 1993 exhibition commemorating the five hundredth anniversary of the birth of Paracelsus, an influential Renaissance physician and medical reformer. The site contains an essay, "Paracelsus and the Medical Revolution of the Renaissance," written by Allen G. Debus, Professor of History of Science and Medicine at the University of Chicago.

THEATER
The Oxford Shakespeare
http://www.bartleby.com/70/

This online version of the 1914 book contains the full text of Shakespeare's 37 plays and 154 sonnets.

Renaissance Drama from Its Medieval Origins to the Closing of the Theatres

http://athena.english.vt.edu/~jmooney/renmats/drama.htm

A brief overview of English theater compiled by a professor of English at Virginia Polytechnic Institute and State University. Contains information about theater history and about Shakespeare, Marlowe, and other dramatists.

WOMEN

Monastic Matrix: A Scholarly Resource for the Study of Women's Religious Communities from 400 to 1600

http://monasticmatrix.org/

Maintained through the Department of History at the University of Southern California, this site includes information that relates to "women's religious life, activities and patronage." All of the religious communities mentioned are searchable by name, region, date, and other access points. Primary documents, a bibliography, and a visual library also are included.

Women in World History Curriculum's Website

http://womeninworldhistory.com/

The site provides information and resources about women's history in what it describes as a "global, non-U.S., context." It features biographies, essays on women in history, and a list of links to other women's history Web sites.

Women Who Ruled: Queens, Goddesses, Amazons, 1500-1650

http://www.fathom.com/course/28701919

An online exhibition of paintings, sculptures, illustrations and other art objects depicting the many women who ruled European states and kingdoms in the Renaissance and Baroque periods. The site is maintained by the Michigan University Museum of Art.

SUBSCRIPTION-BASED RESOURCES

The following online references are posted on the World Wide Web but are available only to paid subscribers. Many public, college, and university libraries subscribe to these sites; readers can ask reference librarians if these sites are available at their local libraries.

GENERAL
Oxford Reference Online

http://www.oxfordreference.com

A virtual reference library of more than 120 dictionaries and reference books published by Oxford University Press. *Oxford Reference Online* contains information about a broad range of subjects, including art, architecture, military history, science, religion, philosophy, and literature. The site also features English language and bilingual dictionaries, as well as collections of quotations and proverbs.

Oxford Scholarship Online

www.oxfordscholarship.com

Oxford Scholarship Online currently contains the electronic versions of more than 700 books about economics, finance, philosophy, political science, and religion that are published by the Oxford University Press. The site features full text of these books, advanced searching capabilities, and links to other online sources.

ART
Grove Art Online

www.groveart.com

This authoritative and comprehensive site provides information about the visual arts from prehistory to the present. In addition to its more than 130,000 art images, the site contains articles on fine arts, architecture, China, South America, Africa and other world cultures, as well as biographies and links to hundreds of museum and gallery web sites.

HISTORY
Greenwood Daily Life Online

http://dailylife.greenwood.com/

The site focuses on what its creator, Greenwood Publishing Group, describes as "the billions of men and women history often forgets, but whose everyday lives created the world we know." It contains information from *The Greenwood Encyclopedia of Daily Life* and other sources describing religious, domestic, economic, intellectual, and educational life. Maps, illustrations, time lines, and teacher lesson plans are also included.

Iter Gateway to the Middle Ages and Renaissance

http://www.itergateway.org/

Iter, a non-profit research group that works to advance the study of the Middle Ages and the Renaissance, has included this page on its Web site. The page enables subscribers to search databases and academic journals for information about this period of history.

MUSIC
Classical Music Library

http://www.classical.com/

This streaming music service contains about 35,000 music tracks, with about 20,000 tracks added monthly. It also features program notes, images, playlists, and links to biographical and humanities databases.

Grove Music Online

www.grovemusic.com

This online version of the highly regarded *The New Grove Dictionary of Music and Musicians* features thousands of articles on musicians, instruments, musical techniques, genres, and styles. In addition to its

articles and biographies, the site provides more than 500 audio clips of music, and links to images, sound, and related Web sites.

Naxos Music Library

www.naxoxusa.com

Naxos Music Library features 75,000 streamed audio music tracks, including selections from Renaissance Era composers. While the music selections are only available to subscribers, the site also provides free information about musical history, including a page describing Renaissance Music from 1400-1600. There is also a free collection of composer biographies and descriptions of musical instruments.

SCIENCE
Access Science: McGraw-Hill Encyclopedia of Science & Technology Online

http://www.accessscience.com/server-java/Arknoid/science/As

This site is an online version of *McGraw Hill Encyclopedia of Science & Technology*, containing all of the articles found in the most recent edition of that reference book. The site includes biographies of 2,000 scientists, definitions of scientific terms, bibliographies, and links to related Web sites.

ELECTRONIC DATABASES

Electronic databases usually do not have their own URLs. Instead, public, college, and university libraries subscribe to these databases and install them on their Web sites, where they are only available to library card holders or specified patrons. Readers can check library Web sites to see if these databases are installed, or can ask reference librarians if these databases are available.

GENERAL
Gale Virtual Reference Library

The database contains more than 100 reference books, including encyclopedias, almanacs, and directories, allowing users to quickly find information about a broad range of subjects.

BIOGRAPHY
Biography Resource Center

The database, produced by Thomson Gale, includes biographies of 200,000 prominent people from throughout the world and from a wide range of disciplines.

Wilson Biographies Illustrated

Produced by H. W. Wilson Co., this database offers more than 100,000 biographies and obituaries of world authors, artists, composers, and other historical figures.

HISTORY
History Reference Center

A product of EBSCO Information Services, the *History Reference Center* is a comprehensive world history database. It contains the contents of more than 650 encyclopedias and other books, the full text of articles published in 50 history magazines, and thousands of historical documents, biographies, photographs, and maps.

World History FullTEXT

A joint product of EBSCO Information Services and ABC-CLIO, this database provides a global view of history with information on a wide range of topics, including anthropology, art, culture, economics, government, heritage, military history, politics, regional issues, and sociology.

World History Online

Facts on File, Inc., a reference book publisher, has placed the contents of many of its encyclopedias, dictionaries and other print materials on this world history database. Users can search by six content categories: Biographies, Subject Entries, Primary Sources, Timeline, Maps and Charts, and Curriculum Content Standards.

LITERATURE
Literature Resource Center

Literature Resource Center, produced by Thomson Gale, includes biographies, bibliographies, and critical analyses of authors from a wide range of literary disciplines, countries, and eras. The database also features plot summaries, the full text of articles from literary journals, critical essays, plot summaries, and links to Web sites.

MagillOnLiteraturePlus

Salem Press has placed many of its literature reference sources on this database, including *Masterplots*, *Cyclopedia of World Authors*, *Cyclopedia of Literary Characters*, and *World Philosophers and Their Works*. The database covers the works of more than 8,500 writers, poets, dramatists, essayists, and philosophers, featuring plot summaries, critical analyses, biographical essays, character profiles, and up-to-date lists of each author's works.

—*Rebecca Kuzins*

CHRONOLOGICAL LIST OF ENTRIES

1450's

Mid-15th century: Foundation of the Saud Dynasty
1450's-1471: Champa Civil Wars
1450's-1529: Thai Wars
1451-1526: Lodī Kings Dominate Northern India
1454: China Subdues Burma
1454-1481: Rise of the Ottoman Empire
April 9, 1454: Peace of Lodi
1455-1485: Wars of the Roses

1456: Publication of Gutenberg's Mazarin Bible
1457-1480's: Spread of Jōdo Shinshū Buddhism
February 11, 1457: Restoration of Zhengtong
April 14, 1457-July 2, 1504: Reign of Stephen the Great
1458-1490: Hungarian Renaissance
1459: Rāo Jodha Founds Jodhpur

1460's

Early 1460's: Labor Shortages Alter Europe's Social Structure
1460-1600: Rise of the Akan Kingdoms
1462: Founding of the Platonic Academy
c. 1462: Kazak Empire Is Established
1462: Regiomontanus Completes the *Epitome* of Ptolemy's *Almagest*
1463-1479: Ottoman-Venetian War
c. 1464-1591: Songhai Empire Dominates the Western Sudan
1465-1487: Reign of Xianzong

July 16, 1465-April, 1559: French-Burgundian and French-Austrian Wars
October 19, 1466: Second Peace of Thorn
1467: End of King Parākramabāhu VI's Reign
1467-1477: Ōnin War
1469-1481: Reign of the Ava King Thihathura
1469-1492: Rule of Lorenzo de' Medici
1469-1508: Ak Koyunlu Dynasty Controls Iraq and Northern Iran
October 19, 1469: Marriage of Ferdinand and Isabella

1470's

1471-1493: Reign of Topa Inca
March 18-22, 1471: Battle of Vijaya
c. 1473: Ashikaga Yoshimasa Builds the Silver Pavilion
1473: Jakob II Fugger Becomes a Merchant
1473-1600: Witch-Hunts and Witch Trials
1474: Great Wall of China Is Built
1474-1479: Castilian War of Succession
Late 15th century: Mombasa, Malindi, and Kilwa Reach Their Height
August 29, 1475: Peace of Picquigny
1477-1482: Work Begins on the Sistine Chapel

1477-1600: Japan's "Age of the Country at War"
June 12, 1477-August 17, 1487: Hungarian War with the Holy Roman Empire
August 17, 1477: Foundation of the Habsburg Dynasty
1478: Muscovite Conquest of Novgorod
1478-1482: Albanian-Turkish Wars End
c. 1478-1519: Leonardo da Vinci Compiles His Notebooks
April 26, 1478: Pazzi Conspiracy
November 1, 1478: Establishment of the Spanish Inquisition

1480's

1480-1502: Destruction of the Golden Horde
After 1480: Ivan the Great Organizes the "Third Rome"
1481-1482: Founding of Elmina
1481-1499: Ludovico Sforza Rules Milan
1481-1512: Reign of Bayezid II and Ottoman Civil Wars
1482-1492: Maximilian I Takes Control of the Low Countries
1483-1485: Richard III Rules England
c. 1485: Portuguese Establish a Foothold in Africa
Beginning 1485: The Tudors Rule England

May, 1485-April 13, 1517: Mamlūk-Ottoman Wars
1486-1487: Pico della Mirandola Writes *Oration on the Dignity of Man*
August, 1487-December, 1488: Dias Rounds the Cape of Good Hope
1488-1505: Reign of Xiaozong
c. 1488-1594: Khmer-Thai Wars
March 5, 1488: Composition of the *Renga* Masterpiece *Minase sangin hyakuin*
1489: ʿĀdil Shah Dynasty Founded
1489: Yorkshire Rebellion

1490's

1490's: Aldus Manutius Founds the Aldine Press
1490's: Decline of the Silk Road
Beginning 1490: Development of the Camera Obscura
c. 1490: Fragmentation of the Bahmani Sultanate
1490-1492: Martin Behaim Builds the First World Globe
1491-1545: Christianity Is Established in the Kingdom of Kongo
1492: Fall of Granada
1492: Jews Are Expelled from Spain
October 12, 1492: Columbus Lands in the Americas
1493-1521: Ponce de León's Voyages
1493-1525: Reign of Huayna Capac
1493-1528: Reign of Mohammed I Askia
August 19, 1493-January 12, 1519: Reign of Maximilian I

1494: Sebastian Brant Publishes *The Ship of Fools*
June 7, 1494: Treaty of Tordesillas
September, 1494-October, 1495: Charles VIII of France Invades Italy
December 1, 1494: Poynings' Law
Beginning c. 1495: Reform of the Spanish Church
1495-1497: Leonardo da Vinci Paints *The Last Supper*
1495-1510: West Indian Uprisings
1497: Cornish Rebellion
Beginning 1497: Danish-Swedish Wars
June 24, 1497-May, 1498: Cabot's Voyages
January, 1498: Portuguese Reach the Swahili Coast
1499: Louis XII of France Seizes Milan
1499-1517: Erasmus Advances Humanism in England
1499-c. 1600: Russo-Polish Wars

1500's

Beginning c. 1500: Coffee, Cacao, Tobacco, and Sugar Are Sold Worldwide
c. 1500: Netherlandish School of Painting
c. 1500: Revival of Classical Themes in Art
c. 1500: Rise of Sarmatism in Poland
1500: Roman Jubilee
1500-1530's: Portugal Begins to Colonize Brazil
Early 16th century: Athapaskans Arrive in the Southwest
Early 16th century: Devotional Bhakti Traditions Emerge

Early 16th century: Fuzuli Writes Poetry in Three Languages
Early 16th century: Rise of the Fur Trade
16th century: China's Population Boom
16th century: Decline of Moundville
16th century: Evolution of the Galleon
16th century: Iroquois Confederacy Is Established
16th century: Proliferation of Firearms
16th century: Rise of the *Shenshi*
16th century: Single-Whip Reform

1510's

1520's

1527-1543: Ethiopia's Early Solomonic Period Ends
1527-1547: Maya Resist Spanish Incursions in Yucatán
1527-1599: Burmese Civil Wars
March 17, 1527: Battle of Khānua
May 6, 1527-February, 1528: Sack of Rome
1528: Castiglione's *Book of the Courtier* Is Published

1528-1536: Narváez's and Cabeza de Vaca's Expeditions
1529-1574: North Africa Recognizes Ottoman Suzerainty
March 7, 1529: Battle of Shimbra-Kure
September 27-October 16, 1529: Siege of Vienna

1530's

1530's-1540's: Paracelsus Presents His Theory of Disease
December 30, 1530: Humāyūn Inherits the Throne in India
1531-1540: Cromwell Reforms British Government
1531-1585: Antwerp Becomes the Commercial Capital of Europe
February 27, 1531: Formation of the Schmalkaldic League
1532: Holbein Settles in London
1532-1536: Temmon Hokke Rebellion
1532-1537: Pizarro Conquers the Incas in Peru
1534-1535: Ottomans Claim Sovereignty over Mesopotamia
April 20, 1534-July, 1543: Cartier and Roberval Search for a Northwest Passage
August 15, 1534: Founding of the Jesuit Order
December 18, 1534: Act of Supremacy

December 23, 1534-1540: Parmigianino Paints *Madonna with the Long Neck*
July, 1535-March, 1540: Henry VIII Dissolves the Monasteries
1536: Turkish Capitulations Begin
1536 and 1543: Acts of Union Between England and Wales
March, 1536: Calvin Publishes *Institutes of the Christian Religion*
October, 1536-June, 1537: Pilgrimage of Grace
1537: Pope Paul III Declares Rights of New World Peoples
September 27-28, 1538: Battle of Préveza
1539: Jiajing Threatens Vietnam
May, 1539: Six Articles of Henry VIII
May 28, 1539-September 10, 1543: De Soto's North American Expedition

1540's

1540-1545: Shēr Shāh Sūr Becomes Emperor of Delhi
February 23, 1540-October, 1542: Coronado's Southwest Expedition
October 20-27, 1541: Holy Roman Empire Attacks Ottomans in Algiers
1542-1543: The New Laws of Spain
June 27, 1542-c. 1600: Spain Explores Alta California
July 15, 1542-1559: Paul III Establishes the *Index of Prohibited Books*
1543: Copernicus Publishes *De Revolutionibus*
1543: Vesalius Publishes *On the Fabric of the Human Body*
Autumn, 1543: Europeans Begin Trade with Japan
1544-1628: Anglo-French Wars

1545-1548: Silver Is Discovered in Spanish America
1545-1563: Council of Trent
February 27, 1545: Battle of Ancrum Moor
1546: Fracastoro Discovers That Contagion Spreads Disease
January 16, 1547: Coronation of Ivan the Terrible
January 28, 1547-July 6, 1553: Reign of Edward VI
1548-1600: Siamese-Burmese Wars
1549: Kett's Rebellion
1549-1552: Father Xavier Introduces Christianity to Japan
1549-1570's: La Pléiade Promotes French Poetry
Mid-16th century: Development of the Caracole Maneuver

1550's

1550's: Tartaglia Publishes *The New Science*
1550's-1567: Japanese Pirates Pillage the Chinese Coast
1550's-c. 1600: Educational Reforms in Europe
1550-1571: Mongols Raid Beijing
1550-1593: Japanese Wars of Unification
January-May, 1551: The Stoglav Convenes
1552: Las Casas Publishes *The Tears of the Indians*
1552: Struggle for the Strait of Hormuz
1553: Servetus Describes the Circulatory System
July, 1553: Coronation of Mary Tudor
September, 1553: First Battle of Kawanakajima
January 25-February 7, 1554: Wyatt's Rebellion
1555-1556: Charles V Abdicates

September 25, 1555: Peace of Augsburg
1556-1605: Reign of Akbar
January 23, 1556: Earthquake in China Kills Thousands
Summer, 1556: Ivan the Terrible Annexes Astrakhan
1557-1582: Livonian War
1558-1593: Burmese-Laotian Wars
1558-1603: Reign of Elizabeth I
January 1-8, 1558: France Regains Calais from England
1559-1561: Süleyman's Sons Wage Civil War
April 3, 1559: Treaty of Cateau-Cambrésis
May, 1559-August, 1561: Scottish Reformation

1560's

c. 1560's: Invention of the "Lead" Pencil
April or May, 1560: Publication of the Geneva Bible
June 12, 1560: Battle of Okehazama
March, 1562-May 2, 1598: French Wars of Religion
1563-1584: Construction of the Escorial
January, 1563: Thirty-nine Articles of the Church of England
January 20, 1564: Peace of Troyes
June, 1564: Tintoretto Paints for the Scuola di San Rocco
1565: Spain Seizes the Philippines
May 18-September 8, 1565: Siege of Malta
September, 1565: St. Augustine Is Founded

1566-1574: Reign of Selim II
July 22, 1566: Pius V Expels the Prostitutes from Rome
1567: Palestrina Publishes the *Pope Marcellus Mass*
1567-1572: Reign of Longqing
July 29, 1567: James VI Becomes King of Scotland
1568: Oda Nobunaga Seizes Kyōto
c. 1568-1571: Ottoman-Russian War
1568-1648: Dutch Wars of Independence
February 23, 1568: Fall of Chitor
1569: Mercator Publishes His World Map
November 9, 1569: Rebellion of the Northern Earls

1570's

February 25, 1570: Pius V Excommunicates Elizabeth I
July, 1570-August, 1571: Siege of Famagusta and Fall of Cyprus
October 7, 1571: Battle of Lepanto
1572-1574: Tycho Brahe Observes a Supernova
August 24-25, 1572: St. Bartholomew's Day Massacre
1573-1620: Reign of Wanli
1574-1595: Reign of Murad III
Mid-1570's: Powhatan Confederacy Is Founded
1575: Tallis and Byrd Publish *Cantiones Sacrae*
March 3, 1575: Mughal Conquest of Bengal

November, 1575: Stephen Báthory Becomes King of Poland
1576: James Burbage Builds The Theatre
1576-1612: Reign of Rudolf II
June 7, 1576-July, 1578: Frobisher's Voyages
1577: Ram Dās Founds Amritsar
1578: First Dalai Lama Becomes Buddhist Spiritual Leader
1578-1590: The Battle for Tabrīz
August 4, 1578: Battle of Ksar el-Kebir
June 17, 1579: Drake Lands in Northern California

Geographical Index

List of Geographical Regions

Category Index

List of Categories

AGRICULTURE

Beginning c. 1500: Coffee, Cacao, Tobacco, and Sugar Are Sold Worldwide, 249

16th cent.: China's Population Boom, 277

16th cent.: Single-Whip Reform, 294

1594-1595: Taikō Kenchi Survey, 852

ANTHROPOLOGY

1460-1600: Rise of the Akan Kingdoms, 41

Early 16th cent.: Athapaskans Arrive in the Southwest, 267

16th cent.: Decline of Moundville, 279

ARCHITECTURE

1459: Rão Jodha Founds Jodhpur, 36

c. 1473: Ashikaga Yoshimasa Builds the Silver Pavilion, 85

1474: Great Wall of China Is Built, 93

1477-1482: Work Begins on the Sistine Chapel, 104

1563-1584: Construction of the Escorial, 680

1576: James Burbage Builds The Theatre, 756

1577: Ram Dās Founds Amritsar, 764

Dec., 1598-May, 1599: The Globe Theatre Is Built, 879

ART

c. 1473: Ashikaga Yoshimasa Builds the Silver Pavilion, 85

1477-1482: Work Begins on the Sistine Chapel, 104

1490's: Aldus Manutius Founds the Aldine Press, 174

1494: Sebastian Brant Publishes *The Ship of Fools*, 211

1495-1497: Leonardo da Vinci Paints *The Last Supper*, 225

c. 1500: Netherlandish School of Painting, 252

c. 1500: Revival of Classical Themes in Art, 256

1508-1520: Raphael Paints His Frescoes, 327

1508-1512 and 1534-1541: Michelangelo Paints the Sistine Chapel, 331

Beginning 1513: Kanō School Flourishes, 352

EXPLORATION AND DISCOVERY

GEOGRAPHY

GEOLOGY

GOVERNMENT AND POLITICS

SCIENCE AND TECHNOLOGY

SOCIAL REFORM

WOMEN'S ISSUES

Great Events from History

Indexes

Personages Index

SUBJECT INDEX